MANUSCRIPTS
IN THE BRITISH ISLES RELATING TO
AUSTRALIA, NEW ZEALAND,
AND THE PACIFIC

SPONSORED BY THE NATIONAL LIBRARY OF AUSTRALIA
AND THE AUSTRALIAN NATIONAL UNIVERSITY

AUSTRALIAN NATIONAL UNIVERSITY PRESS

MANUSCRIPTS
IN THE
BRITISH ISLES
RELATING TO
AUSTRALIA,
NEW ZEALAND,
AND THE
PACIFIC

EDITOR

PHYLLIS MANDER-JONES

 CANBERRA 1972

Printed and manufactured in Australia

Registered in Australia for transmission by post as a book
Library of Congress Catalog Card no. 78-152750
National Library of Australia Card no. and ISBN 0 7081 0450 9

Foreword

The publication of *Manuscripts in the British Isles relating to Australia, New Zealand, and the Pacific* reflects the long and pleasant association between the National Library of Australia and the Australian National University since they agreed in 1964 jointly to sponsor what has always been called informally 'the Mander-Jones project'. Though it falls to us, in our official capacities, to sign this Foreword, we must make it clear to scholars who will gratefully consult this volume that it owes its existence to the initiative of our predecessors, Sir Harold White and Sir Keith Hancock. The launching of the project now completed is not the least of their varied services to scholarship in Australia.

The original proposals for the compilation and publication of a guide such as this were made in 1963 by two historians on the staff of the Australian National University, Dr R. A. Gollan and Mr H. E. Maude. While on study leave in London they had talked to Miss Mander-Jones, who after retirement from a distinguished period of office as Mitchell Librarian, had been London Representative for the Library of New South Wales and later the Joint Copying Project Officer. They had resolved to urge on their return that advantage be taken of her long experience and professional ability to fill a large gap in the relevant information available to historians of Australia and the Pacific. Sir Keith Hancock, then Professor of History in the Research School of Social Sciences at the Australian National University, at once saw the force of these proposals and gave his persuasive authority to securing their realisation. The project would have been too expensive to be undertaken by the University alone; but when Mr (later Sir Harold) White, then National Librarian, expressed his Council's willingness that the Library should share equally in the cost and the task of administration, the work could proceed.

Arrangements for what was then conceived to be a three-year project were worked out in April 1964 between the Library and the University. The latter was represented by the Department of History in the Research School of Social Sciences, with the blessing of the Vice-Chancellor and the Director of the School. These arrangements, with adaptations according to circumstances, have worked harmoniously throughout. The direct financial contributions of our two institutions have been about equal. In the later stages of the extended project the Library made available the services of some of its officers, while the Australian National University Press undertook the publication of the manuscript. It has truly been a joint undertaking.

Foreword

From the beginning both sponsors assumed that Miss Phyllis Mander-Jones would be the Director of the project. Indeed it would not have been launched at that time had she not been available. Her name commanded the professional and personal respect of archivists, librarians, and historians in Australia and the British Isles. Apart from her long experience as Mitchell Librarian, she had recently been concerned in London with the Australian Joint Copying Project (sponsored by the National Library, and the Mitchell Library as a department of the Library of New South Wales), the work of which was closely related to the aims of the new venture. This volume records the results of her appointment. We believe that it will receive and deserve the high compliment which librarians and scholars are accustomed to pay to an indispensable work of reference when they identify it by the name of its author, and we are happy that the National Library and the Australian National University should jointly have sponsored what will be known simply as 'Mander-Jones'.

We leave to the Director the pleasant task of acknowledging in detail the contributions of the many people and institutions who have helped her, and would like to add our thanks to hers. Of those in Canberra who have shared with our predecessors and ourselves the administration of the project we must mention particularly Mr C. A. Burmester, lately Assistant National Librarian; Mrs Pauline Fanning, Chief Librarian, Australian Studies; Dr R. A. Gollan, Professorial Fellow in History; and especially Mr L. F. Fitzhardinge, Reader in History, who was the Department of History's principal representative in matters concerned with the project until Sir Keith Hancock's retirement, and was thereafter closely associated with his successor in all necessary consultations with the National Library.

J. A. La Nauze
Professor of History
Australian National University

A. P. Fleming
National Librarian
National Library of Australia

Canberra, June 1971

Contents

Contents

Contents

Contents

Contents

Contents

Contents

Wales and Isle of Man

Scotland

Northern Ireland

Republic of Ireland

Contents

Introduction

The need for a condensed survey of manuscript sources in the British Isles relating to Australia, New Zealand, and the Pacific has been long apparent. The present volume aims to fill this need, providing a framework for research on specific subjects and for general copying and bibliographical programs.

In 1964, at its inception, the scope of this survey was defined as 'manuscript material in Great Britain and Ireland' relating to Australia and New Zealand, New Guinea, Melanesia, Micronesia, Polynesia, Antarctica, and the sub-Antarctic islands in the southern Pacific and Indian Oceans.

This geographical field is briefly described on the title page as Australia, New Zealand, and the Pacific, the term Pacific covering the oceanic island groups but omitting the coasts of Asia and America and islands of the continental shelf. A few islands outside the limits of the area defined above have been added, the Australian territories, Christmas Island and Cocos Islands, and, because of their importance to voyages of exploration and to science, Juan Fernandez and the Galapagos in the Pacific and islands of the southern Indian Ocean as far west as Kerguelen. Thus the field as originally planned has been fully covered but the term 'manuscript material' must be qualified.

Hand drawn maps, drawings, and paintings have received a brief reference only when found associated with handwritten or typewritten documents. Printed documents found with manuscripts are usually excluded unless they are of extreme rarity. In listing biographical material no mention is made of papers relating to phases of the careers of individuals not concerned with the field of the survey.

Some restriction of coverage of 'manuscript material' has been dictated by the time factor. Pursuit of private papers and business records is often time consuming and it was reluctantly decided not to follow up every lead but to leave this field to future research. Such papers are listed only if well known or discovered by inquiry in likely quarters. Other papers not fully covered are probate records, registers of births, deaths, and marriages, poor law records, and criminal records. Although all are valuable sources of biographical, social, and economic information, relevant references are scattered. Only selected series have been mentioned. For example a few entries have been made for papers relating to assisted emigrants in parish records or in records of Boards of Guardians of Poor Law Unions and for papers concerning convicts transported to Australia found in Quarter Sessions records in county record offices. In the description of records in the Public Record Office a brief entry is included for the records of the Clerks of Assize but none is given for relevant assize papers in records of the Palatinates of Chester, Durham, and Lancaster.

A search has been made for all other manuscripts, biographical, historical, scientific, whether official records or collections of documents in record offices, libraries, institutions, or, to a limited extent, in private possession. Papers of any date are included, although the thirty year rule is usually imposed and in some cases access is denied for an even longer period.

Arrangement of repositories is topographical, London being placed first. Repositories in which nothing has been found are omitted but omission does not always imply that an exhaustive search has been made. Within each description, guides, catalogues, etc., are mentioned whether published or unpublished. The order of entries in such guides or catalogues, or failing them any arrangement in the repository, is followed in the hope that this will facilitate reference, bearing in mind of course that rearrangement may have occurred. Failing any existing arrangement papers are listed alphabetically, chronologically, or in logical order.

Information in a published guide or catalogue is seldom repeated and this is especially the case with regard to the *Guide to the Contents of the Public Record Office*, 3 vols., H.M.S.O. 1963, 1968. Entries in volume three of this Guide and for material received too late for inclusion in that volume are inserted as far as possible in their logical places in our description.

In deciding how much information about papers should be given, the aim has been to indicate the existence and content of documents without unnecessary bibliographical detail and, above all, without evaluation of their importance. Some inequality of emphasis is inevitable. Scattered letters or papers in a collection may need separate entries while lengthy correspondence with particular individuals or series of records may be dismissed in a few lines. Works in which extensive use is made of manuscripts are mentioned but no claim is made that citations are complete. Reference to relevant National Register of Archives Reports is seldom made.

Where the existence of copies was known it has been noted in the text but in the time available it has not been possible to keep this information up to date. An asterisk after an entry indicates that the manuscript or series is included in the Australian Joint Copying Project, though, where more convenient, this is stated in words. Copying under this Project is proceeding rapidly and we have made no effort to keep abreast of current activities. All references to copies are omitted in the description of the holdings of the Public Record Office in London. Inquiries concerning the Australian Joint Copying Project should be addressed to the National Library of Australia in Canberra or to the National Library of Australia Liaison Officer, Australia House, Strand, London.

Every effort has been made to check names and facts as research has proceeded but it is too much to hope that errors are not present. As far as possible the correct forms of names, and, in the case of personal names, dates of birth and death are given in the index; in the text the form given by the manuscript is usually retained.

It is evident that a survey of this kind must be out of date very quickly. Accessions are added to repositories, collections are re-examined and rearranged, manuscripts in private hands go to new owners, new deposits are discovered. Even so, and in spite of omissions, it is hoped that this handbook will draw attention to the main collections of manuscripts in its field. Rather than strive after completeness it has been thought preferable to publish results without delay.

In conclusion it must be emphasised that description of papers does not imply that they can be inspected. The majority are usually available to serious and accredited students, but decision whether papers may be examined must always remain with owners or custodians.

ACKNOWLEDGMENTS

Acknowledgments for help in the preparation of the work are due to a large number of people and to many institutions. Firstly mention must be made of the sympathetic understanding of problems which has characterised administration of the project by Sir Keith Hancock, Sir Harold White, and their successors in the National University and the National Library, Professor J. A. La Nauze and Mr A. P. Fleming.

Members of an advisory panel in England have given valuable advice and provided many necessary introductions. Those who have acted on the panel are Professor Asa Briggs, Vice-Chancellor, the University of Sussex; Dr R. M. Hartwell, Professorial Fellow and Librarian, Nuffield College, Oxford; Dr G. S. R. Kitson Clark, Reader (Constitutional History) and Fellow of Trinity College, Cambridge; Mr A. T. Milne, Secretary and Librarian, the Institute of Historical Research, University of London; and three successive London Liaison Officers of the National Library of Australia, Mr F. W. Torrington, Mr W. D. Thorn, and Mr P. H. Saunders.

Office space for the survey throughout its duration has been provided without cost to the survey. For two years, November 1964 to October 1966 an office was made available by the Institute of Commonwealth Studies, University of London, and since that date by the High Commissioner for Australia. Our debt to both our hosts is gratefully acknowledged.

Information leading to the location of manuscripts has come from many sources. A visiting fellowship, January to June 1964, in the Department of History, Research School of Social Sciences, the Australian National University, enabled the editor to report on knowledge of manuscripts in the British Isles in the field of the survey and scholars and librarians in Australia and New Zealand, too numerous to list in full, helped in the compilation of this report. My assistants and I sincerely thank everyone who provided information either at that time or during the progress of research. Special thanks are due to many members of the Australian National University, particularly to Professor N. G. Butlin, Professor C. M. H. Clark, Professor J. W. Davidson, Mr L. F. Fitzhardinge, Dr R. A. Gollan, Mr H. E. Maude, Professor D. H. Pike, Dr Margaret J. E. Steven (now at the University of Western Australia), and Mr R. A. Langdon, Executive Officer of the Pacific Manuscripts Bureau operating from the Research School of Pacific Studies. Others to whom we are grateful are Dr A. G. Serle and Professor A. G. L. Shaw of Monash University. We also thank Mr K. L. Milne, Agent-General for South Australia, for useful introductions; Dr Averil M. Lysaght, authority on Sir Joseph Banks, for advice on his papers and on zoological and botanical nomenclature; Mr A. G. E. Jones for many historical notes especially on early whaling; and Mr A. de Righi for information on postal history. To other scholars we are indebted for notes on collections of papers. Mr D. W. A. Baker has presented an annotated list of archives of the Colonial Committee of the Church of Scotland now in the National Library of Edinburgh; Mrs B. Thorn and Mrs C. Cameron have compiled reports on records in London and in the counties.

Sincere thanks go to all librarians who have answered our queries. Because of the frequency of our appeals to them we mention Mrs P. Fanning of the staff of the National Library of Australia; Miss S. Mourot, Associate Mitchell Librarian, Sydney; Miss M. Lukis, Librarian of the Battye Library, Perth; and Miss Janet E. Bell, Curator, Hawaiian and Pacific Collection, University of Hawaii.

Special acknowledgement is made of the interest and support given by Sir Harold White when Librarian of the National Library of Australia, and by Mr G. D. Richardson, Principal Librarian of the Library of New South Wales. They have generously arranged that their officers in London should assist with the survey. Mrs P. Millward, Australian Joint Copying Project Officer, who is responsible to both libraries, and Miss M. Miles, London representative of the Library of New South Wales, have supplied reports, Mrs Millward on a number of county collections, and Miss Miles on the archives of several institutions in Dublin. The National Library also seconded two officers as assistant editors, Miss J. A. D. Baskin and Mr J. L. Cleland.

In England it was natural to seek advice from the compilers and editors of *A Guide to Manuscripts Relating to America in Great Britain and Ireland* (1961), B. R. Crick and M. Alman, and of *A Guide to Western Manuscripts and Documents in the British Isles Relating to South and South East Asia* (1965), M. D. Wainwright and N. Matthews under the supervision of J. D. Pearson. Early drafts of the latter guide were given to Mr H. E. Maude, who drew them to the editor's attention, and a complete typescript was lent to the editor in London. The drafts included entries for manuscripts concerning Australia and the Pacific Islands, later found to be too numerous to be printed. Suggestions made by Professor Crick, Mrs Alman, Mr Pearson, Miss Wainwright, and Miss Matthews have been very useful. The survey has also profited by advice from Mr P. Walne, County Archivist, Hertfordshire, editor of a work in progress on sources in the British Isles for the history of Latin America. Thanks are due especially to Dr D. C. M. Platt, who presented a copy of entries for business archives which he had prepared for this work.

No research among manuscripts in the British Isles can afford to disregard the services offered by the National Register of Archives, a branch of the Royal Commission on Historical Manuscripts. Thousands of lists of collections and growing files of name, place, and subject indexes are available in the search room at Quality House, Quality Court, Chancery Lane, where a brochure may be obtained describing services and publications. The latter include the invaluable *Record Repositories in Great Britain*, 4th edition, 1971, *List of Accessions to Repositories, 1954-*, *List of Sources of Business History in the National Register of Archives, 1964-*, *The Prime Minister's Papers, 1801-1902*, 1968. We have made constant use of lists, indexes, and publications and have pleasure in recording our sincere appreciation of the personal interest taken in the progress of the survey by the Secretary of the Royal Commission on Historical Manuscripts, Mr R. H. Ellis, by successive Registrars, Miss W. D. Coates, Lieut.-Colonel R. P. F. White, and Miss F. Ranger, and by members of the staff. Another organisation to which the survey is indebted is the Business Archives Council. Its Honorary Secretary, Major T. L. Ingram, has been especially helpful. The lists of the National Register of Archives (Scotland) operating from the Scottish Record Office, H.M. General Register House, Edinburgh, have been consulted by courtesy of Mr A. Andrews, Curator of Historical Records. In Northern Ireland information is being brought together and papers preserved by Mr K. Darwin, Deputy Keeper of Public Records, Public Record Office of Northern Ireland, Law Courts Building, May Street, Belfast. The help and advice of Mr Andrews and Mr Darwin concerning records in public custody and in private hands are deeply appreciated. In the Republic of Ireland we received generous assistance from many custodians of manuscripts. We must especially acknowledge advice on Irish manuscripts given by Mr P. Henchy, Director of the National Library of Ireland, and Mr B. MacGiolla Choille, Keeper of State Papers at the State Paper Office. The monumental index to manuscripts relating to Ireland and Irishmen, *Manuscript Sources for the History of Irish Civilisation*, edited by Dr Richard J. Hayes, Boston 1965, has been an indispensable guide.

There is one group without whose generous co-operation the survey could not have been compiled, and to whom more than anyone gratitude is due, the archivists, librarians, custodians, and owners of papers in the British Isles. We have studied their guides, catalogues, and schedules but their expert personal guidance has been invaluable. Although their names are too numerous to list, sincere thanks must be expressed to every one of them. Our practice has been to write to each repository or owner enclosing a leaflet explaining our aims together with a list of relevant items which we had heard were in the collection.

Introduction

In practically every case correspondence was followed by visits by one of the staff during which we experienced the kind help which made it possible to bring reports up to date, correct errors, and trace uncatalogued items. Many librarians and archivists took the trouble to criticise the draft reports, which were always submitted. Corrections have been meticulously incorporated but the editor takes sole responsibility for the final entries which were often built up from a number of reports.

Apart from the editor, members of the team working on the survey have laboured for varying periods. In 1964 plans provided for a full time staff of three, the editor, an assistant editor, and a secretary-typist, with part time help from scholars and archivists as opportunity offered. Full time assistant editors have been Mrs J. C. Iltis, November 1964 to April 1965, Miss J. A. D. Baskin, January to December 1967, Mr J. L. Cleland, July 1968 to June 1970, Miss M. E. A. Pamplin, January 1969 to July 1970. Since August 1965 the whole of the ever growing volume of correspondence and the typing of the text has been carried out by Miss J. Pilbeam, who has also assisted in checking names of persons and places. Mrs Iltis, Miss Baskin, and Miss Pamplin reported chiefly on records in London although they also worked in various counties and Miss Baskin supplied notes on papers in the National Library of Scotland. Mr Cleland surveyed the majority of English counties as well as Wales, Northern Ireland, and Eire.

Part time assistants worked usually on papers of particular interest to their own lines of research and nearly all made valuable contributions to the long reports necessary on the vast accumulations in the British Museum and the Public Record Office. Among those who worked extensively in these institutions are Miss J. Bergen, Mrs R. Schofield, Miss R. Arnold, and Miss M. Poole. Mr J. H. M. Honniball reported particularly on the Gladstone papers in the British Museum; the Rev. D. N. Swain on several groups of missionary records and on the Grey papers at Durham; Mrs J. Roth on manuscripts in Cambridge; Dr D. Routledge on papers concerning Fiji; Dr R. M. Pike on manuscripts in the Library at the London School of Economics; Miss M. Titcomb on the Hudson's Bay Company records; Miss G. Renard (Mrs J. S. Marsden) on manuscripts at the Royal Geographical Society; Mrs P. Baird on papers in the Library of the Royal Botanic Gardens at Kew; and Mr J. W. Turner on the records of the Hydrographic Office. Mrs E. Woodrow examined Cabinet records in the Public Record Office and compiled a list of subject headings for the index.

Finally, among acknowledgments, it is a pleasure to express admiration of the efficiency with which the Australian National University Press has resolved the difficulties of translating the work into print.

London, July 1971   PHYLLIS MANDER-JONES

Bibliographical Note

Published works, in which extensive use is made of manuscripts, are cited in the text but no claim is made that citations are complete. Abbreviated titles are used for three works frequently cited:

H.R.N.S.W.: Historical Records of New South Wales, Sydney 1892-1901, 7 vols. in 8.

The Journals . . . of Cook, ed. Beaglehole: *The Journals of Captain James Cook on his Voyage of Discovery*, Edited from the Original Manuscripts by J. C. Beaglehole, Cambridge 1955-67, 3 vols. in 4.

The Banks Letters, ed. Dawson: *The Banks Letters. A Calendar of the Manuscript Correspondence of Sir Joseph Banks preserved in the British Museum, the British Museum (Natural History) and other Collections in Great Britain*, Edited by Warren R. Dawson, London 1958. 'Supplementary Letters of Sir Joseph Banks', Edited by Warren R. Dawson, *Bulletin of the British Museum (Natural History)*, *Historical Series*, vol. 3, no. 2, 1962.

NOTE ON COPIES OF MANUSCRIPTS

The existence of a copy of a manuscript or group of manuscripts has been mentioned frequently in the text. It has not been possible however to trace all copies. When convenient an asterisk is placed after an entry to indicate that the material is included in the Australian Joint Copying Project. Up-to-date information on this project may be obtained from the National Library of Australia, Parkes Place, Canberra, A.C.T., Australia 2600, the Library of New South Wales, Macquarie Street, Sydney, N.S.W., Australia 2000, or from the National Library of Australia Liaison Officer, Australia House, Strand, London W.C.2, United Kingdom.

England

LONDON

ARMY MUSEUMS OGILBY TRUST
Ministry of Defence (Army), Northumberland House, Northumberland Avenue, London, W.C.2

Diary 1809-11 of Ensign Alexander Huey, 73rd Foot, on a voyage to New South Wales and return voyage to England. Typescript of diaries kept on the outward and return voyages in the possession of Lady Macdonald-Tyler, Co. Londonderry, Northern Ireland, q.v.

Diary 1810-40 of Capt. Foster Fyans referring to convict settlement in Australia. Typescript of the original in the possession (1966) of Major D. Neill, Seaford, Macandrew Bay, Dunedin, N.Z.

Wilkinson Papers, including forty letters 1889-1907 from Sir Charles Wentworth Dilke, 2nd Bt, concerning imperial defence, etc.

BANK OF ENGLAND
Threadneedle Street, London, E.C.2

The Stock Ledgers, for which there is a complete series, are the main source for material relating to Australia and New Zealand. Inquirers must know the full name of the holder of the stock and an approximate date, in order to use the material which will provide further genealogical and personal information. Most of the relevant material is after 1850. Access to records over a hundred years old is generally granted to researchers on application to the Secretary of the Bank with letters of introduction from a person of standing. Access to records less than a hundred years old is restricted, but short searches on specific queries may be undertaken by the Bank.

BARING BROTHERS & CO. LTD
8 Bishopsgate, London, E.C.2

The Baring Archives may be consulted to 1889 by permission of the Directors. Application should be made to the Archivist. The archives are arranged in classes and there is a typescript descriptive list. In-letters contained in House Correspondence and in Out-letters connected therewith are filed in Class HC and Class LB respectively. In-letter Books letters are arranged chronologically and each volume is indexed.

HOUSE CORRESPONDENCE

HC 1.70. Letters 1833-66 from Henry Labouchere (created Viscount Taunton 1866) include an assessment of the character of H. C. E. Childers.

HC 1.78. Two open letters 1841, 1843, addressed to Lord Stanley, Secretary of State for the Colonies, about emigration to New South Wales with tables of the monetary and commercial affairs of the colony 1838-40, printed.

HC 6.4. House Correspondence, Australasian.

1. Two memos n.d. [c.1838] concerning Australia: a consideration of the cotton and woollen industries of Great Britain and the value of the Australian colonies in these industries, and an 'Estimate of the Capital necessary for the establishment of a Cotton and Sugar Estate in New South Wales . . . and the profits that may be expected to arise therefrom'.

2. Documents 1844-8 concerning Moreton Bay, including: letters of Charles and James Balfour and Evan Mackenzie, list of squatters at Moreton Bay 1843 with their

holdings, list of goods suitable for the Moreton Bay market, report on the standing of Sir Colin Mackenzie. Baring Brothers granted a credit to two sons of Sir Colin Mackenzie, the eldest being Evan Mackenzie, to whom Baring Brothers were to ship goods and from whom they were to receive wool. The two sons had with others obtained squatting rights in the districts of Moreton Bay and Darling Downs.

3. Documents 1848-9 concerning the Kapunda Copper Mine including seven deeds, summaries of title deeds specifying shares, accounts 1845-9 of the mine, and statement 1844-7 of shipment of ore.

4. Letter 23 Aug. 1852 J. D. Lang, London, to Baring Brothers proposing that Barings take part in the establishment of a company to settle emigrant farmers from Britain in New South Wales and to foster the Australian cotton industry, with statement of Lang's experiments in growing cotton on the coast of New South Wales.

5. Documents 1855-8 concerning the loan to the colony of Victoria for the construction of railways including:

Letter 20 July 1855 Sir Charles Hotham to Thomas Baring inviting Baring Brothers to negotiate a loan for railway construction in Victoria and to act as agent for the colony in the payment of dividends, with official documents Feb.-June 1855 concerning railway progress in Victoria and memo 21 July 1855 by the Colonial Secretary on the financial state of the colony.

Three letters Dec. 1857 to June 1858 Sir Henry Barkly to Thomas Baring concerning the railway loan, the arrival of H. C. E. Childers in Melbourne, the failure of his negotiations, and the political and financial condition of Victoria.

Two letters Dec. 1857, May 1858, C. Ebden, Colonial Treasurer, Victoria, to Baring Brothers making a formal proposal to negotiate the loan and inviting them to become agents in Britain for the colony for the provision of railway material and stock.

Letters 1857-8 John Goodman, merchant of Melbourne, to Baring Brothers concerning railways in Victoria, the proposal for a loan and the state of the goldfields.

Correspondence Feb.-Nov. 1858 between Childers and Baring Brothers concerning Childers's mission to Victoria as Baring's representative, including reports on the progress and ultimate failure of his mission, banks in Melbourne, New Zealand securities, and Childers's account of expenses.

Correspondence Feb.-Mar. 1858 between Baring Brothers and the Union Bank of Australia, London, concerning the latter's taking a part of the forthcoming loan to the colony of Victoria.

Printed Parliamentary Paper, Victoria 1858, concerning the 'Railway loan', two copies. Newspapers and cuttings, mostly Australian, concerning the colony of Victoria and its railways.

6. Letters May-June 1857 from Goodman & Umphelby, bankers, Melbourne, to Baring Brothers concerning railways in Victoria, proposals for Baring's part in raising funds, arrival of railway engineers from England.

7. Letter 25 May 1878 Crown Agents for the Colonies, London, P. G. Julyan to Baring Brothers concerning New Zealand loans and declining Baring's conditions for such loans.

BEAVERBROOK LIBRARY
33 St Bride Street, London, E.C.4

Most collections of books and papers relating to twentieth century politics in this Library are the property of the Trustees of the Beaverbrook Foundations or are on loan to them, but the Lloyd George Papers are the property of Beaverbrook Newspapers. Collections are still being acquired, e.g. the papers of St Loe Strachey, Editor of the *Spectator* 1898-1925, still uncatalogued (May 1969).

Intending readers should write to the Librarian giving the subject of their study. Applicants who do not hold academic appointments listed in reference books must enclose a letter of reference. It is important that applications be made well in advance of the intended visit and that overseas scholars indicate the length of their stay, as space for readers is so limited that at times it is necessary to have an appointments system.

LLOYD GEORGE PAPERS

The private papers 1901-45 of David Lloyd George, Earl Lloyd-George of Dwyfor. The present arrangement is arbitrary, previous attempts to reconstitute original series having failed. Basically the papers are divided into political and personal, by far the greater number being of a political nature. These have been sorted arbitrarily into series A-G, corresponding with various periods of Lloyd George's life, while collections of press cuttings and the personal papers form two further series, H and I.

The documents in series A-G are divided into 'correspondence' and 'papers'. The correspondence is sorted into semi-official, special, foreign, general, and Cabinet notes, and the papers into semi-official, Cabinet, general domestic, general foreign, and speeches. There are minor variations where necessary. Material of the greatest importance for the historian is found in the special correspondence. Most important political figures have special files; usually the correspondence not only of the office holder, but also of his subordinates, will be found under his name. The files are arranged alphabetically by person and contain both in- and out-letters, with a preponderance of the former. The general correspondence contains letters from members of the general public and from other more important individuals not holding official positions.

A detailed descriptive list in fifteen loose-leaf folders, and a 'Guide to the Use of the Lists and Indexes of the Lloyd George Papers', both typescript, are available in the Library. The indexes are on cards by personal name and subject. Series A-E are fully indexed, series F-I are fully indexed only in part; some sections have been indexed only from the list and not from the original documents. Reference numbers comprise the series letter, box, folder, and document number. In addition to the material listed below, which consists mostly of typescript letters, all to or from Lloyd George unless otherwise stated, there are many more references to Australasia in other letters and speeches, particularly in the semi-official correspondence 1915-16, concerning munitions supplies.

C/5/3. Special correspondence 1913, William Morris Hughes, contains letter 12 June 1913 from W. M. Hughes, Attorney General of Australia, introducing Dr Mary Booth.

D/20/2. General correspondence 1915-16. Includes letter 23 Sept. 1915 from Keith Arthur Murdoch, announcing his arrival in London, and enclosing a letter 17 July 1915 from A. Fisher, Melbourne, in which Murdoch is introduced as one of Australia's leading journalists.

E/2/17. Special correspondence 1916, Andrew Bonar Law, Secretary of State for the Colonies 1915-16. Includes letter 17 Oct. 1916 from the Foreign Office referring to the suggestion that Briand, when he interviews Murdoch, should eulogise the Australian troops and express the hope that the Australian Government will send over more troops to France; letter 22 Nov. 1916 from the Colonial Office concerning discontent among Australian troops in France, enclosing a paraphrase telegram 22 Nov. 1916 from the Governor-General of Australia asking for the matter to be remedied; letter 20 Nov. 1916 from Keith A. Murdoch reporting that in accordance

5

with General Headquarters' request Hughes has not allowed soldiers' voting to become known, and stressing the need for the men's respect for Great Britain to be increased.

E/4/2. General correspondence Oct.-Dec. 1916. Includes letter 23 Oct. 1916 from Keith A. Murdoch stating that the majority of army votes have been counted against conscription and that he considers votes from France and Australia will also be unfavourable; also that General Headquarters believes that the publication of this result will prolong the war and suggests that some relief of the Irish situation, and a statement by Lloyd George on the gravity of the situation to be published in Australia would influence the voting.

E/9/3, F/10/1. Special correspondence Feb.-Dec. 1921, Winston S. Churchill, Secretary of State for the Colonies Mar. 1921 to Oct. 1922. Includes correspondence May-Nov. 1921 Governors-General of Australia and New Zealand and others with the Colonial Office, on various matters including reparations recovery, Washington Conference on the limitation of armaments, and Dominion representation at the Hague Conference.

F/28/2,3. Special correspondence 1917-21, William Morris Hughes, Prime Minister of Australia 1915-23. Includes letters relating to the relevance of the Irish question in the Australian political situation, e.g. 17 Aug. 1917 from Hughes mentioning that he is considering whether to prosecute Archbishop Mannix; the collection of war trophies for the Australian National Museum; Versailles Conference; Allied Indemnity Commission; Japan's position in the North Pacific and Australian mandates for certain Pacific Islands; Reparations Commission; the repatriation of Australian soldiers, e.g. 5 Mar. 1919 from Hughes complaining that 'the repatriation of Australian soldiers is proceeding in a most unsatisfactory manner'; Committees on Australian lead and copper; Australian graves in Gallipoli; the position of Nauru, e.g. 9 May 1919 from Hughes giving the history of the Australian capture and occupation of Nauru, discussing Australia's need of phosphates produced there, and summing up her claim to the island; Hughes's belief in the future of airships and his intention to try and persuade Australia to take up the project.

F/32/4,5, F/33/1. Special correspondence 1916-18, Walter H. Long, 1st Viscount Long of Wraxall, Secretary of State for the Colonies 1916 to Jan. 1919. Includes letters relating to the political situation in Australia; Australian representatives at the Imperial Conference; communications between Great Britain and Australia, including copy telegram 21 Aug. 1918 from the Governor-General of Australia stating that arrangements concerning channels of communication should be cleared up or it will be thought that 'the Colonial Office has been eliminated from the affairs of the Commonwealth'; Australian interest in trade between Germany and British colonies.

F/35/3. Special correspondence, Sir Joseph Maclay, 1st Baron Maclay, Shipping Controller 1916 to Mar. 1922. Includes letter 7 Mar. 1919 from Maclay referring to the New Hebrides in which many Scottish people are interested, particularly in missionary effort, and stating that joint French and British control of the islands is proving unsatisfactory, with an unsigned paper Feb. 1919 'Britain and France in the New Hebrides, S.W. Pacific. Arguments for sole control to pass to the British Empire', and appendices consisting of two pamphlets, two maps, and a statement by F. H. L. Paton on Australian interests in the islands; a further letter 22 Mar. 1919 on the importance of the New Hebrides question in which Massey of New Zealand is much interested; letter 22 Mar. 1919 from Lloyd George urging action to expedite repatriation of Australian and New Zealand troops, referring to the great services they have rendered; letter 25 Mar. 1919 in reply, giving details of repatriation and answering Hughes's claim for ex-enemy ships and for increase in tonnage for the Australian trade.

F/36/4. Special correspondence 1918-21, William Ferguson Massey, Prime Minister of New Zealand 1915-23. Includes correspondence concerning war strategy, the purchase of meat in New Zealand by the Imperial Government, and the difficulties caused by the withdrawal of insulated ships from the New Zealand trade; Sir Joseph Ward's service on either the Reparations or Financial Commission; control of Nauru, e.g. letter 9 Apr. 1919 enclosing a report on the phosphate bearing islands in the Pacific; New Zealand's financial position owing to war liabilities.

F/39/1,2. Special correspondence 1919-22, Alfred Milner, 1st Viscount Milner, Secretary of State for the Colonies 1919-21. Includes letters on the control of Nauru, e.g. minute from the British delegate in Paris enclosing a decipher of telegram from Lord Milner proposing that it should remain under British control to which Hughes had agreed, although he was then trying to obtain control for Australia; Hughes's demand that the Prince of Wales should visit Australia before New Zealand, described as 'pure dog in the manger megalomania'; appointment of Baron Forster as Governor-General of Australia.

H/18. Collection of cuttings concerning Australia 1923-44.

H/284 (part). Collection of cuttings concerning New Zealand 1923, 1933-44.

BONAR LAW PAPERS

The private papers, 1901-23, of Andrew Bonar Law, mostly political as opposed to personal papers. The political papers have been artificially grouped in series corresponding with various periods of Bonar Law's life, but no distinguishing letters have been assigned to the series. The correspondence in some series has been further sorted into official, semi-official, general political, special, etc., and the papers into official, Cabinet, etc. The correspondence contains both in- and copy out-letters, mostly typescript to or from Bonar Law unless otherwise stated. A detailed descriptive list in three volumes, and personal name and subject indexes in three looseleaf binders, all typescript, are available in the Library. Reference numbers comprise the box, folder and document number.

12/2/29,32. 6 June, 7 July 1914 James M. Bonn, Suva, concerning dispute about precedence in the Legislative Council of Fiji, and expressing the hope that Bonar Law, when his party comes into power with himself as Prime Minister, will look into things in Fiji 'as the place is practically going worse and worse into debt, and it is a pity to see such a fine place as Fiji not governed properly'.

18/3/45. n.d. and 20 Nov. 1907 Prime Minister of Australia, concerning Bonar Law's speeches on Tariff Reform, mentioning the growth of protection in Australia.

18/8/6. 17 Jan. 1908 to A. Deakin, concerning the Australian tariff and British politics.

30/2/2. 1 Sept. 1913 L. S. Amery, mentioning various matters including the Australian wireless system and Australian constitutional difficulties.

31/1/57. 7 Dec. 1913 L. S. Amery, concerning Australian and New Zealand opinion on Home Rule, he himself being entirely opposed to simple exclusion, preferring a general scheme of devolution.

50/1/3. 1 June 1915 A. L. Stanley, to Colonial Office, gossip about personalities and politics in Australia.

50/1/4. 17 June 1915 Colonial Office memo on the problem of shipments of rifles to Australia.

50/1/23. 22 Oct. 1915 Admiralty, agreeing to surrender fourteen Australian transports.

53/4/15. 6 Nov. 1916 W. M. Hughes, describing the political situation in Australia, the results of the recent General Election and his own political position.

97/5/21. 23 July 1919 War Cabinet Office, stating that Lord Milner has agreed to Australia and New Zealand having copies of the report of the Dardanelles Commission.

99/1/8,9, 99/3/9. Correspondence May-July 1920, with Lord Milner, concerning the Governor-Generalship of Australia.

115/4/13. 10 Jan. 1923 Board of Trade, enclosing a note on the Western Australian Railway.

BLUMENFELD PAPERS

Personal correspondence of R. D. Blumenfeld during his career in journalism. See N.R.A. Report 13874. The collection is not yet sorted and is not open to inspection (Jan. 1970). The correspondence is arranged alphabetically by correspondent and includes two letters May 1907, July 1909 from Alfred Deakin.

BISHOPSGATE INSTITUTE
230 Bishopsgate, London, E.C.2

GEORGE HOWELL COLLECTION

Collection of books, pamphlets, and personal papers of George Howell, Secretary of the London Trades Council 1861-2, Secretary of the Reform League 1864-7 and Liberal M.P. 1885-95. The pamphlets which are bound together by subject include a number written 1846-64 by New Zealand authors dealing with the settler expropriation of Maori lands, the Maori Wars, and the involvement of the British Government in New Zealand political issues. There are also a few pamphlets on Australia 1834-47 dealing with the extension of steam navigation from Singapore to Port Jackson and with the draft of a proposed charter for the 1834 South Australia Commission.

BRITISH AND FOREIGN BIBLE SOCIETY
Bible House, 146 Queen Victoria Street, London, E.C.4

The archives of the British and Foreign Bible Society, founded 1804, cover all parts of the world; the following list indicates which series of records are most likely to contain material relating to Australia. Similarly, the records of the London Secretaries' Association which are deposited with the Society, are also likely to contain relevant material. Both sets of archives are open to bona fide students who should apply to the Archivist.

BRITISH AND FOREIGN BIBLE SOCIETY RECORDS

Library

Manuscript copy *c*.1820 of St John's gospel and part of the Acts of the Apostles translated by Pomare II, King of Tahiti, 1 vol., and letter 19 Mar. 1819 from King Pomare to Secretary of the Society requesting copies of Bible or gospels.

Correspondence 1947-8 with Aldersey Cox of Brisbane relating to the presentation to the Society of Isaac Watts's Bible.

Muniment Room

Minutes of general meetings 1804-91, 3 vols. These contain lists of committee members. Vol.1 has an incomplete index.

Minutes of committee 1807-1939, 117 vols.

Minutes of corresponding committees 1809-15, 1 vol.

Minutes of sub-committees 1810-33, 3 vols.

Minutes of colonial sub-committee 1904-7, with indexes, 1 vol.

Minutes of Australia and New Zealand sub-committee 1919-29, with indexes, 1 vol.

Minutes of overseas dominions sub-committee 1929-33, 1934-9, with indexes, 2 vols.

Papers of estimates sub-committee (New Zealand) 1905-22, 1 vol.

Minutes of editorial sub-committee 1830-1904, kept in Translations Department, 27 vols., rough minutes 1853-5 in Muniment Room, 1 vol.

Papers of foreign depots sub-committee 1933-9, 2 boxes.

Minutes of house sub-committee 1815-1937, 5 vols.

Minutes of depository and printing sub-committee 1817-1905, *c.*14 vols.

Minutes of home organisation 1888-1927, with indexes, 6 vols.

Original in-correspondence

Original home letters 1804-56, 180 boxes.

Original home letters 1902-5, *c.*57 boxes.

Correspondence inwards 1803-21, 8 vols.

Original foreign correspondence inwards 1822-51, 91 vols.

Original foreign letters 1902-5, *c.*39 boxes.

Miscellaneous letters 1931-8, 6 boxes, 1 vol.

Letters and documents 1808-50, 3 vols.

Communications from auxiliary and branch societies and associations of the British and Foreign Bible Society 1831-2, 1 vol.

Out-correspondence

Home correspondence outwards 1827-81, 14 vols.

Home correspondence nos.43-56, 1900-3, 14 vols.

Home correspondence letter books 1903-6, 11 vols.

Letter books A, 1904-6, 4 vols.

Letter books A, nos.47-67, 1919-31, 21 vols.

Letter books B, 1904-5, 5 vols.

Letter books B, 1919-31, 26 vols.

Foreign correspondence outwards 1820, 1 vol.

Correspondence outwards 1820-6, 7 vols.

Foreign correspondence outwards 1827-49, 1851-80, 95 vols.

Foreign correspondence outwards A, 1900-3, 5 vols.

Editorial correspondence, letter books 1832-4, 2 vols.

Editorial correspondence outwards 1832-1908, *c.*27 vols.

Editorial correspondence inwards, letter books 1858-1906, 37 vols.

Editorial department letter registers 1856-60, 1908-12, 1905-26, 22 vols.

Copy correspondence

Three miscellaneous vols., containing copies of correspondence, 1804-5, 1805-9, 1806-10.

Correspondence books containing copies of in- and out-letters, nos.4-12, no.5 missing, 1810-39, 8 vols.

Extracts of correspondence 1881, 1 vol.

Editorial department, extracts from letters 1856-7, 1 vol.

'Account of all the versions and translations printed or executed at the charge of this society', compiled by Thomas Pell Platt, Librarian, 1827-9, 12 vols. Vol.II contains a history of translations of the Scriptures into the Tahitian languages, in the form of quotations from correspondence with missionaries and a few printed extracts from the Society's reports 1816-25.

LONDON SECRETARIES' ASSOCIATION RECORDS

This was an association of secretaries of foreign missionary societies, with head-quarters in London, see J. H. Ritson, *Records of Missionary Secretaries, an Account of the Celebration of the Centenary of the London Secretaries' Association*, London 1920. About thirty societies were represented during the existence of the association, the activities of which were finally merged with those of the Conference of British Missionary Societies. Among members of the Association were William Ellis, Secretary of the London Missionary Society 1833-41, Mesac Thomas, prior to becoming Anglican Bishop of Goulburn, N.S.W., in 1863, Henry H. Montgomery, formerly Bishop of Tasmania 1889-1901, and members of the Moravian La Trobe family.

Minutes of Meetings 1819-20, 1891-1924, 1940-5, 7 vols.

Generally seven meetings were held during the year when topics of mutual interest were discussed; one meeting annually came to be a review of each society's work for the year. Before 1880 the minutes record little more than the chief subject under discussion. No meeting was devoted to discussion of missions in the South Seas, although there are references to the work of the London Missionary Society, the Wesleyan Methodist Missionary Society and the Church Missionary Society in the Pacific and New Zealand. The meeting of Mar. 1839 was a general conversation on the numbers of Roman Catholic missionaries in the southern Pacific, and a criticism of the proceedings of the commander of a French frigate at Tahiti. The volume for minutes of meetings 1911-14 includes a précis of a paper by the Rev. W. O. B. Allen on his impressions formed during a visit to the Australasian colonies, China, and Japan.

BRITISH MUSEUM
Great Russell Street, London, W.C.1

DEPARTMENT OF MANUSCRIPTS

Students must obtain a ticket of admission to the Students' Room in the Depart-ment of Manuscripts by application to the Director's office on a printed form. This is a separate ticket from that required to use the Reading Room for printed books, but both may be applied for on the same form.

The Sloane MSS., purchased in 1753, and the Additional MSS., i.e. 'Additional' to the Sloane collection, the numeration of which they continue, comprise most acquisitions in the Department. Other particular collections bequeathed to the Museum with special endowments are catalogued separately; of these the Egerton MSS. are the only ones to which additions have been made since the original deposit. The Department also holds a few collections on loan from private individuals. Maps and drawings of historical rather than artistic interest are scattered through the collections.

The best summary survey of the contents of the Department, and introduction to the various finding aids is the official publication *The British Museum, The Catalogues of the Manuscript Collections*, T. C. Skeat, revised edition 1962. Full bibliographical details of printed catalogues and indexes are given. The cataloguing of the Sloane and early Additional MSS. is complicated, but the relevant catalogues are listed in detail by Skeat. In November 1969 the catalogue of Additional MSS. after 44835 was not published, but there were proofs of the Catalogue of Additions 1936-45 available, followed by typescript lists covering acquisitions up to the end of 1968,

Add. MS.54564 being the last entry. Summary lists of accessions are printed twice yearly in *The British Museum Quarterly*. Each volume of the printed catalogues has its own index. For accessions 1936-45, Add. MSS.44836-46172, the index was still in galley proof, and entries for later accessions were available only in a rough card index in the Students' Room. When surveying material it has been the general rule to check the catalogue entries initially, to follow this with a further check in the indexes for names and places, and finally to examine manuscripts which appear relevant.

In the following description, the full reference of every item is given, except in the case of Additional MSS. where the reference 'Add. MSS.' is not repeated each time before the number. The type of document is indicated throughout, with the exception of letters, where date, writer and/or recipient immediately follow the reference. Unbound or temporarily bound papers may be unfoliated or have provisional foliation only.

SLOANE MANUSCRIPTS

Sloane MS.45 (2) ff.36-68. 'A general draught of the Islands of Gallapagos', with descriptions by William Ambrose Cowley, n.d. [*c.*1683-6].

Sloane MS.54 Journal Aug. 1683 to Oct. 1686 by William A. Cowley from Cape of Virginia along the west coast of America to Panama, then to the Ladrone Islands, China, Timor, Java, the Cape of Good Hope, and Holland. Another copy is at Sloane MS.1050.

Sloane MS.333 ff.1-22b. Petition *c.*1608 from Pedro Fernandes de Quieros to Philip III, King of Spain, to undertake an expedition to the New Hebrides, English translation.

Sloane MS.3236 Journal 17 Apr. 1681 to 26 June 1691, partly autograph by William Dampier. It contains accounts of journeys and voyages of William Dampier and others in South America and the Pacific, including voyages in the *Cygnet* under Capt. Swan from the coast of Mexico to Mindanao 1686, and under Capt. Read from Mindanao, touching the north-west coast of Australia, 4 Jan. 1688.

Sloane MS.3329 Papers relating to natural history, medicine, etc., collected by Sloane. ff.76-7. Letter 13 June 1715 and scheme of a voyage round the globe for the discovery of Terra Australis Incognita by John Welbe.

Sloane MS.3665 Charts and plans 1688-90 by Capt. J. Kempthorne during his voyage to Bombay including f.64 chart of the Ladrone Isles 1688.

Sloane MS.3986 Miscellaneous, historical, and geographical. ff.43-4. A description of Dampier's *A New Voyage Round the World*, London 1697.

Sloane MS.4044 Letters to Sloane including ff.212-17 letters and proposals 25 Sept. 1715 to 13 Sept. 1716 from John Welbe concerning scheme for the discovery of Terra Australis Incognita, original and manuscript copies.

ADDITIONAL MANUSCRIPTS

5027A Two volumes containing ff.1-89, 118-60 and ff.90-117 respectively.

ff.90-117. Portions of a large general atlas or chart of the world, drawn at Batavia by Dutch artist with initials D.P., 1662-83; ff.100, 114-15 show Endraght's Land on the western coast of Australia.

ff.118-60. Miscellaneous manuscripts in Dutch including a list of the maps on ff.90-117.

5222 Maps and charts, chiefly of parts of the East Indies.

f.12. Chart of the coast of Australia and Van Diemen's Land, showing the islands south of the line and Tasman's voyage of 1644, probably by Thomas Bowrey, Madras 1687. See R. A. Skelton, *Explorers' Maps. Chapters in the Cartographic Record of Geographical Discovery*, London 1960, p.226.

5413 Large chart of the world, probably by Desceliers, *c.*1536-42. ff.25-6. The east portion of the Great Southern Continent called 'Java La Grande'. For further description and dating see *Catalogue of the Manuscript Maps, Charts and Plans of Topographical Drawings* [in the British Museum], 1844, reprinted 1962, 1, pp.24-6, and H. Harrisse, *The Dieppe World Maps 1541-1553*, Göttingen 1899.

5414 Portfolio containing miscellaneous maps and charts.
f.1. Map of the Antarctic regions *c.*1680. Described in *Catalogue of the Manuscript Maps, Charts and Plans of Topographical Drawings*, p.36.
f.27. 'A description of the Islands of Galapagos, delineated exactly according to the prescription of Mr. William Ambrose Cowley, by William Hack', 1685.

5415B Portions of a large outline atlas of the world, *c.*1700 by [?] Philip Jacob Thettott. f.10. Chart of the Philippines and Ladrone Islands with part of New Guinea and part of New Holland, n.d.

7085 'Charts, Plans, Views and Drawings taken on board His Majestys Bark Endeavour in the Years 1768, 1769 and 1770, by Lieutt. Jams Cook, Commander'. Forty-two sketches. The charts and profiles are by Cook, but most of the other drawings are his copies of originals by Parkinson.
f.16. Chart of New Zealand.
f.44. Pencil drawing by Mrs J. King of Aborigines of Fremantle, W.A., 1843.
A list of contents of this volume is in the Bonwick Transcripts in the Mitchell Library, Sydney.

8094-100 Banks Papers
Correspondence 1765-1819 of Sir Joseph Banks, 7 vols. Consists of letters from foreign scientists, botanists and others to Banks with some draft replies. There are many references to voyages especially of Cook, Bougainville, La Pérouse, Baudin, and Flinders in the Pacific, and to collections made by naturalists. See *The Banks Letters*, ed. Dawson.

8945 Papers relating to the navigation of the Indian Seas, 18th cent.
ff.1-2. 'Account of the Rocks Shoals & other Dangers in the Indian N vigation' including some off the west coast of Australia, giving latitude and longitude.
ff.58-9. Letter [5 Mar. 1776] from Cook to Sir John Pringle being a statement of methods used to maintain good health among the crew of H.M.S. *Resolution*, manuscript copy endorsed in Banks's hand.

8946 Tasman's journal 14 Aug. 1642 to 15 June 1643 including drawings of Maoris, Pacific Islanders, etc.; there are also two letters at the beginning of the volume from H. Norris to Dr Solander concerning a Dutch version of the voyage and an English translation of an extract from the journal. For information on this and other Tasman journals see *Abel Janszoon Tasman's Journal of his Discovery of Van Diemen's Land and New Zealand in 1642*, ed. J. E. Heeres, Amsterdam 1898.

8947 Tasman's journal translated into English from the Dutch by Charles Godfrey Woide, 1776. ff.157-8 are 'A Collation of Tasman's Journal with the abstracts published by Valentine, Dalrymple, etc.' and English translation of notes and descriptions accompanying the sketches in Add. MS.8946. A MS. note states that there is a draft translation in Woide's hand, with a covering letter from Woide to Banks in the Alexander Turnbull Library, Wellington.

8951-3 'A log of the Proceedings of and Occurrences on board His Majestys Ship Resolution Upon a Voyage of Discovery towards the St Pole', 23 Nov. 1772 to

21 Mar. 1775, kept by Charles Clerke, 3 vols. Other copies of this log are in Add. MSS.8961-2 and P.R.O.Adm.55/103

8953 ff.101-20. 'Extrait du Voyage fait aux Terres Australes années 1738 & 1739' by Bouvet de Lozier.

8955 Journal 10 Feb. 1776 to 24 Aug. 1779 by Lieut. J. Burney in H.M.S. *Discovery* with notes on charts and addenda to the journal [? to 1780]. Positive microfilm in the University of Hawaii Library.

8958 Papers relating chiefly to New South Wales and the eastern coast of Africa 1811-17.

ff.1-23. Papers including copy journal concerning the crossing of the Blue Mountains by G. Blaxland and his party 1813-16.

f.24. 'Intelligence from the best informed man in New South Wales and one of the oldest settlers there', extract from letter 30 June 1813, Sydney, concerning the prices of wheat and spirits in New South Wales.

f.25. Extract from letter 30 June 1813 concerning Gov. Macquarie's journey to the Blue Mountains.

ff.26-9. A general statement of the inhabitants, land in cultivation and stock as at the general muster in New South Wales 17 Oct. to 16 Nov. 1814.

ff.59-60. Note on Malaspina's voyage 30 July 1789 to 21 Sept. 1794.

8959 Log kept in H.M.S. *Endeavour* 27 May 1768 to 18 July 1771, in two hands. Photostat copy in the Mitchell Library, Sydney.

8960 Complement of H.M.S. *Endeavour* 25 May 1768 to 1 Aug. 1771, giving names, ages, places of birth, dates of entry and discharge.

8961-2 Manuscript copy of log of Charles Clerke (Add. MSS.8951-3), 2 vols.

9345 Sketch book 1768-9 by S. Parkinson in H.M.S. *Endeavour*, mostly pencil and wash sketches; note at beginning of volume reads 'These sketches are by Buchan draughtsman to Mr. Banks'.

9879-81 Notes by Thomas Hardwicke on zoology mainly in the East Indies, but including some references to Australia, c.1815.

9909 Scrapbook containing notes on zoology, mainly in the East Indies including ff.25-6 extracts from Flinders's *A Voyage to Terra Australis*, London 1814, regarding coral reefs.

9944 Relaciones de Viages 1563-9, copies of Spanish documents relating to voyages to the South Seas and New Guinea including the voyage of R. Lopez de Villalobos, Esteuan Rodrigius, Rodrigo de Espinoza, Miguel Lopez de Legaspi, Lope Martinez, Alvaro de Mendaña, Lope Garcia de Castro and Gomez Hernandez Catoira, 1568.

11803 b. 'A Chart of part of the Sea Coast of New South Wales on the East Coast of New Holland from Cape Palmerston to Cape Flattery by Lieut. James Cook, Commander of H.M. Bark the Endeavour, 1770', including Whitsunday Passage, Green and Magnetic Islands, Q'ld.

c. 'A Chart . . . from Cape Morton to Cape Palmerston by Lieut. James Cook . . . 1770', including Wide Bay, Cape Capricorn, Q'ld.

d. Unnamed draft of the above coastlines.

e. Plan of the settlements in New South Wales by C. Grimes, Deputy Surveyor General, 1796, with a list of settlers' names and a key to their holdings, showing acreage.

e.* 'Observations upon the chart of Bass's Straits combined under the direction of Capt. P. G. King, Governor of N.S.W., by Ensign Barrallier', printed.

f. Map of Botany Bay, Port Jackson, and Broken Bay, showing land allotted west as far as Mt Banks, with key; marked in pencil 'Cayley 1805', n.d.

g. 'Chart of Port Dalrymple and the River Tamer on the North Coast of Van Diemen's Land. From the entrance to Crescent Shore as surveyed by Capt Flinders in the Norfolk Colonial Sloop in 1798 . . . by Mr Collins, 1804 . . . [and] by Lt. Coln Paterson, 1805'.

h, i, k, l, m. Five charts of the eastern coast of the North Island, N.Z., from Cavalle Head to Cape Runaway, including Bay of Islands, Hawke's Bay, and Poverty Bay, showing Cook's track in the *Endeavour*, 1769. Three are unnamed draft charts.

12564-3915 Wellesley Papers
   Correspondence and papers of Richard Colley Wellesley, 1st Marquess Wellesley.

13710 Drafts of letters from Lord Wellesley and the Government Secretaries to various persons 1798-1805.

ff.102-3. 19 Apr. 1801 to Gov. King, regarding the escaped convict, Thomas Parnel, 'surgeon', apprehended in Calcutta.

ff.134-5. 31 Mar. 1802 to King thanking him for Capt. John Black's map of Bass Strait; also acknowledging King's letter 29 Sept. and promising to pay regard to Mr Tennant, Commander of the *Earl Cornwallis*.

13712 Drafts of letters 1799-1805 from Lord Wellesley to various persons. ff.151-2. 2 Mar. 1804 to Gov. King concerning a free pardon for Mr Bellasis, formerly of the East India Company's military establishment, Bombay, given management of battery and artillery in New South Wales.

13880 Journal May 1798 to June 1800 by John Washington Price, surgeon, kept on board the transport *Minerva* from Ireland to New South Wales and Bengal, describing the preparation and embarkation at Cork, with a list of the crew, New South Wales Corps detachments, families, and convicts. With drawings of coastal views, fauna, natives, and buildings in Sydney.

13974-5 Copies of official reports and other papers relating to Spanish America, etc., many endorsed by, or addressed to Don Bernardo de Yriarte, member of the Council of the Indies, 17th-18th cent., 2 vols.

13974 ff.184-91. Reports of Pedro Fernandes de Quieros [1612?] and Andres de Medina Davila, printed.

ff.210-25. Draft of introduction, etc., to a projected edition of the voyages of Pedro Fernandes de Quieros and Alvaro de Mendaña, by D. Bernardo de Yriarte, 1784.

13976 'Papeles varios de Indias.' ff.164-76. [*B.M. Cat.* f.163] Description of Juan Fernandez, 1797. f.183. 'Notas de las Yslas que en el ano pasado de 1767 descubrio. . . el Capitan Wallis, mandando el Navio de S.M.B. nombrado el Delphin; con expresion de sus Latitudes, y Longitudes segun el Meridiano de Londres'. [*B.M. Cat.*: f.182 Islands in the South Pacific discovered by Capt. Wallis, 1767.]

ff.184-93. 'Declaracion que hizo en el Ferrol el marinero ingles Pedro Farron de la tripulacion del Delfin al mando del capitan Wallis', Ferrol, 26 Dec. 1768.

13984 Papers relating to Spanish possessions in America, Vol.I. ff.120-33. 'Observaciones sobre el comercio' mentioning the route from Acapulco to the Philippines, n.d. [18th cent.].

13992 Official papers and tracts connected with the Spanish colonies in America, 17th cent. ff.610-23 include papers discussing trade routes to the Philippines.

15331 Chart of the Southern Hemisphere, showing chart of *Endeavour*'s track, after Cook's original, 1775. French, 'Voyage du Capitaine Cook au tour du Pole Antarctique, 1772 à 1775'.

15499 ff.1-12. Short journal by Capt. Samuel Wallis.

ff.13-31. Nineteen charts, mainly of islands, drawn by G. Pinnock, midshipman in H.M.S. *Dolphin* during the voyage of discovery to the South Seas 21 Aug. 1766 to 14 Jan. 1767.

15500 Twenty-two charts with views of headlands and coasts taken during Cook's voyage in the *Resolution* through the Pacific and Southern Ocean 1772-4.

15507 Guard-book containing eighty-four drawings, some coloured, mainly of headlands and islands 1768-70; after Buchan's death most are by Parkinson and some in New Zealand by Spöring. ff.42-3. Incomplete extracts 19 June from journals, being a page from a log book of the *Discovery*, and some other pages with brief comments on New Zealand and Alaska.

15508 Guard-book containing forty-eight drawings by Buchan, Parkinson, and others, made during the voyage of the *Endeavour* 1768-70. Over half are finished wash drawings by J. F. Miller; others are of ethnographic subjects, made after the voyage.

15513-14 Two volumes containing ninety-one drawings by J. Webber during Cook's third voyage in the South Seas 1777-9.

15716 Journal of a voyage 1830-3 towards the South Seas on the *Tula*, commander Capt. John Biscoe, in company with the *Lively*, equipped by Messrs C. and G. Enderby, with related papers.
f.1. Letter 23 Jan. 1846 C. and G. Enderby to the Trustees of the British Museum presenting the journal.
ff.6-50. Journal of the voyage 14 July 1830 to 1 Feb. 1833, the purpose being to find fresh sealing grounds. Entries include: f.25, 28 Feb. 1831, first sight of Australian Antarctic territory; ff.30-1, 30 Oct. 1831, description of Bay of Islands; f.37, 15 Feb. 1832, discovery of Adelaide Is.; f.38, 19 Feb. 1832, naming of Pitts Is.
ff.51-5. Rough pencil sketch of the *Tula* and various headlands, including Adelaide.

15743 Portfolio containing collection of large drawings made by William Hodges during Cook's second voyage 1772-4.

15855 Original book of orders and letters July 1740 to Dec. 1743 of Commodore George Anson during his voyage round the world in the *Centurion*.

16368 g. Sketch of two expeditions sent by Lieut.-Gen. Ralph Darling into the interior of New Holland 1828-30, by Capt. Charles Sturt. Also cutting entitled 'Discovery of the termination of the great interior rivers of Australia: extract of a letter from N.S.W.', n.d. [late Sept. 1830].

16381-3 Southwell Papers
Correspondence and papers of Daniel Southwell, mate of H.M.S. *Sirius*.
16381 ff.13-39. May 1787 to May 1789 to his uncle, the Rev. Weeden Butler, and to his mother, Jane Southwell, describing the voyage to New Holland and then to the Cape of Good Hope.
ff.44-51. 14 Apr. 1790 to Rev. W. Butler stating he is under orders to take charge of the lookout station on South Head while the *Sirius* and *Supply* visit Norfolk Island; describes the wreckage of the *Sirius*.
f.52 Diagram 1790, projection of a column raised as a mark for shipping at the South Head of Port Jackson by Gov. Phillip. (Enclosure to ff.67-76 27 July 1790, Southwell to Rev. W. Butler.)
ff.53-114. July 1790 to Sept. 1791 mainly to his uncle and mother describing the settlements, and his return voyage in the Dutch transport *Waaksamheyd*.
16382 a-d. Journal and log Dec. 1787 to May 1791 of Daniel Southwell in H.M.S. *Sirius*, one of a fleet of ships despatched to form a penal settlement at Botany Bay. Includes account of the journey out, arrival at, and description of Botany Bay, description of the Kilinailau or Carteret Islands, observation of the Aurora Australis and other meteorological details, and an account of Duke of York's Island.
16383 ff.2-146, 161-85. May 1787 to Aug. 1790, copies by Rev. Weeden Butler of the letters of Daniel Southwell to his mother and uncle, containing the account of

the expedition to Botany Bay 1787-90. Originals of letters, with the exception of ff.63-106, 108-22, 12 July 1788, Sydney Cove, are in Add. MS.16381. Occasional words have been altered in the copies.

ff.147-9. A list of words used by the natives of Port Jackson.

ff.151-9. Account of an engagement with the natives at Manly Bay. The journal and letters of Daniel Southwell have been printed in *H.R.N.S.W.* II, pp.661-734.

17101 ff.30-1. 8 Aug. 1817 Queen Pomare of Otaheite, to Capt. Walker of the *King George* requesting spare provisions.

17277 Miscellany containing 51ff. of drawings and sketches made by J. Webber during Cook's third voyage 1776-9.

17542-51 Logs, journals and astronomical observations of the *Discovery*, Capt. G. Vancouver, and the *Chatham*, Lieut. Broughton, during the voyage to the South Seas 1791-5, 10 vols. The logs of the *Discovery* were kept by Lieut. P. Puget.

17552 Various papers 1791-5 relating to the above, especially ff.1-6, 8-9, 12-14 relating to the *Chatham* Dec. 1790 to Aug. 1791.

17583 Miscellaneous papers, Spanish. ff.308-10. Route from Acapulco to Manila, by Bartholome Alcorrea, pilot.

17621 Accounts of various voyages to the Straits of Magellan, Spanish. ff.1-20. Route of the voyage of Hernando de Magellanes from Cabo de San Agustin by Francisco Albo, 29 Nov. 1519 to 4 Sept. 1522, copy made 1783.

17622 Navigation in the South Seas, Spanish.

ff.40-4. Route from Puerto de Cavite in the Bay of Manila to Acapulco taken from D. Jose Gonzalez Cabrera Bueno, *Navegacion Especulativa y Practica*, Manila 1734.

ff.43-4. Return from the Philippines.

ff.93-4. [f.91 *B.M. Cat.*] Route from Spain to the Philippines.

ff.113-16. Unpublished hydrographic observations by D. Alexandro Malaspina, Manila, 1792, including f.115 Marianas.

ff.154-5. 'Viage de Dixon'. This covers Dixon's fur-trading voyages 13 Jan. 1786 to Feb. 1788, while he wintered in the Sandwich Islands and sailed north to Nutka in the spring.

ff.156-7. Extract translated from the *Gazette de France* 8 Oct. 1788 covering La Pérouse's voyages in *La Boussole* and *l'Astrolabe*, from 1 Aug. 1785 until his arrival in Kamschatka Sept. 1787.

17623 Discovery of the Solomon Islands by Hernando Gallego, native of Corñua, 1566, Spanish.

17624 'Yslas Filipinas y Oceano Pacifico', Spanish.

ff.25-63. 'Reflexiones Politicas sobre las Yslas Filipinas y Marianas', by Malaspina.

ff.64-77. 'Examen politico de las Colonias Yngleses en el Mar Pacifico', by Malaspina.

17625 Geographical and other papers, mostly relating to the Philippine Islands.

ff.1-44. Voyage of Pedro Fernandez de Quiros to Terra Australis Incognita by Gaspar Gonzalez de Leza, pilot, 1605. An early 19th cent. copy in two different hands, printed in M. Fernandez de Navarrete, *Viages y Descubrimientos de los Españoles*, Madrid 1825-37, 5 vols.

ff.82-91. Memorial by Pedro Fernandez de Quiros on his discoveries in the Southern Hemisphere; voyage of discovery of Alvaro de Mendaña de Neyra to the Solomon Islands; memorial by Pedro Fernandez de Quiros on the discovery of the southern lands which lie *c.*15°S [New Hebrides].

f.92. Notes on some islands in the Marianas, by Don M. F. de Navarrete, imperfect.

ff.93-5. Map of the Caroline or Palau Is., with description.

ff.104-6. Notes on Murray Island and Torres Strait, from a map made on board *La Claudina* 7 Sept. [?], 19th cent. copy.

17627 A journal of Hernando de la Torre's expedition to the Philippine Islands under the command of F. Garcia de Loaysa, 1525-7, Spanish.

17630 Routes by Alonzo da Riva, 1809, being fifty navigation routes, including several to the Philippine Islands, Spanish.

ff.49-52. Routes from the Philippines to Cadiz, both by Cape Horn and the Cape of Good Hope.

ff.53-5. Route from Manila to Peru, quoting authorities including Cook and Malaspina.

ff.56-62. Navigation south and west of the Philippines; f.57 route from Lima to Manila, f.58 San Blas, California, to Manila and f.59 return.

17631 'Vocabulario Castellano, Nutkeno, Sandwich y Mexicano', by J. E. Santeliz es Pablo, 1791.

17634 Mostly 18th cent. geographical notes in Spanish.

ff.40-64. Miscellaneous notes covering the East Indies and New Guinea, New Holland and Pacific Islands; based on observations taken from, *inter alia*, D'Entrecasteaux, Vancouver, Cook, and Bligh.

ff.65-118. Observations taken on voyages from Cadiz to Lima, Acapulco and the Philippines 1764-94, by D. F. Ali-Ponzoni, including ff.93-110 Manila to Port Jackson, Port Jackson to the Vavau Islands [Tonga], Vavau Islands to Lima, 16 Nov. 1792 to 24 July 1793.

f.243. Extract from a Pacific voyage 1780-1, by Don Francisco Mansell, from the diary of his pilot, Don Josef Basquez.

17636 Geographical collections of Don Felipe Bauza. f.219. Voyage round the world in the *Uranie* and *Physicienne* by Louis de Freycinet and others 1817-20, giving extracts of positions of places in New Holland, Timor, Moluccas, Islas Papous [?New Guinea], Caroline, Mariana and Sandwich Islands, Port Jackson, and others, French.

17637 f.50. Estimated position of the island of Patrocinio seen by *La Pilar*, captain D. Miguel Zapican, Spanish.

ff.50b-51. Extract from the diary of J. Magee, captain of the *Margaret* of Boston, on his voyage from Canton to America, 14 Dec. 1795, Spanish.

f.53. Discovery of an island, 25°S and 166°12′E, by Capt. Ray of the American brig *Hope*, 22 Dec. 1801, Spanish.

f.57b. Eclipse of the sun, Port Jackson [1817], Spanish.

f.127. Geographical observations by Royal Navy officers, Spanish.

f.129b. Extracts from log of *Challenger*, Capt. Fremantle, 9 Nov. 1828 to 31 Dec. 1829, mentioning Swan River, Spanish.

ff.139-41. Table of positions by Capt. Beechey on his Pacific voyage, Spanish.

ff.177-83. Contain mention of Juan Fernandez, Enderby Islands, Fead Islands to the east of New Ireland, and Goodman's Islands [c.1815-25], Spanish.

17642 Coloured plans of towns and bays in the Philippine and other islands of the Indian Archipelago including copy plan of the bay of San Phelipe and Santiago in the Island of Espiritu Santo, New Hebrides, and copy of plan of the bay of San Pedro de Arlanca and the ports of San Lucas and San Juan del Prado in the Tierra de Santiago de los Papuas, both by Capt. Diego de Prado y Tovar.

17647 A. Map of the world with boundary line for Spanish and Portuguese showing discoveries in the Pacific, 17th cent., Portuguese. C. Map [post 1788] showing the Pacific north of the Sandwich Islands from about 15°N, Spanish.

18209 Military plans, 17th-19th cent. f.12. Chart of Gordon River, V.D.L., n.d.

9034 Admiralty papers relating to affairs of commerce in connection with the trade with Spain and Portugal 1706-69, including papers by Capt. Rogers, Capt. G. Shelvocke, and H. Hutchinson relating to the South Seas.

19264 Reflections on the English settlements in New Holland, including routes between English settlements in Asia and New Holland, and between South America and the Philippines, signed Don Francisco Muñoz de San Clemente, 18th cent., Spanish.

19293 Authenticated abstract of thirty official journals of voyages 1699-1740 from the Philippine Islands to New Spain, from originals in the public archives in Manila, 22 Nov. 1742, Spanish.

19294 Extracts in English from Add. MS.19293 [? by Alexander Dalrymple, hydrographer to the East India Co.], 18th cent.

19297 'Of the embocadero and track of the galeon to Manila' from the Marianas; an English translation by Adm. Sir Hyde Parker from the *Cronica di S. Gregorio*, 18th cent.

19301 Journal 23 Aug. 1790 to 28 Dec. 1792 of a voyage from Bombay to the Pelew Islands in the *Panther* by Capt. John McCluer. See J. P. Hockin, *A Supplement to the Account of the Pelew Islands*, London 1803.

19572 'Relacion del Estado del Peru: en el Gobierno del Exmo Senor Virrey Don Manuel de Amat y Jurieu [for Junient]', Lima 1776, Spanish. See B. G. Corney, *The Quest and Occupation of Tahiti*, 1, Hakluyt Society, Series II, Vol.XXXII, 1913-15, pp.1-20, a translation of Part II, Ch.24 of the MS., dealing with the voyages of the *Aguila*, commander Don Domingo Boenechea, to Tahiti, 1772-6.

19953-5 Grey Papers
   Papers presented by Sir George Grey.
   19953-4 Drawings and sketches 1845-53 illustrative of New Zealand*.
 19953 New Zealand pictorial scrapbook 1845-53 by A. Sinclair, Cuthbert Clarke, and J. Merret, containing water-colours and sketches of landscapes and Maoris.
19954 Water-colours, drawings, lithographs, and sketches 1848-53 illustrating New Zealand scenery by C. Heaphy, C. Clarke, G. F. Swainson, C. D. Barraud, J. O. Hamley, C. J. Bosquet, and others, including: ff.83-8. 'The Legend of Hineomoa' by C. D. Barraud with sepia illustrations and Maori motif frames.
f.93 Sketches of Isle of Pines and Loyalty Is. by C. Heaphy.
f.102. Sketches in the New Hebrides by G. F. Swainson.
19955 Cuthbert Clarke's diary 5 Dec. 1849 to 19 Feb. 1850.* Diary of a journey in the suite of Sir George Grey, Governor of New Zealand, from Auckland to Taranaki, including sketches of scenery and natives and a sketch of Bishop Selwyn, 6 Dec. 1849.

20161 List of ships arriving at and departing from St Helena 14 Apr. 1816 to 4 June 1821 including those from and to Australia or whaling grounds, with some passenger lists.

21239 Log Oct. 1786 to Oct. 1787 of Joseph Woodcock in H.M.S. *King George*, Cmdr Nathaniel Portlock, on a voyage round the globe accompanied by the *Queen Charlotte*, Cmdr George Dixon. It covers Owhyee, Sandwich Isles, and N.W. America.
f.1. pencil portrait of Woodcock.

21593 Charts and maps made during voyages of discovery in the South Pacific 1767-99. Besides charts connected with Cook's first voyage to the Pacific there are: 'A Draught of the Straits of Magellan taken on board His Majts Ship Dolphin' by Pickersgill 1767; Survey of Botany and Broken Bays and Port Jackson in New South Wales, Capt. Hunter, n.d.; Southern coast of New South Wales, Bass Strait, and Van Diemen's Land showing the tracks of the *Francis* 1798 and the *Norfolk* 1798-9 from Port Jackson by Flinders, and the track of the whaleboat by G. Bass; 'Sketch of the Parts between Van Diemen's Land and New South Wales. Seen in the Francis schooner in 1798', by Flinders.

22935 Original letters 1760-1813 from eminent botanists to Antoine Gouan, Professor of Botany at Montpellier, French. ff.321-2. 11 Apr. 1788 J. E. Smith, London, mentioning the newly-formed Linnean Society and that Banks had finished the plates for his work on the plants of the Pacific.

23618 Drawings and plans c.1830 executed by or under orders of Lieut.-Col. C. Hamilton-Smith.
No.27. Ports in Australia: Port Phillip and Western Port, Jervis Bay, entrance of Port Hunter, Moreton Bay and Brisbane River, Broken Bay, Botany Bay, Port Macquarie, Twofold Bay, and Port Stephens.
No. 66. Ports in New South Wales: harbour in Port Jackson and Port Hunter.

23920-1 Two guard-books containing 'A Collection of Drawings made in the countries visited by Capt. Cook in his First Voyage also of Prints Published in Hawkesworths Voyages of Biron [Byron] Wallis and Cook as well as Cook's second and third voyages'. The books contain 167 drawings of the first voyage and some of the later voyages by Buchan, Parkinson, Miller, Spöring, Hodges, Cleveley, Webber, and others.

24126 'Manuel hydrographique . . . Marseille 1782', including f.116, short list of Philippine and Mariana Islands.

25612 ff.4-7. 1 Nov. 1808 Matthew Flinders, Isle of France, to M. Barbe de Marbois, Minister of the Public Treasury, Paris, pleading against his unjust imprisonment on the island.

27392 Maps and plans, mostly 18th cent., include a rough map of Bass Strait signed by [Lieut.] J. G[rant].

27885 Part of log 18 Feb. to 23 Sept. 1770 of Cook in *Endeavour*, holograph. An earlier portion is at Add. MS.27955.

27886 Journal 28 Nov. 1771 to 10 Nov. 1774 of Cook in *Resolution* with notes signed by Joseph Gilbert.

27887 Log 30 Nov. 1771 to 28 Dec. 1774 of Cook in *Resolution*, first leaf missing, last leaf Cook's holograph. Fair copy of Add. MS.27956.

27888 Journal, prepared for publication by Cook, of his second voyage round the world in the *Resolution*, holograph.

27889 Holograph fragments of Cook's second voyage, but including at ff.83-96 part of journal 6-21 Oct. 1769 of William Brougham Monkhouse containing account of New Zealand.

27890 Journal 13 July 1772 to 3 Mar. 1774 of Capt. Tobias Furneaux in *Adventure*, copy with Cook's holograph corrections.

27955 'Continuation of the Endeavour Log Book' 5 Nov. 1768 to 8 May 1769, Cook's holograph. A later portion is at Add. MS.27885.

27956 Log 16 Oct. 1773 to 28 July 1775 by Cook in the *Resolution*, holograph.

27958 'The resolution's Quarter Bill. James Cook Esq., Commander', n.d., with f.3, muster table Nov. 1771 to June 1772.

30170 Miscellaneous papers, A-O.
ff.12-13. Account of a survey of the Aurora Isles [Shag Rocks, Antarctica] by the French corvette *L'Atrevida* Jan.-Feb. 1794, French, incomplete.
ff.14-22. Remarks 1821 by Capt. Robert Fildes on the topography and natural history of New South Shetland in the Southern Seas.

30262 Miscellaneous autographs, A-W. ff.11-12. 28 Apr. 1776 R. E. Raspe, Chelsea, to Cook, suggesting mineralogical observations to be made during his third voyage.

30369 Journal 1793-4 of a voyage for whaling and discovery around Cape Horn into the Pacific in the *Rattler* by Lieut. James Colnett, R.N., with maps and coloured views. The journal was printed in 1798.

31158-93 St Vincent Papers

Correspondence, registers, logs, and journals of Adm. Sir John Jervis, subsequently Earl of St Vincent.

31169 Letter book 20 Feb. 1801 to 20 Feb. 1806 to 'Commander-in-Chief' and to others. f.104. 20 Mar. 1801 to Sir Andrew Hamond suggesting that application be made to the French Government for a passport for H.M.S. *Investigator* going out upon discovery, with a reference to Flinders.

31343 Maps and plans of countries in Asia: W/2. New Plymouth and district, N.Z., traced from a photograph taken at South Kensington Museum 1860, showing English cultivation, wild land, native lands, English defences, and native pas occupied; X/2. Coast and river survey n.d. from Nelson to the River Grey, N.Z., John Rochfort, surveyor.

31346 Maps of Australia: A. Plan 1849 of the triangulation of South Australia by Capt. E. C. Frome, R.E.; B. Settled districts of South Australia as divided into counties 1849 by Frome; C. Chart 1855 showing the gold districts of Sandhurst and Castlemaine, Vic., compiled by R. B. Smyth.

31347 Maps of New Zealand: A. Map n.d. of New Zealand; B. Southern part of the province of Auckland 1859 by F. von Hochstetter, showing rapids, waterfalls, hot springs, native settlements.

31360 Sixty-seven charts and maps *c.*1760-80 illustrating the voyages and surveys of Cook and other discoverers.

32439-41 Brown Papers

Correspondence and papers of Robert Brown. Most of the correspondence is relevant, selected papers only are described here.

32439 Relates chiefly to the expedition with Flinders and to Brown's stay in Australia. A number of the letters are printed in *H.R.N.S.W.* IV-VI. Letters include Admiralty letters concerning the appointment of scientists and artists, correspondence of Banks, Brown, Flinders (covering both the expedition and captivity), Gov. King, and Dryander, also:

f.51. 5 Nov. 1801 J. Crossley, Cape of Good Hope, to Rev. Dr Maskelyne, telling of his illness and return.

ff.80-1. Nov. 1802 Flinders to J. Aken, and Aken's report on the condition of H.M.S. *Investigator*, copy.

ff.102-3. 17 July 1803 Flinders, Sydney Cove, to Brown and Bauer arranging for them to remain whilst he returns to England.

ff.140-1. Memorials Sept. 1803 to Banks from woollen manufacturers of York on obtaining wool from New South Wales, and his draft reply.

ff.248-9. 6 Apr. 1806 G. Caley, Parramatta, to Banks on visits to Norfolk Island and his collections.

32440-1 Further correspondence 1813-58 received by Robert Brown while Librarian of the Linnean Society, Keeper of Sir Joseph Banks' Library, and after his appointment at the British Museum. Included are letters from G. Caley, J. B. Leschenault, A. Cunningham, W. Baxter, R. C. Gunn, J. E. Bicheno, and Rev. W. B. Clarke.

ff.298-9. 28 Oct. 1835 P. G. King, Penrith, N.S.W., to Brown on Richard Cunningham's death and the progress of Sydney.

ff.379-82. 27 Feb. 1843 Sir Robert Peel, London, stating that Mrs Flinders's pension could not be increased, and subsequent correspondence, including ff.466-9, 10 Sept. 1858 P. G. King, Sydney, to Brown announcing the granting of pensions to Mrs Flinders from the Governments of New South Wales and Victoria.

32450 W. Plan of allotments, South Melton, near Melbourne, n.d.

32451 B/2. George W. Evans, deputy surveyor to the government, map *c*.1813-14 of New South Wales 'including the new discovered country to the west of the Blue Mountains'.

32641 Journal Dec. 1790 to 16 Feb. 1794 of Archibald Menzies, surgeon R.N., botanist in the *Discovery*, Capt. Vancouver. This journal extends only to the third visit of the expedition to the Sandwich Islands. See G. Vancouver, *A Voyage of Discovery to the North Pacific Ocean and round the World*, London 1798, 3 vols., and A. Menzies, *Hawaii Nei*, [ed. W. F. Wilson], Honolulu 1920.

33100-30 Pelham Papers
 General and official correspondence and papers of Thomas Pelham, Baron Pelham and 2nd Earl of Chichester.

33105 ff.242-3, 260-1. 21 Nov., 12 Dec. 1797 from Sir Jerome Fitzpatrick to John King, Under-Secretary of State for Home Affairs, seeking improved methods of embarkation and better provisions for convicts sent to New South Wales.

33106 ff.138-9, 162-3. 18 Nov. 1798, 8 Jan. 1799 from Fitzpatrick to William Baldwin on safeguarding the health of convicts on hulks.

ff.362-4. 16 Apr. 1800 Fitzpatrick to John King regarding conditions for convicts.

33107 ff.200-3. 30 July 1801 Fitzpatrick to Rev. Charles Lindsay concerning the health and security of convicts shortly to be sent from Ireland to New South Wales in the *Hercules* and *Atlas*, copy.

ff.341-5. 23 Aug. 1801 Fitzpatrick to Pelham drawing attention to conditions of convicts, especially those sentenced to transportation. Also ff.372-4, 403-4, 412-13, letters 27 Aug., 2, 3 Sept. 1801 on the same subject.

ff.476-7. 13 Sept. 1801 William M. Pitt to Pelham concerning the transportation of convicts in gaol at Dorchester.

33108 ff.299-309. 19 Nov. 1801 Patrick Colquhoun to Pelham, with 'suggestions for improving the national police . . . and relieving the country of the expence arising from the conviction, maintenance and transportation of convicts'.

ff.380-1, 444-5. 30 Nov., 11 Dec. 1801 Rev. Brownlow Forde, Ordinary of Newgate Prison, to Pelham suggesting St John's Island in the Gulf of St Lawrence as a more suitable destination for convicts than New South Wales.

ff.411-20. 5 Dec. 1801 William M. Pitt to Pelham detailing a plan for a commission to inquire into the state of the prisons, with an estimate of the expense of conducting hulks.

f.480. 29 Dec. 1801 Capt. John Hunter, London, to Pelham asking that he and other commissioners may be appointed to visit and report on abuses and conditions in New South Wales.

33109 ff.331-6. 9 Aug. 1802 Jeremy Bentham to Sir Charles Bunbury, the Panopticon versus New South Wales, a comparative view of the penitentiary and the new penal colonisation system, with marginal contents, dated 10 Aug. 1802.

33110 ff.38-42. 18 Oct. 1802 Rev. Brownlow Forde to Pelham 'hints for the prevention of crime', with comments on the hulks, which 'neither deter nor reform'.

ff.318-22. Memo 31 Dec. 1802 Sir Richard Ford to Pelham concerning the transportation of convicts to New South Wales, with unfavourable comments on the Panopticon plan.

33115 ff.56-7. Mar. 1802 George III to Pelham with instructions to correct abuses in the hulks, favouring transportation of convicts, as opposed to retaining them in hulks.

33122 ff.40-51. Memorial 21 Apr. 1800 from Jeremy Bentham concerning the site of the proposed penitentiary, including a map, with his signature and memos in pencil.

ff.61-2. List of types of tradesmen, labourers, etc., who sailed as convicts from Portsmouth to New South Wales in the *Canada* and *Minorca* 21 June 1801.

ff.71-6. 1801 on improved conditions for transported convicts.

ff.77-8. Lists 1801 of numbers of convicts which have been and will be sent annually to New South Wales.

ff.89-90. List of all ships taken up by the Transport Board for New South Wales, specifying their cargoes, rates of pay and respective times of sailing.

ff.91-2. Dorset Gaol and House of Correction: summary of the number of criminals in custody with details of trials and sentences 24 June 1801 to 24 June 1802.

ff.180-1. Proposal for transportation of convicts in ships belonging to the government. 33124 ff.109-16. *c.*1800 John Mawe to Pelham on proposed project for a mineralogical expedition to New South Wales.

33209 Dictionary and grammar of the Duke of York Island language by Rev. G. Brown and Rev. B. Danks, with an introduction by Rev. G. Brown, Sydney, 1882, carbon copy.

33233 f.40. Water-colour n.d. of Hobart Town.

33537-64 Bentham Papers
     Correspondence, papers, and works of Jeremy Bentham.

33541 ff.160-5. Correspondence Sept. 1790 mainly between Bentham and Sir John Parnell, Irish Chancellor of the Exchequer, discussing the possibility of establishing a Penitentiary House or Panopticon in Ireland to supersede the present system of transportation of convicts.

ff. 383-4. Feb. 1793 Bentham to Evan Nepean concerning Chapman, a convict sentenced to transportation to Botany Bay.

33542 ff.45-6. 16 Apr. 1795 Sir John Parnell to Bentham preparing a clause in an Act of Parliament to empower the Lord Lieutenant at his discretion to use the money allotted for transporting convicts to employ them at labour.

ff.82-3, 86-7. 10, 12 July 1795 from Sir Charles Bunbury to Bentham regarding the fate of Richard Coates, sentenced to transportation.

33543 ff.423-4. 7 Oct. 1800 Mrs Patterson, Port Jackson, to Mrs B[?] concerned by the number of Irish sent to the colony, and the lack of protection for settlers there [copy?].

ff.601-2. 8 Aug. 1802 Sir Samuel Romilly, Solicitor General, to Bentham admitting astonishment at the law regarding Botany Bay.

ff.603-6. 29 Aug. 1802 Bentham to Etienne Dumont discussing the Panopticon and penal colonisation.

ff.611-18. 3 Sept. 1802 Bentham to Charles Abbot on the illegality of the New South Wales system of penal colonisation, copy.

ff. 619-20. 6 Sept. 1802 Bentham to William Wilberforce asking for facts on conditions in New South Wales.

33544 ff.14-15. 24 Jan. 1803 G. Lee, *Portland* hulk, Langston Harbour, to Sir Henry Mildmay describing, from personal experience, conditions on hulks.

f.37. n.d. James Nield to Bentham transmitting f.32 a letter 13 Feb. 1803, from Sir J. Carter to Sir Henry Mildmay on the state of the convicts.

ff.41-2. 22 Feb. 1803 Bentham to Samuel Bentham mentioning the plans of Lieut.-Col. David Collins to establish another settlement on the south coast of Australia.

33545 ff.443-6. Sept. 1820 [?Bentham to Samuel Bentham], partly in French, possibly several writers. Contains references to botanical collections, Botany Bay and Van Diemen's Land.

33609 Railway map of Australia Dec. 1888, revised to Mar. 1889, by G. Jeffrey and Alfred E. Middleton.

33977-82 Banks Papers
Letters addressed to Sir Joseph Banks, chiefly on botany and other natural history subjects, written from foreign parts, occasionally with drafts of replies. See *The Banks Letters*, ed. Dawson.

34412-71 Auckland Papers
Correspondence and papers of William Eden, 1st Baron Auckland.

34414 ff.473-85. Observations 29 Dec. 1777 submitted by William Smith M.D. to Auckland on the subject of hard labour to be substituted for transportation, printed.

34458 ff.382-4. Correspondence Aug.-Sept. 1812 between Auckland and Lord Sidmouth, the former insisting on the need for more positive action to prevent immoral practices on ships taking female convicts to Botany Bay.

34466 ff.55-8. Memoir 11 June 1783 of the Dutch East India Company presented to the States General, on the interference with their trade in New Guinea by the Portuguese and the support afforded to the latter by the English, French.

ff.130-7. 19 Oct. 1785 'Promemoire' on the subject given by the Portuguese Minister at The Hague to Sir James Harris, English Ambassador, French.

34486 ff.56-9. 6 Oct. c.1863, 30 Sept. c.1866 from Charles Darwin to Samuel Butler suggesting that he might write an interesting description of a colonist's life in New Zealand, and inquiring if he intended to return to New Zealand.

34567-82 Bliss Papers
Correspondence of Rev. Philip Bliss.

34578 ff.76-7. 8 June 1850 Thomas Jackson, Bishop Designate of the projected see of Lyttelton, N.Z., Battersea, to Rev. Bliss stating his pleasure at the interest shown at Oxford in the colony.

ff.156-7. 3 Oct. 1850 Thomas Jackson, Devonport, to Rev. Bliss, reminding him of his promise to buy fifty acres of land in the Canterbury settlement.

34580 f.72. 2 Dec. 185[4] and 34582 ff.193-6, 306, 435-9, 638-41, eight letters 1849-54 Edmund Hobhouse, later Bishop of Nelson, N.Z., to Rev. Bliss, on minor ecclesiastical matters.

34611-30 Macvey Napier Papers
34620 ff.389-90. 20 Sept. 1839 Sir James Stephen to Napier, editor of the *Edinburgh Review*, stating that 'Mr. Wakefield does me the unmerited and undesirable honour of devoting some part of his Journal to my service'.

34625 ff.32-3. 25 Jan. 1845 Stephen to Napier concerning the New Zealand story. ff.436-9. 6 Oct. 1845 Stephen to Napier concerning transportation and convict management in the penal colonies.

34727-47 West Papers
Papers of James West and members of his family.

34744 ff.38-44. Correspondence of Sir Joseph Banks and Dr Daniel Charles Solander concerning their reception at Rio de Janiero on board the *Endeavour* 1768. See *The Banks Letters*, ed. Dawson.

35141 Journal of George Peard, first lieutenant on H.M.S. *Blossom*, Cmdr Frederick William Beechey, during a cruise to the Pacific and Bering Strait 19 May 1825 to 23 May 1828, including a visit to Pitcairn Island. The narrative of John Adams, alias Alexander Smith, a survivor of the mutineers of H.M.S. *Bounty*, was first obtained in full on this occasion and is here given at some length at ff.10b-20. See

London

F. W. Beechey, *Narrative of a Voyage to the Pacific and Beering's Strait to Co-operate with the Polar Expeditions: performed in His Majesty's Ship Blossom . . . in the years 1825, 26, 27, 28*, London 1831.

35142-54 Place Papers
   Papers and correspondence of Francis Place.
35142 ff.240-2. Account of the role played by Francis Place in having his brother-in-law, Mat. Stimson, under sentence of death for highway robbery, transported to Botany Bay.
35149 ff.60-7. Correspondence 7 Apr. 1831 between Francis Place and Major A. W. Beauclerk discussing emigration and the weakness of Wilmot Horton's plan.
ff.148-9. 1 June 1832 Harriet Martineau to Francis Place asking for facts regarding the attitude of the poorer classes towards emigration and transportation.
ff.198-200. 10 Oct. 1832 Francis Place to Henry Wilson disagreeing with Capt. Brenton's ideas for the disposal of poor boys, and suggesting they be sent to the colonies.
35150 ff.92-5. Correspondence 19, 29 Nov. 1835 between Francis Place and Lord Brougham discussing Mr Wilson's scheme for the removal of boys to the colonies 'to be apprenticed to the settlers, under the inspection of magistrates'.

35261 Copies of letters 1815-53 from Edward Gibbon Wakefield and members of his family including Col. William Wakefield and Edward Jerningham Wakefield, mainly relating to New Zealand affairs. They contain first hand descriptions of the country, Wakefield's assessments of the progress of the colony and illustrate the inevitable differences between theory and practice. Albert J. Allom of Parnell, Auckland, N.Z., formerly Wakefield's secretary, transcribed the letters, added occasional notes and sent them to Dr Richard Garnett as material for his biography *Edward Gibbon Wakefield: the Colonization of South Australia and New Zealand*, London 1898.

35349-6278 Hardwicke Papers
   Correspondence and collections of Philip Yorke, 1st Earl of Hardwicke, Philip Yorke, Viscount Royston and 2nd Earl of Hardwicke, Philip Yorke, 3rd Earl of Hardwicke, and Charles Philip Yorke, 4th Earl of Hardwicke.
35350 ff.55-6. 5 Aug. 1774 Daniel C. Solander, London, to the 2nd Lord Hardwicke, describing Capt. Furneaux's voyages in H.M.S. *Adventure* with Cook in H.M.S. *Resolution*, July 1772.
35644 ff.292-6. 10 May 1803 Andrew Doyle, employed by Gov. King in compiling and drawing the natural shrubs of the colony, to Rev. [Cravan?] mentioning the new settlements, farming, native habits, and judicature.
ff.296-7. Memorial c.1803 of Andrew Doyle, emancipated prisoner of New South Wales, to the Dublin Society offering to send drawings of flowers and preserved specimens.
35653 ff.293-4. 26 Apr. 1852 Madame Pauline Fagnet to 4th Earl of Hardwicke concerning the fate of two lottery tickets which she had intended to raffle in order to finance a passage to Australia, and f.294b note 29 Apr. 1852 concerning the tickets.
ff.377-83. Testimonials July-Sept. 1852 of Charles William Johnson desiring an appointment as teacher and superintendent of emigrants in one of the government ships for Australia.
ff.417-18. 19 Nov. 1852 Otway O'Connor Cuffe, Earl of Desart, Under-Secretary of State for the Colonies, to J. D. Powles, Secretary to the London Dock Co., stating H.M. Government did not intend to use the Auckland Islands as a station for convicts, and therefore could not accede to surrendering the lease held by the Southern Whale Fishery and remunerating the Company for its expense.

ff.421-4. Observations 2, 4 Dec. 1852 by the Lord Chancellor and the Solicitor General on the proposed grants of patents for the colonies (Patent Law Amendment Act 1852), copies.

35761 ff.21-2. 19 July 1805 Denis Browne to Alexander Marsden concerning Thomas Gibbons, alias Thomas Fitzgibbon, sentenced to transportation for life.

36297 ff.23-4. c.1848-9 John Stuart Mill to E. G. Wakefield urging him to complete his treatise on colonisation, as an authoritative book on the subject was needed.

36455-83 Broughton Papers
   Correspondence and papers of John Cam Hobhouse, 2nd Bart, Baron Broughton de Gyfford.

36458 ff.454-5. c.1820 complaint from New South Wales on exactions by Gov. Macquarie.

36466 ff.133-4, 191. 7 May, 9 July 1830 Robert Gouger to Hobhouse concerning meetings of the National Colonisation Society. Also ff.290-1 n.d. seeking assistance in obtaining appointment as Secretary to the Board of Commissioners about to be established for the conduct of emigration, and enclosing ff.288-9 a recommendation 23 Feb. 1831 from Francis Place.

36525 ff.35-6. 25 Aug. 1848 G. A. Selwyn, College schooner *Undine*, to Capt. R. H. Fleming, R.N., acknowledging packet of seeds and expressing dismay at the reckless cutting down of trees.

36652 ff.24-32. Dec. 1869 rough census, with detailed statement, of the inhabitants of Pitcairn Island, made by W. Hawkins, petty officer in H.M.S. *Reindeer*, Capt. Edward Nares.

36711-13 Samuel Butler Papers
   Erewhon, autograph, as sent to the press by Samuel Butler 1872, and proof sheets with autograph alterations 1901, and *Erewhon Revisited*, autograph by Samuel Butler 1901.

37015-16 Meryon Papers*
   Correspondence and papers of, or relating to, Charles Meryon.

37015 Correspondence 1855-69 including letters of Meryon to his father Charles Lewis Meryon, M.D., and letters of others relating to Charles Meryon's insanity and death.

37016 ff.85-6. Brief hydrographical notes c.1846 on New Zealand seas 'Annotations de la carte', French.

ff.87-100. Notes on skies for tropical and southern landscapes.

ff.101-25. Sketches and notes on South Sea canoes.

ff.126-87. 'Agenda', a confused mass of notes written by Meryon during the last years of his life, with receipts and other papers, French.

ff.188-203. Sale catalogues of two collections of his etchings sold in London by Messrs Christie, 26 Nov. 1890, 16 July 1891.

37060-6 Farr Papers
   Correspondence and papers of the Farr family of Uford, Southampton, including William Farr, F.R.S.

37060 ff.68-71. 24 Mar. 1790 Capt. James Campbell, Sydney, to Farr commenting on the Aborigines and conditions, 'we every day become more and more sensible of the impossibility of our ever being able to make anything of this country'.

37182-201 Babbage Papers
   Correspondence and papers of Charles Babbage.

37183 ff.301-2. 6 July 1827 from Saxe Bannister, Sydney, concerning Mr [Rümker?].

37194 ff.27-8. 27 Aug. 1847 from Henry Monson, builder, Manchester, seeking assistance in emigrating to New Zealand with his sons. Also ff.63-4, 13 Nov. 1847 acknowledging receipt of books which he will present to the Governor on his arrival. ff.65-71. 15 Nov. 1847 from Edward Beecher with charts of the coral reefs of Point Venus, Tahiti, and Bow Island.

ff.254-5. 29 Feb. 1849 James Bonwick, Glenorchy, Tas., seeking monetary assistance for the passage to Australia of his parents, and giving an account of a recent earthquake in Wellington, N.Z.

37196 f.63. 24 Jan. 1855 from Sir Richard Macdonnell, London, suggesting he visit Australia. Also f.70, 9 Feb. 1855 thanking Babbage for a pamphlet on the ecclesiastical jurisdiction of the Bishop of Adelaide.

37197 ff.149-50. 16 Jan. 1857 from John R. Monson, Port Chalmers, N.Z., considering the new form of government to be premature in a colony as divided as New Zealand.

37198 ff.157-8, 249, 260. Correspondence 14 Feb., 10 Oct., 12 Nov. 1861 between Mrs Mary Graham, Melbourne, and Babbage on monetary matters.

37199 f.362. 2 Apr. 1867 from G. A. Hamilton, Treasury, informing Babbage of the unsuccessful application of Hamilton's son for mastership of the branch Mint at Melbourne.

37327 Journal 20 Feb. to 30 Mar. 1778, 16 Jan. to 1 May 1779, probably by John Law, surgeon in H.M.S. *Discovery*.

37425 f.134. 4 July 1772 Cook to Navy Board reporting on the condition of H.M.S. *Resolution*.

37528 Fair copy of journal 10 Feb. 1776 to 6 June 1778 of Thomas Edgar, master of H.M.S. *Discovery*, and other relevant material, the actual journal beginning 1 Aug. 1776. With three charts.

37631 Clunies Ross Papers

Papers 1824-54 of John Clunies Ross including ff.1-145 concerning his relations with Alexander Hare and settlement on the Cocos Islands; ff.146-233 'Voyages of the *Adventure* and *Beagle*. Supplement to the 2nd, 3rd and appendix volumes of the first edition', satire on Capt. Robert FitzRoy's book provoked by statements in his own and Charles Darwin's account of their visit to the islands, written by Ross.

37689-718 Auckland Papers

Papers of George Eden, 2nd Baron and 1st Earl of Auckland.

37715-17 Letter books 1840-2 called 'China Books' consisting of copies of minutes and letters of Lord Auckland, Governor-General of India, written to British plenipotentiaries and commanders, etc., in China during the 'Opium War'.

37715 ff.50-2. 20 May 1840 to Rear-Adm. the Hon. G. Elliot concerning ships available and mentioning the need for two vessels for New South Wales and New Zealand. ff.111-12, 4 May 1841 to Sir George Gipps thanking him for sending aid to the China Expedition. ff.126-7, 24 June 1847 to Sir William Parker mentioning supplies including coal from New South Wales. See also Add. MS.37717 ff.26-8, 26 Dec. 1841.

37840 MS. copy of government and general orders 23 Feb. 1813 to 21 July 1816 of Lieut.-Gov. Thomas Davey, Hobart.

37842-935 Windham Papers

Correspondence and papers of William Windham.

37885 ff.258-9. 31 Jan. 1807 Transport Office, estimate for a transport to be sent to New South Wales with settlers, convicts, and stores.

37891 Papers relating to the army including ff.3, 191-2, 219, 226 Grose's Corps in New South Wales 1794-1801.

37892-902 Returns of H.M. Forces, including 37892 ff.23-4, 37893 ff.22-3, 37894 ff.23-4, 37895 ff.22-3, 37896 ff.22-3, 37897 ff.23-4, 37898 ff.23-4, 37899 ff.22-3, 37900 ff.22-3, 37901 ff.23-4, 37902 ff.8, 11 Grose's Corps at New South Wales 1794-1807.

37914 ff.121-2. 2 Sept. 1794 James Bunn, Manchester, to Windham imploring his intervention on behalf of Bunn's son sentenced to transportation.

38076 Charts, including f.16. Cocos or Keeling Is., 18th cent.; f.19. Plan of the Tryal Rocks, eighty leagues west of New Holland, 1719; ff.41-2. Touchaheilly Islands and part of a reef seen in June 1790 in H.M.S. *Supply*, Lieut. H. L. Ball commander; f.43. Islands of New Georgia showing the tracks of the *Alexander* 1788, and H.M.S. *Supply* 1790; ff.44-5. Indian Ocean, 18th cent.

38091 ff.32-44. List of ships' logs relating to Cook's voyages 1768-79. Copies of this typescript are in the National Library of Australia and the Mitchell Library, Sydney. ff.191-2. 2 Feb. 1842 from [Rev.] William Williams, Poverty Bay, N.Z., to Dr W. Buckland describing the discovery in New Zealand of bones of the *Dinornis* (Moa). ff.193-210. 1843-45 W. J. Broderip and Prof. R. Owen to Buckland discussing the discovery.

38108-11 Leigh Hunt Papers
38109 ff.132-5. 18 Aug. 1834 E. G. Wakefield to R. Hill concerning proposal to name the capital of South Australia after the 1st Duke of Wellington and the Colonial Office's delay in establishing the colony.
f.140. 25 Nov. 1834 from Wakefield requesting interview with Thornton Hunt on colonisation.

38190-489 Liverpool Papers
38197-381 Official correspondence and papers of the 1st, 2nd, and 3rd Earls of Liverpool.
38229 f.44. 27 June 1793 Gov. Phillip concerning seeds from New South Wales and forwarding statistical returns. See Add. MS.38351.
38244 ff.218-19. 8 Mar. 1810 Gov. Macquarie to Lieut.-Col. Foveaux commending his recent administration of New South Wales, copy.
38234 ff.240-2. 23 Oct. 1810 Lieut.-Col. Foveaux requesting appointment as Lieutenant-Governor of Van Diemen's Land.
38269 ff.379-84. Correspondence 1815-18 concerning a pension for Isabella, widow of Arthur Phillip, formerly Governor of New South Wales.
38299 ff.67-77. 14 Nov., 7 Dec. 1823 T. O. Curling, V.D.L., concerning the economic condition of the colony and migrants' prospects, copy.
38350 ff.262-318. Review of the charters of and Acts concerning the East India, South Sea, and Hudson's Bay companies in connection with the Southern Whale Fishery, and remarks on a Bill proposing to open a trade through the South Seas to China 1791. For further papers c.1800-3 on Parliamentary legislation to encourage the Southern Fishery see also 38356 ff.27, 123-46. Minutes of the Committee of Trade 1786-93 (Add. MSS.38388-94) which have subject indexes at the end of each volume, have references *passim* to the Southern Whale Fishery, mainly concerning the attempt to encourage the fishermen to settle in and operate from England. On this aspect there are numerous references *passim* in Liverpool's official correspondence, particularly in Add. MS.38228. In Add. MSS. there are also a number of letters connected with the Fishery from Samuel Enderby written sometimes on behalf of fellow-merchants: 38218 f.359 n.d. [c.1786]; 38227 f.239, 7 Feb. 1792; 38228 f.373, 13 Mar. 1793; 38229 ff.87-8, 28 Sept. 1793; 38234 ff.124-5, 1 Aug. 1800 requesting permission for whalers to carry cargo under bond to New South Wales; 38236 ff.22-5, 22 Feb. 1802 mentioning two charts which show the trading areas of the different chartered companies and listing the names, owners, and value of the seventy-nine vessels employed in the Southern Whale Fishery in 1802; 38236 ff.233-5,

27 Nov. 1802. For other Add. MSS. references to the Fishery 1786-1802 see 38227 f.18, 38346 ff.75, 274, 38351 ff.261-2, 38352 f.123, 38356 ff.22-6 and 38409 ff.140-2.

38351 f.267. Statistical return 8 Oct. 1792 signed by Gov. Phillip of categories of settlers and persons who had been granted land at Parramatta, N.S.W., and Norfolk Is.; ff.293-304 returns of land grants in New South Wales and Norfolk Is. 1789-92. Also Add. MS.38376 ff.139-40 return 16 Oct. 1792 of land in cultivation in New South Wales and Norfolk Is. (enclosures to Add. MS.38229).

38356 f.227. Chart [c.1800] made aboard the *Lady Nelson*, Bass Strait.

38362 f.224. Petition 4 July 1812 by R. Campbell, merchant and magistrate, to the British Treasury for a return passage to New South Wales and reparation for the expense of travelling to England to give evidence for the Crown in the Bligh case.

38380 ff.290-3. [10?] Oct. 1823 G. Palmer of Palmer, Wilson & Co., to the 2nd Earl enclosing copy of a letter 15 Sept. 1823 from William Barnes urging the establishment of a settlement on the north coast of Australia.

38388-94 Minutes, etc., of the Privy Council Committee of Trade 1786-93.

38390 f.127. Minutes 12-13 Apr. 1787 concerning the establishment of a commission in New South Wales for the trial of pirates.

f.134. Minutes 24 Apr. 1787 concerning approval for the instructions of Gov. Phillip.

38392 ff.122, 133, 136. Minutes 31 May to 3 Aug. 1790 concerning the preparation and approval of a great seal for New South Wales.

38394 f.23. Report 13 Apr. 1787 directing the Advocate General to prepare a commission for the trial of pirates in New South Wales.

38523-4 Leigh Hunt Papers
Correspondence supplementing Add. MSS.38109-11.

38523 ff.149-50. 30 Nov. 1835 E. G. Wakefield to Thornton Hunt on theory of colonisation.

38530 'Journal' of George Gilbert, midshipman in H.M.S. *Resolution* and afterwards H.M.S. *Discovery* on the third Cook voyage.

38734-70 Huskisson Papers
Correspondence and papers of William Huskisson.

38744 ff.314-15. 16 Sept. 1823 S. Enderby and Son, W. Mellish, and D. Bennett and Son to Lieut.-Col. Edward Nicolls, Royal Marines, concerning the advantages to whalers operating near New Zealand if a settlement were established there, copy.

38746 f.251. 16 June 1825 3rd Earl Bathurst to Frederick, Duke of York, Commander-in-Chief, notifying the appointment of Maj.-Gen. Sir Ralph Darling as Governor of New South Wales.

38751 ff.90-4. 19 Sept. 1827 J. Inglis, Secretary of the Van Diemen's Land Co., to J. Pearse; 30 Sept. 1827 Pearse to Huskisson concerning the location of the Company's lands.

38757 ff.232-4. 17 Mar. 1829 R. Therry to Huskisson requesting a colonial appointment, and ff.260-1 n.d. thanking him for his appointment as Commissioner of the New South Wales Court of Requests.

38763 ff.70-4. Memorial n.d. [c.1822] of Lieut.-Col. E. Nicolls, Royal Marines, to Bathurst urging a settlement in New Zealand on military lines, describing the country's resources and especially its potential for flax.

ff.99-100. Memorial n.d. [c.1825] of R. Torrens and others to Huskisson urging a settlement in New Zealand and its exploitation by a chartered company for flax and timber.

38931-9164 Layard Papers
Papers of Sir Austen Henry Layard, Under-Secretary for Foreign Affairs, 1852, 1861-6.

39101-20 Semi-official correspondence with British ambassadors, consuls, etc., 1861-6.

39101 f.208. 25 Oct. 1861 J. G. Paton, Presbyterian missionary, to [?] Kay concerning the proposed Belgian colonisation of Tanna Is., New Hebrides, copy.

39103 f.52. 29 Apr. 1862 J. Barton, consul in Peru, to Layard concerning the proposed introduction into Peru of colonists from the New Hebrides 'by an Englishman named Byrne'.

39106 ff.221, 237. Memos 20, 23 June 1863 A. F. Kinnaird to Layard concerning British recognition of the French occupation of New Caledonia.

39168 Miscellaneous letters and papers, including ff.2-27. 15 Mar. 1861 A. R. Wallace to Thomas Sims, his brother-in-law, mentioning photography, Darwin's book, and including some passing references to Australia. Also two photographs of Wallace.

39285-6 Journals of Capt. Don Domingo de Boenechea, Lieut.-Cmdr Don Tomas Gayangos and Lieut.-Cmdr Don Cayetano de Lángara in three voyages in the *Aguila* from El Callao to Tahiti 1772-3, 1774-5, and 1775-6, with maps, plans, and plates illustrating the journals. All are copies in Spanish made by B. G. Corney from originals in the Archivo General de Indias, Seville. For a translation of the journals and reproductions of the illustrations see B. G. Corney, *The Quest and Occupation of Tahiti by Emissaries of Spain in 1772-6*, Hakluyt Society I, Second Series XXXII, 1913, and II, Second Series XXXVI, 1915.

39822 Correspondence and papers 1765-96 of Larcum Kendall, watchmaker. f.50. 27 May 1775 Kendall to the Commissioners of the Board of Longitude mentioning the chronometer he supplied to Capt. Cook.

39846-7 Samuel Butler Papers
39846 Autograph MS. of the novel *The Way of all Flesh* by Samuel Butler, written 1873-85, and first printed in 1903.
39847 ff.308-10. Dates of events mentioned in *Erewhon* and *Erewhon Revisited*. MSS. of these works are at Add. MSS.36711-13.

39948-9 Huskisson Papers
Official and private correspondence of William Huskisson and his wife.
39948 f.133. 20 Feb. 1831 Roger Therry, Commissioner of the Court of Requests, New South Wales, to Mrs Huskisson, on her husband's death. ff.139-40. 6 Sept. 1832 James Henty, Launceston, V.D.L., to T. Humphry concerning the consignment of natural history specimens from Van Diemen's Land and complaining about the unfair land regulations.
ff.147-9, 150-1. 5 Apr., 17 Aug. 1833 Thomas Henty, Corniston, near Launceston, to William Humphry, describing conditions, 'money is all powerful here', and mentioning opportunities at other settlements.

39954 Owen Papers
Non-scientific correspondence 1838-89 of Sir Richard Owen, superintendent of the natural history departments of the British Museum.
ff.16-582. Include twenty-five letters from Sir William and Mary Ann Martin to Sir Richard and his wife. These cover the period of Sir William's residence in New Zealand as Chief Justice. Also included are ff.280-3 11 Feb. 1853 A. R. Roche, Quebec, to Sir Richard Owen, describing plans for an expedition to the South Seas, 'The New Hebrides Association', in which he hopes to interest the London Missionary Society.

40108-22 Hone Papers
Collections and correspondence of William Hone, bookseller.

40120 ff.422-3, 477-8. 15 Mar. 1836, 9 Apr. 1839, George Fife Angas, Dawlish, Devon, to Hone anxious to establish an Aborigine mission in South Australia and sending a printed appeal from C. Schulters, elder of a Silesian Lutheran congregation, for help in emigrating to South Australia.

40166 Miscellaneous fragments. f.40. 22 Apr. 1865 miner's right issued to Augusta Jane Wells in Crooked River, Vic.

40181-617 Peel Papers

Correspondence and papers, official and private, of Sir Robert Peel. Printed papers, e.g. copies of governors' despatches, parliamentary papers, draft Bills, cuttings, and periodicals are omitted in the following description unless closely related to correspondence noted.

40328-33 Correspondence 1822-41 with Henry Goulburn.

40331 ff.92-3. 13 July 1825 to Goulburn asking for details of the number of convicts sent from Ireland to New South Wales.

ff.106-7. Return 19 July 1825 of the number of convicts sent from Ireland to New South Wales 1815-24, distinguishing males and females and those convicted under the Insurrection Act.

40344-429 General correspondence 1818-41.

40357 ff.35-6. Bill 26 June 1823 for authorising the employment at labour in the colonies of male convicts under sentence of transportation, printed, with f.36b petition of John Grant against this Bill.

ff.37-45. Papers 1822 of John Grant concerning his conviction for accosting and referring to his experiences in New South Wales; these include f.38, '1804, Parramatta, Panegyric of an eminent artist', printed.

ff.48-9. 6 July 1823 from Henry Hobhouse with ff.50-1, 5 July 1823 from Wilmot Horton, ff.71-2, 7 July 1823 Francis Forbes to Wilmot Horton and ff.73-9, 8 July 1823 from Wilmot Horton concerning the New South Wales Bill and proposals to remove restrictions on emancipated colonists.

ff.79-82. Correspondence 8-29 July 1823 with Col. Parry concerning the application of Mary O'Donohoe to join her husband, a stone-cutter transported for life, in New South Wales.

ff.188-92, 198-9. Correspondence 26, 27, 30 July 1823 between Peel, Wilmot Horton, and applicant Ross Cox concerning newspaper reports of establishment of a new police system in New South Wales.

40358 ff.302-3, 309-10, 376-7. Correspondence 20, 21, 31 Oct. 1823 between Peel, Wilmot Horton, and Henry Bathurst, 3rd Earl Bathurst, arranging for the measurement of an arc of the meridian in New South Wales, at the request of Sir Humphrey Davy and the Board of Longitude.

40368 ff.93-4. 1 Sept. 1824 from Edward Eagar sending his pamphlet on the colonies of New South Wales and Van Diemen's Land.

40378 ff.71-2. 13 May 1825 from Wilmot Horton suggesting amendments to the Colonial Convict Bill.

ff.199-200. 24 May 1825 from James Raymond, Irish emigrant to Australia, with f.201 petition for assistance.

40379 ff.202-3. 18 June 1825 from Wilmot Horton sending papers on transportation.

40380 ff.3-6. Correspondence 1, 3 July 1825 with Wilmot Horton on the undesirability of sending 'gentlemen convicts' with seven year sentences to the colonies.

ff.83-6. 13 July 1825 to Lord Bathurst saying that no mode of punishment at home can be devised as a substitute for transportation; ff.313-14 Bathurst's reply.

40381 ff.228-9. c.Sept. 1825 from James Raymond about to depart for New South Wales expressing gratitude for this having been made possible.

40382 ff. 56-9. 10 Oct. 1825 from Wilmot Horton on the desirability of separating 'gentlemen convicts' from others; ff.60-1 Peel's reply rejecting proposed solutions.

40388 ff.41-4. 12 July 1826 to Wilmot Horton about a report that Savery, a convict transported for forgery, had been selected as publisher of the *Hobart Town Gazette* and expressing the view that emigration would never be an effective remedy for diminishing the excessive population at home; ff.54-5 reply 15 July 1826 from Wilmot Horton.

40396 ff.127-8. 6 Apr. 1828 from James Raymond, Sydney, sending a brace of black swans.

40446-52 Correspondence 1841-50 with Sir James Robert George Graham.

40451 ff.70-1, 82-3, 100-3, 118-21. Correspondence Apr.-May 1845 between Peel and Graham on their failure to reach agreement with Charles Buller on New Zealand Co. affairs.

ff.205-8. 20 Aug. 1845 from Graham on the memo of William Walsh, Bishop of Halifax, for the endowment of Roman Catholic clergy in the colonies; ff.211-12 Peel's acknowledgement 21 Aug. 1845.

ff.380-1. 13 Oct. 1845 to Graham with news of the Maori War in New Zealand during May.

ff.386-7. 15 Oct. 1845 from Graham, 'New Zealand is our Algeria'.

40456-8 Correspondence 1841-6 with Thomas Hamilton, 9th Earl of Haddington.

40458 ff. 305-6. 25 Jan. 1846 from Thomas Hamilton, with ff.307-9 memorial and copy letter 8 July 1845 from Charles and George Enderby seeking a grant to use the Auckland Islands as a base for a whale fishery station.

40467-8 Correspondence 1841-5 with Edward George Geoffrey Smith Stanley, Lord Stanley, 14th Earl of Derby.

40467 ff.111-12. 10 Nov. 1841 to Stanley with ff.113-15, 15 June 1841 Henry Edward Michel, Sydney, to his father Gen. J. Michel on the economic distress in the Australian colonies and the roguery of financiers partly caused by the policy of Lord John Russell.

ff.116-19. Correspondence 11, 19 Nov. 1841 on the proposed establishment of a school and college in Van Diemen's Land.

ff.121-4. 25, 26 Nov. 1841 to Stanley on reports of the outfitting of a French expedition which may try to establish a settlement and threaten British sovereignty in New Zealand.

ff.154-5. 30 Dec. 1841 to Stanley 'I think upon the whole that the arguments against the immediate occupation of stations in the Pacific preponderate'.

ff.315-16. c.Dec. 1842 from Stanley on successor to Sir John Franklin in Tasmania, and suggesting Sir John Eardley Wilmot, though knowing him to be a 'muddle brained blockhead'.

ff.345-8. 26 Dec. 1842 from Stanley on the intended strength of the army in 1843 in Britain and the colonies, opposing a reduction in forces in the Australian colonies because of the increased population.

40468 ff.234-7, 245-51, 262-5, 283-92, 322-3. Correspondence Nov. 1844 to Nov. 1845 on policy towards the New Zealand Co.

ff.315-21. Minute 11 Apr. 1845 by Stanley on Gov. FitzRoy's incompetence, advising his immediate recall, printed.

ff.374-5, 387-8. 14 Oct., 28 Nov. 1845 from Stanley concerning encounters with natives at Auckland and commenting on the present inadequacy of colonial defence.

40469-70 Correspondence 1841-9 with William Ewart Gladstone.

40470 ff. 381-90. Correspondence 13, 15, 17 Apr. 1846 concerning the New Zealand Co. and the Government of New Zealand.

ff.438-9. 1 July 1846 to Gladstone informing him of the Queen's consent to the name of Victoria being assigned to one of the divisions of New Zealand.

London

ff.442-3. 24, 28 May 1847 Gladstone to Peel on the recall of Sir John Eardley Wilmot from Van Diemen's Land.

40485-603 General correspondence 1841-50.

40486 ff.316-23. Copy of article by Robert Montgomery Martin 'Principles and Prospects of a Conservative Government' from the *Colonial Magazine and Commercial Maritime Journal* 1841. The tract includes a summary and interpretation of conservative colonial policy. There is further correspondence with Martin, who visited New South Wales *c*.1827.

40489 ff.225-6. 20 Sept. 1841 from Rev. Edward Coleridge enclosing ff.251-2, letter 20 Sept. 1841 from G. A. Selwyn, Bishop elect of New Zealand, pointing out, with reference to New Zealand, the need for further alteration of the Foreigners Consecration Bill; ff.227-8 reply 23 Sept. 1841 refusing the request.

40497 ff.14-15, 377-8. 7, 18 Dec. 1841 to Adm. George Cockburn and Capt. FitzRoy discussing Edward Divett's proposals for steam navigation across the Pacific.

40503 ff.129-30. 28 Feb. 1842 from Buller with ff.131-2 memo from the New Zealand Co. on the Chatham Islands and British policy towards German settlement there under British sovereignty.

40516 ff.164-5. 4 Oct. 1842 from Capt. Frederic Polhill, M.P., stating he would like to be appointed Governor of Van Diemen's Land; ff.166-7 acknowledgement 13 Oct. 1842.

40526 ff.282-3. 11 Apr. 1843 from John Rolleston, vicar of Burton Joyce, thanking Peel for the recommendation of his son to the Governor of New South Wales resulting in the son's appointment as a magistrate.

ff.378-81. 28, 31 Mar. 1843 from John Beecham, secretary of the Wesleyan Missionary Society, and Arthur Tidman, secretary of the London Missionary Society, on the implications of the recent assumption of French authority in Tahiti.

40527 ff.71-4. Correspondence 4, 7 Apr. 1843 between Peel and Buller on the Government's role in colonisation.

f.246. Memorial 28 Apr. 1843 from Margate protestants seeking British intervention in Tahiti.

40547 ff.12-13. 17 June 1844 from William Buckland with ff.14-17 cuttings 1843 of addresses to Sir John Franklin, retiring Lieutenant-Governor of Van Diemen's Land, and ff.17b-18, 23 Oct. 1843 copy of Franklin's reply to the inhabitants of Richmond, Tas.

ff.19-23. Correspondence July 1844 among Buckland, Peel, and Lord Stanley, referring to Sir John Franklin and the suspension of John Montagu as Colonial Secretary in Van Diemen's Land.

40549 ff.159-61, 326-8. Rough notes n.d. and 8 Aug. 1844 relating to the French occupation of the Society Islands.

40550 ff.141-4. 19 Aug. 1844 from E. G. Wakefield, 'the origin of all the misery which has occurred in Tahiti and New Zealand is the missionaries not being confined to their own calling'; ff.145-6 Peel's acknowledgement 29 Aug. 1844.

f.147. 5 Sept. 1844 from Stanley on the same subject.

40552 ff.256-63. 15 Oct. 1844 from Buckland concerning Sir John Franklin, with copy of Franklin's remonstrance 13 Sept. 1844.

40555 ff.330-5. 14 Dec. 1844 from Buller appealing for Peel's intervention in the disputes between the New Zealand Co. and the Colonial Office, with ff.336-7 reply 23 Dec. 1844 granting interview.

40557 ff.31-49, 406-23. Correspondence, memos, and tables Jan. 1845 concerning Navy estimates 1845-6 and Admiralty responsibility in Tahiti, mentioning the new Pacific Station, partly printed.

ff.436-9. 14 Jan. 1845 from Buller with Peel's reply 15 Jan. concerning an interview.

40558 ff.454-5. 31 Jan. 1845 from J. A. Robertson, formerly police magistrate in New South Wales, requesting an interview to discuss his claims against the government for the loss of his position.

40559 ff.27-49. Correspondence 3-10 Feb. 1845 among Peel, Buller, and G. W. Hope, concerning the presentation to the House of Commons of a statement by the directors of the New Zealand Co.

40560 ff.218-19. 21 Feb. 1845 from Sir George Grey informing Peel that he desires to put a question to the House on Tahiti; ff.220-1, 22 Feb. 1845 to Aberdeen with proposed answer and f.221b Aberdeen's approval and comment.

ff.225-6. 21 Feb. 1845 to Buller referring to Buller's letter and memo of 10 Feb. concerning settlement of New Zealand Co. affairs.

40562 ff.72-3. 7 Mar. 1845 from E. G. Wakefield sending ff.74-7 cuttings from the *New Zealand Journal* 1, 15 Feb. 1845 on the Treaty of Waitangi, the New Zealand Co.'s settlements, and Lord Stanley's instructions to Capt. FitzRoy.

40563 ff.46-7. 17 Mar. 1845 from Lieut. John Wood, R.N., seeking an interview in which to prove the New Zealand Co. 'guilty of falsehood and breach of contract'.

40564 ff.357-8. 14 Apr. 1845 from Henry Buckles forwarding ff.359-60 memorial of the South Australian Society requesting a reduction in the import duty on Australian wheat.

ff.481-2. 19 Apr. 1845 from James Hackett, formerly distiller in Tasmania, concerning the 'injustice' done him by Lord Stanley.

40565 f.285. 29 Apr. 1845 from Buller sending a book on New Zealand (no author or title mentioned) and f.286, 30 Apr. 1845 Peel's acknowledgement.

40566 ff.4-9. 1, 10 May 1845 from Buller on Dieffenbach's work on New Zealand and a memorial from the Wellington settlers occasioned by Capt. FitzRoy's proclamation allowing Europeans to purchase land from the natives.

40567 ff.125-6. 16 May 1845 from E. G. Wakefield, Blois, drawing Peel's attention to, and commenting on cutting, ff.127-8, from the *New Zealand Journal* 10 May 1845 concerning a petition from the landowners of Port Nicholson, N.Z.

40569 ff.9-13. Three letters June 1845 from Saxe Bannister seeking Peel's support for his grievances.

ff.23-4. 13 June 1845 from Buller giving notice of proceedings in the House relating to New Zealand.

ff.41-2. 13 June 1845 from E. G. Wakefield, Blois, on reports from New Zealand of 'insane conduct' of Gov. FitzRoy.

40570 ff.198-9. 8 July 1845 from E. G. Wakefield, with f.200 extract of letter 24 Sept. 1844, Nelson, and f.201 cutting n.d. from the *New Zealand Journal* on the appointment of Gov. Grey.

ff.303-4. 12 July 1845 from John Watson enclosing, f.305 memorial 12 July 1845 of the New Zealand Society seeking a more liberal policy towards the settlers.

40571 ff.27-48. Correspondence 18-23 July 1845 among Peel, Henry Aglionby, George Frederick Young, and G. W. Hope on the New Zealand Co.'s claims to land.

ff.49-50. Copy despatch 14 Aug. 1839 from 1st Marquess of Normanby to Capt. Hobson concerning dealings in land with the Maoris and acknowledging New Zealand as an independent state.

ff.103-8. 21 July 1845 from John Young enclosing two letters 20 July 1845 from William Astell and Walter Long to Young indicating their intention to abstain from voting on the New Zealand question.

ff.314-15. 30 July 1845 from James Ellice, Dieppe, alleging the inadvisability of Australia supporting two London banks, with postscript referring to the warlike character of the Maoris.

f.316. 26 July 1845 cutting containing report of the Union Bank of Australia.

ff.333-4. 31 July 1845 from Aglionby enclosing letters, ff.335-45, 31 July 1845 from Sir John Pirie to Peel on the New Zealand Co. negotiations with the British Government and f.346, 3 Aug. 1845 Peel's acknowledgement to Aglionby.

40572 ff.174-5, 176. 12 Aug., 30 Sept. 1845 from William Brown sending his book [*New Zealand and its Aborigines*, London 1845] and Peel's acknowledgement.

ff.177-8. 12 Aug. 1845 from Ellice enclosing letter, ff.179-80, 24 July 1845 Sir Thomas Frankland Lewis to Ellice, stating he has the 'worst possible opinion' of the Bank of Australasia.

ff.201-2. 13 Aug. 1845 from Edward John Eyre sending a copy of his *Journals of Expeditions of Discovery into Central Australia and Overland from Adelaide to King George's Sound in the years 1840-1*, London 1845.

ff.397-8. 22 Aug. 1845 from Ellice with f.399 cutting from the *Colonial Gazette* 16 Aug. 1845 giving an account of the legal action between the Banks of Australia and Australasia.

40573 ff.102-7. Correspondence 27-9 Aug. 1845 between Peel and Hope on the settlement of the New Zealand Co.'s claims.

ff.447-8. 11 Sept. 1845 from Hon. Henry Thomas Lowry Corry, Lord of the Admiralty, arranging to send Peel despatches from the Pacific.

40574 ff.153-4. 20 Sept. 1845 from William Cotton enclosing copy of letter, ff.155-70, 22 Mar. 1845 G. A. Selwyn, H.M.S. *Victoria*, Bay of Plenty, to Rev. Ernest Hawkins, discussing relations between English settlers and the natives of New Zealand.

ff.220-1. 22 Sept. 1845 from Henry Maxwell Lefroy of Farnham, Surrey, residing in Western Australia, with ff.222-3 his printed 'Propositions on the subject of the land system in Australia'.

40576 ff.202-3. 21 Oct. 1844 from Roger Therry, Sydney, asking Peel to recommend him to Stanley for appointment as judge, and enclosing copy of letter 18 Apr. 1828 Peel to Therry in connection with his first appointment in New South Wales.

40589 ff.27-8. 2 Apr. 1846 from John Whytlaw, former merchant of Kororareka [Russell], N.Z., stating that he lost all his possessions in conflicts with the natives and asking for employment in a government department in Britain; forwarding f.29 copy of letter of recommendation 28 Feb. 1846 from Capt. David Robertson, R.N., late commander of H.M.S. *Hazard*.

40592 ff.131-44. Memorial with related correspondence 20, 26 May 1846 of the New Zealand Co. detailing the present state of affairs in the colony.

40595 ff.324-5. 9 July 1846 from Thomas Millard stating he has returned from New Zealand where he was to erect a saw mill, and requesting an interview.

40596 ff.223-4. 20 July 1846 from Charles John Prosser, schoolmaster, seeking assistance with passage money to South Australia.

ff.230-1. 21 July 1846 from Robert D'Oyly requesting a loan since he cannot recover debts owed to him in New Zealand.

40597 ff.29-30. 3 Aug. 1846 from FitzRoy, London, drawing his attention 'to the Bishop's [?] letter. . . which contains unquestionable *facts*, be his opinion right or wrong' and expressing support for Peel's New Zealand policy.

40598 ff.282, 285-6. 26, 27 May 1847 from Sir John Eardley Wilmot, 2nd Bart, arranging for an interview. Also ff.325-7, 6, 8 June 1847 thanking Peel for his role in the Commons debate on 7 June during which it was stated that the present government entertained no charge injurious to the private character of Sir John Eardley Wilmot, 1st Bart.

40600 ff.60-1. 17 Feb. 1848 from George William Hope congratulating Peel on his New Zealand policy and referring to Lord Grey's attitude to Gov. Grey.

ff.362-3. 25 July 1848 from Richard Owen saying he is sending his paper on the osteology of the great birds of New Zealand.

ff.423-6. 28 Aug. 1848 from Sir John Eardley Wilmot, 2nd Bart, on the recall of his father from Van Diemen's Land.

40604-17 General series.

40611-14 Official papers, newspapers, etc., chiefly enclosures in the General Correspondence, but too large for inclusion in the preceding series.

40611 ff.262-3. Memorial 24 Apr. 1843 of friends and supporters of Protestant Evangelical Missions at Lancaster protesting against the French assumption of sovereignty in Tahiti.

40612 f.102. List of imports of wool into England 1841, including figures for New South Wales and Van Diemen's Land.

ff.140-1. Cuttings of farewell addresses Nov. 1843 to Sir John Franklin as Governor of Van Diemen's Land.

40613 ff.63-5. Memorials 26 Apr., 5 May 1843 of supporters and friends of Protestant missions at Chatham and Sittingbourne, seeking government intervention in Tahiti against France.

40862-80 Ripon Papers

Correspondence 1704-1851 of Hon. Frederick John Robinson, Viscount Goderich 1827 and 1st Earl of Ripon 1833.

40862 ff.276-9. Correspondence 11, 13 July 1831 of Lieut.-Gen. Sir Herbert Taylor and Cmdr Walter Windeyer, R.N., and R. W. Hay concerning Windeyer's hopes for an appointment in New South Wales.

40878-80 'Applications for colonial appointments 1832', containing also other correspondence relating to the portfolio for War and the Colonies. Arranged in order of date within the alphabet letter but occasionally in separate sections under the writer's name. Many of the applications and recommendations relate to Australia and New Zealand, e.g. 40878 ff.45-6 James Andrews seeking an appointment in New South Wales or Van Diemen's Land.

41063 ff. 114-15. 1 May 1822 John Adams, Pitcairn Island, last surviving mutineer of H.M.S. *Bounty*, to the inhabitants of Calcutta, per John Grant, editor of the *India Gazette*, thanking them for presents sent in the *Hercules*.

41206-52 Campbell-Bannerman Papers

Correspondence and papers, official and private, of the Right Hon. Sir Henry Campbell-Bannerman.

41215 Correspondence 1871-97 with Herbert John Gladstone. ff.259-60. 19 Apr. 1900 to Gladstone mentioning the Australian Commonwealth Bill, 'I think . . . that we should give the Australians their will of it', typescript copy.

41222 Correspondence 1899-1908 with Sir Robert Threshie Reid, M.P., Baron Loreburn 1906, Earl Loreburn 1911. ff.130-1. 14 Apr. 1900 on Privy Council appeals and the inadvisability of amending the Australian Commonwealth Bill after the recent referendum.

41224-5 Correspondence 1885-1908 with George Frederick Samuel Robinson, 1st Marquess of Ripon.

41225 ff.230-1. 2 Feb. 1908 to Ripon stating that Lord Northcote was anxious to be relieved of his post as Governor-General of Australia, typescript copy.

ff.232-40. Correspondence Feb. 1908 on the selection of a new Governor-General for Australia.

41232-42 General correspondence and papers 1871-1908.

41234 f.259. 18 Feb. 1899 from William Leys, Auckland, commending Campbell-Bannerman's interest in old age pensions and sending a copy of one of his lectures on the subject.

41237 f.58. 15 Nov. 1902 to the United Irish League in Australia acknowledging previous letter (see Add. MS.41241 f.261).

41238 ff.178-9. 12 Dec. 1905 from Alfred Deakin, Prime Minister of Australia, with congratulations 'upon attaining the highest position in the Empire'.

41240 f.293. 14 Apr. 1908 from Robert Muirhead Collins, Australian representative in London, concerning his resignation from office.

41241 f.261. 9 July 1902 from presidents of state branches of the United Irish League in Australia thanking him for his help in their cause.

41346-475 Martin Papers
   Private and official correspondence of the Martin family of Antigua, British West Indies, and afterwards of Lockynge, Berks.

41362-407 Series B. Papers of Sir Henry Martin, Bart, and Adm. Sir Thomas Byam Martin.

41374-8 Reminiscences and miscellaneous memoranda mainly autobiographical of Sir Thomas Martin c.1795-1837.

f.141. Cutting St James Gazette 3 May 1886 concerning identifiable remains found inside a shark caught in Sydney Harbour.

f.199. Note n.d. entitled 'Extension of Electric Telegraph to China and Australia'.

41394-9 Official letter books of Sir Thomas Martin as Comptroller of the Navy 1816-31. Indexed at the end of each volume.

41394 ff.193-7. Correspondence 14-15 June 1819 with C. and J. Johnson concerning naval timber from New Zealand; 30 July 1819 to Macquarie concerning the Dromedary to proceed to New Zealand for timber after landing convicts at New South Wales.

41396 ff.118-19. 6 June 1826 to R. W. Hay on complaints of the conduct of surgeons on convict ships in New South Wales, asking for the names of surgeons 'meddling in the political affairs of the colony'.

41397 ff.32b-33. 19 June 1827 to Wilmot Horton reiterating his objections to Col. Torrens's plan for emigration on the grounds of impracticability.

41398 ff.1-2. 1 Jan. 1829 to Twiss questioning the feasibility of a plan for the Derwent Steam Navigation Company to have a vessel conveyed to Van Diemen's Land by a ship hired by the government for transportation of convicts.

f.131. 13 Mar. 1830 to W. Donlan requesting more samples of canvas and rope made of New Zealand flax.

41399 ff.77b-85. Observations 18 Aug. 1831 by Sir Thomas Martin on the expenses incurred by emigration including f.84 proposed scheme for victualling men wanting to emigrate to New South Wales and f.85b account of the number of convicts transported 1817-29 showing the number who died on the voyage.

41403-6 Miscellaneous naval memoranda 1828-50 of Sir Thomas Martin mainly relating to naval establishments.

41403 ff.52b-53. Table showing the number of convicts transported to New South Wales 1817-24; index complete only to letter F.

41404 ff.40b-41. Table showing the number of convicts transported to New South Wales 1817-32, indexed.

41408-62 Series C. Papers of Adm. Sir William Fanshawe Martin.

41410 Papers 20 Aug. 1856 to Mar. 1859, mostly printed, relating to Home and Foreign defences. There are occasional references throughout this volume to the Pacific and Australia Stations.

ff.10-13. Memo 28 Nov. 1856 J. F. Burgoyne on defences for the foreign possessions of Great Britain. f.12 mentions Australia.

ff.103-17. Memo June 1858 by Sir Richard Dundas for Sir John Pakington on the state of the Navy, mentioning estimates of forces needed for the outbreak of war, and various stations including Australia, New Zealand, and the Pacific, printed. ff.118-19. Memo 29 June 1859 on the state of the Navy, a return showing the number of officers, ships, etc.

ff.139-66. A list of Her Majesty's ships in commission, Mar. 1859, indexed; f.154 Pacific, f.155 East Indies, China, and Australia, f.157 surveying service.

ff.167-229. Papers dealing with foreign stations including instructions for the delivery of packets in the event of war, f.184 Pacific, ff.185-6 Orders to Commander-in-Chief in the Pacific, f.200 Australia, ff.201-2 Orders to Senior Officer in Australia.

41463-73 Series D. Papers of Adm. Sir Henry Byam Martin.

41463 General correspondence 1834-55 of Sir Henry Martin.

ff.117-19. Copies of letters and extracts relating to the Society Islands: f.117, 11 July 1843 S. Herbert, Admiralty, to Rear-Adm. Thomas enclosing instructions from the Secretary of State for Foreign Affairs; f.118, extract of despatch 11 July 1843 Addington to Sir John Barrow concerning the Society Islands and British policy; f.119, 29 Aug. 1844 M. Guizot to Comte de Larnac and 6 Sept. 1844 Lord Aberdeen to Lord Cowley containing extracts of statements concerning British-French relations. ff.120-30. Special instructions by Sir George Seymour for the captains, commanders and officers commanding H.M. ships and vessels employed in the Pacific.

ff.131-9. Copy correspondence Mar.-Aug. 1845 among Cowley, Aberdeen, Addington, Seymour, and Hamilton on the recognition and extent of French sovereignty over Tahiti.

ff.140-491. Correspondence 25 Aug. 1845 to May 1848, mostly copies, concerning French sovereignty in Tahiti, French-British relations in the South Seas, British claims in the Society Islands, and the events leading up to the independence of the Leeward Islands. Some letters also mention Pitcairn Island. Principal correspondents include Queen Pomare and other chiefs, Adm. G. F. Seymour, Gov. Bruat, and other officials, missionaries, etc.

41469 Letter book 17 Nov. 1845 to 5 Nov. 1859 of Sir Henry Martin containing copies of his semi-official letters whilst in command of H.M.S. *Grampus* in the Pacific, and other ships.

ff.1-46. Letters 17 Nov. 1845 to 23 Aug. 1847 most of which are to Seymour with some to Revs. G. Charter, C. Barff, and others. They contain Martin's comments and interpretation of events connected with the French protectorate over Tahiti, the question of the independence of the Leeward Islands, an account of relations with the French, the difficulties of Queen Pomare's position, and events leading up to the independence of the Leeward Islands.

41470 Letter book of Sir Henry Martin containing copies of his official letters 17 Nov. 1845 to 16 Oct. 1847 while in command of H.M.S. *Grampus* in the Pacific. There are translations of some letters into Tahitian by J. Rogerson, missionary at Bora Bora.

41472 Journal 17 Nov. 1845 to 20 Oct. 1848 of Sir Henry Martin while in command of H.M.S. *Grampus* in the Pacific, with occasional ink illustrations.

41494-6 Correspondence of Spencer George Perceval of Severn House, Henbury, Glos., geologist and antiquary.

41495 ff.274-6, 308-9. 17 Mar., 15 Oct. 1877 W. D. Glyde, Adelaide, to Perceval discussing native tools.

41567 Miscellaneous letters and papers, chiefly of Nonconformist divines.

f.41. 30 Apr. 1842 G. Pritchard, London, to his daughter Eliza asking her to make another 'little roundabout' useful for the school-children in Tahiti.

London

f.65. Note 13 July 1836 by John Williams, Norwich, containing extract from a speech delivered by a native at a missionary meeting in Raiatea.

ff.248-9. 24 Oct. 1836 Darwin to Whitley 'at present waiting in London till the Beagle arrives at Woolwich to be paid off', then returning to Cambridge.

41742-6 Macintyre Papers

Historical and autobiographical works of James Johnstone Macintyre, merchant. 41742 Account by Macintyre of his life in Mexico, England, Scotland, and New South Wales, apparently Vol.IV of MS. entitled 'My Life: 1794-1868', written for his daughters; ff.177, 188-99, 204-6, 213-16 contain material specifically relating to his voyage to Australia 1835-40.

41743 ff.1-6. 1 Jan. 1841 Macintyre, London, to J. Hume, M.P., submitting his draft observations on the Australian colonies, originally intended for publication. ff.7-203. 'The physical and historical geography of Australia', by Macintyre, containing criticisms of British colonial policy, especially as regards the land question; ff. 96-111 on the rights of the natives and the reservations of waste lands; ff.112-30 colonisation in relation to steam, discussing the effect the invention will have on colonisation, printed.

41745-6 'Walks on Deck and Rambles on Shore during a Voyage of Circumnavigation of the Globe', narrative by Macintyre of a voyage to Australia via Suez and return via Panama 4 Mar. to 18 Nov. 1853. Incomplete draft prepared for publication, but apparently never printed. 41745 ff.215-78 and 41746 ff.2-103 contain relevant material.

41851-9 Thomas Grenville Papers

41855 ff.104-5. 29 Oct. 1796 W. J. Drury, Yarmouth, to [Lords of the Admiralty] mentioning f.104b Capt. Bligh's 'going directly upon an Enterprize, that would be the most creditable undertaking . . .'.

42000-47 Blore Drawings

Architectural and topographical drawings by Edward Blore, architect and antiquary, mostly unsigned and undated.

42027-9 Designs executed by Blore for various clients including 42028 ff.13-15 designs for Government House, Sydney, c.1832.

42069-82 Hamilton and Greville Papers

Original correspondence and papers of Sir William Hamilton and his nephews Right Hon. C. F. Greville, M.P., and Hon. R. F. Greville.

42071 Correspondence and papers of Hon. C. F. Greville.

(3) Correspondence and papers relating to mineralogical and other scientific subjects: ff.103-4. 30 Mar. 1803 from R. Brown, in sight of Timor, reporting on voyage to date, expressing disappointment at the plants found at New Holland; f.123. 25 Sept. 1805 from G. Humphrey forwarding extracts from his son's letters; ff.125-45. Extracts of letters 17 July 1803 to 19 Aug. 1804 from A. W. H. Humphrey, mineralogist to His Majesty in the settlements at New South Wales. The letters are written from Rio de Janeiro, Sullivan's Bay, Port Phillip, and Hobart Town.

(4) General correspondence 28 Dec. 1750 to 30 Mar. 1809: ff.314-15. 1802 G. W. Evans, Port Jackson, wishing to apply for the situation of Deputy Commissary; ff.356-7, 361-2. 2 Apr. 1808, 30 Mar. 1809 R. Townson, Sydney, detailing the unpopularity of Bligh and Macarthur, lamenting his own situation, and seeking assistance in obtaining a suitable post.

42525-54 Piggot Papers

Historical collections relating to international law, compiled by Sir Francis Taylor Piggot.

42554 ff.117-23. 1 July, 16 Nov. 1918 from V. B. Grapp, Melbourne, concerning the settlement of his claims for reimbursement due to the failure of S.S. *Magdeburg* and S.S. *Lubeck* to complete their freight contracts. Includes ff.119-21 copy of letter 24 June 1918 from Grapp to Sir Robert Garran, typescript.

42575-85 Sherborn Autographs
Original letters and papers, mainly 19th-20th cent., selected from the collection of Charles Davies Sherborn, D.Sc.

42580 f.127. 9 July 1893 Charles Hedley, Sydney, to the editor of *Natural Science* saying he would like to express his views in the magazine on the controversy over 'the permanence of oceans and continents'.

ff.181b-182. 23 June 1891 Rev. Walter Howchin, North Adelaide, to C. D. Sherborn, discussing specimens.

ff.197-8. 9 Aug. 1866 Frederick Wollaston Hutton, Auckland, to T. R. Jones stating he was seeking appointment as a geologist for the Province of Auckland and would like a testimonial.

42583 The following letters are to Richard Owen.

f.3. 5 Nov. 1858 from Bishop Abraham of Wellington, saying he will forward specimens to him at the British Museum.

ff.127-8. 3 Nov. 1848 Sir George Grey, Auckland, stating he has lost a large proportion of his collections in a recent fire, but will endeavour to forward some samples.

ff.204-7. 13 July 1859 Sir William Macarthur, Camden Park, N.S.W., discussing scientific matters of mutual interest.

ff.219-20. 24 Feb. 1860 Mary Ann Martin, Auckland, describing the inhabitants of the Samoan, Loyalty, and Solomon Islands, and the influence of Christianity there.

ff.221-4. 31 Dec. 1860 William Martin, Auckland, discussing the Taranaki War.

42584 ff.48-9. 27 Mar. 1884 Sir Henry Parkes to Owen, introducing Lady Sophia Palmer.

42714 'Memoirs of the early life of John Elliott . . .', 11 Jan. 1759 to 12 Apr. 1782.

f.1b. List of officers and civilians on the quarterdeck of H.M.S. *Resolution* with brief notes on their ages and characters.

ff.7-45. Elliott's account as midshipman in the *Resolution* of Cook's second voyage 1772-4.

42772-846 Rose Papers
Correspondence and papers, official and private, of George Rose, statesman, his son Sir George Henry Rose, and grandson Field-Marshal Hugh Henry Rose, Baron Strathnairn.

42774 General correspondence of George Rose. ff.349b-56. Memo 10 Apr. 1816 on New Holland by Thomas Rowcroft, discussing relations between settlers and convicts.

42780A ff.143-8. Memo 1809 on the need for permanent regulations relating to New South Wales trade.

43039-358 Aberdeen Papers
Correspondence and papers, official and private, of George Gordon, afterwards (1818) Hamilton-Gordon, 4th Earl of Aberdeen.

43072 ff.1-194. Correspondence with Lord Stanley, 14th Earl of Derby.

ff.108-9. 6 Nov. 1844 from Stanley returning letter ff.110-12, 28 Oct. 1844 from Lady Charlotte Bacon seeking Governorship of New Zealand for her husband, Gen. Bacon.

43193-4 Correspondence with 1st Baron Brougham and Vaux.

43194 f.230. 6 June 1854 Saxe Bannister to Brougham appealing for justice.

43229-56 General correspondence 1801-60 of Lord Aberdeen.

43237 ff.99-102. Memo 17 June 1839 John Burnett, formerly Tasmanian Colonial

Secretary, to Lord Normanby requesting a further hearing in order to defend himself against the prejudicial statements made by Sir George Arthur.

43241 ff.219-21. 15 Sept. 1843 from Capt. John Toup Nicolas emphasising the reliance of Queen Pomare on Great Britain and her fear of the French.

ff.222-9. 4 June 1843 Acting Commodore Toup Nicolas, H.M.S. *Vindictive*, Papeete Harbour, to Rear-Adm. Du Petit Thouars, questioning the validity of the French Treaty while awaiting a decision from the British Government, printed.

43242 ff.7-9. 15 Dec. 1843 from Nicolas, Callao, stating that his conduct while in Tahiti entitles him to commendation equal to that of Capt. Sir Thomas Thompson.

ff.217-18. 22 Feb. 1844 Samuel Hill, formerly of the Society Is., to Lord Ashley regretting that Tahiti has fallen under the domination of France, and seeking an interview.

ff.251-2. 2 Apr. 1844 to Nicolas, informing him that he has misapprehended the extent of the obligations of the Government of Great Britain towards Tahiti.

43243 ff.183-4. 4 Sept. 1844 from Nicolas enclosing, ff.185-6, statement of the British naval force employed at Tahiti since the protectorate; with f.187 acknowledgement 7 Sept. 1844.

ff.191-5. 11 Sept. 1844 from Nicolas discussing the causes of hostility between the French and the natives in Tahiti, and mentioning the expulsion of George Pritchard.

ff.333-4. 14 Dec. 1844 from Nicolas forwarding an appeal from Queen Pomare (not enclosed) and informing Aberdeen that she has absented herself from her dominions until the French protectorate is withdrawn.

43244 ff.107-8. 10 Mar. 1845 from Capt. W. B. Hamilton enclosing, f.109, return of ships which have visited Tahiti in 1844.

43247 ff.112-13. 11 Feb. 1850 from Barzillai Quaife, Sydney, concerning validity of certain marriages performed according to the rite of the Church of Scotland.

43249 ff.311-24. 20 Apr. 1853 from Arthur Tidman, Foreign Secretary of the London Missionary Society, protesting against the French treatment of missionaries in Tahiti in violation of the Treaty.

43251 ff.36-7. 10 Aug. 1853 from Capt. Walter Meriton with, ff.38-9, petition 5 Aug. 1853 to Queen Victoria seeking knighthood or peerage as a reward for his important contributions towards navigation around the eastern coast of New Holland in 1816.

43333 Letter book containing copies of general correspondence of Lord Aberdeen as Secretary of State for War and the Colonies 1834-5, 1852-3. f.10. 21 Feb. 1835 to Gov. Arthur informing him of the appointment of John Montagu as Tasmanian Colonial Secretary.

43355-8 Confidential memoranda and papers, printed for the use of the Cabinet during Lord Aberdeen's tenure of office, some with annotations.

43357 ff.124-36. Bill for the Provisional Government of British settlements in the islands of New Zealand, concerning the appointment of Commissioners, n.d., printed draft.

ff.137-40. Bill for regulating the survey and sales of land belonging to the Crown, in the Australian colonies and New Zealand, 1842, printed draft.

f.141. Copy 9 May 1853 of a despatch dated 7 Feb. 1853 from the Duke of Newcastle to Sir William Denison, on the discontinuance of transportation to Van Diemen's Land, printed.

43358 ff.8-54. Printed papers concerning transportation including a history of the subject, its advantages and disadvantages, conclusions, an appendix of tables relating to the number of convicts transported, etc., and a report Nov. 1852 by Lieut.-Col. J. Jebb, C.B., Surveyor-General of Prisons, on 'the convict question'; ff.12b-16 concern attempts to open up new areas in New South Wales and Western Australia for the reception of convicts and f.21b the effects of the gold discoveries.

43383-92 Bright Papers

A selection from the correspondence, official and private, and other papers of John Bright, M.P.

43389 General correspondence 1845-87. ff.285-6. 15 Aug. 1878 from Henry Forbes in New South Wales on the support for Disraeli shown by his compatriots, and possible counter measures.

43510-644 Ripon Papers

Correspondence and papers of George Frederick Samuel Robinson, Viscount Goderich, 2nd Earl of Ripon, Earl de Grey of Wrest and 1st Marquess of Ripon.

43512 ff.84-232. Correspondence with Henry John Temple, 3rd Viscount Palmerston. ff.162-5, 168-9, 179-80. 16, 18, 20 Oct. 1863, 16 Mar. 1864 discussing the advisability of sending additional reinforcements of troops to New Zealand.

43513-15 Correspondence with William Ewart Gladstone and his wife Catherine.

43513 ff.109-14, 119-22, 156-7. 14, 15 Mar., 4 Apr. 1864, 9 Mar. 1865, on the cost of the New Zealand War.

43515 ff.95-6. 11 Dec. 1892 from Gladstone on the Solomon Islands.

ff.98-9. 2 Feb. 1893 to Gladstone giving his support to the Imperial Federation League, but with some reservations.

ff.100-1. 17 Feb. 1893 from Gladstone on the appointment of a Governor of New South Wales 'We of the House of Commons should like to see Duff'.

ff.106-7. 2 May 1893 on making Sir Alfred Stephen a Privy Councillor.

ff.121-3. 13 Oct. 1893 to Gladstone giving reasons why Lord Kintore should remain Governor of South Australia; with f.124 acknowledgement 14 Oct. 1893.

43516 Correspondence with 5th Earl of Rosebery.

ff.55-6. 11 Oct., 12 Nov. 1892 on making Sir Alfred Stephen a Privy Councillor.

ff.64-5, 73-4, 76-8. 15 Dec. 1892, 14, 22, 23 Apr. 1893 dealing with the advisability of establishing a protectorate over the Solomon Islands.

ff.97 100. 22, 23 Mar. 1894 on the need for financial encouragement of the plan for closer and more direct communications between Australia and Canada.

ff.113-19. 18-20 May 1894 discussing the possibility of the Australian colonies raising the question of Samoa at the Ottawa Conference.

ff.159-62, 175, 192. 14, 16 Oct., 20 Nov., 29 Dec. 1894 on candidates for governorships in South Australia and Victoria.

43517-18 Correspondence with Sir Henry Campbell-Bannerman.

ff.15-18. 16, 22 Sept. 1892 on the promotion of Lieut.-Col. V. French, late commander of the local forces in Queensland.

43518 ff.158-9, 160-3. 14, 22 Feb., 13 Mar. 1908, one letter from Campbell-Bannerman, and two from Vaughan Nash, on the choice of a Governor-General for Australia.

43545 ff.196-236 Correspondence with Sir Charles Gavan Duffy.

ff.235-6. 12 Nov. [c.1894] from Duffy inquiring whether Ripon has formulated an answer to a communication from some influential home rulers in Australia which he (Duffy) had sent.

43551 Correspondence with Edward Cardwell, Viscount Cardwell 1874, as Colonial Secretary, mainly letters from Cardwell.

ff.15-269. Include many letters 1864-5 on the withdrawal of troops from New Zealand with references to the strained relations between Sir Duncan Cameron and Sir George Grey.

ff.205-6. 26 July 1865 from Cardwell commenting on the length of Sir George Bowen's despatches.

43552 ff.1-51. Correspondence with 9th Earl of Elgin, as Colonial Secretary.

London

ff.44-51. 2, 4, 12 Mar. 1908 discussions leading up to the choice of Lord Dudley as Governor-General of Australia.

ff.52-241. Correspondence with Robert Offley Ashburton Crewe-Milnes, Earl and Marquess of Crewe.

ff.233-4. 16 Mar. 1909 from Crewe on difficulties of choosing suitable governors for the Australian states.

43553-5 Correspondence with Sydney Charles Buxton chiefly as Under-Secretary for the Colonies. The following letters are from Buxton.

43553 ff.9-10. 4 Oct. 1892 mentioning a ship from Mexico which has been recruiting in the Gilbert Islands.

ff.40-7. 13 Dec. 1892 brief comment on the Solomon Islands and the wisdom of the policy of protection.

ff.81-4. 10 Jan. [1893] making arrangements for the forthcoming meeting with Queensland separationists.

43555 ff.150-2. Correspondence 10, 12 Nov. 1899 between Ripon and Buxton on the 'Samoan Deal'.

43556-8 Correspondence with the Hon. Sir Robert Henry Meade, chiefly as Permanent Under-Secretary for the Colonies. Unless otherwise stated, the following letters are from Meade.

43556 ff.4-9. 2 Sept. 1892 on filling the vacant governorship in Tasmania, and colonial attitudes to the choice of governors.

ff.10-16. 3 Sept. 1892 over the term of office of the Secretary of the Colonial Defence Committee, Maj. Clarke.

ff.20-6. 8 Sept. 1892 stating that there was no annexation of the Gilbert Islands, only the establishment of a protectorate.

ff.71-4. 4 Oct. 1892 on German New Guinea and Uganda.

ff.80-5. 14 Nov. 1892 on the Colonial Defence Committee.

ff.90-3. 19 Nov. 1892 stating he is not in favour of making Bowen a baronet.

ff.221-2. 27 Mar. 1893 concerning cable to the Queensland Government requesting permission for Sir John Pender's telegraph scheme.

ff.233-6. 30 Mar. 1893 against officially rescinding government policy of assistance to old destitute soldiers in the colonies.

ff.246-7. 20 May 1893 on Bank of England consultations with Australian banks.

43557 ff.5-10. 12 Sept. 1893 on choice of governors for Queensland and Tasmania with reference to the salaries offered.

ff.131-2. 22 Oct. 1893 discussing Sir John Pender's cable.

ff.170-8. 29 Aug. 1894 on sending suitable person to Honolulu to assist with negotiations for the Pacific cable.

43558 ff.123-8. 30 May 1895 pointing out the difficulty of finding a suitable governor for New South Wales at the low salary offered.

ff.129-34. 31 May 1895 concerning a telegram sent to New South Wales.

43559-64 Correspondence with Colonial Governors.

43560 ff.1-54. Correspondence with the Earl of Jersey and Sir William Duff, Governors of New South Wales. ff.1-36 correspondence 1892-4 with Jersey on various subjects including a new constitution for Norfolk Island and his own resignation, and ff.37-54 correspondence 1894 with Duff on various subjects including the administration of Norfolk Island and political matters.

ff.55-115. Correspondence 1892-4 with Sir Henry Wylie Norman, Governor of Queensland, on various subjects including separation, elections, and telegraph cables.

ff.116-21. Correspondence 1890-2 with the Earl of Kintore, Governor of South Australia, concerning precedence, and justice in the Northern Territory.

ff.122-6. Correspondence 1892-3 with Sir Robert Hamilton and Viscount Gormanston, Governors of Tasmania, concerning the former's retirement and retrenchment measures adopted by the latter.

ff.127-46. Correspondence 1892-4 with the Earl of Hopetoun, Governor of Victoria, on various matters including the Australia Station and federation.

ff.147-75. Correspondence 1893-4 with Sir William Robinson, Governor of Western Australia, on relations with Sir John Forrest over the Aborigines Protection Board question and Gen. William Booth's plans for obtaining land in Western Australia for the benefit of the unemployed.

ff.176-233. Correspondence 1892-5 with the Earl of Glasgow, Governor of New Zealand, on various subjects including reform of the Legislative Council, elections, defence, the Cook Islands, Samoa, and the arrival of a French Roman Catholic mission in Rarotonga.

43621-40 General correspondence 1849-1909.

43622 ff.33-4. 8 June 1865 from Sir George Grey, Auckland, with complaints concerning the discrepancies between his own and Sir Duncan Cameron's despatches.

43637 ff.1-4. 4 Jan. 1893 from Arnold Morley on introduction of Imperial penny postage.

ff.64-6. Printed memo c.1894 for Ripon left by Robert Reid, Minister of Defence, Victoria, dealing with suggested amendments to the Australian Customs Act.

ff.144-5. 25 June 1895 from Henry Robert Brand, Viscount Hampden, refusing the order of K.C.M.G.

43647-78 Cobden Papers
Correspondence and other papers of Richard Cobden.

43667-71 General correspondence 1836-65.

43671 f.125. 24 Apr. 1864 from Sir Charles Gavan Duffy expressing full support for him over the recent controversy in *The Times*.

43697-701 Unpublished English translation by Walter Farrell, with notes and supplementary material based mainly on printed sources, of Fregattenkapitän Karl August Nerger, S.M.S. *Wolf*, Berlin 1918. The disguised auxiliary cruiser attacked allied and neutral shipping in the Indian, Pacific, and Atlantic Oceans 24 Nov. 1916 to 24 Feb. 1918. The volumes 43697-8 contain descriptions of the capture of such ships as the *Winslow*, *Wairuna*, and *Matunga*, while the *Wolf* was cruising in the Pacific Mar.-Apr. 1917, descriptions of places, remarks on Australian defence, and references to newspaper articles concerning the events in the Pacific.

43722-3 Sturge Papers
Correspondence of Joseph Sturge, M.P., philanthropist.

43722 ff.316-19. 19, 22 Nov. 1858 from Richard Cobden seeking recommendation of a suitable person in Sydney to advise on the fate of his recently orphaned nephews.

43874-967 Dilke Papers
Correspondence, literary MSS. and other papers of Sir Charles Wentworth Dilke, 2nd Bart. See S. L. Gwynn and G. M. Tuckwell, *The Life of the Rt. Hon. Sir Charles W. Dilke, Bart., M.P.*, London 1917, 2 vols., and R. Jenkins, *Sir Charles Dilke: A Victorian Tragedy*, London 1958. The catalogue of Add. MSS.43874-967 covers the first series of Dilke papers but the second, third, and fourth series (Add. MSS.49385-431, 49432-55, 49610-12) are still uncatalogued. All four series are described in a typescript list 'Descriptions of the Dilke papers'. The last three series are of no interest to this survey.

43874 Royal correspondence. ff.109-11. 7 Jan. 1884 from the Duke of Albany voicing a desire to succeed Lord Normanby as Governor of Victoria.

43875-98 General correspondence.

43877 ff.66-73. Correspondence 1869-94 with Sir Henry Parkes concerning the O'Farrell Case 1869, Parkes's forthcoming publication *Fifty Years in the Making of Australian History*, London 1892, 2 vols. and introducing Charles Lyne of Sydney 1894.

f.74. 17 Aug. 1879 from Graham Berry concerning the Reform Bill he has submitted to Parliament, see Add. MS.43934 f.97.

ff.75-8. Correspondence 1900-2 with Sir Edmund Barton including letters 5, 7 May 1900 concerning an opportunity to address members of the House of Commons in order to counter the effects of Sir Julian Salomons's meeting.

ff.79-201. Correspondence 1888-1910 with Deakin on various subjects including legislation, federation, tariffs, the Chinese strike in Sydney, the New Hebrides, Dilke's book, *Problems of Greater Britain*, London 1890, 2 vols., Deakin's book, *Irrigated India, An Australian View of India and Ceylon, their Irrigation and Agriculture*, London 1893.

43881 Correspondence with Granville George Leveson-Gower, 2nd Earl Granville, including ff.204-5 letter 24 Feb. 1885 to Granville reporting on the attitude of the German Ambassador, Count George Herbert von Münster, to the New Guinea problem.

43885-9 Correspondence 1871-1906 with Joseph Chamberlain.

43886 f.267 [*c*.22 Nov. 1884] comments by Dilke, Kimberley, and Chamberlain on Australian federation, typescript copy (probably the original was a scrap of paper passed round at a Cabinet meeting).

43887 ff.2-3. 3 Jan. 1885 from Chamberlain stating his view that the German annexation of New Guinea is very 'unfriendly' but explanation will be requested.

43898 ff.23-4. 1 May 1879 to Frank Harrison Hill, editor of the *Daily News* on the subject of Berry's mission stating that the Victorian Upper House should confine themselves to acting like the House of Lords and not claim financial equality with the Assembly.

43899-908 Family correspondence.

43900-1 Correspondence 1866-7 with Sir Charles Wentworth Dilke, 1st Bart, during travels gathering material for his book *Greater Britain*, London 1868, 2 vols.

43900 ff.215-51. Nov.-Dec. 1866 concerning the voyage, Pitcairn Is. and New Zealand.

43901 ff.1-39. Jan.-Feb. 1867 concerning Australia.

43909-22 General correspondence 1855-1911.

43914 f.107. 22 Mar. 1889 to John Cooksey inquiring about the background of Rev. E. Davis of Sydney.

ff.132-3. 3 June 1889 from Charles H. Pearson, Melbourne, referring to a letter dated 12 Apr. which Dilke wrote to Deakin, and saying he will give a general review of Dilke's case in an article in *The Age*.

ff.185-7. 18 Feb. 1890 from George Melly, M.P., congratulating Dilke on his book and commending in particular the Australian section.

ff.197-8. 12 Mar. 1890 to A. Patchett Martin concerning postage.

ff.201-2. 18 Mar. [1890] from Alfred Edmund Bateman, Board of Trade, suggesting that a paper on Australasian wealth should be read at the Statistical Society.

ff.206-7. 22 Mar. [1890?] from J.C.B. [?] discussing his reviews of Dilke's *Problems of Greater Britain*.

f.210. 29 Mar. 1890 from Henry H. Hayter, Government Statistician, Victoria, concerning Dilke's paper for the Statistical Society.

ff.232-4. 18 Apr. 1890 from Lord Carrington describing the marked hostility in New South Wales to the Naval Tribute Bill.

ff.261-2. 12 July 1890 from Andrew I. Clark, Attorney General, Tasmania, enclosing letter of introduction given him by Deakin and seeking an appointment.

f.306. [c.27 Dec. 1890] to A. Patchett Martin saying he has no personal relation with any other [?] Australasian newspapers, incomplete.

ff.307-9. 30 Dec. 1890 to A. Patchett Martin fearing that the usefulness of the paper on the Imperial Federation League will be limited if proclaimed official.

43915 ff.9-12. 10, 15, 22 Apr. 1891 to A. Patchett Martin on the possibility of writing a joint article for the *Forum* magazine on constitutions, with reference to Upper Houses, referring to a letter from Sir Henry Parkes in which 'he buries the hatchet' and expressing agreement with Martin as to the present chances of federation.

f.26. 1 Aug. [1891] from Lord Kintore sending copy despatch written during his overland journey from Darwin to Adelaide and asking for comments.

ff.174, 181-2. 18 Apr., 23 May 1894 from Sir Saul Samuel asking Dilke to present a petition to the House of Commons regarding damages in the *Costa Rica Packet* case and seeking an interview.

f.278. 13 Aug. 1896 to H. R. Fox Bourne saying he still held the strongest opinion against the labour system in Fiji, typescript copy.

43916 f.143. 16 Aug. 1899 Lord Jellicoe to Lord Jersey telling him that the Australian Premiers were fully informed of the Colonial Office views on the Privy Council.

ff.154-5. 5 Dec. 1899 from John G. Bowrand, Ottawa, expressing his opinion that the Australian Commonwealth Bill repeated the defects of the United States federal system.

ff.166-7. 26 Dec. 1899 from Lord Jersey expecting that Barton would come to watch the progress of the Australian Commonwealth Bill through Parliament.

f.221. [May 1900] from [?] mentioning the second reading of the Australian Commonwealth Bill.

ff.222-3. 12 May 1900 from W. P. Reeves explaining that Seddon's Amendment Act of 1896, which provided that wages current in New Zealand should be paid to all vessels engaged in the coasting trade, was unlikely to affect English shipping companies.

ff.251b-2. 16 Nov. 1900 from Sir John Alexander Cockburn asking Dilke to write a preface to the small volume of speeches which he had delivered at various conferences [*Australian Federation*, with a preface by Hon. C. W. Dilke, London 1901].

43917 ff.103-4. 29 Apr. 1902 from Sir Edward Hutton, Melbourne, sending a copy of the minutes on defence which he had prepared for the Commonwealth Government.

43919 f.39. 15 Mar. 1906 from Lord Knutsford sending ff.40-3 letter 13 June 1890 from Deakin to Knutsford commending Dilke's analysis of the Australian scene in his *Problems of Greater Britain*.

ff.230-5. 16, 21 June 1907 from Sir George Clarke on defence.

43920 ff.114-15. 21 May 1908 from H. A. Guzone inquiring whether Dilke would contribute any articles, perhaps on Australian defence, to the *Standard of Empire*.

f.120. 2 June 1908 from Reginald McKenna awaiting the official comments on Deakin's naval observations.

43922 f.175. 23 Dec. 1910 to Rev. J. Harris inquiring about reports of forcible labour recruitment by French ships in the New Hebrides, typescript copy.

43923 Parliamentary and other official papers of Dilke, including memos prepared for the use of the Cabinet. Printed, but with notes. ff.45-8. Memo 12 July 1885 by Sir Edward Hertslet on the expulsion of Consul Pritchard from Tahiti by the French naval authorities in 1844.

43930-41 Memoirs 1887-1911 of Dilke mainly in the handwriting of his secretary H. K. Hudson, with autograph corrections by Dilke. Much of it is undated since it is in the form of continuous narrative.

43930 ff.189, 200-1. Refers to his visit to Australia and New Zealand.

43931 f.8. Apr. 1869 his speech on questions connected with the trial of O'Farrell, which led to angry correspondence with Henry Parkes.

43934 ff.11-13. Mention interview with Graham Berry, Premier of Victoria; f.62, n.d. [May 1879] describes Sir Arthur Gordon as a man who invented in the name of civilisation and progress a new kind of slavery in Fiji; f.199 referring to Pacific Phosphate Co.'s behaviour in Ocean Is., the Gilbert Is., and Fiji; ff.203-5 referring to indentured labour in Papua and Fiji.

43937 ff.34-8. Summary of events in New Hebrides 1860-83; ff.133-4, 12 June 1883 on the tardy action of the government concerning annexation of New Guinea; f.164, n.d. [Oct. 1883] attack on Lord Derby's Australasian policy; ff.169-71, n.d. [Oct.-Nov. 1883] dealing with Australian concern over French transportation to the New Hebrides and other Pacific islands.

43939 f.26. n.d. [Jan. 1885] on Germany's attitude to Samoa; ff.40-1, 21 Jan. [1885] Cabinet agreement to annexation of New Guinea and f.75, 17 Feb. [1885] its cost.

43941 ff.35-6. [1887] mentioning effects of his support of Australian protests at French occupation of the New Hebrides; ff.69, 88, 122, 156-7, 179 brief references 1888-90 to his correspondence with Deakin and Deakin's views on the question of titles; ff.228-9 [1891] extract from Lord Kintore's letter on his overland journey across Australia and commenting that Kintore's despatch on the subject was a 'great mistake'.

43944-5 Drafts, annotated proof sheets of articles, and notes for various publications, 1878-1910.

43944 ff.48-75. Presidential address 19 Nov. 1907 delivered by Dilke to the Royal Statistical Society making unfavourable comparison between the statistical progress of the mother country and that of the South Sea colonies, commending in particular the contribution made by T. A. Coghlan, printed.

43945 ff.48-60. Lecture 14 Jan. [1907] on imperial defence, given by Dilke at Newcastle, printed.

f.51. Referring to Seddon's proposals for the creation, with some imperial assistance, of a New Zealand force instantly available for imperial service overseas.

f.58. Mentioning soundness of the Australian scheme of a partially paid volunteer force. With ff.62-73 printed copy of this draft.

ff.192-216. Papers by Dilke on indentured and forced labour, part of a collection of papers on inter-racial problems communicated to the first Universal Races Congress 26-9 July 1911, typescript with corrections.

ff.197-8. Mentioning the complete failure of indentured labour in the New Caledonian nickel mines and the small scale French 'kidnapping' of labour in the South Pacific.

ff.203-5. Other examples, taken from New Guinea, New Caledonia, Fiji.

44027-54 Samuel Butler Papers

Correspondence and other papers of, or relating to, Samuel Butler, author.

44027-42 General correspondence 1841-1902 including family and business letters. Many of the letters from Butler are typescript or autograph press copies. H. F. Jones has added a number of notes and made use of the correspondence for *Samuel Butler, Author of Erewhon 1835-1902: A Memoir*, London 1919, 2 vols.

44027 Correspondence 6 Feb. 1841 to 24 Dec. 1873 including ff.70-4, 91-3, 10 May, 28 July 1859 mentioning immigration to New Zealand; f.101 note 15 July 1901 by Butler 'I have destroyed a very large number of letters of mine from N.Z. They were very long, no one can ever conceivably want them & the substance of the greater number of them was printed in "First Impressions of the Canterbury Settlement, N.Z." [*A First Year in Canterbury Settlement*, London 1863] which my people published before I returned from N.Z.'; ff.102-10, 31 May 1861 from Christchurch to his father mentioning money sent and the sheep farm at Rangitata; ff.111-12, 2 Aug. 1861 from his father, T. Butler; ff.113-14 copy of letter n.d. from T. Butler to Sir Julius von Haast mentioning *Handbook of the New Zealand Flora*, London 1864, 2 vols., by J. D. Hooker; ff.115-48 various folios only, correspondence 26 Sept. 1864 to 28 Oct. 1868 with Haast; ff.117-19, 17 Aug. 1865 to his father mentioning sale of property in New Zealand; ff.121-2 copy of letter 6 Oct. 1864 from C. Darwin mentioning controversy in the Christchurch press between Butler and Bishop Abraham, then Bishop of Wellington, N.Z., with copy of Butler's notes; ff.227-8, 23 Feb. 1873 to Haast mentioning the copying of a portrait of Cook at the National Maritime Museum, Greenwich; ff.304-5, 24 Dec. 1873 to Haast sending copy of Butler's *Fair Haven*, London 1873, and saying Leonard Darwin was going to New Zealand.

44028 Correspondence 7 Jan. 1874 to 13 Dec. 1880 including f.17, 2 Aug. 1874 to Haast; ff.217-36, 4 Nov. 1879 to his father mentioning C. P. Pauli, a friend of Butler, at one time sub-editor of Christchurch newspapers.

44029 Correspondence 8 Jan. 1881 to 28 Dec. 1883 including f.157, 31 Dec. 1881 to the New Zealand Trust & Loan Co. concerning dividends of shares in the Company.

44030 Correspondence 2 Jan. 1884 to 30 Dec. 1885 including ff.338-41, 12 Sept. 1885 from Col. A. Lean, Christchurch Club, N.Z., thanking Butler for his book and giving local news.

44031 Correspondence 18 Jan. to 30 Dec. 1886 including ff.13-16, 7 Feb. 1886 from A. Lean of the Christchurch Club mentioning Butler's book, music, etc.; ff.161-2, 4 Nov. 1886 from Haast, London, accepting gift of Butler's books.

44033 Correspondence 31 Jan. 1889 to 31 Dec. 1891 including ff.7-8, 23 Aug. 1913 from A. H. Turnbull, Wellington, N.Z., sending copy of a letter 14 Feb. 1889 from Butler to A. Marks concerning *A First Year in Canterbury Settlement*, and the editing of it by his family.

44034 Correspondence 7 Feb. 1892 to 24 Dec. 1894 including ff.2-3, 7 Feb. 1892 to Mrs Bovill referring to Parramatta and New Zealand; f.13, 22 Feb. 1892 to C. P. Pauli; ff.51-4, 160-3, 177-8, 229-32, 264-7 correspondence 10 July 1892 to 12 Dec. 1893 with A. Lean mentioning literary matters, music, and local news.

44038 Correspondence 1 Jan. to 30 Dec. 1898 including ff.3-72, 2 Jan. to 16 Mar. 1898 concerning the death of Pauli and Butler's relations with him; ff.88-90, 22 Mar. 1898 from G. S. Sale, Professor of Classics, Dunedin University, asking for details of Pauli's death, with reply 14 Apr. 1898.

44040 Correspondence 1 Jan. to 31 Dec. 1900 including f.111, 17 July and f.163, 3 Oct. 1900 from William Rolleston written in England before his return to New Zealand.

44041 Correspondence 1 Jan. to 31 Dec. 1901 including f.192, 18 Nov. 1901 from W. H. Trigg, editor of *The Press*, Christchurch, N.Z., sending a copy of the Jubilee edition of *The Daily Press* and a copy of *The Daily Press* containing an article on *Erewhon Revisited*, London [1921].

44042 Correspondence 1 Jan. to 15 June 1902 including ff.48-9, 82-3, 109, 133-5 correspondence Jan.-Apr. 1902 with O. T. J. Alpers, Christchurch, N.Z., concerning Alpers's review of *Erewhon Revisited* and the complete set of Butler's books which Haast was instructed to place in a library in New Zealand; ff.66-7, 10 Feb. 1902 to the editor of *The Spectator* objecting to the misrepresentation of his intentions in a review of *Erewhon Revisited* and asking that his letter detailing these be published.

44043 Correspondence 1871-85 with E. M. A. Savage containing copies prepared by Butler for publication from the originals preserved in part in Add. MSS.44027-30. See *Letters between Samuel Butler and Miss E. M. A. Savage 1871-1885*, ed. G. Keynes and B. Hill, London 1935.

London

44045-50 Copy B (the first press copy) of Butler's notebooks 1874-1902, with annotations by H. F. Jones and later editorial marks. A selection published by H. F. Jones, *The Note-books of Samuel Butler*, London 1912, and A. T. Bartholomew, *Further Extracts from the Note-books of Samuel Butler*, London 1934.

44051 H. F. Jones, *The Note-books of Samuel Butler*, 1912, with annotations by the editor and page references to the original MSS. (Add. MSS.44045-50), these references being revised and checked in 1930 by G. W. Webb.

44052 Cuttings and other extracts made by Butler *c*.1863-1901 including ff.3-4 articles by J. C. Veel of *The Press*, Christchurch, N.Z., and f.24b Amusements in Australia, from *The Era*, [Sydney?] 26 Nov. 1892 giving reviews of opera and the theatre.

44053-4 H. F. Jones, *Samuel Butler . . . A Memoir*, London 1920, 2 vols., printed copy with notes and chalk markings by A. T. Bartholomew and page references to the notebooks by G. W. Webb.

44086-835 Gladstone Papers

Correspondence and other papers of William Ewart Gladstone. Originally accumulated and housed at Hawarden Castle, Cheshire, these papers were transferred to the British Museum in 1930. A small proportion of the original collection was later returned to Hawarden as unsuitable for retention. The catalogue of the collection *Catalogue of Additions to the Manuscripts. The Gladstone Papers*, 1953, contains a description of the manuscripts in numerical order. Although examination of the manuscripts led to items not indexed, it was impossible to inspect each document and some relevant material may have been missed.

44086-562 Correspondence.

44090 Correspondence 1879-96 with John Campbell Hamilton-Gordon, 7th Earl of Aberdeen.

ff.82-5. 19 Apr. 1887 from Aberdeen concerning his visit to New Zealand and commenting on the loyal attitude of the Irish in the colonies.

f.86. Cutting from *Sydney Daily Telegraph* *c*.1887 describing Aberdeen's visit to Albury.

44096-7 Correspondence 1853-65 with George Arbuthnot at the Treasury.

44097 ff.7-13, 24-32, 61-6, 144-5. Correspondence 6 Jan. 1863 to 13 Apr. 1864 concerning the Sydney Mint and the proposal to make Australian sovereigns legal tender in Britain; includes f.28 letter 19 Dec. 1862 to Thomson Hankey, M.P., signed 'Anglo-Australia', Sydney.

44107 Correspondence 1840-89 with Sir Frederick Rogers, 8th Bart, 1st Baron Blachford 1871. ff.236-8, 263-4, 289-95. Four letters 27 Mar. 1846 to 9 June 1869 concerning the legal problems of the Australian church and the Colonial Bishoprics Fund, including a reference in 1869 to Henry Hutton Parry, Bishop of Barbados, later of Perth.

44118-20 Correspondence 1845-68 [i.e. 1870] with Edward Cardwell, Viscount Cardwell 1874, Secretary of State for War.

44118 ff.172-3. 15 Aug. 1864 from Cardwell on the New Zealand loan.

ff.183-6. 2 Feb. 1865 from Gladstone opposing the granting of pensions to colonial garrisons.

ff.199-207. Three letters Sept., Oct. 1865 from Cardwell on New Zealand affairs and the position of Gov. Grey.

44119 ff.1-10. Jan. 1869 from Cardwell to Lord Granville with recommendations concerning military contributions of the colonies, printed.

ff.21-6. 9 Jan. 1869 from Cardwell regarding distribution of men in the forces.

ff.185-90. Memo 30 Dec. 1870 by Cardwell on proposed Army Organization Bill, printed.

44128-32 Correspondence 1865-95 with Hugh Culling Eardley Childers, Home Secretary.

44131 ff.121-2. Memo 29 July 1884 from Charles William Fremantle, Deputy Master of the Mint, to Childers concerning the vacant mastership of the Melbourne Mint, the delicacy of the position, and the suitability of officers of the Royal Engineers.

44137 ff.228-385. Correspondence 1841-78 with the Rev. Edward Coleridge of Eton College, Commissary of Bishop Selwyn of New Zealand and Bishop Broughton of Australia. This section contains many letters relevant to church problems in New Zealand and Australia, Maori land rights, and missions in Melanesia.

44141-2 Correspondence 1850-86 with Edward Henry Stanley, Lord Stanley 1851, 15th Earl of Derby 1869.

44141 ff.68-9, 89-92, 115, 139-40, 146-8. Correspondence 23 Apr. to 13 Sept. 1883 concerning the Australian demand for British annexation of New Guinea and the islands of the South West Pacific.

ff.75-6, 107-15, 128-31. Correspondence 24 Feb. to 7 June 1883 concerning a public meeting and a loyal address organised by Peter Campbell in Sydney, approving Britain's Irish policy and deprecating Mr Redmond's activities in Australia on behalf of the Irish National League.

ff.82, 126-7. 17 May, 10 July 1883 from Derby concerning the extension of Gov. Phipps's term of office.

44142 ff.14-18, 65, 84-6, 108-9, 115-18. 7 Dec. 1883 to 15 Jan. 1885 from Derby concerning the Australian demand for British annexation of New Guinea and the islands of the South West Pacific; ff.108-9 refer to the suggested bargain with Germany concerning New Guinea and Samoa and ff.115-18 to the offer to buy West New Guinea from Holland.

ff.39-44, 47. 5-28 Jan. 1884 from Derby concerning the application of Prince Leopold, 1st Duke of Albany, for appointment as governor of Victoria or New South Wales.

ff.45-6, 49-53, 56-7. Correspondence 25 Jan. to 24 Mar. 1884 concerning candidates for appointment as governor of Victoria, terminating with the selection of Sir Henry Brougham Loch.

ff.67-72. 22, 25 Aug. 1884 from Derby proposing to appoint Charles Dalton Clifford Lloyd to the mastership of the Australian Mint, and the reaction in Australia to officials from Ireland.

ff.93-4. 23 Oct. 1884 from Derby concerning a parliamentary question about the possible federation of the Australian colonies.

ff.115-18. 1 Mar. 1885 from Derby concerning the proposed appointment of Carrington as Governor of New South Wales.

44162 Correspondence 1836-71 with Sir George Grey, 2nd Bart, of Fallodon, Home Secretary.

ff.155-7. 28 July 1854 from Grey concerning the appointment of Mr Lawley to the government of New South Wales.

ff.158-63. 14, 18 Dec. 1854 from Grey on the 'difficult and troublesome question of the debt to the New Zealand Company charged on the land sales'.

44163-4 Correspondence 1837-55 with Sir James Robert George Graham, 2nd Bart, of Netherby.

44163 ff.143-5. Admiralty memo 1854 relating to the services of Thomas Henry Huxley as assistant surgeon in H.M.S. *Rattlesnake* 1846-50.

44165-80 Correspondence 1850-91 with Granville George Leveson Gower, 2nd Earl Granville, chiefly as Foreign Secretary. See *The Political Correspondence of Mr. Gladstone and Lord Granville 1868-1876*, ed. Agatha Ramm, London 1952, 2 vols., and *1876-1886*, London 1962, 2 vols., which contain some useful cross references to relevant material in the Granville papers (P.R.O. 30/29), and the Foreign Office papers (F.O. 97/621), both in the Public Record Office. The following are letters from Granville to Gladstone.

44166 ff.176-9. 6 Oct. 1869 thanking him for approval of the despatch to Bowen confirming the policy of withdrawing British troops from New Zealand.

ff.184-7. 13 Oct. 1869 with note at end of letter, crossed out, 'Fetherstone and Dillon Bell will arrive in London from New Zealand in December', for loan negotiations.

ff.188-9. 16 Oct. 1869 announcing receipt of 'another violent letter from Lord Russell' objecting to British policy in New Zealand.

44167 ff.21-2. 2 Mar. 1870 thanking Gladstone for his intervention preventing the carrying of a motion against the government for state aid to emigration.

ff.62-3. [?30] June 1870 on the New Zealand loan and mentioning Verdon's belief that separation is likely.

44182 Correspondence 1865-88 with Sir William Brampton Gurdon, private secretary to Gladstone. f.86. Memo 13 June 1873 to Gurdon concerning the departure of the commission to inquire into Fiji.

44213 ff.227-359. Correspondence 1842-82 with Alexander James Beresford Hope, M.P.

ff.230-9. Memo 8-13 Jan. 1846 concerning the new Australian bishoprics and their endowment.

44224-9 Correspondence 1866, 1859-96 with John Wodehouse, 3rd Baron Wodehouse, 1st Earl of Kimberley. Unless otherwise stated, the following are letters from Kimberley to Gladstone.

44224 ff.93-4. 30 Oct. 1870 on naval defence of Australia.

ff.118-19. 23 Mar. 1871 concerning the South Australian and Victorian Bills on marriage with deceased wife's sister.

ff.132-3, 137-40, 150, 234-8, 240-55, 260-1, 266-7, 270-5, 307-8. Correspondence 15 May 1871 to 15 Mar. 1872 and 30 Oct. 1872 concerning differential inter-colonial customs tariffs in Australia and New Zealand and their implications as to trade with foreign countries and defence.

ff.187-94. 26 July 1871 discussing the suggested annexation of Fiji by New South Wales, also stating 'a Hawaiian protectorate seems to me a most proposterous notion'.

ff.232-3. 16 Dec. 1871 on the kidnapping of South West Pacific islanders for labour.

ff.294-5. 7 May 1872 regarding objections to the appointment of Hugh Culling Eardley Childers as governor of Victoria.

44225 ff.6-9, 23, 25-8. Memos 16 Feb. to 21 Mar. 1873 concerning Australian customs tariffs.

ff.10-22, 24, 29-32, 35-7, 45-50, 53-7, 66-70, 138-9, 156-7. Memos 24 Feb. 1873 to 4 Nov. 1874 concerning the annexation of Fiji; ff.192-6, 20 July 1880 Rotumah Island (partly printed); f.157, 4 Nov. 1874 New Guinea.

f.71. Memos 4 Aug. 1873 concerning transfer of Normanby from Queensland to Canada.

ff.184-6, 213-14. Memos 29 June, 31 July 1880 concerning the transfer of Sir Hercules Robinson to Cape Colony.

ff.252-6. Correspondence 25 Oct., 5 Nov. 1880 concerning a complaint by Charles Bradlaugh, M.P., about the prolonged detention of Maori prisoners in New Zealand.

44226 ff.105-9. Memos 4, 9 May 1881 proposing knighthoods for six Colonial Chief Justices, including James Prendergast of New Zealand, Samuel James Way of South Australia, Charles Lilley of Queensland, and John Gorrie of Fiji.

ff.191-3. 14, 15 July 1881 Saul Samuel, Agent General for New South Wales, to Kimberley concerning his government's fear of excessive Irish immigration as a possible result of the Irish Land Bill, copy.

ff.226-9, 263-4. 30 July, 21 Sept. 1881 proposing a baronetcy for Sir Samuel Wilson of Victoria.

44228 ff.8-11. 25 Oct. 1882 proposing a baronetcy for William John Clarke of Victoria.

44237 Correspondence 1846-72 with Sir John Young, 2nd Bart 1848, Baron Lisgar 1870.

ff.334-5. 5 Jan. 1861 from Young inviting Gladstone to a dinner arranged by a deputation of New South Welshmen in London for himself, their governor elect.

ff.336-9. 21 Aug. 1863 from Young concerning the extension of settlement in New South Wales and Queensland, the conduct of Parliament, the Mint, and the moderation of the local press.

ff.342-4. 3 June 1868 Robert Allwood, Lyndhurst, N.S.W., to Young concerning Young's plan (ff.345-8) for the maintenance of the Irish clergy after disestablishment of the Church of Ireland, and with observation on the working of the voluntary system of church support in New South Wales.

44238-40 Correspondence 1839-56 of W. E. Gladstone with his brother-in-law George William Lyttelton, 4th Baron Lyttelton. Unless otherwise stated, the following are letters from Lyttelton to Gladstone.

44238 ff.172-3. 24 Jan. 1846 forwarding a letter from Wakefield and mentioning the Wairau affair.

ff.183-4. 4 July 1846 on the need for measures to remedy the disparity of sexes in Van Diemen's Land and advocating the lengthening of the term of office of colonial governors.

f.188. 14 Aug. 1846 mentioning FitzRoy's pamphlet on New Zealand.

ff.248-9. 26 Apr. 1851 requesting that Gladstone give a careful reading to Sewell's paper on New Zealand.

ff.258-61, 266-7, 278-9. 21 Nov. 1851, 19 Aug., 22 Dec. 1852 on the Canterbury Settlement.

44240 f.364. Cutting from *The Colonies* 29 Apr. 1876 entitled 'Lord Lyttelton and Wakefield'.

44262-3 Correspondence 1832-56 with Henry Pelham Pelham Clinton, Earl of Lincoln, 5th Duke of Newcastle 1851, Secretary of State.

44262 ff.146-7. 3 Feb. 1854 from Gladstone concerning reduction in expenditure of the convict establishment in Van Diemen's Land.

ff.162-3. 16 Dec. 1854 from Newcastle saying that it is unlikely that Parliament will consider any payment to the New Zealand Co. as little could be recovered from the colony.

44263 ff.147-8. 19 June 1862 to Newcastle forwarding a petition from the Provincial Council of Auckland, with ff.149-50 reply 19 June 1862.

44275 Correspondence 1834-50 with Sir Robert Peel, 2nd Bart. ff.279-80. 13 Apr. 1846 to Peel concerning the report of the New Zealand Co. and their proposals for the management of the colony, and ff.281-4 Peel's reply 15 Apr. 1846.

44286-7 Correspondence 1853-97 with George Frederick Samuel Robinson, Viscount Goderich, 2nd Earl of Ripon and 3rd Earl de Grey of Wrest 1859, 1st Marquess of Ripon 1871.

44287 ff.119-22. Correspondence 3-7 Dec. 1892 concerning candidature for appointment as prelates of the Order of St Michael and St George of Bishops Barry, Moorhouse, and Selwyn.

ff.123-4. 10 Dec. 1892 from Ripon with ff.125-36 typescript memo by Sydney Buxton on the establishment of a protectorate over the Solomon Islands.

ff.137-9, 141, 149. Correspondence 2 Jan., 20 Feb., 15 Aug. 1893 concerning the appointment of a governor of New South Wales.

f.157. Telegram 13 Oct. 1893 from Gladstone, and ff.158-61, letter 13 Oct. 1893 from Ripon concerning the appointment of a governor of South Australia.

f.179. 18 Dec. 1893 from Ripon suggesting a knighthood for Sir William Patrick Manning, Mayor of Sydney.

44299 ff.1-196. Correspondence 1828-75 with George Augustus Selwyn, Bishop of New Zealand 1841, and Lichfield 1868. Unless otherwise stated the letters are from Selwyn to Gladstone.

ff.31-2. 26 Jan. 1837 sending a printed appeal for aid to 'the friends of the Church of England, in behalf of their brethren in Australia'.

ff.70-2, 77-80. 19, 20 Jan., 24 May 1841 concerning his brother's refusal of the bishopric of New Zealand.

ff.81-162. 27 Aug. 1841 to 11 Dec. 1867 concerning his own tenure of the bishopric of New Zealand.

ff.177-80. Memo 1 Jan. 1871 by John Coleridge Patteson, Bishop of Melanesia, for the general synod of the church, concerning the removal of natives from islands of the South West Pacific for labour in Queensland and Fiji, copy.

ff.181-2. Extract from a letter 8 July 1871 from Patteson to Selwyn concerning the deportation of the islanders, Norfolk Island school and his own immediate plans for travel.

44319-22 Correspondence 1851-96 with the Hon. Sir Arthur Hamilton-Gordon, 1st Baron Stanmore 1893.

44320 ff.192-6, 199-202. Correspondence 4-31 Dec. 1874 concerning Gordon's appointment as governor of Fiji. ff.256-79. Correspondence 22 Mar. to 9 Nov. 1876 including four letters from Gordon in Fiji concerning his administration and also foreign affairs.

44321 ff.1-36, 114-18. Correspondence 1 Jan. 1877 to 17 May 1878, 1 Jan. to 7 Aug. 1880 including eight letters from Gordon in Fiji.

ff.37-8. 3 Feb. 1878 Carnarvon to Gordon commending Gordon's work, copy.

ff.124-41. Correspondence 3 Sept. 1881 to 6 May 1882 including four letters from Gordon in New Zealand expressing his disgust with the treatment of the Maoris and criticising parliamentary government and the press.

ff.147-9. 18 Sept. 1882 concerning Gordon's visit to Fiji and the success of his native policy there.

ff.157-79. 20 Apr. to 9 Oct. 1883 including five letters from Gordon advising against the annexation of New Guinea, comparing Australian interest there with the desire of settlers in Fiji for annexation by New Zealand, and maintaining the High Commission to be the best machinery for safeguarding British interests in the Western Pacific.

ff.211-15. 23 May, 8 Aug. 1884 Mary Gladstone to Gordon concerning the social influence of governors, referring to Sir Henry Loch and the 2nd Marquess of Normanby, to Bishop Barry, and to the Colonial Federation Conference.

44337 Correspondence 1852-69 with Sir Richard Bethell, 1st Baron Westbury 1861, Lord Chancellor.

ff.139-42. c.14 Oct. 1854 from Gladstone on the Colonial Bishops' Bill.

ff.146-9. 25 Apr. 1855 from Bethell discussing the legal right of the Colonial Church to hold diocesan synods.

44346 Correspondence 1853-5 with James Wilson, M.P., Financial Secretary to the Treasury. ff.15-30. 17 May 1853 from Wilson concerning the formation of a bank to facilitate trade between Australia, India and China.

44350 Correspondence 1828-88 with Sir Charles Alexander Wood, Commissioner of Emigration. The following are letters from Wood to Gladstone.

ff.31-4. 26 Aug. 1848 concerning native affairs in New Zealand.

ff.45-6. 28 Feb. 1850 concerning the New Zealand Co.'s finances.

ff.72-3. 2 Aug. 1854 concerning the new governor of South Australia, Sir Richard MacDonnell.

44352-526 General correspondence. Unless otherwise stated, the following are letters to Gladstone.

44355 ff.100-3. 26 July 1836 Bishop Broughton of Australia to H. Coleridge introducing James Macarthur and mentioning difficulties with Roman Catholics.

44356 ff.107-8. 31 July 1838 John Walpole Willis, Sydney, concerning his censure by John Bede Polding, Roman Catholic Bishop of Australia, for expressing his religious preferences.

ff.215-18. 7 Mar. 1839 G. W. Robertson, editor of the *Sydney Standard*, concerning conditions in New South Wales, criticising the government there and urging the colonisation of New Zealand.

44357 ff.19-20. 7 Sept. 1839 Willis, Sydney, concerning his dispute with Bishop Polding and religious education.

f.21. 3 Mar. 1839 Constantine Henry Phipps, 1st Marquess of Normanby, to Sir George Gipps urging him to use his influence to promote religious toleration in New South Wales, copy.

44360 ff.281-4. 19 Oct. 1843 William Selwyn with extracts from a letter 9 May 1843 written by his son G. A. Selwyn in Auckland, describing his church and school.

44363 ff.62-3. 27 Dec. 1845 Sir Thomas Tancred mentioning that his youngest brother is about to sail for Hobart to join Archdeacon Marriott.

ff.145-6, 150-1, 340-2, 354, 373-4. 14 Jan. to 30 Mar. 1846 Gladstone to Archbishop of Canterbury concerning the government of the Australian church following dispute in Van Diemen's Land.

ff.163-8, 290-7, 308-9, 328-37, 359-60, 371-2. Drafts of despatches 30 Jan. to 30 Mar. 1846 Gladstone to Sir George Grey concerning the government of New Zealand, the New Zealand Co., land titles, Maori rights, Col. William Wakefield's views, and commending Bishop Selwyn of New Zealand.

f.273. 10 Mar. 1846 Gladstone to Lieut.-Col. George Barney offering him appointment as superintendent of North Australia, and possibly later as surveyor-general of New South Wales.

ff.338-9. 21 Mar. 1846 Gladstone to Thomas Cudbert Harington, secretary of the New Zealand Co., concerning land grants at Wellington and Nelson.

ff.357-8. Memo 26 Mar. 1846 from Duke of Wellington concerning the military establishment in New Zealand.

ff.367-70. Draft despatch 30 Mar. 1846 Gladstone to Gov. FitzRoy concerning the Colonial Bishoprics Fund.

44364 ff.47-55, 61-2, 65-6. Draft despatches 30 Apr., 4 May 1846 Gladstone to Gov. Eardley Wilmot, V.D.L., recalling him because of his unsatisfactory administration of the convict system.

ff.56-60, 97-8, 122-3, 192-3, 205-6. 30 Apr. to 16 June 1846 Gladstone to Harington concerning the New Zealand Co.

ff.101-2, 120, 126-7, 245-6. Correspondence 15 May to 29 June 1846 with Archbishop of Canterbury concerning Miss Angela Burdett-Coutts's offer to endow the bishopric of Adelaide, the primacy of the Bishop of Sydney, and the appointment of the first Bishop of Morpeth (Newcastle).

ff.103-5. 16 May 1846 Gladstone to Edward Ellice, M.P., concerning the New Zealand Co., the Maori War, and the proposal to divide the colony.

f.129. 23 May 1846 Duke of Wellington concerning military operations in New Zealand.

ff.134-43. Draft despatches 26 May 1846 Gladstone to Sir George Grey concerning

London

New Zealand affairs, including approval of Grey's Maori policy, the proposed division of the colony, and the New Zealand Co.

ff.150-1. 30 May 1846 Gladstone to William Walter Cargill, M.P., and others concerning New Zealand affairs.

ff.264-7. 8 July 1846 Gladstone to Henry George Grey, 3rd Earl Grey, concerning the transfer of Judge Willis from Sydney to Port Phillip.

44365 ff.25-6. 16 Sept. 1846 Sir George Grey assuring Gladstone of his harmony with Bishop Selwyn of New Zealand.

ff.69-70. 7 Nov. 1846 Bishop Broughton concerning the foundation of new dioceses in Australia and a theological college.

f.123. 9 Mar. 1847 Gladstone to Sir John Eardley Wilmot concerning charges about his moral reputation.

ff.307-11. Correspondence 23, 24 June 1847 with Bishop Nixon concerning the charges against Eardley Wilmot's moral reputation.

f.376. 20 July 1847 Bishop Short of Adelaide concerning the disestablishment of the church.

44368 ff.44-5. 10 Dec. 1848 James Edward Fitzgerald concerning a proposal to re-establish the British whale fishery from the Auckland Islands.

f.257. 30 Oct. 1849 Fitzgerald concerning his intention to work for a New Zealand newspaper.

ff.278-81, 303-8. 24 Nov., 20 Dec. 1849 Charles Bowyer Adderley concerning the framing of an Australian constitutional bill by the Society for the Reform of Colonial Government, and colonial church government.

44369 ff.1, 20. 8, 22 Jan. 1850 Fitzgerald concerning a bill relating to the status of the Church of England in New South Wales which would be a model for other colonies.

ff.67-70. 13 Mar. 1850 Rev. Charles John Abraham concerning an inquiry by the Bishops of Sydney and New Zealand about doctrinal controversies in England.

ff.208-9, 212-13. Correspondence 18, 20 May 1850 with Rev. Henry Venn, secretary of the Church Missionary Society, concerning Australian church government.

ff.330-2, 421-8. 13 July, 19 Nov. 1850 Bishop Broughton of Australia concerning doctrinal controversies, relations with the Roman Catholic Church, the meeting of the provincial synod of bishops in Sydney, and constitutional status of the colonial church.

44370 ff.4-7. Despatch 28 Jan. 1851 Gov. Eyre concerning the failure of the provincial system of government in New Zealand, and of the New Zealand Co. and similar schemes of colonisation.

ff.82-3. 1 May 1851 from Charles Nicholson, Speaker of the Legislative Council of New South Wales, forwarding a copy of a printed declaration and remonstrance against the Australian Colonies Government Act.

ff.126-8. 2 June 1851 Rev. William Montagu Higginson Church concerning an offer by Rev. Lewis Hogg to collect any information required about Australia while there visiting his brother.

ff.243-52. 18 Aug. 1851 Bishop Broughton concerning the royal supremacy and the role of the laity in the government of the colonial church.

44371 ff.92-5. 19 Dec. 1851 J. E. Fitzgerald concerning suggestions for the government of New Zealand and of the church in the colony, the success of the Canterbury Settlement, and the approval of Sir George Grey's Maori policy.

ff.222-3. 2 Mar. 1852 John Archibald Clark, Mayor of Auckland, forwarding a petition opposing the New Zealand Co.'s claims for compensation for their investments from the province of New Ulster.

54

ff.261-2. 29 Mar. [1852?] from Archbishop of Canterbury concerning colonial church government and doctrinal disputes among the Australian dioceses.

44372 ff.45-6, 56-7, 80-7, 92, 98. Correspondence 24, 25 May 1852 between Archbishop of Canterbury and Bishop Broughton concerning the Colonial Church Bill. ff.71-2. Letters 22 May 1852 William Fox, Edward Gibbon Wakefield, Henry Sewell, and Rev. Henry Walford Bellairs suggesting minor amendments to Gladstone's parliamentary remarks about the government of New Zealand.

f.90. 25 May 1852 Rev. Charles John Abraham forwarding a pastoral letter by Bishop Selwyn of New Zealand concerning the constitution of his church and objection to the proposed penal settlement in New Caledonia.

ff.122-3. 29 May 1852 Sir Thomas Tancred reporting greater accord among the clergy in Tasmania.

ff.324-5. 1 Sept. 1852 Bishop Short of Adelaide concerning the royal supremacy and the role of the laity in church government, mentioning the financial plight of the clergy in South Australia.

44373 ff.118-20. 20 Dec. 1852 Bishop Broughton concerning his plans while in England in connection with the constitution of the church in Australia.

ff.194-7. 31 Dec. 1851 Sir Thomas Tancred expecting that the colonies will aspire to something above the 'Yankee type' of institutions, and suggesting the creation of a colonial aristocracy.

ff.341-2. 29 Jan. 1853 Sir John Eardley Wilmot, 2nd Bart, commending Gladstone's conduct in the case of his father's recall from Van Diemen's Land.

44377 ff.120-46. Correspondence 1846-7, 28 Jan. 1854 concerning the dispute over clerical discipline in Van Diemen's Land. Correspondents include Bishop Nixon, Sir John Eardley Wilmot, James Ebenezer Bicheno, and the Rev. Benjamin Harrison.

44382 ff.364-5. 20 Dec. 1854 Sir William Molesworth concerning the constitutions of the legislative bodies of New South Wales and South Australia.

44383 f.122. 3 Mar. 1855 Rev. Charles John Abraham introducing William Swainson, Attorney-General of New Zealand.

44391 ff.287-8. 30 Apr. 1859 Sir George Ferguson Bowen concerning his appointment as Governor of Queensland.

44392 ff.123-4. 10 Aug. 1859 Bowen concerning his offer to Robert George Wyndham Herbert of the post of private secretary in Queensland.

44399 ff.233-4. 19 Nov. 1862 Bowen concerning his visit to Cape York to found a settlement at Port Albany in the Torres Strait.

44403 ff.110-11. 13 Feb. 1865 (see also Add. MS.44405 ff.250-3) James Edward Fitzgerald concerning policy towards the Maoris, urging the withdrawal of British troops from New Zealand, and opposing the division of the colony.

44429 ff.147-8. 2 Feb. 1871 2nd Marquess of Normanby notifying his acceptance of appointment as Governor of Queensland.

44436 f.81. 3 Dec. 1872 Gov. Fergusson concerning the naming of a county in the Northern Territory after Gladstone, the navigability of the Roper River and the attractive hinterland, and nearby goldfields.

44443 ff.276-7. 5 June 1874 Sir Henry Parkes introducing himself and suggesting that the colonies should be raised in status so as to 'form part of the Empire as Australian states', that federation would follow, and that the office of governor should be open to Australians.

ff.308-9. 24 June 1874 Capt. John Moresby, H.M.S. *Basilisk* in the Java Sea, notifying his naming of Mounts Gladstone and Disraeli in New Guinea.

44444 f.236. 29 Aug. 1874 Archibald Michie, Agent General for Victoria and Sir Charles Gavan Duffy forwarding a gift of photographs from the National Gallery in Melbourne.

ff.256-7. 26 Sept. 1874 Sir Henry Parkes claiming that the importance of the Australian colonies is popularly underrated in England, and enclosing 'Statistics showing the relative position and aggregate importance of the Australasian colonies at the close of 1873' (Add. MS.44798 ff.179-80, printed).

44445 ff.97-8. 24 Nov. 1874 John Dunmore Lang forwarding a copy of his latest book and referring to the attitude of Gladstone and Earl Grey to the cessation of transportation to eastern Australia in the 1840s.

44447 f.340. 6 Aug. 1875 Bishop Bromby of Tasmania expressing the appreciation of the Anglican Church and her colonial daughters of Gladstone's writings on church matters.

44448 ff.78-9. 1 Oct. 1875 George Houston Reid regarding the shipping to England of preserved Australian meat.

44449 ff.256-7. 11 Apr. 1876 Sir Henry Parkes forwarding, as a gift, a copy of his speeches during the past twenty-seven years.

44452 ff.187-8. 25 Nov. 1876 from George Houston Reid, offering Gladstone a copy of his *Essay on New South Wales*, Sydney 1876.

44456 ff.16-19. 5 Jan. 1878 Henry T. Pycroft, schoolmaster of Auckland, enclosing part of his translation of classical verse.

ff.224-5. 13 Apr. 1878 Bishop Abraham asking Gladstone to be a pall-bearer at the funeral of Bishop Selwyn.

44457 ff.11-13. 5, 8 June 1878 Bishop Abraham concerning a proposed monument to, and biography of, Bishop Selwyn, and forwarding a printed circular appealing for funds to found a Selwyn College, Cambridge. See also Add. MS.44458 ff.68-9, 17 Oct. 1878.

ff.196-7. 9 Aug. 1878 Rowland Rees, Adelaide, expressing admiration of Gladstone's policies and concerning colonial opinion on the Eastern question.

44458 ff.13-18. 8 Oct. 1878 Sir George Bowen on the recent deadlock in the Victorian Parliament and his own career including his hopes for appointment as governor of New South Wales where he would work for an Australian confederation. See also Add. MS.44459 ff.105-8, 15 Feb. 1879.

44459 f.170. 7 Mar. 1879 Bishop Selwyn of Melanesia concerning [?] his father.

ff.200-1. 19 Mar. 1879 Bishop Abraham (and f.202, 20 Mar. 1879, Tucker to Gladstone) requesting Gladstone to review Rev. Henry William Tucker's biography of George Augustus Selwyn.

44461 ff.70-1. 8 Oct. 1879 Sir Henry Parkes forwarding his article in the *Melbourne Review* suggesting a federation of New South Wales, Victoria, and South Australia.

44466 ff.253-8. 4 Nov. 1880 Sir George Bowen, Mauritius, comparing his own policy towards the Maoris with British policy in South Africa.

ff.263-4. 4 Nov. 1880, London (also Add. MS.44479 ff.176-7, 29 Jan. 1883, Nice), from Sir Charles Gavan Duffy concerning the question of home rule for Ireland.

44470 ff.132-3. 28 June 1881 Robert Dudley Adams, Sydney, 'now sunk down into a man of ships, sheep and shares' forwarding, f.134, a eulogistic paragraph about Gladstone in the *Sydney Morning Herald*.

44482 ff.92-3, 117-19, 159-60. Correspondence 18-21 July 1883 concerning Rev. Alfred Barry's acceptance of appointment as Bishop of Sydney. (See also Add. MS.44485 ff. 7-8, 28-9, 1, 4 Jan. 1884.)

ff.158, 221-3. Correspondence 20, 25 July 1883 concerning James Moorhouse's resignation as Bishop of Melbourne.

44483 ff.92-6. Correspondence 23, 28 Aug. 1883 concerning the proper method of appointment to the bishopric of Sydney.

ff.108-9. 1883 Sir William Fitzherbert and others inviting Gladstone to visit New Zealand to strengthen colonial relations with Great Britain.

ff.222-3. 8 Oct. 1883 Sir Henry Parkes, London, offering him a possum skin rug and (ff.277-8, 24 Oct. 1883) asking his advice as to the competence of Thomas Woolner to sculpt a statue of Queen Victoria to be erected in Sydney.

44487 ff.103-4. 26 July 1884 William Robert Giblin, Premier of Tasmania, forwarding a copy of his speech at the Federation Convention, Sydney, and expressing admiration for England and Gladstone.

44490 ff.102-3. 27 Mar. 1885 David Buchanan, M.P., inquiring about the non-partisan role of the speaker.

44493 ff.99-100. 18 Nov. 1885 Sidney J. Elsom to H. N. Gladstone on the controversy over a speech given by Mr Ackers, M.P., at Sydney. Also ff.109-10, 19 Nov. 1885 Elsom to Gladstone on the same subject.

44498 ff.101-2, 197-9. 2, 13 July 1886 Bishop Bromby objecting to Gladstone's description of Tasmania as 'the home of convicts'.

44499 ff.3-4. Aug. 1886 Sir George Grey, Auckland, enclosing letter from Michael Corrigan, Invercargill, who had written a poem on Gladstone.

44515 ff.208-11, 238-43. 15-20 Aug. 1892 and other correspondence 1872-93 with Sir Thomas Brassey, Governor of Victoria 1895-1900, relating to a proposed appointment and illustrating his many interests including a large experiment in colonisation in Western Australia.

44525 ff.175-8. 19 Apr. 1897 from James F. Hogan, M.P., discussing his forthcoming book on the North Australian Colony [*The Gladstone Colony*, London 1898].

44527-51 Letter books 1835-94 containing copies of letters written by W. E. Gladstone whilst holding office under the Crown. The order is chronological.

44527 f.99. 25 Oct. 1842 to James Macarthur concerning the appointment of Mr Merewether as clerk of the council in New South Wales.

f.100. 25 Oct. 1842 to Lord Stanley recommending Mr Merewether.

f.165. 1 Jan. 1844 to Sir John Johnstone replying to his proposals for Pacific Steam Navigation.

44528 ff.4-198. Almost every folio contains relevant letters 1846-53. Correspondents include Maj. Macarthur, George Douglas Campbell, Lieut.-Col. Sir Frederick Smith, Philip Henry Stanhope, Henry Aglionby, M.P., Sir George Grey, John George Shaw-Lefevre, Henry Goulburn, Bishop Selwyn, George William Lyttelton, 4th Baron Lyttelton, Charles Joseph LaTrobe, John Stephen Hampton, Hon. Sidney Herbert, 1st Baron Herbert, Rev. John William Cunningham, Sir Charles Alexander Wood, Sir Charles FitzRoy, Sir Roderick Murchison, Col. Robert Torrens, Bishop Edward Denison of Salisbury, William Denison, George Arbuthnot in the Treasury, Edward John Eyre, Archdeacon Marriott in Tasmania, Sir John Herschel, and Rev. John Woolley. Subjects include convicts in Van Diemen's Land, the positions of superintendent and chaplain of North Australia, New Zealand Co., representative government for Western Australia, ecclesiastical matters in Australia and New Zealand, the Canterbury Association, the establishment of a Mint in Australia, the government of the New South Wales goldfields, and the place of religion in the University of Sydney.

44529 f.4. 23 Nov. 1853 to Samuel Wilberforce, Bishop of Oxford, concerning the Colonial Church Bill.

f.5. 25 Nov. 1853 to Lord Aberdeen concerning the Crown's patronage of church appointments in the colonies, and referring to the Bishop of Adelaide.

f.13. 7 Dec. 1853 to Sir Charles Hotham, and f.16, 12 Dec. 1853, to James Wilson, M.P., concerning Hotham's need of credit for outfitting himself to be Governor of Victoria.

ff.47-8. 3 Feb. 1854 to Bishop Nixon of Tasmania expressing disapproval of a Tasmanian Bill to regulate ecclesiastical salaries.

London

f.91. 1 May 1854 to H. J. Gladstone concerning letters of introduction to settlers in New Zealand.

f.102. 2 June 1854 to Bishop Nixon of Tasmania expressing his disapproval of the bishop's actions in regard to clerical discipline, and referring to the Colonial Church Bill.

ff.131, 155. 16 Aug., 11 Oct. 1854 to John Robert Godley concerning Godley's holding the position of Agent for Wellington, N.Z., while a civil servant.

f.196. 11 Dec. 1854 to Sir George Grey, M.P., concerning the Treasury's choice of making a monetary payment to the New Zealand Co. or of buying land in New Zealand.

44530 f.2. 21 Dec. 1854 to Sir William Molesworth, 8th Bart, and f.14, 17 Jan. 1855, to Sir George Grey, M.P., concerning the power of veto over Australian legislation on matters of imperial interest.

ff.79-80. 19 Sept. 1859 to Samuel Laing concerning Australia's interest in the telegraph link to Singapore. Also ff.87-8, 5 Oct. 1859 concerning the Panama line to Australia and Messrs Valance's offer.

f.106. 6 Nov. 1859 to Lord Palmerston concerning the Australian [telegraph?] contract.

f.113. 15 Nov. 1859 to Samuel Bright, J.P., concerning a direct route to Australia.

f.127. 6 Dec. 1859 to W. Buchanan, M.P., concerning the 'remission of fines for Australian service'.

ff.136-7. 28 Dec. 1859 and f.139, 3 Jan. 1860, to the Duke of Newcastle concerning the commission for Fiji and his own opposition to Britain's annexation.

f.143. 13 Jan. 1860 to Bishop Nixon of Tasmania concerning withdrawal of state aid to the church.

f.144. 14 Jan. 1860 to Bishop Tufnell of Brisbane forwarding a donation in lieu of attendance at a meeting.

f.149. 24 Jan. 1860 to James Edward Fitzgerald regretting inability to attend Australian dinner, and expressing confidence in Fitzgerald's colonial policy.

44531 f.25. 6 July 1860 to Fitzgerald and Duke of Newcastle concerning Fitzgerald's objection to the New Zealand Bill.

ff.45, 64. 8 Sept., 20 Oct. 1860 to Sir John Young and f.64, 20 Oct. 1864 to C. E. Fortescue concerning Young's appointment as Governor of New South Wales.

f.48. 20 Sept. 1860 to George Augustus Selwyn concerning native affairs and the question of title to land; 22 Sept. 1860 to C. E. Fortescue forwarding Sir Thomas Tancred's letter on native affairs in New Zealand.

f.69. 29 Oct. 1860 to John Robert Godley expressing concern at his ill-health.

f.77. 19 Nov. 1860 to George Augustus Selwyn and Duke of Newcastle concerning the distressing state of New Zealand 'For twenty years I have disbelieved in government from the other end of the world'.

f.110. 23 June 1861 to Selwyn concerning the New Zealand war.

ff.118-19. 11, 13 Feb. 1861 to Lord John Russell concerning 'the pious wish of H.M. the King of the Sandwich Islands' expressed in a note from Bishop Wilberforce of Oxford.

f.136. 25 Mar. 1861 to Rev. Edward Craven, Provost of Eton, concerning a letter from Bishop Abraham, Wellington, N.Z. 'on a subject of distress and perplexity'.

f.137. 29 Mar. 1861 to Rev. M. Hawtrey concerning the New Zealand war.

44532 ff.13, 18, 23. 2, 17, 24 Sept. 1861 to Charles Bowyer Adderley concerning New Zealand and colonial policy towards the Maoris.

f.18. 17 Sept. 1861 to Roger Therry concerning his application for appointment to the judicial committee of the Privy Council.

ff.37, 54. 25 Oct., 29 Nov. 1861 to G. A. Selwyn expressing his continued interest in New Zealand affairs.

f.50. 22 Nov. 1861 to 4th Baron Lyttelton forwarding a letter from G. A. Selwyn.

ff.59-60. 11 Dec. 1861 to Samuel Wilberforce concerning the consecration of the Bishop of Honolulu.

ff.67, 71, 74. 28 Dec. 1861, 4, 10 Jan. 1862 to Mackenzie Wilson concerning his request for an introduction to leading men in New Zealand.

f.121. 11 Apr. 1862 to 5th Duke of Newcastle concerning Newcastle's draft despatch on New Zealand financial affairs.

f.148. 19 June 1862 to 5th Duke of Newcastle and ff.153-4, 25 June 1862 to 1st Baron Norton and James Busby concerning a petition from Auckland Provincial Council for the separation of the province from the government of New Zealand.

ff.152-3, 158. 24 June, 3 July 1862 to George Arbuthnot and ff.174, 187, 29 July, 12 Aug. 1862 to Alfred Latham concerning the question of legal currency in Britain for sovereigns minted in Sydney.

44533 f.79. 17 Jan. 1863 to J. E. Fitzgerald concerning the New Zealand offer to relieve Britain of responsibility towards the Maoris.

f.80. 18 Jan. 1863 to J. E. Fitzgerald introducing Mr Briscoe 'son of my old tutor at Christ Church', an emigrant bound for New Zealand.

f.95. 28 Feb. 1863 to Sir Robert George Wyndham Herbert recently departed for Queensland concerning a deputation on the telegraph to Australia.

f.136. 1 June 1863 to R. Daglish, M.P., concerning the disastrous affairs of the European and Australian Mail Co.

f.152. 27 July 1863 to Earl Grey regarding a proposal to send Sikh troops to New Zealand.

ff.178-9. 20 Oct. 1863 to Sir John Young on the Sydney Mint and seigniorage.

f.183. 27 Nov. 1863 to Arbuthnot on the above subject and a divergence of views on policy with E. W. T. Hamilton, parliamentary agent for New South Wales in England.

44534 f.51. 15 Mar. 1864 to Earl Grey asking for information on New Zealand expenditure.

f.70. 20 Apr. 1864 to G. A. Selwyn sympathising over his difficulties.

f.91. 14, 16 June 1864 to Alexander Dundas Ross Wishart Baillie-Cochrane, concerning a letter from Sir Richard MacDonnell on pensions for colonial governors.

f.99. 11 July 1864 to Sir J. Donaldson regarding new arrangements for Australian postage.

ff.114, 122. 16, 27 Aug. 1864 to Cardwell concerning the New Zealand loan and the transport charge.

f.139. 28 Sept. 1864 to Arbuthnot expressing approval of his handling of 'the New Zealand matter'.

f.172. 19 Dec. 1864 to Mrs [J?] Goalen with a subscription for her son's emigration to Queensland.

44535 ff.29-30, 35, 46, 124, 126, 129, 132, 145, 164. Letters Mar.-Dec. 1865 to Sir William George Anderson, Viscount Cardwell, Earl Grey, and George Alexander Hamilton concerning New Zealand's paying the War Debt, criticism of Sir George Grey and his ministers, and Fitzgerald's recommendation for the removal of troops from New Zealand.

f.48. 19 Mar. 1865 to J. E. Fitzgerald, 'New Zealand may become a model of the true and sound relations between England and a colony of Englishmen'.

f.71. 15 June 1865 to Sir Walter James, also f.73, 17 June 1865 to Thomas Milner Gibson, M.P., and f.129, 26 Sept. 1865 to George Alexander Hamilton concerning payment to the family of the late Adm. Robert FitzRoy, Governor of New Zealand 1843-5.

ff.87, 96. 19, 27 July 1865 to Lord Lyttelton referring to Henry Sewell and the colonists' feelings concerning expenses of the New Zealand war.

44536 f.2. 1 Jan. 1866 to 4th Baron Lyttelton concerning the extremes of the New Zealand war.

ff.27-8. 26 Feb. 1866 to Hugh Culling Eardley Childers referring briefly to the legal tender of coins minted in Sydney.

f.29. 27 Feb. 1866 to Sir Roderick Murchison attesting the good character of Edward John Eyre.

ff.128, 131. 11, 19 Mar. 1869 to Strzelecki concerning Strzelecki's claims to public acknowledgement.

f.140. 7 Apr. 1869 to Sir Thomas Tancred acknowledging the receipt of his pamphlet on New Zealand.

ff.159, 162. 15, 19 May 1869 to Earl Granville concerning the character of Sir Arthur Hamilton-Gordon.

f.165. 21 May 1869 to Earl Granville expressing support of his New Zealand policy.

44537 ff.17, 97. 2 Aug., 15 Oct. 1869 to Lord Granville concerning New Zealand affairs.

44539 f.27. 12 Sept. 1870 to Kimberley concerning 'Mr. Chambers and deceased wife's sister in Australia'.

f.151. 5 Feb., 7 Apr. 1871 to 2nd Marquess of Normanby on leaving England to take up appointment as Governor of New South Wales.

f.174. 9 Mar. 1871 to Kimberley concerning New Zealand.

f.175. 10 Mar. 1871 to Kimberley concerning Fiji.

44540 ff.31, 35. 16, 22 May 1871 to Kimberley concerning differential inter-colonial customs tariffs in Australia and New Zealand.

f.76. 26 July 1871 to Kimberley concerning the annexation of Fiji.

ff.181-2. 28 Nov. 1871 to G. A. Selwyn concerning the death of Bishop Patteson of Melanesia.

44541 f.3. 2 Dec. 1871 to Kimberley concerning the suggested annexation of Fiji.

f.24. 27 Dec. 1871 to John Baptist Cashel Hoey acknowledging the Australian Hansard in which Mr Duffy mentioned Gladstone favourably.

ff.56, 68-9. 25 Jan., 9 Feb. 1872 to Kimberley concerning differential inter-colonial customs duties in Australia and New Zealand.

f.123. 6 May 1872 to Kimberley concerning the suggested appointment of H. C. E. Childers to the governorship of Victoria.

44542 f.62. 30 Dec. 1872 to Kimberley on the Australian church synod and observing the declining quality of the colonial episcopate.

f.78. 30 Jan. 1873 to Sir James Fergusson with congratulations on his transfer to New Zealand and thanks for naming Gladstone county in North Australia.

ff.126-7. 10, 12 June 1873 to Granville and to Kimberley concerning Capt. Goodenough's mission to Fiji and the proposed annexation.

f.133. 2 July 1873 to Lord Enfield concerning the departure of Gen. Smythe for Fiji.

44543 f.55. 24 Jan. 1874 to Kimberley concerning the annexation of Fiji, and New South Wales and New Zealand interests in Polynesia.

44544 f.89. 3 Nov. 1880 to Kimberley concerning the detention of Maori prisoners in New Zealand.

f.167. 9 May 1881 to Kimberley concerning the recommendation of six colonial chief justices for knighthoods and the 'rather infantile state' of Fiji for such an honour.

44545 ff.94-5. 26, 28 Jan. 1882 to Kimberley concerning a bill for the extension of

the jurisdiction of the courts over the Pacific Islands and the Pacific Islanders Bill.
f.141. 20 May 1882 to Kimberley concerning the award of K.C.M.G. for William McArthur as a result of his advocacy of the annexation of Fiji.

f.146. 30 May 1882 to Thomas Woolner concerning busts of Gladstone and other Prime Ministers commissioned by Sir Henry Parkes for New South Wales.

44546 f.43. 5 Dec. 1882 to Madame Olga Novikoff concerning Bishop Patteson, Mr Maclay and the native labour trade.

ff.115-16. 19 May 1883 to Derby concerning the application of Prince Leopold, 1st Duke of Albany, to be Governor of Victoria, and concerning the annexation of New Guinea by 'untrustworthy' Queensland.

f.135. 11 July 1883 to Derby concerning the extension of the term of the 2nd Marquess of Normanby as Governor of Victoria, and the claim of the 1st Duke of Albany to the post.

f.157. 10 Sept. 1883 to Derby on native policy in Queensland and New Guinea.

f.173. 15 Oct. 1883 to Sir Henry Parkes thanking him for a possum skin rug.

f. 181. 26 Oct. 1883 to Sir Henry Parkes assuring him of the competence of Thomas Woolner to sculpt a statue of Queen Victoria.

ff.181-2. 26 Oct. 1883 to the speakers of the Legislative Houses of New Zealand declining their invitation to visit, but recalling his great interest in New Zealand.

44547 ff.10, 91. 8 Dec. 1883, 1 Aug. 1884 to Derby commenting on the annexation of New Guinea and the 'preposterous proposals' of the Australian convention.

f.24. 3 Jan. 1884 to Alfred Barry commending his decision to go to New South Wales.

ff.25, 31. 6, 19 Jan. 1884 to Derby (also ff.34-5, 25, 26 Jan. 1884 to Sir Henry Frederick Ponsonby) concerning the application of the 1st Duke of Albany to be Governor of Victoria, and his possible involvement in a crisis like that over New Guinea.

f.46. 8 Mar. 1884 to 11th Baron Reay, discussing his suggested appointment as Governor of Victoria.

ff.47, 52. 8 Mar. 1884 to Derby suggesting candidates for appointment as Governor of Victoria, including Sir Henry Brougham Loch and Sir Thomas Brassey.

f.75. 25 June 1884 to A. Denison sending a copy of *Salmon at the Antipodes*, by Sir Samuel Wilson, London 1879.

f.83. 12 July 1884 to H. C. E. Childers recommending that the annexation of New Guinea be in conformity with the principles of international law.

ff.106, 152, 156. 5 Sept. to 27 Dec. 1884 to Childers discussing the political element involved in appointments to the mastership of the Australian Mint.

f.107. 9 Sept. 1884 to William Robert Giblin, Premier of Tasmania, thanking him for a copy of his speech on the South Pacific and Australian Federal Council.

ff.118, 128. 1, 23 Oct. 1884 to Derby concerning possible legislation on federation of the Australian colonies.

ff.155-6, 171-2, 184. 26 Dec. 1884 to 6 Mar. 1885 to Granville discussing Australian reaction to an accommodating policy towards German colonisation of New Guinea, and f.173, 3 Feb. 1885, Samoa.

ff.161-2. 13 Jan. 1885 to Granville, and f.163 to Derby, objecting to the proposal of Gov. Loch of Victoria, that West New Guinea should be bought from the Netherlands.

f.169. 27 Jan. 1885 to the Archbishop of Canterbury discussing the attempt by Bishop Moorhouse of Melbourne to alter the title to the ministry.

44548 f.26. 9 June 1885 to Sir Henry Parkes thanking him for his letter illustrating Gladstone's high reputation in New South Wales.

f.97. 9 June 1886 to Harcourt concerning the migration of Scottish crofters and the New Zealand offer.

f.111. 7 July 1886 to Bishop Bromby on the proportion of convict descendants in the population of Tasmania.

ff.112-13. 10 July 1886 to 5th Earl of Rosebery concerning murders in the New Hebrides.

44549 f.51. 12 Dec. 1892 to 1st Marquess of Ripon on the proposal to establish a protectorate over the Solomon Islands, the appointment of Bishop Kennion of Adelaide, as prelate of the Order of St Michael and St George. Also f.63, 23 Feb. 1893 to Archbishop of Canterbury concerning likely Canadian disapproval of a further appointment from Australasia.

f.53. 23 Dec. 1892 to Sir John Morley discussing Sir Henry Parkes's views on bi-cameral legislatures.

f.61. 3 Feb. 1893 to Edward Stanhope, M.P., and f.65, 17 Feb. 1893 to Howard Vincent, declining to receive a deputation from the Imperial Federation League, concerning tariff duties.

f.65. 17 Feb. 1893 to 1st Marquess of Ripon on the appointment of peers to the governorship of New South Wales and recommending Sir Robert William Duff.

f.84. 2 May 1893 to Robert Chalmers thanking him for his *History of Currency in the British Colonies*, London [1893]; and to Ripon on the proposed appointment of Sir Alfred Stephen, former Chief Justice of New South Wales, to the Privy Council.

44563-635 Official Papers. These papers include memoranda, mostly printed, prepared for the use of the Cabinet.

44566 ff.279-88. 1850 to the Bishop of New Zealand from members of the Church of England in the colony outlining a plan for the establishment of a system of church government, printed.

44567 ff.56-63. Memo Mar. 1851 E. G. Wakefield on the military defence of colonies, advocating the despatch to the Cape and New Zealand of 'a dignified unshackled Imperial authority, for the purpose of devising and establishing a new system of relations with the natives based on the principle of no military occupation'.

ff.71-2. 1 May 1851 Charles Nicholson, Speaker of the Legislative Council of New South Wales, transmitting a copy of a printed declaration and remonstrance against the Australian Colonies Government Act.

ff.135-60. Bill c.1851 to set up six provinces in New Zealand.

ff.162-9. c.1851 William Fox, honorary political agent of the colonists of Wellington, voicing the colonists' objections to Gov. Grey's proposed new constitution.

44568 ff.12-15. Memos 13 Jan. 1852 referring to the New Zealand constitution.

ff.109-10. 14 Feb. 1852 Henry Sewell with ff.111-13 extract of a letter from C. Elliott, Nelson, distrustful of Gov. Grey and the proposed constitution.

ff.125-6. Memos c.5 May 1852 on the New Zealand constitution.

ff.189-90. 11 June 1852 objection from the Canterbury Association denying the New Zealand Co.'s right to apply for money for its service to the settlement.

44579 ff.72-3. 5 Oct. 1853 pastoral letter from Bishop Selwyn to his diocese, printed.

44584 ff.125-41. Correspondence 22 Sept. 1854 containing despatches from Sir William Denison and the Bishop of Tasmania to the Duke of Newcastle concerning the position of the Church of England in Van Diemen's Land, printed.

ff.142-3. Prospectus c.1854 of the Association of Members of the Church of England for maintaining in Van Diemen's Land the principles of the Protestant reformation, giving its objects and rules and an account of a committee meeting of the Society, printed.

44585 ff.49-70, 79-97. Memos c.1849-54 concerning the Australian Constitutional Acts.

44589 ff.201-3. Draft Bill Sept. 1859 to provide for the abolition, upon certain terms, of state aid to religion in Tasmania.

44607 ff.91-7. Memo 17 Apr. 1867 E. W. Stafford, Wellington, on native risings, with enclosures, printed.

44615 ff.151-5. Draft Bill 30 Dec. 1870 for amending the law relating to the issue of paper money in Australia, printed.

44618 ff.7-18. Cabinet papers Jan.-Feb. 1872 on the murder of Bishop Patteson at Nukapu, printed.

ff.20-5. 29 Jan. 1872 abuses connected with Polynesian immigration and circumstances which led to the proposed Bill for the punishment of kidnapping in colonial courts, printed.

44629 ff.50-1. 16, 19 July 1883 Thomas Archer, Agent General for Queensland, with message from Sir Thomas McIlwraith voicing dissatisfaction with the Suez Canal plans, and reply from Colonial Office.

ff.148-53. Memos Dec. 1884 of conversations between Bismarck and R. H. Meade on colonial matters including New Guinea and Samoa, printed.

44636-48 Cabinet Minutes. Usually very brief memoranda.

44641 f.55. Copy of telegram 11 Feb. 1873 from Sir Hercules Robinson urging removal of restrictions on intercolonial reciprocity.

44681-714 Literary Manuscripts. Original MSS. of Gladstone's literary works.

44693 ff.172-96. Gladstone's review of Charlotte Mary Yonge's *Life of John Coleridge Patteson, Missionary Bishop of the Melanesian Islands*, London 1874, 2 vols. Printed in *Quarterly Review* Oct. 1874.

44715-835 Miscellanea.

44722-78 Political, theological, and literary memoranda.

44725 f.265. Memo 1835 relating to the committee set up to inquire into the conduct of Gen. Darling as Governor of New South Wales.

44735 ff.141-65, 21 Feb. 1846 education in Van Diemen's Land; ff.191-4, 23 Apr. 1843 transportation; ff.195-204, 231-4, May 1843 formation of a Southern Colony in New Zealand; ff.218-24, 3 May 1846 convict discipline in Van Diemen's Land; ff.262-79, 2 July 1846 policy concerning Van Diemen's Land; ff.282-3 notes of appointments in North Australia and Van Diemen's Land.

44738 ff.1-6, 1850 Australian church legislation; ff.87-102, 1850 Australian Colonies Government Bill.

44739 ff.26-36 draft copy of the 28th report 1850-1 of the New Zealand Co., printed; ff.37-42, 24 July 1851 on the Bill proposed to charge the New Zealand Co.'s debt on the Colonial Revenue; ff.43-4 notes on South Australian Acts.

44741 ff.93-4. Mar. 1853 the Australian Mint.

44777 ff.74-6. 1841 the bishopric of New Zealand.

44790-1 Autobiographical memoranda 1890-7.

44790 'Some of my errors' 1894. ff.135-6 refers to Gladstone's recalling Sir John Eardley Wilmot from Van Diemen's Land, 1845-6.

44796-9 Large miscellaneous MSS.

44798 f.8. Memorial 23 Dec. 1864 of the Provincial Council of Auckland, praying for autonomy.

f.63. Map 4 Dec. 1872 of the Northern Territory enclosed in a letter 2 Dec. 1872 from Sir James Fergusson.

ff.179-80. Printed statistics showing the relative positions and aggregate importance of the Australasian colonies at the close of 1873, enclosed in a letter 20 Sept. 1874 from Sir Henry Parkes.

44894 Documents relating to Sir Francis Drake's voyage of circumnavigation Dec. 1577 to Sept. 1580, transcripts from originals in South America and Spanish collections, Spanish.

45156-7 Harris Papers

Papers of G. P. Harris, Deputy Surveyor-General of Tasmania. These papers were used and extracts printed by R. W. Giblin, *The Early History of Tasmania*, London 1928 and Melbourne 1939, 2 vols.

45156 Correspondence 1803-12 of the Harris family. Mainly letters 15 July 1803 to 23 Aug. 1810 from G. P. Harris on the voyage to Australia in the convict ship *Ocean* and from Port Phillip and Tasmania; also a journal by Harris of his voyage from England to Australia as far as Rio de Janeiro Apr.-July 1803, with a list of officers and tradesmen on H.M.S. *Calcutta* and the *Ocean*; letter 1 Feb. 1811 from W. Hopley, Hobart, to T. Harris on the death of G. P. Harris; letter 23 Nov. 1812 from Harris's widow, Ann, Hobart, to her mother-in-law; chart of King Island, Bass Strait; sketches of the camps at Port Phillip and Sullivan's Cove.

45157 Papers 1808-9 annexed to a memorial by Harris intended to be submitted to the Secretary of State for War and the Colonies concerning a dispute between Harris and Lieut. E. Lord, Acting Lieutenant-Governor of the colony, relating to the respective spheres of authority of the civil and military officers in the discipline of the convicts.

45290-7 Archer Papers

Correspondence and papers of William Archer, literary and dramatic critic, with or relating to persons in the world of letters and the stage. The correspondence was used by C. Archer, *William Archer: Life, Work and Friendships*, London 1931. The papers include:

45295 ff.52-143. Correspondence 26 Mar. 1885 to 27 Mar. 1914 with R. L. Stevenson, England and Samoa.

45442-96 Notebooks of J. G. Frazer, anthropologist. They are described in T. Besterman, *A Bibliography of Sir James George Frazer*, *O.M.*, London 1934, pp.xix-xxi, and much of the material was published by Frazer in *Anthologia Anthropologica*, ed. R. A. Downie, London 1938-9, 4 vols. The volumes include:

45476-7 Anthropological extracts and notes *c.*1846-99, mainly from printed sources, relating to the East Indies, Malaya, and Australasia.

45479-81 Anthropological extracts and notes 1772-1927, mainly from printed sources, relating to New Guinea and Oceania.

45499-505 Genealogical collections 11th-20th cent. concerning the Boys (alias Boyce, etc.) and related families compiled by C. Boyce, M.D. Typescript with manuscript and printed additions, arranged topographically.

45504 ff.63-4. Australasia.

45558-64 Collections of W. Hall Griffin for his *Life of Robert Browning*, London 1910, made mostly *c.*1904.

45558 Transcripts of letters 7 Mar. 1840 to 11 Apr. 1877 mainly from R. Browning to A. Domett, New Zealand poet and statesman. The originals, now Add. MS.45876, have been printed in *Robert Browning and Alfred Domett*, ed. F. G. Kenyon, London 1906.

45559 Extracts from Domett's diary 1872-7. The full text is printed in *The Diary of Alfred Domett*, ed. E. A. Horsman, London 1953, pp.45-207.

45560 ff.1-30. Extracts from Domett's diary 1877-85. The full text is printed by Horsman pp.209-305; ff.31-70 transcripts and extracts of letters 12 Nov. 1842 to 8 Apr. 1874 from J. Arnould, Indian Judge, to Domett.

45561 Domett's visit to Tennyson 3-5 Nov. 1883, being extracts from Domett's diary, printed by Horsman, pp.265-84.

45680 Miscellaneous letters and papers, including ff.114-29 letters 2 Feb. 1866 to

[Sept?] 1892 from R. L. Stevenson in England, Sydney, and Samoa, to G. Saintsbury, mainly on literary subjects.

45750-849 Nightingale Papers

Correspondence, literary MSS. and other papers of Florence Nightingale.

Some of the documents in this collection were printed by Sir Edward Cook, *The Life of Florence Nightingale*, London 1913, Mrs I. B. O'Malley in *Florence Nightingale, 1820-1856*, London 1931, and Mrs Cecil Woodham-Smith in *Florence Nightingale*, London 1950. The collection includes many original Nightingale letters as well as typescript copies of documents selected from archives other than those preserved in the British Museum. Many drafts of letters and literary MSS., etc., are in the hand of Dr J. Sutherland who compiled the collection.

45796-816 General correspondence.

45799 ff.178-207. Letters 21 Sept. to 26 Oct. 1865 from Miss M. S. Rye, Sydney and Victoria, mainly concerning the conditions at the Tarban Creek Lunatic Asylum, Sydney, and referring to the hospital at Ballarat, with further correspondence Dec. 1865 among Florence Nightingale, Lord Shaftesbury, the Officer of the Commissioner in Lunacy, England, and C. M. Webber. Miss Rye went to New Zealand in charge of female emigrants, then to Australia where she collected information about immigration barracks and tried to correct abuses in hospitals, especially at the Tarban Creek Lunatic Asylum.

45816 Plans of hospitals, etc., 1857-89. Include ff.11-22 plans and elevations of Sydney Infirmary drawn by J. Hume, architect, Sydney, 1864 and 1866.

45876 Letters 7 Mar. 1840 to 11 Apr. 1877 from R. Browning and J. Arnould to A. Domett discussing Tennyson and other poets, and their own work. Printed in full in *Robert Browning and Alfred Domett*, ed. F. G. Kenyon, London 1906. Transcripts of some of these letters are at Add. MS.45558.

45982 Miscellaneous letters and papers including ff.87-8 letter 19 Mar. 1830 from J. Buffett, Pitcairn Is., to Capt. F. W. Beechey concerning the affairs of the islanders.

46125-8 Murchison Papers

Correspondence *c.*1820-71 of Sir Roderick Murchison, geologist, mainly of a non-scientific nature. The correspondence is arranged alphabetically. Examples of letters examined are:

46127 ff.50-1. 12 Jan. 1866 from M. Laugel concerning the visit of Prince de Condé, eldest son of Duc d'Aumale, to India, Ceylon, Java, Australia, China, and the Philippines.

ff.142-3. 26 Oct. 1860 from Gov. MacDonnell, Adelaide, referring to a despatch requesting the British Government to extend the limits of South Australia, his opinion of J. M. Stuart and of Mr Chambers who had kept all Stuart's charts and journals and was posing as a patron of science, and a report and map by the Assistant Surveyor General, showing the break in the old horse-shoe of Lake Torrens.

ff.150-3. 3 Aug. 1867 from L. MacKenzie, London, concerning Baron von Mueller and petitions from several influential men in Australia asking that the honour of knighthood be conferred on Mueller.

ff.160-1. 3 Apr. 1841 from W. Macleay, Sydney, introducing Lieut. Emery, who served five years on H.M.S. *Beagle* surveying the Australian coast and was taking to England a large natural history collection.

ff.166-7. 22 Aug. 1861 from J. McMaster, Manchester, asking Murchison's views on the climate and soil of Queensland about which he and friends, who intended emigrating to Queensland, had conflicting information.

ff.182-3. [June?] 1832 from Capt. J. Mangles, R.N., just returned from the Swan

London

River with a collection of petrifactious minerals collected at Perth and other parts of Western Australia.

ff.199-200. Despatch 12 Apr. 1858 from H. Merivale, Colonial Office, acknowledging receipt of letters to Lord Stanley concerning Sir Henry Barkly's despatch on the probable extent and supply of gold in Victoria and two reports by the commissioners appointed to inquire into the mining resources of the colony.

ff.239-40. 28 Aug. 1867 from F. von Mueller, Sydney, referring to the Leichhardt search expedition of 1865 and another to be organised in 1868.

ff.241-2. 17 Apr. 1852 from G. C. Mundy concerning his book *Our Antipodes* saying he had introduced Murchison's note on Australian gold in the third volume, but Murchison's letter predicting the discovery of gold in the first volume had not been revised.

ff.294-5. 12 Mar. 1869 from Rear-Adm. E. Ommaney, London, concerning a memorial to Sir James Clark Ross.

f.475. 10 June 1846, incomplete, from Sir James Clark Ross saying a bottle found near Cape Liptrap was very likely one of the bottles thrown overboard by him on 4 Apr. 1842.

46133 Log 22 Mar. 1882 to 16 Apr. 1884 of H.M.S. *Diamond*, visiting Australia, New Zealand, New Guinea, New Britain, New Hebrides, the Solomon Is., Tonga, Fiji, Norfolk Island, and Samoa, with water-colour sketches and maps of the Australian coastline and the Pacific showing the track of the ship.

46272 Letter n.d. from Capt. R. F. Scott to Sir James Barrie.

46281-345 Burns Papers

A selection from the correspondence, official and private, and other papers of J. E. Burns, P.C., M.P. The papers were used by W. Kent, *John Burns: Labour's Lost Leader*, London 1950.

46282-7 Special correspondence.

46285 Correspondence 1887-1939 with officials of the Dock, Wharf, Riverside, and General Labourers' Union. ff.21, 33-4, 47, 50-2, 58-9. Correspondence and receipts 9 Sept. 1889 to 17 Sept. 1890 concerning donations sent from Australia towards the relief fund for the London Dockers' strike; f.188, 19 Mar. 1907 from B. Tillett to Burns about his visit to Australia where he would meet Mann and Champion.

46286 Correspondence and papers Aug.-Sept. 1889 relating to the London Dockers' strike, followed by correspondence 1889-1906 with officials of the Dock, Wharf, Riverside, and General Labourers' Union and other dockers' unions. f.71. 17 Dec. 1889 from the London Chartered Bank of Australia forwarding £3792; f.72, 9 Jan. 1890 from P. Mennell, correspondent in London for the Melbourne *Age*, concerning surplus of money collected in Melbourne for the English dockers; f.92, Aug.-Sept. 1890 from W. Boynes, England, mentioning a meeting on behalf of the Australian dockers.

46288-304 General correspondence 1874-1942 including correspondence 1899-1900 concerning labour conditions and strikes in Australia.

46362 Miscellaneous letters and papers including J, a description of conditions in Australia c.1840.

46920-7213 Egmont Papers

Papers of the family of Perceval, chiefly collected by John, 1st Earl of Egmont. 47106 Log 8 July 1766 to 19 May 1768 of Robert Molineux, mate in H.M.S. *Dolphin*, on her voyage round the world.

47444-5 Horne Papers

Literary papers of R. H. Horne probably written during the author's stay in Australia 1852-69.

47444 'Theorem on immortality', an unpublished essay on religious and philo-sophical matters.

47445 Miscellaneous papers consisting of a 'Lecture on Insane Kings and other Mad Characters of History' delivered to the Mechanics Institute, Melbourne; a poem 'Ancient Idols', 1868, with two letters relating to the MS. and to Horne; a copy of a poem 'The Last words of Cleanthes' with a letter n.d. from E. Partridge to Mrs Schofield concerning some Horne MSS.

47459 Diary 1 Nov. 1911 to 27 Feb. 1912 of E. A. Wilson of the British Antarctic Expedition.

47559-601 Fox Papers
    Papers of and relating to Charles James Fox.
47568 f.241. Proposal for settling New South Wales 1784, by J. M. Matra.
47569 f.129. Complaints about the administration of New South Wales, 1802, copies.

47714-67 Nightingale Papers
    Correspondence and papers of Florence Nightingale. Some of the documents in this collection, which relates chiefly to the administration of the Florence Nightingale Fund and the foundation of the Training School for Nurses in St Thomas' Hospital, were printed by Sir Edward Cook in *The Life of Florence Nightingale*, London 1913 and also by Mrs C. Woodham-Smith in *Florence Nightingale*, London 1950.
47714-28 Correspondence relating to the Nightingale Fund. Correspondence 1861-1902 with H. Bonham Carter, as Secretary of the Fund.
47714-16 Various ff. 21 Mar. 1867 to 20 June 1871 including correspondence with Sir Henry Parkes, Dr A. Roberts, and E. Deas Thomson, arranging for the recruit-ment of a nursing staff for the Sydney Hospital; also correspondence concerning the management and plans of Sydney Hospital, the selection of the nurses, agreements as to salary, length of service, passage to Sydney; with notes on the nurses chosen, especially Lucy Osburn and a letter by her from Sydney, published in England by H. Carr.
47729-42 Correspondence relating to St Thomas' Hospital.
47729-30 Various ff. 23 Jan. 1863 to 3 Sept. 1868, correspondence with Mrs S. E. Wardroper as Matron of St Thomas', referring to Lady Dowling's scheme for nurses to emigrate to Australia, correspondence of Parkes, Roberts, and Deas Thomson, the management and plans of Sydney Hospital, the selection of the nurses, agree-ments as to salary and conditions, and Lucy Osburn.
47753-9 Miscellaneous special correspondence.
47757 Correspondence relating to nursing in Australia with Sir Henry Parkes 1866-92, Dr A. Roberts 1866-80, W. Hughes 1866, Capt. Mayne, New South Wales Agent General in London, 1866-7, E. Deas Thomson 1867-9, and W. C. Windeyer 1873, concerning the staffing and management of Sydney Hospital; 23 Jan. 1863 from Lady H. M. Dowling to Florence Nightingale concerning a scheme for nurses to go to Australia; 30 Oct. 1867 to 24 Dec. 1885 from L. Osburn, M. Barker, and H. C. Turriff, three of the nurses at Sydney Hospital; 7 Apr. 1891 from E. Noble, Adelaide, and 25 Nov. 1903 from K. Nashe, Adelaide, concerning nursing in Aus-tralia; 20 Feb. 1908 from B. Simpson, née Chant, Matron of Gladesville Hospital for twenty-six years.

47768-72 Franklin Papers
    Papers of Sir John Franklin, his wife, and family.
47768 Letters 19 May 1832 to 26 Mar. 1837 to Franklin from G. W. Crowe, Consul-General in Moorea, and T. C. Robinson, Vice-Consul, including 2 July 1836

from Crowe congratulating Franklin on his appointment to Tasmania, asking to be remembered to Mr Gregory there, and 30 June 1836 mentioning J. Thomas.

47769 Letters and papers 1804-74 of the Franklin and Griffin families including letters 1836-41 to Lady Franklin while in Tasmania.

47966 Copy journal 20 Mar. 1787 to 13 Aug. 1789 by A. Bowes Smyth, surgeon in the convict ship *Lady Penrhyn*. The journal is illustrated and contains additional information about the ship and Botany Bay; f.108, 15 July 1788 refers to a portrait of Cook in the possession of the King of Tahiti. There is another copy in the Mitchell Library, Sydney.

48966-75 Correspondence and papers 1914-50 of S. S. Koteliansky.

48970 ff.160-295. Feb. 1915 to Feb. [1923?] from K. Mansfield to Koteliansky.

48989-9057 Jellicoe Papers
    Papers of J. R. Jellicoe, 1st Earl Jellicoe of Scapa.

49045-57 Correspondence and reports relating to Lord Jellicoe's Empire Mission 1919-20.

49045 Correspondence and papers 1918-20 concerning Australia, New Zealand, India, Canada, and the West Indies; ff.107-24 deal specifically with Australia including a report on naval affairs Aug. 1919; ff.125-84 deal specifically with New Zealand Aug.-Oct. 1919 including letter 25 Sept. 1919 from W. F. Massey, Prime Minister.

49048-51 *Report of the Admiral of the Fleet Viscount Jellicoe of Scapa . . . on naval mission to the Commonwealth of Australia May-Aug. 1919*, Sydney 1919.

49052-4 *Report of the Admiral of the Fleet Viscount Jellicoe of Scapa . . . on naval mission to the Dominion of New Zealand (August-October 1919)*, Wellington 1919.

49064 Letters 1918-22 from K. Mansfield to I. C. Baker.

49086-172 Napier Papers
    These include 49105-47 papers of Lieut.-Gen. Sir Charles Napier, unbound.

49109-15 General correspondence.

49112 Correspondence 1832-41. Includes correspondence 17 July 1834 to 4 June 1835 relating to South Australia (not seen as in very bad condition); 6 Mar. 1838 from Col. Wodehouse, 50th Regiment, Sydney, acknowledging receipt of Napier's book on military law.

49125-30 Letter books 1831-50.

49126 ff.44-8. 30 Aug. 1835 to J. Reddec referring to Napier's appointment as Governor of South Australia, his recent pamphlet on colonisation and the conduct of the Colonial Secretary and other officials.

ff.49-65. 2 July 1835 to his sister Lady Bunbury concerning political economy in new colonies, mentioning South Australia, Tasmania, and Western Australia, and his pamphlet on colonisation.

49127 ff.1-4. 26 Feb. 1836 to Lord Stanhope concerning an article in the *London Review* and the appointment of a governor of South Australia.

ff.41-7. 28 Apr. 1837 to Mr Jones, referring to news on South Australia from Col. Light.

49173-95 Spencer Perceval Papers
    Correspondence and papers of the Hon. S. Perceval, together with papers (chiefly Add. MSS.49191-5) of members of his family, unbound.

49195 ff.84-94. Correspondence Oct.-Nov. 1863 concerning Lieut. J. S. Perceval who was killed at Mauku, N.Z., with a letter 15 Oct. 1863 to his mother describing the voyage from Victoria to New Zealand in command of volunteer troops.

ff.102-3. 28 July 1873 from C. J. Perceval, Nelson, N.Z., to C. D. Perceval informing him of the death of Mrs A. Perceval, [Sydney?], and asking about settlement money which was to be left to his sons.

49199-285 Stanmore Papers

Correspondence, journals, literary manuscripts, and other papers, with the exception of those relating to New Brunswick, which are in the University of New Brunswick, of the Hon. Arthur Hamilton-Gordon, 1st Baron Stanmore. Gordon used these papers in his *Fiji, Records of Private and Public Life 1875-1880*, Edinburgh 1897-1912, 4 vols. Selections from the papers have been microfilmed for the Department of Pacific History, Research School of Pacific Studies in the Australian National University, microfilm also in the Mitchell Library, Sydney.

49199-223 Special correspondence relating chiefly to Gordon's official positions. 49199-218 contain letters and papers mainly concerning Fiji, New Zealand, and the High Commission for the Western Pacific, covering administrative matters and also the policies of various European powers in the Pacific, labour traffic, and policing of the Pacific and New Guinea. A few papers on persons or subjects not falling strictly under the above description are listed below.

49199-202 Chiefly letters 1867-90 to Gordon from the Secretary of State for the Colonies, the Permanent Under-Secretary and other officials, but including some drafts or copies of his replies and other papers.

49199 ff.170-2. 31 May 1877 concerning Gordon's suggestion that he should be made Governor of New South Wales as well as Fiji.

ff.191-8. Copies of Gordon's despatches 1878 concerning proposals for trading and settlements in New Guinea organised by Australian associations.

ff.210-13. 19 Sept. 1878 concerning Thurston. For Gordon's good opinion of Thurston see also 49201 f.123, 18 June 1881.

ff.228-31. Sept. 1878 regarding the trial in Samoa of W. J. Hunt. See also 49200 f.74, Oct. 1878, 49201 ff.125-6, 1881, and ff.321-4, 1883.

49200 Correspondence Oct.-Dec. 1878 including many papers on recruiting especially the cases of the *Iserbrook*, owner Bell (also owner of the *Emma Bell*), and *Australasian Packet*, supercargo 'Jones' alias Tatchell, goldmining in New Guinea, and British authority there.

49201 f.10. Feb. 1879 concerning applications from Australians to settle in Dutch New Guinea.

ff.35, 111-17, 122. Papers 1880-1 concerning proceedings against E. L. Chippendall, owner of a plantation, who allegedly murdered a native in his employ, partly printed.

ff.177-85. Copy despatch 24 July 1882 from Loftus with accompanying papers concerning the schooner *Venture*, Capt. Wolsch.

49202 Correspondence concerning Ceylon except ff.260-89 'Précis of a White Book presented to the Reichstag Jan. 19/85 on the German Land Claims in the Fiji Islands' signed C. S. Scott 26 Jan. 1886.

49203 Letters 1879-1912 from MacGregor chiefly concerning affairs in Fiji with references to Thurston, Mitchell, and Gorrie. ff.298-301, 16 Oct. 1909, concerning Sir Everard im Thurn and the native lands question.

49204 Letters 1875-90 from Thurston including:

ff.24-7. [Aug.?] 1877 discussing the activities of G. A. Woods in Samoa and Woods's correspondence with Vogel.

ff.34-5. 10 July 1878 from Woods in Samoa to Thurston concerning commercial dealings, and position of R. S. Swanston.

ff.37-48. 25 Nov. 1880 concerning land sales at Suva, referring to his secret visit in 1873 to consult chiefs on annexation, and his letter to Granville.

ff.121-7. 17 May 1881 from Tonga concerning the treaty with King George Tupou, and giving his opinion of Baker and his friends.

ff.202-10. Typed copies of letters Nov. 1890 from Tonga concerning Baker's activities during his last days in Tonga.

49205 Letters 1874-83 from Des Voeux, Gorrie, Carew, and Wilkinson.

49206 Correspondence 1880-5 with Hall and Whitaker, premiers of New Zealand.

49207 ff.37-190. Letters 1876-1905 concerning A. E. Havelock and letters from Gordon to Havelock. Letters Mar. 1902 to Feb. 1904 are correspondence with Havelock in Tasmania.

49209 Correspondence 1851-1907 with Gladstone, Salisbury, and Archbishops A. C. Tait and E. W. Benson.

49216 ff.169-216. Letters 1878-90 from Barry containing, besides a brief reference to Fiji, an account of his appointment to Sydney, his term there 1884-7, and references to his work in Australia.

49217-20 Letters 1855-95 from Gordon to Sir Roundell Palmer, 1st Baron Selborne 1872, 1st Earl of Selborne 1882. Letters 1855-95 from Selborne to Gordon are in Lambeth Palace Library MSS.1872-5.

49217-18 Letters 1855-84 including from 49217 f.167 many letters about Fiji, New Zealand, and the position of High Commissioner for the Western Pacific.

49219 Letters chiefly from Ceylon including references to New Guinea and Fiji, especially:

ff.1-4. 5 Jan. 1885 reporting visit by Scratchley on his way to New Guinea, news of the German annexation of part of the island, and criticising the giving to Australia of power over New Guinea.

ff.8-28. Feb.-Mar. 1885 containing references to American and German claims in Fiji.

ff.69-84. 14-29 Apr. 1886 concerning the Bryce-Rusden trial for libel. Reference is made in the letter 29 Apr. to the rumour of Mitchell's appointment to Fiji and Thurston's opinion, see also f.132, 17 Dec. 1886, expressing a more favourable opinion of Mitchell.

49224-32 Family correspondence 1844-89.

49224 ff.234-93. Including letters from Gordon's father-in-law, J. Shaw-Lefevre, many referring to Gordon's appointments, among them:

ff.234-5. 29 Nov. 1872 informing Gordon of Kimberley's intention to offer him the governorship of South Australia.

ff.293-9. 11 July 1881 mentioning *inter alia* Gordon's dislike of his post in New Zealand, disappointment with arrangements made concerning Fiji, and feeling in the House of Commons about the post of High Commissioner for the Western Pacific being held by the Governor of New Zealand.

49225 Letters 1868-82 from Gordon to his wife, some concerning his post in New Zealand and his disappointment in leaving Fiji.

49228-32 Letters 1871-88 from Lady Gordon to her husband; correspondence 1861-88 of Lady Gordon and her sisters including letters from Lady Gordon 1875-9 Fiji, 1881 Melbourne, 1882 New Zealand and Sydney.

49233-42 General correspondence 1841-1912 chiefly in-letters and papers similar to those in special correspondence. There are some drafts of Gordon's replies. See note under 49199-223 for subjects covered.

49233-5 Early correspondence including 49233 ff.189-201 copy of letter 20 Sept. 1849 from C. H. Johnstone to his father giving brief notes on his stay in Hawaii.

49236 Correspondence 1871-6. From 1874 most of the letters and papers relate to Fiji and the Pacific and include:

ff.173-5. Fijian translation of Robinson's address when accepting the cession of Fiji 10 Oct. 1874.

ff.202-6. 6, 8 Mar. 1875 from J. D. Hooker concerning botanical collecting.

ff.213-22. 30 June, 12 July 1875 from Goodenough, H.M.S. *Pearl*, concerning control of labour traffic, also letters 1875 with news of Goodenough's death and his dying wish that it be attributed to a misunderstanding.

49237 Correspondence 1876-8 including letters from Carew, Le Hunte, Leefe, Maudslay, L. Fison, Rev. F. Langham, F. W. Chesson, Liardet, Turner, Swanston, and Th. Weber, German Consul at Apia. Among other letters are:

ff.137-9. 10 Apr. 1878 from Bishop Selwyn, Norfolk Island, concerning the labour traffic, regretting rumours of French annexation of the New Hebrides.

ff.148-50. 26 June 1878 from S. W. Baker, Tonga.

ff.151-4, 167-74, 182-7. June-Sept. 1878 from Sir George Bowen concerning the 'Australasian Colonisation Society' and Gordon's firmness in having 'knocked on the head the schemes of adventurers who proposed to start from here for New Guinea'.

ff.200-1. Copies of statements signed before A. P. Maudslay by Charles Baker 30 Oct. 1878 and P. S. Bloomfield 2 Nov. 1878 concerning money transactions in Tonga involving S. W. Baker.

49238 Correspondence 1879-80 chiefly from Fiji and Pacific Islands during Gordon's absence including letters from W. Seed, W. Fillingham Parr, Rev. F. Langham, L. Fison and Heffernan in Fiji, and from Swanston and Turner in Samoa. Among other letters are:

ff.4-7. Bishop Selwyn's comments on Layard's despatch, 11 Jan. 1879 from Noumea on the undesirability of firing indiscriminately on a place where murder has been committed; ff.43-6, 23 Apr. 1879 from Selwyn, Lichfield.

ff.47-50. 25 Apr. 1879 Gordon to Lord Russell and 28 Apr. 1879 Russell's reply on German influence in the Pacific.

ff.51-3. 29 Apr. 1879 from John Inglis concerning the French in the Pacific and the missions, especially the Presbyterians in the New Hebrides.

ff.175-6. Copy of resolutions of the Methodist New South Wales and Queensland Conference in the case of the Rev. S. W. Baker; ff.208-13, 21 Dec. 1880 from Rev. B. Chapman, General Secretary, Australian Wesleyan Missions, concerning suspension of Baker from ministerial functions.

ff.202-7. 21 Dec. 1880 from John Hill, Rambi, Fiji, reporting the death of his Sydney partner and likelihood of his having to sell his share in London, asking for introductions.

ff.276-8. 27 Dec. 1880 from J. H. Wodehouse, Honolulu, chiefly concerning importation of Polynesian labour.

49239 Letters 1881-3 from Bishop Selwyn, H. F. Symonds, John Hill, Rev. W. Wyatt Gill, Rev. F. Langham, Leefe, and Heffernan, and a number of letters from Commodore Erskine, chiefly about the labour traffic. In addition there are many letters and papers concerning Baker. Also:

ff.37-8, 102-3, 234-8. May 1881, Jan. 1882, Feb.-May 1883 from N. de Miklouho-Maclay chiefly concerning the 'Maclay Coast', letter May 1883 also speaks of the 'slaver' O'Keefe and Holt's allegations.

ff.217-19. 29 Sept. 1882 opinion of New South Wales law officers on the competence of the Supreme Courts of New South Wales and Van Diemen's Land to try cases of murder on the high seas; f.216 memo 21 Sept. 1882 on the legal power of New South Wales to try for murder on the high seas in view of the Act creating the High Commission for the Western Pacific.

49240 Letters 1884-5 chiefly concerning Ceylon.

ff.34-5. 2 Apr. 1884 from Miklouho-Maclay, Sydney, chiefly about the 'Maclay Coast' of New Guinea.

ff.78-84. 4 Feb. 1885 from G. W. Rusden concerning the Bryce case, with draft of Gordon's reply.

London

49241 Letters 1886-7 chiefly concerning Ceylon but including:

ff.41-6, 171-252. Papers concerning land claim and management of the estate of Bua, Fiji , by Wilkinson.

ff.105-7, 179-81. Feb.-June 1887 from Mitchell, Fiji.

49242 Correspondence 1888-1912.

ff.45-9. 1 Nov. 1889 from Leefe, consul at Tonga.

ff.88-95. Draft letter n.d. by Gordon to *The Times* on the resumption of the labour trade in Queensland.

ff.117-18. 23 Aug. 1893 from W. Fillingham Parr written on receiving news of Gordon's elevation to the peerage. 'I am not at all surprised that you should be anxious to hide the name of Sir Arthur Gordon . . .'

ff.144-56. 1 Dec. 1895 from F. A. Jackson, Fiji, concerning the native tax system.

ff.197-211. Allardyce's notes n.d. on the native tax system with Gordon's draft reply to Allardyce concerning a memo of Sir Henry Jackson, Governor of Fiji.

ff.325-6. 2 Oct. 1911 from Colonial Office concerning Gordon's complaint of criticism of his land policy in Fiji by Sir Henry May.

ff.327-9. 24 June 1912 from Colonial Office to 2nd Lord Stanmore transmitting extract of a speech 23 Apr. 1912 by Sir Henry May and resolution of the chiefs expressing sorrow at news of Gordon's death.

49243-52 Letter Books. The dates are not consecutive and no letter books are present for 1871-9, 1883 to July 1884. Gordon kept copies of selected letters. 49245 Feb.-Oct. 1880 contains letters chiefly about Fiji and Western Pacific High Commission affairs; 49246 Nov. 1880 to Dec. 1882 contains letters written in New Zealand, some discussing the difficulties of the High Commission for the Western Pacific.

49253-69 Journals and Diaries *c*.1842-91 with a few entries 1901-2.

49262 1872-4 entries 25, 28 Oct. and 2, 10 Dec. 1874 record discussions with Carnarvon and Gladstone about Gordon's appointment to Fiji; 49263 n.d. entries relate to Fiji; 49264 Jan.-Aug. 1888 includes entries for Gordon's visit to Fiji; 49265 1888-90, ff.1-6, 7 July 1888 comments on Fijians' attitude to courts of justice.

49266 Jan.-Apr. 1892 and Jan.-May 1893 includes at ff.1-17 extracts of letters received and at ff.11-12 a summary of letters from Thurston.

49270-2 Literary Manuscripts and Correspondence.

49271 ff.139-86. Collections for *Fiji, Records of Private and Public Life 1875-1880*, Edinburgh 1897-1912, 4 vols.

ff.195-205. MS. entitled 'Seventeen Years among the Savages' being the story of Pierre Pettice or Pelletier, a cabin boy on the *St Paul* wrecked off the Louisiade Archipelago in 1858, who was found on Night Island off the north east coast of Queensland.

ff.207-28. 'A Child's Journal of a Voyage from Wellington, New Zealand, to London, 1882', being Rachel Nevil Gordon's journal while accompanying her parents to England. Covers their stay in Sydney including a description of the burning of the Exhibition Building in the Botanical Gardens.

49597 Miscellaneous letters and papers including F, letter n.d. from K. Mansfield to M. Gertler.

49600-3 Papers 1908-13 of the Musical League founded 1908.

49602 Correspondence and papers 27 Dec. 1907 to May 1913 including letters from Percy Grainger.

49603 Programs, articles, and cuttings on the Liverpool Festival Sept. 1909 containing many references to Grainger.

49683-962 Balfour Papers

Papers of A. J. Balfour, 1st Earl of Balfour, unbound.

49688-97 Correspondence with Prime Ministers and other statesmen.

49693 Correspondence 10 July 1910 to 22 Dec. 1922 with A. Bonar Law.

ff.216-19. 13-16 Nov. 1915 concerning the *Philomel* with a New Zealand crew serving in the Persian Gulf.

ff.228-32. Telegram 6 June 1916 from the Governor of New Zealand to the Secretary of State for the Colonies about the replacement of a lost ship, with letter 10 June 1916 from Balfour to Bonar Law about this offer.

ff.233-42. 21 July to 30 Oct. 1916 concerning the purchase of ships by W. M. Hughes on behalf of the Australian Government.

49694 Correspondence with S. Baldwin, J. Ramsay Macdonald, and Winston Churchill.

ff.114-33. Account of action in the Dardanelles involving Australian and New Zealand troops, typescript carbon copy.

49697 Correspondence with premiers, statesmen, and governors-general of Canada, Australia, New Zealand, and South Africa, chiefly messages and comments on political affairs.

ff.43-57. Correspondence 9 May 1904 to 21 Jan. 1906 with Lord Northcote referring to the Labour government in Australia, preferential trade, naval expenditure, immigration, etc.

ff.58-70. Correspondence 1-13 May 1916 with W. M. Hughes mainly concerning the loan of a wireless telegraphist for developing Australian communications.

ff.71-84. Messages of greetings, etc., 21 Dec. 1926 and 25 July 1928 from S. M. Bruce, 14 Feb. 1922 to 10 Dec. 1926 from Sir Joseph Cook, 19 Apr. 1919 to Sir Joseph Ward and 9-10 Mar. 1922 from Sir James Allen.

49698-756 Cabinet, Committee of Imperial Defence, and Foreign Affairs.

49698 ff.181-5. *Proposed Draft of Circular Despatch to the Governors of the Self-Governing Colonies, Dec. 1904,* concerning Colonial Conferences 7 July 1904.

49699 ff.84-5 A. J. Balfour, *Thoughts on German Colonies,* War Office, June 1918, referring to German possessions in the Pacific now under mandate of Australia and New Zealand; ff.186-230 'The British Empire and its self-governing members', written by A. J. Balfour for the Imperial Conference, Inter Imperial Relations Committee, 26 Oct. 1926, typescript copies and drafts; ff.232-44 further papers concerning the Imperial Conference and the British Empire Nov. 1926, typescript.

49700-2 Correspondence 1904-16 with Sir George Clarke, Baron Sydenham of Combe.

49700 ff.10-13. 20 May 1904 asking Balfour's opinion on whether he might join two Australian companies, the Life Insurance Association of Australasia and the Advisory Board of Victoria, with reply 30 May 1904 from Sir George Murray.

ff.169-70. 4 Oct. 1904 mentioning Sir William Irvine, Premier of Victoria, when Clarke was Governor of Victoria.

ff.175-8. 27 Oct. 1904 referring to phantom Russian ships sighted in Australian waters.

49701 ff.209-11. 27 May 1905 mentioning the Anglo-Japanese Treaty and the 'White Australia' policy.

49702 ff.104-7. 14 Oct. 1905 referring to the Anglo-Japanese Treaty and possible trouble with Australia, mentioning the Trades Halls of Melbourne and Sydney as trying to influence British foreign policy.

ff.142-3. 14 May 1905 concerning a request by Deakin for advice on a defence scheme for Australian harbours, with ff.144 telegram 11 Nov. 1905 from Deakin to the Imperial Defence Committee asking the Committee to frame such a scheme.

ff.181-2. Telegram 2 Dec. 1905 from the Governor-General of Australia to the Colonial Office concerning the reply of the Imperial Defence Committee.

D

ff.208-11. 20 May 1906 mentioning satisfaction at the Australian defence scheme.
49757-830 Correspondence, chiefly relating to Home Affairs.
49774 Correspondence 13 Nov. 1901 to 8 Nov. 1911 with J. Chamberlain.
ff.26-31. 3-9 Sept. 1902 concerning the next governor-general of Australia, suggesting Marlborough.
ff.49-50. Memo c. July 1903 on French colonial possessions including the New Hebrides.
ff.61-74. 18-24 Feb. 1905 concerning a commercial union with the colonies and the need for a colonial conference to discuss the question fully.
49775 Correspondence 19 May 1888 to 12 Nov. 1926 with Hon. A. Lyttelton and L. S. Amery.
Correspondence with Lyttelton at the Colonial Office includes: ff.17-19, 30 Nov. 1904 concerning the Court of Colonial Appeals; ff.22-6, 31-4, 13 Jan., 1 Feb. 1905 concerning the organisation of Imperial Councils; ff.41-2, 46-50, 27 May, 2 June 1905 referring to 'Colonial Preference' and closer commercial union with the colonies as part of Unionist policy; ff.54-6, 27 Oct. 1905 from B. N. Holland, Colonial Office, concerning despatches from Lords Northcote and Plunket and the date of the Colonial Conference in 1906.
Correspondence with Amery includes: ff.191-4 notes 14 Nov. 1918 by Amery on representation of the Dominions at the Peace Negotiations, a result of W. M. Hughes's protest over recent British action at Versailles; ff.200-1, 16 Apr. 1926 suggesting a sub-committee of the Committee of Civil Research be set up to study the question of scientific research to enable permanent white settlement in tropical Africa and North Australia; ff.202-46, 19 Oct. to 12 Nov. 1926 concerning the international position of the Dominions and enclosing draft memo 1921 by Gen. Smuts on the Constitution of the British Commonwealth and constitutional relations in the Empire, with reply 20 June 1921 from Amery.
49838-69 General correspondence 1872-1929.
49838 ff.84-92. Correspondence Apr. 1881 with J. C. Clarke, Gullendaddy, Boggabri, N.S.W., concerning the death of Balfour's brother, Cecil.
ff.93-100. Further correspondence 20 Aug. 1881, 30 Oct. 1891 concerning his brother's assets and affairs in Australia.

50013-64 Iddesleigh Papers
Correspondence and papers of Sir Stafford Henry Northcote, 1st Earl of Iddesleigh.
50031-3 Family Correspondence 1853-1921.
50033 Royal and other correspondence 1887-1921 of Henry Stafford Northcote, second son of Sir Stafford Northcote, Governor-General of Australia 1904-8.
ff.12-24, 95-6. Correspondence Mar. 1904 to Mar. 1908 concerning Northcote's position as Governor-General of Australia.
ff.98-9. 28 Apr. 1908 from T. J. Carr, Bishop of Melbourne, sending good wishes to Lady Northcote before leaving Australia.
ff.122-5. 30 June 1916 from W. M. Hughes to Lady Northcote mentioning wounded British and Australian troops.
ff.128-9. 7 June 1919 from W. M. Hughes to Lady Northcote congratulating her on the award of D.B.E.
ff.131-2. Memo on gift presented to Lord Northcote in 1907 when he visited the Northern Territory in H.M.S. *Pyramus*.

50078-114 Hutton Papers
Correspondence and papers of Lieut.-Gen. Sir Edward Hutton, Organiser of the Mounted Infantry, Commander of the Military Forces in New South Wales 1893-6, General Officer Commanding the Canadian Militia 1898-1900 and Commander

and Organiser of the Military Forces of the Commonwealth of Australia 1901-4. In 1900 he served in South Africa where he commanded Australian mounted troops.

50078-89 Royal and Special Correspondence 1884-1920.

50078, 50080-9 contain letters and papers concerning Australian defence; 50080 contains correspondence with Lord Minto on the South African War.

50090-1 Family Correspondence 1868-1948.

50091 contains letters and papers concerning Australian defence and the South African War.

50092-9 General Correspondence 1874-1922.

50094-9 contain letters and papers concerning Australian defence; 50097 contains correspondence regarding the participation of Australian troops in the South African War.

50254 Letters to E. B. Taylor, anthropologist, from scientists and other persons, unbound.

15 Dec. 1869 Col. A. Lane Fox concerning boomerangs and their use.

1 Nov. 1886 A. P. Maudslay giving Taylor addresses of people in Fiji who would provide information on native customs.

50275-357 Arnold-Forster Papers

Correspondence and papers of H. O. Arnold-Forster. The papers, together with additional material, were used by M. Arnold-Forster in *The Right Honourable Hugh Oakeley Arnold-Forster: A Memoir. By his Wife*, London 1910. Many of the individual volumes contain original letters, as well as typescript and manuscript copies, together with cuttings, offprints, pamphlets, Blue Books, memoranda, reports, Command Papers, frequently annotated with notes, corrections, and amendments.

50275-99 Papers as Secretary to the Admiralty 1900-3, unbound.

50294 ff.8-16. 12 Feb. 1902 suggested scheme of colonial contributions to place before colonial premiers, typescript.

ff.17-47. Miscellaneous papers July 1902 on the formation of a separate Australian navy.

50300-34 Papers as Secretary of State for War 1903-5, unbound.

50307 ff.86-7. Minute Jan. 1904 on a New Zealand proposal for an Imperial Reserve Force.

50318 ff.165-6. Return Mar. 1904 showing numbers of the Australian military forces available.

50823 Piano arrangements of the tune *Country Gardens* by Percy Grainger 1918.

50831-41 Sydenham Papers

Correspondence and papers of Sir George Sydenham Clarke, Baron Sydenham of Combe, Governor of Victoria 1901-4. For details of his career see his autobiography, *My Working Life*, London 1927.

50831-4 Letters 1892-1913 to Sir Valentine Chirol, author and journalist.

50831 ff.61-270. 30 Dec. 1901 to 11 Nov. 1903 from Government House, Melbourne, and 2 Apr. to 29 Dec. 1904 from London, containing many references to Australian politics, with cuttings from Australian newspapers.

50832 ff.1-34. 1 Jan. to 13 Sept. 1905 containing several references to Australia. The remainder of the letters are written from Bombay.

50835 Correspondence 1892-1909 chiefly while Secretary of the Committee of Imperial Defence.

ff.122-3. 5 June 1909 from Lord Kitchener to Clarke concerning an invitation from A. Deakin to Kitchener to visit Australia in 1909.

50836 Memo as Secretary of the Committee of Imperial Defence with some copies of letters 1904-7.

ff.78-84. Notes c.1906 on the general administration, etc., of the Australian army, typescript carbon copy.

50844 Letters 15 June 1921 to Aug. 1922 from K. Mansfield to Mary Annette, Countess Russell, the authoress, written from Switzerland, France, Spain and England.

50867-87 Musical MSS., mostly autograph, of Percy Grainger 1890-1950.

51024-41 Diaries of Capt. R. F. Scott, R.N., C.V.O., as leader of the British Antarctic Expedition 1910-13. Mainly printed in *Scott's Last Expedition*, ed. L. Huxley, London 1913. (Not to be consulted or photographed without permission of Peter Scott, Esq., Slimbridge, Glos.)

51042 Photographs of members of the British Antarctic Expedition 1911-12.

51071-204 Cecil Papers
   Correspondence and papers of Lord Edgar Cecil, Viscount Cecil of Chelwood, in temporary binding.
51072 Correspondence with politicians including L. S. Amery 1912-45.
ff.226-38. 26 Oct. 1926 from Amery to Cecil containing an account of the co-operative schemes of the Electrolytic Zinc Co. of Australia by H. W. Gepp, head of the Australian Development and Migration Commission, with account and letter 12 Aug. 1926 addressed to Lord Stonehaven, and reply 1 Nov. 1926 from Cecil.
ff.239-40. 22 Nov. 1926 from Amery including a scheme initiated by the National Union of Students to make possible world tours by university and public school men with the object of getting first hand experience of the opportunities offered by Canada, Australia and New Zealand.
51097 Miscellaneous correspondence 4 Mar. 1924 to 23 Dec. 1925 mainly official, relating to foreign affairs.
Memo 6 Mar. 1925 for Lord Parmoor to sign protocols of the League of Nations on behalf of His Majesty's Government, the Commonwealth of Australia, and India, typescript.
Note 15 July 1925 prepared by Sir Frederick Lugard for the League of Nations on forced labour, with reference to New Guinea.
51098 Miscellaneous correspondence 5 Jan. 1926 to 15 Feb. 1927 mainly official, relating to foreign affairs.
ff.111-13. 25 Sept. 1926 from the New Zealand Delegation to the League of Nations, approving of Cecil's leadership of the Empire Delegation to the League, with reply of the same date.
f.131. Copy of letter 14 Oct. 1926 to S. M. Bruce.
ff.138, 140. 18 Oct. 1926 from Bruce, London, saying he is unable to attend a meeting of the British Universities' League of Nations Society, with reply 20 Oct. 1926.
51118 Minutes of the British Empire Delegations' Conference held June-Aug. 1927 at Geneva to discuss naval armament, at which the Commonwealth of Australia was represented by Sir Joseph Cook and New Zealand by Sir James Parr, Adm. Earl Jellicoe, and Rear-Adm. A. F. Beal, dup. typescript.
51119 Conference for the Limitation of Naval Armament held June-Aug. 1927 at Geneva between the United States of America, Japan and the British Empire, dup. typescripts.
ff.33-45 include British and Dominion ships, displacements under Washington standard conditions, prepared by the British delegation and including Australian and New Zealand vessels.
51120 Conference for the Limitation of Naval Armament, Technical Committee held June-July 1927 at Geneva, at which the Australian representative was Capt.

H. J. Feakes, R.A.N., and the New Zealand representatives were Rear-Adm. A. F. Beal and Earl Jellicoe.

51150 Memoranda relative to the British Commonwealth Relations Conference, Toronto, 11-21 Sept. 1933.

52461-3 Correspondence 1916-17 between Gen. Sir Archibald Murray, G.C.M.G., as Commander-in-Chief, Mediterranean and Egyptian Force, and Gen. Sir William Robertson, G.C.B., as Chief of the Imperial General Staff.

52461 31 Jan. to 29 Aug. 1916 containing many references to Australian and New Zealand troops and their activities; also letters Feb. 1916 from Gen. W. R. Birdwood and Brig.-Gen. C. B. B. White, concerning the formation of Australian and New Zealand Divisions and the lack of discipline among the troops.

52462 Correspondence 12 Sept. 1916 to 21 June 1917.

52463 Privately printed edition of this correspondence, *Egypt 1916-17*, London 1932.

52512-21 Campbell-Bannerman Papers
  Correspondence and papers of Sir Henry Campbell-Bannerman, unbound.

52515-16 Letters 1906-8 from V. A. Bruce, 9th Earl of Elgin, Colonial Secretary, and 1906-7 from W. Churchill, as Under-Secretary for the Colonies.

52515 Notes Mar. 1906 on Hon. A. Lyttelton's proposal for an Imperial Council with a permanent commission attached to it, typescript carbon copy; 19 May 1906 from Lord Elgin on the constitution of the Colonial Conference.

52516 Letters 16, 23 Jan. 1907 concerning an Australian dinner party and Australian representation at the Colonial Conference; memo May 1907 from the Prime Minister of Canada to Elgin concerning steamship services between Canada and Australia, with a covering letter 17 May 1907 from Elgin to Campbell-Bannerman; 28 Dec. 1907 from Elgin enclosing a letter from F. S. Hopwood concerning the New South Wales Government's request for the extension of Sir Harry Rawson's term of office as Governor of New South Wales; 28 Jan. 1908 B. H. Holland to Nash concerning the resignation of Lord Northcote as Governor-General of Australia, with another letter 13 Feb. 1908 on the same enclosing copy of a telegram 12 Feb. 1908 from Northcote; 21 Feb. 1908 from Elgin concerning a replacement for Northcote; 21, 24 Jan. 1907 from W. Churchill concerning the presence of State Premiers of Australia at the Colonial Conference.

52517-19 General correspondence 1892-1908.

52519 6 May 1907 concerning the Colonial Conference, steamship subsidies and trade between Canada, Australia, New Zealand, and Britain, signed W.R., typescript.

52537 Letters 5 Apr. 1915 to 9 Jan. 1916, mostly copies, from Capt. F. H. Mitchell to his wife and to his mother, written during the Dardanelles campaign, unbound. They describe the landing and evacuation of the Peninsula with many references to Australian and New Zealand troops, Generals Birdwood and White, and other Australian and New Zealand military leaders.

52623-773 Diaries and correspondence 1908-37 of Sir Sidney Cockerell, Director of the Fitzwilliam Museum, Cambridge. Diaries 1932-7 (52670-2) and all letters by living writers are not available for inspection.

52770 Correspondence 1936-47 of Cockerell as Adviser to the Felton Bequest, National Gallery of Victoria, Melbourne.

52888-9 R. V. Williams, musical scores and sketches of the film music for 'Scott of the Antarctic' 1948-9 and 'The Loves of Joanna Godden' 1947.

52916-23 Letters from authors, poets, and artists to S. Schiff, writer under the name 'Stephen Hudson', and his wife Violet.

London

52919 ff.112-82. Letters [1920?] to Aug. 1922 from K. Mansfield mainly concerning families, work, health, and movements in Europe.

ADDITIONAL CHARTERS

Add. Ch.37766 Counterpart deed of conveyance 6 June 1835 of land at Port Phillip, by native chiefs to John Batman, founder of the colony of Victoria.

EGERTON MSS.

Eg. MS.902 'Navegaciones antiguas y modernas á la Mar del Sur y otras partes del globo', collected by Don Joseph Antonio de Armona, 1772, manuscript copies. ff.1-2. Navegaciones de Fernandez de Quiros, y descubrimientos en la Mar del Sur, 1595-1613. Extracts from the Archivo Real de Simancas.

Eg. MS.1816 Papers relating to early voyages of the Spanish to America and the South Sea 1518-1621. Transcribed, chiefly from copies in the public archives at Seville, for Martin Fernandez de Navarrete, partly in his handwriting, and mostly printed in his *Viages y Descubrimientos*, Spanish. Includes the voyages of Miguel de Legaspi 1565, Pedro Fernandez de Quiros 1605, Joris van Speilbergen 1615, notes on New Guinea 1544, Francisco de Cáceres 15[?], and notes by Maestro Fray Ygacio Muñoz 1595. At the end of the volume is a corrected draft of a summary of the voyage to the Southern Hemisphere by the corvettes *Descubierta* and *Atrevida* under the command of Don Alexandro Malaspina 1789-94.

Eg. MS.2177A Journal 10 Feb. 1776 to 6 Jan. 1779 in H.M.S. *Resolution* by Cook, holograph. Photocopy in the Mitchell Library, Sydney.

Eg. MS.2177B ff.1-4. Journal in H.M.S. *Resolution* 28 Nov. 1778 to 6 Jan. 1779 and fragment of log continuing journal 7-17 Jan. 1779, both holograph by Cook. ff.5-12. Secret instructions 6 July 1776 for Cook, commander of H.M.S. *Resolution*, signed by the Lords of the Admiralty. Copy in the Mitchell Library, Sydney.

Eg. MSS.2178-9 Journal 10 Feb. 1776 to 17 Jan. 1779 in H.M.S. *Resolution*. As rewritten for publication by John Douglas with introduction giving a review of previous voyages in the Pacific; argument by W. Wales 20 Apr. 1784 to prove that Cook sought for Cape Circumcision under the proper meridian; notes 18 May 1784 by Henry Roberts on map compiled by him on Cook's instructions and later instructions of the Lord Commissioners of the Admiralty. Published as *A Voyage to the Pacific Ocean. Undertaken, by the Command of His Majesty, for making Discoveries in the Northern Hemisphere*, ed. John Douglas, London 1784.

Eg. MS.2180 Letters 1776-84 to J. Douglas chiefly concerning publication of the journals of Cook's second and third voyages, including 4 Jan. to 23 June 1776 James Cook, 16 Dec. 1780 to July 1784 Capt. James King, 22 Jan. 1782 to 29 June 1784 Lieut. Henry Roberts, 9 Nov. 1782 and 30 Mar. 1784 Sir Joseph Banks, 11 Nov. 1783 to 24 July 1784 Thomas Pennant and 11 Feb. to 5 Aug. 1784 William Wales.

Eg. MS.2591 Journal 10 Feb. 1776 to 29 Nov. 1779 in H.M.S. *Discovery* entitled 'Some Account of a Voyage to South Seas In 1776-1777-1778. Written by David Samwell Surgeon of the Discovery' with silhouette portrait of Samwell. Printed illustrations include engraved portrait of Samwell 1798 and engraved views of Pacific Islanders. *A Narrative of the death of Captain James Cook to which are added some particulars concerning his life and character*, by David Samwell, London 1786, is bound with the journal. This differs considerably from the MS. account of Cook's death, ff.196-225.

Eg. MS.2851 Correspondence of botanists, chiefly French and English, consisting for the most part of letters 1784-1860 from Philip Barker Webb to W. B. A. Moquin-Tandon. It includes letters 14 Oct. 1796 from Archibald Menzies and 20 May 1815 from Robert Brown, and an incomplete list of specimens of plants of Australia, collected 1817-29 by Allan Cunningham and sent to Professor de Candolle Aug. 1834, with note by Candolle. There are several references to Australian plants and to naturalists who had visited Australia.

Eg. MS.2854 Portolano executed in Italy c.1540, probably by Battista Agnese. ff.3b-4. Chart of the Indian Ocean showing part of the coast line below the Tropic of Capricorn in the latitude of Western Australia. ff.13b-14. General map of the world showing Magellan's route around the world in the *Victoria* 1519-22 and the Spanish trade route across the Isthmus of Panama to Europe.

Eg. MS.2856 Portolano made by 'Georgio Sideri dicto Calapoda Cretensis . . . nel anno domini 1562 die 18 Freuer'. ff.2b-3. Map of the world showing the Pacific Ocean. f.3b. Map of the Pacific Ocean.

Eg. MSS.3291B f.207, 3291C ff.13-69b. Papers 1885-92 relating to the defence of Australia among papers of Reginald Earle Welby, Baron Welby, mostly printed.

HARGRAVE MSS.

Harg. MS.494 Genealogical, legal, and other papers including ff.66-102 copies of papers relating to the East India Company, the South Sea Company, and the Hudson's Bay Company, giving their limits in relation to one another, and to the Southern Whale Fishery, with a copy of remarks signed by T. Russell, India Board, 28 Mar. 1791.

HARLEY MSS.

Harl. MS.3450 Portolano containing charts 1578 drawn by John Martines of Messina. f.5. Chart of the Sea of China and the Eastern Archipelago with part of the coast of New Holland called 'Meridionale, discoperta novamente'.

Harl. MS.4034 Copy by W. Hacke of a set of charts and sailing directions taken by Capt. B. Sharp from a Spanish prize in 1681, mainly charts of the Pacific coast of America. f.295. Map 1669 of the Marquesas showing the discoveries of Mendaña in 1595 and of Quiros in 1606. f.296. Map n.d. of the Pacific Ocean showing parts of New Guinea, the Gulf of Carpentaria and Tasmania. Another volume of charts of South America by W. Hacke entitled 'Captain Bartholomew Sharp's South Sea Waggoner' is at Sloane MS.44, but does not include the charts listed above.

Harl. MS.4225 'A Journal kept by an Ingenious Englishman on board the *Nicholas* of London John Eaton Comander in a voyage from Gorgona Island to the City of Batavia on the island of Java', 22 Dec. 1684 to Dec. 1685.

ROYAL MSS.

Royal MS.20E ix Portolano or 'Boke of Idrography', by John Rotz, 1542 including f.30 a map of the world showing the East Indies, the coast of Java and a coastline in the latitude of Australia.

STOWE MSS.

Stowe MS.794 Journal 28 May 1793 to 21 Oct. 1794 in the *Chesterfield*, Matthew

B. Alt commander. In various hands. Part 1 is a journal 28 May to 11 Sept. 1793 of voyage made in company with the *Shaw Hormuzear*, William Bampton commander from Norfolk Island through Torres Strait to Timor. An abridgement of Bampton's journal of this voyage has been printed in M. Flinders, *A Voyage to Terra Australis*, London 1814. Part 2 is journal 20 Dec. 1793 to 21 Oct. 1794 while the *Chesterfield* was cruising in the South Atlantic Ocean.

LOANS

Loan 57 Bathurst Papers
  Formerly in Public Record Office P.R.O.30/62.

57/55. Private letters 1824 from various correspondents in Ceylon, Mauritius, New South Wales, and Van Diemen's Land. The volume, which is not consistently foliated, includes letters:

25 Nov. 1824 J. J. Gordon Bremer, H.M.S. *Tamar* at sea, asking for promotion for his son and referring to his own work in establishing a colony at Melville Island.
23 July [?] from [?] recommending Mr McIntyre for a grant of land in Van Diemen's Land.

17 Apr. 1824 J. Wilmot Horton sending an official communication to the Governor of New South Wales to be delivered to Mr McIntyre on his arrival there.
18 Aug. 1823 J. Wilmot Horton to Thomas P. Macqueen concerning his grant of land in New South Wales.

19 July 1824 Pat Murray to his brother Maj.-Gen. Sir George Murray concerning Peter McIntyre late tenant of Achinnar in Glenartney going to New South Wales, asking him to give McIntyre letters of introduction to Sir Thomas Brisbane.

28 Nov. 1824 Northampton concerning Edward Abbott lately returned from Van Diemen's Land.

26 Jan. 1824 John Owen, Pembrokeshire, mentioning Mr Bates, just appointed Commissioner of Excise and Collector of Duties for Van Diemen's Land, and asking that his brother Charles Owen be considered for a similar post in New South Wales.
6 Dec. 1823 W. Wilberforce, Yoxall Lodge, nr Lichfield, concerning the lack of clergymen in Van Diemen's Land with extract from Mr Bigge's report giving details of this.

PRINT ROOM

Students must obtain a ticket of admission to the Print Room in addition to a general reader's ticket.

199* B1-4 Banks Collection of Drawings and Water Colours. This includes drawings n.d. of New Zealand, New Caledonia, New Georgia, and Otaheite, made during an expedition commanded by Capt. Charles Clerke, and possibly by Clerke himself; also drawings c.1777-9 of fishes and birds by John Webber and an unknown artist during Cook's third voyage. For bird drawings see A. Lysaght, 'Some Eighteenth Century Bird Paintings in the Library of Sir Joseph Banks', *Bulletin of the British Museum (Natural History), Historical Series*, vol.1, no.6, 1959.

Webber [margin annotation]

DEPARTMENT OF ETHNOGRAPHY

In December 1970 the Department moved to 6 Burlington Gardens, W.1. Information contained in documents kept in the Department is available to qualified students at the discretion of the Director. The correspondence files include notes and photographs, some of which have been extracted and kept as 'ethnographic documents' in special files. There is a card index to such documents. The following are examples:

Australia

900-1 Letters 1905-7 from Graham Officer, Kallara Station, Louth, N.S.W., concerning his gift of Aboriginal implements.

903 Descriptions of objects from the Mitchell and Burke districts of Northern Queensland, including weapons of the Dalleburra tribe, given by Robert Christison. Also 916 Notes on the Dalleburra tribe by R. Christison, typescript.

904 Letters 15 Sept., 25 Nov. 1914 from Lawrence Hargrave concerning relics at Woollahra Point, Sydney, N.S.W.

906b, 908, 922 Notes on Aborigines by Mrs Daisy Bates, Ooldea.

907, 920, 923 Letters 1925-9 from J. S. Litchfield, Darwin, concerning Aboriginal objects; letter 1 Sept. 1926 describes the initiation of Aboriginal boys, typescript carbon copy.

915 Letters 26 Jan., 12 Feb. 1856 from J. S. Prout to J. Barnard Davis concerning his paintings of natives of Australia, Tasmania, and New Zealand. If Davis purchased all the paintings Prout would place with them autograph letters by Tasmanian Aborigines, 'Some Notices of Natives of Van Diemen's Land at Flinders's Island in 1845 under the protection of Mr. Robinson', by Robert Clark, catechist, and a painted board issued by Lieut.-Gov. Arthur illustrating 'the humane wishes and promises of the Governor' to the Aborigines, the board having been given to Prout by G. A. Robinson. See N. J. B. Plomley, 'A list of Aboriginal material in collections in Europe', *Records of the Queen Victoria Museum*, Launceston, New Series 15. The autographs of natives and Clark's 'Notices' are with Prout's letters. The painted board given by Prout to Davis is now in the Museum of Archaeology and Ethnology, Cambridge.

925 Letter 1949 from J. F. Jones, Burnie, Tas., describing hammer stones.

New Guinea

991 Questionnaire with report 22 Jan. 1965 by B. A. L. Cranstone on the use of Pandanus nuts in Tifalmin Valley, New Guinea, 1963-4.

1000 The Robert Mond Collection, collected and described by Dr B. Malinowski, typescript carbon marked 'uncorrected copy'.

1009 Notes 1922 on collection from the Trobriand Islands by Dr B. Malinowski, typescript.

1003 Letter n.d. from W. Stalker reporting on the natives of the Kei Islands.

1008 Letter 23 Oct. 1911 from A. K. Chignell describing objects he is sending from a prehistoric site at Wanigera, via Tufi, North Eastern District, Papua.

1013 Photographs of Fijian rock-carvings by B. and S. Fahnestock.

Oceania

1079 W. Fowler, canoes and their construction in the Solomon Islands, typescript, with photographs.

1087 E. L. G. Thomas, notes on the ethnography of Buka, Solomon Islands, with tables of vocabularies English, Buka, and New Guinea and New Ireland languages, typescript.

1088 Northcote Jack, ethnographic account of Rennell Islands.

1117 Ethnographical Museum, Academy of Sciences, Leningrad, list of ethnological material from Polynesia, giving names of collectors, typescript.

1120 List of the more important Capt. Cook relics in the British Museum, Department of Ethnography, 1937, typescript.

1120 A, B. Photographs of objects believed by J. Edge Partington to have been collected by Capt. James Cook, New Zealand, Hawaii, north-west coast of America. Department negatives XXXVIII/28-50.

1121 Ethnographical Museum, Academy of Sciences, Leningrad, the Hawaiian collections, typescript with photographs. History and lists of the following collections:

Coll.505, presented to Major Bohm, officer commanding the port and fort of Petropavlosk in Kamchatka by the survivors of Capt. Cook's third journey, sent by Bohm to the Museum in 1780.

Coll.517, brought to St Petersburg by Mr Buldakow, Director of the Russo-American Company in 1810 on behalf of Baranow, Governor of the Russian colonies in North America and in the Pacific Ocean; contains the royal dress presented to Baranow by King Kamehameha I.

Coll.736, presented to the Admiralty Museum in St Petersburg by Russian travellers and explorers, eighteenth to mid-nineteenth century.

Coll.570, presented by Lisiansky in 1804 after his voyage round the world in the *Newa*.

1129 W. H. Eagle, nine 35mm. film strips of Easter Island archaeology with detailed notebook and cuttings, presented Oct. 1953.

The Department files of drawings and photographs are arranged by area. The files of drawings include Portfolio 4118, a box containing drawings and paintings of Tasmanian Aborigines by Prout, Thomas and Alfred Bock, Robert Dowling, and W. B. Gould, plus etchings by Duterrau. There is also a painting of a Tasmanian Aboriginal by Duterrau. Most files of drawings depict ethnographical objects and are kept in folders.

BRITISH MUSEUM (NATURAL HISTORY)
Cromwell Road, London, S.W.7

Vol.I, pp.1-76 of *History of the Collections Contained in the Natural History Departments of the British Museum*, London 1904-12, 2 vols. in 3, includes a description of the Museum's libraries, pp.23-53 being a 'List of Important Books, Manuscripts and Drawings'. In January 1970 a further work was in the press, 'A Short History of the Libraries and List of Manuscripts and Drawings in the British Museum (Natural History)', by F. C. Sawyer, *Bulletin of the British Museum (Natural History), Historical Series*, vol.4, no.1. A set of *Catalogue of the Books, Manuscripts, Maps and Drawings in the British Museum (Natural History)*, London 1903-40, 8 vols., has been cut up and pasted on cards and an author card catalogue is maintained, supplementing the printed catalogue. Entries in the printed catalogue of the Museum's libraries and its supplement are sometimes fuller than in *History of the Collections* or in 'A Short History'. Each department of the Museum has its own library and catalogue, the catalogues cited above being union catalogues. Call numbers for manuscripts are not yet all fixed and it is sufficient to indicate the library in which the manuscript is held: L General Library, B Botany, E Entomology, M Mineralogy, P Palaeontology, Z Zoology.

For documents relating to the Pacific voyages of Captain James Cook see also *The Journals . . . of Cook*, ed. Beaglehole. For papers of Sir Joseph Banks see also *The Banks Letters*, ed. Dawson, with supplements, and *The Endeavour Journal of Joseph Banks 1761-1771*, ed. J. C. Beaglehole, Sydney 1962, 2 vols., vol.1, pp.127-47.

As well as material on mineralogy the library in the Department of Mineralogy holds material on oceanography, a selection of which is listed below. Notes are held also on observations carried out on the following ships: H.M.S. *Egeria* 1887-8; H.M.S. *Iris* 1912, New Zealand coast to coast of New South Wales; H.M.S. *Myrmidon* 1887, north coast of Australia; U.S.S. *Nero* 1899-1900, trans-Pacific track; H.M.S. *Penguin* 1896, Funafuti and Fiji; U.S.S. *Tuscarora* 1873-8, Pacific Ocean.

Only a selection of the important collections of drawings and paintings is listed below. Separate paintings and collections also include: J. Cotton, water-colour of the garden warbler 1834 (Z); A. Garrett, water-colours of South Sea fishes with notes (Z); M. Hitchcock, water-colours of insects and plants of Fiji 1895-6 (E); F. Jensen, vegetation of Lifu 1876 (B); W. Smyth, H.M.S. *Blossom*, drawings of vertebrates 1825-8 (Z); J. Webber, water-colour of *Pringlea antiscorbutica* (B).

Anderson, W. Notes on birds observed during Cook's second voyage and descriptions of plants and animals of the third voyage (Z and B).

Andrews, C. W. Four notebooks 1897-8 relating to Andrews's visit to Christmas Island, some details in the notebooks not being incorporated in his *Monograph on Christmas Island*, British Museum (Natural History), 1900; twenty-three letters 1897-8 from Andrews to C. D. Sherborn (Z).

Atkinson, E. L. Notebook containing data on parasitic Protozoa and two notebooks on worms collected during the British Antarctic Expedition 1910-13 (Z).

Banks, Sir Joseph

Some manuscripts and drawings from the library formed by Sir Joseph Banks are in the British Museum but a large number are in the libraries of the Botanical and Zoological Departments of the British Museum (Natural History). The correspondence and papers are scattered. See *The Endeavour Journal of Joseph Banks*, ed. J. C. Beaglehole, London 1962, vol.1, pp.127-39.
Journal of Banks kept during Cook's first voyage, transcript (B).
Correspondence of Banks. One volume of original correspondence put together from various sources in the British Museum (Natural History) and twenty volumes of transcripts (B). Letters from A. Cunningham*.
Four lists, in an unknown hand, of bird skins collected during the voyages of Cook and others, formerly catalogued under Solander. From the Banksian Library (Z).

Bannerman, D. A. Notebooks on the birds and ornithological literature of the eastern Polynesian islands (Z).

Barclay, G. Journal of a voyage round the world 1836-41, H.M.S. *Sulphur*, 3 vols. (B).

Bauer, F. L. Forty-nine water-colours of animals and two hundred and three water-colours of plants collected when accompanying Flinders to Australia 1801-5 (Z and B).

Bloxam, A. Natural history notes made during the voyage of the *Blonde* 1824-5 and correspondence concerning the notes 1890-8 (L).

Bower, T. H. B. Two notebooks on birds collected in north and north-west Australia *c.*1886, used by G. M. Mathews, *South Australia Ornithologist*, vol.2, 1915-16 (Z).

Brown, R. Papers

Correspondence, 3 vols. (B). Arranged alphabetically by name of correspondent with list of correspondents in each volume. Typescripts of some letters in the Mitchell Library, Sydney. Documents are numbered and include:
Vol.1/17 statement by Sir Joseph Banks as to Cook's second voyage, transcript by R. Brown; 1/53-61 letters 1844-8 from J. E. Bicheno containing comments on the government of Van Diemen's Land and on conditions in the colony; 1/59 letter 26 Mar. 1847 refers *inter alia* to Prout; 1/109-12 letters 1803-17 from G. Caley, microfilmed for the Mitchell Library, Sydney; 1/122-4 letters 1831 and n.d. from

London

Allan Cunningham, letter 1/122, 17 Apr. 1831 refers to collections he had made at Moreton Bay 1829 and on Norfolk Island in 1830; 1/196-200 letters 1841-5 from Sir George Grey referring *inter alia* to Eyre.

Vol.2/3-13 letters 1824-6 from P. P. King, some concerning Cunningham's paper including 2/12 letter 26 Dec. [1854?] North Shore, Sydney, concerning exhibits for the Paris Exhibition and giving colonial news including news of rebellion on the gold-fields; 2/74-86 letters 1814-49 from members of the Macleay family chiefly from W. S. Macleay 1824-54, 2/80 letter 29 May 1839 from W. S. Macleay giving his favourable impressions of the colony, 2/81 letter 7 Apr. 1840 from W. S. Macleay describing a journey to Illawarra and the garden at Elizabeth Bay; 2/248-52 letters 1820-3 and one letter 11 Sept. 1840 from W. Swainson offering his herbarium to the British Museum.

Vol.3/100-48 correspondence 1800-54 of Robert Brown, 3/100-16, 1800-3 arrangements for Brown to accompany Flinders, voyage to Australia, etc.; 3/117-26, 1805 on arrangements for the return voyage on the *Investigator* and arrival in England including 3/125-6 statements of natural history specimens collected and statement of the expense of removing the specimens from H.M.S. *Investigator* at Liverpool to the Customs House, London; 3/121-31 papers concerning the services of Matthew Flinders; 3/132-48 correspondence 1847-54 concerning Mrs Flinders's pension.

Journal 1800-4 kept during a visit to Ireland and on the voyage under Flinders (B). The section Dec. 1801 to Jan. 1802 relating to the visit to King George Sound and to the voyage along the southern coast of Western Australia has been microfilmed for the Battye Library, Perth, W.A. The journal includes a volume 14 Sept. to 28 Oct. 1804 describing tours in New South Wales.

Catalogue of the species in his own and the Banksian herbarium, including plants collected during the voyage of H.M.S. *Investigator* and while Brown was in Australia 1801-5 (B). Microfilms of this catalogue are in the herbarium of each Australian state accompanied by a typescript list of genera compiled by N. Burbidge.

'Catalogus Plantarum in vicinitate Newcastle & ad ripas fluviorum Hunteri, Patersoni, Gullielmi ab Oct. 14 ad Novr. 20 an: 1804, observatorum a R.B.' (B).

Collection of descriptions of New Holland plants (B).

Notes on zoological collections made during the voyage of H.M.S. *Investigator* and in Australia 1801-5 (Z).

Miscellaneous papers including: list of seeds collected on the east and north coasts of New Holland 30 July 1802 to 4 Mar. 1803; list of plants from Moreton Bay collected by Fraser 1829; list of plants from Swan River; new or doubtful plants collected by Fraser during second expedition to the western interior of New South Wales; list of specimens collected 1823 by Baxter on the south-west coast of New Holland; note on two islands of Kent's Group; a few remarks on Port Dalrymple given to Gov. King 6 Sept. 1804 (B).

Caley, G. Journals of journeys in New South Wales 1801-5, 1 box, transcripts and microfilms in the Mitchell Library, Sydney; descriptions of plants of New South Wales 1801-4, 1 vol. (B).

Carter, T. Two field notebooks 1887-1922 on the birds of north-west and south-west Australia (Z).

Challenger, H.M.S. 1873-6. Manuscripts include the diaries of Sir John Murray, J. J. Wild, R. von Willemoes-Suhm, the ship's log, soundings book, records relating to the publication of reports and numerous notes by various authors on the plants, animals, and deep sea deposits collected. There is also an album presented to Sir John Murray and containing signed photographs of contributors to the reports (M).

Chapman, F. Lists of Foraminifera from Funafuti with typescript lists *c.*1902-10 (Z).

Cunningham, A. Papers* (B)

Transcripts of some papers in the Mitchell Library, Sydney. See also Ida Lee, *Early Explorers of Australia*, London 1925.

'Journal of the proceedings of Mr. James Bowie and Mr. Allan Cunningham' 1814-15 with continuations by Cunningham to 1819 (B).

Letters 1817-19 to Sir Joseph Banks and W. T. Aiton.

Lists of seeds and specimens including seeds collected on board H.M. cutter *Mermaid* 1818 and specimens of plants collected on board H.M. Sloop *Bathurst*, 20 May 1821 to 25 April 1822.

'Original MS. of appendix to P. P. King's "Survey" ii pp. 497-533' dated 'New So. Wales July 1822'.

Folder labelled 'Australia etc.' containing letter 16 July 1822 to R. Brown; copy of letter 16 May 1839 R. Brown to Cunningham; 'Catalogue of plants observed upon the Shore of Australia' 1819-21; the same 1819-22 but not identical, possibly neither item in Cunningham's hand; lists of specimens of plants collected 1819-27.

Cunningham, R. Index *c.*1830 to J. J. Labillardière, *Novae Hollandiae Plantarum Specimen*, Paris 1804-6, 2 vols., and R. Brown, *Prodromus Florae Novae Hollandiae*, London 1810 (L).

Darwin, C. R. Lists and notes 1832-45 by C. R. Darwin, J. E. Gray, and T. Bell relating to the Reptilia and Amphibia obtained by Darwin during the voyage of the *Beagle* also one sheet list of Cirripedia (Z).

Deschamps, L. A. Journals 1791-1801 kept on *La Recherche* under d'Entrecasteaux and during travels in Java, with drawings and sketches, including sketches of plants and animals observed during the whole of his travels (B and Z).

Drury, Dru. Letter book 1761-83, some letters refer to Banks, Solander, and R. Forster; volume of miscellaneous papers including agreements with ships' captains, letters from various correspondents among which are four letters 1800-3 from J. W. Lewin, New South Wales, and three lists of articles supplied to J. W. Lewin, photostats in the Mitchell Library, Sydney; two diary notebooks July 1794 to Apr. 1796, Sept. 1801 to June 1805, the latter containing some notes on Sir Joseph Banks and J. W. Lewin (E).

Dryander, J. Catalogue of the drawings of animals in the library of Sir Joseph Banks arranged in systematic order; Catalogue of drawings of birds by W. W. Ellis and J. Webber and of specimens from Cook's third voyage, formerly catalogued under Solander (Z).

Dunstan, B. Notebooks, lists of collections, locality index, and catalogue of figures of specimens of Queensland type fossils, also correspondence 1913-23 with R. J. Tillyard concerning fossil insects (P).

Ellis, W. W. 115 water-colour and pencil drawings of birds and fish made during Capt. Cook's third voyage (Z). See A. Lysaght, 'Some Eighteenth Century Bird Paintings in the Library of Sir Joseph Banks', *Bulletin of the British Museum (Natural History)*, *Historical Series*, vol.1, no.6, 1959.

Engleheart, H. Magnified drawings of Australian and Ceylonese zoophytes, 2 vols. with a set of tracings of the drawings and a list of sea-weeds and zoophytes collected and arranged by Mrs L. Grey and the Rev. H. Engleheart (Z).

Forster, J. G. A. Catalogue of the drawings and collections of animals made on Cook's second voyage, two parts in one vol., pt 1 an annotated list of the drawings, pt 2 a list of specimens with localities. Formerly catalogued under J. Dryander (Z). 261 water-colour and pencil drawings of animals and plants made during Cook's second voyage, 4 vols. with unpublished outline engravings of some drawings (Z and B).

Gould, J. Letters, notes, and drawings c.1848-68 relating to Australian mammals and birds by J. Gould and others. The letters include 6 Feb. 1848 from J. McGillivray, 31 Jan. 1851 J. Gould to Sir William Jardine and 29 Sept. 1857 J. R. Elsey, photo-copy in the National Library of Australia. There are also several letters from Krefft (Z).

Günther Collection. The papers of A. Günther including correspondence arranged by name of correspondent among which are letters 1874-89 from Sir Walter Lawry Buller and 1861-77 J. L. G. Krefft. There is also a group of letters c.1870-98 labelled 'Overseas Travellers' including letters from correspondents in Australia and New Zealand (L).

Guppy, H. B. Notes c.1890 on the rocks, plants, and animals of the Solomon Islands and six boxes of notes relating to rocks, plants, and soundings of the Antarctic regions, Indian Ocean, and South Pacific (M).

Harris, C. M. and Webster, F. B. Galapagos Islands, report, records, and notes relating to the expedition 17 Mar. to 11 May 1897 from Hyde Park, Mass., U.S.A., also photographs and drawings (Z).

Hinds, R. B. Diary 1835-40 as naturalist in H.M.S. *Sulphur*, 2 vols. Sections in vols.1 and 2 concerning Hawaii are published in 'The Sandwich Islands . . .', transcribed and ed. E. A. Kay, *Hawaiian Journal of History*, vol.2, pp.102-35, 1968. Vol.2 contains sections on the Marquesas, Bow Island, Tahiti, Fiji, and New Ireland (L).

Hooker, Sir Joseph Dalton. Lists of plants collected 1839-43 while surgeon and naturalist in the *Erebus*, with notes and drawings (B); twenty-eight water-colours and pencil sketches 1839-43 of Antarctic fish, some used by Sir John Richardson in illustrating his *Zoology* (with J. E. Gray, London 1844-75, 2 vols.) of the voyage (Z); Collection of sketches and outline drawings 1840-1 of invertebrate animals (M).

Hubrecht, A. A. W. Notes 1906 relating to specimens of Nemertina collected in the Antarctic regions during the British Expedition 1898-1900 *Southern Cross* and British National Antarctic Expedition 1901-4 *Discovery* (Z).

Laishley, R. Notebook containing extracts from his autobiography (L); volume of water-colour and pencil drawings illustrating the natural history of New Zealand with a manuscript entitled 'Gleanings of Natural History in New Zealand' (Z).

Lowe, P. R. Check lists of birds collected during the cruise of the *Zenaida* 1906-7 and third cruise 1907-8 with notes and figures (Z).

MacGillivray, J. Catalogue of the Radiata and Mollusca collected during the voyage of the *Rattlesnake* 1846-50 (Z). See Correspondence in Keeper of Zoology's Room, Foreign Letters, vol.II no.126 letter 1855 from Sydney advising the despatch of jars of specimens from Fiji and the Solomons.

Maconochie, A. Reports on Norfolk Island (B).

Murray, Sir John. See H.M.S. *Challenger*. The Murray Library in the Department of Mineralogy is devoted to oceanography.

Neill, J. Sixty-seven water-colours of mammals, reptiles, and fish found at King George Sound, W.A., and in its neighbourhood 1839-42, accompanied by notes. Some were used to illustrate E. J. Eyre, *Journals of Expeditions of Discovery into Central Australia*, London 1845, 2 vols (Z).

New South Wales. Seventy water-colours of animals and plants made near Port Jackson, some used for the plates of J. White, *Journal of a Voyage to New South Wales*,

London 1790. These have been erroneously attributed to T. Watling who did not arrive in the colony until 1792. Formerly catalogued under Watling.

Owen Collection (L)

Sir Richard Owen's papers and copies of his printed works. There is a typescript list in which printed works and manuscripts are numbered in one sequence. Many of the former are annotated by Owen and letters and memoranda have been inserted. The Museum also holds Owen's collection of drawings of zoological and palaeontological subjects including the original drawings and water-colours for illustrations in his published works. There are 520 folios among which the following drawings of Australian subjects have been noted: 226, 315, 416, 430-8, 449, 452-6, 464-73. No.472 is a coloured anatomical drawing of a Platypus signed J. W. Lewin 1810.

25. Fifteen pocket notebooks Oct. 1830 to Nov. 1839 including notes of Australian interest among which is a memo that Frederick Bennett leaves Oct. 1833 in the *Tuscan*, Capt. Stavers, on a voyage to the South Seas to last two or three years. Later notes are that he was seen diligently collecting in the Sandwich Islands and that he returned to England 25 Nov. 1836.

33. Notes made while dissecting the Pearly Nautilus, successive drafts for portions of the memoir, author's interleaved copy with memos and other notes and water-colour drawings from which the plates were engraved.

59. 'Autograph Manuscripts'. The contents of the volume include 'Rough notes for the article on Crustacea in the Zoology of Captain Beechey's Voyage &c' and completed manuscript for the same.

62. Owen correspondence, 27 vols. chiefly letters to Owen arranged alphabetically by names of writers and including correspondence of William Clift. The letters deal chiefly with natural history subjects, especially collections sent to the Museum. Many letters 1836-89 relate to Australia, New Zealand, and Pacific islands, some describing colonial conditions. Correspondents include Dr G. Bennett (letters 1844-88 microfilms, photoprints, and typescripts in the Mitchell Library, Sydney) and his son G. F. Bennett, Sir Walter Buller, J. B. Davis, J. D. Enys, R. D. Fitzgerald, W. L. R. Gipps, C. Gould and J. Gould, J. R. Gowan, Sir George Grey, N.Z., R. C. Gunn, J. von Haast, J. Hector, Lieut. F. Helpman, government schooner *Champion*, C. S. Hill, Capt. J. Everard Home, F. Huddleston, J. B. Jukes, P. P. King, F. J. Knox, G. Krefft, Sir William Macarthur, F. McCoy, J. D. Macdonald, assistant surgeon H.M.S. *Herald*, G. Macleay, Sir Thomas L. Mitchell, von Mueller, S. R. Pittard, E. P. Ramsay, W. Swainson, Rev. R. Taylor, J. P. Verreaux, Col. W. Wakefield and F. Wakefield, F. G. Waterhouse, J. Watts concerning F. Isaacs, C. S. Wilkinson, W. Williams.

63. Natural history manuscripts including scientific correspondence addressed to Sir Everard Home. Among the manuscripts are items numbered 68-87, notes on Australian animals with letters 1830-1 from Dumaresq, F. Bauer, and A. Cunningham.

102, 103. 102 'Rules for Collecting and preserving Specimens of Plants', an inscription on p.1 reads 'By Dr. Solander; his autograph' and verso of sheet 4 bears an inscription 'Doctor Solander's Method of preserving Plants'; 103 'To dry Plants in Sand &c by Mr. Brown', a note in another hand reads 'Not Brown's autograph'.

Parkinson, S. Drawings of plants and animals collected during Cook's first voyage, three vols. of animals (Z) and eighteen vols. of plants (B). Some drawings were unfinished and completed drawings were made from them by various artists. The Museum holds the 742 copper plates and complete set of proofs executed for Sir Joseph Banks, also a portrait of Parkinson.

Raper, G. Seventy-two drawings of the scenery and natural history of New South

London

Wales, Norfolk Island, and Lord Howe Island 1787-92 (Z). Colour transparencies of twenty-nine water-colours of birds are in the Mitchell Library, Sydney.

Riley, Alexander. Letter 26 Nov. 1804, Port Dalrymple, to Lieut.-Gov. Paterson relating to hardware in his charge, contemporary copy (B).

Royal Society of London. Account of the petrological, botanical, and zoological collections made in Kerguelen's Land and Rodriguez during the transit of Venus expeditions 1874-5, see *Philosophical Transactions*, vol.168, 1879 (L).

Shortridge, G. C. Letters 1904-6 to Oldfield Thomas while collecting specimens in Western Australia for the British Museum. Microfilm in Battye Library, Perth, W.A. In Personal Correspondence file of Oldfield Thomas in Mammals Section.

Smith, E. D. Fifty-six original water-colours for illustrations to R. Sweet, *Flora Australasica*, London 1827-8 (B).

Solander, D. C. Manuscripts
A descriptive slip catalogue, systematically arranged, in two parts: Animals, to include all species then known, 2 vols (Z); Plants, being a catalogue of the Banks Herbarium, 25 vols. (B).

List of plants, collected by W. Anderson during Cook's third voyage, in the order in which they were arranged in the drying books (B).

Notes of plants and animals collected during Cook's first voyage, the notes made when specimens were collected, the plants in the order in which they were laid in the drying books, descriptions written up during the voyage, and completed lists of local faunas and floras (B and Z).

Sowerby, J. A Sowerby collection of correspondence, papers, drawings, and prints, uncatalogued Jan. 1970. It may repay examination.

Stalker, W. Three notebooks relating to the birds of New Guinea, c.1909 (Z).

Teale, Sir Edmund Oswald. Details of the Teale collection of Australian fossils (P).

Thornhill, W. B. Notebook containing drawings of Lagenidae with short notes c.1895-1900, see H. Sidebottom, 'Lagenae of the South-West Pacific Ocean', *Quekett's Microscopical Club Journal*, Ser.2, vols.11-12, 1912-13. Sidebottom's album of drawings is also held (Z).

Wallace, A. R. Two notebooks giving localities for his collections of birds and other material in the Malay Archipelago 1855-61 (Z). The Museum also holds a portrait of A. R. Wallace.

Watling, T. Collection of 512 water-colour drawings of the natives, animals, plants, and scenery, with maps, in the neighbourhood of Port Jackson, N.S.W., c.1792-4. The works of at least three artists are represented, only drawings by T. Watling are signed (Z). Microfilm in the Mitchell Library, Sydney.

Wilkins, Sir Hubert. Two typescript copies with manuscript notes of his *Undiscovered Australia*, London 1928 (L).

Wilson, E. A. A quantity of notes and drawings of marine mammals c.1901-11, also sketches of whales, dolphins, and seals made during the British Antarctic Expedition 1910-13 (Z).

Wood, A. C. Account of a voyage to the Fiji Islands, Australia, New Zealand, and notes on birds observed, Nov. 1923, a copy of a letter, typescript (Z).

ROBERT BROOKS & CO. LTD
Adelaide House, King William Street, London, E.C.4

Some of the firm's records relate to Australia. They include: journals 1822-8, 2 vols.; ledgers 1826-32, 2 vols.; letter book 1841-3; acceptance book and cash book 1855-6. There is also a bundle of loose letters mainly from Robert Towns & Co., Sydney, relating to a cotton plantation on the Logan River, Queensland.*

Miscellaneous papers relating to Australia include other papers concerning Robert Towns and letters 1875-7 from or concerning T. R. Icely.

CABLE AND WIRELESS LTD
Mercury House, Theobald's Road, London, W.C.1

This company was formed in 1929 by the amalgamation of Western Telegraph Co. and Eastern Telegraph Co. The Eastern (Extension Australasia and China) Telegraph Co., whose operations included the laying of part of the Pacific Cable was itself an amalgamation of a number of older companies. All inquiries about the archives of companies absorbed by Cable and Wireless Ltd should be directed to the Secretary.

The assets of all Australian external communication services, previously owned by Cable and Wireless Ltd and Amalgamated Wireless (A/sia) Ltd, were acquired by the Overseas Telecommunications Commission, Sydney, N.S.W., which was established by an Act of 1946.

Volume of fifty Australian agreements 24 Jan. 1868 to 1 Jan. 1917 bound together after the merger of Eastern and Western Telegraph in 1929, with list of contents at the front. The following examples show the range of operations:

24 Jan. 1868, Government of Tasmania with Tel. Con. & Main Co. Ltd for Tasmania-Victoria submarine telegraph cable.

3 Jan. 1870, Tel. Con. & Main Co. Ltd with Aust. Tel. Co. Ltd for Singapore-Batavia, and Java-Timor-Darwin submarine telegraph cables.

24 June 1875, Governments of New South Wales and New Zealand with E. Ex. A/sia & C. Tel. Co. for New Zealand-Australia submarine cable.

6 May 1879, H.M. Queen with E. Ex. A/sia & C. Tel. Co. Ltd for Penang-Port Darwin submarine cable.

19 July 1888, Tel. Con. & Main Co. Ltd with E. Ex. A/sia & C. Tel. Co. Ltd for Banjoewangie and Western Australia cable.

9 Jan. 1889, E. Ex. A/sia & C. Tel. Co. Ltd with Colonial Office for concessions and land in Broome.

14 Apr. 1900, Government of South Africa with E. Ex. A/sia & C. Tel. Co. Ltd for Durban-Australia cable and reduced rates Europe-Australia.

2 July 1900, Tel. Con. & Main Co. Ltd with E. Ex. A/sia & C. Tel. Co. Ltd for contracts for Mauritius-Rodrigues-Cocos-Fremantle-Glenelg cable.

22 Nov. 1901, George Clunies Ross with E. Ex. A/sia & C. Tel. Co. Ltd for lease of land, Direction Island telegraph station.

3 Apr. 1913, E. Ex. A/sia & C. Tel. Co. Ltd with South Australia Commissioner of Crown Lands for surrender of rights to land in Adelaide.

The Public Relations Officer, Cable and Wireless Ltd, holds further material of historical interest, including personal records, cuttings, reminiscences of employees, some printed archives, and rare books and pamphlets. The manuscript material is filed under such topics as: Broome, W.A.; Bamfield-N.Z.-Australian cable; *Emden*; and Pacific Cable Board. The collection of Hugh Greig at Fanning Island, for example, includes photographs, menus, reminiscences, and his engagement agreement dated 1904. Printed items include the memorandum and articles of association of the British Australian Telegraph Co. Ltd, incorporated Jan. 1870, and souvenir brochures. *Reminiscences of a Hard Case* by H.W.N.S., Singapore 1937, describes in detail the laying of the cable to Darwin.

London

CHURCH MISSIONARY SOCIETY

157 Waterloo Road, London, S.E.1

The archives of the Society more than fifty years old may be consulted for research purposes by approved students. Selected records have been microfilmed for Australia and New Zealand and copies of a typescript 'Guide to the Microfilmed Archives relating to the Australian and New Zealand Missions 1808-1884', prepared in 1959 by M. S. Hitchings, are available in libraries holding microfilms. Since 1959 some reorganisation has taken place and new call numbers have been allotted to certain series. Where this has happened the new references are given before the entries; old references which appear on the microfilms and in M. S. Hitchings's list are given in brackets after the entry. For biographical material on missionaries see *The Register of Missionaries*, c.1904.

The New Zealand mission began in 1814 and the Australian in 1825, the former being known as the Australasian Mission until 1841, when the home society's work in Australia ceased. All records of the Australian mission to 1841 are found among New Zealand mission records in London. In 1884 the mission to the Maoris became the responsibility of the church in New Zealand and material in London of interest to the New Zealand historian declines.

MINUTES

Committee Minutes 1799- .

The minutes of various committees and subcommittees are entered in the same volumes in chronological order. Early volumes contain lengthy extracts from correspondence.

Subcommittee Minutes 1799-1818, 1 vol.

Minutes of the following subcommittees: Accounts 1808-17, Correspondence 1799-1818, Funds 1812-15, Special Committees 1799-1815. Minutes of these subcommittees are continued in Committee Minutes.

Indexes to Minutes.

Indexes 1799-1907 and Précis Indexes 1863-1900.

Subcommittee Minutes. Alphabetical index to names and subjects.

Copies of Sydney Corresponding Committee Minutes 1821-41 (CN/o1).

These are copies, with some gaps, of the minutes of meetings held in Sydney, sent to England and arranged in the order in which they were received. Up to about 1830 the Sydney Committee seems to have arranged its agenda to deal with all business at one meeting. From c.1830 on, it held separate meetings to deal with New Holland and New Zealand affairs; but, particularly towards the end of the period, this is not invariably so, and both departments may be dealt with at the one meeting. The series contains, beside the record of meetings, copies of many letters and is particularly important for material relating to the establishment and development of the mission to Aborigines in New Holland.

Copies of Minutes of Missionaries' Meetings held in New Zealand 1823-77 (CN/o4).

Reports, accounts and copies of correspondence are included. The mission is called Australasia Mission 1823-45 and New Zealand Mission from 1846. Minutes of New Zealand District Committee Meetings are included from c.1840-66. Central Committee Minutes cover 1847-56 and Missionaries' Conference Minutes 1863-77.

Committee of Native Institution, Australia Minutes 1821-35 (CN/o13).

Minutes, Correspondence and Other Papers concerning Land Questions 1845-76 (CN/o15).

CORRESPONDENCE AND REPORTS

In-letters

Early Correspondence 1809-11 (CN/E).
Sixteen letters from Marsden, Hall and King.

G/AC3. Home letters, in- 1817-67, 105 boxes (CH/o). Letters to the Society's secretaries including letters from government departments and missionaries not on their stations. First approaches by prospective missionaries are almost invariably here.

Sydney Corresponding Committee Secretaries to Home Secretaries 1821-45 (CN/02).

Correspondence between Sydney Corresponding Committee, missionaries, and others 1820-52 (CN/05). New Holland Mission 1821-37 including some New Zealand correspondence; correspondence 1837-52 mainly New Zealand.

Missionaries' joint reports 1836-58 (CN/06). Annual and semi-annual reports arranged chronologically.

Correspondence between missionaries and New Zealand Mission Secretary 1831-64 (CN/07).

Letters from New Zealand Mission Secretaries to Home Secretaries 1826-69 (CN/08).

Correspondence concerning C.M.S. Auxiliary in Australia 1821-35 (CN/012).

Government and official correspondence 1823-64 (CN/014).

Miscellaneous papers 1820-55 (CN/016).

Miscellaneous letters to Home Secretaries 1821-68 (CN/017).

Papers of missionaries and lay workers on their stations arranged alphabetically (CN/019-0100).

New Zealand letters 1822-60, typescript (CN/0101). Mainly from H. Williams but also from Burrows, Clarke, Davis, Grey, etc. Many letters deal with land questions.

Mission Books 1820-80, 28 vols. (CN/M). Fair copies made in London of the salient matters of in-letters. They were made for the convenience of secretaries and committees dealing with business arising from correspondence. Separate name indexes exist which include a few form headings, e.g. Estimates, Accounts.

Z27. Unofficial papers mainly relating to Norfolk Island 1874-87 (U/N).

Out-letters

G/AC1. Home letter books 1824-75, 23 vols. (CH/L).
General 'home' out-letters of C.M.S. secretaries including letters to government departments and to missionaries other than those on their stations. The letters are press copies pasted into the volumes, not always in strict chronological order.

Copies of letters to missionaries (CN/I).

Miscellaneous Correspondence

Miscellaneous General Secretary's papers to New Zealand c.1835-75. A set of papers consisting of copies of various letters, original letters and drafts of memoranda. The originals of copies are to be found mainly in New Zealand Mission in-letters and copies in Mission Books. Many letters deal with Bishop Selwyn's relations with C.M.S. missionaries, with H. Williams and the land question, and with reorganisation of the New Zealand Mission 1852.

Bishops' correspondence 1830-80 (CN/03). Letters to C.M.S. secretaries and correspondence with missionaries including: W. G. Broughton 1830-44, G. A. Selwyn 1842-67, W. G. Cowie 1871-9, S. T. Neville 1874, A. B. Suter 1868-80, W. Williams 1868-80, E. C. Stuart 1877-80, C. J. Abraham 1861-7, O. Hadfield 1871-80.

G/Y/N1. Kempthorne papers 1843-8 (H/N2).

Miscellaneous foreign letters 1845-74 (C) including thirty-five items of Pacific interest.

G/AC5. Post-1880 material relating to the New Zealand Mission 1924-39 (H/N).

G/Y/AU1. Miscellaneous material relating to more than one mission (H/HZ). Letters, mainly concerning Australia and India, from Rev. R. W. Stewart and E. Stock on their tour of the colonies, with printed documents 1892-3.

ACCOUNTS, STATISTICS

Estimates and accounts 1823-80 (CN/09). Station estimates 1834-48, incomplete; various accounts for stores, etc., 1827-35, the only item for 1835 being New Holland Mission, Wellington Valley, N.S.W.; various accounts for stores, property, etc., 1834-79, incomplete.

Statistics 1872-80 (CN/010). Mainly lists of missionaries and native pastors with numbers of communicants.

Medical certificates 1847-74 (CN/011).

MISCELLANEOUS PRINTED MATERIAL

Newspapers, pamphlets, cuttings mainly relating to New Zealand, photographs of Norfolk Island.

COLLEGE OF ARMS
Queen Victoria Street, London, E.C.4

The College of Arms is a source for information concerning grants of arms, and for genealogical information. Arms may be either official, e.g. 1836 the first grant of arms in Australia, to the Anglican diocese of Australia, or they may be private. The pedigree entries cover both armigerous families which emigrated and families which became armigerous after their arrival in Australia or elsewhere. All inquiries should, in the first instance, be addressed to The Officer in Waiting, and before any search is undertaken a fee must be agreed.

COMMONWEALTH AND CONTINENTAL CHURCH SOCIETY
7 York Buildings, Adelphi, London, W.C.2

In 1835 the Western Australia Missionary Society was established. The Society's work expanded rapidly and in 1836 the title Australian Church Missionary Society was adopted. This amalgamated with the Newfoundland Church Society in 1837 and became the Colonial Church Society, later Empire and Continental Church Society and then Commonwealth and Continental Church Society. Since 1920 financial support for the church in Australia has been channelled through the Bush Church Aid Society. The Society's correspondence was destroyed during World War II but printed Annual Reports 1834-1929 and Minutes since 1839 are held, although Minutes 1843-50 are missing. Extracts only have been microfilmed for the Australian Joint Copying Project.

CONGREGATIONAL COUNCIL FOR WORLD MISSION
Livingstone House, 11 Carteret Street, London, S.W.1

COMMONWEALTH MISSIONARY SOCIETY

The Commonwealth Missionary Society continues the work of the Colonial Missionary Society founded in 1836. Before 1836 the London Missionary Society carried out this work and its records contain early papers relating to the work. The Society was incorporated in 1897, before which date it functioned as a Committee of the Congregational Union of England and Wales. In 1956 the Society became the Commonwealth Missionary Society and is now one of the societies which form the Congregational Council for World Mission.

MINUTES

Minutes 1836-69, 1899; Rough Minutes 1836-52; Ministerial Committee Minutes 1917-60; Finance Committee Minutes 1913-50.

The Minutes include statements of policy and news of the work of the Society's agents or of ministers in Australian states and New Zealand receiving assistance from the Society. Ministerial Committee Minutes deal with appointments and these minutes and those of the Finance Committee include information on Australia and New Zealand.

CORRESPONDENCE

The Society's correspondence has been destroyed. Extracts from letters, financial statements, lists of churches and ministers are given in appendices to the printed Annual Reports, sets of which are scarce. The set at Livingstone House runs from 1-70, 1837-1906, 11-13, 1847-9 being extracted from the periodical *British Missions*. Reports 1907 to date were published in *The Evangelical British Missionary* 1907-8, *The British Missionary* 1909-56, *Commonwealth News* 1957- . Reports and extracts from letters appear also in *The Colonial Chronicle, a Quarterly Record of the Transactions of the Colonial Missionary Society* and *Home Missionary Magazine*.

LONDON MISSIONARY SOCIETY

The archives of the London Missionary Society are arranged in box files by area and form. Under each mission area records consist of in-letters, reports, private or semi-official journals, personal papers and 'odds'. Typescript catalogues of in-letters have been made and are filed in loose-leaf binders, carbon copies of sections being placed in the boxes of records which they list. See R. Lovett, *History of the London Missionary Society 1795-1895*, London 1899, 2 vols., N. Goodall, *History of the London Missionary Society 1895-1945*, London 1954, and J. Sibree, *London Missionary Society, A Register of Missionaries, Deputations etc. from 1796-1923*, 4th ed., London 1923. The Society's minutes and selected records relating to Australia and the South Seas have been microfilmed for the Australian Joint Copying Project.

BOARD MINUTES

Minutes of the meetings of the Directors of the Society 1795-1918, indexed, 54 boxes.

COMMITTEE MINUTES

South Seas and West Indies. Minutes of the Western Committee Jan. 1835 to Mar. 1836, indexed, 1 box.

South Seas. Minutes of the Western Committee, later called the Southern Committee, South Seas Department, book 3, Feb. 1845 to Mar. 1852, and 5-9, June 1868 to Sept. 1917, indexed, 4 boxes.

Candidates. Minutes of the Committee of Examination, later called the Candidates Committee, which dealt with appointments. Book 1, May 1799 to June 1816, not indexed, books 2-16, June 1816 to Sept. 1918, indexed, 13 boxes.

Foreign Occasional. Ad hoc committees, concerned primarily with India and China and later Africa. The material on Australasia, Papua, and the Pacific is easily located, as all but book 1, 1882-1904, are indexed. Books 1840-5, and 1-3, 1882-1918, 2 boxes.

Ship. Book 1, 1864-1916, not indexed, book 2, 1917- , indexed, 1 box.

Arthington Trust. The Trust supported missionary work in Africa, India, China, and Papua. The books are indexed, so the few references to Papua can be located. Books 1-2, 1905-19. Finance Sub-committee, book 1, 1906-17, 1 box.

Home Occasional. Ad hoc committees, e.g. Committee appointed to consider the misrepresentations in a public journal of the conduct of the directors in the case of Tahiti, 1844. Book 1, 1841-52, indexed, book 2, 1852-72, not indexed, book 3, 1872-86, not indexed but includes the minutes of the New Guinea Steamer Committee, books 4-5, 1887-1920, indexed.

Special. Sydney Ship Committee 1908-21. Sub-committee minutes 1892-1909; p.70 Report of the Sub-committee on the work of Rev. J. King, organising agent for Australasia.

LETTERS

Western Outgoing Letters: South Seas and West Indies, 4 boxes. Letter books of duplicates 1823-35, boxes 2-4 indexed.

Western (later Southern) Outgoing Letters: South Seas, 29 boxes. Letter books of duplicates 1835-1914, indexed.

Home Office Letters 1795-1876, 12 boxes. In-letters of the Society from correspondents in the British Isles. There is a typescript calendar which gives a summary of the subject matter as well as the name of the writer and date and place of origin.
Boxes 1-2 contain chiefly letters relating to the _Duff_ 1796-1801.
Folder 6 in box 2 includes a letter 12 Jan. 1812 J. Hardcastle to Wilberforce concerning Marsden's proposal for a ship in the South Seas, a proposal supported in letters 1814 from T. Haweis filed in box 3.
Box 3, folders 5-6 contain letters about Pitcairn and boxes 4-6 include letters from William Ellis 1827-9, 1835, and John Williams 1835, 1837.
Boxes 8-9 include correspondence 1844-5 between the Society and representatives of the British and French Governments concerning relations with the French in Tahiti. Boxes 10-12 include letters 1850-71.

Home Office Letters 1795-1896, 3 boxes. These boxes contain chiefly in-letters that should be filed in the above series, and later may be incorporated in it. Some papers, committee reports, and drafts of out-letters are included. The following notes give an indication of subjects covered:
Box 1. Letter 15 Nov. 1796 Capt. James Wilson, Rio de Janeiro; letter 6 Aug. 1799 S. Greatheed to John Eyre concerning captured missionaries of the _Duff_; papers and committee reports 1796-1800 concerning missions to the South Seas; drafts of letters to New South Wales 1799-1817; letter 11 Jan. 1796 T. Haweis concerning the outfitting of the brig _Sally_ for the Southern Whale Fishery; report June 1796 T. Haweis, R. Cowie, and J. Hardcastle on the Sandwich and Marquesas Islands.
Box 2. Letter 2 May 1829 Capt. J. W. Hill, Liverpool, offering his services at Pitcairn Island; 1 Mar. 1837 J. R. Pattison, Launceston, regarding the wreck of the _Charles Eaton_ and proposing to leave missionaries on Murray Island; correspondence with Lieut. Armit, R.N., of the Colonising Association.
Box 3. Letters 1863-92 concerning New Guinea including letter 2 Aug. 1892 from James Chalmers; letters concerning the _John Williams III_; letter 16 Sept. 1885 William Lane, Tas., regarding his life and missionary work in Samoa.

Candidates Papers 1796-1899, boxes 1-25.

Theological college reports, character testimonials, personal notes, health certificates, reports on proposed wives, and related correspondence of applicants to the Society. The papers are filed alphabetically by the candidate's name and a name index to the contents is held in each box.

Answers to printed questions 1835-85, boxes 26-8.

Answers to theological questions, and those relating to social background and education, are filed chronologically. A name index is held in each box.

MISCELLANEOUS BOXES

Home Personal. Box 3, Papers of R. W. Thompson including notebook relating to Australia and New Guinea 1892-6.

Home Personal. Box 5, William Ellis, private letters to missionaries 1832-8, indexed, including letters to D. Darling, J. M. Orsmond, and G. Pritchard, Tahiti, to C. Barff and G. Platt, Samoa, and to F. Miller, Hobart.

Home Odds. Box 6, notes of a lecture given by Sir William Macgregor on Papua and the Pacific, Sheffield, 1919; boxes 10-12, papers relating to the Tyerman and Bennet Deputation 1821-9 including correspondence 1821-2 relating to Australia and New Zealand discussing *inter alia* Threlkeld and his mission to the Aborigines, with copies of correspondence 1824 with Sir Thomas Brisbane concerning Threlkeld and a letter 1824 by Bennet from Sydney; box 13, A. N. Johnson Deputation to Australia 1907, correspondence and papers.

AUSTRALIA

Letters from Australia 1797-1919, 23 boxes; boxes 1-3, 1797-1836, indexed, boxes 4-7, 1845-69, sorted into subjects, boxes 8-23, letters have cover sheets summarising contents.

Journals Australia 1800-42, 1 box, indexed. Journals of W. Shelley, R. Hassall, L. E. Threlkeld, and R. C. Morgan.

PAPUA

Letters from Papua 1872-1919, 16 boxes, contents lists to boxes 2-8, 1877-1900, boxes 1 and 9-16 sorted into subject folders but not indexed.

Reports Papua 1882-1919, 3 boxes, not indexed.

Journals Papua 1871-1901, 3 boxes, name index in box 1. Journals of A. W. Murray, S. McFarlane, W. G. Lawes, F. W. Walker, H. M. Dauncey, R. Bruce, A. Pearse, and H. P. Schlencker.

Papua Personal, 1 box. Letters 1895-1901 from James Chalmers including letters to Gowan; correspondence 1880-1906 of J. J. K. Hutchin including letters from Chalmers, Holmes, and Lawrence; typescript extracts from H. M. Dauncey's diary 1888-97; cuttings and papers on Sir Hubert Murray and C. W. Abel; letters 1893-1903 W. G. Lawes to his wife with a photograph of Lawes.

Papua Odds, 2 boxes. Box 1 contains cuttings concerning the death of James Chalmers; translations of psalms into Keapara and Kerepunu by C. Beharell; St Mark translated into Tarara by a Papuan teacher; notes on early mission days in Papua by R. Lister Turner. Box 2 contains a description of Port Moresby 1875 by W. Wyatt Gill, typescript; C. W. Abel papers mainly relating to industrial work in Papua and the Kwato Extension Association.

London

Papua Miscellaneous Papers

John Henry Holmes Papers. J. H. Holmes ('Homu') served in Papua from 1893 until 1917, living in turn in the Fly River district, Jokea in the Elema district, Orokolo, and Uriki in the Purari Delta. He was the first to describe the language and ethnography of the Gulf and Purari Papuans in a number of published papers and three books about his experiences. The papers consist of diaries 1893-1901, Aug.-Dec. 1906, 1915, 14 vols.; typescript expanded select entries Aug. 1893 to July 1895; autobiographical stories, typescript and miscellaneous talks on missionary activities in Papua; anthropological papers, typed notes, and manuscripts interspersed with correspondence with A. C. Haddon; typescript entitled 'Darkness and Dawn' published as *Way Back in Papua*, London 1926, and cuttings about *In Primitive New Guinea*, London 1924.

Edwin Pryce Jones Papers. E. P. Jones worked with J. H. Holmes at Jokea, Papua, from 1899. The following three items were found with the Holmes papers: letters 1899-1900 to his wife in England kept as a diary, some missing; anthropology notebook; notebook of journal entries, those of 1918-23 entitled 'Orokola notes'.

SOUTH SEAS

Letters from the South Seas 1796-1919, 59 boxes, boxes 1-45, 1796-1899, indexed with a contents list held in each box, boxes 46-59, 1900-19, letters have cover sheets summarising contents.

Reports South Seas 1866-1919, 8 boxes, not indexed, but sorted and filed chronologically.

Journals South Seas 1796-1899, 12 boxes. Index to all the writers in box 1. Besides original MSS., there are extracts only, typescript or manuscript, of some journals.

South Seas Personal, 4 boxes.

Box 1.

Rev. W. W. Gill's MS. book 1846-72; W. Wyatt Gill papers.

Diary of George Turner 1837-40; 'Fifty five years mission work in Samoa', written on his retirement 1884-91.

Charles Barff, 'Recollections to replace lost papers'. These include an account of Buzacott's work and the mythology of Huahine.

William Harbutt personal papers.

Diary of Alfred Saville 1862-71.

William F. Wilson, 'The Rev. Charles Wilson of Tahiti' with notes about his ancestors in Scotland and descendants in Tahiti, Sydney, Samoa, Fanning Island, Honolulu, England and Canada, 1925, typescript.

S. J. Whitmee's notes on Capt. Fowler of *John Williams II*.

Letters of Mr and Mrs William Mills 1838-52, originals and typescript copies.

Eromanga, by George Turner 1885.

Letters 18 Apr. 1900, J. E. Newell to T. E. B. Wilson; 26 Feb. 1901 James H. Cullen to T. E. B. Wilson.

Letters 8 Oct. 1892 Sarah E. Chalmers to E. B. Savage; 2 Jan. 1882 Louisa Spicer to Rev. Thomas Powell; 18 July 1864 Ariifaaite, Papeete, to Charles Barff.

Personal instructions given to the Rev. Henry Nisbet 1840, copy of original in private hands.

Letter 1818 from Pomare II to William Pascoe Crook.

Letter 1854 from Isaiah Papehia to Samuel Boothroyd 1854.

Letters from George Gill 1844, Aaron Buzacott 1839 and C. Barff 1867.

Letter from W. G. Lawes, Niue, to Alfred Saville concerning 'Bully' Hayes and blackbirding, copy.

Notes of Dr Hiram Bingham and his wife Minerva Clarissa of Apaiang, Gilbert Islands, and later of Honolulu.

Goward correspondence 1890s.

Two letters 1867 from Alfred T. Saville, Niue.

Two letters 1838, 1846 from Queen Pomare.

Box 2.

Papers relating to John Williams, his wife Mary, and some material on their sons, Samuel T. Williams and John C. Williams. As yet there is no index but the main contents are original and manuscript copies of letters 1817-39 from John Williams, some to his parents, a few letters to John Williams and letters connected with his murder from Mary Williams and others. There is also a photocopy of a printed circular by George Baxter to accompany two prints depicting his reception at Tanna and his murder on Eromanga.

Box 3.

Material on Elizabeth Moore of Samoa.

Letters 1895-7 from Chief Malietoa to Rev. W. E. Goward, with translations.

Personal papers of Robert Clark Morgan. There are ten letters to Capt. Morgan 1838-49 written during the period when he was captain of the *Camden* and later *John Williams I*, containing instructions from the directors of the London Missionary Society and expressions of appreciation from the Samoan Mission.

Box 4.

The Funafuti diaries 26 Oct. 1912 to Dec. 1915 by Sarah E. Joliffe.

Character studies of local inhabitants, Funafuti, Ellice Islands [1914?].

Portraits n.d. of Dr Alexander Macdonald and his wife Selina Dorcas, Samoa 1837-50.

Diaries 1842-57 of Rev. William Harbutt and his wife Mary Jane on the island of Upolu, Samoa. Original manuscripts and copied extracts.

Notes on Aaron Buzacott.

Notes by H. T. Gill on Isaiah, a Cook Islander who visited England 1853-6, and his father Papehia. Notes by S. J. Whitmee on Elikana, an Ellice Islander.

Notes on some *Duff* missionaries and others; James Harris, L. E. Threlkeld and his relations with Marsden, King Te Moana of Nuku Hiva, and William Pascoe Crook; also Henry Nott, William Puckey, Francis Oakes of Parramatta, Rowland Hassall, and the Hassall family.

South Seas Odds, 16 boxes.

Box 1.

Sleigh papers, Loyalty Islands, comprising diaries 1865-79 and other personal papers; correspondence mainly between Sleigh and the French authorities; letters from the London Missionary Society and from other missions in the Pacific; family papers 1860-93.

Boxes 2-3.

Ships. Miscellaneous papers, photographs and cuttings 1790-1919 including material on the earlier *John Williams* ships, an account 1794 of outfitting the *Sally* for the Southern Whale Fishery and a draft account of the voyage of the *Prince William Henry* to the Pacific 1794-9; disbursements of the missionary ship *Camden* 1840, 1841. Box 2 contains papers relating to the *Duff* and miscellaneous material on the *John Williams* ships.

Box 4.

Deputation to the Samoan Mission, Report 1888, typescript. German cuttings translated, concerning Leopold Mohn and Julius Hones in the Tubuai Islands 1851-1936. Hymn composed by Sadaraka, a native teacher at Mangaia.

London

W. W. Bolton 2 May 1944, centennial address on the death of Henry Nott, typescript.

S. J. Whitmee, two papers on Samoa and the three Treaty powers.

J. E. Newell, Apia, 11 Aug. 1899 to J. G. Rogers.

Extracts from Vailima letters by Robert Louis Stevenson 1890-2, typescript, also cuttings and photographs.

Alex Hough 1909, paper on Samoa.

The story of the *Margaret Brender* 1869, typescript.

The stone of Tangiia by A. Townley Gill, Rarotonga.

The story of my father's watch, by Rev. S. T. Williams, son of John Williams, 1900, typescript.

Letter 1846 from Queen Pomare to [Tamateni?], Tahitian.

Papers of pupils of the South Sea Seminary 1830.

Notes on the Gill family, missionaries in Papua.

One of the original copies of Pratt's Samoan Grammar (in G. Pratt's handwriting?).

Report from J. M. Orsmond, Tahiti (the Orsmond MS.) 1849, typescript copy.

H. P. Bralsford, 'Rarotongan dictionary', typescript.

'E tuahua enua. No te ui Ariki', 1869, MS. notebook, Rarotongan.

Box 5.

The book of Jerimiah [*sic*] with Mr Platt's corrections 1835 (for first Tahitian Bible).

Papers about the Rev. George Pritchard, Tahiti, late consul in Samoa.

Letter 3 July 1817 from Pomare II to Samuel Marsden, printed translation of an original in the Kroepelien Collection, Oslo.

Niue Island Church Book 1858-1917. Church meetings, church members including the dates of their deaths, census to 1908.

W. Crosfield, Missionary journey in the South Seas 1897. 34pp. devoted to the Australian colonies and 77pp. to Papua-New Guinea.

Letters from Orsmond, Threlkeld, Williams, and others, Raiatea 1819-21, printed.

Box 6.

John Davies, 'Brief narrative of the Tahitian Mission', c.1830. MS. in Davies's handwriting with notes on left hand pages in writing of Henry Nott, 2 vols. Subsequently edited by C. W. Newbury and published for the Hakluyt Society in 1961.

Native Affairs Book 1840-66 (Tahitian affairs 1844-60). Letters and minutes annotated by Teuira Henry.

Boxes 8-10.

F. Lenwood deputation papers.

Box 11.

Bickham Escott, High Commissioner for the Western Pacific, to the Colonial Office concerning annual grant to the missions, Gilbert and Ellice Islands 1916.

Correspondence on R. E. G. Grenfell of the American Board of Commissions for Foreign Missions barred from the Gilbert and Ellice Islands for disgraceful conduct 1916.

Paper concerning mission work in Nauru passing from American Missions to the London Missionary Society 1917.

Reports on education by the London Missionary Society 1912.

Testimony by native pastors against native dances, obscene pastimes, and government corruption on Tabiteuea and Nonouti, Southern Gilberts, with correspondence.

Inquiry by Arthur Grimble and the government into the administration of the Southern Gilberts and the effect of the missions there.

Arthur Grimble and the land question.

A defence prepared at the request of His Excellency Governor Solf by the staff of the London Missionary Society in German Samoa, Malua, London Mission Press, 1901.

Letter comparing Churchward's *New Samoan Grammar*, Melbourne 1923, with the work of Pratt and Newell.

Statement of the case of the Rev. John Jones, expelled by the French from Mare, Loyalty Islands, 1899, printed.

Letter concerning teachers from the South Seas in New Guinea 1916.

Proposed extension of the South Sea Mission to the northern New Hebrides, Kingsmill Group, New Caledonia, and New Guinea.

Cook Island papers 1914-19.

Box 12.

Minute books: Cook Islands 1845-74, 1 vol., Loyalty Islands 1857-77, 1878-87, 2 vols.; also account books: Lifu, Loyalty Islands, 1858-1901, 1 vol.; Nengone, Loyalty Islands, Mission Treasurer's account 1858-71, 1 vol.

Box 13.

John Williams IV papers including references to the New Guinea mission 1875-97.

Box 14.

Samoan District Council Minutes 1836-51, 1 vol. indexed; Niue and English vocabulary by G. P. [Pratt?] 1861; Fraternal Association in Rarotonga, minute books 1839-41, 1842-5, 2 vols.

Box 15.

Miscellaneous correspondence and notes on Tahiti collected for publications; talk 'Missions in the South Seas' by R. L. Stevenson prepared for a meeting of the Presbyterian Church of New South Wales, Sydney, 1893; notes on Thomas Gilbert.

Box 16.

Ships. Sketches and photographs; material relating to the *Duff* including copies of correspondence in the India Office Records; specifications for the *Royal Admiral*.

James Edward Newell Papers

J. E. Newell served in Samoa from 1881 until his death, first at Savaii and from 1887 at the Malua Seminary. He visited England in 1891-3, 1902, and 1910, and Sydney in 1883-4, where he married his second wife, Honor Jane, daughter of Rev. W. W. Gill.

Diaries 1870-88, 1891-1908, incomplete, 32 vols.

Letters from Newell: out-letter books, carbon copies, 1882-98, 6 vols., mainly concerned with administration but with some personal letters including one to R. L. Stevenson (no.1, 1893-8); folder of *c.*50 loose letters 1899-1910 including letter to *Sydney Morning Herald* 1899 concerning Cardinal Moran and the Samoan Protestant missionaries, and three bundles of accounts; letters 1898-1910 to his sons, mainly personal and family matters.

Letters to Newell: letters 1883-1910 in English including one folder of letters from the London Missionary Society, London, 1900-6; letters 1888-1910 in Samoan; other letters 1872-1910 including three from James Chalmers ('Tamate') and one from Dr Wilhelm Solf, Governor of Samoa, to Mrs Newell.

Official reports etc. Decennial reviews of the Samoan Mission 1881-90, 1891-1900; Malua Institution report 1909; Samoa Christian Endeavour Union report May 1906; rough statistics for Samoa, Gilbert and Ellice Islands 1881-1909; examination papers in Samoan.

Miscellaneous talks and articles, anthropological and linguistic notes, papers concerning R. L. Stevenson, letters and cuttings, some on Cardinal Moran.

EUROPE

Holland. Box 1 folders 1, 2, 4, 5, ten letters 1799-1828 mainly from Bernardus Ledeboer, Netherlands Society secretary, commenting on events in the South Seas, with occasional references to Batavia.

London

Germany, Scandinavia, Switzerland. Box 2 folders 1-4, several letters 1799-1843 relating to the work of the Society in the South Seas including letters 17 Mar. 1838 G. Wermelskirch, Dresden, mentioning plans for sending two missionaries to South Australia.

France. Box 3 folders 3, 5, 6, letters relating to Tahiti.

BOUND VOLUMES

Thomas Blossom, Life 1847, xerox of a manuscript copy 1895 held at Hull Reference Library, Local History Department.

David Bogue, Missionary lectures 1817 transcribed by Robert Moffat.

Autobiography of Mrs Alexander Chisholm, written for her children's children. Typescript copy of a manuscript lent to the Society by R. G. Chisholm.

W. Crosfield, Missionary journey in the South Seas 1897. Typescript copy of manuscript which is in South Seas Odds box 5.

Joseph King, Polynesia, past present and future 1914. Typescript intended as the second edition of *Christianity in Polynesia*, Sydney 1899, with correspondence concerning publication.

Joseph Mullens, 'A Brief History of the South Sea Mission', 1878.

The Journal of Lillie Saville 1866-7. Typescript copy of a manuscript given to the Society by Margaret Thornton.

Robert Thomson, 'History of Tahiti', which he dictated to his wife. Original manuscript but incomplete at the time of his death in 1851.

Samuel James Whitmee, 'Recollections of a long life'. Typescript copy of a manuscript lent to the Society by P. A. B. Whitmee.

MISSIONARY PORTRAITS 1798-1844

Miniatures of thirty missionaries to the South Seas, labelled and listed. Most are painted by Sarah Newell, and others are the work of J. W. Childe, C. Penny, R. Kirkpatrick, and W. T. Strutt. From its inception the Society kept a pictorial record of all missionaries, and the collection is catalogued and described, with biographical notes on the portrait painters, by I. M. Fletcher in 'Missionary portraits 1798-1844', typescript 1960-2.

PHOTOGRAPH AND PICTURE COLLECTION

South Seas, 3 boxes, and Papua, 3 boxes. Pictures, mainly photographs, of missionaries and the peoples with whom, and places where, they worked. The majority of photographs were taken c.1900 and are not of a high quality.

CONGREGATIONAL LIBRARY
Memorial Hall Trust, 16 Farringdon Street, London, E.C.4

In 1971, 16 Farringdon Street was being rebuilt and the Congregational Library was temporarily housed at Lown Hall, Howard Road, Cricklewood. It is hoped the Library will return to Farringdon Street.

Directory of Congregational Biography, Ministerial, c.1640-1962. A card index giving biographical information with references. Some early Puritan and Presbyterian Dissenters of the sixteenth and seventeenth centuries are included, also missionaries of the London Missionary Society and Colonial Missionary Society born and/or trained or holding pastoral charges in Great Britain. Typescript copy of some 30,000 master cards in the custody of the compiler, the Rev. C. E. Surman, 4 Holly

Lane, Erdington, Birmingham. Another set of the cards is in Dr Williams's Library, but those in the Congregational Library carry additional information.

Some representative Congregational laymen c.1640-1962, typescript volume forming Part II of the above Directory. Some colonial laymen are included.

CORPORATION OF LONDON RECORDS OFFICE
Guildhall, London, E.C.2

ADMINISTRATIVE RECORDS

Journals of the Court of Common Council 1416 to date.

From the nineteenth century the Common Council performed the ordinary functions of a municipal council. The annual printed *Minutes of the Proceedings of the Court of Common Council*, with indexes, serve as a précis and guide to the proceedings, reports, letters, and accounts contained in the Journals. As subjects covered include petitions, Thames navigation, payments, donations to a variety of causes at home and abroad, poor laws, Australian references are likely although none were found in the five years examined.

JUDICIAL RECORDS

Sessions records within the period of transportation to Australia 1784-1868 supplement other convict records. Newgate was the gaol for both the City of London and the County of Middlesex but the records of Middlesex cases, which were filed and minuted separately, are now held in the Greater London Record Office (Middlesex) q.v. The following volumes have been microfilmed*: Indexes to persons indicted 1756-92, Gaol Delivery Books 1783-93, Convict Lists 1829-40, and Transportation Account 1829-40.

Sessions Files

Gaol Delivery, Oyer and Terminer 1785-1834, c.390 rolls. Indictments, recognizances, writs, jury panels, and other such documents.

Indexes to persons indicted 1756-1834, 3 vols. Under each letter of the alphabet there are lists arranged chronologically. The lists, which give name and date, and an abbreviated indication of the offence and sometimes of the sentence, serve as a key to the rolled files.

Sessions Minute Books

Gaol Delivery, Oyer and Terminer (Fair Entry Books) 1783-1834, 12 vols. Each session is divided into Gaol Delivery, giving names of justices, jurors, and those tried, with a note of their offences and sentences, and where appropriate, Oyer and Terminer, giving names of jurors and recognizances brought forward, and the Gaol Calendar, giving names of prisoners arranged by sentence. Most transportation sentences are 'beyond the seas' although some specify 'the eastern coast of New South Wales and adjacent islands'.

Rough Entry Books for all sessions 1784-1834, 15 vols.; also 1 vol. 1830-4 of Gaol Delivery.

Sessions Papers

Bundles of informations, depositions, examinations, petitions, returns, 1784-5, 1786-9, Jan.-Sept. 1818, Oct.-Dec. 1818, Jan. 1825, Oct. 1828, Sept.-Oct. 1835.

Sessions, Miscellaneous

Convict Lists 1829-40, 12 books. 'Rough lists' of convicts on board particular ships for transportation to Australia, giving names, ages in many cases, the initial letter of the hulks from which they were transferred, the place of sentence, date, and term to be served. The lists are arranged chronologically by ship and include prisoners sentenced in all parts of the British Isles as well as at courts martial in Bermuda and various West Indian stations, Upper and Lower Canada.

Transportation Account 1829-40, 1 vol. This account relates to the same voyages as the convict lists above and was transferred from the Public Record Office in 1955. It contains clerks' charges for drawing up documents and other contracts connected with the transportation of convicts, arranged chronologically by ship.

MISCELLANEOUS PAPERS

MS. box 6.2. Letters of Lieut. William Lawson and related papers 1817-24 including three documents stating he has received no regimental pay in Australia; six letters 1819-24 from Lawson to his agent John Sloper in London giving details of his affairs; letters 1824 to his son Nelson; other family letters 1824; letter 9 Aug. 1824 John Marsh to Sloper offering his services as a wool broker; letter 9 Oct. 1821 Garling, Sydney, to Lawson; letter 15 Nov. 1823 James Quilter, London, to Lawson concerning the will of Hannah, mother of William Lawson. There is a microfilm in the Mitchell Library, Sydney, see *Old Ironbark, Some Unpublished Correspondence (1817-1824) from and to William Lawson, Explorer and Pioneer of Veteran Hall, N.S.W.*, introd. and ed. William Beard, Sydney 1967.

MAJOR H. CROSSMAN
13 Blake Gardens, London, S.W.6

Letter books 8 Mar. 1852 to 11 Mar. 1854 and 12 June 1854 to 3 July 1855 of Lieut. William Crossman (later Sir William). They contain copies of official letters to Capt. E. Y. W. Henderson, Comptroller General of Convicts, Western Australia, concerning the building of the Albany road and other public works, chiefly in the Albany district. Microfilms in the Battye Library, Perth. The originals cannot be inspected while Major Crossman is a serving Army officer.

H.M. CUSTOMS AND EXCISE
The Library, King's Beam House, Mark Lane, London, E.C.3

In earliest times customs revenue was administered at the Exchequer although the collection of certain duties was often wholly or partly farmed out to individuals. In 1671 the Crown resumed direct control and a board of Commissioners was appointed to manage the collection of duties in England and Wales. Scotland had separate Commissioners from the Act of Union 1707 until 1823 except for a short period 1723-42. Ireland also remained separate until the Act of 1823 established two Boards, one of Customs and one of Excise, both for the whole of the United Kingdom. From 1849 to 1909 the Board of Excise was part of the Board of Inland Revenue. From 1909 both customs and excise have been administered by the Board of Customs and Excise, established in its present form in that year.

The records of the Board of Commissioners fall naturally into two broad groups, the records of headquarters at Custom House, London, and the records of the outports. Under the Public Records Act 1958 both groups were required to be centralised and handed over to the Public Record Office having been processed in accordance with Public Record Office requirements, although provision was made for the retention by the Department of certain records for longer periods on good reason being shown. The Commissioners of Customs and Excise have availed themselves of this provision and by agreement with the Public Record Office and with the approval of the Lord Chancellor, are retaining certain classes for a hundred years. Other classes are being held pending final listing and indexing. A single classification scheme has been adopted for all the records, and lists of all classes are produced in the style of the Public Record Office. There are such lists for all the classes described below.

In 1883 the system of keeping official records on files was introduced and it gradually supplemented or replaced the traditional volumes of minutes, correspondence, etc. Few of these files have been retained, but those which are selected for preservation are processed by the Departmental Records Officers and transferred in due course to the Archives.

Three fires at successive Custom Houses in London, culminating in that of 1814, destroyed many of the early central records. Consequently there are very few continuous series prior to that date. The documents at Head Office include a large number of 'plantation' records. When the Customs Commission originally took responsibility for plantation affairs these ports came under the jurisdiction of the Western department but by the end of the eighteenth century there was a separate plantation clerk and assistant plantation clerk. The plantation records which are the main obvious source of information concerning Australasia in this collection have been sorted and arranged in one class (Customs 34).

Most outport records were not deposited in the London Custom House until the years immediately following the Public Records Act 1958, when the majority of the important records were transferred. The registers of British shipping, which are still kept by the ports themselves, are the major exception to this. These are not registers of arrival and sailing, but of property rights and shares in ships. They date mostly from the introduction in 1786 of the modern system of registration. Although registers are not deposited, lists of the surviving registers in each port are available. It is also hoped that the information contained in the registers will eventually be put on computer cards in London. Information in the registers may be of interest to this survey in so far as it relates to ships trading with Australia and the Pacific, or wrecked off the coasts there.

The Scottish records of the Department remain in Scotland. All headquarters records relating exclusively to Scotland are now held at H.M. General Register House, Edinburgh, but in general all Scottish outport records are still in the ports.

In addition to the archives, the Library has volumes of printed Bills of Entry for the Ports of London and Liverpool. The series for London runs from 1817-1937 and that for Liverpool from 1820-1937. Both series have gaps, but they remain the only considerable collections of such bills in the United Kingdom. Bills 'A' and 'B', 'Ships Reports', and 'Imports, Exports and Shipping of London', were printed daily, and Bill 'C', 'Imports, Exports and Shipping of Liverpool', originally twice a week, but later daily. The bills have been bound into annual volumes in these groups. The most useful are the Imports, Exports and Shipping Lists which detail the cargoes of imports and exports, giving information under goods and under ports of origin or destination, and naming the agent.

HEADQUARTERS RECORDS

Customs 1-27 Classes at the Public Record Office.

Customs 28 Board and Secretariat: Minute Books 1734-1885, 335 vols.

Only ten books have survived for 1734-1814 so that there are large gaps for these years. After 1814 there is a continuous series. Indexes to the volumes cover mainly personal names but are unreliable. The minutes record the Board's general business. It appears that the Board of six Commissioners originally dealt with most matters of policy and administration itself, but during the nineteenth century, less and less administrative routine and establishment matters came before it.

Customs 29 Board and Secretariat: Minute Entry Books 1696-1904, 55 vols.

29/1-15. Minute Entry Books 1696-1869. These were originally compiled for Sir William Musgrave, Commissioner 1763-86, and continued into the nineteenth century. The series is often referred to as 'Musgrave'. This digest is the only complete chronological record of the Board's administration throughout the period. The information in the notes and extracts is recorded under alphabetically arranged subject headings, e.g. Colonies, Convict Ships, Transports. There is an index to these headings in each volume. The entry books serve as a useful introduction to the general minutes of the Board.

Customs 30 Board and Secretariat: Out-letter Entry Books: Extra-Departmental 1812-1910, 588 vols.

These have not been examined in detail but would repay investigation for further information on particular topics or to obtain background to entries in the minutes. In particular, the report books, the memorial books, and the Treasury letters are likely to be useful. A summary of the class is given below. It should be noted that the books include some in-letters.

30/1-8. Private office 1845-1900. Correspondence of the Chairman mainly with the Chancellor of the Exchequer and Members of Parliament, indexed.

30/9-14. Board to Privy Council and Treasury: General 1812-14. Certain memorials and letters to the Privy Council Office and Treasury, indexed except 30/9, 10, Jan.-Dec. 1812.

30/15-194. Board to Privy Council and Treasury: Report Books 1812-69, indexed, except 30/16, 17, May-Sept. 1812.

30/195-224. Board to Privy Council and Treasury: Treasury letters 1814-82, indexed.

30/225-58. Board to Privy Council and Treasury: Memorial Books 1826-69, indexed.

30/259-74. Board to Privy Council and Treasury: Irish affairs 1824-48, indexed.

30/275-82. Board to Privy Council and Treasury: Scottish affairs 1824-48, indexed.

30/283-395. Board to Public Offices 1814-82, indexed.

30/396-588. Miscellaneous Letter Books 1868-1910, indexed.

Customs 31 Board and Secretariat: Out-letter Entry Books: Intra-Departmental 1700-1910, 669 vols.

The books in this class are often referred to as 'cut-out books' from the practice of cutting out the bottom right-hand corner of the index pages, which are indexed by ports, to facilitate reference. They have not been examined in detail but it is probable that there is occasional mention of goods imported from Australia and other matters of interest. A summary of the class is given below.

31/1. Abstract of Customs general orders 1700-76, indexed.

31/2-270. Board to Collectors: Western Ports 1787-1909, indexed.

31/271-495. Board to Collectors: Northern Ports 1812-1910, indexed.

31/496-504. Board to Outport officials and others 1814-82, indexed.

31/505-12. Board to Assistant Commissioners: Ireland 1812-30, indexed.

31/513-71. Board to Assistant Commissioners: Scotland 1823-72, indexed.

31/572-628. Board to Collectors: Ireland 1830-72, indexed.

31/629-69. Board to Collectors: Scotland and Ireland 1869-1910, indexed.

Customs 32 Board and Secretariat: In-letter Entry Books: Extra and Intra-Departmental 1707-1882, 202 vols.

These have not been examined closely, but like classes 30 and 31 may be worth investigation in particular instances. The Registers of Cases Referred are particularly likely to be useful. A summary of the class is given below. These entry books include some out-letters.

32/1-2. Privy Council and Treasury to Board: Orders and Warrants 1707-1813, indexed.

32/3-75. Privy Council and Treasury to Board: Registers of Cases referred 1811-82, partly indexed.

32/76-98. Irish affairs 1823-44, partly indexed.

32/99-103. Scottish affairs 1823-49, indexed.

32/104-70. Reports about the inspection of Ports 1828-57, indexed.

32/171-99. Registers of papers received from Northern Ports 1833-49, 29 vols., indexed.

32/200-1. Registers of confidential papers received 1845-82.

32/202. Miscellaneous in-letter book of Hon. S. Spring Rice 1851-8.

Customs 34 Board and Secretariat: Papers relating to Plantations c.1750-1890, 916 vols. and bundles.

Volumes not listed below do not relate to the field of this survey.

34/1. Minute Entry Book: Plantation Clerk 1828-58, indexed.

34/2-19. Out-letter Entry Books: Extra-Departmental Reports to the Treasury 1819-55, indexed.

34/20-30. Out-letter Entry Books: Extra-Departmental: Letters to Public Offices and Private Individuals 1816-55, indexed.

34/31-73. Out-letter Entry Books: Intra-Departmental: Board to Collectors 1814-90, indexed.

34/74-8. In-letter Entry Books: Extra and Intra-Departmental 1811-79. The four volumes relevant to this survey are 34/76A-78, Plantation Reference Books 1843-5, 1858-66, 1875-6 and 1877-9. They are registers of movements of papers, the papers themselves being no longer extant, unless a few are to be found in the 'promiscuous' bundles listed below.

34/79-86. General Plantation Receipts and Disbursements 1767-1851.

34/116-49. Ages, Capacities, Revenue, and Trade 1827-53. The volume for 1850 is missing. These are annual returns made by ports, giving information about the establishment, duties received, expenditure, staple articles exported, and vessels entering and leaving.

34/150. Index to Plantation Correspondence 1846-55. This is a chronological register of in-letters, giving the date of the incoming correspondence or Board's orders, and the subject. Most of the original correspondence to which this index refers is no longer extant, but it is possible that some papers will be found in the bundles listed below under names of colonies or 'promiscuous'. There may be related correspondence also in the entry books listed above (34/2-73). The register shows clearly the wide variety of matters concerning the colonies which engaged the Board's attention.

E

London

34/154-8. Plantation Establishment 1805-52.

34/154, 1805-52 contains admissions of Plantation officers with dates. There is an index of names. Former appointments of each officer are also given. 34/155-8 (1828-52) contains admissions in the Australian colonies and New Zealand.

34/161-2. Plantation Vacancies 1816-51.

34/163-6. Plantation Officers: Pensions 1857-77, indexed.

34/169-71. Seizures 1828-53, indexed.

34/172. Stores Supplied 1814-54.

34/173. Particulars of reports to Treasury and Council 1830-45.

34/174-916. Promiscuous Bundles c.1748-c.1855. The papers in these bundles are original miscellaneous subject files sorted and arranged in folders or 'bundles' by H. Atten, Librarian, c.1900-15. Within the folders the files of papers have been numbered and in many cases there is a brief list on the outside covers of the contents of the folders, with 'selected' papers particularly noted. The papers are mainly in-letters from Collectors and other officials in the colonies, with copies or related correspondence and memoranda. They are not in strict chronological order either within the original subject file, or within the folder. Papers on a variety of subjects are included, but the majority deal with establishment matters. No detailed list has yet been made (1970). Relevant territories are 613-35, New South Wales 1823-60; 636-43, New Zealand 1833-55; 787-92, South Australia 1832-54; 794-801, Tasmania 1826-56; 848, Van Diemen's Land 1834-52; 849-61, Victoria 1833-57. 836-916 are Various Promiscuous Bundles 1769-1855.

Customs 48 Excise Board and Secretariat: Excise and Treasury: Entry Books of Correspondence with Treasury 1668-1839, 142 vols.

The volumes are indexed except 48/141, 142, 1835, 1839. The indexes consist mainly of personal names of petitioners and memorialists. Copies of petitions and memorials with covering letters from the Commissioners to the Treasury and other related correspondence are entered. Several volumes were examined but no reference to Australasia found. However it is possible that there are relevant entries dealing with goods imported from these colonies in the later years.

OUTPORT RECORDS

Customs 50-101 Records of the Outports in England and Wales excluding London

A list of these outport records is printed in the *Appendix to the Second Report of the Royal Commission on Public Records*, II, Part II, pp.242-8 (Cd.7545/1914), but is incomplete. Some introduction to the records by R. C. Jarvis, 'Local Archives of H.M. Customs', is printed in the *Bulletin of the Society of Local Archivists*, 9, pp.1-14, 1952. Students interested in the archives of particular ports should apply to the Librarian of H.M. Customs for further information. Many classes will have records relating generally to colonial and plantation trade and shipping and to whale fisheries in the eighteenth and nineteenth centuries, but references of special interest will be scattered and incidental.

Customs 102 Port of London

102/1-70. Bench Officers' Minute Books 1795-c.1850. The earlier minutes survived the fire of 1814 and the whole series forms an important record of transactions taking place in the famous Long Room of the London Custom House. They record all the general business of the Port of London and there are occasional references to Australia.

MINISTRY OF DEFENCE,
NAVAL HISTORICAL BRANCH
The Naval Library, Empress State Building,
Lillie Road, London, S.W.6

The main body of Admiralty records is deposited at the Public Record Office but this library, formerly called the Admiralty Library, holds a collection of ships' logs, journals, charts, maps, and progress books. A typescript list of the manuscripts is available. Documents are made available for reference purposes and applications to see them should be made to the Librarian. Selected manuscripts have been microfilmed for Australian libraries.

MANUSCRIPTS

MS.14. List 1838 of latitudes and longitudes of maritime places and points of high land by Henry Raper.

MS.18. Journal 1719-21 of Capt. George Shelvocke in command of the *Speedwell* on a privateering voyage to the South Seas, with the *Success* under Capt. John Clipperton. See G. Shelvocke, *A Voyage Round the World by the Way of the Great South Sea, performed in the years 1719-22*, London 1726.

MS.23. Private journal 1852-5 of John MacGillivray, naturalist, being observations made during surveying voyage of H.M.S. *Herald*, Capt. H. Mangles Denham commander, 2 vols.

MS.72. Journal May-Sept. 1793 of Capt. William Bampton of the *Shaw Hormuzeer* sailing from Norfolk Is. towards Batavia, in company with the *Chesterfield* whaler. The ships sailed through Torres Strait and made observations on Tate, Nepean, and Chesterfield Islands. Log of H.M. cutter *Mermaid*, Lieut. P. P. King, commander, Jan. 1818 to Jan. 1821, 8 parts, incomplete, with journal Sept. 1817 to July 1818, 3 parts.

MS.73/2. Log Jan. 1821 to Nov. 1822 of H.M.S. surveying vessel *Bathurst*, Lieut. P. P. King, commander, incomplete.

MSS.73/4, 74/3. Vocabularies of various Pacific Islands, by John MacGillivray, rough or abstract vocabularies of San Cristoval (Bauro) and Guadacanal in the Solomons and of islands in the New Hebrides.

MS.74/8. Extract 14 Feb. to 13 Mar. 1779 from the journal of Capt. Charles Clerke, R.N.

MS.74/9. Log 1849-51 of H.M.S. *Herald*, Capt. Sir Henry Kellett, surveying the Pacific, with an account of visits to the Sandwich Islands, 4 vols.

MS.77. Log and proceedings 1840 of H.M.S. *Terror* commanded by Francis R. M. Crozier, and despatched to locate the south magnetic pole.

MS.79. Log 30 July 1818 to 4 Oct. 1819 of H.M. cutter *Mermaid*, Lieut. P. P. King commander. Logs 15 June 1820 to 11 June 1821 of H.M. cutter *Mermaid* and brig *Bathurst*.

MS.87. Log and proceedings 1852-4 of H.M.S. *Trincomalee* mainly along the west coast of South America, by W. Dawson.

MS.125. Admiralty Court Book containing lists of officials of Admiralty Courts overseas c.1840-1900, 2 vols. Includes a typescript sheet listing Colonial Courts authorised to act as Prize Courts under the Prize Courts Act 1894.

MS.145. Log 28 Mar. to 13 Oct. 1867 of Henry Crawford, midshipman, in H.M.S. *Virago* to Sydney via Cape of Good Hope, and 14 Oct. 1867 to 14 Nov. 1868 of

London

Crawford in H.M.S. *Challenger* sailing from Sydney to Auckland, and around the islands of Fiji and Samoa.

MS.159. Log 15 June to 31 Aug. 1864 kept by midshipman G. Wilson of H.M.S. *Victory*, Capt. Francis Scott. Voyages from Sydney to Auckland and other North Island ports.

MS.160. Log 30 July 1866 to 25 Dec. 1868 kept by midshipman G. Wilson of H.M.S. *Brisk*, Capt. Charles W. Hope. Voyages from Sydney to Auckland, and around the coasts of New Zealand.

MS.168. Papers 19th cent. of Adm. Sir Robert Smart. Notes and correspondence including a description of the 'Island of Disappointment' discovered by Cmdr John Byron in 1765, and the islands of King George and Prince of Wales.

MS.172. In- and out-letter books 2 Mar. 1804 to 11 Oct. 1805, of Capt. Francis Fayerman of H.M.S. *Athenian*, in command of an East India convoy to Canton, which was instructed to take the route through Bass Strait.

MS.180. Personal papers of Adm. Edward Edwards relating to the mutineers of H.M.S. *Bounty* and the voyage of H.M.S. *Pandora*.

MS.182. Journal 5 Feb. 1898 to 19 Aug. 1901 of Sir Edward Seymour, Commander in Chief of the China Squadron, 8 parts.

Journal 1804-8 of James Snead, seaman, typescript. Begins with a short account of a voyage to Canton and back in the *Neptune* East Indiaman, and includes 'sentiments of an officer on board the *Neptune* with respects to Bass Strait'.

LISTS OF SHIPS

Captains and Ships 1688-1832, 5 vols. Dates of entry and discharge from service of captains, listing the ships they commanded, within the period covered by each volume, indexed.

Ships and Captains 1688-1859, 12 vols. Supplements the former volumes by listing all ships and the term for which each captain served, indexed.

Progress Books c.1697-c.1912, 10 vols. in 15. A complete list of all ships in the Royal Navy, with particulars of origin, type, repairs, and fate of each ship, indexed.

List of the Navy 1660-1886. Within the period covered by each volume, and these often overlap, a list of ships of the Royal Navy gives details of when and by whom each ship was built, its dimensions, and number of men and guns, indexed.

List of H.M. ships lost from all causes other than by the enemy 1800-91.

Register of the Royal Navy of Great Britain 1801-10, by William Goddard, with dimensions, pedigree, reported trials, condition, and fate of ships.

Returns prepared for the Committee on finance between March and July 1848, with name, date of building, builder, and cost of repairs.

Ships laid off 1856-1900. Giving name, date where paid, and an appendix listing H.M. ships lost since 1840 with particulars.

Admiralty Register. Showing the names of new ships and vessels ordered to be built by the program 1859-60, with rate, tons, and where building, indexed.

List of ships in H.M. Navy that have been sold or taken to pieces since 1 Jan. 1874, two typescript copies.

Memoranda 1889, 1893-6, 5 vols. Annual volumes, each indexed, listing ships ordered to be built, sold, and taken to pieces.

MAPS, CHARTS, AND ILLUSTRATIONS

Most of the entries in the card catalogue indicate whether maps and charts are in manuscript, but the typescript shelf list of atlases and charts is more useful.

Vf 9/2. Hobson's Bay, Port Phillip, as surveyed by Frederick Shortland Oct. 1836.

Vf 9/3. Port Phillip as surveyed by Lieut. Thomas Symonds and Frederick Shortland of H.M.S. *Rattlesnake*.

Vo 42. Atlas containing track charts of various voyages made by H.M. ships 1840-60. Nine charts cover routes through the Pacific.

Vz 1/16. French chart of the Pacific 1742.

Vz 8/55. Chart of the Palliser Islands, by P. B. Henry n.d.

Vz 8/57. Spanish chart n.d. of the Solomon Isles, with the track of the *Princesa* 1781.

Vz 8/61. Black and white sketch n.d. of the Bishop of Oznaburg Isle, by Capt. Samuel Wallis.

Vz 11/55. Sketches and charts drawn on Cook's second voyage 1772-4, by Peter Fannin, master of H.M.S. *Adventure*.

PORTFOLIOS

A checklist on cards covers the portfolio series which consist mostly of sketches, photographs, and charts.

A 25. View of the wreck of H.M.S. *Buffalo* at Mercury Bay, N.Z., 28 July 1840.

D 45. Photograph n.d. of the working drawings of the *Endeavour* Bark, James Cook, commander.

D 46. Photograph of draught of H.M. armed store ship *Supply*, her body taken off and fitted in the single deck, with dimensions, Deptford Yard, 3 May [1702?], [P.] Hayes.

G 11. Photograph taken by Bolton G. Corney, of the memorial at Point Venus in Tahiti placed there 3 June 1769 by Capt. James Cook.

G 43. Photographs taken by Engineer Commander Samuel J. Bird, R.N., whilst serving on the Pacific Station in H.M.S. *Myrmidon* 1872-6. These include Hilo Bay, Hawaii, and various Hawaiian ferns.

I (6). Unfinished sketch of Capt. Cook's interview with the natives on landing at Van Diemen's Land 29 Jan. 1777, probably by J. Webber. *Webber*

I (8). Collection of eight photographs of Pitcairn Island, taken in 1913 by Cmdr Francis Brooker, R.N.

PICTURES

A bundle of papers relating to pictures and their location in various departments of the Admiralty.

PHOTOGRAPHS

Ships' Photographs c.1886-1945, 17 vols. with typescript index.

Photographs of Naval Stations, three almost identical vols. including views of Auckland and Sydney.

CAPTURED ENEMY DOCUMENTS

The following microfilms of German Naval Archives were transferred from the Public Record Office in June 1966. Application to see them should be made to the Head of the Naval Historical Branch, Old War Office Building, Whitehall, S.W.1.

Australian Government Selection (G.F.M.29) 1854-1944, 46 reels. Selected files of the Reichs-Marine-Amt, the Admiralstab der Marine, Abteilung B, and the Oberkommando der Marine/Seekriegsleitung relating to the Far East, Eastern Asia, South Seas, and Pacific Islands, and Australia; also to German raiders operating in southern waters during the Second World War.

University of Hawaii Selection (G.F.M.28) 1867-1916, 25 reels. Selected files of the Reichs-Marine-Amt and the Admiralstab der Marine, Abteilung B relating to East Asia, Australia, and South Sea islands.

A. DE RIGHI, ESQ.
41 Doughty Street, London, W.C.1

Collection of letters assembled primarily for their philatelic interest but including many of historical value. Mr de Righi has permitted copies of these to be made for Australian libraries and lists of names of correspondents are available in the National Library of Australia. With the letters are some miscellaneous documents. The following examples indicate the interest of the letters to the field of this survey:

17 Oct. 1805, A. L. S. Bowden, Hobart, to Charles Fox, London.

1810, Charles Mackintosh, 73rd Regiment, Sydney, referring to Methodist Missionary activities in Samoa.

1 Oct. 1834, John Foster, Fosterville, Ross, V.D.L., to John Hartley, Settle, Yorks., concerning bills drawn by his brother, describing his own pastoral activities and commenting on Hobart and Launceston.

10 July 1838, Mrs James Lord, Hobart, to Rev. J. B. Naylor, Headmaster of the Queen's Orphan School, asking for a girl to be allowed to enter her service.

1851, Ivor Crowther, Bathurst, N.S.W., to A. Hanger Leather, Sydney, about gold diggings.

DR WILLIAMS'S LIBRARY
14 Gordon Square, London, W.C.1

An historical and theological library founded in 1716 by Daniel Williams, the nonconformist divine, and particularly well endowed with material relating to Dissenters. The manuscript collections are catalogued in a Handlist of Manuscripts, typescript. There is also an index of personal names.

12.46. Robert Millar Papers 1793-1818. Correspondence with and about members of the Unitarian Movement giving an account of the Scottish Martyrs and their associates, especially Palmer and Ellis but also Muir, Boston, Skirving, and Margarot. Letters 1789-1802 from Theophilus Lindsey to Millar including reports of the political and commercial activities of the Scottish Martyrs and their associates in Australia.

Letters 1802-4 from Hannah Lindsey to Millar concerning Palmer, Ellis, and Boston, the wreck of *El Plumier*, and the death of Palmer.

Letters Millar to Palmer, copies: 5 Sept. 1791 on Ellis; Jan. 1804 on Palmer's character.

Letter 24 Sept. 1790 William Christie to Millar on Palmer's conduct at Woodston.

Letters 1789-95 Palmer to Millar including letter 25 Oct. 1795 from Sydney, copy.

12.79-80. J. T. Rutt, *The Life and Correspondence of Joseph Priestley*, London 1831, 2 vols. Original letters inserted include: 7 Feb. 1794 Palmer, *Hanislaus* hulk, to Rutt; 18 Dec. 1795 Muir, Sydney, to Rev. Shields.

24.80. Correspondence 1785-7 between James Purves and Palmer. Eleven letters, also discussion of the letters and their history with quotations from Alexander Gordon.

Directory of Congregational Biography, Ministerial, c.1640-1956, typescript copy of master cards in the custody of the compiler, the Rev. C. E. Surman, 4 Holly Lane, Erdington, Birmingham. Another and fuller set c.1640-1962 is in the Congregational Library, q.v.

ENGLISH CARPENTARIA ASSOCIATION

Acting Secretary: Mr J. Evans, 2a Templar Street, London, S.E.5

The diocese of Carpentaria was established in 1903. The English Carpentaria Association has not kept correspondence further back than 1962. The Association published a quarterly magazine *The Carpentarian* July 1927 to Oct. 1938 containing extracts from correspondence of bishops and others. *The Carpentarian* is now replaced by *The English Carpentarian* 1943- .

Minutes 5 Dec. 1908- .

Year books 1956-7- , partly duplicated typescript.

Kennett, William I. Letter 1 Oct. 1867, typescript copy, containing descriptions of Somerset, York Peninsula, and the customs and language of Aborigines; account of a voyage 1866 in the *Lord Raglan*, London to Sydney; a continuation 1 Sept. 1867- of an account of life at Somerset.

Calendar, typescript, of selected articles in the *Anglican* 1855-6 with typescript copies of articles, also a typescript revision of an article 'A Journey North' by L. Britain, the *Anglican*, 1953.

FAIRBRIDGE SOCIETY INC.

119 N.E. Wing, Bush House, Aldwych, London, W.C.2

Records of the Society (Child Emigration Society until 1949) include:

Copy letter book containing letters 1912-15 from G. D. Jefferson, Secretary of the Society, to Kingsley Fairbridge in Western Australia.

Book of photographs of parties of children going out to Australia, children named and other details given, 1912-52.

Minutes 1925- .

Individual case files 1913- .

Printed Annual Reports 1923- .

FAWCETT LIBRARY

27 Wilfred Street, London, S.W.1

The Fawcett Library contains material on the interests, activities, and achievements of women at all times and in all countries. It contains some 20,000 books and many serials, pamphlets and cuttings. It also has a growing collection of autograph letters and the records of several societies now defunct. The Library is open to members of the Fawcett Library and Society and, for a small fee, to members of the public.

WOMEN'S SERVICE LIBRARY AUTOGRAPH COLLECTION

Vol.2. General Women's Movement including Emigration, Married Women's Property, Local Government, etc.

London

Part A, 1800-86. Includes letters to and from Maria Rye chiefly concerning her Female Middle Class Emigration Society. The following letters were noted: 26 July 1862 Mme Bodichon to Lord Shaftesbury acknowledging £25 for Maria Rye's journey to Australia in connection with female emigration and stating hopes of raising £400 to ensure her at least two years' livelihood in advance; 26 Sept. 1862 Maria Rye to Mme Bodichon concerning the sale of her law stationer's business and her inability to induce Sir Rowland Hill to reduce ocean post to 1d; 20 May 1865 Maria Rye, Redfern, N.S.W., to Mme Bodichon concerning moral difficulties of life in colonies and efforts to reform conditions in hospitals and workhouses.

Part B, 1887-1909.

22 Feb. 1907 Mrs Emily Crawford to Miss Palliser stating that they had succeeded in getting the passage money to Australia reduced to £6, enabling them to send out young persons who had to earn their living.

Part C, 1910- .

14 Dec. 1943 Mrs Ibbott, Mayor of Heidelberg (first woman mayor in Victoria), to Mrs How-Martyn stating her view that more women should stand for local councils before expecting to be elected to Parliament.

Vol. 3. Emancipation of Women.

Part A, British Commonwealth. Includes letters chiefly twentieth century, from women members of Parliament and members of Cabinets in Australia and New Zealand.

PAPERS OF MRS HOW-MARTYN

Mrs Edith How-Martyn, Secretary of the Women's Freedom League and Founder of the Suffragette Fellowship, spent some years in Australia and New Zealand. Her papers include scrapbooks 1940-8 dealing chiefly with women's affairs and suffrage in Australia and New Zealand, the volumes or bundles being labelled, e.g. 'Diaries and scrapbooks on tours in Australia 1947/8 and New Zealand 1940/1', 'Australia. Women in Parliament. Councils' 1941-3.

PAPERS OF VIDA GOLDSTEIN

There is a microfilm in the State Library of Victoria. The papers include diaries of visits to England and America 1902, 1910, and 1919. Vida Goldstein was an Australian suffragette.

NOTES COLLECTED FOR NORMAN MACKENZIE

A collection of typescript or stencilled papers, broadcasts, articles, and notes prepared by various individuals and organisations for Norman Mackenzie's book *Women in Australia*, Melbourne 1962. The collection also includes annual reports and journals from women's organisations, judgments from arbitration court cases, press cuttings, etc., some of which have been catalogued separately and can be found through the subject catalogue under headings relating to Australia.

EMIGRATION RECORDS

In 1963 the Women's Migration and Oversea Appointments Society ceased to exist and some of its records were passed to the Fawcett Library. These include the records of that society under its various names and the records of earlier defunct women's migration societies. Una Monk, *New Horizons: a Hundred Years of Women's Migration*, London 1963, a history of these societies, is based on the records described below as well as on other printed material. The following records 1862-6 have been microfilmed for the National Library of Australia and the Mitchell Library, Sydney: letter books 1862-82, minutes 1896-1901, Finance Committee minutes 1885-6, cuttings 1880s and 1890s, addresses 1861 by Maria Rye and 1863 by J. E. Lewin and four reports 1861-86 of the Female Middle Class Emigration Society. The two addresses and four reports are printed.

Female Middle Class Emigration Society 1862-86

This Society was founded by Miss Maria Rye and Miss Jane Lewin to assist unemployed educated women to emigrate and to find suitable employment in the colonies of Australia, New Zealand, South Africa, and Canada. Some assistance was also given to women going to other countries.

The extant records of the Society consist of two letter books, one unlabelled 1862-76, and the other labelled 'Letter Book no.3' 1877-82. They contain office copies of letters received from women who had emigrated to Australia, New Zealand, and South Africa under the Society's auspices to work as governesses, or occasionally as clerks. There are also letters from the Society's New Zealand contact, Miss Harriet H. Herbert. The letters reflect the educational and economic state of the colonies for twenty years as seen by a large number of literate women.

British Women's Emigration Association 1884-1919

Formerly known as the United Englishwomen's Emigration Association and also as the United British Women's Emigration Association, this Association was formed in 1884 by Miss Louisa Hubbard to take over the work of the defunct Women's Emigration Society. During the 1890s it also took over the work of the Colonial Emigration Society which had earlier absorbed the work of the Female Middle Class Emigration Society. The Association's aims were to assist the emigration of women, to improve the standard of selection of women emigrants, and to secure proper protection for them on their journeys and upon arrival. Although the Association continued, as the early societies had done, to assist the emigration of educated women, the selection and protection of domestic workers came to form the larger part of the work.

Minute Book May 1896 to Dec. 1901.

Council Minutes Jan. 1915 to July 1919. See also Council minutes under the Society for the Oversea Settlement of British Women.

Sub-Committee for Diffusing Information Mar. 1903 to July 1905.

Finance Committee Minute Book, United Englishwomen's Emigration Association Mar. 1885 to Mar. 1886.

Factory Scheme Sub-Committee Dec. 1903 to Nov. 1904.

Hostel Minute Book Apr. 1909 to Nov. 1912. Relates to the Society's Colonial Training College situated first at Leaton and then at Stoke Prior.

Advisory Committee Apr.-Sept. 1914.

Colonial Intelligence League 1911-19

The Colonial Intelligence League came into being in 1910 as a committee closely connected with the British Women's Emigration Association and the South African Colonisation Society but became a separate organisation in 1911. The aim of the League was to further and develop the emigration of better class women by collecting and making available information about the colonies and employment. It also provided some accommodation in Canada and training for domestic work.

Council Minutes June 1912 to June 1919.

Executive Committee Minutes Oct. 1913 to June 1919.

Finance and Settlement Sub-Committee Minutes Nov. 1913 to July 1915, Nov. 1915 to Dec. 1919.

Literature Sub-Committee Nov. 1913 to July 1915.

County Organisation Sub-Committee Mar. 1912 to 9 July 1914.

London

Women's Migration and Oversea Appointments Society 1920-64

Until 1962 this was the Society for the Oversea Settlement of British Women formed in 1920 when the British Women's Emigration Association, the South African Colonisation Society, and the Colonial Intelligence League combined. The Society received an annual government grant to cover administrative costs and in return advised the Oversea Settlement Department of the Colonial Office on broad questions of policy relating to the overseas settlement and emigration of women, selected women for emigration, ensured their protection and reception upon arrival, and assisted them to find employment and accommodation. It was particularly concerned during the early years with the emigration of ex-service women under the free passage scheme and later with the selection of girls for the Market Harborough hostel which trained domestics for Australia. The Society had constant contact with the Australian and New Zealand High Commissions in London. It was disbanded in 1963.

Council Minutes July 1919 to June 1937, some minutes apparently missing. The first volume also contains Minutes of the Joint Council of Women's Emigration Societies Apr. 1917 to July 1919.

Executive Minutes Jan. 1920 to Mar. 1958.

Finance Committee Minutes Dec. 1919 to Apr. 1952.

Australia and New Zealand Committee Minutes June 1928 to Nov. 1933.

Schoolgirls Tour Committee Minutes, including tours to Australia and New Zealand June 1927 to Nov. 1938.

Training Centre Committee Minutes Mar. 1929 to May 1930.

Training Hostel Sub-Committee Minutes May 1930 to Mar. 1931.

Junior Branch Sub-Committee Minutes July 1925 to Sept. 1930.

Staff Sub-Committee Minutes Mar.-June 1930.

Publicity Sub-Committee Minutes Oct. 1935 to Mar. 1939.

Press Cuttings

There are three volumes of cuttings and leaflets relating to emigration. One marked 'News Cuttings' 1881-1914 contains cuttings and leaflets many relating to Australia and New Zealand, and also some letters. These include the following:

From Miss H. Hart, Dunedin, N.Z., 1880 about the sending of women to New Zealand.

From Crown Agents for the Colonies 6 Mar. 1885 to Miss Ross about nominated passages to Western Australia and the need for emigrants with capital only.

From Hon. Mrs Ellen Joyce 16 Dec. 1914 about the proposed publication of a pamphlet on emigration to Australia which may have occasioned an attack on the Government by the Labour Party by referring to the part the Queen was playing in women's emigration. A copy of the pamphlet 'Openings for unemployed women in Australia' is in the volume.

Oversea Settlement Office

Folder marked 'Conference, Round Table 25.6.1920'. Minutes of a conference between the Oversea Settlement Office, the Society for the Oversea Settlement of British Women, the Victoria League, and others, about female emigration to Australia and New Zealand. Also contains letters about arrangements and the agenda for the conference.

Folder marked 'S63 Oversea Settlement Committee Advisory Committee Minutes 29.10.1931-'. Contains minutes of the War Service Advisory Committee 30 June 1920 relating to the assisted emigration of ex-service women and letters on the same subject and includes letter 15 Feb. 1921 from Miss Nancy Morris, Sydney, N.S.W., about the type of emigrants who should be encouraged to go to Australia and commenting on the economic situation.

FREEMAN, FOX AND PARTNERS
25 Victoria Street, London, S.W.1

Sydney Harbour Bridge

Correspondence relating to visits to Australia by Sir Ralph Freeman and to the United Kingdom by L. Ennis before construction 1926-7. B.B.C. talk and lectures to University Engineering Societies 1932-8, drafts and original paper to Institute of Civil Engineers 1935, and calculations for steel superstructure for various designs n.d., all by Sir Ralph Freeman.

Auckland Harbour Bridge

Reports 1951 by Freeman, Fox and Partners on the proposed bridge with three reports 1963-4 by Freeman, Fox and Partners on traffic analysis, working and proposed extension of the bridge.

GENERAL POST OFFICE
St Martin's-le-Grand, London, E.C.1

This large collection of archives will remain with the Department at present, but no decision has yet been made as to its future. Sorting, cataloguing and listing on Public Record Office lines is in progress, but detailed lists of all classes are not yet complete and material in uncatalogued classes may be located only from rough lists. It is only possible to give approximate dates for the classes in the description below; the total number of pieces and individual references for items cannot be given at this stage. The documents range from the seventeenth to the twentieth century and cover all aspects of Post Office organisation, administration, and services, including telegraph, telephone, and wireless as well as mail services.

Official business was generally transacted by means of minutes and reports, between the Secretary to the Post Office and the Postmaster General. Most of these are submissions from the former to the latter, but there are some minutes from other officials and some replies of the Postmaster General. With these documents there are also enclosures and papers leading up to, and resulting from, the minutes and reports. For each series of minutes or reports there are two classes: 'documents' containing such original minutes, reports, and papers as have survived, and 'volumes' containing copies of, or references to, all minutes and reports including those which have been destroyed and recording the Postmaster General's decision on each case. Introduced in 1794, the Postmaster General's Minute series (Post 30 and 35) originally comprised mainly minutes on personnel aspects of Post Office organisation in England, Wales and Scotland, and of the packet boat and overseas mail arrangements. From 1790 such matters had been recorded in the Postmaster General's Report series (Post 40 and 42) which, after 1794, continued to comprise reports on the more important cases. In 1811 a separate Packet Minute series (Post 29 and 34) was started, a Packet Report series (Post 39 and 41) also being used from 1807 until 1837. The reason for the existence of these parallel series of records is not apparent, but it seems that the use of reports to submit matters for the attention of the Postmaster General was peculiar to one particular Secretary to the Post Office, Sir Francis Freeling. Following the introduction of a separate series of Packet Minutes, separate series were created for Irish and Scottish Minutes. From 1921 all administrative papers were grouped into a single General Minute series (Post 33 and 38), and subjects hitherto contained in the Packet Minute series will be found there after that date.

General guides to the history of the Post Office in Britain, based on the archives, are Howard Robinson's *The British Post Office, a History*, Princeton 1948, which has an extensive bibliography, *Britain's Post Office*, London 1953, and *Carrying British Mails Overseas*, London 1964. A useful series of printed Parliamentary Papers relating to the Post Office 1806-1959, is available. Most volumes are indexed and there are manuscript General Indexes 1806-1915, 2 vols., which facilitate the location of papers relating to Australasia in this period. In addition there is among the records an uncatalogued manuscript 'Short History of the development of the early postal systems of the Australian colonies' by J. G. Hendy, Custodian of the Post Office Records, 31 May 1904, 1 vol. This contains a chapter on the packet service including remarks on the service with New Zealand and chapters on developments in the various colonies.

Post 1 Treasury Letter Books 1686-1931, 831 vols.

Post 30 Postmaster General's Minutes: Documents 1794-1920, 4760 boxes.

Until about 1837, when the parallel Report series faded out, the documents in this class mainly concern nominations for appointments and other matters of a routine nature, but also include some papers on general policy and procedure. The later papers refer to a wide variety of matters including those formerly recorded in the Report series.

Post 35 Postmaster General's Minutes: Volumes 1794-1920, 1708 vols.

There are cumulative indexes under department, place, name, and subject headings. 35/1-196, 1794-1860 also have indexes in each volume. Spot checks in these indexes indicate that although the volumes record many papers which have not survived these do not include much relating to Australasia that is not in Post 30.

Post 29 Packet Minutes: Documents 1811-1920, 1467 boxes.

The packet boat service was the responsibility of the Post Office except for 1837-60 when control was transferred to the Admiralty. The Packet Minute series (Post 29 and 34) comprise minutes concerning this service and overseas mail services generally. The class list for Post 29 is in two versions, one numerical and the other alphabetical by place and subject headings.

The matters covered by these papers are extremely varied. The material includes letters, memoranda, and proceedings relating to the development of a direct packet service between the United Kingdom and Sydney and to the contracts which were made with shipping companies to maintain this service, e.g. 29/52 1775Z/1849 concerning the contract with H. & C. Toulmin and including a copy of the original articles of agreement.

Post 34 Packet Minutes: Volumes 1811-1920, 228 vols.

34/1-205, 1811-59 are indexed by subject. After this there are cumulative indexes. 34/45, Jan.-Apr. 1844 was checked and a number of relevant minutes not in Post 29 were found, e.g. 5 Feb. submitting that the offer of Messrs Marshall and Eldridge to contract for mails to Sydney be refused since the experimental contract with Messrs Toulmin was proving adequate.

Post 33 General Minutes: Documents 1921-40, 5583 boxes.

Post 38 General Minutes: Volumes 1921-40, 265 vols.

Post 40 Postmaster General's Reports: Documents 1791-1841, c.655 boxes.

Post 42 Postmaster General's Reports: Volumes 1790-1841, 141 vols.

Post 39 Packet Reports: Documents 1807-37, 33 boxes.

The Packet Report series (Post 39 and 41) which developed from the Postmaster General's Report series in 1807 contain reports on the packet boat and overseas mail services starting four years earlier than the parallel Minute series but fading out about 1837. Although a large number of reports are shown as missing in the class list for Post 39 many will be found filed with later reports on the same subject. The indexed volumes in Post 41 form the only guide to the contents of this class.

Post 41 Packet Reports: Volumes 1807-37, 6 vols.

Each volume is indexed. The indexes were checked and the only relevant entry found was in 41/3 under 'Miscellaneous', a report 17 Apr. 1819 from Francis Freeling concerning a plan by John Paine for the establishment of a more frequent and certain communication between the United Kingdom and New South Wales, by which he would make five voyages in two years. Freeling recommended that negotiations should not be entered into and commented 'I have ascertained from the inspector of ship letters that the total amount of ship letter postage between this country and New South Wales does not amount to above £500 or at most £600 per annum'.

Post 43 Overseas Mails: Organisation and Services, Packet Boats and Shipping 1683-1942, 212 pieces.

Post 44 Overseas Mails: Organisation and Services, Colonial Post Offices 1763-1867, 54 pieces.

44/18. Select Committee of the Legislative Council of New South Wales, Report 1843. This contains the postal resolution made by the Select Committee which decided that the Post Office should not be regarded as a source of revenue, but that savings effected by the establishment of additional offices should be expended for the benefit of the community. Photostat in the National Library of Australia.

44/19-23. Post Office Commission of Enquiry Reports 1845-7. Following a Treasury instruction 29 Aug. 1844 the General Post Office in London sent two postal officials R. Richard Smith and E. D. James to make detailed reports on the working of the postal services in the Australian colonies and in New Zealand. At the time the services in Australia were run by the various colonies and showed considerable administrative variations. The Treasury was considering bringing them under General Post Office control and accordingly the Commissioners were asked to report on the administration, cost and possible rationalisation of the services. Although the New Zealand postal services were largely under the control of the General Post Office, the Commissioners' terms of reference were similar for that colony, which was highly disorganised as a result of the first Maori War. The Commissioners' handwritten reports, all addressed to Lieut.-Col. W. L. Maberly, Secretary to the Post Office, are a valuable guide to the early history of the Post Office in Australasia. Each report deals with developments in the colony under consideration, its staffing and administration, postal routes, revenue and expenditure, the number of letters sent and received, and makes suggestions for administrative reforms. Copies of reports on the Australian colonies are in the National Library of Australia, those for New South Wales and Van Diemen's Land being transcripts and those for South Australia and Western Australia being photostats.

44/13-17. Appendices to Post Office Commission of Enquiry Reports 1841-7. These papers sent in to the Commission include statement of salaries and accounts; various returns, e.g. list of post offices in the colony, giving place, date of establishment and name of postmaster, list of persons enjoying franking privileges; specimen forms, e.g. of mail contracts; stamp impressions; copies of local ordinances relating to postal arrangements.

Post 45 Overseas Mails: Organisation and Services, Packet Agencies 1843-70

Includes Southampton Packet Agent's Eastward of Suez Order Book 1846-69, 1 vol. containing copies of memoranda to naval agents east of Suez relating to various matters connected with the conveyance and delivery of mail. Several entries relate to Australia and New Zealand.

Post 47 Overseas Mails: Organisation and Services, Conventions and Conferences c.1810-1947

Includes printed Reports of the following Postal and Telegraphic Conferences between the Australasian colonies: Adelaide 1890, Brisbane 1893, Wellington 1894, Sydney 1896, Hobart 1898, and Sydney 1900, 6 vols. Related papers, e.g. minutes of proceedings, debates, reports of permanent heads of departments, and papers laid before the Conference, are printed with the reports.

Post 48 Overseas Mails: Organisation and Services, Letter Books c.1796-1940

'Admiralty Agents' Letter Books 1855-70. Letters and reports mainly from agents and ships' captains to the Admiralty Superintendent of Packets at Southampton. This office was abolished in 1870 when its duties respecting mail packets were transferred to the Post Office. The volumes are not indexed; within the volumes the letters are in rough chronological order. The agents report on the performance of the contracts, the equipment of the packets, on delays and wrecks and other matters concerned with the safe conveyance of mails.

'Admiralty Agents' Post Office Letter Books 1860-70. Letters from the Secretary to the Post Office to the Admiralty Superintendent of Packets at Southampton, with a few related papers. Within the volumes, which are indexed, the letters are in rough chronological order.

'Contract Packet' Letter Books 1860-1920. Copies of letters from the Secretary to the Post Office to the various shipping companies with mail contracts concerning the conveyance of mails. The volumes are indexed by companies, most of the entries relating to Australasia being found under the Peninsular and Oriental Company. From 1871 to 1920 only volumes for every fifth year have been preserved.

'Colonial Postmasters' Letter Books 1849-1920. Copies of letters from the Secretary to the Post Office to colonial postmasters. The volumes are indexed under places, the Australasian colonies sometimes grouped together, and sometimes entered separately under the chief town. From 1870 to 1920 only volumes for every fifth year have been preserved. The letters relate to missing mail, dead letters, postage stamps, mail timetables, the money order system, and other general postal matters.

'Agents' Letter Books 1849-1902. Copies of letters from the Secretary to the Post Office, to postmasters and packet agents both at home and abroad. From 1870-1902 only every fifth volume has been preserved. The volumes are indexed under places but do not include the Australasian colonies. Relevant material in this series is apparently only slight.

Post 51 Overseas Mail: Contracts, Sea c.1755-1931

Most of the documents are printed articles of agreement between the Admiralty or Postmaster General and the shipping companies for the conveyance of mail overseas. With the articles of agreement there are in some cases printed copies of correspondence and Treasury minutes submitted for the approval of Parliament.

Post 96-101 Private Collections

The following private collections have not yet been fully sorted and listed but may possibly contain material of Australasian interest:

John Palmer, Surveyor and Comptroller of the Mails 1786-92, 1772-1845.

Lord Walsingham, Joint Postmaster General 1787-94, 1762-92.

Sir Francis Freeling, Secretary 1798-1836, 1796-1826.

Marquess of Salisbury, Joint Postmaster General 1816-23, 1820-3.

Sir Rowland Hill, Secretary 1854-64, 1839-69. This includes letters written during Hill's visit to South Australia in 1839.

Sir John Tilley, Secretary 1864-80, 1853-74.

Post 105 Inland and Overseas Mails: Organisation, Public Notices and Instructions to Post-masters c.1790-c.1900

This large collection of printed documents is not yet fully sorted and listed, but there is a typescript list of the numbered notices and instructions for 1840-1900, arranged chronologically. They relate to a wide variety of Post Office business including overseas mail arrangements.

GENERAL REGISTER OFFICE
Somerset House, London, W.C.2

BIRTHS, MARRIAGES, AND DEATHS

The records resulting from the Registration and Marriage Acts of 1836 which provided for the central registration of births, marriages, and deaths as from 1 July 1837, must be clearly distinguished from all ecclesiastical records of baptisms, weddings, and burials. Much detailed information concerning the registers of births, marriages, and deaths kept in the United Kingdom, in other Commonwealth countries (including Australia, New Zealand, New Guinea, and the New Hebrides Condominium), and in the Irish Republic, is given in the General Register Office's *Abstract of Arrangements respecting the Registration of Births, Marriages and Deaths*, London, H.M.S.O., 1952. But this publication is now out of print and difficult to obtain. It is also out of date on a number of points; it should be noted particularly that the Non-Parochial Registers are now in the Public Record Office, q.v.

Copies of all local births, deaths, and marriages entered in the register books deposited with the Superintendent Registrars of all civil registration districts in England and Wales since 1 July 1837, are in the General Register Office. Consolidated quarterly indexes, arranged alphabetically, are available for inspection in the public search rooms. For births, the mother's maiden name is not given before c.1911, and for deaths, the age of the deceased may not appear after c.1911. Certificates of births, marriages, and deaths may be obtained on payment of the statutory fee. Limited searches are also made in these records on payment of a fee, but when application is made, care should be taken to give as many relevant particulars as possible in order that the entry may be identified.

CENSUS

Census returns for 1871 and at ten yearly intervals thereafter, are in the custody of the Registrar General. Decennial returns 1801-61 are in the Public Record Office q.v. The later returns are useful for discovering the age and place of birth of individuals, provided the place of residence at the time of the census is known. They are not fully open for public consultation, but limited searches or checks on behalf of correspondents may be undertaken in certain circumstances on payment of a fee.

London

GEOLOGICAL SOCIETY OF LONDON
Burlington House, London, W.1

The main collection of manuscripts in the Society's Library consists of the correspondence with Sir Roderick Murchison. The collection is not on open access, but bona fide research workers may apply to the Secretaries of the Society for special arrangements to be made. The letters are sorted alphabetically by correspondent in box files up to the letter R. Letters S-Z and a few unidentified letters have not yet been filed (Oct. 1969). There are letters from Sir Charles Lyell, Sir Frederick McCoy, and Sir Richard Owen but none of these apparently relate to the field of this survey. The following letters were noted:

Henry Barkly, Melbourne, 17 May 1860 on the geology of Australia.

James Crawford and John Auld, Otago, 29 Oct. 1861 concerning the geological survey of Otago.

James Hector, Edinburgh, 17 Jan., 22 Oct. 1861 concerning the New Zealand survey.

Phillip [S?] King, 'on the road to Argyle, N.S.W.', 24 Jan. 1834 concerning the visit of Murchison's relative accompanying King on a journey to Lake George.

Hugh Miller, Witness Office, 5 Mar. 1845 mentioning geological specimens from New Zealand, 'which of late has been giving promise of very wonderful remains'.

F. Odernheimer, Wiesbaden, 22 June 1853 concerning his mineralogical survey in Australia.

J. Nicol, Worcester, 9 July 1854 'You should send McCoy to Australia where he might do some good work and not stir up mischief between old friends. Anyhow the question is settled beyond their power to change'.

W. Pentland 31 May 1831 referring to fossils from Moorea and kangaroo fossils from the New Holland Caves.

MRS M. GILLON
56 Chester Row, London, S.W.1

Domville Taylor's journal Aug.-Sept. 1845 of an expedition in search of Leichhardt with sketch map of route; sketchbook and separate sketches illustrating the expedition, station life, and contracts with Aborigines. There is a microfilm in the Mitchell Library, Sydney.

MISS M. L. GRAHAM
25 Park Close, Ilchester Place, London, W.14

PAPERS OF JOHN BENJAMIN GRAHAM*

Graham arrived in Adelaide in 1839, built up a prosperous store and was able to invest in the Burra Creek Copper Mines.

Diaries 1841-2, 1848-51, 1858, 7 vols. Graham returned to England in 1848. The diary for 1858 records a voyage to Australia and return.

Diary 1848-9 by John Adams, Adelaide, stepfather of J. B. Graham.

Letters 1848-70 from Henry Ayers. Ayers acted as Graham's agent 1848-67 and continued to act for him in some business matters until 4 Jan. 1870.

Letters 1858-66 from Henry Rymill, Adelaide; letters 1867-76 from Henry and Frank Rymill acting as agents for J. B. Graham especially in the management of his station Canowie; letters 1877-1910 from H. and F. Rymill to H. R. Graham, son of J. B. Graham.

Correspondence and papers 1910, 1925-6 concerning the stations Canowie and Curnamona, including: printed pamphlet entitled *Memorandum and Articles of Association of Canowie Pastoral Company Limited Incorporated the 19th day of September 1874*; manager's and overseer's reports 1870-7 on Canowie; Canowie Pastoral Company Limited Annual Reports 1895-9, 1902, 1905, 1908, printed; Canowie quarterly accounts, biennial statements, valuations, stock returns 1854-1901; for 1882-93 the valuations and returns are also present for Curnamona station.

South Australian Mining Association and Burra Burra Copper Mines papers. Letter 27 Dec. 1847 signed 'Eureka'; two letters c.Sept. 1868 from John Darlington to Chairman and Directors of the South Australian Mining Association, the second being a long report (both letters partly illegible).

Plan 1889 of Glen Warwick and Baratta Stations, printed, and manuscript sheet giving estimated receipts and expenditure Glen Warwick and Baratta runs.

GREATER LONDON RECORD OFFICE (LONDON)
County Hall, London, S.E.1

There are typescript catalogues of almost all the records held by the Greater London Council at County Hall. See *Guide to the Records in the London County Record Office. Part 1, Records of the Predecessors of the London County Council except the Board of Guardians*, 1962.

BOARDS OF GUARDIANS RECORDS

The records of the Boards of Guardians in the metropolitan area passed to the London County Council in 1930. A card index was made but is being superseded by new lists. Where parishes were unaffected by the Act of 1834 creating Boards of Guardians, the records of relief are kept with parish records as listed below. Relevant material is most likely to be found in the minutes of the Boards. Minutes of the committees and sub-committees of the Boards rarely relate to emigration, although special committees sometimes do. Particularly in the early twentieth century, there are registers showing the movements, including emigration, of children from the various workhouses and homes. To suggest the extent of the records likely to contain material on emigration, relevant records of a few Boards are listed. Call numbers are given for records to which call numbers have so far been assigned (Feb. 1969).

B.B.G. Bermondsey

1-19, St Mary Magdalen (later incorporated in St Olave's Union) Board Minutes 1836-70; 20-1, St Mary Rotherhithe Board Minutes 1838-55; 22-83, St Olave's Union Board Minutes 1836-1904; 182-3, St Olave's Union, Emigration and Placing Out Committee Minutes 28 Apr. 1890 to 24 Mar. 1892.

Be.B.G. Bethnal Green

1-92, Board Minutes 1836-1930; 222-9, Special Committee and Sub-Committee Minutes 1891-1930.

Ca.B.G. Camberwell

1-72, Board Minutes 1835-1930; 141-4, Special Committee Minutes 1885-1929; 200, Register of children boarded out, emigrated 1893-1926; 206, Register of children at Peckham children's home, adopted 1896-1930 and emigrated 3 Aug. 1893 to 13 Oct. 1927.

London

Fulham

Fulham and Hammersmith, Board Minutes 1845-1901; Fulham, Board Minutes, 1902-30; Register of children emigrated 1899 to July 1928.

Lambeth

Board Minutes 1836-1930, with separate indexes, 1877-9 missing; Register of children emigrated, vol.1, 1900-23.

Paddington

Board Minutes 1845-1930.

Stepney

Stepney, Board Minutes 1925-30; Limehouse, Board Minutes 1836-1925, with separate indexes from 1875; Mile End Old Town, Board Minutes 1857-1926 with index; St George in the East, Board Minutes 1836-1924 with index; Whitechapel, Board Minutes 1837-1926 with index; Register of children emigrated 1911-15, 1 vol.

Wandsworth

Board Minutes 1836-1930, indexed.

CUB. CENTRAL UNEMPLOYED BODY FOR LONDON

Records 1904-30, including those of its predecessor, the Central Committee for Unemployed, and those of the Hollesley Bay Labour Colony 1904-38. The Central Unemployed Body, set up in 1905, provided for the establishment of a distress committee of the council of every metropolitan borough, financed partly from voluntary subscription, partly from the rates.

5. Emigration Sub-Committee Minutes Jan.-Oct. 1905, not indexed and of general interest only.

27-31. Emigration Committee Minutes Dec. 1905-1915, partly indexed. Business relates mainly to Australia, with correspondence, reports, and accounts from Australian agencies.

32. Emigration Committee report file no.4a, 23 Sept. 1912 to 24 Nov. 1913. Statistics and financial statements.

132. Emigration register Oct. 1909, no details given.

133. Sailing register 1912-15, arranged by borough with an index of names. Each entry gives name in full, age, number, and relationship of dependents, destination, date of sailing, occupation, special qualifications in agriculture, forestry, livestock, fruit and vegetable farming (including experience at Hollesley Bay), whether sent to agents or friends, cost of outfit, cost of passage, landing money, total expenditure, and remarks (usually limited to the sex of the dependents). The destination of most was Australia or New Zealand although some were travelling to Canada.

134-7. Register of emigration loans and repayments 1905/6-1914/15. Under each letter of the alphabet names are arranged chronologically by year. Each entry gives case number, name, borough, and financial details; destination is not stated.

167. Hollesley Bay Labour Colony subject file 6. Proposal to hand over the colony to the Australian Imperial Force 1917.

201. Hollesley Bay Labour Colony. Personal cards of inmates 1905-19 and after. Cards arranged alphabetically under boroughs.

PARISH RECORDS

P89/MRY1. St Marylebone, Directors and Guardians of the Poor

518. Committee Minutes vol. 37, 1 Sept. 1826 to 3 May 1828: deputation to wait upon Colonial Secretary William Huskisson (p.251); their report that Huskisson

agreeable to the emigration of female paupers of good character so long as expenses are defrayed from the poor rate (p.258); Rev. Dr Spry in touch with Col. Cockburn of the Colonial Office, fitting out females willing to emigrate (p.266).

521. Committee Minutes vol.40, 23 Dec. 1831 to 24 May 1833: general meeting to consider sending paupers to Van Diemen's Land (p.70); report on twenty-four females fitted out and ready to sail, with £10 allowed towards their passage (p.133); further landing allowance of 10/– per head to be paid to the governor (p.138).

527. Committee Minutes vol.46, 5 Feb. 1841 to 22 July 1842: letter of thanks to an alderman who provided information on the emigration of females to Australia (pp.8-9).

532. Committee Minutes vol.51, 7 Apr. 1848 to 6 July 1849: embarkation order for thirteen girls sailing to Adelaide in the *Ramillies*, with their names and ages, rules and regulations to be observed during the voyage, articles to be furnished to each girl at an estimated cost of £3.15.6 (pp.163-6); letter from the Colonial Land and Emigration Commissioners on the character of further candidates for emigration (pp.201-3).

534. Committee Minutes vol.53, 2 Aug. 1850 to 7 Nov. 1851: communication from Mr Page, 70 Wimpole Street, on behalf of George Whitney and family, desirous of going to Australia (p.22).

551. Index to Committee Minutes vols.16-53. As the index may be deficient the Committee meeting books would probably repay further searching.

P91/LEN. Shoreditch, St Leonard, Trustees under the Act for the better relief and employment of the poor

14-27. Minute Books 1826-33 with no index, 1833-46 indexed, 1846-53 incomplete, damaged, or with no index. There appear to be few Australian references. In 1827 it was unanimously carried that nine girls be fitted out to emigrate to Van Diemen's Land, and unanimously carried that £20 be made available so that the four children of a pauper woman named Pickard, convicted of a felony and sentenced to fourteen years transportation, could accompany her to Australia.

P83/MRY1. Islington, St Mary, Commissioners concerned with employment, poor relief

749-50. Minutes 1816-41, 1848-58.

ST THOMAS' HOSPITAL, NIGHTINGALE TRAINING SCHOOL RECORDS

The Nightingale Training School archive consists of the administrative records of the Nightingale Training School and the Nightingale Collection.

H.I./ST/NTS. Administrative Records of the Nightingale Training School

A typescript calendar of the records, with index, has a brief introduction stating that £44,000 was collected by public subscription in gratitude for Florence Nightingale's work in the Crimean War and that on 13 Mar. 1860 the Secretary of the Nightingale Fund Council, A. H. Clough, wrote on behalf of the Council to the President, Treasurer and Governors of St Thomas' Hospital concerning the founding of a training school for nurses, this being Florence Nightingale's idea of how the fund could best be used. She admired the work of reorganisation begun in 1855 at St Thomas' by Mrs Wardroper, Matron.

A feature of the Nightingale Training School was that nurses were trained not merely for St Thomas' but with the clear intention that they should be sent out in groups to other institutions to undertake nursing reform. One such group was sent to Sydney, N.S.W., in 1867 under the leadership of Lucy Osburn, see Sir Zachary Cope, *Six Disciples of Florence Nightingale*, London 1961, and M. P. Susman, 'Lucy

Osburn and her First Nightingale Nurses', *Medical Journal of Australia*, May 1965.
Class A. Administration, including Matron's correspondence, etc., 1913- .
A3. Matron's Reports. A3/4, 5, 7, 11-14, 1879-89 include brief details of the careers
of Lucy Osburn and Mary Barker after their return to England. A3/6 gives informa-
tion on Lucy Osburn's contingent for New South Wales.
A16/8. Matron's correspondence concerning a copy of a bust of Florence Nightingale
for Australia.
Class C. Probationers, mainly registers.
C1/1-5. Probationers' Admission and Discharge Registers July 1860 to July 1920,
C4/1-32 Probationers' Record Books July 1860 to Mar. 1950, C5/1-6, 1860-1954
Indexes to C4/1-32 (the last vol. in Matron's Office), C7/1-4 Time Books 1862-99
include records relating to Lucy Osburn and her group of five nurses. C1/1-5 and
C4/1-32 are arranged chronologically by date of admission and give details of age,
training, character, and subsequent appointments, C4/1-32 being the more detailed
records. C4/1 Probationers' Record Book 1860-71 includes Lucy Osburn (entered
in the index as Asburn, Lucy) and her five nurses: (1) Mary Barker, (93) Elizabeth
Ann Blundell, (96) Betsy Annie Chant (later Mrs Simpson), (103) Annie Miller,
(111) Haldane C. Turriff, (115) Lucy Osburn.
Class D. Accounts.
Class Y. Miscellanea.
App.A. Records of the Nightingale Fellowship.
App.B. Records of the Nightingale Fund Council.
Note: The same classification has been used as for other St Thomas' Hospital records
which are deposited in the Greater London Record Office. In this classification B
relates to patients' administration. Records less than seventy years old in some series
may not be consulted without the consent of the Matron.

The Nightingale Collection

See the following lists:
Calendars of letters to and from Florence Nightingale arranged chronologically,
typescript.
Calendar of letters of related interest, typescript.
Supplementary Calendar, typescript.
Alphabetical card indexes of the above calendars under correspondents and subjects.

The collection relates to Florence Nightingale's organisation of nursing in general.
Correspondence constitutes the major part of the collection and consists of letters from
Florence Nightingale 1854-1900, letters to her 1853-1907 and letters 1855-1910 not
from or to her but on subjects related to those in the first two series. There are also
a few miscellaneous printed and manuscript items. Objects connected with Florence
Nightingale, such as clothes, books, etc., have not been deposited.
Letters from Florence Nightingale:
68/7. 4 Apr. 1868 to J. J. Frederick concerning *inter alia* the difficulty of obtaining
probationers and referring to the trained group sent lately to New South Wales
and to applications from India and the colonies for matrons and head nurses.
70/13. 30 Nov. 1870 to H. Bonham Carter referring *inter alia* to Lucy Osburn's
desiring to leave Sydney.
78/3. 6 Sept. 1878 to W. Clark congratulating him on his stirring up the colonies
with his plans, with note 'to my father William Clark, on his appointment to advise
the Government on a scheme for the drainage of Sydney, N.S.W., signed A. M.
Clark'.
SU157. 10 Sept. 1867 from Florence Nightingale to Sir J. McNeill concerning the

organisation of nursing in India and outlining the aim of beginning as in New South Wales by sending a small trained and efficient staff to take charge of one hospital to attempt the work of nursing and training nurses; 'a Lady Superintendent and four Head Nurses' were to be sent to Sydney for a three year engagement, giving details of salaries and free passage by Panama.

Letters to Florence Nightingale:

V5-7/66. 17 Oct. 1866 from R. R. Winter concerning Lucy Osburn and training for medical work in Delhi; 23 Oct. 1866 from Lucy Osburn giving her reasons for declining work in Delhi; 3 Nov. 1866 from R. R. Winter regretting Lucy Osburn's decision not to go to India.

V45/89. 24 July 1889 from Alfred Roberts, Prince Alfred Hospital, N.S.W., was trying to develop a high moral and professional standard among nurses, had abundant applicants for three year training, asking Florence Nightingale for a bust of herself for the nurses.

Bonham Carter Papers

Papers *c.*1861-*c.*1916 of Henry Bonham Carter as Secretary of the Nightingale Fund, 33 packets. A brief typescript list and a detailed manuscript calendar have been prepared. The Bonham Carter Papers form a separate group within the Nightingale Collection.

Pkt.8/179-95. Papers 1867-8 connected with Lucy Osburn's appointment to Sydney, N.S.W., including letters about her agreement concerning term of service, from Henry Carr, Lucy Osburn, J. E. Manning, Hon. Secretary, Sydney Infirmary, and notes on the Sydney Infirmary by Alfred Roberts.

Pkt.9/1. 2 June 1868 from Lucy Osburn, Camden Park, commenting on her hosts and on her life in New South Wales.

Pkt.9/19. 19 June 1868 from Mrs Wardroper, one of her nurses having had a letter from Haldane Turriff giving news from Sydney.

Pkt.10/33-4. 7 Sept. 1869 from Lucy Osburn commenting on nurses; 13 July 1869 from J. E. Manning thanking Bonham Carter for the statuette of Florence Nightingale to be placed in the Board Room.

Pkt.19/20-1. 6 Sept. 1871 from Lucy Osburn concerning friction between the English nurses and Australian trainees; item 21 is a copy of the *Sydney Morning Herald* 21 Sept. 1871, questions in the New South Wales Parliament about the Sydney Infirmary.

PRIVATE RECORDS

O/63. Documents 1837-44 relating to the estate of John Whitby, Middlesex, including papers 1843-4 concerning George Whitby, licensed victualler, Hobart Town, formerly a convict.

Q/WIL. Collection of G. Willis.

165. Letter 18 May 1845 Sir John Franklin, H.M.S. *Erebus* off Greenhithe, to Sir Henry Willock, chairman of the East India Company, recommending Sergeant James as Advocate General in India, on account of his application as Solicitor General in Van Diemen's Land.

384. List of names and qualities of Kamehameha II, King of the Sandwich Islands, and his suite, visiting England, with notes on their clothing needs, 3 June 1824, in the writing of Sir Henry Ellis.

385. Letter 30 June 1859 from Kamehameha [IV], King of the Sandwich Islands, to Manley Hopkins about a carriage and carriage horses.

448. Facsimile of Tichborne estate mortgage debenture for £100, Sir Roger Charles Doughty Tichborne, Harley Lodge, West Brompton, mortgagor.

London

GREATER LONDON RECORD OFFICE (MIDDLESEX)

1 Queen Anne's Gate Buildings, Dartmouth Street, London, S.W.1

Selected Sessions Records, Hoare, and Shordiche papers have been microfilmed for the Australian Joint Copying Project.

SESSIONS RECORDS

The most useful introduction to this mass of bulky and complicated material is the official *Guide to the Middlesex Sessions Records 1540-1889*, 1965. The sessions derive from four separate Commissions: (1) Commission of the Peace for the County of Middlesex (2) Commission of Oyer and Terminer (Middlesex) (3) Commission of Gaol Delivery of Newgate (Middlesex) (4) Commission of the Peace for the City and Liberty of Westminster. (2) and (3) were normally the province of the Judges of Assize representing the King in the counties, but since the royal courts sat within the limits of the county of Middlesex, no assizes as such were held, and special arrangements were made. In Middlesex the Commission of Oyer and Terminer was directed to the King's Bench and Common Pleas with a few of the local Justices of the Peace, but the distinction between its specific commission to inquire into more serious offences and the Commission of the Peace to deal with more general misdemeanours was not maintained; in fact the two sessions were almost one court, and the sessions records were combined.

The Commission of Gaol Delivery of Newgate (the common prison for the City of London and Middlesex) was delivered to the Lord Mayor and Aldermen of London with, until the mid-eighteenth century, some Middlesex Justices of Oyer and Terminer, the sessions being held in the Old Bailey. Up to 1754 the Middlesex Clerk of the Peace kept the records dealing with prisoners from his county but after that date the Clerk of the Court retained all records; however, the Middlesex records were maintained as a separate series and eventually transferred to the Middlesex Record Office. The contemporary publications *The Whole Proceedings on the King's Commission of the Peace, Oyer and Terminer and Gaol Delivery for the City of London and also the Gaol Delivery for the County of Middlesex, held at Justice Hall in the Old Bailey*, 'published by authority', and covering 1729-1913, contain, as the title indicates, accounts of trials at the Gaol Delivery sessions for Middlesex (only later vols. indexed). There is a good set easily available in the Guildhall Library, London.

The City and Liberty of Westminster was included within the traditional county of Middlesex and sessions of the peace were held separately until 1844 when the Middlesex Sessions were ordered to be held for Westminster by adjournment. The pre-1844 Westminster records eventually came into the custody of Middlesex.

Most of the series of judicial sessions records for 1784-1868 provide information concerning individuals tried, convicted, and transported to Australia, although frequently the sentence of transportation is for a given number of years, but to no specified destination. The most important series are:

MJ/SBB. Sessions Books (briefly recording the work of each session) 1639-1889.

MJ/SR. Sessions Rolls (writs and jury lists, bills of indictment, recognizances) 1549-1889.

MJ/SP. Sessions Papers (lists of prisoners, appeals, petitions, informations, and examinations of accused and witnesses) 1666-1889.

MJ/SPT. Papers concerning transportation, including orders for transportation and bonds from contractors for transporting convicts, 1720-1867, e.g. a note that certain named prisoners be transported to the eastern coast of New South Wales, 1787.

OB/SB. Gaol Delivery Books (Fair Entry Books) 1754-1834.

OB/SR. Gaol Delivery Rolls 1756-1834, e.g. series of records relating to trial for theft of George Barrington at Old Bailey in Sept. 1790 and sentence of transportation to Australia.

OB/SP. Gaol Delivery Papers 1755-92.

WJ/SBB. Westminster Sessions Books 1641-1844.

WJ/SR. Westminster Sessions Rolls 1620-1844.

WJ/SP. Westminster Sessions Papers 1689-1844.

MJ/CJ. Calendars of Indictments (alphabetical lists of indictments for trespass and felony for each session of the peace and gaol delivery, but no indictment for felony after 1757) 1684-1797.

MJ/CB. Books of Calendars (including indictments and recognizances; separate vols. for Westminster adjourned sessions 1846-60), 1833-89.

OB/CJ. Alphabetical index to indictments of Middlesex prisoners tried at sessions of gaol delivery at Newgate 1754-1832.

OB/CP. Newgate Calendars (printed calendars, in annual volumes, of London and Middlesex prisoners for trial at the sessions held at the Old Bailey, giving name, age, and trade of prisoner, his offence, the name of the justice committing and date of committal, with sentence added in manuscript) 1820-2, 1830-53, e.g. records relating to offence, committal, and sentence of Elizabeth Callaghan who was transported to Australia and later as Eliza Thompson, married John Batman.

BOARDS OF GUARDIANS RECORDS

The records of the following Unions are deposited and there is a typescript list of each series. Those most likely to have information on emigration to Australia and New Zealand are:

BG/B Brentford Union

1-71. Minutes 1836-1930, indexed. For example 12 May 1852 'Capt'n Hemsley gave notice that on Wednesday 26th inst. he should submit to the Board for their consideration the following proposition—"The propriety of assisting the labouring Poor of good character & others seeking relief from the Poor Rate to emigrate to the colonies in New South Wales". Resolved that the Board be specially summoned for that day to consider the same.'

196-201. Childrens' Committee Minute Books 1915-30, indexed. Containing reports on children after sent abroad.

216. Emigration Register 1891-1927. This gives personal details of individuals emigrated to Canada, Australia, and New Zealand with the name of the society through which they emigrated and other remarks such as the ship on which they sailed, the date, and the cost.

BG/E Edmonton Union

1-94. Minutes 1837-1930, partly indexed.

97-104. Schools' and Childrens' Committee Minute Books 1911-30, partly indexed.

155. File entitled 'Emigration of Chase Farm schoolchildren', 1925. Clerk to the Guardians file of in and out-letters relating to emigration to Canada, Australia, and New Zealand, giving details of the children proposed and containing information on various schemes for emigration, e.g. the Dreadnought Scheme for boys.

BG/H Hendon Union

1-78. Minutes 1835-1930, partly indexed.

BG/U Uxbridge Union

1-28. Minutes 1836-1930, not indexed.

London

BG/W Willesden Union
1-34. Minutes 1896-1930, printed series indexed.
127/6. Local Government Board Order 24 Mar. 1914 authorising expenditure by Willesden parish of £5 towards the emigration of Alfred Burr, a poor child, to South Australia.

OTHER OFFICIAL RECORDS

The Local Government Act 1929, and Poor Law Act 1930, transferred the responsibility for the care of destitute children from the Boards of Guardians to the County Council which could procure the emigration of destitute children provided it gave its consent before a petty sessions. The Public Health Committee, known as the Public Health, Housing and Public Assistance Committee, Jan.-Dec. 1930, and as the Public Health and Assistance Committee Jan. 1931 to Mar. 1935, was, under the Middlesex scheme, to 'arrange for the emigration of suitable persons who are desirous of emigrating'. No departmental files on the subject have survived, and a spot check of the series of Committee Minutes 1930-48, only partially indexed, revealed very scanty references to emigration in general. Likewise the printed reports from the Committee to the full County Council for this period, unindexed, appear to contain nothing of interest.

PRIVATE RECORDS

Shordiche Papers
425/2-10. Correspondence and papers of George Dick Shordiche, mainly while abroad 1845-52, including letter 7 Dec. 1851 to his mother written from Melbourne, Vic., describing his success at Mount Alexander Gold Diggings and letter 9 May 1852 to Mrs Parrin from Forest Creek Gold Diggings describing his experiences there (both transcribed); also photograph portrait n.d. of George Charles [?Dick] Shordiche 'supposed murdered', Forest Creek Gold Diggings.
726/20, 21. Typescript notes and article on Shordiche family of Ickenham, Mddx., n.d. [20th cent.].

Fuller, Smith, and Turner Papers
891/1/2/2159-82. Original bundle of correspondence 1829-39 of Douglas Thompson of Chiswick concerning lands at Swan River Settlement, W.A., belonging to his son Douglas Thompson, jun.; especially letter 1830 from Douglas Thompson, jun., at Swan River to his father describing the country, the conditions and his land, and letters and papers 1836-9 of Douglas Thompson, sen., concerning the death of his son, accidently drowned, and the land to which he was entitled.

Round Settled Estate Papers
617/274/6-8, 27-34. Bills and correspondence 1841 for fitting out Thomas Samuel Wegg to go to Van Diemen's Land, and two letters 1841 from John Samuel Wegg (alias Thomas), Launceston, V.D.L., asking for money as he could not get a job there.

Gurney Papers
538 Box 43/7. Administration of effects 30 May 1879 of Henry Gurney, late of Auckland, N.Z., farmer, died intestate.

Miscellaneous
290/8. Deed of conveyance 1858 Elizabeth Haynes, spinster of Bethnal Green to Thomas Haynes of Bethnal Green and Thomas Porter of Hackney Road, of all the real and personal estate in Australia of her brother, John Thomas Haynes, late of Adelaide (d.1844).
653. Ticket of leave 1838 Thomas Canning, N.S.W.

GUILDHALL LIBRARY
Basinghall Street, London, E.C.2

See Philip E. Jones and Raymond Smith, *A Guide to the Records in the Corporation of London Records Room and the Guildhall Library Muniment Room*, London 1951. The Library has catalogues of manuscripts arranged by classification and accession order.

MS.3041 BOWREY PAPERS

Thomas Bowrey, merchant of Wapping, traded for nineteen years from the Persian Gulf to Borneo and Sumatra before returning to England in 1689. He met Dampier in Achin in 1688 and Defoe was a correspondent. Among the papers are drafts or notes of schemes to enlarge South Sea and East India trade including:

3041/2. A Petition to the Committee of the House of Commons appointed to consider Greenland trade for the right to 'solo fishing for whales in all seas beyond the Cape of Good Hope exclusive to all others'.

3041/8. Proof sheets of Bowrey's *A Dictionary: English and Malayo*, London 1701, in the preface of which he speaks of 'New Guinea, part of Hollandia Nova . . . that wonderful large Island . . . which probably may be part of Terra Australis and likely to reach near to Terra del Fuego'.

MSS.11021-96, 11107-40D GIBBS PAPERS

The firm of Antony Gibbs & Sons Ltd, merchants and foreign bankers of Bishopsgate, was established in 1808. In 1853 the collateral firm of Gibbs, Bright & Co., Bristol/Liverpool, whose interests were primarily in shipping, opened a house in Melbourne, styled Bright Bros. & Co. and treated it as a branch of the Liverpool house. Further branches were opened at Brisbane (1862), Sydney (1875), Dunedin (1881), and later throughout Australia. In 1881 the name was changed to Gibbs, Bright & Co. Nearly all the business archives of the Liverpool house are directly relevant. Some of the business archives of the London head office listed below are of marginal interest only, particularly as many of the volumes of correspondence have no indexes. Other series, particularly of accounts, and the family archives and manuscripts have been excluded from this list although they have passing references to Australian affairs.

11036. Out-letter books, private, 1845-82 of Henry H. Gibbs, afterwards 1st Baron Aldenham, 4 vols.

11038. Copy-book 1854-5 of in-letters addressed to William Gibbs, mainly from his nephew Henry H. Gibbs. Some pages illegible, marginal interest.

11038C. London head office, confidential information book 1883-1905 on merchant firms both inland and foreign, including reports on over eighty Australian or New Zealand firms.

11039. Out-letter book 1874-1936 of Alban George Henry Gibbs, afterwards 2nd Baron Aldenham, not indexed, includes a few letters in connection with the visit of Vicary Gibbs to Australia, 1883-4.

11040. Private letters to partners 1884-1919, 5 vols. Vols.1, 3 fully indexed, vol.4 indexed to p.60, vols.2, 5 not indexed. Frequent references to Australian affairs, Australian firms, letters to partners George Montagu Merivale, Sydney, and Charles Edward, Reginald and Samuel Bright, Melbourne.

11041. Directors' general out-letter books, private, 1907-34, 6 vols. indexed. Marginal interest only.

11042. Directors' general out-letter books, special 1881-1922, indexed, vol.2 indexed roughly. More of Australian interest than in 11041 above.

London

11044. Out-letter books, private, 1884-1911 of Francis Amboor Keating, manager of the Australian branch at Melbourne, 2 vols., incomplete.

11045. Out-letter books, general, 1905-11 of F. A. Keating, 4 vols.

11050. Papers, correspondence and accounts 1897-8 concerning the relations of, and business done by the company's Australian branch, Gibbs, Bright & Co. of Melbourne, with the New Zealand Exploration Co. Ltd of Cornhill, London, and of Paris, 3 sheaves in 1 parcel. List of documents enclosed.

11051. Letter book 1897-8 of Gibbs, Bright & Co. of Melbourne, relating to business done with the New Zealand Exploration Co.

11053-4. London head office, general ledgers, first series 1815-82, 29 vols., second series 1883-1918, 30 vols. Each volume is indexed. Australian entries occur from vol.14, 1854-5, and throw light on relationship between the Australian branches and head office.

11067. Correspondence and papers 1852-75 relating to private, i.e. partnership, agreements.

11068. Miscellaneous, chiefly foreign agreements, with papers appertaining 1891-1940, 3 guard files, indexed. Agencies for overseas firms in Australia or Australian firms overseas, also other agreements.

11069C. Liverpool house, private and confidential reports 1884-1908 on the financial position of other banking and merchant firms, inland and foreign, including Australian, arranged alphabetically.

11071. Liverpool house, private ledgers 1833-1903, 3 vols. Volumes 2, 3 have entries relating to Australia.

11072. Liverpool house, private journal 1871-82. A few Australian entries.

11073. Bristol and Liverpool houses, deed of covenant 19 Aug. 1853 George Gibbs and Robert Bright of Bristol, merchants, Samuel and Tyndall Bright of Liverpool, merchants, and others with the Liverpool and Australian Navigation Company, 1 bound vol., twenty-three signatures and wafer seals on silk ribbon.

11077. Liverpool house, bills of sale of merchant ships, with papers appertaining 1839-63. Mainly the Canada run but including the certificate of sale of *Jenny* registered Melbourne 19 Aug. 1855 signed by Henry Dickson and H. C. E. Childers and partners Charles Bright and William Hamilton Hart.

11082. Liverpool house, deeds 1869 between the surviving partners of the firm Bright Brothers & Co. and the executors of Robert Bright, a deceased partner.

11083. Liverpool house, Gibbs, Bright & Co. memoranda, agreements, correspondence, accounts, and other papers 1881-1903 relating to the liquidation by Antony Gibbs, Sons & Co., of the old firm of Gibbs, Bright & Co., including Bright Brothers of Australia.

11084. Liverpool house, miscellaneous papers 1836-1903. Documents include: bill of sale 24 July 1854 of *Great Britain*; insurance documents 1850, 1853 *Great Britain*, *Admiral Ian Evertsen*, *Wassenaar*; explanations by Melbourne branch of list of queries on their accounts by Liverpool house 21 Mar. 1855; cheques and money orders 1866 from Brisbane, Dunedin, Melbourne; bottomry bond signed by Evan Davies, Brisbane, master of *Maryborough*, John George Brown, solicitor's clerk, Brisbane, George Horsley, clerk to Bright Bros., Daniel F. Roberts, notary public; duplicate agreement 1854 between Gibbs, Bright & Co. and the Liverpool & Australian Navigation Company; indenture agreements 1855 B. R. Mathews, Garrett Kilkelly; papers 1871 on the lease of premises in Brisbane; partnership agreements 1864 Frederick Hart, 1875 Simpson & North.

11086. Melbourne house, Gibbs, Bright & Co., letters, telegrams and other papers 1883-7 chiefly from Amby Downs station, southern Queensland, concerning sheep farming and the wool trade.

11093. Letters 1918-20 from managers and partners of the Australian houses in Melbourne and Sydney, particularly Alfred Ernest Bright, Hon. Sir Alfred William Meeks, James Edward Hayne, addressed to Francis Amboor Keating, London; also memos and letters from P. Deane of the Prime Minister's office to Keating regarding the post-war political and economic situation in Australia, especially Queensland, during the election period in 1920.

11107-8. Liverpool and Bristol houses and Australian branches, Melbourne, Sydney, Newcastle, Brisbane, and Adelaide, annual accounts 1881-1909, 1910-24. Perth accounts included from 1910.

11110. Gibbs, Bright & Co., Australasian private letter books 1910-27, 10 vols.

11110A. Private letters 1883-4 from the Hon. Vicary Gibbs, son of 1st Baron Aldenham, whilst serving with the Australian branches, chiefly addressed to his elder brother, the Hon. Alban George Henry Gibbs.

11111. London head office, general private out-letter book 1911-30 touching the Australian branches and their business.

11140B. Chartering accounts and ledgers, 2 vols., including entries relating to Australia.

MSS.11657-99 GLOBE INSURANCE CO. ARCHIVES

11687. Deed of settlement 19 Dec. 1839 Australasian Colonial and General Life Assurance and Annuity Company.

MS.11891 DIARY

1 Aug. 1841 to 3 Apr. 1842 (during the opium wars) of a London tea merchant, possibly George Dent, grocer and tea dealer of 55 Blackman Street, Borough, at Macao, on a voyage from Macao to Sydney, via Manila and Hobart, on board the *Lord Amherst*. The authorship is suggested by internal evidence.

C. HOARE AND CO.
37 Fleet Street, London, E.C.4

This bank has no special connection with Australia, although individuals with Australian connections, e.g., Mesac Thomas, Bishop of Goulburn, were customers. Ledgers recording details of each customer's transactions with the bank have been kept since the bank was established in 1672. A card index to the ledgers is maintained, in some cases this gives personal details such as addresses.

HOUSE OF LORDS RECORD OFFICE
Westminster, London, S.W.1

The House of Lords Record Office is the general archive of Parliament, the repository for the records of Parliament as a whole as well as for the domestic records of the Upper House. Today these records number over two million pieces and are preserved in the Victoria Tower at the Houses of Parliament. They include practically all the surviving records of the House of Commons, which possesses no record office of its own; these are consulted in the search room of the Record Office, as are also the few series actually deposited in the House of Commons Library.

London

The office is open to the public throughout the year, Mondays to Fridays, whether Parliament is sitting or not. Persons wishing to consult the records are asked to give previous notice to the Clerk of the Records by letter or telephone informing him of the subject of their search. No special passes are required. Typed and photographic copies of documents can be provided at a reasonable charge, subject to the needs of parliamentary business.

General guides to the records include M. F. Bond, *The Records of Parliament: a Guide for Genealogists and Local Historians*, Canterbury 1964. Among the guides to parliamentary procedure which help to explain the creation of the various classes of records are G. F. M. Campion, *Introduction to the Procedure of the House of Commons*, London 3rd ed., 1958, and M. F. Bond, 'Materials for Transport History amongst the Records of Parliament' in *Journal of Transport History* IV, May 1959. *The List of Main Classes of Records*, 1966, H.L.R.O. Memorandum I sets out these classes very clearly. *The Use of Finding Aids in the Search Room*, 1965, H.L.R.O. Memorandum 25, describes most of the various guides, lists and indexes available; but in addition there is a two volume 'Draft Guide to the Contents of the Record Office', typescript, available in the Search Room, to be printed shortly. The Record Office *Annual Reports*, issued in February of each year, contain useful information on current accessions and a list of the more important subjects which have been studied in the office. Current *Annual Reports* and other *Memoranda* may be obtained without charge on application to the Clerk of the Records.

Record Office holdings fall into four main groups: (1) Records of the House of Lords; (2) Records of the House of Commons; (3) Miscellaneous; (4) Historical. These groupings, based on provenance, will be used in the forthcoming *Guide to the Contents of the Record Office* and have therefore been used in the following description. *The List of Main Classes of Records* merely lists alphabetically the classes of records housed in the Record Office. Certain printed series are included in the present description. Some are records of the greatest importance because no originals survive, and because of their extreme rarity, while others serve as guides and finding aids to the great mass of original documents.

Detailed lists of documents in the Main Series and Public Petitions, compiled in the course of research for this survey but too long to be included, have been deposited in the National Library of Australia, Canberra, the Mitchell Library, Sydney, the Alexander Turnbull Library, Wellington, N.Z., and the Library, Australia House, London.

1. RECORDS OF THE HOUSE OF LORDS

JOURNALS

For description see *Journals, Minutes and Committee Books of the House of Lords*, 1955, H.L.R.O. Memorandum 13.

The journals give a day to day record of business transacted and list all papers laid before the House, although they do not necessarily include the text of bills, amendments, reports, or papers. The appropriate volume provides an outline account of parliamentary business concerning the subject in hand, and specifies individual records deposited, with the date of deposit. The original records, if they have survived, to which the journals and their indexes provide a key, are to be found filed chronologically in the Main Papers series; if they have been lost or destroyed, the only record of the transaction is that in the journals. *The Collected Indices of the Journals of the House*, 1510-   , give page references to the printed *Journals*.

Original Journals 1510-   , c.400 vols. With MS. indexes 1510-1628, 1660-1829. Printed *Journals* 1510-1829, 61 vols., 1830-   , c.140 vols. From 1820 there are sessional indexes in each volume, and there are also collected indexes, decennial after 1863, for the entire period 1510- .

For description see H.L.R.O. Memorandum 13. These papers are the primary records of proceedings from which the journals are compiled.

MS. Minutes 1621-1826, 177 vols., are a useful supplement to the journals as they sometimes contain considerably more information.

Printed *Minutes* 1824- , *c.*150 vols., supersede the MS. minutes from 1827. They approximate to the printed *Journals* except that they contain supplements announcing forthcoming business which provide the only record of parliamentary business intended but never undertaken.

COMMITTEE RECORDS

For description see H.L.R.O. Memorandum 13.

Appointment Books 1621-1861, 138 vols., giving names of committee members, witnesses, etc., rarely contain matter not entered in the journals.

Minutes of Proceedings of Committees of the Whole House, are kept separately 1828-55, 8 vols. Before 1828 they appear in the manuscript minutes and after 1855 in the minutes and journals.

Minutes of Proceedings, Select and Standing Committees (other than Committees for Privileges) 1661-1837, 86 vols., incorporate printed summaries of evidence 1793-1817. After 1837 there are various series of minutes according to the type of committee, e.g. on Public Bills 1837-1913, 82 vols., on Unopposed Private Bills 1839-1912, 73 vols. From 1792 minutes of proceedings contain short indexes. There is also a manuscript Index to Proceedings 1800-46 in two volumes which contains the following relevant entries:

1824 Australian Company's Bill.
1846 Australian Agricultural Company.
1837-8 Committee to enquire into the present state of the Islands of New Zealand and the expediency of regulating the settlement of British subjects therein.
1846 New Zealand Company.

Verbatim evidence given before Committees on opposed bills (excluding divorce bill evidence) survives in an incomplete series from 1771. Before 1835 it is filed with the Main Papers and from that date is kept in a continuous sequence, to which there is no index. During 1825-50 evidence before committees, and documents produced, were frequently printed in full in the *Journals* and *Appendices*.

Reports of Committees may be found entered in the *Journals*, and the originals are filed amongst the Main Papers.

ACTS

A series of some 60,000 original Acts is held in the Record Office. Although these quite often contain matter not found in the printed versions, no Acts are listed here as they can be traced easily through the printed series.

BILLS

The original bills are filed in the Main Papers and are included in the manuscript lists of these papers. However, it has not been possible to include in these lists documents from three classes of private bills, relating to naturalisation (until 1844), to divorce (until 1857), and to estates, which are an important source of biographical and genealogical information. For these, reference must be made to the *Journal* indexes. The naturalisation bills often cover a number of people and, since the *Journal* indexes mention only the first person named in each bill, these papers in particular would repay further examination.

JUDICIAL RECORDS

Judicial proceedings, appeals, cases in error, and peerage claims are recorded in summary form in the journals and in greater detail in the manuscript minutes. The original documents are filed in the Main Papers but have not been listed in this entry. Searchers with a particular case in mind would be advised to examine the records further.

PRINTED LORDS SESSIONAL PAPERS

The House of Lords printed papers were bound and indexed in the nineteenth century in the same way as those of the Commons q.v. Since each House 'communicated' most documents to the other, a large number of Lords papers are in the Commons volumes, with Commons numbers, and it is unnecessary to use the Lords series except for papers not communicated. Very few sets of Lords *Sessional Papers* have been preserved. Certain papers laid before the House between 1788 and 1805 were bound into a series of 48 vols., the most important of these being listed in P. & G. Ford, *Hansard's Catalogue and Breviate of Parliamentary Papers 1696-1834*, Oxford 1953, pp.xi-xiii. Since 1801 printed papers have been gathered and bound at the end of each session as *Sessional Papers of the House of Lords*. From 1801 until 1885 the papers are indexed in three volumes of *General Indexes*, the entries being arranged alphabetically by short title. For 1886-1920 there are separate *Tables and Indexes* to the *Sessional Papers*, 34 vols. From 1921 to date the general tables of contents have been prefixed to the bound series of papers but not issued separately.

MAIN PAPERS

See *Guide to House of Lords Papers and Petitions*, 1959, H.L.R.O. Memorandum 20. 'Main Papers' is the name customarily given to the single continuous series in which the bulk of the original documents preserved in the House of Lords are chronologically arranged. The records, 1497 to date, consist of all the papers presented to the House and laid on the Table, petitions, peerage claims, and the bill papers, judicial records, and certain committee records described above. They are preserved in bound volumes for 1497-1704 and from 1705 to date in *c*.8000 box files. Up to 1870 documents of unusual size and format have been kept separately as the Parchment Collection. There is a manuscript list of this collection but no relevant entries were found.

From 1801 many of the papers laid before the House including Command, House, and Act papers, together with bills and other material, have been collected and printed in a single series of *Sessional Papers*. Important papers 1826-44 were also printed as appendices to the *Journals*. Thus the *Collected Indexes* to the *Sessional Papers* 1801 to date, can be used to trace the originals of parliamentary papers perhaps more conveniently than the more comprehensive *Journal Indexes* in which all entries are duplicated.

A *Calendar of Manuscripts 1497-1693* in 13 vols., was begun by the Historical Manuscripts Commission 1870-94. Documents are listed, described, and often printed *in extenso*. It was continued by the House of Lords as a new series, *Manuscripts of the House of Lords 1693-1714* in 11 vols. 1900-63. Manuscript lists of documents after 1714 are still being compiled, with brief entries only. By Dec. 1968 documents to 1879 had been listed in some forty-four volumes.

The usual form of reference to documents is by date of presentation, as recorded in the *Journals*, and short title. Examination of the manuscript lists indicates material relating in particular to transportation, emigration, colonial legislation, the Australian colonies, New Zealand, Pacific Islands, the church in the colonies, and, up to 1848, whale fishing. Some unlisted papers after 1879 may be found from the *Journals* if, as in many cases, the number of the paper is marked in pencil against the entry.

OTHER CLASSES

Further series which might be consulted for specific purposes include:
Crown Office Records 1461- .
Parliament Office Papers 1609- . P.O.39/1 letter 18 Dec. 1862 from the President, N.S.W. Legislative Council to the Clerk of the Parliaments about standing orders.

2. RECORDS OF THE HOUSE OF COMMONS

A duplicated handlist 'Records of the House of Commons', 1968, is available for consultation in the search room.

Nearly all the original records of the House of Commons were destroyed in the fire of 1834, apart from the Journals, and a few sixteenth and seventeenth century papers mixed with the Main Papers of the House of Lords.

JOURNALS

These journals are similar to the journals of the House of Lords, recording daily business in the same way. But, because they often contain summaries or transcripts of documents laid before the House, now no longer extant, they are a particularly valuable source of information. It would appear that the Journals contain the only record of the reports of the Select Committee on Returns . . . respecting Convicts, 1779, before which Sir Joseph Banks recommended transportation to Botany Bay; and of the Select Committee on the Punishment of Convicts [in the Hulks] by Hard Labour, 1778, before which Dr Solander gave evidence. *The Collected Indices of the Journals of the House of Commons*, 1547- , give page references to specific volumes of printed *Journals* on which subjects appear.
Original Journals 1547-1800, 241 vols.
Printed *Journals* 1547- , *c.*224 vols. Each volume has a detailed index of its contents.

PRIVATE BILL RECORDS

It seems that most private bills relating to Australia and New Zealand were unopposed and very few papers exist.
Petitions 1857- . There are very few before 1904.
Examiners' Evidence and Reports 1847-99.
Deposited Plans 1794- , MS. index.
Minutes of Evidence before Committee 1835-99. MS. index, containing an entry relating to the Australian Agricultural Company 1857. There is subsequent material in the House of Commons Private Bill Office.

PRINTED COMMONS SESSIONAL PAPERS

The volumes of printed papers are of the greatest importance, since the unprinted papers, 1851 to date, in the custody of the House of Commons Library are not generally available for consultation, and virtually no original papers before that date survive. In 1776 the House of Commons began reprinting certain papers and assembling them in bound volumes. This *First Series*, 1803, 15 vols. and index, contains papers 1715-1800. Further volumes of separate printed papers 1731-1800, the Abbot Collection, 110 vols., were gathered on the orders of the Speaker, Charles Abbot, afterwards Lord Colchester. Since 1801 printed papers have been gathered and bound at the end of each session, as *Sessional Papers of the House of Commons*. In the official bound sets, the pages of each volume have been numbered through in manuscript, and the volumes numbered consecutively. It is to these manuscript page numbers that the cumulative *General Indexes* refer and not to the printed page numbers of the various papers gathered into the volumes.

Hansard's Catalogue and Breviate of Parliamentary Papers 1696-1834, a reprinted facsimile edited by P. & G. Ford, Oxford 1953, serves as a subject index to the *Sessional Papers* to 1834. This does not include any material relevant to this survey. P. & G. Ford have produced further breviates and select lists covering papers 1833-1939, and a *Guide to Parliamentary Papers*, Oxford, 2nd ed. 1959. Other check lists have been compiled by W. R. Powell, 1962, and K. A. C. Parsons, 1958. An examination of the *Catalogue of Papers Printed by Order of the House of Commons, 1731-1800*, 1807 (the Abbot Collection) showed entries for bills relating to transportation 1779 and 1784, reports on transportation 1784-5, and accounts and papers concerning the Greenland and Southern Whale Fisheries 1786, settlements in New South Wales 1790-1, and convicts 1792; also letters from Gov. Phillip concerning New South Wales 1792.

PUBLIC PETITIONS

Public petitions are noted in the *Journals* but do not appear in the printed series of *Sessional Papers*, and only since 1949 have the originals been preserved. However from 1833 a Select Committee has been appointed at the start of each session to which are referred all petitions presented to the Commons, excepting those which relate to private bills. In the *Reports* of the Committee many petitions are printed in full, others in abstract, and the number of signatories and other details are given. The only complete set of *Reports* is kept in the House of Commons Library but may be consulted in the House of Lords Record Office. Examination of a general index to the *Reports* 1833-52, found in H.C., *Accounts and Papers* LIV, 1854-5, revealed a number of relevant items, listed alphabetically under subject or petitioner.

Subjects of petitions 1835-52 include: the colonisation and government of Australia, convicts, corn duties, church establishment, emigration, land questions including Portland Bay land purchase and native land rights in New Zealand, mails, steam communication, abolition of transportation, Treaty of Waitangi, Gov. Arthur and Gov. Darling, Sir John Franklin, Judge Willis, Queen Pomare of Tahiti, and many other matters relating to the Australian colonies, New Zealand, and the Pacific.

OTHER CLASSES

Certain of the following groups of records remain in the custody of their originating departments but many are available for consultation and may be of interest in specialised research. Inquiries should be addressed to the Clerk of the Records.

Clerk of the House 1888-1938.

Public Bill Office 1833- .

Journal Office 1680-   ; the records include manuscript evidence on disputed election hearings 1869-1906.

Committee and Private Bill Office 1818-   .

Accountant's Office 1818-   .

3. MISCELLANEOUS

Includes Shaw-Lefevre MSS. 1764-1860, for which there is a manuscript handlist available in the Search Room. Sir John George Shaw-Lefevre was Under-Secretary for the Colonies 1833, Poor Law Commissioner, and Commissioner for South Australia 1834, a member of the Emigration Committee 1843, and Clerk of the Parliaments 1855-75. The papers are both official and personal. They include letters addressed to him as Poor Law Commissioner 1835-41 and various letters relating to the South Australian Commission 1835-41.

4. HISTORICAL

Includes Samuel Papers 1883-1962, for which see H. S. Cobb, *The Samuel Papers*, 1966, H.L.R.O. Memorandum 35. Herbert Louis Samuel, 1st Viscount Samuel, was a Liberal politician.

A/32. Captain Cook Memorial Committee papers 1909-14 containing original correspondence and extracts from magazines and cuttings relating to the Committee formed to secure the erection of a memorial in London to Capt. Cook. They include letter 14 Apr. 1910 from Lord Brassey concerning efforts to raise funds in Australia for a memorial, and letter 20 July 1914 from Lord Brassey regretting his absence from the unveiling of the monument.

HUDSON'S BAY COMPANY
Beaver House, Great Trinity Lane, London, E.C.4

Applications for permission to consult the archives of the company must be supported by two letters of recommendation and addressed to the Secretary. Students granted access to the archives must give notice in writing of acceptance of the Company's conditions. Except under special circumstances determined by the Governor and Committee, archives may be consulted only up to and including 1870.

The Hudson's Bay Record Society issues a series of volumes containing selected documents accompanied by introductions. Sets of this series are filed in a number of libraries in Australia and New Zealand. Volumes XXI and XXII contain E. E. Rich's *History of the Hudson's Bay Company 1670-1870*, London 1958-9. The Company publishes a quarterly journal, *The Beaver*, Winnipeg.

A station in Honolulu existed 1833-61, having been created on the advice of Sir George Simpson. Honolulu had been used by the Company's vessels for repair and transhipment of mail and cargo before 1833 and references to the Sandwich Islands occur in the records, the Company's affairs in Hawaii at this time being managed by Richard Charlton. Later agents and assistant agents were George Pelly, Alexander Simpson, George Traill Allan, Dugald Mactavish, David McLoughlin, Robert Clouston, and James Bissett. Additional staff included Joseph Hardisty.

Apart from Vol.II of the *History* mentioned above covering 1763-1870, Hudson's Bay Record Society publications containing documents or references relating to Hawaii are Vols.IV, VI, VII, *McLoughlin's Fort Vancouver Letters 1825-1946*, series 1-3, 1941-4; Vol.X, *Simpson's 1828 Journey to the Columbia*, 1947; and Vol.XIX, *Eden Colvile's Letters 1849-52*, 1956. References to the Sandwich Islands also occur in *Letters of Dr. John McLoughlin written at Fort Vancouver 1829-1832*, ed. Dr Burt Brown Barker, Portland, Oregon, 1948 (letter book in the possession of the editor); Herbert Beaver, *Reports and Letters . . . 1836-1838 Chaplain to the Hudson's Bay Company and Missionary to the Indians at Fort Vancouver*, ed. T. E. Jessett, Portland, Oregon, 1959; A. G. Morton, *A History of the Canadian West to 1870-71*, London 1939; and J. S. Galbraith, *The Hudson's Bay Company as an Imperial Factor, 1821-1869*, Toronto 1957. Articles on Hawaii in *The Beaver* appear in the issues for Sept. 1941, Spring 1964, and Autumn 1965.

A typescript catalogue is practically complete for records to 1870. For post records there is a typescript summary catalogue.

In the 1920s a beginning was made with a scheme for typing extracts from the

F

London

records. These extracts are on foolscap and filed in loose leaf binders in two series: 'Annals' (extracts from London records), 19 vols.; 'Factory Journals' (extracts from Post Journals), 7 vols. There are typescript indexes to these extracts.

Records relating to Hawaii are found in the following sections:

A. London Office Records, including minute books, correspondence, accounts, contracts, wills, deeds.

B. Records of the Hudson's Bay Company posts, journals, letters, accounts, etc.

C. Records of ships owned or chartered by the Hudson's Bay Company.

D. Journals, correspondence, etc., of governors of Rupert's Land.

E. Records, mainly originating from Canada, which do not fit into Section B or any other section.

A1. Minutes of the Governing Committee in London 1833-61. These consist chiefly of letters received and decisions, discussion is not recorded, some volumes indexed.

A6. Letter books, copies of letters from the Governing Committee in London to officers of the Company 1833-61, some volumes indexed.

A11/61-3. Letters 1835-61 from the Sandwich Islands to London. They concern sales of cargoes of the Company's ships, bills of exchange, and business of the post but give general news, reports of commercial and political conditions, of the movements of shipping, and especially news of whaling vessels.

61. Letters 1835-40 from G. Pelly, some with statements of his current account with the Company. Enclosed in letters 1835-6 are two printed lists of vessels at Oahu 6 July to 22 Nov. 1835 and 1 Jan. to 1 Aug. 1836.

62. Several hundred letters 1843-52 from G. Pelly, G. T. Allan, and D. Mactavish. Letters 10 Aug. 1843 and 2 Jan. 1844 refer to the visit of Adm. Thomas and his reversal of the actions of Lord George Paulet and to the visit of a French warship a few days before 2 Jan. 1844. Sandwich Islands post accounts are with some letters and enclosed with letter 20 Oct. 1845 is a copy of account of H.M. Kamehameha III with the Company. With letters 1845 are copies of statements of dealings with Rear Adm. Sir George Seymour and copies of correspondence with William Miller, British Consul-General. Documents 1846 include a group recording decisions of the Company to establish the Sandwich Islands post.

63. Several hundred letters 1853-61 from R. Clouston and, after his death at sea in 1858, from J. Hardisty and J. Bissett. Among enclosures to the letters are statements of accounts. Attached to letter 17 Dec. 1859 is a printed extract from a newspaper endorsed 28 Feb. 1860, entitled 'Table showing the number barrels of oil and Lbs of Bone taken by the North Pacific Whaling Fleet for the years 1852-1859, (including only vessels that have returned to the Sandwich Islands) and giving the average for each season'.

B191c. Sandwich Islands, in-letters 1844-61. Only a few letters have been preserved.

B191d. Sandwich Islands, account books 1-12, 1836-53.

B191e. Sandwich Islands, reports on districts. The sole item is a map of property leased in 1846 for a 'second seat' in Hawaii.

B191z. Miscellanea 1834-67. Papers 1835-60 relating to land, miscellaneous accounts 1834-67.

B223b/1-43. Correspondence books 1825-60, copies of out-letters from Fort Vancouver, Columbia, some volumes indexed.

B223c/1-2. Correspondence inward 1826-60, Fort Vancouver, Columbia.

For some letters in B223b-c relating to the Sandwich Islands to 1846 see *McLoughlin's Fort Vancouver Letters 1825-1846*, Series 1-3, 1941-4.

B226b/1-19. Correspondence books 1844-61, copies of out-letters from Fort Victoria, Vancouver Island, some volumes indexed.

B226c/1-2. Correspondence inward 1848-69, Fort Victoria, Vancouver Island.

C1. Logs of the Company's vessels. A detailed loose leaf catalogue is available.

D3/2. Gov. George Simpson, Journal 1841. Draft of part of his journal of his voyage round the world 1841-2. See his *Narrative of a Journey Round the World . . . 1841 and 1842*, London 1847, 2 vols.

D4/1-127. Gov. George Simpson. Correspondence books 1821-60, copies of out-letters but including some in-letters, also Simpson's official reports to the Governor and Committee in London, some volumes indexed.

D5/1-52. Gov. George Simpson. Correspondence inward 1821-60.

E25/1. Thomas Lowe, Journal 1841-2 of a voyage from London to the Sandwich Island and Fort Tako, north west coast of America. Entries 12 Feb. to 17 Mar. 1842, pp.52-65, describe Honolulu, the beginning of the entry headed Fort Tako 1 June 1842, pp.65-7, describes the five day visit to Maui.

IMPERIAL WAR MUSEUM
Records Section, Lambeth Road, London, S.E.1

Most of the material in the Imperial War Museum is post-1914, although there are some records relating to the Boer War. A large proportion of the collections has still to be catalogued (Jan. 1970) but it is unlikely that there is any material relating specifically to the field of this survey. The documents are mostly personal journals and diaries of British serving officers in the two World Wars.

International Military Tribunals, Far East, 1946-8, 187 vols. and boxes. Formerly in the Public Record Office, F.O.648, transferred 1966. Copies of records relating to the trials of Japanese War Criminals held in Tokyo Apr. 1946 to Dec. 1948, the originals being preserved in the custody of the International Court at The Hague. F.O.648/103. Prosecution papers relating to the conspiracy to obtain domination in Pacific areas, and the expansion of aggression in Asia and the Pacific areas. F.O.648/155. Charges against Japanese war criminals charged under the War Crimes Act 1945 by Australian military authorities.

De Chair Papers

DeC.1c. Memoirs or Journal of Midshipman de Chair, H.M.S. *Alexandra*, June-Oct. 1882.

DeC.2, 3a-b, 4-5. 'A Life worth Living', memoirs to 1914 by Adm. Sir Dudley de Chair, written 1931-47, also memoirs 1914-23, 4 vols. In 1968 two further volumes, typescript, of memoirs for 1924-30 when Sir Dudley was Governor of New South Wales, were in the possession of Commander H. G. D. de Chair, Boxmoor, Herts.*

DeC.6-7. Two diaries 1911, 1915.

DeC.10. Correspondence 1882-1921.

INDIA OFFICE LIBRARY
Orbit House, 197 Blackfriars Road, London, S.E.1

S. C. Sutton, *A Guide to the India Office Library*, London 1967, 2nd ed., and A. J. Arberry, *The India Office Library: A Historical Sketch*, London 1967, 2nd ed., contain detailed descriptions of the resources of the Library. The Librarian's *Annual Report* includes a section 'Accessions' recording *inter alia* manuscripts acquired during the year. Until 1967 it also included a section 'Use' noting publications and theses for higher degrees based wholly or partly on material in the Library; this has now been discontinued as it proved impossible to make the list comprehensive. A leaflet *Recent Accessions of Private Archives* revised and reprinted 1969, lists collections acquired for the European Manuscripts section during the post-war period and includes some pre-war deposits not mentioned elsewhere.

The manuscripts are classified European or Oriental according to the language in which they are written. The following are the relevant printed catalogues for manuscripts received before 1937:

Vol.II Part I, S. C. Hill, *Catalogue of the Orme Collection*, London 1916, indexed.

Vol.II Part II, G. R. Kaye, *Catalogue of the Minor Collections and Miscellaneous MSS.* Section I, nos.1-538, London 1937. Section II, nos.539-842, E. H. Johnston (printed but not published; available in the Catalogue Hall). A joint index to Sections I and II is in preparation.

The manuscripts received after 1937 are recorded on a card index in the Catalogue Hall. The entries are mainly for personal names but there are some for subjects and places. Where handlists of the contents of collections have been compiled, the card index is marked 'H', and where catalogues have been compiled it is marked 'C'. A reproduction of these cards, as at the end of 1963, has been published in one volume by G. K. Hall, Boston, Mass., 1964.

All manuscript accessions both before and after 1937, except special collections, are referred to as 'MSS. Eur.'. Official access rules apply, i.e. a collection is made available for consultation only when corresponding official papers are thirty years old.

In addition to papers listed below, a few official, semi-official, and personal letters to and from individuals in Australia and New Zealand are to be found in the volumes of correspondence in a number of collections of vice-regal papers.

Orme Collection. Part of the material collected by the historian Robert Orme in preparation for his *History of the Military Transactions of the British Nation in Indostan from the year 1745*, London 1763-78.

XIX, 5. Vellum bound volume containing:

pp.43-52. Extract from a work not named [possibly an account of Jacob Roggeveen's Voyage] containing a description of the discovery of Easter Island and the sighting of land called New Zealand, English, n.d.

pp.53-63. Copy of a memorial by de Quiros concerning the 'settling and discovery of the fourth part of the World, Australia Incognita', English c.1610. Printed with other papers by de Quiros in Dalrymple's *Collection of Voyages, chiefly in the Southern Atlantick Ocean*, London 1775.

MSS. Eur. F85. Henry Lawrence Collection. Papers of Sir Henry Montgomery Lawrence, Indian Army officer and administrator 1823-57.

Handlist, typescript.

F85/69. Letters 1836-40 to and from Honoria Lawrence including letter 26 Mar. 1840 from M. Irwin, Perth, W.A. Copy in the Battye Library, Perth, W.A.

F85/70. Letters 1841-3 to and from Honoria Lawrence including letter 13 July 1841 from M. Irwin, Perth, W.A. Copy in the Battye Library, Perth, W.A.

MSS. Eur. D588. David Scott Letters. Papers of David Scott, Director of the East India Company 1788-1805, Chairman 1796-7, 1801-2.

Handlist, typescript.

p.36 (a). MS. map of Western Port, Vic., covering Phillip Island, French Island, and the surrounding coastline of the mainland, with names of settlers and local topographical names, undated. Scale approx. 5 miles = 1 inch.

MSS. Eur. E299. Moorsom Papers. Papers of Capt. Wayne Robert Moorsom.

E299/29/1-16. Correspondence 1875-7 between members of the Moorsom family concerning the illness and death of C. D. Moorsom at Tauranga, N.Z.

E299/30/1-3. Letters c.1868 from Constantine McDougall Moorsom, Tauranga, to his family.

E299/60/173. Cuttings c.1863-70 concerning New Zealand, some concerning the Maori War.

MSS. Eur. F83. Elgin Collection. Papers of James Bruce, 8th Earl of Elgin and 12th Earl of Kincardine, Viceroy and Governor-General of India 1862-3.

'Catalogue of the Viceregal Papers of the Eighth Earl of Elgin', M. C. Mountford, 1957, typescript.

F83/12. Copy letters Apr. 1862 to Sept. 1863 from Elgin to the Governor of Madras, Sir William Denison, 1 vol.

F83/19. Original letters Mar. 1862 to Oct. 1863 from Denison to Elgin, 1 vol. Letter 30 Apr. 1862 contains a memo regarding the export of horses to India from Australia by Frederick Barlee.

F83/29. Original letters 1862-3 from Commander-in-Chief, Sir Hugh Rose, to Elgin, 1 vol. Letters 19, 20 Aug. 1863 relate to the sending of native troops to New Zealand.

MSS. Eur. F78. Wood Collection. Papers of Sir Charles Wood, 1st Viscount Halifax, Secretary of State for India 1859-66.

Handlist, typescript.

F78/56/Bdle. 6 no.18. Original letters May-Aug. 1863 from Gov.-Gen. Elgin to Wood. Letter 30 Aug. 1863, with enclosures 17-24 Aug. 1863, relates to the sending of native troops to New Zealand.

MSS. Eur. F90. John Lawrence Collection. Papers of John Laird Mair Lawrence, 1st Baron Lawrence, Viceroy and Governor-General of India 1864-9.

Handlist, typescript.

F90. Original letters 1864-8 from Sir William Denison, Governor of Madras, to Lawrence, 1 vol.

F90. Original letters 1864-8 from Lawrence to Denison, 1 vol.

INDIA OFFICE RECORDS
Orbit House, 197 Blackfriars Road, London, S.E.1

Australia, New Zealand, and the Pacific, although generally of fringe interest to the East India Company, at times impinged on its history, particularly with regard to trade, shipping, emigration, and the problem of convicts. Source material on these themes is to be found scattered through the official archives, 1600-1858, which are in the keeping of the India Office Records.

The original records of the India Office also include those of the Board of Control 1784-1858 and the Burma Office 1937-47, as well as those of the India Office proper 1858-1947. They may be divided into two broad groups: (1) the archive accumulations produced by the home administration of the Company and of the India Office in London (2) copies of records termed 'Proceedings' produced by the administrations in India and other parts of the East, and sent to London for information. This distinction has not, however, always been strictly maintained; there are also artificial series, constructed in the nineteenth century, which contain documents drawn from both groups. The complex administrative history of the Company and the work of India Office officials in the nineteenth and early twentieth centuries, on which the present series are based, explain why classes and series of records are sometimes broken up and are not therefore immediately obvious to the searcher. A new scheme of classification has been applied to the records to reveal the archival structure of the series and to provide a framework for reference and production, but the work is still incomplete. A description of the records and classification scheme is given by Joan C. Lancaster in *Archivum* XV, 1965.

It is expected that a general introduction describing the records constituting each of the classes in the classification scheme, together with a summary of the contents of all the series, will appear (Joan C. Lancaster, *A Brief Guide to the India Office Records 1600-1947*) and that supplementary departmental and series guides will be published. Meanwhile, Sir William Foster, *Guide to the India Office Records 1600-1858*, London 1919 (lithograph reprint 1966) is the only general guide showing the relationship between the records and the administrative history of the Company. A survey of the various finding-aids at present available is Joan C. Lancaster, *A Guide to the Lists and Catalogues of the India Office Records*, London 1966, which also explains how to requisition documents. There is *List of General Records 1599-1879*, 1902, with supplement 'India Office Papers: Miscellaneous Lists', typescript [*c.*1957]. Both concern mainly the records resulting from the home administration in London and are now gradually being superseded by the new departmental guides. Other existing catalogues, lists, and indexes of sections of the records are mentioned in appropriate places below. It should be noted that the artificial class 'Z, Registers and Indexes, 1702-1950' contains both contemporary lists and indexes, where it has been possible to abstract these physically from the main record series, and modern compilations. The general map collection, which includes printed and manuscript maps, charts, plans, and surveys, is coded 'W', 'X', and 'Y' in the classification scheme, but the majority are at present catalogued quite distinctly.

All finding aids, original records, and maps are consulted in the Catalogue Hall and Reading Room shared with the Library, except large maps which are produced in the special map room. Documents less than thirty years old are not available for inspection.

B. COURT OF DIRECTORS AND COURT OF PROPRIETORS: MINUTES, ETC.

See handlist 'Minutes etc. of the Courts of Directors and Proprietors', typescript, 1967.

B/1-236. Minutes of the Court of Directors 1599-1858, 236 vols.

The volumes also contain the minutes of the Court of Proprietors until Apr. 1833. The minutes are brief, recording the receipt of correspondence, memorials, reports and recommendations from individuals and committees, and decisions taken. Up to Apr. 1810 there are annual indexes. In addition there are two separate series of indexes 1790-1827 (Z/B/1-5) and 1813-58 (Z/B/6-96). All are in the nature of summaries of contents arranged chronologically under alphabetical headings. The second series is less well set out and probably less complete than the first; it was compiled from a set of minutes no longer extant, but a key in each volume makes reference possible for the period after 1827 for which no other index exists.

D. GENERAL COMMITTEES AND OFFICES (CORRESPONDENCE COMMITTEE, SECRETARY'S & EXAMINER'S OFFICE) MINUTES, ETC.

See handlist 'Minutes etc. of the General Committees and Offices', n.d. (extract from *List of General Records*, 1902).

D. Minutes of the Committee of Correspondence 1784-1834, 16 vols.

These may give more detailed context information on subjects recorded in the

Court Minutes, since the committee handled much important business at this period, advising the Directors not only on routine matters such as requests for leave, but also on a variety of commercial matters. The volumes themselves are not indexed; a series entitled 'References to the Committee of Correspondence' 1704-1833 (Z/D/1-13) contains lists of papers submitted to the Committee, and for 1810-33 there is a separate series of indexes (Z/D/14-27) although one volume 1828-30 is missing. Both are personal name indexes arranged alphabetically under a year or group of years.

D. Correspondence Reports 1719-1834, gaps 1820-1, 1823-5, 72 vols., 6 missing.

These volumes contain reports and resolutions of the Committee. Each volume has only a personal name index (1769-). For example an entry in the index for the volume for Apr. 1805 to Jan. 1806 under 'Cottrell, Sir Stephen', refers back to the Committee's consideration on 5 June 1805 of Sir Stephen Cottrell's letter transmitting an extract of a letter from the Governor of New South Wales to Lord Camden. This contained a suggestion with respect to vessels built in New South Wales being permitted to export seal skins and trepang to China, and to import from China produce for the use of the colony.

D. Memoranda of the Correspondence Committee 1700-1858, 58 vols.

These volumes are artificial collections of various notes, memoranda, and other papers of the Committee taken from two earlier series 'Court Papers' and 'Court Miscellanies'. They are not indexed or paginated but a check of the volumes covering the relevant period is worthwhile if references have been found in the minutes.

E. GENERAL CORRESPONDENCE

See handlist 'General Correspondence', typescript [1967].

E/1. Home Correspondence (Secretary's Office) 1602-1859

Correspondence between London and other parts of the Western world.

E/1/1-195. Miscellaneous letters received 1701-1858, 195 vols. These are the original in-letters received by the Court of Directors from various individuals, both employees and outsiders. They are an amalgamation of two earlier series 'Correspondence Papers' and 'Court Miscellanies'. The letters are bound chronologically and each volume has a more recent index of persons and ships, with a very few other entries. They are mainly memorials and petitions.

E/1/196-314. Miscellanies 1699-1859, 119 vols. These consist of copies of home letters out. Vols.196-244, 1699-1809, have tables of contents, and vols.248, 253, 255 covering 1813, 1817, 1819, indexes. There is a separate series of contemporary indexes 1805-59 (Z/E/1/1-44). There are also four volumes containing contemporary lists of miscellanies 1817-59 (Z/E/1/45-8).

E/2. Correspondence with the Board of Control 1784-1858

E/2/1-28. Copies of letters from the Company to the Board 1784-1858, 28 vols. Vol.28 contains copies of enclosures 1817-27 forming an appendix to the main series. Vols.1-6, 1784 to May 1821, have tables of contents; the rest have indexes except vols.23-4, Oct. 1855-7 and vol.27, Apr.-Sept. 1858.

E/2/29-54. Copies of letters from the Board to the Company 1784-1858, 26 vols. Vols.51-4 contain copies of enclosures 1818-37 forming an appendix to the main series. Vols.29-32, 1784 to Feb. 1818 have tables of contents; the rest are indexed.

E/4. Correspondence with India (Examiner's Office) 1703-1858

This includes both the original letters received by the Company from the governments of the presidencies and original drafts of despatches or out-letters from London; together they constitute the official correspondence between the two ends of the administration. The letters received are entirely un-indexed but they may be used in conjunction with the despatches which have modern indexes, since the despatches give exact references to letters answered. Both the letters received and the despatches are arranged chronologically without regard to department, although within the letters themselves the subjects dealt with are grouped in paragraphs, and as new departments were instituted from the late eighteenth century onwards a corresponding series of letters was commenced. Within the departments the use of short separate letters each dealing with a particular subject was much increased after 1830 but the general letters continue. From about 1830 there are duplicate series of letters received and despatches which were kept at the Board of Control, arranged by departments. These 'Board's Copies' are now found under the appropriate department in section 'L'. The departmental arrangement, and the fact that they are mostly indexed, means that they may be useful; on the other hand, they do not cover the late eighteenth century, and the contemporary indexes in the volumes are not so convenient to use as the modern indexes mentioned above. Letters received and despatches have therefore been listed in this section and not under 'L'. A further series of draft despatches is described under F/3. The correspondence with India covers the whole range of the Company's business and interests. References to New South Wales, mainly concerning trade (legal and illegal), individual merchants, ships and convicts are scattered, the subjects almost always recorded also in the Court of Directors' minutes, since the Court discussed letters in and draft letters out.

F. BOARD OF CONTROL

See handlist 'Board of Control', n.d. (extract from *List of General Records* 1902).

The Board of Commissioners for the Affairs of India, usually called the Board of Control, was established by Act of Parliament in 1784. Originally composed of six Privy Councillors, the Board was widened in 1793 to include two non-Privy Council members. The Board, as official representative of the Government, generally supervised the administration of the Company in India, approving the Directors' despatches to India and sometimes initiating its own; it also dealt with other government departments concerning Indian matters and was responsible for making returns to Parliament when called for. In 1858 it absorbed the remaining functions of the East India Company and the President became the First Secretary of State for India in Council. Many of the records duplicated those of the Company and were retained by the India Office in preference to the latter.

F/1. Minutes 1784-1858, 7 vols.

Up to 1816 the minutes note draft despatches, copies of minutes, memorials, correspondence received, and decisions taken, most of this business coming from, or being referred to, the Court of Directors of the Company. The last meeting of the Board was held on 24 June 1816. After that date the papers were signed in circulation and the minutes refer only to Establishment matters. Each volume has its own index.

F/2. Letter Books 1784-1858, 20 vols.

These contain copies of letters despatched, and after May 1840, copies of letters received, by the Board. Each volume has an index.

F/2. Letters, etc. 1822-58, 20 vols.

Original letters received with draft replies bound into volumes arranged according to subject. The three registers of correspondence coded under Z/F/2 relate to Public

Department Home Correspondence, letters in and out, 1836-47, 1855-8 which no longer survives among the Board's records.

F/3. Draft Despatches

See also E/4. Described in Foster's *Guide* (p.22) as 'Draft Paragraphs submitted to the Board of Control' the draft despatches represent the second stage in the procedure of despatches from the Company at home to its representatives in India. A proposed despatch had already been submitted unofficially to the Board and returned to the Company with amendments or suggestions. Since most of these 'Previous Communications' have been destroyed, these copies of second or official drafts retained as record files by the Board for tracing negotiations previous to despatches, are particularly useful. They are marked up with the Board's final approval or emendation. They include copies of any correspondence which may have taken place between the Court and the Board on the matter and often give the register number of the Board's collections of papers referring to the matter where these survive. There are separate series of volumes for Bengal, Madras, and Bombay and within the presidencies the drafts are arranged strictly chronologically without concern for the department involved. It seems likely that the volumes after 1814 were destroyed. The exception is the series of draft commercial despatches to all presidencies which survive for 1812-34. The series of registers (Z/F/3) refers to the later drafts 1814-58.

Bengal 1784-1814, 32 vols., 1 missing. There is a gap Sept. 1796 to Dec. 1797. For Oct. 1799 to Sept. 1811 each volume has an index. As an example, relevant draft despatches in vol.12, Oct. 1800 to Sept. 1801, are: 24 Mar. 1801 approving measures taken for preventing convicts from New South Wales establishing themselves in any part of the East Indies, and instructing that everything possible be done to stop further intercourse, except that indispensable for the conveyance of supplies to New South Wales; 24 Mar. 1801 reiteration of prohibition on sending convicts from Bengal to Botany Bay; 20 Apr., 3 July 1801 concerning a payment to Capt. Flinders on his survey of the coast of New Holland in the *Investigator* to be used as Table Money for himself and his officers.

Madras 1784-1814, 22 vols. For Jan. 1798 to Sept. 1811 each volume has an index.

Bombay 1784-1814, 14 vols. For Jan. 1798 to Nov. 1807 and Dec. 1810 to Sept. 1811 each volume has an index.

Commercial to all Presidencies 1812-34, 8 vols., each with an index.

F/4. Board's Collections 1796-1858, 2730 vols.

Collections of earlier date than 1796 were destroyed and there are many gaps in the existing series caused by the destruction of unimportant collections. The collections contain the papers on which the various drafts to all presidencies were founded, that is, the documents enclosed, referred to, or cited in letters received. They were registered and arranged by the number and date of the draft answering despatch. The series of registers 1794-1858 (Z/F/4/1-18) arranged on this system is the key to obtaining particular collections.

G. FACTORY RECORDS

See *List of Factory Records*, 1896.

This is an artificial group of material which was collected and sorted under the various factories both within and outside India. It contains many of the seventeenth and eighteenth century records of the Company including correspondence, consultations, and diaries, some series being continued in other sections.

London

The following factory records have been noted mainly for the information they contain on the early history of the Dutch in the East Indies (see also section 'I').

G/4. Borneo 1648-1814, 1 vol.*

G/10. Celebes 1613-74, 1 vol.*

G/21. Java 1595-1815, 72 vols.*

G/34. Straits Settlement 1769, 1795-1805, 1830, 196 vols.*

G/34/11-134. Prince of Wales Island, Public Consultations 1805-30, 122 vols. These are similar to the Public Consultations of Bengal, Madras and Bombay [Section 'P'] and contain direct references to New South Wales. There are indexes 1809-30, arranged under stereotype headings. Vol.25, 1809, contains a request from the Bengal Government that any information respecting a rebellion in New South Wales may be communicated, with the reply that no intelligence of it has been received; vol.53, 1815, has an acknowledgement by the Supreme Government of the receipt of European convicts escaped from New South Wales, and several entries relating to John Porter, a convict from New South Wales.

G/35. Sumatra 1615-1795, 162 vols.*

H. HOME MISCELLANEOUS SERIES

See S. C. Hill, *Catalogue of the Home Miscellaneous Series*, London 1927. This is an indexed and detailed guide to a very mixed collection of documents of various origins, including some Board of Control records, accumulated at East India House in the seventeenth and eighteenth centuries and bound into volumes, with additions, in the nineteenth century. It covers the whole of the history of the Company and includes many papers originating in the East as well as genuine 'home' papers.

Vol.379 (7), pp.459-73. Extracts from Bengal Consultations 23 June 1790 to 30 Mar. 1791 concerning the supply of provisions to Botany Bay and New South Wales by Messrs Lambert and Ross, and R. Biddulph.

Vol.494 (6), pp.461-501. Copy of a bill for opening the trade of New South Wales under licences for the East India Company and the South Sea Company [1807].

I. EUROPEANS IN INDIA

See handlist 'Europeans in India', typescript [1967].

I/3. Transcripts and translations of Dutch and Portuguese Records at The Hague 1600-1700

These are not records of the East India Company. They were obtained by F. C. Danvers, Registrar and Superintendent of Records 1884-90. Those listed below refer mainly to contacts between the Dutch and English in the East Indies, and have been included here for the light they throw on the discoveries and explorations of the Australian coast by the Dutch. There are no indexes to this material, but F. C. Danvers, *Dutch Activities in the East, 17th Century: being a report on the records relating to the East in the State Archives in The Hague*, ed. Nihar Ranjan Ray, Calcutta 1945, is a useful introduction.

I/3/1-86. Letters from India 1600-99, with translations 1600-70, 86 vols.*

I/3/87-94. Letters from the Dutch East India Company to India 1614-1700. With translations 1614-1700, 8 vols.*

I/3/95-106. Letters from the Governor-General at Batavia to various factories 1617-99, with translations 1617-43, 12 vols.*

L. DEPARTMENTS

See handlists 'India Office Papers: Miscellaneous Lists', typescript, *c.*1957.

This large collection contains a mass of complex records, ranging from the seventeenth to the mid-twentieth century. They have been arranged under the various India Office departments. Those listed below are the most important to this survey. It is not necessary to describe the first three in detail. In each case they contain series of home correspondence, correspondence with India (Board's copies of letters from, and despatches to, the three presidencies), and departmental papers. The correspondence is useful in that it is often fuller than that in duplicate series elsewhere in the India Office Records. The departmental papers or files after c.1880 may be easily consulted with the help of the annual indexes and registers which are included in the Handlists and classified under 'Z'. Spot checks in the indexes and registers of the Economic Department and the Public and Judicial Department show that after 1900 the important questions of Indian emigration to Australia, New Zealand, and the Pacific, and of the status of Indians in these countries, occur frequently.

L/E. Economic 1786-1950, 4074 vols.

L/P&J. Public & Judicial 1795-1950, 3866 vols., 1262 boxes.

L/P&S. Political & Secret 1778-1950, 4141 vols., 880 boxes.

L/Mar. Marine 1605-1931, 1897 vols.

See *List of Marine Records 1600-c.1882*, 1896.

The large collections of records relating to the maritime affairs of the East India Company and the India Office are mainly to be found under this heading. They are divided into three sections, the two relevant being Ships' Logs and Marine Miscellaneous.

L/Mar/B/1-818. Ships' Logs 1702-1856, 818 vols. The section in the list describing these logs is detailed, giving the first and last dates in each log, the name of the ship and its captain, and a brief note on the direction of the voyage. The official logs were kept in a special book form supplied by the Company. A few ledgers and receipt books are extant, but in 1860 there was a general destruction of journals and books other than the logs. The logs contain mostly navigation details and comments but also, often, lists of officers, crew, and passengers on board, and information on cargo carried. Logs include the journal 1796-8 of Second Officer Godsell of the *Duff*.* Another example is the log of the *Royal Admiral* journeying to Port Jackson and Whampoa 1792-3 giving the number of passengers, soldiers, and convicts received on board, cargo to be delivered to Port Jackson, and an account of the newly discovered reef off the north-west coast of New Caledonia. Thirty-five ships voyaging to Australia and the Pacific in 1788-1833 were noted from the list. The references are given in chronological order, but in the volumes, the logs themselves are bound by ships.

L/Mar/C/1-900. Marine Miscellaneous 1600-1879, 900 vols. This is an artificial series of miscellaneous papers on marine matters, only very summarily described in the list. Work is in progress on the series.

27-48. Minutes of the Committee of Shipping 1803-34, mostly indexed. These contain information on the use of ships engaged by the government for the conveyance of convicts to New South Wales or Van Diemen's Land to bring back tea from China on the Company's account.

509. List of ships abroad 1807-32. Printed lists on backed sheets bound into one volume (pages loose and torn). They give dates of sailing, name, managing owners, commanders, tonnage, places to which consigned, and schedules of time appointed. There are numerous additions in manuscript, some noting the arrival of Botany Bay ships not included on the printed sheet as regular or chartered ships, e.g. 'Arrived 7 Sept. 1816 *Northampton* Botany Bay ship from Canton'.

147

London

P. PROCEEDINGS

All Proceedings (46324 vols.) or Consultations as they are usually called until the mid-nineteenth century, are copies of the proceedings of the Presidents and Councils sent contemporaneously to the Company in London, or to the India Office, for information. From the late eighteenth century the business was divided into departments, separate records being kept for each. Proceedings for Bengal are described below. Similar but fewer references are to be found in the Proceedings for Madras, Bombay, and India.

BENGAL

See *List of Proceedings etc.: Bengal 1704-1858*, 1899; *List of Proceedings etc.: Bengal 1859-1897*, 1899.

P. Public, Commercial and Shipping Consultations 1789-1800, 58 vols.

Include annual indexes (Z/P/43-53). The indexes are very general, arranged under an alphabetical list of subjects repeated in each volume, e.g. Board of Trade, Company's Servants, Europe Ships, Individuals, Marine. In the seven index volumes checked, occasional references to Botany Bay ships were found, leading to the proceedings recording the arrival and departure of the ships at Calcutta. Nothing else of interest was found but since trade with New South Wales is a regular feature of the commerce reports, it is likely that there are scattered references to it in these Proceedings.

P. Commercial Consultations 1801-34, 288 vols.

Include annual indexes (Z/P/9-42). The arrangement is similar to the consultations above and the same remarks apply.

P. Commercial Reports 1795-1858, 57 vols.

These are reports on the external commerce of Bengal for the whole period, also covering internal commerce between 1812 and 1836. The first volume in the series covers 1795-1802; the papers for these years are badly bound together out of strict chronological order. Subsequently the volumes are annual. The later papers are printed. There are no indexes. Copies of the annual reports made by the Reporter General of External Commerce for the commercial year, which ended on 31 May, were forwarded to the Court of Directors together with copies of relevant summaries, abstracts, statements, and comparative tables, analysing the total trade of Bengal. The texts of the reports usually have a useful general comment on the trade with New South Wales, e.g. Report 10 Sept. 1800: 'The late prohibition respecting the export of Bengal Rum to Port Jackson (because the article which produced the greatest profit) will probably deter the private merchants of Calcutta from sending any more ships to the colony. The entire failure of the speculation to New Guinea is the cause of the Imports being so very small in comparison with the average of the three preceding years'. With the accompanying statistics, these reports are the major source for discovering the nature and fluctuations of the trade between Bengal and New South Wales.

P. Law Consultations 1777-1834, 53 vols., 1 missing, 1786-93.

The main series of Law Proceedings does not officially start until 1794 when it was resolved that 'all matters and business relative to the Courts of Quarter Sessions and the correspondence with the Justices be recorded in a separate set of consultations in the Public Department', but the practice had been instituted some years earlier. The volumes, which are annual after 1794, each have a brief contents list arranged chronologically. They are a particularly valuable source of information on the transportation of European convicts to New South Wales between 1800 and 1830.

P. Public Consultations 1704-1858, 893 vols., 1 missing, July-Dec. 1858.

In June 1818 the Public Department changed its title to General Department but the later consultations are still inaccurately called 'Public' in the handlist. The volumes have annual indexes, a few with the actual consultations, but the majority in a physically separate series (Z/P/539-627).

P. General Proceedings 1859-97, 62 vols.

Include four separate annual indexes 1862-4, 1866 (Z/P/151-3B). This is a continuation of the previous series. The volumes are printed; the entries are arranged by months and the indexes (tables of contents before 1879) are also monthly. Some of the entries to which the indexes refer are regarded as 'Matters of Routine—Papers not printed' in which case they do not appear among the Proceedings sent to London. Contact with Australia appears to have been slight in this period, but statistics of Australian colonies were sent spasmodically to Bengal, e.g. in Oct. 1866 statistics for Tasmania were received.

J. W. JERVOIS, ESQ.
24 Byfeld Gardens, London, S.W.13

The papers of Sir William Francis Drummond Jervois, Governor of South Australia 1877-83 and of New Zealand 1883-9, are in the possession of various members of the family in England. In 1969 they were in the custody of Mr and Mrs J. W. Jervois who were willing to consider applications by serious students for permission to inspect them.

Relatively few papers relate to Sir William Jervois's terms in Australia and New Zealand but some New Zealand papers are of substantial importance. There are also scrapbooks containing chiefly cuttings from newspapers relating to both colonies and there is a volume of duplicates of Colonial Office papers relating to New Zealand.

Most of the papers have been xeroxed for Professor R. W. Winks, Department of History, Yale University, New Haven, Connecticut, U.S.A. for use in preparation of a biography. Professor Winks is willing to answer inquiries and hopes to place his copies finally in Rhodes House, Oxford.

KEATS MEMORIAL HOUSE
Keats Grove, London, N.W.3

Letter 13 Apr. 1841 from Charles Armitage Brown to his son in New Plymouth, N.Z., mentioning goods being shipped out and other matters.

Notebook containing rough notes about the journey to New Zealand 1841 made by Charles Armitage Brown.

KLEINWORT, BENSON LTD
20 Fenchurch Street, London, E.C.3

The two merchant houses Kleinwort and Benson were established in the late eighteenth century. The Kleinworts specialised in international banking and trade finance, the Bensons in investment banking and in raising new capital for industrial and commercial undertakings at home and overseas. The two houses came together in 1961 and the merchant banking activities were merged in Kleinwort, Benson Ltd. A large body of the records of both houses, some dating back to 1865, is preserved in a special building at The Lawn, Old Bath Road, Speen, Newbury, Berkshire. Application for permission to consult records should be made to the Secretary of the

Company at 20 Fenchurch Street, London, E.C.3. Records more recent than fifty years old are not usually available.

Correspondence. Some correspondence over fifty years old is available.

Account Books, Ledgers, Kleinwort. A series of fourteen volumes 1865-1919 is devoted to the East Indies, China, Japan, Australia. The area covered by individual volumes varies and the volumes overlap in date.

Account Books, Ledgers, Benson. General Ledgers 1875-   , 30 vols.; Clients' Ledgers 1868-   , 16 vols.; Stock Ledgers 1888-   , 5 vols.

Monthly Balance Books, Kleinwort, 1865-1922, 11 vols. Australia is included. Monthly balances and recapitulation figures are given.

Reserve, Bad, and Doubtful Debts, Kleinwort. Australian firms are included in vols.1, 2, 1859-90, both with indexes.

Credit Information Books, Kleinwort, contain information on financial standing and commercial activities. Two vols. 1878-1910 with indexes and two tin boxes 1910-30 cover the Cape, East Indies, China, Japan, Australia, and New Zealand.

Accounts in loose leaf form, Kleinwort, relating to the East and to Australia, in tin boxes.

Merchants' Trust Company Ltd, Minute Books and Ledgers and thirty reports of meetings of shareholders, 1891-1920.

New Zealand Mines Trust Limited (Puket tin dredging, Waihi investments and exploration), Minute Books, Ledgers, and Reports, 1905-   .

LAMBETH PALACE LIBRARY
Lambeth Palace Road, London, S.E.1

The Library of the Archbishops of Canterbury, founded as a public library in 1610, contains, besides printed books, the archives of the Archbishop of Canterbury, official ecclesiastical archives of the Church of England, Fulham papers, which are papers of the Bishops of London, and other manuscript accessions. The Library is open to students at the discretion of the Library Committee and new readers are asked to provide a letter of introduction. Special permission is needed for access to some categories of manuscripts.

RECORDS OF THE ARCHBISHOPS

Registers, chronologically arranged documents of such official acts as consecrations of bishops, institutions of livings, visitations, licences to preach. They contain permissions to officiate in England under the Colonial Clergy Act 1874.

Moore Papers

The Moore Papers include a group containing letters and papers of Richard Johnson and Samuel Marsden*:

Diary of a voyage to Australia 1786 and of subsequent experiences in Sydney. Dated Sydney 6 Apr. 1794, unsigned but written by Johnson.

Copies by Johnson of his letters to Viscount Dundas and to various officials in Sydney.

Copy of a further diary by Johnson, Sydney, 6 Aug. 1794.

Letter 4 May 1792 Samuel Marsden, Sydney, to William Wilberforce describing the religious state of New South Wales and the quarrels between Johnson and the Lieutenant-Governor.

Letter n.d. to William Wilberforce relating to the erection of a place of worship. Unsigned but endorsed with Johnson's name.

Plan and elevation of a church built by Johnson.

Letter 8 May 1793 Johnson, Port Jackson, to 'Your Lordship' describing the religious state of Sydney and his activities. With cover addressed to Abp Moore.

Longley Papers

See N.R.A. Report 1962.

Vol.2. Letters and papers 1846-62 mainly personal including correspondence with F. R. Nixon, F. A. Marriott, and G. A. Selwyn.

Vol.3. Official letters and papers 1862-8 concerning colonial bishoprics, with contents list.

Vol.4. Official letters and papers 1864-8 including ff.237-40 letter 1867 Longley to H. L. Jenner on the ritualistic movement.

Vol.6. Official letters and papers of the first Lambeth Conference 1867 including letters from Australian and New Zealand bishops and ff.322-3 resolution of the fourth synod of the diocese of Wellington 1867.

Vol.7. Letters and papers 1867-8 mainly personal including ff.199-202 letter 1865 from G. A. Selwyn about a bishop for Dunedin.

Vol.9. Photograph album of the first Lambeth Conference.

Tait Papers

See N.R.A. Report 1961 for an outline catalogue and index to names of correspondents in vols.76-104. There is a typescript index to names of correspondents to vols.105-60 and vols.169-201 are indexed on cards. A manuscript register lists letters in chronological order from 30 Jan. 1857 to 1882, letters in later years being arranged in alphabetical order. This letter register covers the 290 vols.

Miscellaneous correspondence:

Vols.82-100 include letters 1865-6 from Baroness Burdett-Coutts, letters 1868-82 from bishops in Australia and New Zealand.

Vol.103. Correspondence c.1850-78 of Catherine Tait including ff.295, 298 letters from G. A. Selwyn.

Vol.104. Correspondence and miscellaneous papers collected by R. T. Davidson preparatory to collaborating with W. Benham in *Life of Archibald Campbell Tait Archbishop of Canterbury*, London 1891, 2 vols. ff.101, 122, letters from A. Short.

Official correspondence:

Vol.169, 1870 Foreign, includes papers relating to the Colonial Church Bill 1866, see also vol.173 for the Colonial Church Bill 1871, papers relating to the appointment and status of bishops in the colonial church and letters relating to New Zealand.

Vol.170, 1879 Foreign, includes correspondence concerning the bishoprics of Dunedin, N.Z., Grafton and Armidale, N.S.W.

Vol.171, 1870 Foreign, includes correspondence concerning episcopal organisation in Australia and about the dioceses of Bathurst and Adelaide.

Vol.178, 1871 Foreign, includes papers concerning the Melbourne Church Assembly, the new diocese of Queensland, the proposed tribunal to hear appeals of Australian Church tribunals on doctrine and ritual, the appointment of the bishop of Honolulu, letters concerning New Zealand.

Vol.194, 1873 Foreign, includes correspondence concerning the dioceses of Brisbane and Melbourne and letter from A. Willis enclosing the new charter of incorporation of the church in Hawaii.

Vols.196, 198-200, 1874 Home, include correspondence concerning Croasdaile Bowen of Christchurch, N.Z., Mrs Mina Jury, missions, and G. W. Spooner, Tokomairiro, N.Z.

Vol.201, 1874 Foreign, includes correspondence concerning the dioceses of Brisbane, Dunedin, and Ballarat, also on the Colonial Clergy Act 1874 and letter enclosing Acts passed by the Melbourne Church Assembly.

London

Vols.202-90. Item numbers are given within Home or Foreign Correspondence in each year for relevant letters:

1875 Home/188, F. H. Wyld on Dr Colenso's position and teaching.

1875 Colonial Letters/10, Dunedin bishopric.

1876 Foreign/4, Auckland; /46 Perth, appointment to the see.

1877 Foreign/15, Christchurch, N.Z.

1878 Foreign/18, Honolulu; /30 New Zealand; /34 Queensland; last item Waiapu.

1879 Foreign/1, Armidale, N.S.W.; /7 Fiji, letter concerning the field for an English Mission in Fiji.

1880 Foreign/16, Dunedin, N.Z.; /32 Melbourne; /46 Sydney; /47 Tasmania.

1881 Home/58, Rev. W. H. Cooper concerning lectures on Australia.

1882 Foreign/1, Adelaide; /17 Maoris, visit to England; /24 Riverina, N.S.W., formation of bishopric.

Benson Papers

Correspondence is listed in a contemporary, handwritten 'Register of letters of Archbishop Tait 1881-1882 and Archbishop Benson 1883-1896'. The letters are held in boxes arranged by year, there being a home and foreign series for each year. Within these series numbered bundles of letters are arranged alphabetically according to the name of the principal correspondent or the subject. There are also a few boxes containing miscellaneous subject bundles. Almost all boxes contain several bundles of letters relating to Australia and New Zealand and letters on Fiji occur in 1886 Foreign Box 5d/13, 1887 Foreign Box 6f/13, 1889 Foreign Box 8f/F1, M2; Norfolk Island in 1884 Home Box 3c/155; Melanesia in 1892 Foreign Box 11g/M5, 1893 Home Box 12c/T3, W12, 1894 Foreign Box 13d/M2; Hawaii in 1886 Foreign Box 5d/18. Bundles on other subjects noted are as follows:

1883 Home Box 2d/172, J. R. Selwyn on relations of home and colonial church, 2d/206, about Colonial Bishoprics Fund.

1884 Home Box 3b/63, emigration.

1885 Foreign Box 4a/14, Jenner challenges jurisdiction of the Bishop of London by holding confirmations at Bruges.

1886 Foreign Box 5d/14, Aborigines.

1887 Home Box 6c/10, Dr Barnardo's Homes.

1888 Home Box 7a/C22, Colonial Clergy Act, 7a/C28d, colonial bishops taking the oath to the see of Canterbury; 7b/E15, Church Emigration Society.

1888 Foreign Box 7e/D2, church in the colonies.

1889 Home Box 8a/C38-9, Colonial Clergy Act.

1891 Home Box 10a/C33, Colonial Bishoprics Fund, 10a/C34, fitness of persons appointed as colonial bishops; 10b/D14, oaths of colonial bishops.

1894 Home Box 13b/M10, Missionary Conference.

1896 Home Box 15a/C16, Colonial Clergy Act; 15b/M6, appointment of missionary bishops.

1884 Box 22, Colonial Clergy missionaries: 1893 Honolulu. Box of unnumbered bundles including papers relevant to the setting up of a Board of Missions, the Colonial Clergy Act, correspondence and papers relating to Honolulu, among them letters returned to Lambeth on the death of Bishop Bickersteth, letters relating to the episcopal jurisdiction of Honolulu 1898-1900 and letters concerning the transfer of the Hawaiian Mission to the American Church in 1900 with pamphlets and cuttings.

1880s Box 32, Emigration, Miscellaneous.

Temple Papers

The papers 1897-1902 are arranged and catalogued and the catalogue will be duplicated by the National Register of Archives. There is also a contemporary manuscript register. The arrangement is by year, there being a home and foreign series for each year. Papers include:

Vol.2, 1897 Home, Colonial Clergy Act; vol.6, 1897 Home, Archdeacon Scott's nephew a clergyman in New Zealand.

Vol.7, 1897 Foreign, Vogan on the church's lack of concern for the Aborigines; vol.8, 1897 Foreign, New Guinea.

Vol.9, 1898 Home, Boards of Missions.

Vol.18, 1898 Foreign, Appeals by Brisbane Grammar School; Honolulu.

Vol.21, 1899 Home, Colonial Clergy Act.

Vol.32, 1899 Foreign, Australian Aborigines; Honolulu; Melanesian Mission.

Vol.41, 1900 Foreign, Honolulu; episcopal jurisdiction of Tonga.

Vol.43, 1901 Home, Church Emigration Society; Colonial Clergy Act.

Vol.50, 1901 Foreign, Honolulu.

Vol.59, 1902 Foreign, Boards of Missions and the Society for the Promotion of Christian Knowledge; Melbourne.

Davidson Papers

A typescript list is available. The papers 1891-1928 are arranged in two series: first a series of bundles and boxes of material relating to specific subjects and covering a number of years under each subject, second a series of smaller bundles arranged chronologically by year and alphabetically within each year. Material in the first series includes Australia 1905-11, 1 box; New Zealand 1903, 1910, 1924 in a box with other subjects with the initial N. In the second series papers on Australia occur in 1891, 1895, 1897-1900, 1903-14, 1918, 1926-7; on New Zealand in 1905-6, 1909; on Fiji and New Guinea in 1907, 1912; on Fiji in 1909, 1914; on the New Hebrides in 1907 and on Polynesia in 1908-9. Other subjects noted are: Dr J. T. Marriott, Dean of Bathurst, in 1904-5; Aborigines in Western Australia, Labour Party in Australia, Colonial Bishoprics Fund in 1906; Bush Brotherhood 1907, 1927; Colonial Bishoprics Fund 1907; establishment of the Kingsley Fairbridge Scheme 1910.

RECORDS OF THE VICAR GENERAL

Act Books

The Act Books are a chronological record or day book of the business passing through the Vicar General's hands. An index to names and places appears in *Index to the Act Books of the Archbishops of Canterbury 1663-1859*, Index Library vol.55, 1929, and vol.63, 1938.

Papers

VM Marriage allegations 1660-1864. Microfilms in the National Library of Australia.

VZ 11 Papers relating to colonial dioceses include the following records, the first three of which are recorded in Archbishops' Registers and Act Books.

VZ 11/1a, d. Appointment and resignation of colonial bishops.

VZ 11/2. Ordination papers for the colonies 1867.

VZ 11/3. Colonial consents to officiate in England 1857.

VZ 11/4. Miscellaneous papers relating to colonial sees 1803-1927.

VZ 11/5. Foreign chaplaincies.

FACULTY OFFICE PAPERS

FM Papers relating to the issue of Marriage Licences.

FM 1 Marriage allegations 1632-1864. Microfilms in the National Library of Australia.

FIII/11 Calendars of foreign notaries. These list the notaries practising overseas giving date of appointment and reference to the muniment books FI.

London

Papers of the Bishops of London. There is a typescript list and see also the introduction to, and arrangement of, W. W. Manross, *The Fulham Papers in the Lambeth Palace Library, American Colonial Section*, Oxford 1965.

FP 334-86. Letter books 1830-51 of Bishop Blomfield should repay examination.

FP 458. Fiji 1904-7, correspondence and papers chiefly concerning the appointment of a Bishop of the Western Pacific based on Fiji. The correspondence and papers are tied into bundles, one for each year. The 1906 bundle includes a few letters and papers 1901 concerning missions in the Pacific and the possibility of Fiji being placed under the Bishop of Honolulu. There is also a packet labelled 'Polynesia Bishoprics 1906-7'.

FP Additional Box 32. Australia, New Zealand, Tasmania, Honolulu, Fiji.

The papers include letters and pamphlets 1867-70 concerning H. L. Jenner and the ritualism controversy; papers 1874-84 relating to the needs of the Anglican residents of Fiji including letters from E. A. Liardet, G. R. Le Hunte, Rev. W. Floyd and from bishops in New Zealand and Tasmania, also correspondence 1883-4 of the Society for the Propagation of the Gospel concerning the offer of £10,000 by the Hon. John Campbell, N.S.W., to endow a Fijian see and relations between Fiji and New South Wales; papers 1863-70 relating to Honolulu and Hawaiian and Melanesian missions; letters 1869-70 some from C. Perry, Bishop of Melbourne, concerning disproportionately large grants to African provinces, also letters discussing episcopal communication between Sydney and Fiji.

There is also a group of letters 1828-30:

Letter 1828, copy*, from Sir George Arthur to C. J. Blomfield, Bishop of London, urging increase of numbers of chaplains and schoolmasters in Van Diemen's Land, introducing Mr [William?] Rayner and describing the arrival of chaplain Browne who shared his berth with the runagate Ikey Solomon.

Letter 1830, copy, from Blomfield to W. G. Broughton despatching Mr Dickinson.

Letter 1830 from Sir George Murray about persons to be sent to New South Wales.

There is a typescript catalogue compiled in 1961 and a card index of more recent accessions. No manuscripts relating to the field of this survey were found in H. J. Todd, *Catalogue of Manuscripts*, London 1812. The following manuscripts have been noted:

MSS.1374-88 Burdett-Coutts Papers

The papers are concerned mainly with the development of the colonial church and its legal status in relation to the Church of England. Angela Georgina Burdett-Coutts, Baroness Burdett-Coutts of Highgate and Brookfield, endowed the sees of Capetown and Adelaide in 1847. The main files relating to Australasia and the Pacific are:

1374. Ecclesiastical correspondence 1864-7 includes *Appeal to Wilberforce for a Mission to the Sandwich Islands*, 1864.

1375. Correspondence 1864-8 mainly with bishops. f.227 letter 1868 from G. A. Selwyn[?].

1380-1. Miscellaneous correspondence 1865-6, 1866-8 mainly concerned with the controversy over the relationship between colonial churches and the church in England.

1382. Miscellaneous papers 1865-9 mainly legal and concerning colonial churches, ff.1-28 endowment of Adelaide; ff.38-9 petition 14 Dec. 1866 from Sydney opposing the Colonial Bishoprics Bill.

1383. Miscellaneous papers 1842-67 concerning colonial bishoprics.

1384. Papers concerning Baroness Burdett-Coutts's endowment of colonial bishoprics.

1385. Correspondence 1846-68 with and about the colonial church, ff.1-114 Adelaide; ff.115-24 Brisbane; ff.125-34 Newcastle; ff.135-63 New Zealand.

MS.1562 Papers of Joshua Watson

ff.1-2. Extract from letter 1851 [from wife of the Bishop of New Zealand] describing teaching of Maoris.

ff.34-5. Letter 1843 from J. M. Rodwell describing the activities of G. A. Selwyn.

ff.36-9. Extract from letter 1845 from Mrs William Martin, N.Z.

ff.40-2. Letters 1844-6 from Sarah Selwyn and G. A. Selwyn.

ff.49-57. Letter 1852 from W. Tyrrell.

MSS.1618-19 Claude Jenkins Papers, editorial correspondence of the *Church Quarterly Review*, includes a few letters from Australian bishops.

MS.1727 Miscellaneous Letters and Papers. Includes letters from bishops mostly addressed to J. Jackson, Bishop of London, mainly interesting as autographs and including letters c.1864-77 from bishops in Australia and New Zealand. ff.50-76, papers 1853-1904 of Edmund Hobhouse, Bishop of Nelson.

MS.1751 Miscellaneous Guard-book 1820-1932. Letters and papers of P. C. Claughton include letters from: ff.77-8 M. B. Hale 1862, ff.92-3 G. A. Selwyn 1863 and ff.98-9 E. W. Tufnell 1867.

MS.1809 Correspondence of Charles Pourtales Golightly includes ff.81-6 letters 1878-81 from G. H. Stanton, Bishop of North Queensland.

MSS.1861-75 Selborne Papers

See E. G. W. Bill, *Catalogue of the Papers of Roundell Palmer (1812-1895) First Earl of Selborne*, London 1967. The papers were used by Lord Selborne in *Memorials Family and Personal, 1766-1865, Memorials Personal and Political, 1865-1895*, London 1896-8, 4 vols.

1861. f.97 letter 1844 from G. A. Selwyn.

1862. f.172 letter 1868 from G. A. Selwyn.

1868. ff.218-25, 235-8, 245 letters 1883 from Sir Henry Parkes.

1870. ff.37-44 letters 1887 from C. Perry.

1872-5. Letters 1855-95 from Lord Selborne to Sir Arthur Hamilton-Gordon, 1st Baron Stanmore. The letters were exchanged for Gordon's letters to Selborne in 1916. Especially from 1874, particularly in MSS.1872-4, many letters discuss Gordon's problems in his official positions in Fiji, as High Commissioner of the Western Pacific and in New Zealand. For Gordon's letters 1855-95 to Selborne see B.M. Add. MSS.49217-20.

MSS.2184-213 Howley Papers including some of his widow's papers. Archbishop Howley's papers as Bishop of London are in the archives of the United Society for the Propagation of the Gospel q.v. His papers as Archbishop of Canterbury should repay examination but a list of the papers seen 1969 listed only a letter from Bishop Nixon in MS.2203.

MS.2218 ff.65-90. Letters of Archbishop Sumner to Labouchere.

LAMBETH CONFERENCE PAPERS

1867 and c. every ten years. Access is subject to forty years limitation and permission to consult the papers must be obtained from the Librarian.

LINNEAN SOCIETY
Burlington House, Piccadilly, London, W.1

Non-members may consult the Library by presenting a satisfactory reference or letter of introduction. An alphabetical name catalogue of manuscripts in loose-leaf binders is in progress and there are old indexes to correspondence 1790-1869 in an exercise book. There is also an exercise book containing a 'General Index 1790-1879', an index to correspondence 1870-9 and a list of miscellaneous papers. Notes of letters and manuscripts of Australian interest, compiled by Miss I. Leeson in 1927 are filed in the Mitchell Library, Sydney, which also has some transcripts. Selected papers have been microfilmed for the Australian Joint Copying Project.

ARCHIVES

Letters of interest from a policy, scientific, or historical point of view are filed and include:

John Lewis, Swan River, 29 Apr. 1836 concerning a cask of botanical specimens bequeathed to the Linnean Society by Alexander Collie, surgeon R.N., who died at King George Sound 8 Nov. 1835, also letter 7 Aug. 1837 from London agent.

Dr John Lhotsky, Soho, biographical sketch of Ferdinand Bauer. Manuscript of paper communicated to the Society by the Secretary 18 June 1839, see *Linnean Society of London Procs.* I, Nov. 1838 to June 1848, pp.39-40, also letter 17 Mar. 1839 to Lhotsky from Franz Bauer, Kew, correcting Lhotsky's manuscript biography of his brother.

Sir John Eardley Eardley Wilmot, 16 Feb. 1846, written as President of the Royal Society of Van Diemen's Land asking for books.

Rev. William Woolls, Parramatta, 18 Dec. 1860 concerning articles he has sent.

Miscellaneous papers are numbered. They include lists of animals and birds from Australia given to Mr Leadbeater 'to be set up' 1818-21 (Nos.18, 36); descriptions of specimens from New Guinea by W. E. Leach, M.D. (No.22); and decisions concerning the arrears of George Bennett 1856 (No.55).

COLLECTIONS OF PAPERS

Ellis Manuscripts, 2 vols., 2 boxes. See *Catalogue of the Manuscripts of the Linnean Society of London, Part IV Calendar of Ellis Manuscripts*, London 1948. The correspondence and miscellaneous papers of John Ellis, F.R.S., include references in letters 1771 to Ellis from James Badenach, Dr William Brownrigg and James See to the arrival of the *Endeavour* and to seeds brought back by Solander; also six letters 1774 from Daniel Solander.

Macleay Correspondence presented by Sir George Macleay in 1886, 3 boxes. There is a list of letters in chronological order and the contents of the boxes are arranged alphabetically by name of writers. The letters are addressed partly to A. Macleay and partly to W. S. Macleay. Typescript copies of many of the letters of Australian interest are in the Mitchell Library, Sydney. The letters include:

Rev. James Backhouse, 1837, 1843, concerning plants.

Sir Joseph Banks, seven letters 1805-18.

Rt Rev. Frederic Barker, Bishop of Sydney and Metropolitan of Australia, 1856 concerning a proposed school in Sydney for clergymen's daughters, with a printed appeal for subscriptions.

Edward Barnard, Dec. 1824 concerning conditions at Sydney, a house available to the Colonial Secretary, his salary, etc.

Capt. Biden, 9 Apr. 1825 copy of letter concerning the appointment of Mr Rowe, assistant surgeon on the *Princess Charlotte*.

Bory St Vincent, 2 May 1825 concerning the collection of natural history objects in Australia.

Vice-Adm. Sir Courtenay Boyle, Navy Office, 8 Jan. 1825 urging Macleay to accept appointment in New South Wales, and 17 Mar. 1825 concerning the appointment of Mr Rutherford as surgeon.

Robert Brown, three letters 1840 mentioning John Lyall's going to Sydney and Mr Marsh, nephew of Benjamin Brodie, also asking for plants.

Rev. Buckland, Oxford, 1843 forwarding Professor Owen's report on mastodon remains sent by Sir Thomas Mitchell from the Darling Downs and concerning letter from Rev. T. Williams who had sent boxes of bones of a huge bird. Enclosures: letter from W. J. Broderip describing the bones and extract of letter from Professor Owen.

Charles Campbell, Duntroon, 1846 concerning the death of his father and his feelings towards Macleay.

Rev. W. B. Clarke, six letters 1843-52 on geological subjects.

Allan Cunningham, off Watson's Bay, on paper watermarked 1827, had seen a rare orchid in the grounds of Wentworth's cottage, The Retreat; was willing to take care of packet for Robert Brown.

Charles Darwin, May 1839 introducing Syms Corrington, an emigrant to Australia, who had been his servant on the *Beagle* and prepared his specimens.

Sir William Denison, Aug. 1855 concerning guns.

William Henry Fitton, two letters 1825, 1842 concerning the possible emigration of his son.

G. W. Sandels Gethethjerte, Sydney, 27 Feb. 1844 referring to the Australian Subscription Library and deprecating projected innovations.

Sir George Gipps, 20 May 1846 accepting Macleay's resignation as Speaker in the Legislative Council.

Dr J. E. Gray, two letters 18 June 1841, 15 Nov. 1844 concerning *inter alia* the purchase by the British Museum of Gould's collections and the publication of Clark Ross's voyages.

Thomas Cudbert Harington, of the New Zealand Company. Printed testimonials 1842-3 from Sir Ralph Darling and others connected with his claim for increased salary while assistant to the Colonial Secretary of New South Wales, also letters 1858-9.

Rev. C. J. Hoare, Apr. 1829 introducing Archdeacon Broughton.

Sir James Everard Home, Sept. [1825?] asking for specimens and July 1845, H.M.S. *North Star*, Sydney, concerning the *Fly*, Capt. King and Gov. FitzRoy.

Sir William Jackson Hooker and Sir Joseph Dalton Hooker, letters 1817-24, 1832 to be delivered by Cunningham, 31 Mar. 1845 and Sept. 1845 concerning the curatorship of Sydney Botanic Gardens, the claims of Kidd and Leichhardt.

G. Howitt, Melbourne, two letters 1844 describing plants round Melbourne.

T. H. Huxley, Dec. 1850 describing his voyage home, concerning the publication of results of the voyage under Owen Stanley, the lodging of Stanley's collection in the British Museum, he might have been tempted to live in New South Wales.

J. Innes, Feb. 1825 recommending his son George at Bathurst, who was suffering losses of stock through the depredations of Aborigines.

David Jones, 18 Aug. 1857 concerning the closing of a road between his property and that of William Brown.

Robert L. King, Parramatta, 31 Dec. 1857 concerning his resignation from the Museum and his study of the genus *Eucalyptus*.

P. P. King, n.d. concerning a butterfly (wing enclosed).

William Lithgow, St Leonard's Lodge, 1859 refers to 'the hermitage where I have lived upwards of four years without having ever once visited the great world of Sydney'.

Robert Lowe, part of letter asking advice on houses in George Street, Sydney; had severed his connection with *The Times*.

London

Duncan Macarthur, three letters 1825 concerning A. Macleay's departure for New South Wales and giving advice on sheep to take out.

John Macarthur, two letters n.d. concerning emancipists, acquisition of land to secure privileges. One letter invited A. Macleay and his son to stay.

A. Macleay, 28 Dec. 1824 to Earl Bathurst, accepting the post of Colonial Secretary in New South Wales and asking for an appointment for his eldest son, also Bathurst's refusal 3 Jan. 1825.

E. Macleay, Mrs A. Macleay, Sydney, n.d. to W. S. Macleay, part of letter mentioning purchase of an estate, the grant at Elizabeth Bay and formation of the garden, and social events in Sydney; also 31 July 1837 concerning bad treatment of A. Macleay by the Governor. W. S. Macleay, 1839 to Shuckard concerning his voyage out; also two letters from Shuckard; also draft of letter 30 July 1845 from W. S. Macleay resigning trusteeship and membership of the Australian Club because of the treatment of Robert Lowe, and copy of a letter n.d. to James Macarthur criticising his actions.

F. J. McCrae, 331 Castlereagh Street, Sydney, 22 Feb. 1846 recommending a sea voyage for John Macleay. Intended to operate on Jane Macpherson 'tomorrow'.

J. A. I. Pancher, Tahiti, 1853 acknowledging a box of plants for the French Government gardens of which he was in charge and concerning his botanical studies.

Sir William Parry, 12 Aug. 1833 concerning a petition from the Port Stephens district.

Sir James Clark Ross, *Erebus* at Sydney, 27 Feb. 1844 invitation to dine on board and meet King.

Phillip [S.?] Sims, 9 Aug. 1841 concerning an article by him in the *Sydney Morning Herald* on Ross's voyage.

Sir John Sinclair, 30 Jan. 1825 concerning Macleay's appointment in New South Wales, suggesting the colony's staple product should be wine, that the true silver rabbit, to be had in Lincolnshire, would be an asset to the colony and that the Carlisle Codlin would be a desirable apple to introduce; had heard from Sir Thomas Brisbane about stock subscribed for in the colony.

A. Smith, 1843 introducing Dr Dawson going to Sydney as principal medical officer, also 1848 introducing Dr Shanks to succeed Dawson. Asks for reptiles.

J. de C. Sowerby, Aug. 1847 expressing pleasure at news of Sydney Botanic Garden.

Sir Alfred Stephen, 16 May 1846 concerning A. Macleay's resignation of the Speakership, with draft of reply.

Adm. Sir James Stirling, 2 Dec. 1834, 20 Mar. 1835 asking for information on his grant at Bathurst.

Samuel Wilson, Dec. 1841 memo for D. Poole, Tahiti. Had conducted researches into the 'Traditionary History of the Polynesian Islands'. Miscellanea in Box 3 include accounts, some with illustrated bill heads, also:

List of shareholders 31 Dec. 1842.

Plan of Allandale Estate, farm of 5 acres no.325.

Plan of cabins of the *Duncan Dunbar*, 1500 tons, Henry Neatby commander.

The Smith Papers, 26 vols. See *Catalogue of the Manuscripts of the Linnean Society of London, Part I*, London 1934. The papers of Sir James Edward Smith, M.D., F.R.S., first President of the Royal Society, include letters from and relating to Sir Joseph Banks; fourteen letters 1806-25 from Robert Brown, a number of letters from other famous botanists concerning plant collecting in Australia and Pacific islands, many letters 1798-1825 from A. Macleay, eleven letters 1805-25 from Archibald Menzies, twenty-two letters from Thomas Pennant, 27 Oct. 1798 concerns wool-bearing animals.

Society for Promoting Natural History Records

This Society was founded in 1782. On 30 May 1822 a meeting of the Society resolved to hand all its assets to the Linnean Society of London. Records include Minute Books, rules with signatures of members, printed rules with lists of members, and a volume entitled 'Entering Book' in which a few letters and reports were transcribed.

Vol.II of the Minute Books contains a number of entries 1789-97, recording exhibition at meetings of objects from Australia and the Pacific. Between July and Dec. 1789 members saw exhibits sent by John White, surgeon, and other items were shown by Archibald Menzies, Everard Home, T. Wilson, Mr Winlaw, and Mr Spence. At the meeting of 8 Apr. 1793 H. Wood showed two drawings of 'natives of Botany Bay', a man and a woman, by Capt. Rye, made when a lieutenant on 'one of the ships that carried out the convicts'. At the meeting on 14 Dec. 1795 a letter was read from Capt. Paterson at 'Sidney Cove'. The letter is transcribed at the end of the minutes for this meeting. It is written 2 May 1794 to William Forsyth by the *William* leaving for the 'Southern Whale fishing'. The letter describes exploration on the Hawkesbury, discovery of the Grose, and the state of the colony.

Among records of the Society there is a separate 4to paper bearing a copy of part of a letter 23 Aug. 1790 from Norfolk Island. It is marked in a recent hand 'from Paterson' but Paterson did not arrive on the island till Oct. 1791. The letter describes the recall of King, arrival of Ross, and wreck of the *Sirius* in Mar. 1790, also the subsequent killing of large numbers of mutton birds to save the inhabitants from starvation.

Members of the Society with Australian and Pacific connections, with dates of their election are: Francis Grose 1785 and Everard Home 1783. Among honorary members are George Bass 1797, Archibald Menzies 1787, William Paterson 1785, John White 1789.

Swainson Correspondence, 5 vols. See catalogue in *Linnean Society of London Procs.*, 112th Session 1899-1900, pp.25-61. The correspondence of William Swainson includes letters from Sir Joseph Banks 1816-19, Allan Cunningham 1821-31, Richard Cunningham 1833, John Gould 1830-7, A. Macleay and W. S. Macleay 1816-38. Also letters from: Andrew Bloxam, *Blonde*, Valparaiso, 18 Sept. 1825, had visited the Sandwich Islands; also six letters 1825-6 several referring to collections from the Sandwich Islands.

Jabez Bunting, 1840 concerning missionary work in New Zealand.

D. Coates, 1840 concerning missionary work in New Zealand.

James Drummond, Swan River, 1 Nov. 1837 concerning collecting.

T. J. Ewing, Hobart, 9 Dec. 1837 on Tasmanian birds.

Sir William Jackson Hooker, a number of letters 1816-39. In letter 9 Mar. 1831 he gives his opinions of James Drummond.

T. J. Lempriere, six letters 1829-39 referring to cost of living and prospects for Swainson's son in the colony.

Sir John Richardson, a number of letters 1830-40. Letters in 1830 refer to James Drummond and in 1840 to his debt to Mr Lempriere in Van Diemen's Land.

Thomas Winter, Hobart, n.d. concerning the Tasmanian crow.

Thomas Woolcombe, Devonport, N.Z., 1840 concerning the Plymouth Company of New Zealand.

There are also letters from friends in England concerning Swainson's emigration to New Zealand in 1837, a letter 15 May 1839 from the British Museum declining to purchase his collection, and a manuscript 'found among Swainson's papers' entitled 'On the Botany of Tahiti' read before the Wellington Philosophical Society 1870 by W. B. D. Mantell, see *Trans. N.Z. Institute*, vi, App.

London

William Archer, original drawings of Tasmanian Orchideae by William Archer, F.L.S., of Cheshunt, Tas., 1848-56, with manuscript notes by Archer. Water-colours mounted in a folio vol.

James Backhouse, an enumeration of plants noticed by James Backhouse on visits to Moreton Bay and Lake Macquarie in 1836. In the same volume pp.50-1, 54-81 are parts of a draft list of Australian plants including plants from New South Wales, Van Diemen's Land, Norfolk Island, and a note on Swan River and South Australia.

Ferdinand Bauer, eight letters 1802-4 in German to his brother Franz, from the *Investigator*, Timor and Sydney.

Ferdinand Bauer, coloured drawing of *Lambertia formosa*, see Sir James Smith, 'The Characters of twenty new genera of plants', *Linnean Society of London Trans.* IV, pp.213-23. Bauer's drawing is the original for Tab.xx. On p.223 there is a note that the plate is 'from a Drawing made in New South Wales and corrected from wild Specimens'.

Ferdinand Bauer, *Illustrationes florae Novae Hollandiae*, London 1813, Sir James Smith's copy with manuscript index at end.

Emilia F. Noel, Wild Flowers of Western Australia. Water-colour sketches, named, 1939. One of six small 8vo vols. presented by Miss Noel in 1949.

Daniel Solander, manuscript on shells, Humphrey's copy.

George Suttor, 'Notes on the Forest Trees of Australia'. Received 14 June, read 20 June 1843, unpublished.

Alfred Russel Wallace, Journals 1856-61, 4 vols., Lists of Australian birds and hardy plants, notebook on 'Butterflies of Malay Archipelago' and notebook 1855-9.

THE EARL OF LIVERPOOL
Flat 111, 24 John Islip Street, London, S.W.1

The papers of the Earls of Liverpool (second creation) are in the possession of the Earl of Liverpool but are not available for inspection. They include:

Letters 1863-7 of Cecil George Savile Foljambe, created Viscount Hawkesbury and First Earl of Liverpool 1905. The letters were written to his mother, Viscountess Milton, while a midshipman on H.M.S. *Curaçoa* and describe service with the naval brigade in New Zealand 1863-4 and experiences on cruises to Sydney, Hobart, Adelaide, Melbourne, to various parts of New Zealand and to the Pacific islands. The letters, omitting personal passages and using exclusively the diary contained in them, were published, C. G. S. Foljambe, *Three Years on the Australian Station, For Private Circulation*, London 1868. See also *The Philatelist*, Dec. 1967, pp.72-4 and Jan. 1968, pp.110-11.

Papers of Sir Arthur William de Brito Savile Foljambe, Second Earl of Liverpool including papers relating to his term of office as Governor and Governor-General of New Zealand 1912-20. In later years Lord Liverpool retained a keen interest in New Zealand and in its army.

LLOYD'S
London, E.C.3

Application for permission to consult records should be made to the Librarian and Curator. Records include:

Underwriter's risk books, giving date, insurance taken out, name of ship, ports of embarkation and disembarkation, nature of goods insured, broker, amount insured, rate of insurance, and premiums paid. Details of claims and settlements are included in some volumes. The risk books form a miscellaneous collection from underwriters connected with Lloyd's and include references to voyages made to Australia and the Pacific.

Lloyd's List 1743- . Printed list of ship arrivals and sailings arranged under port and giving date of arrival and sailing, port of embarkation or destination, and name of master. Also gives details of wrecks, founderings, and vessels sighted. Complete sets of *Lloyd's List* are rare.

MELANESIAN MISSION
121 Kennington Road, London, S.E.11

The Melanesian Mission was initiated in 1849 by George Augustus Selwyn, first Bishop of New Zealand, and its headquarters are in Auckland, N.Z. The London office is mainly concerned with forwarding supplies and raising finance. The minutes and correspondence of the Mission in Britain are not available for inspection, but the London office contains other items of interest about which inquiries should be made in writing to the General Secretary.

Draft letter n.d. Commodore Goodenough to the Admiralty objecting to and making comments on Parliamentary Paper Cd. 1114 concerning Goodenough's role in the cession of Fiji to Britain. Letter 20 Oct. 1875 Admiralty to Mrs Goodenough transmitting copy letter 26 Oct. 1875 from the Under-Secretary of State for the Colonies concerning the Earl of Carnarvon's reaction to the late Commodore Goodenough's views. Goodenough's personal journal 28 Mar. 1861 to 11 Jan. 1862 being mainly a record of a voyage up the China coast.

Handwritten copies of letters 1887-8 Dr Henry Welchman of Bugotu, [New Hebrides?] to his mother.

Journals 1889-1908 of Dr Henry Welchman, 12 vols. These give a general day to day account of life in the Melanesian Islands, recording treatment of diseases and incidents in his life as missionary and teacher.

Letters 1868-70 from Bishop Hobhouse to Bishop Patteson, typescript copies and originals, lent by Miss D. Hobhouse. These letters are written from Reading and mainly give news of events in England and of Bishop Selwyn at Lichfield. They include a typescript page headed 'Norfolk Island 3 Nov. 1863'.

List of workers on the Melanesian Mission from the time of Bishop Selwyn.

'Chapter VI George Augustus Selwyn Pioneer and Statesman', no author given.

Letter Apr. 1847 from J. C. Patteson to Joan [?].

Bishop Patteson's Greek Testament with manuscript notes.

Typescript copies of letters 15 Jan. 1946 to 13 Sept. 1949 from Nell Fagan and other women missionaries in Melanesia to Miss M. Rice.

Printed material includes:
The Southern Cross Log 1895-1918, 11 vols. New Series 1923-9, 1 vol. Auckland and Sydney.
Southern Cross Log 1901-2, 1911-66, printed for English supporters of the Mission, 22 vols.
Annual Reports 1901-39 (1917, 1923 missing), 27 vols.
Bound volumes of occasional papers printed by the Mission include, in volumes issued from time to time, reports 1864-1900, occasional papers 1892-6 and *The Island*

London

Voyage 1874-95, a printed journal of the Bishop and other missionaries describing travel and progress of the Mission.

METHODIST MISSIONARY SOCIETY
25 Marylebone Road, London, N.W.1

The Society has almost complete records for which there are brief typescript lists called 'Box Lists'. An account of the Society is given in G. G. Findlay and W. W. Holdsworth, *The History of the Wesleyan Methodist Missionary Society*, London 1921-4, 5 vols. A list entitled *Ministers and Probationers of the Methodist Church, formerly Wesleyan, Primitive and United Methodist* is published from time to time. It includes an alphabetical list of deceased ministers giving date of commencement of ministry and date of death.

The Australasian Conference of the Methodist Church was formed in 1855 and took over the Pacific field so that the bulk of the records in London relating to that field cease at that date, although a few references and relevant documents occur in continuing records, particularly committee minutes and out-letters. The records and papers relating to Australia, New Zealand, and the Pacific Islands are found among minutes, in-letters, out-letters, candidates' papers, ship records, legal records, personal papers, minutes of meetings of former branches of the Methodist Church, and some broken runs of the periodical publications issued by these branches. Most of this material was listed in 1957 by a New Zealand scholar, Mrs M. H. Alington, and microfilmed for Australia and New Zealand. In 1958 additional papers and miscellanea were listed and microfilmed. Photocopies of all lists can be consulted at the National Library of Australia and other libraries holding microfilms. There are sixty-nine reels of microfilm and larger negatives of selected portraits and sketches. Material listed by Mrs Alington is on reels 1-54 and additional material on reels 55-69.

Transcripts of some of the Society's early records relating to Australia made by James Bonwick are now in the Mitchell Library, Sydney, together with photostats of correspondence before 1938 relating to Australasia and the Pacific Islands. Since the latter were made, the records have been reorganised. See also under In-letters, Fiji, below.

MINUTES, LONDON

Committee Minutes 1798-   . The main series of minutes of meetings in London. Notes of references to Australia, New Zealand, and the Pacific Islands 1798-1865 are given in Mrs Alington's list. The earliest volume 1798, 1804-16 is called Missionary Committee Minute Book. There is a second version of the minutes 1814-15 apparently founded on the volume 1798, 1804-16 in a second minute book entitled 'Minutes of the Executive Missionary Committee and copies of letters on missionary business. Begun Sept. 2, 1814. By James Buckley, Secretary'. In this volume the 1814-15 minutes are followed by minutes and copies of out-letters to 26 Feb. 1819.

Other minutes of meetings in London are Rough Minute Books 1808-84, 10 vols. Minutes of secretaries' (or officers') meetings 1-18, 1838-1952 (1891-7 missing) and minutes of various committees, including Finance Committee minutes 1825-1931, 7 vols.

DISTRICT MINUTES 1822-55

These are minutes of meetings of committees in various districts overseas accompanied by annual reports. Minutes and reports for 1829-32 are not extant.

Australia, Van Diemen's Land, and New Zealand. Nearly complete runs, 1822-55 and Perth Circuit report 30 Sept. 1859, also Swan River 1862 and a bundle of papers on the formation of Conference 1854. With the minutes are nearly complete runs of annual reports from New South Wales 1824-52/3, New Zealand 1834-52/3, Van Diemen's Land 1836-52/3, and from Victoria and South Australia 1851-5. There is a bundle of accounts for 1838.

Fiji and Friendly Islands. Nearly complete runs, Friendly Islands 1827-55, Fiji 1836-54. With the minutes are annual reports for the Friendly Islands 1833-52 and for Fiji 1836-54. There is a bundle of accounts for the Fiji district 1838-40 and a statement of accounts for Fiji 1844. The minutes of Fiji district meetings at Rewa 7 May 1839, Lakemba 6 July 1839, Viwa 14 Aug. 1844 and 21-9 June 1852 are in the Mitchell Library, Sydney, and the Society holds negative photostats.

IN-LETTERS

Although in-letters are arranged by districts in which missionaries were stationed, their subject matter is not confined to the particular district. The Australian letters, for example, include letters concerning New Zealand, the Fijian, and the Friendly Islands. Letters listed by Mrs Alington cover 1812-c.1889. The main series is filed in boxes:

Australia 1812-89. Letters 1837-42 include papers concerning the mission to the Aborigines, letters 1851-9 include three private letters from Joseph Albiston 1854-5.

Tasmania 1823-57, 1861-76.

New Zealand 1819-82. Attached to letter 26 May 1859 from T. Buddle, Onehunga, are nos.1-2, Apr.-May 1859 of *Te Haeata*, Akarana.

Friendly Islands 1822-75. Early letters include some 1831-5 from J. Watkin to J. Entwisle; Parliamentary Paper, *Sir C. Mitchell . . . Recent disturbances in . . . Tonga . . . July 1887*; letters and papers 1837-48 from the Friendly Islands and letters 1841 concerning difficulties in Samoa, the French visit to Vavau, and French possessions in Oceania and including letters from Richard Burdsall Lyth and Peter Turner.

Fiji c.190 letters 1835-84. The main series from Fiji has been presented to the Mitchell Library, Sydney. The Society has five boxes of negative photostats of the original letters. A few letters have been found since these photostats were made.

Samoa 1834-70.

New Britain 1878-81.

A few additional letters were found after Mrs Alington had completed her list and will be sorted eventually into their proper files. When found they were placed in five folders labelled Australia, Tasmania, New Zealand, Friendly Islands, and Fiji. The letters in these five folders are microfilmed in reel 55 and contained when filmed:

Folder 1, Australia. Twenty-six letters 1838-85.

Folder 2, Tasmania. Three letters 1832, two from Jane B. Waterhouse and one from Jabez Bunting Waterhouse, Hobart, to Rev. Jabez Bunting, London.

Folder 3, New Zealand. Nine letters 1835-69 including letters from J. Wallis and J. H. Bumby.

Folder 4, Friendly Islands. One letter 1848 from R. Amos to Rev. J. E. Coulson, Boston. Also a printed map of the Friendly Islands 1854.

Folder 5, Fiji. Eight letters 1840-7.

OUT-LETTERS

Copies of out-letters are in chronological order in volumes, each of which has an

London

index. Mrs Alington's list gives notes of letters concerning Australia, New Zealand, and Pacific Islands contained in volumes covering 1814-67.

Out-letters 1814-19 are to be found in the second committee minute book 2 Sept. 1814 to 26 Feb. 1819, see Minutes (London) above. There is also a separate extra volume of out-letters 1816-20. An 1820 letter book on thin paper is illegible and not microfilmed. Elijah Hoole's letter book 1834-61 occurs among out-letters.

CANDIDATES' PAPERS

These give brief biographical information about missionaries especially up to the time of their acceptance by the Society and include:

Minutes of meetings of the Preachers of the London Districts for examination of missionary candidates 1829-41, and minutes of the Discipline Committee 1843-64, 1 vol.

Bundles of letters of recommendation, letters from candidates 1833-69, 1 box.

Volume labelled 'Missionary candidates' 1844-56.

Book of rough notes on candidates 1836-9.

Examination of missionary candidates 1840-6, 1850, 7 vols.

Letter 30 June 1846 from the Bristol District concerning George Daniel.

There are also lists of missionaries not so far microfilmed for Australia and New Zealand:

'List of Missionaries & their Stations' 1785-1828, 1 vol. The title has been added in pencil on the flyleaf. The missionaries are in numerical order and there is a name index.

Lists of missionaries 1785-1860 arranged by district, 1 vol. Most of the volume is blank, a few pages filled for each district, the title of each section being written in pencil. A list of 'Missionaries sent to Australia & South Seas' 1814-53 is included.

'A Record of Missionaries &c. sent out by the Wesleyan Missionary Society from 1769 to 1863 showing their Destination; dates of Departure & Arrival; Return, Time & Place of Death &c., preceded by an Alphabetical List', 1 vol. The title page is original and a note has been added stating that the list is 'superseded'.

Folder containing typescript lists and statistics of missionaries to c.1910.

SHIP RECORDS

Minutes of the Ship Committee 1842-55, minutes of meeting 27 July 1841 inserted in front, 1 vol. The 1841 meeting refers to 'proceedings of the Ship Committee at their three meetings in May 1841'. The volume ends with the handing over of the management of the ship to the Australasian Missionary Committee.

Extracts from the minutes of the Ship Committee 1845-8, also extracts from the minutes of the Australasian Missionary Committee and from those of the Home General Committee and Finance Sub-Committee 1856-62, 14 items, not microfilmed.

Papers relating to the *Triton*, built in 1838, bought by the Wesleyan Missionary Committee in 1839, and used in the South Seas Mission until 1847, including log books 1839-47 of voyages in the South Seas; papers concerning the outfit and management of the ship including a file giving dimensions, sails, etc.; papers concerning crew and passengers with instructions to Capt. Beatty and passengers, also papers 1840-5 concerning Capt. G. Buck and Mrs Buck; papers 1839-46 concerning provisions and stores; 'The work and voyage of the Triton' by Walter Lawry, Sydney, 1844.

Papers relating to the *John Wesley I* including letters and papers 1845-6 concerning the building of the ship, plan, list of sails, and accounts; log book 1846-59 of voyages to the Friendly Islands and Fiji; letters and papers 1846-64 concerning the management of the ship; letters and papers concerning the transfer of the ship to the Australasian Conference in 1856.

Papers relating to the *John Wesley II* including agreement for building 24 Oct. 1866.

Miscellaneous papers concerning other ships, including inventory 1837 of the *Heber* of Bristol, printed, a list of the crew of the *Heber* on a voyage to New South Wales and India 1837-8 and a copy of the *Sunderland Herald* 6 Dec. 1861 containing a notice to mariners.

LEGAL RECORDS

These include 'Draft Petition to His Excellency The Governor of New South Wales', n.d., requesting removal of the chapel in Macquarie Street to a more favourable site; 'Gift of land in Feejee by Mr. J. B. Williams, 1857', deed of John Brown Williams, U.S. consul in New Zealand and commercial agent for the Fiji Islands, accompanied by a letter 12 Jan. 1857 from J. B. Williams, Fiji; many copies of deeds relating to land in New Zealand 1829-50. There are also: 'Copy of a deed dated 20 Nov 1895, transferring United Methodist Free Church property in New Zealand to the newly formed united church in that colony'; and 'Copy of deed of conveyance to representatives of the Methodist Conference of O'Brian's Bridge Wesleyan Methodist Mission Chapel, District of Glenorchy, Van Diemen's Land. Dated 28th April 1831'.

PERSONAL PAPERS

Eight boxes called 'Biographical'.

Boxes 1-4. James Calvert Papers 1838-92. Calvert was a missionary in Fiji 1838-66. Box 1 contains his journals Mar. 1838-86 (broken series), biographical notes, Mary Calvert's journal June 1863 to May 1866, a few letters to Calvert and miscellaneous private papers. Box 2 contains notebooks and miscellaneous papers including notebooks on Fiji, a bundle of notes and copies of letters 1839-86 and manuscript periodicals 'The Lakemba Note' 5 June 1845 to 7 Dec. 1847, 'The Vewa Record', 1, 24 May 1850 to 1 May 1854, 'The Nandy Chronicle', 3, 6 May 1852. Box 3 contains personal papers and correspondence including letters: 1839-48 Calvert to J. Hunt, 1861-6 to G. S. Rowe, 1837-50 James and Mary Calvert (née Fowler) to Philip Fowler and family; other letters from James and Mary Calvert, also letter books c.1854-64. Also in Box 3 are letters including: 1844 R. B. Lyth to J. Hunt, 1848 Hunt to Capt. Worth, 1851 Mary Ann Lyth to Mr Farmer, 1855 Elizabeth Brooking to Mrs Farmer, 1855, 1858 to J. Thomas. Box 4 contains cuttings 1855-1916 on Fiji.

Box 5. John Hunt Papers 1833-68. Hunt was a missionary in Fiji 1838-48. The papers include journals 1838-47 and correspondence 1833-68.

Box 6. Papers of John H. Bumby, R. B. Lyth, Joseph Orton; extracts from the 1829 journal of Nathaniel Turner, missionary in Fiji 1828-31; Henry Hanson Turton, memo on the *Triton* and a memoir (1861) of John Polglase, missionary in Fiji 1851-60, by J. S. Fordham, missionary in Fiji 1853-62.

The papers of J. H. Bumby consist of twenty-two letters from or about Bumby in New Zealand 1838-57.

The papers of R. B. Lyth, missionary in Fiji 1836-55 include letter books Dec. 1836 to Sept. 1855 and letters and other papers 1843-7. There is also a microfilm of R. B. Lyth's letters 1829-56 to his family and a letter 12 Dec. 1952 from M. L. Early to Miss Longstaff giving biographical information about the wife of R. B.

London

Lyth. The originals of the letters on the microfilm are in the possession of Mrs D. V. Crawford, Loughborough, Leics. q.v.

The papers of J. Orton consist of a journal 1795 to Jan. 1832 containing biographical notes and four small notebooks on South Sea Islands (mostly Friendly Islands) labelled 'probably Jos. Orton'. No.4 gives an account of the Chevalier Dillon's behaviour.

The H. H. Turton papers connected with the *Triton* are 'Tritonia: or memoranda of the first voyage of the Wesleyan missionary ship "Triton" from England to New Zealand in 1839-40. To which are added Hints for intending missionaries and emigrants. By a New Zealand missionary', with a second incomplete copy.

Boxes 7-12. John Thomas Papers 1821-75. These are the papers of John Thomas, missionary in Tonga and Fiji 1825-60 and those of his wife Sarah (née Hartshorn). They include journals of J. Thomas, volumes of his writings on Tonga; photographs, prints and drawings, and an inventory of the papers.

MISCELLANEA

Correspondence with Government Departments. 14 Oct. 1861 H. M. Denham, R.N., to the Society concerning exploring expedition to the Fiji Islands and correspondence 1827-77 between the Colonial Office and the Society concerning Van Diemen's Land, New Zealand, and the South Sea Islands.

Other papers. Copy of report of the trial 'The King against Dillon', Hobart, 24 Apr. 1827 copied from the *Hobart Town Gazette* 28 Apr. 1827, letter 23 Sept. 1850 King George of Tonga to his son. The Society also holds a letter 1841 from John Thomas, Tonga, in the Steele collection Box 4, and notes and transcripts: summary of business relating to foreign missions in the Minutes of Conference 1790-1900; articles, notes, photographs, 1832-42 relating to the Rev. Charles Tucker in the Friendly Islands.

Portraits, sketches, etc.
Four framed portraits, Rev. Samuel Leigh, Rev. J. H. Bumby, Rev. J. Hunt and Rev. Dr F. Langham.
Three framed pictures, Hongi and Waikato, oil paintings; Rev. J. Waterhouse superintending the landing of missionaries at Taranaki, N.Z., Baxter print, 1844; the *Triton*, water-colour, with a plan and cross section of the vessel.
Portfolio of drawings, etc., containing a folder labelled 'Australasia' and including water-colours of Bruair and Warnbela, Australian Aborigines, signed Browne; two water-colours 1823 by S. Leigh of the New Zealand King Tabooha and his brother George; Tamati Waka Nene, New Zealand chief, water-colour; also views 1842 of mission stations in New Zealand, of the Wesleyan mission premises Somosomo, Fiji, by Mrs R. B. Lyth, and of Macquarie Harbour, the last a water-colour signed T. J. Lempriere.

MS. map of Fiji Islands, c.1840, on parchment.
Photographs of missionaries, of King George of Tonga, Thakombau, etc.

Sets of missionary journals and a small collection of printed books. Some are rare and a microfilm copy has been made of selected items.

MINUTES, ETC., OF FORMER BRANCHES OF THE METHODIST CHURCH

Methodist New Connexion. Minutes 8 Aug. 1844 to 12 June 1883, 6 Feb. 1896 to 18 June 1908, 4 vols. This branch started work in Australia about 1844 and in New Zealand in 1865.

Bible Christians. Minutes 15 Aug. 1861 to 28 July 1873, July 1882 to 27 July 1891, 3 Nov. 1903 to 22 Oct. 1909, 3 vols. *The Bible Christian Magazine, being a continuation of the Arminian Magazine* 32-86, London 1853-1907, incomplete. This branch started work in Australia in 1850 and in New Zealand in 1877.

United Methodist Free Church. To 1857 called Wesleyan Methodist Association. Minutes 5 Oct. 1869 to 6 June 1883, 16 Oct. 1900 to 10 June 1908. Report of the home and foreign missions, vols.22-51, 1878-1907. *The Missionary Echo of the United Methodist Free Churches* 1-39, London 1894-1932. This branch started work in Tasmania in 1838, in Australia in 1849, and in New Zealand in 1864.

United Methodist Church. The above three branches were united in this church in 1907. Minutes 20 Oct. 1908 to 23 Oct. 1923, 4 June 1925 to 26 Apr. 1927, 2 vols. Report of the missions (home and foreign) vol.1 [1908]-1932.

NATIONAL MARITIME MUSEUM
Greenwich, London, S.E.10

A summary catalogue of manuscripts is maintained and some calendars and indexes have been prepared, see also K. Lindsay-MacDougall, *A Guide to the Manuscripts at the National Maritime Museum*, 1960. For documents relating to the Pacific voyages of Captain James Cook see *The Journals . . . of Cook*, ed. Beaglehole.

NATURAL COLLECTIONS

OFFICIAL RECORDS, ADMIRALTY

Records deposited by arrangement with the Admiralty and the Public Record Office. A great part of Admiralty orders and Navy Board Letters is duplicated in department letter books at the Public Record Office and some sections of series listed below as ADM/A-F and J are in the Public Record Office. Particular documents cited in the following entries are examples only.

ADM/A Navy Board In-letters, Admiralty Orders, General, 1688-1815, 1356 vols.

ADM/B, ADM/BP Admiralty In-letters from Navy Board, General, 1738-1831, 136 vols.

ADM/C Victualling Board In-letters, Admiralty Orders, 1707-1815, 400 vols.

ADM/D, ADM/DP Admiralty In-letters from Victualling Commissioners, 1703-1809 and 1809-22, 51 vols. and 56 bundles.

ADM/E Sick and Hurt Board In-letters, Admiralty Orders, General, 1702-1806, 54 vols.

For the remainder of the series see under Transport Board below, ADM/ET. The Transport Board took over responsibility for sick and hurt seamen in 1806.

ADM/E44A, Jan. 1784 to Dec. 1793, includes among other relevant documents 22 Mar. 1787, Phillip granted extra portable soup; 24 July 1789, bill drawn by Hunter, *Sirius*, for quarters for the sick sent ashore at the Cape; 16, 22 Oct. 1790, Capt. Edwards, H.M.S. *Pandora*, supplied with Peruvian bark, rob of lemons, portable soup, common black tea.

ADM/ET Transport Board In-letters, Admiralty Orders, General, 1807-15, 9 vols.

ADM/ET/59. 26 Nov. 1813 Sir John Jamison, physician, R.N., granted two years' leave of absence on half pay to enable him to visit his property in New South Wales.

ADM/F, ADM/FP Admiralty In-letters from Sick and Hurt Commissioners, 1742-1806, 35 vols. and 49 bundles.

ADM/G Victualling Board In-letters, Abstract of Admiralty Orders, 1694-1819, 26 vols.

ADM/J Admiralty Out-letters to Navy Board, Ticket Office Orders, 1774-1815, 106 vols.

London

ADM/J/3931. Aug. 1786 to Apr. 1787 includes letters and orders Oct.-Dec. 1786 relating to *Sirius* and *Supply*.

ADM/L Lieutenants' Logs 1678-1809, 5025 vols.

Some captains' logs are included but most captains' and masters' logs are in the Public Record Office.

ADM/OT Navy Board, In-letters, Treasury Orders, Transports, 1783-9, 1 vol.

Includes documents concerning supplies and accommodation for marines and convicts in the First Fleet to New South Wales.

ADM/RP Navy Board, In-letters, Admiralty Orders, Transports, 1793-7, loose papers in five solander cases.

OFFICIAL RECORDS, MERCHANT NAVY

The official records were centralised under the Registry of Shipping and Seamen in 1872. There are good personnel records from 1850 when the Board of Trade assumed responsibility for the organisation of merchant seamen. A selection of records is deposited on loan by the Registry of Shipping and Seamen.

RSS/1 Registry of Ships at British Ports, 1814-26, 12 vols.

RSS/2 London Registers. Foreign going ships, 1787-1800, Coasting ships 1786-1801, 6 vols., 2 vols.

RSS/3 Plantation and Colonial Registers. Annual lists, 1807-11, 1817-20, 1824-6, 1836-7, 1844-5, 1852, 1855, Copies of certificates of British registry 1812, 1817, 1821, 1825, 1828, 1832, 1835, 1838, 1844, 1854, 7 vols., 11 vols.

Annual lists give an account of the numbers of vessels in colonial ports on 31 Dec. of each year listing ships lost or re-registered and giving year and number of the certificate of registry, master's name, tonnage, and crew numbers.

Copies of certificate of British registry give details of ownership, where built, serving officers and physical description. The register for 1824 contains only one ship, *Australian*, at Hobart. Over half the ships in the 1840 register are from Australian and New Zealand ports, about ninety-two from Sydney, twenty-eight from Bruni Island and Hobart Town, sixteen from Launceston, eight from Adelaide, four from Melbourne, and two from Russell, N.Z.

RSS/10 Log Books and Crew Lists, 1884-1940, 37 logs.

Includes a few logs of ships bound for Australia or engaged in voyages to the Antarctic.

RSS/11 Certificates of Competency of Service, 1850-1921, 55 certificates.

RSS/12 Miscellaneous Documents and Specimen Forms

RSS/12/C. Documents 1851-4 relating to the mercantile marine service of Arthur Orton, later claimant in the Tichborne case.*

RSS/13 Official Logs, Cutty Sark, 14 Feb. 1870 to 21 Oct. 1874, 5 books.

RSS/14 Crew Lists, Cutty Sark, 1870-95, 21 lists.

BOT/W Board of Trade Registers and Indexes of Wrecks, 1855-98, 30 vols.

On loan from the Board of Trade. Arranged roughly alphabetically in chronological volumes, many with indexes.

OFFICIAL RECORDS, ROYAL NAVY DOCKYARDS

Chatham Dockyard 1672-1900, *c.*1000 vols.
Portsmouth Dockyard 1693-1900, *c.*450 vols.

Both these collections contain material of general interest on such subjects as the fitting of ships destined for the Australia and Pacific Stations and the supply of equipment to ships or to the colonial governments.

SEMI-PUBLIC RECORDS

LLY *Lloyd's Register of Shipping*

Surveyors' reports and plans of ships which date from the publication of the re-constituted Register of Shipping in 1834. At first the papers were arranged chrono-logically under the ports of survey, with plans separated from reports, and with an index of ships' names, LLY/IND/1-8. After 1914 the system was altered and papers were arranged alphabetically by name of ship. Surveyors were appointed to foreign ports from the mid-nineteenth century, including Australian and New Zealand ports from 1871-3, and their reports were sent to London. Only the first and any subsequent report which covered some important alteration, together with plans, if any, have been preserved. Lloyd's records are deposited on loan and include: LLY/1104 Auckland 1876-91; LLY/1108 Brisbane 1891; LLY/1110 Dunedin 1883-5; LLY/1111 Fremantle 1897-8; LLY/1125 Hobart 1876-9; LLY/1127 Melbourne 1872-96; LLY/1152 Sydney 1872-82; LLY/1157 Wellington 1889.

LLY/W *Lloyd's Records of Ships Wrecked 1901-* , 474 boxes.

Reports and correspondence kept under the name of the ship at the time of the casualty, filed alphabetically within the groups, which became due for transference from time to time. Reports were previously filed under ports of survey. There is a complete list of files which are housed in numbered boxes. Files usually include first entry reports, plans and correspondence, the place and number of the last report and a brief statement of the circumstances of the loss.

PERSONAL PAPERS

Aldrich, Adm. Pelham. ALD/1 Extracts from his log 1872-5 as first lieutenant in the *Challenger*.

Barlow, Vice-Adm. C. J. BAR/3 Captain's journal 1889-92, H.M.S. *Orlando*, Hobart, Auckland, Sydney.

Baynes Papers include BAY/104 Letters received, also notes and memoranda, from Adm. Sir Joseph Nias among which, in a statement of his service as captain of H.M.S. *Herald*, is an account of service in New Zealand 1840.

Bedford, Adm. Sir Frederick George Denham. BED/6 Diary 1879 of H.M.S. *Triumph* including a visit in April to the Hawaiian Islands.

Bellasis Papers. Papers of Richard Aldworth Oliver.

BEL/52 Collection of Admiral's general orders and memoranda 1840-50 with index, including memos from J. E. Erskine, *Havannah*, Sydney: 6 May 1849 giving an extract of a report of Lieut. C. B. Yule, *Bramble*, to Owen Stanley on a shoal north of Port Jackson; 11 Jan. 1850 enclosing letters from the New South Wales Colonial Secretary and Jacob Inder & Co., traders, about the piratical seizure of the schooner *Ellen* by her crew when en route for Moreton Bay; also from J. E. Erskine, *Havannah*, Wellington, 2 Feb. 1850 listing the mutineers who landed the passengers, master, mate, and steward in New Zealand.

BEL/53 Letter book 1847-51, H.M. sloop *Fly*, Cmdr R. A. Oliver, with index, con-cerning chart making in New Zealand waters, including despatch 10 June 1850 about the situation in the New Hebrides.

BEL/54 Private journal 1848-9 of R. A. Oliver describing arrival in New Zealand, skirmishes with the Maoris Sept. 1849 and criticising Wakefield's theories. Unfinished.

Bethune, Capt. Henry L. BET/8 Log and journal Nov. 1883 to Feb. 1886 kept by

London

Bethune in H.M.S. *Constance* visiting Easter Island, Pitcairn, Hawaii, and other Pacific islands.

Blake, Capt. William Hans. BLK/1 Diary May-Aug. 1867 describing the visit of H.M.S. *Falcon* to Tahiti and return to Australia; BLK/5 Letter book, *Falcon* 1866-7; BLK/7 Collection of certificates, letters and orders 1846-74 relating to his career and referring to his service in New Zealand 1860, also report of the inquiry 4 Aug. 1867 into the capture and destruction of the brig *Curlew* and schooners *Mary Ida* and *Kate* by natives of the New Hebrides.

Bond, Rear-Adm. Francis Godolphin. BND/1 Letters including forty from Bligh with two draft replies by Bond. Three of Bligh's letters relate to the *Bounty* mutiny and twenty-eight to the second breadfruit expedition. These letters and notes are published in *Fresh Light on Bligh*, ed. G. Mackaness, Sydney 1953, Australian Historical Monograph no.29, copy at BND/3.

Bougainville, Louis Antoine de. BOG/3 Notes collected by Bougainville for his article on navigation, mostly concerning Arctic exploration but containing references to John Forster, who translated Bougainville's account of his voyage of circumnavigation 1766-9, and to Cook.

Bridge, Adm. Sir Cyprian. BRI/1-10, 12-13, 16 Papers while in command of the *Espiègle*, Australia Station, 1881-9, and commander-in-chief Australia Station 1894-8 including journals 1895-8, letter books 1881-5, letters and telegrams sent early 1898 and letters received 1895-8.

Carteret, Rear-Adm. Philip. CAR/5 Letters and notes about the *Swallow* including letters from Byron and a few pages from a rough log of the *Swallow* 1766-9; CAR/10b Notes on some points from Dalrymple's *Historical Collection of . . . voyages . . . in the South Pacific Ocean*, London 1770.

Cochrane Collection. COO/3/A Papers 1830 of Vice-Adm. W. Fitzwilliam Owen relative to survey work in Western Australia.

Dare, Capt. Joseph Stafford. DRE/5 Journals 1887 as mate in the barque *John Gambles*, Liverpool, Sydney, Newcastle and return, and 1888 in the *Astoria* to Newcastle.

Doughty, Rear-Adm. Frederic Proby. DTY/4-7 Captain's letter books 1882-6 H.M.S. *Constance* also Captain's order book 1883-6; DTY/8 Log 1852 of H.M.S. *Portland* on a visit to Pitcairn; DTY/11 Captain's journal 1882-3 H.M.S. *Constance*; DTY/12 Log book of H.M.S. *Constance*; DTY/15 the case against Lieut. T. Smith-Dorrien, first lieutenant-commander H.M.S. *Constance* 1884-5.

Edgell, Vice-Adm. Harry Edmund. EDG/1 Official out-letters 1855-6, H.M.S. *Tribune* including letter 10 Apr. 1857 reporting a stop at Honolulu for coaling.

Fisher, Rev. George. FIS/25 Observations of horizontal vibrations made in Cape Town, Sydney, Dunheved, and Victoria 1858.

Flinders, Capt. Matthew. Collection deposited on indefinite loan by Sir William Matthew Flinders Petrie and including besides maps, charts, and sketches:

FLI/1-14 Papers of Matthew Flinders, personal letters among which are thirty-five letters 1804-15 from M. Pitot; official letters 1801-12; copies of Flinders's letters 1795-1808 from a private letter book; journal and letter book 1806-7 incomplete; service, personal, legal, and business papers and technical memoranda.

FLI/8a Portion of a journal relating to the voyage in the *Providence* with Bligh.

FLI/9a Narrative of voyages in *Tom Thumb* Sept. 1795 to Apr. 1796, George's River and Port Hacking.

FLI/9b Narrative of expedition to Furneaux Island in the colonial schooner *Francis* Mar. 1798, copy, original in the State Library of Victoria.

FLI/25-31 Papers of Mrs Ann Flinders, letters 1799-1812 from Matthew Flinders, letters from Sir Joseph Banks and others and drafts of letters c.1820-32 by Mrs Ann Flinders mostly undated.

FLI/101-10 Papers of Professor Sir William M. Flinders Petrie, correspondence 1875-80 with J. J. Shillinglaw about a projected book on Flinders, correspondence 1873-80 with his mother mostly about her father Matthew Flinders, notes and memoirs of Flinders, photographs, articles, etc.

Franklin, Sir John. FRN/1-26 Letters 1828-9 to his niece referring to his Arctic expeditions with occasional references to the South Seas.

Fraser, John, marine artist. FSR/3 Letters to John Fraser from his brother William Fraser, 14 June 1887 *Halcione*, Port Nelson, N.Z., and 14 Dec. 1888 barque *Merope*, Newcastle, N.S.W.

Fremantle, Adm. the Hon. Sir Edmund Robert. FRE/107a Bundle of private letters Feb. 1864 to May 1866 to his family while commander in H.M.S. *Eclipse*, Australia and New Zealand stations; FRE/107b, 117, 118a, 123, 125 letters received and letter books 1866-73 with notes and recollections relating to 1864-6 and FRE/unnumbered, loose papers 1865 relating to Coromandel, N.Z., copies.

Hamilton, Capt. Henry George. HTN/93a Forty letters 1839-43 to his family while sheep farming in New South Wales including six during his passage out in the *Union*, letters from Sydney after arrival, Camden, other places and Collaroy containing many references to George and Patrick Leslie; HTN/93b Further letters and extracts, copies.

Hamilton, Adm. Sir Louis Henry. HTN/217 Account of the mission to Australia Dec. 1945 to Apr. 1948 as a member of the Commonwealth Naval Board, typescript; HTN/226 Loose papers 1947 relating to the Commonwealth Defence Board.

Henderson, Vice-Adm. William Hannam. HEN/1/6 Correspondence 1869-70 as lieutenant in *Liverpool*, Flying Squadron cruise; HEN/1/10 Correspondence 1881-5 when commander in *Nelson*, flagship on Australia Station, also photograph album and copies of printed papers and articles in *Naval Review* 1923-4 on the Flying Squadron cruise.

Invernairn of Strathnairn, Lady Elspeth, née Tullis. IVR/1-11 include letters 1906-14 from Shackleton, three pen and ink sketches by E. A. Wilson and cuttings and miscellanea concerning the *Discovery* 1902, etc.

Kennedy, Capt. James B., R.N.R. KEN/1 Logs of three voyages in *Medway* 1849-52 England to Australia with description of taking emigrants to Port Phillip, log of *Aries* 1853-4 England to Australia; KEN/5 Logs 1862-3 *Racer* England to Melbourne, Melbourne to Calcutta, Melbourne to England; KEN/10 Letter book 1862-6 *Racer*; KEN/14 Account book 1857-67.

McClintock, Adm. Sir Leopold. McL/46 Letters and papers 1900 in the Antarctic.

Mackay, Dr Andrew. MKY/8 Letters 1787-1805 from Maskelyne, some relating to a proposal for Mackay to go on an expedition to Australia.

Maclear, Adm. John F. L. P. MAC/1 Magnetic journal Dec. 1872 to July 1876 H.M.S. *Challenger*; MAC/2-5 Captain's out-letter book 1878-82, journals 1879-81, work book 1879-81, H.M.S. *Alert* during her surveying voyage round the world and in Pacific and Australian waters 1879-81.

Malcolm, Vice-Adm. Sir Charles. MAL/5 In- and out-letter book 1829-37 including letter 27 Apr. 1831 to Lieut.-Gen. Darling and letter 12 Aug. 1830 from Sir Edward Owen giving news *inter alia* of settlers at Swan River, W.A.

London

May, Adm. Sir William Henry. MAY/5 Official log and journal 1869-70 H.M.S. *Liffey* during the world cruise of the Flying Squadron.

Montagu, John, 4th Earl of Sandwich. SAN/1-6 Notebooks of officers' appointments 1771-82, notes of biographical interest are written against some of the names including notes of P. Carteret, Tobias Furneaux and appointments of officers, mates, boatswains, etc., in Capt. Cook's ships.

North, Frederick. NOR/2-3 Journal H.M.S. *Alert* 1880-2; NOR/4 Photograph album. North was paymaster in the *Alert*.

Hornby, Adm. Sir Phipps. PHI/1 Admiral's journal Sept. 1847 to Mar. 1849 while in command of the Pacific Squadron. Most entries relate to South America but there are entries relating to Tahiti, the Sandwich and Navigator's Islands, entries 1 May 1848 special instructions *inter alia* for conduct of ships' officers and crews in Pacific Islands, 24 May 1848 Foreign Office instruction on redressing outrages, 27, 28 Sept. 1848 Capt. Worth, *Calypso* investigates murder at Fiji, reports on service in Pacific; PHI/2/1 Letter and order book Sept. 1847 to May 1851; PHI/2/2 Squadron letters 1847-51. Out-letter book; PHI/3/6 Loose papers including papers on the Sandwich and Society Islands and Capt. Fanshawe's last report on Pitcairn, despatches and documents 1847-9 concerning Pacific Islands; PHI/3/15 Letters from the Admiralty, Flag Officer's ruling 1848 concerning the Galapagos Islands, relations with French squadron 1848; PHI/3/16 Report 1851 on Pacific Islands, signed Barazer, in French.

Phipps Hornby, Adm. Sir Geoffrey Thomas. PHI/133a-d Scrapbooks of cuttings chiefly about the cruise of the Flying Squadron 1869-70.

Phipps Hornby, Adm. Robert Stewart. PHI/208 Letter book 1901-3, *Pylades*, Australian waters.

Phipps Hornby, Cmdr Windham Mark. PHI/305 Journal 1900 of a voyage to Australia kept by his father-in-law Mr Corbet, with photographs.

Purcell-Buret, Capt. Theobald John Claud. PUR/2-3 Diaries Jan.-June 1940, troop ship *Andes*, Marseilles, Hong Kong, New Zealand, for the first contingent of colonial troops.

Riou, Capt. Edward. RIO/1 Log of the *Guardian* 21 Apr. 1789 to 5 May 1790; RIO/3a-b Copy of memoirs written *c.*1856 by his niece.

Sharpe, Vice-Adm. Philip Ruffle. SHP/1-2, 13 Jottings 1831-53. Sharpe served under Owen Stanley on the *Rattlesnake*.

Smith-Dorrien, Adm. Arthur Hale. SMD/1 Scrapbooks, vol.1, 1865-87 contains sketches, water-colours, photographs, cuttings, and manuscript notes including some on Queen Emma, Sandwich Islands, expedition 1874 H.M.S. *Volage* to Kerguelen and visit 1877 of H.M.S. *Shah* to Pitcairn.

Stokes, Adm. John Lort. STK/1-55 Papers relating to H.M.S. *Beagle* consist of official logs 1837-43 when surveying on the Australian coast, out-letter book 1841-3, nautical remarks Bass Strait and Tasmania, miscellaneous papers including letters, account books, and an album of pictorial material. Papers relating to H.M.S. *Acheron* consist of official log 1848-50 when surveying on the New Zealand coast, out-letter books 1848-51, notebooks, captain's orders, and miscellaneous papers. There is also the official log Aug.-Dec. 1851 of H.M.S. *Havannah*, Sydney to Spithead. Other papers are STK/46 Account of the Australian diggings 1851. STK/50-2 Letters received 1853-4, 1846-58 of which STK/51, 1854, includes letters from Capt. J. E. Erskine, late of *Havannah*, about the French occupation of New Caledonia and from Edward Eyre about a proposed expedition to Central Australia, also an account of the first voyage of the *Himalaya*. The collection includes some printed material with cuttings.

Wemyss, Vice-Adm. E. W. E. WEM/7 Photograph album illustrating places visited by H.M.S. *Cambrian* during her Australian tour 1909-11.

Yorke, C. YOR/5/F3 Letter 1811 from Matthew Flinders to Yorke as First Lord of the Admiralty.

HISTORICAL NOTES

Notes, logs, remark books, often collected in the course of writing books, include collections by Capt. H. T. A. Bosanquet, H.M.S. *Paluma* in Queensland waters 1893-4 with notes on naval survey work; by Cicely Fox-Smith and Basil Lubbock on sailing ships; by Cmdr J. A. Rupert Jones, R.N.R., on surveyors and explorers.

ARTIFICIAL COLLECTIONS

British Records Association. BRA/766 Indenture 1831 for an apprentice to William Mellish, owner of *Sir Andrew Hammond*, employed in the Southern Whale Fishery.

Robert Edward Barker Collection. BRK/4-5 G. W. Anderson, *A New, Authentic and Complete Collection of Voyages Round the World*, London 1784, 2 vols. has some manuscripts inserted including letters from Capt. James Cook; BRK/6-7 Log 1828-31, 1833 H.M.S. *Challenger* kept by J. M. R. Ince; BRK/10-11 Log H.M.S. *Fly* 1842-3.

George Gabb Collection of Letters by Scientists, 17th-19th cent. GAB/7 W. J. Hooker 16 Sept. 1839 to Gov. Franklin introducing his son J. D. Hooker.

Green Papers, GRN, containing records of the Blackwall yard including logs of ships in the Melbourne passenger trade, *Newcastle* 1875-7, *Star of Devon* 1877, *Lord Warden* 1879-83, *Windsor Castle* 1865-74, all kept by C. Cooke, master.

Sir Thomas Phillips Collection including PHB/P/13 letters and documents 1753-1819 connected with Capt. W. Bligh and others, also letter 1804 from Bligh in the Croker Collection.

Wellcome Collection. WEL/39 Log 1903-4 Antarctic ship *Terra Nova*, Capt. J. McKay, kept by Chief Officer A. P. Jackson, England, New Zealand, Antarctic; WEL/45 Log 1744-59 *Royal George*, Capt. Thomas Field, England to India and return with notes on navigation and the coast of New Holland.

Ship Lists 1509-1922, LRN/7-21 some giving dimensions and tonnage, some arranged by rates.

Personnel, R.N. PRN/2 List of Lord High Admirals 1660-1915; PRN/5 Promotions of lieutenants.

Watch Station and Quarter Bills include LOG/W12 bill 1838 of H.M.S. *Fly* kept by T. Anson; LOG/W/21 Watch station and quarter bill c.1849-51 H.M.S. *Fly*, Capt. R. A. Oliver, New Zealand Station.

HISTORY, PERSONAL RECORDS

Personal records include letter books, order books, signal notebooks, general notebooks, and also journals and diaries:

JOD/15 Journal 1873-4 Sir George Strong Nares, H.M.S. *Challenger*, Cape of Good Hope to Melbourne, with description of flora and fauna, Marion Island, Prince Edward Island, Heard Island, Kerguelen Island.

JOD/16 Journal 1829-31, R. Guthrie, surgeon R.N., H.M.S. *Seringapatam* containing descriptive essays on some places visited among Pacific Islands.

JOD/19-20 Journals of Capt. Cook's first and second voyages, see *The Journals . . . of Cook*, ed. Beaglehole, I and II. Microfilms of both journals and photocopy of the journal of the second voyage in the National Library of Australia.

JOD/26 Medical journal 1845-54, T. M. Philson, assistant surgeon and C. Pine,

London

surgeon H.M.S. *British Sovereign*, Sydney to Auckland, and H.M.S. *Castor*, Auckland to Sydney.

JOD/36 A narrative of Commodore Anson's voyage Sept. 1740 to June 1744 by L. Millechamp with drawings of birds and animals.

JOD/42 Journal 1844-7, Lieut. T. Davies, H.M.S. *America* in the Pacific, mainly of South American interest but the ship visited the Hawaiian Islands in Oct. 1845.

JOD/44 Diary Apr.-June 1877, J. Rorke, second cabin passenger on the clipper *Loch Vennacher*, Greenock to Melbourne.

JOD/54 Abstract journals and logs kept by Capt. J. S. Roberts as midshipman and fourth officer in East India ships and cable ships: *Highflyer* 1869-71 London to Melbourne and return; S.S. *Khedive* 1885 Malta, Glenelg, Sydney, King George Sound, Plymouth.

JOD/56 Narrative account 1772-3 of the voyage of the *Resolution* by R. Pickersgill.

JOD/57 Log 1766-7 of the *Dolphin*, Capt. S. Wallis, kept by R. Pickersgill, England to Tahiti.

JOD/58 Journal 1764-6, John Byron, *Dolphin*, unsigned contemporary copy.* From marginal notes it would appear that this was the text used by Hawkesworth.

JOD/75 Journal Feb.-June 1850 Francis C. Taylor, emigrant in the *Stag*, Deptford to South Australia.

JOD/78 Diary 1893-4 Mrs M. C. MacGillivray, passenger in the clipper *Torrens*, London to Adelaide.

JOD/79 Journal Jan.-May 1853, J. Lovell in barque *Elizabeth* taking emigrants from Bristol to Melbourne.*

JOD/81-2 Notebook and journal 1886, S. W. Pring, passenger in *Ben Cruachan*, London to Sydney, also brief log and short diary of the return voyage.

Logs by Royal Navy Officers

About three hundred volumes, catalogued alphabetically by ships' names. Most of the logs were kept by midshipmen.

LOG/N/B/3. Journal 1874-6 H.M.S. *Barracouta*, E. D. Ommanney, visiting Australia, Fiji, Samoa.

LOG/N/C/38. Master's remark book Jan.-Dec. 1865 H.M.S. *Curaçoa*, J. E. Scudamore master, Australia and Pacific Islands.

LOG/N/E/1. Log and journal 1874-6 H.M.S. *Barracouta*, Lieut. A. MacLeod, Australia, Fiji, Samoa, New Caledonia.

LOG/N/M/9. Log and journal 1890-1 H.M.S. *Curaçoa*, A. W. Richmond, naval cadet, to Australia and New Zealand.

LOG/N/N/2. Logs 1881-5 H.M.S. *Nelson* and H.M.S. *Espiègle* on the Australia Station.

LOG/N/P/1. Logs and descriptive journal 1854-5 A. V. Maccall, clerk's assistant, *Pique* and *Amphitrite* visiting the Marquesas, Sandwich Islands, and Pitcairn.

LOG/N/R/3, 9, 10. Logs and journal 1872-4 H.M.S. *Rosario* J. T. Daly, Australia, New Zealand, Pacific Islands. In R/3 the journal describes the Solomons which the *Rosario* visited to collect evidence of the loss of the schooner *Lavinia*.

Logs by Officers of the East India Company

Mostly duplicates of official journals deposited at East India House.

LOG/C/35. *Tigris*, Indian Navy, 1836 by Cmdr W. Igglesden, Bombay to Murray Island and back to trace the fate of the passengers and crew of the *Charles Eaton*.

Logs by Officers of Merchant Ships

LOG/M/5, 6. *Clarence* 1870-2, London to Melbourne and return.

LOG/M/9. *City of Poonah* 1852-3, London to Port Phillip, Calcutta.

LOG/M/13. *Port Jackson*, barque, ocean training ship 1913-14, Australia and round the world.

LOG/M/19. *Active*, whaler 1838-42, whaling voyage to the South Seas and north of New Zealand.

LOG/M/20. *Recovery* 1828-31 and *Matilde* 1832-6, whaling voyage.

LOG/M/25. *Kelso* 1849-50, New Zealand. The log is accompanied by other documents belonging to the writer, W. Locke.

LOG/M/27. *Quilpue* 1905, Liverpool to Melbourne.

LOG/M/30. *Great Britain* 1854 to Jan. 1855, Liverpool to Melbourne.

LOG/M/33. *Carlisle Castle* 1880-4, England to Melbourne with lists of passengers, officers and cargoes, also pencil sketches of other ships.

LOG/M/35. *Erik* 1876 a whaling cruise, log kept by gunner T. F. Miller with photographs.

LOG/M/42. *John Melhuish* 1853-4 London, Port Phillip, Sydney, incomplete.

HISTORY, NARRATIVE

HIS/10 Anson's voyage round the world, lecture given 1951 by F. Maggs, typescript.

HIS/16 Narrative on the Tristan da Cunha Islands *c*.1834 compiled to illustrate the picture by W. J. Huggins of the *Fairlie* taking on board the crew of the brig *Nassau* wrecked when homeward bound from Australia and quoting the journal of Williams, chief mate of the *Nassau*.

BGR/2 Memoir of J. Trevenen by Adm. C. V. Penrose, see Rev. J. Penrose, *Lives of Vice-Admiral Sir Charles Vinicombe Penrose K.C.B. and Captain James Trevenen*, London 1850, and C. V. Penrose, *A Memoir of James Trevenen*, ed. Christopher Lloyd and R. C. Anderson, London 1959.

SPB Shipbuilding, includes reports on trials of R.N. vessels and a little on the introduction of steam power. SPB/12 Canoes of Oceania by J. Hornell, 1936, typescript and galley proofs, see A. C. Haddon and J. Hornell, *Canoes of Oceania*, Honolulu 1936, B. P. Bishop Museum Special Publication 27.

NWT/4 *Loch Garry* Magazine, manuscript, compiled Feb.-Mar. 1877 on a voyage from Melbourne to Glasgow.

AGC Biography, autographed letters include:

AGC/1/6. Notes 28 Sept. 1740 on Anson's voyage.

AGC/2 Holograph draft 1770 by James Cook of order for survey of surgeon's stores.

AGC/5 Letter *c*.1830 Capt. Basil Hall, R.N., to Lord Stuart of Rothesay about a projected voyage of circumnavigation.

AGC/8 Draft list 1776 by Nevil Maskelyne of instruments lent to Cook.

AGC/13 Letter 20 Sept. 1902 Sir Ernest Shackleton, Winter Quarters, South Victoria Land, to Mr Lethbridge.

AGC/16 Eight letters 1774-91 Lieut. James Ward, R.N.

AGC/25 Letter 13 May 1799 Adm. Lord Collingwood to Capt. King, H.M.S. *Sirius*.

AGC/39 Songs by Charles and Thomas Dibdin including Tom Truelove's knell sung in 'Great News on a Trip to the Antipodes'.

AGC/54 Letter 1 Sept. 1858 T. C. Spaulding, master of whaler *Anger*.

London

BGY Biographical Data include:

BGY/1/2. *Superb* Gazette, part of diary 1880 and diary 1883-4 by Mrs Berridge on *Superb*, photographs including groups on *Walmer Castle*, *Highflyer* and *Superb*.

BGY/3 Henry Green of Blackwall; BGY/3-6 papers relating to the *Highflyer*; BGY/7 copy of agreement re command of the *Melbourne*.

BGY/4/10. Testimonial 28 Dec. 1856 to Dr James Harris, surgeon *Donald Mackay*, signed by passengers.

BGY/8 Collection of certificates of discharge and testimonials 1879-1912 given to Capt. Henry Norman, *Cutty Sark* and *Titanic*.

BGY/S/1. Letters 1882 Walter Stock, on board *Hereford* and from Australia.

ADL Administration and law, a group of documents including examples of printed forms used in the Royal Navy and merchant service. Among other papers are:

ADL/1/B/11. Account of the wreck of H.M.S. *Orpheus* off the coast of New Zealand 1863.

ADL/1/B/18. Navy Board order 4 Mar. 1825 to Capt. Hammond, *Wellesley*, to test and report on New Zealand flax wheel rope supplied to the ship.

ADL/3/B. Sir James Clark Ross, commissions including that as captain, *Erebus* 1839.

ADL/5/B/19. *Lincolnshire*, contract ticket 23 Dec. 1868, Mrs Stallard, three children and servant £150 London to Melbourne.

ADL/6/A/15. Discharge certificate June 1883 Harry Upjohn signed by A. Moore, master of the *Cutty Sark*.

SCN/1/5. Survey 1837 by Richard Thompson of the population of Pitcairn.

NOT/1/4. F. V. Smythe, article on Dunbar wharf, Limehouse, and the firm of Duncan Dunbar, 19th cent., typescript.

FL/14 Letter 17 Oct. 1800 Matthew Flinders to his parents.

FD/35 Cmdr L. B. Denham, track chart 1877 H.M.S. *Opal* to Pitcairn.

FD/46 Documents deposited 1874 by Capt. G. S. Nares, H.M.S. *Challenger* at Kerguelen, other documents connected with Nares's expedition and photograph of epitaph by Sir Ernest Shackleton on three members of his 1914-17 expedition to the Antarctic.

FD/54 Admiralty commission Oct. 1780 for William Harvey to the *Resolution* confirming commission 15 Feb. 1770 given by Capt. C. Clerke.

TRN/15 Transcript of letter 31 May 1836, Thomas Birkby, to his father describing his voyage to Australia in 1834 and life in Australia.

In 1969 uncatalogued accessions included a diary 1861-4 kept by a marine in H.M.S. *Charybdis*; logs, papers, etc., of the firm of Devitt and Moore and of other shipowners.

Photographic copies include a microfilm MRF/17, Sir Joseph Banks's journal of his voyage round the world 1768-71. For some years the original of this transcript of Banks's *Endeavour* journal was on loan to the Museum from Lord Stanley of Alderley. Lord Stanley has reclaimed the journal and it has been sold at Sotheby's.

The Museum has many paintings, some of which are hung in the galleries, and large collections of drawings, prints, charts, maps and plans of ships. Admiralty records, Ships' Covers Series I 1849, 1861-1927 formerly P.R.O. Adm. 138 and Ships' Building Specifications, hull and machinery, formerly P.R.O. Adm. 170 are with plans.

NATIONAL WESTMINSTER BANK LTD
41 Lothbury, London, E.C.2

This bank holds the records of many constituent banks and much of its manuscript material is still uncatalogued (Jan. 1970). It is likely that more documents relevant to the field of this survey will be found. Inquiries for further information should be addressed to the Archivist. The following have been noted among the records of Stilwell and Sons, merged with the Westminster Bank in 1923.

Deeds and documents 1836-8 relating to property in New South Wales sold by William Kent to John Miller (Dossier 1306).

Power of attorney 14 Mar. 1863 from Rev. Henry Tingcombe to John Pakenham Stilwell concerning estate in New South Wales (Dossier 1313). Further related papers in the National Library of Australia.

OVERSEAS BISHOPRICS FUND
Church House, Dean's Yard, Westminster, London, S.W.1

The records of the Fund are not open to the general public. Application must be made in writing to the Honorary Secretary.

Founded on 1 June 1841, prior to 1959 the Fund was known as the Colonial Bishoprics Fund. The Rev. E. Hawkins, Secretary of the Society for the Propagation of the Gospel, was the first secretary. The records relate to the changing status of the church, the problems of financing the church and obtaining the necessary letters patent for new sees from the Colonial Office. Among the papers there is some information of interest to the social historian especially that provided by Bishop Broughton and others relating to the need to divide the diocese of Australia. The small collection of letters by C. J. Abraham, first Bishop of Wellington, is of particular interest for comment on public opinion concerning the conduct of the Maori Wars and a visit to Taranaki in the 1860s.

New Zealand, Tasmania, Mauritius, 1 box. Mainly letters connected with the endowment and foundation of new bishoprics together with statistics on the growth of the church. Includes letters on various bishoprics in New Zealand and on the bishopric of Tasmania. Of special interest are five letters 1860-1 from C. J. Abraham to Hawkins.*

Australia A-M, 1 box. Letters dealing with the foundation of the dioceses of Adelaide, Ballarat, Bathurst, Bendigo, Brisbane, Bunbury, Carpentaria, and Melbourne and including letters 1845-6 on the division of the diocese of Australia and the formation of the sees of Melbourne and Adelaide; letters from W. G. Broughton, Mr Justice Coleridge and W. E. Gladstone.

Australia N-W, 1 box. Letters dealing with the dioceses of Newcastle, New Guinea, North Queensland, North-West Australia, Perth, Riverina, Rockhampton, St Arnaud, Sydney, and Willochra.

Miscellaneous, 1 box. Correspondence 1842 between the Archbishop of Canterbury and Lord Stanley on colonial Bishops' salaries. Return of colonial Bishops and their salaries 1855 and 1865, and various parliamentary papers 1865 relating to the colonial church.

Colonial Bishoprics Fund out-letter books 1841-83, 3 vols., incomplete indexes.

Additional Colonial Bishoprics Journal 1841-1911, 2 vols. Contains records of meetings of the Fund's committee and copies of important letters.

Colonial Bishoprics, copies of letters patent 1793-1865, 2 vols.

London

Cash books 1841- ; General Account 1841-*c*.1852, 1 vol.; List of Subscribers 1843-5, 1 vol.; Ledgers 1841-*c*.1930, 6 vols.

PENINSULAR AND ORIENTAL STEAM NAVIGATION COMPANY
122 Leadenhall Street, London, E.C.3

The company has established a museum and surviving non-current records are housed under the care of the Curator, to whom application should be made for permission to consult them. For information on records of later date application should be made to the Assistant Secretary. A few miscellaneous Orient Line records are preserved including a fine collection of cuttings.

About 1965 many volumes, including records and published works, were listed and about 880 volumes were assigned numbers which are given in brackets after entries below.

For published works on the P.&O.S.N.Co. see Boyd Cable, *A Hundred Year History of the P.&O. . . . 1837-1937*, London 1937, D. Divine, *These Splendid Ships*, London 1960, G. F. Kerr, *Business in Great Waters, the War History of the P.&O. 1939-45*, London 1951.

Files of historical photographs and negatives are maintained under the supervision of the Curator of the Museum.

MINUTES, CHARTERS, ETC.

Reports of Proceedings and Chairman's Addresses at Annual Meetings 1841-1961, printed.

Charters 1-9, 1840-1901, printed (877); 1-10, 1840-1922, printed (878); 10th Supplemental Charter 1922 and Trust Deeds 1922-3, printed and typescript (874).

Minutes of Board Meetings, Peninsular Steam Navigation Company and the Transatlantic Steam Company 1840 to July 1841, 2 vols.; 23 Mar. 1840 to 28 Aug. 1840, 28 Aug. 1840 to 6 July 1841, 2 vols. (626 a, b). Minute in 1840 states that from 23 Apr. 1840 the new Company will be called the Peninsular and Oriental Steam Navigation Company.

Minute Books 1-5, 2 Sept. 1840 to 13 Oct. 1858 (777 a-e). Minute Book 1 is not indexed. The first mention of Australia noted occurs in Minute Book 1, 28 May 1846, 'Read, letters from the Australian Steam Committee, dated 13, 23 & 29 May, making certain enquiries with reference to a Steam Communication being established between Singapore & Australia'. Minute Books 2-5 are indexed and there are frequent references to communications with Australia.

Various decisions of the Management Committee from May 1898 to May 1906, alphabetically arranged, with appendix May 1906 to May 1909, printed (870). Cover marked 'Private, Board Room'. Each entry gives the date of the relevant minute. Entries relating to Australia and New Zealand include entries under Adelaide Agency, Agreements, Commonwealth of Australia, Freight, Gold, Melbourne Agency, Perth Agency, Pursers, Refrigerated Cargo, Sydney Agency, Western Australia, Wines.

Acts of Parliament: Post Office Acts to 1837 (849); Post Office Acts to 1838 (355); Act to Amend the Passengers' Act 1855, 13 July 1863 (854); Post Office Act 1908 (525); Post Office Amendment Act 1935 (526), printed.

P. & O. Steam Navigation Company

A number of letter books and a folder of early correspondence exist. Most volumes are provided with indexes. Some seem unlikely to contain references to Australia but are listed here as they may repay examination: letter books 1838-43, 2 vols. (785 a, b); folder of correspondence, chiefly original in-letters and other papers 1840-53, mainly concerning the purchase of the *Oriental* 1840, purchase of other companies, etc. (filed 1969 in large black solander case marked G); letter books entitled Peninsular and Levant 1855-7, 2 vols. (782 a, b); letters from agents re Eastern Service 1867-8, 6 vols. (808); miscellaneous letters and papers from agents, etc. 1875-6 (846); 'Passengers' Letters', copies of in-letters 1885-1913 (865) chiefly letters of appreciation of comfort of troops in transit; P.&O. centenary telegrams and letters of congratulation 1937 (843). The following volumes contain references to Australia or seem likely to do so:

Letters re Mail Contracts (Australian) 1849-56 (789).

Egypt letter books, 3 vols. (784 a-c). No.1, 1843-9, no.2, 1862-5, badly damaged by water and mostly illegible, no.3, 1865-8. A brief examination of no.3 revealed: letter 26 Jan. 1866 to the Company's agent at Alexandria enclosing a copy of an extract of a letter from the Company's agent in Melbourne suggesting an abatement in rate of shipping freight at present charged on Australian gold.

Letter 3 July 1866 to the Company's superintendent at Suez censuring him for undue detention of goods en route for Australia and stating that the Company has received letters of complaint from Australia.

Letter book 1849-56 containing copies of letters between the Company and the government concerning contracts for mails to Australia and the East (789).

Letter book entitled on spine 'Australian Line' containing copies of letters to agents at Batavia, King George Sound, Adelaide, Melbourne and Sydney, 8 Nov. 1851 to 16 Oct. 1858 (875).

Letter books, 2 vols. (786 a, b). The two volumes contain copies of in-letters and out-letters 1847-70 to and from ships' captains and inspectors. In the front of the volume covering 1853-70 is a 'Report on the Anchorage (in Gage Roads) Swan River by R. D. Guthrie, Nautical Inspector'.

Letter book 1860-75 (787). Copies of letters and circulars to commanders concerning the management of ships.

Letter books, 'Letters to Government' 1866-93, 6 vols. labelled 6, 9, 12, 14, 15 and 17, copies of out-letters (778 a-f) containing occasional reference to Australian affairs, coal at King George Sound, details of mail despatch, and landing procedures.

Letter books, 'Letters from Government' 1866-80, 5 vols. labelled 5-9. Copies of in-letters (779 a-e).

'Letters from Government' 1868-93, 8 vols. Original in-letters June-Sept. 1868, Jan. 1873 to Nov. 1874, Aug. 1875 to Nov. 1876, 1892-3 and one vol. 1869-75 (780 a-h).

Indexes to Admiralty letter books, 4 vols.: no.3 out-letters, no.3 in-letters, no.4 out-letters, no.4 in-letters, n.d. (866 a-d).

Letter book entitled on spine 'Docks' containing original letters, notes and documents 1869-*c*.1888 concerning docks, including the major Australian and New Zealand docks and giving dimensions, charges, and conditions (876).

Letter book entitled on spine 'Contracts and Tenders No.3, 1872 to 1883' and on front cover 'Contracts and Tenders, Naval and Engineering Dept.'. Copies of in- and out-letters (869).

London

'Foreign Letters', letter books Oct. 1893 to Sept. 1895, 5 vols. labelled 50-4, copies of out-letters to agents (781 a-e). Some letters are long and detailed, letters to agents in Adelaide, Melbourne, and Sydney contain material on meat, butter and fruit marketing and on shipment of refrigerated goods.

Correspondence, notes, etc., between Sir Thomas Sutherland, Lord Inchcape and Charles G. Deane concerning new ships c.1907-23 (888).

MAIL CONTRACTS

Parliamentary and other papers concerning mail contracts 1835-1907, printed.

GENERAL ORDERS, INSTRUCTIONS, REGULATIONS

Instructions for the use of commanders, Australian Line 1921, 1948, 1954 and other volumes of orders, etc., 1860-1937, printed.

SHIPS

Nautical Reports Sept. 1848 to Mar. 1955, 36 vols. Reports digested from ships' logs, ship index in each volume.

Programs for movements of ships 1874-99; proposed movements of mail steamers 1877; mail services 1889-1917, 1920-8. These are printed records. Later movements may be traced in various printed handbooks of sailings etc. Printed time tables exist 1950 to date. There are also printed lists of passages engaged and of passage rates.

Register and Dimensions of Ships, 3 vols. 1852-6, 1859-85, 1886-1922 (841 a-c).

Other records include: New Ships, Repairs, etc. 1866-85 (872); Capacities of Steamers 1879-89 (871); Expenses for New Ships 1898-1925 (873); Load Lines c.1909-c.1949 (867 a, b); General Particulars of the Fleet of the P.&O.S.N.Co. c.1950 (652).

There are also volumes on specifications and particulars of various ships and volumes containing letters and papers connected with the loss of or accidents to ships usually one volume to each ship concerned, e.g. a volume entitled Reports and Proceedings of the Nautical Committee Jan. 1849 to July 1874 (788) includes references to accidents to *Benares*.

PERSONNEL

Salary Book 1852-c.1885.

Salary Books 1854 to 'from 1941' (811-19). Other salary books (836-40). New revised rates of pay, Europeans and natives Aug. 1932 (821).

List of Commanders, Officers, and Engineers 1891; List of Commanders, etc. 1940 (655); Staff on War Service, 2nd World War (833); List of Commanders, etc. 1955 (591).

Other volumes of staff records include:

Muster Roll, Sydney Agency 1880-1917, 2 vols. Pages are endorsed with dates on which the record was sent to London. Names, places of birth, ratings, dates of appointment, wages per month, and allowances are given. (In 1969 these two vols. were filed in large black solander case marked G.)

Staff Records A-Z, 2 vols. (826 a, b); Shore Staff 1936-   (828) and about a dozen volumes of Retired Lists, Reports, etc. c.1873-c.1916 various dates (820, 822-5, 829-32).

MISCELLANEA

Old documents 1847-1929 (627), bound with typescript index, some items are printed.

Includes, loose at end, letter 27 July 1900 from Sir James Mackay to Sir Thomas Sutherland with enclosure concerning Australian quarantine and Sutherland's reply 2 Aug. 1900, typescript copy and 'Memo re Australian quarantine' 2 Aug. 1900, typescript.

Statement of the position and operations of the Company 1866 (558), 2 copies.

Report to the Board of Directors by the Committee appointed by the Board's Minute of 5 January 1875 (882). Refers to effect on the Profit and Loss Account of reduction of the Australian subsidy.

Weekly Reports for the Board Dec. 1892 to Sept. 1899, 4 vols. (783 a-d). At regular intervals there are statements on the freight rates to Australia from London and from Sydney and Melbourne to London, details of cargoes available, and state of the market.

Memoranda, F. R. Kendall. A ledger with index, only a few pages used (848). Entries include a list of employees at the Sydney Agency 1867 with rates of pay; notes on mails Australian Line and on 'Calendar Monthly Services' showing cost of monthly service to Australia via Suez and Galle from the Return published by the Postal Conference; note on comparative distances of various routes King George Sound to Melbourne; notes on cost of 1 oz. gold in London, on average rate per mile for inter colonial passages between various places in Australia and New Zealand. At the end of the volume are a few cuttings c.1925.

Notebook of Gordon Baylis on the work of the Repairs Department contains *inter alia* notes on repairs to ships on the Australian run including repairs in dock in Sydney.

'Syndicate for airship-traffic with the Netherlands-Indies, Memorandum', mimeographed, n.d. but part of the memorandum covers 1931-3. Marked 'Confidential'.

Lists of P.&O. ships and officers 1851, 1951.

Gribble's Tables of Bearings and Distance 1851, with inset showing proposed movements of P.&O. mail steamers 1858 (766), printed.

Papers connected with the First and Second World Wars include papers concerning S.S. *Borda* and papers and notes on P.&O. troopers (834 and black solander case marked G).

Volumes and boxes of cuttings c.1842-1963.

Program of ball and supper in Museum Great Room, Sydney, 26 Aug. 1852. Printed on silk and framed. A memento of the pioneer voyage of the *Chusan*.

Capt. W. F. Norie, Certificates and letters 1850-71. The papers include some photographs (646).

Robert Methven, *The Log of a Merchant Officer viewed with Reference to the Education of Young Officers and the Youth of the Merchant Service*, London 1854. Illustrated from sketches by the author and with inserted typescript summary of a biography of R. Methven, who commanded ships on the Australian run, including the *Bombay* 1862 (772).

F. R. Kendall, letters 17 Feb. 1858 to 13 Jan. 1866 to his mother, typescript (645). An inscription on the front flyleaf is signed H. M. Kendall, Shanghai, and states that the letters are those from his father when he went out East to Bombay and to Australia, then to Singapore and Hong Kong. Several inserted typescript pages entitled 'Journal from May 14th to July 24th, 1859' describe the author's visit to Australia; letters 21 Apr., 12 July 1859 also describe this visit. Papers inserted at the end of the typescript refer to Lieut. E. N. Kendall, R.N., d.1845, Superintendent of the P.&O. at Southampton, and to his proposal for the Company to extend steam navigation to Australia.

John Spurge, log 18 Apr. to 10 Aug. 1889 on a voyage to Australia and back, S.S. *Carthage* (648). The manuscript contains no description of Australian ports of call, which include King George Sound and Sydney, but the details of the voyage are of interest.

W. W. Lloyd, P.&O. Pencillings, original pen and ink drawings and published work entitled *P.&O. Pencillings*, London 1891, containing reproductions of black and white water-colours of life on P.&O. ships (587) n.d.

Sydney to London by P.&O. Royal Mail Steamers, n.d., issued by Macdonald, Hamilton, Sydney.

ORIENT STEAM NAVIGATION COMPANY LTD

Practically all Orient Line records were destroyed by enemy action during World War II. A few manuscript, typescript, and printed miscellanea have been preserved, some of them of great value for the study of the Company's history. There is a fine collection of cuttings in bound volumes *c.*1887-1959. Manuscripts in volumes include:

Index Book of Orient Line Personalities and Places *c.*1863-1905 (659). An exercise book with alphabetical entries.

Lieut. John Isherwood, Orient Line Fleet. Photograph of MS. with drawings of ships.

S. Sindall, Orient Line Flags, typescript signed and dated Apr. 1935 (651).

Miscellanea filed in boxes are chiefly printed but include some manuscript and typescript notes, e.g. Box 5 contains memoranda of Sir Alan Anderson's trip to Australia 1926 and R. J. Best's trip to Australia, reports on publicity and impressions 1930.

MRS M. POWNALL
9 Sprimont Place, London, S.W.3

WATERHOUSE FAMILY LETTERS

The letters 1797-1803 are in two albums, one containing chiefly letters 1800-3 from George Bass to his father-in-law, William Waterhouse, concerning the venture in the *Venus*, the other chiefly correspondence between Bass, his wife, and mother.

8 Jan. 1800 Bass to W. Waterhouse concerning the venture in the *Venus* with postscript on Waterhouse's share. Postscript in *H.R.N.S.W.* IV, p.587, note.

9, 13 Jan. 1801 Elizabeth Bass to her father.

30 June 1801 Bass, *Venus*, Cape of Good Hope, to W. Waterhouse. *H.R.N.S.W.* IV, pp.420-1.

19 Aug. 1801 W. Waterhouse to Bass concerning disappointing news of the voyage.

4 Oct. 1801 Bass, *Venus*, Port Jackson, to H. Waterhouse. *H.R.N.S.W.* IV, pp.586-8.

30 Jan. 1802 Bass, *Venus*, Matavai Bay, Otaheite, to W. Waterhouse, *H.R.N.S.W.* IV, pp.689-91.

20 May 1802 Bass, *Venus*, off Morokai, Sandwich Is., to W. Waterhouse.

5 Jan. 1803 Bass, *Venus*, Port Jackson, to James Sykes.

5 Jan. 1803 Bass, *Venus*, Sydney Cove, to W. Waterhouse stating that the pork voyage had been their first successful venture, that Gov. King gave a letter to commanding officers sailing to Spanish ports in South America, and that he (Bass) was anxious to procure cattle for salting also live cattle for introduction into the colony, the

guanacos and pacos of Chile also being desirable. After leaving the Spanish coast Bass proposed to go to Otaheite; he had some idea of selling the brig to the Spaniards who 'cannot fail to admire her beauty and strength', Bishop had been totally useless.

6 July 1797 Mrs Elizabeth Bass to her son George, *inter alia* regrets that he has decided to give up the navy.

Letter n.d. [1797] Bass to his mother, describing his voyage southward in the whale-boat, stating that he would accompany his friend Flinders on a voyage to explore the strait he was sure existed and hoped to collect something valuable for Sir Joseph Banks, and to present something to the Linnean Society of which Col. Paterson had written to him from England. This letter is in very bad repair and incomplete.

15 Feb. 1799 Js. Innes, H.M.S. *Vigilant*, to Bass, surgeon H.M.S. *Reliance*, Botany Bay, N.S.W. Sent by Mr Palmer.

15 Feb. 1799 Matthew Flinders to Bass, a long letter about charts of Port Dalrymple and the Derwent and about their friendship. The letter is enclosed in a cover on which is a short message from his mother to Bass warning him against the writer of the letter.

8 Oct. 1800 Bass to W. Waterhouse informing him he has married Elizabeth Water-house that day at St James church. Also letter n.d. Henry Waterhouse to his father saying he has given away Betsy.

Letter n.d. [1880] Bass to Mrs Waterhouse telling her that Betsy was very ill and desired her mother and one of her sisters.

8, 9 Jan. 1801 Bass's farewell letters to his mother, Capt. Waterhouse, and his wife.

The remainder of the letters 1801-3 consist of correspondence between Bass and his wife, letters to Bass from H. Moore, Craven Coffee House, Strand; R. Shepherd-son, Canton; J. Innes; W. Waterhouse; W. Kent, *Buffalo*; two letters from Bass to his mother and to a friend; letter 16 May 1803 from Gov. King's wife to Mrs Bass giving news of Bass's departure from Sydney; letter 9 Dec. 1803 W. Waterhouse to his daughter Mrs George Bass; letter 9 Aug. 1803 Flinders, *Porpoise*, Port Jackson, to Mrs George Bass. There is also a memo 20 May 1802 by Bass written off Morokai, Sandwich Is., giving a report on the proceedings of the *Venus*.

Copies of some of the items listed above and of additional Bass and Waterhouse papers are in the Mitchell Library, Sydney.

PRINCIPAL PROBATE REGISTRY
Somerset House, London, W.C.2

The Probate Act of 1857 transferred probate business from various ecclesiastical jurisdictions to one civil authority, the Probate, Divorce and Admiralty Division of the High Court of Justice, and copies of all wills and administrations after Jan. 1858 wherever proved or granted in England and Wales (Scotland, Northern Ireland, and Eire are excluded) are deposited in Somerset House. An annual index of wills and administrations less than one hundred years old, giving name, address, and brief summary of the estate, is maintained on the open shelves in the Main Hall. Registry staff will undertake searches in this index in reply to postal inquiries, on payment of a fee. The documents are produced for inspection in the Main Hall on payment of a small fee for each item.

The wills and administrations proved or granted in the most important of the earlier ecclesiastical courts, the Prerogative Court of Canterbury which were at one time deposited in Somerset House, have now (1970) been transferred to the Public Record Office q.v.

London

PUBLIC RECORD OFFICE
Chancery Lane, London, W.C.2

Students wishing to be admitted to the Public Record Office must obtain a reader's ticket valid for three years, or a temporary permit, valid for one week. This description of documents in the Public Record Office follows as closely as possible the pattern and terminology of the *Guide to the Contents of the Public Record Office*, London, H.M.S.O., 1963-8, 3 vols. Reference to this work is briefly by title, volume, and page number only. Volumes I and II deal respectively with 'Legal Records', and 'State Papers and Departmental Records', deposited before August 1960. Volume III continues both volumes with 'Documents Transferred 1960-1966' and also contains corrigenda and addenda to the two previous volumes. The preface and introductions to this work are an essential introduction to the history and classification of the records and facilities for their use.

Also available in the Public Record Office is the 'Summary of Records', 2 vols., duplicated typescript, which lists all classes in each group giving dates covered and number of pieces. Part I lists Legal Records and Part II State Papers and Departmental Records; together they form a complete list of all groups and provide a means of quick reference to names of classes. The Summary is a tool for internal use and is not intended for publication. In 1970 Part I remains as at 1962; Part II is revised from time to time, the last revision being early 1969.

The various printed, typescript, and manuscript class lists, indexes, and calendars, sets of which are on the open shelves in the Public Record Office are intended primarily for students searching the records in person. The Public Record Office lists and indexes which have been officially published are listed, together with handbooks, catalogues, and guides, in *Government Publications, Sectional List No.24 British National Archives*, revised to March 1968, London H.M.S.O. 1968. Some of the earlier publications which became out of print have been re-issued by the Kraus Reprint Corporation, New York, and additional lists and indexes still in typescript are being published by Kraus under the same arrangement as that for the re-issue of printed *Lists and Indexes*. Also, the List and Index Society, C/o Swift Ltd, 5-9 Dyers Buildings, London, E.C.1, distributes, to members only, bound copies of unpublished Public Record Office lists and indexes reproduced by photographic processes. At the Public Record Office a 'Card Index of Lists and Indexes' is maintained and available to searchers. In addition a special 'Card Catalogue of Maps and Plans' is being compiled; this relates to maps and plans from many groups of records and includes an index of surveyors and draughtsmen. A program of publication based on these cards is planned.

In the following description all relevant handbooks, lists, and indexes, both published and unpublished, are mentioned under each group. Those which relate to the whole group are listed before the class descriptions, those relating to one particular class only are under the class heading. Inventories and indexes compiled by the departments themselves and transferred to the Public Record Office with the departmental records are usually given class numbers, but in order to facilitate production they have been physically removed from the class, put together in one series of index volumes and given serial index numbers. To avoid confusion and unnecessarily long references, these IND numbers have been omitted in the following description, but they must be found from the class lists and used when calling for the index volumes.

In the space available here it is impossible to give more than an outline of the records relating to Australasia and the Pacific. An attempt has been made to list courts and departments the records of which relate to these areas and to note all relevant classes. In general, notes on subjects covered are included only as examples. Inevitably in such a vast accumulation of records, further research in classes, and possibly in groups, not described may well reveal further material, but the following entries will direct students to the main sources for the area. These entries supplement information in the *Guide to the Contents of the Public Record Office*, which must be used in conjunction with them.

Selected material in the Public Record Office has already been microfilmed or is being microfilmed for the Australian Joint Copying Project. No indication is here given of classes wholly or partly copied as any note is almost immediately out of date. Information about the filming of Public Record Office holdings is available from Australia House, London, and from the authorities in Australia controlling the Australian Joint Copying Project under whose sponsorship a handbook to microfilms prepared under the project is being compiled (1971).

CLERKS OF ASSIZE

The records of the Clerks of Assize cover both civil and criminal cases heard before the Justices of Assize in the counties, these cases usually, though not necessarily, being of a more serious nature than those heard at the Quarter Sessions. The existing records vary in date and completeness. Minute books may contain either crown or civil cases, or both. Those for the Oxford Circuit (Assizes 1) do not appear to contain any crown cases. Crown books give more details of the crime than the minutes. The earlier ones include copies of orders for transportation for the late eighteenth century when the destination is frequently referred to as 'the eastern coast of N.S.W. or some of the islands adjacent' and these state that the securities and contracts mentioned are to be 'filed amongst the records of the court'. Lists of orders for transportation after each sessions replace these full copies of orders in the mid-nineteenth century. Crown books also contain lists of recognizances to answer, to prosecute, and to give evidence, and notes of examinations, informations, depositions, confessions, and convictions. Indictments consist of rolls or files of loose documents including original bills of indictment (presentments of jurors) for both felonies and misdemeanours, giving details, e.g. age, place of origin, trade, and much information about the crime. They also include lists of jurors, recognizances to appear, examinations, and informations of accused and witnesses. Depositions have been destroyed, except those earlier than 1800, and those relating to trials for murder, sedition, treason, riot, conspiracies to effect political changes, or any other trials of general or historical interest. Gaol books list persons 'delivered', crimes, convictions, and sentences, noting in the late eighteenth century, transportation to New South Wales, and later, to such place as may be directed.

The documents are filed under the eight circuits as re-arranged in 1876. Before this date there were six circuits. The *Guide to the Contents of the Public Record Office* I, pp.127-31, indicates under which circuit the pre-1876 assize records for each county are now found. Within each circuit documents are arranged by date of assize and then by county or place of sessions.

See Class List of the Records of the Clerks of Assize, 1957, typescript. This list is published as Vol.6 in the List and Index Society Series.

CENTRAL CRIMINAL COURT

See Class List of the Records of the Central Criminal Court, giving sessions, names of defendants and charges, typescript.

Crim.1 Depositions 1839-1922, 207 bundles.

As for Assizes, these depositions are selected, relating to trials for murder, sedition, treason, riot, and conspiracies to effect political changes, or to any other trials of general or historical interest.

HIGH COURT OF ADMIRALTY

See the following lists:

Class List of the Records of the High Court of Admiralty, 1960, 2 vols., typescript. The first volume, covering H.C.A.1-40 is published as Vol.27 in the List and Index Society series.

High Court of Admiralty: Descriptive List of Means of Reference, 2 vols., typescript. Index to Certain Records of the High Court of Admiralty, 1949, typescript, covering H.C.A.30, 49/1-45 and 32/92-3.

List of High Court of Admiralty 1, c.1960, 2 vols., typescript. Published as Vols.46-7 in the List and Index Society series.

High Court of Admiralty. Instance Papers: Index. (Early Series, Series I-V.)

High Court of Admiralty. Prize Papers: Index 1793-1815.

CRIMINAL

H.C.A.1 Oyer and Terminer Records 1535-1834, 101 bundles.

Containing minutes, indictments, precepts, warrants, and examination books, the records cover the criminal jurisdiction of the High Court of Admiralty. Vice-Admiralty Courts in the colonies had to send reports of trials to the High Court of Admiralty and these may be found in the indictment files (1/1-28, 89-96, 32, 64, 99). Other reports may remain among the records of the Colonial Office.

Records of cases may be found through the List of High Court of Admiralty 1. The second volume is an alphabetical index of persons and ships with occasional geographical entries.

APPOINTMENTS

H.C.A.50 Admiralty Muniment Books Eliz.I to 1873, 24 vols.

The index is in H.C.A.51/2. Volumes contain entries made chronologically and include copies of commissions for the establishing of Vice-Admiralty Courts in New South Wales 1787, Van Diemen's Land 1825, Western Australia 1831, South Australia 1841, New Zealand 1841, Victoria 1851, Queensland 1859, and Fiji 1875; patents under the seal of the High Court of Admiralty appointing Vice-Admirals (usually the Governors of each colony), Judges (usually the principal judicial officer), Registrars, and Marshals.

While the setting up of a Vice-Admiralty Court and appointment of Vice-Admiral were almost simultaneous for the territories above, only in New South Wales was the first Judge appointed at the same time. Elsewhere some years elapsed before this appointment or the appointment of other officers to the court, indicating that the initial setting up of a court may have been in part a formality. In Western Australia, Judge, Marshal, and Registrar were appointed in 1865, in South Australia the first Judge in 1843 but Marshal and Registrar in 1863, in Victoria, Judge and Registrar in 1856 and Marshal in 1859, in Queensland, all three officials in 1861, in New Zealand the first Judge in 1865, in Fiji the first Judge in 1876, in Van Diemen's Land the first Judge in 1851. 51/2 contains no record of appointments of Registrar and Marshal in Van Diemen's Land, New Zealand, or Fiji.

The Vice-Admiralty Courts Act 1863 made it unnecessary for the Admiralty to issue commissions to fill vacancies in Vice-Admiralty Courts as from this date the Governor and chief judicial officer *ex officio* filled the positions of Vice-Admiral and

Judge respectively, should these fall vacant, until formal Admiralty appointment. Notifications of appointments, however, continue to be recorded in this class.

H.C.A.51 Indexes to Admiralty Muniment Books Eliz.I to 1955, 2 vols.

The two indexes which constitute this class largely contain duplicate information, but the second can be used as a record of High Court of Admiralty appointments by area.

51/2. Index to H.C.A.50 prepared *c.*1863 and updated thereafter, organised on a geographical basis. Apart from England itself there are headings such as New South Wales, New Zealand, under each of which appointments to one office such as Vice-Admiral, Judge, Registrar, are grouped together. Dates of appointment are given as well as references to the volumes of H.C.A.50. Reference, with date, is also given to the commissions empowering the setting up of a Vice-Admiralty Court. There is also a table of contents and appendices listing Vice-Admiralties.

VICE-ADMIRALTY COURTS

H.C.A.49 Proceedings 1636-1875, 106 bundles.

This class includes prize and instance papers, assignation books, bonds for letters of marque, the bulk of the records relating to the West Indies and Africa. The following have been noted:

49/100. Proceedings of Vice-Admiralty Court in New South Wales on four prize cases: Dec. 1799, capture of Spanish ship *Plomer* bound for Lima by the *Betsy* (Obadiah Clarke), *Barbara* (Jetho. Gardener), *Resolution* (William Irish) in company with the *Venus* (Ellis) on 7 July 1799; 27 Feb. 1800 capture of Spanish ship *Euphemia* bound from Lima to coast of California by the *Betsy* (Obadiah Clarke) on 6 Nov. 1799; 26, 27 Nov. 1804 capture of the *Swift* of Batavian Republic bound from Batavia to Amboyna by the *Policy* (Charles Sparrowe Foster) on 12 Sept. 1804; 18, 19 Nov. 1806 capture of Spanish ship *Santa Anna* bound from Saint Blas to Callao on the coast of Peru by *Port au Prince* (Isaac Duck) on 20 June 1806.

PREROGATIVE COURT OF CANTERBURY

This group contains wills and administrations proved or granted in the Prerogative Court of Canterbury before the Probate Act of 1857 came into effect. Although wills of all persons dying abroad or at sea and of all persons holding property in more than one diocese should have been proved in the Prerogative Court of Canterbury, this did not always happen. Such wills are often found in diocesan, archidiaconal, or 'pecular' collections deposited in ecclesiastical archives or local record offices; see A. J. Camp, *Wills and their Whereabouts*, Canterbury 1963. The British Record Society has published the indexes to the Prerogative Court of Canterbury wills 1383-1700, London 1893-1960, 12 vols., but there are no further printed lists. Students using this material are advised that it is essential to have the date of death of persons concerned, and if possible, their place of origin and other information on family connections, before commencing searches.

Prob.1 Special Wills 1587-1853, 28 items.
Prob.3 Inventories 1702, 1718-82, 61 bundles.
Prob.6 Act Books, Administrations 1559-1858, 233 vols.
Prob.7 Act Books, Limited Administrations 1810-58, 71 vols.
Prob.8 Act Books, Probates 1526-1858, 57 vols.
Prob.9 Act Books, Limited Probates 1526-1858, 250 vols.
Prob.10 Original Wills 1484-1858, 7456 boxes.
Prob.11 Registered Copy Wills 1384-1858, 2263 vols.

London

This is an index to Prob.11.

ADMIRALTY

Classes containing information on individuals and ships are not all described below. Among classes not mentioned and containing biographical information are Accounting Departments, Adm.22-4, 27, 29, 25-6, 139, 43-5, 48, 141-2, 154; Admiralty and Secretariat, Adm.9, 6, 118; Chatham Chest, Adm.82; Greenwich Hospital, Adm.65-7, 69, 161-6, 73; Material Departments, Adm.93; Medical Departments, Adm.102; Navy Board, Adm.107; Royal Marines, Adm.96, 157-9, 192. For a note on how to trace officers and ratings see the introduction to Lists and Indexes XVIII. Material Departments, Adm.83-94, 135-6, 95, 176, 195 relate to the physical history of H.M. ships.

It is probable that some records from the latter part of the nineteenth century onwards, notably from the Medical and Victualling Departments, have been destroyed. References to letters and related papers in Adm.1 Board of Admiralty and Secretariat Papers, and in Adm.12 Indexes and compilations, Series III, will provide information on the more important aspects of the work of these departments after the closing date of their individual records.

See the following lists:

Lists and Indexes XVIII, *List of Admiralty Records*, vol.1, 1904, reprint New York 1963.

Lists and Indexes: Supplementary Series VI, *List of Admiralty Records to 1913*, vol.1 Accounting Departments—Dockyard Records, vol.2 Greenwich Hospital—Transport Department, reprint New York 1966-7.

Supplementary List, 2 vols., typescript, working copies of Supplementary Series VI with later additions.

Table of heads and sections under which the correspondence of the Admiralty Board is digested (cover title: 'Digest Heads and Sections'), printed, no imprint. (A typescript copy of this table entitled 'Digest Tables', dated 1935 and corrected to 28 Feb. 1951 contains useful notes on Admiralty records.)

Lists of Admiralty ships employed on missions of discovery 1669-1860, compiled by B. Poulter, typescript, 1929. Contents: Ships employed on Scientific Missions 1669-1800, arranged chronologically, Ships employed on Missions of Discovery 1800-60, arranged alphabetically, names of stations being added in manuscript.

Chaplains of the Royal Navy 1626-1903, compiled by Rev. A. G. Kealy, Portsmouth, photographic copy. There is also on the Search Room shelves a photographic copy of a manuscript list by Rev. A. G. Kealy, 'Chaplains of the Royal Navy 1626-1816', dated 1887.

Return of officers' services 1846 (Adm.9), indexed. Photographic copy of a list of names with manuscript notes, bound 1956.

Admiralty: Medical Department: registers, hospital muster books, etc. (Adm.102), typescript, 1923.

Indexes and Lists presented by Miss E. H. B. Fairbrother in 1928, manuscript and typescript, listing mainly information concerning individuals or ships and including: I. General Note [concerning the Fairbrother Lists and Indexes] . . . Admiralty Accountant General's Department, Marine Pay Office, Medical Department, Navy Board, Secretary's Department, and Victualling Department lists and notes. A manuscript note in the volume states that 'The Lists now bound up in the present volumes are described by the compiler as forming somewhat an expansion of G. Fothergill, *The Records of Naval Men*, Walton-on-Thames, 1910'.

II. Admiralty: Accountant General's Department, Navy Board and Secretary's Department, indexes relating to commissions, appointments, and services (Adm. 1/1-5, 167-80, 4280-1; 6/61-72, 182; 30/31; 33/41-90B).

IV. Admiralty: Chatham Chest, Accountant General's Department and Secretary's Department, index of Chaplains.

VI. Medical Department Registers, Medical Journals, lists and indexes (Adm.101). Contains lists of convict ships, emigrant ships, and select medical journals with indexes of surgeons.

X. British Museum Add. MS.11603: indexes of officers of the Royal Navy with a rough index of additional names noted in Accountant General's Department Ships' Musters Series IV.

XI. British Museum Add. MS.11603: (list of officers of the Royal Navy from the Restoration in 1660 to . . . 1750) and Beatson's Political Index for 1788 and 1806: seniority list and index of officers of the Royal Navy.

XIV. List of ships lost 1759-1815 (compiled from Adm.14/36-165), typescript copy 1939.

Adm.168 Contract and Purchase Department, Adm.170 Ship Department, Ships' Building Specifications (Hull and Machinery), typescript 1962. List of documents now preserved in the National Maritime Museum. This volume also contains an index of ships' drawings in the National Maritime Museum.

Other particular lists and indexes are listed under relevant classes.

List of classes described

Accounting Departments: 16-20, 117, 115, 30-9, 41, 46-7, 49, 171
Admiralty and Secretariat: 1-2, 116, 3, 167, 156, 178, 194, 5, 8, 6-7, 13, 10-12, 50-5
Greenwich Hospital: 80
Historical Section: 137
Medical Departments: 97, 132-3, 98-9, 101, 104-5
Navy Board: 106
Station Records: 122, 125, 127, 172
Transport Department: 108
Victualling Departments: 109, 134, 110-12, 114
Various: 177

ACCOUNTING DEPARTMENTS

For Adm.14-15 In-letters 1693-1835 and Out-letters 1807-30 see *Guide to the Contents of the Public Record Office* II, p. 16.

ACCOUNTS

Adm.16 Treasurer's 1681-1836, 188 vols.

Examples of the scattered relevant references are: 16/120, repurchasing by contractors of stores originally purchased for Botany Bay 1787; 16/121, disbursements for transports 1788.

Adm.17 Various 1615-1850, 226 vols.

17/7-12, 1759-1836, include entries for payment of allowances to Mrs James Cook during the absence of her husband, to John Webber, William Hodges, and Lieut. Henry Roberts for work on paintings, drawings, and charts for the publication of Cook's voyages, payment of Lieut. William Collins's expenses from the Cape of Good Hope to London with despatches from Gov. Phillip.

17/15-27, 1790-1832, Consuls' accounts including a fee from the consul, Sandwich Islands, for the subsistence, medical care, and clothing of distressed seamen.

London

Adm.18 Bill Books 1642-1831, 155 vols.

18/116-17 include entries for Capt. James Cook and his officers.

18/120, 1791-4, includes entries for allowances to officers of the First Fleet and of the settlement of New South Wales equal to the wages of various servants maintained by the officers.

18/135-7, 1822-30, include entries for bills from captains of ships in Australian and Pacific waters.

Adm.19 Journal 1826-60, 35 vols.

In addition to general entries for transport and victualling services, relevant entries relate to bills drawn by commissaries in the colonies, and bills and accounts of captains and persons of ships in or bound for Pacific waters.

Adm.20 Treasurer's Ledgers 1660-1836, 357 vols.

Adm.117 Ships' Ledgers 1872-7, 1880-4, 1036 vols.

See Record and Establishment Books (Adm.115) and Ships' Ledgers (Adm.117), typescript, 1952.

REGISTERS

As noted in the introductory note to the Admiralty group many classes of Accounting Departments give biographical information. Special note should also be made of:

Adm.115 Record and Establishment Books 1857-73, 1090 vols.

For list see Adm.117.

Adm.30 Various 1689-1836, 71 vols.

Examples of relevant volumes are:

30/44, 1750-1800, stores lists of pursers including those of the *Endeavour, Adventure,* and *Dolphin.*

30/48, 1814-19, includes muster books, accounts, and correspondence of the colonial brig *Emu.*

30/49, 1813-18, contains the muster books of the colonial brig *Kangaroo.*

30/50, 1813-18, contains pay list of the *Kangaroo*, also the commander's entry book of correspondence and lists of crew and supernumeraries.

SHIPS' PAY BOOKS

See the following lists:
Admiralty: Accountant General's Department: ships' pay books: controller's and ticket office (Adm.31-2), typescript, 1960.
Admiralty: Accountant General's Department: ships' pay books: treasurer's. Series I-III (Adm.33-5) 1669-1832, 3 vols., typescript, 1959-60.

For Adm.31-5 Ships' Pay Books see *Guide to the Contents of the Public Record Office* II, p.18.

SHIPS' MUSTERS

See the following lists:
Muster Books. Index of Ships' Musters Series I-II, Adm.36-7, 3 vols., typescript.
List of Admiralty Accountant General's Department Ships' Musters Series III, Adm.38, typescript, 1924.
Admiralty Records, Musters, Series IV, includes Adm.39, 119, 41, MS.

For Ships' Musters Adm.36-9, 41, see *Guide to the Contents of the Public Record Office* II, p.18. In searching the indexes listed above, the Australian Joint Copying Project's

'Ships of the Royal Navy in Australian and Pacific Waters' is useful. It is hoped (1971) that this will be stencilled, see below under Admiralty and Secretariat, Adm.8.

MISCELLANEA

As noted above in the introductory note to the Admiralty group, many classes give biographical information. The following classes should also be noted:

Adm.46 Admiralty Orders 1832-56, 197 vols.

Adm.47 Record Books 1832-56, 25 vols.

Adm.49 Various 1658-1862, 176 vols. and bundles.

Adm.171 Medal Rolls 1793-1914, 59 vols.

171/16, 1845-7, 1860, 1866, Medal roll for the First and Second Maori Wars.
171/52, 1899-1902, Sea Transport Medal awarded to senior officers and certain others of the mercantile marine who served in transporting troops to the South African War and the Boxer Rebellion in China.

ADMIRALTY AND SECRETARIAT

Adm.1 Papers 1660-1943, 9749 vols.

See the following lists:
Adm.1, In-letters [and papers. List of Adm.1, 5691-9443, 1858-1938], typescript. Admiralty Secretary's Department In-letters preserved in the Public Record Office. Index to Captains' Letters 1793-1815, Adm.1, A-P. 4 vols. manuscript with type-script title-page, 1930. (A continuation of a similar compilation 1698-1792 in Adm. 10/8 Indexes and Compilations Series I.)
In-letters (Adm.1/3506-21) relating to the Royal Naval College, Portsmouth 1808-36, lists of names of candidates and parents prepared 1951 by P. A. Penfold from material compiled by Miss Fairbrother.

Up to 1839 there are sections for various types of correspondents. After that date, commencing Adm.1/5495, the New General Series begins, many papers having been weeded. Beginning 1/5495 each piece contains material relating to a particular subject or from similar correspondents and there are no sections such as Adm. 1/1435-2378 Captains' letters 1698-1839. During the 1914-18 War even volume arrangement of related papers was abandoned and files are in chronological order only. The description below of subjects and correspondents in Adm.1/1-5494 also indicates subjects and correspondents in the New General Series, allowing for the emergence of new subjects and correspondents and the fading of the importance of others. The series of volumes mentioned are relevant examples.

1/1-607, Admirals' despatches arranged by station, including 1/19-53, 1807-39, Brazil Station and 1/160-220, 1744-1839, East Indies Station.

1/1435-2738, 1698-1839, Captains' letters, arranged alphabetically by names of captains and chronologically within each letter of the alphabet. The letters are those sent direct to the Admiralty and, even if covering the same subject as those trans-mitted in Admirals' despatches, are often fuller or vary in content.

1/2739-3231, 1791-1839, Lieutenants' letters arranged like captains' letters and similar in content.

1/3246-457, 1787-1839, Letters from officers of marines arranged under commandants at Chatham, etc.; Field Officers 1/3317-324, 1802-39, include scattered letters from New South Wales. Many volumes may contain biographical information or refer-ences to employment of marines on hulks or on transports.

London

1/3542-4, 1795-1826, letters received from the Minute Branch include estimates of seamen needed for ships analysed by stations. 1/3544, 1824, contains many papers relating to the return to Hawaii in the *Blonde* of the bodies of the King and Queen.

1/3545-654, 1673-1738, 1832, letters from the Navy Board often concerning equipment of ships and occasionally conveyance of convicts to Australia. For letters 1738-1832 see Adm.106/2178-297.

1/3729-74, 1704-1839, letters from the Transport Department include requests for convoy and protection of transports going to Australia.

1/3775-809, 1822-39, letters from the Victualling Department include a significant number concerning transfer of surplus medical stores from ships to New South Wales colonial authorities. Earlier letters may be found in Adm.110, Out-letters of the Victualling Department.

1/3814-24, letters relating to the colonies. 1/3824, 1787-92, contains letters concerning New South Wales and includes marines' effective list 1788 and returns of men wishing to remain in the colony.

1/3825-48, 1719-1839, letters from consuls. A number of references to New Zealand occur.

1/3878-910, 1740-1839, letters from Doctors' Commons relate chiefly to Vice-Admiralty Court proceedings.

1/3930-87, 1697-1834, Intelligence, include lists of foreign ships encountered on stations, abstracts of ships and complements proposed to be employed in particular years, and abstracts of ships' dispositions.

1/3992-6, 1793-1839, letters from Lloyd's, chiefly acknowledging information from the Admiralty or sending information about the loss of ships, about safety of shipwrecked crews and about new banks and reefs.

1/3999-4035, 1703-1839, letters from the Ordnance Office.

1/4080-277, 1689-1839, letters from Secretaries of State including those for Home Affairs and the Colonies.

1/4280-2, 1718-1839, letters from societies. 1/4282, 1828-39, letters from the British Museum, Royal Society, and Marine Society, some of which concern donations by the Admiralty or meteorological, tidal, or astronomical information.

1/4283-313, 1698-1839, letters from the Treasury.

1/4366-5113, 1801-39, promiscuous letters arranged alphabetically by initials of names of correspondents and chronologically within each letter of the alphabet.

1/5253-494, 1680-1839, reports of courts martial. See also Adm.156.

1/5489-94, 1755-1809, letters relating to marines.

Adm.2 Out-letters 1656-1859, 1756 vols.

2/1-168, 1665-1815, orders and instructions. For later out-letters see Adm.13.

2/169-376, 1689-1815, letters from Lords of the Admiralty with separate series of volumes for ships, establishments, accounts, etc.

2/377-1044, 1689-1815, Admiralty Secretary's letters with separate series of volumes for public offices, admirals, captains, lieutenants, commanding officers of squadrons, etc.

2/1045-393, 1689-1815, series of volumes concerning or addressed to Vice-Admiralty Courts, consuls, courts martial, marines (series extending to 1845), pocket series and secret orders.

2/1394- , 1816- , the modern series of letter books with divisions for the following branches: Appointment, Legal, Military, Political and Secret, and Miscellaneous, also containing a few volumes of earlier date.

Adm.116 Cases 1852-1939, 3494 vols.

See list: Secretary's Department, Cases, Adm.116, typescript and duplicated, 1958.

Adm.3 Minutes 1689-1881, 286 vols.

Decisions minuted include movement of ships and men, orders for special expeditions, creation of new commands.

Adm.167 Board Minutes, Memoranda 1869-1938, 102 vols.

167/28-91, 1895-1934, are a continuation of Adm.3.

Adm.156 Court Martial Records 1890-1936, 191 files.

Cases extracted from Adm.1, 116, 137, 167.

Adm.178 Papers and Cases, Supplementary Series 1891-1941, 178 files and vols.

Includes items extracted from Adm.1, 116, 167.

Adm.194 Courts Martial Register 1812-1916, 45 vols.

Closed for one hundred years.

ORIGINAL PATENTS

Adm.5 Vice-Admiralty, etc. 1746-1862, 78 cases.

These include appointments of Vice-Admiralty Courts: 5/58, Van Diemen's Land 1825; 5/59, Western Australia 1831; 5/62, South Australia 1841; 5/63, New Zealand 1841; 5/72-3, Victoria 1857; and 5/75, Queensland 1860.

REGISTERS, RETURNS, AND CERTIFICATES

Adm.8 List Books 1673-1813, 1821-93, 172 vols.

Monthly lists with sections under stations and special categories as the need arose. Relevant entries are under East Indies, Brazil, China, South America, Pacific, Australia, Particular Service (e.g. forming a settlement on the west coast of New Holland), Surveying Service, Ordered Home, Prison Ships, Store Ships, etc., and there are also abstracts of monthly lists. Adm.7/229-96 and 560-1 partly fill the gap 1814-20. An index to selected ships has been prepared from Adm.8 and Adm.7 under the Australian Joint Copying Project and is provisionally entitled 'Ships of the Royal Navy in Australian and Pacific Waters'. It is intended (1971) that it should be stencilled.

Adm.6 Various 1673-1859, 428 vols.

See the following lists:

Index to Admiralty commission and warrant books 1695-1835, 1735-42, compiled by D. H. W. Young, 4 vols., typescript, 1958-9.

Index to Admiralty Secretary's commission and warrant books 1742-58 (Adm.6/16-18), 1758-80 (Adm.6/19-22), manuscript.

This class contains a mass of biographical material described in *Guide to the Contents of the Public Record Office* II, p. 21. The commission and warrant books 1695-1849 include 6/20 containing warrants for Cook's officers, carpenters, etc., on the *Endeavour*. There is also a group of papers relating to convict ships: 6/416 description book of the *Crocodile* 1850-2; 6/418-19 register and index of convicts on the *Cumberland* 1830-3; 6/421-3 registers and index of convicts on the *Dolphin* and *Dolphin*'s description book 1819-34.

Adm.7 Miscellanea 1563-1892, 1904, 1911, 781 vols.

Miscellaneous records, some of biographical interest.

7/229-96, 1796-1829, Board Room Journals are earlier volumes of the series in Adm.13/105-79.

Adm.13 Supplementary 1803-1902, 250 vols.

Records for the most part supplementing or continuing some of the preceding classes.

13/2-6, 1830-78, Port and standing instructions to commanding officers of stations including Australia, Pacific, East Indies, and China. The papers cover the creation of the Pacific and Australia stations. There are also sailing orders and many references to whaling.

13/28-40, 1859-69, Correspondence of the Military Branch concerning foreign stations continuing records in Adm.2/1583-616, 1816-59, covering conveyance of troops to and from Australia and New Zealand, the movement of men on the Pacific Station, taking possession of islands in the Pacific.

13/105-79, 1842-80, Board Room Journals. The journals form a useful guide to the movement of ships and include periodical reports of the whereabouts of all ships on particular stations. The class can be used as a guide to despatches relating to movements in Adm.1, Admirals' and Captains' despatches and also to order books in Adm.3, 167, and 46. For earlier volumes of journals see Adm.7/229-96.

INDEXES AND COMPILATIONS

Adm.10 Series I 1660-1851, 15 vols.

Adm.11 Series II 1741-1869, 72 vols.

Adm.10-11 are chiefly indexes to officers' services.

Adm.12 Series III 1660-1934, 1688 vols.

See list: Digests and Indexes Series III (Adm.12), typescript.

Adm.12 contains digests and indexes of Adm.1-3, 13, 116. 12/9 List of Admirals' Despatches, East Indies 1813-47 is particularly useful because East Indies Station records, Adm.127, cover only 1808-10 and 1838 onwards.

LOG BOOKS, ETC.

A guide to relevant logs of ships is provided by the list prepared under the Australian Joint Copying Project and provisionally entitled 'Ships of the Royal Navy in Australian and Pacific Waters', see above under Adm.8.

Adm.50 Admirals' Journals 1702-1911, 413 vols.

See List of Admirals' Journals (Adm.50) arranged alphabetically *c.*1744-*c.*1855 and by station 1855-*c.*1910, typescript.

Adm.51 Captains' Logs 1669-1852, 4563 vols.

See Admiralty: alphabetical list of captains' logs (Adm.51), 2 vols., typescript.
All lieutenants' logs and duplicates of captains' logs sent to Deptford in 1911 are now in the National Maritime Museum.

Adm.52 Masters' Logs 1672-1840, 4660 vols.

See Alphabetical list of masters' logs (Adm.52), 2 vols., typescript.

Adm.53 Ships' Logs 1799-1936, 100696 vols.

See the following lists:

Admiralty, list of ships' logs (Adm.53) *c.*1800-1885, 3 vols., manuscript.
Logs to 1913, 3 vols., typescript.
Admiralty: ships' logs (Adm.53) 1914-38, 10 vols., typescript.

Adm.54 Supplementary, Series I Masters' Logs 1837-71, 339 vols.

See list: Admiralty: ships' logs, supplementary Series I (Adm.54) masters' logs (1837-71), Series II (Adm.55) logs and journals of ships on explorations (1766-1861), typescript.

Note: the captains' logs of the ships in Series II are to be found (generally under 'Explorations') in the first volume of Captains' Logs.

Adm.55 Supplementary, Series II Explorations 1766-1861, 162 vols.

For a list see Adm.54. A List of Ships' Logs, etc. relating to Capt. Cook's voyages 1768-79 in the Public Record Office, the British Museum, the Admiralty Library and private collections is also available. Copies are in B.M. Add. MS.38091 ff.32-44; also copies in the National Library of Australia and the Mitchell Library, Sydney.

GREENWICH HOSPITAL

Many classes contain biographical material.

Adm.80 Various 1639-1919, 171 vols.

Miscellanea containing, besides biographical material, 80/119, 1846-54, papers relating *inter alia* to the duties of naval officers on foreign stations, mainly the Pacific Station.

HISTORICAL SECTION

See Admiralty 1914-18 War Histories (list of pieces with subject index), typescript.

Adm.137 1914-18 War Histories 1914-20, 3062 vols.

Papers collected to form the basis of the *History of the Great War: Naval Operations*, London 1920-31, 5 vols.

MEDICAL DEPARTMENTS

Adm. 97 In-letters 1702-1862, 259 vols.

The letters relate to staff, equipment, pay, etc. Entries for Cook occur in 97/86-7 and later volumes include requests for posts on convict ships and reports of conditions. Registers, digests, and indexes are in Adm.132-3 and out-letters 1742-1833 in Adm.98.

Adm.99 Minutes 1698-1816, 281 vols.

Relevant entries relate chiefly to transports for convicts and troops.

REGISTERS

Adm.101 Medical Journals 1785-1856, 127 bundles.

Besides Miss Fairbrother's Index and List VI there is a manuscript list of convict ships, emigrant ships and selected journals (Adm. 101) bound with T. J. Preston, *Report on Journals of Medical Officers examined at the Public Record Office . . . 1793 to 1856*, London, H.M.S.O., 1903. App. to Statistical Report on the Health of the Navy . . . 1902.

101/1-75, 1816-56, journals on convict ships, mostly proceeding to Australia.

101/76-9, 1825-53, journals on emigrant ships, mostly bound for Australia and New Zealand.

101/80-127, 1785-1856, are selected journals of which the following are relevant: 101/94/3 *Cockatrice* 1852; 101/95/4 *Curaçoa* 1841-2; 101/96/5 *Dido* 1855; 101/98/4

London

Emu 1814-15; 101/105/5 *Juno* 1856; 101/112/3 *Pandora* 1852; 101/114/4 *President* 1853-5; 101/122/1 *Talbot* 1844-5; 101/127/1 *Warspite* 1825-6.

Adm.104 Various 1774-1886, 29 vols.

Including lists of surgeons and assistant surgeons. 104/11, 1774-1886, is an index to services of surgeons and assistant surgeons in 104/12-28.

Adm.105 Miscellanea 1696-1867, 1871, 74 vols.

Reports of medical officers and reports on officers contain much biographical information.

105/36, 1836-51, reports on diseases on convict ships.

105/69, 1822-52, index to 105/1-12.

NAVY BOARD

Adm.106 Navy Board Records 1658-1837, 3577 vols. and bundles.

See the following lists:
Index to Navy Board nos.3021-34 (Bounty Papers), typescript.
Tables of Heads of Sections under which the correspondence of the Navy Board is digested. no imprint.

Apart from the considerable amount of biographical information included, the records contain information about ships sent to Australia and the Pacific, logs, pay books, crew lists, supplies, e.g. references to the requirements of Capt. Cook and his officers. Some entries concern conveyance of convicts to Botany Bay.

STATION RECORDS

See list: Admiralty Station Records, typescript, 1960.

Station Records sometimes duplicate material filed elsewhere but arrangement by area gives them particular value. The stations commanding Pacific waters until the establishment of the Australia Station were the East Indies Station and the Pacific Station, formerly the South America Station. The China Station became separate in 1864 but before that date it had been the senior division of the East Indies Station. The common boundary between the East Indies and Pacific Stations was the 170th degree of west longitude. The Australia Station was established in 1859 (see Adm.1/5716, letters from Admiralty to Secretariat, memo 25 Mar. 1859 giving the boundaries of the new station). In 1903 the boundaries of the Australia Station were extended to take in New Guinea and Pacific islands north to the Carolines and east to Tahiti (see Commonwealth of Australia, Parliament, statute no.8 1903 and Adm.1/7671 correspondence with Colonial Office beginning 28 Apr. 1903 and continuing to 1904 by which time the Admiralty had varied the boundaries of the Australia Station chiefly to include Cocos or Keeling Islands and Christmas Island within the China Station).

AUSTRALIA

Adm.122 Correspondence, etc. 1855-96, 27 vols.

122/1-6, 1866-91, general service.
122/7-8, 1874-84, New Guinea.
122/9-10, 1868-84, New South Wales.
122/11, 1868-84, Queensland.
122/12-15, 1855-89, Samoa.
122/16, 1862-76, Somerset and Thursday Island.
122/17, 1874-84, South Australia.

122/18, 1859, 1875-84, Tasmania.

122/19, 1868-84, Victoria.

122/20, 1870-83, 1887, Western Australia.

122/21, 1884-6, correspondence concerning the schooner *Albert* alias *Dours*.

122/22-3, 1873-84, coal.

122/24, 1885-9, gunboat *Gayundah*.

122/25-6, 1870-90, naval ordnance store.

122/27, 1856-96, photostats of material in the Mitchell Library, Sydney, dealing with Norfolk Island.

Later material is to be found in the New Zealand National Archives, Wellington, and in the Commonwealth Archives, Canberra. For descriptions of these collections see J. L. Cleland and P. Mander-Jones, articles on Australia Station records in *Journal of Pacific History* 1 & 2, 1966 & 1967.

CHINA

Adm.125 Correspondence 1828-1936, 148 vols.

The correspondence includes a considerable amount relating to the Pacific, Australia, and New Zealand, in particular communications with Australia, coal supplies, protection of British interests in the Pacific, guano, protection of vessels from United States privateers, the 'slave trade' in the Pacific, reports on islands visited and the 1868 Australian commercial expedition to eastern Asia. Some of the later records relate to Australian and New Zealand ships and men employed on the China Station. Records of the Australian squadron 1856-8 are in 125/135.

125/131, 1830-9, relates to the Cocos or Keeling and Seychelles groups of islands. Indexes 1856-1914, are at Adm.126.

EAST INDIES

Adm.127 Correspondence 1808-10, 1838-1930, 71 vols.

Relatively little relating to the Pacific has been found in this class. There are scattered references to communications with the Pacific, the acquisition of stores from Sydney, and returns of courts martial which include some on the Pacific Station.

PACIFIC

The Pacific Station was created as a separate entity in 1837 and Valparaiso was named as its headquarters. From 1848, and especially from 1865, ships in the Pacific squadron used Esquimalt harbour, and correspondence, memoranda, and reports accumulated by the Commander-in-Chief of the Station were left at Esquimalt when the base was transferred to Canada in 1910. In 1911 the Provincial Secretary, British Columbia, applied through the then Commander-in-Chief for copies of documents of local historical interest in the Station Records and permission was given by the Admiralty for copies to be made. These copies, if indeed they were made, have not been found in the Archives of British Columbia. In 1914 'early' records of the Pacific Station were sent to the Admiralty from Esquimalt and in 1937 part of these 'early' records, bound in three volumes, was placed 'on permanent loan' in the Archives of British Columbia (*British Columbia Historical Quarterly* 1, 1937, p. 260). Three volumes of 'early' records were retained by the Admiralty and are now in the Public Record Office, Adm.172/1-3. Meanwhile, in 1923, the Admiralty placed forty volumes (now bound in thirty-nine volumes) of the records which had been at Esquimalt, on deposit in the Public Archives of Canada, Ottawa. Adm. 155/1 is an index to volumes 1-20 (formerly volumes 1-22) of this deposit and covers the records of Admirals Stephenson, Palliser, and Bickford 1893-1903. This information

197

on Pacific Station Records was kindly supplied in 1968 by the Dominion Archivist, Public Archives of Canada, by the Provincial Librarian and Archivist, Provincial Archives, Victoria, British Columbia, and by Mr B. M. Gough, also from correspondence files at the Public Record Office, Inspecting Officers—Admiralty, General, 1934-45, Commonwealth Relations Office, General, 1927-37, and CA/1/4, 1959. For details of the records see B. M. Gough, 'The Records of the Royal Navy's Pacific Station', *Journal of Pacific History* 4, 1969, pp. 146-53.

The Archives of British Columbia have three volumes filed with the 1937 'permanent loan' from the Admiralty. Volumes 1 and 2 are Station Records containing documents relating to British Columbia 1848-59 and were apparently transferred direct from Esquimalt [1911-12?]. Volume 3 is entitled 'Vancouver Island, Naval Letters . . . 1863 . . . 1864'. It consists of copies of letters signed by the Governor with one letter signed by his secretary and may have come from the records of the Governors of British Columbia.

Adm.172 Correspondence 1843-58, 4 vols.

172/1, 1843, 1853, correspondence and reports concerning the contract mail service with copies of contracts.

172/2, 1845-58, hydrographical information compiled on the station from reports by ships' officers.

172/3, 1845-57, Navigator's, Friendly, and Fiji Islands, correspondence and reports.

172/4, 1844-5, in-letters of Rear-Adm. G. F. Seymour, some of which relate to Tahiti. This volume comes from the private papers of Rear-Adm. Seymour.

TRANSPORT DEPARTMENT

Adm.108 Records 1773-1837, 188 vols.

This class contains the records of the Transport Board 1794-1817 and the transport service provided by other branches of the Admiralty before and after that date. It contains information of a fairly routine nature relating to the provision of transports for moving troops and convicts, a considerable amount of which relates to Australia.

108/1-18, 1817-29, in-letters from the Admiralty and Treasury.

108/19-30, 1795-1806, out-letters to Secretaries of State and other departments.

108/31-147, 1798-1829, minutes with indexes to vols.66-77 which are in the main a record of in- and out-letters.

108/148-88, 1793-1837, miscellaneous items which include 148-57, 1793-1830, ships' ledgers, 158-67, 1795-1832, freight ledgers, and 182-3, 1814, 1821, printed rules for agents and for masters of hired transports.

VICTUALLING DEPARTMENTS

Adm.109 In-letters 1793-1849, 232 vols.

Letters from the Admiralty, Navy Board, Treasury, and other departments, the Solicitor, victualling yards and stations, ships' captains and surgeons, some relating to the victualling of ships and New South Wales. There are entries for stores for ships on the Pacific and China Stations obtained from New South Wales.

Adm.134 Register of Letters Received 1822-49, 45 vols.

Adm.110 Out-letters 1683-1831, 84 vols.

Many letters relate to the field of this survey and include letters concerning the victualling of H.M. ships, convict ships, transports, and New South Wales, also letters concerning bills drawn for supplies, travelling expenses. 110/82-4, 1814-31 are registers and abstracts of letters.

Adm.111 Minutes 1701-1832, 307 vols.

Minutes chiefly concern the accounts of H.M. ships including transports and convict ships, the Commissary, New South Wales, and bills drawn by officers.

Adm.112 Accounts, etc. 1660-1831, 212 vols.

There are scattered references to stores for ships bound for the Pacific and for the settlement at New South Wales and to bills of exchange drawn for stores at Sydney and elsewhere.

Adm.114 Miscellanea 1698-1860, 55 bundles.

114/16-22, 1824-39, 1847-56, expeditions to the Arctic and Australia including entries relating to the equipment and supply of ships for expeditions to the Pacific and Antarctic.

114/23-4, 1840-6, concern expeditions to China with references to stores purchased in New South Wales from Aspinall Brown & Co. and others.

VARIOUS

Adm.177 Navy Lists: Confidential Edition 1914-18, 18 vols.

Only sections were published during the war years.

CABINET OFFICE

For a description of the organisation, functions, and history of the Cabinet Office and a general introduction to the records see Handbook No.11, *The Records of the Cabinet Office to 1922*, 1966. The Cabinet Office subject indexes mentioned as searching aids on p.25 of Handbook No.11 are concerned almost exclusively with general policy and are of limited help in locating material relating specifically to Australia, New Zealand, and the Pacific. It has not been possible in some classes to summarise the relevant material but copies of detailed lists of such papers in Cab.23, 24, 37, 38, 41, 42, and 58, too long to be included, have been deposited in the National Library of Australia, Canberra, the Mitchell Library, Sydney, the Alexander Turnbull Library, Wellington, N.Z., and the Library, Australia House, London. The lists for Cab.37, 38, and 42 are complementary to the published Handbooks Nos.4, 9, and 6, noting only such material not clearly listed there as relevant to Australasia and the Pacific. Subjects covered in papers relating to Australia, New Zealand, and the Pacific in all these classes include Imperial, Economic, and Defence Conferences, Pacific policy, Imperial preference, dominion legislation and consultation, shipping and naval policy, emigration.

See the following lists:

Handbook No.11, *The Records of the Cabinet Office to 1922*, 1966.
Handbook No.4, *List of Cabinet Office Papers 1880-1914*, 1964.
Handbook No.9, *List of Cabinet Papers, 1915 and 1916*, 1966.
Handbook No.6, *List of Papers of the Committee of Imperial Defence to 1914*, 1964.
List of Cabinet Office Records, 1960, with later additions, typescript.

List of Classes described

Cabinet: 23, 24, 21, 1, 37, 41
Committees: 22, 42, 27, 19
  Committee of Imperial Defence: 2-6, 38, 17-18, 16, 35, 34

London

Committee of Imperial Defence, Colonial/Oversea Defence Committee: 7-11, 36
Conferences: 29-32
Historical Section: 45
Economic Advisory Council: 58

CABINET

Cab.23 Minutes 1916-38, 94 vols.

See index 'Cabinet Office Minutes, Subject Index (Cab.23) Dec. 1916-Mar. 1918', published as Vol.40 of the List and Index Society Series.

Minutes and conclusions of the War Cabinet, Dec. 1916 to Oct. 1919, and the Cabinet from Nov. 1919; also minutes of the Imperial War Cabinet 1917-18, notes of conversations on secret military matters 1918, and conclusions of Conferences of Ministers 1919-22. Sometimes Cabinet papers from Cab.24 (G.T. or C.P. series) or from Cab.27 (Committees) are reproduced as appendices to the conclusions and reference is frequently made in the conclusions to the relevant paper in the C.P. series. Early meetings in this class occasionally contain full manuscript notes of the discussion, but the majority record only a very brief comment on the discussion together with the conclusion reached. Up to the end of the War Cabinet the reference comprises the class number followed by volume number and number of the meeting, e.g. 23/1/12; after Oct. 1919 it comprises the meeting number followed by year number and number of the conclusion, e.g. 6(19)5. For a description of the types of papers in this class see Handbook No.11, pp.11-14, 27-8.

Cab.24 Memoranda 1915-38, 281 vols.

The subject index to C.P. papers (Cab.24) 1915-21 is published as Vols.29 and 41 in the List and Index Society Series.

The main series of papers (with indexes) circulated to the War Cabinet (G.T. series) and to the Cabinet (C.P. series). The class also contains a small series of papers, G. War series, reproduced in Cab.42, and a series of reports summarising the political and general situation abroad.

Cab.21 Registered Files 1916-38, 768 files.

See Handbook No.11, Appendix A, pp.37-50, containing a selective list of Cabinet Committees established between Dec. 1916 and the end of 1922 for which records have been preserved. Appendix A lists records drawn from Cab.21, and 27, with a few from Cab.24. See also list on Search Room shelves.

21/36 restriction of shipping, including Australian shipping routes 1917; 21/62 peace terms, and administrative organisation of the Empire 1917; 21/69 Commission on Dardanelles and Gallipoli operations 1915, 1917; 21/71, 78 Imperial War Cabinet on peace terms 1917; 21/95 food and shipping problems 1917; 21/98 Imperial Cabinet meetings, notes 1918; 21/108 trade with the enemy mentioning Australia, New Zealand, and Fanning and Washington Islands 1918; 21/111 Australian Purchases Committee, copper and lead 1918; 21/140 British Empire Delegation, Paris, 1919; 21/142 relations of British Secretariat, British Empire Delegation and Departmental Missions, Paris, 1919; 21/143 Peace Conference, British Empire Delegation 1919; 21/183 meat situation 1920; 21/187 Imperial naval policy 1921; 21/198 Empire Press Union, cable and wireless facilities 1921; 21/217 history of the British Empire Delegation 1921; 21/218 Washington Conference 1921; 21/219 memorials on battlefields 1921; 21/235 cables landed at Yap, Caroline Islands 1922; 21/260-3 national and Imperial defence 1923, including Dominion air forces and defence co-operation; 21/272 Pacific naval bases 1923; 21/295 inter-Imperial relations, co-operation and consultation 1926; 21/299 shipping, war measures 1927;

21/311 Dominion support and neutrality 1928; 21/312-13 Imperial Wireless and Cable Conference 1928; 21/315 Imperial defence 1928; 21/336-8 Imperial Conference 1930; 21/339 London Naval Treaty 1930; 21/342 London Naval Conference, colonial constitutional questions 1930; 21/361 Australia, appointment of Governor 1932; 21/362-7 Imperial Economic Conference, Ottawa, 1932; 21/368-9 Imperial defence 1929-33; 21/374 Monetary and Economic Conference 1933; 21/386 defences of Australia 1934; 21/393 world shipping situation 1934; 21/397 defence of Australia 1935; 21/398 Imperial defence, Hankey's mission to the Dominions 1935; 21/401 competition between the United Kingdom and Australian steel and munitions industries for New Zealand orders 1935; 21/402 Singapore naval base, Pacific defence 1935; 21/404-5 London Naval Conference 1935; 21/414 New Zealand: co-operation in defence 1936; 21/434 Defence Requirements Committee 1936; 21/440 defence policy, Dominions' munitions manufacture 1936; 21/449 food supply in war, Australian and New Zealand economy 1936; 21/486 Australia, 150th anniversary celebrations 1938-9; 21/487 New Zealand, liaison officer to Cabinet Office 1937; 21/488 Dominion co-operation 1938-9; 21/489-91 Dominion collaboration: meeting of Ministers in London 1939; 21/492 status of Dominion High Commissioners 1930-5; 21/493-4 British Commonwealth consultation on international affairs 1935-9; 21/495-7 Imperial defence: Australian and New Zealand assistance 1938-9; 21/498-9 Dominions air training scheme 1936, 1939; 21/500-2 New Zealand defence measures 1936-9; 21/503 New Zealand, trade questions 1934-9; 21/504-6 trade discussions with W. Nash, New Zealand Minister of Finance and Customs, London, 1939; 21/668-72 supply of war materials from the Dominions 1937-9; 21/677 supply of munitions to the Dominions 1937; 21/700-1 Imperial defence policy, annual review 1934-8.

Cab.1 Miscellaneous Records 1866-1922, 29 vols.

Mostly printed memoranda. Photocopies of most of these papers are in Cab.37. Noted here are a few papers which do not appear in Cab.37 or 24 and which relate to Australasia and the Pacific.

1/3/54 preferential trade with the colonies 1902; 1/4/7 free trade and the colonies 1903; 1/5/27 Australian attitudes towards the Japanese 1905; 1/10/30 report on the opening of the war 1914, mentioning Australia and New Zealand in the Pacific; 1/11/2 colonial governments' trade policies during the war 1914; 1/12/10, 46 Dardanelles, Gallipoli 1915; 1/21/1 release of Irish untried prisoners 1916, p.2 Dominion attitudes; 1/22/10 restrictions of imports 1916, mentioning Australia and New Zealand; 1/22/13 available manpower 1917, with tables, suggesting 6th Australian Division and 2nd New Zealand; 1/22/29 restrictions on supplies to allied governments 1917, p.3 colonies agree; 1/23/2 coloured troops and labour 1917, p.3 Fiji; 1/23/10 post war economic adjustment 1917, Dominions and preference; 1/23/15 nationalisation of shipping 1917, pp.13-15 inter-Imperial shipping; 1/24/3 position of shipping during 1917; 1/24/21 wheat from Australia 1917; 1/26/4 food supply, p.6 Australian meat; 1/27/2 German colonies 1918; 1/27/16 anti-dumping legislation 1918, pp.1-2 Australia; 1/27/24, p.4 German overseas possessions 1918; 1/27/26 peace negotiations, projected League of Nations, Pacific Commission; 1/28/8, 10 Peace Conference, British Empire Delegation 1919; 1/28/15 Peace Conference, p.13 German Pacific colonies, (3) British Empire interests; 1/33/4, p.323 Pacific, Australian, and New Zealand defence, threat from Japan 1912; 1/33/6 Dardanelles 1915, including letter 9 May from Jack Churchill describing fighting terrain.

Cab.37 Photographic Copies of Cabinet Papers 1880-1916, 162 vols.

The collection is compiled from various official and private sources and contains

London

almost all the papers in Cab.1. Many papers listed in Handbooks Nos.4 and 9 relate to Australasia and the Pacific and a detailed list supplementary to the Handbook has been prepared (see introduction to group).

Cab.41 Photographic Copies of Cabinet Letters in Royal Archives 1868-1916, 37 vols.

The descriptive list 'Prime Ministers' Letters at Windsor' is published as Vol.5 in the List and Index Society Series. Discussion of topics in the letters is brief and frequently only the decision made is listed.

COMMITTEES

Cab.22 War Council, Dardanelles Committee, and the War Committee 1914-16, 82 folders.

Minutes and papers all photocopied and chronologically rearranged in Cab.42.

Cab.42 Photographic Copies of Papers of the War Council, Dardanelles Committee, and the War Committee 1915-16, 26 vols.

A list is contained in Handbook No.9 and a detailed list supplementary to the Handbook with special regard to Australasia and the Pacific has been prepared (see introduction to group).

Cab.27 Committees: General Series 1915-38, 663 files.

Minutes and papers for Cabinet Committees on various subjects. See Handbook No.11, Appendix A, pp.37-50, containing a selective list of Cabinet Committees established between Dec. 1916 and the end of 1922 for which records have been preserved. See also list on Search Room shelves.

27/43. Indemnity 1918. Report, proceedings and memoranda, with brief mention of Australia and the Pacific colonies (W. M. Hughes in the Chair).

27/44. Economic Defence and Development 1918. (38) Retention of Imperial Control over Nauru Island 1918; (40) Phosphate Rock 1918, mentioning Nauru; (61) Food and Freight Policy 1918, wheat from Australia; (63) Dumping 1918, Australian legislation; (64) Nauru 1918; (81) Empire Cotton-Growing Committee 1918, with Australian Government representative.

27/52. Peace Celebrations 1919.

27/68. Ireland 1919. Vol.I, report and proceedings, Dominion feelings, distrust of British policy.

27/69. Ireland 1919. Vol.II, memoranda. (3) The Dominions and Ireland, mentioning Mannix, Ryan, and Gavan Duffy.

27/71. Finance 1919. 9(14) and App.B, Australian navy, fear of Japanese aggression; 14 The Bread Subsidy, Australian wheat prices; 15(6) Meat Supplies, Australasian meat and prices; 19(5) Australian Government and repayments.

27/88. Sugar and Wheat 1920. Third meeting (7) Australian sugar.

27/98. League of Nations 1920. (6) Mandates, pp.46-54 'B' and 'C' Mandates, Pacific Islands, Japanese objections to 'White Australia' policy; (9) pp.61-3 Permanent Commission of Control.

27/106. Decontrol of Food 1920, with references to Australasian imports and Australian drought 1919.

27/114-29. Unemployment 1920. 2/114 Minutes, with references to emigration; 27/115(14) Emigration; (40) Overseas Settlement Committee, agricultural workers to Australia and New Zealand; 27/116(51) Emigration; (61) State-aided Emigration; 27/119(241) Oversea Settlement and Unemployment; 27/122(354) New Zealand, Cornish tin-miners; 27/124(48) Empire Settlement and Development; (491) Overseas Trade, including Australia; 27/129(477) Overseas Settlement.

27/112. Imperial Cabinet papers 1921, concerning matters of policy and defence to be discussed by the Imperial Cabinet.

27/142. Observation of Armistice Day 1921.

27/164. Reduction of National Expenditure 1922, Part I, p.7 (13) Japan in the Pacific, threat to Australia and New Zealand.

27/166. Part V, Department of Overseas Trade: Estimates.

27/174. Overseas Settlement 1922, discussing various schemes for assisted passages and land settlement in the Dominions.

27/179. Trade Policy 1922 (10) Imports and Exports, including Australia; (12) Empire Migration and Settlement; (13) Empire Development Schemes, p.2 proposed unification of Australian railway gauges; (20) Measures for Promoting Overseas Trade, p.4 Australia, Trade Commissioners; (22) Training Centres for British Emigrants, urging Dominion Governments to establish farm training centres; and other general papers on overseas trade.

27/330. Compulsory Arbitration in International Disputes 1926, p.6 Australia and New Zealand opposed; App. Imperial Conference, pp.11-12 views of Dominions.

27/336. Equal Franchise 1926-7, with table, including Australia and New Zealand, and mentioning the Australian compulsory vote.

27/356. Beam Wireless 1927. Report, proceedings and memoranda, including P.M.G.'s memo, interim report of Imperial Communications Sub-Committee; telegraphic correspondence with the Dominions and proposed conference.

27/366. Competition between Beam Wireless and Cable Companies 1928, including Australian and Pacific communication.

27/417. Agricultural Policy 1930, wheat prices, including Australia.

27/428. Wheat Quota 1930. Memo on the operation of the Wheat Commission during the War, Australian wheat.

27/435. Trade Policy 1930, tables of industrial exports including exports to Australia and New Zealand.

27/492. Ottawa Legislation 1932 including Ottawa Agreements on imports; Part II United Kingdom and Australia; Part III United Kingdom and New Zealand.

27/495. Meat Policy 1932, imports from Australia and New Zealand.

27/567. Proceedings of a Conference between United Kingdom and Dominion Representatives on the Meat Situation 1934.

27/596. Political and Economic Relations with Japan 1935-6, referring to Australasia and the Pacific and Far East political situation.

27/634. British Shipping in the Far East 1937, mainly Singapore, Hong Kong and Anglo-Japanese relations, but also, by implication, Pacific and Australasian defence.

Cab.19 Dardanelles and Mesopotamia Special Commissions 1916, 1917, 1919, 33 folders.

Documents relating to the two Special Commissions appointed to inquire into the conduct of operations in those theatres of war, including copies of statements and other documents submitted, minutes of evidence and reports.

COMMITTEE OF IMPERIAL DEFENCE

A detailed description of the organisation, functions, and history of this body is contained in Handbook No.6. For a description of its sub-committees see Handbook No.11.

Cab.2 Minutes 1902-39, 9 vols.

London

Cab.3-6 Memoranda 1901-39, 53 vols.

These minutes and memoranda up to 1914 are reproduced in Cab.38, and listed in Handbook No.6. There is material relevant to Australasia and the Pacific in Cab.4 (B series, Miscellaneous) and Cab.5 (C series, Colonial Defence), which are now subject to a thirty year closure.

Cab.38 Photographic Copies of Minutes and Memoranda 1888-1914, 28 vols.

The copies are mostly from Cab.2-6, but some papers are from Cab.17 and 18; all are arranged in a single chronological order. Handbook No.6 is a full guide; a detailed list supplementary to the Handbook with special regard to Australasia and the Pacific has been prepared (see introduction to the group).

Cab.17 Correspondence and Miscellaneous Papers 1902-18, 199 files.

17/1-10. Naval matters; 17/1 distribution of naval forces n.d.; 17/3 protection of ocean trade in war 1902-12; 17/5 plans for combined operations in war 1905; 17/9 Commonwealth co-operation in the naval defence of the Empire 1912-13.

17/39-51. Colonies; 17/48 Australia, naval and military matters 1905-10.

17/52-76. Foreign countries; 17/56 France: New Hebrides 1904-5; 17/67, 74 renewal of Anglo-Japanese Alliance 1905-6.

17/77-9. Colonial and Imperial Conferences 1907-11.

17/84-90. Treatment of enemy and neutral ships in time of war; 17/86 British and Colonial ports 1910-12.

17/93-102. Committee of Imperial Defence: organisation; 17/101 Dominion representation 1912-13.

17/123-73. Dardanelles.

Cab.18 Miscellaneous Volumes 1875-1915, 99 vols.

18/7 New South Wales, report of the Royal Commission on Military Service 1892; 18/8 Colonial Conference 1887; 18/9 Conference of Colonial Premiers 1897; 18/10 Colonial Conference 1902; 18/11 Colonial Conference 1907; 18/12 Imperial Conference 1911; 18/29-37 returns of resources of Australian colonies 1886-91; 18/38-45 returns of resources of miscellaneous colonies 1886-93; 18/54-99 returns of resources of colonies 1894-1919.

Cab.16 Ad Hoc Sub-Committees 1905-22, 44 vols.

16/5. Military needs of Empire 1908, pp.33, 35 imports and exports, Australia and Germany, also Polynesia.

16/9B. Appendices to naval policy 1909, pp.219-22 protection of trade including Australian wheat.

16/11. Neutral and enemy merchant ships 1909.

16/14. Submarine cables 1911.

16/18. Trade with the enemy 1912.

16/24. Maintenance of oversea commerce in time of war 1912.

16/29. Insurance of shipping in time of war 1914, pp.370-1 Australia.

16/30. Supplies in time of war 1914, referring to Australia and New Zealand.

16/32. Empire wireless communications 1914.

16/36. Territorial changes. Reports, memoranda (T.C.). The first report deals with German Pacific colonies and proposals concerning the exchange of the New Hebrides for other French islands. Islands mentioned include Cook, Pitcairn, Caroline, Pellew, Marshall, and the Marianas, Nauru, Samoa, and German New Guinea.

Memoranda T.C.1-45 relate to the Pacific as follows: T.C.5 Australian and New Zealand interests, especially New Hebrides; T.C.8 New Hebrides; T.C.11 Japanese occupation of Pacific Islands; T.C.15 British trade interests, including New Guinea and Samoa; T.C.16 Australia and Japan; T.C.17 Rapa and Manga Reva Islands: hydrographic survey; T.C.21 British trade interests, including New Guinea, Solomon, Caroline, and Marshall Islands; T.C.22 Japanese claims; T.C.25 French harbours in the Pacific, including report on Society Islands, Tuamotu, and Marquesas Islands; T.C.27 German colonies 1917; T.C.29 territorial changes, including Pacific; T.C.32 air-route to India, Australian extension; T.C.41 air-route to Australia.

Cab.35 Imperial Communications Committee 1919-24, 14 vols.

Memoranda, minutes, and report concerning policy on telegraphy, cables, etc.

Cab.34 Standing Sub-Committee 1921-2, 1 vol.

Includes memoranda relating to British interests in Australasia and the Pacific, the Singapore naval base, Dominion Air Forces, Imperial naval policy and co-operation, the Anglo-Japanese Alliance, Australasia and the Pacific, military and air disarmament.

COMMITTEE OF IMPERIAL DEFENCE, COLONIAL/OVERSEA DEFENCE COMMITTEE

Cab.7 Minutes, etc. 1878-1922, 9 vols.

7/1. Secret and confidential reports and correspondence 1878-9.

7/1/1. Reports on temporary defences, (2) Australian colonies, Tasmania, and New Zealand, (5) correspondence with Admiralty and War Office, p.5 South Australia.

7/1/2. Correspondence on defences of colonies, including naval defence of New Zealand, and coaling station at King George Sound, W.A.; further correspondence on King George Sound and the West Australian mails.

7/1/3. Further correspondence, including defences of South Australia and the use of torpedoes.

7/2-4. Reports of Royal Commission on Defence of British Possessions and Commerce Abroad (Carnarvon Commission), 1881-2.

7/5. War Office memoranda on defences, including Cocos (Keeling) Islands, Fiji, Falkland Islands, King George Sound, Torres Strait.

7/6. Various reports on defences 1877-1900. 7/6/1 III Coaling stations, p.3 King George Sound, p.4 Falkland Islands; App.A, p.12 trade with Australasia, defences for coaling stations; B King George Sound; 7/6/2 Defence Committee meeting Aug. 1883; memorandum on defence 1884, p.14 Thursday Island; 7/6/3 correspondence on defence of colonial possessions and garrisons abroad 1884.

7/7. Minute Book Nov. 1879 to Dec. 1899.

7/8. Minutes Apr. 1900 to May 1916.

7/9. Oversea Defence Committee minutes Feb. 1919 to Nov. 1922, including 1919: aeroplanes to colonies and protectorates; guns for vessel of High Commissioner for Western Pacific; re-organisation of defence force; 1920: Falkland Islands: oil fuel storage; re-arming of local forces in colonies and protectorates.

Cab.8 Memoranda 1885-1922, 9 vols.

8/1-6. Papers in M series 1-504, 1885 to Feb. 1922, contents lists in volumes.

8/7. Unnumbered papers 1919-20; 8/7/33 Falkland Islands; 8/7/34 Western Pacific; 8/7/35 Fiji; 8/7/38 Falkland Islands; 8/7/48 Colonies and Protectorates, Falkland Islands, Fiji, Fanning Island, British Solomons, and Gilbert and Ellice Islands.

London

8/8-9. Memoranda, O.D.C.1-120, 1920-2, with various papers on imperial and local defence.

Cab.9 Remarks 1887-1922, 18 vols.

Remarks on specific schemes of colonial defence. Each volume contains a list of contents.

Cab.10 Minutes by the Committee 1912-22, 7 folders.

10/1/2. Norfolk Island, protection of cable landing place 1912.

10/3/10. Australia, defence scheme of the Commonwealth 1914; 10/3/11 Fiji, ordinance for defence force 1914.

10/4-7. Minutes 1919-22 on various defence matters.

Cab.11 Defence Schemes 1885-1921, 169 folders.

11/1 defence schemes: instructions 1899-1910; 11/21-2 New Zealand 1871-1913; 11/23-5 Australia 1895-1913; 11/26 Tasmania 1878-98; 11/44-5 Falkland Islands, strategic value 1886-1908; 11/46-8 Fiji Islands 1887-1914; 11/118-20 colonial defence 1887-1914; 11/121-6 colonial forces 1898-1913; 11/127-32 oversea garrisons 1888-1912; 11/133-6 colonial naval and military expenditure 1879-1912; 11/137-41 Committee on Colonial Military Expenditure, report 1888-9; 11/142-5 colonial military law 1863-1913; 11/146-69 port regulations, stores, armaments 1880-1912.

Cab.36 Joint Oversea and Home Ports Defence Committee 1920-2, 2 folders.

36/1/2. pp.3-4 naval threat from Japanese to ports, including Melbourne and Sydney.

36/2/1. J.D.C.6, 7 Disposal of surplus naval guns: offer to Dominions.

CONFERENCES

Cab.29 International Conferences 1916-38, 161 files.

Minutes and papers relating to the Peace Conference and other conferences.

29/28/2. Minutes of the British Empire Delegation 1919-22.

29/79. Notes of plenary sessions of the Peace Conference 1919.

29/80. 'The Dominions and the Peace Conference: a history by Clement Jones'; 29/100 memo of the British Empire Delegation 1920; 29/101 bulletins of the British Empire Delegation 1920.

29/117-35. London Naval Conference 1929-30; 29/133-5 delegations of the British Commonwealth.

29/139. Lausanne Conference 1932, including meetings of British Commonwealth delegations.

29/140-5. Monetary and Economic Conference, London, 1933; 29/143-5 British Commonwealth delegations.

29/147-58. London Naval Conference 1935-6; 29/151 conversations with the Dominions and India; 29/158 British Commonwealth delegations.

Cab.30 Washington (Disarmament) Conference 1921-2, 33 vols.

30/1-7. Minutes, memoranda of the British Empire Delegation Oct. 1921 to Feb. 1922, with index to plenary session notes; 30/13-18 Minutes 1921-2 of the Committee on Pacific and Far Eastern Questions (with index); 30/27 Notes of conversations between the British Empire Delegation and foreign delegations; 30/28 Conference resolutions (B.E.D. series); 30/30 Draft mandates, for approval by the League of Nations; 30/31 Sir Maurice Hankey's conference circulars; 30/32 British Empire Delegation circulars.

Cab.31 Genoa (International Economic) Conference 1922, 13 vols.

31/1-5. Minutes, memoranda of the British Empire Delegation.

Cab.32 Imperial Conferences 1917-37, 137 vols.

32/1/1-2. Minutes 1917 and 1918 of the Imperial War Conferences.

32/2-6. Notes, minutes, memoranda of the Imperial Conference 1921.

32/7-22. Imperial Conference, London, 1923.

32/23-37. Imperial Economic Conference, London, 1923.

32/38-64. Imperial Conference, London, 1926.

32/65-7. Imperial Wireless and Cable Conference 1928.

32/68. Committee on the Organisation of Communication Services 1928-9.

32/69. Conference on the Operation of Dominion Legislation, London, 1929.

32/70-100. Imperial Conference, London, 1930.

32/101-16. Imperial Economic Conference, Ottawa, 1932.

32/117-23. Committee on Economic Consultation and Co-operation 1933.

32/124. Economic Discussions with Australian Ministers Mar.-Apr. 1935.

32/125. Commonwealth Prime Ministers' Meetings, London, Apr.-May 1935.

32/126. Economic Discussions between United Kingdom and Dominion Ministers, London, May-July 1935.

32/127-37. Imperial Conference, London, 1937. (32/137 Polar Questions, closed 1969.)

HISTORICAL SECTION

Cab.45 Correspondence and Papers, 291 vols.

Papers used in the compilation of published war histories and Official War Histories. The compilations are in Cab.44.

AUSTRALIAN OPERATIONS (from German Archives 1923)

45/171. Questions submitted by the Australian Official Historian.

45/172. Information collected by Capt. J. J. W. Herbertson.

45/173. Information supplied by Herr Archivrat Stenger.

DARDANELLES 1914-19

45/215. German account, despatches concerning Dardanelles defence and naval operations, 1914-15.

45/216. Commander A. St. V. Keyes, R.N.: 'Y' Beach, 25 Apr. 1915.

45/217. Questions and answers from the Ottoman General Staff about the Dardanelles operations, 1919.

GALLIPOLI 1915

45/232. Extracts from Australian Historical Mission diary.

45/233. ANZAC: composition of the Corps and reports on the Campaign, including one by Gen. Birdwood.

45/246. Maj.-Gen. Cunliffe-Owen, ANZAC: landing at Gaba Tepe and the subsequent operations, Apr.-May 1915.

45/251. Sapper T. C. Farmer, 1st Co. N.Z. Engineers: three months in Gallipoli, Apr.-July 1915.

ECONOMIC ADVISORY COUNCIL

Cab.58 Minutes, Memoranda and Reports 1925-38, 208 files.

The Committee of Civil Research was formed in June 1925 to carry out economic, scientific and statistical research in relation to civil policy and administration, acting in a purely advisory capacity. In Jan. 1930 it became the Economic Advisory Council, with Sir Francis Hemming as Secretary and including on the committee J. M. (later Lord) Keynes. A history of the Committee and the Council and the standing sub-committees during its existence 1925-39 is in 58/16.

58/1-2. Minutes 1925-32.

58/3-16. Memoranda.

58/17-23. Minutes and memoranda 1931-9 of the Standing Committee on Economic Information.

58/95-208. Minutes, memoranda, reports of the Sub-committees of the Economic Advisory Council 1925-38.

CAPTURED ENEMY DOCUMENTS

The classes in this group contain microfilms of the documents of the German Foreign Ministry captured during the Second World War. Useful guides to this mass of microfilm are *A Catalogue of Files and Microfilms of the German Foreign Ministry Archives 1867-1920*, American Historical Association Committee for the Study of War Documents, 1959, lithograph, and *A Catalog of Files and Microfilms of the German Foreign Ministry Archives 1920-1945*, The Hoover Institution, Stanford University, California 1962-6, lithograph, 3 vols. The films were made in the course of a number of study projects, some official, e.g. G.F.M.4 and 5, and some, including the class of Australian Joint Copying Project microfilms described below, undertaken by private institutions and individuals. The original documents are now all returned to the West German Government. Films of German Naval Archives captured at the same time and noted in *Guide to the Contents of the Public Record Office* II, p.48, have been transferred to the Ministry of Defence, Naval Historical Branch; application to see these films should be made to The Head of the Naval Historical Branch, Old War Office Building, Whitehall, S.W.1.

See Class List of German Foreign Ministry microfilms *c.*1957, 4 vols., typescript.

G.F.M.4 and 5 Projects L and M 1863-1945

The films in these two classes were produced by the German War Documents Project set up by the British and American Governments, joined later by the French Government. Most of the material relating to Australia, New Zealand, and the Pacific in these two classes is included in G.F.M.23, but some material 1920-39 was not refilmed, positives being made from the official films and sent to Australia. A large number of the films in G.F.M.4 and 5 have been retained by the Foreign Office.

G.F.M.10-14 University of California Selection, Series I, etc.

These classes described in *Guide to the Contents of the Public Record Office* II, p.46, contain selections of microfilms made for various American Universities, and include material on the Pacific. Positives of relevant South Sea material have been sent to Australia.

G.F.M.23 Commonwealth National Library, Canberra, and Mitchell Library, Sydney, Selection 1875-1944, 14 reels.

The papers described in the class list are mainly earlier than 1914, and relate to Australia, New Zealand, and the Pacific area. A further twenty-six reels of supplementary material, mostly files 1887-1944 relating to Australia and New Zealand and dealing with such subjects as politics, industry, shipping, immigration, and propaganda, are available in Australia. The negatives of both series were made for the Australian Joint Copying Project.

COLONIAL OFFICE

In the early twentieth century the records in this group were arranged topographically as far as possible, classes being put together in separate series under individual colonies arranged alphabetically. Classes which did not fit into this arrangement, i.e. classes relating to specific subjects, or to the colonies generally, were formed into series under the heading 'General'. Many of the series and classes are continued in the Commonwealth Relations Office group with the reference D.O.

Within the series arranged topographically the arrangement of the classes is usually similar, any deviations are noted where they occur. The chief class under each colony is the Original Correspondence consisting of despatches, reports, and other papers from Governors, letters from public offices in the United Kingdom, and letters from individuals, societies, companies in the United Kingdom and the colony. The volumes generally have brief contents lists or indexes. Until the end of the eighteenth century comments were not attached to the letters but thereafter it gradually became customary for minutes to be written on the letters themselves and later still, for these minutes to be written on separate sheets and attached to the letters. By the mid-1830s drafts of replies began to be attached to the letters; these are particularly important to the researcher after 1872, when entry books of out-letters ceased to be kept.

The Original Correspondence was not at first registered. Précis books were kept until 1814 but do not cover all colonies. They are found under Colonies General, Entry Books, Series I (C.O.324) and among the records of particular colonies. (See Handbook No.3, R. B. Pugh, *The Records of the Colonial and Dominions Offices*, pp.20-1.) The earliest registers proper, found in the class Registers, General (C.O. 326/77-84) date from 1810 and relate chiefly to war matters though there are scattered references to colonial affairs. The modern type of registers was begun in the 1820s and is found in C.O.326/85-359. These registers recorded all in-correspondence except letters from potential immigrants which were no longer registered after *c*.1835. General registers ceased in 1849 and after this date separate registers were kept for each colony. The correspondence was usually entered in three distinct sections: despatches from Governors, correspondence from public offices, and correspondence from individuals and private organisations; the date, name of writer or office, number of communication, and, in most cases, a brief summary of the subject matter, are given.

Letters and other communications from the Colonial Office were, until 1872, copied into a series of Entry Books of which there is generally one class for each colony. The copying of all out-letters and other communications was abandoned in 1872, and a series of Out-letter Registers kept in their place. Like the Registers of Original Correspondence these were brief records of the date, correspondent, and serial number with a brief summary of the contents arranged in three main groups: communications to Governors, to public offices and to individuals in private organisations. Drafts of out-letters bound in with the volumes of Original Correspondence can be used in conjunction with the Entry Books or, after 1872, Out-letter Registers. The registers of in- and out-correspondence are of particular value where the original letters or drafts have been destroyed under statutory regulation. A stamp against the entry in the register shows where this has occurred.

Under each colony there are also classes of formal documents, most of which are printed, including acts, sessional papers, gazettes, public service lists, blue books, and other statistics. They are not included in the following descriptions unless in manuscript form. There are also considerable files of early newspapers published in the various colonies grouped with the Blue Books in the Miscellanea classes.

London

These are not described here, but are listed by A. R. Hewitt, *Union List of Commonwealth Newspapers in London, Oxford and Cambridge*, London 1960.

Classes under the heading 'General' such as Colonies General, Confidential Print, Honours, Patronage are similar to the classes arranged under 'Colonies'. There are separate classes for Original Correspondence, Entry Books, Registers of Correspondence, and Miscellanea. It should be noted that these subject or general classes contain much that is of importance to the study of individual colonies.

Three major published series of documents include material from the Colonial Office records relating to Australasia: *Historical Records of New South Wales*, Sydney 1889-1901, 7 vols. in 8, *Historical Records of New Zealand*, Wellington 1908, 1914, 2 vols., *Historical Records of Australia*, Melbourne 1914-25, 33 vols.

See the following lists:

Handbook No.3, R. B. Pugh, *The Records of the Colonial and Dominions Offices*, 1964.
Handbook No.8, *List of Colonial Office Confidential Print to 1916*, 1966.
Lists and Indexes XXXVI, *List of Colonial Office Records*, 1911, reprint New York 1963.
Comprehensive List of Colonial Office Records A-Z, 10 vols., 1948-55, typescript.
Supplementary List, 2 vols., 1948-55, typescript.

The Comprehensive List arranged alphabetically by colonies, contains all the classes grouped topographically under 'Colonies' and relevant parts of some 'General' classes. The Supplementary List contains all the 'General' classes. Together these lists replace all earlier lists except that given below.
Catalogue of the Maps, Plans and Charts in the Library of the Colonial Office, 1910.

List of classes described

COLONIES

Auckland Islands: 394, 330
Australia (General): 418, 557, 11
Australia (Commonwealth): 706-7
Australia, North: 395
Australia, South: 13, 331, 514, 396, 15, 17
Australia, Western: 18, 332, 353, 397, 19
Australia and New Zealand: 644-5
Fiji: 83, 419, 515, 400, 85, 459
New Guinea, British (Papua): 422, 578-9, 436
New Hebrides: 914
New South Wales: 201, 360, 369, 202-3, 206-7
New Zealand Company: 208
New Zealand: 209, 361, 365, 406, 211, 213
Pacific, Western: 225, 492-3
Queensland: 234, 424, 450, 423
Tasmania: 280, 370-1, 408, 281-2, 284
Victoria: 309, 374, 513, 411, 311

GENERAL

Supplementary: 537
Accounts Branch: 431, 622, 621, 701
Appointments: 877, 918
Chief Clerk: 523, 863, 864
Claims, 1914-18 War: 848
Colonial Empire Marketing Board: 868

Colonies General: 323-4, 381, 378-9, 432, 652, 694, 570, 854, 862, 816, 380, 325
Confidential Print: 881, 886, 885
Correspondence, Indexes: 714
Dominions: 532, 708-9
Dominions (War 1914-18): 616, 752-3
Dominions (War 1914-18): Prisoners: 693, 754-5
Dominions (War 1914-18): Trade: 687, 756-7
Emigration: 384, 428, 485, 385, 386
Empire Marketing Board: 758-60
Governors' Pensions: 449
Honours: 448, 728-9
Imperial Service Order: 524, 834-5
Maps and Plans: 700
Overseas Settlement: 721, 791-2
Patronage: 429-30
Personnel: 850
Precedence: 851
Registers: 326, 382, 668, 383, 600
Order of St Michael and St George: 447, 845, 734, 844, 745

COLONIES

AUCKLAND ISLANDS

See also Correspondence, Indexes C.O.714 and classes under New Zealand.

C.O.394 Entry Book 1850-2, 1 vol.

C.O.330 Register of Correspondence 1850-3, 1 vol.

Register of the in-letters relating to the Islands found under New Zealand, C.O.209/134.

AUSTRALIA, GENERAL

See also Supplementary C.O.537 and classes under Australia (Commonwealth) and Colonies General.

C.O.418 Original Correspondence 1889-1922, 226 vols.

In-letters, with minutes and draft replies, relating particularly to the Federal Council of Australasia in which South Australia, Western Australia, Queensland, Tasmania, Victoria, and Fiji participated, and to Federation of the Australian colonies. In-correspondence 1901-22 relating to the Commonwealth of Australia, its states and territories, is also included. Original correspondence for the colonies before 1889 will be found under the individual colonies. For correspondence after 1922 see Dominions C.O.532.

C.O.557 Register of Correspondence 1889-1900, 1 vol.

Register of in-letters in C.O.418. For registers 1901-8 see Australia and New Zealand C.O.644 and for registers 1909-22 see Australia (Commonwealth) C.O.706.

C.O.11 Memoranda 1842-58, 1 vol.

The following items are included: draft of warrants to the Australian Agricultural Co.; papers about the occupation of Crown Lands, the disallowance of the New South Wales Acts, ecclesiastical establishments, the surrender of mineral rights to the Crown, a war steamer for Sydney and Moreton Bay; minute on the severance of Norfolk Island from the Diocese of Sydney.

London

AUSTRALIA (COMMONWEALTH)

See also Supplementary C.O.537.

C.O.706 Register of Correspondence 1909-22, 9 vols.

Register of in-letters found in Australia (General) C.O.418. For register 1889-1900 see Australia (General) C.O.557 and for registers 1901-8 see Australia and New Zealand C.O.644.

C.O.707 Register of Out-letters 1909-22, 7 vols.

For registers of out-letters 1889-1900 see Colonies General C.O.379 and for registers 1901-8 see Australia and New Zealand C.O.645.

AUSTRALIA, NORTH

C.O.395 Entry Books 1846, 2 vols.

Despatches containing instructions for the establishment of the colony of North Australia, land grants to settlers and convicts, funds, appointments to public offices, and finally the revocation of the letters patent by which the colony was established. In-correspondence is found under New South Wales C.O.201.

AUSTRALIA, SOUTH

See also Supplementary C.O.537, Correspondence, Indexes C.O.714 and classes under Australia (General), Colonies General and Emigration.

C.O.13 Original Correspondence 1831-1900, 155 vols.

The letters include some from the South Australian Commissioners and the South Australian Association. There are also papers leading up to the annexation in 1863 of what is now the Northern Territory and its subsequent administration.

C.O.331 Register of Correspondence 1849-1900, 12 vols.

For earlier registers see C.O.326.

C.O.514 Register of Out-letters 1873-1900, 2 vols.

C.O.396 Entry Books 1834-73, 16 vols.

CO.15 Sessional Papers 1836-1925, 226 vols.

15/1-5, 12-13 contain papers of the Executive Council 1836-56 and of the Legislative Council 1943-51 in manuscript.

C.O.17 Miscellanea 1836-1925, 101 vols.

17/12-42 Blue Books of Statistics 1840-66 in manuscript.

AUSTRALIA, WESTERN

See also Supplementary C.O.537, Correspondence, Indexes C.O.714 and classes under Australia (General) and Colonies General.

C.O.18 Original Correspondence 1828-1900, 228 vols.

C.O.332 Register of Correspondence 1849-1900, 14 vols.

For earlier registers see C.O.326.

C.O.353 Register of Out-letters 1873-1900, 3 vols.

C.O.397 Entry Books 1828-73, 29 vols.

C.O.19 Acts 1844-1925, 31 vols.

19/1 Acts 1844-8 in manuscript.

AUSTRALIA AND NEW ZEALAND

C.O.644 Register of Correspondence 1901-8, 4 vols.

Register of in-letters in Original Correspondence classes under Australia (General) C.O.418 and New Zealand C.O.209. For later registers see Australia (Commonwealth) C.O.706 and New Zealand C.O.361.

C.O.645 Register of Out-letters 1901-8, 3 vols.

For later registers of out-letters see Australia (Commonwealth) C.O.707 and New Zealand C.O.365.

FIJI

Much material concerning Fiji before the machinery of government was properly established in the Crown Colony in 1875 is found in the Admiralty and Foreign Office groups. Papers for the period before 1871 are also found in Colonial Office records for New South Wales and Victoria; these include papers reflecting the interest of the Australian colonies in the prospects of Fiji during the cotton boom of the 1860s. See also classes under Australia (General), Colonies General, especially C.O.380, Correspondence, Indexes C.O.714, and Supplementary C.O.537.

C.O.83 Original Correspondence 1860-3, 1872-1946, 244 vols.

Original letters addressed to the Colonial Office with regard to Fiji, together with enclosures, departmental minutes, ensuing inter-departmental correspondence, and draft replies. Five volumes of early correspondence are of particular significance: 83/1, 1860-3 containing letters relating to the establishment of the Smythe Commission, together with Smythe's report and that of Seemann on the flora and agricultural potential of Fiji; 83/2-4, 1872-3 containing correspondence, mainly originating with the Admiralty and Foreign Office regarding the labour traffic, the propriety of formally recognising the Cakobau government and the setting up of the Goodenough-Layard Commission; 83/5, 1874 containing the Goodenough-Layard report, Sir Hercules Robinson's negotiation of the cession, and the setting up of the machinery of government.

C.O.419 Register of Correspondence 1860-3, 1872-1939, 20 vols.

C.O.515 Register of Out-letters 1874-1926, 9 vols.

C.O.400 Entry Books 1859-62, 1 vol.

This volume contains correspondence concerning the Smythe mission which is not available elsewhere.

C.O.85 Sessional Papers 1875-1950, 61 vols.

85/1, 4, 6, 10 papers of the Executive Council 1875-1905, and 85/2, 3 papers of the Legislative Council 1875-86 in manuscript.

C.O.459 Miscellanea 1874-1940, 66 vols.

Mainly printed Blue Books but also containing: 459/1A original deed of cession signed by Cakobau and Sir Hercules Robinson 1874; 459/53 Wilkinson's original transcript of the deed into Fijian 1874.

GILBERT AND ELLICE ISLANDS

For correspondence see classes under Pacific, Western.

NAURU

For correspondence 1914-21 see classes under Pacific, Western and for later correspondence see classes under Dominions.

London

NEW GUINEA, BRITISH (PAPUA)

For later papers see classes under Australia (General); see also classes under Colonies General.

C.O.422 Original Correspondence 1884-1900, 15 vols.

This correspondence including despatches from the Special Commissioners, Administrator, and later Lieutenant-Governor, with minutes and draft replies, covers all aspects of the administration and the activities of the Germans, Dutch, private companies, missionaries, and other individuals in the area.

C.O.578 Register of Correspondence 1884-1900, 2 vols.

For later registers see Australia and New Zealand C.O.644.

C.O.579 Register of Out-letters 1884-1900, 1 vol.

For later registers see Australia and New Zealand C.O.645.

C.O.436 Sessional Papers 1888-1925, 7 vols.

436/1 minutes of the Executive Council 1888-98 in manuscript.

NEW HEBRIDES

For correspondence see classes under Pacific, Western.

C.O.914 Joint Regulations 1907-23, 1 vol.

Copies and originals of regulations approved by British and French High Commissioners for use in the Condominium, arising from a convention, 1906 for the settlement of land claims, etc.

NEW SOUTH WALES

Since New South Wales originally administered eastern Australia and New Zealand, the records of Tasmania to 1825, New Zealand to 1841, Victoria to 1851, and Queensland to 1859 are to be found in the classes described below. The records of Norfolk Island and Lord Howe Island, still administered by New South Wales, are also included. For classes for the period 1901-22 see Australia (General) and for classes after 1922 see Dominions. See also Supplementary C.O.537, Correspondence, Indexes C.O.714 and classes under Colonies General.

C.O.201 Original Correspondence 1784-1900, 629 vols.

M. E. Deane's Index to C.O.201/146-9, 159-60, 170, 180, 190, 199, 208, 217, and 237 covering the period 1823-33, typescript, 1930, is an index to some of the miscellaneous volumes, and volumes concerning settlers, in this class for which contemporary indexes were not compiled. It indexes the names of writers, arranged in rough alphabetical order under the year in which the letter was written, and gives a brief indication of the contents of the letters. Bound copies are available at the Public Record Office, in the National Library of Australia, the Mitchell Library, Sydney, and the State Library of Victoria.

These despatches and in-letters, sometimes accompanied by reports, orders, regulations, and statistical returns, relate in detail to all aspects of the administration of the colony up to 1856 when responsible government was introduced. Even after that date, when the need for formal communications lessened, the subjects covered range widely.

A stray letter from the Colonial Land and Emigration Office and a draft letter to the Treasury 21 Dec. 1854 concerning payments for emigrants' passages on the *Abdullah* which should be in 201/480 are under New Zealand C.O.209/4.

C.O.360 Register of Correspondence 1849-1900, 16 vols.

For earlier registers see Registers C.O.326. A précis of in-correspondence 1800-5 is in C.O.202/2-4 below and a précis of in-correspondence 1805-9 in C.O.324/66 under Colonies General.

C.O.369 Register of Out-letters 1873-1900, 4 vols.

C.O.202 Entry Books 1786-1873, 78 vols.

202/2-4 contain a précis of inward correspondence 1800-5; for a précis of outward correspondence 1801-11 see Colonies General 324/66.

C.O.203 Acts 1829-1925, 85 vols.

203/1-16 Acts 1829-50 in manuscript.

C.O.206 Miscellanea 1803-1925, 187 vols.

206/61, 1810-44, includes précis and memoranda on the history of the settlements in New South Wales and Van Diemen's Land with statistical returns 1825-35, convict returns 1831 and 1834, return of convicts transported to New South Wales to 1810, agricultural and vital statistics 1830, abstract of quit rents 1834, and cost of defence in New South Wales 1834.

206/62, 1841-5, includes miscellaneous memoranda on the Roman Catholic religion, legal appointments, Port Phillip and Port Essington, North Australian squatters, and a paper by Buller on representative government.

206/63-99 Blue Books 1822-59 in manuscript.

C.O.207 Entry Books relating to Convicts 1788-1868, 8 vols.

Records of the Superintendent of Convicts returned to the Colonial Office in London.

NEW ZEALAND COMPANY

C.O.208 Original Correspondence 1837-61, 309 vols.

In- and out-letters, registers and business records of the New Zealand Company including some accounts from New Zealand as well as the papers of the home office of the Company. Registers of emigrants, journals of ships' surgeons, a register of applications for passages and a register of land transfers have been preserved. 208/307 is Col. Wakefield's journal 1839-42 and 208/308 his letter book 1845-8. 208/133-46 are various reference books, registers and indexes to correspondence in this class. Duplicate copies of many of the more important papers are in the New Zealand National Archives in Wellington.

NEW ZEALAND

Material relating to New Zealand up to 1841 is also to be found under New South Wales. For registers of in- and out-correspondence 1901-8 see Australia and New Zealand C.O.644 and 645. For all correspondence relating to New Zealand after 1922 and for relations between New Zealand and other dominions, Fiji and the Western Pacific High Commission 1902-22 see Dominions C.O.532. See also New Zealand Company C.O.208, Auckland Islands C.O.394, 330, Supplementary C.O.537, Correspondence, Indexes C.O.714 and classes under Colonies General.

C.O.209 Original Correspondence 1830-1922, 313 vols.

C.O.361 Register of Correspondence 1849-1900, 1902-22, 21 vols.

For earlier registers see Registers C.O.326.

London

C.O.365 Register of Out-letters 1873-1900, 1909-22, 9 vols.

C.O.406 Entry Books 1837-72, 28 vols.

C.O.211 Sessional Papers 1841-1925, 347 vols.
211/1-3a minutes of the Executive and Legislative Councils 1841-53 in manuscript.

C.O.213 Miscellanea 1840-1925, 107 vols.
213/26-8 Blue Books 1840-54 in manuscript.

NORTHERN TERRITORY
See Australia, South.

PACIFIC, WESTERN

The jurisdiction of the Western Pacific High Commission extends over the Gilbert and Ellice Islands, the New Hebrides Condominium, the British Solomon Islands, Tonga, and all other islands in the Western Pacific not administered by Australia, New Zealand, Fiji, France, or other powers. Since the High Commissioner is the sole channel of communication between these islands and the United Kingdom, there are no separate classes of original correspondence for them. See also Supplementary C.O.537 and classes under Colonies General.

C.O.225 Original Correspondence 1878-1946, 340 vols.

These despatches and in-letters include, in addition to the routine material on administration, material on relations with other powers in the Pacific and on the two World Wars. Various files are closed for fifty years.

C.O.492 Register of Correspondence 1878-1940, 23 vols.

C.O.493 Register of Out-letters 1879-1926, 7 vols.

QUEENSLAND

See also Supplementary C.O.537, Correspondence, Indexes C.O.714, and classes under New South Wales, Australia (General), and Colonies General.

C.O.234 Original Correspondence 1859-1900, 71 vols.

C.O.424 Register of Correspondence 1859-1900, 8 vols.

C.O.450 Register of Out-letters 1873-1900, 2 vols.

C.O.423 Entry Books 1859-73, 4 vols.

SOLOMON ISLANDS PROTECTORATE, BRITISH

For correspondence relating to the Protectorate see classes under Pacific, Western. For that part of the Solomon Islands administered by Australia see classes under Australia (General) and Dominions.

TASMANIA

See also Supplementary C.O.537, Correspondence, Indexes C.O.714 and classes under New South Wales, Australia (General) and Colonies General.

C.O.280 Original Correspondence 1824-1900, 403 vols.
280/2 is a volume of papers concerning the Australian Agricultural Co.

C.O.370 Register of Correspondence 1849-1900, 13 vols.

C.O.371 Register of Out-letters 1873-1900, 2 vols.

C.O.408 Entry Books 1825-72, 46 vols.

C.O.281 Acts 1830-1924, 35 vols.

281/1-7 Acts 1830-71 in manuscript.

C.O.282 Sessional Papers 1825-1925, 204 vols.

282/1-5, 7-20, 22-3, 31 contain papers of the Executive Council 1825-56 in manuscript.

C.O.284 Miscellanea 1822-1925, 146 vols.

284/44-78. Blue Books 1827-55 in manuscript. 284/50 includes a manuscript report on Aborigines living at Oyster Cove Station Jan. 1858 to May 1859.

TONGA

For correspondence see classes under Pacific, Western.

VICTORIA

See also Supplementary C.O.537, Correspondence, Indexes C.O.714 and classes under New South Wales, Australia (General) and Colonies General.

M. E. Deane's Index to the despatches relating to Victoria 1851-60, typescript 1929-30, was compiled from both in- and out-despatches preserved in Melbourne and is an index to persons, places and subjects mentioned in the despatches. It also serves as an index to the governors' despatches in C.O.309, the copies of despatches in C.O.411 and the War Office out-despatches 1851-4 in W.O.6. Bound copies are available at the Public Record Office, the National Library of Australia, the Mitchell Library and the State Library of Victoria.

C.O.309 Original Correspondence 1851-1900, 150 vols.

In addition to routine matters the governors' confidential despatches contain particularly interesting comments on the political developments of the period. Many communications relating to the period after 1873 have been destroyed.

C.O.374 Register of Correspondence 1852-1900, 14 vols.

C.O.513 Register of Out-letters 1873-1900, 4 vols.

C.O.411 Entry Books 1851-72, 13 vols.

C.O.311 Sessional Papers 1851-1925, 312 vols.

311/2-13 papers of the Executive and Legislative Councils 1851-6 in manuscript.

GENERAL

SUPPLEMENTARY

C.O.537 Correspondence 1759-1929, 1208 vols. and files.

This class is mainly composed of secret despatches and telegrams withheld from the various Colony classes of Original Correspondence and from the Colonies General, Original Correspondence at the time when they were bound up. Much of the material relates to defence and dates from the last quarter of the nineteenth century and from the twentieth century. Registers to this class are under Colonies General C.O.694.

Most of the volumes in this class are general, but some contain only papers relating to individual dominions or colonies. The following are relevant:

537/91-4, 456-61, 1138-53 Australia 1841-58, 1870-97, 1903-12, 1918-22; 537/462-4, 1154 New South Wales 1903-13, 1917; 537/465 South Australia 1887; 537/121-2,

London

1173-6 New Zealand 1870-97, 1915-20; 537/115, 413-15, 703-5 Fiji 1874-97, 1907-14, 1920-4; 537/136, 414, 447-52, 963-82 Pacific, Western 1876-97, 1900-14, 1919-26.

ACCOUNTS BRANCH

References to financial matters will also be found in the Original Correspondence and Entry Books of the various colonies and in the Original Correspondence and Entry Books of specific subject classes, e.g. Governors' Pensions C.O.449 and Emigration C.O.384 and 385, also under Colonies General C.O.323, 324 and 381 and Supplementary C.O.537.

C.O.431 Original Correspondence 1868-1925, 152 vols.

Correspondence with colonial governors, the Treasury and other public offices and individuals on financial matters. These include annual estimates of expenditure for the Colonial Office and individual colonies, grants-in-aid, bills of exchange, costs of punitive expeditions, and salaries and passage allowances for governors-general, governors, and other officials.

C.O.622 Registers of Correspondence 1868-1921, 18 vols.

C.O.621 Entry Books and Registers of Out-letters 1868-1908, 19 vols.

The Entry Books cover the years 1868-72 and the Registers 1871-1908.

C.O.701 Miscellanea 1794-1913, 28 vols.

Contingent Fund Accounts, Free Fund Account, Colonial Office estimates, salary lists, pensions, and other entry books and ledgers relating to colonial warrants, letters patent, and King's Messengers are included in this class.

701/1-5, 1795-1868, include some papers on payment of losses by shipwreck on voyages to the colonies.

701/22, 1911-12, is a volume entitled 'Queries and observations upon the account of the High Commissioner for the Western Pacific'.

APPOINTMENTS

C.O.877 Original Correspondence 1920-43, 22 pieces.

Earlier papers are in Colonies General C.O.323, and Patronage C.O.429. Relevant letters concern recruitment and training for the Colonial Service from the dominions and colonies, and assistance in recruiting suitable people employed in the Colonial Service for posts in the Dominions. Closed for fifty years.

C.O.918 Registers of Correspondence 1920-39, 7 vols.

CHIEF CLERK

For the history of the Chief Clerk's Department see Handbook No.3, R. B. Pugh, *The Records of the Colonial and Dominions Offices*, pp.10-11. For records of the Chief Clerk before 1901, except 1843-8, see Colonies General. See also Honours, Precedence and Order of St Michael and St George.

C.O.523 Original Correspondence 1843-8, 1901-31, 92 vols.

523/1A, 1843-8, relates to the internal management of the Colonial Office and financial matters relating to the Governors' commissions, commissions for trying offences, etc. The later volumes relate chiefly to honours, formal business and ceremonial, particularly colonial representation at Coronations, colonial appointments to the Privy Council, decorations, medals, seals, flags, and the drafting of Governors' instructions and annexation documents.

C.O.863 Register of Correspondence 1902-31, 8 vols.

C.O.864 Register of Out-letters 1902-33, 4 vols.

CLAIMS, 1914-18 WAR

C.O.848 Original Correspondence 1920-38, 7 boxes.

These papers concern losses in war, enemy debts, and reparation claims. Custodians of Enemy Property were appointed in the colonies and some of the correspondence is with them. Closed for fifty years. No registers have been deposited (May 1969).

COLONIAL EMPIRE MARKETING BOARD

The Board was set up in 1937 to promote the development and sale of colonial products but it was closed in 1939.

C.O.868 Original Correspondence 1938-9, 7 boxes.

COLONIES, GENERAL

The classes under this heading relate to two or more colonies or to all colonies in general. They are in part the records of the general departments of the Colonial Office including the Chief Clerk's Office; for a description of these departments see Handbook No.3, R. B. Pugh, *The Records of the Colonial and Dominions Offices*, pp.10-11. There is an emphasis in these papers on the formal aspects of colonial administration.

C.O.323 Original Correspondence 1689-1943, 1868 vols.

Various files are closed for fifty and a hundred years. Examples of material found in this class are:

323/34-95. Law Officers' reports and opinions on colonial matters, with related papers, 1784-1860.

323/97-116. Applications for passports 1796-1818.

323/117-41. Applications for appointments in the Colonial Office and the colonies generally 1819-35, and in the convict services 1856-61.

323/146, 149, 155-7, 162. Private letters 1825-30 to Hay from or about groups of colonies including New South Wales, Tasmania, and Swan River. Many concern patronage but there are other private letters from Darling on the condition of the colony, e.g. 323/146, 1825-6, and reports on conditions in other colonies.

323/165-75. Private letters 1831-5 to Hay including a few relating to positions in Australia, New Zealand, and the Pacific Islands.

323/176-1868, 1801-1925. Despatches from Governors (after 1871) and letters from public offices and individuals on relations between the various colonies, between the colonies and Great Britain, and between the Empire and foreign countries.

C.O.324 Entry Books, Series I 1662-1872, 175 vols.

Commissions, instructions, petitions, orders-in-council, warrants, letters patent, Law Officers' opinions, correspondence. Examples noted are: 324/46, 1797-1801, includes a warrant for using the existing New South Wales seal until a new one is prepared; 324/65, 1797-1807, includes opinions on cases of murder and assault in New South Wales; 324/66 contains a précis of inward and outward correspondence 1801-11 from New South Wales and other colonies on land grants, the state of the colony, appointments, the suspension of D'Arcy Wentworth; 324/85-7 contains private letters 1825-36 from Hay to colonies including New South Wales, Tasmania, and Swan River; 324/94, 1825-36, includes a few scattered letters relating to various subjects such as intending settlers in Australia and the obtaining of seeds and plants from Swan River.

324/103-5. Colonial and military circulars to Governors and others 1794-1820, 1826-40.

324/112-49, 151-2, 154. Domestic letters from Secretary of State to public offices and individuals 1798-1860.

324/150, 153, 155-75. Letters from Chief Clerk, Military Chief Clerk, and others, and registers of domestic in-letters and despatches 1847-72. The out-letters immediately following 324/171 are in C.O.379/1.

C.O.381 Entry Books, Series II 1740, 1791-1872, 93 vols.

Chiefly the formal documents associated with the establishment and administration of the colonies, including the erection of dioceses, the appointment of governors, colonial officers, bishops, members of legislative bodies, and instructions to governors and administrators. After 1872 only the drafts of such documents (C.O.380) are available.

Relevant volumes noted are: 381/4 Australia 1843-56; 381/5 North Australia 1846; 381/6-7 South Australia 1836-70; 381/8-9 Western Australia 1838-72; 381/26 various colonies including New South Wales, Van Diemen's Land and Swan River 1830-42; 381/55-6 New South Wales 1837-72; 381/57-8 New Zealand 1839-69; 381/66 Queensland 1859-71; 381/72 Tasmania 1870; 381/78 Van Diemen's Land 1837-69; 381/79 Victoria 1850-70; 381/85-7 warrants for all colonies 1801-16.

C.O.378 Register of Correspondence 1852-1939, 149 vols.

Up to 1849 some correspondence is registered under Registers C.O.326. 378/34, 1926, is also a register of out-letters.

C.O.379 Register of Out-letters 1871-1925, 24 vols.

379/1, 1871-2, contains copies of out-letters for 1871 and Jan.-Feb. 1872, being the volume immediately following C.O.324/171 as well as the beginning of the out-letter register. The register of out-letters for 1926 is at C.O.378/34.

C.O.432 Register of General Miscellaneous Correspondence 1860-70, 2 vols.

For a description of these registers see Handbook No.3, R. B. Pugh, *The Records of the Colonial and Dominions Offices*, pp.26-7. They cover material found in C.O.323.

C.O.652 Register of 'Unregistered' Correspondence 1886-1927, 4 vols.

See Handbook No.3, R. B. Pugh, *The Records of the Colonial and Dominions Offices*, p.29. The registers are arranged in alphabetical order under names; they index letters, mainly from private individuals, which were not fully registered.

C.O.694 Register of Secret Correspondence 1865-1928, 28 vols.

Indexes of secret in-letters and telegrams under Supplementary C.O.537.

C.O.570 Secret Entry Books and Registers of Out-letters 1870-95, 2 vols.

Entry Books up to 1872 and Registers from 1872 of secret out-letters and telegrams addressed to or concerning all colonies except those in the Mediterranean and Eastern departments.

C.O.854 Circular Despatches 1808-1956, 156 vols.

See Handbook No.3, R. B. Pugh, *The Records of the Colonial and Dominions Offices*. Other circular despatches will be found in C.O.323/244, 152, 261 and C.O.324/103-5.

C.O.862 Register of Replies to Circular Despatches 1858-1931, 25 vols.

A brief entry for the subject of the circular, and its date with an indication of which colonies replied and of when and how the answers were disposed, with lists of circulars sent except the lists for 1881 and 1900 which are in C.O.854. Some replies from Australia are in Supplementary C.O.537/156.

C.O.816 Original Letters Patent, Warrants 1834-82, 7 docs.

C.O.380 Draft Letters Patent, Commissions, Royal Instructions, Warrants 1764-1925, 215 vols.

These volumes of drafts, which are indexed under the above headings in date order, contain letters patent erecting colonies and dioceses, commissions of instructions for governors, warrants for appointments to legislative bodies, the bench and public offices, and charters of public companies and banks.

Relevant volumes noted are: 380/12 Various colonies including New South Wales 1786-97; 380/104-6 New South Wales and Van Diemen's Land 1835-54; 380/107 New South Wales, Tasmania and Norfolk Island 1855-9; 380/108-9 New South Wales and Tasmania 1860-73; 380/110-11 Victoria 1850-73; 380/112-14 Queensland 1859-73; 380/115 New South Wales, Tasmania, Victoria, Queensland 1874-82; 380/116-20 Western Australia and South Australia 1830-73; 380/121 Western Australia, South Australia, and New Zealand 1874-82; 380/122-6 New Zealand 1839-73; 380/127 Fiji and Western Pacific 1875-82; 380/130-2 Miscellaneous 1807-82; 380/140 New South Wales and Van Diemen's Land 1790-1829; 380/142 Index 1787-1842; 380/160 New Zealand, Fiji, and Western Pacific 1883-1905; 380/161 Australia 1900-5, New South Wales and Victoria 1883-1905; 380/162 South Australia, Western Australia, and Tasmania 1883-1905; 380/163 Queensland, British New Guinea 1883-1905; 380/181 Fiji and Western Pacific 1906-25.

C.O.325 Miscellanea 1744-1877, 53 vols.

See Handbook No.3, R. B. Pugh, *The Records of the Colonial and Dominions Offices*. The following volumes were noted:

325/16. Returns of colonial appointments, Ceylon, New South Wales 1817.

325/20. Lists of those holding office in each colony with salaries 1834.

325/21-2. Registers of applications for colonial appointments 1820-32.

325/23. Registers of applications for colonial appointments in the convict service 1855-8.

325/24, 28. Colonial statistical returns 1832-9. 325/28 includes visitation reports of Archdeacons Scott and Broughton on Tasmania 1826-30, accompanied by governors' despatches.

325/32. Précis of cases relating to the Cape of Good Hope, Ceylon, New South Wales etc., 1825-6.

325/33. Private papers, Cape of Good Hope, New South Wales 1826-7.

325/35. Private papers, miscellaneous 1826.

325/36. Regulations respecting grants of land in the Australian colonies 1826-31.

325/38. Précis and memoranda, Australia 1827-48.

325/40. Précis and memoranda, state of the Roman Catholic Church in the colonies 1833-51.

325/43. Relations with New Zealand Co. 1840-5; Western Australian minerals, Port Gregory or Champion Bay suggested as a touching point for steamship service between Java and Australia *c*.1850.

CONFIDENTIAL PRINT

Handbook No.8 *List of Colonial Office Confidential Print to 1916* contains a short introduction and a list of the print arranged in sections corresponding with the classification of the print in series. The list gives reference, date, description and number of pages of each paper.

C.O.881 Australia 1833-1923, 15 vols.

This class includes Australia as a whole and the individual colonies, also New Guinea, New Zealand, and the South and West Pacific.

C.O.886 Dominions 1907-25, 11 vols.

C.O.885 Miscellaneous 1839-1933, 34 vols.

CORRESPONDENCE

C.O.714 Indexes 1795-1870, 165 vols.

Indexes to the correspondence of the Colonial Office compiled in the mid-nineteenth century, see Handbook No.3, R. B. Pugh, *The Records of the Colonial and Dominions Offices*, p.43. In general under each colony there are separate volumes of Governors' correspondence, domestic correspondence, general correspondence, and alphabetical indexes of subjects for each colony. The two first are arranged chronologically under the colony or office originating the correspondence. The alphabetical indexes contain brief entries describing the correspondence in date order under subject headings which are enumerated at the beginning of each volume. Relevant volumes noted are: 714/5 Auckland Islands 1846-55; 714/6 Australia (General) 1845; 714/7-10 South Australia 1835-66; 714/11-15 Western Australia 1828-66; 714/53 Emigration 1850-7; 714/113-18 New South Wales 1812-70; 714/119-22 New Zealand 1840-70; 714/130 Queensland 1859-66; 714/148-53 Tasmania 1820-66; 714/162-3 Victoria 1851-66.

DOMINIONS

The Dominions Division, established in 1907, dealt with matters relating to the Dominions and, for practical reasons, to certain other territories including the Western Pacific High Commission area and Fiji. The classes under this heading include papers concerning all or several of the Dominions, and continue the various classes for individual Dominions when these series were closed in 1922, except those for the Western Pacific High Commission and Fiji where the records continued to be filed under those headings. See also classes under Colonies General.

C.O.532 Original Correspondence 1907-25, 335 vols.

In-letters to 1922 relating to matters concerning two or more colonies, e.g. laws, international agreements made by the United Kingdom affecting the Empire, parliamentary affairs, colonial conferences, defence, trade, and communications. After 1922 correspondence relating specifically to Australia and New Zealand is found here. This class is continued in Commonwealth Relations Office, D.O.35.

C.O.708 Register of Correspondence 1907-26, 37 vols.

C.O.709 Register of Out-letters 1907-26, 12 vols.

DOMINIONS (WAR OF 1914-18)

C.O.616 Original Correspondence 1914-19, 82 vols.

In-letters, minutes and draft replies about the progress of the war, the Dominion contingents, munition workers for the United Kingdom from the colonies, supplies for the armies, donations to the United Kingdom War Relief Funds and other causes, and some trade matters including the black listing of companies known or suspected to be trading with the enemy and additions to the lists of prohibited exports.

C.O.752 Register of Correspondence 1914-19, 8 vols.

C.O.753 Register of Out-letters 1914-19, 5 vols.

DOMINIONS (WAR OF 1914-18): PRISONERS

C.O.693 Original Correspondence 1917-19, 10 vols.

Correspondence concerning Germans interned in the Dominions, their treatment, movements, and repatriation, and also correspondence on military courts for the trial of prisoners of war.

C.O.754 Register of Correspondence 1917-19, 2 vols.

C.O.755 Register of Out-letters 1916-19, 4 vols.

DOMINIONS (WAR OF 1914-18): TRADE

C.O.687 Original Correspondence 1916-19, 68 vols.

Correspondence on trade among the United Kingdom, the Dominions, and the colonies, Empire trade with allied and neutral countries, and investigations into attempted trade with enemy sympathisers. Some trade matters are also dealt with in Dominions C.O.532.

C.O.756 Register of Correspondence 1916-19, 4 vols.

C.O.757 Register of Out-letters 1916-19, 4 vols.

EMIGRATION

C.O.384 Original Correspondence 1817-96, 193 vols.

In-letters from public offices including the Agent General for Emigration and the Land Board, and from individuals. They include general policy letters on emigration to the various colonies in Australia and to New Zealand, and administrative matters such as selection of emigrant agents, their salaries and expenses, and the chartering, equipment, and despatch of ships. They also include letters from individuals, parishes, and societies, and from naval and military personnel about land grants.

384/28 contains letters 1830-1 from individuals, arranged alphabetically, many of which concern suggested schemes for emigration, or alterations to existing systems; there are separate sections for writers such as R. Gouger whose section contains letters and pamphlets about emigration generally, child emigration and the South Australian Land Co.

384/108-54, 1876-85, contain despatches from Fiji, New South Wales, Queensland, and other colonies on indentured Indian, Chinese, and Pacific Island labour.

There is a gap in the records for 1857-72. Before 1872 the letters are domestic only. After that date they include despatches from the colonies; earlier despatches are in the Original Correspondence class under the various colony headings. Papers on emigration 1857-72 and after 1896 will be found under the colony concerned and under Colonies General. Papers after 1918 will be found under Overseas Settlement.

C.O.428 Register of Correspondence 1850-96, 14 vols.

An index to emigration correspondence 1850-7 is under Correspondence C.O. 714/53.

C.O.485 Register of Out-letters 1872-1903, 9 vols.

C.O.385 Entry Books 1814-71, 30 vols.

385/3-4. Registers of intending emigrants to whom information had been sent 1831-3.

385/5. Out-letters to New South Wales 1832-3.

385/6. Out-letters to Tasmania 1832-3.

385/11. Out-letters on bounties 1831-2.

385/30. Out-letters concerning the sending of emigrants to the disturbed parts of New Zealand 1862-71.

Other volumes contain letters referring to loans to emigrants, expenses incurred in shipping emigrants, salaries of emigration officers, and cases of distressed emigrants.

C.O.386 Land and Emigration Commission 1833-94, 193 vols.

386/1-9. In-letters 1838-78 to the Land and Emigration Commissioners. 386/1 contains letters from Gawler during his voyage to South Australia about the conditions for emigrants on his ship, and his first despatches from the colony concerning the general situation and finance.

386/10-42. Entry books of correspondence 1833-46 to the Colonial Office and others, from public bodies, offices and individuals, e.g. the South Australian Association 1833-5, Light and Kingston 1836, the South Australian Commission 1837-8, the South Australian Colonisation Office 1838-46, the Emigration Commission 1839-46, and the Agent General for Emigration 1837-9.

386/43-119. Letters 1838-76 to the Colonial Office from the Land and Emigration Commission on land policy generally, sales of land, bounties, and the encouragement of emigration.

386/120. Private letter book of Sir Frederick Rogers 1852-60.

386/121-36. Letters 1837-73 to Emigration Agents, Colonial Secretaries from the Colonial Land and Emigration Office on the despatch and equipment of emigrant ships, gratuities for surgeon superintendents and matrons, child emigration, German emigration, land, and exploration. 386/126, 1849-50, contains details of paid passages to Adelaide.

386/137-93, 1835-94, include registers of correspondence, land orders, registers and indexes of emigrant labourers' applications for free passages to South Australia 1836-41, registers of births and deaths of emigrants at sea 1847-69, lists of ships chartered, with statistics of emigrants and details of ships' departures and destinations 1847-67, and registers of ships' surgeons 1854-94.

EMPIRE MARKETING BOARD

The Board was set up in 1926 to promote the marketing of Empire products in Britain and to foster intra-imperial trade. It was dissolved in 1933.

C.O.758 Original Correspondence 1922-34, 107 boxes.

C.O.759 Card Index, 134 packets.

759/1-72 contain the name index and 759/73-134 the subject index.

C.O.760 Minutes and Papers 1926-33, 39 vols.

GOVERNORS' PENSIONS

C.O.449 Original Correspondence 1863-1925, 10 vols.

Claims and related correspondence concerning pensions for colonial governors. 449/1, 1863-5, contains material on negotiations leading up to the Governors' Pensions Act 1865; subsequent volumes contain material on legislation amending the Act. Registers to this class are in Colonies General C.O.378. Out-letters and registers are in Colonies General C.O.324, 381, 379. For correspondence 1925-31 see Colonies General C.O.323 and for correspondence after 1931 see Personnel C.O.850.

HONOURS

For the period before 1858 see classes under Colonies General. See also classes under individual colonies, Chief Clerk, Imperial Service Order and Order of St Michael and St George.

C.O.448 Original Correspondence 1858-1943, 68 vols.

In-letters and telegrams from the colonies and dominions making recommendations for honours, in most cases accompanied by brief histories of the individuals concerned, with minutes and draft replies on the recommendation. Also letters on the administration of the honours system and on the cancellation of honours. Various files closed for fifty years.

C.O.728 Register of Correspondence 1859-1939, 18 vols.

After 1930 these registers also refer to the correspondence of the Order of St Michael and St George C.O.447. Various files closed for fifty years.

C.O.729 Register of Out-letters 1872-1934, 4 vols.

Various files closed for fifty years.

IMPERIAL SERVICE ORDER

C.O.524 Original Correspondence 1902-32, 14 vols.

C.O.834 Register of Correspondence 1902-26, 2 vols.

C.O.835 Register of Out-letters 1902-26, 2 vols.

MAPS AND PLANS

C.O.700 Maps 17th-19th cent., c.1600 maps.

For a description of the maps in this class see *Catalogue of the Maps, Plans and Charts in the Library of the Colonial Office*, London 1910. Most maps listed in this catalogue up to 1885 are in this class, the remainder being still in the Colonial Office Library. The catalogue is in alphabetical order of country. In addition to headings such as Australia, Fiji Islands, New Guinea, see the general headings Eastern, Miscellaneous, Pacific, and The World. For other maps and plans among the Colonial Office records searchers should consult the general card index of maps described in the general introduction to the Public Record Office.

OVERSEAS SETTLEMENT

C.O.721 Original Correspondence 1918-25, 118 vols.

In-letters from Dominion governments, High Commissioners and Agents General on settlement within the Empire and on the administration of the Empire Settlement Act 1922.

C.O.791 Register of Correspondence 1918-26, 10 vols.

C.O.792 Daily Register of Correspondence 1919-27, 4 vols.

PATRONAGE

See also Appointments C.O.877 and Personnel C.O.850. There is also a considerable amount of material in Colonies General C.O.323 and in classes under individual colonies.

London

C.O.429 Original Correspondence 1867-70, 1881-1919, 131 vols.

In-letters relating to applications for appointments. Applications are from people in the colonies seeking positions or preferment, and from people in Great Britain seeking positions in the Colonial Office or colonies.

C.O.430 Register of Correspondence 1867-70, 1887-1918, 20 vols.

Index of in-letters. 430/7, 1896-1901, contains confidential applications arranged under the names of the various colonies; 430/8, 1896-1904, lists private recommendations. For 1881-6 see registers under Colonies General.

PERSONNEL

C.O.850 Original Correspondence 1932-40, 181 boxes.

PRECEDENCE

See also classes under Colonies General, Dominions, and Chief Clerk, and also classes under individual colonies.

C.O.851 Original Correspondence 1873-85, 1 box.

Copies of documents on problems of precedence arising in the colonies.

REGISTERS

For an account of these registers see Handbook No.3, R. B. Pugh, *The Records of the Colonial and Dominions Offices*, pp. 21-3, 30, 41.

C.O.326 General 1623-1849, 358 vols.

Separate classes of registers for individual colonies do not exist before 1849, but are to be found in this general class.

326/77-82, 1810-16, relate chiefly to war matters but contain some scattered references to the colonies.

326/85-358, 1822-49, contain entries of correspondence from Governors, public offices, and individuals relating to the colonies. Letters from intending emigrants are entered only to the mid-1830s.

C.O.382 Daily Correspondence 1849-1929, 82 vols.

Registers of all correspondence received in the Colonial Office. The entries at first include a brief statement of the subject matter but in 1873 this was omitted for despatches from the colonies. 382/63, 1909, includes out-letters.

C.O.668 Daily Correspondence, Out-letters 1901-10, 9 vols.

Registers of out-letters similar in form to C.O.382. For 1909 see 382/63.

C.O.383 Acts 1781-1892, 93 vols.

Registers of Acts received from the colonies, the Acts being arranged in classes under individual colonies. Relevant volumes noted are: 383/32 Fiji 1875-91; 383/61 New Guinea 1888-91; 383/62 New South Wales, Tasmania, Victoria, Western Australia, South Australia, New Zealand 1841-56; 383/63 New South Wales 1856-66, Tasmania 1857-65, Western Australia 1857-65, Victoria 1857-67, South Australia 1857-67, Queensland 1860-6; 383/64 Western Australia 1866-70, Queensland 1866-74, New South Wales 1866-75, Tasmania 1866-77, South Australia 1867-77, Victoria 1868-77; 383/65 New South Wales 1875-92; 383/66-8 New Zealand 1856-91; 383/77 Queensland 1875-92; 383/85 Tasmania 1878-91; 383/92 Victoria 1878-91.

C.O.600 Printing 1864-1914, 26 vols.
Registers of documents, including Confidential Print, sent to the printer.

ST MICHAEL AND ST GEORGE, ORDER OF

C.O.447 Original Correspondence 1836-1932, 129 vols. and files.
447/9-10, 1868-9, contain miscellaneous memoranda on the extension of the Order to all colonies. 447/125-9 are files of papers.

C.O.845 Register of Correspondence 1869-1930, 5 vols.
After 1930 the correspondence is registered in Honours C.O.728.

C.O.734 Entry Books and Register of Out-letters 1838-1934, 7 vols.

C.O.844 Original Warrants and Letters Patent 1852-99, 8 vols.

C.O.745 Miscellanea 1818-1940, 5 vols.

COMMONWEALTH RELATIONS OFFICE

See the following lists:
Handbook No.3, R. B. Pugh, *The Records of the Colonial and Dominions Offices,* 1964.
List of Commonwealth Relations Office, 2 vols., typescript. Arranged in alphabetical order of country except the list of Confidential Print D.O.114-16.

DOMINIONS

D.O.35 Original Correspondence 1926-53, 1231 boxes.
Continues C.O.532. Various files closed for fifty and a hundred years.

D.O.3 Register of Correspondence 1927-36, 133 vols.
Continues C.O.708. Part closed for fifty years.

D.O.4 Register of Out-letters 1927-9, 3 vols.
Continues C.O.709.

HONOURS (DOMINIONS)

D.O.36 Original Correspondence 1927-9, 2 vols.
Continues C.O.448. Part closed for a hundred years.

IMPERIAL SERVICE ORDER (DOMINIONS)

D.O.81 Original Correspondence 1927-9, 1 vol.
Continues C.O.524.

OVERSEAS SETTLEMENT

D.O.57 Original Correspondence 1926-36, 189 boxes.
Continues C.O.721.

D.O.5 Register of Correspondence 1927-36, 12 vols.
Continues C.O.791.

D.O.6 Register of Daily Correspondence 1928-9, 3 vols.
Continues C.O.792.

ST MICHAEL AND ST GEORGE, ORDER OF (DOMINIONS)

D.O.89 Original Correspondence 1927-8, 1 vol.
Continues C.O.447.

London

CONFIDENTIAL PRINT

D.O.114 Dominions 1924-51, 119 vols.
  Continues C.O.886. Part closed for fifty and part for a hundred years.

D.O.115 Australia 1928-36, 3 vols.
  Continues C.O.881.

BOARD OF CUSTOMS AND EXCISE

For notes on the history of the Board and a general introduction to the records see H.M. Customs and Excise. The records in the custody of that department and the records deposited in the Public Record Office have been treated for reference purposes as one group, the Public Record Office classification scheme being imposed throughout. Classes 1-49 are headquarters (London Customs House) records and of these, classes 1-27, 44, and 45 are in the Public Record Office. They comprise ledgers and other statistical compilations prepared until 1871 in the office of the Inspector General of Imports and Exports, and later in the Statistical Office, establishment salary registers, a few miscellaneous entry and seizure books, annual reports of the Board, and a series of registered Excise papers. The lists mentioned below cover these classes only, but as lists of the classes at H.M. Customs and Excise are completed they will be sent to the Public Record Office for the use of students.

See the following lists, published together as Vol.20 of the List and Index Society series:

Class List of the Records of the Board of Customs and Excise to 1837, 1922, typescript.
Class List of Customs Records after 1837, 1929, typescript.

Customs 4 Ledgers of Imports, under Countries 1809-99, 94 vols.

In the earlier volumes New Holland is included in Asia; in the later volumes there are separate entries for the Australian states, New Zealand, and the Pacific or South Sea Islands, under Australasia. For 1830-69 the entries indicate whether the goods were brought in British or foreign ships.

Customs 5 Ledgers of Imports, under Articles 1792-1899, 162 vols.

Under each heading there is further subdivision by the country or state from which the goods were imported. For 1821-70 the entries indicate whether the goods were brought in British or foreign ships.

Customs 6 Ledgers of Imports into the Colonies, under Countries 1832-53, 22 vols.

The Australian colonies are grouped together following Ceylon, and New Zealand follows this section.

Customs 7 Ledgers of Imports into the Colonies, under Articles 1832-53, 22 vols.

Under each article there is further subdivision by colonies, the Australian following the African colonies. The summaries in these ledgers indicate the wide variety of articles imported into the colonies.

Customs 8 Ledgers of Exports of British Merchandise, under Countries 1812-99, 140 vols.

In the earlier volumes New Holland is included under Asia; in the later volumes the British settlements in Australia, New Zealand, and the South Sea Islands are listed separately under Asia. Until 1869 the entries show whether the goods were carried in British or foreign ships.

Customs 9 Ledgers of Exports of British Merchandise, under Articles 1812-99, 109 vols.

Under each article, the arrangement is by the countries to which it was exported.

Customs 10 Ledgers of Exports of Foreign and Colonial Merchandise, under Countries 1809-99, 97 vols.

These show the quantity and official value of the goods, under the countries to which they were exported, there being a section for the Australian colonies, New Zealand and the South Sea Islands. Until 1870 there are entries showing whether the exports were shipped in British or foreign vessels.

Customs 11 Ledgers of Exports of Foreign and Colonial Merchandise, under Articles 1809-99, 127 vols.

Under the heading of each article the arrangement is by the countries to which the articles were exported.

Customs 12 Ledgers of Exports from Colonies, under Countries 1832-53, 22 vols.

These are arranged primarily by the countries to which the goods were exported, there being sections for the British settlements in Australia and New Zealand. Within this framework the articles are listed in alphabetical order. These volumes show very clearly the extent of the trade between the colonies themselves in Australia and New Zealand.

Customs 13 Ledgers of Exports from Colonies, under Articles 1832-53, 22 vols.

Under the heading of each article there is further arrangement by the colonies from which the article was exported.

Customs 14 Ledgers of Imports and Exports, Scotland 1755-1827, 39 vols.

These ledgers show imports and exports, distinguishing in the latter case between British and foreign and colonial merchandise. The entries are arranged under the countries from which the goods were imported or to which they were exported. The Australian colonies are found under Asia.

Customs 15 Ledgers of Imports and Exports, Ireland 1698-1829, 140 vols.

These ledgers are arranged under the various countries to which goods were imported or from which goods were exported, the countries being grouped geographically with the Australian colonies under Asia. Exports of British merchandise, and of foreign and colonial merchandise are distinguished. From 1825-9 there is a duplicate series arranged alphabetically under the articles imported or exported. For 1829 there were no imports from New South Wales or Van Diemen's Land, but exports are listed.

Customs 17 States of Navigation, Commerce, and Revenue 1772-1808, 30 vols.

The volumes contain annual statistical tables prepared by the Inspector General of Customs giving detailed information on these subjects. The last volume 1808-9 was checked. The commerce table appears to be the only one in which statistics are given for New Holland. In other tables it is included in the general heading 'Asia'.

Customs 23 Abstracts of Imports, under Ports 1873-99, 94 vols.

The articles are listed alphabetically under each port in the United Kingdom. Monthly statistics given for each commodity show the quantity, value, and place from which it has been imported. Both free and dutiable goods are shown. Detailed comparative information is therefore easily obtained from this series.

Customs 24 Abstracts of Exports, under Ports 1882-99, 18 vols.

The articles are listed alphabetically under each port. The quantity and value are given, and the countries to which the goods are exported, but the statistics are not broken down into monthly figures. Both free and dutiable goods are listed.

London

Customs 21 Miscellaneous Books 1715-1857, 92 vols. numbered 1-96.

21/1-15. Entry books, early 19th cent. to 1857. 5 vols. are missing. The period covered by the extant books is Apr. 1816 to Dec. 1818, May 1822 to Dec. 1857. A contemporary manuscript index (21/14) covers vols.1-7, but of these only vols.3 and 4, 1816-18, survive. The entry books contain copies of letters and reports received and sent by the Commissioners of Customs to other officials, including the Treasury and the Board of Trade, and to individuals, e.g. 2 May 1817, copy of a memo forwarded to S. R. Lushington in explanation of an account of timber imported from foreign ports and British colonies.

EXCHEQUER AND AUDIT DEPARTMENT

The Exchequer and Audit Department was established in 1866 taking over the functions of the Comptroller General of the Exchequer and the Commissioners of Audit. Certain records of the Comptroller of the Exchequer are found here but some earlier related documents are in classes of Exchequer records, see *Guide to the Contents of the Public Record Office*, I, pp.45-113, especially pp.107-8. The Commissioners of Audit were created in 1785 and their duties included acting as Comptrollers of Army Accounts from 1785-1835 and, from 1832, acting as Commissioners for Accounts in Ireland. The records associated with both these functions are in this group.

See the following lists:

Lists and Indexes XLVI, *Lists of the Records of the Treasury, the Paymaster General's Office, the Exchequer and Audit Department*, London 1922, reprint New York 1963. Class List of the Records of the Exchequer and Audit Office after 1837, 1962, typescript.

A.O.1 Declared Accounts (in Rolls) 1536-1828, 2541 rolls.

See Lists and Indexes II, *List and Index of Declared Accounts from the Pipe Office and the Audit Office*, London 1893, reprint New York 1963.

Accounts of various branches of government audited and declared before the Chancellor of the Exchequer and two or more Lords Commissioners of the Treasury. Included in this class are accounts from the Governors, Commissaries, and Agents of New South Wales, Norfolk Island, and Van Diemen's Land and accounts for army pensions.

Originally, two copies of accounts were prepared for declaration, one being returned to the Audit Office after declaration and the other to the Pipe Office. But this system appears to have been altered before the end of the eighteenth century and no papers relevant to this survey have been found in the Pipe Office records. Before being returned to the Audit Office the accounts were registered in the Treasury in volumes called Auditors' States of Account (T.38). The keeping of accounts in rolls was discontinued in 1829 and after that date the accounts in volume form are to be found in A.O.2. See also A.O.20 and 22.

A.O.2 Declared and Passed Accounts (in Books) 1803-48, 92 vols.

These accounts continue those in A.O.1 and also contain accounts signed and passed by the Commissioners of the Audit, only found here as they were apparently not declared until 1829. In addition to the accounts cited in A.O.1, this class also includes accounts from Western Australia, New Zealand, and the Convict Hulk Establishment. 2/71 contains an account for the conveyance of convicts to New South Wales. There are also details of bills drawn on behalf of the colonies in the accounts of the Paymaster General of H.M. Forces. See also A.O.20 and A.O.22.

A.O.20 Accounts Declared before the Chancellor of the Exchequer 1849-66, 124 vols.

A continuation of accounts declared before the Chancellor of the Exchequer in A.O.1 and 2. This class contains the accounts of consuls at Apia, Fiji, Manila, Sydney, Tahiti, and Woahoo, commissaries, Treasury Chests, convict services, ordnance store keepers, and also civil lists of the various colonies, the Guardian of Juvenile Immigrants in Western Australia, the Convict Hulk Establishment, the Master of the Mint, and the Colonial Office.

20/121-4. Abstracts of accounts 1855-66 declared by the Chancellor of the Exchequer including those from the colonies and from consuls as well as English home departments.

A.O.22 Signed and Passed Accounts 1848-1912, 137 vols.

Accounts passed by Audit but not declared before the Chancellor of the Exchequer although they were approved, as are all the other accounts, by Treasury Warrant. Earlier accounts of this kind are to be found in A.O.2. Accounts in this class include those of the colonial treasurers, the Crown Agents for the Colonies, the Colonial Land and Emigration Commissioners, and from 1867 the accounts of consuls in the Pacific, branches of the Royal Mint in Australia, and accounts similar to those found until 1866 in A.O.20.

A.O.3 Accounts, Various 1539-1886, 1430 rolls and vols.

Accounts, statement books, reports on accounts, vouchers subsidiary to the accounts in A.O.1, 2, 20, 22. Some are a great deal more detailed than the declared accounts while others are very brief abstracts of information. There are papers for the various colonies including statement books of the collectors of revenue for duties, court fines, commissaries, consuls in the Pacific, the Crown Agents and Emigration Commissioners, and details of salaries, pensions, and superannuation payments for various departments and services. See also A.O.19.

A.O.19 Accounts Current c.1829-1906, 123 bundles.

The detailed accounts from which the abstract accounts in A.O.2, 20, 22 were prepared. Others are in A.O.3. They include accounts from the Australian and New Zealand colonies for the civil list, the Colonial Colonisation Commissioners, commissariats, convict service, Crown Revenue, Guardians of Juvenile Immigrants, Public Accounts Service Account, and also from the Treasury Chests at Akaroa, Lyttelton, Otago, Port Victoria, and Wellington, accounts for the Colonial Land and Emigration Commissioners, colonial trusts, commissariats abroad, the Convict Hulk Establishment, the Agents General for Crown Colonies, and the Australian branches of the Royal Mint. An indexed list of the contents of A.O.19 is to be found in the Class List.

A.O.21 Authorities for Expenditure 1836-66, 4 bundles.

Authorities for expenditure relating to salaries, pensions, and contingent expenses chiefly of the Treasury, Audit Office, and Paymaster General's Office. Authorities for the salaries of consuls include consuls in the Pacific.

A.O.4 Registers of Accounts Received 1765-1834, 1845-68, 27 vols.

Registers of accounts from, amongst others, the colonies and consuls, convict services, the Agents General for Crown Colonies, and the Emigration Commissioners, showing when the accounts were received, the name of the inspector to whom allocated, observations. 4/22 is a brief index to these registers for 1845-68.

A.O.5 Registers of Papers Received 1806-1918, 86 vols.

Registers of letters received by the Commissioners of Audit 1806-67, the Comptroller General of the Exchequer 1840-67 and the Exchequer and Audit Department 1867-1918. The letters relate to queries about accounts with related papers from colonial treasuries, commissariats abroad, the convict service, the War Office, and the Admiralty. The volumes are indexed by the corresponding department or colony and by subject. 5/18-22 are separate subject indexes of letters received 1838-48.

A.O.6 Minutes 1785-1867, 147 vols.

Brief entries of the Minutes of the Commissioners of Audit. Most of the volumes are indexed. They record the passing of accounts and the formal receipt or approval of the despatch of letters relating to matters such as queried accounts, payments, and modes of accounting. They cover all subjects described under other classes and can be used, in addition to the various registers, as a guide to the dates when particular matters were dealt with in the Exchequer and Audit Department.

A.O.7 Out-letters, General 1785-1867, 91 vols.

Entry books of out-letters, many of which are recorded formally in A.O.6, to departments and officials including the Treasury, Colonial Office, War Office, Admiralty, and Navy Office, colonial governors, treasurers and commissaries, and the Crown Agents for the Colonies querying accounts, payments, vouchers, and other matters associated with the balancing and passing of accounts. See also A.O.8 and 23.

A.O.8 Reports and Letters to the Treasury 1801-67, 89 vols.

Reports and letters to the Treasury similar in content to those in A.O.7 including reports on colonial, commissary, and consular accounts, and letters requesting information on authorities to expend money, or proposed changes in votes. See also A.O.23.

A.O.9 In-letters, Office of Comptroller General of the Exchequer 1840-67, 11 bundles.

The indexes in A.O.5 cover this class.

A.O.10 Reports to the Board 1785-1867, 106 vols.

Reports to the Commissioners of Audit from the staff of the Audit Office informing the board on various matters, e.g. accounts ready to be audited, observations on preliminary inspections of accounts, queries to be raised and action to be taken. The accounts in question include those from governors, colonial treasurers, commissaries, the Emigration Commissioners, heads of the convict service in the colonies, and the Crown Agents for the Colonies.

A.O.15 Enrolment Books 1563-1927, 184 vols.

Enrolments of all letters patent, warrants, commissions, letters of attorney, probates of wills required for the execution of the Department's duties. 15/168, 1814-32, contains probates and letters of administration, many of which relate to Australia.

A.O.16 Miscellanea 1568-1910, 196 vols.

16/44 includes King's Warrants 1787-1806 for expenditure by W. Chinnery, Agent for New South Wales, and later volumes include warrants for expenditure, instructions to colonial governors, treasurers, auditors, commissaries, and agents concerning the revenue and expenditure of the colonies and the modes of accounting for these.

A.O.17 Absorbed Departments 1580-1867, 499 vols.

Records of three extinct departments: the Comptroller of Army Accounts, the Comptroller General of the Exchequer, and the Commissioners for Accounts, Ireland. The Comptroller of Army Accounts contain general reports, miscellaneous reports 1808-34, and reports on foreign stations 1808-29 including New South Wales and Van Diemen's Land. 17/250, 254 correspondence books of the Comptroller of the Exchequer 1839, 1844-7 include entries relating to Exchequer Bills and warrants for colonial expenses. 17/338-499 contain accounts 1774-1832 from the Commissioners for Accounts, Ireland, with scattered references to the transportation of convicts. There are also papers relating to salaries and other payments.

A.O.23 Reports and Letters 1867-90, 23 vols.

Out-letter books continuing the material in A.O.7 and 8.

FOREIGN OFFICE

See the following lists:

Lists and Indexes LII, *List of Foreign Office Records to 1878*, London 1929, reprint New York 1963. Superseding Lists and Indexes XLI, 1914.

Lists and Indexes: Supplementary Series XIII, *List of Foreign Office Records (1879-1913)*, 8 vols., New York 1964-6. Vols.1-4 General Correspondence 1879-1905 arranged alphabetically by country; vol.5 Various Classes 1879-1905; vols.6-8 Embassy and Consular Archives (1879-1913) arranged alphabetically by country. Vol.5 includes a revision of the list of F.O.93, superseding LII, pp.293-302.

List of Classes described

General Correspondence:

> General Correspondence before 1906: Listed alphabetically by country in *Guide to the Contents of the Public Record Office* II, pp.124-7; also classes 97, 84, 566, 802, 804
>
> General Correspondence after 1906: 368-9, 627, 371-2, 662, 409, 833
>
> Other Classes: 83

Treaties: 93-4

Embassy and Consular Archives: Listed alphabetically by country in *Guide to the Contents of the Public Record Office* II, pp.130-51, III, pp.52-67.

Archives of Commissions: 317, 897

Confidential Print: Listed alphabetically by country in *Guide to the Contents of the Public Record Office* II, pp.154-8, III, p.69.

Chief Clerk's Department: 366

Passport Office: 737, 655

Cabinet Papers: 899

Peace Conference of 1919-20: 374, 373, 608, 893

War of 1939-45: 916

Miscellaneous: 96

Private Collections: 361, 519, 633, 350, 343, 358, 352, 363, 323, 800

GENERAL CORRESPONDENCE

The general correspondence is divided into three sections: Correspondence before 1906, Correspondence after 1906, and Other Classes. Embassy and Consular Archives are complementary to General Correspondence.

See the following lists:

Registers and Indexes of Correspondence, typescript and duplicated typescript, containing lists of F.O.802, 566, 622, 804, 409.

Indexes 1906-19, on cards. The cards are arranged alphabetically within each year. They also cover a mass of papers received in 1920 because, so far as the political papers are concerned, a new filing system was not introduced until well into 1920. The references on these cards normally give the index registry and file numbers and the year.

London

Index to Cases. MS. photocopy, shelved with the lists of F.O. Records. This copy of an index compiled in the Foreign Office relates to the 'Case' volumes which are to be found in General Correspondence F.O.1-84, 97 and 99-110. It covers the whole period of this correspondence to 1905 and has been continued into the period covered by the classes F.O.367-72, 382, 383 and 395. The first part of the volume is an index, under persons and subjects, to the second part of the volume which follows the Foreign Office alphabetical arrangement under countries but includes F.O.84 Slave Trade and F.O.83 Great Britain and General. F.O.97 Supplement to General Correspondence is not included in the alphabetical arrangement, but references to it will be found under various countries. A few references to Miscellanea are similarly noted but these do not appear to have been generally included in this index. Public Record Office call numbers have been added except in the few instances where it has not been possible to identify the volume.

GENERAL CORRESPONDENCE BEFORE 1906

Relevant documents have been noted in classes for correspondence with the following countries: America, Central, and Guatemala, America, United States of, Argentine Republic, Borneo, Chile, China, Columbia and New Granada, Ecuador, France, Germany (see also Prussia and Germany), Holland and Netherlands, Italy, Japan, Norway, Pacific Islands, Paraguay, Peru, Portugal, Prussia and Germany, Russia, Spain, and Sweden. The following notes on some classes give examples of special subjects.

F.O.5 America, United States of 1793-1905, 2625 vols.

Early nineteenth century records relate to such subjects as the quantity of spirits imported into New South Wales by American vessels; later papers concern the arrival in America of the Irish rebels, Meagher, O'Donohoe, and Mitchel, pardons for Americans transported to Tasmania for their part in the Canadian rebellion, the annexation of New Zealand and its effects on American fisheries and interests in the South Seas, and the alleged activities of the American consul in New Zealand inciting the Maoris to revolt. There is a considerable amount of material in this class additional to the correspondence in F.O.58, particularly correspondence with Hawaii after its annexation by the United States in 1898. Papers from San Francisco early in 1897 relate to the United Brotherhood of the South Seas.

F.O.27 France 1781-1905, 3772 vols.

Includes correspondence on French expeditions to Australia and the Pacific, the search for La Pérouse, imprisonment of Matthew Flinders, the formation of colonies in the Pacific, French penal settlements, etc. Much of this is in the correspondence of the consuls at New Caledonia and Tahiti 1869-1905. Early correspondence with the Tahitian consulate is in F.O.58, but after Tahiti becomes French territory, it is in F.O.27. Other correspondence 1880-1905 relates to the escape of recidivists from the penal settlement in New Caledonia to Australia and New Zealand.

F.O.58 Pacific Islands 1822-1905, 345 vols.

Subjects range from the regulation of relations between Great Britain and independent governments established in the islands and Britain's relations with the European powers with regard to their designs on territorial acquisitions, to matters involving injuries or supposed injuries to the rights of British subjects. Copies of treaties and conventions, proclamations, and other official publications of island governments and newspapers are attached to despatches. 58/1-2 deal with New Zealand 1838-41, the appointment of a Resident and the subsequent signing of the

234

Treaty of Waitangi. Following volumes contain the correspondence of consuls in the Pacific Islands and of the Western Pacific High Commissioner. The many volumes listed as 'Various' contain letters from missionaries, captains of British and American naval vessels, rulers of various islands and petitions from native chiefs. There is correspondence relating to New Guinea, e.g. in 58/245-9 and 312; the last covers Jan.-June 1897 and contains correspondence on various islands, on the United Brotherhood of the South Sea Islands (a report from the consul at San Francisco which was missing from the series of San Francisco correspondence in F.O.5) and a printed paper entitled 'Australian Station'. Other volumes deal with labour traffic and the sale of arms and spirits in the Pacific. Correspondence in this class is supplemented by other classes of general correspondence, especially with countries with territorial interests in the Pacific Islands, and also by F.O.97.

F.O.64 Prussia and Germany 1781-1905, 1654 vols.

Much of the correspondence relating to the Pacific is not bound in the general series, but is bound together in volumes dealing with the area. These volumes are:

64/1107-10, Fiji land claims 1875-85.

64/1144-52, 1208, 1323, Colonial policy, annexation in New Guinea, the Pacific 1876-93.

64/1232, *Certified protocols of the Samoan Conference involving Germany, Britain and the United States of America*, 1889.

64/1404, Extradition from German protectorates 1887-96.

64/1502, 1505, 1532, 1560, 1583, 1604, 1626, British consul, Samoa 1900-5. Correspondence of this consulate 1844-99 is in F.O.58.

64/1591, Claims in the Mariana Islands of John Turner Harrison, a British subject who was deprived of his rights of lease over certain islands when Spain sold the Marianas to Germany in 1900, 1900-3.

64/1614, Concessionary rights of the Eastern Extension Telegraph Company in the Carolines and other places 1899-1904.

64/1631, Various: Pacific and Diplomatic 1905. Correspondence among Burns, Philp & Co. of Sydney, the German Government, Colonial Office, Foreign Office, Australian Government, and others concerning trade restrictions imposed by Germany in the Caroline and Marshall Islands, with notes on other Pacific Islands. A letter 24 Jan. 1908 on the settlement of the Burns, Philp claim is in F.O.800/19.

F.O.72 Spain 1781-1905, 2234 vols.

Correspondence noted is mainly found in volumes dealing with consuls at Manila 1844-98, especially information concerning ships trading among the Philippines, Australia, and New Zealand, and shipwrecks in the Marianas, Torres Strait, and other places. 72/761, 1849, includes an account of the discovery of Barbara Crawford, saved by Aborigines of Cape York from the cutter *America* wrecked on its passage through Torres Strait to Port Essington. There is correspondence with and concerning Andrew Cheyne, a trader in the Pelew Islands 1861-7, and on the arrest of W. H. Hayes at Manila 1875. Other subjects include expeditions to New Guinea, immigration, Spanish naval forces in the Pacific, the Queensland Acclimatisation Society, Caroline Islands, Fiji, and merino sheep for New South Wales. Volumes on specific subjects include:

72/5, 1785. Letters and papers from consuls at various places in Spain which include a *cedula* or *ordonnance* 10 Mar. 1785 to establish a Philippine Company with the aim of maintaining trade between America and Asia, via Cape Horn, touching at Spanish ports in the South Seas, and letter 16 May 1785 enclosing prospectus for the establishment of a new company in the Philippines.

72/1588, 1666, 1807-9. Correspondence 1874-87, concerning the sovereignty of Spain over the 'Caroline or Pelew Islands' and other matters relating to Pacific Islands and natives including reports of H.M. ships. The peace treaty 11 Aug. 1883 concluded between two Pelew Islands chieftains at the instance of Capt. C. A. G. Bridge, R.N., captain of H.M.S. *Espiègle*, is at F.O.323/2, Private Collections, Miscellaneous.

F.O.97 Supplement to General Correspondence 1780-1905, 621 vols.

97/39, 1859-63. Depredations of United States ships on guano islands, collusive wrecking, applications by persons in Australia and New Zealand to work certain guano islands in the Pacific.

97/101-2, 1855-6, 1860. Coolie emigration.

97/249, 1824-59. Proceedings of the Dutch and British authorities in the Eastern seas, with printed copies of a treaty 17 Mar. 1824 between Great Britain and the Netherlands respecting territory and commerce in the East Indies, discussions 1841-6 on the proceedings of the Dutch authorities in the Eastern Archipelago and the execution of the treaty of 1824.

97/449, 451, 453, 488, 490-1, 495, 498, 500-4, 563-4, 1873-90. Marriages abroad, arranged by country, including Pacific Islands. See F.O.802/239 for register and index.

97/546, 1887-94. New Zealand land claims.

97/589, 1890-2. Imprisonment of J. R. Mills in the Honolulu State Prison on a charge of murder.

97/613, 1899-1900. Confidential archives of the Apia Consulate.

97/621, 1880-5. Granville Papers. Miscellaneous correspondence including letters relating to Hawaii.

F.O.84 Slave Trade 1816-92, 2276 vols.

Correspondence with consuls abroad and with commissioners at the several stations appointed to carry out the articles of the Slave Trade Conventions with various nations. Volumes known to contain relevant correspondence are given below; further correspondence may be found from the index, F.O.802/530 and registers F.O.802/503-28. The correspondence deals mainly with Africa, but subjects covered include the Pacific Islands, mail services, naval reports of the East India Station, kidnapping, Commodore Wilson's report on the labour trade, Marquis de Rays's scheme for the colonisation of the Western Pacific, and affairs in New Guinea.

84/1090, 1321. Navigator's Islands 1859, 1872.

84/1352, 1471, 1501, 1533, 1591, 1614. New Caledonia or Noumea 1872, 1877-9, 1881-2.

F.O.566 Registers of General Correspondence 1817-1922, 1874 vols.

In these registers correspondence for each country is entered in separate volumes according to broad classifications such as 'Diplomatic', 'Consular', 'Commercial', 'Treaty'. Some early registers will be found in F.O.95 Miscellanea, Series I.

F.O.802 Registers (Library Series) and Indexes of General Correspondence 1808-90, 678 vols.

The registers relating to France and the United States of America go back to 1761 and 1793 respectively. This Library Series was compiled after 1890 when the correspondence up to this date had been weeded. The registers describe all papers in the volumes of general correspondence, and the indexes are full indexes of subjects, places and persons. Microfilm copies of F.O.802 are at F.O.605.

F.O.804 Indexes to General Correspondence 1891-1905, 59 vols.

Full indexes to the 'unweeded' correspondence and to F.O.566. Photographic copies of F.O.804 are at F.O.733.

GENERAL CORRESPONDENCE AFTER 1906

F.O.368 Commercial 1906-19, 2269 vols.

Subdivided each year under country, general, and miscellaneous, which is again divided by specific headings, e.g. Sugar Convention, Suez Canal.

F.O.369 Consular 1906-41, 2718 vols.

Subdivided each year under country, including Pacific Islands to 1913.

F.O.627 Dominions Information 1929-33, 58 vols.

This class concerns inter-imperial relations as affecting foreign countries, e.g. the appointment of Dominion diplomatic representatives in foreign countries, economic emancipation of British Dominions.

F.O.371 Political 1906-41, 30309 vols.

To 1920 arranged each year under country and subjects, e.g. contract labour, arms traffic, war. Pacific Islands and affairs of the New Hebrides are listed 1906-13. A new arrangement was introduced in 1920 whereby countries and subjects are arranged each year, alphabetically under an area division: Central, Eastern, Far Eastern, Northern, American, Western, and African.

F.O.372 Treaty 1906-37, 3242 vols.

Subdivided each year under country and subject headings, with large miscellaneous sections. Many shipping cases are included. Country subdivisions are not used after 1923.

F.O.662. Numerical (Central) Registers of General Correspondence 1906-20, 69 vols.

These are daily opening registers and show the department to which the correspondence was sent.

F.O.409 Indexes (Printed Series) to General Correspondence 1920-50, 109 vols.

These are subject indexes, compiled annually.

F.O.833 Foreign Trade Department 1891-1919, 18 pieces.

British trade abroad has always been the joint concern of the Foreign Office and Board of Trade and until 1917 there was a Commercial Department of the Foreign Office to act as the channel between British Diplomatists and consuls abroad, and the Board of Trade at home. In that year the Department of Overseas Trade was formed, with its own permanent head and Parliamentary Under-Secretary. There is a typescript list entitled 'Various Classes (including F.O.833, Foreign Trade Dept.)'. 833/4-15 are registers (833/1-3 being vacant). Three earlier indexes, Commercial Department 1891-1905 are at F.O.804/57-9 and contain many entries relating to Australia and the Pacific. They also give references to the series of commercial registers 1891-1905 in F.O.566.

OTHER CLASSES

F.O.83 Great Britain and General 1745-1946, 2523 vols.

A large collection of correspondence which does not fit into the series of correspondence arranged by country and which deals with subjects which could apply to

London

all countries, e.g. consular reports, mails, telegraph. There is a typescript list covering 83/583-2523. F.O.802/235, 1822-90, indexes guano islands and other cases and F.O.802/239, 1814-93, indexes marriages abroad. 83/2314, 1829-76, contains Law Officers' reports, Pacific Islands including New Zealand. Many other departmental indexes in F.O.802, 566, and 804 may indicate documents on relevant matters. The series of marriages at British embassies and legations covers the periods 1814-72 and 1891-1905; those for 1873-90 are in F.O.97. The correspondence is arranged within each volume by countries, including Pacific Islands.

TREATIES

See the following lists:

List of Foreign Office Treaties, Protocols of Treaties (F.O.93), typescript and manuscript.

List of Foreign Office Treaties, Ratifications of Treaties, photocopies of typescript.

F.O.93 Protocols of Treaties 1788-1962, 149 boxes.

Numbered manuscript and printed documents relating to various countries, arranged in alphabetical order by country. Documents relating to the Pacific Islands and Australasia concern trade, postal arrangements, spheres of influence and are filed in the following: 93/33 France 1827-1907; 93/36 Germany 1886-1904; 93/46 no.55 Holland and Netherlands 16 May 1855, convention, boundaries of New Guinea; 93/49 Japan 1894-1900; 93/59 Mexico 1 Feb. 1904; 93/71 Pacific Islands no.1 20 Apr. 1900, agreement with the King of Niue (Savage Island), British protectorate, etc.; 93/73 no.4, 19 July 1890 Paraguay; 93/76 no.9, 15 Dec. 1902, Peru; 93/83 Samoa 1873, 1879; 93/85 Sandwich Islands 1843-77 including treaty *re* whaling; 93/99 no.35, 8 Jan. 1886, Spain, declaration on Caroline and Pelew Islands; 93/101 no.39, 14 Oct. 1902 Sweden and Norway award, Samoan claims arbitration; 93/106 Tonga 1878-1900.

F.O.94 Ratification of Treaties 1782-1957, 1859 boxes.

From 1929-57 many conventions and treaties listed under Australia and New Zealand in 94/1091-852 concern universal post, safety of life at sea, whaling, sugar, tin, and constitutional matters. The following documents concerning conventions, chiefly on trade and boundaries, have also been noted: 94/439 Hawaii 1851, 1852; 94/763 Netherlands 1895 *re* boundaries in New Guinea; 94/779, 784, 904 France 1897, 1898, 1911. Volumes on other subjects are: 94/873, 980-1 *re* New Hebrides 1906, 1914, 1922; 94/792-3 Germany 1899 *re* Samoa, Tonga, Solomon Islands; 94/794-6 United States and Germany 1899-1900 *re* Samoa; 94/805 Tonga 1900; 94/855 Mexico, postal rates with New Zealand 1904; 94/934 Norway, *re* commercial treaty of 1826, 1912; 94/1055 Great Britain and Dominions 1928-9 treaty, renunciation of war.

EMBASSY AND CONSULAR ARCHIVES

See Public Record Office, Foreign Office Embassy and Consular Archives, typescript (c.1900), 15 vols. arranged alphabetically by country.

Embassy and Consular Archives transferred to the Public Record Office are listed alphabetically by country in *Guide to the Contents of the Public Record Office* II, pp.130-51, and III, pp.52-67. See also description in II, p.123.

Papers relevant to Australasia and the Pacific are too numerous to list here. Papers on trade, emigration, and shipping in the Pacific have been noted in classes for many countries including America, United States of, Argentine Republic, Brazil, Chile, France, Germany, Greece, Italy, and Japan. Classes for Norway, Russia, and Sweden contain papers on Antarctic exploration, territorial claims, and whaling. The records of the consulate for Fiji and Tonga 1858-76 are now in the Central Archives of Fiji and the Western Pacific High Commission in Suva, see *Journal of Pacific History* 3, 1968, p.218. Among French consular records are F.O.687 Papeete, Correspondence, Registers 1818-1948 with detailed typescript list. In 1937 selected records of this consulate were placed by the Foreign Office in the Mitchell Library, Sydney, including correspondence 1826-43 and *c.*1858-88, annual reports and shipping papers 1841-87.

Examples of relevant subjects have been noted in the following classes:

America, United States of, F.O.703 Baltimore, Letter Books and Registers, colonising expedition to the Pacific 1897.

Argentine Republic, F.O.446 Buenos Aires, Letters and Papers, repatriation of colonists of the New Australia Settlement 1894-9.

Chile, F.O.132 Correspondence, Tasmanian prisoners 1835-6, French occupation of the Society Islands 1843; F.O.162 Punta Arenas Correspondence and F.O.805 Registers, South Georgia Exploring Co., whaling in the South Shetlands; F.O.596 Valparaiso, Correspondence; and F.O.814 Registers, Antarctic Expedition of Sir Ernest Shackleton.

Guatemala, F.O.252 Correspondence, emigration of Gilbert Islanders to Guatemala 1893.

Peru, F.O.177 Correspondence, various attempts to export alpacas to Australia, e.g. the project of Tasmanian colonists who chartered the *Prince Regent* in 1853 and Charles Ledger's project, reported in his letter 1 Apr. 1856.

ARCHIVES OF COMMISSIONS

F.O.317 Miscellaneous 1868-92, 5 vols.

317/1, 1868-9. Royal Commission for inquiring into the laws of naturalisation and allegiance: Lord Tenterden's minutes.

317/3, 1881-2. Commissions to revise the instructions to British naval officers engaged in the suppression of the Slave Trade: minutes.

F.O.897 Mixed Arbitral Tribunals: Anglo-American Pecuniary Claims 1923, 3 vols.

An Arbitral Convention of 4 Apr. 1908 between Great Britain and the United States provided for differences of a legal nature to be referred to the Permanent Court of Arbitration at The Hague. The three volumes in this class contain specimen claims including 897/3 Fiji land claims Oct. 1923.

CONFIDENTIAL PRINT

See Foreign Office, List of Confidential Print, typescript.

The National Library of Australia is obtaining a complete set of all Foreign Office Confidential Print either in original or photocopy. There is a numerical list of the class at F.O.881 and a list arranged by country is given in *Guide to the Contents of the Public Record Office* II, pp.154-8.

CHIEF CLERK'S DEPARTMENT

F.O.366 Archives 1719-1940, 1137 vols.

The records are divided into: Accounts, Correspondence and Papers, Ledgers. Papers include appointments and expenses of British consuls.

366/739. Index to register of in- and out-letters 1891-6 includes references to Samoa and the Australian Government. The registers are in F.O.566/735-6.

London

PASSPORT OFFICE

See Foreign Office, Passport Office (List), typescript.

Documents relevant to the field of this survey may be found in classes listed in *Guide to the Contents of the Public Record Office* II, p.158, and in the classses listed below:

F.O.737 Representative Case Papers 1920-54, 23 files.

Application forms for passports, renewals, exit and travel permits, and correspondence and papers of a routine character concerning *inter alia* consular inquiries on the granting of diplomatic visas.

F.O.655 Representative Examples of Passports Issued 1809-1921, 1852 pieces.

These include examples for New South Wales 1894-1914, Victoria 1895-1920, South Australia 1899 and 1902, Western Australia 1912-15, Queensland 1912, New Zealand 1904, 1914-16, Tahiti 1908, and Hawaii 1916.

CABINET PAPERS

See the following lists:

F.O.Various classes, F.O.899 Cabinet Papers, typescript.
List of Cabinet Papers 1880-1914, London, H.M.S.O., 1964.
List of Cabinet Papers 1915 and 1916, London, H.M.S.O., 1966.

F.O.899 Cabinet Papers 1900-18, 20 vols.

Papers and memoranda prepared by the Foreign Office for the information of the Cabinet. Photocopies of the papers up to the end of 1916 are in Cab.37. A few papers 1917-18 in F.O.899 are not included in the numbered series of Cabinet Papers (Cab.24). This class also contains five volumes of summaries of foreign press reports 1915-17.

PEACE CONFERENCE OF 1919-20

See the following lists:

F.O. Conference (F.O.373-4, 839-40 and 893), typescript.
Peace Conference 1919-1920, F.O.608, with subject index, typescript.

The two subjects with which Australia was mainly concerned were White Australia and the future of the Pacific Islands in which W. M. Hughes opposed President Wilson. They are discussed in C. Hartley Gratton's *The United States and the South West Pacific*, Melbourne 1961, ch.12.

F.O.374 Acts of the Conference 1922-35, 20 boxes.

These include minutes of meetings of the British Empire Delegation Jan.-June 1919.

F.O.373 Handbooks 1918-19, 7 boxes.

These were prepared by the Historical Section of the Foreign Office for the use of officials attending the Conference and were subsequently issued to the public in a modified form.

373/3 no.35 *German Colonisation* refers to New Guinea and Samoa; no.66 *British New Guinea*.

373/7 no.132b *Treatment of Natives in German Colonies* deals mainly with Africa but also refers to New Guinea; no.138 *Galapagos Islands*; no.140 *Cocos Islands*; no.141 *Easter Island*; no.142 *Discoveries and Acquisitions in the Pacific*; no.143 *British Possessions in the Pacific*; no.144 *French Possessions in the Pacific*; no.145 *German Possessions in the Pacific*; no.146a *New Hebrides*.

F.O.608 Correspondence 1919-20, 281 vols.

Correspondence and papers of the British delegation which include the following: 608/126 German colonies; 608/133 Germany, Dr Solf; 608/174 America, independence movements in Hawaii and Porto Rico; 608/175 Oceania and Miscellaneous, Political, German claims in the Antarctic, future of the New Hebrides, future of New Guinea, status of Germans in Samoa; 608/211 Far East, political relations between Japan and Australia, coloured labour for New Zealand; 608/224 Oceania and Miscellaneous, Economic, includes files on minerals and phosphate in German Pacific possessions, Pacific Phosphate Company claims and Papuan tariffs; 608/240-1 German colonies; 608/248 Memoranda, Western Pacific.

F.O. 893 Conference of Ambassadors, Paris 1920-30, 33 vols.

WAR OF 1939-45

F.O.916 Consular (War) Department. Prisoners of War and Internees 1940-6, 2566 files.

Reports from various sources on prisoners of war and internment camps in enemy and enemy occupied countries and on the treatment of British subjects, both military and civilian. Other matters dealt with include welfare, exchanges, repatriation, escapes, deaths.

MISCELLANEOUS

F.O.96 Miscellanea, Series II 1816-1929 and 1937, 218 bundles.

96/173, 1869. Trade returns of consular fees, including returns from Tahiti and Manila.

96/181, 1887. Petition of the Federal Assembly of the Presbyterian Churches of Australia and Tasmania for the withdrawal of French troops from the New Hebrides, signed at Melbourne 23 Sept. 1887.

PRIVATE COLLECTIONS

See F.O. Private Collections (List), typescript.

Many collections of private papers dealing directly with foreign affairs are included in the Foreign Office group. Frequently they contain records similar to those in Consular and Embassy Archives. A number of collections transferred to the Public Record Office since Aug. 1960 are placed together in F.O.800. Some of these were not available when this description was compiled either because of the thirty year rule or because they were on loan to the Foreign Office. Papers retained by, or on loan to, the Foreign Office (1969) include 800/256-63 Chamberlain Papers, 800/152-4 Oliphant Papers, and 800/272-9 Sargent Papers.

F.O.361 Clarendon Papers 1867-70, 1 vol.

The papers of the 4th Earl of Clarendon include a letter 7 Oct. 1869 from Granville referring *inter alia* to the withdrawal of the last regiment from New Zealand.

F.O.519 Cowley Papers 1774, 1802-c.1935, 304 vols.

A collection of papers mainly accumulated by Henry Wellesley, 1st Baron Cowley, and his son Henry Richard Charles Wellesley, 1st Earl and 2nd Baron Cowley, during their diplomatic careers. Correspondence of interest relates to the Pacific Islands and is found among the 1st Earl's papers for the period he was in France. It consists of semi-official and private correspondence 1852-71 mainly from the Earl of Clarendon 1853-69 and from other Foreign Office ministers supplementing French Embassy Archives for the period. Many of the papers have been published in *The Paris Embassy during the Second Empire. Selections from the papers of Henry Richard Charles*

London

Wellesley, 1st Earl Cowley, Ambassador at Paris, 1852-67, edited by his son Col. the Hon. F. A. Wellesley, London 1928. Among the miscellaneous papers of the Hon. F. A. Wellesley is a bundle of private letters written to Lord and Lady Augustus Loftus 1853-96 which includes several while Loftus was Governor of New South Wales.

F.O.633 Cromer Papers 1872-1928, 43 vols.

Private and official correspondence of Evelyn Baring, 1st Earl of Cromer as Chief Secretary to the Viceroy of India, Commissioner of the Egyptian Public Debt and later Minister Plenipotentiary in Egypt, also covering the period when he was active at home in parliamentary and political affairs. The correspondence includes the following letters to Lord Cromer: 633/2, 25 May 1880, from Alfred de Rothschild suggesting that Europeans should be encouraged to settle in the Dominions; 633/7, 9 June, 7 Dec. 1894, from Lord Kimberley and 10 May 1894 from Lord Lansdowne on German interests in the Pacific; 633/23, 14 Oct. 1914, from Hubert Church and reply 17 Oct. 1914 on Edward Gibbon Wakefield's work in New Zealand, and 15 Dec. 1914 from Oliver Bainbridge on the brutal treatment of natives in Samoa, New Guinea, the Solomon Islands, and the Bismarck Archipelago.

F.O.350 Jordan Papers 1901-19, 16 vols.

Sir John Newell Jordan, Minister Resident in Korea 1901-6 and envoy to China 1906-20. His letters from China have references to Dr George Morrison. 350/16 includes a letter 15 Feb. 1918 from Ronald Macleay of the Far Eastern Department of the Foreign Office to Jordan discussing Jordan's attempts to arrange the deportation of enemy subjects to Australia, plans which were later abandoned.

F.O.343 Malet Papers 1884-95, 13 vols.

Private correspondence of Sir Edward Baldwin Malet as Ambassador to the German Court 1884-95 including scattered letters relating to German territory in north New Guinea, the secret negotiations between the United States, Great Britain, and Germany on Hawaii, Tonga, and Samoa 1885, German interests in the Caroline Islands and Samoa 1886 and 1893, and the Samoan Conference at Berlin 1889.

F.O.358 Simmons Papers 1857-96, 6 bundles.

Private letters, reports formerly belonging to Gen. Sir J. L. A. Simmons, R.E. They relate chiefly to the Russo-Turkish War of 1876-80 and include 358/6 letter 30 Jan. 1896 from William Everett, Intelligence Division to Simmons sending notes on naval and military policy in the event of war with France, suggesting *inter alia* that any expedition which may be considered against Saigon and New Caledonia could be fitted out in India and Australia.

F.O.352 Stratford Canning Papers 1778-1863, 66 bundles.

Original correspondence, draft letters and miscellaneous diplomatic papers of Stratford Canning, afterwards Lord Stratford de Redcliffe. The papers deal mainly with Turkey, but among the papers for 1820-3 when he was Minister to the United States are: 352/8-9 documents *c.*1824 on trade with the United States Pacific coast.

F.O.363 Tenterden Papers 1873-82, 5 vols.

Letters to the 3rd Lord Tenterden, Under-Secretary of State for Foreign Affairs 1873-82, and drafts of letters from him including the following in 363/4: letter 6 Apr. 1875 from Edward Thornton, British Legation, Washington, saying that British trade may be driven out of the Hawaiian Islands by the Hawaiian Reciprocity Treaty; correspondence and cuttings Mar.-May 1876 relating to the incident of

H.M.S. *Barracouta* at Samoa and antagonism towards Col. A. B. Steinberger, the special agent of President Grant in Samoa; also two letters 23 Feb., 23 Mar. 1875 concerning John Mitchel.

F.O.323 Miscellaneous 1836-87, 8 bundles.

323/2. Treaty of Peace between two chieftains of the Pelew Islands 12 Aug. 1883, prefaced by a memo of Sir Cyprian Arthur George Bridge, captain H.M.S. *Espiègle*, at whose instance the treaty was signed.

F.O.800/6-20 Lascelles Papers

Papers of Sir Frank Cavendish Lascelles, Ambassador to Russia 1894 and to Germany 1896-1908, including the folowing letters:

800/9. 17 Feb. 1897 and Feb.-Mar. 1899 from Lascelles to F. H. Villiers on Samoan affairs.

800/10. 3 Apr., 13 May 1901 from F. H. Villiers and 6 Apr. 1901 from Lascelles concerning the possession of the Tasman Islands, part of the Howe group.

800/11. 12 Jan. 1908 from E. B. Malet asking Lascelles to help Mr Campbell, a representative of Burns, Philp & Co. going to Berlin at the suggestion of the Germans.

800/13. 21 Nov. 1906 from Lady Northcote, Government House, Melbourne, asking for exhibits for a proposed exhibition of women's work to be held in Australia, and 1 July 1907 thanking him for exhibits; 4 Apr. 1901 from Arthur Larcom concerning the complaint of the Samoan Estate Co. against the Hamburg Plantation Co. and against Dr Solf for not recognising the Company's leases.

800/19. 24 Jan. 1908 from Lascelles to E. B. Malet on the settlement of the Burns, Philp claim. The letters for 1906 in this volume have many references to the colonial scandal and its consequences within Germany.

F.O.800/25-8 Fergusson Papers

Correspondence of Sir James Fergusson, Under-Secretary in the Foreign Office 1886-91. The correspondence includes:

800/25. Letters and notes 12 Mar. 1888 on parliamentary questions on Raiatea, 3 May 1888 Chinese in Australia, and 10 May 1888 the Convention of 1879 concerning Samoa.

800/26. Letter 31 Mar. 1890 from J. Holford Plant, missionary at Norfolk Island, to L. Knowles concerning the Solomon Islands and Florida Island and the feelings of the natives towards the French and Germans.

F.O.800/29-31 Langley Papers

Sir Walter Langley was Assistant Under-Secretary of State 1886-1919. Among his correspondence are letters Oct.-Nov. 1888 on inquiries by John Walsh concerning Mary R. Martin who died in New Zealand in 1887, and correspondence and notes Mar. 1892 and 3 May 1894 on the formation of a commercial league among self governing colonies referring to an amendment of the Australian Customs Act.

F.O.800/35-112 Grey Papers

Papers of Sir Edward Grey, Viscount Grey of Falloden, Secretary of State for Foreign Affairs Dec. 1905 to Dec. 1916. There is an index to his papers which lists correspondence on subjects such as Alfred Deakin's proposals on the Monroe Doctrine and the Pacific, colonial and imperial conferences, the New Hebrides, German possessions in the Pacific, Dr George (Chinese) Morrison, occupation of the Pacific Islands, the Dardanelles Campaign, W. M. Hughes, and proposals for a commercial treaty between Australia and Japan.

London

F.O.800/115-46 Lansdowne Papers

Papers of the 5th Marquess of Lansdowne, Secretary of State for Foreign Affairs 1900-5, including letter 17 July 1902 to M. Cambon, and memo 19 Aug. 1903 on the New Hebrides and on the colonial question.

F.O.800/159-91 Bertie Papers

Francis Leveson Bertie, 1st Viscount Bertie of Thame was Assistant Under-Secretary for Foreign Affairs 1894-1903 and Ambassador to Paris 1905-18. These papers include 800/165 correspondence May-June 1908 on a proposal to award the Legion of Honour to Dame Nellie Melba.

F.O.800/200-17 Balfour Papers

The papers of the 1st Earl of Balfour, Secretary of State for Foreign Affairs Dec. 1916 to Oct. 1919, cover 1916-22 and include:

800/200. Letter 16 Apr. 1918 concerning the economic situation in Egypt and referring to the development of commercial connections among Australia, New Zealand, and Egypt.

800/201. Letters 9, 28 Feb. 1917 concerning German colonies and *inter alia* protest by Australia and New Zealand against their retrocession to Germany.

800/208. Copy of letter 16 May 1917 from Balfour concerning government control exercised by Britain over vessels of British register, referring to ships requisitioned from the Pacific and the Australian and New Zealand coasting trades, the maintenance of only essential Pacific services and the deficiency of the Australian railway system which impeded the release of vessels from existing trade.

800/209. Letter 16 Aug. 1917 from Lord Northcliffe while on a mission to the United States containing a strongly worded protest from the Australian Prime Minister, W. M. Hughes, on the proposal to requisition ships being built at New York for Australia, also two letters 5 Mar. 1917 concerning colonial representatives attending War Cabinet meetings.

800/211. Correspondence with officials and others in the United States of America 1917-18 includes several letters which concern Australia's opinions on the fate of the German colonies and on the anti-conscription movement. Miscellaneous papers in 800/214 also contain references to the German colonies and to imperial trade relations.

800/215, 216. Include correspondence Feb.-May 1919 on the question of Japanese immigration, mandates over Pacific Islands, especially Nauru, the use of indentured labour in Samoa, and the position of the Dominions when Britain is at war.

F.O.800/232 Bulwer Papers

Private papers of Sir Henry L. Bulwer, Ambassador to Washington 1850-1. Memoranda 1848-51 deal mainly with Central America but include a memo 6 Sept. 1849 by Vice-Adm. Lord Dundonald, H.M.S. *Wellesley*, Halifax, on the coal mines at Sydney and Picton and their importance in the event of a war between Great Britain and the United States.

F.O.800/264 Henderson Papers

Correspondence of Sir Nevile Meyrick Henderson including letter 25 Mar. 1927 to S. M. Bruce, Prime Minister of Australia, on the wrongs caused by the Treaty of Versailles.

F.O.800/280-4 Henderson Papers

Correspondence of the Right Hon. Arthur Henderson, Foreign Secretary 1929-31 including 800/280, letter 29 Aug. 1929 from Lord Passfield, Dominions Office, on the Optional Clause of the League of Nations and the dissatisfaction of Australia and South Africa over the formula concerning international disputes.

F.O.800/336-81 Nicolson Papers

Sir Arthur Nicolson, 11th Baronet and 1st Baron Carnock, was Assistant Private Secretary to Lord Granville 1872 and Under-Secretary of State for Foreign Affairs 1910-16. The correspondence covers 1889-1916. 800/381 has two letters from A. J. Bigge, Baron Stamfordham, Private Secretary to King George V, 20 Mar. 1916 on a gift of money from New South Wales to France, and 20 May 1916 on the importance of W. M. Hughes's presence at the Paris Peace Conference; also letters 18 Jan. 1916 from Government House, Cairo, anticipating Nicolson's talk with Hughes, and 28 Mar. 1916 from Lt.-Col. Sir A. H. McMahon, Cairo, saying that the Prince of Wales's visit to Cairo had given great pleasure to the Australian and New Zealand troops.

GENERAL REGISTER OFFICE

CENSUS RECORDS

R.G.9 Census Returns 1861, 4542 books.

Enumerators' schedules of returns made by heads of households giving the names, age, sex, occupation, and place of birth of individuals. In order to use these returns to obtain information about a particular person, it is necessary to know that person's place of residence at the time of the census. Census returns for 1841 and 1851 are among the Home Office records (H.O.107). Limited searches only in the census records are undertaken by Public Record Office staff on payment of a fee. Later returns are kept at the General Register Office, Somerset House.

NON-PAROCHIAL REGISTERS AND RECORDS

These records were originally deposited in the General Register Office by virtue of the Non-Parochial Registers Act 1840 and the Births and Deaths Registration Act 1858. The Acts followed Reports by Royal Commissions in 1838 and 1857 authenticating most of the registers and records.

All except one of the non-parochial registers relate solely to England and Wales. Almost all are from Protestant Nonconformist Churches. They do not include registers of the established Anglican Church for which application should be made to the incumbent of the local parish church, or of the Roman Catholic Church (except a very few for the north of England) for which application should be made to the priest in charge of the appropriate church. There are no Jewish registers included in this deposit; information concerning these should be obtained from the Jewish Historical Society of England. A small number of the registers are from inter-denominational institutions, e.g. the City of London burial ground at Bunhill Fields. Most non-parochial registers are for 1775-1837, but a few continue to 1858. E. Welch's article 'Nonconformist Registers', *Journal of the Society of Archivists* II, 9, Apr. 1964, pp.411-17, describes these records in more detail.

Since there is no general index, it is necessary to know the approximate locality in which a particular event took place and also, if possible, the denomination of the church or chapel where it was likely to be registered, before searching the records for genealogical information. Extended and speculative searches cannot be undertaken by Public Record Office staff, but short specific searches will be undertaken on payment of a fee.

See *Lists of Non-Parochial Registers and Records in the Custody of the Registrar General of Births, Deaths and Marriages*, London, H.M.S.O., 1859. Copies in the Reading

London

Rooms at the Public Record Office are marked up in manuscript with the Public Record Office class number. The list of R.G.4 is also published as Vol.42 in the List and Index Society Series.

R.G.4 Registers: Authenticated: Main Series 1567-1858, 4680 vols.

R.G.5 Certificates 1742-1840, 207 files.

The registers were compiled from these original certificates when they were in the registry of births for Presbyterians, Independents, and Baptists at Dr Williams's Library, London, and the metropolitan registry for Wesleyan Methodists at Paternoster Row. There are indexes in R.G.4.

R.G.6 Registers: Authenticated: Society of Friends Series 1613-1841, 1673 vols.

There is an index to these registers in the Library of the Religious Society of Friends, London.

R.G.8 Registers: Unauthenticated: Miscellaneous Series 1646-1900, 110 vols.

MINISTRY OF HEALTH

The Ministry of Health group includes several classes of records inherited from predecessor bodies, all of which were concerned with the relief of the poor and unemployed, and consequently with pauper emigration as one solution to the problem.

See the following lists:
Class List of the Records of the Ministry of Health, 1954, 2 vols., typescript.
Detailed List, Ministry of Health: Poor Law Union Papers M.H.12, 1952, 2 vols., typescript.

GENERAL BOARD OF HEALTH AND LOCAL GOVERNMENT ACT OFFICE

M.H.13 Correspondence 1847-71, 272 vols.

13/252 contains sections of correspondence with the Colonial Office 1855-8, and Emigration Office 1853-4. The former contains a printed return to the House of Commons 17 Feb. 1858 of vessels in British colonies placed in quarantine during the ten years 1845-54 inclusive, with the original returns from the Australian colonies and New Zealand forwarded by the Colonial Office. The Emigration Office papers include letters July-Sept. 1854 from J. G. Sparke, M.D., Government Medical Inspector of Emigrants at the Port of London concerning inadequate precautions taken against cholera and other diseases in certain vessels conveying emigrants to Australia.

POOR LAW COMMISSION, POOR LAW BOARD AND LOCAL GOVERNMENT BOARD

M.H.12 Poor Law Union Papers 1834-1950, 16741 vols.

References to emigration are scattered through the papers which also deal with schools, workhouses, the legal settlement of paupers, and elections of Guardians.

M.H.15 Index of Subjects 1836-1920, 107 vols.

The Index relates to the correspondence and papers in M.H.12 and 19. Each volume has a section 'Emigration' usually divided into 'expenses' and 'miscellaneous'. The entries give, in addition to a summary of the content of the letter, the year, the number of the letter and the number of the Union, or an indication that it is Government Office correspondence. In order to find the name of the Union involved, it is necessary to refer to the detailed class list of M.H.12 which lists the Unions in numerical order.

M.H.19 Government Offices, Correspondence and Papers 1834-1908, 280 boxes.

Correspondence of the central authority for Poor Law, public health and local government services with other Government departments. Most of the papers are arranged by departments in alphabetical order but some volumes relate to specific subjects. The indexes are in M.H.20.

19/5-11. Colonial Office 1835-92. 19/5 nominally covers the period 1834-74, but papers 1840-70 inclusive are missing. Papers 1835-9 contain material concerning emigration to the Australian colonies, much of this being from J. D. Pinnock, Colonial Office, appointed in 1835 as Government Agent for Emigration, resident in London.

19/22. Emigration Office 1836-76. Papers for 1857-62 are missing. The volume includes a number of letters concerning emigration to Australia, as well as papers concerning more general questions such as the emigration of persons with infectious diseases and statistics of emigrants to various colonies.

M.H.20 Government Offices, Registers of Correspondence 1837-1920, 85 vols.

These are indexes to M.H.19. 20/1-3 are General 1837-55; the other volumes are arranged alphabetically by departments, 20/10-14 being Colonial Office 1882-1920. Some of the papers to which reference is made have been destroyed.

POOR LAW HEALTH AND POOR LAW SERVICES

M.H.64 Poor Law Instruments 1916-32, 28 vols.

These copy authorisations to local Guardians of the Poor to expend money on Poor Law business, were issued until 1919 by the Local Government Board and thereafter by the Ministry of Health. They gave official sanction of expenditure to assist the emigration of poor persons as well as to make alterations to Union Institutions, to raise loans, and to acquire and sell property. The documents in the volumes are arranged chronologically but there are no indexes. No copy instruments survive before 1916.

HOME OFFICE

In 1782 a Secretary of State for Home Affairs was appointed with exclusive jurisdiction over internal business. The new Secretary's department immediately became responsible for colonial affairs and remained so until 1801 despite the appointment of a Secretary of State for War and the Colonies in 1794. Consequently a number of papers relating to the establishment and control of the settlements in New South Wales are found in this group. Much that is of background interest to the transportation system has not been included in this description, e.g. papers on the state of the country and on the administration of the courts and gaols in H.O.20. H.O.109-13 and 127 relating to prison administration have been transferred to the Prison Commission.

See the following lists:

Lists and Indexes XLIII, *List of State Papers Domestic 1547-1792 and Home Office Records 1782-1837*, London 1914, reprint New York 1963.

Class List of the Records of the Home Office and Signet Office to 1837, reproduction of pp.93-146 of Lists and Indexes XLIII, with additional typed pages and MS. additions and corrections.

Class Lists of the Records of the Home Office and Signet Office from 1837, 1957, typescript; continuation of Lists and Indexes XLIII.

London

CRIMINAL

H.O.140 Calendars of Prisoners 1868-1948, 531 vols.

Detailed lists, mostly printed, of prisoners tried at Assizes and Quarter Sessions. For similar lists see H.O.16 and 77. Closed for one hundred years.

H.O.6 Circuit Letters 1816-40, 25 bundles.

Reports, letters, and memorials from judges, recorders, and others recommending remissions of sentences, also lists of convicts and letters on transportation and convict discipline.
6/23. Return of convict deaths in New South Wales for 1838.

H.O.7 Convicts, Miscellaneous 1785-1835, 3 vols.

7/2. Miscellaneous correspondence 1823-35 relating to convict matters. It includes a letter from Francis Forbes about transportation, a report of proceedings to inquire into charges made by Rev. John Vincent against the Surgeon Superintendent and the Master of the convict ship *Elizabeth*, and a return of convict deaths in New South Wales for 1829 and 1830.

H.O.8 Convict Prisons 1824-76, 207 vols.

Lists of convicts on hulks and in prisons giving details of age, offences and convictions, surgeons' reports, and behaviour. The remarks column shows date of transportation where appropriate.

H.O.9 Convict Prisons, Miscellaneous Registers 1802-49, 16 vols.

Mainly registers of the convicts on hulks with varying details of offence, conviction, character, behaviour in gaol, and in some cases date and place of transportation. 9/16 is a letter book relating to the establishment of the hulks 1847-9.

H.O.10 Convicts, New South Wales and Tasmania 1788-1859, 64 vols.

Lists of convicts in these colonies giving details of sentences, employment and settlement, lists of pardons, and returns of general musters in New South Wales including the 1828 census. No details are given in the class list for 10/36 and 10/37 except the date 1837; 10/36 is a general muster c.1821-3 and 10/37 a general muster and classified list of landholders c.1806.

H.O.11 Convict Transportation Registers 1787-1870, 21 vols.

Convicts are listed under the name of the ship in which they were transported. The ships are listed in order of their sailing date. Some details of convictions and sentences are given.

11/20 consists of two indexes, the ships which were sent to each colony 1787-1870, and an alphabetical list of all the convict ships giving their sailing date and destination.

11/21 is a statistical summary of the number of convicts transported Jan. 1787 to Mar. 1870. Details include the number of males and females on each ship, yearly totals and, from 1848, establishments from which the convicts were sent, indicating whether the males held tickets of leave or conditional pardons.

H.O.12 Criminal Papers, Old Series 1849-71, 196 boxes.

Original in-letters, memorials, and other papers relating to criminal matters, which have been preserved. Indexes to this class are in H.O.14. Subjects include the chartering of ships for the transport of convicts, their despatch from the United Kingdom and arrival at their destination, the treatment of female convicts on voyages, inquiries about individual convicts, reports on juvenile immigrants to Western Australia and applications for passages for families of transported men. Similar papers of an earlier date are in P.C.1.

H.O.13 Criminal Papers, Entry Books 1782-1871, 111 vols.

Out-letters on criminal matters including the movement of prisoners within and without the United Kingdom, the disposal of effects of dead prisoners, instructions for assigning convicts about to be transported, and other similar administrative matters; also appeals against sentences, remissions, and to the end of 1849 warrants and pardons. The volumes are indexed by name of individual or departmental recipient.

H.O.14 Criminal Papers, Registers 1849-70, 37 vols.

Indexes to H.O.12 arranged under such headings as 'Admiralty', 'Colonial Office', 'Hulks', 'Special Subjects', and names of individual gaols. From 1855 letters and warrants issued from the Home Office are included in the registers. A list of papers preserved and of numbers destroyed is included in each volume. The entries give the date and a brief statement of the subject of the letters received.

H.O.15 Criminal Papers, Warrant Books 1850-98, 30 vols.

These continue the entries of warrants in H.O.13 and include warrants for removal of convicts from prisons to hulks, conditional pardons for prisoners embarked for penal settlements and pardons for convicts in penal settlements. Personal names are indexed roughly alphabetically in each volume under such headings as 'Free pardons', 'Conditional pardons'.

H.O.26 Criminal Registers, Series I 1791-1849, 56 vols.

Registers of all persons charged with indictable offences in Middlesex showing the result of the trial, the sentence if convicted, whether it was executed or commuted, and other personal details. The arrangement is roughly alphabetical by name.

H.O.27 Criminal Registers, Series II 1805-92, 223 vols.

Similar to H.O.26, covering the rest of England and Wales and including Middlesex after 1850.

H.O.25 Entry Books, Public Departments 1850-71, 13 vols.

Out-letters on criminal matters to other Government departments including information on ships chartered for the transportation of convicts and the sending of families of convicts to penal settlements.

H.O.130 Miscellaneous Books 1798, 1824-6, 4 vols.

130/1. Trial of prisoners at Winchester at a Special Commission of Assize 1830. This contains a detailed list of prisoners with results of the trial, and statistical summaries of the trial and of the prisoners' backgrounds.

H.O.77 Newgate Calendar 1782-1853, 60 vols.

Detailed printed lists of prisoners to be tried at Newgate, with manuscript additions stating, from July 1822 onwards, the results of trials. Each issue has an alphabetical index to committals at the front and a manuscript index under subjects, e.g. Middlesex verdicts, London arraignments, at the back.

London

H.O.16 Old Bailey Sessions 1815-49, 9 vols.

H.O.17 Petitions, Series I 1819-39, 131 bundles.

Original petitions of convicts appealing against sentences or for reduction thereof, with accompanying papers.

H.O.18 Petitions, Series II 1839-54, 381 bundles.

Similar to H.O.17.

H.O.19 Petitions, Registers 1797-1853, 12 vols.

Alphabetical list referring to the original petitions in H.O.17 and 18 giving the results of the petitions. Details of where and when individuals were convicted and their sentences are also given.

H.O.21 Prisons, Entry Books, Series I 1812-84, 15 vols.

Out-letters and instructions to governors and inspectors of the prisons of Millbank, Parkhurst, Pentonville, Portland, etc. Subjects include the cost of superintending the embarkation of prisoners on transports, the selection of the prisoners for Gibraltar to replace those going to New South Wales, and the appointment of religious instructors and matrons for convict ships. There is a contents list of letters in date order in each volume.

H.O.22 Prisons, Entry Books, Series II 1849-1921, 82 vols.

Letters to prison inspectors and officials of county prisons, similar to H.O.21. Some letters refer to reports on the disposal in England of convicts awaiting transportation. The volumes have contents lists of letters in date order under regions. Closed for a hundred years.

H.O.23 Prisons, Registers of County Prisons 1847-66, 20 vols.

Detailed lists of prisoners under the names of the gaols in which they were kept. There are rough alphabetical indexes in each volume.

H.O.24 Prisons, Registers and Returns 1838-75, 29 vols.

Similar to H.O.23 but also including prison returns for England and Wales 1860-9 giving statistical information about prisoners.

VARIOUS

H.O.107 Census Papers, Population Returns 1841, 1851, 2535 boxes.

H.O.28 Admiralty, Correspondence and Papers 1782-1840, 63 vols.

Original in-letters and draft out-letters with allied papers. They include letters on the settlement in New South Wales and related subjects, e.g. 28/7 copy of Capt. Bligh's report 1790 on the mutiny of the *Bounty*, letters on the transportation of convicts, the health of prisoners on the hulks, whaling, and voyages of exploration.

H.O.29 Admiralty, Entry Books 1779-1836, 7 vols.

Similar in subject matter to H.O.28. These include correspondence on convict hulks, transportation, pardons, convicts returning from penal settlements before the expiration of their sentences, instructions to commanders of ships of war concerning vessels employed in whaling, the obtaining of breadfruit, store ships for New South Wales, the powers of Governors, and bills drawn for colonial purposes or for expenses connected with voyages of exploration.

H.O.31 Council Office, Correspondence and Papers 1782-1840, 18 bundles.

Orders in Council, proceedings, and correspondence. 31/1, 1782-94, includes orders for convicts to be transported, an order approving the draft of instructions for the governors of New South Wales and an order approving a great seal for New South Wales. 31/14 Committee of the Privy Council for Trade 1785-9, contains papers on New Zealand hemp, the Southern Whale Fishery, and coinage for New South Wales. There is also correspondence on these and similar subjects.

H.O.32 Foreign Office, Correspondence and Papers 1782-1845, 20 vols.

Only a few of these in-letters appear to relate to Australasia. 32/2, 1790-2, includes letters concerning the activities of the French in the Pacific.

H.O.48 Law Officers, Reports and Correspondence 1782-1871, 54 vols.

These include opinions on various agricultural riots and may therefore be of interest for information on cases in which labourers were transported. 48/28 reports and correspondence 1830-3 was checked but nothing of interest found.

H.O.49 Law Officers, Letter Books 1762-1871, 11 vols.

Entry books of letters to the Law Officers, except 49/4 which contains entries of letters from them to the Home Office. 49/7 was checked and the following entries found: ff.66-80, 98 correspondence June-Aug. 1818 concerning the *Chapman* convict ship to Sydney from Ireland, ff.252, 314, letters 24 Aug. 1824, 12 Feb. 1827 concerning the death of Thomas Perryman, Bay of Islands, N.Z.

H.O.34 Public Offices, Correspondence and Papers 1836-98, 88 vols.

Out-letters to various government departments, each volume with an index arranged under departments and subjects. Relevant entries are to be found under headings such as 'Colonial Office', 'Council Office and Board of Trade', 'Convicts', 'Admiralty', 'Transport and Victualling'. Subjects include the convict service overseas, emigration, postal services, savings banks, colonial legislation on subjects of interest to the Home Office, Irish police for the colonies, and the visit of the King of the Sandwich Islands to Birmingham and Manchester.

H.O.35 Treasury and Customs, Correspondence and Papers 1781-1854, 33 vols.

In-letters and drafts of out-letters, including colonial correspondence up to 1800, e.g. 35/1, 1781-90, letter 18 Aug. 1786 asking the Commissioners of Treasury to take necessary measures to provide ships, provisions, implements and other necessaries for the First Fleet, with a plan for the establishment of the settlement and estimates of requirements. Other papers in 35/1, 7, 9-22 relate to the establishment of the settlement, the despatch of ships, convicts, stores and equipment, and bills drawn by Governors and others. Examples of other matters discussed in the correspondence are: proposal and plan by W. Richards for the regulating of convicts under sentence of transportation; 35/17, 1797, letter enclosing a statement of the expenses of Norfolk Island and a letter from the Commissioners of Transport concerning articles procured for settlers in New South Wales, with account. Relevant letters after 1806 relate chiefly to the convict service in the Australian colonies.

H.O.36 Treasury Entry Books 1776-1871, 37 vols.

Entry books of out-letters sent to the Treasury. Indexes in each volume show relevant material under such headings as 'Criminal letters, memorials etc., transmitted' and 'Botany Bay'. Many letters relate to the payment of gratuities to masters or surgeon superintendents of convict ships and to the convict service generally; there are also letters about the purchase of stores for New South Wales in Batavia, the Cape of Good Hope and other places.

H.O.30 War and Colonial Office Correspondence and Papers 1794-1840, 5 bundles.

In-letters, except 30/5 which is an entry book of out-letters 1815-36. 30/3, 1801-38, was checked and letters on the following subjects found: the appointment of an Agent General for Emigration to control the funds for the conveyance of settlers to the Australian colonies and all other matters relating to emigration; the transmission of remarks on the system of secondary punishment in Van Diemen's Land; the transmission of a statement by George Loveless, a convict in Van Diemen's Land, about a London Trades Union.

H.O.40 Disturbances, Correspondence, etc. 1812-55, 59 bundles.

Original correspondence and other papers relating to riots and disturbances. 40/27, 1817-34, was checked and the following entries found: ff.506-7, letter 16 Jan. 1831 from J. H. Mair, High Wycombe, Bucks., concerning sentences of transportation and death passed at Assizes and referring to certain papermakers among those sentenced to death who may make valuable settlers in New South Wales; ff.508-9, list 13 Jan. 1831 of prisoners recommended for mercy, returned by J. H. Mair, 16 Jan. 1831.

H.O.41 Disturbances, Entry Books 1816-98, 33 vols.

Entries of out-letters, warrants, etc., relating to riots and disturbances. 41/8 Sept.-Dec. 1830 was checked but nothing of interest found.

H.O.43 Domestic and General, Entry Books 1782-1898, 206 vols.

Only scattered references to Australasian material were found in these out-letters. There are indexes from 1792 onwards. These show relevant material under various headings, e.g. 'Foreign', the recovery of escaped convicts should they arrive at Dutch Ports in the Isle of Sunda, and requests for the friendly reception for ships from New South Wales wishing to purchase livestock in the same area, and 'Criminal', detailed lists of convicts, to be laid before the King for his declaration of their places of imprisonment overseas.

H.O.45 Domestic and General, Registered Papers 1841-1934, 16015 boxes.

See the following lists, published as Vols.22, 23, 30, and 39 of the List and Index Society series:
Subject indexes to Registered Papers 'Old Series', H.O.45, 1841-55, 2 vols., photocopy of manuscript.
Subject indexes to Registered Papers 'Old Series', H.O.45, 1856-71, 1 vol., typescript.
Subject index to Registered Papers, H.O.45, 1871-1934, 7 vols., typescript.

Original in-letters and papers selected for preservation. Up to 1871 they comprise the Old Series on domestic matters. The series begun in 1871 includes criminal papers which before that date are to be found in H.O.12 but after 1878 most of the criminal and some other papers are in H.O.144. Reference to H.O.45 may be made from the Daily Registers (H.O.46) and from the Subject Indexes listed above which show material under the headings 'Convicts', 'Transportation', 'Emigration' and under names of gaols, e.g. 'Parkhurst'.

H.O.46 Daily Registers 1841-1934, 295 vols.

Registers of correspondence received each day. They include indexes of names and special subjects and lists of papers preserved and destroyed. Entries relating to passages for wives of transported convicts and suggestions that no more convicts be sent to Van Diemen's Land were noted under 'Special Subjects', entries relating to emigration under 'Colonial Office', and numerous references under 'Convicts'.

H.O.138 Register of Papers Issued 1871-3, 6 vols.

Subdivisions under the heading 'Convict Prisons' include New South Wales,

Tasmania, and Western Australia. Under these can be found entries for papers relating to the transfer of the control of transported convicts from Imperial to Colonial authorities, financial estimates for the Colonial Service in the various colonies, and pardons.

H.O.144 Registered Papers, Supplementary 1879-1932, 17223 boxes.

Papers on criminal and certain other subjects. Closed for one hundred years.

H.O.74 Entry Books, Commissions 1836-71, 4 vols.

74/1. Letters 1836-45 to the Criminal Law Commission.

H.O.73 Expired Commissions 1786-1894, 70 bundles and vols.

73/16. Papers and books relating to the Select Committee on Gaols, 1835-7.

H.O.47 Judges' Reports 1784-1829, 75 vols.

Letters and reports from judges on cases and criminals and petitions for commutation of sentences and free pardons.

H.O.38 Warrant Books, General Series 1782-1921, 72 vols.

Entries of warrants, appointments to offices, licences to plead, and licences for many other matters. There is a classified index in each volume, under headings such as 'Warrants', 'Pardons', 'Offices'. Sample entries found relate to a seal for New South Wales, the power of the Governor of New South Wales to remit sentences, the appointment of Governors, and the commutation of death sentences to transportation.

SCOTLAND

H.O.102 Correspondence and Papers 1782-1853, 66 vols.

Original letters and papers, petitions, and circuit letters on criminal matters.

H.O.104 Criminal Entry Books 1762-1849, 12 vols.

Out-letters, indexed by name of person under 'Free Pardons', 'Conditional Pardons', 'References', 'Respites', and 'Warrants Particular'.

IRELAND

H.O.100 Correspondence and Papers 1782-1851, 264 vols. and bundles.

Original letters and papers including scattered letters on the transportation of convicts.

H.O.122 General Letter Books 1782-1871, 24 vols.

Entries of out-letters, indexed under broad headings, e.g. 'Civil', 'Military'. Some relate to the chartering of ships for the transport of convicts, and to requests for assistance to emigrate to Australia.

PAYMASTER GENERAL'S OFFICE

In this description no mention has been made of the following classes which are brief records of pay or pensions for army, navy, and civil officers, their widows and dependants, or are records containing other information chiefly of biographical interest which can be approached only by names of individuals: P.M.G.3-6, 9-13, 15-16, 18-20, 22, 24-5, 33, 35, 48, 50-1, 57, 69-71. Earlier records of the pensions and allowances referred to in P.M.G.15-16, 18-20, 24-5 are found in Adm.22, 23, 25.

See the following lists:

Lists and Indexes XLVI *Lists of the Records of the Treasury, the Paymaster General's Office, the Exchequer and Audit Department*, London 1922, reprint New York 1963.

London

Class List of the Records of the Paymaster General's Office preserved in the Public Record Office, 1937, typescript.

ARMY ESTABLISHMENT

P.M.G.1 Letters 1784-1867, 115 vols.

Except for 1/1 this class consists of entry books of out-letters relating to pay, allowances, supplies, and army services generally.

1/1. The volume 1822-3 includes a group of private letters from Sir Thomas Brisbane to William Petrie Craufurd of the Paymaster General's Office in London. The letters concern Brisbane's personal affairs, the state of the colony, his plans for it, and their implementation.

1/2-25. Common letter books 1804-39 containing letters to and from Deputy Paymaster General, Commissariats, agents, other departments, and individuals concerning army expenditure, salaries, allowances, and pensions. Relevant entries in the indexes to each volume are chiefly under individual names or regiments.

1/26-45. Treasury letter books 1808-39 relating to queries on expenditure and including some letters on individuals' pay and pensions. Relevant entries in the indexes to each volume are chiefly under individual names or regiments.

1/46-103. War Office letter books 1784-1834 concerning such matters as instructions to Commissariat officers in the colonies, sums expended in the colonies on pay and allowances, stores, and queries concerning payments.

1/106-15. Registers of letters received 1842-67 with a brief summary of the contents.

P.M.G.2 Ledgers 1757-1840, 254 vols.

Yearly and half yearly accounts of the expenditure and receipts of the regiments and garrisons. Relevant entries may be found in the volumes called 'General', 'Army Extraordinaries', 'Garrisons Abroad' and 'Regimental'. The regimental number must be known to make effective use of many of the volumes.

P.M.G.14 Miscellaneous Books 1720-1861, 192 vols.

A collection of accounts, ledgers, cash books, entry books, registers, warrant books, and letter books relating to the Army Establishment.

14/77-85. Army Extraordinaries 1801-4, 1820-36. A note at the beginning of 14/85 explains the constitution of Army Extraordinaries and the mode of expenditure and repayment. These volumes contain accounts of extraordinary expenses of the Army incurred and paid for, also advances and repayments for expenses of any branch of the public service at foreign stations including advances to agents for the various colonies. Examples are: 14/79, 1822-3, containing records of sums advanced to S. Brooksbank on account of New South Wales bills, and of subsequent repayments, and of an advance to Col. Arthur to defray the expenses of his conveyance to Van Diemen's Land; 14/85, 1836, containing records of advances to John Marshall for defraying the expenses of the conveyance of emigrants to New South Wales and Van Diemen's Land to be repaid from the emigration funds of the colonies to the military chests at those stations, repayment to the Treasurer of the Ordinance for the cost of a fire engine for New South Wales, payments to His Majesty's Stationery Office for stationery for Van Diemen's Land, and to the Receiver-General of the Post Office in respect of sums paid into military chests abroad.

Other volumes in this class which may contain biographical information on army personnel are entry books of royal warrants for half pay, etc., 1720-1817, ledgers for regiments, staff, and garrisons on foreign stations 1804-24, entry books and registers of powers of attorney 1721-1841 (also in P.M.G.51) and a volume on law cases relating to the administration of effects, disputes over payments of wages to agents, and similar matters.

CIVIL ESTABLISHMENT

P.M.G.27 Consolidated Fund 1811-1929, 67 vols.

27/2, 1834-5, contains records of superannuation and retired allowances paid to consuls. Later records are in P.M.G.28.

P.M.G.28 Superannuation and Retired Allowances 1834-1925, 97 vols.

Registers of payments of superannuation, retired, and special allowances to staff of civil establishments. Entries relate to the civil establishment of Western Australia 1835-7, the Convict Hulk Establishment, and convict establishment abroad, governors of colonies, consuls (earlier records are in P.M.G.27), emigration agents, the Mint, and the British Antarctic Expedition 1910-13.

MISCELLANEOUS

P.M.G.49 Main Account Ledgers 1834-1921, 98 vols.

49/1-71. Ledgers of votes and deposit accounts 1837-1921, those for 1837-48 relating to army and navy establishments only. They include broad entries for payments of money into military chests abroad, balances or deficits of commissary chest accounts, and advances to colonial agents.

49/72-98. Ledgers for the civil establishment and miscellaneous accounts 1834-48 including expenses of colonial settlements, emigration, and convict services, and travel expenses and allowances of governors and other colonial officials.

P.M.G.51 Power of Attorney Registers c.1790-1899, 17 vols.

Registers of powers of attorney, assignments, and so on, relating mainly to naval, military, and civil officers and their dependants. See also P.M.G.14.

P.M.G.54 Special Claims 1834-47, 7 vols.

Registers of special payments made to departments, officials, and private individuals for works, services, and special expenses. Arrangement is alphabetical, chiefly by name of the official or individual concerned with some entries under the names of the branches of government. Particulars of the claim and payment made are shown. Entries are mostly for travelling expenses of officials and individuals travelling on government business including colonial governors, bishops, and consuls, and payments of salaries and allowances, but also include payments for stores sent from one colony to another, expenses of the convict service, sums to defray the charges of government of the colonies, and other miscellaneous items.

P.M.G.66 Paymaster General of the Forces: Minute Books 1804-36, 6 vols.

NAVAL ESTABLISHMENT

P.M.G.73 Miscellanea 1821-37, 2 vols.

73/2. Book containing the addresses of naval officers on retired and half pay including chaplains, pursers, and masters, and also of Royal Marine officers on unattached, retired full, and reserved half pay, 1837.

PRISON COMMISSION

See Class List of Prison Commission Records, 1958, typescript.

Pri.Com.1 Sessions Papers, Old Bailey 1801-1904, 156 vols.

Printed proceedings of the Commissioners of Oyer and Terminer and Gaol Delivery for London and Middlesex and from 1834 the parts of Essex, Kent and

Surrey within the jurisdiction of the Central Criminal Court. The printed proceedings of the Admiralty Session 1807-8 are included in this class. There is an index to the names of the prisoners tried at the end of each issue and a cumulated index at the back of each volume.

Pri.Com.2 Prison Books 1770-1894, 429 vols.

Registers of prisoners, photograph albums, minute books of the following prisons: Chatham, Dorchester, Gibraltar, Millbank, Newgate, Parkhurst, Pentonville, Portland, Portsmouth, Shorncliffe, Westminster Penitentiary, Woking, Wormwood Scrubs, and some hulks. Particulars of prisoners are given in detail in the registers which are indexed roughly alphabetically.

Pri.Com.5 Old Captions and Transfer Papers 1843-71, 52 boxes.

Court orders for the imprisonment of convicts, transfer papers for the removal of convicts to prisons, and certificates of transportation, each containing the penal record and other particulars of the prisoners. Reference to these can be made through the registers in Pri.Com.6.

Pri.Com.6 Registers and Indexes 1824-85, 20 vols.

Registers to Pri.Com.3 and 4 and indexes to the Old Captions (Pri.Com.5).

Pri.Com.7 Registered Files, Series I 1838-1933, 738 files.

The papers, selected for permanent preservation from those created in the offices of the Prison Commissioners, are arranged in three groups dealing with the administration of prisons, the pay and conditions of service of the staff, and the custody and treatment of convicts. Warrants for prisons and hulks as places of confinement for people awaiting transportation are included in the small amount of material which has survived for the period before 1877.

PRIVY COUNCIL OFFICE

By the eighteenth century the Privy Council had become primarily a body which validated decisions reached elsewhere. However it did retain some executive functions including certain responsibilities with regard to convicts sentenced to transportation. It also retained certain judicial powers, acting as a court of final resort in Admiralty jurisdiction and in all civil and criminal appeals from the courts of the Crown's dominions overseas, exercised through its Judicial Committee. (See *Guide to the Contents of the Public Record Office* I, p.165.) This right of appeal has been gradually restricted or abolished by dominion legislation.

See the following lists:
Class List of the Records of the Privy Council Office [excluding P.C.1], 1958, typescript.
List of Unbound Papers [of the Privy Council Office P.C.1], 4 vols., manuscript and typescript. This list is published as Vols.24, 35, 36 in the List and Index Society Series.

P.C.1 Papers, Mainly Unbound 1481-1946, 4559 bundles.

The Unbound Papers supplement the Registers (P.C.2) and the Minutes (P.C.4) which record only those matters which came before the Council or its Committee. They are of varied character and include petitions and letters from individuals to the Council, reports and memorials from government departments and Committees of the Council, law officers' opinions, papers in appeal cases, orders and minutes of the Council, proclamations, precedents. Subjects covered include colonies, prisoners and convicts, charters to companies, universities and other institutions, public health and quarantine, the Southern Whale Fishery, trade, embargoes, and neutral property. Many papers to 1783 relating to colonial affairs were published in calendar form by J. Munro, *Acts of the Privy Council, Colonial Series, Vol.VI, The Unbound Papers*, London 1912.

The papers listed below were noted from the 'List of Unbound Papers'. Further documents relating to convicts and transportation will be found in 34/A93, 37/A112, 40/A133, 64/B31, 65/B33, 2715-18 (lists of convicts embarked on the *Eden* 1840, *Tortoise* 1841, *Elphinstone* 1842, *Anson* 1843), 3499, 3534, 3565, 3583, 3672A, 3745, 3827, 3904, 3917, 3938, 3943, 3973, 3981, 4005.

1/19/A27. Three papers Nov. 1792 seeking the judges' opinion on the court martial of William Muspratt, one of the alleged mutineers of the *Bounty*.

1/23/A41. Draft minute book 1795 recording: 9 Apr. embargo taken off the *Joseph*, and 13, 15 Sept., 13, 14 Oct. transportation of convicts.

1/35/A94. Petition of the Committee for Managing the Missionary Society, for leave to export to the South Seas, received 30 July 1796 with permission 3 Aug. 1796, to export three tons of bar iron to Otaheite.

1/43/A148. Admiralty memorial proposing increased pay for the surgeons' mates of prison ships and gun boats, ordered 27 Nov. 1798.

1/43/A150. Letter 18 Nov. 1798 from Lord Castlereagh changing the sentence of Christopher Coleman from death to transportation for life, and enclosing a copy of the report from the judges, 14 Nov. 1798.

1/43/A156. Admiralty memorial concerning increased pay for the commanders of prison ships, received 26 Apr. 1799.

1/57. Draft of additional instructions to the Governors of His Majesty's plantations directing them to restrain the issue of paper bills of credit in the colonies, received 26 Sept. 1782.

1/61/B15 part 1. Admiralty representation 21 Nov. 1786 proposing that four more companies of marines be raised for the intended settlement at Botany Bay, received 22 Nov. 1786; report 3 May 1786 for granting certain premiums for the encouragement of the Southern Whale Fishery; memorial concerning an additional officer for a man-of-war accompanying transports to Botany Bay, received 14 Dec. 1786.

1/62/B16. Admiralty memorial 27 Mar. 1787 and Order in Council 4 Apr. 1787 concerning the establishment of a Vice-Admiralty Court in New South Wales; letter 20 Apr. 1787 from Lord Sydney transmitting draft of instructions for Gov. Phillip.

1/62/B18. Order 23 June 1789 referring to the Committee of Council for Trade a draft instruction to Gov. Phillip *re* lands in New South Wales; order 8 Aug. 1789 approving an additional instruction.

1/62/B19. Order 21 May 1790 to the Committee of Council for Trade concerning a great seal for New South Wales.

1/63/B22. Papers 1791 relating to the Southern Whale Fishery.

1/64/B29. Letters 10 Jan., 27 May 1794 from Henry Dundas to the Lord President of the Council relating to the appointment of John Hunter to New South Wales; report 12 June 1794 of the Committee for Trade on the draft of instructions for John Hunter.

1/67-92. Papers 1819-44 relating to convicts and prisons. In-letters addressed to the Home Office, but referred to the Privy Council, including letters from departments and individuals responsible for the transportation of convicts and petitions from prisoners' wives to be allowed to accompany them. In each bundle the papers are arranged in small packages under months with some loose memoranda. Similar papers are found in H.O.12.

1/1717. Proposed supplementary charter 1861 of the Chartered Bank of India, Australia, and China.

1/1781-3. Peninsular and Oriental Co. petition 1875 for supplementary charter, petition and appendices 1873-5 George Bain v. the Company.

1/1807. Draft charter n.d. of the South Australian Banking Co.

1/1901. Letters 1841 from the Treasury giving approval to the confirmation of New South Wales Acts 13 and 19.

1/1902. Papers 1823-73 relating to the case of Saxe Bannister, Attorney-General in New South Wales 1823-6.

1/1903. Papers 1888 concerning the suspension of Chief Justice Onslow, Western Australia, printed.

1/3482. Draft Order in Council 18 Mar. 1800 appointing the place to which certain convicts shall be transported.

1/3527. Draft Order in Council 31 May 1801 appointing the place to which certain convicts shall be conveyed; memorial of Benjamin Rotch praying that a certificate of British Registry may be granted to the *Hannah and Eliza* belonging to Milford and bound for the Southern Whale Fishery, received 21 Apr. 1801; draft Order in Council 21 May 1801 granting a register to the *Hannah and Eliza*; other papers concerning Benjamin Rotch and the Southern Whale Fishery are in 1/3482, 3578, 3610, 3645, 3650, 3689, 3750.

1/3535. Minutes 30 Dec. 1807 mentioning the extension of the limits of the Southern Whale Fishery.

1/3541. Order in Council 3 Feb. 1802 approving commission and instructions for Gov. King.

1/3654. Petition of Charles Enderby for the embargo to be taken off the *Minerva* bound for the South Seas, received 11 May 1805.

1/3656. Draft instructions 9 May 1805 to William Bligh as Governor of New South Wales; Order in Council 9 May 1805 appointing the place to which certain convicts shall be sent.

1/3658. Draft commission for William Bligh as Governor, received 30 Apr. 1805, read and approved 1 May 1805.

1/3746. Report 22 Nov. 1806 on John Palmer's appeal against Simeon Lord; order 26 Nov. 1806 allowing John Palmer to appeal against Simeon Lord; other papers concerning this case are in 1/3672C, 3790, 3872.

1/3878. Commission and instructions 2 May 1809 for Gov. Macquarie.

1/3885. Draft Order in Council 2 Aug. 1809 appointing the place to which certain convicts shall be conveyed; report of H.M. Advocate, Attorney and Solicitor General on transportation from Jersey, received 8 Aug. 1809.

1/3967, 3968, 3970. Papers including letter 1812 concerning the plundering of a village at Tippoona, Bay of Islands, N.Z.

1/3983. Petition of Price Darlos that directions be given for the crew and passengers to depart in the *James Hay* to New South Wales, received 3 Oct. 1812; letter from Lord Bathurst to the Lord President with a list of male convicts, received 10 Oct. 1812.

1/4012. Petition to dismiss appeal for want of prosecution, Simeon Lord, appellant, Arthur Hogue, respondent, received 19 Aug. 1813; petition of appeal from a decree of the Governor of New South Wales, William Campbell, appellant, Simeon Lord, respondent, received 30 Aug. 1813.

1/4030. Letter 19 Jan. 1815 from the Admiralty concerning four convicts escaped from Norfolk Island but delivered up at St Helena.

1/4083. Papers 1815-33 relating to convicts, 5 boxes.

1/4183. Petition 20 May 1820 of Henry Mitchison, merchant, London, for leave to export twenty sheep to New South Wales in the *Skelton*; letter 26 May 1820 from Henry Goulburn transmitting a memorial by gentlemen, clergy, merchants, landholders, and other free inhabitants of New South Wales for relief from certain restrictions.

1/4200. Commission and instruction for Gov. Brisbane, approved 22 Jan. 1821, incomplete.

1/4211. Request 12 Dec. 1821 from Rev. R. Aitkins, Hanley, that permission be granted to Hanson Moreton to accompany his brother to New South Wales.

1/4272. Order in Council 19 Oct. 1824 empowering the Judges of the Supreme Courts of New South Wales and Van Diemen's Land to make and alter rules and orders relating to their respective courts.

1/4285. Papers 2 Mar. 1825 relating to substitution of British coinage for Spanish dollars in the colonies, incomplete.

1/4287. Drafts of a commission and instructions 14 June 1825 for Gov. Darling; Order in Council 14 June 1825 for the preparation of a great seal for Van Diemen's Land; draft Order in Council for erecting the island of Van Diemen's Land into a separate colony.

1/4288. Admiralty memorial 27 July 1825 proposing that they may be empowered to appoint a Vice-Admiralty Court in Van Diemen's Land, with Order in Council 2 Aug. 1825.

1/4303. Report 5 June 1826 of the Committee of Council for Trade recommending that a charter of incorporation be granted to the New Zealand Company.

1/4314. Order in Council 30 Jan. 1827 requiring the appellant in the appeal of Campbell *v.* Cox from New South Wales to bring in his case.

1/4315. Petition 5 Feb. 1827 of William Campbell concerning his appeal against John Macarthur.

1/4317. Draft Order in Council 14 Apr. 1827 regulating the trade of His Majesty's possessions, within the limits of the East India Company's charter.

1/4318. Order in Council 23 May 1827 approving committee report recommending dismissal of the petition of William Campbell; committee report 26 May 1827 on the appeal of Edward Eager, formerly of New South Wales, against Samuel Pinder Henry.

1/4327. Papers 1827-8 relating to the alleged employment of Henry Savery, convict, by the *Hobart Town Gazette*.

1/4350. Letter 6 Mar. 1829 from R. W. Hay, enclosing copy of letter from the Lieutenant-Governor of Malta to Sir George Murray relating to the transportation of seven Greeks to New South Wales or Van Diemen's Land.

1/4351. Copy despatch 20 Sept. 1828 from Lieut.-Gov. Arthur reporting the arrival of the convict ship *Bengal Merchant* in Van Diemen's Land.

London

1/4381. Draft Order in Council 4 Feb. 1831 empowering certain officers to make laws for Western Australia.

1/4449. Copy despatch 7 Feb. 1835 from Gov. Bourke recommending conditional pardon for two convicts, and a ticket of leave for another.

1/4466. Papers Apr.-May 1843 relating to convict discipline in Norfolk Island and Van Diemen's Land and the replacement of Capt. Maconochie as Superintendent of Norfolk Island.

P.C.2 Registers 1540-1960, 760 vols.

Registers of the Privy Council contain minutes of its proceedings, orders, certain proclamations and the reports of committees with the papers accompanying them, sometimes entered at length, sometimes in abstract only. Decisions of the Council took the form of orders and letters, all of which were entered in the Registers. If a petition was rejected or the Council not called on to take action, there is no entry in the Register. The volumes are fully indexed. The subjects dealt with include convicts (there are detailed lists of convicts whose destination was determined by an Order in Council), marines, whale fishery, instructions to Governors of New South Wales, Botany Bay, commissioners. 2/377-9 form an alphabetically arranged type-script index to Orders in Council, etc., undated, but noted in list as 'made in the reign of Queen Victoria'. These include entries for the appointments of colonial officials, establishment of chartered companies, and various colonial Acts.

P.C.4 Minutes 1670-1808, 1826-1928, 27 vols.

The minutes are valuable as a record of the grounds on which petitions were rejected, and for abstracts of papers that have vanished. The original petitions and letters to the Council are likely to be found among the Unbound Papers, P.C.1. The Minutes were abolished in 1928 when they became an abstract of the Registers. From 1795 most of the volumes are indexed; subjects include New South Wales, Victoria, South Australia, Western Australia, Tasmania, Fiji, colonial Acts, charters, and appeals.

For a description of this class see R. B. Pugh, 'Privy Council Minutes newly transferred to the Public Record Office', *Bulletin of the Institute of Historical Research* XXII, 65, May 1949, pp.11-21.

P.C.8 Original Correspondence 1860-1936, 1269 files.

The papers selected for preservation cover practically the whole range of work of the Privy Council Office, but do not include files of the Education, Medical, or Agricultural Department. When successive files are opened on the same case, they are tied together with the latest paper on top bearing the file number quoted in the list; the file cover shows previous or subsequent paper numbers. Files consist of a file cover (giving number, subject, from whom received), précis, minutes, originals, drafts and copies of letters, cases and affidavits, and other related documents. Subjects relevant to the field of this guide include charters for companies, banks, and universities, Acts, and the registration of medical practitioners. Examples of files noted are: 8/544 charter, Australian Mining Co. 1901; 8/647 supplementary charter, University of New Zealand 1905-7; 8/1086 coinage, proclamation discontinuing Sydney Mint 1926.

P.C.9 Registers 1860-1935, 78 vols.

For the purposes of tracing documents preserved in P.C.8 these registers are of little value, but they do give some indication of the subject matter of documents no longer extant, the numbers of which are noted on file covers in P.C.8.

P.C.7 Letter Books 1825-99, 54 vols.

These are entry books of out-letters; after 1900 carbon copies of out-letters were put inside files of correspondence and although letter books were still continued for a number of years they have not been preserved. Letters are mainly to government departments and concern the drafting of orders, acknowledgement of petitions and memorials, granting of charters. Subjects of letters include currency, appeals, charters, free ports, convicts, transportation, trade, New South Wales, Western Australia, South Australia, Victoria, Van Diemen's Land, New Zealand, quarantine matters (some letters in reply to petitions to export sheep and machinery to New South Wales and Victoria), the escorting of Dutch ships to Batavia. Each volume is indexed.

P.C.5 Plantation Books 1678-1806, 16 vols.

5/14-16, 1784-1806, include some commissions and instructions issued to Governors Phillip, Hunter, King, and Bligh.

P.C.6 Miscellaneous Books 1660-1900, 19 vols.

6/4-6 are Daily Registers, General, Apr. 1839 to June 1860. They are registers of documents put before the Council and give date of entry, subject, date received, date of the paper (letter, petition, or report), date of minutes and memoranda. Subjects include charters, convicts, free ports, trade, Australia, South Australia, New South Wales, Victoria, Western Australia, Van Diemen's Land, North Australian settlements, New Zealand, Tahiti, and Norfolk Island.

PUBLIC RECORD OFFICE

The Public Record Office group contains the domestic records of this institution, collections of transcripts from various sources and documents acquired by gift, deposit, or purchase, formerly in a separate group called Gifts and Deposits. Gifts and Deposits are now in one class, P.R.O.30. The call number for documents formerly called Gifts and Deposits must always include the prefix P.R.O.30, e.g. the call number for List of Anglican deans, archdeacons, and canons in Allan Papers is P.R.O.30/2/3/13. There are class lists for all the collections described except where it is specifically stated that there is none. These class lists are published as Vols.10, 11, 12 in the List and Index Society Series.

DOCUMENTS ACQUIRED BY GIFT, DEPOSIT, OR PURCHASE

P.R.O.30/2 Allan Papers 19th cent., 8 boxes and vols.

A collection of notes and cuttings relating to the ecclesiastical history of the whole world, made by Maj.-Gen. Alexander S. Allan. The material covers both the Roman Catholic and Anglican Churches. Information relevant to the field of this survey is included in many general notebooks and lists covering the British colonies, e.g. 2/3/13. Lists of Anglican deans, archdeacons, and canons in the British Colonies 19th century. Only two notebooks relate solely to Australasia:

2/2/5. Notebook entitled 'Notitia Ecclesiastica' containing brief rough notes on Roman Catholic bishops in Australia, New Zealand, and Oceania, c.1876-81.

2/7/22. Notebook listing the Roman Catholic sees and apostolic vicariates in Australia, New Zealand, and Oceania, and giving details of the incumbents c.1833-70.

P.R.O.30/48 Cardwell Papers 1834-1911, 54 boxes.

Papers of Edward Cardwell, Viscount Cardwell, Secretary for the Colonies 1864-6 and Secretary of State for War 1868-74. The following notes result from a search of the correspondence arising from Cardwell's period at the Colonial Office and also

London

his correspondence with Earl Granville while the latter was Secretary of State for the Colonies Dec. 1868 to July 1870.

48/Box 5/28. War Office Correspondence and Memoranda.

ff.64-7, 70-9, 86-9 eight letters 25 Sept. to 5 Dec. 1869 from Cardwell and Granville concerning the proposed withdrawal of the 18th Regiment from New Zealand, the actions of Gov. Bowen and the feasibility of returning Sir George Grey to the colony; ff.94-7 letter 12 Dec. 1869 from Granville concerning Cardwell's correspondence with Sir George Grey about the legislative separation of the islands of New Zealand; ff.112-14 letter 29 Dec. 1869 from Granville about troops for the colonies.

48/Box 7/45. Colonial Office Correspondence and Memoranda, Miscellaneous. f.4, letter 22 Oct. 1864 from Palmerston congratulating Cardwell on the more peaceful state of New Zealand.

P.R.O.30/6 Carnarvon Papers 1833-98, 173 vols.

Papers of Henry Howard Molyneux Herbert, 4th Earl of Carnarvon, Under-Secretary of State for the Colonies Feb. 1858 to June 1859, Secretary of State for the Colonies June 1866 to Mar. 1867 and Feb. 1874 to Jan. 1878. In Sept. 1879 he was appointed Chairman of the Colonial Defence Commission.

The volumes usually have lists of contents indicating the subjects dealt with and numbers assigned to individual letters. The latter are given below in brackets.

6/1-3. Correspondence, the Queen and her personal staff Feb. 1874 to Jan. 1878.

6/1, Feb. 1874 to July 1875, includes many letters concerning the annexation of Fiji. Letters 1874 include: (44) from Carnarvon praising the ability of Sir Hercules Robinson; (50-2, 69-71) concerning the presentation of a yacht to Thakombau; (61, 63-4) proposed change of the name Fiji. Letters 1875 include: (80-4, 86-7, 135, 141) concerning the presentation of a war club by Thakombau to the Queen, the last two dealing with the loan of the club to the Colonial Institute; (123) from Carnarvon forwarding photographs of Australian natives of the Clarence River, and (125) the Queen's acknowledgement remarking that they are hideous but interesting; (145-51) concerning the epidemic of measles in Fiji.

6/2, July 1875 to July 1876, includes letters concerning: (10, 30) the measles epidemic in Fiji and Norfolk Island; (13, 19) references to the death of Goodenough and the Queen's wish to express sympathy to his widow, her goddaughter; (23-4) photographs of Fiji which the Queen desires to purchase; (33-4, 45-6) the Queen's desire to enable the brother of her faithful servant John Brown to visit his aged mother from New Zealand; (101) expressing the Queen's interest in whether Gordon has taken measures to prevent the natives of Fiji 'being swept away by worthless adventurers'; (111-12) the opening of the New Zealand telegraph line.

6/3, July 1876 to Jan. 1878, includes letters concerning: (165-8) statues of the Royal Family for the Melbourne Public Library, Sir Redmond Barry's request for a copy of the Albert Memorial Book for the Library; (176) from Carnarvon describing the new parliamentary buildings in Melbourne as magnificent; (181) referring to a report on Norfolk Island and the Pitcairn Islanders. There are also letters about Fiji, including (110-11) discussing the site for the capital.

6/4. Correspondence, the Prince of Wales and his personal staff Mar. 1874 to Jan. 1878. (29-30) concerning statues of the Prince and Princess of Wales for Melbourne Public Library; (108-9) concerning the proposed visit of the Prince of Wales to Australia.

6/5-13. Correspondence, Cabinet, 1874-8.

6/5, First Lord of the Admiralty Feb. 1874 to Feb. 1878, includes ff.1-3 correspondence concerning Goodenough's mission to Fiji; ff.21-3, 34-5, 42-3, 54-61 further correspondence concerning the annexation of Fiji and subsequent need to increase the strength of the Australia Station there; ff.71-9 correspondence concerning the *Rosario* as a training ship for New Zealand.

6/6, Lord Chancellor May 1874 to Aug. 1877. Includes: (1) to Carnarvon concerning the 'Kidnapping Bill'; (9) to Carnarvon concerning the annexation of Fiji; (14) from Carnarvon resisting pressure from the Australian colonies for annexation of New Guinea and condemning precipitous acquisition of land by companies or individuals; (45) from Carnarvon regarding the Lacepede Islands and the establishment of a court in the Pacific; (56) to Carnarvon enclosing a letter (missing) from Sir George Bowen describing Australian feeling about the New Guinea crisis with (57) a copy of Carnarvon's reply.

6/7, Chancellor of the Exchequer Mar. 1874 to Jan. 1878. Includes: (43, 52, 54, 56, 60, 88, 89) Feb. 1875 to Jan. 1876 correspondence concerning the proposal for a guaranteed loan to New Zealand; (48) from Carnarvon asking for sanction for sappers for Fiji; (49-50) letters from and to Carnarvon concerning guaranteed loan to Fiji.

6/8, Foreign Secretary Feb. 1874 to Jan 1878. Includes: (3-4) from Carnarvon suggesting Goodenough be warned not to compromise H.M. Government until the whole matter of Fiji has been considered; (29) stating that the Queen thinks it would be a mistake to change the name of Fiji; (34) from Derby, 'we shall want New Guinea some day for ourselves'; (54) from Derby sending a despatch from Lord Lyons on New Guinea, suggesting a protectorate over islands nearest Australia.

6/11, Prime Minister Feb. 1874 to Jan. 1878. Includes: (13, 14, 16, 19) July-Nov. 1874 concerning the annexation of Fiji and the appointment of the governor; (60) from Carnarvon saying that the War Office opposes return of troops to the Australian colonies; (61) concerning a baronetcy for Sir Charles Clifford; (108-10) concerning the International Exhibition at Melbourne and the proposed visit of the Prince of Wales to Australia.

6/12, Secretary for War Mar. 1874 to Jan. 1878. Five letters Dec. 1874 to Mar. 1875 concerning the need for a detachment of Royal Engineers in Fiji; 23 Feb. 1875 to Carnarvon regarding a legal officer for Fiji; correspondence Oct. 1875 concerning returns of the effective strength of the British Army in the colonies; correspondence Dec. 1875 to Apr. 1876 concerning the Victorian Government's proposal about troops for the colony; 28 Dec. 1876 to Carnarvon discussing the position of general officers in the colonies and their rank after the Colonial Secretary; 14 Feb. 1877 from Carnarvon mentioning Australian defence; letter n.d. [May 1877?] to Carnarvon raising the question of handing over War Office property to the colonies; 8 Nov. 1877 to Carnarvon, with Carnarvon's reply of the same date, concerning the proposed committee on colonial defence.

6/14-17. Correspondence, Official, 1874-8.

6/14, The Commander-in-Chief and the Royal Family and their personal staffs Feb. 1874 to Oct. 1877. (98) to the Commander-in-Chief about sending one or two regiments to Australia; (117-19, 123-5) from the Commander-in-Chief concerning Western Australia's request for officers to advise on defences and fortifications, Sir William Jervois and Col. Scratchley being selected; (140) on behalf of the Duke of Edinburgh asking to see the address from Melbourne on the occasion of his marriage.

6/16, The Speaker, Law Officers and others May 1874 to Feb. 1878. 13 May 1876 from the Speaker introducing Jess Young, late observer and naturalist of Elder's exploring expedition which crossed the Australian continent; Dec. 1877 to Feb. 1878 correspondence with Sir Hercules Robinson concerning the constitutional crisis in New South Wales. Among correspondence with Law Officers there is a letter 27 Apr. 1875 from Carnarvon concerning an amended clause in the Pacific Islands Bill.

6/17, Under-Secretaries, Foreign Office, War Office May 1874 to Jan. 1878. 2 May

London

1875 from Carnarvon expressing the hope that the clause in the Pacific Islands Bill setting up a consular court will be retained in spite of expense involved; 24 Mar. 1875 to Carnarvon expressing concern at the rapid growth of New Zealand's debt guaranteed by the Treasury, with 25 Mar. 1875 Carnarvon's reassuring reply; 31 Oct. 1877 from Carnarvon enclosing Gordon's latest despatch (missing) from Samoa, Carnarvon opposing annexation but fearing the effect of German occupation on Australian opinion; 31 Oct. 1877 to Carnarvon conveying Lord Derby's strong opposition to annexation based on a desire to forestall Germany.

6/23-41. Correspondence with colonial governors 1874-8.

6/25. Correspondence Mar. 1874 to Feb. 1878 with governors of the Australian colonies.

(1-6) Mar.-Oct. 1874 correspondence with Weld, W.A., including letters concerning the proposal for a telegraphic line to Western Australia and letters from Weld reporting the desire of the colonists for responsible government.

(7-22) Feb. 1874 to Aug. 1876 correspondence with Robinson, W.A., including (11a) despatch to Robinson criticising Weld's approval of agitation for responsible government and (17) from Robinson reporting on the present indifference in the colony to responsible government.

(24-34) Mar.-Oct. 1874 correspondence with Normanby, Q'ld, including (24) from Normanby reporting on party politics and the rush to the Palmer goldfields, (25, 32) concerning the Aborigines and Anti-Slavery Societies and their objection to native police, (30) to Normanby concerning his transfer to New Zealand warning him to be careful in dealing with the South Pacific Trading Company and the annexation of Fiji, (34) Normanby's reply.

(35-43) Nov. 1874 to Apr. 1875 correspondence with Cairns, Q'ld, and S.A., concerning his retirement on account of ill health. (44-6) letters from Du Cane, Tas., concerning his retirement.

(47-51) Jan. 1875 to May 1877 correspondence with Weld, Tas., including letters from Weld defending his approval of agitation for responsible government in Western Australia, mentioning his part in New Zealand affairs and reporting on politics in Tasmania.

(52-84) Mar. 1874 to Feb. 1878 correspondence with Robinson, N.S.W., including (65) from Robinson reporting that he has purchased a yacht as Her Majesty's gift to the King of Fiji, and mentioning a political crisis in New South Wales, enclosing cuttings; (69) from Carnarvon expressing regret at the withdrawal of troops from the Australian colonies and suggesting in confidence that, if the colonies provided the money, troops might be returned; (70, 72, 77, 78) further correspondence 1874-6 on this subject, Carnarvon urging the proposal be dropped owing to difficulties of recruitment.

(85-124) Mar. 1874 to Nov. 1877 correspondence with Bowen, Vic., including reports on politics and defence and letters describing his visit to America in 1875 and return to Victoria through the Pacific and New Zealand; (87) from Bowen mentioning that Gavan Duffy is returning to Ireland and reporting a conversation in which Duffy expressed sympathy with the confederation of the Empire; (99) from Carnarvon dealing with defence and raising the question of federation of the Australasian colonies; (104) from Bowen approving federation and discussing the loyalty of the colonies and the views of the Victorian Parliament on defence.

6/39. Correspondence with governors of New Zealand and Fiji Mar. 1874 to Feb. 1878.

(1-9, 11-15) Mar. 1874 to Mar. 1875, correspondence with Fergusson, N.Z., concerning New Zealand and Pacific Islands affairs especially the cession of Fiji including (1) informing Carnarvon of New Zealand opinion of American designs on

Pango Pango in the Navigator's Group, of a New Zealand plan for establishing trade relations with the islands of the Pacific by means of a guaranteed company, and discussing the claims of Vogel and McLean to the honour of K.C.M.G.

(10, 16-47) Dec. 1874 to Dec. 1877, correspondence with Lord Normanby discussing New Zealand affairs including the abolition of Provincial Councils and criticism of Sir George Grey's policy.

(48-115) Oct. 1874 to Feb. 1878, correspondence with Gordon including Gordon's remarks on Sir Hercules Robinson's report on Fiji, Gordon on the High Commissionership, his first impressions in Fiji, and opinion of Layard, his favourable opinion of natives and whites, the efficient organisation of the Wesleyans, and the distress of white settlers following the fall in cotton prices; (93, 102, 110) from Gordon concerning Samoa and Tonga; (96) from Gordon announcing his intention to resign because his wife disliked Fiji, his expenses were high, and his life too rough; (103) Gordon suggests he be made Governor of New South Wales to enable him to continue his work in Fiji.

6/42-7. Correspondence, Colonial, Miscellaneous 1874-8, arranged alphabetically.

6/42, ff.43-7, 89-90, letters Nov. 1874 to Sept. 1875 from Lord Belmore concerning Sir James Martin; ff.48-52 correspondence Dec. 1874 with the Austrian Ambassador in London concerning Dr Julius Haast; ff.193-9 correspondence Nov. 1877 with Sir Redmond Barry concerning his request for an Albert Memorial book for Melbourne Public Library.

6/43, ff.19-24, correspondence July 1874 with Viscount Canterbury concerning the annexation of Fiji; ff.211-13, 217, 220-2, 232-3, correspondence Apr.-Sept. 1875 with Sir Gavan Duffy mentioning the prerogative of pardon question; ff.236-8, 2 Dec. 1874 from Du Cane, Tas., on his retirement.

6/44, ff.2-29, letters Nov. 1873 to Apr. 1874 from Goodenough; ff.176-8 letter 19 July 1875 from E. Knatchbull-Hugessen, M.P., enclosing letter 10 Apr. 1875 from A. J. Buisson, clerk of the consular office in Fiji, complaining about the conduct of E. March while consul; ff.172-6 correspondence July-Oct. 1875 with Beresford Hope, M.P., forwarding protest by Charles Campbell, N.S.W., against the Colonial Marriages Bill; ff.233-42 further correspondence Feb.-Mar. 1877 with Knatchbull-Hugessen and Hope on this Bill.

6/45, ff.90-5, correspondence Sept. 1875 to Jan. 1876 with Layard, Fiji; ff.162-3, 26 June 1874, from Sir Arthur Milne on the question of whether a naval or army officer could perform the duties of Colonial Secretary in Fiji; ff.199-202, 227, 259-62, 1875-6 concerning the annexation of New Guinea.

6/46, f.7, 5 Jan. 1876, from J. Horatio Nelson seeking an introduction for Capt. Spencer Churchill; f.36, 31 Dec. 1874 to Sir Henry Parkes regarding J. Martin's back pay and thanking him for his assistance to Robinson during his visit to Fiji; f.41, 21 May 1875 to Parkes thanking him for photographs of Aborigines; ff.64-5, 31 July 1875 from Parkes stating his confidence in a federation for the Australian colonies and his desire to strengthen the bonds of Empire; ff.233-4, [Oct.] 1877 from Lionel H. Rice concerning Queensland's poll tax on Chinese immigrants and asking to be received as a member of a deputation from the colony opposing it.

6/47, ff.57-60, minute 18 Nov. 1874 to Sir William Foster Stawell conveying Carnarvon's regret that troops were withdrawn from the Australian colonies and suggesting their return to Victoria if that colony would meet the expense; ff.90-2, 1 Sept. 1875 from Lord Stanley concerning Lieut. Robert Henry Armit's proposal to form a limited liability company to colonise New Guinea; ff.200-1, 25 Feb. 1874 from Sir George Frederic Verdon, Vic., congratulating Carnarvon on becoming Secretary of State for the Colonies and assuring him that Australasia feels safer under a Conservative Government; ff.20-4, 207-46 correspondence 1874-7 with

K

London

Vogel in London and New Zealand including mention of the Pacific Islanders Protection Bill; ff.264-6, 15 May 1874 from George Palmer, London, suggesting a memorial to Col. Light.

6/48-51. Correspondence, memoranda, 1874-7, often undated.

6/48, pp.101-3, 105-8 minutes 1875 on Fiji; pp.109-17 Colonial Office Confidential Print, *Australia No.39. Printed . . . June 4, 1874*, on Fiji; pp.119-61 paper entitled 'Suggestions for increasing the British population in the Cape Colony', n.d., p.119 refers to child emigration to New Zealand 1874, p.151 suggests that Australia and Canada should also have access to the National Schools.

6/50, f.161, 23 Mar. 1875 concerning pearl fishing off the northern coast of Queensland; f.170, n.d. concerning New Guinea; ff.178-81, extract from letter 18 Oct. 1877 from Layard to Lord Derby concerning a visit to the New Hebrides and the labour traffic; f.183, memo on Layard's despatch to the Foreign Office concerning the labour traffic. There are also memos on Fiji, New South Wales border tariff and postal communication, and correspondence from Victoria and South Australia.

6/51, ff.1-2, on Fiji; f.3, on Vogel's proposal for a trading company in the Pacific. Other memos on the labour traffic and on Fiji include f.10, concerning letters from Goodenough and Robinson, f.11, on a report from Goodenough and Layard, ff.14-15, on Seemann's mission to Fiji in 1860, ff.17-18, on reports 1870 from Capt. Challis and from Britton on Fiji. Further memos on the Australian colonies include f.34, May 1874 on a letter from Bowen, Vic., f.51, on Australian statistics, f.52, Nov. 1875, f.172, 1877 on colonial stocks, the former on a conversation with Vogel, f.169, July 1877 on a conversation with McAlister, Q'ld, concerning the Chinese Taxation Bill, ff.170-1, on a deputation from Agents General on the General Post Office new mail system.

6/52. Correspondence and papers, Colonial Defence Commission 1879-81. Letters, memoranda, minutes to and from Carnarvon, arising from his chairmanship of the Royal Commission investigating ways and means of defending the principal colonial ports and coaling stations in the event of war.

6/65. Correspondence, Miscellaneous June-Oct. 1885.

(63) 6 Sept. 1885 to Sir Robert Herbert reporting a conversation with Cardinal Moran, Abp of Sydney, concerning the inequality of educational opportunity for Roman Catholic children in the Australian colonies, and the development of the denominational schools system.

6/66. Correspondence, Miscellaneous Oct. 1885 to Jan. 1886.

(75) Minute 30 Nov. 1885 by Prof. Mahaffy, Trinity College, Dublin, urging intervention by Carnarvon to ensure that Irish candidates are properly considered for educational posts in Australia and specifically for the chair of mathematics at the University of Adelaide, with (76) Dec. 1885 Carnarvon to Sir Arthur Blyth, Agent General for South Australia, asking him to comply with Mahaffy's request, and (77) 2 Dec. 1885 from Blyth promising to assist and advising that a Dublin graduate was Dean of the Professorial Board at the University of Adelaide.

6/69-131. Publications, Colonial Office Confidential Print, etc.

6/93-4, 1875-7, includes C.O. Confidential Print, Australia 52-62 being papers relating to New Guinea, Norfolk Island, and Fiji.

6/97-8, 1874-7, includes C.O. Confidential Print, Miscellaneous 20, 22, 27, 33 relating to Australasia.

6/122, 1870-7, C.O. Confidential Print on the defence of commercial harbours and coaling stations 1877, f.20, King George Sound, f.24b, statistics on Britain's trade with Australasia.

6/124, 1878-9, C.O. Confidential Print, correspondence and reports concerning defence of the colonies, ff.75-8, correspondence and memo Dec. 1877 to June 1878 concerning South Australia.

6/125, 1881, Colonial Defence Commission Papers including report 16 June 1881 on the defence of Fiji.

6/126, Colonial Defence Commission Third Report 1882, pp.17-18, Thursday Is., p.25, Fanning Is., p.26, Fiji, p.492, Appendix 7 correspondence including tables on Australian defence.

6/131, 1862-89, Various Departments including the Second Report of the Defence Commission with correspondence which deals mainly with the Australian colonies and New Zealand, and C.O. Confidential Print, Miscellaneous 47, being a summary of the reports of the Defence Commission Feb. 1883, pp.14-15, Australia.

6/132-3. Papers as Under-Secretary of State for the Colonies, Colonial Memoranda 1858-9.

6/132. (66) Board of Trade minute 19 Aug. 1858 against the federation of the Australian colonies; (67) memo 24 Apr. 185[?] on a private letter from Denison to Col. Gore Browne in New Zealand on federation and the state of the government in New Zealand; (68-115) other minutes and memoranda Mar.-Aug. 1858 relating to matters in Australia and New Zealand including procedure on the death or absence of governors, provisional government in South Australia, Maoris, the work of Browne in New Zealand, New Zealand military affairs, the Christchurch-Lyttelton railway, the possible separation of Moreton Bay from New South Wales, the Reform Bill in Victoria, payment of troops in Victoria, convicts in Western Australia, Capt. Sturt's report on the North Australia Exploring Expedition, and postal communications in Australia and New Zealand.

6/133. The numbers in this volume are continued from 6/132.

(282-3) note 7 May 1858 on South Australian Act relating to marriage with deceased wife's sister; (307-8) letter n.d. from the Bishop of New Zealand respecting his claims to jurisdiction over Norfolk Island; (309-11) note 9 Mar. 185[?] addressed to Lord Stanley on same subject; (343-5) note 22 Feb. 1859 on Pritchard's proposal for the cession of Fiji.

6/134-59. Correspondence as Secretary of State for the Colonies 1866-7, arranged alphabetically.

6/134, ff.12-19, 15, 28 Dec. 1866 from Sir Thomas Dyke Acland, Essex, on the Pitcairn Islanders.

6/135, ff.402-29, correspondence 21 Sept. 1866 to 23 Mar. 1867 with Bowen on matters in Queensland, including 'inconvertible legal tender notes', the intercolonial conference at Melbourne, trade, and federation.

6/136, ff.747-50, 21 July 1866 from Bowen to Cardwell concerning the financial crisis in Australia and the issue of inconvertible legal tender.

6/137, ff.922-9, 30 Jan. 1867 from Sir Daniel Cooper, N.S.W., requesting Carnarvon to arrange a meeting to form an association of colonials in England.

6/138, ff.136-7, 19 Oct. 1866 to Lord Derby on his memorandum on the Victorian application for an iron-plated ship.

6/140, ff.497-502, 505-6, correspondence 17-23 Oct. 1866 with the Bishop of Ely about affairs in Perth.

6/142, ff.737-51, correspondence 20 Oct., 12 Dec. 1866 with F. Gisborne about the proposed telegraph to Australia.

6/148, ff.354-7, correspondence 2 Nov. 1866 with Sir Edward Lugard on questions of military contributions in Victoria.

6/153, ff.1449-52, 26 June 1866 from the Bishop of Western Australia complaining of the Governor's treatment of the clergy.

6/154, ff.1672-9, 18 Oct. 1866 correspondence with Rogers on mails and Victorian defence.

6/157, ff.525-40, 8 Sept. to 7 Oct. 1866 from Verdon, Treasurer of Victoria, on Victoria's iron-clad ship and the colony's contribution of £25,000 towards it.

6/159, ff.1003, 1016-17, 12-15 Sept. 1866 from Sir Henry Edward Young on the differences between the Governor and Bishop of Western Australia.

6/160-5. Colonial Papers, Registered Series 1866-7.

6/160, July 1866 to Mar. 1867, includes ff.46-7, memos on telegraphic communications; *passim* colonial defence including naval defence and Victoria's contribution towards an iron-clad ship; ff.82-96, minute 1 Nov. 1866 to Sir George Grey reprimanding him for his conduct over charges against him connected with Maori Wars; ff.113-14, memo 22 Nov. 1866 on a conversation with Mr Hart of South Australia; ff.116-17, memo 7 Nov. 1866 on convicts in Western Australia.

6/166-8. Papers, chiefly Confidential Print, from various sources 1866-79.

6/166, ff.84-8, House of Commons paper July 1857 containing correspondence on colonial Church affairs in Canada and Australia.

6/167, f.313, Treasury estimate 1866 of sum required in year ending 31 Mar. 1867 for the aid of the Pitcairners on Norfolk Island.

6/168, ff.521-7, 536-42, memos on colonial defence.

6/169. Cabinet memoranda 1866-7. ff.9-14, n.d. Australian suffrage; ff.52-70, opinion of Carnarvon's colleagues on Verdon's scheme for the naval defences of Victoria.

6/172. Colonial Papers 1866-7. ff.811-16, petition from the Bishops of New Zealand with related correspondence 10 Aug. 1865 to 31 Jan. 1866.

6/173. Miscellaneous Papers 1866-79. f.996, memo on Comptroller Newland recalled from Western Australia, included in patronage memo July 1866.

P.R.O.30/8 Chatham Papers, 373 vols.

No Class List giving dates of pieces is available for this collection. There is a typescript list of volumes which gives the names of writers of letters in each volume, the correspondence in each section being arranged alphabetically by author; this list is published as Vol.8 in the List and Index Society Series. The collection includes a large number of letters addressed to William Pitt, jnr, miscellaneous papers, petitions, and additional papers sorted by subject, e.g. papers relating to the Admiralty and Navy. The following items have been noted in the volumes of general correspondence but it is possible that other papers will be found elsewhere.

8/169, ff.112-16, letter 20 Apr. 1792 from James George Prossor with enclosures containing hints concerning agriculture applicable to the settlement at New South Wales 'the result of long Experience and true Information being given to me, some of them by near and Dear Relatives of unimpeached Truth and many Corroberated by my own Observation and Experience'.

8/171, ff.18-45, twelve letters from William Richards, jnr, Sept. 1786 to Oct. 1792 concerning his scheme for conveying convicts to Botany Bay; ff.97-8, letter 3 Dec. 1786 from Duke of Richmond concerning convicts for Botany Bay.

P.R.O.30/61 Childers Papers 1870-91, 1 vol.

Correspondence, mainly from the Queen and her Private Secretary to Hugh Childers. The only letter concerning the field of this survey is at ff.21-2, 3 Apr. 1881, from the Private Secretary to Lyttelton [for Childers] in which he discourages a friend of Lyttelton's from wearing a Victorian Volunteer medal at Court, mentioning the fuss made when a New Zealand medal was recognised. The bulk of the Childers Papers are at the Royal Commonwealth Society, q.v.

P.R.O.30/28 Doctors' Commons Records 1796-1857, 23 vols. and bundles.

These are legal records and include reports, cases and opinions, and Admiralty bill books.

28/1-12. Doctors' Commons reports *c.*1800-34. 28/9 report book 1825-6 was checked and the following entries found: copy letters 10 Aug., 23 Sept. 1826 to Earl Bathurst concerning the right of the Archdeacon of New South Wales to act as King's Visitor to churches and schools in that colony; copy letters 12 Apr. 1826 to Secretary Canning concerning Rev. Dr Poynter's observations relating to the claim of Rev. J. Daniel on the French Government.

28/13-16. Doctors' Commons cases and opinions 1796-1834.

28/18-22. Admiralty bill books 1816-57 (gap 1850-6). These contain accounts of expenses involved in Admiralty instance and prize courts cases. 28/19 was checked and no relevant entries found but other volumes may contain relevant material.

P.R.O.30/29 Granville Papers 1604-1909, 429 boxes and vols.

Papers of the 1st and 2nd Earls Granville and their families. The 2nd Earl was Secretary of State for the Colonies Dec. 1868 to July 1870 and Secretary of State for Foreign Affairs 1851-2, 1870-4, and 1880-5. A few private Granville papers relating to Hawaii 1880-5 are in the group of Foreign Office records at F.O.97/621. See also *The Political Correspondence of Mr. Gladstone and Lord Granville 1868-1876*, ed. Agatha Ramm, London 1952, 2 vols., and *1876-1886*, London 1962, 2 vols.

All entries in the following description are from the papers of the 2nd Earl except 29/7/12. Folio numbers are given where the volumes or documents have been numbered.

29/7/12. Letters from Hon. Frederick Gerald Byng to 1st Earl Granville. Include letters May-Nov. 1824 concerning the visit of the King and Queen of Hawaii and suite to England.

29/23. Correspondence, Cabinet and Political, *c.*1840-57. Include two undated minutes: J. Jebb on the convict system, and W. Gregory on the expedition to North Australia.

29/26A. Correspondence, Cabinet and Political, 1876-8.
17 Feb. 1877 from Lord Blachford stating that Lord Grey was responsible for the introduction of responsible government in New Zealand.
10 Aug., 14 Sept. 1877 Gordon reports on Fiji, matters of revenue, his opinion of the natives and white settlers.

29/27A. Correspondence, Cabinet and Political, 1879-83.
28 Mar. 1879 from Francis Knollys asking on behalf of the Prince of Wales for an assurance that Granville will serve as a Royal Commissioner for the proposed Australasian Exhibition.
3 July 1879 Gordon asking Granville to accept a copy of his account of 'the campaign of Fiji'.
17 May 1883 from Lord Derby asking whether the Duke of Albany might be governor of Victoria if he cannot go to Canada as he wishes.

29/28A. Correspondence, Cabinet and Political, 1850-99.
ff.1355-8, 18 Oct. 1886 from Stanhope forwarding an extract of despatch 34, 16 July 1886 from Douglas proposing to name certain township lands in New Guinea after Granville.
ff.1373-4, memo n.d. 'Substance of the proposals made by Rear-Admiral Tryon to the Australasian colonies as to Colonial Naval Defence, in a circular letter of 24 Dec. 1885' with notes on the opinions of the colonies.

London

29/39. Correspondence, the Queen and her personal staff, June-Dec. 1881. 5, 7 July, 8 Aug. 1881 concerning the visit of the King of Hawaii to Queen Victoria.

29/51. Correspondence, Cabinet, Duke of Argyll, 1869-73.
8, 20 Nov. 1868 concerning Sir Bartle Frere's memo on New Zealand and the proposal to send surplus troops in India to New Zealand.

29/55. Correspondence, Cabinet, Clarendon and Kimberley, 1869-74.
ff.164-5, 18 June 1869 from Kimberley on emigrants to Western Australia.
ff.247-8, 16 Dec. 1871 from Kimberley enclosing a memo by Herbert on Fiji, and giving his own comments.

29/57. Correspondence, Cabinet, Gladstone, Nov. 1868 to June 1870.
ff.16-20, 24, 29 Mar. 1869 from Gladstone referring to Strzelecki's claim for a financial reward for exploration in Australia.
ff.35-7, 21 May 1869 from Gladstone approving of Granville's refusal to delay the departure of the last British regiment from New Zealand.
ff.93-5, 2 Aug. 1869 from Gladstone concerning New Zealand with Kinnaird's note on disaffection there.
ff.144-5, 20 Sept. 1869 from Granville on a despatch to be sent to Sir George Bowen, Governor of New Zealand, concerning a new decoration.
f.280, 12 May 1870 from Gladstone on the New Zealand loan.

29/61. Correspondence, Cabinet, Gladstone, 1872.
11 Jan. 1872 from Gladstone referring to the kidnapping of South Sea islanders by the *Hope* alias *Anna* and stating that the *Victoria* should police the South Seas.
22 Oct. 1872 from Gladstone mentioning a vote in the House of Commons intended to force the annexation of Fiji.

29/62. Correspondence, Cabinet, Gladstone, Jan. 1873 to Mar. 1874.
10 June 1873 from Gladstone referring to Goodenough's mission.

29/119. Correspondence, Cabinet, Childers, 1884-5.
29 Sept. 1884 from Childers concerning the alarm of the Australian colonies should Germany annex New Guinea and stressing the loyalty of Australians.
2 Feb. 1885 from Childers concerning the German claim in Fiji, with his letter 29 Jan. to Derby and Derby's reply 31 Jan.

29/120. Correspondence, Cabinet, Derby, 1883-5.
2 July 1883 from Derby on British interests in New Guinea.
5 Oct. 1883 from Granville on French convicts in the Pacific.
16 Sept. 1884 from Derby on the annexation of New Guinea.
6 Oct. 1884 from Derby, copy of cabinet decision announcing the declaration of a British protectorate along the whole of the south coast of New Guinea and contiguous islands.
11 Dec. 1884 from Granville asking a question about Samoa and Tonga.
11 Dec. 1884 two letters from Derby concerning New Guinea, Samoa, and Tonga.
20 Dec. 1884 Herbert to Spring-Rice stating that Derby is prepared to proclaim a British protectorate over the north coast of New Guinea as far as the Huon Gulf if Granville approves.
7 Jan. 1885 Loch to Derby, telegram no.4, secret.
10 Jan. 1885 from Derby concerning agreement with Holland and Germany on New Guinea.
15 Jan. 1885 concerning the governorship of New South Wales, with Lorne's letter 14 Jan. 1885 to Derby.
18 Jan. 1885 from Derby concerning the Dutch position in New Guinea.
6 Mar. 1885 from Granville on New Guinea giving his reasons for agreeing with Germany on the boundary, with Derby's reply 6 Mar. 1885.

29/128. Correspondence, Cabinet, Gladstone, 1884. Includes letters 2, 5 Sept., 25, 31 Dec. 1884 from Gladstone on New Guinea.

29/129. Correspondence, Cabinet, Gladstone, Jan.-June 1885.

13 Jan. 1885 from Gladstone stating reasons for disapproving Loch's suggestion of negotiation with the Dutch on the purchase of part of New Guinea.

29, 31 Jan. 1885 from Gladstone on New Guinea.

3 Feb. 1885 from Gladstone concerning the German annexation of New Guinea and referring to Samoa, with related papers.

5-6 Feb. 1885 from Gladstone reporting his general conversation on colonies with Bismarck at Lord Rosebery's; memo 5 Mar. 1885 on back.

6 Mar. 1885 from Gladstone urging the importance of settling the New Guinea boundary so that colonial questions may not prejudice a settlement in Egypt.

29/135. Correspondence, Cabinet, Kimberley, 1880-3.

ff.8-9, 22, 24 Aug. 1880 from Kimberley on the annexation of Samoa.

ff.165-70, 17 Jan. 1883 note from Kimberley concerning United States' intentions in Hawaii, stating he does not see 'that we are called upon to do anything as the case now stands'. With Foreign Office Confidential Print 4696, *Memorandum respecting American Designs on the Hawaiian Islands*, printed 8 Jan. 1883.

29/147. Correspondence, Official, 1880-5.

7 Dec. 1884 R. H. Meade's memo of a conversation with Dr Busch concerning Britain's attitude to the recent German annexations and her intentions towards Samoa and New Guinea.

20-7 Dec. 1884 from Meade in Berlin concerning the unexpected German annexation on 19 Dec. of New Guinea as far as the Huon Gulf.

10 Jan. 1885 from Meade concerning New Guinea and Samoa.

29/154. Correspondence, United States of America, 1880-5.

12 Apr. 1881 from Sir Edward Thornton, British Minister at Washington, reporting a confidential conversation with the French envoy giving an account of an interview with Blaine in which reference was made to the King of Hawaii's visit to San Francisco and the latter's suspected intention of selling his kingdom to a European power.

29/198. Correspondence, Drafts, including Hawaii, 1880-5.

7 Sept. 1882 Granville to R. F. Synge acknowledging receipt of a letter from King Kalakaua of Hawaii.

29/219-382. Foreign Office Confidential Print, with some additional printed material, e.g. Parliamentary Papers.

A number of the Confidential Prints in 29/258 'Slave Trade' and 29/321 'Pacific Islands' relate to the South Sea Islands 1868-85.

29/382, containing miscellaneous material, includes a despatch from the Governor of New Zealand with a memo by Sir Julius Vogel on the Federation of the British Empire, presented to Parliament July 1885, and a despatch from the Secretary of State to the Governors of the Australian colonies on the subject of a Bill for the Constitution of a Federal Council for Australasia, presented to Parliament Aug. 1885.

P.R.O.30/45 Hatton Papers 1779-1854, 1 vol.

Papers of several Home Secretaries, but principally Viscount Sidmouth, Home Secretary 1812-22. Most common are petitions for mitigation of sentence from convicted persons, some of whom had been sentenced to transportation. Several petitions originated in the Australian colonies but the great majority of them were written in the United Kingdom shortly after conviction. There is no index but the papers are arranged in roughly chronological order.

London

P.R.O.30/57 Kitchener Papers 1877-1938, 124 folders.

Papers of the first Earl Kitchener of Khartoum include correspondence and memoranda relating to the history of Australia and New Zealand. These had their origin in Kitchener's period as Chief of Staff to Lord Roberts during the Boer War, his tour of inspection of the armed forces of Australia and New Zealand 1909-10, his membership of the Imperial Defence Committee 1910-12, and his service as Secretary of State for War 1914-16.

57/16-22. Boer War Correspondence 1899-1903. Mainly letters to Kitchener from Lord Roberts, other serving officers, and English politicians, mostly concerning problems of supply and equipment, tactics employed and the progress of the war; 57/17 contains a copy of Kitchener's speech when unveiling a memorial at Bathurst, N.S.W., to those who died in the war paying tribute to the loyalty of Australians to the Empire.

57/39. Far Eastern and Australian Tour, Miscellaneous Correspondence, 1909-10 includes:

TT8. Kitchener's speech undated to 'Your Excellencies, Mr. Prime Minister and Gentlemen', typescript.

TT9. Fragment of Kitchener's speech, undated, to British officers after his tour assuring them of a warm welcome in Australia by all but 'a very small and unimportant section of the community', typescript.

TT10. Kitchener's speech to the Grand Masonic Lodge of New South Wales explaining his reasons for visiting Australia and expressing his belief in the power of Masonry to assist in the defence of the country and as a link between people in many parts of the world, typescript.

TT14. Letter 2 Mar. 1910 from Kitchener to Sir Joseph Ward advising him that he did not intend to submit a special memo on the defence of New Zealand as his Australian report was also relevant to conditions there but enclosing a confidential report on defence installations in New Zealand; TT16 Ward's reply.

TT15. Letter 1 Dec. 1909 from A. Deakin to Kitchener welcoming him to Australia, introducing him to Gen. Hood and recommending Col. Kirkpatrick.

TT20. Letter 3 Aug. 1910 from Col. Kirkpatrick to Kitchener describing the progress made in the implementation of his recommendations in Australia.

57/40. Australian Tour Newspaper Cuttings 1910.

57/41. Imperial Defence Committee Correspondence and Reports 1910-12. Include VV9 letter 23 July 1912 Lord Lascelles to Kitchener reviewing political developments in New Zealand since Kitchener's tour and acquainting him with the implementation of his proposal to train men up to the age of twenty-five.

57/51-8. War on the Western Front 1915-18. Correspondence, reports and memoranda including: WV61 letter 2 June 1916 Birdwood to Kitchener reporting the visit to the Australian troops of W. M. Hughes.

57/61-5. The Dardanelles Expedition 1915-16. Packets of correspondence and memos and a volume of extracts from secret telegrams. The principal correspondents are the generals W. R. Birdwood, I. Hamilton, J. G. Maxwell, A. G. Hunter-Weston, J. H. Byng, and the politicians W. Churchill, H. H. Asquith, and Bonar Law. The letters from the generals are of particular interest for the information they provide about the evolution of tactics, the ability and morale of the troops, the conditions on Gallipoli, events of importance, and their opinions of one another, e.g.: WL97, 6 Apr. 1915, Birdwood to Kitchener on his changed views about Gallipoli, his pessimism, his attempts to persuade Hamilton to change the plan and land all the troops on the Asia Minor side. Kitchener's correspondence with the politicians deals with the appointment of officers for the campaign, the conduct of the expedition, the reinforcements to be provided, and the tour of inspection made by the Secretary of State for War just before the evacuation.

57/73-4. Manpower and Recruiting Correspondence, Memoranda and Reports 1914-16. Only two documents relate to Australian affairs:
WS64. 'How universal service was introduced into Australia', an unsigned speech by an English officer in Australia during Kitchener's tour; it describes how 'Australia went Kitchener mad' and sketches the obstacles, social and political, in the path of army reform, typescript.
WS71. Parade State for the Second Australian Division at its inspection by Kitchener on 31 Mar. 1916, signed T. A. Blamey.

P.R.O.30/56 Northcote Papers 1904-8, 1 vol.

Correspondence between Lord Northcote, Governor-General of Australia 1904-8 and Lord Elgin, Secretary of State for Colonies, A. J. Balfour, and J. Chamberlain. It contains:

Balfour to Northcote, five letters including 1 Jan. 1905 commenting on tariffs in Australia; 30 June 1905 discussing Northcote's suggestion that funds be diverted from naval expenditure to promoting emigration to Australia.

Chamberlain to Northcote, sixteen letters including letters on imperial preference; 24 Apr. 1904 expresses the hope that office will modify the extreme views of members of the Labour Party and approves of British emigration as a means of minimising danger from Asia; 7 Oct., 23 Dec. 1904 mentions his high opinion of Watson and Deakin; 16 Aug. 1905 mentions Deakin's ability and this letter and letter 30 Nov. 1905 refer to Wise; letters 1906-8 discuss the federal constitution.

Elgin to Northcote, thirteen letters including 6 Apr. 1906 on the status of consuls, the New Hebrides controversy; 12 Apr. 1906 on the right of the home government to be consulted on such matters as legislation dealing with coloured labour; 9 Aug. 1906 opposes Carruthers's efforts to get all the state premiers invited to the Colonial Conference; 6 Apr. 1906, 30 Sept. 1907, and 20 Mar. 1908 mention Deakin and several letters deal with the control of award of honours.

P.R.O.30/22 Russell Papers 1804-1913, 118 boxes and vols.

Papers of Lord John Russell, later Earl Russell, Secretary of State for the Colonies Apr. 1839 to Aug. 1841 and Feb.-Oct. 1855 and Prime Minister July 1846 to Feb. 1851 and Oct. 1865 to June 1866. The correspondence and papers noted below relate only to the period of his official career 1839-66; papers covering his earlier and later years may include additional correspondence relating to Australasian and Pacific affairs. See also *The Early Correspondence of Lord John Russell 1805-40*, ed. F. A. R. Russell, London 1913, 2 vols. and *The Later Correspondence of Lord John Russell 1840-1878*, ed. G. P. Gooch, London 1925, 2 vols.

22/3B. f.411, 9 May 1838 from Lord Glenelg sending copy of a despatch from the Lieutenant-Governor of Van Diemen's Land dealing with the employment of convicts on public works, should assignment cease; ff.510-11, 20 June 1838 from Sir William Molesworth agreeing generally with Lord Howick's proposals for abolishing the present system of transportation but opposing the establishment of penitentiaries on Norfolk Island and at Port Arthur.

22/3C. ff.954-72, Papers on the transportation of convicts including remarks by the Bishop of Australia; ff.984-5 memo by Russell on transportation, consisting of seven proposals recommending the abolition of assignment and the discontinuance of transportation for seven years; f.1213 return 29 Aug. 1839 showing present distribution of infantry of the line at home and abroad and plans for their redeployment.

London

22/3D. ff.1280-6, 3 Sept. 1839 from Lord Normanby on being succeeded by Russell as Secretary of State for the Colonies, presenting a synopsis of pressing colonial problems, and mentioning that many questions concerning the Australian colonies had been postponed by the passing of an Act for the temporary government of New South Wales, while others arising from the modification of the convict system were the subject of continuing discussions, also advising Russell to be wary in dealing with 'that association of Durham and others' which had been selling land in New Zealand before they had actually acquired it; ff.1562-3, 6 June 1840 from the Archbishop of Canterbury regarding the plan of the Society for Promoting Christian Knowledge for granting £10,000 to endow colonial bishoprics including one in New Zealand, asking that ecclesiastical authorities be allowed to select the bishops and urging that bishops should also be appointed to Van Diemen's Land.

22/4A. f.130, 27 Feb. 1841 from the Earl of Devon on behalf of friends in Devonshire about ecclesiastical affairs in New Zealand; ff.242-3, 246-7, two letters 22 Apr. 1841 from the Archbishop of Canterbury, or on his behalf, concerning Selwyn's candidature for the bishopric of New Zealand.

22/4B. ff.524-5, 19 Aug. 1841 from the Archbishop of Canterbury acknowledging Russell's letter respecting the disposal of lands in New Zealand; ff.564-5, 10 Sept. 1841 from Stanley concerning the application for an increase in salary by Dr Polding, Vicar Apostolic of New South Wales, whom he suspected of engaging with Dr Ullathorne in a propaganda campaign on behalf of his church, while on extended leave of absence from the colony.

22/4C. f.774, 18 Sept. 1843 from Sir James Stephen stating that Sir James Stirling would accept the Lieutenant-Governorship of New Zealand should Captain Hobson's incapacity prove 'incurable'; ff.878-9, 26 June 1844 from the New Zealand Company asking Russell to explain his intentions when agreeing with the Company in Nov. 1840 to grant it four acres of land for each £1 spent in the colony since his successor as Secretary of State for the Colonies was refusing to abide by their understanding of the agreement, with ff.880-3, reply from Russell 29 June 1844.

22/4E. ff.1314-15, 3 Nov. 1845 from Edward Wakefield urging a parliamentary discussion of events in New Zealand where the cruel and illegal actions of Gov. FitzRoy had inspired a native uprising.

22/5C. ff.1131-2, 27 Sept. 1846 from Lord Grey expressing his horror at the nature of the Norfolk Island convict settlement and urging its immediate break up.

22/5D. f.1403, 16 Oct. 1846 from Lord Grey respecting the severe fighting in New Zealand and the need to send reinforcements there.

22/5F. ff.1742-3, n.d. from Lord Grey deploring the fact that Gladstone's draft Bill did not provide for a general legislature for the whole of New Zealand.

22/6H. ff.2084-96, memo Dec. 1847 by Lord Auckland on the comparative naval strengths of Britain and France in various places including the Pacific.

22/7A. ff.325-30, 24 Feb. 1848 from Lord Grey proposing to set up a Committee of the Privy Council on difficult colonial problems such as the New Zealand constitution.

22/7B. ff.425-6, 9 Mar. 1848 from Lord Grey expressing his strong dissatisfaction with Sir Charles FitzRoy; ff.433-4, letter 10 Mar. 1848 from Lord Grey describing his amended plan for setting up a committee of the Board of Trade to deal with difficult colonial questions.

22/7D. ff.1391-4, 18 Nov. 1848 from Lord Grey about a post for J. Gregory deprived of the treasuryship of Van Diemen's Land when Russell was Secretary of State for the Colonies; ff.1419-20, 25 Nov. 1848 from Sir Charles Wood concerning the disposition of British naval vessels in the Pacific; ff.1431-2, 29 Nov. 1848 from Lord

Grey referring to the decorations awarded to officers who served in New Zealand; ff.1530-1, 24 Dec. 1848 and ff.1542-3, 29 Dec. 1848 from Lord Grey proposing that the colonies should pay for their own barracks and referring specifically to a barracks hospital for New South Wales.

22/7E. ff.1660-1, n.d. [1848-9] from S. Loyd [*sic*] recommending Col. Torrens whose standing with the Colonial Office was in jeopardy.

22/7F. ff.1969-83, draft in confidential print of the amended report on the Australian legislatures 29 Mar. 1849; ff.2044-5, 9 Apr. 1849 from Lord Grey requesting that Russell read the report on the Australian constitutions.

22/8A. ff.89-92, draft 19 Aug. 1849 by Russell assessing the value of the colonies and suggesting that they be permitted to send members to the House of Commons in proportion to their contribution to the cost of the imperial army and navy; ff.99-101, 23 Aug. 1849 from Lord Grey commenting on Russell's draft, agreeing that the colonies were valuable and should be retained, but doubting the practicability of the proposal to have colonial representatives in the Commons; ff.228-32, 22 Sept. 1849 from Lord Grey concerning his lack of success at the Colonial Office, stating that his unpopularity at home was increasing the difficulties of governors abroad and commenting on his inability to perform duties to his own satisfaction and his willingness to resign or to carry on in a reformed Colonial Office.

22/8B. ff.379-80, 15 Oct. 1849 from Lord Grey in reply to Russell's proposals for reforming the Colonial Office, opposing the omission of the clause in the Australian Colonies Bill permitting them to amend their constitutions; ff.510-11, 1 Nov. 1849 from Lord Grey enclosing his draft despatch to New South Wales on the convict question, stating his opinion that the colonists had been unreasonable in their reversals of opinion about transportation; ff.577-8, 21 Nov. 1849 from Lord Grey disapproving of Russell's alterations to the despatch on convicts and doubting whether colonial representatives could be added to Parliament.

22/8C. ff.625-6, 10 Dec. 1849 from Lord Grey regarding representative government for Cape Colony and enclosing the papers on the Australian constitutions 'in case you wish to refer to them'; ff.661-4, 14 Dec. 1849 from Lord Grey affirming the value of Sir James Stephen's work in preparing the Australian constitutions and remonstrating against Russell's refusal to appoint him to a paid post in the Board of Trade; ff.691-2, 20 Dec. 1849 from Lord Grey commenting on the news of the hostile reception of a convict ship in New South Wales; ff.699-700, 23 Dec. 1849 from Lord Grey advising that Sir George Grey had at first favoured the revocation of the Order in Council permitting transportation to New South Wales but agreed after discussion to modify the despatch to be sent to the colony; ff.855-6, 11 Jan. 1850 from Lord Grey on colonial affairs generally and enclosing a despatch which he proposed to send to New Zealand if Russell approved.

22/8D. ff.1146-7, 27 Mar. 1850 from Lord Grey enclosing a despatch (on the scheme for a colonial House of Lords) from South Australia and a letter from Under-Secretary Hawes respecting it; ff.1212-3, 21 Apr. 1850 from Lord Grey regretting the late arrival of a despatch from Van Diemen's Land which he had hoped to present to Parliament with the other despatches from the Australian colonies; ff.1269-70, 2 May 1850 from Russell to Sir Lucien O'Brien assuring him that no further restraint had been placed on his brother than had been rendered necessary by his 'peculiar character' in the penal colony.

22/9E. ff.60-1, 9 Aug. 1850 from Jno. Bear, Melbourne, recalling that he was planting vineyards in Victoria during Russell's term in the Colonial Office, and advising him of the despatch of wines for his own use and for the national exhibition.

London

22/9G part I. ff.46-7, 4 Oct. 1851 from Lord Grey enclosing a draft of his reply to FitzRoy on 'gold-finding business' and opposing the suggestion that more forces be sent to New South Wales.

22/9H. ff.185-6, 22 Nov. 1851 from Lord Grey enclosing papers concerning gold discoveries in New South Wales and approving of the establishment of a Mint in Sydney.

22/9J part I. ff.101-19, memo 11 Dec. 1851 by J. F. Burgoyne on the defence of Great Britain including references to the Australian settlements.

22/9J part II. ff.417-24, draft memo 31 Dec. 1851 by Russell on political negotiations with the Duke of Newcastle, the latter disapproving of Lord Grey's colonial policy, particularly the policy followed regarding New Zealand.

22/10A part II. ff.249-52, draft 1 Jan. 1852 and ff.253-5, letter 15 Jan. 1852 from Russell to the Duke of Newcastle defending the colonial policy of his government in granting representative government to the colonies.

22/10C. ff.790-3, two letters 29, 30 May 1852 from Lord Grey disapproving of the changes made by Sir John Pakington in the New Zealand Constitution Bill, his own efforts to have it modified and his view that, as a result of the gold discoveries, convicts would soon be in demand in Van Diemen's Land.

22/10E. ff.1338-9, 3 Oct. 1852 from Lord Grey mentioning that he had once offered the governorship of New South Wales to Lord Elgin.

22/11A. ff.186-7, 22 Aug. 1853 from the Duke of Newcastle favouring Sir George Grey for the governorship of Cape Colony.

22/11D. ff.1256-7, 18 July 1854 from George Gawler stating his determination to have a full settlement with the government before Sir George Grey left for Cape Colony.

22/11E. ff.1439-10, 20 Sept. 1854 from F. L. Arthur reporting the death of his father Sir George Arthur who had received many favours from Russell; ff.1588-9, 21 Oct. 1854 from Sir George Grey discussing colonial church legislation; ff.1616-19, 30 Oct. 1854 from Sir George Grey enclosing F. Rogers's report on the Australian Constitutional Acts, with minutes by Merivale and F. Peel.

22/11F. ff.1930-1, 1946-7, 1969-70, copies of correspondence 14-18 Dec. 1854 between Gladstone and Sir George Grey on the means of settling the debt to the New Zealand Company now charged against the colony's land sales.

22/12C. ff.695-8, 13 Mar. 1855 from Sir George Grey commenting on the riots in Victoria and the unpopularity of the Victorian colonial secretary and disapproving of some of the actions of Sir Charles Hotham, also referring to the constitution for Van Diemen's Land; ff.750-3, 20 Mar. 1855 from Sir George Grey approving of Hotham's measures for quelling the Victorian riots but critical of his character, also discussing the Victorian constitution and the influx of ex-convicts into the colony; ff.809-13, 26 Mar. 1855 from Sir George Grey reporting that the constitution for Van Diemen's Land was ready for the Royal Assent but that the South Australian proposals presented serious difficulties and would have to be returned.

22/12E. ff.1106-7, 11 May 1855 from Sir George Grey enclosing Merivale's proposals respecting the New Zealand Company and asking about Gov. Grey's plan on the same subject; ff.1188-92, 22 June 1855 from C. Adderley, M.P., regarding the negotiations between the government and the New Zealand Company, with draft of the proposed agreement, and minute by Russell; ff.1207-8, 26 June 1855 Russell's draft to G. Lewis enclosing his amendments to the agreement with the New Zealand Company.

22/13A. ff.10-11, 2 Jan. 1856 from H. Labouchere expressing his hopes for a more moderate South Australian constitution and his belief that its colonial branches should be independent of the Church of England.

22/13C. ff.975-6, 12 June 1857 from Johnson Hicks, Melbourne, expressing his appreciation of Russell's political career.

22/16B. ff.729-31, 18 Apr. 1866 from E. Cardwell discussing the proposal to set up a committee to consider the question of the legislative separation of the islands of New Zealand, with Russell's reply 20 Apr. 1866.

22/25. 11 Nov. 1861 from Sir George Grey respecting the application for the consecration of a bishop of the Sandwich Islands.

22/117. Letter Book, Colonies May-July 1855. Contains: letter 4 July 1855 to the Archbishop of Canterbury respecting the appointment of a bishop to Western Australia and the recommendation of M. Hale, also agreeing to the need for the Society for the Propagation of the Gospel to consider the position of the Bishop of New Zealand now that the House of Commons would no longer provide funds to support him; copy letter 4 July 1855 to Gov. Hotham, Vic., recognising the difficulties confronting him and assuring him of the support of the Crown.

BOARD OF TRADE

The Board of Trade officially adopted this title only in 1861. Until then it was known as the Committee of Council on Trade and Plantations, established by Order in Council in 1784 and reconstructed in 1786. The Board still operates under the Order of 1786. In the mid-nineteenth century the Board became an executive rather than an advisory body and in the early 1860s its work was split between a number of specialised departments, e.g. Commercial, Finance, and Establishment Departments; the early records under General are continued in these sections. For a brief historical note on the Board see *Guide to the Contents of the Public Record Office* II, pp.267-8. Further 'Notes on the Board of Trade', n.d., bound negative photocopies of typescript and 'The Board of Trade. Its Constitution and Development', n.d., bound photocopies of typescript, both tracing the history of the various departments, are on the open shelves in the Public Record Office.

See the following lists:

Lists and Indexes: Supplementary Series XI, *List of Board of Trade Records to 1913*, New York 1964. Superseding Lists and Indexes XLVI, 1922.
Class List of the Records of the Board of Trade, 3 vols., typescript.
'Board of Trade Records 1846-85', typescript, contains subject lists for the following classes: B.T.1, 11, 13, 15, 22 and M.T.9.

List of Classes described

General: 1, 3-6
General Department: 63
Commercial Department: 11, 35, 12, 36
Establishment Department: 13-14, 20-1
Finance Department: 15-18, 62, 83
Railway Department: 22
Registry: 19
Companies Department: 58
Companies Registration Office: 41, 31, 95, 34
Statistical Department: 24, 26-7, 32, 70
Registry of Shipping and Seamen: 98
Department of Overseas Trade: 59-61, 90

London

B.T.1 In-letters and Files 1791-1863, 569 vols. and boxes.

1/1-461 contain the original letters and papers sent to the Board 1791-1845, each paper being marked with the letter and number by which it is referred to in the minutes (B.T.5). The papers are usually, but not always or consistently, bound chronologically in the volumes. They include petitions, memorials, and general correspondence from private individuals, and official communications from other government departments. They deal mainly with matters relating to trade and commerce, fisheries, and merchant shipping, e.g. 1/75, Mar.-Apr. 1813 contains a petition signed by the Enderbys concerning the Southern Whale Fishery; 1/411, May-June 1843 contains, among other letters on New Zealand flax, a letter 7 June 1843 from N. J. J. Donlan complaining about the unfavourable report of the Admiralty on his manufacture of sailcloth from New Zealand flax; if he received no more encouragement he would renew negotiations for the sale of his discoveries to a foreign nation which would result in the flax's remaining useless to the settlement and in the colony's becoming a burden, and eventually an abandoned settlement, of England.

1/462-560 continuing the volumes of in-letters, contain the files of the General Department 1846-63 selected for preservation. In addition to commercial questions, navigation, and merchant shipping, these also relate to company charters, licences to limited liability companies to hold land, and copyright matters.

Registers and indexes of both series of papers are in B.T.4. The subject indexes in B.T.19 cover the later files. Many files relate to general colonial matters, e.g. legislation and trade. Files relating directly to Australia, New Zealand, and the Pacific deal with such matters as seals for colonies, bank and company charters, Acts concerning shipping, tariffs and duties.

B.T.3 Out-letters 1786-1863, 64 vols.

These are entry books and bound copies of letters sent from the Board dealing with various commercial and trade matters. Many merely give the Board's opinion on such matters or request the decision of other departments. Each volume is indexed by recipients, grouped, where appropriate, into departments, e.g. Treasury, Colonial Office, Customs.

B.T.4 Registers and Indexes 1808-64, 40 vols.

These relate to in-letters and files, those still extant now being in classes B.T.1 and 6. 4/1-8, 1806-35, are registers only, but they are a useful key to the mass of unindexed material in the volumes of in-letters up to 1846. The later registers and indexes are valuable because they indicate material which has not been preserved.

B.T.5 Minutes 1784-1940, 146 vols. and bundles.

In 1853 the system of keeping minute books was abolished and a system of departmental registration of papers introduced. From July 1839 only the original rough unbound minutes have been preserved. In the volumes up to that date there are sometimes, but not always, references to the volumes of in-letters and to the individual papers in them. These earlier minute books have indexes but the sheets of rough minutes are not indexed.

B.T.6 Miscellanea 1697-1876, 292 vols. and bundles.

Many of the papers recorded in the registers (B.T.4) are in this class. They consist of original letters, reports, accounts, and returns sent to the Board, with a number of registers and entry books.

6/58. First Committee Papers (i.e. papers of the Committee of Privy Council for the consideration of all matters relating to Trade and Foreign Plantations, appointed in 1786), New South Wales 1792-1806. The volume is foliated but the individual miscellaneous papers are not numbered. There is no index. The documents include: return of lands granted and leased 1792-1800; returns of lands granted since 30 May 1793, and 13 Dec. 1794, both giving names and descriptions of settlers, acreage granted, location and date of grant; returns of ships entering and leaving Port Jackson, with descriptions of the quantity and quality of the cargo on each vessel and details of ships registry 1792-1805; account 7 Dec. 1799 of a Spanish ship captured off the coast of Peru and condemned as legal prize at a Vice-Admiralty Court at Sydney; statement by Gov. King 6 Dec. 1804 certifying that Robert Campbell was permitted to put on board the *Lady Barlow* (registered in Calcutta) oil and skins caught within the limits of New South Wales by British subjects and to proceed to London with them, bond having been given not to take on board any article that was the produce of the East India Company's possessions, with a duplicate bond signed by R. Campbell; return of schooners and sloops belonging to and employed by individuals in New South Wales, 20 Feb. 1804, giving the names of the vessels, owners' names, tonnage, where built, and where employed, generally on the Hawkesbury River, or the Coal River (Canada), and in Bass Strait.

6/88. First Committee Papers with continuations, America, West Indies, and New South Wales, 1805-7. The volume is foliated but the papers themselves are not numbered. Papers relating to New South Wales are at f.181 to end of volume. They include a group of papers concerning the carrying of goods produced in New South Wales in the *Lady Barlow* to England 1804-6 including extracts of letters from Gov. King to Lord Hobart, a letter 18 July 1805 from Charles, Samuel, and George Enderby, and Thomas and John Mather complaining that the exporting to England of oils and skins from the fishery being established by the colonists of New South Wales was undermining the Southern Whale Fishery, and a copy of Robert Campbell's memorial 10 Aug. 1805 (see Margaret Steven, *Merchant Campbell, 1769-1846. A Study of Colonial Trade*, Melbourne 1965, ch.V). The paper from Sir Joseph Banks, 4 June 1806 'Some remarks on the present state of the Colony of Sidney [*sic*] in New South Wales and on the means most likely to render it a productive instead of an expensive settlement' (printed, *H.R.N.S.W.*, VI, pp.86-91) is explained by a memo 14 Aug. 1806 from Sir George Shee, Downing Street, endorsed 'The papers alluded to in the within Note have been several times under the Consideration of the Committee of Trade and have lately been sent by Lord Auckland into the hands of Sir Joseph Banks, who has stated his observations fully on the settlement of New South Wales but nothing has yet been decided thereon'. The memo concerns correspondence respecting 'the intercourse of the Americans on the shores of New Holland for the purpose of fishing and traffic'.

The volume also contains the following items: correspondence Sept. 1806 concerning further indulgences to Col. Macarthur with regard to his sheep; return of ships entering Port Jackson June-Dec. 1806; memorial 23 Jan. 1807 from William Jacob on the trade between New South Wales and the western coast of America; paper undated and unsigned, on the settlement of New South Wales, the fisheries established there and ships built there; account of ships cleared outwards from England for the Southern Whale Fishery 1800-6; account n.d. [probably 1807] of vessels employed in the whale fishery by adventurers in New South Wales; letter 2 June 1807 from Samuel Enderby stating that in his own opinion and that of other old adventurers in the British Southern Whale Fishery the encouragement of a seal fishery from New South Wales could be prejudicial and dangerous to the existence of the Southern Whale Fishery; copy of draft Bill 1807 for opening the trade of New South Wales under licences from the East India Company.

London

6/93. First Committee Papers with continuations, Southern and Greenland Whale Fisheries, 1786. The volume is not paginated or foliated, but the papers are numbered. There is an index in 6/115.

6/95. First Committee Papers with continuations, Southern Whale Fishery, 1787-92. This volume is foliated and the individual papers numbered. There is no index. The volume also contains documents relating to the American and Greenland Whale Fisheries, not indicated by the description in the class list.

6/115. Index to First Committee Papers 1782-6. This covers some of the volumes of First Committee Papers. The only relevant section is that which refers to 6/93. The references are to the paper numbers.

6/153-72. Orders in Council referring to Colony Laws 1802-43. These are the Orders in Council and Minutes of the Colonial Secretary referring local colonial Acts to the Committee in Council to consider and report their opinion, with related papers, e.g. copies of legal opinions. Several volumes were checked. They are arranged chronologically and usually Acts from the same colony are grouped together. There are no indexes. None relating to the Australian colonies was found, all apparently being Canadian or West Indian Acts.

6/180-2. Reports of the Committee of Trade 1784-93. All three volumes are indexed. 6/181, 1784-7, contains the following reports: 13 Apr. 1787 for directing the Advocate General to prepare a commission for the trial of pirates in New South Wales, 24 Apr. 1787 on the draft instructions for Gov. Phillip, 3 May 1786 for granting certain premiums for the encouragement of the Southern Whale Fishery. 6/182, 1787-93, has the following reports: 3 Aug. 1790 proposing a device for a great seal for New South Wales and its adjacent islands (cf. *H.R.N.S.W.* I Part 2, pp.340, 389), 19 Apr. 1791 on certain proposals concerning the removal of persons concerned in the Southern Whale Fishery from Nova Scotia to Great Britain. 6/180, 1784-93 contains nothing relevant that is not included in the other two volumes.

6/230. Trade Statistics: Russia Trade, Whale Fishery, Customs Accounts 1782-1800. ff.69-100 concern the Whale Fishery. They include an account 1785-1800 of the quantities of whale oil, whale fins, and seal skins imported, distinguishing Southern Whale Fishery from other imports. There are also annual tables showing the bounty paid, the number and tonnage of vessels employed, and some related correspondence.

6/249, 287-8. Trade Minutes, Colony Laws 1827-35, 1847-54. These constitute a brief record of the colonial Acts, usually forwarded by the Colonial Office or the Treasury, read in Committee. 6/249, 1827-35, unindexed, is little more than a list of Acts read, with occasionally a comment 'operation' meaning that its operation is approved. 6/288, 1852-4, indexed, was also checked. The comments and amendments given are fuller, e.g. 21 Feb. 1854 Western Australia Ordinances 14 and 15 read 'Return the Acts and Papers and state that my Lords see no objection to the Acts in question being submitted for Royal allowance'. On 18 Aug. 1854 a letter from the Colonial Office was read transmitting Acts for consideration, including No. 11 of 1853 for regulating the gauge of railways, repealing the 1852 Act. The Committee advised that H.M.'s assent be witheld on account of a petition received from the Lieutenant-Governor of Victoria objecting, on the grounds that different gauges have been authorised and are being built in that colony; the Committee, considering it of the greatest importance that the colonies should have a uniform gauge, refer the question of the comparative merits of the two gauges to Sir George Grey, enclosing a memo on this subject by Capt. Galton. Minutes 11 Sept. and 8 Nov. 1854 contain comments on a despatch from the Lieutenant-Governor of South Australia respecting the collection of customs duties in New South Wales and Victoria on goods brought from South Australia by the River Murray.

6/250. Trade Minutes, Miscellaneous, c.1808-25. The volume, which is indexed, contains an entry 19 Aug. 1809 referring to a report of Customs respecting the registry of Indian built ships (cf. papers concerning *Lady Barlow* in 6/58 and 88), a minute 27 Nov. 1813 referring to a letter from Messrs Chas., Sam. and Geo. Enderby requesting a clause may be introduced into the New South Whale Fishery Act concerning the oath of fidelity taken by masters of Southern Whale ships, and an entry 10 Apr. 1823 referring to documents required to be produced on the entry of foreign vessels or articles of foreign merchandise into the ports of H.M. dominions and required to be signed by a British consul. These minutes also appear in the full series of minutes (B.T.5) and tie up with the in-letters in B.T.1.

6/251. Miscellaneous Information respecting Trade 1830. A large volume containing cuttings of general interest, pasted on the sheets, arranged under places and subjects in alphabetical order. The cuttings range only from A-L. There is an index.

6/253-61. Miscellanies c.1811-24. Apparently original bundles 1-242 of in-papers now bound into volumes. 6/261, 1823-4, was checked. There is no index. The volume is not foliated or paginated and the papers are un-numbered. The only relevant item noticed was an undated list of 'acts relating to subjects connected with consular business' which includes two referring to log books of vessels employed in the Greenland and Southern Whale Fisheries to be produced to British consuls and subscribed by them (cf.6/250).

6/262-78. Miscellaneous Papers c.1779-1846. The volumes are not indexed, foliated or paginated and the papers are un-numbered. Samples taken were 6/265, 1785-1806, in which the manifest 31 Dec. 1804 of the *Lady Barlow* bound from Sydney Cove to London with a cargo of elephant oil, dried fur seal skins, and she-oak, was found, and 6/278, 1844-6, which contains several letters and papers Apr. 1843 to Dec. 1844 concerning the application of James Cumming to establish a trading factory at Port Essington, the development of the port and the use of the Torres Strait route in general, a printed report of the Colonial Land and Emigration Commissioners 1843, and a report of Customs 7 Feb. 1844 with other papers on the application by the French consul-general concerning imports of wine and other commodities in French vessels into New South Wales.

6/282-4. Colonial Acts, Drafts of Minutes sent to the Privy Council Office and the Colonial Office 1815-55.

6/283, 1841-7, was checked. It contains unbound sheets of draft minutes arranged in approximate chronological order giving a summary of the Committee's decision, e.g. 8 Apr. 1847 'The Lords of the Council have caused the devices for a public Seal for New Zealand (and other colonies) to be prepared accordingly and they humbly take leave to present the same for yr. Majesty's Royal approbation'.

6/286. Reports on Colonial Acts, Charters, 1843-50. This volume contains bound fair copies of the draft minutes in 6/282-4. The minute is often to the effect that they should be 'left to their operation', or specially confirmed and enacted. An entry 21 July 1847 recommends that a charter of incorporation be granted to the Southern Whale Fishery Company on the petition of Charles Enderby and others.

GENERAL DEPARTMENT

B.T.63 Correspondence and Papers 1928-40, 26 boxes.

Most of the files up to 1934 relate to the administration of the Merchandise Marks Act, one of the duties which the department took over on its foundation in 1928. It also dealt with general questions relating to the supply, price and sale of foodstuffs. The only relevant file found from the list was 63/21, G 664 discussion between United Kingdom and Australian ministers on trade policy 1936.

London

COMMERCIAL DEPARTMENT

B.T.11 Correspondence and Papers 1866-1946, 1750 boxes and pieces.

Only a very few files before 1902 have survived and there is a gap for 1912-14. Those surviving include files relating to Australian and New Zealand commercial registrations and trade agreements.

B.T.35 Indexes and Registers of Correspondence 1897-1902, 1910, 1918, 28 vols.

Most of the papers prior to 1902 to which these relate have not survived. After 1903 this series of registers and indexes has been destroyed except the volumes for 1910 and 1918 which have been kept as specimens. 35/2 register 1897 and 35/10 index 1900 were checked. From these it appears that many of the in-papers which have not survived were printed and not of great interest, e.g. statistical returns and cuttings from local newspapers concerning tariff alterations and arrangements.

B.T.12 Out-letters 1864-1921, 160 vols.

This series of entry books and bound copies of letters sent from the department is not complete. The volumes are indexed by recipients and subjects up to 1885. The correspondence covers the whole business of the Commercial Department and relates to trade circulars, passenger returns, emigration and immigration returns, company charters.

B.T.36 Indexes to Out-letters 1897-1908, 13 vols.

36/11, 1907, was scanned and indicates that there is material in the later volumes of out-letters.

ESTABLISHMENT DEPARTMENT

B.T.13 Correspondence and Papers 1865-1963, 168 boxes.

These surviving original papers of the department deal mainly with purely establishment matters, e.g. staff, organisation of departments, appointment of committees, but there are some more general files relating to exhibitions, commercial and trade schemes and agreements. 13/47, F 22569 relates to Board of Trade resolutions concerning the Imperial Conference 1911, and to memos suggesting the interchange of civil servants between New Zealand and the United Kingdom. There is a series of files concerning the Australian meat supply to the United Kingdom during the war years 1914-18; this includes files on the report of the Royal Commission on the Australian Meat Export Trade 1915 and on the termination of the contract for meat supplies from Australia 1919. Files of the same period relate to meat and cheese supplies from New Zealand. There are also other more general files, e.g. proposals for the extension of the Trade Commissioner Service within the Empire 1917, and British Empire Statistical Conference Report 1920.

B.T.14 Registers of Correspondence 1865-1917, 9 vols.

The registers for 1905-12 are missing. All incoming letters for the period are registered; the volumes are therefore useful for discovering the subject matter of the files which have been destroyed. The entries in the registers are marked 'destroyed' where applicable. The registers are indexed by the authors of the letters received. Date, number in letter book, action, and references to further communications are all given. 14/1, 1865-76 and 14/6, 1900-4 were checked. The letters relate mainly to staff matters, superannuation, sick leave, examinations, travel allowances, and no specifically Australasian material was found.

B.T.20 Out-letters 1865-1921, 48 vols.

B.T.21 Indexes to Out-letters 1865-1921, 8 vols.

FINANCE DEPARTMENT

B.T.15 Correspondence and Papers 1865-1955, 181 boxes.

These are the surviving in-letters and papers of the department which had administrative functions as well as financial duties taken over from the General and Marine Departments in 1865. Subject indexes to the papers up to 1895 are in B.T.19. There are a number of files dealing with general colonial matters such as colonial lights, ships registered in colonies, and distressed British seamen in colonial ports. These have not been listed in detail but the few files relating directly to Australia and New Zealand are given below. The F number is the file reference, the figure following the stroke indicating the year.

15/4, F 8017/68 Provisions landed on the Auckland Islands for the benefit of persons who may be shipwrecked.

15/10, F 389/74 Contribution of £600 towards the cost of maintenance of Somerset Settlement (Torres Straits).

15/19, F 1581/81 Maintenance of the humane establishment (Somerset Settlement) at Torres Straits.

15/35, F 13025/94 Question whether Board of Trade acceptances to the National Bank of Australia are exempt from stamp duty.

15/47, F 11098/1903 Memorandum and articles of association of the Council of Western Australian Mine Owners.

B.T.16 Indexes and Registers of Correspondence 1864-1919, 171 vols.

The registers for 1864 and 1865 are missing. From 1903 only sample registers and indexes 1910 and 1919 have been kept. 16/22 index 1870 was checked and the only entries found were two relating to the despatch of a supply of books and forms to New Zealand and New Caledonia. It seems that the subject matter of the papers referred to in these registers and indexes, but no longer preserved in B.T.15, was of a trivial nature.

B.T.17 Out-letters 1864-1919, 226 vols.

These are bound copies of letters and circulars sent out to other departments and to individuals. Only the volume for 1866 is indexed. It was searched but nothing of direct interest was found. In addition to salaries, expenses, and allowances of various kinds, many of the letters refer to lighthouse dues and accounts (including colonial lighthouses).

B.T.18 Indexes to Out-letters 1869-1918, 50 vols.

18/17, 1885, 18/32, 1900, and 18/50, 1918 were checked. All contained several references to correspondence with officials and individuals in Australia and New Zealand concerning minor financial matters, e.g. accounts for stores sent out, payments by the Bank of England to banks in Australia and New Zealand, payments of wages and expenses to individuals on ships, or to relatives of deceased crew members.

B.T.62 Comptroller of Trading Accounts, Correspondence and Papers 1918-30, 26 boxes.

The Comptroller of Trading Accounts Department was set up under the Finance Department to administer the accounts of the various trading services under the control of the Board of Trade during and immediately after the War. The class includes six files 1920-1 relating to Australian zinc concentrate supplies and the scheme for the manufacture of spelter from them, a file 1920 on the shortage of meat cargoes delivered at United Kingdom and foreign ports from Queensland, one 1921 on the recovery of certain food costs from the Queensland Government, and three files 1921-4 on wage increases under the 'Rise and Fall' clause of meat contracts in Queensland, North Australia, Western Australia, and Port Darwin.

B.T.83 Comptroller of Trading Accounts, Out-letters 1919-22, 8 vols.

The volumes are not indexed. 83/3, 1920 was checked and letters on the subjects similar to those mentioned in B.T.62 found, e.g. letters Jan.-Feb. to various banks concerning money to be credited to the Victorian Government on the Australian meat supplies accounts, 2 Jan. to the Controller of Non-Ferrous Raw Materials about payment for a consignment of refined spelter from Sydney, and 6 Feb. to A. T. M. Sharpe, Zinc Products Association Pty Ltd, about the insurance of a shipment of Australian zinc concentrates and arrangements for coastal shipment from Port Pirie to Outer Harbour, S.A.

RAILWAY DEPARTMENT

B.T.22 Correspondence and Papers 1867-1900, 58 boxes and pieces.

After 1867 the Railway Department performed certain secondary functions concerned with charters, the Companies Act, copyright, life assurance companies, patents, and trade marks. The records in this class relate only to these subjects. The registers and indexes to them were transferred, with the records relating directly to transport matters, to the Ministry of Transport, and are now in M.T.7. Subject indexes to the papers preserved 1867-95 are in B.T.19. Only one file relates directly to Australia: 22/34, R 4907/84 Board's sanction of proposed reduction in capital of Port Phillip and Colonial Gold Mining Co., 1884. Other files deal generally with copyright and merchandise marks in the colonies.

REGISTRY

B.T.19 Indexes to Papers Retained 1846-95, 21 vols.

These are modern typescript subject indexes to the papers selected for preservation in B.T.1, 11, 13, 15, 22 and M.T.9, 10, classes which relate to the General, Commercial, Establishment, Finance, Railway, Marine, and Harbour Departments of the Board of Trade respectively. The indexes cover ten year periods and within the period are arranged alphabetically by the keyword or name in the description of the subject.

COMPANIES DEPARTMENT

B.T.58 Correspondence and Papers 1865-1962, 347 boxes and pieces.

See Class List, 'B.T.58 Companies Department: Correspondence and Papers', *c.*1961, typescript.

This class includes a few papers earlier than 1904 taken over from the Commercial, Railway, and Finance Departments which successively performed duties of the Board of Trade under the Companies Acts. Examples of files relating directly to Australasia are:

58/7, COS/808A. Council of Western Australian Mine Owners, memorandum and articles of association 1900-3.

58/10, COS/1192A. Refusal of Board of Trade to include 'Chartered' in registered title of London Chartered Bank of Australia Ltd 1893-1910.

58/48, COS/3020. The Van Diemen's Land Co. petition for supplemental charter to enable the company to reduce the share capital and to issue debentures 1914.

58/107, COS/1229. South Australian Co., old charter papers, Board's approval of repayment to shareholders, new regulations for payment of interim dividends,

proposed amendment to the number of directors, resolution to wind up, and alteration to deed of settlement 1927.

58/288, COS/9315/39. Great Boulder Proprietary Gold Mines Ltd, application for
appointment of inspector 1939-40.

COMPANIES REGISTRATION OFFICE

Under an Act of 1844 it became possible for Joint Stock Companies to acquire
corporate privileges by registration alone, without obtaining special Acts of Parliament or Royal charters; at the same time the process of registration became the
responsibility of the Board of Trade. A separate Companies Registration Office was
created in 1904.

B.T.41 Files of Joint Stock Companies Registered under the 1844 and 1856 Acts 1844-c.1860,
920 boxes.

See Class List, 'B.T.41 Files of Joint Stock Companies registered under the 1844
and 1856 Acts', typescript.

These are the files for 1844-c.1860 of all companies, both active and defunct,
which were registered under the Act of 1844 and the Act of 1856 which repealed the
1844 legislation and required all companies completely registered, but not those
provisionally registered, to re-register. Files of companies so registered which
survived after 1860 are, if later dissolved, in B.T.31, or if still active, on the existing
Companies' Register (see Board of Trade, Companies Registration Office). The
documents are in two series 'General' and 'Railway' and within each series have
been arranged alphabetically by company title. The class list follows this pattern
giving the title required for both provisional and complete registration and in some
cases other documents required by the Registrar during the company's existence or
in connection with its winding-up. The class list shows a good number of companies
connected with Australasia.

B.T.31 Files of Dissolved Companies 1856-1948, 33943 boxes.

See the following lists:

Class List, 'B.T.31 Files of Dissolved Companies', 12 vols., typescript. These volumes
(C15-25b) list the files in the blocks in which they were transferred from the Companies Registration Office, giving the year of incorporation, name of the company
and the company number. There is a summary of the contents of each transfer at
the beginning of the first volume.

Alphabetical index to companies incorporated 1856-1900, registered in London, and
voluntarily dissolved 1933-48, typescript.

Index to Companies Registered 1856-1920. Privately printed for the Board of Trade,
2 vols.; one alphabetical sequence by legal title of the company, for the two volumes.

Index to Companies on the Register 30 June 1930, 1 vol., as above.

Index to Companies on the Register 30 June 1937, 1 vol., as above.

31/1-31740 are files of companies of all kinds incorporated 1856-1931 and dissolved
1856-1932, with a few dissolved 1933-48. 31/31741-33943 are files of companies
incorporated up to 1943 and dissolved 1933-43. The documents are arranged by
company number, i.e. chronologically, within the blocks in which they were transferred. Under the provisions of a schedule of destruction 1950 the annual returns in
these files were weeded out except the first, last, and every intermediate fifth; more-
over a one per cent sample was preserved of entire files. In 1959 and 1960 it was
decided that all documents of public and non-exempt private companies should be
preserved except certain annual returns of which only the first, last, and every intermediate tenth should be preserved, but that all files of exempt private companies

should be destroyed except a one per cent sample to be preserved. These exempt private company files, both destroyed and preserved, are indexed in B.T.95. The class list is annotated to indicate action taken under the destruction measures.

The files of public and non-exempt companies contain balance sheets, returns of directors, shareholders, but in most cases those of exempt private companies contain little more than the annual returns.

B.T.95 Classified Index 'Classi Sheets' to Dissolved Exempt Private Companies 1888-1940, 295 pieces.

The index is arranged in company numerical order and gives particulars of the companies involved. The original files (in B.T.31) have been destroyed except a sample one in every hundred.

B.T.34 Dissolved Companies, Liquidators' Accounts 1890-1932, 5221 pieces.

See Class List, 'B.T.34 Dissolved Companies, Liquidators' Accounts', typescript.

Accounts were not required to be forwarded to the Registrar of Companies by liquidators before the Companies (Winding Up) Act 1890. Liquidators' Accounts after 1932 are in B.T.31.

STATISTICAL DEPARTMENT

B.T.24 Out-letters 1832-8, 1 vol.

Only this one volume of out-letters survives for 1832-72 with the exception of some correspondence 1840-4 when the department was amalgamated with the Railway Department, which will be found through the registers in M.T.7. The volume is indexed by recipients. It does not appear to contain any specifically Australasian references; a letter 2 Aug. 1833 to R. W. Hay concerns efforts to stimulate governors of all British colonies to co-operate in making the tables of revenue, population and commerce in the United Kingdom and its dependencies more satisfactory.

B.T.26 Passenger Lists, Inwards 1878-88, 1890-1955, 1347 boxes.

See Class List in 'B.T.26, 27 Statistical Department, Passenger Lists', typescript.

Copies of official returns by ships' masters of all passengers brought to the United Kingdom in ships from places out of Europe and not within the Mediterranean Sea. Most of the returns before 1890 have been destroyed. The documents are arranged under ports of arrival and chronologically within each port. The class list has an introductory note explaining the anomalies which occur in this arrangement, e.g. certain ports at certain dates are not listed separately but included in other port headings. The returns give, in addition to the date of entry to Britain, the passenger's age, occupation, country of last permanent residence, and country of intended future residence.

B.T.27 Passenger Lists, Outwards 1890-1960, 1922 boxes.

See Class List in 'B.T.26, 27 Statistical Department, Passenger Lists', typescript.

Copies of official lists of all passengers leaving the United Kingdom on ships bound for places out of Europe and not within the Mediterranean Sea. Pre-1890 lists have been destroyed. The documents are arranged and classified similarly to those in B.T.26.

B.T.32 Registers of Passenger Lists 1906-51, 15 vols.

These registers, compiled at the Board of Trade, record the lists of passengers, both in and out, received there (B.T.26-7). The lists are recorded by name of ships under the ports within each year. Up to Oct. 1908 only Southampton, Bristol, and Weymouth are included. The early entries contain notes of the dates of arrival and departure of ships, but the later entries give only the date of receipt of the list.

B.T.70 Correspondence and Papers 1918-39, 65 boxes.

No files previous to 1918 have survived for the department as a separate entity, but a few papers may be found through the registers in M.T.7 for 1840-4 when it was amalgamated with the Railway Department, and in B.T.11 for 1872-1918 when it was merged with the Commercial Department. Many of the files in this class refer to various census of production, labour statistics, industrial development returns, and emigration and immigration statistics. Several relate to imperial matters, e.g. 70/2, S 594/21 Report and resolutions adopted by the British Empire Statistical Conference (1920), 1921. Only three relate specifically to Australia and New Zealand: 70/21, S 497/29 Observations of the New Zealand Government on international wool statistics 1921; 70/60, S 987/37 High Commissioner for Australia and Papua trade accounts revision 1937; 70/60, S 1374/37 Australia, balance of payments 1928/9-1935/6.

REGISTRY OF SHIPPING AND SEAMEN

The Registry came into existence in 1835 and since 1854 has worked together with the Merchant Marine Offices under the direction of the Board of Trade. Some records, e.g. registers of ships and seamen, and ships' logs are still (May 1969) at the General Register and Record Office of Shipping and Seamen, Cardiff (q.v.).

B.T.98 Agreements and Crew Lists, Series I c.1747-1860, 6944 pieces.

See Class List, 'B.T.98 Agreements and Crew Lists, Series I', typescript.

98/1-139 are muster rolls c.1747-1853. They are arranged by port of ship's registry within each year or group of years and within that in roughly chronological order if the returns are loose.

98/140-6944 are agreements and crew lists 1835-60, mainly lists. Up to 1856 they are arranged by port of registry within each year or group of years and then roughly alphabetically by ship's name. After 1856 the arrangement is numerical by ship's official number regardless of port of registry or ship's name. In the earlier series a section 'Colonial' follows the United Kingdom ports.

DEPARTMENT OF OVERSEAS TRADE

B.T.59 Overseas Trade and Development Council Papers 1930-9, 29 boxes.

This general class of files, minutes of meetings and other memoranda of the Council has only one item of direct interest: 59/21, DC520 Manchester Chamber of Commerce, mission to Australia 1935.

B.T.60 Correspondence and Papers 1918-46, 97 boxes.

B.T.61 Establishment Files 1918-46, 82 boxes.

B.T.90 Advisory Committee to the Department of Overseas Trade, Minutes and Papers 1918-30, 26 files.

MINISTRY OF TRANSPORT

The department was formed in 1919 when, in addition to exercising new functions, it also took over the powers and duties previously exercised by the Board of Trade and other departments, relating to harbours, docks and piers, waterways and inland navigation, roads, bridges and ferries, canals, tramways, and railways. With the duties, certain relevant records were transferred; consequently there are Board of Trade and Admiralty records as well as records of the Ministry of Transport itself. There are class lists for all the classes cited below. Where these are detailed subject lists this has been stated.

List of Classes described

Admiralty and Board of Trade Harbour Departments: 10, 2-3
Admiralty Transport Department: 23, 31-2
Board of Trade Marine Department: 9, 4-5, 15
Ministry of Shipping: 25
Board of Trade Railway Department: 7

ADMIRALTY AND BOARD OF TRADE HARBOUR DEPARTMENTS

M.T.10 Correspondence and Papers 1864-1919, 2074 boxes.

See Class and Subject List, 5 vols., typescript.

This class is a selection of Board of Trade Harbour Department files which have been thought worthy of preservation. It continues the Admiralty Harbour Department Correspondence and Papers *c.*1842-65 (M.T.19) which has no files of special Australasian interest. Both classes contain papers relating to general colonial matters, e.g. navigation, prize courts. Further correspondence relating to the subjects of these files and to matters for which files have not been retained may be found in M.T.2 and 3. Many files in this class deal with Bills and Acts, local and Commonwealth bye-laws, regulations, regular reports of harbour masters, marine boards, and notices to mariners, much of the material being printed and available elsewhere. In addition, many other matters relating to foreshores, harbours, lights, navigation, pilotage, and wireless telegraphy are covered.

M.T.2 Out-letters 1848-1919, 456 vols.

Vols. 1-23, 1848-62, are entry books and bound copies of letters written by the Admiralty Harbour Departments, and vols. 24-256, 1864-1919, the same written by the Board of Trade Harbour Department. The volumes themselves are not indexed but there are three volumes of separate indexes for 1913, 1915-16 in M.T.3. These out-letters deal with such matters as harbours and lights. They may relate to the same subjects as the files of correspondence and papers in M.T.10.

M.T.3 Indexes to Out-letters 1913, 1915-16, 3 vols.

ADMIRALTY TRANSPORT DEPARTMENT

M.T.23 Correspondence and Papers 1795-1917, 820 boxes.

See Class and Subject List, 3 vols., typescript.

This department dealt with the transport by sea of all military forces and their supplies until 1917 when it was incorporated in the newly formed Ministry of Shipping. Earlier records are under Admiralty (Adm.108) and later records in M.T.25. The files in this class are only those selected for preservation. There are many general files dealing with a variety of colonial transport matters such as staff, administration, the fitting out of ships, mails, freights, and wartime measures. After 1900 there are many relating particularly to Australia and New Zealand.

M.T.31 Letter Books 1857-69, 13 vols.

These are entry books of out-letters, each volume separately indexed. Included are letters to freight troop ships and convict ships.

M.T.32 Surgeon Superintendents' Journals of Convict Ships 1858-67, 12 vols.

The journals of the Surgeon Superintendents in charge of convicts contain the rules and regulations to be observed, lists of convicts' names, details of diet, and medical reports. Similar journals 1816-56 are in Adm.101/1-75.

BOARD OF TRADE MARINE DEPARTMENT

The Marine Department was created as a separate branch of the Board of Trade in 1850, and until 1939, it was responsible for the administration of the legislation dealing with merchant shipping and related matters. Papers relating to merchant shipping before 1852 are still with the Board of Trade records (B.T.1) as are the indexes to all Marine Department papers up to 1895 (B.T.19).

M.T.9 Correspondence and Papers 1854-1959, 2688 boxes and pieces.

See the following lists:

Class List 1854-1902, 1 vol., typescript. This is a subject list from 1885.
Subject List 1903-38, 1 vol., typescript.
'Board of Trade Records 1846-85', 1 vol., typescript. This describes the contents of the files before 1885.

This class is a selection of files thought worthy of preservation. Almost all the papers for 1852-5, and many for 1856-7, have been lost. Further correspondence relating to the subjects of these files and to matters for which files have not been retained may be found in M.T.4 and 5. There are many concerning general colonial matters, e.g. vessels, lighthouses, shipwrecks, emigration, and many dealing with legislation, regular reports of marine boards, rules and regulations, passenger certificates, certificates of competency of masters and mates, and other matters, much of which is printed and available elsewhere.

M.T.4 Out-letters 1851-1939, 1424 vols.

The volumes are entry books and bound copies of letters of the Board of Trade Marine Department except the last volume which contains out-letters of the Ministry of Shipping from Oct. 1939. They are indexed up to Dec. 1866 except vols. 113-15, 118-21, 124-9 relating to wrecks 1864-6. Further indexes and registers of correspondence 1864-1918 are in M.T.5. The letters, mostly addressed to local marine boards, shipping masters and collectors of customs, deal with surveys and examinations of passenger ships, collisions at sea, rewards for services, and similar matters. They should be used together with the files of papers and correspondence in M.T.9.

M.T.5 Indexes to Out-letters and Registers of Correspondence 1864-1918, 58 vols.

This class includes two special indexes of wrecks 5/4, 6, 1866-7, and two registers 5/12, 14, 1873-4. The entries in the registers are marked up with direct references to files on the same subjects, some of which are now in M.T.9 but most of which are no longer extant.

M.T.15 Consultative Marine: Correspondence and Papers 1867-1964, 1029 boxes and pieces.

See Class and Subject List, 1 vol., typescript.

The Consultative Marine Branch within the Marine Department of the Board of Trade was created in 1876. It comprised specialists in particular fields of ship survey work and much of its activity related to the safety of ships at sea. The only file relevant to this survey is 15/251, M.5302/1916 containing surveyor's observations on the import of boilers to Western Australia by the United States. Many of the technical papers of the Branch are now to be found in M.T.9.

London

MINISTRY OF SHIPPING

M.T.25 Correspondence and Papers 1917-28, 88 boxes.

See Class and Subject List, 1964, 1 vol., typescript.

The Ministry of Shipping was established in Feb. 1917 and dissolved in Apr. 1921. Its chief function was to control the use of ships in support of the war effort, the new Ministry taking over these functions from the Admiralty Transport Department. The following files were noted. The last number is the file reference, the figure following the stroke indicating the year.

25/12. 32773/1918 Return showing vessels withdrawn from Australian waters since the outbreak of war.

25/12. 40132/1919 Scheme for the demobilisation of the Australian forces.

25/51. 50326/1920 Particulars of New Zealand personnel evacuated from the United Kingdom.

25/63. 42373/1921 Deportation or repatriation of ex-enemy subjects from Australia and China, and their lost possessions abroad.

BOARD OF TRADE RAILWAY DEPARTMENT

M.T.7 Indexes and Registers of Correspondence 1840-1919, 324 vols.

These relate to both the correspondence and papers dealing directly with transport matters, which were transferred to the Ministry of Transport, and also to the correspondence and papers resulting from the Board of Trade's secondary functions in connection with charters, the Companies Act, copyright, and patents, which were retained by the Board (B.T.22). Only the latter class contains material of Australasian interest and these indexes and registers are only of importance after 1885 since there is a subject index (B.T.19) to the documents for the years before this in B.T.22.

TREASURY

See the following lists:

Lists and Indexes XLVI, *Lists of the Records of the Treasury, the Paymaster General's Office, the Exchequer and Audit Department,* London 1922, reprint New York 1963.

Lists and Indexes: Supplementary Series XII, List of Treasury Records 1838-1850 in preparation (May 1969).

Class List of Treasury Records from 1838, typescript.

List of Classes described

In-letters and Files: 1, 98, 2, 3, 108, 4, 160-3

Out-letters: 5, 6, 111, 7, 114, 9, 11, 97, 117, 12, 27, 13-16, 130, 155, 18-22, 142, 23, 28, 24

Minutes: 29

Accounts: 30-2, 35, 38-9

Registers: 46

Miscellanea: 61-2, 60, 58, 57, 64, 52-4, 56, 165

Expired Commissions: 92

Private Office Papers and Private Collections: 168, 170, 171-2

IN-LETTERS AND FILES

See the following lists:

List of Treasury In-letters, 3 vols., manuscript and typescript.

Subject Index to Treasury Long Papers, manuscript.

List of Registers and Indexes to Treasury Board Papers, T.2, 3, 108, photocopies and typescript.

Subject Indexes to T.160-4, 11 vols.

T.1 Treasury Board Papers 1557-1920, 12626 vols.

Original correspondence to the Board from government departments in England and the colonies, and from individuals, together with copies of despatches, reports, minutes, and drafts which relate to the matters under consideration. Until the various colonies became self-governing the papers reflect all aspects of financial and economic control of the colonies and their establishments and after self-government they reflect the continued close financial, economic, and monetary ties of the Empire.

Papers for the late eighteenth century concern the arrangements for the foundation of the penal colony in New South Wales, the organisation and despatch of the First Fleet and subsequent development in the colony. Later papers cover a wide range of subjects relating to Australia, New Zealand, Fiji, New Hebrides, New Caledonia, Pitcairn, Tonga, and other Western Pacific High Commission islands. These subjects include: accounts, Acts, agriculture, appointments, salaries and allowances of the civil establishments, Australian and Antarctic exploring expeditions, bonds and securities, buildings, bank charters and general banking matters, bounties, clergy, coal mines, colonial agents in England, Colonial Treasury and Audit Offices, church and school establishments, companies, convicts, currency, customs and excise, defence, emigration, annual estimates and expenditure for the various colonies, equipment and supplies, Exchequer bills, financial instructions to governors, treasurers and auditors, guano, hospitals, land, lighthouses, loans, note issues, postal and telegraph matters, quit rents, railways, the Australian branches of the Royal Mint, the Royal Navy, royalties on Australian goldfields, shipment of specie and bullion, statistics, trade, troops in the colonies, Vice-Admiralty Courts, and whaling and fisheries.

For Treasury Board Papers after 1920 see T.160-3. The minutes of the Treasury Board 1870-1920 are found in this class with the papers to which they relate. Earlier minutes are in T.29 and 99.

Particular papers in T.1 can be found only by obtaining references from the registers in T.2 and 108, or from other Treasury classes, and by checking these references in, firstly, the skeleton registers in T.3 and, secondly, the List of Treasury In-letters. Having acquired the date and running number of papers from the registers or other Treasury classes the searcher must consult the skeleton registers in T.3 to ascertain whether the paper has remained at its original number or whether it has been moved forward to join allied papers at a later date and number. Only after checking here can the searcher finally consult the List of Treasury In-letters to find the piece (box) number, and the paper number, both of which must be quoted when calling for an individual item. Various files in this class are closed for one hundred years.

1/3411-4404 contain certain groups of Treasury Board Papers dealing with particular matters over a considerable length of time and are known as 'Long Papers'. A manuscript subject index of these papers is available.

T.98 Treasury Board Papers, Supplementary 1599-1800, 3 vols.

These are similar to the papers in T.1.

T.2 Registers of Papers 1777-1920, 502 vols.

Brief entries of the papers in T.1. The registers are in two series, an alphabetical and a numerical one, the former being subdivided after 1817 into 'Individuals' and 'Public Offices'; in the latter section relevant entries are found under such headings as Home Office, Colonial Office, Colonial Agents. For the new numbers of papers which have been carried forward and filed with later papers see T.3.

T.3 Skeleton Registers 1783-1920, 110 vols.

These indicate which of the Treasury Board Papers in T.1 have been carried forward and filed with related papers of a later date, and the new number under which they may be found. They are also a guide to the constitution of the 'Long Papers' in T.1.

T.108 Subject Registers 1852-1920, 25 vols.

Registers, arranged by subject, of the Treasury Board Papers in T.1. See also T.64/93 Index to Treasury Registered Papers dealing with colonial affairs 1832-4, Pt 3.

T.4 Reference Books 1680-1819, 43 vols.

The books for the late eighteenth and early nineteenth centuries consist of brief entries of correspondent, date, subject, and the department to which the letters and petitions have been referred for attention. Entries include papers transmitted to the Treasury Solicitor or King's Proctor concerning wills, administration of estates, prize matters, papers transmitted to the Colonial Office concerning financial matters in the colonies, and papers transmitted to the Admiralty concerning the cost of sending emigrants and convicts to the colonies.

T.160 Finance Files 1920-42, 1113 boxes.
T.161 Supply Files 1920-42, 1085 boxes.
T.162 Establishment Files 1920-42, 647 boxes.
T.163 General Files 1920-42, 129 boxes.

These four classes continue the Treasury Board papers in T.1, and the various classes of out-letters. Various files in T.160-2 are closed for fifty years.

OUT-LETTERS

See List of Treasury Out-letters, T.5-28, 97, 101-55, 157-8, 1959, typescript.

The earliest volumes of out-letters from the Treasury are to be found in T.27 General 1668-1920 and T.28 Various 1763-1885 from which, later, were formed separate classes of considerable groups of letters to particular departments on particular subjects. The earliest of these separate classes is T.9 Council 1793-1922. If the numbers of letters no longer warranted a separate letter book the class was absorbed back into 'General' or 'Various' or was combined with another class. Generally, up to 1885 the volumes are in the form of entry books; after that date they are bound copies of letters sent. Some of the entry books begin with copies of routine letters followed by lists of the departments or persons to whom they were sent or, if sent to only one department or official, the dates on which they were sent with a note of any altered details. The classes of out-letters cease about 1920 and out-letters from these classes are thereafter to be found on files in classes T.160-3. Most volumes are indexed up to 1913.

Papers in the Treasury Board Papers (T.1) associated with these out-letters can be traced from the file number at the head of each letter, which, with the date, can be checked in the Skeleton Registers and then found in the List of Treasury In-letters.

T.5 Admiralty 1849-1920, 58 vols.

The despatch of convicts and supplies, proposals for new postal services to Australia via Singapore and Panama and for communications by steamer between Australia and China, arms and equipment, salaries and allowances, coaling stations for the Australian Squadron, and the disposal of instruments belonging to the observatory at Parramatta are examples of the non-routine subjects with which these volumes deal. In the earlier volumes there is a separate index for the hire of convict ships showing the number of convicts to be despatched, to which colonies, and also what stores are to be sent.

T.6 Auditors 1810-1921, 42 vols.

Letters to the Auditor of the Exchequer, the Commissioners of Audit, and the Comptroller and Auditor General successively. They include papers concerning colonial accounts, Bills drawn in the colonies, salaries and allowances of colonial officials, vouchers of colonial expenditure, and other colonial matters.

T.111 Bank of England 1917-21, 4 vols.

Correspondence on Treasury Bills, Exchequer Bills, loans, etc. Scattered letters relate to bullion held to the Bank of England account in the Bank of New Zealand, Wellington, and loans and repayments to dominion and colonial governments.

T.7 Colonial Affairs 1849-1921, 44 vols.

Letters to the Colonial Office on all aspects of finance and economic control including salaries, pensions and allowances, postal services and other communications, maintenance of convicts and surplus stores for the convict service, colonial debentures and bonds, annual estimates and expenditure, legislation relating to economic matters, investment of balance in hand held in London on behalf of the various colonies, emigration, branches of the Royal Mint, and guano licences.

T.114 Commissions (Temporary) 1914-20, 7 vols.

114/2. Papers 1916-17 relating to the Wheat Supplies Commission contain some references to purchases of wheat from Australia.

T.9 Council 1793-1922, 44 vols.

Copies of Orders in Council to 1830 and, from 1810, copies of out-letters to the Council Office relating to the Orders in Council. Also contains letters to the Board of Trade 1889-1907 which have some scattered references to such matters as the Australian branches of the Royal Mint.

T.11 Customs 1667-1922, 137 vols.

The volumes for 1801-49 concern both Customs and Excise. For Excise to 1800 and from 1849-1909 see T.27 and 22. Letters in this class include some concerning the staffing, salaries, allowances and pensions of the Customs services in the Australian colonies, and the payment of duties by colonial notes.

T.97 Finance 1886-1913, 14 vols.

Letters to the Mint, National Debt Commissioners, Public Works Loans Commissioners, Bank of England, and others. For later correspondence relating to the Mint and the Bank of England see T.130 and 111 respectively. Included are letters on the administration and working of the Australian branches of the Royal Mint, on loans and debentures, note issues, coinage, bullion accounts, and other matters.

T.117 Ministry of Food 1917-21, 2 vols.

The volumes contain scattered references to purchases of products from the dominions and colonies including surplus cheese from Australia and New Zealand, and tallow from Australia.

T.12 Foreign Office 1857-1920, 47 vols.

The volumes include letters concerning arrangements for the despatch and forwarding of mails to Australia, New Zealand, and the Pacific through foreign ports, the arrangement of new shipping routes for mails and contracts for the Pacific mail service, negotiations with foreign countries relating to the telegraph, and the establishment of telegraphic stations. Letters also relate to the establishment and maintenance of consular offices in the Pacific Islands, stores for foreign ships in British waters, and the estates of deceased British subjects in foreign areas of the Pacific.

T.27 General 1668-1920, 260 vols.

Early volumes in this class contain out-letters on all subjects but gradually separate classes of documents were formed at various dates for particular departments or special subjects.

Headings under which relevant entries can be found in the indexes to the various volumes include Admiralty, Colonial Agents, Colonial Office, Emigration Commissioners, Foreign Office, Home Office, Master of the Mint, Australia, and the various colonies or states, also subject entries including 'superannuation', 'renewable orders', 'gratuities to masters of convict ships', 'governors and officers commanding', and 'lighthouses'.

T.13 Home Office 1835-1920, 31 vols.

Scattered letters relate to the convict services, prisons, staff, clothing, and equipment.

T.14 Ireland 1669-1921, 112 vols.

Letters to Irish Government departments, local authorities, and individuals. There are only scattered letters of interest and these relate chiefly to the transportation and maintenance of convicts, and to emigration.

T.15 Law, General 1807-1913, 52 vols.

Letters to the Treasury Solicitor and other law officers. These include correspondence concerning expenses for witnesses including those brought from Australia to appear in cases, instructions to the Treasury Solicitor to arrange for legal advice, terms of contracts for victualling and clothing convicts and for transporting them, also many letters relating to deceased estates which can be located through the indexes in each volume.

T.16 Law, King's (Queen's) Proctor 1857-1913, 13 vols.

Letters to the King's Proctor and, after 1876, the Treasury Solicitor (in his capacity as King's Proctor) and other officials concerning intestates' estates. The volumes have indexes of personal names. For earlier correspondence see T.15.

T.130 Mint 1914-24, 2 vols.

For earlier correspondence see T.97 and 22. Included are letters concerning the minting of coins for dominion and colonial governments, the administration of the branches of the Mint in Australia, auditing of Australian bullion accounts, and payments for gold.

T.155 Overseas Trade 1919-22, 1 vol.

Correspondence concerned with the administration of United Kingdom trade posts abroad, with some papers on other matters including a memo on changes in prices in various countries 1918/19 to 1919/20, including prices in Australia and New Zealand.

T.18 Parliamentary 1875-1922, 18 vols.

Letters include some to the Parliamentary Counsel on the drafting of legislation relating to the colonies, e.g. 18/11, 1898-1900, contains a letter asking the Parliamentary Counsel to contact the Colonial Office with a view to assisting with the Australian Commonwealth Bill.

T.19 Post Office 1850-1920, 57 vols.

Includes letters on postal services to Australia, New Zealand, and the Pacific including parcel post, cost of services, postal rates, contracts for mail, telegraphic services, and postal agreements among the various colonies and foreign countries. For earlier correspondence see T.22.

T.20 Stationery Office 1849-1922, 20 vols.

There are scattered letters concerning stationery for the various colonies and for the convict service in Australia. For earlier correspondence see T.22.

T.21 Superannuation 1857-1920, 111 vols.

Indexed volumes of letters relating to pensions.

T.22 Taxes 1704-1921, 62 vols.

Includes correspondence 1820-49 with, or relating to, the Post Office, Mint, and Stationery Office continued in T.19, 130, 20 respectively.

T.142 Board of Trade 1914-20, 9 vols.

For earlier volumes see T.9. The class includes some correspondence concerning trade and shipping arrangements with the dominions, meat supplies from Australia and New Zealand, and some correspondence concerning the salaries of members of the Imperial Trans-Antarctic Expedition 1914-17.

T.23 Treasurers Abroad 1856-1913, 7 vols.

Letters relate to business connected with the administration of the Treasury Chest in the various colonies, including regulations, staffing, mode of accounting, annual surveys, and arrangements for the abolition of the Chest.

T.28 Various 1763-1885, 113 vols.

Out-letters to various correspondents of which the following contain relevant material.

28/8-37, 1811-35, and 28/92-106, 1837-56. Naval and military departments. Subjects include transport to and from Australia, subsistence, and supplies.

28/41-59, 1796-1859. Secretaries of State including the Secretary of State for Home Affairs and the Secretary of State for the Colonies. Subjects include revenue and expenditure, salaries, allowances and pensions, supplies and stores, advance of funds to the Colonial agent, customs and excise, currency, emigration, banking ordinance, public works, bounties.

T.24 War Departments 1855-1920, 63 vols.

Scattered letters deal with colonial defence and the training of colonial troops in Britain.

MINUTES

T.29 Minute Books 1667-1870, 632 vols.

Minutes of the Treasury Board, those for 1848-70 being only selected minutes. Later minutes are in T.1. The subjects covered are similar to those described under T.1.

ACCOUNTS

T.30 Accounts General, Yearly 1688-1854, 46 vols.

The annual balanced accounts of income and expenditure.

London

T.31 Quarterly Accounts 1701-1855, 450 vols.

The quarterly accounts from which the accounts in T.30 were made up.

T.32 Quarterly Expenditure 1800-55, 38 vols.

Details of the accounts of the spending departments which are not shown in T.30 or 31 after 1787.

T.35 General, Various 1636-1865, 53 vols.

A miscellaneous collection of summaries or abstracts of accounts, estimates, etc. There are occasional very brief entries under the heading 'Extraordinaries' for sums of money for the various colonies.

T.38 Departmental Accounts 1558-1881, 825 pieces.

Accounts and ledgers of government departments and other services including the following:

38/6. Departmental Audits (not Treasury) Ledger Account, 1809-20. Includes entry for sums to enable Barnard, agent for New South Wales, to meet demands made in respect of the colony.

38/79-115, 118-19. Auditors' states of accounts, 1783-1856, which are copies of the accounts in A.O.1, 2, 20, 22 and correspondence with the Commissioners for Auditing Public Accounts.

38/120-53. Civil Contingencies Ledgers, 1815-58. Scattered entries for payments of travel expenses of governors and other distinguished persons, additional expenses of surveying voyages and exploring expeditions, and payments for publication of the results of such expeditions, expenses of consuls, the purchase of provisions, and supplies for convicts on board transports and other matters.

38/154-251. Civil List, 1699-1819; 38/252 Civil List Ledger, 1840-54. Scattered entries for grants to settlements in Australia and New Zealand, for exploring expeditions, emigration, and convict services.

38/310-38. Returns of the convict hulks 1802-18, and Reports to the House of Commons 1831.

38/491-9. Treasury Fees and Fee Books 1837-50. Amongst other items, these record payments to colonial agents for ordinary and emigration purposes, freight on specie, gratuities to masters and surgeons of convict ships, and fees for the administration of wills of convicts.

38/741-4. Special service and miscellaneous accounts 1783-1821, including entries for expenses of King's messengers in carrying colonial despatches for moving convicts; 38/742, 1794-1802, contains accounts relating to the expense of maintaining Benelong and expenses incurred by Bligh in shipping a breadfruit tree.

38/748-73. Supply Books 1702-1855. Records of the grants of supply for the public service and issues made in respect of them. There are entries for the expenses of the antipodean settlements, Bills drawn by colonial governors, salaries and expenses of the consular service, the Mint, emigration services, convict services, and exploring expeditions.

T.39 Treasury Chest 1838-78, 143 vols.

39/1-79. Accounts of foreign and colonial stations 1846-76. Accounts for New South Wales are in 39/53-7, Victoria in 39/56-7, Tasmania in 39/70-2, South Australia in 39/1, 57, Western Australia in 39/2-3, North Australia in 39/24 and New Zealand in 39/58-62.

39/80-108. Miscellaneous Accounts 1838-72, relating to the colonies, the convict service, commuted pensions, and accounts of advances and repayments by colonial accountants.

39/109-43. Ledgers 1843-78. Entries will be found under such headings as Balances, Treasury Bills, Profit and Loss, Consignment of Specie, Commissariat notes, Ordinance effectives, Navy effectives, and Convict Establishments in the colonies.

REGISTERS

T.46 Victualling Lists 1763-95, 23 bundles.

46/22. Lists of people victualled at Teneriffe, Rio de Janeiro, and the Cape of Good Hope 1787 en route for the new settlement in New South Wales, naming marines, wives and children, men and women convicts, and convicts' children.

MISCELLANEA

T.61 Disposition Books 1679-1856, 77 vols.

Entries of Letters of Direction indicating the particular account upon which payments as listed in the Order Books (T.60) were to be drawn, including annual entries for the colonies in Australia and New Zealand.

T.62 Maps and Plans, Series I 1668-1837, 134 docs.

A miscellaneous collection of maps and plans which in general accompanied letters and reports to be found among the Treasury Board Papers.

62/120. Tasmania: Hobart Town, Governor's house, 1828.

62/121. Tasmania: Sullivan's Cove, 1828.

T.60 Order Books 1667-1831, 44 vols.

Entries of the Orders upon the Tellers of the Exchequer which were drawn by the Auditor of the Receipt as directed by Treasury Warrants (T.56-7).

T.58 Letters and Orders to Paymaster General 1834-70, 29 vols.

Scattered general references to payments for expenses of the colonies and of emigration and for expenses of convicts on the hulks.

T.57 Royal Orders and Warrants Thereon 1834-1959, 7 vols.

Entry books of Royal Orders for the payment of money with notes of the Treasury warrants issued thereon. Relevant entries include funds to maintain convicts in New South Wales and Van Diemen's Land, and funds for the exploration of north west Australia.

T.64 Various 1547-1874, 402 vols.

A miscellaneous collection of reports, correspondence, accounts. The following volumes were noted:

64/30-5, 1807-9. Reports of the Comptroller of Army Accounts.

64/83, 1813-27. New South Wales despatches, regulations, government orders, and memoranda including port regulations for Port Jackson 1819 and Hobart 1818, regulations for vessels going to Newcastle, revenue for the Female Orphan Institute, Parramatta, account of the New South Wales Police Fund Dec. 1817 to June 1819, and copies of despatches from Darling concerning the issuing of additional shares in the Bank of New South Wales and estimates of the value of government work performed by convicts.

64/92, 1811-16. Bills of governors and other colonial officials including many from New South Wales and Van Diemen's Land referred to the Secretary of State for the Colonies.

London

64/93, 1832-4. Index to Treasury Registered Papers dealing with colonial affairs. Part 3 labelled 'Trinidad' includes references to letters from the Australian colonies dealing with financial and establishment matters in Treasury Board Papers (T.1).

T.52 Warrants, King's 1667-1857, 122 vols.

Entry books of letters patent, privy seals, Royal sign manual warrants relating to such subjects as salaries, pensions, payments of money, and administration of estates. Scattered warrants of interest concern the maintenance of convicts on the hulks, the charges of the Civil Establishment of various colonies, money for the contingent use of regiments, amongst them those stationed in Australia or New Zealand, and the disposal of forfeited property of felons.

T.53 Warrants Relating to Money 1676-1839, 68 vols.

Entry books of warrants from Treasury to the Auditor of the Receipt to pay money or issue debentures. These are overall authorities for funds for various departments and include only very scattered references to individual sums for the convict service, and salaries and pensions of some colonial officials.

T.54 Warrants Not Relating to Money 1667-1849, 58 vols.

Entry books of warrants from Treasury for matters other than those concerned with the payment of moneys including instructions to Colonial Governors, Accountants, and others concerning the revenue and expenditure of the colonies and the mode of accounting for them, appointments, salaries, warrants for buying and selling, advances to various undertakings, and warrants for paying balances after accounts have been audited. They also contain lists in alphabetical order of compassionate allowances.

T.56 Warrants, Various 1620-1863, 51 vols.

Warrants for payments of money including, in volumes for Army Extraordinaries, advances to the Crown Agent for the Colonies, Bills drawn on the colonies, advances to officials going to the colonies, advances on account of emigration, payments for equipment, stores, and stationery.

T.165 Blue Notes 1880-1934, 61 vols.

The Blue Notes, which are printed, were prepared annually as briefs for Ministers as background information on the establishment and functions of government departments and special activities for use in discussions in the Committee of Supply. Relevant notes cover the Colonial Office, convict establishments in England and the colonies, grants-in-aid of expenditure in certain colonies, and the transit of Venus 1874. The notes outline the history and functions of the subject, the establishment, salaries and allowances and in the case of the convict services, clothing, stores, and diets for the convicts.

EXPIRED COMMISSIONS

T.92 Revenue Enquiries 1765-1854, 260 bundles.

92/166. Commission on Colonial Revenue 1830. Index to Treasury minutes 1829-32 relating to this Commission.

PRIVATE OFFICE PAPERS AND PRIVATE COLLECTIONS

T.168 Hamilton Papers 1858-1913, 74 items.

Papers of George Alexander Hamilton and Sir Edward Walter Hamilton both of whom served in the Treasury, both achieving the rank of Permanent Secretary. There are scattered papers of interest including such subjects as postal services to

Australia via Panama, colonial defence, loans to the colonies for railways, the establishment of a settlement at Cape York for the relief of shipwrecked vessels and a memo on 'Advances towards free trade or protection since 1860 in foreign countries and the colonies' including New South Wales and Victoria.

T.170 Bradbury Papers 1870-1922, 144 items.

Working papers, memoranda, and notes used by Sir John Bradbury, Financial Adviser and Joint Permanent Secretary to the Treasury. Only scattered papers are relevant, chiefly on loans to the Australian Commonwealth and states.

T.171 Chancellor of the Exchequer's Office, Budget and Finance Bill Papers 1859-1925, 1937, 339 pieces.

Bound collections of papers which have accumulated during the preparation of each Budget. There are gaps 1895-1901 and 1903-6. There are some references to the Colonial Office.

T.172 Chancellor of the Exchequer's Office, Miscellaneous Papers 1792-1925, 1858 pieces.

General correspondence and papers from the Chancellor's Office; not all the papers of the Office have survived. Similar and complementary material to that found in the pre-1920 papers is to be found in the Hamilton Papers (T.168), the Bradbury Papers (T.170) and Chancellor of the Exchequer's Office, Budget and Finance Bill Papers (T.171). The following items were noted:

172/28, 1908. Proposed financial arrangements between the Imperial Government and the Australian Government.

172/34, 1910. British Ornithologists Union, exploration of the Great Snow Mountains, Dutch New Guinea.

172/51, 1911. Sir Ernest Shackleton's Antarctic Expedition 1907-9, request for a grant towards publication of scientific results.

172/215, 1915. Conference with the High Commissioners and Agents General of the self-governing dominions.

172/369, 1916. Purchase of ships by Australia, Excess Profits Duty.

172/616, 1917. Australia, financial position.

172/793, 1918. New Zealand meat supplies, withdrawal of refrigerated tonnage from the New Zealand trade.

172/941, 1850. Licence in Mortmain for the purchase of land in the City of London by the Bank of New South Wales.

172/944, 1853-63. Royal Mint in Australia.

172/1156, 1920, 172/1233, 1922. Representations and negotiations from Australia for a Commonwealth loan.

172/1163A, 1920. Australian debts.

172/1271, 1922. Preference on Australian dried fruits. Also some papers on Imperial preference, Imperial Economic Conference.

TREASURY SOLICITOR AND H.M.
PROCURATOR GENERAL

Until 1842 the Treasury Solicitor acted solely for the Treasury, but since then he has acted as solicitor and legal adviser to a growing number of government departments, and as solicitor to those departments which have a legal adviser but no solicitor. Included amongst these are the Colonial Office and Commonwealth Relations Office. Since 1876 the office of H.M. Procurator General has been held with that of Treasury Solicitor. Formerly H.M. Procurator General had many duties under Admiralty, ecclesiastical and prerogative law, but his main duties now are concerned in peacetime with matrimonial causes, and in wartime with prize proceedings both in the United Kingdom and overseas.

No detailed descriptions have been made of the following classes containing papers of biographical interest which can be used only by tracing names of individuals in the indexes: T.S.2 Letter Books, Treasury 1806-59, 1899-1919, including scattered letters on forfeited property of convicted felons and on deceased estates; T.S.7 King's (Queen's) Proctor, Accounts 1845-53, including accounts and expenses of reports on deceased estates; T.S.8, 9 King's (Queen's) Proctor, Reports, Series I and II 1804-44, containing entry books of memorials and correspondence on intestacies and wills; T.S.11 Treasury Solicitor's and King's (Queen's) Proctor, Papers 1584-1856, dealing with state trials and cases on wills, deceased estates, etc.

See the following lists:

Class List of Treasury Solicitor's Records, 1938, typescript.

Calendar of Treasury Solicitor's Papers 1584-c.1856, 6 vols., including 2 index vols., typescript.

TREASURY SOLICITOR

T.S.3 Miscellaneous Letter Books 1813-61, 1898-1924, 44 vols.

The earlier volumes relate to such subjects as the administration of estates, War Office business, lunatics, ecclesiastical and criminal matters, e.g. 3/13, Apr.-Dec. 1823 contains letters relating to claims against defaulting paymasters in New South Wales. The volumes from 1898-1924 concern prize matters and the prosecution of German war criminals.

T.S.4 Journals of Proceedings 1828-65, 38 vols.

These are records of work undertaken by the Treasury Solicitor and show briefly letters received and sent and actions taken. They relate to matters such as mutinies, form of charter parties for the hire of transports going to Australia, port regulations in the colonies, Vice-Admiralty commissions in the colonies, and wills.

T.S.5 Report Books 1806-99, 1919, 88 vols.

Entry books and press-copy books of reports and letters to the Treasury and other departments excluding the Admiralty, Home Office, War Office, and Office of Works. Under the heading 'Colonial matters' in the indexes can be found a few entries for such items as costs in the trial of a seaman in Fiji, guano licences, estates of United Kingdom citizens dying in the colonies, and the engrossing of documents of various kinds involving colonial or dominion countries. There are also reports and letters on wills, bankruptcies, and trials to which reference can be made through the indexes under the name of the individual concerned.

T.S.6 Report Books, Admiralty 1816-28, 1868, 15 vols.

Entry books of reports made to the Admiralty and, until 1832, to the Navy Board, by the Solicitor to the Admiralty. There are a few scattered papers relating to such subjects as commissions for the trial in the colonies of offences committed at sea, and the hiring of transports for the movement of soldiers and convicts.

KING'S (QUEEN'S) PROCTOR

T.S.13 Prize and Prize Bounty Cases, Decrees and Affidavits 1914-28, 858 bundles.

See List of Records in T.S.13, typescript.

Writs, claims, correspondence, and legal case papers are included in this class.

T.S.14 War Trade Intelligence Department Records 1914-19, 55 vols.

These records were transferred to H.M. Procurator General for Prize Court purposes when the Department was closed. The volumes include minutes of various committees and war trade statistics.

T.S.15 Assignation Books 1827-73, 5 vols.

Notes of proceedings in appeals from Admiralty Instance and Prize Courts, and from Vice-Admiralty Courts including those in the colonies. 15/1 and 5 contain isolated cases of interest.

WAR OFFICE

From 1801-54 the Secretary of State for War also carried out the business of the colonies, and records for this period have been divided as far as practicable between the War Office and the Colonial Office. When it appears that records have remained with the Colonial Office this is stated in the description of the relevant class below. Troops in the colonies were under the control of the Governor, but were administratively controlled from London. Thus much correspondence, especially before 1840, relating to troops and defence will be found among the Governors' despatches in Colonial Office records while documents such as returns and court martial proceedings will be found among War Office papers.

See the following lists:

Lists and Indexes XXVIII, *List of War Office Records*, I, London 1908, reprint New York 1963.

Lists and Indexes LIII, *Alphabetical Guide to War Office and Other Military Records Preserved in the Public Record Office*, London 1931, reprint New York 1963.

Lists and Indexes: Supplementary Series VIII, *List of War Office Records*, New York 1968.

There are lists to all classes described below except those closed for one hundred years. The lists are bound sometimes separately, sometimes several together in numerical order, and sometimes grouped together under a heading. They have not been detailed but special lists and indexes are noted under the class headings.

List of Classes described

Correspondence: 1, 40-1, 43, 32, 141, 139, 31, 107, 3-4, 6
Returns: 17, 73, 10-12, 76, 22, 97, 25, 108, 114
Miscellanea: 106, 28, 78, 30, 26, 33, 162-3, 180
War 1914-18: 95, 153-4, 157-8
War 1939-45: 167
Ministry of Defence (Army): 181
Private Collections: 77, 133, 80, 105, 110
Ordnance Office: 44-9, 52, 54-5
Judge Advocate General's Office: 71-2, 86, 89-92, 81-2, 93
Commissariat Department: 57-62

CORRESPONDENCE

W.O.1 In-letters 1732-1868, 1138 vols.

Original despatches, letters and papers to the Secretary at War and later to the Secretary of State for War.

Colonies and Dependencies. Most of the correspondence relating to Australia and New Zealand covers 1841-55. Correspondence prior to 1841 is mainly in Colonial

London

Office records, especially C.O.201, 324, 537 and other classes under Colonies, General. Correspondence from the Australian colonies and New Zealand and relating to them deals with defence, barracks, allowances, encouragement of pensioners to become settlers, sending of troops to New Zealand, validity of courts martial of Maoris under military law, military convicts.

1/431-4, 1841-5, Australia, includes correspondence from New South Wales, Tasmania, South Australia, Western Australia, and New Zealand. 1/433 contains a large section for New Zealand; 1/435-6, 1846-53, South Australia; 1/437, 1846-54, Western Australia; 1/519-25, 1846-55, New South Wales; 1/526-35, 1846-55, New Zealand; 1/574-6, 1846-55, Tasmania; 1/577-8, 1851-5, Victoria (see also 1/519-25); 1/595-601, 1838-53, miscellaneous, containing some Victorian correspondence.

Public Departments. Correspondence from public departments extends only to 1815. There are scattered relevant letters from the Commander-in-Chief, Treasury, Transport Office, and Secretary of State, e.g. 1/803, 1806-7, Transport Board, which includes letter 6 Jan. 1807 from John C. Spence, master of the *Duke of Portland* complaining of the conduct of Capt. Cummings, New South Wales Corps, in charge of the convict guard; letter 7 Aug. 1807 from the Transport Board on the *Recovery* and *Sinclair* preparing for the conveyance of stores to New South Wales and having accommodation for thirty-four cabin passengers; letter 21 Aug. 1807 from the East India Company concerning the use of ships to convey convicts and stores to New South Wales and returning to England loaded with cargo from India. Letters from other departments may be found from the *Alphabetical Guide*. From 1841-55 correspondence from departments is found in classes listed under the headings Colonies and Dependencies.

Miscellaneous. Series 2 and 3 of this section are arranged alphabetically, but Series 1 is made up of a variety of volumes, e.g. 1/893, 1797-9, East India Company, including: letter 19 July 1798 to the Colonial Office sending copy of a minute of the Court of Directors on a request by the Colonial Office that the *Minerva*, having transferred convicts to New South Wales, be allowed by the Company to proceed to Bengal and there load a cargo of sugar, indigo, cotton; letter 28 Oct. 1799 saying the Company will take measures to prevent the importation of spirits to New South Wales from the East Indies, with memo on the amount of rum exported to New South Wales 1796-8. 1/910, 1803-5, Prisoners of War, including copies of correspondence Feb.-Aug. 1804 between Matthew Flinders, Governor De Caen, and the Admiralty on Flinders's imprisonment at Mauritius, with a covering letter 24 Aug. 1804 from the Admiralty. 1/952, 1816-18, Establishments, including distribution of troops, with explanatory notes, estimates, returns, abstracts, which refer to New South Wales. 1/970, 1854, General correspondence, divided into government departments, concerning a variety of subjects such as arrangements for regiments in Australia, Ordnance establishments in New South Wales, Victoria, and South Australia, and various returns referring to Australia.

W.O.40 Selected Unnumbered Papers 1753-1815, 32 bundles.

In-letters and reports addressed to the Secretary at War.

40/16. Claims 1802-5 of eight non-commissioned officers and men of the New South Wales Corps who were taken as prisoners to Mount Avido in South America in Aug. 1798 by mutineers from the *Lady Shore* carrying convicts and soldiers to New South Wales. Among the documents is a return 27 Mar. 1797 of a detachment of the New South Wales Corps embarked on the *Lady Shore* under Ensign Minchin showing the names of the mutineers.

40/26. Documents 1807 concerning the vaccination of convicts on hulks.

40/28. Letter 23 Dec. 1808 and other correspondence 1808 on the embarkation of the 73rd Regiment to relieve the New South Wales Corps.

W.O.41 Selected 'A' Papers 1810-22, 98 vols.

In-letters relating to accounts, dealing chiefly with payments for prisoners of war, militia, volunteers, also including scattered references to payments of troops ordered to New South Wales. 41/76-98 are registers and show the subject of each paper and its disposal.

W.O.43 Selected 'V.O.S.' and 'O.S.' Papers 1809-57, 107 bundles.

See Catalogue of War Office Old Series and Very Old Series at the Public Record Office; photoprints of printed numerical lists and indexes 1904 and 1906, with a report on the weeding of the papers, 1904.

The papers include files 1838-55 in 43/24, 48, 58, 71, 83 on the emigration of pensioners, the disbandment of the New South Wales Veteran Company, and indulgences to be granted to its members should they settle in the colony; also colonial military expenditure 1826-32. Files on the New Zealand Fencibles Nov. 1846 to Dec. 1847, including nominal lists, are in 43/89. Among the New South Wales papers there are memorials 1819-35 in 43/51 on the case of Capt. Robison, New South Wales Veteran Company.

W.O.32 Registered Papers, General Series 1855-1958, 5969 boxes and files.

These papers selected for permanent preservation at the War Office relate to all aspects of War Office business. There is a partial and selective index, typescript, arranged alphabetically by places and subjects. This shows that there are papers relating to Australia and New Zealand. Various files are closed for fifty and seventy-five years.

W.O.141 Registered Papers, Special Series 1914-17, 3 boxes.

Documents removed from the General Series in W.O.32, closed for one hundred years, no list available.

W.O.139 Subject Indexes 1826-1901, 13 vols.

Registers giving a digest of the Department's correspondence with reference to the papers preserved in W.O.32.

W.O.31 Memoranda Papers, Commander-in-Chief 1793-1870, 1565 bundles.

There are scattered papers relating to officers serving in New South Wales.

W.O.107 Quartermaster General, Papers 1763-1919, 68 boxes.

This class contains papers relating to various expeditions including the Maori Wars and the Dardanelles expedition of the First World War. 107/7 contains manuscript and printed copies of the journals of Lieut.-Col. D. J. Gamble, Deputy Quartermaster General, New Zealand, Dec. 1861 to Feb. 1865. Other copies of these journals are in W.O.30/132 and 33/16. With the manuscript journals are copies of returns, plans, etc. 107/44 contains private correspondence of British officers 1915 and deals with supplies, the withdrawal, and other matters concerning the 1915-16 campaign in the Dardanelles.

W.O.3 Out-letters, Commander-in-Chief 1765-1868, 617 vols.

These entry books of the Commander-in-Chief and Adjutant-General include scattered letters relating to Australasia and the Pacific in most of the various series which make up the class. The letters deal mainly with routine matters. The volumes are indexed.

London

W.O.4 Secretary at War 1684-1861, 1053 vols.

These entry books include various series containing scattered references to Australia and New Zealand, e.g. General, 4/138, 140 include letters relating to the New South Wales Corps and 73rd Regiment, some of which are printed in *H.R.N.S.W.* I, part 2.

There are also two series dealing specifically with Australia and New Zealand. 4/284-90, 1847-53, Colonies. Including letters relating to the Australian colonies and New Zealand sent to officers and public departments and dealing with the emigration of military pensioners, especially to New Zealand, problems of supervision after they have settled, pensioners as guards on convict ships, sending of military convicts to Western Australia.

4/845-6, 1789-1810, New South Wales Corps. Letter books containing copies of letters dealing with all aspects of the New South Wales Corps.

W.O.2 Indexes of Correspondence 1759-1858, 107 vols.

Index headings General Administration, Regimental, Warrants, and Miscellaneous include entries for the New South Wales Corps and 73rd Regiment. Under the heading Letters to Soldiers are routine letters to Commanding Officers asking for information on soldiers in response to requests from relations and others. Entries under Accounts and Medical may repay examination.

W.O.6 Secretary of State 1793-1859, 214 vols.

Letter Books. The series Colonies and Dependencies 1832-58 and Public Departments 1794-1815 include letter books entitled Eastern Colonies covering the Australian colonies and New Zealand. Subjects covered are similar to those in W.O.1 and 43. All volumes have indexes.

RETURNS

Further classes of personal and service records, returns of establishments, and medals and awards which would repay searching are described in the *Guide to the Contents of the Public Record Office* II, pp.308-13: W.O.64-6, 69, 42, 67, 24, 27, 100-2, 116, 23, 121, 131, 120, 97, 117-19, and III, p.28: W.O.145-6.

W.O.17 Monthly Returns 1759-1865, 2812 vols.

Most returns give names of officers only. Examples are:

17/241. Returns 1790-1809 of the Marines and New South Wales Corps serving in New South Wales, the only complete years being 1797, 1799 and 1802. Returns Mar. 1791 to May 1792 are in 17/2294.

17/1222-33. Returns 1854-65 for New South Wales and its dependencies.

17/1234-61. Returns 1837-65 for Western Australia. There do not appear to be separate returns for other states.

17/2295-337. Returns 1810-53 of regiments in Australian colonies and New Zealand. The return of the 73rd Regiment, Mar. 1810 includes the names of officers who volunteered from the 102nd to the 73rd Regiment and names of officers of the Invalid Company formed out of the 102nd Foot in New South Wales.

17/2338-55. Returns 1847-65 for New Zealand.

17/2747, 2764-8. Returns 1835-55 of Royal Engineers including detachments in the Australian colonies and New Zealand.

W.O.73 Monthly Returns, Distribution of the Army 1859-1938, 141 vols.

Printed summarised returns, showing distribution of the army and giving other statistical information. Closed for five years.

W.O.10 Artillery, Muster Books and Pay Lists 1708-1878, 2876 vols.

W.O.11 Engineers, Muster Books and Pay Lists 1816-78, 432 vols.

W.O.12 General, Muster Books and Pay Lists 1732-1878, 13305 vols.

Inserted at the beginning of the list of W.O.12 are typescript notes on War Office searches for information on private soldiers and non-commissioned officers, showing what records to consult in order to find birthplace, marriage, and children; also information on recruits and soldiers serving in India, and the information to be found from Monthly Returns and Depot Musters.

Musters and pay lists of regiments serving in Australia and New Zealand may be found from the list. Musters of the New South Wales Corps cover 1789-1815. The earliest muster 5 June to 24 Dec. 1789 in 12/11028 lists names of recruits, by whom recruited and dates of commissions and attestations. Later musters of the Corps are at 12/9899-907. Monthly pay lists and musters of the New South Wales Veteran Company 1810-23 are in 12/11228-9.

W.O.76 Officers' Services, Records of 1755-1954, 550 vols.

This series supplements the returns of services in W.O.25 Registers, Various. The records give officers, various ranks and services, with certain personal particulars.

W.O.22 Pension Returns, Royal Hospital Chelsea 1842-83, 300 vols.

22/226, Pensioners as guards on convict ships to Western Australia 1862-7; 22/227, South Australia 1876-80; 22/248-55, Colonies, Miscellaneous 1845-75; 22/256-7, Colonies, Miscellaneous, Admiralty and Marine pensioners 1845-54, 1871-5; 22/258-63, Consuls' accounts 1854-80 including payments by consuls in Tahiti and the Sandwich Islands to pensioners; 22/272-5, New South Wales 1849-80; 22/276-93, New Zealand 1848-80; 22/297, Queensland 1876-80; 22/298, Tasmania 1876-80; 22/300, Victoria 1876-80.

W.O.97 Royal Hospital Chelsea, Soldiers' Documents 1760-1900, 4231 boxes.

97/853, 1760-1854, contains documents for soldiers of the 73rd Regiment among which are several documents for men transferred from the New South Wales Corps.

97/1141, 1760-1854, includes documents of the Colonial Veteran Corps.

97/1361, 1855-72, Royal Engineers includes documents for men who served in New Zealand, Western Australia, and Victoria.

W.O.25 Registers, Various 1660-1938, 3992 vols.

Certain files in this class closed for one hundred years. The following registers contain relevant information:

25/1-121. Commission Books 1660-1873, 2 series.

25/122-208. Notification Books 1708-1848.

25/209-32. Succession Books, General 1754-1808, 2 series, e.g. 25/219 includes entries for the New South Wales Corps 1805-8.

25/266-688. Description and Succession Books 1756-1900, e.g. 25/642-3, New South Wales Corps 1808-16, 25/404, 48th Foot 1817-24.

25/689-702. Staff Pay Books, etc. 1792-1870.

25/703-43. Staff Returns 1792-1856, e.g. 25/733, 1841-2, foreign stations including New South Wales and Van Diemen's Land.

25/744-870. Returns of Officers' Services 1796-1835; for an index of names see Miss E. H. B. Fairbrother, Indexes and Lists XII, War Office 25/780-805, Index of Officers giving their Services, 1928, manuscript.

25/871-1120. Service Returns No.1, e.g. 25/1070 New South Wales Corps, non-commissioned officers and men liable to service abroad 1806.

London

25/1121-1131. Service Returns No.3, e.g. 25/1130 New South Wales Corps or 102nd Foot, non-commissioned officers and men 1783-1810.

25/1145-95. Embarkation and Disembarkation Returns, e.g. 25/1151 including detachments of the 50th Foot going to New South Wales and Van Diemen's Land 1834; 25/3502, Royal Artillery 1789-1869 including returns for officers going to Australia and New Zealand; 25/3503-4, 1815-57, returns for the 48th, 57th, 39th, 17th, and 4th Foot and for individual officers of the New South Wales Veteran Company 1817-19.

25/1196-358. Muster Master General's Index of Casualties 1797-1817, e.g. 25/1342 New South Wales Corps Dec. 1798-1817.

25/1359-2410. Casualty Returns 1809-72, e.g. 25/1824, 48th Regiment Dec. 1817 to Dec. 1824; 25/2170 non-commissioned officers and men of the New South Wales Corps 1810-17; 25/2243, officers, non-commissioned officers and men of the New South Wales Veteran Company June 1826 to Aug. 1830.

25/2963-78. Deaths and Effects 1810-59.

25/2979-3019. Half Pay and Retired Pay 1712-1870.

25/3020-125. Widows' Pensions and Bounty 1735-1856.

25/3126-37. Miscellaneous Pensions 1795-1856.

25/3138-79. Contingencies and Extraordinaries 1684-1830.

25/3180-95. Commissary General of Musters 1704-94.

25/3206-45. Miscellaneous Lists and Returns 1684-1886, e.g. 25/3239 includes report of the marriage of Lieut. Henry Hill, 57th Foot, 19 Feb. 1831 to Julia Thomas at St Philip's, Sydney. For an index of names see Miss E. H. B. Fairbrother, Indexes and Lists XIII including W.O.25/3239-40, 1928, manuscript.

W.O.108 South African War, Papers 1899-1905, 84 vols.

108/1. Papers 1899-1904 concerning the departure of troops including Australian and New Zealand forces.

108/2 includes nominal rolls of colonial contingents 1900.

108/29 includes correspondence relating to Australians 1901-3.

W.O.114 Strength Returns of the Army 1890-1920, 54 vols.

114/25-42. Weekly returns of the British Army and dominion contingents in the British Isles 1914-20.

MISCELLANEA

Classes W.O.123, 74, 103, 95 described in *Guide to the Contents of the Public Record Office* II, pp.318-22 may also be relevant.

W.O.106 Directorate of Military Operations and Intelligence, Papers 1837, 1870-1939, 1594 boxes.

The following papers were noted; there are also papers 1914-22 on defence and operational plans in the Dardanelles, Egypt, Palestine, France, and other theatres of war.

106/43-4. Papers dealing with Imperial Conferences 1897, 1902, 1911, 1917, and 1923.

106/45. Papers July 1910 on the general principles affecting overseas dominions in matters of defence.

106/70-7. China, Boxer Rising.

106/293. Report 23 Nov. 1908 on Australian military defence by Capt. G. R. D. Churchill, 19th Punjabis, recently attached to the Australian military forces.

W.O.28 Headquarters Records 1746-1901, 347 vols.

This class includes copies of and extracts from orders issued at various head-quarters overseas. The orders are arranged by country and deal with military expenditure, appointments and discharges, transfers, the assembling and findings of courts martial.

28/266. Western Australia 1842-53.

28/287. New South Wales Nov. 1841 to Oct. 1848, Van Diemen's Land Nov. 1843 to Oct. 1848, New Zealand Jan.-June 1848.

28/288. New Zealand Oct. 1847 to Feb. 1855, Victoria Nov. 1852 to June 1854.

28/291. Van Diemen's Land Nov. 1841 to Jan. 1843, May 1849 to Dec. 1855, New South Wales July 1849.

28/302, 346. Boxer Rebellion 1900-1 includes a few references to the Australian naval contingent.

W.O.78 Maps and Plans 1627-1953, 5430 pieces.

78/5427-8 include maps showing the existing armament at Adelaide 1896, Sydney, Broken Bay, and Cronulla 1897, Auckland Harbour and approaches 1914, Port Lyttelton, Port Levy, and Pigeon Bay 1911, Otago Harbour 1911 and Cook Strait 1890.

W.O.30 Miscellanea 1684-1903, 132 vols.

Sample volumes are:

30/36-42. Registers 1785-1847 of warrants including those issued in the Australian colonies and in New Zealand referring mainly to mutiny and desertion and the convening of district and garrison courts martial.

30/112. Correspondence July-Aug. 1849 on the proposed change in the method of furnishing reliefs in the east in view of strength reduction. The proposal was that regiments should first serve in India and then proceed to one of the Australian colonies, New Zealand, or the Cape before returning to England.

30/132. Reports and journals 3 Jan. 1863 to 16 Aug. 1866 of Lieut.-Col. D. J. Gamble, Deputy Quartermaster-General in New Zealand, with maps and plans, partly included in W.O.33/16. Manuscript and printed copies in W.O.107/7.

W.O.26 Miscellany Books 1760-1817, 42 vols.

Entry books of Royal warrants, e.g. 26/33 copy of a warrant 5 June 1789 for raising a corps of foot under the command of Major Grose.

W.O.33 Reports and Miscellaneous Papers 1853-1939, 1528 vols.

The typescript Class List contains many entries concerning military operations in New Zealand 1860-5 including journals of Lieut.-Col. D. J. Gamble (see W.O. 30/132), defence of Australian colonies and French possessions in the Pacific, especially the New Hebrides 1905.

W.O.162 Adjutant-General 1847-1952, 98 vols.

Files and volumes on organisation, mobilisation, and recruitment.

162/67-73. Dardanelles May-Dec. 1915.

162/94-8. Medals and conditions of service of South African and overseas contingents 1899-1900.

London

W.O.163 War Office Council and Army Council 1870-1938, 46 vols.

Minutes and decisions of the War Office Council, established under the War Office Act 1870 and of the Army Council, created by Letters Patent 6 Feb. 1904 to supersede it, also of meetings of military members Aug. 1914 to Jan. 1916.

W.O.180 Royal Hospital Chelsea, Invaliding Board 1800-1915, 78 vols.

Board papers 1800-87, minute books 1823-1915, discharges 1801-21, and Appeal Board papers 1829-75.

WAR 1914-18

W.O.95 War Diaries 1914-22, 5487 boxes.

Diaries of all Australian and New Zealand divisions, brigades, battalions, corps, batteries, casualty clearing stations, tunnelling companies, sanitary sections, supply columns, lines of communications of troops, and the New Zealand Western Pacific Expeditionary Force are included. W.O.154 contains a supplement to this class.

W.O.153 Maps and Plans 1914-20, 1215 pieces.

Assembled from various sources, many having been extracted from war diaries. They cover the theatres of war and the Army of Occupation including the Dardanelles, Gallipoli, and Egypt.

W.O.154 War Diaries, Supplementary 1914-20, 342 folders.

Documents removed from the main series in W.O.95. Closed for one hundred years.

W.O.157 Intelligence Summaries 1914-21, 1307 vols.

Summaries of information and reports on military, economic and political matters in Europe, Africa, the Middle East, and the Far East. Specific Corps mentioned in the Class List include the 1st and 2nd Anzac Corps in the Dardanelles and France Apr. 1915 to Dec. 1917, and the Australian Corps and New Zealand Division in France, Belgium, and Germany May 1916 to Nov. 1918.

W.O.158 Correspondence and Papers of Military Headquarters 1909-29, 895 pieces.

Letters and papers relating to operations in Europe, Africa and the Middle East. Specific Corps mentioned in the Class List include the Australian Electrical and Mining Corps Oct. 1916 to Sept. 1918 in France, Belgium, and Germany, and New Zealand and Australian Divisional Headquarters in the Dardanelles Apr.-Sept. 1915.

WAR 1939-45

W.O.167 War Diaries, British Expeditionary Force 1939-41, 1446 files.

Daily records of events, reports on operations, intelligence summaries, etc., of Headquarters, Divisional, Regimental, and other unit commanders of the British Expeditionary Force in France from Sept. 1939 to June 1940. No list available. Closed for one hundred years.

MINISTRY OF DEFENCE (ARMY)

W.O.181 Directorate of Military Survey, Papers 1887-1942, 306 files.

Unregistered branch files of the Geographical Section, General Staff, which became the Directorate of Military Survey in 1943. Various files closed for fifty and one hundred years.

181/19. International Commission for Air Navigation projection for polar air maps 1922-30.

181/106-7. Australia 1909-14, 1933.

181/108. New Guinea, Anglo-German boundary 1909-10.

181/109. New Guinea, Australian-Dutch boundary 1933-4.

181/110. Fiji 1908-15.

181/135-63. Colonial Survey Committee, mainly Africa 1909-41.

PRIVATE COLLECTIONS

W.O.77 Archer Papers 1814-28, 1837-8, 7 vols.

Entry books of out-letters, semi-official and private, kept by Thomas Archer, Principal Clerk 1835-54, in the Commissariat Department of the Treasury. They include the following papers:

77/1 letters 11 Apr. 1814 to the Transport Office and 20 Apr. 1814 to Capt. Bristow asking when the *Devonshire* will sail for New South Wales; 77/3 memo c.Feb. 1815 for the Storekeeper-General on various stations including New South Wales; 77/5 letter 15 Oct. 1815 to David Allan, N.S.W., saying he cannot accept Allan's son as a clerk and telling of changes in the Commissariat Department; 77/6 letter 16 Jan. 1817 to David Allan introducing Mr Murray, proceeding to New South Wales with 48th Regiment; 77/7 letter 31 Jan. 1838 to William Miller, N.S.W., asking him to help Charles Weaver who is going to New South Wales to practise law and letter 27 Feb. 1838 to Miller concerning an error in the abstracts of Ordinaries sent by Miller. This class supplements out-letters in W.O.58.

W.O.133 Brownrigg Papers 1792-1820, 17 vols.

Out-letter books of Gen. Sir Robert Brownrigg, military secretary to the Commander-in-Chief and Governor of Ceylon, 1811-20. Those written while military secretary include scattered letters concerning New South Wales, e.g. 133/3 Miscellaneous, including letter 7 Mar. 1797, to Maj. Paterson informing him that the New South Wales Corps is to be increased and may be required for actual service and letter 7 Mar. 1797 to Maj.-Gen. Fox regarding three foreigners enlisted in the New South Wales Corps; 133/6 Miscellaneous, including letter 14 Apr. 1799 to the Right Hon. C. Greville on an ensigncy in the New South Wales Corps for Francis Barrallier, and letter 2 May 1799 to Greville concerning Barrallier's proceeding to New South Wales.

W.O.80 Murray Papers 1804-59, 13 packets.

Correspondence and memoranda of Sir George Murray as Lieutenant-Governor of Upper Canada 1815, Commander-in-Chief in Ireland 1825-8, Secretary of State for War and the Colonies 1828-30, and Master General of the Ordnance 1834-5, 1841-6. 80/2 correspondence with the Duke of Wellington includes two letters 2 Aug. 1828 from Wellington asking Murray to appoint J. E. Manning as registrar of the Supreme Court of New South Wales and 6 Nov. 1828 enclosing acceptance 5 Nov. 1828 by Rev. W. G. Broughton of the Archdeaconry of New South Wales. Other correspondence in W.O.80/4 includes a letter 4 Oct. 1841 from Henry Goulburn to Murray concerning Mr Davies, Assistant Treasurer at Launceston, and five letters 5 Nov. 1841 to 4 July 1844 from Lord Stanley concerning Sir Thomas Mitchell and his position in New South Wales, with a letter 9 Feb. 1844 from Mitchell, Sydney, submitting his claims to be appointed the successor to Sir George Gipps and asking for recommendation to Lord Stanley.

W.O.105 Roberts Papers 1835-1913, 40 boxes and 8 folders.

These papers relate mainly to the period when Lord Roberts was Commander-in-Chief in South Africa. 105/5-23 despatches and reports of operations in South Africa 1899-1902 by the Commander-in-Chief and Commanders in the field contain many references to Australian and New Zealand troops. Other South African material such as confidential correspondence, papers, and telegrams are in 105/24-39. Among the addenda items in 105/41-8 are 105/45 papers on defence and the re-organisation of the army, including a printed copy of a speech made in the Australian Senate by Senator Lieut.-Col. the Hon. C. St.C. Cameron on the need for military service in the Commonwealth, 105/47 notes on the strategic development of the Pacific, unsigned, c.1906 and 105/48 a printed petition presented to King Edward VII by Charles Edward Morphett of Adelaide on behalf of the South Australian Bush-men's Corps which served in South Africa 5 Apr. 1900 to 30 Apr. 1901, with letter 28 Dec. 1904 from [J?] Bowers to Lord Roberts returning the petition.

W.O.110 W. H. Smith Papers 1881-8, 10 boxes.

Correspondence and papers of the Right Hon. William Henry Smith, M.P., mainly accumulated while he was Secretary of State for War 1885-7. 110/7 is an indexed register of letters showing those destroyed and has several references to correspondence with the Hon. Edward Stanhope and others, e.g. 110/5, 6 contain correspondence 26-30 Nov. 1886 with Stanhope on a proposal to give Queen's Commissions to officers of the Colonial Military Forces and on the appointment of administrators in the colonies in the absence of the Governors, enclosing a list of the rules applying to such appointments in Australia, New Zealand, and Fiji. 110/6 also contains a letter 16 Aug. 1886 from J. H. Tuke of the Emigration Information Office, referring to emigration to Australia and New Zealand. 110/8 includes a printed memo on the defence of British possessions and commerce abroad with papers on the subject referred to the Defence Committee by the Secretary of State 9 Aug. 1883 referring briefly to Thursday Island, Fiji, and Port Refuge in the Cocos Islands as coaling stations.

ORDNANCE OFFICE

W.O.44 In-letters 1682-1873, 732 vols.

See List of and Index to, the Board of Ordnance (W.O.44), typescript. Arranged in sections: index to inventions (44/620-40), indexes to services (44/686-700), index to the papers preserved in the Public Record Office (44/1-619, 641-85, 701-32), list of books in Ordnance Correspondence Misc.85.

The letters are arranged in several series, first by country including 44/165-90 New South Wales, Tasmania, and Western Australia, and then under various head-ings such as Admiralty, Secretary of State, War Office, Artillery, Barracks Eastern, Engineers, Inventions, Pensioners, Services, and Miscellaneous.

The index to the papers preserved at the Public Record Office gives many refer-ences to Australian and New Zealand material for volumes under all these headings, but it is not complete, e.g. documents in 44/165-6, 169-70, 173, 178, 188-9 are not included.

W.O.45 Reference Books 1783-1870, 298 vols.

Registers of the in-letters to the Board of Ordnance 1783-1856 and the Master-General 1844-70.

W.O.46 Out-letters 1660-1861, 169 vols.

46/44, 1858-61, letters to the Inspector-General of Fortifications including letters relating to Australia and New Zealand.

46/109, 1857-60, Passages.

W.O.47 Minutes 1644-1856, 2897 vols.

47/121-2357. Board's minute books 1809-55. The early volumes relating to New South Wales usually deal with the supply of all types of provisions, clothing, stationery, and medicines. Later minutes also deal with such matters as promotions and appointments, employment on particular jobs, erection of barracks, and convicts.

47/2549-759. Extracts of minutes, series II, 1786-1856, including indexes 1810-31.

47/2760-850. Pensions minutes 1808-34.

Indexes to the Board's minutes 1819-52 are listed under this class but have no detailed class number, only the index serial number. Each index volume is arranged by person, subject, and place and gives references to 47/121-2357.

W.O.48 Ledgers 1660-1847, 357 vols.

48/201-14. Treasurer's ledgers, foreign 1832-46, include amounts for purchase of furniture, lodgings, pay of storekeepers and others, storage of arms and ammunition in Australia and New Zealand. The volumes are indexed.

48/240-53. Treasurer's ledgers, military account 1832-47, cover additional pay, allowances, pensions in Australia and New Zealand. The volumes are indexed.

48/344-7. Voluntary accounts ledgers 1828-45, include entries for Colonial Agents, Lords of the Treasury and others for supplies for mounted police in New South Wales, stores for convicts and convict ships, stores for the South Australian exploring expedition Apr. 1844. The volumes are indexed.

There are scattered relevant entries in 48/228-39 Treasurer's ledgers, Commissariat 1834-56 and in 48/317-24 Expenditure ledgers 1830-1.

W.O.49 Accounts, Various 1592-1858, 293 vols.

This class includes a series of abstracts of colonial estimates, 1843-54. 49/183 contains estimates of expenditure on account of pay of the military corps stationed in the colonies, e.g. Royal Engineers at Sydney and Hobart 1843-51 and in New Zealand 1846-51; 49/184-7 include estimates of Ordnance and Barrack establishment expenditure at Sydney, Hobart, Adelaide, Perth, Auckland, and Wellington 1849-54; 49/166 includes documents on repairs to be carried out on Ordnance works and buildings in New South Wales and Tasmania 1842-3; 49/274 includes allowances made to storekeepers at Sydney June 1843 to Mar. 1847, Hobart Mar. 1846 to Mar. 1847, Adelaide Mar.-Dec. 1847, and to the Ordnance Clerk at Auckland Mar. 1845 and Mar. 1847.

W.O.52 Bill Books, Series III 1783-1859, 782 vols.

The bill books supplement the ledgers. They cover expenditure on foreign establishments, shipping and transport, travelling, repairing of arms, command pay for Royal Engineers and Royal Artillery in the colonies.

W.O.54 Registers 1594-1871, 947 vols.

The contents of this class are detailed in *Guide to the Contents of the Public Record Office* II, pp.327-9. Many of the series concern Australia and New Zealand, e.g. 54/259 returns of Engineer Officers showing stations 1847-50, 54/756-947 appointment papers 1809-55. For an index of names to 54/734 Returns of Barrack Masters 1835-50 see Miss E. H. B. Fairbrother, Indexes and Lists XIII including W.O.54/734, 1928, manuscript.

W.O.55 Miscellanea 1568-1923, 3038 vols.

Documents in many series in this class include papers relating to Australia and New Zealand. Examples are:

London

55/231-82. Colonial reports 1808-59. 55/253 Tasmania 1828-9; 55/263 New South Wales 1837; and scattered throughout 55/266-81, 1839-59.

55/318-24. Miscellaneous reports 1689-1855 include reports from Australian colonies; supplementary reports on various subjects also relate to Australian colonies.

55/852-6. Engineers' papers 1835-53 Australia, New Zealand (from 1840), and Norfolk Island.

55/971-1023. Engineers' papers 1785-1856 miscellaneous.

55/2844. Statements of lands and buildings Sydney 1841, 55/2869 Adelaide 1853, 55/2875 Auckland 1851, 55/2989 New South Wales 1851, 55/3026 Tasmania 1851.

JUDGE ADVOCATE GENERAL'S OFFICE

Papers relating to courts martial occur also in other classes of War Office records. Copies of sentences of courts martial are occasionally found in W.O.1 In-letters from the Judge Advocate General; letters of the Commander-in-Chief in W.O.3 deal *inter-alia* with charges against officers and courts martial, e.g. 3/541-68, 1833-57, all relate to courts martial; W.O.4/845-6, 1789-1810, are entry books of the Secretary at War dealing with the New South Wales Corps; W.O.30/36-42 contain routine warrants dealing with district and garrison courts martial; W.O.57/35 and 58/116 contain some New South Wales courts martial documents; W.O.84 Charge Books 1857-92, 1908-33, and W.O.85 Deputation Books 1751-1910 appear to deal mainly with courts martial in England and Ireland and have not been included in the description below. W.O.81-2, 86, 90-3 are closed for one hundred years.

W.O.71 Courts Martial Proceedings 1668-1850, 1879, 1914-56, 1251 vols.

The List available of these proceedings covers only 1668-1850. Other volumes are a recent addition to the class; because of their dates they are unlikely to be relevant to this survey. Class closed for one hundred years.

W.O.72 Courts Martial, Letters and Miscellaneous Documents 1696-1850, 103 bundles.

Original in-letters with enclosures, reports, and other miscellaneous documents sent to the Judge Advocate General relating to courts martial held in England and abroad, e.g. 72/35, 1810-11, original letters, evidence, reports, lists of witnesses relating to the court martial of Lieut.-Col. Johnston.

W.O.86 District Courts Martial 1829-1913, 60 vols.

Registers of district courts martial including those held in Australia and New Zealand, giving name and rank, regiment, when and where held, nature of charge, and sentence, often transportation to New South Wales. The entries are mainly for privates and non-commissioned officers. Closed for one hundred years.

W.O.89 General Courts Martial 1666-1760, 1812-29, 5 vols.

89/4-5 are registers of general regimental courts martial 1812-29, held in England and abroad, including some held in New South Wales and Tasmania 1819-29. They give name and rank, regiment, where and when tried, substance of the charge, and the sentence.

W.O.90 General Courts Martial, Abroad 1779-1920, 7 vols.

Registers of general courts martial held abroad 1796-1865, are in 90/1-3 and include those held in Australia and New Zealand 1800-65. The information is similar to that in W.O.86 and 89. Closed for one hundred years.

W.O.91 General Courts Martial, Confirmed at Home 1806-1904, 51 vols.

Entries are in order of the date laid before the sovereign, the length of time between the actual court martial and that date varying considerably. Class closed for one hundred years.

W.O.92 General Courts Martial, Registers 1666-1704, 1806-1917, 3 vols.

Registers of general courts martial laid before the sovereign and confirmed at home including those held in Australia and New Zealand. Many soldiers tried for desertion were sentenced to transportation to New South Wales. Closed for one hundred years.

W.O.81 Courts Martial, Letter Books 1715-1900, 133 vols.

These include scattered relevant letters, e.g. 81/43-4, July 1810 to July 1811 and have copies of correspondence with Bligh and Lieut.-Col. Johnston concerning papers and witnesses for the court martial of Johnston; 81/45 includes letters 9 Oct. 1811 to Lieut.-Col. Torrens concerning the memorial 2 Dec. 1811 of James Williamson, late Deputy Commissary-General in New South Wales, to R. Wharton on the expenses of Capt. Finucane at Johnston's trial and, n.d., to G. Harrison concerning the memorial of Walter S. Davidson and the summoning of the same as witness for his defence by Lieut.-Col. Johnston. The volumes have alphabetical indexes of names and titles of persons to whom letters are addressed. Closed for one hundred years.

W.O.82 Courts Martial, Office Day Books 1817-99, 24 vols.

Registers of letters received concerning courts martial giving name of writer, date sent, received, and answered, and a brief note on the subject matter. Letters registered in these volumes are in W.O.72. Closed for one hundred years.

W.O.93 Courts Martial, Miscellaneous Records 17th cent. to 1922, 15 vols.

These records include alphabetical indexes to the confirmations of courts martial in W.O.91 and 92. Closed for one hundred years.

COMMISSARIAT DEPARTMENT

W.O.57 In-letters 1806-17, 58 bundles.

This class includes entry books of letters 1806-16 from the Treasury, the later volumes of which include some letters to Deputy-Commissary Allan, N.S.W., dealing with stores, clothing, rations, appointment of a clerk, articles for the Surveyor General's Department. There are also original letters to the Commissary-in-Chief from commissariat officers at stations abroad, e.g. 57/35 contains original correspondence 1810 from William Broughton and 1813-15 from David Allan, while officers of the Commissariat Department at Sydney. No correspondence for 1811-12 was found in this bundle. Among the enclosures to Broughton's letter 30 June 1810 is an account of contingent expenses incurred by Col. L. Macquarie and his personal staff 25 Dec. 1809 to 24 June 1810, copies of bills drawn on the Treasury, and warrants, receipts, and vouchers. Other documents include a letter 13 Nov. 1810 from John Palmer enclosing copy of commission of appointment 12 Apr. 1790 as Commissary of stores and provisions in New South Wales. Enclosures to letters from D. Allan include general statements of the inhabitants of New South Wales as at the general musters 27 Sept. 1813 and 16 Nov. 1814, an estimate of the quantity of wheat required for rations Dec. 1814 to Dec. 1815, and statements of land under cultivation. Other documents in 57/35 deal with the court martial 1814 of Leonard Fosbrook, Deputy Commissary in Tasmania, the issue of corn rations during scarcity, and returns of government cattle.

The in-letters of the Commissariat Department 1817-54 are among the Treasury Board papers in T.1 and are noted in the registers of those papers T.2, 3, 108.

London

W.O.58 Out-letters 1793-1888, 178 vols.

Miscellaneous correspondence on appointments and salaries, e.g. 58/37 includes entries for passages to New South Wales and Tasmania, tenders for supplies for New South Wales and approval of accounts made in Tasmania, but most of the relevant correspondence of this kind is in 58/116-24, letters to Commissariat officers abroad (Australia and New Zealand) 1819-58. 58/116-20 contain letters Feb. 1819 to Nov. 1843 for New South Wales (including New Zealand), Tasmania, Western Australia, and South Australia, 58/121-2 letters Nov. 1843 to July 1853 New South Wales, Western Australia, and South Australia and 58/123-4 letters May 1843 to Jan. 1858 Tasmania and New Zealand. All the volumes have indexes and some give dates of acknowledgement and date despatched. 58/45-62 letters to Government Departments 1809-56 contain references to the Australian states and New Zealand. They deal with topics similar to those in 58/116-24 as well as the erection of barracks, repairs to buildings, expenditure, immigration. 58/46-9 auditors' letter books 1814-56 contain statements of the various Commissariat establishments, including those in New South Wales and Tasmania, giving name, rank, rate of pay, period of employment, and remarks. Also included are statements of casualties at these stations. See also Archer Papers W.O.77.

W.O.59 Minutes 1816-54, 76 vols.

Entry books of Treasury minutes drawn up from original letters and reports received from Commissariat officers and others. The numbers given in the margins refer to the originals which are among Treasury Board papers at T.1. There is an index at the end of each volume and together with the minutes they form an index to the originals. During the period covered by these minutes, the Commissariat was carried on as a separate department of the Treasury. Letters and reports from Commissariat officers in Australia and New Zealand are included.

W.O.60 Accounts 1774-1858, 112 vols.

60/49. Military Chest returns, foreign accounts branch 1832-6 including stations in New South Wales, Tasmania, and Western Australia. The returns give date of letter and registration number, period of the return, description and total amount of coins received and paid, and the balance and reports of surveys, but not the source of the funds.

W.O.61 Registers 1791-1889, 135 vols.

The four series comprising this class are detailed in *Guide to the Contents of the Public Record Office* II, p.333. All four series contain relevant material.

W.O.62 Miscellanea 1798-1859, 50 vols.

Many of the documents in this series deal with the activities of the Commissariat at the time of the Crimean War. 62/50 contains regulations connected with the Commissariat Department on foreign stations. Entries in this volume for South Australia, Western Australia, and New Zealand are only slight but those for New South Wales and Tasmania, especially the former, are detailed, e.g. the existing regulations connected with the Commissariat Department in New South Wales condensed and collected at Sydney up to 31 Dec. 1839 are given on various pages.

RELIGIOUS SOCIETY OF FRIENDS
The Library, Friends House, Euston Road, London, N.W.1

Most local archives relating to Australia and New Zealand are in the custody of the officers of the Society of Friends in Australia and New Zealand. However some copies of minutes and some original records and annual reports are scattered through-out the official correspondence, miscellaneous and private papers held in Friends House Library. A card index of persons, places, and subjects is maintained and there are detailed inventories for some collections. Some journals and correspondence are primarily of religious interest, others, such as those of Daniel Wheeler, James Backhouse, William Benson, Ann F. Jackson, and E. Maria Bishop contain detailed descriptions of people and places. A typescript biographical dictionary of Friends is continually supplemented by new entries and notes of sources of information. Selected records have been microfilmed for the Australian Joint Copying Project.

MINUTES AND TESTIMONIES

The London Yearly Meeting was responsible, through committees of its standing representative body (Meeting for Sufferings), for general oversight and corres-pondence with Friends overseas, including those professing with the Society in the Australian colonies and New Zealand. The first such corresponding committee of Meeting for Sufferings, appointed in 1817, was called the Continental Committee. In 1903, however, Meeting for Sufferings transferred responsibility for corres-pondence with Friends in Australia to a newly-formed Australia Committee. Matters relating to New Zealand were in 1905 handed to this committee which was renamed the Australasian Committee. The name was changed again in 1930 to Australia and New Zealand Committee. Friends in Australia had been formed into a General Meeting (having the status of a Quarterly Meeting, though gathering annually), in 1901; Friends in New Zealand were similarly organised in 1913. In 1964 both General Meetings were reorganised as independent Yearly Meetings. From this date Monthly Meetings in Australia were renamed Regional Meetings.

London Yearly Meeting Minutes 1834-56.

The Minutes are printed as *Proceedings* 1857 to date. Both manuscript and printed minutes are indexed, typescript to 1856, printed 1857-1906, typescript in preparation 1907 to date, and include the most important minutes of Meeting for Sufferings relating to Australia and New Zealand, as well as the reports of the Continental Committee and the Australia Committee. The report of the 1874-5 Deputation to Australia appears in Yearly Meeting *Proceedings* 1876. Brief sketches of the early history of the various meetings and meeting houses in Australia and New Zealand are found in Yearly Meeting *Proceedings* 1887.

London Meeting for Sufferings Minutes, indexed. Cumulative typescript index in course of preparation. Minutes 1828-1916 contain Australasian references.

Continental Committee Minutes 1817-1905, indexed.

Australia (afterwards Australasian, then Australia and New Zealand) Committee Minutes 1903-19, 4 vols., indexed in cumulative typescript.

Testimonies concerning ministers deceased 1728-1872, 7 vols.

Memorials of Quaker ministers presented to Yearly Meetings appear in these volumes. However, from 1862 selected testimonies, and from 1873 all testimonies, are printed in Yearly Meeting *Proceedings*, and it is here that most ministers of Australian and New Zealand interest appear. A typescript index of testimonials 1728 to date is in Friends House Library.

CORRESPONDENCE AND PAPERS

Casual correspondence 1785-1881, 1 vol., indexed.

Official correspondence, mainly epistles, sent to and from the London Meeting and those professing with the Society in Van Diemen's Land, South Australia and Sydney. Epistles to Van Diemen's Land 1835-55, from Van Diemen's Land 1838-52;

to South Australia 1842-54; to Sydney (sometimes included with Van Diemen's Land) 1842- .

Epistles to and from Australia and New Zealand 1867-1909. Over forty epistles, most of them printed, MS. box 14.

Other epistles can be found scattered throughout the correspondence and other collections listed below. There is no single series of official correspondence between the Meeting for Sufferings and its Committees and Friends in Australia and New Zealand, or visiting Friends travelling under official auspices. Letters often remained with the personal papers of correspondents, office bearers or other members of the Society.

Miscellaneous Correspondence and Papers, portfolio 8.

Chiefly letters to London and including official, semi-official, and private letters. 8/1-48, 63-88 appear to be papers of the Continental Committee and include papers c.1840 relating to the Meeting at Adelaide and letters and papers 1845-66 relating to the Meetings in South Australia, Van Diemen's Land, Sydney and Brisbane; letters 6 Dec. 1858, 7 Nov. 1859 from Elinor Clifton, Australind. There is also a letter 8/125, 1911 from J. F. Jackson, N.Z., about sources for a history of Friends in New Zealand.

Accounts, temporary box 85.

A box of packets of accounts includes the following:
J. J. Neave Expenses Account 1877-99.

Australian Friend and other Australian matters.

Ann F. Jackson Expenses Account 1886-1903 and other New Zealand matters.

Portfolio Series

The Portfolio Series comprises about forty volumes mostly miscellaneous in character. For portfolio 8 see above.

Portfolio 6/59. Liberation minute 1867 for J. J. Neave to visit Australia. After visiting every Australian colony and New Zealand, Neave and his family settled in Sydney.

Portfolio 17/103. Business letter 1834 from Backhouse and Walker, Hobart.

Portfolio 17/115-16. Letters 1839-40 from John Tawell to Meeting for Sufferings re a meeting house at Sydney.

Portfolio 18/14. 'Report of a visit to the penal settlement of Port Arthur and the Aboriginal settlement on Flinders Island etc. by James Backhouse and George Washington Walker . . . 1832', manuscript copy. See J. Backhouse, *A Narrative of a Visit to the Australian Colonies*, London 1843.

Portfolio 19/164. Letter 10 June 1847 from 'T.M.' Hobart Town, to Edward J. Scott re T.M.'s resignation from the Society in Van Diemen's Land.

Portfolio 25/67. Letter 22 Apr. 1907 from William Benson, Sydney, concerning the letters of Margaret Fox.

Portfolio 28/93. Copy of letter 1833 James Backhouse to John Cadbury.

Portfolio 30/72. Letter 1844 James Backhouse, York, concerning illustrations for his books on Australia and Africa.

Portfolio 40/70. Letter 28 Mar. 1908 C. H. Robey to C. J. Holdsworth, clerk of the Australasian Committee, concerning the *Australian Friend*.

Portfolio 42/80-3. Letters 1835-7 Daniel Wheeler, *Henry Freeling* and Sydney.

Manuscript Boxes

The series of Manuscript Boxes was begun between the two world wars in the first instance for single items or small collections. Manuscript boxes 14-28 comprise, in the main, papers accumulated by the Continental Committee and later by the

Australian Committee (afterwards Australasian and later still Australia and New Zealand Committee). Box 14 contains correspondence with Australia and New Zealand and is listed above under Epistles to and from Australia and New Zealand 1867-1909.

MS. box 1/9. 'The Days of our Fathers' by an Old Timer, an account of John Barton Hack of South Australia, typescript.

MS. box 2/4. Elizabeth B. Rutter, Account of Friends Hostel, Wellington.

MS. box 5. Nine letters 1888-1912 J. J. Neave to Francis and Felicia Hopkins, Rockhampton.

MS. box 5/23. Joseph Taylor, circular letters. Ten typed or duplicated letters written during a visit in 1911 to all Australian states and New Zealand, containing descriptions of places and Friends and including comments on the continual strikes and the successes of the Christian Scientists and Theosophists in Australia.

MS. box 15. Early twentieth century letters from Henrietta Brown and E. Maria Bishop to E. R. Ransome from many parts of Australia.
Six letters 1901 from Sarah Jane Lury to the Australia Committee during a religious visit to New Zealand.
E. Maria Bishop, journal and letters. Journal 1901-2, and thirty-four journal letters 1900-2 of a visit to all Australian states including description of landscape and local vegetation.
Tasmania, official correspondence and documents 1869-1900 including letters from F. Cotton, J. B. Cotton, J. B. Mather, and J. F. Mather.

MS. box 16. Letters 1880-90 from William and Katherine Jones to the Continental Committee written from Japan, United States of America, New Zealand, and Australia.
Letters 1910 from Charlotte Ransome, member of the Continental Committee.
Deputation to Australia 1874-5 papers, official and private letters from the Deputation, also a set of personal notes on Friends in Australia and New Zealand intended for 'private perusal' giving biographical information on Friends, e.g. the May family at Mount Barker, S.A.
E. R. Ransome papers relating to Australia and New Zealand including notes on the Friends' School, Hobart, the 1874-5 Deputation and the Australasian Committee 1906, also letters 1902, 1906 to C. J. Holdsworth.
Correspondence 1901-2 relating to the Australia General Meeting 1902 including letters from John Morland and Joshua Rowntree.
Melbourne General Meeting, official correspondence 1868-1902 with the Continental Committee.

MS. box 17. Alfred H. Brown correspondence and papers 1905-16. A. H. Brown visited Australia and New Zealand 1912-14 and returned to Hobart again in 1915. He sent back to London numerous reports on the general situation in Australia with particular reference to the peace testimony of Friends in relation to the Defence Acts and the Australian Freedom League. One report is entitled 'Japan-Australia-and New Zealand: report for English Friends, Australian and New Zealand Friends and peace workers' 1913. Other reports and much of his correspondence concern Friends' School, Hobart.
Edward A. Annett and A. M. Annett correspondence 1906-7. Over twenty-two letters written to the Australasian Committee during a religious visit to New Zealand. These are primarily of religious interest but contain some personal information about Friends in New Zealand.
Herbert and Mary Grace Corder, circular letters 1911. Letters, primarily of New

Zealand interest, to the Australasian Committee during a religious visit to Australia and New Zealand.

MS. box 18. Australian letters. South Australia 1868-1903; Sydney 1868-1904; Brisbane 1888-1902; use of the Melbourne Meeting House 1901.
Hobart Town Monthly Meeting, Minutes 1833-4, list of members.
Melbourne Meeting House, correspondence 1901.

MS. box 21. Friends' School, Hobart, correspondence and other papers 1870-1907 including correspondence relating to the school 1886-1902 with letters 1898-1900 of J. F. Hills.

MS. box 23. Friends' School, Hobart, deed of trust and specifications for extensions to buildings.

MS. box 24. New Zealand, official correspondence and documents 1870-1937 including notes and memoranda by Meeting for Sufferings and the Australia and New Zealand Committee concerning the Society in New Zealand, with information from New Zealand, lists of Friends in different provinces, epistles, circulars, and letters on the setting up of a Friends' School in New Zealand.
Rockhampton official correspondence 1875-1902 mainly letters by F. Hopkins, Friends' correspondent at Rockhampton. Subjects include the Deputation of 1874-5, possible immigration of South Russian Mennonites and Scandinavians, and the troubles of the Society in Brisbane.

MS. box 27. Australia and New Zealand, official papers 1874-1935, mainly lists of Friends with addresses including South Australia 1879, 1888-98, 1901; Brisbane 1888-1902; Sydney 1888, 1892, 1898-1900; Rockhampton 1901; Irish Friends in Australia 1899. Some lists include occupations and further notes and there is considerable biographical detail in R. P. King's notes on Sydney Friends 1886 and in Impressions of Deputation to Australasian Meetings 1933. Other documents include letter from T. S. Davy 1885 concerning T. Houston's visit to Australia; copy of a letter 1837 to Backhouse and Walker by a convict confined on Goat Island; printed pamphlets and papers concerning the opening of the new Friends' Meeting House, Auckland, 1913.
Tasmanian letters 1835-70.

MS. box 29. Charles J. Holdsworth collection. C. J. Holdsworth was clerk of the Australasian Committee 1906-14. His papers include letters from Friends in New Zealand, letters from English Friends relating to New Zealand, minutes of New Zealand Monthly Meetings, and cuttings from New Zealand papers.

Lettered Manuscript Boxes

The lettered series of manuscript boxes was created chiefly in the first decade of the twentieth century.

Box L. Certificate liberating Backhouse and Walker for service in New Holland, Van Diemen's Land, and South Africa 1831.

Box Q. Wellington, N.Z., Conference 1909. Autograph album together with circulars relating to the Conference.

Box R. List of Friends 1854. 'List of Friends and those connected with them in the Australian colonies, Van Diemen's Land, New Zealand and South Africa'. A manuscript note says 'Compiled by Robert Lindsey and Frederick Mackie'.
Letters Apr. 1834 to June 1840 G. W. Walker to G. Richardson from Hobart, Sydney, and South Africa, the last also referring to Australia. (In Richardson MSS. Miscellaneous letters vol.16 pp.57-63.)

Box T. Letters from Lucy Fryer Morland 1920. L. F. Morland made four visits to Australia, New Zealand and South Africa, and her circular letters linked Friends throughout the world.

Box W. E. R. Ransome, notes on the history of Friends in Australia and New Zealand 1910, giving sources of information on Australian meetings, organisation and very brief biographical notes.

Daniel Wheeler Collection

An inventory is in course of preparation. Two volumes contain letters, papers, and extracts from the journals of Daniel Wheeler, volume 2 covering his journeys with his son Charles 1833-7, visiting Australia and the South Seas in the *Henry Freeling*. The papers include a long series of informative letters from Charles Wheeler to his brothers and sisters in Russia. Printed items include engravings by Austin and Rodius, also engravings of Pacific Islands, many taken from Cook's voyages, maps of the Pacific, and contemporary newspapers including *Ke Kumu Hawaii* 1834-6, published by the Mission Press, Oahu. Among Daniel Wheeler's 'travelling minutes' in a 'Certificate Case' are birth certificates of his sons, certificate of his marriage to Jane Brady, certificates, some in Tahitian, authorising his travels in Australia and the Pacific. There is also a 'Daniel Wheeler South Sea Day Book' on the *Henry Freeling* covering the voyages from the departure from London Nov. 1833 to arrival in Sydney Feb. 1837, where the ship was sold. Barter transactions made during the voyages with London Missionary Society missionaries are recorded. Photocopies of two letters 1837 from Daniel Wheeler are in Photostat box and a letter 18 Mar. 1836 from Daniel Wheeler to William Manley is in MS. vol.101/66.

James Backhouse Collection

James Backhouse visited Australasia and South Africa during the years 1831-8, his companion being George Washington Walker, who subsequently settled in Hobart.

Letter Books: 1, 1831-5 (MS. vol.S48); 2, 1835-67 (MS. vol.57); 4, 1837-41 (MS. vol.S69); 5, 1841-68 (MS. vol.58).

Journal Letter Transcripts 1831-3, 2 vols. (temporary box 61/1).

Account Book 1831-40 (MS. vol.S355).

Correspondence 1831-56 (Case 101). Over eighty letters relate to Australia and include correspondence with the Colonial Office, letters to his mother and family, letters from Gov. Arthur, Maj. Bayliss and John Douglas, a statistical return of punishments at Macquarie Harbour 1826-32. Some letters concern the Aboriginal establishment at Flinders Island, other letters concern Daniel and Charles Wheeler, Alexander Macleay, Backhouse's visit to Norfolk Island and Port Phillip 1837-8. There are letters from Walker 1844, Maconochie 1844, Sturt 1848, Joseph May, Mount Barker, 1850, Fred Mackie from Norwich 1852 and Hobart 1857, Francis Cotton, V.D.L., 1853 describing his son's experiences at the gold diggings. The papers include a poem 'The Norfolk Island Exile' by a Prisoner.

Lindsey MSS.

Robert Lindsey of Brighouse, after nearly five years in America, visited Australasia with Frederick Mackie 1852-6. He returned to America and visited Australasia a second time in 1860-1, accompanied on this journey by his wife Sarah. Their journals, although primarily of religious interest, briefly describe people and places.

Australasian Itinerary 1852-5 (MS. vol.S228).

Memorandum Journal vol.10, 5 Oct. 1851 to 23 May 1856, containing a condensed account of the first Australasian journey (MS. vol.S240). Vol.15, Dec. 1859 to Jan.

London

1861, vol.16, Jan. 1861 to Apr. 1863, include descriptions of Hawaii and the Pacific voyage (MS. vols.S244-5).

Australasian Letters 1852-5 (MS. vols.S241-3).

Sarah Lindsey, 'American Memorandums', vols.3-4. Sarah Lindsey's letters home copied by members of her family (MS. vols.233-4).

Miscellaneous Personal Papers

William Benson, Journals, 7 vols. During 1866-8 W. Benson, with John and Charles Holdsworth and a tutor, Mr Bell, visited all the Australian colonies. This was not a religious visit although the young man had connections with members of the Society of Friends in every colony. They visited Sydney, Wollongong, Melbourne, Ballarat and other Victorian diggings, Hobart and various Tasmanian townships, and South Australia including Mount Gambier, Mount Barker, Mount Remarkable, Angaston, Port Augusta, and Adelaide. The descriptive journals are illustrated with sketches of buildings, e.g. Sydney University, Richmond Church, V.D.L., places, botanical and zoological specimens, and maps (MS. vols.S286-92).

Alfred Wright, 'Stones of Memorial', autobiography 1895, 3 vols. Wright was a member of the 1874-5 Deputation to Australia and his writings are primarily of religious interest. The voyage and the Deputation to Australia and New Zealand are described in vol.1, his second visit to Australasia in 1890-2 in vol.3 (MS. vols. S347-9).

Isaac Sharp MSS. Diaries, 105 vols. Vols.33-40, 1880-2, transcripts and vols.53-60, 1880-2, original manuscripts, relate to Sharp's religious visit to Australia, vols.61-2, 1882, and parts of vols.59 and 60 relate to New Zealand; accounts and receipts 1877-84 include a section on the visit to Australia and New Zealand 1880-2, accompanied by J. J. Neave, with related correspondence; letters to the Continental Committee during his travels; memo on journeys, 1884.

Gibson MSS., a collection of autographs including 'Plants named after Friends' (Gibson 4/57); letter 25 Mar. 1845 from John Tawell, Aylesbury, to H. C. Backhouse (Gibson 4/135).

Wilfrid E. Littleboy, journal letters written to his parents while travelling in Australia, 1909. The letters are numbered 1-30 (MS. vol.72).

Correspondence 1889-95 of J. H. Tuke concerning emigration to Australia and Canada (MS. vol.S254).

Correspondence mainly between Ann Fletcher Jackson and E. R. Ransome 1886-1905 (uncatalogued). Ann Fletcher Jackson and her husband Thomas settled in New Zealand in 1879. From then until her death in 1903 Mrs Jackson travelled extensively throughout New Zealand, visiting isolated Friends and groups, and corresponding regularly with E. R. Ransome, clerk of the Continental Committee, for thirty-three years. In 1888-9, accompanied by her son J. Fletcher Jackson, she paid a religious visit to all the Australian colonies except Western Australia. The majority of the letters are by A. F. Jackson or her son Fletcher. Besides providing information on the early Society and its members, the letters give a vivid account of day to day life in New Zealand. The letters from Australia (Mount Barker, Adelaide, Hobart, Sydney, Brisbane, Rockhampton, and Melbourne 1888-9) are confined more to Society affairs. A number of letters from A. F. Jackson expressing her anxieties at the state of the Society in Brisbane were destroyed at her request.

John Cadbury, Jnr. Four letters 1863-4 to E. and H. Newman. (Case 101. The vol. is called 'The Pritchard Letters, Henry Newman Letter Book'.) The letters include a long verse letter describing the voyage from Plymouth to Australia and letters from Berisland and Brisbane describing life in Australia.

MISS E. G. ROSS
37 Fitz-George Avenue, London, W.14

Collection of private papers of Admiral Sir James Clark Ross including:

Verses entitled 'To Captain Ross on the presentation to him of a Flag by a Lady previously to his departure for the South Pole'. The verses are signed 'E.G.' and the date '10th July 1839' is added in pencil.

Instructions from the Admiralty dated 14 Sept. 1839.

Three letters to Capt. J. C. Ross from Capt. F. R. M. Crozier with notes of the progress of observations. Two letters are written soon after leaving England [Oct.?] 1839 and 20 Nov. [1839]. The third letter 'Saturday Evg' [1840] implies arrival in the Antarctic, 'I think when we land on the Pack we should have some gruel with us in case of surf setting in'.

ROYAL AERONAUTICAL SOCIETY
4 Hamilton Place, London, W.1

LAWRENCE HARGRAVE PAPERS

Most of these papers were transferred to the Museum of Applied Arts and Sciences, Sydney, in Nov. 1963, but the Society retains a few papers relating to Hargrave, including two photograph albums and a packet of papers 1885-99 in Hargrave's hand, being papers read by him to the Royal Society of New South Wales.

ROYAL ANTHROPOLOGICAL INSTITUTE OF GREAT BRITAIN AND IRELAND
21 Bedford Square, London, W.C.1

The Royal Anthropological Institute was founded in 1843 as the Ethnological Society of London, which merged in 1871 with the Anthropological Society of London, formed in 1863, to become the Anthropological Institute of Great Britain and Ireland. The word 'Royal' was added in 1908. Application to consult any item should be made in writing to the Librarian. The catalogue of manuscripts consists of typescript descriptions, arranged numerically in folders, with index. Most of the manuscripts are unbound. There is also a catalogue of the collection of portraits and paintings, typescript. Papers connected with expeditions, if held by the Institute, are included in the catalogue of manuscripts. The Institute holds a manuscript bibliography of Dr A. C. Haddon.

MS.6. 'Vocabulary of the Aboriginal dialect called Wirradhurri spoken in the Wellington district . . . of New Holland collected by James Günther, 1839'.

MS.12. Grammar n.d. of the Binandele language, Mamba River, British New Guinea including Gouin exercises and translations and Binandele-English dictionary, Anon., mimeographed.

MS.25. 'Genealogies and histories of the Matanitu or tribal governments of central Viti Levu, Great Fiji, by Adolph B. Brewster, late Commissioner of Colo (Tholo), North and East Provinces, Fiji, 1923', typescript with illus., tables, and map. A holograph note by Sir Everard im Thurn 23 May 1937 on front endpaper reads: 'A. B. Brewster's ethnological notes on Fiji, thrown out from his book by the publisher and made up in book form for me, 25 Sept. 1923', see A. B. Brewster, *The Hill Tribes of Fiji*, London 1923.

MS.25A. Genealogies and histories of Matanitu or tribal governments of central

London

Viti Levu, Great Fiji. Original native documents 1890-5 and other manuscripts 1919-25.

MS.31. Tedi River tribes by Aliston Blyth 1922. Typescript carbon copy with letter 22 July 1922 from Blyth at Kokoda to A. R. Hinks of the Royal Geographical Society.

MS.34. Explanation of some of the Australian class names, the correlation of the classes and the relation between them and the languages, by John Mathew, Coburg, Vic., 1926, typescript. Tables, map, also letter 19 Oct. 1926 to the Secretary of the Royal Anthropological Institute with comments on the paper by M. Thomas.

MS.38. Aboriginal vocabulary, comprising the Ballarat, Bacchus Marsh, Melbourne, and Gippsland dialects with a selection of dialogues and familiar phrases, by Col. W. Champ, Pentridge 1862, 2 vols. Title on vol.2 reads 'Supplement to the aboriginal vocabulary, comprising the Mount Gambian and Wonnin dialects'. Includes Mitchell's vocabularies of words having the same meaning in different parts of Australia.

MS.90-8. Arthur Bernard Deacon collection. A. B. Deacon took a degree at Cambridge in 1925, after which he was appointed to the Anthony Wilkins travelling studentship to undertake anthropological investigation in the New Hebrides. He worked at Maleku, Fiji, in 1926 where he died 12 Mar. 1927. The papers consist of notebooks 1926-7, correspondence 1926, glossaries of native terms, genealogies, geometrical figures, linguistic notes, drawings, and miscellaneous notes by A. B. Deacon and Camilla H. Wedgwood. The genealogies and glossaries were compiled by C. H. Wedgwood from Deacon's notes c.1934. Manuscript and typescript.

MS.99. Notes and extracts collected by Leon Marillier on various topics including marriage customs in Polynesia, Melanesia, Australia, and Micronesia, and death customs in Tonga, Samoa, Hervey Islands, New Guinea, and Australia.

MS.116. Personal papers of Edward Horace Man including letter 27 Apr. 1891 from Rev. Edward Henry Thompson, Franklin, Tas., to his Uncle Harry, giving details of his parochial and other activities in Tasmania, with cutting about Man from a local Tasmanian paper.

MS.147. 'Notae ethnographicae', 1859-65, by John Barnard Davis. Includes list of ethnological objects collected by the late George Augustus Robinson and purchased from his widow 29 Mar. 1867, mainly of Tasmanian interest.

MS.157. 'Sex and custom'. Notes etc. by Joseph Daniel Unwin c.1913-14, arranged in 214 folders, many relating to Pacific Islanders, manuscript and typescript.

MS.159. English-native vocabulary of the Woolner dialect, Adelaide River, North Australia, by J. W. Ogilvie Bennett, Adelaide 1869. Published anonymously as *Vocabulary of the Woolner District Dialect*, Adelaide 1869, and reprinted in E. M. Curr, *The Australian Race*, London 1886.

MS.161. Ponape notes, Anon., n.d., 2 vols., including vocabulary, names of sea animals, and Ponape stories.

MS.165. Extracts from printed accounts of voyages of exploration in the Pacific in the 18th century.

MS.166. Bibliographical material in classified form collected by Robert Wood Williamson relating to Samoa and other Pacific Islands, with list of headings on folders by Miss M. Campbell. 76 drawers of folders.

MS.169. 'Aboriginals. Commonwealth Government's policy in respect of North and Central Australia. Memorandum sent by Mr Scullin, Premier of the Australian Commonwealth at the time of the Imperial Conference, 1930, in reply to representations from the Royal Anthropological Institute', mimeographed. See *Man* 92, May 1931, pp.84-6, 'A letter from the Prime Minister of the Commonwealth, the Rt. Hon. J. H. Scullin'.

MS.182. The Easter Island monuments and tablets by Rev. Francis A. Allan, 1904.

MS.184. Rites and customs of Australian Aborigines by Brab I. Purcell, Melbourne, 1893. Read before the Royal Geographical Society, Sydney, Jan. 1893.

MS.187. Notes on Aboriginal paintings discovered by Frederick S. Brockman while leading the North West Kimberley Exploring Expedition, W.A., 1901, typescript.

MS.189. Anthropological Institute of Great Britain and Ireland, Wellcome Medal. 1938. The Aborigines of Arnhem Land and the problems of administration, by D. F. Thomson, typescript carbon copy. Bound with it are Report of expedition to Arnhem Land, Northern Territory of Australia, typescript, and *Recommendations of policy in native affairs in the Northern Territory of Australia*, Canberra 1938. 1958. An adjustment movement in Arnhem Land, Northern Territory of Australia, by Ronald Murray Berndt, Perth 1958, typescript carbon copy with illus., diags., and bibl.

MS.205. Register of objects from the Pacific in geographical order, by James Edge-Partington, 1896. Some of the objects were reproduced in *An Album of the Weapons, Tools, Ornaments . . . of the Natives of the Pacific Islands* issued for private circulation by J. Edge-Partington and Charles Heape, Manchester 1890-8.

MS.207. Genealogies of Samoan families, Samoan Affairs Office, Pago Pago 1956, typescript carbon copy. A note attached reads 'These genealogies were found in longhand script in the files of the Department of Education in Pago Pago, American Samoa, during 1955. It is believed that they may have formed part of a manuscript draft by William Churchill. This typescript copy is one of four prepared in 1956 by the Samoan Affairs Office in Pago Pago . . .'

MSS.219-40. Anthropological and other papers of Sir Everard Ferdinand im Thurn, Lieutenant Governor and Colonial Secretary Ceylon 1901-4 and Governor of Fiji and High Commissioner of the Western Pacific 1904-10. Most of the papers deal with Fiji and include:
MS.219. Diary Sept. 1904-10, typescript with manuscript and printed insertions.
MS.220. Correspondence with A. B. Brewster and related papers on Fiji 1913-23, manuscript and typescript carbon copies.
MS.221. Correspondence with Bolton Glanvil Corney 1916, 1919-22 concerning the early history of Fiji, manuscript and typescript carbon copies.
MS.222. B. Glanvil Corney's notebooks containing manuscript extracts from newspapers and journals, including the *Sydney Gazette*, and from original documents concerning trade and shipping in the Pacific, especially Fiji.
MSS.223-37. Miscellaneous papers consisting of notes by im Thurn and others, printed Parliamentary papers, pamphlets, extracts from newspapers and journals, including the *Sydney Gazette* 1802-29, mainly relating to Fiji but also dealing with other Pacific Islands, voyages in the Pacific, Thaddeus von Bellingshausen, Capt. David Porter, and the U.S. frigate *Essex*, and including, in MS.229, typescript copies of letters 1865-6 from Robert G. W. Herbert, first Premier of Queensland, to his family in England.
MS.240. Warrant, K.B.E. and other documents including address from the Municipal Council of Suva on the retirement of im Thurn as Governor and Commander-in-Chief, Fiji, and admission, M.A., University of Sydney 1914.

MS.241. Dieri legends (South Australia) collected and edited by H. K. Fry, typescript with manuscript corrections, annotations, and sketches.

MS.243. Pencil sketches of animals and plants by school boys at Lakemba, Fiji, 1911.

MS.254. 'Some modern Maoris: a review discussion'. Summary of a paper communicated to the Maori Research Conference, May 1953, by Alice Joan Metge, Auckland University College, Department of Anthropology, mimeographed.

MS.255. 'Urbanisation and the pattern of Maori life': text of a paper delivered by Alice J. Metge at the 8th New Zealand Science Congress held in Auckland, May 1954, mimeographed.

MS.256. 'The urban Maori': an address delivered by Alice J. Metge to the Anthropology and Maori Race Section of the Auckland Institute and Museum, Oct. 1953, mimeographed.

MS.261. Genealogies compiled by Brenda Zara Seligman including British New Guinea, Keita, and Lambeth genealogies and Massim and Mekeo (New Guinea) genealogies, 6 vols.

Uncatalogued. Papers of Vice-Admiral Henry Boyle Townsend Somerville. In 1889-96 Somerville took part in hydrographic surveying service in Australia and the Western Pacific and in 1897-1900 in the Eastern Pacific Ocean in H.M.S. *Egeria*. See his 'Songs and specimens of the language of New Georgia, Solomon Islands . . . with introductory notice of Melanesian and New Georgia songs by S. H. Ray', reprint from *Journal of the Anthropological Institute*, May 1897, London 1897.

Vice-Admiral Somerville bequeathed his archaeological MSS. to the Institute. He was particularly interested in orientation in ancient monuments and it is likely that some papers relating to the Pacific area may be found among the MSS.

Portraits and paintings include five water-colours of Tasmanian Aborigines by Thomas Bock, and an oil-painting of a group of natives of Tasmania by R. Dowling, the heads copied from portraits by Bock. There is also a plaster bust of a female native of Tasmania entitled: 'Truganinny wife of Woureddy by B.I.M. [B. I. Murray?] Hobart 1836'. H. L. Roth, *The Aborigines of Tasmania*, Halifax 1899, p.xviii mentions busts of both Woureddy and Truganinny in the Institute but no bust of Woureddy can be traced. See *Journal of the Royal Anthropological Institute*, 1961, 91-2, pp.223-4, N. J. B. Plomley, 'Tasmanian Aboriginal material in collections in Europe'.

ROYAL ARTILLERY INSTITUTION
Woolwich, London, S.E.18

The Library of the Royal Artillery Institution is a private one. All inquiries should be addressed to the Secretary. The proceedings of the Institution 1858-98 have been published as *Minutes of Proceedings of the R.A.I.*, vols.1-25, continued 1899-1905 as *Proceedings of the R.A.I.*, vols.26-32, and 1905 to date as *Journal of the R.A.I.*, vol.32- . There are card catalogues to the manuscript material and military documents.

M/MS/295. Report and notes 1843 on the coast and harbours of the middle and southern islands of New Zealand by Capt. W. M. Smith, with covering letter. The result of an expedition of exploration Sept.-Nov. 1842 when in the employ of the New Zealand Company. See *Minutes of Proceedings of the R.A.I.*, p.21.

MS/119. Australian Corps Heavy Artillery, operations from 8 Aug. to 18 Sept. 1918, by Major J. N. Kennedy. Typescript with maps, 2 vols.

MS/271. Cutting, *New Zealand Herald*, 12 Nov. 1960, giving an account of the battle of Rangariri 1863, with covering letter 1 Feb. 1961 from Mrs Nona Morris.

The Library also has a number of rare printed books relating to the military history of Australia and New Zealand.

ROYAL COLLEGE OF SURGEONS OF ENGLAND
Lincoln's Inn Fields, London, W.C.2

The manuscripts are listed by Victor G. Plarr, *A Catalogue of Manuscripts in the Library of the Royal College of Surgeons of England*, London 1928. The arrangement is alphabetical in one series covering authors, subjects, and titles of documents. The Librarian's copy is interleaved with additions and amendments. There is no other finding aid to the manuscripts. The portraits, paintings and drawings are described by William LeFanu, *A Catalogue of the Portraits, and other Paintings, Drawings and Sculpture in the Royal College of Surgeons of England*, Edinburgh & London 1960.

The Hunterian Collection of paintings contains a portrait of Omai, unsigned and undated, but attributed to William Hodges, R.A., reproduced in A. Bury, *Antiques Review*, 1954 no.7 fig.11. The Hunterian Museum also contains a number of specimens some of which come from Australia. Others were destroyed with much else, during the 1939-45 War.

For manuscripts relating to Charles Darwin's voyage in the *Beagle*, which belong to the Royal College of Surgeons, see The Darwin Memorial, Down House, Downe, Nr Orpington, Kent.

Cab.VIII 1(a). Folder of letters to Richard Owen arranged alphabetically by author includes the following:

Edward Samuel Picard Bedford, parsonage, Hobart, 7 Feb. 1835 sending Echidna, Platypus, Native Cats, and a few specimens of Mollusca, with comments.

C. G. Cotton, St John's College, Bishop's Auckland, N.Z., 29 Feb. 1846 concerning specimens of Kiwi from Hokianga and mentioning that 'the disturbed state of this Country has long ago turned the thoughts of the Natives away from such pursuits', i.e. collecting specimens.

[?] Gregory, Melbourne, 30 July 1842 concerning specimens.

James Everard Home, jnr, Wellington, 21 Feb. 1847 concerning the preservation of specimens in spirits; Wellington, 6 May 1847 sending an account of the habits of the worm called Palolo in the Navigator's Islands 'as I received it from the missionaries at Upolu'; Wellington, 13 May 1847 concerning the great perch from New Zealand.

W. Gilchrist Whitson, 24 Mar. 1837 about instructions for bringing home specimens from New Holland.

Ronald C. Gunn, Launceston, 23 Nov. 1843 about specimens sent.

Edmund Hobson, n.d., asking whether the zoological features of Van Diemen's Land differ from those of New Holland sufficiently to render the appointment of a naturalist to that island important in the illustration of the natural history of that part of the world, and mentioning his brother at Port Phillip who had sent a cask of animals from that part of New Holland.

Cab.VIII 1(b). Letters and papers to Richard Owen from George Bennett.* General account of specimens of comparative anatomy and natural history collected and presented to the Museum of the College by George Bennett 17 May 1834, with a note by Richard Owen. The specimens include some from Australia, e.g. a new species of leech from ponds in the Yass Plains, N.S.W.

Notes on the habits of the spermaceti whale n.d.

Letters concerning his scientific pursuits and specimens of all kinds including whale, lyrebirds, flying fish 1833-9, chiefly written from Sydney but including 25 Aug. 1833 Singapore, 24 Feb. 1834 St Helena, 25 May 1835 at sea. In the letters 16 Aug. and 20 Oct. 1835 Bennett refers to his appointments in New South Wales.

275 H.5(33). 'List of Skeletons of Quadrupeds and Birds Collected by Mr. Gould during his expedition in Australia', n.d.; it includes one cranium of a native of the Western Coast, fifteen skeletons of mammalia, twenty-two crania of mammalia and one hundred and forty-one entire skeletons of birds, all named.

275 L.3(26). Notebook containing translation of letter from Rudolf von Willemoes-Suhm on the *Challenger*, Sydney, to Carl Theodor Ernst von Siebold, Apr. 1874. It describes the journey out to the Antarctic, the soundings taken, species found, and includes a description of the stay on Kerguelen Island. Printed in *Zeitschrift für wissenschaftliche Zoologie*, 24, 1874.

275 L.9. Official letters relating to the Museum, arranged chronologically; they include a letter 9 Jan. 1816 from Duncan Mackenzie sending a cranium of a native of New South Wales to be placed in the Museum, and a letter from the London Hospital asking for an account of appearances on the inspection of the body of Terah Poo, the Otaheitan. With copy reply sent 6 Aug. 1816 by William Clift.

276 G.46. Copy of Dr George Shaw's Catalogue of part of the Natural History Collection preserved in spirit, in the Hunterian Museum, 1806. This copy by William Clift has the note by him 'This Catalogue or list was made by Dr. Shaw while the Collection remained in Castle Street before its removal to Lincoln's Inn Fields'. The catalogue refers chiefly to Sir Joseph Banks's collections from New Holland.

276 J.54. Scientific correspondence in a portfolio so labelled; this includes a letter 25 June 1834 from Thomas Lloyd to Richard Owen concerning 'Marriner's account of his captivity in the Tonga Islands' containing an account of an enormous alligator which came ashore and destroyed many persons and animals.

The following items described in the catalogue could not be located in the College archives, Feb. 1969:

Photographs of original drawings of Tasmanian Aborigines by Alfred Bock in the Tasmanian Museum, Hobart, n.d. but pre-1891.

Engrossed letter n.d. from the Royal Australasian College of Surgeons.

ROYAL COMMONWEALTH SOCIETY
18 Northumberland Avenue, London, W.C.2

A typescript catalogue of manuscripts is maintained. Fuller descriptions of some items and collections appear in Library Notes, New Series No.1, Jan. 1957- , duplicated typescript.

MANUSCRIPTS ORIGINATING IN THE COURSE OF THE SOCIETY'S BUSINESS

Autographs I, routine correspondence preserved chiefly for the signatures. A second collection, Autographs II consists of signatures only. See Library Notes, N.S.126, June 1967.

Walter Frewen Lord Prize Essays. See Library Notes, N.S.47, 53, 68, Nov. 1960, May 1961, Aug. 1962. Winning essays, typescript. Subjects include the New Hebrides, imperial defence, and emigration, especially to New Zealand.

Library Talks. Library talks commenced in February 1958. The majority have been recorded on tape and typescript transcripts made. A list of talks 1958 to July 1962 is given in Library Notes, N.S.68, Aug. 1962. In the typescript Catalogue of Manuscripts the list is continued to 1969.

Royal Commonwealth Society

Papers printed in the *Proceedings of the Royal Colonial Institute* are not listed here and copies or transcripts of manuscripts held elsewhere are omitted. Some papers not listed may contain material of marginal interest to this survey, e.g. the papers of Sir George Arthur relating chiefly to Honduras. Other material omitted below consists of drawings, maps and photographs, e.g. Australian natural history paintings intended as bookmarks sold by John Sands (MSS.8) see Library Notes, N.S.120, Dec. 1966; Browne, two sketches of diggings (MSS.8); J. M. Cantle, fifteen water-colours of Australian birds (MSS.8); S. T. Gill, water-colour of a native sepulchre near Missunga Plains, 8 May 1842 (MSS.8) see Library Notes, N.S.9, Sept. 1957, also two sepia paintings of the Flinders Ranges, S.A. (MSS.82); Maj.-Gen. H. G. Robley, drawings and photographs of Maoris (MSS.89); Map of New Holland as explored by Captain Cook (MSS.8); Map of Port Phillip 1836 (MSS.87); Sir Henry A. Wickham, sketch for a chart of the Conflict Group, east of New Guinea (MSS.9).

MSS.11 General

Angas, G. F. Letter 18 Jan. 1869 to S. W. Silver, interested in working as an illustrator for Cassell's *Illustrated Travel.*

Eddy, C. W. Colonies in their commercial relation to the mother-country, 1870, with press cuttings.

Gourley, W. C. Two essays: 'A great contrast in colonisation (Anglo-Saxon *v.* German) Feb. 1926', and 'The United Kingdom & Dominions Representation Delegation system', 1913, revised 1926, typescript.

Grey, H., 3rd Earl. Note on Australian bishops, apparently for a speech *c.*1847 with notes on transportation; also notes on transportation of convicts to the colonies 1847-9, relevant to the first chapter of Grey's *Colonial Policy of Lord John Russell's Administration*, II, London 1853, probably working notes for writing this book.

Harding, Sir Edward John. A folder containing letters 1912-17, see Library Notes N.S.115, 117, 119, 121, 123, 125, 127, July, Sept., Nov. 1966, Jan., Mar., May, July 1967. Letters on pp.49-214 cover Australia and New Zealand during Harding's tour as Secretary to the Royal Commission on the Natural Resources. The tour returned via Pago Pago and Hawaii.

Imperial Conferences 1897, 1926. Autographs of delegates to and officials at the 1897 Conference and photograph of the official group 1926, signed by the seven Prime Ministers.

Rainbow, A. E. Developments in colonial status in the British Empire 1900-22, typescript, 1923.

Shelton, P. H., Montreal. Greater Britain, 1954-6, typescript.

Smith, Col. F. H. Papers on migration and imperial defence, typescript and manuscript.

MSS.11c99 General, Biography

Childers Papers. Thirteen boxes of papers with calendar. The papers refer mainly to Childers's political career in England and to members of his family, especially his younger son Rowland, see N.R.A. Report 11163 which arranges the papers in twenty-eight sections including:

6. Diaries of H. C. E. Childers 1847-50, 1860-7, 10 vols. 6/2 journal 1850 of his voyage to Melbourne.

8. Diaries of Emily, née Walker, wife of H. C. E. Childers, 8 vols., 1852-69 with gaps, but including 1852, 1853, 1855-6 relating to her life in Victoria.

London

16-18. Rowland Childers papers including at 18 over one hundred letters 1878-86 from Victoria written by R. Childers or by other correspondents. Some of R. Childers's letters are about sheep farming and with them is a map of Yanko Station, Jerilderie, N.S.W., 1880.

Dunn Papers. See Library Notes, N.S.49, Jan. 1961. Papers of E. J. Dunn, geologist including autobiography and autobiographical notes, among which are summary notes on 'Men I have Met', R. O'Hara Burke, von Mueller, T. Baines, and others; some miscellaneous correspondence with a letter of reminiscences 1911 from S. B. J. Skertchly and two letters 1929 and 1930 from James Park, Otago; printed items and a folder of photographs, chiefly portraits and photographs of the interior of Dunn's house 'Roseneath', Kew, Vic.

Frome Collection. Photographs of paintings and drawings including water-colours and pen and pencil drawings of South Australia. The originals are in the Art Gallery of South Australia, Adelaide.

Young Papers. Papers with card index by Ethel Young and nine letters. The Library also has Miss Young's 'A Patriarch of Empire, the Memoir of Sir Frederick Young, K.C.M.G.', typescript, based on the Young Papers. The collection of papers includes a letter 1 June 1871 from Florence Nightingale, typescript copy, which discusses the benefits of state aided colonisation and is reproduced in full in Library Notes, N.S.114, June 1966.

MSS.8 Australia

Australian letters 1834-5 chiefly to Alexander Macleay. Six letters including letters from J. T. Gellibrand, Hobart, J. O. Clunie, Moreton Bay, and T. P. McQueen, Segenhoe. For the two letters from J. O. Clunie see Library Notes, N.S.142, Oct. 1968.

Backhouse, J., and Walker, G. W. Four reports 1833-5 on Port Arthur, incomplete, Flinders Island and Norfolk Island, probably contemporary copies.

Bell, W. Notes on the *Eucalyptus globulus* or Australian Blue Gum Tree, *c.*1873 or 1874 with covering letters to C. W. Eddy, Royal Colonial Institute.

Bonwick, J. 'The Writing of Colonial History', typescript with manuscript corrections. Lecture given to the Royal Colonial Institute 26 Mar. 1895. Summary published in *Procs. Roy. Col. Inst.* 26, 1894-5. Transcribed without the introductory remarks on history in general, in Library Notes, N.S.111, 112, Mar., Apr. 1966.

Convict Transportation Documents 1839-43. See Library Notes, N.S.39, Mar. 1960. Eight documents, printed forms completed in manuscript. Some items microfilmed 1960 for the Tasmanian State Archives. The documents are lists of convicts on the *Barossa* 1839, *Margaret* 1842, and *Lord Petre* 1843; also charter parties and lists of stores for the *Margaret* and *Lord Petre*.

Crichton family. Letters 1823-48. Box containing forty-four letters of members of the Crichton family, James Crichton of Thorn, Blairgowan, Perthshire (d.1844) and his four sons John, Robert, James, and William, and his daughter Anne. Letters 28-44, 1841-8, are mainly from or about Australia to which several members of the family emigrated and engaged in sheep grazing. See Library Notes, N.S.147, 8, Mar., Apr. 1969, 151, July 1969. There is also a volume of typed transcripts of the letters and miscellaneous material not transcribed consisting of letters, biographical cuttings, and photographs.

Despard, Maj.-Gen. H. Letter book 1846-54, see Library Notes, N.S.70, Oct. 1962. Over 300 letters dealing mainly with regimental affairs and written while Despard was Colonel Commanding the 99th Regiment in Sydney 1846-8, Hobart 1848-54 and on special duties to keep order on the Victorian goldfields 1853.

Fitzgerald, S. C. Unpublished novel, 'Madeline Blake', typescript.

Frome, E. C. Two rough pencil sketches of plans of Government Houses in Sydney and Hobart with brief descriptions.

General Association for the Australian Colonies. Minute Book, etc. 1855-62. The volume is prefaced by a printed article by J. S. O'Halloran, 'Reminiscences of the Australian Association' from *Colonies and India* 1884, and contains minutes, correspondence, printed reports, and other publications. In the back is a list of names and addresses of members.

Gordon, A. L. 'Argemone'. Manuscript copy of poem, 1869, unpublished until F. M. Robb's edition of Gordon's *Poems* in 1912; also introductory notes by a contemporary, initialled 'W.N.', n.d.

Gyles, T. B. 'The pioneer: prelude and story . . . by "Tom", Benson Gyles'. A long epic on the discovery and growth of Australia and several shorter poems. Also personal correspondence with Col. Archer Crust.

Murdoch Family. Papers of Peter Murdoch and G. B. Murdoch. The papers of P. Murdoch include 'Journal of the Commissioners for the Survey and Valuation of Crown Lands in Van Diemen's Land' 8 Apr. to 8 Dec. 1826 in which the entries are in places somewhat fuller than those for the same period in the official copy of the Journals in the Tasmanian State Archives, see *Journals of the Land Commissioners for Van Diemen's Land 1826-28*, ed. Anne McKay, Hobart 1962. Other papers are connected with P. Murdoch's administration at Emu Plains and the convict system in general. There are also deeds of various dates 1837-63 mentioning his property in Van Diemen's Land. The papers of G. B. Murdoch include three receipts 1880-9 for payment on shares in companies in Australia and printed documents concerning coal mining and railways in New South Wales. See Library Notes, N.S.157, 8, Jan., Feb. 1970.

Simpson, D. H. 'The Portraiture of Tasman, a survey of alleged likenesses of the navigator and discoverer in the Royal Commonwealth Society and elsewhere', 1965, typescript. Includes photographs, documents, and correspondence. See Library Notes, N.S.52, Apr. 1961. Copies, without illustrations and documents, in the National Library of Australia, the Mitchell Library, Sydney, and the Alexander Turnbull Library, Wellington, N.Z.

Smith, J., Melbourne, Vic. On the land legislation of the Australian colonies, 1872.

Townend, G. P. and Smith, R. S. Monumental inscriptions in Australia, typescript. Transcriptions 1913-22 of headstones in cemeteries in New South Wales and Victoria.

Westall, W. The original drawings executed during Flinders's surveys 1801-3 are now in the National Library of Australia. For an illustrated and annotated catalogue see *Drawings by William Westall*, ed. T. M. Perry and D. H. Simpson, London 1962, and Library Notes, N.S.103, July 1965. The Society has photographs of drawings and paintings not reproduced in its 1962 volume. These are mounted in an album with portraits and photographs of a bust of Westall. It also has a letter 26 June 1810 from Westall to the Secretary of the Admiralty complaining of the unwillingness of the Admiralty to purchase a third painting of Australia, view of Cape Townsend.

Wilmoth, L. J. John Gardiner, pioneer and overlander, typescript, 1936, with portraits and inserted manuscript copies of documents: letter 13 Nov. 1835 G. F. Storey to Dr Pilkington on the alleged poisoning of Edward Eagle, Mrs Gardiner's brother; Mary Gardiner's account of a voyage from Sydney to Port Phillip, Mar. 1837, from the original in the possession of William Austin, Croydon, Vic.; copy of original deed in possession of Canon P. St. J. Wilson, Brighton, Vic., granting land in Morven, V.D.L., to John Smith 30 June 1823.

M

London

MSS.81 Western Australia

The Observer, Fremantle, W.A. No.3, Sat. 19 May 1832, edited by Charles Macfaull. Apparently an unique copy, see Library Notes, N.S.107, 109, Nov. 1965, Jan. 1966.

Viveash, S. W. Diary 1838-51, typescript prepared by Canon A. Burton with introduction and index. Some extracts are quoted in Canon Burton, 'Life on the Swan 85 years ago', *Western Australian Historical Society Journal*, 1, pt.2, 1928.

Wollaston, J. R. Diaries 1840-56, 3 vols., typescript, arranged with additional material and indexed by Canon A. Burton. Two of the journals have been published, *Wollaston's Picton Journal*, Perth 1948; *Wollaston's Albany Journal*, Perth 1954.

MSS.82 South Australia

Burr, T. 'Classified list of Minerals discovered in the Province of South Australia to the close of the year 1844 . . . To which is subjoined a summary of the geology of the located districts'. The Library also has Burr's manuscript 'On the Interior', a physical description of South Australia 14 Dec. 1842.

Gouger, R. Papers, including documents showing appreciation of Gouger's services in South Australia, see Library Notes, N.S.65, May 1962. There is also correspondence 1952 concerning the Old Gum Tree, Glenelg. The Society also has a pencil sketch by Mary Hindmarsh of Gouger's temporary residence 1836-7, see Library Notes, N.S.9, Sept. 1957 and a pencil sketch by J. M. Skipper of the 'Proclamation Tree'.

South Australia Land Grant 1839, parchment copy of original grant 'No.382' accompanied by a sketch map of the property with authenticating declarations 1875, grantees G. F. Angas and H. Kingscote of London and J. R. Todd of Middlesex.

South Australian Company. Summary of report 1879 on the Company's farm lands, lithograph with map.

South Australian maps, some manuscript. Eight maps and plans 1838-42 including Sturt's examination of the country to the north of Adelaide, with descriptive notes 1838 and Sketch of Encounter Bay by B. T. Finniss, Apr. 1838. There are also sixteen coloured maps showing blocks of land sold and a 'Rough Sketch of the Settled Portions of the Province of South Australia . . . quite inaccurate. A copy permitted to be made for Mr. Morphett solely for his own use . . . 1842'.

MSS.84 New Guinea

Album containing thirty-nine photographs, some panorama, taken Nov. 1884 when Commodore Erskine proclaimed the British Protectorate. Nine illustrations in Charles Lyne, *New Guinea*, London 1885, are poorly reproduced from or based on the same originals.

MSS.85 Queensland

Price C. Vocabulary of the Coonambella tribe written in an exercise book. An introductory note dated 1885, Townsville, refers to James Morrel, a 'sailor boy' who was shipwrecked and lived among the Aborigines for fifteen years, also to others who had opportunities of learning the Aboriginal dialect.

Roth, Henry Ling. Papers on North Queensland exploration relating to the Pioneer River 1862 and the Mackay District *c*.1877.

MSS.86 New South Wales

Darling Papers. Extract from the Governor's Instructions under the Sign Manual 17 July 1825, contemporary copy; Minute 96 of the Executive Council 10 Oct. 1831 authorising the establishment of a public library, signed 'R. Darling', contemporary copy; Order convening a meeting of the Executive Council at Sydney, 17 Mar. 1836.

Lang, Rev. J. D. Letter 30 Jan. 1826, Sydney, to Affleck Moodie concerning a quarrel with Commissary General Wemyss over the building of a Scots Church, possibly contemporary copy.

Oxley, J. 'Journal of a second expedition into the interior or terra incognita of New South Wales for purposes of tracing the source of the Macquarie River' 30 May to 5 Nov. 1818, with Oxley's signature. Also diary of Mr Evans 8-18 July, signed G. W. Evans. Official copies given to the Society by the Colonial Office in 1915. Published, with only trifling differences, J. Oxley, *Journals of Two Expeditions*, London 1820.

MSS.87 *Victoria*

Ballarat Anti-Convict Petition *c.*1864, 1 roll. 'Address from the Women of Ballarat and Ballarat East in the Colony of Victoria to the Women of England'. See Library Notes, N.S.59, Nov. 1961.

Brassey, T., 1st Earl. Trade and resources of Victoria. Address delivered before the London Chamber of Commerce 7 June 1898, typescript.

Fawkner, J. P. Letter 2 May 1836, Pascoevale, Port Phillip, to Alexander Simen of the *Caledonia*. Refers to Collins's visit to Port Phillip in 1803, describes the proceedings of the settlement in 1835 and its bright prospects. Possibly a contemporary copy.

First judicial decision given in Victoria, 2 May 1836, facsimile copy. A series of petty disputes between Batman and Fawkner.

MSS.88 *Tasmania*

Hull, H. M. 'The Aborigines of Tasmania', n.d., probably *c.*1873. See Library Notes, N.S.91, July 1964.

Woolley, C. A. Three prints of photographs of the last Tasmanian Aborigines from negatives taken in 1866.

MSS.89 *New Zealand*

'Among the Maoris'. Unsigned journal 1898-9 of a visit by an English woman to the tribal areas, North Island, N.Z., typescript with water-colours and photographs.

Armour, presentation to Maori Chief 1836, delivery form and receipt 4 Nov. 1837, signed with Patuone's mark. See Library Notes, N.S.110, Feb. 1966.

Hocken, T. M. Letter 10 May 1890, Dunedin, to S. Edwards regarding a Maori name for the town of Gore, N.Z.

'Parakaia te Pouepa', report in Maori of a meeting of Chiefs 1861 at Otaki to discuss setting up a Maori king, most chiefs being in favour of Col. T. G. Browne as Queen Victoria's representative, xerox copy of original in possession of Miss Alice B. Adams, Exmouth, Devon.

Wakefield, E. G. Three letters 1849 to G. F. Young, M.P.; also a printed prospectus of the Society for the Reform of Colonial Government. See Library Notes, N.S.105, Sept. 1965.

Young, G. F. Four letters to colonists in New Zealand 1842-6: 13 Nov. 1842, 22 Mar. 1846 to James Kelham, 13 Nov. 1842 to Henry St Hall, 13 Nov. 1842 to Capt. Arthur Wakefield, typescript copies.

MSS.9 *Pacific*

Albemarle Family. Pacific album 1899. Contains photographs of Government House, Sydney, and a photographic record of a South Sea cruise in 1899, apparently on S.S. *Waikare*. The Samoan photographs include two pictures of R. L. Stevenson and some record of military operations there in 1899. The album also contains various manuscript notes and signatures of Tongan and Samoan notabilities.

Alfred, barque, log 1828-9 of a whaling voyage leaving Port Jackson 11 Sept. 1828. Some time was spent off Malaita, Solomon Is., returning via Santa Cruz Islands and Tikopia.

Cantrell, E. G. Recollections; also typed transcript of Malayan portion with notes. From 1910-14 Cantrell was in Samoa where he went to teach tapping and curing to Chinese labourers on the Aleisa Estate. The forty pages relating to this part of his life give information on the Chinese community in Samoa, and on relations with the German settlers. See Library Notes, N.S.98, 99, Feb., Mar. 1965.

Powell Papers. See Library Notes, N.S.64, 66, Apr., June 1962. W. Powell travelled extensively in the Pacific as a young man and explored New Britain 1877-80. In 1885 he became Consul for the Navigator's Islands and Deputy Commissioner for the Western Pacific. In 1888 he was appointed Consul at Stettin whence he attended a conference on Samoa at Berlin, Apr.-June 1889. His Pacific papers include documents on his consular appointments, papers connected with his travels 1873-80, among which is a copy of a contract to take George Turner to New Guinea to collect botanical specimens for the Sydney Botanical Gardens, a memo on the Powell Trading Association Ltd, correspondence and cuttings on the annexation of New Guinea and on his book *Wanderings in a Wild Country*, London 1883, letters and reports chiefly on Samoa 1885-6 with which are several letters 1886 from Thurston. There is also an album of Powell's photographs, many of Pacific interest.

Welchman, Dr and Brittain, Rev. A. H. Album of views of Melanesia with manuscript list of contents. The photographs were taken on a tour of Melanesia by Bishop Henry Hutchinson Montgomery in 1892 when Bishop Selwyn was ill. Bishop Montgomery's *The Light of Melanesia*, London 1896, describes the tour and mentions that some 120 photographs were taken by Dr Welchman, Rev. Brittain, and himself.

MSS.91 Fiji

Riaz, T. D. Letters 1962-5 and photographs of Fiji including letters concerning graves on Korowaga Hill, with some biographical information on those buried there; photographs and letter describing Riaz's experiment in the production of wheat in Fiji 1948 and 1965; photograph of monument to a cannibal chief, with descriptive note by Riaz.

Original paintings and photographs

Besides the drawings listed under Manuscript Collection, the Society holds a small collection of paintings among which are water-colours of Fiji, New Zealand views, and views of Anzac positions at Gallipoli. In 1969 a collection of albums of photographs was found, the photographs almost certainly connected with the work of A. H. Fisher for the Visual Instruction Committee of the Colonial Office. Vols. XXIV and XXIX contain Australian photographs, vols.XXVI-XXVIII New Zealand, and vol.XXVII an incomplete series of Pacific Islands photographs. See Library Notes, N.S.149, 150, May, June 1969.

ROYAL ENTOMOLOGICAL SOCIETY OF LONDON
41 Queen's Gate, London, S.W.7

Bona fide students and inquirers may use the Library on application to the Registrar of the Society. There are no printed lists or catalogues but card indexes arranged alphabetically by author, to correspondence and manuscripts do exist. The manuscripts, which have no references, include those listed below.

Documents relating to Commander James John Walker, R.N., M.A., F.L.S., President of the Royal Entomological Society 1919-20:

Narrative journal Feb. 1890 to July 1893 of the surveying voyage of H.M.S. *Penguin*, 3 vols. bound together. The journal deals mainly with entomological and natural history subjects at the various stopping places which include Darwin, Baudin Island, Roebuck Bay, Abrolhos Islands, Fremantle, Perth, Hobart, Williamstown, Melbourne, Adelaide, Albany, Dampier Archipelago, Cossack, and Holothuria Reef.

'Entomological notebook kept during a voyage', n.d. It is not a complete or continuous account of the voyage, the text being in three sections covering Port Said to Colombo, Colombo to Bigge Island, and Baudin Island to Fremantle. Some general remarks on the voyage are included. From internal evidence it appears to relate to the voyage of H.M.S. *Penguin* 1890-3.

'Australian journal and observations on natural history', Dec. 1899 to July 1902, 1 vol. The volume is labelled 'H.M.S. Ringarooma' but it is clear from the journal that Walker travelled out in the P.&O. ship *Oceana* via the Cocos Islands, King George Sound, and Albany, Adelaide, and Melbourne arriving Sydney 9 Feb. 1900. In Sydney he was stationed on H.M.S. *Katoomba* and H.M.S. *Royal Arthur*. The journal gives detailed descriptions of his many expeditions in search of entomological and botanical specimens in Australia, particularly in the vicinity of Sydney, in the New Hebrides, and in New Zealand.

ROYAL GEOGRAPHICAL SOCIETY
Kensington Gore, London, S.W.7

Access to the archives and library of the Society is normally restricted to Fellows. Requests for information should be addressed to the Director. For the history of the Society see H. R. Mill, *The Record of the Royal Geographical Society 1830-1930*, London 1930, and C. R. Markham, *The Fifty Years' Work of the Royal Geographical Society*, London 1881 (also published in *Journal of the Royal Geographical Society*, vol.L, 1880). Organisation of the archives is proceeding and a card index is being prepared listing names of persons and geographical areas occurring in the correspondence and miscellaneous papers.

MINUTE BOOKS

Permission to consult the Minute Books must be obtained from the Director.

Council Minutes Oct. 1830 to Mar. 1947, 23 vols. with Index Vols.1-17.

Committee Minute Books Mar. 1841 to Mar. 1956, some early vols. missing; Minutes of Evening Meetings Nov. 1930 to May 1941. Raleigh Club and The Geographical Club (predecessors of the Royal Geographical Society), Minute Books and papers 1826-30.

LETTER BOOKS

Letter books 1841-1916 including Antarctic letter book Oct. 1899 to Sept. 1902.

CORRESPONDENCE

In-letters 1831-1920 arranged in chronological blocks, within which letters are filed alphabetically. There are also several separate series including Antarctic expeditions, Great Barrier Reef Expedition, papers of Sir Clements R. Markham.

OBSERVATION FILES

Geographical, meteorological, and astronomical observations, longitude tables, etc., contributed by explorers and seamen and including, e.g. observations from

London

S.S. *Antarctic*, observations by Dr W. M. Strong in New Guinea 1905-6, and observations by Michael Terry in Central Australia 1928. These are often related to correspondence in the correspondence files and/or papers in the Journal MSS.

MISCELLANEOUS PAPERS

Some of these are called 'Library MSS.', 'Museum Drawer', 'Library Cases'.

Corney, B. Glanvil. Papers, some printed. Manuscripts include 'side lights on an incident in Capt. Cook's first voyage of circumnavigation', a notebook containing a Fijian vocabulary for medical officers and some Easter Island material.

James, E. A. Fifteen journals 1900-34, including 'World Tour 1925-6' with printed and water-colour illustrations; 'World Tour 1929-30', vols.1-2 New Zealand and Fiji; 'Around the Southern Hemisphere 1934', 2 vols.

National Antarctic Expedition 1901. Box files *c.*1898-1903 containing loose papers and correspondence relating to the organisation and personnel of the expedition including Capt. Scott's reports and material relating to *Morning* and *Discovery*, cuttings, and rough minute book of the Antarctic Expedition Committee 13 July 1900.

Routledge, Scoresby. Papers and manuscripts relating to Easter Island; also logs of the Expedition Yacht *Mana*, Southampton to the South Pacific Islands 20 Feb. 1913 to 31 July 1916. On loan.

Library MSS.

Alexander, C. B. A white and coloured policy for a new Australian state in north and north-western Australia, typescript; also correspondence with the Royal Geographical Society Oct.-Nov. 1939.

British Graham Land Expedition, receipts and payments account from the inception of the expedition to 2 Nov. 1938.

British Ornithologists' Union Expedition to New Guinea 1908-11, Leader W. Goodfellow, papers, mainly correspondence.

Colbeck, Capt. W. Official record of S.S. *Morning*, relief ship to *Discovery*, 9 Jan. 1903, off Possession Island.

Cook, Capt. J. Letter 17 Sept. 1771 to J. Walter, Whitby, describing his discoveries in the South Seas, photographic copy; four photographs and one rubbing of memorials to Cook.

Crosfield, M. C. Journal and geological field notes with rough sketches, British Association Expedition to Australia, Java, Ceylon; vol.1 Australia, vol.2 Thursday Island onwards. Found filed with Journal MSS. Feb. 1968.

Crozier, Capt. F. R. M. Papers and letter 1840-1.

Darwin, C. R. Letter 6 Feb. 1874 requesting books on the Sandwich Islands for a 'history of Infanticide in the Sandwich Islands' and 'Note on block of rock seen on Iceberg in 61 South Lat.' 1839.

Des Graz, C. L. M. 'Journal, impressions et remarques pendant le voyage des corvettes *l'Astrolabe* et *la Zélée*', 3 vols., 7 Sept. 1837 to 22 June 1840, a variant draft of the journal 7 Sept. 1837 to 6 Feb. 1838 including pen and ink sketches, 'Tableau comparatif des idiomes des différentes peuplades visitées par l'expédition', French and fifteen native languages of Pacific Islands, Australia, and New Zealand, eulogy of Dumont d'Urville, and some account of the expedition.

Discovery. Two letters 1939 and cuttings, also notes on Antarctic exploration.

D'Urville, Capt. Dumont. Letter 20 Feb. 1840 to Sir John Franklin's A.D.C. for insertion in the Hobart newspapers, being an account of the discoveries of d'Urville's expedition, and thanks to Sir John Franklin and the people of Hobart.

Filliter, E. Day to day record and descriptive pieces written on a journey to Papua and New Guinea accompanying Rev. B. Butcher and his family May-Nov. 1932.

Flinders, M. Letter 1801 to T. Franklin.

Harper, R. From Hermitage, N.Z., to West Coast by Fyfe's Pass, a first crossing c.1928-9, leader A. P. Harper.

Harvey, J. H. Some notes on the family of Dampier, 10 Jan. 1942.

Hides, J. G. and others. Reports of aerial reconnaissances in Papua 1934-6 with covering letters from the Government Secretary, Territory of Papua.

Leichhardt, L. Documents concerning the expedition to Port Essington 1846, concerning his unsuccessful attempt to cross the continent in 1847 and letter 27 May 1867 from von Mueller reporting progress of the Ladies Leichhardt Search Expedition.

Mackintosh, Capt. A. Diary of sledge journey laying depots for relief of Sir Ernest Shackleton and his party, crossing from the Weddell Sea, 25 Jan. to 15 Apr. 1915, copy by C. Evans.

Maconochie, A. Photostats of letters 1833-6 concerning the Chair of Geography, University of London, and his resignation in order to go to Van Diemen's Land; letter 22 June 1837, Hobart, including a sketch on the structure of Van Diemen's Land and on the natives at Port Phillip; preliminary statement Mar. 1839 on his differences with Franklin including copies of letters from Sir Alfred Stephen, F. M. Innes, J. C. Macdougall, and G. Robertson, also original letters from G. Robertson 22 Mar. 1839 and J. C. Macdougall 28 Mar. 1839.

Markham, Sir Clements R. List of Antarctic Medallists of the Royal Geographical Society 1904, with some details of investitures and expeditions.

Marshall, Dr E. S. Personal diary 25 Dec. 1909 to 18 Mar. 1911, British Expedition to Dutch New Guinea; also extracts from Marshall's letters concerning the New Guinea Expedition; correspondence of Marshall and Dudley Everitt with photographs; correspondence referring to Marshall's Antarctic journal and papers.

Murray, G. Journal 1898 of Deep Sea Expedition, S.S. *Oceana*; notebook, few entries only; journal 6 Aug. to 2 Oct. 1901 aboard S.S. *Discovery* from Cowes to Cape Town; notebook containing pencil and water-colour marine biological drawings initialled 'E.A.W.', i.e. Dr E. A. Wilson, and a note on the density of surface water signed E. H. Shackleton; correspondence 1881-1919.

North Australian Expedition. Six packets of papers 1853-4 and printed prospectus 12 Nov. 1860 of new colony to be formed on the River Victoria in Northern Australia (packet 5). Packets 1-2, 4-5 include letters from Sturt, Baines, Lort Stokes, G. M. Waterhouse, Trelawny Saunders, Sir George Grey, J. S. Wilson, and G. Cathcart; also other papers. Packet 3 contains papers and correspondence 1853-4 concerning proposal by E. Haug for an expedition to the interior of Australia.

Parkhill, A. Speech 17 Feb. 1936 on the arrival of Lincoln Ellsworth at Melbourne after his Antarctic flight. Copy of *Little America Times* (Antarctic newspaper) 1934.

Ross, Sir James Clark. Letter n.d., received 2 Aug. 1842, H.M.S. *Erebus*, reporting to Admiralty on his second Antarctic voyage. This letter formerly in correspondence files.

Scott, Capt. R. F. Letters 1886-1913 from Scott, his wife, and parents, some concerning his death, with cuttings 1913; notebook kept by J. W. Lovibond containing record of hair, eye, and skin colour of members of Scott's 1901-4 expedition.

London

Shackleton, Sir Ernest. Correspondence 1908-9 at the conclusion of the *Nimrod* expedition, also papers 1914-16 on the Imperial Trans-Antarctic Expedition and the proposed relief expedition by *Aurora*.

Shackleton, H. Letter 12 June 1916 referring to his son's plan to rescue the twenty-two men stranded on Elephant Island.

Smith, W., master of *William of Blyth*. Copy of memorial 1821 to the Lords Commissioners of the Admiralty concerning the discovery of the South Shetland Islands in 1819. Also a photostat of printed pamphlet *Notes on South Shetland*, London 1822.

Terry, M. Appendices 1934 to a paper on his expedition to Central Australia in 1933.

Thurston, Sir John B. Diary of the first expedition across Fiji, commencing 22 July 1865 at Levuka, with sketches and a few pages of notes on Fiji affairs.

Wilsden, Lieut. F. W. Easter Island, H.M.S. *Orama*, 11 July 1915, with photographs.

Museum Drawer

Beachy Island. Records and lists of stores left at Beachy Island by Belcher 1854, McClintock 1858, and Young 1875, found by Capt. Alex. Fairweather, S.S. *Terra Nova* and forwarded with explanatory letter 5 Nov. 1885.

Discovery. British National Antarctic Expedition 1901-4, four logs, also deck log Aug. 1901 to Feb. 1902.

Palmer, Surgeon J. L. Water-colour sketches 1853 of an Easter Islander and of a Pitcairn woman, Dorcas Young, in island costume aboard H.M.S. *Portland*.

Pitcairn Papers. List of families on Pitcairn Mar. 1884; letter 20 Dec. 1884 J. R. McCoy, Pitcairn, to Capt. F. P. Doughty, H.M.S. *Satellite*; laws and regulations; letter 9 Apr. 1831 Capt. A. A. Sandilands, H.M.S. *Comet*, with list of names and ages of islanders moved to Otaheite; two letters Dec. 1832 and Jan. 1833 from J. Hill, Pitcairn; extract of letter 20 May 1833 Capt. Fremantle, H.M.S. *Challenger*, at sea.

Scott, Capt. R. F. Copy of two pages from diary Jan. to Oct. 1911.

Shackleton, Sir Ernest H. Sketch map drawn on menu card by Shackleton to illustrate proposed Antarctic journey 7 May 1914; signatures of members of *Quest* Expedition 16 Oct. 1921.

Library Cases

Aldrich, Adm. P. Journal in H.M.S. *Challenger* 1872-4, written in a log book marked H.M.S. *Resolute*, unused 1849 by Aldrich's uncle, illustrated with water-colours.

Allen, G. H. Log H.M.S. *Herald* 21 Jan. 1848 to 18 June 1851, Pacific survey and three summer voyages through Behring Straits.

Balfour, Lieut. Andrew F. Journals, logs, and remark books 1873-96 kept during service in H.M. ships *Challenger*, *Stork*, and *Penguin* in Pacific, Antarctic, China, and Banda Seas.

Bernacchi, Cmdr L. C. Private diary 14 Feb. to 4 Nov. 1904 kept in S.S. *Discovery* on National Antarctic Expedition, with sketch maps, photographs and rough notes.

Biscoe, J. Journals 1830-2 of a voyage towards the South Pole in the brig *Tula* with the cutter *Lively* in company. Both vessels belonged to C. Enderby.

Jackson, A. P. Chief Officer *Terra Nova*. Log 1903-4 of *Terra Nova* during expedition sent to the relief of Capt. R. F. Scott. The log contains occasional sketches of crew members in the margins.

Markham, Sir Clements R. Log H.M.S. *Collingwood* from 3 Dec. 1846, kept by C. R.

Markham, midshipman, Pacific Station; 'My Life in the Navy', loose papers including sketches in H.M.S. *Superb* 1849; also other papers.

Moore, W., Chief Mate *Eliza Scott*, schooner, Capt. John Balleny. Log 12 July 1838 to 17 Sept. 1839 of *Eliza Scott* from London to New Zealand. Presented to the Society by C. Enderby.

Ninnis, A. H. Journals, charts, photographs, and other papers relating to A. H. Ninnis's commission as Purser in S.S. *Aurora* on the Imperial Trans-Antarctic Expedition 1914-16, and the Antarctic Relief Expedition 1916-17. The papers include letters on Antarctic exploration, discussing proposals for an expedition in 1923.

Richards, R. R. A., Chief Paymaster H.M.S. *Challenger*. Diary kept on voyage round the world 1872-6, copy.

Shackleton, Sir Ernest H. Memorial Committee Minute Book.

Vereker, Cmdr the Hon. F. C. P. Journals and logs 1865-86 illustrated with watercolours and charts relating especially to his service in R.N. survey ships 1865-7, 1867-70 and 1870-2 in the East Indies, Pacific, and China Sea.

Wilson, Dr D. P. Log and private journal 23 Oct. 1839 to 19 Mar. 1843 with illustrations in ink and water-colour kept while ship's surgeon on the second voyage of the South Seas whaler *Gipsy*.

JOURNAL MANUSCRIPTS

Journal Manuscripts are chiefly papers offered for publication in the Society's *Journal* or *Proceedings*. Not all were published, some were published in part only, or lacking drawings and maps. Editorial changes were made in almost all cases. The Society obtained one or more reports on each manuscript and referees include eminent scientists and geographers whose letters, kept with relevant manuscripts, are frequently of value in themselves. Since 1893 decennial indexes to the *Journal* or *Proceedings* and later the *Geographical Journal* have been published. For a list of papers published to 1880 see C. R. Markham, *The Fifty Years Work of the Royal Geographical Society*, London 1881, pp.152-242, also published in the *Journal* vol.L, 1880.

In 1967, sorting of Journal Manuscripts by continental area was begun, papers about each area being arranged alphabetically by author. Lack of space does not permit the inclusion here of a list of Journal Manuscripts but a list has been made of such papers and copies are deposited in the Royal Geographical Society, London, the National Library of Australia, Canberra, the Mitchell Library, Sydney, the Alexander Turnbull Library, Wellington, N.Z., and the Library, Australia House, London.

MAPS AND PICTORIAL MATERIAL

Manuscript maps and charts are filed in the Map Room. Paintings, sketches, and photographs, framed and unframed include:

Antarctic. Three oil paintings, one by E. Seapo and one by E. L. Greenfield; sketch book of Lieut. G. Gerran Phillips, H.M.S. *Terror* 1839-42; water-colours and pencil panoramas executed during the *Discovery* expedition by E. A. Wilson; portraits of Sir James C. Ross, F. R. M. Crozier, Sir Ernest Shackleton, Sir Douglas Mawson, and Capt. R. F. Scott.

Australia. Oil paintings of Sydney and North Australia by T. Baines and four volumes of his sketches in North Australia, also oil paintings in Timor, of *Messenger*, *Tom Tough*, and *Blue Jacket* and a portrait of the wife of Capt. Drysdale.

Pacific. Portrait of Capt. J. Cook; oil painting of Trobriand Islanders by E. Silas.

London

ROYAL HORTICULTURAL SOCIETY

The Lindley Library, Vincent Square, London, S.W.1

The Society was founded by Sir Joseph Banks and others in 1804 as the Horticultural Society of London. The Library contains, in addition to the large number of books and pamphlets on horticulture, botany, and allied subjects, a small collection of manuscripts, mostly drawings and travellers' diaries. Many manuscripts were dispersed about 1860 before the Society was revived by Royal patronage. There are no guides to the manuscripts; the reference numbers given are the location numbers.

76.1 B. Journal Sept. 1824 to Mar. 1826 by James McRae of a plant and seed collecting expedition on H.M.S. *Blonde* to the Sandwich Islands and other places in the Pacific Ocean. The journal contains a list of instructions to McRae issued by the Horticultural Society 16 Sept. 1824. There are accounts of specimens sent home by McRae on this expedition in *Transactions of the Horticultural Society of London*, VI-VII, 1826-30.

56.1 B. Notes by Ronald C. Gunn on the flora of Van Diemen's Land, n.d. but received by J. Lindley 1838. These are the collector's notes to accompany specimens sent to Lindley, giving details of the areas in which the specimens were found. Inserted loose are further remarks, Launceston, 21 June 1833.

41.2 H. Eighty drawings by Pierre Jean François Turpin of Australian flora, illustrating Jacques Julien Houton de Labillardière's *Sertum Austro-Caledonicum*, Paris 1824. The original drawings are interleaved with the plates.

ROYAL INSTITUTE OF INTERNATIONAL AFFAIRS

10 St James's Square, London, S.W.1

Records of General Meetings 1940-61 and of Private Discussion Meetings 1946-60 relating to South and South East Asia, Australia, and the Pacific area are listed in *A Guide to Western Manuscripts and Documents in the British Isles relating to South and South East Asia*, London 1965. It is stated that application for permission to see the records listed should be made to the Meetings Secretary.

INSTITUTE OF PACIFIC RELATIONS

A private international organisation founded in 1925. There was an International Secretariat in New York and constituent autonomous bodies in a number of countries, some being separate organisations, e.g. American Institute of Pacific Relations. In England work for the Institute was carried out by the Royal Institute of International Affairs and in Australia, Canada, and New Zealand by the Australian, Canadian, and New Zealand Institutes of International Affairs.

The Institute carried out an extensive publications program and held thirteen conferences. Many mimeographed data and conference papers listed in published proceedings of the conferences are held in the Royal Institute of International Affairs. Only one unprinted paper relating to the field of this survey apart from conference papers has been found in the card catalogue of the Royal Institute of International Relations: 'Institute of Pacific Relations, Peopling of Australia', report of Chairman of Meeting of the Institute of Pacific Relations and other Societies, Temple Court, 20 Aug. 1929, typescript.

ROYAL INSTITUTION OF GREAT BRITAIN
21 Albemarle Street, London, W.1

The collection of manuscripts includes papers of six nineteenth century scientists: Count von Rumford (Sir Benjamin Thompson), Sir Humphrey Davy, Michael Faraday, John Tyndall, Sir William Crookes, and Sir James Dewar. It also includes the papers of Sir William Bragg. All these men were closely connected with the Institution. The manuscripts are not yet finally catalogued and there are no published guides or catalogues. A report 1963 by the Librarian K. D. C. Vernon containing a brief description of the first five of the accumulations mentioned, with a list of some of the manuscripts in the Institution, can be seen at the National Register of Archives (N.R.A. Report Sci 9522A). Access to the manuscripts is open to scholars giving advance notice to the Archivist of what they wish to consult, and their purpose.

Michael Faraday

This collection includes the manuscript of Faraday's diaries, i.e. his 'Experimental Notes' 1831-62, the typescript of his 'Experimental Researches', many of his manuscript lecture notebooks and much of his correspondence with leading scientists and other public figures all over the world. There are typed transcripts of many of the letters in several volumes, including two large portfolios.

The papers include a botanical note 6 Apr. 1838 in Faraday's hand, but unsigned, endorsed 'Ward's cases', referring to a box of ferns sent to New Holland, 4 June 1833, and to another case of plants sent to New Holland, mentioning Norfolk Island pines and 'Mr. Smith's letter', n.d.

John Tyndall

The papers are well arranged and preserved. Typed transcripts of some of the correspondence have been made and bound in ten volumes, each with personal name index. Most of the original letters have been preserved separately in boxes. They are mainly in-letters to Tyndall with some copy or draft out-letters. They include letters from Sir Joseph Hooker, Charles Darwin, T. H. Huxley, and Sir John Herschel. It was not possible to make a detailed search, but a spot check in vol.IX of the transcripts, containing the correspondence between Tyndall and Huxley showed a letter 4 Dec. 1851 from the latter referring to his preference for a professorship in Sydney rather than Toronto, and to Tyndall's prospects of going to Sydney.

Sir William Bragg

Sir William's papers were officially deposited with the Royal Institution by his son, Sir Lawrence, in 1964 but at present (Feb. 1969) they are still kept by Sir Lawrence in his own room at the Institution pending sorting, listing, and arranging. The following is a brief summary of the more important items in the collection:

Notebook while a student at Trinity College, Cambridge, 1881-4.

Records in notebooks of his reading and preparation for lectures in his early years at Adelaide University. Associated with these notebooks is a very interesting collection of letters to Richard Threlfall, Professor of Physics at Sydney 1886-98, to whom he wrote for advice. These letters were presented to the Institution by Sir Richard's son, R. E. Threlfall in 1962.

Notebooks covering the start of his early researches at Adelaide.

Letters from Ernest Rutherford, Professor of Physics at McGill University, Montreal, 1896-1907, in reply to Bragg's lengthy letters setting out his early ideas and research into radioactivity. The latter are now in the Cambridge University Library.

Notebooks recording research at Leeds University 1909-15, at first following up the work on ionisation which he had been doing at Adelaide, and later branching out into x-ray crystallography.

London

Notebooks covering researches into organic structures at University College, London, and the Royal Institution, post 1918.

Correspondence about x-ray analysis, especially its beginning in 1912-14 and correspondence about crystal specimens for analysis 1922-33.

The manuscripts of his account of his life from his earliest recollections to his going to Australia in 1885.

An almost complete set of reprints of his original papers and addresses, the manuscripts of his original papers, and addresses and cuttings, almost complete for 1906-42.

Sir Lawrence Bragg

Sir Lawrence has a number of personal and family papers, papers relating to the work on x-ray crystallography which he pursued jointly with his father, and some material relating to his grandfather, Sir Charles Todd. The last is not extensive but includes notebooks, cuttings, and correspondence relating to the Overland Telegraph. Other Todd papers are scattered among various members of the family, but the majority have been destroyed. In Dec. 1969 papers with Sir Lawrence's sister, Mrs Caroe, 15 Campden Hill Square, London, W.8, included: correspondence 1872 during the building of the Overland Line, being eleven letters from Alice Todd, three from her children, and two from Charles Todd, miscellaneous family letters 1885-92, copy of letter of appointment Feb. 1855 of Charles Todd to his post in Adelaide with instructions from Airy to Todd, letter Oct. 1855 from Charles Todd to his parents describing the voyage out to Australia and his impressions of Adelaide, and several photographs.

Sir Lawrence's collection of papers, letters, diaries, and notebooks referring to his own work will eventually be sorted, listed, and transferred to the Royal Institution.

ROYAL SOCIETY
6 Carlton House Terrace, London, S.W.1

Application for permission to examine documents should be made to the Librarian. The main guide to the Society's large collection of archives and other manuscripts is an author index on cards. Some series and groups of documents are catalogued or have contents lists usually arranged by author. For a description of catalogues see R. K. Bluhm, 'A Guide to the Archives of the Royal Society and to Other Manuscripts in its Possession', *Notes and Records of the Royal Society*, 12, no.1, pp.21-39, Aug. 1956. For references to correspondence connected with Capt. James Cook see *The Journals . . . of Cook*, ed. Beaglehole, and for correspondence of Sir Joseph Banks see *The Banks Letters*, ed. Dawson.

MINUTES 1660-

The Journal Book, minutes 1660-, with duplicate set 1660-1826.

Council Minutes 1663-, with duplicate set 1663-1822.

Committee Minute Books, *ad hoc* Committees, nineteenth and twentieth centuries.

CORRESPONDENCE

In-letters 1800-99 called Miscellaneous Correspondence, 6435 items in 17 volumes.

Entries in the card catalogue are under names of writers and give a summary of contents. Letters of Australian interest noted include MC6.250, 351, MC7.119, 269, letters 1862-5 from the Colonial Office concerning the proposal to provide a powerful telescope at Melbourne Observatory; MC14.254, 257, 284, letters 1887-8 from the Colonial Office concerning the proposed Antarctic expedition; various letters from Rev. W. B. Clarke, J. D. Hooker, and F. von Mueller.

New letter book, copies of out-letters 1885-20th cent., 73 vols. This correspondence is uncatalogued but may repay examination.

LETTERS AND PAPERS 1741-1806

3651 items in 127 vols. Letters and papers communicated to the Society, the greater number published in *Philosophical Transactions* and easily traced through its indexes. There is also a manuscript catalogue with printed cumulative author index. An example of these letters is LP5.115 letter 30 Nov. 1768 James Cook, Rio de Janeiro.

PHILOSOPHICAL TRANSACTIONS MANUSCRIPTS 1807-65

*c.*600 items in 75 vols. and box files. Relevant papers are mainly on Australian natural history and include papers by Sir Everard Home, e.g. PT2.19 on the wombat.

ARCHIVED PAPERS

83 vols. and box files. Papers communicated to the Society but not published in *Philosophical Transactions* or published in abstract only, entries under authors' names in the card catalogue. The papers include AP11.5a-j, letters 1822-5 from Sir Thomas Brisbane concerning observations at Parramatta and C. C. L. Rümker.

DOMESTIC ARCHIVES

7 vols. each with brief contents list. Include DM4.65-111, letters and papers 1828-31 on the dispute between Sir Thomas Brisbane and C. C. L. Rümker concerning observatories in New South Wales.

METEOROLOGICAL ARCHIVES

352 items in volumes and box files. They include: MA367-78 Antarctica 1898-9; MA62 Hobart Town 1822; MA61 Macquarie Harbour 1822; MA57-8 Parramatta 1822-3; MA146 Port Jackson by William Dawes 1788-91; MA60 Port Macquarie 1822; MA59 Tasmania 1840-1; MA379-93 Melbourne 1857-68; MA63 Honolulu 1836; MA97 H.M.S. *Alligator* moored near Port Essington 1838-9; MA56 *Royal George* daily observations by Sir Thomas Brisbane, England to New South Wales 1821; MA84 H.M.S. *Sulphur* in Australian waters 1837.

BLAGDEN CORRESPONDENCE

Contains letter from Sir Joseph Banks, two letters Aug., Oct. 1774 concerning Omai and two letters 25 Nov. 1814 referring to discoveries in New South Wales and 28 Feb. 1815 concerning frost and snow in Van Diemen's Land.

HERSCHEL CORRESPONDENCE

25 vols. with typescript catalogue. Includes letters from Sir Redmond Barry and Sir Francis Beaufort, concerning the climate of northern Australia and observations at Parramatta and Brisbane; Sir Thomas Brisbane; W. B. Clarke; Melbourne Observatory; Robert FitzRoy, *Beagle*; Sir John Franklin, Hobart; Alexander Macleay; H. A. Severn, the Mint, Sydney; C. C. L. Rümker; E. M. Ward, Sydney.

RUTHERFORD OF NELSON CORRESPONDENCE

9 vols. Photocopies of correspondence collected from all over the world, edited in 1956 by Dr Ernest Marsden for the Rutherford Memorial Committee of the Royal Society.

SABINE CORRESPONDENCE

5 vols. with typescript catalogue. A number of letters 1835-68 are to Capt. James Clark Ross mainly about Antarctic exploration and allied subjects from various writers including Gen. Sir Edward Sabine 1840-6, Sir George Gipps 14 July 1841,

London

W. Hobson, Auckland, 15 Oct., 8 Nov. 1841, J. D. Hooker 28 Mar. 1839, W. Macleay 13 Oct. 1841.

The following letters to Sabine have also been noted:

26 Dec. 1863 to 20 Mar. 1868, R. L. J. Ellery, Observatory, Melbourne.

22 July 1862, J. H. Kay, Melbourne, concerning the observatory and telescope, and G. F. Verdon.

14 Sept. 1857, 18 Aug. 1858, G. Balthasar von Neumayer, Melbourne, concerning the magnetic survey of Victoria and the observatory.

1829, C. C. L. Rümker, memo on chronometers and remarks n.d. on a passage from New South Wales to England.

19 Oct. 1856, W. Scoresby, *Royal Charter*, Hobson's Bay, sending results of observations.

14 Nov. 1860, W. Scott, Observatory, Sydney.

n.d. [1862?], A. B. Smith, Melbourne, on the voting of money for use by G. F. Verdon.

11 Aug. 1865, E. C. Symonds, Treasury, Melbourne, to W. P. Wilson about funds for an equatorial telescope.

25 Apr. 1866 to 27 Nov. 1867, G. F. Verdon, Treasury, Melbourne, and other papers.

1861-7, Professor W. P. Wilson, University of Melbourne, mainly about the observatory.

SCHUSTER CORRESPONDENCE

Includes letters 1906-34 from Ernest Rutherford.

MANUSCRIPTS, GENERAL

A typescript 'revised catalogue' refers, where appropriate, to more detailed entries in *Catalogues of the Miscellaneous Manuscripts and of the Manuscript Letters in the Possession of the Royal Society*, Part 1 by J. O. Halliwell, Part 2 by W. E. Shuckard, London 1840. Among Manuscripts General is a volume of letters and papers of the family of Sir Joseph Banks, one of three volumes of which the other two have been broken up, placed in Miscellaneous Manuscripts and provided with entries in the card catalogue. The remaining volume is uncatalogued but no papers have been found in it relating to Australasia or the Pacific.

MS110-16. Astronomical observations 1823-5 at Parramatta, 7 vols.

MS170. Documents relating to J. A. Lloyd's paper on the difference of level of the Atlantic and Pacific Oceans, printed in *Philosophical Transactions* 1830. In-letters 1800-99, Miscellaneous Correspondence, q.v. include a letter 28 June 1821 from Sir Francis Beaufort concerning two plates illustrating this paper.

MS214. Cook Medal Papers, including letters from Sir Joseph Banks and from Mrs Cook.

MS410. *Challenger* Publications Committee Papers.

MS547, 591-3. Letters and papers concerning the British National Antarctic Expedition 1901-4, uncatalogued MSS.594, 595, and 622 also relate to Antarctic expeditions.

MS646-7. Council Minutes 1765-7 and extracts 1766-71 relating to the transit of Venus.

MISCELLANEOUS MANUSCRIPTS

17 vols.

MM3.14. A. Dalrymple 17 Dec. 1767 on the transit of Venus.

MM5.39. Memorial [15 Feb.] 1768 by the Royal Society to the King, asking for financial assistance towards observing the transit of Venus 1769 in northern latitudes and south of the Equator.

MM6.60. Sir Joseph Banks 30 Mar. 1787 to the Earl of Liverpool on the advantages of sending a vessel from England rather than a transport from Botany Bay to obtain breadfruit for the West Indies.

MM6.64. Sir Joseph Banks 4 July 1795 to Foreign Office concerning a present of plants to the Russian Grand Duchess embarked on *Venus*; the plants were from specimens brought by Bligh from Tahiti, and New Zealand flax brought back by Banks and others.

MM6.71. Sir Joseph Banks 20 Oct. 1810 to Admiralty welcoming Flinders's promotion to the rank of post captain and hoping it might compensate in part for his unjust confinement.

MM7.7-160. Letters and papers of the Board of Longitude, many relating to Pacific voyages, e.g. 8 July 1779 Maskelyne to Banks concerning calculations by W. Wales of the latitudes and longitudes of places visited by Wallis and Banks; C. Green's log of the *Endeavour*; Wallis's log of the *Dolphin*, papers relating to Capt. Cook's voyages to the Pacific, list of instruments for making astronomical observations at Botany Bay 1786.

MM10.11. Table n.d. showing the index errors of thermometers by comparison with the standard thermometer of the observatory, Ross Bank, V.D.L.

MM10.32. Notices n.d. of the Aurora Australis 1-31 Mar. 1841, made on board H.M.S. *Erebus*.

MM10.185. J. Robertson, catalogue of birds collected on board H.M.S. *Terror* between the Cape of Good Hope and Van Diemen's Land.

MM11.92. Memorial of Lieut. T. E. L. Moore, late of H.M. barque *Pagoda* on a voyage of magnetic observations in south polar seas 1844-5.

MM11.156. Letter 20 Sept. 1841 from Admiralty enclosing meteorological observations made at Port Arthur, V.D.L.

MM12.66-8. Southern Telescope Committee letters, originals of correspondence published in *Correspondence Concerning the Great Melbourne Telescope*, London 1871.

MM14.36. Extract from Admiralty instructions 16 Sept. 1839 to Capt. J. C. Ross.

MM14.33. James Macdonald, Prahran, Vic., on comets, 6 Aug. 1862.

MM14.37. Copy of letter 26 Sept. 1839 to *The Times* signed 'Cui Bono' and concerning the mistake in the Antarctic voyage of *Terror* and *Erebus*.

MM14.70, 80-3. Letters 1864-5, some copies, concerning the Great Melbourne Telescope.

MM14.119. J. Wood Beilby, Mordialloc, Vic., sketch of a new theory of the oceanic tides, 27 Mar. 1869, and a draft of the Society's reply.

MM14.130. List of volumes of observations, Flagstaff Observatory, Melbourne, 1858-63.

MM15.27. W. B. Clarke, The Royal Society's 'Obligation' to the Society 22 July 1876, holograph.

ROYAL SOCIETY OF ARTS
John Adam Street, London, W.C.2

The Royal Society of Arts, founded in 1754, extended its interests to the colonies in 1755, and two years later set up a Standing Committee of Colonies and Trade. Most of the material of Australasian and Pacific interest occurs in the early nineteenth century in connection with the Society's awards or premiums made for the advancement of the practical arts. Papers and correspondence in connection with the awards are printed in full in the *Transactions*, and after 1851, the *Journal*, with the originals retained in MS. transactions until 1852, but incomplete after that date. A summary of the same material is also found in the Committee Minutes, most usually the minutes of the Committee on Colonies and Trade. The minutes also are printed in part in the *Transactions* or *Journal*.

MINUTES

Society Minutes 1754 to date.

Council Minutes 1846 to date.

Committee Minutes 1758 to date.

The use of twentieth century Council and Committee Minutes is restricted. Only the Committee Minutes, which have contemporary indexes, contain relevant material, particularly the minutes of the Committee of Colonies and Trade. Sample entries are listed below, but all Australasian references can be traced through the printed indexes to the *Transactions*.

Committee Minutes 1821-2. Colonies and Trade 8 Mar. 1822: pp.410, 412-13, gold medal to J. Macarthur for greatest quantity of fine wool and his claims for the finest sample, also Ceres silver medal for fine wool to T. Raine whose sea elephant oil from Macquarie Is. tested; pp.416-17 report by W. Salisbury, Brompton, on New Zealand flax of which a Mr Williams at Sydney already has a large plantation.

Committee Minutes 1822-3. Colonies and Trade 12 Mar. 1823: pp.392-5 Gregory Blaxland's claim for premium for wine; 5 Apr. 1823: pp.396-7 T. Kent's extract from mimosa bark for tanning.

Committee Minutes 1844-5. Colonies and Trade 9 Jan. 1845, pp.155-60 Edward Macarthur's replies to questions about soil type, mode of planting of dried fruits and wines; Agriculture 19 May 1845, pp.11-13 Mrs T. Allom, Bloomsbury, designing apparatus for sending bees to New Zealand in the care of Rev. Charles Waring Saxton, and silver Isis medal recommended.

TRANSACTIONS

Manuscript transactions 1770-1852 contain the originals of papers and correspondence in the printed *Transactions* 1783-1851; the latter being fully indexed. Relevant material in the period before the printed series begins concerns the Society's offer of a premium for the introduction of the breadfruit tree from the Pacific into the West Indies 1777. The topics listed under Committee Minutes are matched by material in the *Transactions* and, after 1852, in the printed *Journal*, of which few of the original papers have been preserved.

CORRESPONDENCE

Loose archives (chiefly letters received) 1754-1847.

Letter books (copies of letters sent) 1770-97, 1816-50.

Loose archives (letters received) 1848 to date.

Loose archives, General Committee Papers 1855-1911.

To most of the correspondence and certain other papers up to 1848 there is a card index by author and subject, the subject entries classified first by the Society's standing committees. An index to correspondence after 1851 has not yet been prepared. There appears to be very little relevant materia l, but the following entries were noted:

B2/155, f.22. Letter 9 May 1844 from M. Saunders stating that J. Cooper, jnr, is unable to attend the Committee considering Lieut.-Col. Edward Macarthur's wines.

GCP51/2a/36. Letter from Samuel Davenport concerning South Australian products for display in the Great Exhibition of 1851.

ST JOSEPH'S FOREIGN MISSIONARY SOCIETY
St Joseph's College, Mill Hill, London, N.W.7

The Society, founded by Bishop Vaughan in 1866 to train priests for foreign missions, has been entirely responsible for the Roman Catholic mission to the Maoris in New Zealand since 1887. The official decree of Propaganda establishing the mission was dated June 1887 but in December of the previous year, after repeated requests from Bishop Luck of Auckland, two Mill Hill priests had arrived and established the first mission station at Matata, Bay of Plenty. Since that date, stations have multiplied throughout North Auckland.

The original records of the Society are of a confidential nature, but permission to consult them may be granted to bona fide students, on application to The Archivist, St Joseph's College. The relevant records noted are:

File labelled 'New Zealand (T4)' containing various papers and correspondence 1882-1932 of the Superior-General and Vicar-General. These include letters 1882-4 to and from Fr Patterson, a friend of Bishop Vaughan who preached and spoke on behalf of the Society in New Zealand and Australia; Bishop Luck's appeal 1884 to Mill Hill for priests to serve the Maoris in the Auckland Diocese; typescript note on the history of the Maori Mission in New Zealand 1838-1943.

Box file labelled 'N. Zealand 1892-1903(21)' containing mainly in-letters to the Superior-General and Vicar-General arranged chronologically. The file also contains an envelope marked 'letters written after the death of Cardinal Vaughan' which all appear to be dated 1931 and to deal with administrative matters of the Maori Mission.

Volume entitled 'New Zealand Maori Mission (CB19)' containing mainly copies of letters 1890-1902 from Bishop Vaughan, Superior-General, and Father Francis Henry, Vicar-General, to the Bishops of Auckland and to Mill Hill priests and others there. Inside, loose, there is a copy of the agreement 28 Mar. 1900 between the Bishop of Auckland and the Society, and several other papers.

St Joseph's College Library has a complete bound set of the quarterly publication *St Joseph's Foreign Missionary Advocate* from its inception in 1883 until 1936 when publication in England ceased. These volumes are not indexed but contain regular and numerous articles and news items on the development of the Maori Church in New Zealand. There is also a collection of photographs at St Joseph's College which includes those priests who have served in New Zealand, from the original two Fathers, Becker and Madan, to the present time.

ST MARYLEBONE PUBLIC LIBRARY
Marylebone Road, London, N.W.1

Album entitled 'The Barkly Papers', mostly letters to Sir Henry Barkly. The volume has not yet (1971) been given a reference number or catalogued in detail; there appear to be letters covering the whole of Sir Henry's adult life but they are not arranged chronologically. The following relevant examples were noted:

30 June 1856 from Sir Rowland Hill proposing a meeting with Sir Henry to discuss matters connected with Melbourne Post Office.

26 Sept. 1861 from W. J. Hooker concerning his work on Australian flora, men-

tioning the encouragement he had received from Mueller, Sir John Young, and others.

14 Apr. 1857 from William [?Hovitt], London, referring to the Land Fund in Australia as a means of getting the unemployed out to the Australian colonies.

SALVATION ARMY
101 Queen Victoria Street, London, E.C.4

Most records were destroyed during the war 1939-45. Post-war case papers are retained for a period and then weeded and probably destroyed after about seven years. Those retained may be inspected in certain cases with special permission.

SCOTT AND BOWNE LTD
50 Upper Brook Street, London, W.1

After exporting Scott's emulsion to Australia for many years, Scott and Bowne Ltd formed a subsidiary Scott and Bowne (Australasia) Ltd in 1907. Since then both companies have diversified and now manufacture a range of chemical products. The following records are extant, all except the Sales Record Book being records of Scott and Bowne (Australasia) Ltd.

Sales Record Book 1897-1907 giving quantity and value of exports of Scott's emulsion to Australia.
Production Registers 1907- .
Minute Books 1907- .
Annual Profit and Loss Accounts and Balance Sheets 1907- .

SIMMS MOTOR AND ELECTRONICS CORPORATION LTD
Oak Lane, Finchley, London, N.2

In the custody of the Public Relations Officer there is early material relating to F. R. Simms. This includes: 1893/5, letter 21 Feb. 1893 from F. Simms of the firm H. G. Simms, formerly W. H. Simms, Christchurch, N.Z., accepting agency for both islands. Further Simms material is deposited with the Veteran Car Club.

The Public Relations Officer also holds material presented to the Company by a former employee, E. A. Church. This includes: 8/EAC/8/27 cutting from *The New Zealand Motor World*, July 1953 containing an article on Robert Mitford Hankinson, his work with Simms in the United Kingdom and as agent and manager in New Zealand.

SION COLLEGE
Victoria Embankment, London, E.C.4

The Library of Sion College, founded in 1624, contains 100,000 volumes including much medieval material. From 1710 to 1836 the Library received a copy of every printed book as a copyright library.

There is a collection of manuscripts for which there is a catalogue, a search of which did not reveal any material relating to Australia and the Pacific.

The Library also contains a large collection of pamphlets, including sermons of clergymen who served in Australia and New Zealand.

SOCIETY OF JESUS
114 Mount Street, London, W.1

The Society's archives of the English province include the two letters described below. Since Australia was attached to the Irish province of the Society further relevant records will be found in the custody of the Very Rev. Fr Provincial, 85 Eglinton Road, Dublin 4.

Arch. Prov. Ang. B22. Copy letter 10 July 1858 from Daniel O'Connell, Sydney, to Cardinal Wiseman asking for a rector for the College of St John the Evangelist, Sydney University. With copy reply 8 Oct. 1858 from Joseph Johnson to Cardinal Wiseman saying he had no Jesuit fathers available.

Arch. Prov. Ang. India 1902-11, no.110. Letter 27 Sept. 1843 from N. Lythian, S.J., London, to Rev. Thomas Glover in Rome suggesting that a college of the Society might be established at Swan River.

SOCIETY FOR PROMOTING CHRISTIAN KNOWLEDGE
Holy Trinity Church, Marylebone Road, London, N.W.1

The Society, founded in Jan. 1698, retained strong links with the colonies throughout the eighteenth and nineteenth centuries even though its sister foundation, the Society for the Propagation of the Gospel (see United Society for the Propagation of the Gospel) assumed official responsibility for the church in the colonies in 1701. The links were originally maintained through the translation, publication and provision of literature, but in the nineteenth century also by the provision of financial grants for all church purposes. The Society extended its activities to Australia in 1825, New Zealand in 1840, Hawaii in 1861, Melanesia in 1872 and Polynesia in 1884.

The archives of the Society were used for two histories: W. O. B. Allen and E. MacClure, *Two Hundred Years: The History of the Society for Promoting Christian Knowledge, 1698-1898*, London 1898, and W. K. Lowther Clarke, *A History of the S.P.C.K.*, London 1959. There is a card index. The records are open for inspection by students by appointment.

REPORTS

R/1 Annual Reports 1704-   . Before 1889 several reports are bound together but after that date each report is a volume in itself. The volumes are not indexed, but contain lists of contents from which scattered references to the work of the Society in Australasia and the Pacific can be gleaned, although these are very few in the early period. In addition to these proceedings, there are various appendices containing reports of committees, a list of District Committees, a catalogue of books and tracts issued and of grants for the building of churches.

MINUTES

GM/1-75. General Board Minutes 1699-1925, 75 vols., indexed.

GM/1b-32b. General Board Duplicate Minute Books, Series 2. 1699-75, 1756-69, 1774-1859, 32 vols.

S/m/1-38. Standing Committee Minutes 1825-99, 38 vols. All the volumes are indexed, vols.8-10 by name and committee, vols.11-23 by name, and vols.24-38 by subject.

PF/m/1-7. Foreign Translation Committee Minutes 1834-1925, 7 vols. Volumes 4-7 are indexed. Although the Committee was primarily concerned with translations

347

into European languages and Arabic, there are many references to Australia, and to Maori and Mota translations.

CC/m/1-3. Minutes of the Committee of Correspondence with District and Diocesan Committees 1811-25, 3 vols. These committees were formed to provide a suitable framework for the circulation of books and tracts, and there is the occasional reference to the supply of material for use in New South Wales.

Emigration Committee Minutes 1882-   , 5 vols. to 1915.

The Society made grants of books for emigrants to appropriate ships from 1836 onwards, and later made provision for the appointment of voyage chaplains to accompany unmarried women on voyages and for the emigrants once land was reached. Entries in the minute books relate to the organisation of these matters, with many short reports from chaplains on ships going to Australia and New Zealand.

Ladies Emigration Committee Minutes 1897-1921, 2 vols., indexed.

This committee acted as a consultative body, with the object of making the emigration of women and girls both safe and beneficial. The minutes refer mainly to the organisation of protected parties to Canada, with few references to Australia.

EB/m/20-4. Education Book Grant Committee Minutes 1907-24, 5 vols., indexed. Applicant, place, type, amount, and date of grants are given in brief tabulated form. A number of entries refer to Australia and New Zealand.

FINANCE

CC/l/1. District Committees and Booksellers' Letter Book 1910-19, indexed. Contains some accounts with booksellers in Australia and New Zealand.

FT3 Cash Account Books. FT3/02-4, 1813-30, 3 vols.; FT3/1-14, 1829-1923, 14 vols. Indexed by name and subject and containing occasional relevant entries.

Uncatalogued Money Grants voted 1840-1924, 2 vols. More detailed than the cash account books these volumes detail date, place, amount, and purpose of many grants made to Australia, New Zealand, and the Pacific. They are not indexed.

CORRESPONDENCE

CR1/1-26. Abstract Letter Books. Containing abstracts of letters received and sent 1699-1701, 1708-83, 26 vols.

CR2/1-6. Original Letters Received 1698-1860, 6 files.

CR2/7-9. Miscellaneous Letters c.1740-1825, 3 vols.

CS3/1-16. Letter Books containing copies of letters sent 1698-1917, indexed.

Back numbers of these are periodically destroyed, and only one volume was seen, 25 Jan. to 13 Apr. 1916, which contains several letters to Australia and New Zealand.

PITCAIRN ISLAND PAPERS

MP/c/1-2. Pitcairn Island Fund Committee Letter Book 1853-9, 2 vols. This committee came into existence Dec. 1852, to provide funds for the passage home of Rev. George H. Nobbs, Chaplain of Pitcairn Island, and the supply of clothing, furniture, and other needful articles. Vol.2 contains some original correspondence 1857.

MP/m/1. Pitcairn Island Fund Committee's Minute Book 1852-9.

MP/p/1. Letters and Papers, 1 box.

MP/r/1. The Pitcairn Island Register from the destruction of the *Bounty*, up to the present time, kept by John Buffett, snr, 1790-1854. Edited by Sir Charles Lucas, and published as *The Pitcairn Island Register Book*, London 1929.

BOARD OF TRADE, COMPANIES REGISTRATION OFFICE
Companies House, 55-71 City Road, London, E.C.1

Files of all live companies from c.1860 and files of companies dissolved since 1948 are available for public inspection. Those of live companies before c.1860 have been transferred to the Public Record Office, now in B.T.41; those of companies dissolved before 1948 have also been transferred, now in B.T.31, 95, and 34. The files at Companies House relate both to companies registered in England and Wales and to companies incorporated overseas which have an established place of business in England and Wales. The records include the documents necessary for incorporation and registration, e.g. articles and memoranda of association, annual returns, balance sheets, and records of changes in structure during the life of the company, and, where applicable, documents concerned with winding-up or liquidation.

Four indexes to the files, all arranged alphabetically by company titles are available in the public search room: (1) Live companies e.g. Australian Pastoral Co. Ltd, Australian Pearl Co. Ltd, (2) Companies registered and dissolved since 1948, and companies dissolved after 1963, e.g. Australian Wine Importers Ltd, (3) Companies registered under Insurance Acts, e.g. Australian Mutual Provident Society, (4) Companies incorporated outside Great Britain which have an established place of business in Great Britain, e.g. Australian Associated Press Pty Ltd, New Zealand Shipping Co. Ltd. From these indexes the company number must be found as it is essential to call for a file by its registered number. A small fee is payable for each file searched.

Records of companies registered in Scotland are with the Registrar of Companies, 102 George Street, Edinburgh 2. These files are indicated in the indexes by the prefix 'E' before the company number.

CORPORATION OF TRINITY HOUSE
Tower Hill, London, E.C.3

The Corporation of Trinity House is the general lighthouse authority for England, Wales, and the Channel Islands and the chief pilotage authority for England and Wales. It is also represented on harbour boards and on other bodies concerned with the sea. It advises authorities overseas, and its Elder Brethren act as nautical assessors to advise wreck commissioners and judges in the Admiralty and other courts.

Its records as they existed before 1941 are described in the Eighth Report of the Historical Manuscripts Commission, Appendix 1, 1881, reissue 1907. When Trinity House was destroyed by enemy action in 1941 the letter books and select entries were lost. The minute books have survived and may be consulted at the discretion of the Corporation. Each volume has an index. The Eighth Report of the Historical Manuscripts Commission gives details of records to the early eighteenth century. Nineteenth century minute books include entries recording requests for advice from the Australian colonies and from New Zealand. Examples of such entries are:

5 Nov. 1835, concerning letters about lighthouses at the ports of Hobart Town and Launceston.

6 June 1843, concerning letter from Capt. Robert FitzRoy resigning as an Elder Brother.

7 Nov. 1843, concerning the question raised by the Board of Trade whether pilotage fees for steam vessels in Van Diemen's Land should be less than for sailing vessels.

25 Nov. 1879, concerning a report from Mr Douglass, made in compliance with a request from the Board of Trade, about fees received by him for assistance in pro-

349

curing apparatus for New South Wales; 20 Apr., 4 May, and 7 Dec. 1880, concerning correspondence with the Board of Trade about advice and assistance from Mr Douglass in obtaining equipment for Macquarie lighthouse, Sydney.

The destruction of the letter books and select entries means the loss of a large body of material. As far as is known few Brethren had connections with Australia, New Zealand, or the Pacific Islands. Capt. William Raven, commander of the *Buffalo*, was admitted as a Younger Brother on 6 Nov. 1800 and as an Elder Brother on 13 Nov. 1806. Biographical data on Capt. Effingham Lawrence, father of the Tasmanian pioneer, William Effingham Lawrence, was contained in a letter from Capt. Effingham Lawrence to the Court of the Corporation 12 Nov. 1796 supporting his election as Elder Brother, which took place on 22 Nov. 1796. Historical notes on Capt. William Raven, William Effingham Lawrence, and his father were compiled by Capt. W. R. Chaplin, Elder Brother. Copies of these notes have been placed in the National Library of Australia, Canberra, the Mitchell Library, Sydney, and the State Library of Tasmania, Hobart.

TRUST AND AGENCY CO. OF AUSTRALASIA LTD
Winchester House, Old Broad Street, London, E.C.2

This Company was formed in 1860 to advance money on mortgage to Australian settlers. The decline in the demand for mortgages in Australasia during the prosperous years of the early twentieth century meant that this part of the Company's business was considerably reduced, especially after 1909 when attention was increasingly directed to the Argentine. The records include:

Board Minutes 1860- .
Ledgers 1860- .
Cash Books 1860- .
Journals 1860- .

UNILEVER LTD
Unilever House, Blackfriars, London, E.C.4

Among the records of Unilever Ltd are parcels of papers relating to the business of the firm in Australia and the Pacific Islands. The parcels are numbered. Application for permission to examine the papers should be made to The Chief Press Officer, Information Department, Unilever Ltd.

TT 3734 112A. Sunlight Works, Sydney, 1906-23. Letters between Lever and Meek on the affairs of the Sydney company, and Pacific plantations, difficulties during 1906-10, possibility of co-partnership for Meek, visit of Meek to England, share prices and dividends, political career of W. A. Holman, decimal coinage, possibility of importing Chinese or Indian labour into the copra islands.

TT 3734 144. Messrs Lever Bros., Sydney, 1899-1915. Letters between Lever and John Hope and P. & T. Gray about soap making, freight charges for soap making machinery, cask making, staff, salaries and soap works matters and Hope's career. Correspondence, all of a personal nature, between Lever and Hope continued for many years.

TT 3739 144. Messrs Fulton and Greenhalgh's journey to the Pacific, 1902. This file contains only the letters arranging bookings for the journey.

TT 3742 164A. Pacific Islands Co. 1902-4.

TT 3743 164A2. Pacific Islands Co. 1905-10.

TT 3743 164B. Papers Feb.-Oct. 1910. These include papers concerning the Pacific

Phosphate Co., draft letter to the Colonial Office about land on Ocean Is., agenda of Board Meetings, notices to members, correspondence.

TT 3743 164C. Papers Oct. 1910 to Oct. 1911. These include papers and correspondence relating to Ocean Island, a translation by George Haller on the South Seas Phosphate Co., original in German, letter from Elschner at Nauru about his position there, and letters between Theet and Dickinson.

TT 3744 164D-E. Pacific Islands Co. 1911-12, 1912-15.

TT 3747 195(i). Fanning and Washington Islands 1903. The papers include correspondence concerning the freehold and ownership of the islands with a description of Fanning Is. by Buller and letter from the Colonial Office on copra exports from the islands.

TT 3748 195(ii). Fanning and Washington Islands 1903-4. Letters to and from Lever and solicitors, and reports on the islands.

TT 3775 1882. Pacific Islands Co. 1902-24.

TT 3783 5904. Pacific Phosphate Co. 1910-13.

UNITED SOCIETY FOR THE PROPAGATION OF THE GOSPEL
15 Tufton Street, London, S.W.1

The Society for the Propagation of the Gospel in Foreign Parts was incorporated in 1701 by Royal Charter. Its name was changed in 1965. The Society's connections with Australia begin in 1787 when it supplied religious books and tracts to the Rev. Richard Johnson, chaplain to the settlement of New South Wales. The first official mention of S.P.G. dealings with New South Wales was in 1790 and concerns some books received from the Society for Promoting Christian Knowledge 'For the use of the corps about to embark for New South Wales', see S.P.G. Journal vol.1, 15 Jan. 1790. The Journal entry for 15 Mar. 1793 records in full a copy of a letter from Rev. R. Johnson, Government Chaplain at Port Jackson, dated 21 Mar. 1792. At this time Johnson was negotiating with S.P.G. for schoolmasters. The Society continued to pay for schoolmasters from 1793-1834. Between 1793 and 1900 the Society supported 435 missionaries in Australia and the Pacific, see C. F. Pascoe, *Two Hundred Years of the S.P.G., An Historical Account of the Society . . . 1701-1900*, London 1901, pp.466-7.

The Society's records are of more than ecclesiastical interest. For example, the Australian correspondence, especially that of Bishop W. G. Broughton (see 'C' MSS.), provides basic material on the changing status of the colonial church, its relationship with the state, and the problems associated with government financial aid.

Classified Digest of the Records of the Society . . . 1701-1892, London 1893, Anon. but known to be by C. F. Pascoe, describes manuscripts to 1890 and is an earlier edition of his *Two Hundred Years of the S.P.G. . . . 1701-1900*. Both contain a missionary roll. The following are also useful: H. P. Thompson, *Into All Lands: The History of the Society for the Propagation of the Gospel in Foreign Parts 1701-1950*, London 1951; J. W. Lydekker, *The Archives of the S.P.G.*, London 1936, pamphlet S.P.G. World Wide Series, no.2. The greater part of the Society's records is arranged systematically, but the task is by no means complete and all that is held is not yet listed in the inventories. A guide to the archives of the Society is in preparation. The general rule is that all records are open to students forty years after the date of accession. The Journal 1783-1901, Minutes of the Standing Committee 1833-1900, *Annual*

London

Reports 1783-1900 and correspondence and papers relating to Australia in MSS. called C,D,E,CLS or F, and X were microfilmed for Professor S. C. McCulloch who deposited the microfilms in the Library of Congress, see S. C. McCulloch, 'S.P.G. Documentary Material on Australia 1788-1900', *Journal of the Rutgers University Library*, vol.19, no.2, June 1956, pp.49-58. Sets of positives are in the National Library of Australia and the Mitchell Library, Sydney. Some selective microfilming of Australian and New Zealand papers and of J. C. Patteson papers has also been done. The *Annual Reports* contain, besides a review of the year, excerpts from selected missionary reports.

JOURNALS AND MINUTES

In the eighteenth century the Journal of the meetings of the Society as a whole is the most important source for the history of the Society's work. Not only does it give an account of policy and decisions, but many important letters from missionaries have been extracted or copied in full. The contemporary indexes for each volume are not exhaustive. The powers of a small committee, which met informally to prepare business, increased markedly, especially between 1819 and 1833. At the General Meeting on 1 Feb. 1833, it was agreed that the whole of the preparatory business be conducted by this committee, by this time called the Standing Committee. In 1882 a Supplementary Charter was granted and the Standing Committee became the executive body of the Society.

There is a fair copy of the Journal of the Society 1701-1864 and a signed 'rough' copy 1714-1964. Appendices to the Journal contain copies of many important letters, A 1701-1810, C 1804-54, D 1842-60. From 1882 the Minutes of the Standing Committee are the Society's proceedings.

CORRESPONDENCE AND REPORTS

Arranged in alphabetical series. A and B MSS. relate to America.

C MSS. Letters and documents, mainly in-letters, arranged geographically and within areas by dates, 1789-1924, 18 boxes.

Australia. Includes correspondence from Dr George Gaskin 1789, S. Marsden 1805-33, R. Hill 1821-34, Archdeacon T. H. Scott 1824-9, J. Vincent 1828, the South Australian Mission 1835-6, the Western Australian Mission 1835-6. The remainder concerns mainly problems connected with finance of schoolmasters and ministers, but social conditions are touched upon. Calendared.

Rev. F. W. Wilkinson 1828-31. Incomplete calendar.

W. G. Broughton, Bishop of Australia, 1831-43, 1844-9. Letters and journals.

Arthur correspondence 1823-38. Photocopies of correspondence of Sir George Arthur as Lieutenant-Governor of Van Diemen's Land, with a typescript calendar. Originals in the Mitchell Library, Sydney.

Dioceses of Sydney and Queensland 1837-49. Incomplete calendars.

Diocese of Melbourne, letters of Bishop Perry 1847-9, Tasmania 1839-42, Western Australia 1837-47, Newcastle 1847-9, Norfolk Island 1842. Incomplete calendars. Diocese of Tasmania 1842-9, 1883-9.

South Australia 1934-49, 1847-59. Incomplete calendars.

Documents 1821-98 concerning Australia and including candidates' papers.

Government papers 1827-48 concerning Australia, covering provision of chaplains and questions of government aid. Incomplete calendars.

Miscellaneous 1857-1924. Letters from the Bishops of Newcastle, Grafton, Armidale, Goulburn, and Perth concerning grants from the Colonial Bishoprics Fund.

New Zealand. Letters concern new settlements, affairs of the New Zealand Church Society, its relations with the New Zealand Company. Included are letters from

J. R. Godley, G. A. Selwyn, W. A. Selwyn, J. F. Churton, and J. F. Wickstead, the journals of Bishop Selwyn 1843-8, letters and journals 1841-9, letters 1866-75 of the Colonial Bishoprics Council concerning the foundation of the Dunedin bishopric, and letter 1844 from J. T. Moody, Pitcairn Island. Incomplete calendars. Letters 1855-71 from Bishop J. C. Patteson of Melanesia to his father and sisters, arranged in order of date and in folders which list the principal contents.

D and E MSS. Series begun in 1850 containing letters and reports received from abroad. It was intended that D should be a series of letters and papers and that E should be a series of annual reports. In practice E contains many letters and some reports are filed in D. Both series are bound in volumes except nine boxes in E called E/Pre and some post 1929 E files. D and E volumes are being paged and each item listed.

D MSS. Letters and papers received from abroad 1850-1925, are divided geographically by dioceses and bound in volumes each usually covering a group of dioceses. To 1874 there are six volumes, some covering dioceses in Australia and New Zealand and some also including Melanesia and Honolulu, some letters dating from 1840. After 1874 the following series exist: 1875-80 Australasia, 6 vols.; 1881-6 Australasia and the Pacific, 6 vols.; 1887-93 Australasia, 7 vols.; 1894-1925 Australasia and the Pacific, 31 vols.

E MSS. Annual reports from missionaries. All missionaries did not send annual reports but in many cases there are good runs. The reports were required to give a wide range of information including description of parsonage, church affairs, finance of churches and schools. The reports from Adelaide in 1858 contain much material on the Poonindie native training institution. E/Pre, nine boxes have been added to E volumes, boxes being distinguished by capital letters. Box B 1845-6 includes Australian material among replies to questionnaires 1845-6 and Box J contains reports 1834-8 from Australia, New Zealand, and Pitcairn. For 1856, 1858-66 there are volumes of reports from Australia and New Zealand, some volumes including Norfolk Island, Melanesia, and Honolulu. From 1866 material relating to Australia and the Pacific is bound into forty general volumes, covering years or groups of years. Within the volumes the Australasian and Pacific reports and letters are usually, but not always, kept together. From 1905-29 there is one volume for each year and thereafter the system becomes more complex, being a collection of bound volumes, box files, and dossiers.

From 1849-81 the Society had an Emigrant's Chaplain at Liverpool and some of his later reports filed in E MSS. may repay examination.

CLS MSS. Copies of important letters sent are listed as F by Lydekker but Pascoe does not refer to them. The volumes are arranged geographically and divided by dioceses in alphabetical order. See also X MSS.138, 144-53, 154, 157. Australia July 1837 to Aug. 1871, Feb. 1872- ; Adelaide Mar. 1847 to 1900; Melbourne Oct. 1847 to 1900; Newcastle Oct. 1847 to 1903; Queensland May 1900- ; Western Australia Feb. 1901 to Dec. 1921, Jan. 1922- ; New Zealand Sept. 1842 to Apr. 1900, May 1900 to July 1912, Sept. 1913 to Aug. 1929; Tasmania Mar. 1844 to May 1915; Australasia 1932-5, 1936-9, 1940-2, 1943-5, 4 boxes.

CLR MSS. 1833-1928. Copies of the most important letters received, i.e. those read before the Society, have been kept since 1833. They are listed as G by Lydekker and referred to by Pascoe as H-M. The volumes are arranged geographically and subdivided by dioceses. Most volumes contain indexes. The series is now discontinued. See also X MSS.130, 133-7, 154. Australia Dec. 1834 to Nov. 1899, 4 vols., Dec. 1899- ; Adelaide June 1846 to Jan. 1861, Feb. 1861- , 2 vols.; Melbourne Feb. 1847- ; Newcastle Sept. 1847 to 1899; Perth Dec. 1846 to Dec. 1914; Queensland Mar. 1899-   ; Western Australia Sept. 1914-   ; New Zealand Aug. 1841-   , 3 vols.; New Zealand and Polynesia June 1913-   ; Tasmania Apr. 1842-   ; Honolulu Jan. 1871 to Mar. 1910.

X MSS. Miscellaneous manuscripts and volumes. The series is in process of organisation. Most volumes or parcels of material have been given a serial number. The following include material relating to Australia, New Zealand, and the Pacific.

12. Colonial Office papers 1839. The volume contains a copy of parliamentary papers setting out expenses of the ecclesiastical establishments throughout the colonies.

79. Sub-committee Australia 1844-7; Emigrants' Spiritual Aid 1849-50; Jubilee Committee 1851.

106-9. Candidates' correspondence books 1827-8, 1828-9, 1829-31, 1846-55, 1860, fragmentary.

110-14. Missionary applications, lists with notes 1848-52 and other candidates' lists and testimonials 1837-68; 113, Candidates' lists 1848-68 with incomplete index.

115. Candidates' Committee proceedings 1839-46, and Board of Examiners minutes 1846-8, contemporary index.

116-22b. 1848-73 Board of Examiners minutes, contemporary indexes.

123. Board of Examiners and Chaplaincies Committee 1878-81.

126. Missionaries book 1869-87, a page for each missionary giving date accepted, place sent, terms of agreement, instructions.

128. Secretary's day book 1854-61.

130, 133-8, 144-54. List of letters received 1840-1, précis of letters received and sent 1840-c.1866; 133, Précis of letters received Australia, New Zealand and Cape of Good Hope 1847-50; 154, copies of letters received and sent 1822-7 including government letters.

157. Out-letters 1822, 1839-46, incomplete contemporary indexes.

Copies of out-letters, 1 box, containing Secretary's letter books 1841-63.

193-202. Missionary accounts, records of salaries due and paid to colonial missionaries and schoolmasters 1782-1851, 10 vols., incomplete contemporary indexes of places and persons.

205. Candidates' Sub-committee minutes 1904-52, 5 vols.

230. Application Sub-committee reports 1865-1900, printed.

230. Application Grants Committee reports 1901-29, 3 vols., printed.

234. Letters of Rev. Edmund Hobhouse on his journey to the United States with S.P.G. delegates 1853.

FULHAM PAPERS

Papers 1813-28 of William Howley, Bishop of London, presented to the Society by the Bishop of London 1869, 4 vols. The papers of William Howley, Archbishop of Canterbury 1828-48, and some of his widow's papers are in the Lambeth Palace Library.

Vol.1, letters received, includes letters c.1825 from Rev. R. Hill, Macquarie, Lord Bathurst, Marsden, T. H. Scott, W. Walker, G. Erskine, and Rev. R. Mansfield concerning religious matters in New South Wales and Van Diemen's Land.

CANDIDATES' TESTIMONIALS

Testimonials c.1870-1949, 62 boxes. The series is not complete, items having been removed to the succeeding series, Personal Dossiers, 1949- , which include missionary reports, previously Series E.

Unsuccessful candidates' testimonials c.1827-1906, 15 boxes.

PHOTOGRAPH ALBUMS

Includes an album covering Australasia.

MISCELLANEOUS PAPERS

Diaries of Matthew Blagdon Hale, 1st Bishop of Perth, Jan. 1854 to Dec. 1875, 1 vol. with index, typescript.

The complete journal of J. R. Wollaston of Western Australia, 6 vols. 1840-56, with index, typescript.

Papers of Prebendary Tucker and Bishop Montgomery 1879-1901, one box, containing also a few letters 1900 from Rev. W. H. Cooper, former missionary in Australia, New Zealand, and Canada.

Bishop Montgomery papers, 3 boxes, one of which is not available to students until 1975.

Autograph Book. The volume includes a letter 28 July 1862 from H. J. C. Harper, Christchurch, and a facsimile letter Epiphany 1848 from G. A. Selwyn, N.Z., to his father from Tonga Tabu.

Panorama St John's College, Auckland, N.Z., lithograph c.1845, eight sections unsigned.

UNIVERSITY OF LONDON LIBRARY
Senate House, Malet Street, London, W.C.1

Extensive notes on authorship and subject matter are to be found in R. A. Rye, *Catalogue of the Manuscripts and Autograph Letters in the University Library*, 1921, *Supplement 1921-1930*, 1930, and subsequent typescript supplements. There is also a typescript catalogue of facsimiles.

MANUSCRIPTS

I.H.R. MS.400. Includes abstracts of printed papers regarding the conduct of the French in the Society Islands 1822-45.

AUTOGRAPH LETTERS

AL3. Sir Joseph Banks, Soho Square, 21 Aug. 1815 concerning 'the undertaking now in hand for exploring the rapid currents of the Zaira', with remarks on the *Bounty* and the 'Peopling of Pitcairn's Island'.

AL31. William Cobbett, Norwich, 15 Mar. 1830 to Mr Akerman, 183 Fleet Street containing minute instructions for the preparation of the petition against Wilmot Horton's emigration project, which appeared in the Register on 20 Mar. 1830.

AL218. William Wilberforce, Iver, Bucks., 2 Aug. 1823 asking for 'Mr. Peele's [later Sir Robert Peel, then Home Secretary] consideration of the application of several highly respectable people in favour of Geo. Fish', convicted at Hull, 'that instead of being transported for seven years according to his sentence, he may be placed in the Penitentiary'.

IMPERIAL COLLEGE OF SCIENCE AND TECHNOLOGY
South Kensington, London, S.W.7

The correspondence and scientific papers of Thomas Henry Huxley, F.R.S., are preserved in the College archives: part of Huxley's working library is also kept there. There are two collections of manuscript material: the Huxley Manuscripts (HM) given at various times by Huxley or his widow to the Royal College of Science, now one of the constituent bodies of Imperial College, and the Huxley Papers (HP) purchased from Mrs Rosalind Huxley in 1937.

HUXLEY MANUSCRIPTS (HM)

See Mrs J. Pingree, 'T. H. Huxley: List of his scientific papers', 1968, duplicated typescript.

Documents of the voyage of H.M.S. *Rattlesnake* 1846-50. T. H. Huxley was appointed Assistant Surgeon for the voyage Dec. 1846 to Nov. 1850 which surveyed the Great Barrier Reef, and islands in Torres Strait, the Gulf of Papua and the Louisiade Archipelago. These documents are some of the scientific records which he made; they include diaries, notebooks and drawings. The notes are very detailed as are also many of the sketches and diagrams of marine specimens, natural features and native peoples. All the volumes have been rebound and most of the drawings have been remounted. Other related records are in the Huxley Papers.

Scientific Notebooks, Papers, and Correspondence. These include both manuscript and printed papers, notebooks, letters and memoranda arranged in sections according to subject.

Drawings and Photographs. These are arranged in sets according to subject. Many drawings illustrate laboratory work; some are highly finished, others are rough sketches only. They frequently illustrate notes in the scientific Papers. Box H includes photographs of Australian Aborigines and Maoris.

Personal Correspondence. This consists of letters 1847-54 between Thomas Huxley and his fiancée Henrietta Heathorn and letters 1855-95 between the two of them after marriage. Huxley met his future wife in Sydney in 1846 and she remained there until she left to marry him in England. Among the letters are descriptions and sketches of the Bathurst goldfields in 1852. They are catalogued by Mrs J. Pingree, 'T. H. Huxley: Correspondence with Henrietta Heathorn 1847-54', 1969, duplicated typescript.

HUXLEY PAPERS

See Warren R. Dawson, *The Huxley Papers, a Descriptive Catalogue*, London 1946. The papers include correspondence, personal papers, scientific papers and drawings. There are a number of letters concerning the voyage of the *Rattlesnake* and other letters of Australian interest. Among the drawings are forty-six pencil drawings and four water-colours some done in Sydney and its neighbourhood, 1850.

INSTITUTE OF COMMONWEALTH STUDIES
27 Russell Square, London, W.C.1

JEBB COLLECTION

Letters and papers *c.*1904-18 of Richard Jebb. The correspondence, much of which is typescript, is arranged alphabetically by correspondent. A typescript list of the material is available. In addition to the letters listed below there are a number of general interest on such matters as imperial federation, imperial naval and military policy, tariffs and trade, the Imperial Conference 1911, the Imperial War Conference 1917, and the Royal Colonial Institute. Correspondence between Jebb and Deakin is in the National Library of Australia.

27 Aug. 1913 from Col. James Allen discussing naval policy in Canada and New Zealand.

27 Oct. 1912 from John Allen concerning the naval policies of the two New Zealand political parties, with copy reply 9 Dec. 1912.

4 June 1918 from L. S. Amery about the Pacific Cable[?].

28 June 1907 from A. R. Atkinson concerning *inter alia* the status of New Zealand.

23 Aug. 1912 from R. Muirhead Collins sending duplicated speech on Australian navy and imperial defence.

17 Dec. 1907, 29 Sept. 1909 from W. R. Creswell concerning Australian naval policy.

22 Jan. 1912 to Lionel Curtis on the federal movement in Australia.

1 Feb. 1913 from G. E. Foster giving details of proposed visit to Australia.

28 July 1911 from Sir Samuel Griffith concerning the appointment of Sir James Garrick as Agent General while holding a position in the Queensland Cabinet.

18 Nov. 1907 from E. Grigg on his visit to New Zealand and Australia.

2 July, 26 Sept. 1913 to Arthur Hawkes on Australian naval policy.

16 Mar. 1908 from Viscount Milner mentioning Chinese migration to Western Australia.

20 June 1907 from Bishop Neligan of Auckland on the New Zealand church and education, and visits of the Navy to New Zealand.

29 Oct. [?1913] from G. H. Scholefield on new naval proposals for New Zealand with enclosed cutting.

16 July 1906 from H. H. on Australian wine being exported to Canada.

LONDON SCHOOL OF ECONOMICS
British Library of Political and Economic Science, Houghton Street, London, W.C.2

CANNAN COLLECTION

Personal papers, correspondence and collection of printed works of economist Edwin Cannan, 143 vols.

Vol.1031 ff.37-8. Letter 4 Mar. 1931 from William Barrett of Melbourne residing in London, regarding Cannan's suggestion that Australia could benefit by shipping her gold reserves to England. With Cannan's reply of same date, arguing that gold reserves are of little value to Australia if not used for purposes of international trade.

DALTON PAPERS

Papers of economist and Labour politician Hugh Dalton, Baron Dalton.

Diaries. Vols.55-6. Notes on a visit to New Zealand 1938, typescript. The visit lasted for two weeks during which time he met Labour Government leaders, trades union organisers, and Reserve Bank of New Zealand officials. The notes give details of the attempts of the Savage administration to overcome the aftermath of the depression, outline government policies on finance, social security, and public works, and comment on the personalities of some New Zealand politicians and financial leaders. The gist of Dalton's conversations with Leslie Lefeaux, Peter Fraser, George Lawn, and Walter Nash, is briefly recorded.

JEBB PAPERS

Correspondence and memoranda, chiefly relating to prisons, of Sir Joshua Jebb, Commissioner of Pentonville prison and Chairman of the Directors of Convict Prisons 1850-63, 11 box files.

London

Most of the correspondence and memoranda were written between 1840-63. Photostats of a large proportion of the material relevant to Australia are in the Mitchell Library, Sydney. The papers contain information and discussion on the transportation system, the selection of ticket of leave men, the role of Western Australia as a convict settlement, and the decision to abolish transportation.

LETTER COLLECTION

Vol.IV, item 26. 26 July 1834 from Francis Place to [?] desiring the post of secretary to the Board of Commissioners to be set up under the South Australia Act.

Vol.V, item 26. 2 Jan. 1903 from Louis Alexander Mountbatten, 1st Marquess of Milford Haven, Chief of the Naval Intelligence Department, to Maj.-Gen. John Barton Sterling, expressing distaste for the demand by Australia that, in return for her contribution towards the naval budget, she has the right to choose the destination in war of ships of the British Navy on the Australia Station. The letter contains additional notes by Sterling 3 Jan. 1903 which discuss the issue.

MACDONALD COLLECTION

Letters and manuscript material 1895-1923 of J. Ramsay Macdonald and wife Margaret concerned with shop fines, the employment of women, and other social questions, 8 vols.

Vol.I, item 2. 1 Sept. 1896 from W. Pember-Reeves, New Zealand Agent General in London, to Margaret Macdonald stating that fines in shops and factories were not widely used in New Zealand.

Vol.V, item 22. 23 Aug. 1908 from Lilian Locke Burns at Charters Towers, Q'ld, to Margaret Macdonald describing the position of women's political organisations in Australia, arguing that the Australian Labour parties were in a state of stagnation, and noting that new radical political organisations may emerge.

MALINOWSKI PAPERS

Correspondence, lectures, manuscripts of books and articles, field notebooks, and miscellaneous notes 1910-42 of anthropologist Bronislaw Malinowski, 7 cases. The majority were written between 1938-42. The papers are still largely unsorted and uncatalogued but contain manuscript notes, lectures, and correspondence relating to Malinowski's field investigations in the Pacific Islands and notably in the Trobriands and New Guinea.

MILL TAYLOR COLLECTION

Manuscripts, correspondence, and miscellaneous papers 1822-1918 of, or related to, John Stuart Mill and Harriet Taylor and other members of their families, 59 vols. and 10 boxes.

Vol.I, item 44, Vol.II, item 163, Vol.XXI, items 335-41, Vol.XXVII, items 45-51, Vol.XXIX, item 246. Seventeen letters 1859-93 between Harriet Taylor and Arthur Hardy, brother-in-law by her first marriage, concerning family matters. Arthur Hardy emigrated to South Australia in 1838 and lived at Mount Lofty. The Library also possesses twenty-seven letters 1839-69 (MS.652) to Arthur Hardy and his son Marmaduke Hardy from their relations in England. Most are concerned with family matters but show that Arthur Hardy conducted many English commercial transactions through his relations, e.g.: 15 Nov. 1838 from John Taylor, Arthur Hardy's brother-in-law, mentioning that he had sent seeds to Hardy, and giving wool price quotations; 6 May 1841 from John Taylor sending bills of lading for forty-six cases of wine and three bales of wool shipped to South Australia; 21 July 1845 from D. Taylor and Sons, London, mentioning sale of wool sent over by Arthur Hardy;

22 Dec. 1847 from John Taylor mentioning that the sample of lead which Arthur Hardy had sent to England for assaying was of reasonable quality but did not contain a large silver content; 13 Nov. 1847 from John Taylor mentioning the sale of copper ore sent by Arthur Hardy to England.

NIGHTINGALE COLLECTION

Florence Nightingale's published works 1851-79, 29 vols.

Vol.10, item 1. 'Note on the Aboriginal Races of Australia', paper read Sept. 1864 to the annual meeting of the National Association of Social Science, discussing the work of Bishop Salvado of Port Victoria amongst Aborigines at the Benedictine mission of New Norcia.

PASSFIELD TRUST PAPERS

Private papers 1853-1947 of Sidney and Beatrice Webb (Lord and Lady Passfield) including Beatrice Webb's diary, correspondence with and between Beatrice and Sidney Webb, financial papers, and papers arising out of their public activities. The papers are not the property of the Library and permission must be obtained from the Passfield Trustees before they can be consulted.

Vol.19, ff.65-109. Beatrice Webb's account in her diary of the three month visit which she and her husband made to New South Wales, Queensland, and South Australia in 1898, as part of a fact-finding tour of America, Australia, and New Zealand. See *The Webbs' Australian Diary 1898*, ed. A. G. Austin, Melbourne 1965, and *Visit to New Zealand in 1898—Beatrice Webb's Diary with Entries by Sidney Webb*, Wellington 1959.

PEMBER REEVES COLLECTION

Collection of in-letters 1895-1908 to William Pember Reeves, New Zealand Agent General in London, 1 vol.

During his period as Agent General, Pember Reeves maintained a correspondence with a number of prominent men in New Zealand, notably Edward Tregear and Mark Cohen. These letters are particularly concerned with the New Zealand labour movement and with the workings of arbitration legislation.

Letters from Edward Tregear
Twenty-nine letters 22 Apr. 1896 to 19 Apr. 1907, outlining some of his political beliefs and giving graphic descriptions of New Zealand election campaigns, party platforms, and political leaders. The most notable are:
Item 2. 8 Dec. 1896, description of the general election of 1896.
Item 7. 17 Jan. 1897, description of personality of R. J. Seddon.
Item 11. 15 Sept. 1897, suggestion that Pember Reeves should return to engage in New Zealand politics.
Items 13, 14. 1 Apr., 30 June 1898, description of Tregear's 1500 mile journey in the North Cape region of New Zealand.
Item 16. 11 Jan. 1900, description of the poor organisation of the New Zealand Boer War contingent.
Item 18. 14 July 1900, details of Tregear's trip to Fiji and Tonga with R. J. Seddon.
Item 22. 7 May 1901, discussion of trade union and labour matters in New Zealand.
Item 24. 5 Dec. 1902, details of 1902 general election.
Item 25. 28 Feb. 1903, discussion of the reasons why George Fisher was elected to the New Zealand Parliament.
Item 28. 18 July 1906, outlining his past relationship with R. J. Seddon and examining the state of New Zealand politics after Seddon's death.

London

Letters from Mark Cohen

Twenty-three letters 3 July 1896 to 18 July 1908. Cohen frequently met New Zealand political and labour leaders. The most notable letters are:

Item 32. 29 Jan. 1897, description of the general election of 1896.

Item 35. 18 Dec. 1899, description of November election 1899 containing an account of the political failings of the Liberal Party.

Item 42. 26 Feb. 1906, analysis of Seddon's political policies.

Other letters

Forty-four letters from New Zealand politicians and visitors to New Zealand including correspondence from Sir Joseph Ward, Sir William Russell, Sir Frederick Revans Chapman, F. Waldegrave, John McLachlan, R. J. Seddon, Ben Tillett, Sir John McKenzie, and James Mackay. The most notable letters are:

Item 55. 18 Jan. 1897 from Sir Joseph Ward explaining his political position.

Item 63. 10 Aug. 1897 from Ben Tillett, British Labour leader, in Sydney, describing his visit to New Zealand.

Item 66. 16 Feb. 1898 from Sir John McKenzie, Minister of Lands, stating that he was tired of the back-stabbing process of politics.

Item 83. 3 Feb. 1904 from R. J. Seddon stating that he opposed the importation of Chinese labour into South Africa.

Fourteen letters 24 Aug. 1896 to 8 July 1906 from F. Waldegrave giving descriptions of the New Zealand political scene.

Co-operative Settlement in Queensland 1895.

Item 96. Unsigned memo describing the failure of the several communities established in Queensland under 'The Co-operative Communities Land Settlement Act' of 1893.

LANSBURY PAPERS

Vol.20. In- and out-correspondence and memoranda 1929-30, containing letters relating to emigration and land development in Australia including ff.74-5 extract from address by J. E. Fenton, Feb. 1930.

LOW PAPERS

Guard-books and other volumes of newspapers containing cartoons by Sir David Low, early 20th cent. These include *The Canterbury Times*, 1 vol., *The Spectator*, 3 vols., *The Sydney Bulletin*, 2 vols., and *The Exhibition Sketcher*, 1 vol.

OTHER MANUSCRIPTS

Misc.213. 'Colonisation in the Pacific: a study in Imperial enterprise', Leila Thomas 1922, typescript.

Misc.262. Volume containing miscellaneous entries and notes c.1830 on the trade of New South Wales, the East Indies, and South America. The notes consist mainly of an item entitled 'Memo regarding the trade of New South Wales' by Mr Thornton suggesting means by which the trader can make a substantial profit as a result of trading between England, Rio de Janeiro, Sydney, the Pacific Islands, the Philippines, and Mauritius.

LONDON SCHOOL OF HYGIENE AND TROPICAL MEDICINE
Keppel Street, London, W.C.1

Applications for use of manuscripts should be made to the Librarian. There is a dictionary catalogue of books, pamphlets, and manuscripts to 1965 published by G. K. Hall & Co. Later accessions are similarly catalogued on cards. From a brief check of obvious geographical headings in the catalogue there appear to be very few manuscripts relating to the field of this guide but the following were noted.

F. W. O'Connor, Medical Researches in the Western Pacific, being a report on the results of the expedition sent from the London School of Medicine to the Ellice, Tokelau, and Samoan Islands 1921-2, unedited manuscript.

P. A. Buxton, The Control of Mosquitoes in Apia, Samoa, c.1925, typescript.

NEW COLLEGE, LONDON
527 Finchley Road, London, N.W.3

The records of this Congregational theological college, dating from the eighteenth century, are mainly concerned with the administration of the various constituent colleges and the care of English congregations. The registers of students give information about those who went out to Australia, New Zealand, and the Pacific as ministers or missionaries. In addition two letters were noted:

419/41. n.d. Rev. Thomas Binney, Ginnagallah, near Sydney [to James Gibson] referring to grants he has made to chapels there, to his chairmanship of the annual assembly of the Tasmanian Congregational Union, to his own address on the Bishop of Adelaide's idea of union, to the movement to effect ecclesiastical reforms in South Australia, and to his sons who are settled in Australia. The address was later enlarged into a book *Lights and Shadows of Church Life in Australia*, London 1860, see *Memorial of the late Rev. Thomas Binney LL.D.*, ed. Rev. J. Stoughton, London 1874.

435/4. 9 Mar. 1859 Rev. T. Binney, Hobart, to H. Rutt discussing financial matters and referring to assistance he has given to Congregationalists in Australia, to his controversy with the Bishop of Adelaide, his friendship with Dr Perry, Bishop of Melbourne, and favourable impression of Sir Henry Barkly at Melbourne.

SCHOOL OF ORIENTAL AND AFRICAN STUDIES
London, W.C.1

The Library maintains a card catalogue of printed books and manuscripts in three divisions, author, title, and subject. The catalogue to Easter 1962 has been photolithographed, Boston 1963, 22 vols. Vol.22 is a catalogue of manuscripts and microfilms. A check has been made of the following sections: Australian Dialects, Easter Island, English, Malayo-Polynesian, Micronesian.

Since cataloguing is still in progress and re-arrangement has taken place it is not easy to identify some of the documents microfilmed for the Australian Joint Copying Project.

MARSDEN COLLECTION

The collection of oriental books of William Marsden presented to King's College, London, in 1835 and now in the School of Oriental and African Studies. Manuscripts include:

MS.9882. Vocabularies of the language of Tonga or the Friendly Islands, compiled at Tongatabu, and of the language of New Caledonia, by officers of the French frigates *L'Espérance* and *La Recherche*, with some documents in French on the crews of the ships and instructions for their voyage 1793. 9 parts.

MS.12023. D. C. Solander, Vocabulary of the language of Tahiti, English and Tahitian.

MS.12153. Vocabularies of the languages of Tahiti, Prince's Island, Sulu, Samarang,

361

N

London

New Holland, New Zealand, Savu compiled by Sir Joseph Banks. Some vocabularies are in Banks's handwriting and on some Banks has written notes, e.g. 'Otahiti Words from Mr. Monkhouse' and on the New Zealand section, 'The South part as taken by Mr. Parkinson in Queen Charlot's Sound'.

MS.12156. Vocabularies of the languages of Otaheite, New Zealand, Savu, Prince's Island, Samarang, Sulu, Madagascar, the Mandingos, the Eskimos, Malabar, and Peru, 'Vocabularies of the Taheitian and some other languages compiled during Cook's first voyage', and from other sources. Some manuscripts in this volume appear to be copies of manuscripts in MS.12153.

MS.12892. Sir Joseph Banks, 'Observationes de Otaheite &c'. This title and the manuscript are in Banks's handwriting. A label in another hand reads 'Names & Descriptions of Persons & Places, with other memoranda, made by Sr Jos. Banks at Taheiti &c when visited in Cook's First voyage (1769)'.

MS.41645/a-d. (a-c) Notebooks of William Dawes, one dated 1790, entitled by another hand 'Grammatical forms and vocabularies of languages spoken in the neighbourhood of Sydney', (d) Short vocabularies of the natives of Van Diemen's Land, collected by the officers of the French frigates *La Recherche* and *L'Espérance* in 1792.

RAY PAPERS

Sydney Herbert Ray, authority on Oceanic languages, visited Torres Straits, New Guinea, and Borneo with the Cambridge Anthropological Expedition 1898-9. The papers include manuscript notes apparently used for his published works and many notes and manuscripts collected by Ray. Most of the papers have been placed in sixteen boxes for the contents of which a handlist is available. Papers at present (1970) in an additional parcel will probably form boxes 17 and 18.

Among the papers in the boxes are vocabularies and notes of languages in Polynesia, Melanesia, and Micronesia by S. H. Ray, F. W. Christian, and others. Some at least formed Accessions 40789 and 40794 and a few papers from Accession 40789 are in the parcel. Also in various boxes are vocabularies of dialects of New Guinea (including Bailala River, Benedele, Bogadjim, Elema, Kukukuku) by Copeland King and others. Some of these are in boxes 1, 5, 8. They formed Accession 40799. Other extensive studies in the boxes are:

Boxes 2-3. S. H. Ray, Papuan vocabularies.

Box 2. C. O. Lelean, Fijian vocabularies. Part of Accession 40800.

Box 3. S. H. Ray, Comparative vocabulary of Oceanic words, some parts in parcel. Formerly Accession 40790.

Box 4. A. Capell, Notes on Eromanga words.

Box 6. R. H. Rickard, Dictionary and grammar of the New Britain dialect, 3 vols., the first dated 1879. Accession 40791.

Box 11. H. B. T. Somerville and S. C. Weigall, Words and phrases in Roviana and Marovo with their English equivalents.

The additional parcel contains a vocabulary for a comprehensive study of Melanesian languages by Ray, vocabularies of Solomon Islands languages from G. Friederici's MSS. and letters 1891-3 from R. H. Rickard, O. Michelsen, L. Fison, W. Gunn, R. H. Mathews.

RAY MANUSCRIPTS

Selections from the Ray Papers.

MS.40801. S. H. Ray and others, Notes on the vocabulary and epigraphy of the Easter Island tablet. 5 parts.

MS.68121. Catalogue of printed books and manuscripts relating to languages and the science of language and belonging to S. H. Ray, 9 vols. in 2 portfolios. Both portfolios contain much information relevant to the field of this guide.

L.II.6.2. Accession 38227. Vocabularies of native dialects of British New Guinea; Appendices to Annual Reports on the administration of the territory of New Guinea 1889-96 bound in 1 volume and provided with manuscript notes by S. H. Ray. Shelved with printed books.

OTHER MANUSCRIPTS

MS.18945. A collection of official documents belonging to Henry Dundas, 1st Viscount Melville including correspondence June-July 1808 concerning Lieut.-Col. Lachlan Macquarie's letter transmitting the claim of certain officers of the 73rd Regiment for non-effective and other allowances from 25 June 1805 to 20 June 1806.

MS.40894/1-2. C. G. Seligmann and G. Pim, Vocabulary of the language of the Otati tribe in neighbourhood of Cape Granville, Cape York Peninsula, Q'ld, obtained from Caroma, a woman of Otati tribe, who knew a fair amount of English and had for years been associated with Pim, 1898; a short vocabulary of the dialect of the natives of Raffles Bay.

MS.50494. W. G. Ivens, 'A grammar of the language of Pangkumu, Malekula Island, New Hebrides, Melanesia', and 'A grammar of the language of Loh, Torres Islands, Melanesia'.

MS.183038. Index to A. Dalrymple's collection of maps, charts, and plans including some of Australia, New Guinea, and Pacific Islands; also a list of six volumes of memoirs.

MS.184245. G. C. W. C. Wheeler, 'The Mono-Alu people of Bougainville Strait', West Solomon Islands, c.1943, typescript. The manuscript notes for the typescript are at MS.170822.

UNIVERSITY COLLEGE
The Library, Gower Street, London, W.C.1

There is a card index to College correspondence, autograph letters, and some of the holdings of the Mocatta Library. The larger collections of papers are catalogued or indexed separately as described below.

JEREMY BENTHAM MANUSCRIPTS

Papers of Jeremy Bentham, jurist and social reformer, 177 boxes. See A. Taylor Milne, *Catalogue of the Manuscripts of Jeremy Bentham in the Library of University College, London*, London 1937, 2nd ed. 1962. Most of the papers are simply rough drafts and notes arranged in folders, roughly according to subject, but with considerable overlapping. Bentham, advocating his Panopticon, categorises New South Wales as the 'true Bastile' and comments on conditions in the colony; he also makes more general observations on Australia in connection with colonisation and pacificism. There are many papers concerning the Panopticon and the convict system in New South Wales. Other papers include:

Box 8, folder 8. Proposal 11 Aug. 1831 for the formation of a joint stock company by the name of the Colonisation Company, on an entirely new principle, including comments on colonisation of Australia. 23 Aug. 1831, Edward Gibbon Wakefield on the Colonisation Society's plan.

Box 25, folders 4, 5, 7, 10. General principles of international law, with reference to pacificism and emancipation, colonies, and the navy, 1786-9.

London

Box 169, folder 35. Journal *c.*1795 of James Martin who escaped from Botany Bay on 20 Mar. 1791. Original and copy.

SOCIETY FOR THE DIFFUSION OF USEFUL KNOWLEDGE PAPERS

See Monica C. Grobel, 'The Society for the Diffusion of Useful Knowledge', Ph.D. thesis, University of London, 1933, 4 vols. The bibliography serves as a catalogue to the papers and detailed references are contained in footnotes throughout.

Letters 1827-45, 26 boxes. Arranged in box files by year, alphabetically filed within the year and including:

Correspondence 1830 concerning *The New Zealanders*, London 1830, a compilation by George Lillie Craik, which incorporated the journal of the shipwrecked mariner, John Rutherford, including letters 18 Feb. 1830 D. Jardine, 1830 H. Bellenden Ker, Mar.-Apr. 1830 Charles Knight, 18 Jan. 1831 John Rutherford.

Letters May 1830 to Nov. 1841 from W. B. Clarke concerning a series of plans of cities published by the Society.

Letters soliciting publications from the Society: 3 Aug. 1836 Alexander Maconochie to help establish itinerant libraries in Van Diemen's Land; [4 Nov.] 1836 J. B. Shepherdson appointed by G. F. Angas to organise schools of industry in South Australia; 14 Sept. 1837 G. W. Robertson of the Protestant South Australian Emigration Community; 13 Dec. 1837 J. Gawthorn, 7 Dec. 1837 Thomas Edgworth, and 1837 Edward Strutt, recommending the request of William Waterfield of the Colonial Missionary Society; 6 Sept. 1839 T. M. Partridge enclosing a report of the Literary Society and Public Library of New Zealand; 31 Mar. 1840 Thomas Heath, L.M.S. missionary at Manono, Samoa, enclosing issue of *O Le Sulu Samoa* [*Samoan Torch*], also describing death of John Williams, visits to New Hebrides, New Caledonia, and Sydney; 14 Nov. 1845 J. Knowles, secretary, Port Nicholson [N.Z.] Mechanics' Institute, enclosing half-yearly report.

Letters concerning the grant of £10 worth of books to the South Australian Company through J. Hindmarsh: 1836 Thomas Coates, 1836 Rowland Hill, 27 May 1836 Henry Jickling, 6 June 1836 J. Hindmarsh.

Correspondence concerning the use of a map of the county of Wellington, W.A., prepared by the Society to show a proposed new settlement near Port Leschenault called Australind: 10 Aug. 1840 T. J. Buckton, Secretary, Western Australian Company, asking for 1000 copies and enclosing prospectus of the Company and terms of land sales; 10 Aug. 1840 Society's reply (copy) with certain objections; 12 Aug. 1840 T. J. Buckton accepting Society's terms; 14 Aug. 1840 F. Beaufort agreeing to proposed changes in map.

Other miscellaneous letters are: 21 Oct. 1830 A. C. Kilgour suggesting preparation of a guide to the colonies to assist emigration; [?6 June 1839] A. Maconochie, Hobart Town, introducing Frederick Maitland Innes and describing him in some detail; 28, 30 Dec. 1839 F. M. Innes offering to write a small volume on Van Diemen's Land; 27 May 1839 J. Lhotsky offering his services and submitting for publication in *Penny Magazine* a tract on physical education; 19 Jan. 1840 Francis Beaufort concerning map of Australia; 1841 William B. Carter for Secretary, New Zealand Company, answering Society's inquiry about the settlement at Port Nicholson, recommending maps and chart published by Wyld, Charing Cross, and Arrowsmith. There may be further correspondence from F. M. Innes who contributed to the Society's publications.

Biographical Dictionary letters, 4 boxes. Letters concerning a projected publication of the Society arranged alphabetically in box files.

29 Apr. 1842 T. Hewitt Key reconsidering his previous recommendation of J. Lhotsky and endorsed with comments about Lhotsky.

29 Oct., 2, 6, 29 Nov. 1841 J. Lhotsky offering to contribute to the dictionary and to undertake translations, with remarks on his experience and his present distressed state.

General Committee Minutes 1826-46, 3 vols.
A few references are found in vol.3 to some of the requests listed under letters. See pp.33-4, 54, 62, 70, 109, 205, 235. See also p.75, 'Illustrations of the present state and future prospects of New South Wales', laid on table.

Minutes of Sub Committees 1827-34, 2 vols., indexed.
Vol.1, p.62, Dr Thomson proposing a history of the Coral Islands; vol.1, pp.96-7, 261, 271, vol.2, pp.5, 13, 23, 44, purchase of Rutherford's journal, preparation of *The New Zealanders*.

BROUGHAM PAPERS

Correspondence of Henry Peter Brougham, 1st Baron Brougham and Vaux. These letters are still being catalogued (Dec. 1969) but there is a large card index of personal names already in existence. This shows that the collection includes relevant letters from John Brougham, P. R. Brougham, two of Henry's nephews who emigrated to Australia, and from George Fife Angas, Philip P. Blyth, Fielding Browne, James Dowling, Charles Few, Matthew Davenport Hill, and Saxe Bannister.

FREDERICK HUTH & CO. LTD RECORDS

A firm of merchant bankers with world-wide connections, dissolved in 1936, which had dealings with Australia, particularly in connection with the importation of wool.

Letter books, English letters Oct. 1827 to Sept. 1851, 67 vols. This is out-correspondence, indexed by name of recipient, with place and date. Many letters are illegible. Australian entries appear from c.1840, e.g. vol. for 1 July to 30 Sept. 1845, to Rev. G. K. Rusden, Maitland, N.S.W., and Samuel Stocks Jnr & Co., Adelaide; vol. for 1 July to 30 Sept. 1851 to Augustus Dreutler, Sydney, Flower Salting & Co., Sydney, J. B. & G. Were, Sydney and Melbourne, and Were Todd & Co., Adelaide. There is also a small series of Spanish letters from 1812-13, an extensive series of German letters, together numbering 112 volumes, of negligible Australian interest, and a volume of letters Jan.-July 1839, not indexed, from the Liverpool branch to the London branch, which may contain references to Australian affairs.

Journals 1822-50 with gaps, c.12 vols. A few references to Australian accounts appear in 1843-50.

Bills receivable 1820-51, 20 vols. Australian references from 1840.

Bills payable 1820-51, 20 vols. Australian references from 1840.

Accounts current, English, 1840-3, 1844-6, 2 vols., indexed. Examples of Australian references found are: vol. for 1840-3 Australian Fire & Life Insurance Co., Sydney, Thomas Breillat, Sydney, Henry Ferris, Sydney, Flower Salting & Co., Sydney, H. Meinertzhagen, Sydney, Henry Moore, Sydney, C. W. Roemer, Sydney, Rev. G. K. Rusden, Maitland, N.S.W., Salting & Garrard, Sydney, A. W. Scott, Sydney, P. Scott, Sydney, Samuel Stocks Jnr & Co., Adelaide, Anthony Williams, Hobart. There are also series of foreign, Spanish, and German current accounts, and the current account of the Liverpool branch which is not indexed.

Insurance ledgers, A 1819-21, C 1828-33, D 1834-8, E 1838-9, K 1850-1, 5 vols. Indexed, usually by the names of ships. These may contain entries of Australian interest.

Cash books, Glyn Hallifax Mills & Co., bankers, 1814-49, 13 vols. 1837-8 and 1845-6 missing, not indexed.

Sales and returns, 1834-50, 1849-52, 1856-61, 3 vols., indexed by name of firm and by ship.

London

Ledgers B 1821-5, D 1829-30, F 1836-40, 3 vols.

Cash book 1898-9 [1898-1901?].

Loose correspondence

29 Dec. 1848 William Millard, for James Blackmore Wilcocks of the Office for Government Emigration, Colonial Passenger and General Emigration Agency, Plymouth. The agency acted for the Colonial Land & Emigration Commissioners, New Zealand Company, South Australian Company, the India and Australian Royal Mail Steam Packet Co. and others.

2 Feb. 1843 Fried Boss, London, to Mr Meinertzhagen, 10 Moorgate Street, London, in German.

16 Mar. 1849 William Tarrach, Southwark, applying for employment because 'some of your clerks have left your office for Australia'.

22 July 1843 T. Beasley, Torquay, on sherries from Victoria.

CHADWICK PAPERS

Papers of Sir Edwin Chadwick, sanitary and public health reformer, and secretary to the Poor Law Commission in 1834. The correspondence is arranged alphabetically in folders and the other papers arranged by subject. Although Chadwick was interested in emigration and in many social and reform movements affecting the colonies, there appears to be little material relating specifically to Australasia and the Pacific in this collection. The correspondence includes:

Letters thanking Chadwick for the proofs of his 'Sanitation in the Colonies' from Australasian Agents General in London: 11 Jan. 1887 Sir Arthur Blyth, South Australia, 14 Jan. 1887 Sir Saul Samuel, New South Wales, 7 Jan. [1887] Sir Francis Henry Dillon Bell, New Zealand; another letter 19 Apr. 1886 from Blyth acknowledging receipt of a collection of papers on drainage and sanitation; letter 14 Feb. 1845 from John Robertson, Manchester, concerning the sale of tattooed New Zealand heads.

PACIFIC STEAM NAVIGATION CO. PAPERS

'Statements and documents relative to the establishment of steam navigation in the Pacific', typewritten copy of a brochure privately printed by William Wheelwright London 1838 to promote the formation of the company. Includes a supporting letter by Capt. Robert FitzRoy.

ROYAL MAIL STEAM PACKET CO. PAPERS

The collection includes daily minutes 1843-54, reports and accounts 1842-1903, mail contracts 1840-76, and other financial records.

AUSTRALASIAN PACIFIC MAIL STEAM PACKET CO. PAPERS

Minutes of the Court of Directors, Apr. 1852 to July 1861, indexed.

MOCATTA LIBRARY

Library of the Jewish Historical Society of England, housed in University College.

Harold Boas correspondence

Correspondence of Harold Boas, F.R.A.I.A., F.A.P.I., Perth, W.A., with Anglo-Jewish associates met while Jewish representative, Y.M.C.A., with A.I.F. in France and England 1916-20. The letters are filed alphabetically by correspondent, occasionally by subject, with drafts or typescript copies of Boas's replies. They include:

24 Oct. 1947 to Sir Robert Waley Cohen and 2 Dec. 1947 from him.

11 Oct. 1950 from Dr Israel Feldman.

23 July 1917 from Rev. A. A. Green, London.

Correspondence 10 Sept. 1947 to 13 June 1948 with Sir Basil and Lady Henriques concerning their visit to Australia under the auspices of the British Council, and earlier letters from July 1946. Also copies of *Fratres*, circular letters sent by Henriques to members of the Bernhard Baron St George's Jewish Settlement, with personal endorsements, and a brochure describing the Settlement.

Correspondence 26 Aug. 1938 to 13 Apr. 1946 with Hebrew University, Jerusalem, including letters to and from Prof. and Mrs Norman Bentwich who visited Australia in 1938, Dr Chaim Wardi, who visited Australia in 1939, with references to Dr Steinberg's scheme for the settlement of refugees in Western Australia, Dr Fischel, who visited Australia in 1940, M. Zacharin of the Jewish Council to Combat Fascism & Anti-Semitism concerning the visit of Dr Sambursky, and A. M. Cohen, Australian representative of the Jewish National and University Library.

4 Mar. 1919 Invitation and menu of the Maccabaeans' dinner in honour of Monash, London.

Seventeen letters with replies 1918-19 Dr Claude Montefiore, founder of Liberal Judaism, concerning Boas's position as Jewish representative, Y.M.C.A.

Seventeen letters with replies 20 Aug. 1918 to 15 Oct. 1959 Hon. Lily Montagu, O.B.E., J.P., founder of the World Union of Progressive Judaism.

Ten letters with replies 25 Sept. 1930 to 9 Sept. 1943 Dr Israel Mattuck, Rabbi, Liberal Jewish Synagogue, London, concerning the establishment of Liberal congregations in Australia.

Correspondence 31 Oct. 1938 to 2 Jan. 1939 Dr Benzion Shein concerning his visit to Australia.

Correspondence 5 Mar. 1924 to 30 July 1925 concerning Jewish War Memorial, U.K.

Four letters with replies 14 Nov., 5 Dec. 1917 Israel Zandwill concerning arrangements to meet Major D. I. Friedman, Australian Jewish Chaplain.

Laws and Regulations of the Melbourne Synagogue. Kahal kodesh she'erit Yisra'el, 5608, pr. William Clarke, Melbourne 1948.

VETERAN CAR CLUB OF GREAT BRITAIN
14 Fitzhardinge Street, Portman Square, London, W.1

Application to consult the records should be made to the Secretary.

SIMMS PAPERS

Papers relating to F. R. Simms. Further papers are in the custody of the Public Relations Officer, Simms Motor and Electronics Corporation Ltd, Oak Lane, Finchley, London, N.2.

179/41/5. Letter 6 Mar. 1894 from the Secretary, Victorian Railways, Australia, to Daimler Motor Syndicate Ltd concerning a sample automatic ticket machine.

207/47/9. Provisional agreement 13 Sept. 1893 between the Syndicate and Swinburne and Co. Ltd for the sole agency of Daimler Motors except for launch driving in Western Australia.

264/7/9-11, 22-3, 25-6, 30, 33, 35-7. Correspondence 1896 between Sir J. Somers Vine and F. R. Simms about the exhibition at the Imperial Institute, and about the possible establishment of a car-hire business in Western Australia by George Gray, mining engineer.

422. Correspondence of Simms and Co. in a leather bound volume entitled 'The B.M.I. 1891', including: request 11 July 1892 from Jules Renard and Co., Sydney, Melbourne and Antwerp for the agency of motor boats in Australia; correspondence 1891 between F. R. Simms and his partner Alfred Hendriks and H. Stecher of

London

Henry Noon and Co., Sydney, sole agent of British Daimler Motor Co. in Australia and New Zealand.

Papers of John Pollitt, d.1958. The second accession of these papers is indicated as P2.

3/86. Letter 27 June 1899 from J. W. Burstall, High Street, Hull, to Yorkshire Motor Car Manufacturing Co. Ltd, requesting a catalogue and asking if the company had an agent in Melbourne.

3/100. Letter 29 June 1899 from J. W. Burstall to Y.M.C.M. Co. Ltd asking if his brother's firm, Burstall and Smith, 387 Little Collins Street, Melbourne, might be made agents in Australia, and saying that the business was likely to be in complete cars rather than chassis for bodying.

3/145. Letter 9 Aug. 1899 from B. C. Burstall, Burstall and Smith, to Y.M.C.M. Co. Ltd, stating his interest in the development of motor cars and saying that his firm would prefer to import chassis only.

3/149. Letter 16 Aug. 1899 from Burstall and Smith to Y.M.C.M. Co. Ltd enclosing a copy of 3/145 concerning motor car industry.

3/160. Letter 12 Sept. 1899 from [?] to Y.M.C.M. Co. Ltd saying that Burstall and Smith had received the company's catalogue and were confident they could secure a good business if they were made agents.

5/3. Letter 11 July 1948 from John W. Andrews, Auckland, to John Pollitt giving an account of his experience in the motor trade in New Zealand.

5/4. Letter 16 Apr. 1949 from G. H. Brooks, Port Lincoln, S.A., to John Pollitt referring to a car made by Lewis Cycle Works.

P2/3/1/1. Letter 2 Aug. 1899 from Lewis Cycle Works, Freeman Street, Adelaide, to Y.M.C.M. Co. Ltd requesting prices and particulars of vehicles.

P2/3/1/2. Letter 22 Aug. 1899 from Edward L. Holmes, temporary manager of Thomson Motor Patents Company, 60 Queen Street, Melbourne, to Y.M.C.M. Co. Ltd requesting a catalogue and price list, stating that the company was formed to exploit Thomson Motor Patents in Australia 'but it will be some time before any are manufactured'; in the meantime they might meet a large demand for motor vehicles by selling the company's products.

P2/5/1. Letter 3 Feb. 1950 from C. W. Lewis, Lewis Cycle Works Ltd, Adelaide, to Y.M.C.M. Co. Ltd giving details of the origin and development of his firm.

VICTORIA AND ALBERT MUSEUM
The Library, Cromwell Road, London, S.W.7

The Library houses a large collection made by John Forster including material collected as biographer of Dickens. The collection consists of printed books, paintings, pamphlets, and manuscripts. *The Catalogue of the Paintings, Manuscripts, Autograph Letters, Pamphlets etc. bequeathed by John Forster Esq. LL.D.*, London 1893, is indexed by sections, that for manuscripts by writer only. The manuscripts, especially the correspondence, may repay further examination. The index section for pamphlets has subject headings which show a number of relevant pamphlets, e.g. The Australian Patriotic Association to C. Buller on the continuance of transportation, Sydney, 1843; on emigration to Australia 1848; and on steam communications with the Australian colonies and New Zealand 1850.

WELLCOME INSTITUTE OF THE HISTORY OF MEDICINE

183 Euston Road, London, N.W.1

The Library holds more than 5000 Western and about the same number of Oriental manuscripts. There is an author card-catalogue to the former, with indexes to subjects, places, languages, etc. Entries are provided with notes, sometimes extensive, on authorship, subject, collation, and provenance. The first volume of this catalogue has already been published, *Catalogue of Western Manuscripts on Medicine and Science. Part 1: MSS. written before 1650*, London 1962. It was compiled by the present Keeper of Western Manuscripts and former Librarian, S. A. J. Moorat. A catalogue of the post-1650 manuscripts is in preparation (Apr. 1969). The Wellcome Library also has about 100,000 autograph letters arranged alphabetically by author in folders.

WESTERN MANUSCRIPTS

Rev. George Brown, missionary in Samoa 1860-75. 'A South Sea Island Native Practitioner', typescript, *c*.1900, containing notes on medicinal plants used in Samoa.

Alan Deed Brunwin. 'Some observations on the Santonin treatment of dysentery', with letter, Suva 1908, printed in *Journal of Tropical Medicine and Hygiene* 11, 1908, p.278.

Fleetwood Buckle. Diaries of Buckle as a doctor in the Royal Navy, June 1866 to Dec. 1870, 10 vols. These are small card-case memoranda books containing brief notes of his duties, lists of those sick, jottings about the voyages and placed visited, and occasional pencil sketches of scenery and coastlines. The volume Aug.-Dec. 1869 covers the visit of H.M.S. *Liverpool* to Tasmania and Victoria, and includes a sketch of the coast seventy miles south of Sydney. The volume July-Dec. 1870 describes the ship's calls at New Zealand and Pitcairn Island.

Sir James Cantlie, founder of the Royal Society of Tropical Medicine and Hygiene. Papers 1888 in connection with an inquiry into the life history of Eurasians, including an unfinished paper on the subject by Cantlie and a number of completed questionnaires with covering letters from medical officers and others in China, Malaya, and New Zealand. Letters and forms were received from, among others, Patrick Joseph Carrol, T. J. Trimnel, Alfred Ginders, George H. Davies, and Thomas Watt Bell in New Zealand, and Frederick W. Taplin in Point Macleay, S.A. Report on the conditions under which leprosy occurs in China, Indo-China, Malaya, the Malay Archipelago, and Oceania, 1894. Part 2, relating to leprosy in the Pacific, is missing. The complete report is published in *Transactions of the Epidemiological Society*, 1897-8.

Jane Foster and others. Collection of cookery 'receipts' with a few medical 'receipts', 1739-94; signed inside cover 'Francis Watkins Esq., Parramatta, New South Wales', *c*.1825.

John Murray Gibbes. Essay 'Reincarnation = Evolution', written in the Australian bush where Gibbes had retired to meditate and produce this theory, 1904.

Jacques Julien Houton de Labillardière. ff.v-vii. Fragment of a work in Latin on the flora of Tasmania and of Carteret Bay, New Ireland, 1792. The notes were taken during the expedition of D'Entrecasteaux in search of La Pérouse, which arrived in Tasmania 23 Apr. 1792, and, after visits to various Pacific Islands, reached Amboyna 6 Sept. 1792.

Denis Gascoigne Lillie, marine zoologist to Scott's Antarctic Expedition 1910-13. Notebooks compiled from lectures while Lillie was a student at Birmingham University and later St John's College, Cambridge. They are usually written in pencil and copiously illustrated with pen and pencil drawings sometimes coloured in crayon. The lectures are on zoology 1903-10, 9 vols., geology 1905-10, 9 vols., and botany 1910, 4 vols.

Notes on fish, fishing, and trawling, 1910. Rough notes mostly in pencil, illustrated with sketches and diagrams, perhaps compiled before his departure on Capt. Scott's *Terra Nova* in June 1910.

Biological log Nov. 1910 to June 1913. Original log in pencil.

Fair copy by Lillie in ink, of biological log, but last entry 28 Jan. 1911.

Whale log Nov. 1910 to June 1913. Fair copy by Lillie in ink, illustrated by pencil sketches of various types of whales. The log covers the Antarctic cruise Nov. 1910 to Mar. 1911, winter cruise July-Nov. 1911, Antarctic cruise no.2 Dec. 1911 to Apr. 1912, Antarctic cruise no.3 Dec. 1912 to Feb. 1913, homeward voyage Mar.-June 1913.

Address to the Tasmanian branch of the British Medical Association 'On the application of Mendel's principle of heredity', with diagrams in ink, Hobart 1913.

John Lillie, grandfather of Denis Gascoigne Lillie. Lectures on science delivered at the Mechanics' Institutes at Launceston and Hobart 1842-55, 12 parts; lectures on science delivered at the Mechanics' Institute, Hobart, 1851-4. Unbound in cloth slip case with a photograph of the author in a leather case with cover.

Robert McCormick

Rough draft of 'Diary whilst fitting out for Antarctic Expedition 1839', Feb.-Oct. 1839. The first forty-six leaves are wanting. McCormick served as surgeon and naturalist in H.M.S. *Erebus* during the Antarctic Expedition 1839-43 under Capt. James Clark Ross.

Rough journal, H.M.S. *Erebus*, Sept. 1839 to July 1843, 15 parts, pp.521-7 in part 5 missing.

Meteorological register, H.M.S. *Erebus*, Oct. 1839 to July 1843.

Ornithological memoranda, Oct. 1839 to June 1843, including notes 19 May 1841 on seals caught and an *Ornithorhynchus* from Tasmania.

Richard Robert Madden, Colonial Secretary of Western Australia 1847-50. Collection of material relating to spiritualism, witchcraft, mesmerism, and clairvoyance c.1860, 5 parts. A note by his son Thomas More Madden, states that these chapters were intended for a third volume of his *Phantasmata*, London 1857, 2 vols.

William Brougham Monkhouse, surgeon to H.M.S. *Endeavour* 1768-70 during Cook's first voyage. Notes taken of William Hunter's lectures on anatomy c.1755.

Joseph Oliver. Collection of homilies and prayers, notes on geography, astrology, and astronomy c.1795-1810. 'New discoveries by English navigators' describes the voyages of Wallis in the *Dolphin* and Carteret in the *Swallow* 1766, with particular detail about Wallis at Tahiti, of Cook in the *Endeavour* 1768-71, and of Cook and Clerke in the *Resolution* and *Discovery* 1776-9. The geographical notes ignore the Pacific discoveries although there is a note on New Holland.

Sir Raymond Edward Priestley. Notes on animal, bird, plant and insect life in the Antarctic made during the Shackleton Expedition 1908-9, to which Priestley was geologist, and the Scott Expedition 1910-12, to which he was scientist with the Northern party; typescript.

Nathaniel Rogers. Obituary of eminent persons and private friends 1826-69, 2 vols. Brief, but personal, notices of persons, some later entries accompanied by tinted photographs, including George Bennet of the London Missionary Society, Robert Torrens, William Jackson Hooker, and others.

Robert Neal Rudmose-Brown. Account of the expedition of the Scottish Antarctic ship *Scotia* to which Rudmose-Brown was naturalist.

Oliver Smithson. 'Mossman Fever', with letter, Brisbane 1910, printed in *Journal of Tropical Medicine and Hygiene*, 14, 1910, p.251.

George Charles Wallich. Collection of material on marine biology by, or connected with, Wallich 1860-98, 9 vols. Wallich entered the Indian Medical Service in 1838 and surveyed the Atlantic bottom in the *Bulldog* in 1860. He laboured under a strong sense of grievance for he believed that his discoveries in marine biology had been deliberately ignored, and later plagiarised. Although his experience was in the Atlantic, his papers all contain sections disputing the claims made for the *Challenger* Expedition.

AUTOGRAPH LETTERS

Some letters in this collection are routine communications interesting only for their signatures, others are interesting for their contents as well. A random check of 150 names with Australasian connections uncovered only the following correspondents: Sir Anthony Brownless, Melbourne University 16 Jan. 1884; W. B. Clarke, River Darling, N.S.W., July 1866; Sir William Thomas Denison, Government House, Sydney, Aug. 1858; a substantial collection by Joseph Dalton Hooker including letters 26 Nov. 1844 to Messrs Reeves concerning prospectuses for *Flora Antarctica*, and 18 May 1866 to Thomas Baines concerning his pictures of the Northern Territory Expedition.

WELLINGTON MUSEUM
Apsley House, Hyde Park Corner, London, W.1

The papers of the 1st Duke of Wellington are in the possession of the present Duke. A large number chiefly concerned with the public life of the 1st Duke are at Apsley House. See Historical Manuscripts Commission, *The Prime Ministers' Papers 1801-1902*, London 1968. These papers, especially bundles of correspondence 1806-52 accumulated after his withdrawal from India in 1805, should repay examination.

ARCHDIOCESE OF WESTMINSTER
Archbishop's House, Ambrosden Avenue, London, S.W.1

The Roman Catholic archives in the Archbishop's House are the records of the Vicars Apostolic of the London District from the sixteenth century until the reorganisation of the hierarchy in 1850, and thereafter of the Archbishops of Westminster. The collection contains no long continuous series of official records, but consists mainly of correspondence, working papers, and memoranda of individuals, with a number of printed pamphlets and treatises. The major part of the collection has been sorted into artificial sections labelled A-H, and there is a temporary draft catalogue for these sections. In addition there are papers relating to the incumbencies of Cardinal Wiseman and Cardinal Vaughan, which are still being sorted and listed, but which are available for inspection. The records after 1903 are still unsorted and are not yet available for inspection.

The mission in New Holland started under the jurisdiction of the Vicar Apostolic of London (1817) although for a while it was theoretically subject to the jurisdiction of the Vicar Apostolic of the Cape of Good Hope (1819-35). In 1835 Bishop J. B. Polding arrived as first Vicar Apostolic of New Holland, and in 1842 when the first episcopal sees were created in Australia, he was made the first Archbishop.

The relevant material found is listed below in detail because it is so scattered and of such a miscellaneous nature, and because the cataloguing and arrangement of the records is not yet organised. It is possible that there are other references which were not discovered during this search.

A large group of miscellaneous manuscripts, mainly in-letters to the Vicars Apostolic, with some draft and copy out-letters and some printed matter, 1501-1847. After 1799 the papers are loose, filed chronologically in boxes.

Bishop Poynter

Two letters 12 Dec. 1817, 16 Nov. 1818 from J. Flynn, Prefect Apostolic of New Holland; other letters concerning Flynn and his position are dated 28 Feb., 23 Aug., 8 Dec., n.d. 1817, and 24 July, 3 Aug., 19 Aug., 17 Dec., 24 Dec. 1818.

Letters 23 Aug. 1822, 26 May, 11 Oct. 1823, 19 Jan., 12 June, 11 Oct. 1824, 19 Sept. 1825, 10 Jan., 16 Jan., 16 Feb., 19 Apr., 15 Nov. 1826 from P. Conolly discussing various general, moral, and educational problems in New South Wales, his difficulties with Dr Slater [Vicar Apostolic of the Cape of Good Hope, residing in Mauritius], Samuel Coote in Van Diemen's Land, and Rev. Therry, R.C. Chaplain in Sydney. Other letters noted are:

18 Jan. 1820 James Buckley to Poynter concerning his passage to the West Indies in a government ship mentioning that 'Mr. Morris had informed me that two priests had obtained a free passage to Botany Bay by the orders of Lord Bathurst and were to be treated on the footing of captains, adding that he [Mr Morris] had seen the orders himself'.

14 Oct. 1822 Governor of New South Wales to Roman Catholic chaplains, Rev. Conolly and Rev. Therry, giving advice and instructions, printed.

28 Aug. 1823, 7 Oct. 1824 R. Wilmot Horton to Lieutenant Governor of Van Diemen's Land, and Governor to P. Conolly, recommending Samuel Coote for work in Van Diemen's Land, copies.

28 Aug. 1823 Wilmot Horton to Poynter stating that Coote might pass his books free when he left for Van Diemen's Land.

16 Sept. 1823 Samuel Coote to Poynter asking for letters of introduction.

12 June 1824 S. Coote, V.D.L., to Poynter concerning his movements.

24 June 1824 R. Wilmot Horton to Poynter concerning the appointment of two clergymen for New South Wales.

8 June 1825 Cutting from *Sydney Gazette* containing acknowledgement by the R.C. chaplain [Rev. Therry] Sydney, to James Burke of Airds, N.S.W., for his offer of land in Campbelltown, with comments on the education and general position of Catholics in New South Wales.

20 June 1825 Archdeacon Scott, Parramatta, to Poynter enclosing cutting and disagreeing with Therry's statements.

6 July 1825 J. J. Therry, Sydney, to Poynter enclosing printed extracts from *The Australian* asking for financial help for Catholics in New South Wales.

15 July 1825 R. Wilmot Horton to Poynter summoning him to discuss R.C. clergymen for New South Wales.

19 July 1825 [?] to Poynter requesting him to find two suitable clergymen for New South Wales.

6 Oct. 1825 R. Hay to Poynter concerning allowances and outfit for two clergymen to go to New South Wales.

19 Oct. 1825 T. Doyle, Bishop in Ireland, to Poynter saying he had no priests available to send as missionaries to New South Wales.

2, 5 Nov. 1825 Two official letters from Rome commissioning Roger Murphy to go as missionary to New South Wales, Latin.

16 Dec. 1825 [?1826] [?] to Poynter concerning two clergymen for New South Wales. n.d. [?1826] List of clergymen and chapels required for New South Wales.

3 Apr. 1826 Poynter to Rev. Therry and Archdeacon Scott concerning Therry's conduct, indicating Lord Bathurst's determination to remove him from New South Wales, two drafts.

3 Apr. 1826 Poynter to R. Hay concerning Coote, copy. Reply 11 Apr. 1826 stating Lord Bathurst had directed Governor of Van Diemen's Land to stop Coote exercising functions of a R.C. clergyman, copy.

26 May 1826 R. Hay to Poynter giving Lord Bathurst's consent to the two clergymen mentioned by Dr Kelly going to New South Wales.

13 June 1826 Bishop Kelly to Poynter about Roger Murphy and Daniel Power leaving from Cork for New South Wales.

4, 10 July 1826 R. Hay to Poynter advising him of movements of ship on which Murphy and Power are to travel.

5 July 1826 R. Hay to Poynter advising him that P. Conolly may not have increase in salary.

10 Aug. 1826 John Birdsall, Cheltenham, to Poynter concerning latter's application to the General Chapter at Downside for missionaries for Australia.

12 Aug. 1826 Poynter to Murphy and Power, Sydney, requesting them to refrain from political activities in Australia, draft.

12 Aug. 1826 R. Hay to Poynter stating Lord Bathurst's decision to cancel Murphy's appointment.

Bishop Bramston

26 Apr. 1834 Bramston to Rome concerning appointment of John Polding as first Vicar Apostolic of New Holland, official draft in Latin.

17 May 1834 Official letter from Rome to Bramston concerning the appointment of John Polding, Latin.

23 Aug. 1834 Official letter from Rome to Bramston concerning the elevation of New Holland to status of Vicariate Apostolic, Latin.

Bishop Griffiths

5, 7 Mar. 1845 Bishop Willson, V.D.L., to Controller General, and Controller General to Sir Eardley Wilmot, concerning supply of books for R.C. convicts under coercive labour, copies.

21 Sept. 1845 [?] to Griffiths concerning allowances for R.C. priests going to Van Diemen's Land.

29 Sept. 1845 [?] to Griffiths concerning Willson's request for books for convicts in Van Diemen's Land.

SECTION B. SUPPLEMENTARY SERIES

Another miscellaneous group of documents including a number of fair and draft letter books of the nineteenth century.

B3. Volume of letters 1817-27 from Bishop Gradwell, Rector of the English College in Rome, chiefly to Bishop Poynter in London. This includes: 21 Apr. 1818 Gradwell to Poynter stating that Dr Collingridge had reported unfavourably on Flynn to Propaganda.

B30. Volume of letters 1817-27 to Bishop Gradwell in Rome. This includes:

7 Oct. 1825 Poynter to Gradwell concerning the despatch of two more Catholic clergymen to New South Wales.

5 May 1826 Poynter to Gradwell mentioning *inter alia* Therry's indiscretion in New South Wales.

London

130. Box of miscellaneous papers, mostly in-letters 1824-69. These include:

130/1/11. 17 June 1848 Archbishop Polding, Sydney, to Secretary of State for Colonies concerning his application for land to establish an institution for the education of Catholic clergymen under his own superintendence, copy.

130/1/30. 3 Dec. 1849 Bishop Pompallier, Vicar Apostolic of Auckland, written on board *Oceania* near Algoa Bay on his way to New Zealand, mainly describing the journey.

130/1/34. 21 Feb. 1852 J. M. B. Serra, Bishop of Port Victoria and Bishop Administrator of Perth, concerning the suspension of Dr Brady, Bishop of Perth, his schismatic behaviour in 'this wild country' and his anticipated departure for Madras.

130/4/9. 14 May 1849 J. B. Pompallier, Bishop of Maronea and Apostolic Administrator of Auckland, written in London, describing the Catholic mission in New Zealand, and dwelling on the need for more missionaries.

140. 'Roman letters'. Two boxes of papers, decrees, and rescripts from Propaganda, unofficial letters from Vatican officials, drafts of letters to Rome 1818-64. These include:

8 June 1850 Official decree from Rome appointing Joseph M. Benedictus Serra coadjutor to the Bishop of Perth, with right of future succession, Latin.

13 Sept. 1850 John Brady, Bishop of Perth and Vicar Apostolic, written from Rome in his own handwriting, naming Bishop Serra his chargé d'affaires in things temporal in Perth, French.

20 Sept., 13, 20 Nov. 1850 Three letters referring to Dr Brady and Bishop Serra, Italian, Latin and French, Italian.

28 Nov. 1850 To Fr Urguhard in Western Australia, ordering him to Europe immediately, having put the temporal affairs of the diocese in the hands of Bishop Serra, copy, French. Official letter referring to same, Latin and French.

V1/63. Box of undated papers. These include:

n.d. [*c.*1900] Six draft letters of Vaughan relating to Fiji and the Gilbert and Ellice Islands, referring to the policy of the Deputy Commissioner of the Gilbert and Ellice Islands and to a dispute with the French missions about the demarcation of the Vicariate, English and Italian.

n.d. [*c.*1900] Two draft letters concerning relations between the Catholic and Protestant missions in New Guinea, English and Italian.

R. WILLCOCKS, ESQ.
7 Shooters Hill Road, Blackheath, London, S.E.3

Copies of the following letters have been made for the Australian Joint Copying Project.

2 Dec. 1772 from Palsy, Landerneau, France, to Jean Motteux & Co., London, containing news of reports on Kerguelen's expedition 1772 in search of the 'South Land', officers of the *Gros Ventre* having complained that Kerguelen had not gone to her assistance when attacked.

8 July 1774 from Palsy, L'Orient, France, to Jean Motteux & Co., London, reporting the arrival of the *Beaumont* from China and stating that the *Beaumont* met Captain Cook's frigate at the Cape of Good Hope and reported the killing of some of Cook's men by the 'same Folcks' who had killed and eaten Marion and his crew.

25 Dec. 1807 from Lieut.-Gov. Collins, Hobart, to Cox & Son, London, commenting on his account with them, on the allowance he made to Mrs Collins, on payment for the new uniform he had ordered and on funds due to him since his mother's death.

23 Oct. 1848 from J. McDouall Stuart, Port Lincoln, to an unnamed correspondent concerning Sturt's expedition to Central Australia, concerning the discovery of a lode of copper at Port Lincoln and Stuart's desire to form a Port Lincoln Company, asking for a loan for this purpose.

ZOOLOGICAL SOCIETY OF LONDON
Regent's Park, London, N.W.1

The Society was founded in 1826 by Sir Thomas Stamford Raffles. A selection of the administrative documents and official correspondence of the Society has been preserved, together with some collections of paintings and drawings. This material is housed in the Society's Zoological Library. Application for permission to consult these papers should be made to the Secretary, stating the purpose for which it is required. No material from the private files of the Society may be published without permission in writing from the Secretary. The following letters of special interest have been noted:

Morton Allport, Hobart, two letters 10 Aug., 6 Nov. 1869 concerning the scientific importance and success of the introduction of salmon into the rivers of Tasmania.

George Bennett, Sydney, 6 Sept. 1870 concerning specimens of *Ceratodus forsteri*, a reptilian fish sent to the British Museum, mentioning that two specimens had just been received by Mr Kennedy of Sydney University from a relative in Northern Australia who procured them in Mary's Creek, near his residence, and also concerning three specimens of Wood Hen sent to the Society; Sydney 20 Feb. 1871 stating that he had sent a pair of Wood Hens from Howe's Island and that Charles Moore, Director of the Botanical Gardens, had sent a White Kangaroo Rat, with comments on the Gardens.

Lewis Adolphus Bernays, Vice-President of the Queensland Acclimatisation Society, 15 May 1869 sending a package of seeds, 10 Aug. 1870 declining to exchange specimens since 'it has never been the policy of the Society to import to Queensland either birds or animals unless they were calculated to produce direct results in the way of keeping down insect life or improving the food of the colonists'.

William Henry Catlett, New South Wales Zoological Society, Sydney, 15 Nov. 1890 mentioning that Capt. Murray of S.S. *Parramatta* had brought an English squirrel from the London Zoo for the Gardens, and advising that he was sending a pair of American foxes purchased from America by Sir James Hector in New Zealand to destroy the rabbits there, but prevented by the New Zealand Government.

G. P. Clifford, Manager, Otago Acclimatisation Society, copy letter 2 Apr. 1870 concerning an *Apteryx* and a Kakapo, rare New Zealand birds, 'I would mention that in return for what we have sent we shall be thankful for either game or insect-eating birds, the object of our Society being to introduce that which is useful and not that which is curious'.

John Gould, three letters 5 Feb., 5, 19 Nov. 1851 concerning the exhibition of his humming birds in the Society's Gardens, with account of the receipts for 1851.

Albert Carl Ludwig Gotthilf Gunther, three letters 20 Mar., 5 Apr., 7 Sept. 1870 about the *Ceratodus* discovered by Krefft; 13 Dec. 1870 about salmon from Tasmania.

James Hector, copy letter Wellington 9 Sept. 1868, addressed to the British Museum, advising that he has entrusted to Sir George Grey two live specimens of *Hatteria* to be handed over to the Society's Gardens.

William Hillier, Earl of Onslow, two letters 21 June, 8 July 1892 concerning a pair of Keas, New Zealand parrots, sent to the Society and one letter 27 Jan. 1893 concerning their wrong labelling in the Society's Gardens; 23 Jan. enclosing a report on the suitability of Little Barrier Island as a bird reserve, and asking if the Society can take any action to show that scientific men in England would greatly deplore the inevitable extinction of the curious avifauna of New Zealand, with a printed memo by Lord Onslow deploring the diminution of, and suggesting measures for the preservation of, native New Zealand birds; 24 May 1895 suggesting that the Society makes representations to J. G. Ward, New Zealand Treasurer and Postmaster General, while he is in the United Kingdom, on the rapid extinction of the wingless and other birds of New Zealand.

William Saville Kent, 28 Mar. 1884 stating that he had unexpectedly been offered the post of Inspector of Fisheries to the Government of Tasmania, Hobart, 29 Sept. 1886 forwarding a copy of his monthly report, mentioning the good prospects for the oyster fishery of the colony and his hopes to return to England in 1887.

Edward Pearson Ramsay, four letters 13 July, 6 Sept., 4 Nov. 1870, 27 Jan. 1871 concerning the *Ceratodus* in which he became interested on a visit to Queensland to examine sugar growing interests.

G. S. Sale, 10 Sept. 1870 offering a Kakapo 'the only specimen that has been brought to England alive' to the Society for £50 with copy letter, undated, containing instructions for the care of the Kakapo.

South Australian Banking Company, Mar. 1856 to May 1857, copy correspondence concerning money fraudulently obtained from the Company by John Houston using a forged letter from D. W. Mitchell, Secretary of the Society.

George Sprigg, Secretary of the Acclimatisation Society of Victoria, 26 Aug. 1863 enclosing copies of all correspondence and details of actions taken by his Society to procure specimens of *Didunculus strigorostus*, a rare pigeon inhabiting the Navigator's Islands.

J. Vidgen, Hon. Sec., Queensland Acclimatisation Society, 30 Aug. 1869 advising of a shipment of birds to England and acknowledging receipt of a number of small English birds and rooks 'the sparrows have however taken possession of the Supreme Court Building and the Town Hall in the centre of our City [Brisbane] and are evidently on excellent terms with themselves'.

Alfred Russel Wallace, Sourabaya, Sept. 1861 concerning his stay on the island of Bourn [?Borneo] and commenting on its affinities with the Celebes rather than with the Moluccas; eight letters (one part, n.d.) Feb.-May 1862 concerning his purchase of Paradise Birds in Singapore for the Society and his expenses in connection with this, the letter 31 Mar. 1862 announcing the safe arrival in England 'I suppose for the first time of the Birds of Paradise'; 19 June 1875 inquiring about a paper on the Galapagos Islands supposedly in preparation by the Society and asking for copies of the lists made out of birds, reptiles, etc.; 17 Sept. 1880 mentioning his set of skins of South Australian birds with some Indian, Chinese, and European, obtained by exchange, almost all being labelled with name and locality.

Henry Wright, printed report 17 Oct. 1892 on Little Barrier or Hauturu Island with particular reference to its suitability as a native bird preservation area.

BEDFORDSHIRE

BEDFORD COUNTY RECORD OFFICE
Shire Hall, Bedford

See *Guide to the Bedfordshire Record Office*, 1957, with two *Supplements*, 1962, 1966.

BOARDS OF GUARDIANS RECORDS

Relevant material in Poor Law Union letter books, some of which have contemporary indexes and for some of which there are modern subject indexes, includes:

PUBC 1. Bedford, Correspondence, Out-letters 1835-1919, 20 vols. 1/4 contains scattered references to emigration in Australia.

PUBC 2. Bedford, Correspondence, In-letters 1835-89, 13 vols. Eight volumes 1835-65 contain contemporary contents lists which point to about forty items relating to emigration to Australia. The correspondence, mainly addressed to the Clerk of the Bedford Union from the Secretary of the Poor Law Commission Office, London, and the Secretary of the Colonial Land and Emigration Commission, London, deals with the availability of vessels for Australia, contracts for the conveyance of emigrants, financial arrangements, the general cases of emigration of women, children, paupers, and the families of convicts, qualifications for selection, lists of assisted emigrants and a number of letters concerning the emigration of named individuals. Emigration is to New South Wales, Port Phillip, Van Diemen's Land, and particularly South Australia.

PRIVATE RECORDS

Some papers of Australian interest described below are printed in Bedfordshire Historical Record Society, *Publications*, vol.40, 'Some letters from Bedfordshire Pioneers', ed. Andrew Underwood.

AD.1191. Letter 20 Jan. 1844 from John Feazey, sheep farmer, Melbourne, Vic., to his mother at Wilden, describing station life.*

BD.1392/2. Letter 6 Apr. 1851 from George Witt, doctor and ex-mayor of Bedford, Sydney, to Thomas Barnard, Bedford.*

BS.1548-9. Probate of Henry Marshall, Bedford, 1877-80, one codicil referring to property in New Zealand.*

CRT.150/24. Letters 1831-9 from Australian convict, Richard Dillingham, copies.

G/DDA Bute Estate Papers. Contain eleven items 1841-6 referring to pastoral activities of J. C. S. McDouall in New South Wales and New Zealand, mainly letters from McDouall and his father W. McDouall to the Marquess of Bute.

H/WS Wilshere Papers. Estate papers c.1502-1867 and papers 1789-1825 of William Wilshere as Chairman of Bedfordshire Quarter Sessions. Among the latter about thirteen relevant items 1818-22 were sighted, principally requests to higher authority for removal to the hulks of convicts sentenced to transportation.

HY.574. Copy probate will of Thomas Fyshe Palmer.* One of the codicils was added on the *Surprise* before the voyage to Botany Bay, 1793-4.

L.5/1006. Letter Nov. 1864 from Joel Croxford, prospector, 'Ironbarks Gold Fields', New South Wales, to his brother and niece at Silsoe.

L.30/11/122/62, 229. De Grey papers, letters from Jemima, Marchioness Grey and Baroness Lucas, to her daughter Amabel 14 July 1774 referring to the return of the *Adventure* to the Cape and the account of preceding events in New Zealand waters reported by Capt. Furneaux; 12 Jan. 1780 lamenting the death of Capt. Cook and referring to accounts in the papers.

SA.454. Mortgage on property of Thomas Potter Macqueen in New South Wales included in a deed of appointment and conveyance 22 May 1841.*

W1 Whitbread Papers 1792-1815

W1/4831-48. Papers 1811-13 relating to Jorgen Jorgenson, mainly his letters to Whitbread seeking an interview and financial assistance.

W1/4984-5005. Papers 1809-14 'Prisons and Hulks', mainly correspondence with Whitbread, particularly on conditions aboard the hulks, and, to a lesser extent, in New South Wales, including some reports. There are also letters on individual convict cases, including a petition by Jorgen Jorgenson. W1/4985 is a copy of a twenty-two page letter from Edward Abbott to Philip Gidley King 13 Feb. 1808, Sydney, giving an account of affairs in New South Wales at the time of the deposition of Gov. Bligh.

W1/5007. Letter 14 Dec. 1793 from Lauderdale, Grey, and Sheridan to Dundas (Lord Melville) querying the legality of the sentences of transportation imposed on Thomas Muir and Thomas Fyshe Palmer.

W1/5009. Letter 14 Aug. 1797 to Samuel Whitbread from Palmer in Sydney saying that the deaths of Jos. Gerrald and Skirving were due to privations and suggesting the matter be brought before Parliament.

WJ Wade and Jackson, solicitors, Shefford, Deeds

WJ/607. Mortgage Oct. 1858, not executed, mentioning Gerard Phillips, Sydney, gentleman, and William Northwood, Baltic Wharf, Sussex St, Sydney, timber merchant, part of original town grant near Market Wharf, Sussex St, Sydney.*

X.256/2-3. Letter 8 Apr. 1842 from Charles Cartwright, convict in government employ, Wollongong Stockade, Illawarra, N.S.W., to his wife Elizabeth at Millbrook; letter 14 July 1844 to his wife, father, and mother, discussing the possibility of his wife's joining him on his obtaining his freedom twelve months later.*

X.263/1. Log of *Sir William Bensley* from Deptford to New South Wales, via Cape of Good Hope and return journey calling at Calcutta, carrying male convicts on outward voyage and ballast on return, 12 Aug. 1816 to 16 June 1818.*

X.263/2. List of women and children with their places of origin, 27 Apr. to 14 May 1819, probably the convicts transported on the *Lord Wellington*. The list shows numbers from each county, but not names of individuals.*

X.275/1. Letter 6 June 1866 from Priscilla Dodson, member of sheep farming family, Gympie, Q'ld, to her aunt, Ann Stapleton at Elstow.*

X.275/10-12. Cuttings of articles and illustration 'Two Pioneers' from the *Adelaide Observer* 1 Aug. 1914 and from *Bedfordshire Times* c.27 Oct. 1914.*

X.275/19. Letter 1893 from Priscilla Hurley, daughter of Priscilla Dodson, Gympie, Q'ld, to Ann Stapleton.*

X.290/323. Terms upon which land was granted to settlers in New South Wales and Van Diemen's Land, 1827.

X.345/28. Letter 25 Sept. 1892 Albert H. Culpin, Sydney, to his father Rev. Ben Culpin, minister at Shillington Congregational Church. A wharf labourer for the New Zealand Company, he refers to the Broken Hill strike and maritime disturbances.

BERKSHIRE

MRS M. MACMILLAN
Yew Tree Cottage, Long Wittenham, Abingdon

BARKLY FAMILY PAPERS

See M. Macmillan, *Sir Henry Barkly, Mediator and Moderator, 1815-1898*, Cape Town 1970. The papers of Sir Henry Barkly consist of letters c.1826-36 to his father and family and papers and private correspondence connected with his terms as Governor of British colonies including Victoria, among which are letters from the Duke of Newcastle and drafts of Barkly's letters to Newcastle and Cardwell frankly discussing political issues in Victoria. A draft letter 26 June 1863 Barkly to Newcastle also discusses the character of J. O'Shanassy. Among Barkly's Victorian correspondence is a letter 4 June 1863 from Gardner D. Engleheart concerning the case of Leonard Mason and enclosing copies of a letter 27 Apr. 1863 from Engleheart to Capt. Timmins and of a petition to Barkly from Mason's family praying for his pardon. Drafts of Barkly's private letters 1864-5 to Cardwell concerning Victoria are drafts of letters written from Mauritius discussing the conferring of baronetcies on Australians, transportation of convicts, and the coaling of ships in Melbourne after carrying convicts to Western Australia, the possibility of separation of the Australian colonies from Great Britain and advice on the conduct of governors towards their ministers.

SIR THOMAS SIMSON PRATT PAPERS

The papers of Sir Thomas Simson Pratt include his commissions, correspondence concerning the conferring upon him of the Order of the Bath and the appointment of commissioners to consider defence 1858, addresses. There is also a considerable amount of correspondence, chiefly letters from his wife and daughter to his son Thomas 1843-63. A few letters written from Bath in 1859 refer to Pratt's appointment to command the British forces in Australia and c.forty-three letters 1860-3 are written from Victoria, chiefly from Melbourne, by his wife and daughter Anne, who became the second Lady Barkly. Letters written 1860-1 contain many references to the campaign in New Zealand and to Pratt's difficulties there.

CAPTAIN T. G. S. WARD
Lammas Eyot, Long Wittenham, Abingdon

Captain Ward has a large collection of ship letters, to and from Australia, New Zealand, and Great Britain, of primarily philatelic value but including many of historic interest. From time to time he has allowed copies to be made of selected letters for Australian and New Zealand libraries. The following examples give some idea of the scope of the collection:

Private correspondence includes letters from members of prominent families, e.g. Leslie, N.S.W.; Stephen, N.S.W. and Tas. Commercial correspondence includes 13 Mar. 1804 Lieut. C. Menzies, Port Jackson; 6 Mar. 1826 R. Campbell, Sydney; letters 1830-59 from Dr Lhotsky, Salting and Garrard, H. Meinertzhagen, all of Sydney, to Frederick Huth & Co., London; letters from Macnab Bros. and Co., Sydney, to Barry Bros., London, exporters of brandy; from Lyall, Scott & Co., Sydney, and from Acraman, Main, Lindsay & Co., Adelaide, to Hoare & Co., London, concerning wine. There is also a letter 6 Dec. 1837 from the Derwent Bank, Hobart, signed C. Swanston. Religious correspondence includes letters 1830-58 from Campbell & Co., Sydney, to the London Missionary Society and letters to the Society from correspondents in Hobart, Adelaide, and Melbourne.

REV. H. SELWYN FRY
The Vicarage, Stanford in the Vale, Faringdon

SELWYN PAPERS

Papers of George Augustus Selwyn, Primate of New Zealand and Bishop of Lichfield, of his wife Sarah Harriet and of his son John Richardson Selwyn, Bishop of Melanesia.

Diocese of New Zealand, Register Book of the Acts of the Bishop 1841-52. Two copies containing record of the consecration of G. A. Selwyn as Bishop of New Zealand 17 Oct. 1841, copy of his Letters Patent, copies of valedictory letters from the Archbishop of Canterbury, from the Colonial Office and from the Church Missionary Society and records of his acts beginning with his departure from England 26 Dec. 1841 and ending 12 Dec. 1852.

Letter book of G. A. Selwyn containing copies of a few letters c.1847-59.

Autobiography c.1820-67 of Sarah Harriet Selwyn, wife of Bishop G. A. Selwyn.

Original correspondence, c.250 letters consisting of correspondence of Bishop G. A. Selwyn, his wife and Bishop J. R. Selwyn. The letters have been placed in folders, containing:

Letters 1838-78 from Bishop G. A. Selwyn to his father and others including long letters 1843-9, one incomplete, from New Zealand and Pacific Islands illustrated with pen and ink sketches.

Letters 1850-76 from Bishop G. A. Selwyn to his wife, several mentioning the Maori Wars and Gov. Grey.

Letters c.1842-67 to Bishop G. A. Selwyn.

Letters 1853-67 to Bishop G. A. Selwyn from correspondents in New Zealand.

Letters 1839-77 to Bishop G. A. Selwyn, about fifty letters of lesser interest.

Miscellaneous letters and papers 1838-78 relating to Bishop G. A. Selwyn, to the labour traffic and the church in New Zealand, including: letters 1848 William Williams, Auckland; 1868 Capt. Hope, H.M.S. Brisk; 1851 C. J. Abraham, Auckland; 1870 Rev. R. H. Codrington, Norfolk Island; 1871 Lieut. T. C. Tilly, R.N., agent for the Melanesian Mission, Auckland; extract from journal 1871 by Capt. Jacob, Melanesian Mission schooner Southern Cross.

Letters c.1857-77 from Bishop J. R. Selwyn to his parents including a few letters from Norfolk Island and New Zealand.

Correspondence of Bishop J. R. Selwyn, chiefly letters c.1860-98 to his mother, many from Norfolk Island and including his journal 13 Apr. to 15 June 1876; other correspondence c.1880-90 of Bishop J. R. Selwyn with his mother and family.

Accounts and papers 1868-72 of Bishop G. A. Selwyn, including cuttings.

Photographs of Bishop G. A. Selwyn and his wife, obituary of Bishop G. A. Selwyn, three water-colours by Bishop G. A. Selwyn, two of Purewa near Auckland and one entitled 'Natives, Island of Waiheke', a collection of family photographs and portraits including drawings and prints of Sir John and Lady Richardson, genealogical notes by the Rev. R. H. Codrington, printed, and family trees.

Form for the Consecration of the Church of St. Barnabas, Norfolk Island, built in memory of John Coleridge Patteson D.D., First Bishop in Melanesia. St. Andrew's Day 1880, Melanesian Mission Press, Norfolk Island. With manuscript inscriptions. The form of service is printed in Mota and English.

Rev. H. Selwyn Fry

Norfolk Island newspaper *O Sala Ususur*, July 1898. Copy inscribed 'Mrs. Selwyn'. Portrait of Bishop G. A. Selwyn by George Richmond, R.A., crayon and water-colour. Engravings of this portrait were published and it is the original drawing for a portrait in oils in the possession of Major John Selwyn, Pinkney's Green, Berkshire.

BERKSHIRE RECORD OFFICE
Shire Hall, Reading

See *Guide to the Berkshire Record Office*, 1952. A loose-leaf catalogue and card indexes of subjects and personal names are maintained. There is also a temporary list of accessions on cards and a card index to subjects of manuscripts not yet catalogued. The published *Guide* and loose-leaf catalogue describe official records, estate and family records, parish records, transferred records, and maps. All records listed below have been microfilmed for the Australian Joint Copying Project.

PARISH RECORDS

D/P132 Tilehurst Parish Records
D/P132/28. Miscellaneous, including printed material on emigration to Western and South Australia 1829, 1835.

PRIVATE RECORDS

D/EBp Bouverie Pusey Family Papers
D/EBp/F20. Family papers including letter 28 Aug. 1854 from the Colonial Office to P. Pusey enclosing letter 19 Apr. 1854 from Lieut.-Gov. Sir William Denison, Van Diemen's Land, to the Duke of Newcastle requesting authority for the purchase of agricultural implements.

D/EBy Benyon Family Correspondence
D/EBy/C43. Miscellaneous correspondence including letter 5 Oct. 1836 from a correspondent at Reading to R. Benyon de Beauvoir of Englefield House enclosing letters 25 Mar. 1836 from Thomas Mills, Sydney, to his wife and to Messrs Eastaff and Benyon and Rev. Williams protesting his innocence of the crime for which he was transported.

D/ECb Cooke, Cooper and Barry, solicitors, Deposit
D/ECb/B86. Papers 1880-3 relating to the marriage settlement of the Rev. Henry Le Grand Boyce and to the identification of John Waltham Boyce, Bundaberg, Q'ld, including a statement by J. W. Boyce giving his life story.
D/ECb/B93. Papers relating to the marriage settlement of John Hulme 1824 including letters of administration 31 May 1880 of William Carnaby Hulme, late of Bendigo, Vic., died 7 Mar. 1858.

D/ECh Carleton, Holmes and Co., solicitors, London, Deposit. Buscot Estate Papers
D/ECh/T41. Letter 21 Mar. 1864 from R. C. Crawford, Hill End, N.S.W., concerning affairs in New South Wales and containing a brief mention of the Maori War.

D/EDd Dundas, Crawford, and Willis Family Papers
D/EDd/F2. Volume interleaved with Crawford family and miscellaneous correspondence. Letters to James Coutts Crawford include: 6 June 1839 Lord Camperdown introducing his nephew; 1849 Henry Keppel, a passenger in the *Rattlesnake*, giving news of the *Bramble* and mentioning that Capt. Yule had suggested offering a passage to the widow of Charles Edward Stanley; 20 Apr. 1853 Henry Bell, Wellington, N.Z., with news of Mrs Crawford's death, also news of land regulations and elections; 18 Feb. 1858 E. J. Wakefield concerning a possible purchase of land on Watt's Peninsula; 11 Dec. 1861 A. Fitzgibbon, Nelson, on civil engineering in the area.

Berkshire

Letters 1861-77 to J. C. Crawford include letters from the following correspondents in New Zealand: I. E. Featherston, F. A. Weld, D. Monsy, F. Whitaker, W. Wells, and W. L. Campbell at Hawkes Bay. In the family correspondence there is also a letter 31 Oct. 1848 to Sophia, wife of James Coutts Crawford, and several letters 1872-87 containing news of Miramar, the property in New Zealand.

D/ELl Lenthall Family Papers
D/ELl/F9. Fourteen photographs of the Lenthall family in Australia.

D/EPb Pleydell-Bouverie Family Papers
D/EPb/C59. Correspondence of the 3rd Earl of Radnor 1853-6 concerning his sponsorship of Mary Ann Sherwood as an emigrant to Melbourne.

D/EPg Broome Pinniger, solicitor, Newbury, Deposit
  The records include printed maps 1840-1 of New Zealand and Wellington.

D/ESv(M) Stevens Family of Bradfield Papers
D/ESv(M)/F112-14, 118, 120, 124. Letter books of T. Stevens 1860-81, some with indexes. F112, 1860-2 includes letters to Bishop Harper, Lord Lyttelton, and J. R. Godley on appointments of clergy and a schoolmaster to posts in Invercargill, Otago, and other places in New Zealand, with letters to candidates, T. Stevens being Bishop Harper's Commissary; F113, Jan.-July 1863 includes letters concerning G. G. Scott's plans for building Christchurch Cathedral and letters of appointment of clergy and schoolmasters in Otago; F114, Feb.-Oct. 1864, F118, Jan.-July 1868 and F120, Apr.-Dec. 1870 include letters to the Bishop of Christchurch concerning the appointment of clergy and concerning the Cathedral; F124, May 1880 to Feb. 1881 includes letters concerning appointments of masters to Christ's College, N.Z.

D/EWl Walter Family Papers, deposited by Cooke, Cooper and Barry, solicitors
D/EWl/T62. Documents 1861-81 concerning the Barklamb family in Benalla, Vic.

D/Ex(160) Reynolds Family of Faringdon Papers
  One bundle in this box of papers, uncatalogued 1967, is labelled 'Australian Papers' and includes papers 1838-9, 1850-6, relating to money due to Robert Huntley and his wife, Balmain, Sydney, among them letters from Braidwood, Gundagai, and Balmain.

D/Ex(169) Williams Family of Warfield Papers
  A box of papers, uncatalogued 1967, includes a few letters 1843-8 to the Hon. Thomas Williams, M.L.C., Adelaide, and a letter book 1847-59 of Thomas Williams in which is an incomplete letter Jan. 1847 written from South Australia concerning land there and mentioning wool shipped from Port Lincoln.

T/Z1. Photocopy of J. Mason's account 1838 of his transportation to Australia in 1831 and of his life there.

THE DUKE OF WELLINGTON
Stratfield Saye House, nr Reading

  A collection of documents, personal and private in character, connected with the 1st Duke of Wellington and including six letters 1826-9 from W. G. Broughton and one letter 1826 to the 1st Duchess of Wellington concerning him. These letters have been microfilmed for the Mitchell Library, Sydney. Five letters 1826-7 relate to Broughton's life in England. The other two letters are:

25 Mar. 1829 concerning final arrangements for his embarkation.

25 May 1829 from Sheerness, on the eve of his departure for New South Wales, expressing his gratitude to the Duke of Wellington and enclosing a prayer for him.

BUCKINGHAMSHIRE

MRS A. T. PEPPERCORN
Bendrose Grange Cottage, Amersham Common

Reminiscences of John Watts of Budgelaing.* The reminiscences are typed and bound in a small leather quarto volume and are illustrated with photographic views and portraits of John Watts, Arthur Hodgson, L. A. Steiger, and Robert Ramsay. The first stud sheep for Eton Vale were purchased from L. A. Steiger. Budgelaing is now Felton, Darling Downs. John Watts left England for South Australia in 1840 and returned in 1843. Later he accepted an offer to manage Budgelaing and sailed for Sydney in 1846. He left the colony for England in 1868 but visited it again twice. For a time he managed Eton Vale for Arthur Hodgson and finally owned a half share.

BUCKINGHAMSHIRE RECORD OFFICE
County Hall, Aylesbury

PRIVATE RECORDS

D/MH Earl of Buckinghamshire Papers

Hobart Papers (War Office). Private papers relating to the term of Robert, Lord Hobart, later 4th Earl of Buckinghamshire, as Secretary of State for War and the Colonies 1801-4 including the following letters:

17 Nov. 1802, John Hunter, suggesting a commission of investigation into New South Wales, to be taken there in a ship commanded by him.

28 Dec. 1802, Lord St Vincent, concerning the burden laid on the Navy by the transportation of convicts, stores and settlers to New South Wales.

1 Mar. 1803, Capt. William O. B. Drury, H.M.S. *Neptune*, Spithead, applying for the governorship of New South Wales.

19 July 1803, from two aspiring emigrants asking for assistance to go to New South Wales as free settlers.

D/LE Hartwell Papers

Correspondence of Dr John Lee of Hartwell House, nr Aylesbury, astronomer, which includes the following letters:

19 Apr. 1842 to 23 Jan. 1848, Charles Smith, Melbourne, describing his voyage to Australia, conditions and events in the colony, family matters, and sending natural history specimens.

22 June 1847 to 15 Dec. 1858, John L. Smith, Walworth and Melbourne, describing his departure for Australia, events and conditions in the colony, domestic and financial matters, his partnership with Mason, and the disappearance of Henry Marsh. Also two replies 5 Oct. 1847, 21 Apr. 1848 from John Lee.

28 Sept. 1840 to 7 Nov. 1843, Christian Carl Ludwig Rümker, Hamburg, about his failure to receive payment for the sale of his property in New South Wales, and about astronomical matters. Also from Rümker 31 July 1842 to Benjamin Smith and from John Lee and others concerning Rümker's property in New South Wales.

30 Aug. 1849, Capt. Philip King, Bridport, concerning the cost of an observatory and residence at Parramatta.

30 May 1853, George Witt, Sydney, on domestic matters.

7 Aug. 1861, Miss B. N. Parkes, London, seeking subscriptions for fund to send young ladies to Australia as governesses.

26 Sept. 1865, William Stratford Lee, Fremantle, expressing contrition for disgrace he has brought on family and friends.

Buckinghamshire

Fremantle Papers

Additional papers are in the possession of Commander the Hon. J. T. Fremantle (April 1970).

Captain Stephen G. Fremantle Papers

Boxes 213-14, 216-18. Papers mainly relating to his command of H.M.S. *Juno* and including: log books 1854-7; papers 1854-8 re courts martial; the taking possession of the Cocos Islands 1857-8; copy proclamation 1856 Gouverneur du Boujet as to immigrants to New Caledonia; papers 1852-6 re discipline of the Australia Station; draft report n.d. of visit to Samoa group of islands; orders, letters 1857 paying off of H.M.S. *Juno*.

Box 228. Extract from journal of Acting Lieut. G. W. Gregorie while employed as agent in the removal of Pitcairn Islanders, with copy of his report to the Governor General at Sydney, and covering letter 1856 to Capt. S. G. Fremantle.

Box 43(L), (M). Correspondence of Stephen G. Fremantle: letters 1847-57 to his mother Lady Elizabeth Fremantle, mostly from the Australia Station, containing accounts of his life in Sydney and visit to Pitcairn Island; 1847-56 to his sister Emma.

Sir Thomas Francis Fremantle Papers

Boxes 97, 136, 154. Papers 1842 including manuscript and printed copies of letters and summary of case re proposed colonisation of New Zealand involving the Manukau and Waitemata Co. and the New Zealand Co. Letter 24 May 1860 Sir William Denison to Capt. S. G. Fremantle giving details of unsettled conditions among the Maoris and an account of current New South Wales politics. Papers re service affairs of Capt. S. G. Fremantle including copy of report 1855 by Capt. H. M. Denham, H.M.S. *Herald*, on exploration of Western Pacific, and original letters 1855, 1857-8 from Denham. Printed pamphlet by Capt. S. G. Fremantle, defending his conduct in regard to courts martial involving officers of H.M.S. *Juno* 1853-8.

DR M. A. T. ROGERS
Learing, Hitcham Road, Burnham

J. E. THOROLD ROGERS PAPERS*

The papers of J. E. Thorold Rogers, the agricultural economist, include:

Letter 14 Apr. 1858, J. W. Rogers promising to send a long letter telling of his adventures until he settled down as Judge of the Court of Mines and Chairman of General Sessions, Ballarat, and introducing William Champ, son of his friend Champ, ex-Colonial Secretary of Van Diemen's Land, and now Inspector-General of Prisons, Victoria.

The following letters among the correspondence of J. E. Thorold Rogers contain references to Australia:

26 June 1875, Sir George Ferguson Bowen, Athenaeum, London, assuring Rogers that his works were frequently referred to in the Parliaments and journals of the colonies and fully appreciated and that Rogers had rendered important services to the cause of free trade.

22 May 1862, Richard Cobden referring to a long and interesting letter he had received from Bowen, Governor of Queensland, and asking if a periodical could be established at Oxford to advocate Adam Smith's ideas, carry them to their logical conclusions, oppose feudalism from a 'politico-economical' point of view, and show up the colonial system as an anachronism.

3 Mar. 1864, J. E. Thorold Rogers to Cobden commenting on the visit of the Government Commissioner from Queensland who was in England working on a 'very

sensible colonial emigration scheme', 20,000 or more emigrants having been sent to Queensland.

HUGHENDEN MANOR
National Trust, High Wycombe

Papers of Benjamin Disraeli, Earl of Beaconsfield, and his family. A handlist of the papers, 1961, is available.

Political Papers
XXI General Correspondence
124-30. Correspondence 1847-50 Col. Robert Torrens discussing immigration to the colonies with a reference to his pamphlet on a plan for the Irish peoples to be encouraged to emigrate to South Australia.
361. Two letters 1878 Sir George Grey, Prime Minister of New Zealand.
394-6. Three letters 1867 Sir Charles Gavan Duffy.

CAMBRIDGESHIRE

CAMBRIDGE UNIVERSITY LIBRARY
West Road, Cambridge

A Catalogue of the Manuscripts Preserved in the Library of the University of Cambridge, 1856-7, 6 vols., covers all Western manuscripts in the 'two letter' classes, e.g. Mm. vi.48, and Additional Manuscripts to Add.337. There is an Accessions Register recording all Additional Manuscripts and fuller descriptions of many manuscripts, compiled for ultimate use in a published catalogue, may be seen on request. A *Summary Guide to Accessions of Western Manuscripts (other than Medieval) since 1867*, Cambridge 1966, is primarily a guide to the main series of Additional Manuscripts but includes brief particulars of other collections of Western manuscripts. A card index to Western manuscripts after 1500 covers the 'two letter' classes and Additional Manuscripts and is chiefly an index of personal names. A subject index on cards with entries under each heading arranged in accession order, is also maintained. Published or typescript handlists amplify the manuscript and typescript descriptions mentioned above. In the following list of manuscripts relating to the field of this survey, Additional Manuscript numbers, so far assigned, are given in brackets. One of the items listed, the papers of William Gooch, is in a 'two letter' class and this number is also given in brackets.

BALDWIN PAPERS

The papers of Stanley Baldwin, 1st Earl Baldwin of Bewdley. Vol.57 includes correspondence 1929-30 with Lord Beaverbrook about his 'Empire Crusade' and 'United Empire Party', also correspondence concerning other subjects connected with the Empire. Vols.90-8, 'Empire Affairs', include, especially in Vols.92-3, papers 1923-5 on imperial trade and foreign policy; Vol.94 contains files 1926 on the Australian shipping service and files 1924, 1927-8 on overseas settlement and the economic mission to Australia; Vols.96-8 contain letters 1923-39 from dominion governors and other prominent persons, also letters 1925-35, 1938, mainly concerning the Ottawa Conference 1932. Papers which are the property of H.M. Government, including papers 1923-5 of the Committee of Imperial Defence and Cabinet Papers have been withdrawn from the original files and are not available.

CREWE PAPERS

Papers of the Marquess of Crewe. Some have been listed and indexed.

C. General Correspondence, 61 boxes.

C/7. Includes correspondence 1908-27 with Lord Chelmsford among which is correspondence with the Public Library of New South Wales concerning the gift of the 'Tasman Map' by H.R.H. Princess George of Greece. A letter 18 Feb. 1927 from J. T. Lang thanking the Marquess of Crewe for sending the map is in C/30.

C/13. Contains a letter 27 Sept. 1909 from Deakin enclosing a minute from Sir Francis Campbell and letter 15 Dec. 1909 to Deakin.

C/17. Includes a letter 17 June 1908 concerning the Immigration League of Australia; C/26 includes correspondence 1908-9 with Henniker Heaton and C/34, 44, 58, 61 include correspondence on Australian, New Zealand, and colonial affairs; correspondence 1908-12 on Indian immigration to Crown Colonies is in C/44.

M. Miscellaneous Papers, 21 boxes.

M/9. Includes papers 1909 on the proposed Imperial Court of Appeal and concerning the reaction of the Colonial Office to German attempts to secure control of tantalite mines in Western Australia.

M/15. Includes the First Report of the Dardanelles Commission and M/18 contains Committee of Imperial Defence papers 1909-16.

S. Speeches, 3 boxes.

S/1-2. Speeches 1908-9 on dominion affairs; notes for a speech 15 Mar. 1910 on Sir George Reid, also correspondence and notes for a speech May 1913 at the Colonial Institute.

DARWIN PAPERS

See *Handlist of Darwin Papers at the University Library, Cambridge*, 1960. There are manuscript lists which include papers deposited after 1960, among which are letters concerning the voyage of the *Beagle* and some letters from Australian correspondents.

29-39, notes, lists of specimens and letters 1832-6 written on board H.M.S. *Beagle*; 69, notes and correspondence include notes on the South West Pacific by Lieut. Charles Smith and letters 1869 from F. Müller; 92, includes papers concerning Samuel Butler's attack on Darwin; 94-5, 100-4, correspondence with Sir Joseph Dalton Hooker; 97, includes letters 1831-6 from Hooker chiefly connected with the voyage of the *Beagle*; 106-7, include letters 1865-73 from Samuel Butler and 1862-81 from A. R. Wallace.

WILLIAM GOOCH PAPERS (Mm.vi.48)

'Letters, Memoranda and Journal containing the History of Mr. William Gooch, Astronomer of the Daedalus Transport: from the time of his entering College in 1786, to his premature end in 1792, when he was murdered by the Savages of Woahoo'. The papers include letters 1791-2 from Gooch to his parents, and 1793-4 from Maskelyne to Gooch's father. The 'Journal' consists of extracts made by his father from the original journal. There are a few rough pen and pencil sketches and at the end of the volume are papers formerly in the possession of Sir Joseph Banks, one paper giving a detailed account of the murder.

HADDON PAPERS

The papers of A. C. Haddon c.1870-1930, transferred from the Cambridge University Museum of Archaeology and Ethnology, consist chiefly of correspondence and field notes of Haddon and others. In 1970 they were temporarily arranged in numbered envelopes, numbers running in blocks of thousands, not all numbers used. A preliminary typescript list has been made.

1-999. Papers, correspondence and diaries of A. C. Haddon. 6, correspondence with Chinnery and Beaver on New Guinea; 17, documents and photographs connected with Haddon's trip across Australia in 1923; 26, correspondence with Seligman and general correspondence on physical anthropology especially with regard to Torres Strait.

1000-99. Torres Strait.

2000-99. New Guinea but including 2002, a manuscript book on New Caledonia written in 1878 by Atkinson, given to Haddon by [? J.] C. S. Bruce; 2003, notes by Seligman on the physical anthropology of Mekeo and other places; 2072-3, Torres Strait papers. Other envelopes contain correspondence with Chinnery, Wirz, Holmes, and others.

3000-99. Chiefly correspondence about publications but including 3005, letter from Chinnery enclosing his recommended policy for Aborigines of the Northern Territory of Australia and 3068-72, notes, drawings, and papers on canoes.

10001-85. Hornell collection including material on navigation, canoes, and string figures, also Hornell's diaries relating to his work in the Pacific and elsewhere.

12000-81. Rivers papers. 12001, notebooks of the 1914 expedition to the New Hebrides; 12009, notes on Torres Strait; 12014, pencil drawings made by Torres Strait Islanders; 12019, cuttings and correspondence on Fiji.

16000-15. Deacon papers include notes and correspondence on Malekula and on linguistics.

JARDINE, MATHESON & COMPANY ARCHIVE

Permission to consult the archive must be obtained from Messrs Matheson & Co. Ltd, 3 Lombard Street, London, E.C.3, and from the University Librarian. This permission is normally given to serious students who, when making application, must send a reference from the university or institute under whose auspices they are making the research, and information must be given as to the purpose of the research and the period to be covered. Microfilming is not permitted, and permission to have photographic copies is given only subject to the consent of Matheson & Co. Ltd.

Some documents are missing and others have been damaged by damp or insects but the archive is practically complete for the period covered. The firm has published privately, *Jardine, Matheson & Company, an Historical Sketch, being an Account to Show the Circumstances in which the Company Came into Being and How it was Consolidated over the Last Century*, [?1968]. A guide entitled 'Jardine, Matheson Archive, Introductory Notes and Summary of Contents' has been made. Xerox copies of this guide can be obtained.

The archive is arranged in four sections, I Accounts Records, II Correspondence, III Prices Current and Market Reports, IV Books sent to Cambridge in 1950. A 'Calendar & Index' has been made to a part of section II, called IIA and comprising unbound in-letters. The 'Calendar & Index' is in two parts, the 'Calendar' on foolscap sheets and the 'Index' on slips.

I Accounts, ledgers 1798-1886, journals, cash books, invoice books *c.*1810-*c.*1912. Entries include information on trade with Australian firms.

II Correspondence *c.*1800 to early twentieth century. The correspondence is arranged in eight series lettered A-H, A Unbound In-letters, B Letter Books, C Bound volumes of In-letters, D Telegram Books, E Documents, F Diaries, G Duplicates,

Cambridgeshire

H Miscellanea. Most correspondence with Australasia and the Pacific deals with importation from China of tea, sugar, rice, matting, rattan chairs, silk and exportation to China of wool, flour, gold, and South Sea products, especially sandalwood and bêche-de-mer. It is likely that IIC, D and G may repay examination but the following notes refer only to IIA and IIB.

IIA Unbound in-letters *c*.1820-*c*.1890. Arranged in five groups, IIA 1 being the largest and most general, subdivided by place of origin, e.g. IIA 1/2 America, IIA 1/3 Australasia, IIA 1/6 East Indies, IIA 1/10 London. IIA 2 is called Local, IIA 3 Formosa, Korea, Japan, IIA 4 Unplaced. Group 5 contains private letters and is subdivided by place of origin, e.g. IIA 5/1/2 America. Relevant letters have been found chiefly in IIA 1/2 and IIA 1/3 but also in other groups. In the 'Calendar & Index' to IIA an individual number is given to each letter, e.g. IIA 1/3/4821, and all individual numbers for letters from a correspondent are given on his slip in the 'Index'. Private letters are distinguished by the letter P, e.g. IIA 1/3/P29. There are some supplementary letters distinguished by the letter S. As individual numbers of all letters from a correspondent can be found from his 'Index' slip, the numbers are not given for the examples listed below. These examples are designed to show the scope of the correspondence. The number of letters from the correspondents listed vary from five from John Bell to *c*.650 from James Henty and James Henty and Co.

Australian Agricultural Co., Newcastle, 1863-72.

Bank of Australasia, Sydney, 1856-79.

Bell, John, Hobart, 1830-5.

Bickley & Co., Fremantle, 1856-75. 9 Aug. 1865 concerning the shipment of six horses, the proceeds of their sale to be invested in teas.

Bingle & Co., Newcastle, 1865-73, Bingle, White & Co., 1873-*c*.1880 concerning shipping of coal to Hong Kong.

Bird, Mrs Patricia and Janet Thomson Bird, chiefly from Melbourne, 1861-81, concerning remittances from the estate of Mrs Bird's deceased son Alexander in China and concerning the two women's difficulties.

Brown & Co., Hobart and Sydney, 1850-81. 21 Jan. 1851 states that Brown & Co. have been given power of attorney for Jardine, Matheson & Co. to claim on the estate of Charles Swanston; 19 Mar. 1875 requests a quantity of Chinese vermilion; 16 Feb. 1877 mentions the loss of the steamer *Singapore* off the Queensland coast.

Campbell, Robert, Sydney, 1824-51.

Capper, C. E., Wellington, N.Z., of the firm of W. & G. Turnbull, 1878-80.

Cargills & McLean, Dunedin, 1863-74 including several letters concerning the sale of S.S. *Albion* by Jardine, Matheson & Co., the mortgage on her held by Henty and Charles Hoyt; 12 Aug. 1871 reporting total loss of the *Hindu* off the coast of New Zealand. A circular letter 1 July 1874 states that in future the firm will be known as Cargills, Gibbs & Co. Dunedin and Invercargill and Cargills, Joachim & Co. London.

Cargills, Gibbs & Co. 1874-81.

Carter, T. & H. & Co., Fremantle, 1860-70. 29 Dec. 1862 inquires if there was a market for horses; 20 May 1870 asks if there was a market for salt fish and several letters refer to the use of lead ore and old metal as ballast; 16 Aug. 1870 refers to rumours of the discovery of gold, which would stop the collection of sandalwood.

Cole, G. W. 1832-*c*.1862 from the Sandwich Islands, Australasia, the East Indies, Lintin, Coast, and London. Letters from the Sandwich Islands 13 Sept. to 18 Nov. 1832 refer to cargoes of whale oil and furs and to various ships. Letters include 11 Mar. 1833 announcing his arrival in Sydney, saying he had put himself in the hands of Edwards & Hunter and asking that his oil be insured; 24 May 1833 expressing satisfaction with Australia and hoping to settle his affairs in England and return there. Other letters from Sydney 1833-5 say he was enjoying whaling and later letters 1859-62 concern the sale of the *Zingari* by Jardine, Matheson & Co. and introduce James Hawthorn and J. H. Clough.

Daniell, King & Co., Sydney, 1865-71. 30 June 1871 mentions the retirement of A. C. Daniell, the firm continues as George King & Co.

Downie & Murphy, Melbourne, 1859-61. Some letters mention passages for Chinese returning from Australia and export of coal and copper.

Edwards & Hunter, Sydney, 1833-40. Letters in 1833 refer to the *Agnes*, 18 Jan. 1833 contains a description of her voyage from Manila to Sydney; 14 Feb. 1842 contains a description of New South Wales, mentions new buildings in Sydney, thanks Jardine for his hospitality and help and says writer is sending him shoes, cheese, and bacon.

Gilchrist, Watt & Co., Sydney, 1854-64.

Glyde, G. & Son, Perth, 1872-81.

Harper, Robert & Co., Melbourne, 1878-81 concerning the rice market.

Henty, James, and James Henty & Co., Melbourne, *c.*650 letters 1853-81. Some letters refer to shipments of gold; 28 Feb. 1870 requests information on prospects of the sale of New Zealand Kauri sawn timber in China; 17 May 1872 reports the discovery of tin and copper; 16 July 1872 gives a large order for China silk; 14 May 1875 criticises the extensive immigration of Chinese into Queensland; 29 Nov. 1876 reports the finding of large deposits of guano on Pacific Islands; 17 Apr. 1877 passes on an order for teas from Neill & Co., Dunedin, N.Z.; 23 Jan. 1878 states that business is at a standstill owing to the political situation and that there has been a drought for two years; 8 July 1879 sends sample of South Sea Islands ivory nuts which bring £25-30 a ton in London; 11 Nov. 1879 besides referring to trade in teas, nut oil, bêche-de-mer, and shark fins, says that their interest in Neill & Co. has ceased; in later letters other firms mentioned as connected with James Henty & Co. are Alfred Shaw & Co., Brisbane, Alfred Lamb & Co. and Lamb, Parbury & Co.; 18 June 1881 reports smallpox in Sydney and quarantine of ships from China; 27 Sept. 1881 reports the government seizure of the shipment of gunpowder on the *Ocean.*

King, George & Co., Sydney, 1871-81. 28 Mar. 1876 refers to the market in Australia for sugar from China.

Lamb, Alfred & Co., Sydney, 1875-81.

Lawrence, James, Melbourne, 1868-72 concerning shipments of coal.

Marmion, W. E. & Co. Ltd, Fremantle, 1875-81.

Monger, John Henry, Perth and York, W.A., 1870-81. 23 Apr. 1870 states that they are indebted to G. Shenton for their introduction to Jardine, Matheson & Co. Some letters ask that the proceeds of the sale of sandalwood be invested in tea, some ask that the proceeds be remitted to Dalgety, Du Croz & Co., London. 6 July 1876 gives details of sandalwood shipped for themselves and for Shenton and Glyde & Son, also mentions rumour of the discovery of a forest of sandalwood in northern Queensland. In the 1880s reference is made to the prohibition of cutting of sandalwood.

Moore, Henry, Sydney, 1840-81. 13 Feb. 1840 contains instructions to Capt. J. S. Rounce, *Thomas King*, for voyage to China and return. In 1860-72 Henry Moore acts for Jardine, Matheson in the sale of property in Maitland belonging to the late Captain Larkins. 18 July 1865 concerns arrangement with A. Henry of Erromanga to ship sandalwood. From 1867 references occur to decline in the supply of sandalwood.

Neill & Co., Dunedin, 1871-*c.*1881. Reference is made to their connection with Russell, Ritchie & Co., Cargills & McLean and James Henty & Co.

Cambridgeshire

Paddon, James, 1845-54 from Sydney and the New Hebrides concerning the sandal-wood trade. 20 Mar. 1851 states that he and Capt. Towns on the Isle of Pines are the only people collecting sandalwood in the Pacific Islands.

Pearce, Edward, Wellington, N.Z., 1865-81 concerning trade in timber and other New Zealand products.

Russell, George Gray & Co., Dunedin, 1870-3.

Russell, Ritchie & Co., Dunedin and Timaru, successors to George Gray Russell & Co., 1873-8. They are connected with Neill & Co. and Cargills & McLean.

Saw, Henry, Perth, 1862-70. Proceeds from the sale of sandalwood are to be sent to W. A. Shaw, Fenchurch Street, London, later to McDonald, Finsbury Circus, London, or bartered for tea and sugar. 27 June 1870 inquires if there is a market for silver grey rabbit skins as Saw has a large number on his run.

Scott and Gale, Geraldton, 1862-73. The firm is connected with Carter & Co., Fremantle, and James McDonald & Co., London. 24 Jan. 1872 describes flood damage in the Greenough and Irwin areas.

Swanston, Charles, Hobart, 1832-47. 28 Jan. 1832 refers to the departure of Hamilton for London, to Swanston's succeeding him as director of the Derwent Bank and to the power of attorney and instructions to himself and Capt. Montagu as agents for Jardine, Matheson & Co. in Van Diemen's Land; 9 Dec. 1846 refers to the loss of the *Prima Donna* and to his proposal to charter a vessel and send his son on her to Hong Kong.

Thacker & Co., Sydney, 1845-54, and Thacker, Daniell & Co., Sydney, 1853-63. Reference is made in 1845-7 to their chartering the *Alfred, Regia* and *Statesman*, the last to pick up sandalwood at Anatam from Capt. Paddon, the proceeds of the sale of sandalwood to be invested in sugar and tea. 23 Feb. 1850 concerning an experimental cargo of cured beef; 29 Apr. 1850 stating that Paddon is very ill and owes them money, referring also to Capt. Towns on the Isle of Pines collecting sandalwood; letters in 1851 describe the discovery of gold in the Wellington, Bathurst, and Port Phillip districts and the effects of this discovery; 4 June 1851 suggests importing Chinese labourers with their wives and children; 27 June 1852 asks Jardine, Matheson & Co. to engage a Chinese cook, carpenter, and overseer for Edward Hamilton of Collaroy and suggests wages, rations, and conditions of contracts; 13 May 1853 concerning their proposal to open a branch in Melbourne, George King to be a partner in a firm to be named Thacker, Daniell & Co.; 2 Nov. 1853 concerning damage to the *Arabia* at Tanna, the expected arrival of Daniell from England and the proposed departure of John Thacker and family from England; 9 Mar. 1854 refers to their one year contract with Capt. Paddon, New Hebrides, for supply of sandalwood; 15 Nov. 1854 reports difficulty over missing deeds in the sale of three houses in Elizabeth Street, Sydney, owned by the late Dr Gutzlaff; 13 Jan. 1859 discusses prices of teas sold for Robert Towns, Dent & Co. and Griffiths, Fanning & Co. Letters in the 1850s report the superiority of Melbourne gold, failures of firms in Melbourne, Sydney and in the interior of New South Wales.

Towns, Robert, Sydney, 1850-4. The letters mention connections with Capt. Paddon and Towns's trading in sandalwood. There are references to Towns's chartering the *Statesman*, Capt. Hodge, in 1853, De Salis being a part owner, and Towns's doubts about Capt. Hodge and his delays.

Turnbull, W. & G., Wellington, N.Z., 1878-80.

Wallace, Robert B., Newcastle, 1867-75, concerning coal shipments.

Ward, Joseph & Co., Newcastle, 1865-7.

'Private' letters 1837-82 5/1/3 include letters from C. Swanston, J. Thacker, Capt. J. Larkins and James Henty & Co. Thacker's letter 2 July 1844 tells of quarrels with his partners, and letter 20 Nov. 1844 mentions assisting Capt. Larkins in the purchase of the *Corsair*; Capt. Larkins's letters 1844-5 include 10 Oct. 1844 from Sydney saying he did not trust Swanston; 23 July 1845 describes his dealings in tea, sugar, cigars, wheat, and sandalwood, mentions that he was taking M. D. Hunter & Co. to court and hoped to recover £2000 from them; the James Henty & Co. letters are signed by James Balfour and written from Geelong; 15 Oct. 1855 says a branch was opened at Geelong ten months before and describes the country, the richness of the gold deposits, and the tea market.

IIB Letter books *c.*1800 to early 1900s, 737 vols.

Most letter books have indexes. There are eight series of letter books all of which might repay examination. The series richest in letters relating to Australasia and the Pacific are IIB 1 India 1800-83 and IIB 2 Europe 1810-98. The other series are 3 Coast 1842-83, 4 Local 1842-82, 5 Miscellaneous 1850s-1880s, 6 Private *c.*1818-1880s, 7 Insurance 1820-59, 8 Press copy letter books. In this last series 8/6 contains letters 1883-5 to Australasia but is illegible. All series should repay examination. The following are a few examples of letters:

IIB 1. India letter books 1880-83, 67 vols. Letters chiefly to India, East Indies, Australia.

Vol.18, July 1834 to Feb. 1835. 3 Nov. 1834 to Lieut. G. W. Cole saying they were glad his whaling venture was a success, his Sandwich Island cotton had sold for a mere trifle, the rope was still at Lintin; 12 Dec. 1834 to Edwards & Hunter, Sydney, saying they were still trying to sell the *Lady Hayes* for £5000, if not sold she was to return via Java and pick up a cargo of rice.

Vol.28, Jan.-June 1841. 23 Apr. 1841 to Alexander Kerr & Co., Hobart, saying tea was scarce and ships lying idle.

Vol.36, Jan.-June 1845. 25 Feb. 1845 to Messrs Otadui & Co., Manila, introducing Capt. Larkins, brig *Sarah*, and guaranteeing his bills.

IIB 2. Europe letter books 1810-98, 58 vols.

Letters mainly to Europe but also to America and Australia.

Vol.4, Jan.-June 1843. 23 Jan. 1843 to Lamb & Parbury, Sydney, acknowledging their letter of 12 Oct. and noting that the *Dawson* will bring sandalwood, proceeds to go to the credit of Thacker, Mason & Co.; 23 Jan. 1843 to James Alexander Esq., C/o Messrs Gilchrist & Alexander, Sydney, stating that sandalwood 'lately imported from your quarter' is not equal to Malabar Coast.

Vol.5, July 1843 to Mar. 1844. 5 July 1843 to Charles Swanston, Hobart, commenting on the large quantity of sandalwood from 'your quarter' and the South Sea Islands during the past year and the consequent drop in price.

Vol.6, Apr. 1844 to Feb. 1845. 6 Apr. 1844 to Dudley Sinclair, New Zealand, stating their tortoise shell ex *Osprey* has been sold for 223 dollars; 6 Jan. 1845 to George Pelly, Oahu, Sandwich Islands, regarding the difficulty of selling pickled salmon in Hong Kong.

Vol.7, Mar. to Dec. 1845 includes letters concerning sandalwood and Capt. Paddon, also a letter to Paddon. Letters 16-17 Nov. to Thacker say that New Zealand gum and varnish made from it are unsaleable and that so far there is no sale for sulphur from New Zealand or the New Hebrides.

Vol.9, 1847, contains many letters to Thacker & Co., Sydney, on trade in sandalwood, also 20 Feb. 1847 to George Pelly, Honolulu, acknowledging his letter announcing despatch of sheet lead and sandalwood for sale in Hong Kong, and 4 Nov. 1847 to C. & C. F. Beck, Adelaide, advising the arrival of the *Swallow* with South Seas sandalwood.

Vol.10, 1848, contains further letters to Thacker and Pelly on similar subjects.

Cambridgeshire

III Prices Current and Market Reports, 83 boxes.

The documents are for the most part printed but include in Box 44, manuscript or printed lists with prices added in manuscript 1834-8 from Edwards & Hunter, Sydney, giving prices of teas, coffee, tobacco and sugar and export prices of salt beef and pork, wool, kangaroo skins. Printed prices current and market reports cover c.1835-80.

IV Books sent to Cambridge in 1950 include Accounts Current 1808-1920, some of which may be of Australasian or Pacific interest.

LUDLOW PAPERS

Correspondence and papers of the Ludlow family include letters 1837-49 from César des Graz. Twelve letters 1837-40 (Add.7450/39) were written during the voyage of the *Astrolabe*. Among these are 14 Feb. 1838 from Tahiti referring to Pritchard and Moerenhout, 17 Dec. 1839 from Hobart and 17 Feb. 1840 written during the cruise in the Antarctic.

OWEN LETTERS

Letters to Sir Richard Owen (Add.5354) include a letter 2 Mar. 1887 from Sir Walter Buller concerning a fossil he is sending from New Zealand.

RUTHERFORD PAPERS

The correspondence and papers of Lord Rutherford (Add.7653), transferred from the Cavendish Laboratory, include letters 1904-16 and later letters from Sir William Bragg, Adelaide, some concerning early research into radioactivity.

SEDGWICK PAPERS

The papers and geological correspondence of Adam Sedgwick (Add.7652) have been transferred from the Sedgwick Museum. There is a typescript list. The correspondence includes letters c.1840-54 from the Rev. W. B. Clarke and letters c.1854-7 from R. Brough Smith.

STEPHEN PAPERS

Correspondence and personal papers of Sir James Stephen and Sir James Fitzjames Stephen (Add.7349), diary 1846 of Sir James Stephen (Add.7511).

Add.7349/5. Letter 3 July 1855 from Sir George Stephen to Sir James Stephen written on board the *Oliver Lang* off the Australian coast describes the voyage, arrival in Melbourne, the city, living conditions, the surrounding country and his own prospects.

Add.7511. Diary 1 Jan. to 6 Sept. 1846 of Sir James Stephen contains references to Lord Lyttelton and to business with the Australian colonies and New Zealand. Examples of subjects mentioned are: 5 Jan. description of his parting with his cousin G. Milner Stephen and assessment of his character; 7 Jan. visit from Maconochie and discussion of his proposed 'mark system' for prisoners in Van Diemen's Land; 14 Jan. church establishment in New South Wales; 23 Feb. Sir Charles FitzRoy's visit to the Colonial Office with assessment of his character; 6 Mar. North Australia; 27 Apr. Van Diemen's Land, stating his conviction that Wilmot should be recalled; 28 June comment on Gladstone, '. . . yet he recalled Sir Eardley Wilmot, and for that let him be held in homage'; 5 July meeting with Denison, new Governor of Van Diemen's Land.

Papers of Sir James Stephen deposited 1970 by Professor G. S. Graham, King's College, London. Uncatalogued April 1970.

The papers consist of transcripts and some original papers, the transcripts having been made for Caroline Emelia Stephen, *The Right Honourable Sir James Stephen, K.C.B., LLD. . . . Letters. With biographical notes by his daughter*, Gloucester 1906.

Journals and Letters

Seven volumes of transcripts numbered 8-14. Vol.8 contains a transcript of Stephen's personal diary 1 Jan. to 6 Sept. 1846. Vols.9-14 contain transcripts of or extracts from letters from Sir James Stephen, Vols.9-10 containing letters 1807-58 to various correspondents, each volume having an index, Vols. 11-13 containing letters 1816-39 to his wife and Vol.16 letters 1841-59 to his son.

In addition to these seven bound volumes there is a folder of unbound transcripts of letters 1836-57 from Stephen with a few letters to him. The letters are to or from various correspondents and are apparently part of the missing Volumes 1-7 of the above series. They include:

8 Feb. 1845, Stephen to Lord Grey concerning the New Zealand Company and 25 Feb. 1845 Grey's reply.

1 May 1849, 'Extract' from report of a Committee of the Privy Council suggesting that one of the Governors of the Australian colonies should hold a commission appointing him Governor-General of Australia, 'We think he should be authorised to convene a body to be called the General Assembly of Australia'.

27 July 1853, Stephen to the Earl of Harrowby and 29 Aug. 1853 Stephen to the Duke of Newcastle concerning the 'Colonial Church Regulation Bill'.

Folder of fifty-two original letters 1834-53 from the 3rd Earl Grey to Stephen.

The correspondence between Grey and Stephen has been partly surveyed from the copies among the Grey Papers kept in the Department of Palaeography and Diplomatic, University of Durham, by J. M. Ward in 'Retirement of a Titan', *Journal of Modern History*, xxxi, No.3, Sept. 1959. The letters include correspondence 1849-50 concerning the Privy Council report on the government of the Australian colonies. There is also a letter 2 Sept. 1846 concerning the establishment of a whaling station on the Auckland Islands, transportation and the need for labour in the colonies.

Folder of letters from Lord Glenelg 1835-6, 18 letters.

The papers include several other folders of miscellaneous letters among which are original letters by Stephen, Stanley, Glenelg, and Gladstone. Examples are:

Feb. 1845, Stephen to Grey concerning attacks on Stephen by the New Zealand Company. There is a copy of this letter in the folder of unbound transcripts 1836-57 dated 8 Feb. 1845.

17 May 1847, Gladstone to Stephen asking about Dougan's information on Van Diemen's Land and that given by Archdeacon Marriott.

30 Oct. 1894, J. Bryce to L. Stephen giving dates of Stephen's appointments.

Dr Martin's Papers

Papers consisting chiefly of drafts of and notes for a life of Stephen compiled by Dr Evelyn Christian Martin. The notes include a transcript of Stephen's journal 1 Jan. to 6 Sept. 1846 and there is a photograph of a sketch of Stephen as a young man. Among the folders of notes one folder contains references and notes extracted from Public Record Office material relating to Australia and another contains papers dealing with Stephen's connection with the Church Missionary Society. There are also notes on letters which appear to be those in the Stephen Papers described above, as well as other notes from sources especially on 'Colonial Department Organisation', as well as lists of contemporary pamphlets and periodicals.

TEMPLEWOOD PAPERS

The political papers of Sir Samuel Hoare, Viscount Templewood, 115 boxes.

Cambridgeshire

Access is unrestricted with the exception of papers of an official nature thirty years old or less, Committee of Imperial Defence papers of any date, certain Royal correspondence, some post-war files which include items of a confidential and personal nature. A handlist has been made and there is a card index to correspondence. The papers include some personal and family papers but the main section is grouped under the heading General Political and covers 1905-60. It seems possible the papers might repay a search for relevant material but the index to the handlist does not reveal any such papers.

WARD LETTERS

Letters to John Ward, diplomatist, c.1815-85 (Add.6157) include a few letters 1839-48 concerning New Zealand from F. Baring, Durham, Buller, and Hutt.

PAPERS TO BE TRANSFERRED FROM THE CAMBRIDGE MUSEUM OF ARCHAEOLOGY AND ETHNOLOGY

The following were ready for transfer in January 1970:

Brewster Collection

The collection includes a field notebook 1894-5 of A. B. Brewster and miscellaneous papers, e.g. letter 14 Apr. 1875 from R. S. Swanston, Sydney, to Langham; first hand account of instructions given by Sir Hercules Robinson to Swanston on board H.M.S. *Pearl* during the cession of Fiji to Great Britain; correspondence 1894-6 between E. J. Turpin and J. B. Thurston; short account chiefly by Turpin of events in Fiji 1796-1867; various notes on Fijian affairs by G. Gerrish and C. R. Swayne; notes on Bully Hayes; Jimmy the Devil's attack on H.M.S. *Fremantle*, Capt. Croker 1840; a Samoan and a Rotuman legend; Brewster's account of the *Seeadler* 1917 and Graf von Luckner's account of his exploits in the *Seeadler* with photographs.

H.M.S. *Dido*

Papers 1871-4 connected with H.M.S. *Dido*, Capt. W. C. Chapman, including reports on naval personnel, on labour on plantations in Fiji; précis of the trial of John Renny, George Renny, and Vaughan 1873 on a charge of the murder of a Fijian; register of kidnapped Polynesians returned to their homes by H.M.S. *Dido*; letter 24 Aug. 1874 Capt. Chapman to Lieut. J. H. Martin.

P. D. Montague. Diary 26 Dec. 1913 to 4 Jan. 1914, notebooks and drawings during his expedition to New Caledonia; also catalogue of the collection made during the expedition.

New Hebrides

'History of the Paciffic' by a European settler in the New Hebrides, n.d. but apparently written during the 1880s, describing the New Hebrides and giving an account of J. Paddon, his farm, his trading and whaling ventures. The account of Tanna includes evidence of Capt. Cook's visit, notes on anchorages, on ships and crews lost at various times. Entries 8 Oct. to 18 Dec. 1883 list deaths of natives.

Robley Papers. Notebook on Maori art, drawings of Maoris and of Maori subjects.

H. D. Skinner. Papers on the material culture of Maoris.

Stanmore Collection

Papers collected by Sir Arthur Gordon, later 1st Baron Stanmore. The papers consist of 'Genealogies and Histories of Central Viti Levu' by A. B. Brewster, typescript with photographs, also Fijian legends and tales in Fijian in the handwriting of E. B. Heffernan, clerk to Gordon. The latter papers have been referred to as the Im Thurn Papers but are now known as Stanmore Papers.

Von Hügel Collection

Diaries 1874-7 of Baron Anatole von Hügel's visit to Australia, New Zealand, and

the Pacific are being retained for the present in the Cambridge Museum of Archaeology and Ethnology pending possible publication of the Fiji diary. In January
1970 the following papers were ready for transfer:

Photographs, seven albums illustrating Fijian scenery, villages, canoes, native
constabulary, and ceremonies, and including portraits of Fijians, many of which
are named, one album of photographs from Australia, New Zealand, Fiji, Samoa,
Rotuma, and Tonga, and various folders containing duplicates of photographs in
these albums.

List of Aborigines settled at Coranderrk, Vic., their approximate ages and former
places of abode or tribes.

CAMBRIDGE UNIVERSITY MUSEUM OF
ARCHAEOLOGY AND ETHNOLOGY
Downing Street, Cambridge

The Museum has correspondence, papers, and photographs relating to its
collections. Some papers are filed in a 'Documents Box' in the Haddon Library
storeroom.

DOCUMENTS BOX

Examples of papers relating to the field of this survey:

Bruce Collection. Notes on items collected in 1891 by Bruce on the Batavia River,
Q'ld.

Hillier Collection. Letter 17 Nov. 1908 Hillier to Baron von Hügel listing items
in the collection from the Hermannsburg Mission, Central Australia.

Radcliffe Brown Collection. List giving tribal and geographical provenance of
specimens from Western Australia.

COLLECTIONS

Haddon Collection. A. C. Haddon's correspondence and papers have been transferred to the University Library but his collection of photographs is retained by
the Museum. It includes prints of the Dick Collection from Port Macquarie, N.S.W.,
taken early in the nineteenth century; photographs of rock art in western New South
Wales and near Kyogle; three photographs 1865-80 by F. Bonney of Darling River
Aborigines; photographs by Sir Baldwin Spencer of Arunta Aborigines.

Von Hügel Collection. Von Hügel's photographs connected with his visit 1874-7
to Australia, New Zealand, Pacific Islands, and Java are to be transferred to the
University Library; a number of Lindt's photographs of Clarence River Aborigines
will be retained by the Museum (1970). Von Hügel's diaries 1874-7 are being retained (1970) pending possible publication of the Fiji diary but it is intended that
they shall be placed eventually in the University Library.

Stanmore Collection. Manuscripts collected by Sir Arthur Gordon have been
transferred to the University Library but the Museum retains two albums containing
chiefly water-colours by Constance Frederica Gordon Cumming executed in Fiji
1875-7 (Z4151-2) and illustrating pottery, weapons, houses, and scenes, but containing also some drawings made in Tahiti and New Zealand and photographs of
Gordon and family and Fijian personalities. There are also twenty-three large water-
colours of Fiji scenes by Constance Gordon Cumming with notes by the artist,
photographs of sketches in Fiji 1875-7 by A. J. L. Gordon and two of his mono-
chrome sketches, one depicting three male Fijians and the other a village scene,
spear throwing in progress.

Cambridgeshire

MISCELLANEA

Australian Aborigines. A drawing of an Aboriginal by G. F. Angas, a collection of photographs including prints of the Kerry collection and a copy of 'Governor Arthur's Proclamation' to the Aborigines of Van Diemen's Land illustrating justice (Z15076).

Cook Collection. Copy of accession notes on the Cook Collection deposited in Trinity College c.1771. The collection has been placed on loan from Trinity College and the Museum correspondence 1924 contains letters concerning the 1771 deposit and the 1924 loan.

Cruise of H.M.S. *Herald*. Photographs of water-colours by J. Glen Wilson, the originals in the possession of Capt. H. M. Denham, C.M.G.

CENTRE OF SOUTH ASIAN STUDIES
Laundress Lane, Cambridge

REID/BELL COLLECTION

Item 7 contains papers 1833-9 connected with a farm near Hobart, V.D.L., owned by Capt. William Bell. The papers include a bill of exchange 2 Aug. 1833 to A. J. Betts & Co., Hobart, from a firm in Calcutta; three accounts of Capt. W. Bell, one being his account 31 Mar. 1839 with Learmonth & Co.; an extract of a letter 20 June 1836 from W. Bell to T. Learmonth about the expenses of his farm; letter 24 Oct. 1836 J. Learmonth, Hobart, to Bell; a few papers 1839 connected with the estate of W. Bell.

OGILVY PAPERS

The papers may repay examination. A brief note accompanying them mentions that William Ogilvy, writer in the East India Company, was in Sydney, N.S.W., c.1832 boarding with Mrs Lord.

CHURCHILL COLLEGE
Cambridge

Application for permission to consult the following papers should be made to the Archivist, Churchill College.

SIR JOHN COCKCROFT ARCHIVES

The archives include correspondence 1952-67 about the Australian National University.

ADMIRAL LORD KEYES ARCHIVES

The archives include correspondence 1916-17 concerning the Dardanelles expedition; papers 1940-5 relating to the operations in the Pacific; correspondence and papers Nov. 1944 connected with Lord Keyes's speech on Sydney dockyard; papers 1945 concerning the Empire Defence League.

ADMIRAL SIR JAMES FOWNES SOMERVILLE ARCHIVES

The archives include diaries, the diary for 1915 recording experiences as Fleet Wireless Officer during the Dardanelles campaign; orders, despatches, and other papers 1915 connected with the Dardanelles campaign; papers relating to the Dardanelles Commission; papers of the Colonial Defence Committee; diaries 1943-5; Eastern Fleet correspondence 1942-4.

FITZWILLIAM MUSEUM
Trumpington Street, Cambridge

The library maintains a catalogue of authors and recipients of letters.

Correspondence of Sir Joseph Banks, *c.*300 letters, mainly letters to Banks but including seven letters by him.* There is a brief typescript list. Letters from Banks include 31 Mar. 1796 to Major William Price concerning the capture of the collection of Labillardière. In the same folder is a letter 15 June 1798 to an unnamed correspondent concerning the restitution of objects of natural history collected during La Pérouse's expedition. Letters to Banks and other papers include a printed extract from *The Athenaeum* 3609, 26 Dec. 1796, pp.908-9, being a commentary on Banks's Journal of Cook's first voyage; a folder of one hundred and two letters 1782-1802 from Dryander containing very brief mention of the South Seas, including Van Diemen's Land and Tahiti; letter 3 Mar. 1799 from W. R. Notcutt, Bristol, mentioning that he would like specimens of coal from Botany Bay.

Letter 22 Nov. 1893 from Robert Louis Stevenson, Vailima, Samoa, to Samuel Smiles.

PEPYSIAN LIBRARY, MAGDALENE COLLEGE
Cambridge

See *Bibliotheca Pepysiana, A Descriptive Catalogue of the Library of Samuel Pepys, Part I,* '*Sea*' *Manuscripts*, by Dr J. R. Tanner, London 1914; also Navy Records Society Publications Vols.26, 27, 36, 57, 60.

MS.2826. The Voyage of William Ambrosia Cowley, mariner, from the Cape of Virginia, along the west coast of America to Panama, then to the Ladrone Islands, China, Timor, Java, the Cape of Good Hope, and Holland. See William Hacke, *A Collection of Original Voyages*, London 1699. Cf. also British Museum, Sloane MSS.54 and 1050.

NEWTON LIBRARY
Department of Zoology, Downing Street, Cambridge

The Newton Library includes papers and correspondence concerning the work of John Gould and other scientists interested in the birds of Australia and Pacific Islands.* The following description is made by permission of Professor Torkel Weis-Fogh, Head of the Department of Zoology.

PAPERS OF JOHN GOULD

Most of the papers were formerly in the Cambridge Philosophical Society, and are now on loan to the Newton Library. The papers consist of:

Collection of original manuscript notes and sketches for the *Birds of Australia*. At the top of each sheet there is often an illustration of a bird's head, and below this, in the margin are headings such as Latin name, English name, locality with appropriate notes. Longer notes follow and occasionally include rough sketches. See A. McEvey, 'John Gould's ability in drawing birds', *Art Bulletin of Victoria*, 1967-8, pp.13-24; also A. McEvey, 'Collections of John Gould Manuscripts and Drawings', *La Trobe Library Journal*, 1 No.2, Oct. 1968, pp.17-31.

Notebook including five letters 1835-49 from Gould to Sir William Jardine, three from London 28 Sept. 1835, 3 Nov. 1837, 30 Apr. 1838 describing his cabin in the *Parsee*, one from Maitland, N.S.W., 28 Sept. 1839 and one from London 5 Jan. [1849?].

Cambridgeshire

'General List of Birds inhabiting Australia and the Adjacent Islands'.

'List of Swan River Birds'.

Two general lists of Australian birds.

CORRESPONDENCE OF ALFRED NEWTON

There is a card index to the correspondence, which includes the following letters of Australian and Pacific interest chiefly relating to Gould's works on Australian birds.

Allcock, T. 22 Feb. 1858 (New.79).

Briggs, J. J. 28 Dec. 1858, discussion on Melbourne ducks, with one sheet of two water-colours (New.154).

Gould, John. 1 Aug. 1856 (New.11), 8 Feb. 1859 (New.154), 26 Mar. 1859 (New.168), 22 Mar. 1861 (New.173).

Prince, E. 25 Sept., 30 Nov. 1865 (New.194, 205).

Salvin, O. 16 Nov. 1857, expressing his dislike for Sclater, 'he is of the Gould genus so look out' (New.47).

Sclater, P. L. 24 Dec. [1858], on Newton's suggestion Gould agrees to change the name of the humming bird (New.152).

Tristram, H. B. 19 June 1876, intends writing on bird life in South Pacific (New.301).

Wallace, A. R. 25 Aug. 1875, invited to Malay Archipelago (New.297).

ST JOHN'S COLLEGE
Cambridge
The Library holds the following manuscripts:

SAMUEL BUTLER COLLECTION

See H. F. Jones and A. J. Bartholomew, *The Samuel Butler Collection at Saint John's College, Cambridge, a Catalogue and a Commentary*, Cambridge 1921. The Library's copy is interleaved and has manuscript additions. See also H. F. Jones, *Samuel Butler, Author of 'Erewhon', 1835-1902, a Memoir*, London 1919, 2 vols. The collection includes autograph letters among which is a fragment containing a part of the article 'Our Emigrant', see *The Eagle*, II, 1861, pp.101-13, and XXXV, 1914, p.115. The fragment is signed by Butler and written to the editor of *The Eagle*.

WHYTEHEAD PAPERS

See *Poetical Remains and Letters of Thomas Whytehead*, London 1877. The papers include letters 1823-43, poems and miscellaneous papers of Thomas Whytehead, who sailed Dec. 1841 with Bishop G. A. Selwyn as a missionary to New Zealand. Eight letters 1841-3 from Thomas Whytehead, some of them copies, written chiefly to his family, describe the voyage to New Zealand and life there. A letter 21 Mar. 1843 from Bishop Selwyn and an extract 18 Mar. 1843 from the journal of the Rev. W. C. Cotton refer to Whytehead's death. Among the papers is Thomas Whytehead's translation of a hymn into Maori, verses to Mrs Selwyn and a list of Bishop Selwyn's party on the *Tomatin*. Papers of the Rev. R. Y. Whytehead include a biographical note on Thomas Whytehead.

OTHER MANUSCRIPTS

Other manuscripts include a letter 19 Aug. 1905 from Henry Lowther Clarke, Archbishop of Melbourne, to the Master of St John's and among letters 1792-1833

of William Wilberforce is a letter 25 June 1829 from William Wilberforce to Sir
Edward and Lady Parry expressing good wishes on their departure for Australia.

SCOTT POLAR RESEARCH INSTITUTE
Lensfield Road, Cambridge

The Institute is a sub-department in the Department of Geography, Cambridge
University; the library includes, besides printed material, files of unpublished scientific papers, an extensive photographic collection, and a large number of maps,
manuscripts, and paintings. The catalogue of manuscripts, typed on slips filed in
loose-leaf binders, is arranged alphabetically under names of writers, and when
necessary under names of expeditions and ships. There is also a 'Manuscript Accession Register' typed on slips filed in loose-leaf binders. Current accessions are
described in *Annual Reports* and in the *Polar Record*. A description of selected manuscripts entitled 'The Manuscript Collection of the Scott Polar Research Institute,
Cambridge' by Ann Savours, appeared in *Archives, Journal of the British Records
Association*, 4, No.22, 1959, pp.102-8. The Institute supplements its collection of
manuscripts with copies of manuscripts held elsewhere.

RECORDS OF EXPEDITIONS TO THE ANTARCTIC

British Expedition 1839-43, leader J. C. Ross, letters and journals, logs of *Erebus* and
Nimrod; meteorological logs 1840-3 of F. R. M. Crozier, H.M. sloop *Terror* (MSS.547-
8); letter n.d. [18 Sept. 1843?] J. D. Hooker to J. E. Gray, British Museum, in
reply to an invitation from Gray (MS.590).

British Expedition 1898-1900, leader C. E. Borchgrevink, journals and meteorological record kept by L. C. Bernacchi (MS.353/1).

British National Antarctic Expedition 1901-4, leader R. F. Scott, Scott's journal
(M.S.352); Wilson's diaries (MSS.232/1-3) published with reproductions of many
of his paintings in *Diary of the Discovery Expedition to the Antarctic Regions 1901-1904*,
ed. Ann Savours, London 1966; plans of the *Discovery* (MSS.371, 415-17); journals
of other members of the expedition (MSS.342, 346, 353/2, 366/4-7, 774/1).

Scottish National Antarctic Expedition 1902-4, log kept on the *Scotia* 1903-4 by
R. N. Rudmose Brown (MS.826).

British Antarctic Expedition 1907-9, leader E. H. Shackleton, journals and notebooks
of R. E. Priestley (MSS.298/1-3) and F. Wild, typescript copy (MS.437), meteorological log Mar. 1908 to Feb. 1909 (MS.374).

British Antarctic Expedition 1910-13, leader R. F. Scott, Wilson's diaries (MSS.
234/1-4, 505/1, 715/2), extracts from some of these and from his 1901-4 diaries
(MSS.232/1-3) together with reproductions of many of his paintings published in
Edward Wilson's Birds of the Antarctic, ed. Brian Roberts, London 1967; the manuscript
of Cherry Garrard's *The Worst Journey in the World, Antarctic, 1910-1913*, London
1922, 2 vols. (MS.873); notebooks and papers of Cherry Garrard and others (MS.
763); maps and surveys (MS.280); journals of other members of the expedition
(MSS.196, 198, 230, 279, 280/8, 11, 298/6-14, 402, 774/2, 825/1-2); log of the *Terra
Nova* (MSS.129, 280/12-13); journal and log of cruise of the *Terra Nova* by Patrick
Keohane (MSS.825/1-2); maps and surveys (MS.280).

British Imperial Trans-Antarctic Expedition 1914-17, leader Sir Ernest Shackleton,
journals of R. W. James (MS.370), F. A. Worsley (MSS.296-7, 384, 733/1-2),
A. Keith Jack, abridged typescript (MS.448). Worsley's MSS.296, 733/1-2 have
been published as *Shackleton's Boat Journey*, London 1933, microfilms of the original
journals in the Mitchell Library, Sydney.

Cambridgeshire

British Expedition 1920-2, journals and notebooks of T. W. Bagshawe and M. C. Lester (MSS.339, 358), charts by M. C. Lester (MS.358).

Shackleton-Rowett Antarctic Expedition 1921-2, leader Sir Ernest Shackleton, journals of D. G. Jeffrey (MS.250) and H. Wilkins (MS.215).

British Graham Land Expedition 1934-7, leader J. R. Rymill, journals and notebooks of members of the expedition (MSS.29-37, 236-7, 429, 432/5); survey sheets and compilations (MS.183).

Falkland Islands Dependencies Survey 1947-50, Fuchs's journal, Base E, Stonington Island (MS.187).

Norwegian-British-Swedish Antarctic Expedition 1949-52, leader J. Giaever (MSS. 190-1, 201, 284-5, 368), maps and surveys (MSS.192, 204, 213, 217, 231, 268, 281, 363, 380).

British Commonwealth Trans-Antarctic Expedition 1955-8, leader V. E. Fuchs, and others, plans for the expedition (MS.622).

Maps and Surveys include original map material from the South Georgia Surveys 1951-7, leader V. D. Carse (MSS.195, 444-5).

OTHER MANUSCRIPTS RELATING TO THE ANTARCTIC

MS.100 H. R. Mill Bequest and MS.367 H. R. Mill Gift. The correspondence and unpublished papers of Hugh Robert Mill, Antarctic historian. The 'Bequest' comprises over three hundred letters from over one hundred correspondents including L. C. Bernacchi, C. E. Borchgrevink, W. S. Bruce, F. Debenham, Sir Joseph Dalton Hooker, chiefly answering Mill's questions about the British Antarctic Expedition 1839-43, Sir Douglas Mawson, Sir John Murray, R. F. Scott, Sir Ernest Shackleton, and Lady Shackleton; also typed extracts from R. C. Mossman's journal. The 'Gift' consists of papers amassed by Mill while writing his *Life of Sir Ernest Shackleton*, London 1923.

MS.101 W. S. Bruce Collection, the papers and correspondence of W. S. Bruce. The bulk of the collection consists of nearly four hundred letters 1893-1918 between Bruce and others interested in polar exploration. Correspondents include Sir Douglas Mawson. There are also typescript copies of documents relating to the early history of the South Shetland Islands, and parts of Bruce's journal of the Scottish National Antarctic Expedition 1902-4, and the printed but unpublished log of the *Scotia*.

MS.395 Back Collection. The papers and journals of Sir George Back have been on loan to the Institute since 1955. They cover 1820-50 and include c.fifty-five letters 1819-39 to and from Sir John Franklin and six letters 1823-51 from Sir James Clark Ross.

MS.397 R. T. Gould Papers. The writings and polar correspondence of R. T. Gould partly dealing with problems of research into the early history of the Antarctic.

MS.559 Lady Kathleen Scott, correspondence 1911-19 with various friends including letters concerning Antarctic Expedition affairs.

MS.678 E. N. Webb, Feb. 1964 letter to G. de Q. Robin comparing his experiences during the Australian Antarctic Expedition of 1911-14 with Shackleton's Ross Sea Shore party of 1914-17.

FRANKLIN PAPERS, LEFROY BEQUEST (MS.248)

The Institute has a list of the Lefroy bequest compiled by Miss F. J. Woodward. In its catalogue of manuscripts, entries for the papers in the Lefroy bequest are based on Miss Woodward's notes. Certain papers in the bequest were considered better placed in other institutions and the Institute has a correspondence file containing information on this distribution, the only papers of Australian or Pacific interest distributed appearing to be letters 1861-2 of Lady Jane Franklin and Sophia Cracroft from Hawaii and later letters connected with Hawaii, given to the Library of the University of Hawaii in 1952. References to and quotations from manuscripts in the Lefroy bequest occur in: K. Fitzpatrick, *Sir John Franklin in Tasmania, 1837-1843*, Melbourne 1949; F. J. Woodward, *Portrait of Jane*, London 1951; A. L. Korn, *The Victorian Visitors*, Honolulu 1958.

Selections of MS.248 have been microfilmed for the Australian Joint Copying Project. Copies of papers relating to Tasmania have been made for the Royal Society of Tasmania, see *Some Private Correspondence of Sir John and Lady Jane Franklin*, ed. Dr G. Mackaness, Sydney 1947, Aus. Hist. Monog.XV.

Lady Jane Franklin Papers

248/84-96. Journals, voyage to Van Diemen's Land 1836-7 and in Van Diemen's Land 1838-43. Vols.6-7, Feb.-July 1841 cover her visit to New Zealand.

248/97. Notes on the convict system of Van Diemen's Land 1840.

248/121-6. Journals, travels in America and the Pacific 1860-2. Vol.3, 9 Apr. to 16 June 1861 covers the first visit to the Sandwich Islands and contains nine cuttings after p.22; Vol.5, 2 Dec. 1861 to 23 Mar. 1862 covers the second trip to the Sandwich Islands.

248/128-36. Journals and diaries 24 Sept. 1862 to Apr. 1865. 248/130, diary Jan.-Dec. 1863, pp.51, 92, 100, 181, 187, 194, 197, 318 contain mention of her prize essays on Tasmania organised through the Rev. J. P. Gell; 248/131-3 diary 1864, from p.164 in Vol.1 there are references to casting a statue of Franklin for Australia and pp.26, 50 in Vol.2 contain the first references to Queen Emma's visit to England; 248/135-6 journal 13 July to 6 Nov. 1865 mainly concerns Queen Emma's visit to England.

248/156-8. Rough journals in Van Diemen's Land 1837-44. Vol.2 includes notes for the journey to Port Phillip and Sydney and a list of visitors at Port Phillip 4 Apr. 1839.

248/164. Journal 25 Apr. to 8 May 1861 concerns the first visit to the Sandwich Islands.

248/167. Outline statement on the career of Sir John Franklin 1800-44.

248/170-223. Correspondence includes: 248/170/1-6, letters to John Griffin, Nos.4-6, 6 Jan., 8 Dec. 1837 and 12 Oct. 1841 relate to Tasmania, Nos.4, 5 being copies; 171/1-5 to Mrs Leeves, No.5, 20 Aug. 1841 relates to Tasmania; 172/1-72, 1829-39 to Sir John Franklin; 174/1-23, 1837-43 to Mary Simpkinson; 175/1-6, 1840-2 to J. C. Ross, some are copies; 202, notes on Sir John Franklin's boyhood; 206/1-6 letters 1852-3 from various bodies in Van Diemen's Land, copies; 223, letter 1842 to Sir John Franklin; 227, 12 Oct. 1865 letter from Queen Emma.

Sophia Cracroft Papers

248/239. Journal on departure from Van Diemen's Land 1843-4.

248/246/1-8. Letters 1839-44 to her brother Thomas; 247/73-83, 1860-2 to her mother and sisters; 253, 5 Sept. 1881 to the King of Hawaii, draft.

Sir John Franklin Papers

248/291. Journal 8 Apr. to 18 May 1841, Van Diemen's Land.

248/292/1-9. Memos 1839-43 on the administration of Van Diemen's Land.

248/293. Observations 1840 on a voyage of the *Investigator* 1801-3.

248/295-498. Correspondence includes: 248/295/1-3, letters 1840-3 to Sir Francis Beaufort; 296/1-19, 1814-45 to R. Brown; 300, 1824 to Mrs Flinders, copy; 303/1-86, 1829-45 to Lady Jane Franklin; 306/1-5, 1838-41 to Sir George Gipps; 316/1-11, 1840-3 to J. C. Ross containing frank comments on affairs in Van Diemen's Land;

Cambridgeshire

317, 1840 to Lord John Russell; 319, 14 Apr. 1839 to Mrs Simpkinson referring to plans for Lady Jane Franklin to travel overland from Port Phillip to Sydney; 321/1-2, 1844 to Lord Stanley; 330, 1838 draft letter concerning the dismissal of Maconochie; 332, 1800 from D. Allenby to W. Franklin; 362/1-2, 1843 from L. Cotton concerning the treatment of convicts in Van Diemen's Land; 364/1-26, 1827-45 from F. R. M. Crozier to J. C. Ross; 373/1-2, 1840-1 from Sir Hugh Elliott; 383/1-7, 1810-12 from Matthew Flinders; 384/1-3, 1801-5 from Matthew Flinders to T. Franklin; 386, two letters 1814, 1815 from R. M. Fowler, commander of the *Porpoise*; 248/390, 13 Sept. 1843 from E. I. Franklin (afterwards Mrs J. P. Gell) to J. C. Ross; 396/1-2, 1836, 1839 from Mrs E. Fry concerning prison discipline in Van Diemen's Land; 400/1-4, 1839-41 from J. Gould; 401/1-2, 1836, 1842 from Charles Grant, 1st Baron Glenelg; 411/1-16, 1812-41 from J. Griffin to Lady Jane Franklin and to Sir John Franklin; 422/1-4, c.1842 from F. H. Henslowe, private secretary to Sir John Franklin; 423/1-2, 1838-9 from Sir John Herschel, the last concerning plans for Ross's Antarctic expedition; 426, 1846 to Lady Jane Franklin from Sir Joseph D. Hooker concerning Tasmanian flora; 440, 1848 to Lady Jane Franklin from Maconochie; 467/3-5, 1834-42 from J. C. Ross; 498, 1844 from the Earl of Derby referring to Franklin's despatch complaining of his subordinates.

PARRY PAPERS

The papers (MS.438) contain, besides papers relating to the Arctic, correspondence of Sir William Edward Parry including letters written to his family while he was commissioner for the Australian Agricultural Company 1829-34. There are also letters from his wife I. L. Parry during the same period. All letters 1829-34 concern family news and private life in Australia, chiefly at Port Stephens but including references to visits to Sydney and to Australian Agricultural Company business.

Among the papers are journals by I. L. Parry, 4 vols. including Vol.3, Oct. 1830 to Dec. 1832, Vol.4, Dec. 1832 till their departure for England in 1834, containing personal notes on day to day life at Port Stephens and during visits to Sydney, also fourteen drawings in water-colour and pencil by I. L. Parry or copied from her originals. They are chiefly views of Port Stephens including a front elevation of Tahlee House with key to rooms. One drawing depicts the 'Coal Works at Newcastle showing the steamer *Sophia Jane*'. The drawings are titled and dated on the back and are either signed or bear a note that the drawing is a copy.

PAINTINGS, PORTRAITS, AND DRAWINGS

The Institute has many paintings, portraits, and drawings. It maintains a typed catalogue on slips in loose-leaf binders arranged alphabetically by names of artists. Anonymous items are arranged by subject.

Six water-colours by J. K. Davis, painted during the British Antarctic Expedition 1839-43 and showing the ships and scenes when members of the expedition landed at various points, one water-colour depicting New Year's Day festivities.

Paintings by G. Marston, British Antarctic Expedition 1907-9.

Water-colours by E. A. Wilson and A. Cherry Garrard, British Antarctic Expedition 1910-13. Garrard is represented by two water-colours, Wilson by a large collection.

Portraits include oil paintings of Sir John Franklin by various artists and a pencil drawing of Sir John Franklin by Negelen, two silhouettes of Sir William E. Parry and portraits of him by C. Skottowe and T. Phillips, oil paintings of R. F. Scott and a pencil sketch of R. F. Scott by E. A. Wilson, a charcoal portrait of Sir Ernest H. Shackleton.

SELWYN COLLEGE
Cambridge

Four boxes of papers relating to Bishop G. A. Selwyn, Bishop Patteson and others. A brief inventory of the boxes may be consulted on application to the Librarian.

Box containing Bishop Selwyn's diary 1843-4 and including notes and sketches; letter 17 Oct. 1857 from Bishop Selwyn, '*Southern Cross* at Sea' to 'My very dear Boys' describing the voyage through Melanesian island groups with water-colour sketches and maps; letters of Bishop Selwyn including extracts from his letter to his mother 11 Jan. 1843, Waimate, Bay of Islands, and to his father describing the voyage of the *Undine*. There are also various other letters among them a letter 31 Aug. 1843 from Jack Kitson, Nelson, N.Z., to Rev. Harry Dupuis.

Box labelled 'Addresses presented to George Augustus Selwyn'. Most of the addresses were presented by churches and church bodies in New Zealand in 1868.

Box containing letters 1842-64 by Mrs G. A. Selwyn and two sketches of the *Southern Cross*.

Box labelled 'Documents relating to the Selwyn Family, Mrs. G. A. Selwyn, Bp. Patteson, Sir William Martin'. The documents include a small photograph of Bishop G. A. Selwyn; copy of a letter dated 'Tonga Tabu Epiphany 1848' from Bishop G. A. Selwyn to his father written on H.M.S. *Dido* and other letters and documents concerning Bishop G. A. Selwyn. An envelope labelled 'Bp. Patteson' contains among other papers: letter 3 Sept. 1861, Patteson, H.M.S. *Cordelia*, to Lady Martin; letter 26 May 1868, Patteson, Norfolk Island, to Capt. Hope concerning the labour trade; letter 27 Feb. 1869, Patteson, Norfolk Island, to Bishop Abraham, typescript copy; 'some reminiscences of Bishop Abraham, Precentor of Lichfield Cathedral from 1876 to 1890, by a Vicar Choral in 1906', typescript; papers relating to the death of Patteson at Nukapu and the punitive visit to the island by H.M.S. *Rosario*, Capt. A. H. Markham, with correspondence between Selwyn and Markham; three addresses to Sir William Martin on his departure from New Zealand in 1874.

CAMBRIDGESHIRE AND ISLE OF ELY COUNTY RECORD OFFICE
Shire Hall, Castle Hill, Cambridge

PRIVATE RECORDS

R57/24/18(b)12. Letters 1837 from Ann Gore, Gilmour, Lake Bathurst, N.S.W., 3 letters.

Holworthy Papers. This large collection includes two items of Australian interest:

279/F2. Part of diary 16 Dec. 1877 to 1878 by J. M. Holworthy, St Vincent to Melbourne, chiefly a journal of the voyage on the S.S. *Lusitania* (see the Melbourne *Argus* 23 Jan. 1878) but containing brief impressions of Melbourne and Adelaide.

279/T46. Small group of papers concerning Hampton Properties Ltd, a gold mining company near Kalgoorlie, 1899-1919.

MRS J. ROTH
61 Maids' Causeway, Cambridge

Notes and photographs collected 1928-57 by George Kingsley Roth on the material culture, sociology, and administration of Fiji. Pottery, housebuilding, mat and bark-

Cambridgeshire

cloth making, and ceremonial are recorded in detail from notes collected in various parts of Fiji, mostly in the Fijian language. Mrs Roth intends to place the papers in the Cambridge University Library.

CHESHIRE

CHESHIRE RECORD OFFICE
The Castle, Chester

The inventories of papers in the Cheshire Record Office are kept in loose-leaf binders. There is a card index to these inventories consisting of names, subjects, and places.

QUARTER SESSIONS RECORDS

The records include:

Orders by Quarter Sessions and Chester Sessions for transportation of convicts 1747, 1803-29, 4 bundles.

Orders by Secretary of State for transportation of convicts to the hulks 1802-40, 4 bundles.

Reports and returns of convicts transported and under sentence of transportation 1802-56, 6 bundles.

Circulars and correspondence on transportation of convicts 1802-51, 1 bundle.

Miscellaneous 1726-1857, 78 docs.

PRIVATE RECORDS

DBE Bennett Collection

DBE 15. Notes assembled from various sources on the genealogy of the Whittell family of Chester and London including the family of Dr Henry Rawes Whittell, who sailed for Australia in 1838. Notebook with some letters inserted which include queries about the Australian branch of the family.

DBE 29, pp.92-109. Genealogical notes on the Woolfield family of Birmingham and Papatoetoe with ten letters c.1854 from the Papatoetoe branch. The letters relate chiefly to the family but several comment on the life of settlers in New Zealand.

DSA Stanley of Alderley Family Correspondence

DSA 75. Notebook 19th cent. compiled by Owen Stanley's mother Catherine, relating to her children.

DSA 79. Letters including twenty-four 1846-9 to Owen Stanley concerning family matters including the death of his brother Charles in Tasmania.

DSA 92. Correspondence of Charles Edward Stanley and his wife Elizabeth (Eliza). Letters 12 May 1847 'Hobarton' from Elizabeth to her mother-in-law concerning the mails, Denison's health and his reaction to the affair of Miss Webb, 19 Oct. 1852 Newlands, Parramatta, Capt. P. P. King to Elizabeth mentioning the publication of *The Voyage of H.M.S. Rattlesnake*, London 1852, references to a mortgage by Owen, religion and education in the colony, the death of his sister Hannah Macarthur and her daughter, Denison, the gold rush and its consequences, and other news.

Five letters 1 Jan. to 28 Feb. 1853 T. H. Huxley to Elizabeth concerning MacGillivray's *The Voyage of H.M.S. Rattlesnake* and Huxley's review of it.

DSA 134/1. Letters 1825-43 to Louisa Dorothea Stanley from Catherine Stanley including: letter 28 Nov. 1834 about the arrival home from Australia of W. E. Parry and his family, their impressions of Australia and the specimens Isabella had brought back with her; letter Oct. [1843?] reporting that Owen Stanley was at Gibraltar.

DSA 134/2. Correspondence 1844-61 of Catherine Stanley containing various references to Stanley including letter 16 Apr. 1848 from the Bishop of Tasmania written on his voyage to Australia and letter 1849 concerning the death of Charles in Tasmania.

DSA 204. Correspondence 1837-50 of and about Owen Stanley and correspondence 1832-49 of Charles Edward Stanley.

DWS Wilson of Sandbach Collection

DWS 16. Petition July 1849 by passengers in emigrant ship *Cheapside* about tea.

DWS 19. Journal 1850-1 of John Ayre, surgeon, R.N., M.R.C.S., on the emigrant ship *Duchess of Northumberland* with a report of a Court of Enquiry into the case of Lucy Wells and James Millard which appears to relate to the voyage of the *Cheapside* 1849-50; also four loose letters relating to treatments given on the *Duchess of Northumberland* and on other ships while in port in England. See also note under DWS 23/2.

DWS 21/4. Accounts, personal correspondence, and papers relating to a journey round the world by Mr and Mrs M. Wilson. The collection includes thirty-four accounts Mar.-Aug. 1889 chiefly from hotels but also from commercial firms in Australia and New Zealand; also tickets and timetables.

DWS 23/2. Volume containing private journal June-Oct. 1849 of Dr John Ayre, surgeon in emigrant ship *Cheapside* bound for Adelaide with free passengers; further reports on the case of Lucy Wells and James Millard; journal 21-7 Dec. 1849 of a voyage from Sydney to Port Phillip; a sickness list of a voyage from Sydney to Calcutta; journal and treatment journal for a voyage to Moreton Bay with emigrants arriving 31 Jan. 1851; miscellaneous notes and course of ship on journey from Port Phillip to London in the *Tasman* 1850; other miscellaneous notes and letters relating to these or other unidentified voyages.

CHESTER CITY RECORD OFFICE
Town Hall, Chester

Catalogues are in loose-leaf binders and cover the official records and also non-official accessions. There are card indexes by name, place and subject to these descriptions and there is also a card index in progress to the *Cheshire Sheaf*, which from time to time prints material in the Archives Office.

PRIVATE RECORDS

CR 31 Brown Family of Upton, Chester

Letters 1853-76 from John Brown in Australia and New Zealand include letters 1853-62 from Melbourne, Ballarat, and nearby diggings with some description of the growth of Ballarat and his lack of success; letters 1863-71 from various goldfields in New Zealand; letters 1871-5 from Gippsland, Foster and Melbourne, Vic.; 1876 and 1884 from Sydney after returning from Queensland. There is also a cutting from *World News* 20 Jan. 1907 and a letter 29 May 1907 from the firm of Archibald C. Tuthill of Cobram, Vic., concerning John Brown's estate.

Cheshire

CR 36/44. Copy of extract of will 31 Mar. 1905 of Edward Davies, Melbourne, bequeathing £5 annually to the Blue Coat School, Chester, for a prize to be given annually for general purposes and every fourth year for an essay on 'Imperial Federation', copies of which were to be sent to the Gordon Institute, Melbourne, and the Melbourne Orphanage. Copies of prize winning essays from Chester and the Melbourne Orphanage are included, also letters and accounts 1905-38.

D/JWW Documents from Joliffe, Wickham and Wood, solicitors, Chester D/JWW 685-8, 690-1. Printed material and correspondence 1900-3 concerning the South Australian Development Syndicate Ltd and the Murninnie Mine on Spencer Gulf, S.A.

G/Ch 14-16. Deeds 1833-46 relating to Port Pool Meadow, one of the parties being Philip Oakden, formerly of Liverpool, then in Launceston, V.D.L.

VISCOUNTESS ASHBROOK
Arley Hall, Northwich

EGERTON-WARBURTON FAMILY PAPERS

There are two groups of letters; those of George Egerton-Warburton of Western Australia and those of his brother Peter Egerton-Warburton of South Australia.

Letters 1839-85 principally of George Egerton-Warburton but also of his wife Augusta, c.100 items. Most of the letters are addressed to his mother, but also to his father until his death in 1847, and to his brother Rowland in Cheshire. The letters are written almost entirely from King George Sound and the St Werburghs property which George Egerton-Warburton founded there.

Arriving in Hobart in 1839 he was transferred with his regiment to King George Sound, took up land while serving and left the army in 1845 to farm at St Werburghs. He had command of the convict establishment at Albany 1852-5 until retrenchment terminated the appointment, after which he turned increasingly to developing pastoral and wool growing interests. The letters give considerable detail at every stage of plans, progress, financial affairs and investments, and life in the district and the colony, as well as family news. There are frequent references to his brother Peter Egerton-Warburton, his arrival from India in 1853, his affairs after settling in Adelaide, and his exploration. Towards the end of the period a particular interest was the building of a chapel at St Werburghs aided by a gift of £500 from his brother, concerning which there were negotiations with Bishop Hale of Perth.

Letters 1857-87 of Peter Egerton-Warburton and members of his family mainly to his brother Rowland but also his mother, 27 items. Written almost entirely after his retirement as commissioner of police in South Australia, the letters contain frequent references to his vines and wine production at Beaumont near Adelaide with mention of preparing table raisins, making olive oil, and seeking a recipe for the drying of figs. In 1887 he refers to a visit of Sir Samuel Davenport to his brother in Cheshire. Other matters included are family affairs, his wife's health, and his general situation and financial position. There are occasional comments on general South Australian affairs. A letter 7 Oct. 1872 from his wife Alicia refers to the start of his east-west journey and there are letters of his son Richard and daughter Ethel who married the eldest son of Bishop Short of Adelaide. The correspondence includes a genealogical note giving dates and place of birth of members of the family.

CORNWALL

REV. R. E. MARSDEN
Pendeen Vicarage, Penzance

SAMUEL MARSDEN PAPERS*

The papers include biographical notes and letters concerning the biography of Samuel Marsden. Among the notes are extracts from the Act Book of the Diocese of Canterbury 4 Mar. and 24 May 1793, Marsden's appointment to New South Wales· As well as correspondence c.1839-76 between members of the family chiefly about property, and family letters c.1819-32, there are a few letters from Marsden 1810-26 to friends, some of which describe his plans to visit New Zealand 1812-13. Legal documents include papers 1839-1902 on land on the Bell River and Molong Creek, copy of the conveyance 8 June 1802 of a farm, Thomas Rynan to Rev. S. Marsden, and a number of papers connected with the estates of members of the Marsden family. There is also a large collection of cuttings concerning Samuel Marsden and the Betts family and a number of pamphlets and leaflets including Mary Betts (née Marsden), *Lines Written on the 100th Anniversary of the Birthday of the Rev. Samuel Marsden*, Sydney 1871, and Church Missionary Society, *Missionary Papers* 111, 1816, containing Marsden's account of his first Sunday in New Zealand. Portraits and photographs, chiefly portraits of Marsden and members of his family, include a crayon drawing of Samuel Marsden, a painting of S. E. Marsden as a boy, and a water-colour of the second parsonage at Parramatta. There are also a number of personal effects among which is a diary 14 June to 19 Aug. 1827 of a voyage from England on the *Nimrod*, possibly by J. Marsden.

SAMUEL EDWARD MARSDEN PAPERS*

The papers of S. E. Marsden, Bishop of Bathurst, include addresses of welcome, letters concerning his commissions, and the Notarial Act on his consecration as Bishop 29 Jan. 1869 as well as other biographical papers. There are a few letters from S. E. Marsden: c.1842-84 to his mother, one 3 Nov. 1884 from Melbourne, and 1844-89 to his sister. Most of the correspondence consists of letters c.1842-1907 to S. E. Marsden, the majority from friends and bishops, including *inter alia* letter 9 Mar. 1869 from the Archbishop of Canterbury, letters 1870-85 from the Bishop of Sydney, 24 Nov. 1874, 6 Nov. 1886 and 5 May 1887 from the Bishop of Melbourne, 19 July 1883 from the Bishop of Newcastle, N.S.W., 7 Aug. 1885 from the Bishop of Tasmania, and 7 Sept. 1898 from the Bishop of Ballarat.

MISS G. CARLYON
Tregrehan, St Austell

Correspondence 1848-53 of Col. Edward Carlyon concerning the emigration of his son Pomeroy to Australia, including negotiations to obtain a travelling companion, and notifications of Pomeroy's death on the goldfields in 1853. Also a letter 2 May 1848 Richard Rodda, Angaston, descriptive of South Australia.

CORNWALL COUNTY LIBRARY
County Hall, Truro

The following items are contained in a copy, held in the Library, of a *History of the Family of Bonython of Bonython*, prepared by H. Farnham Burke, London 1901:

Five letters 1894, 1903, 1911-13 J. Langdon Bonython to a cousin Mr Evelyn

Rashleigh concerned mainly with Bonython family history, the Rashleigh home of Menabilly and his interest in purchasing Bonython in Cornwall, the house and land around it. There are also references to South Australian agricultural affairs and Federal politics. Tipped into the volume are cuttings 10 July 1912 from *The Critic* relating to the first official visit of Lord and Lady Denman to South Australia including a photograph of the Mayor of Adelaide, J. Lavington Bonython, and cutting 11 July 1912 from the *Adelaide Advertiser* relating to the same visit. There are also photographs of the Bonython houses Carclew and Carminow and a photograph of the Governor General Sir Ronald Munro-Ferguson and a group in front of Carminow.

CORNWALL COUNTY RECORD OFFICE
County Hall, Truro

PRIVATE RECORDS

AD 56/1. Letter 22 Apr. 1850 W. Blewett, Gwinear, Cornwall, to his son and daughter in the Port Phillip area, Vic.

DDLR Deeds and Papers of the Lawrence Family
   These include information on pedigrees of the Bligh family.

DDX 26/5. Papers of F. C. Cann 1887-1919 relating to mining mainly in Queensland include: publications 1913-19 of State Departments of Mines; letters 1919 from Fred Wegg Horne, Eden, N.S.W., seeking to interest Cann in alluvial gold workings on the west coast of the South Island, N.Z.; typescript report 27 Mar. 1920 F. C. Cann to the Burma Queensland Co. Ltd on their wolfram mining properties in Queensland; letters 1918 from A. F. MacLaren, managing director of the Thermo-Electric Ore Reduction Corporation Ltd, London, to F. C. Cann at Wolfram Camp, Q'ld, concerning the company's mines there.

DDX 116/61. Papers of R. B. Evans including report 2 Mar. 1887 on the Shotover and Skippers District goldfield with favourable comments on the likely success of large scale quartz mining.

22M Vyvyan Family Papers
22M/FC/40/8. Sixty-four letters 1857-68 including eight letters by J. Henry Vyvyan to his uncle Sir Richard Rawlinson Vyvyan, Bt, describing conditions in New Zealand, land regulations, copper mining, the difficulties of his farming life, and the obstacles to his return to England. The bulk of the remaining letters are from his uncle or his father Rev. Vyell Vyvyan about family affairs, and also persuading him to return to Cornwall.

CUMBERLAND

CUMBERLAND, WESTMORLAND AND CARLISLE RECORD OFFICE
The Castle, Carlisle

PRIVATE RECORDS

D/BS Scott Family
Eighteen letters 1819-49, 1852, addressed to Miss Scott of Sandgate Hall, Penrith, from various friends in Sydney.

D/Ken Graham, Dalton & Kennedy of High Crosby
Twenty-four letters 1829-37 from Georgina Molloy in Western Australia and South
Australia to her mother Mrs Dalton Kennedy of Crosby Lodge, Cumberland, and
elsewhere describing her experiences as an immigrant. The earlier letters give an
account of the voyage from England to Australia. The bundle also contains a sketch
map c.1833 of the situation of the Molloy's ranch by the Vasse River, Geographe
Bay; a tracing of a chart of Swan River surveyed by James Stirling in 1827 and
published 1829; and first and second editions of *Extracts of Letters from Swan River*,
London 1830.

DX/67/37 Magden Family
Four letters 1854-5, 1859 from Stephen Magden of Melbourne, Tarrangower and
Quartz Reef, Pleasant Creek, Vic., to his father Robson Magden of Nenthead,
Alston, descriptive of living conditions, prospects and gold mining.
Letter 1866 from Greymouth, N.Z., to his brother Robson Magden of Alston.
Seven letters 1866-76 of Stephen Magden, Samuel and Margaret White, from
Ipswich, Brickfields, Normandy Reserve, and Dinner Camp, Q'ld.
Letter 1886 from Robson and Mary Urwin, Adelaide, to their uncle and aunt at
Alston.

DERBYSHIRE

DERBY CENTRAL LIBRARY
Wardwick, Derby

BROOKHILL HALL COLLECTION

Correspondence 1824-8, 1831, 1847, 1877-8 of Lieut. William Sacheverell Coke.
The letters are principally from Coke to his father and uncle. They describe his
voyage in the *Regalia* to Cork to pick up an additional 130 convicts and then, after
delays, to New South Wales via Rio de Janeiro and include: 8 Nov. 1825 giving
an account of conditions and pay for a lieutenant going to New South Wales in
charge of a convict ship; 23 Dec. 1825 written on board the *Regalia* before sailing
for Ireland describing the general dissatisfaction on board and appealing for help
in his own financial difficulties; 20 Apr. 1826 giving an account of a plot to murder
the soldiers and crew and take the ship to South America; 24 Mar. 1827, Newcastle,
N.S.W., describing native life and customs and giving an account of Newcastle and
farming conditions there; Apr.-Aug. 1827 from Newcastle describing social life,
climate, vegetation, and life and conditions in the barracks, and giving an account
of court procedure; 10 Feb., 14 May 1828, Sydney Barracks, referring to the settlement at Swan River, and giving a long account of personal troubles.

Miscellaneous correspondence of later years includes: 16 May 1831 R. W. B.
Brown, Cape Town, describing journey to Perth with references to life in the colony;
29 Oct. 1877, 2 Sept. 1878 H. H. Hayter, Office of Government Statistician, Vic.,
to W. S. Coke thanking him for information regarding the officer who commanded
the first settlement at Western Port, for the names of officers in charge of other early
Australian settlements and other material.

Other miscellaneous items include: diary of W. S. Coke 5 Feb. to 21 Sept. 1827;
letter 26 July 1827 Robert Dawson, manager of the Australian Company Settlement,

Derbyshire

Port Stephens, to Lieut. [Coke?] asking him to remove Corporal Evans and to send a better disciplinarian; portion of a letter 7 Aug. 1827 by Charles [Sturt?] referring to his wish to conduct an expedition to explore the waters of the interior; letter 23 Apr. 1828 George Sleeman, newly appointed Commandant, Raffles Bay, to Coke; copy of permit 17 Aug. 1828 signed by C. Sturt, Acting Major of Brigade, for Lieut. Coke to proceed from Sydney to Van Diemen's Land for passage to England.

CATTON PAPERS

This is a collection of about 10,000 items dating back to the twelfth century and relating to the history of the Horton, Wilmot, and Wilmot Horton families. It includes papers of Sir Robert John Wilmot Horton, Under-Secretary of State for War and the Colonies 1821-8. Relevant material was noted in the following sections of the collection: Unbound Letters, Catton ABC, Numbered Volumes, and Subject Volumes.

Unbound Letters. In this series of chronologically arranged unnumbered correspondence thirty-five items 1822-30, 1834 were noted, consisting of miscellaneous correspondence addressed to Wilmot Horton from about thirty correspondents and relating to colonial appointments in New South Wales and Van Diemen's Land, emigration, the obtaining of free passages, letters of introduction, grants of land, petitions, and with occasional letters relating to official policy such as those by T. Potter Macqueen and J. D. Lang. Other correspondents include George Villiers on the Cape Company, H. B. M. Vavasour, G. Watson Taylor with reference to John Macarthur, T. Fowell Buxton, George Galway Miller, T. H. Scott regarding Marsden's charges against Henry Grattan Douglass, Rev. Edward Stanley, George Anson from near Valparaiso after six months' voyage in the Sandwich Islands and Edward Miller Mundy.

Catton ABC. A series of boxes containing volumes of letters arranged alphabetically by correspondent among which were noted 321 items addressed mainly to Wilmot Horton from twenty-one correspondents.
Principal correspondents are:

Sir George Arthur. Letters 1823-4, 1828-9, the bulk written in England and dated 1823. They relate to Honduras matters including the cases of several individuals and of Mr Meredith of Van Diemen's Land, to Arthur's preparations for departure to Van Diemen's Land and his suggestions for appointments. Seven letters 1824 from Hobart concern the voyage out, appointments, the need for legislative and executive authority and separation from New South Wales, with a list of those who should be considered for positions when this is effected and mentioning currency problems and bushrangers.

Saxe Bannister. Correspondence and documents 1823-31, after his resignation as Attorney General of New South Wales, concerning his claim for moneys due and reflections made on his conduct in New South Wales. Apart from the letters to Wilmot Horton there are letters of Bannister to Sir George Murray, R. W. Hay, Lord Goderich, and Lord Bathurst and correspondence on the case between Wilmot Horton, William Tooke, and Hay. One letter 29 Aug. 1829 to Wilmot Horton contains enclosures, among them a history of the case from 1824.

John Thomas Bigge. Letters 1822-5 relating to his commissions of inquiry in New South Wales and the Cape Colony, with emphasis on the former. Thirty-two letters written from Albany, England, mainly in 1822 refer to the forwarding and preparation of the several parts of his report on New South Wales and the laying of these before Parliament. Later correspondence refers to legislation subsequent to the reports and to individuals including Sir Thomas Brisbane, Col. Arthur, Mr Eagar and Lieut.-Gov. Sorell. There are items of correspondence 1822-4 relating to Port Macquarie, between F. Goulburn, Capt. F. Allman, the Commandant, and Bigge. Correspondence after 1823 is mainly from Cape Town and relates to the inquiry undertaken with Major Colebrooke, but New South Wales matters continue to be discussed.

Sir Thomas Brisbane. Letters 1824-5 addressed to Wilmot Horton including memo 8 Mar. 1824 on government establishments at Port Macquarie, Bathurst, Emu Plains, and allowances, salaries, and stores of superintendents; copies of circulars seeking information on the convicts in various government establishments and from clergymen and magistrates on those seeking land; letter with reference to the Australian Agricultural Company; group of correspondence among Brisbane, F. Goulburn, Maj. Ovens, and Hannibal Macarthur on the latter's seeking further convict labour, including lists of his applications and of convicts assigned; abstract of trials 1819-24 before the Court of Criminal Jurisdiction.

William Carter. Letters 1825-8, 1831 mainly of William Carter, Sydney, but also from his father in England. Wilmot Horton appears to have secured a legal appointment on behalf of the father and recommended Carter to Francis Forbes.

Francis Forbes. Letters 1822-8. Those written prior to his departure for New South Wales in 1823 to take up the position of Chief Justice refer to the Bigge reports, the selection of judges for colonial courts, and his work on the New South Wales Bill. Many of the eleven letters 1824-8 written from Sydney are lengthy. They describe the work of the Supreme Court, trial procedure, differences between the Governor and the Colonial Secretary, troubles with the Aborigines, the formation of the Legislative Council, liberty of the press, Moreton Bay, the trade of the colony, utilisation of the labour of settlers and convicts, Howell's case, Capt. King's grievance against Sir Thomas Brisbane, Macarthur's case, Col. Dumaresq, the suicide of Mr Mills, juries in the Supreme Court, the case of Mr Douglass and personal affairs.

Robert Gouger. Letters 1830 relating to the National Colonisation Society and its schemes and invitations to Wilmot Horton to participate.

John Macarthur. Letters 1822-7 written in London relating particularly to the New South Wales Bill 1823-4, but also to the use of free and convict labour, emigration, land valuation, land policy, quit rents, his father's intentions regarding agricultural development in the colony and suggestion of giving land grants to servants of the East India Company, the Marsden-Douglass case, the Australasian Company including a printed prospectus, and penitentiaries in New South Wales.

Stirling and Hutt. Copies of papers n.d. of James Stirling, William Hutt, and Col. Torrens on emigration and land economics in association with the National Colonisation Society.

Robert Torrens. Letters 1826-31, 1837, but mainly 1826-8, addressed to Wilmot Horton concerning Torrens's views on the emigration of the working classes of Great Britain and Ireland and his scheme of emigration without public expense, his own employment, and possible position on the new Colonial Land Board.

Minor correspondents noted in Catton ABC are: T. Fowell Buxton, George Canning, Henry Goulburn from Dublin concerning his brother in New South Wales, H. Hatherton, Henry Hobhouse, William Huskisson, J. D. Lang relating to convicts and the sale of land and emigration, R. M. Matheson, Palmerston, Robert Peel, Sir Herbert Taylor, and William Wilberforce.

Numbered Volumes. In this series of 117 'volumes' of correspondence forty-one items 1824-37 were noted as follows:

Derbyshire

19/874. Letter 1 Feb. 1836 E. Power to Wilmot Horton on the Australian Company wishing to start in Ceylon.

21/937. Copy of letter 21 Aug. 1828 by Wilmot Horton with reference to the death of Mr Mills in New South Wales.

22/955-6. A letter of Mr Black to Wilmot Horton on quit rents and from Lord Howick with reference to Mr Tennant's views on colonisation.

28/1187, 1189-91, 1193-6, 1202, 1205-6, 1208, 1210, 1213. Letters 1825-36 including letters of 1834 from Lieut.-Gov. Arthur, and Gov. Bourke referring to Wilmot Horton's son, Bourke's removal of William Carter from the Supreme Court, his visit to Potter Macqueen's property in the northern districts, and a letter of Francis Forbes also mentioning Wilmot Horton's son and the cessation of trade between India and Sydney.

40/1356. Letter 21 Nov. 1832 Henry Forbes, Madras, with reference to his brother lately come from New South Wales.

50/1564. Terms 20 Jan. 1837 on which crown lands will be disposed of in New South Wales and Van Diemen's Land.

51/1565. Cutting 18 Feb. 1837 from the *Sydney Times* on the report of the Select Committee on the sale of land in the colonies.

76. Copies of confidential letters on official subjects *c*.1824-6, generally indecipherable.

81/2503. Letter 22 Jan. 1830 H. Dumaresq, N.S.W., referring to a petition he is sending to Sir George Murray on the need for more exports, land regulations, King George Sound, the press and libel sanctions, and Sturt's expedition to trace the Murrumbidgee.

90/2558. Cutting *re* South Australia Commissioners' dinner on board the *Coromandel*.

95/26-7. Letter June 1831 from James Busby, late collector of internal revenue in New South Wales, on the need for labourers in New South Wales, with a study of the present situation.

104/2638. Letter n.d. Wilmot Horton to Sir Robert Peel on the economics of assisted emigration.

109/2927. Letter 30 Aug. 1830 Wilmot Horton to C. Tennant referring to his retirement from the National Colonisation Society, with Tennant's reply.

112/2952. A group of correspondence 1836 relating to emigration.

Subject Volumes. A series of volumes of papers collected by subject. The following were noted under the heading 'Emigration'.

Letter 20 Feb. 1835 Gov. Bourke on H.M.S. *Hyacinth*, Twofold Bay, to Wilmot Horton sending 'Return of the number of free persons who have arrived in New South Wales from 1st January 1832 to 31st December 1834 assisted under the arrangements sanctioned, under His Majesty's Government for promoting emigration', and other papers.

Government Papers 1827-33, printed.

Printed copy of paper of 3 Mar. 1827 submitted to the Emigrant Committee by Wilmot Horton with manuscript additions.

Opinions in favour of emigration extracted from various sources, 1827.

Copies of papers on emigration 1704-1830.

Copies of extracts of letters on emigration, 1826.

MILLER MUNDY MSS.

A collection of about 2000 items mainly family correspondence and legal documents including forty letters 1834-89 mostly dated in the 1840s, relating to Alfred Miller Mundy, Colonial Secretary of South Australia. The letters are almost entirely to him while he was with the 21st North British Fusiliers in Van Diemen's Land, at Port Phillip, and in Adelaide. Many letters are from members of the family. There is a letter from Lord Stanley *re* a proposed appointment, presumably to South Australia; letters 1845 from Sir George Grey to Mrs Mundy describing the voyage to New Zealand and Government House, 1849 to Alfred Miller Mundy expressing sympathy for the loss of his son, to whom Grey was godfather, also 1850 describing the state of New Zealand, referring to the marriage of Eyre and to progress with the Maoris. There is also a letter from Bishop Short of Adelaide concerning the death and burial of the son. Two lengthy letters 1845, 1847 from Sir John Hindmarsh, Heligoland, comment on South Australian affairs and politics, and letters 1859 express sympathy at the death of Lady Hindmarsh. There are descriptive letters from Adelaide by Mary Stephen 1 Oct. 1849 to Mrs Miller Mundy and 1844 by Alfred Miller Mundy.

DERBYSHIRE RECORD OFFICE
County Offices, Matlock

For a general account of the Derbyshire Record Office and incoming material see *Derbyshire Archaeological Journal* LXXXII, 1962, and annual articles.

PRIVATE RECORDS

D239 Fitzherbert MSS.

This collection is under process of arrangement and description and the following references are taken from N.R.A. Report 4879:

Box 9. Business and personal letters *c.*1778-1850 addressed to W. S. Perrin and later to Sir Henry Fitzherbert. There are many hundreds of these letters tied in bundles and roughly dated. None have been examined in detail. A few letters were noticed from Sir Joseph Banks to W. S. Perrin, including one from the *Endeavour*, South America.

Box 44. Papers 1852 relating to emigrants to Australia from the Ashbourne district.

Box 59. Two letters 1821, 1826 addressed to Sir Henry Fitzherbert from Mr Buxton describing settlement of the Buxton family in Van Diemen's Land.

Descriptive work in the Record Office to March 1970 has brought to light a letter 26 Aug. 1838 Richard Groombridge, a blacksmith who emigrated to Brown River, Tas., to relatives in Kent, giving details of his voyage out and employment including whaling. He also gives details of other immigrants from Kent.

D567. Two letters 1923, 1934 from George Davies, a Derby Socialist who emigrated to Portland, near Whangerei, North Auckland, giving details of his life in New Zealand, the state of the New Zealand economy and details of the agriculture of the region.

247B Dixon Family Papers

Letters 1863-81 principally to Dr Frank Dixon of Buxton from his brother James Dickson at Dunedin and from James R. Hamilton in Dunedin, N.Z., Sydney, and Melbourne. Three letters 1863 from James Dickson refer to his departure from Glasgow, arrival at Dunedin under agreement as a road surveyor, and work and prospects there. A group of four letters 1863-6 from James Hamilton of the Marine Engineers Office winds up Dickson's affairs on his death, mentioning costs of burial, care of the grave, and exhumation of the coffin. The main group of correspondence consists of sixteen letters 1874-9 presumably from the same J. R. Hamilton referring to family affairs, the sending of various gifts including a possum rug and brooches of colonial gold or kangaroo claws, the children's education, business affairs in Melbourne and Sydney, and his commercial success in what appears to be the book trade.

COLONEL P. V. W. GELL
Hopton Hall, Wirksworth

The muniments include the papers of the Rev. John Philip Gell, of Eleanor Isabella his wife, only child of Sir John Franklin, papers of Sir John and Lady Franklin and of Philip Lyttelton Gell. Selected papers relating to Australia have been microfilmed for the Australian Joint Copying Project. N.R.A. Report 5438 lists some but not all of the following papers.

JOHN PHILIP GELL PAPERS

Notebook 1835-41 including personal accounts for his outfit for the journey to Van Diemen's Land in 1839.

Diary 9 Nov. 1839 to 27 Mar. 1840 describing his voyage to Van Diemen's Land on the convict ship *Runnymede*.

Letters 1838-49 from J. P. Gell.

Letters 1877-98 to J. P. Gell including thirty-four about Tasmania.

Papers 1839-84 concerning the Queen's School and Christ's College, Tas., including a précis of the papers, copies of correspondence, and a printed pamphlet, *Christ's College, Tasmania 1838-1905*, with a supplement 1906.

Papers concerning Sir John Franklin's estates in Van Diemen's Land and South Australia including a deed of arrangement 29 Oct. 1855, Rev. J. P. Gell and Lady Franklin, and correspondence with R. C. Gunn, Launceston. The South Australian papers concern a farm, Myponga, and lands at Port Lincoln and include correspondence with Henry Gawler, Adelaide.

Miscellanea including a drawing of the 'Tasmanian Museum' 16 Mar. 1842, marriage certificate of J. P. Gell and E. I. Franklin and obituary of J. P. Gell.

ELEANOR ISABELLA GELL PAPERS

Diaries 1836-44, 3 vols.

Letters 1837-43 from Eleanor Isabella Franklin, fourteen letters to her relations in England and three letters 1846 to J. P. Gell. A typed copy of a letter 11 Nov. 1836 from the *Fairlea* to her aunt Miss Franklin is filed with typed copies of letters 1800-62 from Sir John Franklin, see below.

Letter 29 Apr. 1848 to Sir John Franklin sent by a relief expedition, mentioning Van Diemen's Land.

Letters 1837-42 to Eleanor Isabella Franklin from Sir John and Lady Jane Franklin, and undated letters from Lady Jane; also one letter [1843?] from Mrs Mary Richardson.

Miscellanea including an invitation to a ball 1 June 1842 from Capt. Ross and Capt. Crozier and officers of H.M.S. *Erebus* and H.M.S. *Terror*, and drafts of notes from E. I. Franklin to accompany her farewell gifts to Capt. Ross and Capt. Crozier.

ARTHUR DANIEL GELL PAPERS

Diary 1845 describing his visit to his brother J. P. Gell in Hobart.

Letter 30 Oct. 1848 to A. L. Elder concerning his affairs in South Australia on the eve of his departure for New Zealand.

Letter 1 Oct. 1849 from Lady Richardson to Mrs Gell enclosing part of a letter she had received from Miss Eyre concerning news of A. D. Gell's death at sea.

Illustration of a memorial to A. D. Gell in Trinity Church, Adelaide, S.A.

Typescript copies of letters 1800-62 from or concerning Franklin including a letter 2 May 1801 from Matthew Flinders to Thomas Franklin.

Handwritten copies made by Philip Lyttelton Gell in 1897 of letters from Franklin to his family 1820-39. The originals were 'preserved by Rev. Arthur Wright'.

Letters 1936-8 from Franklin to Mrs Hannah Booth and letter 15 June 1844 to J. P. Gell.

Four drafts of official letters 1837-40 from Franklin.

Typed copies of letters 1842-3 from Franklin to G. T. W. B. Boyes, copied from the originals in the possession of Mr Boyes's son.

Letters from Franklin to Dr Richardson include eleven letters 1837-43 referring to affairs in Van Diemen's Land, Maconochie, Montagu, Lord Stanley, the press, Ross's expedition to the Antarctic, the visit of d'Urville, and difficulties with Sir John Eardley-Wilmot. Other letters of Australian interest are:

Apr. 1824 concerning plans for an expedition to Australia by Col. Dumaresq and the possibility of Richardson's accepting a job in Australia; 6 Apr. 1829 concerning an offer to Franklin from the 'Australian Land Company' of an appointment at a salary of £2000; 19 Apr. 1830 concerning a meeting of the directors of the Van Diemen's Land Company and the prospect of their offering Richardson an appointment; 11 June 1830 reporting the decision of the directors; 16 May 1836 concerning Franklin's efforts to get Dr Stevens appointed surgeon on the ship on which he is going to Van Diemen's Land.

Letter 23 May 1845 Franklin to Rev. J. P. Gell, discussing *inter alia* reasons for Gell remaining to complete his work in Van Diemen's Land.

Letters to Sir John Franklin:
1812-40 from members of his family; 13 Jan. 1812 Matthew Flinders; 24 Nov. 1836 Capt. W. E. Parry recommending Mr Macquoid, High Sheriff of New South Wales; 19 Aug. 1837 J. Hindmarsh; note in French from d'Urville; 28 July 1842 J. W. Carter; 10 June 1845, 13 Feb. 1847 Rev. J. P. Gell, Hobart, the latter thanking Franklin for his gift of £500 to the College.

Miscellaneous correspondence relating to Sir John Franklin:
13 May 1836 Twopenny to Sir John Richardson asking him to recommend a young man named Stuart to Franklin for employment in Van Diemen's Land.

Miscellanea: small volume containing autographs cut from letters, notes, and papers. The papers include extracts from letters concerning the reception of Sir John Franklin in Van Diemen's Land and his farewell; an agreement, signed, between Sir John Franklin and Charles Ferguson, master of the barque *Rajah* to convey Sir John, his family and servants to England; a silk programme Fourth Tasmanian Anniversary Regatta 1841 and satin programme, Centenary Regatta 1938; letter 25 [July?] 1899 Arthur Wright, Coningsby Rectory, Lincoln, enclosing a 'key' to the plan of old Government House, Hobart, and promising to send a cardboard model. (This model is now in the possession of Col. P. V. W. Gell.)

The papers include letters from Lady Jane Franklin, a letter to her [1844?] from Sophia Cracroft and a letter Oct. 1852 from J. H. Kay, Van Diemen's Land, concerning funds collected there for an expedition in search of Sir John Franklin. Miscellanea include recollections of Lady Jane Franklin by Philip Lyttelton Gell.

Derbyshire

PHILIP LYTTELTON GELL PAPERS

The business papers include papers concerning companies in Australia: British Exploration of Australia Ltd, Australian Smelting Corporation, The Millionaire Ltd, Pilbarra Asbestos Company (Australia), Consolidated Deep Leads Ltd (Australia), London & Western Australian Exploration Company.

DEVON

D. F. O. DANGAR, ESQ.
Gurrow Point, Dittisham, nr Dartmouth

Letter 1840 R. Campbell & Co., Sydney, to Henry Dangar, Neotsfield, Hunter River, concerning his account and usual charges on transactions in the colony also mentioning that his arrangement with R. Campbell & Co. about his wool was a good one.*

DEVON RECORD OFFICE
County Hall, Topsham Road, Exeter

See *Devon Record Office, Brief Guide, Part 1, Official and Ecclesiastical*, [1968]. This publication includes, pp.52-73, a table showing records held arranged by parishes listed in alphabetical order. Private collections deposited are given accession numbers followed by the letter M. Typescript Accession Lists are compiled and there are card indexes of personal and place names and, to a certain extent, of subjects. Accession Lists may at first be very brief but are detailed when work on a collection is completed.

OFFICIAL COUNTY COUNCIL RECORDS

Treasurer's Accounts include a packet for 1821-5 concerning transportation of convicts from Exeter Gaol to hulks or to ships about to proceed to New South Wales. Apparently the packet has been preserved by chance. Papers concerning each consignment of male or female convicts, consist of a Treasury order authorising the County Treasurer to pay the costs of transportation, a receipt for delivery of the convicts listing their names and a receipt for money expended signed by the contractor for transport, sometimes stating that the sum is reckoned at 10d. a mile.

PRIVATE RECORDS

152M Sidmouth Papers (Addington of Upottery)
All papers are not fully sorted. Box 1814 includes:
Letter 3 Nov. 1814 from Rev. Adam Clarke to Lord Sidmouth asking for protection or passport necessary for Samuel Leigh, who has agreed to go to New South Wales as a missionary and notes of arrangements to be made for Leigh's salary, and pension prospects.
Note 20 Mar. 1814 by George William Evans, Sydney, headed 'Sketch of a tour of discovery' and describing a tour across the Blue Mountains to the Macquarie River. With the above paper is a manuscript map entitled 'A Sketch of New South Wales including the New Discovered Country to the West of the Blue Mountains . . . 1813 . . . 1814 by George William Evans'.

352M Please and Ponsford Families (Topsham) Papers

352M/T24. Counterpart lease for two years 30 Oct. 1877 from George John Ponsford, Christchurch, N.Z., to William Robinson, Christchurch, N.Z., coppersmith, of Lot 7, town reserves, Christchurch.

352M/T25. Draft appointment of attorney 1879. George Ponsford, Christchurch, N.Z., gentleman, to William Widdowson, Christchurch, retired builder.

352M/T26. Agreement to lease property 21 Dec. 1881, George Ponsford to George Brown of shop and house in Manchester St, Christchurch.

877M/F1. 'Journal of our voyage in the ship *Selkirkshire* from Glasgow to Rockhampton, 1882' by Frances, wife of James Parsons Thomson, medical officer, formerly on the staff of Newcastle-upon-Tyne Infirmary. The ship carried *c.*400 Scottish emigrants bound for Australia. The journal ends at sea before the voyage was completed. Photocopy in the National Library of Australia.

B961M Kennaway Papers, 3rd and 4th Deposits
Business and legal papers include:

B961M/B15-16. Correspondence and papers, chiefly papers 1888-95 of Sir John H. Kennaway concerning the winding-up of the Bank of South Australia including printed notices to shareholders 'Summary of the Statement of Affairs at the 6th Day of December 1894 . . .' and cuttings.

1148M Acland of Broad Clyst Papers
Boxes 6, 8, 11 include a few papers of Australian and New Zealand interest. In Box 6 is a letter 22 June 1869 from Laidley Mort, Sydney, to Sir Charles Acland, 12th Bt, describing his farming activities and his business in Sydney; the letter refers to Garnett's experiences in the colony and mentions that he is now part owner of a station at Mt Enniskillen on the Barcoo River. Box 8 contains a letter 20 Feb. 1850 from Bishop G. A. Selwyn, St John's College, Auckland, to Sir Thomas D. Acland stating that the *Actaeon* had a long voyage fatal to Veitch's plants but the cases have been sent back to him filled with plants from New Zealand; Nares has accompanied Selwyn on a cruise in the *Undine* to New Caledonia and other islands. Box 11(2) includes a letter 10 Nov. 1841 from George R. Farmer to Sir Thomas D. Acland concerning flax in New Zealand, and a packet 're Colleges, Churches and Chapels' containing *inter alia* an 'Appeal on behalf of Christ's College Tasmania', printed at St Helier, Jersey.

1052M Grendon Family Papers
1052M/F43-51. Family letters 1837-1933 include F47-9 letters 1859 from A. Ford, Christchurch, N.Z. The letters state that the writer is with her husband in New Zealand after a voyage of 109 days. Her early impressions are described.

1262M Fortescue of Filleigh MSS.
1262M/FC52. Letters 1889-90 from J. W. Fortescue, New Zealand, to his father and to 'Susan' giving political news.

EXETER CITY LIBRARY
Castle Street, Exeter

For the records of the Borough of Exeter see Historical Manuscripts Commission Report on the Records of the City of Exeter, 1916. For deposited collections there is a catalogue of accessions on slips in loose-leaf binders; duplicates of the slips are also filed in chronological order in separate binders for parishes. A name index on cards is maintained.

Devon

Transportation Orders 1802-43, 1 box.
Bonds and contracts for transportations to New South Wales 1787-9.

PRIVATE RECORDS

49/9 Penny and Harward, solicitors, Tiverton, MSS.
49/9/3. Deeds and papers concerning the Dunsford family of Tiverton. Items 3/234-51, 1851-83, concern members of the family in Victoria, John Bear, John Pinney Bear, Thomas Hutchings Bear, Ann Bear, William Henry Dunsford, and include 3/234 will 26 Sept. 1851 of John Bear, Collins Street, Melbourne, settler, 3/240 balance sheets 1859-82 of the colonial estate of W. H. Dunsford and 3/242 letters 1860-4 to F. Dunsford from J. P. Bear concerning family affairs.

Chichester of Arlington Court (National Trust) MSS.
50/11. Miscellaneous papers, printed and manuscript, concerning emigration to New Zealand and Australia, including a printed paper endorsed in manuscript 'London 23 May 1839' addressed to William Jerman, signed John Marshall, Australian Emigration Agent, and giving particulars for Australian Packet Ships and 'Conditional Nearly-Free Passages', and other papers connected with the emigration of William Jerman, blacksmith. Another item in 50/11 includes papers 1839 concerning the sending of Capt. Hobson to New Zealand, one letter stating that he had no connection with the New Zealand Company.

Acland Papers
51/12/4. Several letters 1880-93 from J. B. D. Acland, his wife and daughter written from Christchurch, N.Z., and Rangitata, N.Z., mentioning conditions on stations and politics.

Lethbridge Letters
Letters concerning Devonshire families resident abroad, addressed to Sir Roper Lethbridge on the occasion of his Presidential Address to the Devonshire Association, Exeter, 1901, 3 vols. with index of names and places. Names of Australian and New Zealand families include Acland, N.Z.; Belfield, N.Z.; Cutmore, Q'ld; Eales, N.S.W.; Holman, N.Z.; Norrish, W.A., Roope, Vic.; Seward, W.A.; Sparke, N.S.W. The collection also includes a letter from P. G. Bond, Plymouth, concerning the Colton family, S.A. Thomas Colton married Susan Bond, whose brother Edward traded for some years in a schooner on the Australian coast and was lost at sea in 1860 in the brig *Ensign*.

PLYMOUTH CITY LIBRARIES
Central Library, Tavistock Road, Plymouth

See *Plymouth Records 1. A Guide to the Archives Department of Plymouth City Libraries, Part I*, 1962. It is recommended to readers to make an appointment to see the records. Many municipal and private records were destroyed by enemy action in 1941. The Archives Department lists records in other hands and has listed all the Anglican parish records of Plymouth and district, all Nonconformist records of Plymouth and some business and charity archives.

PRIVATE RECORDS

Broadbent and Huddart MSS.
Archives of G. H. Sellick, solicitor, deposited by successor firm, Broadbent and Huddart, solicitors.
16. Petherbridge family papers, including 16/2, schedule of property in Weymouth

and Currie Street, Adelaide, S.A., belonging to William, John, Benjamin, and Alfred Petherbridge, 1859, printed.

16/7. Correspondence and two conveyances about land in Town Acre 138, Adelaide, belonging to A. R. Petherbridge, 1883.

Vosper Letters

A few letters 1885-1900 from F. C. B. Vosper, M.L.A., editor of the *Australian Sunday Times*, written to his father in England. Two letters 1885 are from H.M. Training Ship *Devonport*, five letters 1886-90 from Queensland and three letters 1895-1900 from Western Australia. There are also two letters 1901 from his widow and a small pamphlet *Legalised Robbery. An exhaustive account of the liquidation swindles perpetrated at Charters Towers*, Charters Towers 1891. Microfilm in the Battye Library, Perth, W.A.

V. BONHAM-CARTER, ESQ.
Broomhall, East Anstey, nr Tiverton

Biography* of Oswald Bloxsome and copies of the diary of his journey to Australia 1838 in the barque *Florentia*. Mr V. Bonham-Carter has presented the original manuscript of a first part of the diary to the National Library of Australia. The second part ending 3 Aug. 1838 with arrival in Sydney has been lent for copying in Australia by the owner Mr O. Bloxsome, Delubra, Mandubbera, Queensland. The biography, written by H. S. Bloxsome of this address contains digressions on attacks by Aborigines and on prominent contemporaries, e.g. Robert Lowe, Oswald Brierly, and Stuart Russell.

MRS N. CLOVER
Normount, Torquay

KIDMAN PAPERS*

Photograph of Elizabeth Mary, née Nunn, wife of George Kidman, mother of George, Frederick, Thomas, Sackville, Sidney, and Charles. Married secondly Stephen Starr, by whom there were three daughters.

Photograph, carte de visite, 1873, J. H. Nixon, artist photographer, Wellington, S.A. The staff of Mt Gipps Station, N.S.W., including Sidney Kidman aged 16.

Photographic copy of receipt 'N.S.W. Silverton, 28th July 1884' signed Sidney Kidman 'I have this day sold Mr. James Poole 10 stears . . . for value received in consideration of 1/14 in Broking Hill Mine on Mt. Gipps'. With covering letter 14 Feb. 1968, H. Gooch, 62 Currie Street, Adelaide, to Mrs Nelson Clover stating that the original receipt is in the Charles Rasp Library at Broken Hill, N.S.W.

Letter 31 Mar. 1898 from Sackville Kidman, Broken Hill, to Fred Nunn, typescript copy. It concerns the possibility of employment for F. Nunn and his sons, conditions on Kidman stations, the mail coaching plant in Western Australia running under the name of Cobb & Co., also family news.

Copy of verses, 'Kidman's Boys, dedicated to Sir Sidney Kidman on the occasion of his 75th Birthday which was celebrated by his employees, in a "Rodeo" held at Adelaide, on 3rd September 1932', printed.

Autograph of Sidney Kidman, Eringa, Kapunda, 18 Dec. 1901.

Two lists of Kidman stations, one written in an exercise book by H. J. Bird, showing name of company, name of station, area, carrying capacity for sheep, cattle or horses and state in which located, the second being a typescript list with less detail.

Letter 6 Apr. 1954 H. J. Bird, Adelaide, to Mrs Nelson Clover describing the visit of Queen Elizabeth II and Prince Philip to the Flying Doctor Base at Broken Hill in 1954, also commenting on the Traeger portable transceiver, School of the Air, and drought conditions on Kidman stations. Enclosed is a typescript copy of an article on the Flying Doctor Service and on social services for the outback.

Collections of magazine articles and cuttings concerning Sir Sidney Kidman.

Description of Kidman stations, typescript. A general description (1969) of cattle stations and sheep stations giving average size of holding, average size of paddocks, distances for out stations, water supplies, seasonal tasks, staff, machinery, grasses.

DORSET

V. MONTAGU, ESQ.
Mapperton, Beaminster

SANDWICH PAPERS

A fee of £5 per day is charged to students using the records at Mapperton (Jan. 1970).

The papers include those of the fourth Earl, some of which are printed in *The Sandwich Papers*, Navy Records Society, 1932-6, 4 vols. The numbers quoted below are taken from N.R.A. Report 5472.

8. Thirty-eight envelopes of letters and papers c.1766-88 of Lord Sandwich as First Lord of the Admiralty, concerning naval affairs at home and abroad (some printed by the Navy Records Society).

10. Naval memoranda and correspondence 1768-9.

12. Naval papers c.1770-80 of the fourth Earl, memoranda not wanted for the Navy Records Society publication, 1 box.

13. Naval memoranda and correspondence 1771.

16. Ten bundles and four loose papers c.1771-82 concerning naval matters.

18. Green box file including:
Two letters concerning the publication of the narrative of the first voyage of Cook 1771-3.
Letters 1774-80 of Daines Barrington relating to Forster's narrative of the second voyage of Cook; also Forster's account.
Papers and correspondence 1781-4 relative to the publication of the narrative of Cook's last voyage, 30 letters.
Correspondence 1779-80 of Sir James Harris with Lord Sandwich relating to the death of Cook, 6 letters.
Miscellaneous letters 1773-90 including three letters 1776 from Cook (missing 1958), 9 letters.
Papers relating to Cook's second voyage 1772, 6 docs.

268. Autograph letters including correspondence from Banks, Cook, and Maskelyne.

Letters and papers relating to the second and third voyages of Cook have been referred to and printed in *The Journals of . . . Cook*, ed. Beaglehole. These papers 1771-82 include three letters 11 July, 23 Oct., 26 Nov. 1776 from Cook to Sandwich.

DORSET MILITARY MUSEUM
The Keep, Bridport Road, Dorchester

Stations and Services of the 39th Regiment of Infantry, 1701-1939. Pages 15-25 describe the Regiment's period in Australia and include a list of ships carrying detachments 8 Nov. 1825 to 17 Sept. 1827 with note of the officers in charge. The Regiment received orders to transfer to India in July 1832. There is a list of the stations in Australia and the number of officers and men at each. References are made to: Capt. Wakefield's establishment of a settlement at King George Sound in the latter part of 1826, Capt. Smyth's establishment of Fort Wellington at Raffles Bay in 1827, the Regiment's action in suppressing bushrangers in the Bathurst area, Capt. Forbes's command of the Mounted Police, the journeys of exploration of Capt. Charles Sturt and others, relations with the civil government, and the administration of the colony of New South Wales by Col. Lindesay between the departure of Gov. Darling and the arrival of Gov. Bourke.

Capt. John Douglas Forbes and Lieut. the Hon. Lauderdale Maule. Account of a journey north to the Liverpool Range, then west across the Goulburn and Hunter Rivers and south-west to the upper Macquarie River and thence to Bathurst and return to Sydney, 15 June to 24 July 1830.

Diary of the proceedings of a detachment of the Mounted Police led by Capt. Forbes and Lieut. Maule on an expedition in search of a gang of bushrangers supposed to be settled in the interior of New South Wales, 29 Mar. to 30 May 1832. The diary gives daily details, rates of travel, bearings of remarkable topographical features, and daily latitude and longitude. The detachment set out from Bathurst, passed through Mudgee, reached the Namoi on 1 May, and travelled up the left hand bank of the Gwydir. On 19 May the party turned back to the Namoi and returned to Sydney by steamboat with a stop at Newcastle. There are frequent references to the Aborigines.

Capt. Charles Sturt. Account of Sturt's career compiled in 1930 by P. R. Phipps, typescript with associated cuttings.

DORSET RECORD OFFICE
County Hall, Dorchester

For an account of the Record Office and indication of holdings see *Archives* VII, No.36, Oct. 1966, pp.207-14.

QUARTER SESSIONS RECORDS

Orders 1730-92 for the transportation of convicts, and contractors' bonds and contracts for transportation including one 25 Jan. 1787 for transportation to New South Wales; also receipts for convicts delivered on board vessels and related correspondence.

DORCHESTER GAOL RECORDS

10946. Register of Prisoners containing entry Mar. 1834 for the Tolpuddle Martyrs.

PARISH RECORDS

Beaminster Parish Records
P57/OV29. Eight bills 1852 for the outfit of Jane Frampton, an emigrant to Adelaide, S.A.

Buckland Newton Parish Records
P18/OV34. Correspondence 1848-52 concerning emigration of paupers to Australia in 1849 with lists of outfits for eight emigrants, bills and receipts for rail fares and

carriage, and a copy of the Poor Law Board conditions in their orders 1848 sanctioning the emigration of poor persons.

Corfe Castle Parish Records

P11/OV212. Copy of despatches, reports, and correspondence 1834-5 concerning the selection and sending of female emigrants to New South Wales and Van Diemen's Land, printed.

Stalbridge Parish Records

P308/VE1. References in vestry minutes 1839, 1847-8 to persons emigrating to Australia.

Wareham Parish Records

P63/OV18. Among entries in the vestry minutes for 1848 there are three references to raising money for emigration including the emigration of Joseph Jacobs and his family to South Australia.

PRIVATE RECORDS

D10 Weld (Lulworth Castle) MSS.

D10/C292, 306, 308, 310. Correspondence including three letters 1858, 1884, Palmer, Eland and Nettleship, London, to Joseph Weld, jnr, Hampshire, *re* his New Zealand property; 29 Mar. 1873 G. H. Brown, Wharfdale Station, Oxford, N.Z., to Joseph Weld II concerning relations with the Maoris and life on a sheep farm; two letters 1876, 1878 F. Weld, Government House, Hobart Town, to Joseph Weld II with references to family affairs, rising New Zealand land values, sporting life and Melbourne Cup Day; 1865 John Vaughan to Joseph Weld II mentioning selling American and buying New Zealand property.

D16 Weld (Chideock) MSS.

D16/C59. Letter 5 Feb. 1859 Charles Weld to Laura Phillips with congratulations on the betrothal of Frederick Weld to her daughter.

D16/C60. Correspondence, Sir Frederick Weld. Includes letter 15 Nov. 1864 F. Weld, Flaxbourne, N.Z., to his wife with estate directions, references to horses and speculation whether he would be asked to form a ministry.

D16/F19. Family papers, 19th cent., Charles Weld. Poems, prose, plays, including a printed ballad and a letter n.d. Emma Agnes Petre, to Charles Weld.

D16/F35. Family papers, Sir Frederick Weld. Letters 1875 of T. P. Henning to F. Weld in Perth concerning the Weld pedigree; copies of letters 1875 F. Weld to the editor of *Burke's Landed Gentry* supplying information; 18 May 1883 Straits Settlements, statement on the history of the Weld family.

D43 Colfox Papers

D43/C26. Letter 15 Jan. 1831 M. Stevens, principal turnkey, H.M. Gaol, Hobart Town, V.D.L., to Thomas Collins Colfox seeking remission of sentence, including a petition 1824 to Sir Robert Peel from Hannah Stevens his mother.

D128 Dampier (Hilfield) MSS.

D128/T20. Copy of power of attorney 29 Aug. 1839 Thomas Maber Sparks, about to leave for Australia, to Messrs Saml Sparks and Wm Sparks. Power of attorney 4 Feb. 1843 Octavius Batten Sparks, late of Bath, now of Monaro, N.S.W., to the same.

D239 Battiscombe MSS.

D239/F13. Letters and documents 1854-87 referring to appointments of Lieut. Albert Battiscombe.

D239/F14. Diary 1860-1 Lieut. Albert Battiscombe of *Pelorus* Naval Brigade at Camp Waitara, N.Z., during the Maori War, describing engagements with the enemy, Maori defences and battle tactics, Maori settlements, way of life and traditions, with some drawings and cuttings.

D257 Battiscombe MSS.

D257/F3. Commendations 1846-61 of Rear-Adm. Albert H. W. Battiscombe including those of his service in New Zealand.

Photocopy 232. Letter 1836 from John Hardy, transported to Australia in 1834, and letter 1869 to him; with transcripts and notes 1966 by R. Legg.

Tolpuddle Martyrs Centenary

Material gathered 1933 by A. C. Cox including correspondence with Walter M. Citrine, General Secretary of the Trades Union Congress General Council, concerning the Tolpuddle Martyrs Centenary Celebrations; T.U.C. publications for the celebration and a paper 1934 by W. Maitland Walker 'An impartial appreciation of the Tolpuddle Martyrs'.

THE HON. MRS G. MARTEN
Crichel House, Wimborne

Private papers concerning Charles Sturt's expedition to Central Australia in 1844-6.* See C. Sturt, *Narrative of an Expedition into Central Australia . . . 1844, 5 and 6*, London 1849, 2 vols., and 'A Condensed Account of an Exploration in the Interior of Australia', *Journal of the Royal Geographical Society of London*, 17, 1847.

Letter of Instructions from Gov. Grey with a 'Return of the number of men and animals, as well as provisions I propose to take into the Interior'.

Journal 11 Aug. 1845 to 12 Jan. 1846 apparently kept during the expedition with separate extra drafts of some passages.

Piesse's return of provisions and letter to Sturt 29 Jan. 1846.

'Vocabulary of the Dialect Spoken by Murray River Tribes, May 1844' and 'Specimens of the Language of the Natives of the Upper Darling'.

Letters concerning the expedition including letters of appreciation, four rough drawings and two charts, letter 16 Feb. 1847 Piesse to Sturt from Calcutta and drafts of notes by Sturt on the mines and the general revenue of South Australia, also a draft of his 'notice of the province of South Australia' published with his *Narrative*, London 1849, 2 vols.

DURHAM

DURHAM COUNTY RECORD OFFICE
County Hall, Durham

PRIVATE RECORDS

D/HO Hodgkin Papers

The papers of a Quaker family including papers relating to a visit to Australia and New Zealand 1866-8 by J. B. Hodgkin. See typescript list. Among the papers are:

Durham

D/HO/C32/37. Letter 18 Nov. 1866 from J. B. Pease, Darlington, to J. B. Hodgkin giving advice on his visit to Australia in the light of the writer's experiences.

D/HO/F60-2. Letter books 1866-8 of J. B. Hodgkin, copy-books of letters written on the *Yorkshire* arriving in Hobson's Bay, sailing to New Zealand on the *Albion*, visiting Christchurch and other places, returning to Melbourne and describing the return voyage to England. Many of the letters are written from Australia.

D/HO/C25/1. Letter 15 Dec. 1896 from Viscount Hampden, Governor of New South Wales, to T. F. Buxton introducing T. Hodgkin.

D/HO/C33/9. Invitation 7 Dec. 1896 to a dance from T. F. Buxton, Governor of South Australia, to J. E. Hodgkin.

D/LO Londonderry Papers

   See typescript list.

D/LO/C. Political and personal correspondence of the 7th Marquess of Londonderry includes D/LO/C236 letters 1922-7 containing reference to emigration of the unemployed and D/LO/C237 letters 1932-8 among which is D/LO/C237/10 correspondence 1937 with Amery on German colonies.

D/X Miscellanea

D/X245/7. Three letters 1856-7 from G. Lawson to his wife, 7 Jan. 1856 from Liverpool advising emigrants against the Black Ball Line, 4 Apr. 1856, Melbourne, describing the voyage, 24 May 1857, Ballarat, containing a few remarks about the diggings and mentioning that his brothers Joseph and Thomas were about thirty miles away.

DURHAM LIGHT INFANTRY MUSEUM AND ARTS CENTRE
Aykeley Heads, Durham

Shuttleworth, Maj. Charles Ughtred, Diary 1864-5, 2 vols., describing the part played by the 68th Durham Light Infantry in the Maori War.

The Museum also has water-colours 1864 by Lieut. H. G. Robley, 68th, and Capt. William Algernon Kay depicting scenes at Gate Pa, Tauranga, and Te Papa Cemetery; also a water-colour of a Maori chief by Robley and a photograph of members of the 68th taken shortly before the Gate Pa battle.

UNIVERSITY OF DURHAM
Department of Palaeography and Diplomatic, South Road, Durham

BACKHOUSE PAPERS

   Letters from James Backhouse

215. 26 Mar. 1849 to H. Backhouse suggesting that 'our dedicated relative' write a simple and brief letter to Friends in Australia.

216. 6 Apr. 1849 to H. C. Backhouse suggesting letter to Friends in Australia, 'The main body of them is in Hobart Town'. Other groups in Van Diemen's Land, New South Wales, Port Phillip and South Australia are described. In Australind 'resides a solitary Friend . . . Elinor Clifton'.

217. 20 Apr. 1849 to H. C. Backhouse concerning Dr G. F. Story and T. Mason, Friends of Hobart Town, who were to visit South Australia. Mason emigrated to New Zealand but had gone to Van Diemen's Land to avoid troubles with the Maoris.

EARL GREY PAPERS

   Formerly the Grey of Howick collection in the Prior's Kitchen, Durham. See

Ronald P. Doig, *Earl Grey Papers, an Introductory Survey*, Private Libraries Association 1961. This work describes the scope of the collection, its contents and arrangement, and the extent of card indexing. Duplicated typescript lists of Earl Grey Papers available are:

List of Political and Public Correspondence of the 2nd Earl Grey 1787-1843.

List of Personal and Family Correspondence of the 2nd Earl Grey 1762-1875.

List of Correspondence of the 3rd Earl Grey 1818-1894.

List of Enclosures in the Correspondence of the 3rd Earl Grey.

There are card indexes to the correspondence of the 2nd and 3rd Earls. The papers of the 3rd Earl have been used by Professor J. M. Ward in his *Earl Grey and the Australian Colonies 1846-1857*, Melbourne 1957.

Papers of the 2nd Earl Grey

The papers include correspondence with Prime Ministers, which may repay examination.

Correspondence of the 3rd Earl Grey

Selected letters have been microfilmed for the State Library of South Australia. The arrangement of correspondence is alphabetical under names or titles of correspondents but there are also separate sections for Colonial Papers and War Office Papers. Colonial Papers are again divided under the subheadings Australia, Emigration, New South Wales, New Zealand, Tasmania, and Transportation. The card index, as well as listing names of correspondents, contains lists of papers in these sections and cross references to names of correspondents whose letters relate to the subjects. There are also cross references from names of places including South Australia, Victoria and Western Australia to the entries under Colonial Papers, Australia.

Adelaide, Bishop of, Augustus Short, 13 Mar. 1847 concerning his appointment to the diocese of Adelaide.

Aglionby, H., 30 Sept. 1844 enclosing cuttings on debenture issue and proclamations of Gov. FitzRoy, N.Z., 26 Mar., 8 May 1844.

Anglesey, Sir Henry William Paget, 1st Marquess, correspondence including memo 14 May 1851 by Grey 'on Sir Jn Burgoyne's memo. respecting the employment of sappers and miners in Australia'.

Ashburton, Francis Baring, 3rd Baron, copy of letter 4 Oct. 1849 Grey to Ashburton on representative government in New Zealand.

Auckland, George Eden, 2nd Baron and 1st Earl, letters 1846-8 include 25 Aug. 1846 enclosing copy of extract from letter 26 Apr. 1846 Prof. Airy, Astronomer Royal, to Sir Robert Peel, concerning the observatory at Parramatta, also referring to the magnetic observatory in Van Diemen's Land. Other letters contain a few references to New Zealand and the Pacific.

Ball, J. T., 27 Feb. 1869 with printed paper on Protestant churches in colonies, presented to Established Church (Ireland) Commission.

Bath and Wells, Bishop of, Robert John Eden, 3rd Baron Auckland, letters 1846-7 mainly on appointments to colonial bishoprics.

Bell, Sir Francis Dillon, 7 Mar. 1870 enclosing copy of New Zealand Commissioners Act 32-3 Vict.LIX, printed.

Bourke, Maj.-Gen. Sir Richard, 11 Aug. 1833, 31 Jan. 1836, 17 July 1838, for enclosures see Colonial Papers, New South Wales; copies of letters 23 Oct., 29 Nov. 1832, Grey to Bourke.

Browne, Lt.-Col. Sir Thomas Gore, letters 1851-61; copies of letters 14 Nov. 1851, 31 Oct. 1860, Grey to Browne.

Buller, C., letters 1838-48 to Grey enclosing memos 1846-7 on affairs of the New Zealand Company including minute 19 June 1847 by Stephen.

Burrell, C. G., 31 Jan. 1836 accepting place of landing waiter in Australia.

Burrell, H. R., 28 Oct. 1852 containing complaint against J. D. Lang concerning purchase by Burrell of land at Moreton Bay and enclosing copy of Lang's receipt.

Busby, J., 7 Sept. 1861, 1 July 1864 on New Zealand.

Campbell, Maj. J., 18 Oct. 1837 on the New Zealand Association; copy of letter 1 Nov. 1837 Grey to Campbell.

Canterbury, John Henry Thomas Manners-Sutton, 3rd Viscount, 5 July 1873 on the Colonial Church Bill.

Canterbury, Archbishop of, William Howley, letters 1846-7 on appointment of colonial bishops; copies of letters 1846-7 Grey to Howley on Australian bishoprics.

Carlingford, Chichester Samuel Parkinson-Fortescue, 1st Baron, 8 Nov. 1860 on New Zealand, 27 July 1863, 13 May 1868.

Chapman, H. S., 28 July 1853 enclosing memo 'on the present state of the Executive Councils, and . . . the new legislative councils of the Australian colonies'.

Colonial Papers, Australia. Manuscript memos and printed papers with manuscript notes chiefly 1838-57. The subjects dealt with include lands, steam communication, a printed draft report 21 Feb. 1849 by James Stephen on Australian legislatures, memo n.d. by Tulloch on military labourers for Western Australia, and a group of papers on the administration of the Colonial Office 1829-c.1849.

Colonial Papers, Emigration. Emigration, New South Wales, 1831-2, papers including memos on Arthur's despatches on land and emigration, report of Commissioners for Emigration, as submitted in Feb. 1832, State of the Poor South of England; also notes on classes of emigrants and a discussion in the House of Commons.

Colonial Papers, New South Wales. Among the papers are: memo 22 Nov. 1832 by R. Roberts on behalf of Mr Girard of New South Wales with letter 26 Nov. 1832 from Roberts; for Grey's reply 29 Nov. 1832 see Lord Howick's Private Letter Book pp.178-81; correspondence and memos on the government of New South Wales and on land questions there during Bourke's term as Governor; copies of two letters 29, 31 Dec. 1851 J. N. Hardy to E. Deas Thomson on gold digging; notes n.d. by Grey from speech by Lowe on New South Wales.

Colonial Papers, New Zealand. These include papers and correspondence 1837 on draft New Zealand Bill; letter 18 Nov. 1845 T. C. Harington asking Earl Grey to be a governor of the New Zealand Company; paper 1846 by T. C. Harington; report 24 Aug. 1846, special committee of Court of Directors of the New Zealand Company concerning the dissolution of the Company; other New Zealand papers 1846-51, 1861-9.

Colonial Papers, Tasmania. Paper 12 May 1838 by Grey on assignment of land in Van Diemen's Land; printed report on the state of prison discipline in Van Diemen's Land by Capt. Maconochie, H.M.S.O., 1838.

Colonial Papers, Transportation. Papers on transportation 1838 by Grey and 1st Earl Russell, chiefly printed but including minute of a conversation 1852 between Grey and S. King at the Colonial Office.

Compton, R., 12 Jan. 1861 on employment in Australia.

Cooling, R. H., 26 Aug. 1864 enclosing cutting on transportation to Western Australia.

Cox, C. A., correspondence 1853 among Cox, J. W. Cowell, and Grey on the New Zealand Company, and letter 1887 to Grey.

Dangar, H., 18 May 1853 on transportation, enclosing two cuttings from the *Sydney Morning Herald*.

David, J. C. A., 13 Aug. 1857 on convicts in Australia.

Denison, Lt.-Gen. Sir William Thomas, letters 1847-70, including letters 1847-53 Grey to Denison with some copies; enclosures include letters Denison to Rev. W.

Murray and La Trobe to Denison, also returns Aug.-Nov. 1851, Dec. 1851 of 'Persons who have left Van Diemen's Land for the Colonies on New Holland', and cuttings on the Australasian League.

Derby, Edward George Geoffrey Smith Stanley, 14th Earl, letters 1846-67 including letter 22 Mar. 1846 from Sir John Eardley-Wilmot to Derby, copies of letters 21 Mar. 1846 J. L. Pedder to Eardley-Wilmot and 19 Mar. 1845 Pedder and others to Editor of *The Naval and Military Gazette*.

Donaldson, Sir Stuart Alexander, 10 May 1858 on the first session of Parliament, New South Wales, with copy of letter 30 July 1858 Grey to Donaldson.

Dumas, A. G., letters 1852-3 with enclosures: to letter 4 Mar. 1852 cutting on J. D. Lang's departure from Australia; to letter 27 Apr. 1852 cuttings on the New South Wales Anti-Transportation League, printed lists of employers of convicts etc.; to letter July 1852 cutting from *Moreton Bay Courier* containing letter by Dumas defending Grey's colonial policy; to letter 9 May 1853 copies of correspondence on Dumas's request for transfer to another colony.

Elliot, Sir Thomas Frederick, letters 1832-57 including letter 22 Apr. [1848] on emigration, for enclosures see Colonial Papers, Australia, and Colonial Papers, New South Wales, also Shaftesbury to Grey 18 Apr. 1848.

Eversley, Charles Shaw-Lefevre, 1st Viscount, 30 Nov., 8 Dec. 1844 on evidence before the New Zealand Committee of Francis A. Molesworth, brother of Sir William Molesworth.

Eyre, E. J., letters 1846-51; copies of two letters 9 Nov. 1846, 30 Dec. 1851 Grey to Eyre.

Farrer, W. J., letters 1866 on Colonial Bishoprics Bill, enclosed in letter 7 May 1866 are copies of letters from Baroness Burdett-Coutts 1865-6.

Featherston, I. E., 22 Mar. 1870 enclosing printed memo 7 Jan. 1870 by W. Gisborne, on the decision of the Imperial Government to remove the last regiment from New Zealand.

Fitzgerald, Capt. C., letters 1849-56 including enclosure to letter 15 Aug. 1853, a cutting concerning a public meeting at Perth on transportation; copies of letters 1846-52 Grey to Fitzgerald.

Fitzgerald, J. P., M.D., letters 1849-94 include letters from New Zealand with a few references in later letters.

FitzRoy, Sir Charles Augustus, letters 1850-2; copies of letters 1848-52 Grey to FitzRoy.

Franklyn, H. M., editor of the *Victorian Review*, Melbourne, 1 Oct. 1879, 1 Apr., 16 Nov. 1880.

Gairdner, G., 28 Nov. 1857, 27, 28 July 1858 on Australian colonies.

Gardner, W. A., 15 Sept. 1851, copy, also letter 20 Sept. 1853 concerning conditions in Van Diemen's Land.

Gipps, Sir George, 20, 24 Dec. 1846.

Glenelg, Charles Grant, 1st Baron, letters 1831-58 mainly on Canada; copies of letters 1835-8 Grey to Glenelg, several items on New South Wales.

Gordon, Gen. Sir James Willoughby, letters and memos 1831-49 including a few items of relevance to Australia especially memo 28 May 1849 on the reduction of the military force in Australia.

Grey, Sir George, Governor, letters 1847-60, copies of letters 1846-52 from Earl Grey; among enclosures are copies of despatches and extract from report 3 June 1853 from Major Kenny on the progress and present condition of the New Zealand Fencibles 20 May 1853; copy of letter 20 Oct. 1847 from Earl Grey includes two enclosures: letter 6 Jan. 1847 W. Swainson to 3rd Earl Grey and memorial 6 Jan. 1847 Swainson to 1st Earl Russell.

Durham

Grey, Sir George, Colonial Secretary, letters and notes 1836-82, several items outside his term as Colonial Secretary refer to Australian matters.

Halifax, Charles Wood, 1st Viscount, letters 1830-85 including a few c.1851 relating to New Zealand.

Hampton, John Somerset Pakington, 1st Baron, 4 Dec. 1852 enclosing memo from inhabitants of Western Australia on steamships.

Harington, T. C., 18 Nov. 1845 to Grey.

Hawes, Sir Benjamin, letters and memos, from 1847 including some relating to Australia and New Zealand.

Hay, Sir John, 22 Dec. 1875 acknowledging Grey's *Parliamentary Government considered with reference to a Reform of Parliament*, London 1858.

Head, Rev. Oswald, 30 Nov. 1837 enclosing a copy of petition from T. Henderson, master mason of South Shields on behalf of his son Thomas against sentence of transportation for stealing.

Henderson, Lt.-Col. Sir Edmund Yeamans Walcott, 4 July 1869.

Henderson, Vice-Adm. G., 11 Sept. 1853 on transportation, quoting extracts from letter 5 Nov. 1855 from his son, Sir Edmund Y. W. Henderson, enclosing copy of letter Capt. Charles Fitzgerald to Sir Edmund.

Hutt, Sir William, copy of letter 8 Mar. 1847 Grey to Hutt on emigration in general.

Jebb, Maj.-Gen. Sir Joshua, letters 1852-63; copy of paragraph from letter 9 Dec. 1852 concerning contracts in Van Diemen's Land; copy of letter 5 Dec. 1850 Lt.-Col. Sir Edmund Y. W. Henderson to Jebb on Western Australia.

Kempthorne, S., Secretary of the Colonists' Protection League, N.Z., 27 Aug. 1873; copy of letter 15 Apr. 1874 Grey to Kempthorne.

Lang, J. D., 11 Apr. 1837 on an appointment in New South Wales for Rev. R. Watson, Presbyterian minister.

La Trobe, C. J., 21 Nov. 1851; copies of letters 25 Jan., 27 Nov. 1851 Grey to La Trobe; paper marked 'Feb. 19/51 letter to Mr LaTrobe written at the request of Mr Hodges recommending Mr Arnold', letter of which this was apparently a cover is missing.

Leitner, H., 13 Aug., 29 Oct. 1892; draft Mar. 1894 by Grey 'Cancelled sketch of a letter to Mr Leitner on Colonial Federation'.

Lisgar, John Young, 1st Baron, 23 May 1866.

Macarthur, Lt.-Gen. Sir Edward, letters 1831-8 with enclosures 1837-8 on emigration especially from Dorset and on military establishments in New South Wales; copy of letter 21 May 1851 Grey to Macarthur.

Macarthur, J., 17 May 1861 enclosing cutting on Maori War from *Sydney Morning Herald* 20 Mar. 1861.

Maconochie, Capt. A., letters 28 Jan. to 16 Mar. 1839, 6 Feb. 1858; two letters 1839 on transportation.

Macqueen, T. P., 27 Feb., 11 Oct. 1831, 3 Apr. 1832 on emigration; copies 13 Jan. 1831, 19 Jan. 1832 Grey to Macqueen on emigration.

Melbourne, Bishop of, Charles Perry, letters 1847-51; enclosure to letter 27 Nov. 1849 copy extract of letter Perry to T. Turner on transportation; copies of letters 1847-52 from Grey.

Merivale, H., letters 1847-60; copy of letter 23 Oct. 1847 Grey to Merivale.

Murdoch, Sir Thomas William Clinton, 13 Apr. 1852 enclosing memo by Grey on emigration to Australia, 11 Apr. 1852 in which Grey defends the Colonial Land and Emigration Commission against attack by Charles Dickens in *Household Words*.

Murray, Gen. Sir George, 19 Jan., 3 Feb. 1837, 21 Mar. 1838; copy letter 5 July 1832 Grey to Murray.

Panmure, William Maule, 1st Baron, 23 Feb. 1832 enclosing extract from letter 1 Oct. 1831 Dr Boyter to Panmure on trade and agriculture in New Zealand.

Parkes, Sir Henry, letters 1872-4; copies of letters 1872-4 to Parkes.

Parkes, J., letters 8 Aug. 1841 to 21 Feb. 1856 on Van Diemen's Land and New Zealand.

Poole, G. H., 12 Aug. 1853 enclosing memo on colonisation in the form of a letter to Grey.

Pownall, Very Rev. G., 20 May 1863 on convicts in Western Australia.

Richardson, J., copy of letter 23 Dec. 1853 Grey to Richardson and others with printed circular letter Aug. 1853 to members of the Legislative Council of New South Wales and related papers.

Richmond, C. W., letter 19 Sept. 1861 concerning the charge brought against Richmond by Dr I. E. Featherston.

Roberts, R., copy of letter 29 Nov. 1832 Grey to Roberts being a reply to Roberts's letter and memorial to Grey on behalf of Mr Girard of New South Wales.

Roebuck, J. A., letters 15, 18 Nov. 1844 concerning the evidence of F. A. Molesworth to the New Zealand Committee.

Sanford, H. A., letters 11 Aug. 1863 to 15 Jan. 1864 on transportation to Western Australia.

Scrope, G. J. P., 21 Feb., 2, 10, 14 Dec. 1831 on emigration; copy of letter 14 Dec. 1831 Grey to Scrope.

Sewell, H., letters 1869-72; enclosure to letter 22 Dec. 1869 pamphlet *The Case of New Zealand . . . A letter from Henry Sewell . . . to Edward Wilson*, London 1869, with inscription by J. A. Youl; letters 1869-73 Grey to Sewell, eight of these are originals, returned to Grey by Sewell's son Rev. W. Sewell with covering letter 25 Oct. 1879.

Shaftesbury, Anthony Ashley-Cooper, 7th Earl, letters 1848-69, some on emigration.

Sherbrooke, Robert Lowe, 1st Viscount, 2 Dec. 1867.

Sholl, R. J., 11 Jan. 1856, 23 Feb. 1863 on transportation to Western Australia.

Smith, J. A., 23 July 1852, 28 Feb. 1853 on the New Zealand Company.

Stephen, Sir George, 25 Aug. 1864, 23 Jan., 25 Sept. 1865; copy of letter 27 Oct. 1864 Grey to Stephen.

Stephen, Sir James, letters 1831-53 including Australian and New Zealand material; copies of letters 1833-51 Grey to Stephen.

Stephen, Sir James Fitzjames, 23 June, 13 July 1873 on the legal position of colonial churches.

Strzelecki, Sir Paul Edmund de, 14 Jan. 1847 enclosing paper on mineral ores in Canada, Australia, New Zealand; copies of letters 23 Oct., 10 Nov. 1848 Grey to Strzelecki.

Tasmania, Bishop of, Francis Russell Nixon, 21 Dec. 1846, 22 Mar., 11 Nov., 30 Dec. 1847.

Therry, Sir Roger, 24 Sept. 1832 on memorial on behalf of Roman Catholics in New South Wales; copy of letter 2 Apr. 1833 Grey to Therry.

Tulloch, Maj.-Gen. Sir Alexander Murray, letters 1836-58; copy of letter 22 Sept. 1847 from Grey; extract from letter 11 Nov. 1847 Grey to Tulloch with papers on military settlement.

Wakefield, E., 22 Apr. 1845 enclosing letter 22 Apr. 1845 from Sir William Fox to Wakefield on attack on Bay of Islands settlement, N.Z.; also letter 18 Apr. 1849 deprecating E. G. Wakefield's attack on Grey and duplicate copy; copy of letter 20 Apr. 1849 Grey to E. Wakefield.

Wakefield, E. G., 5 Sept. 1831, 3 May 1837; extracts from letter 7 June 1852 E. G. Wakefield to J. R. Godley copied in manuscript from the *Lyttelton Times* 30 Oct. 1852; copy of letter 7 Sept. 1831 Grey to E. G. Wakefield.

Durham

War Office papers including some material *c.*1835-6 on troops in New South Wales and Van Diemen's Land.

Wellington, Arthur Wellesley, 1st Duke, letters 1839-52; copies of letters 1839-52 Grey to Wellington, a few relate to New Zealand military affairs.

Youl, Sir James Arndell, 6 Oct. 1869 from Youl, H. Sewell, and H. Blaine as secretaries to delegation from colonies with representative or responsible government; letters Dec. 1869 Grey to Youl and others; printed circular letter 23 Dec. 1869 Youl and others to colonial governments.

Young, Sir Henry Edward Fox, letters 1846-54, some containing enclosures concerning South Australia; letter 10 July 1851 encloses cutting from *South Australian Gazette* 3 July 1851 with article 'Gold' by Rev. W. B. Clarke; copies of letters 1847-51 Grey to Young.

Letters from the following may also repay examination, many accompanied by copies of letters from Grey.

4th Earl of Aberdeen; 8th Duke of Argyll; J. B. Sumner, Abp of Canterbury; Viscount Cardwell; W. E. Gladstone; Adm. the Hon. Sir Frederick William Grey; J. Hume; 1st Baron Monteagle; 1st Marquess of Normanby; 1st Baron Raglan; 1st Earl of Ripon; L. Sullivan; 1st Baron Taunton.

3rd Earl Grey Subject Files

Files on Australia, Colonial Affairs, and New Zealand contain chiefly cuttings, copies of speeches by Grey and a bundle of notes 1841-6 by Grey from official publications on New Zealand.

Manuscript Volumes, including Registers

This list does not include volumes concerning estate matters. The volumes, apart from 'Lord Howick's Private Letter Book' are not yet indexed.

'Lord Howick's Private Letter Book', Colonial Office letter book containing copies of letters Jan. 1831 to June 1833 sent by Howick; index and summary at back.

Register of letters received and written 1 Jan. 1855 to 24 Nov. 1858.

Registers of letters received and written 25 Nov. 1867 to 23 Sept. 1894, 4 vols. The fourth volume also contains a list of addresses and various memoranda.

Registers of letters Nos.1-2115, July 1846 to Feb. 1852, with index at back. These letters were evidently kept in the Colonial Office.

'Colonial memorandums': notes *c.*1845-51 by 3rd Earl Grey on despatches, with an index of places; enclosed is a paper headed 'Distribution of Business' showing the officials responsible for various aspects of colonial work.

Register of applications for employment [in the colonies] 1846-51. Details of the application and generally of the applicant are given; enclosed is a list of applications for colonial governorships and legal posts.

The 3rd Earl Grey's Journal 25 Aug. 1827 to 24 July 1871, 29 vols. The 'Journal' notes private and public activities. A brief examination of a sample volume 1847-9 revealed descriptions of debates in the House of Commons, proceedings at Cabinet meetings, discussions of Grey's motives, brief references to business at the Colonial Office and Board of Trade, to Australian and New Zealand affairs, and frequent references to discussions on emigration.

The 3rd Earl Grey's Diary 1857-94, 38 vols. The 'Diary' contains private memoranda.

D.1. Volume containing original correspondence 1826-34 between Gen. Charles Grey and his brother Adm. Sir Frederick William Grey; it includes letter 30 Nov. 1826 from Archdeacon Scott, Sydney, sending news of Grey's family from England.

Pamphlets

The following items have been noted:

Speech of . . . Earl Grey, on Emigration to Australia, delivered in the House of Lords, on

Thursday, August 10th, 1848, and Reply on the same subject to Lord Monteagle, London 1848 (2 copies).
Speech of . . . Earl Grey, on the withdrawal of Troops from New Zealand. In the House of Lords, Monday, March 7, 1870, London [1870].

ESSEX

ESSEX RECORD OFFICE
County Hall, Chelmsford

See *Guide to the Essex Record Office*, 1969.

QUARTER SESSIONS RECORDS

The following series of records illustrate the type of information to be found on individuals transported. For a useful secondary source on Australian convict material in these records see T/Z 38/39 below.

Q/SPb Process Books of Indictments 1681-94, 1709-1918, 31 vols.

These give a note of every indictment session by session supplying name, abode, and occupation of defendant, offence, plea, verdict, and sentence. Individuals sentenced to transportation may be readily located as there is an index of defendants in each volume.

Q/SPb 17, p.135. Indictments entered for the Session 23 Apr. 1805 of John Cook and William Boyton, labourers of Braintree, for Grand Larceny, their pleas of guilty and not guilty respectively, and the sentence of both to transportation beyond the seas for seven years.

Q/SR Sessions Rolls 1556 to date (incomplete), 1953 rolls.

Q/SR 920. The documents for each Session are in a single roll or bundle. In this roll, for the Session 23 Apr. 1805, most of the numbered indictments referred to in Q/SPb 17 above may be found and further details of the case obtained. It concerned the theft from Joseph Savill of four bushels of beans on 12 Jan. 1805 to the value of sixteen shillings and of a further six bushels in the previous December.

Q/SBb Sessions Bundles: Later Series 1694-1921, 860 bundles.

Q/SBb 399/97. Examination of the witness William Pasfield taken 17 Apr. 1805 giving the story of the theft of beans by Cook and Boyton in some detail making it clear that it was a case of persistent theft.

Q/CR Clerk of the Peace. Parliamentary Returns 1787-1857

Q/CR 9/5. Returns of transportation orders for each Session 1844-53 giving name, age, crime, and sentence (seven, ten, or fourteen years). The average number transported annually was between thirty and fifty individuals.

Q/CR 9/7. Draft and copy returns, with correspondence, of expenses of prosecution at the Central Criminal Court, Assizes, and Quarter Sessions, and of conveying convicts sentenced to transportation to Portsmouth. The correspondence includes a letter 12 Oct. 1835 from the Home Department, calling to the attention of magistrates at Quarter Sessions an Act of the last Session making moneys available from the Consolidated Fund for payment of expenses of criminal prosecutions, previously paid out of County Rates, and expenses of transportation of convicts to the hulks.

Essex

D/DBF 166. Will 25 Sept. 1868 of John Vaughan, late of Hotham Creek, Pimpara, Q'ld, probate granted 27 May 1885, and papers including letters 1885-97 relating to the subsequent careers in Queensland of the children.

D/DEs Scott, Watlington, and Perry Family Papers (Harlow, Chigwell, and Matching Deeds)

D/DEs F4, 7. Cash book 1848-62 kept on behalf of Charles Perry, Bishop of Melbourne. Legal documents including copies of marriage settlement 1841 and will 1846 of Charles Perry and agreement 1853 for purchase of church and parsonage house constructed or coated with iron to be sent to Melbourne.

D/DEs T92A. Copies of wills and settlements of the Perry Family including settlement on the marriage of the Rev. George Perry with Miss Elizabeth Smith and appointment 23 May 1885 of J. W. Perry Watlington as trustee of the settlement for Bishop Charles Perry.

D/DP Petre Family Estate and Family Papers

D/DP E127-9, 174. Legal documents and correspondence 1839-c.1842 including: deed 2 May 1839 transferring the lands and prospects in New Zealand of the New Zealand Colonisation Association, together with the ship *Tory* and her cargo to the New Zealand Land Co.; letter 3 Dec. 1840 F. A. Molesworth, Wellington, N.Z., to J. Coverdale about the allotment of lands in New Zealand; power of attorney 1842 William Henry Francis Lord Petre to Charles Clifford and William Vavasour to manage his estates in Wellington and Nelson, N.Z.; power of attorney n.d. William Bernard Lord Petre to Nathaniel Levin *re* lease and conveyance of New Zealand lands; letter n.d. John Morrison, London, to Lord Petre at Thorndon saying that the deer which Lord Petre had given for New Zealand had been shipped to J. A. Weld on the *Dona Anita*.

D/DP F198. Cuttings 1850 reporting an address of thanks to Lord Petre from the Catholics of Wellington, N.Z., for his help in obtaining a pastor for them.

D/DSe Sperling Family Correspondence

D/DSe 3. Letter 4 Mar. 1810 2nd Duke of Northumberland to James Brogden, M.P., including comments on the proceedings against Gov. Bligh in New South Wales and support for Johnston; letter 13 Jan. 1816 to James Brogden including suggestions for hemp growing and the convict settlement at Botany Bay.

D/DTa F2. Power of attorney 1876 from a member of the Tabor family resident in Australia, concerning George Tabor Kemp, grazier of Dirck Creek, Richmond River, N.S.W.

D/DU 190/25. Letters 1866-1903 addressed to Mrs Rose Robertson of South Kensington, later Mrs Rose Player Frowd, mostly from relations in Australia.

D/DU 559 Alexander Miller White, solicitors, Deposit

D/DU 559/19. Company Prospectuses, reports, cuttings 1899, concerning Alexander Wallace's investments, printed. Companies include Australian Hardwoods (Jarrah) Ltd and Imperial Jarrah Wood Corp., W.A.

D/DU 559/20. Letters 1896 from Arthur O. Wallace to his father Dr Alexander Wallace about his work as a boundary rider at Hartwood sheep station, near Deniliquin, N.S.W.

D/DU 572 George Drought Warburton Papers

D/DU 572/8. Letters 1848 from W. H. G. Kingston, novelist, writer of *How to Emigrate*, London 1850, to G. D. Warburton proposing to send schoolmasters to the distant outstations of Australia and Canada and regretting that transportation to Australia is to be resumed.

T/Z 38/39. M. H. Dunwell, Brentwood College of Education, 'True Patriots from

Essex: An investigation into transportation of convicts from the County of Essex to New South Wales during the period 1787-1809 with particular reference to transportees of the First Fleet', typescript 1965. Section II lists 130 convicts tried at Quarter Sessions and transported from Essex to New South Wales 1785-1824, and also a list from H.O.11 in the Public Record Office, London, of c.200 convicts tried at the Essex Assizes. Case histories are also included of two convicts, Henry Abrahams and Anthony Rope.

GLOUCESTERSHIRE

BRISTOL ARCHIVES OFFICE
The Council House, Bristol 1

A guide is in preparation.

PRIVATE RECORDS

07889 Papers of Sir George Chick

The papers include four letters and a small number of legal papers 1847-61, relating to James Bennett Gibbs, a gold digger of Adelaide and Avoca, including two letters written by him to a benefactor in Bristol and letters to him returned as undeliverable.

09862 Bristol Incorporation of the Poor, Deeds of St Peter's Hospital. 6 a-e. Five contracts for the passage of paupers to Van Diemen's Land and New South Wales 1833.

12161 Player Family Papers 1719-1881
19. Will and probate 14 Jan. 1869 of Henry John Player, Mansfield, Vic., storekeeper.
20. Certified copy of entry 27 Dec. 1878 in register of deaths, Henry John Player, d. Jan. 1869.
21. Power of attorney 25 Feb. 1879 from executors of the will of H. J. Player to Edmund Player, Park Street, Bristol, to obtain letters of administration.

14152/30 Letter Dec. 1847 from C. G. Masey, Paterson River, N.S.W., to his father Edward Masey containing personal news, news of his cattle and horses, of visits to the Macleay River and Lake Macquarie.

14581 Haynes Collection. HA/M1/8. Engine drivers' certificate of competence 1897, Richard Murray, Eastern Goldfield, W.A.

17563 Roslyn (Red Lodge) MSS. 10. Regulations for the disposal of land in the new colony of South Australia 14 July 1835. The regulations appoint and name the Colonisation Commissioners. A list is given of contemporary published works on Australia recommended to prospective colonists.

19839 Churchus, Gregory, and Pitt Family MSS.
26-7. Letters 1840-1 from Daniel Rutter Long, *Himalaya*, Plymouth, bound for Melbourne, to Isaac Pitt, Cirencester, addressed to 'dear brother and sister' giving details of the voyage from London and embarkation of emigrants at Plymouth; to Mrs Elizabeth Long, Witney, Oxon., his mother, giving family news and description of the state of trade, mentioning land jobbers, money-making, Aborigines.
28. Letter 1849 Susannah Maria Long, eldest daughter of D. R. Long, mentioning that her father was convinced that gold exists in Australia.

20535 Prideaux Family Papers. 365. Bill of exchange 1861 issued by the Union Bank of Australia in favour of Francis Grevile Prideaux.

UNIVERSITY OF BRISTOL
The Library, Queen's Road, Bristol 8

HALE PAPERS*

The papers of Bishop Matthew Blagden Hale, Archdeacon of Adelaide, S.A. 1847-57, Bishop of Perth, W.A., 1857-75, Bishop of Brisbane 1875-85, include besides cuttings, printed items and works of Bishop Hale, printed and manuscript.

130/4-14. Diaries 1851, 1852, 1855, 1860, 1876-80, 1883-4.

130/20. Extracts from diary 1851.

130/108-11. Four letters from the Archbishop of Canterbury to Bishop Hale, Brisbane.

130/129. Letters Patent creating the see of Western Australia, separating it from Adelaide and appointing M. B. Hale first Bishop, copy.

130/130. Act of consecration 25 July 1857 of M. B. Hale as Bishop of Perth.

130/133-230. Papers relating to the Poonindie Mission to the Aborigines at Port Lincoln, S.A., including 133-66 correspondence, 167-74 drafts of reports from Archdeacon Hale to the South Australian Government, 175-84 printed reports 1849-75 also printed account of the mission 1858 by G. W. Hawkes, 185-208 correspondence, 209-14 cuttings, 215-30 letters from Aborigines and nominal rolls of Aborigines.

MISS L. M. M. WINTOUR
C/o The Midland Bank Ltd, 89 Henleaze Road, Bristol

JEFFCOTT AND KERMODE FAMILY LETTERS

Letters written chiefly to John Moore Jeffcott, Advocate, High Bailiff of Castletown, Isle of Man, by his cousins Sir John William Jeffcott and William Jeffcott, by his relative William Kermode of Mona Vale, V.D.L., and by Robert Quayle Kermode. The letters include:

Sir John William Jeffcott to J. M. Jeffcott: 6 Sept. 1834 from Dublin; 4 Mar. 1837 from Mona Vale regretting that he could not say goodbye in person, he was staying at the house of the father of 'your cousin Robert Kermode', was very favourably impressed with Van Diemen's Land and had spent nearly two months travelling in it with Robert Kermode, gives some description of Mona Vale.

5 Nov. 1837 Sir John William Jeffcott, Adelaide, to William Kermode, Mona Vale, giving his first impressions of South Australia and saying he intended to return to Van Diemen's Land as soon as possible; he recounts the affair of Mr Brown, Emigration Agent, and mentions other difficulties.

9 Jan. 1831 William Jeffcott, Dublin, to his aunt Mrs Jeffcott.

7 Dec. 1837 William Jeffcott, Dublin, to J. M. Jeffcott mentioning that his brother John was 'Chief Justice of Australia', referring also to John's engagement to Anne Kermode and to his unfortunate duel in 1833.

William Kermode to J. M. Jeffcott: 1 Feb. and 20 Mar. 1838 Mona Vale, V.D.L., chiefly concerning the death of Sir John William Jeffcott and his papers, the letter of 1 Feb. 1838 referring also to William Kermode's good relations with Sir John and Lady Franklin and to affairs in Van Diemen's Land; 1 June 1843, Hobart Town, stating that he had had several letters from William Jeffcott, and reporting that he came to Hobart for a land sale; 19 Dec. 1846, Mona Vale, V.D.L., mentioning that

La Trobe had visited him; 13 Mar. 1851, Mona Vale, mentioning the unpopularity of Sir William Denison and that Robert had been asked to be a member of the new legislature.

26 Apr. 1838 William Kermode to Gov. Hindmarsh asking for the return of Sir John William Jeffcott's private papers, copy in the handwriting of William Kermode.

Anne Quayle Kermode (née Moore, Mrs William Kermode) Mona Vale; 31 Jan. 1834 to Mrs John Crellin, Isle of Man; 10 Apr. 1837 to Mrs J. L. Crellin, Isle of Man.

23 Apr. 1835 Robert Quayle Kermode, Liverpool, to J. M. Jeffcott.

21 July 1853 Robert Quayle Kermode, Hobart Town, to J. M. Jeffcott with obituaries of Robert Quayle Kermode, one a manuscript copy of an obituary, *Sydney Morning Herald* 17 May 1870.

Robert Crellin Kermode, Mona Vale, to Mrs Jeffcott (widow of J. M. Jeffcott) 28 May 1911 and 5 Jan. 1912. The writer is the second son of Robert Quayle Kermode and his first wife. His letter 28 May 1911 mentions the prevalence of potato blight in northern Tasmania, and that of 5 Jan. 1912, typescript, mentions his recent visit to Adelaide.

23 Mar. 1969 Miss L. M. M. Wintour concerning the duel between Sir John William Jeffcott and Dr Hennis.

With the above papers are biographical notes, chiefly in typescript, on the Kermode and Archer families in Tasmania and a notebook containing manuscript copies of records in India Office papers relating to E. M. Jeffcott and Sir William Jeffcott, including his will.

GLOUCESTERSHIRE RECORDS OFFICE
Shire Hall, Gloucester

PARISH RECORDS

See *Guide to the Parish Records of Bristol and Gloucestershire*, 1963, Bristol and Glos. Archaeological Society, Records Section Vol.V.

P47a OV8/1. Bisley Parish Records

Papers concerning assistance to emigrants 1837-9 including transactions with the Poor Law Commission for sending sixty-eight persons to Australia, Aug. 1837, raising loan, presentation to the Emigrant Surgeon and Inspector of account for clothing, provisions, conveyance for average persons at £15 each; printed pamphlet 1838 over the signature of John Marshall, Emigrant Agent, London.

P124 CW4/4. Dursley Parish Records

Correspondence 5 Aug. 1840 with the Poor Law Commission, Somerset House, concerning the raising of £25 by the Vestry to send Henry Clark, wife and child to Australia, with circulars and forms concerning assistance for emigration.

P125 IN4/15. Dymock Parish Records

Three letters Aug. 1914 from John Nicholas, Toronto, N.S.W., to the vicar with enclosed photographs, asking for information about gravestones in the churchyard at Dymock. John Nicholas emigrated to New South Wales in 1877 with six children, the letters are personal and discursive without giving biographical information or comment on life in New South Wales.

PRIVATE AND NONCONFORMIST RECORDS

D326 Estate and Family Papers of Sir Anselm Guise, Bt

D326/F62. Copy of a letter 1854 from Henry Edwards, Merri Merri Creek, near Melbourne. The document is a journal rather than a letter. It describes the voyage out in 1853 in the *Ganges* and comments on Melbourne and the surrounding country. The main part of the document describes botanical and zoological specimens.

D540/T63. Mortgages 1866-7 raised by Donald Cameron, Tasmania, on land in England.

D543 George Eaton Stranger, surgeon's log and journal 1836-41. The log on the South Australian Company's ship *Sarah and Elizabeth* contains comment on the voyage to South Australia where Stranger practised medicine on Kangaroo Island. He began the return journey to England on the *Solway* which was wrecked on the Australian coast without loss of life, and reached England Oct. 1838 on the barque *Seppings*. The log and journal to this date occupy pp.1-173 of the manuscript; pp.174-217 contain his journal in England to 1841.

D654 Goldingham and Jotcham MSS.

D654/11/21/F9. Letters of administration and will of Joseph Wheeler, Castlemaine, Vic., 1883.

D1022/21. Letter 17 Aug. 1771 from Capt. James Cook to Capt. John Walker, Whitby, describing the voyage to Tahiti, the transit of Venus and return voyage. Copy in the Mitchell Library, Sydney.

D1436. Letters 1879-81, four letters and copy of one letter, from William George, a stockman on Gurdy Creek, Grantville, Vic., describing Grantville, his work and wages and commenting on conditions in the country and on the government.

D1628. Letters 1841-63 from Victor de Tremerreue written from France and New Zealand and concerning a legacy. The letters contain no information about New Zealand.

D1799 Dyrham Park Archives
D1799/C158. Letter 1934 from Mary M. Blathwayt, Temuka, N.Z., giving genealogical details of the New Zealand branch of the Blathwayt family, engaged chiefly in sheep farming.

D2424. Shortwood Baptist Church, Nailsworth, Register of members 1716-1837. Notes against many names state that these members emigrated.

D2455 Hicks Beach MSS.
    Papers deposited in 1969 by Earl St Aldwyn. The following references are from N.R.A. Report 3526.
PCC/62 (233, 308). Papers and correspondence 1878-80 of Sir Michael Hicks Beach with Governors of Australian states and New Zealand concerning political crisis in Victoria and New Zealand.
PCC/12 (2747). Letters 1889-97 J. W. Fortescue from New Zealand.
PCC/37 (2803). Letters 1913-14 Susan Hicks Beach from India, the East Indies, and Sydney.

D1889 Graham-Clarke MSS.
    This deposit is not yet fully catalogued (May 1970) but includes correspondence and papers *c*.1846-79 concerning W. G. Eagles's emigration to Australia and his life there, his claim on his father's estate, and the education of his son C. H. B. Eagles.

M. P. J. HAYWARD, ESQ.
Hayward's End, Stonehouse

Frederick Hayward, 'Incidents in my Australian Life', a description of life on a sheep station 1846-56, typescript. The original manuscript was presented to the Archives Section, State Library of South Australia in 1927.

Frederick Hayward, journal 1858 of a voyage Melbourne to Southampton and journal 1859 of a voyage London to Melbourne.

Martinus Peter Hayward, diaries 1863-4 of his voyages Plymouth to Melbourne and return to London.

Testimonial 1857 to M. P. Hayward as candidate for the post of Emigration Agent in England for South Australia, a paper roll with several hundred signatures.

MISS M. MEASURES
Beechcroft, Brownshill, Stroud

Diary 15 Dec. 1865 to 31 Dec. 1870, with a few later notes, kept by the wife of Capt. Thomas Henry Sherwood at Unumgar Station at the head of the south arm of the Richmond River, N.S.W. For the history of Unumgar Station see R. L. Dawson, 'Pioneering Days on the Richmond River', *Roy. Aust. Hist. Soc. Journal and Proceedings* 19, 1934, pp.175-90.

The entries in the diary are brief, usually one line a day but they vividly record daily life and work on the station, mentioning the names of visitors, the employment and rations of Aborigines, visits by Capt. Sherwood to Ipswich, Gympie, Kyogle, and Casino and by Capt. and Mrs Sherwood to Ipswich, Brisbane, and other stations, killing of meat, arrival of mails. At the beginning of the volume is a table headed 'Children's heights Unumgar' giving dates of birth, names, and heights of the five children of Capt. and Mrs Sherwood 1864-76. It seems probable that this is the period during which Capt. Sherwood owned Unumgar.

MRS G. NIXON-ECKERSALL
Morton Grange, Thornbury

Barkly family papers including a family tree, manuscript reminiscences of his early life by Sir Henry Barkly, and a volume of cuttings probably compiled by the second Lady Barkly and containing a number of newspaper articles on conditions in Victoria during Sir Henry's term as Governor.

HAMPSHIRE

ROYAL NAVAL HOSPITAL
Haslar, Gosport

The Library of the Royal Naval Hospital, Haslar, holds a number of surgeons' journals. A copy of a list compiled by Surgeon Commander A. H. H. Vizard, R.N., Aug. 1921 is in the Library. It is entitled 'Description of Medical Officers' Journals about 1856-1900 retained in office'. Selected journals have been microfilmed for the Australian Joint Copying Project.

East Indies and China Station
51-2. J. Buckley 1870-1, H.M.S. *Rinaldo*, giving notes on the China Station. 51, 1871 mentions King George Sound. 52 covers 10 May to 31 Dec. 1870.

57. G. L. King 1861-2, H.M.S. *Sphinx*, covering the Philippines, Pelew Islands, and the Marianas.

58. T. Coghlan 1863, H.M.S. *Sphinx*, including twenty-five water-colours of the Philippines, Pelew Islands and Guam.

61. A. B. Messer 1867, H.M.S. *Perseus*, referring to a short voyage to Manila and the Pelew Islands.

72. J. P. Caddy 1858-60, H.M.S. *Pylades*, including journals on the East India, China and Pacific Stations with limited reference to New South Wales.

108. G. Goodman 1875, H.M.S. *Dido*, covering the South Seas, New Zealand, and Australia and the introduction of measles into Fiji.

109-10. A. B. Messer 1874-5, H.M.S. *Pearl*, covering an outbreak of enteric fever in the *Pearl* and *Barracouta*, commenting on sewerage at Sydney, covering also a visit to the Pacific Islands and including an inquiry into the reputedly poisonous nature of the arrows of the South Sea Islanders.

111. G. Goodman 1872, H.M.S. *Basilisk*, covering the Australian coast and notes on South Sea Islands.

112. P. Comrie 1874, H.M.S. *Basilisk*, covering New Guinea and the homeward voyage.

113. A. B. Messer 1863-4, H.M.S. *Curaçoa*, covering the Naval Brigade in New Zealand.

114. R. Edwards 1861, H.M.S. *Pelorus*, covering the Naval Brigade in New Zealand.

115. W. Fasken 1862, H.M.S. *Fawn*, an illustrated journal including a chart of Polynesia and a water-colour of the Queen's House, Wallis Island.

Australia Station

116-17. W. Reid 1876, 1879, H.M.S. *Wolverene*. 116, 1876 includes a description of the ship, diet, and diseases recorded; 117, 1879 covers the Pacific Islands and includes notes on South Sea Islands and on diet.

118. G. Mair 1880, H.M.S. *Danaë* giving notes on the Samoan group and on diseases.

119-20. H. Slade 1864, 1862, H.M.S. *Miranda*. 119, 1864 reviews the wounded of the Naval Brigade in New Zealand; 120, 1862 covers Sydney, New Zealand, and Fiji.

121. D. Hilston 1862-3, H.M.S. *Harrier*, covers the Naval Brigade in New Zealand.

122-3. A. Rattray 1865, 1867, H.M.S. *Salamander*. 122 covers the east coast of Australia and discusses diet and climate and contains maps; 123 covers Australia, New Zealand, and homeward.

Home Station and Irregulars

136-8. Journals 1852-63 of H.M. ships and of H.M. convict ships and hired ships conveying convicts to Van Diemen's Land, Norfolk Island, and Western Australia. A list of journals is available with the microfilm copies.

Pacific Station

146. W. Hoggan 1875, H.M.S. *Repulse*, containing notes on sea lions, and covering Hawaii.

156. J. C. Messer 1869, H.M.S. *Charybdis*, containing notes on the Pacific Station with brief mention of diseases contracted in New Zealand and New South Wales.

R. CREAGH-OSBORNE, ESQ.
Little Lords Mead, Broad Lane, Lymington

Journals 1837 of Capt. Richard Crozier, H.M.S. *Victor*, while in South Australian waters. A microfilm of the journals is in the Archives Section of the State Library of South Australia.

PORTSMOUTH CITY RECORD OFFICE
Guildhall, Portsmouth

PRIVATE RECORDS

16A Hewett Collection

16A/146/1-65. Personal letters, and copies, of the Hewett family with a few miscellaneous papers 1855-1924 including letters to Anderson J. Hewett 1896-1906 some addressed to him in New Zealand.

SOUTHAMPTON CIVIC RECORD OFFICE
Civic Centre, Southampton

See *Southampton Records 1. Guide to the Records of the Corporation and Absorbed Authorities in the Civic Record Office*, 1964. Typescript catalogues in loose-leaf folders include: Corporation Records (with separate catalogues for Quarter Sessions Records), Absorbed Authorities, Parish Records, Deposits (with some separate catalogues).

SESSIONS RECORDS

The main series of Sessions Records are filed at SC/9. In Southampton the office of clerk of the peace remained for many years in the hands of a local solicitor: see Page and Moody Deposit, D/PM, below.

PARISH RECORDS

PR5 St Mary Parish Records

These include Churchwardens' Accounts, Rates, and Vestry Minutes 1831-9, with receipts 1840-6. The Vestry Meeting 1 Apr. 1834 records a proposal made to assist emigration to Australia, following a letter dated 19 Mar. 1834 from the Court of Guardians asking that consideration be given to granting to the Court a portion of the rates 'to carry into execution the recommendation & benevolent design of His Majesty's Government to send out to New South Wales a certain number of Young Women of unexceptional character . . .'.

PRIVATE RECORDS

D/MW Moberly and Wharton, solicitors, Deposit.

A typescript catalogue in progress (1968).

Papers of W. V. Jackson, deceased, 2 boxes. From the papers it appears that W. V. Jackson of Southampton resided in Wellington, N.Z., at intervals to 1891 when he returned permanently to England. The papers concerning Jackson's New Zealand affairs include:

Extracts from will of W. V. Jackson 16 Mar. 1891.

Letter 17 Oct. 1856 from Copland, Barnes & Co. authorising W. V. Jackson to act as agent for provisioning the fleet of the Royal Mail Steam Packet Co.

Small bundle of papers 1874-6 concerning the foundation of the Colonial Bank of New Zealand and W. V. Jackson's investment in the Bank.

Account Book of W. V. Jackson's property in New Zealand with letters and cuttings inserted.

Papers 1863-6 recording the death of J. M. Carter in the district of Mount Grey, N.Z.

D/PM Page and Moody Deposit

This firm of solicitors took a prominent part in public life and many official records including the Quarter Sessions Records noted below are preserved in their archives. There is a typescript catalogue.

Records of convicts transported to Australia have been sighted or seem likely to occur in the following Quarter Sessions Records:

D/PM5/2. Judicial Proceedings, bundles and files.

D/PM5/2/3/1-23, 4/1-10, 5/1-24. Files of draft indictments 1779-c.1840. Other draft indictments are in D/PM5/2/9, 11, 16, 17.

D/PM5/2/6/1-10. A bundle of papers 1804-26 about prisoners.

D/PM5/2/7/1-56. A bundle of informations and warrants 1823-9 among which is 7/39 return of convicts sentenced to transportation 27 Jan. 1829, being a return from Southampton Gaol listing four male convicts with a report on their conduct in gaol.

D/PM5/2/8/5-6. Returns of convicts sentenced to transportation 26 Mar., 30 Apr. 1827.

D/PM5/2/11/11. Draft return of two convicts sentenced to transportation 25 Jan. 1826.

UNIVERSITY OF SOUTHAMPTON
The Library, Highfield, Southampton

An Accessions Register provides some guide to manuscripts and archives in the Library.

MOGG PAPERS

Diary 1811-68, 6 vols., with notes and one or two printed books. William Mogg, a naval purser, kept a private journal from the time he joined the navy until 1868. In 1817 he was appointed clerk in charge of stores on H.M. brig *Investigator* and was to remain for four years in close association with her captain, George Thomas. In an appendix to volume 1 of his diary, Mogg gives particulars of Thomas's adventurous career, taken from Thomas's diary. Thomas was apprenticed 2 June 1796 to Welham Clarke, commander of the *Commerce* in the Southern Whale Fishery. Within eighteen months of leaving England the vessel was wrecked in the Pacific but captain and crew were saved by a merchant ship under American colours from which he and another boy were set ashore on an uninhabited island in the 'Indian Archipelago'. See L. E. Tavener, 'George Thomas, Master, Royal Navy', *Mariner's Mirror*, 36, 1950, pp. 117-21.

ROYAL MARINES MUSEUM
Royal Marines Barracks, Eastney, Southsea

The archives are in the charge of the Royal Marines Historian and are available by special arrangement. The Museum is in process of building up official and private records, the former being subject to the thirty year rule. They do not include service documents of individual ranks, which, with official correspondence, are held by the Public Record Office where official corps records now in the Museum will be placed eventually. Prior application to inspect private records must be made to the Historian. Such records include:

List of names of Marines and some wives who comprised the detachments at Victoria, Port Essington 1837-50.

Five letters 1844-7 written by Capt. John Macarthur, R.M., during his service at Port Essington, typescript copies of originals in the Public Record Office.

The Royal Marines and New Zealand, compiled 1962 in R.M. Barracks from available records.

HAMPSHIRE RECORD OFFICE
The Castle, Winchester

A card catalogue is maintained arranged by accession number. Class lists, type-script, are made for selected series and collections, sometimes duplicating the cards, sometimes in more detail. There is a typescript List of Catalogues.

PRIVATE RECORDS

4M52 Lempriere Collection

The collection consists of deeds and papers 18th and 19th cents. of the Channel Islands families, Lempriere and Dumaresq, with a few papers of the related Curry and Beuzeville families. Among the papers are letters concerning property in Hampshire and the careers of members of the families, and private correspondence.
4M52/257. Declaration of trust 19 Dec. 1862 by Robert George Wyndham Herbert of Brisbane of £5000 advanced by Algernon Lempriere for sheep farming in Queensland to be arranged in partnership with Walter Scott.
4M52/368-81. Genealogical Papers, include 4M52/374b, on Lempriere of Pelham, mentioning Algernon Thomas Lempriere who was private secretary and A.D.C. for upwards of two years to Sir George Ferguson Bowen, Governor of Queensland, afterwards of New Zealand; 4M52/375, undated tree of the descendants of Thomas Lempriere, 'Banker at Verdun (taken prisoner of war) afterwards of Tasmania'.

4M58 Solicitor's Deposit
4M58/9. Mortgage 24 July 1862 by Thomas Twisden Hodges, late of Melbourne, Vic., now of Ashford Lodge, Petersfield, and Rosa Wilson Hodges his wife, for securing £1000.

HEREFORDSHIRE

HEREFORD COUNTY RECORD OFFICE
Old Barracks, Harold Street, Hereford

QUARTER SESSIONS RECORDS

Q/RAS/19-21. Records of Enrolment and Deposit, Sheriff's Appointments.

Documents 1834-6 relating to the appointment of Assistant Gaoler for conveying to the hulks those under sentence of transportation, including tenders for the contract. The successful contractor agreed to 7d. a mile per convict, a group of less than six to cost 8d. per convict.

PRIVATE RECORDS

A95 Pateshall Collection
A95/V/N. Papers of Admiral Nicholas Lechmere Pateshall.
A95/V/N/2, 3. Lieut. Pateshall's account 29 Oct. 1802 to 24 July 1804 of a voyage round the world on board H.M.S. *Calcutta*, Daniel Woodriffe Commander. After sailing a number of convicts were released from irons including some 'Herefordshire friends', and details follow of ports of call. On 9 Oct. 1803 the vessel entered Port Phillip Bay. The account of the settlement there includes description of the Aborigines

and native animals. There are two copies of the journal, possibly both in the hand of Pateshall's sister.

A95/V/N/1, 160-75, 191. Documents relating to Pateshall's career and to the *Calcutta* voyage.

A100 British Records Association Deposit

Messrs Wigan and Co., solicitors, Strand, London.

A100/64. Indenture 17 Nov. 1880 between Annsybella Martha Clive of Perrystone near Ross, Herefordshire, widow, and Edward Henry Clive, Sir Walter Rockliffe Farquhar, and Harrie Morton Farquhar. Annsybella's husband George Clive had mortgaged Tipperary properties in 1848 and 1854 and applied the sums raised to acquiring property in New South Wales. On his death in 1880 his Australian estates were bequeathed to his wife who agreed to these being created additional securities for the original principal and interest. The Australian estates consisted of lands within the stations at Collaroy, Bow, Commeallah and Collyblue.

A100/65. Assignment 29 May 1904 by Mrs A. M. Clive to her son General E. H. Clive of shares in the Collaroy Company Limited.

B47 Foxley Collection

Papers of John Davenport, Sheriff of Staffordshire.

B47 p.55. Four letters 1853-5 of F. G. Newbold to John Davenport, his uncle George Davenport and his aunt Davenport. Letter 1853 describes the wreck on 24 Aug. 1853 of the *Meridian* on the island of Amsterdam in the southern Indian Ocean. Bound for Australia in this ship he was rescued and taken to Mauritius. Arriving ultimately in Australia the letters give an account of his life and work on Billa Billa station near Calandoon, 500 miles from Sydney, a station owned by Messrs Easton and Robertson. Reference is made to Mr Lutwyche, a companion on board the *Meridian*, as a barrister hoping for a judgeship in Sydney.

D52 Cotterell Papers

Five letters and statements Aug.-Oct. 1838 by William Leigh addressed to Sir John Grey Cotterell, Gamons, Hereford, *re* the sending of his son Thomas Cotterell to South Australia on board the *Catharine Stewart Forbes*. Sir John put up a sum of £2000 and Leigh acted as his agent in apportioning the funds. Leigh refers to his seeking letters of introduction and gives an account of the dinner attended by Mr Gleddon, the South Australian Agent in London, and G. Morphett 'brother of my Agent in South Australia'. This meeting assured him of the prospects of settlement in South Australia. There is later reference to an order being sent to Morphett for him to select on behalf of Tom rather than to wait for the latter's arrival in the colony. Tom, however, ultimately settled in Canada.

D96 Messrs R. & C. B. Masefield, solicitors, Deposit

D96 p.1. Bundle 81. Certificate of title 6 July 1891 of Audley Baskerville Mynors to a piece of land in the Parish of Cedar in Queensland; deed of covenant 1875 and declaration of trust of thirty shares in the Union Bank of Australia between Rev. Edward Higgins of Bosbury House, Hereford, and Joseph Higgins Whatley of Great Malvern, Worcs.; also memo that certificate of thirty shares in the Union Bank of Australia was sent to R. B. Mynors on 13 Jan. 1885.

G2 Biddulph Collection

Letters from the *Tom of London*, Capt. Mudie, master, while whale hunting in the South Seas.

J54 Jay Family Papers

J54/309. Letter 12 June 1856 W. Andrew, Kirkham, Yorks., concerning Andrew's brother who had married the previous December and gone out to New Zealand sheep farming.

HERTFORDSHIRE

MRS M. HILL
Crossway, Upper Hall Park, Berkhamstead

Letters from Frederick Charles Cope to his friend Izaak Walton, chief accountant of the Imperial Continental Gas Association, including:

24 Dec. 1860, Melbourne, describing Melbourne, the straitened circumstances in which he and his family had been living, the difficulties of finding employment, and containing fragmentary references to the matters which had led to his dismissal from the I.C.G.A.; 13 Aug. 1862, Ararat, Vic., describing his present financial good fortune through appointment as Clerk of the Courts with descriptive references to Ararat and the gold diggings, and to his son Godfrey then on a station at Yea owned by a Mr Close. There is also a letter 18 Oct. 1863 from Godfrey Cope, Lake Hindmarsh, to Walton describing station conditions including hours of work, itemising of clothing costs, and an inquiry as to chances of employment.

COMMANDER H. G. D. DE CHAIR
Maintop, Felden Lane, Boxmoor

Reminiscences of Admiral Sir Dudley Rawson Stratford de Chair, while Governor of New South Wales 1924-30, 2 vols., typescript.* The reminiscences describe vice-regal life from a personal point of view and include a section (chapters VII and VIII, pp.86-102) on the constitutional struggle initiated by Lang to abolish the Legislative Council. There is also a copy of a letter 6 May 1927 from L. S. Amery. The two volumes form volumes VI and VII of the Memoirs of Admiral Sir Dudley de Chair, other volumes of which have been placed by Commander de Chair in the Imperial War Museum, Lambeth Road, London, S.E.1., q.v.

Journal* 24 Oct. 1927 to 9 Apr. 1929 of H. G. D. de Chair as Lieutenant in H.M.S. *Laburnum* and Journal 13 Apr. 1929 to 8 Apr. 1930 as A.D.C. to Sir Dudley de Chair, Governor of New South Wales. The *Laburnum* was on the New Zealand Station and visited Fiji, Samoa, and the Society Islands, June to Oct. 1928.

Journal* 8 Apr. to 11 July 1930 of H. G. D. de Chair recording part of the journey of Sir Dudley de Chair and party returning from Sydney, N.S.W., to England via the East Indies and the Far East.

In Feb. 1970 Commander de Chair was about to place both the two volumes of Sir Dudley's reminiscences and his own journals in the Imperial War Museum.

THE MARQUESS OF SALISBURY
Hatfield House, Hatfield

The main collection of the papers of Robert Arthur Talbot Gascoyne-Cecil, 3rd Marquess of Salisbury, is deposited in the Library, Christ Church, Oxford, q.v. Among papers at Hatfield House are three volumes of his journal of a voyage round the world 1851-3. The third volume ends in New Zealand in July 1852, before he left Auckland to visit other places in New Zealand, then returned to Sydney to embark for the voyage home across the Pacific and round Cape Horn. It appears that a journal after July 1852 was either not written or has not been preserved. Also at Hatfield House is a volume containing a manuscript copy of the journal 1851-2.

Vol.1, 12 July to 18 Sept. 1851 describes the voyage from its commencement on

443

9 July 1851, arrival in Cape Town and first impressions. Vol.2, 19 Sept. 1851 to 22 May 1852, continues the journal at the Cape, describes the journey to Australia and experiences in South Australia, Victoria, and Van Diemen's Land. Vol.3, 1 June to 22 July 1852, contains an account of the visit to New South Wales, the voyage to Auckland and impressions of New Zealand. Letters, some of which are copies and some originals, among the papers at Christ Church, describe the voyage and include letters giving some account of the remainder of Lord Robert Cecil's stay in New Zealand, his return to Sydney, and journey back to England.

The journal and letters supplement each other, the journal being generally more detailed. There are vivid descriptions of shipboard conditions and of fellow passengers. Ships to Australian ports and to New Zealand were the *Amazon*, Cape Town to Adelaide, arriving 30 Jan. 1852, the same vessel to Melbourne, arriving 24 Mar. after a twelve day passage, the *Mariposa* from Melbourne to Launceston, leaving Melbourne 8 Apr., the *Water Lily* from Hobart to Sydney, 22 May to 1 June, and the *Raven* from Sydney to Auckland, arriving 14 July after a voyage of thirteen days. The visit to South Australia included a voyage in a mail cart to join Mr Hughes and accompany him to his property Bundaleer, also a visit to the copper mines. In Victoria there was a visit to the goldfields, see *Lord Robert Cecil's Gold Fields Diary*, introduction and notes by Sir Ernest Scott, Melbourne 1935. In Van Diemen's Land, besides the overland journey from Launceston to Hobart, there were trips into the country with Sir William Denison. Travels in New South Wales included a journey by the steamboat *Rose* to the Hunter River District. There is comment on the gold rush, misgovernment in South Australia, the convict system, relations with the Aborigines and Maoris, the Church of England, and dissenting religious organisations. The characters and opinions of officials, clergy, and settlers are assessed.

HERTFORDSHIRE COUNTY RECORD OFFICE
County Hall, Hertford

Part I of a projected Guide has been published, *A Guide to the Hertfordshire Record Office, Part I, Quarter Sessions, etc.*, 1961. A second volume dealing with other official records, ecclesiastical records and deposited and purchased records is planned. Typescript schedules of collections of papers including official records, are maintained. A card subject index to schedules is being compiled.

QUARTER SESSIONS RECORDS

Q.S.Misc.B66/1-8. Papers relating to transportation of convicts 1742-98. These include County Treasurer's payments 1797-8 to the Deputy Clerk of Assize for transportation costs.

Q.S.Misc.B109/2-3. Drafts and copies of Treasury returns 1838-41 of expenses of conveying prisoners under sentence of transportation to various depots and prisons.

SHERIFF'S OFFICE RECORDS

SH14 Writs and Case Papers

Inventories and printed Bills of Sale are often attached to the papers. An inventory SH14/5/25 sets out the goods and chattels of the notorious John Tawell, publicly hanged at Aylesbury in 1845 for poisoning his mistress. See Percy C. Birtchnell, *A Short History of Berkhamsted*, privately printed 1960, p.97. John Tawell, an excommunicated Quaker, had been transported for fourteen years for uttering a forged cheque; he had received a ticket of leave and had a drug and grocery shop in Sydney, where he had made a fortune speculating in shipping and oil.

PARISH RECORDS

D/P34 Digswell Parish Records

D/P34/29/1-2. Admission and Discharge Book, No.5 Australian Military Hospital, Digswell House, and a book of photographs of the hospital 1917.

PRIVATE AND NONCONFORMIST RECORDS

F Documents deposited by Lieut.-Col. F. D. E. Fremantle, Bayford House, Hertford

F841-907. Hotel bills, small account book and correspondence 1888-9 with Shaw Savill & Albion Line, including telegrams, one from Hobart, connected with a tour by Mrs F. C. Hanbury to Tokyo, Australia, New Zealand, Ceylon.

Q Records of the Hertford Meeting of the Society of Friends

Q124. Correspondence 1846-58 with Monthly Meeting in Adelaide and Hobart, chiefly letters from Australia: two letters 1846 from Joseph May, Mount Barker Monthly Meeting; copy of minute 7 Mar. 1847 that Margaret May, dissatisfied with the tenets of the Society had married a person not then a member; letter 18 June 1852 from Joseph May states that his son William is leaving in the *Martin Luther* for England; two letters n.d., 1853 from Edward May, Adelaide; letter 1856 from William May, Mount Barker, stating his sister Rachel Ann had married Frederick Mackie a member of the Norwich Monthly Meeting and that they had gone to Hobart; letter 1858 from George W. Walker, Hobart.

Acc.166 Title Deeds of High Cannons, acquired by the County Council

Acc.166/27507. Bond of indemnity 24 Jan. 1841, Mary Winter and others including Arthur Thomas Le Mesurier Winter, late of Hobart Town but then of Stanley Hill, and James Winter of Hobart Town.

Acc.166/27510. Letter 21 Feb. 1844 from Charlotte Newcome identifying the handwriting of James Winter, her brother, with letter 4 Dec. 1842 from James.

Acc.345 Documents 1800-1926 relating to Southend Farm, Barley

Acc.345/26714. Release 21 Nov. 1854 by trustees to purchaser, one of the trustees being James Neale late of Barley, carpenter, then of German Town, Australia, an emigrant.

Acc.345/26719-20. Power of attorney from James Neale, German Town, certified by Alexander Fraser, Notary Public, Geelong, Vic., 6 Mar. 1858 and copy of affidavit by Martin Bone, Kildare, Geelong, bricklayer, showing James Neale to have been alive at Geelong 14 June 1858.

Acc.536 Passingham and Hill MSS.

Acc.536/82964. New South Wales Gold Mines, rough minute book of board of meetings 1852-4.

Acc.599 Martin Leake Family Papers

Acc.599/85011-63. Papers of Henry Martin Leake, R.N., who died before 1840 in Australia, including 85011-21, correspondence 1912-22 of Lieut.-Col. William Leake with the Admiralty, N.S.W. Registrar General and Somerset House seeking information on H. M. Leake; 85032-9, bills for H. M. Leake's four children and receipt for passage money for the boys' journey to Sydney 1831-2; 85041, letters of attorney 1 Jan. 1830 from H. M. Leake, Portsmouth, to his father; 85060, letter 20 Mar. 1832 from H. M. Leake, Sydney, to his father saying he hoped for permission from the Admiralty to remain and obtain a grant of land, his sons Henry and George being then resident 150 miles from Sydney.

Acc.599/85843-955. Papers of William Plunkett including 85940-50, papers 1836-60 relating to his son William who died 20 Jan. 1860 on his way to New Zealand on the *Clontarf* bound from London to Canterbury.

Hertfordshire

Acc.599/87116. Letter June 1917 from Lieut.-Col. Arthur Martin Leake, France, mentioning speech by W. M. Hughes.

Acc.941 Bulwer Lytton Papers

Four deposits have been made, three of which consist chiefly of estate papers. The fourth, Acc.941, includes the papers of Edward George Earle Lytton Bulwer-Lytton, 1st Baron Lytton, as Secretary of State for the Colonies 1858-9. They are uncatalogued but the Record Office has a photocopy of an inventory, typescript and manuscript, compiled c.1953, which includes some papers at Knebworth but not all the papers deposited in Acc.941.

Papers of 1st Baron Lytton as Secretary of State for the Colonies 1858-9, 2 boxes. Box 1. Correspondence with Governors and packets labelled 'Correspondence with Lord Carnarvon', 'Australia', and 'Miscellaneous'.

Packets of correspondence with Governors include:

Sir Henry Barkly. Copy of extracts of letters to Sir John Pakington describing the goldfields and other industries, and political conditions; also three letters to Lytton concerning the defence of the Australian colonies, John Thomas Smith, Mayor of Melbourne, and Andrew Clarke, Surveyor General.

Sir William Denison. Letters concerning Plunkett's resignation as President of the Legislative Council, the separation of Moreton Bay from New South Wales, the desire of the New South Wales Government to secure steam postal communication, the policing of Pacific Islands, the New Zealand Waste Lands Acts 1856 and 1858, and free grants made under them.

'Correspondence with Lord Carnarvon' packet includes a letter to Lytton recommending Fitzgerald, the New Zealand colonist, as Governor of Moreton Bay if Bowen refuses the position.

'Australia' packet includes a paper on the naval defence of Australia; draft of a bill, Waste Lands (Australia) Acts Repeal 2 May 1855, printed; Australian Mail Service, special report of the Permanent Committee to the members of the Australian General Association, printed; draft of letter from Lytton to Bowen informing him that the Queen approved his appointment and giving draft instructions; six letters 1860-4 from Bowen reporting on affairs in Queensland; correspondence with Merivale includes a copy of letter n.d. from Lytton to Merivale asking for a report on Lees as Chief Justice of Moreton Bay with favourable report by Merivale and copy of Lytton's farewell letter 18 June 1859 to the Colonial Office.

'Miscellaneous' packet 1851-66 includes letters 1859 from Denison concerning elections in New South Wales and other news from the colony.

Box 2. Miscellaneous Papers 1858-9. Volume containing a register of letters, a letter book, and packets of correspondence.

Letter book includes 15 Oct. 1858 to Derby and 22 Nov. 1858 to Barkly concerning the mayor of Melbourne; two letters Oct. 1858 concern the question of precedence of governors, bishops and generals in the colonies; n.d. [14 Dec. 1858?] to Disraeli returning Ellice's letter concerning his appointment with postscript recommending that Moreton Bay be made a separate colony; 26 Mar. 1859 to Sir John Young asking his decision on his nomination for Moreton Bay; letters Apr.-May 1859 to the Queen and to Bowen concerning Bowen's appointment as Governor of Moreton Bay and concerning a new name for the colony; 18 June 1859 to Merivale expressing Lytton's thanks to the officials at the Colonial Office.

Packet 'Correspondence with the Queen, the Prince Consort and Members of Cabinet' includes 13 Sept. 1858 from Derby referring *inter alia* to the impossibility of giving precedence to the mayor of Melbourne, his wife having been a convict;

446

draft of letter 9 Feb. 1859 to the Queen naming Tufnell as Bishop of Brisbane; 28 Apr. 1859 from the Queen concerning the naming of Queensland.

Packet 'Letters from individuals' includes 20 Apr. and 3 May 1859 from Bowen applying for the governorship of Moreton Bay, acknowledging Lytton's suggestions and making recommendations; 2 Feb. 1859 from Edmund Dutton asking for introductions to the Governor of New Zealand and officials there to enable him to procure statistical and geological information; 17 Jan. 1859 seeking introductions to the Governors of New South Wales and New Zealand on behalf of Cesar Godeffroy; 8 June 1858 recommending Mr Wilson, solicitor, proceeding to New Zealand; 23 June 1858 supporting Eyre's claims to promotion.

C. V. W. DE FALBE, ESQ.
Thundridge House, nr Ware

Family letters relating chiefly to the de Falbe family in Denmark but including some letters of Australian interest, e.g. letter 12 Oct. 1846 Ludwig Leichhardt, Stroud, N.S.W., to Miss Emmeline Macarthur afterwards Emmeline de Falbe.

HUNTINGDONSHIRE

HUNTINGDONSHIRE COUNTY RECORD OFFICE
County Buildings, Huntingdon

See *Guide to the Huntingdonshire Record Office*, 1958.

PRIVATE RECORDS

ddM Manchester (Duke of) MSS.

ddM 8/1(108). Correspondence and accounts 1858-72 relating to the Duke of Manchester's estates in New Zealand.

ddM 8/2(109). Miscellaneous letters and cuttings 1869-77 including some from Australia and New Zealand concerning self government.

ddM 10/22(139). Papers 1855-65 on an irrigation scheme for the development of a cotton industry in Queensland.

ddM 20/3(240). Letters 1870-1 concerning the National Emigration League.

ddM 20/9(346). Papers 1882 on colonial, including Australian, affairs.

M17/18. Address of welcome 1880 to the Duke of Manchester, President of the Colonial Institute, from the mayors and corporations of Singleton, Dubbo, Gunnedah, and Camatanakan, N.S.W., on the occasion of his visit.

Bundle of letters 1880 concerning the loss of Clanwilliam Mead, son of the Rector of St Neots, Hunts., in the bush near Palparara.

X197/14. Will 1891 of Sydney Linton, Bishop of the Riverina, N.S.W.

KENT

CANTERBURY CATHEDRAL LIBRARY AND CITY RECORD OFFICE
The Precincts, Canterbury

Cataloguing of the archives is in progress (1967).

CATHEDRAL RECORDS

Chapter Minutes

The only relevant references are as follows: 1847 Midsummer Chapter, to grant licences of alibi for the consecration of the Rev. Charles Perry, D.D., to the Bishopric of Melbourne, Rev. William Tyrrell, D.D., to the Bishopric of Newcastle, and Rev. Augustus Short, D.D., to the Bishopric of Adelaide; 30 Mar. 1878 invitation to American and colonial bishops to Canterbury on the occasion of the Pan Anglican Congress 1878; 13 Jan. 1883 resignation of the Bishop of Tasmania, the Chapter considering it in their power to accept it; 29 Aug. 1891 Dr Beaney's bequest of £1000 to Dean and Chapter on condition that his executors be allowed to erect a tablet in his memory; 27 Apr., 28 May 1892 concerning the erection of the tablet and payment of the bequest.

CITY RECORDS

City Sessions 1823-46. The records of proceedings contain some transportation orders.

Treasurer of the County Stock. County Rate Bills (Sessions and Gaol Business 1829-32) contain receipted accounts for moving convicts to hulks at Sheerness or transports at Chatham and Blackwall.

CANTERBURY PUBLIC LIBRARY
Canterbury

The Public Library is housed in the building formerly known as the Beaney Institute, built with the assistance of a legacy from the Hon. Dr James George Beaney, born in Canterbury and later a surgeon in Melbourne. It contains a collection of papers and other items relating to Beaney, some of which were borrowed in 1967 by the Australian Medical Association, Victorian branch, for an exhibition in Melbourne, including illuminated addresses, medals, a testimonial accompanying the gift of £300 to Beaney in 1866 after the Mary Lewis manslaughter case, and two portraits of Beaney, one in theatrical costume.

KENT ARCHIVES OFFICE
County Hall, Maidstone

See *Guide to the Kent County Archives Office*, 1958, and the series *Kentish Sources*. A *Supplement* to the *Guide* covering most accessions 1957-68 is expected shortly (1970). Loose-leaf catalogues are maintained of Borough and Petty Sessions, Taxation Commissions, Lieutenancy Records, Parish Records, Turnpike, Highway Board, Poor Law Records, and Unofficial Estate and Family Archives. There are also Calendars of Wills and Administrations.

PC/M MAIDSTONE GAOL RECORDS

Volumes supplementing information found in the Quarter and General Sessions Records include:

Convict Book 1805-33. Register arranged annually by sheriffs, of all convicts, giving names, dates when payments began, where convicts were sent, and dates of removal; it includes many references to transferring prisoners to the hulks and to transportation.

PRIVATE RECORDS

U23 Wykeham-Martin MSS.
U23 Z1. *Terms upon which land is granted to settlers in New South Wales and Van Diemen's Land*, Colonial Office, Apr. 1827; *Information for the use of . . . settlers for the new settlement in Western Australia*, Colonial Office, Feb. 1829; together with a covering letter Mar. 1829 concerning the government's view on the emigration of paupers to the colonies.

U24 Mann (Cornwallis) MSS.
U24 C16. Letters 1831-7 to the Cornwallis family of Nizells in Hildenborough including eleven from James Trimmer 1831-3 giving news of his nephews Arthur, William, and Spencer who had settled in Western Australia. The letters deal chiefly with farming near Perth and York and the shortage of food. There are also descriptions of James Trimmer dining with Sir James Stirling and his sending flax seed to his nephews.

U36 Manorial documents and deeds c.1250-1927 presented by various donors through the British Records Association
U36 T952. Two deeds 1856-7 granting Lawrenny and Oriensey estates in Van Diemen's Land to Edward Lord.
U36 E124. Papers 1919-33 relating to the Stone-Wigg family including letters of administration with will annexed of the Right Rev. Montagu John Stone-Wigg of Colonna, Burwood, N.S.W., formerly Bishop of New Guinea.
U36 E152. Letter 20 Dec. 1814 from W. R. Wulbier advising that the positions of Barrack Master, Engineer, and Superintendent of the Government Herds are vacant in New South Wales.

U47 Documents from various owners, presented or deposited through the Kent Archaeological Society
U47/11 T556/1. Letters of administration 1860 of John Elgar Spencer of Wanganui, N.Z.
U47/22 T161. Probates of wills, certificates, deeds of covenants 1811-32 relating to the Blaxland family.

U82 Monckton Collection. Deeds and other papers 1470-1932 of Maidstone and district presented by Messrs Monckton Son and Collis, solicitors
U82 C425. Includes death certificate of Kate Bishop who died in Auckland, N.Z., 1908.

U145 Faunce-Delaune MSS. Papers of the Delaune, Thornycroft, Pincke, and Faunce families
U145 C35/1. Letter 1839 from Bonham Faunce while in the army and stationed at Hobart, to his mother Brydges Faunce describing his life there.

U194 Family papers of the Gambier and Howe families and other miscellaneous documents 1280, 1569-1899
U194 F10/1. Notebook of Rev. J. E. Gambier begun at Cookham 1773 containing entries chiefly copied from elsewhere including a description of Omiah dated 'London Aug. 11 1774'.

U295 Colyer-Fergusson MSS. Papers of the Colyer-Fergusson and Somes families 1627-1932
U295 F13. Correspondence 1820-44 mainly addressed to Joseph Somes concerning

449

the Parliamentary elections for Dartmouth with reference to a charge made against him as chairman of the New Zealand Company.

U295 Z1. Joseph Somes and Somes Bros. 'Some ships owned by them used as troopships and transports and others possibly connected with the colonization of New Zealand: collated and written by H. Fildes', Wellington 1932, notebook. Inside there are two loose letters 1 Feb. 1939 from E. H. Scholefield and 31 Oct. 1937 from Horace Fildes concerning Somes's ship, with cuttings on the same subject, a photograph 1932 of Mr and Mrs H. E. M. Fildes, and a copy of report 1937 of the New Zealand General Assembly Library.

U310 Norman MSS. Papers 1578-1930 of the Norman family

U310 B16. Papers 1830 concerning transactions carried out by Messrs Norman under a power of attorney from Elisa C. Broughton, Hamilton Hume, and others, relating to the estate of the Rev. John Kennedy (referred to in one of the papers as the Rev. W. Kennedy) and his wife Mary.

U310 B26. Report and copies of letters 1826-30 relating to share transactions between Mr Hindson and I. Seely of Sydney, and Edward Barnard and Richard Norman.

U310 B31/7. Copies of a memorandum of agreement 1829 by G. W. Norman and Richard Norman to give letters of credit to Thomas Horne the younger in Van Diemen's Land.

U310 C36. Seven letters 1827-30 from Archdeacon Thomas Hobbes Scott to G. W. Norman and Richard Norman chiefly dealing with the state of the colony, the affairs of the Church and School Corporation, the Australian Agricultural Company, personal and business matters and his impending resignation. There is also a set of notes about personalities including John Jamison, D'Arcy Wentworth, [S. T.] Campbell, John and Gregory Blaxland, and William Lawson.

U310 C126. Three letters from Col. Edward Macarthur and one from James Macarthur to G. W. Norman; 22 Apr. 1839 from E. Macarthur concerning Herman Norman; 1 Jan., 31 Aug. 1852 from Parramatta and Sydney dealing with family matters, Macarthur's voyage from England, communications between Sydney and Parramatta, the gold rush and its effect on the colonies of New South Wales and Victoria; 6 Mar. 1852 from James Macarthur, Sydney, mentioning his brother Edward, commenting further on the gold rush and advising that a box of samples of copper ore from the Wallah Wallah mines near Yass is being sent to Norman.

U310 O2. Declaration and other papers 1842 concerning G. W. Norman's providing money as a security for the faithful performance by Edward Barnard of the duties of Agent General for the Crown Colonies.

U310 P33. Chart of Van Diemen's Land from the best authorities and from surveys by G. W. Evans, Surveyor General, Hobart Town 1821, printed.

U310 Z5. *Outlines of a plan formed under the auspices of government for locating settlers at Swan River Western Australia*, by T. Peel [1856].

U350 Dering MSS.

U350 F10-14. Military and official papers 1882-1921 of Sir Henry E. Dering, Bt.

U350 F13. Papers 1916-17 relating to Dering's obtaining the post of Assistant Provost Marshal to the 3rd Australian Division, the 'estaminet affair' which resulted in his recall to London, and his subsequent efforts to obtain a similar posting to the United States Army. The papers include letters from W. R. Birdwood, G.O.C., Australian and New Zealand Army Corps.

U564 Chilston MSS. Letters and papers of Aretas Akers-Douglas, 1st Viscount Chilston

U564 C219/1. 1 Nov. 1886 from Sir Robert Nicholas Fowler, M.P., Wellington, N.Z.

U564 C321. Letters from Viscount Knutsford, Secretary of State for Colonies 1887-92.

U564 C321/11-13, 15, 19-20, 64, 69-140. Letters 1888-92 concerning Stavely Hill's wish for a colonial governorship, preferably Queensland, and Knutsford's inability to comply because Hill did not meet with the approval of Lord Henry Bruce.

U564 C321/14. 21 Nov. [1888] concerning the difficulties of finding governors for Queensland and South Australia.

U564 C575. Letters from Charles Style Akers in Australia to his brother Rev. Aretas Akers. The letters listed below contain family and personal matters in addition to the subjects described. The letters not listed deal only with personal and family matters.

U564 C575/2. 24 Sept. 1849, the danger of sending money and letters by convict ship.

U564 C575/4. 21 Mar. 1852, botany and flora of Norfolk Island, a visit to Phillip Island and his return to Norfolk Island.

U564 C575/5. 8 Oct. 1853, bad weather, the good life in Australia, high wages, and the need for immigrants.

U564 C575/6. 26 Nov. to 1 Dec. 1853, fever in Hobart, development of Melbourne, bad workmanship on buildings, drunkenness, prices, wages, the good life in Australia, and the making of fortunes.

U564 C575/7. 3 Aug. 1854, farming in Australia and his hope of returning home.

U564 C576. 12 May 1855 C. S. Akers to his father Aretas Akers, snr, about his proposed journey home in *Ocean Chief* clipper.

U619 Chapman MSS. Deeds and papers 1593-1895 of the Chapman family

U619 C1. Letter 1819 from Lachlan Macquarie to James Chapman mentioning the appointment of Bigge, the Secretary of State's censure of his (Macquarie's) conduct, and the regulations he had made for the colony.

U713 Deeds of Gravesend and district and additional papers 1292-1892

U713 F5. Copies of letters 1818-35 from David Fryett of Westminster to his brother Richard in Hobart chiefly concerning financial troubles and requests for help, with frequent expressions of intent to visit or settle in Van Diemen's Land.

U840 Pratt MSS. Deeds, papers, and correspondence deposited by the Marquess Camden

U840 O22/17. Letter 17 May 1805 William Bligh to 2nd Earl Camden, Secretary of State for War and the Colonies, concerning the naval rank of Governor of New South Wales.

U840 O92. Petition 18 Nov. 1804 of John William, a settler at Prospect Hill, N.S.W., now on board H.M.S. *Swiftsure* at St Helena wishing to return to his family but forced to serve before the mast.

U929 Holworthy Collection

U929 F10/1. Letter 1879 C. J. Holworthy, Wellington.

U929 F11-12. Letter books 1874-87, 1887-91 of J. M. Holworthy connected with his exporting business to Australia.

U929 F15. Documents 1891-3 re the failure of Robert Jolley & Co., Melbourne, and J. M. Holworthy & Co.

U929 F17. Diary 1881 of voyage London to Christchurch, N.Z.

U929 F19. Order of discharge 1886 F. W. Holworthy, importer, Dunedin, N.Z., a bankrupt.

U951 Knatchbull MSS. Accounts, letters, and papers deposited by Lord Brabourne

U951 C1/65. 25 Mar. 1831 Lord Melbourne to Sir Edward Knatchbull concerning the employment of convicts in the dockyards as opposed to their transportation.

U951 C168/1-3. *Sydney Morning Herald* 19 Jan. 1843, *True Sun* 27 Jan., 28 Feb. 1844 containing accounts of the trial and execution of John, half brother of Sir Edward Knatchbull, 9th Bt, for the murder of Ellen Jamieson in Australia.

U951 Z26-48. Banks MSS. Miscellanea

U951 Z30/1-2. Journal of Joseph Banks on the *Endeavour*, copy by S. S. Banks 1771-5, see *The Endeavour Journal of Joseph Banks, 1768-1771*, ed. J. C. Beaglehole, I, pp.141-3.

U951 Z32. Diplomas and letters from learned societies and individuals including 32/59, 62, 23 Feb., 11 June 1818 from Van Hultham requesting seeds from Australia and New Zealand, and letters on patronage, some concerning people who assisted Cook at Kamchatka.

U1045 Deeds and papers 1320-1904 of Ashford and other parishes deposited by Hallett & Co., solicitors, Ashford

U1045 T69. Rugden Farm, Wittersham, Kent, deeds and plan. Eight baptismal, marriage, and burial certificates of the Winton family, Wittersham 1815-75. Eight birth, baptismal, and death certificates of the Winton family, South Australia, 1843-75.

U1127 Smith Masters MSS.

U1127 C91. Personal correspondence 1850-8 of Cowburn family including one letter 30 June [?] from James L. Brown, Honolulu, on personal matters, the anniversary celebrations of the young prince, and a conversation with the King.

U1371 C57-8, 85-8. Letters 1856-82 to Lady Rose and Henry Weigall from his family at Kynaston, Vic.

DARWIN MEMORIAL
Down House, Downe, Orpington

The maintenance of Down House, the home of Charles Darwin, as a national memorial open to the public, has been the responsibility of the Royal College of Surgeons since 1953. The manuscripts, museum pieces, and paintings on display are listed in *A Historical and Descriptive Catalogue of the Darwin Memorial at Down House, Downe, Kent*, Edinburgh & London 1969, pamphlet; the manuscripts include the following items which relate to the voyage of the *Beagle* described in later life by Darwin as 'by far the most important event in my life, and has determined my whole career'.

Autograph journal or diary by Charles Darwin on the voyage of H.M.S. *Beagle* 1831-6, 1 vol. See *Charles Darwin's Diary of the Voyage of H.M.S. 'Beagle'*, edited from the manuscript by Nora Barlow, Cambridge 1933. The journal covers the whole journey; pp.604-724 of the manuscript relate to the passage from the Galapagos Islands through Polynesia and Tahiti, New Zealand, New South Wales, Van Diemen's Land, King George Sound to the Cocos Islands, Sept. 1835 to Apr. 1836.

Eighteen small pocket-books, undated. During his travels Darwin made rough pencil notes in these books. Many are illegible, trivial jottings relating to supplies and equipment; but many record first-hand his observations and impressions while on inland expeditions. The journal was largely compiled from these notes. Two note-books refer specifically to the Pacific and Australia; that for New Zealand is lost. See *Charles Darwin and the Voyage of the Beagle*, notebooks and letters edited by Nora Barlow, London 1945.

Lists, undated, in Darwin's handwriting of 3907 specimens preserved in spirit of wine and sent home during the voyage of the *Beagle*, six notebooks stitched together in threes.

Letters written by Darwin to family, friends and colleagues, mostly while on the *Beagle*, 1831-9, 1 vol. These include: 27 Dec. 1835, Bay of Islands, to his sister Caroline describing his stay in Tahiti and New Zealand; 28 Jan. 1836, Sydney, to his sister Susan describing New South Wales; 14 Feb. 1836, Hobart, to his sister Catherine. These three letters are printed in *Charles Darwin and the Voyage of the Beagle*. Darwin's correspondence is now widely scattered but much of it has been printed. Very few letters addressed to Darwin survive. He himself systematically destroyed almost all the letters received before 1862, and retained only the most important of those received after that date.

DAVID SALOMON'S HOUSE
Southborough, Tunbridge Wells

See M. D. Brown, *Catalogue of Mementos*, Jewish Historical Society, 1968.

Letter 1852 from B. S. A. Gompertz concerning J. B. Montefiore's activities in Australia.

Two letters 1852-3 from Laura Montefiore, Victoria.

Letter 1852 from Sidney Montefiore, Melbourne.

Letter 1853 from Justina Montefiore, Melbourne.

LANCASHIRE

LIVERPOOL CITY LIBRARIES
Record Office and Local History Department
William Brown Street, Liverpool

Lists of archive deposits are arranged in class order and are maintained in loose-leaf binders. There is a sheaf Index to Archive Lists.

380 BOW C. T. BOWRING & CO. LTD

The records of this firm which began business in Liverpool in 1835 as shipowners, general merchants, insurance brokers, and underwriters, are deposited on indefinite loan by Messrs C. T. Bowring & Co. Ltd, 52 Leadenhall Street, London, by courtesy of Mr Peter Bowring. See A. C. Wardle, *Benjamin Bowring and his Descendants*, London 1938.

380 BOW 2/5. Account Book 1872-80 records private accounts and includes, p.133, an entry May 1879 for the purchase of £700 New Zealand Government Consolidated 5% Bonds.

380 COM INCORPORATED LIVERPOOL CHAMBER OF COMMERCE

Minute Books include Minutes of the Council 1860-90 and of various committees to 1930.

380 COM 1/2. Minutes of the Council 1883-90 include entries: 6 Feb. 1889 concerning an address 'The Colonies & Trade' by the Right Hon. Baron de Worms; 15 Nov. 1889 minute on Australian mail arrangements as affecting East Indian mail arrangements.

380 COM 2/11/3. Minutes of the Australian and New Zealand Committee, entry

for 16 July 1923 records report by Col. Hawkins on his visit to Australia and New Zealand and ignorance of the colonists of the port facilities at Liverpool.

380 MD 1-27 ACCOUNTS AND PAPERS OF HENRY ELD SYMONDS

Part of a deposit by Messrs Whitely & Co. (solicitors). Selections have been microfilmed for the Australian Joint Copying Project. Symonds traded principally with Australia and South America. Some papers relate to New Zealand. The papers include:

380 MD 1. Mortgage 1 July 1854 mentioning among children of H. E. Symonds, J. A. Symonds, Melbourne, agriculturalist.

380 MD 2-21. Accounts and correspondence 1856-60 including material on shipping ventures. 380 MD 13, 14, 16, 17 contain accounts or correspondence of Every & Co.; Learmonth, Gilfillan & Co.; Creeth, Hicks & Creeth; Ronald Gibbs & Co.; Aspinall, Sutherland & Co.; W. Younghusband & Co.

380 MD 22-6. Accounts and correspondence 1850-63 of the executors of H. E. Symonds.

920 GRE GREGSON COLLECTION

920 GRE 2/17. Unbound letters including correspondence 1773-82 of Mathew Gregson with or concerning D. Samwell, surgeon who sailed with Cook on his third voyage to the Pacific. Samwell's letters Feb.-July 1776 describe preparations for sailing and those dated Oct. 1780 to 1782 given some account of the voyage.*

920 MD 283-6 HENRY THRELFALL WILSON PAPERS

920 MD 283. Poster advertising White Star vessels sailing from Port Phillip.

920 MD 284. Ledger of H. T. Wilson, entries mainly 1853-5.

920 MD 285. Contract 9 May 1855 to Pilkington and Wilson to convey mail from Liverpool to Adelaide, Sydney and Melbourne.

920 MD 403-4. Journal of Sir William Bower Forwood, 20 Nov. 1857 to 28 Jan. 1858 of a voyage Liverpool to Melbourne in the *Red Jacket* and journal 30 Mar. to 15 May 1858 of a voyage Sydney to Valparaiso in the barque *Queen of Avon*; also meteorological observations.

920 ROS ROSCOE PAPERS

920 ROS 4261. Letter 8 Oct. 1814 T. Rushton, Sydney, sending money to his three daughters in Liverpool.

920 ROS 4269. Letter 31 Oct. 1815 T. Rushton, Sydney.

920 ROS 4499. Letter 28 Jan. 1825 Sir J. E. Smith, Norwich, giving news of McLeay who was leaving to become Colonial Secretary in New South Wales and taking with him a large family.

OCEAN MANAGEMENT SERVICES LTD
India Buildings, Liverpool 2

See F. E. Hyde with the assistance of J. R. Harris, *Blue Funnel, a History of Alfred Holt and Company of Liverpool from 1865 to 1914*, Liverpool 1957, and S. W. Roskill, *A Merchant Fleet in War, Alfred Holt & Co. 1939-1945*, London 1962.

Ocean Steamship Co. Ltd, Minutes of Annual General Meetings 1865- .

Ocean Steamship Co. Ltd, Voyage Books.

Correspondence between John Swire, Alfred Holt, Philip Holt, and Albert Crompton 1879-80.

Papers relating to Roxburgh, Colin Scott & Co., Aitken Lilburn & Co., John Swire and Sons and the start of the Australian trade.

UNIVERSITY OF LIVERPOOL
The Library, Ashton Street, P.O. Box 123, Liverpool 3

There is an alphabetical name index to manuscript collections in the Library in a loose-leaf file.

THOMAS MELLARD READE COLLECTION

Letters to Reade filed alphabetically by writer, include:

25 Apr., 12 Sept. 1883 J. Anderson, London, concerning laying of cable for the Eastern Telegraph Co.

25 Nov. 1901 I. Wolfe Barry, London, concerning the telegraph cable.

25 Sept. 1888 O. Fisher, Cambridge, concerning the Tarawera eruption.

29 Dec. 1887, 12 Jan. 1888 H. B. Guppy concerning his geological notes, chiefly on the Solomon Islands.

6 Oct. 1888 F. Hesse, London, of the Eastern Extension Australasia and China Telegraph Co. Ltd on repair of Java-Australia cables.

1901-6 J. M. Maclaren, London, various places in the British Isles and India, nineteen letters some referring to the writer's knowledge of the geology of Australia and New Zealand.

CO-OPERATIVE UNION LTD
Holyoake House, Manchester 4

ROBERT OWEN CORRESPONDENCE

Five letters 19 Mar. to 19 July 1830 from Robert Gouger sending notices of meeting and seeking to interest Owen in a society, later the National Colonisation Society.

Four official communications 17 Feb. to 23 June 1835 concerning Robert Owen's appeal on behalf of the six labourers convicted at the Dorset Assizes of administering false oaths. There is a memo of Robert Owen's reply to one letter. Also a memorial 23 June 1835 of the working classes *re* remission of penalty of six convicts from Dorset.

Letter 11 Aug. 1839 from James Lindsay suggesting co-operation between the Scots and the New Zealand (Emigration) Co. for the better colonisation of New Zealand.

GEORGE JACOB HOLYOAKE COLLECTION

The collection includes among letters to G. J. Holyoake:

Five letters 1854-73 from Horatio and Henry Thomas Holyoake, Ballarat and Melbourne, the former speaking of his gold prospecting experiences and on 22 Apr. 1855 of the fight with the troopers at Ballarat, and the latter of his marriage to Jane Phiddian, employment as a master saddler in Melbourne and defence of G. J. Holyoake in the *Argus*.

Seven letters 1860-97, six from Gerald Supple describing Melbourne and telling of trial, imprisonment, reprieve, and release on a charge of murder; despatch from Lord Canterbury, Governor of Victoria, to the Earl of Kimberley at the Colonial Office relating to Supple.

Four letters 1885-93 from Sir Henry Parkes referring in 1885 to his reception in Sydney after an overseas tour, New South Wales politics, and the prospects of creating a federal Australia. He and Holyoake were boys together in Birmingham.

Letter 3 Feb. 1851 of William Hornblower, Birmingham, containing family news and the information that John Griffin Hornblower was now doing well in Australia.

JOHN RYLANDS LIBRARY
Deansgate, Manchester 3

The English manuscripts in the John Rylands Library are described in *Handlists* published 1928-51. See also *Publications of the John Rylands Library* and supplementary lists, duplicated typescript. For current accessions see the *Bulletin of the John Rylands Library*.

ENG.MS.53. A voyage for whaling and discovery round Cape Horn into the Pacific Ocean in the merchant ship *Rattler* by Lieut. James Colnett 1793-4.

ENG.MSS.349, 372-87, 393-99, 401. Part of the autograph collection of Rev. Thomas Raffles, Liverpool; for an account of this collection, maintained and continued by his son, see 6th Report of the Royal Commission on Historical Manuscripts, Pt.I, pp.468-75.

ENG.MS.349/309. Letter 2 Nov. 1852 William Howe, missionary, Papeete, Tahiti, concerning the restrictions on Protestant ministers ordered by the French government and enclosing the following letters with translations or descriptions: 9 Feb. 1816 Pomare, King of Tahiti, to the missionaries at Uaeva in Moorea with a literal translation by William Ellis; 1844 Pomare II, King of Tahiti; 28 Apr. 1848 Gov. Lavaud to W. Howe, in French; 1852 Gov. Bonard to W. Howe, in French; four letters 1851-2 Pomare Aimata, Queen of Tahiti, one with translation.

ENG.MSS.372-86. 'Original letters, authors' mainly to Rev. Thomas Raffles, many accompanied by engraved portraits. The letters include:

ENG.MS.373/147. Letter 23 May 1839 George Bennet *re* autograph transcription of part of I Samuel by King Pomare. (The transcript is at ENG.MS.401.)

ENG.MS.373/172. Two letters 1834, 1836 Thomas Binney.

ENG.MS.376/612. Letter 28 Apr. 1828 Rev. William Ellis.

ENG.MS.376/679. Letters from Rev. Richard Fletcher: 6 Nov. 1837, Manchester, asking Raffles to give the charge at the approaching ordination of Henry Royle appointed missionary in the South Seas; 26 Aug. 1853 announcing his intention of going to Australia; printed letter 10 Aug. 1853 to the Church assembled in Grosvenor Street Chapel, Manchester, on the Australian mission which he had been invited to attend.

ENG.MS.378/1004. Letter n.d. William Howe announcing his arrival from Tahiti.

ENG.MS.382/1647. Note 26 Oct. 1841 of George Pritchard containing a text in two languages.

ENG.MS.386/3075. Letter 6 Jan. 1837 Rev. John Williams, London, asking Raffles to allow his Sunday School teachers to distribute literature.

ENG.MS.386a/4042. Letter 19 Dec. 1835 Rev. George Young, Whitby, referring in part to the writer's *Life and Voyages of Captain James Cook*, London 1836, of which a printed notice is attached.

ENG.MS.387. 'Original letters, missionaries'. A collection of letters and miscellaneous papers, mainly 1820-40, usually addressed to Rev. Thomas Raffles by missionaries from various areas including the South Seas, and to a minor extent Australia. Engraved portraits or views accompany many letters. About fifty relevant items include: prayer 1843 of Apalaamo of Tutuila, Samoa; prospectus 4 Mar. 1820 of the London Missionary Society project to send a deputation to the South Seas; letters 1826 from William Ellis; letter 1860 from Rev. W. W. Gill and a prospectus of his *Gems from the Coral Islands*, London [1863, new ed.?]; copy of *Requirements and Rules for the Parramatta Sunday School Teachers*, Parramatta, Missionary Press, Aug. 1816; letters from William Howe including one 1843 from Eimeo; letter 25 Aug. 1848 George Platt, Raiatea, to Rev. R. G. Milne; note from Rev. Henry Nott with a prayer of King Pomare; letter 24 Dec. 1846 John Rodgerson, Borabora, to the Rev. R. G. Milne; letter 1827 Rev. Samuel Marsden; printed account of the Mission Printing Office on Upolu, Samoa.

ENG.MSS.393-99. Calendar of documents relating to 'authors' in ENG.MSS.372-86 and 'missionaries' in ENG.MS.387, giving a brief description of material, 7 vols. ENG.MS.401. Part of I Samuel with a fly-leaf note Feb. 1831 saying it was transcribed by King Pomare 1819 from the translation made by the Rev. John Nott, missionary, by whom it was presented to George Bennet in 1823 at Matavai in the South Seas. (See ENG.MS.373/147.)

ENG.MS.867. Typescript autobiography of A. H. Gibson of Ngaio, N.Z., chiefly dealing with his experiences in New Zealand from 1879. A letter 4 Aug. 1935 by the author states that a copy is also deposited in the Alexander Turnbull Library, Wellington, N.Z. In Oct. 1878 A. H. Gibson sailed for New Zealand with his father Robert Henry Gibson.

Crawford and Balcarres Papers
Correspondence relating to the Rusden family includes:
26/2. Maria (née Pennington), Countess of Crawford. Personal correspondence including: letter 8 May 1830 from Anne Rusden, Leith Hill Place, thanking her for the favour of Col. Lindsay in assisting her son to go abroad.
40/2. Lieut.-Gen. James Lindsay of Balcarres. Personal correspondence including: five letters 1830-42 from Frank Townsend Rusden, Leith Hill Place and Hunter River, N.S.W.; thirteen letters 1832-47 Rev. George Keylock Rusden, Leith Hill, on board the *James Harris*, Sydney, but mainly from the parsonage, Maitland, N.S.W.; ten items 1830-42 relating to Rev. G. K. Rusden and family.
42/2. Anne (née Trotter) wife of Lieut.-Gen. James Lindsay. Personal correspondence including: four letters 1832-42 from Anne Rusden; letter 1833 from Rev. G. K. Rusden.

MANCHESTER PUBLIC LIBRARIES
Central Library, Archives Department, Manchester 2
RECORDS OF THE MANCHESTER REGIMENT

The records of the Manchester Regiment, formerly the 63rd Regiment of Foot and the 96th Regiment of Foot, were previously kept in the Regimental Museum but are now deposited in the Library. See Col. H. C. Wylly, *History of the Manchester Regiment*, London 1923-5, 2 vols.

M 25/2/1/1. Record of Services of the 63rd Regiment of Foot 1758-1910. A brief record is given of the Regiment's term in Australia May 1828 to Mar. 1834. There is a list of the Regiment and its distribution.

M 25/2/1/6. Record of Services of the 96th Regiment of Foot 1824-1914. A brief record is given of the Regiment's term in Australia and New Zealand July 1839 to Feb. 1849.

M 25/6/6. Address July 1848 to Lieut.-Col. Cumberland, commanding 96th Regiment, from the citizens of Hobart expressing regret at the departure of the Regiment for Launceston.

M 25/D/1/A/3c. Miscellaneous papers including a list of New Zealand medals awarded to the 96th Foot. Also printed descriptions of New Zealand awards 1845-66.

M 25/D/1/A/6a, b. Report 15 Mar. 1845 by Lieut. Edward Barclay to Lieut.-Col. C. B. Cumberland on the attack by Maoris on Kororareka, Bay of Islands, 11 Mar. 1845. With additional report by Ensign I. Campbell.

M 25/D/1/A/8. Nominal roll of officers and non-commissioned officers and men of the 96th Foot who were entitled to the medal for the New Zealand War 1845-7.

M 25/D/1/A/16-17. Papers 1830-4 including letters from J. Burnett and Sir George Arthur relating to Major James W. Fairtlough.

M 25/D/1/E/29. Correspondence 1952-3 between J. K. Collins, formerly Captain, 2nd Battalion, the Manchester Regiment, and the Northlands Regiment (New Zealand) concerning the action at Ruapekapeka Pa 1845.

GARDNER PAPERS

M 72/24/1-3. Documents 1850, 1855, 1922 relating to Richard Gardner, son of Robert Gardner.

M 72/25/1-17. Legal documents 1850-2; agreements between Robert Gardner of Manchester and his son William Atkinson Gardner of Launceston, V.D.L., relating to property in Van Diemen's Land and the partnership of Gardner, Bazley & Co.; indenture and memorandum of agreement involving the same parties with Georgiana Oakden and Theodore Bryant Bartley of Launceston in connection with the sale and purchase of land, shares, cattle.

MISCELLANEOUS

M 83/2. Album containing postcards 1901 of Hawaii. Photographs including one in 1893 of John Marriott and a party of Samoan teachers and their wives who sailed in the *John Williams* for New Guinea.

Owen MS.12. Letter book containing letters 1853-4 from John Owen, Melbourne.

THE EARL OF DERBY
Knowsley Hall, Prescot

The papers and correspondence of the 14th Earl of Derby have been listed, N.R.A. Report 1057. In 1969-70 the papers were in the care of Mr Robert Blake, Provost, Queen's College, Oxford. The papers fall into two main categories, official papers created during Lord Derby's tenure of offices under the Crown and as political leader, and correspondence consisting of General Correspondence, Special Correspondence, and Letter Books. General Correspondence consists of series of letters, some series arranged alphabetically by name of writer, some arranged chronologically. Special Correspondence consists of bundles of letters, each usually containing letters from a single person. Letter books are arranged chronologically.

Boxes 14-60. Official Papers

14/2. Miscellaneous papers relating to colonial business 1827-34.

19/5. Miscellaneous colonial papers 1834 and other papers.

21. Papers relating to the colonies, especially Canada 1838-54, and including a letter book relating to Catholic bishoprics in the colonies 1841-51 and printed secret and confidential memos on colonial honours 1844.

22/3. Memos on ecclesiastical affairs in the colonies 1841-2.

23/6. Aborigines Society 26 Jan. 1842.

24/2. Memos on Australia and New Zealand. Subjects covered include alienation of crown lands, transportation of convicts, Van Diemen's Land boys from Parkhurst, resolution of the Commercial Association Mar. 1842, military forces in Australia.

27/1-5. Cabinet memoranda 1841-5; 27/1, 1841 including memo on emigration to New South Wales; 27/2, 1842 including memo on Port Essington; 27/3, 1843 including memos on Australian sugar cultivation and the introduction of Chinese labourers; 27/5, 1845 memos on Charles Buller and the New Zealand Company, transportation, Capt. FitzRoy's conduct in New Zealand and a new convict settlement.

29/5. Aborigines Protection Society 1845.

30/2. Bill for sale of crown lands in Australia and New Zealand.

32. Miscellaneous printed and private papers including New Zealand papers.

39/2. Government business 1852 including the case of Smith O'Brien and his companions.

39/7. Government business 1852 including transportation, printed and confidential.

45. Confidential printed papers with some manuscripts 1852 including papers on convicts, transportation and discovery of gold in Australia.

47/2. Government business 1859 including Fiji.

Boxes 61-114. General Correspondence

Seven series of in-letters bound into volumes or tied into bundles 1827-58, 1833-4, 1858-9, 1866-8. Letters 1827-9 are bound in volumes, the rest are in bundles.

Boxes 115-64. Special Correspondence

The following bundles or series of bundles should repay examination:

115/5-6, Sir Robert John Wilmot Horton 1825, 1833-4; 117/8, T. Spring-Rice, 1st Baron Monteagle 1830-53; 122, W. Smith O'Brien 1831; 125, D. O'Connell 1831; 127/4, Sir George Gipps 1831-46; 129/1-4, Sir Robert Peel 1832-45; 130/12-13, Lord John Russell, 1st Earl Russell 1831-52, 1867; 131/5-6, Henry 3rd Earl Grey 1833-57, 1864-6; 131/8-9, Sir James Stephen 1833, 1844-5; 132/3, Lieut.-Gen. Sir George Arthur 1834-45; 133/2, Arthur 1st Duke of Wellington 1838-52; 135/5, Lieut.-Gen. Sir Edward Macarthur 1841-5; 135/6, Sir Eardley Wilmot and J. E. E. Wilmot 1841-7; 135/9, W. E. Gladstone 1841-63; 138/8, Capt. later Vice-Adm. Robert FitzRoy 1841-51; 138/12, Charles Buller 1842-5; 140/1, Lieut.-Col. George Gawler 1842-56; 140/3, Elizabeth Fry 1842-3; 141/8, F. R. Nixon, Bishop of Tasmania, 1842-5; 161/1-3, 15th Earl of Derby, styled Lord Stanley 1851-69 (further papers of the 15th Earl of Derby are in the Liverpool City Libraries, Record Office and Local History Department, pending listing, Feb. 1970); 162/1, Sir Edward Bulwer Lytton, 1st Baron Lytton, 1858-9; 163/5-6, 4th Earl of Carnarvon 1866-7; 163/7, 3rd Marquess of Salisbury 1866-7; 164/6, Gathorne-Hardy 1867.

Boxes 166-97. Letter Books 1827-69.

Box 198 contains Index to Cabinet Correspondence 1866-8.

Letters of John Gould and two volumes of original drawings, also one volume 'Gould and Richter's original Drawings of Australian Animals' are at Knowsley Hall, see A. McEvey, 'Collections of John Gould Manuscripts and Drawings', *La Trobe Library Journal*, Vol.1, No.2, Oct. 1968, especially p.27.

LANCASHIRE RECORD OFFICE
Sessions House, Preston

See Guide to the *Lancashire Record Office*, 1962.

QUARTER SESSIONS RECORDS

QGT Gaol, Transportation. Bonds 1836, 1838-9, 1841-3, for the transport of convicts from Lancashire prisons to the General Penitentiary at Millbank and to the hulks.

PALATINATE OF LANCASTER RECORDS

DDCm/1/14-55. Miscellanea. Assize Papers. Orders 1819-42 for the commutation of death sentences to transportation. Individuals are named with a brief mention of crime committed and reference to their transportation to New South Wales, Van Diemen's Land, or beyond the seas.

DDX 255/9. Calendar of crown prisoners 31 Mar. 1794 in Lancaster Castle and their sentences.

PRIVATE RECORDS

DDB1 Blundell of Crosby

53/5A. Journal 23 July to 15 Nov. 1840 of a voyage from Gravesend to Sydney by F. Smythe addressed to his sister C. M. Smythe, describing activities on board and including daily latitude and longitude and distances sailed.

DDHt Houghton (Lowton) MSS.

Papers 1864-84 relating to Alice Robert Houghton Fitzsimmons of Castlemaine, Vic., including her will 31 Mar. 1864 and papers and correspondence 1882-4 connected with her death and her property and that of her husband in Australia.

DDPd Pedder Muniments

26/392. Certificate 19 Nov. 1852 of a notary public at Sydney of a declaration made by Sarah, wife of Thomas Gough, blacksmith, of Parramatta, N.S.W., and widow of William Lowthwaite with declarations concerning the latter who died 21 Nov. 1851.

DDX 75/132. Letter 8 Feb. 1893 from Rev. J. E. Newell returning from furlough in England written on board S.S. *Oroya* bound for Australia with references to Mr Wolstenholme, a free church minister, and Rev. Bussell.

DDX 76 Papers c.1900-58 of Professor R. J. A. Berry

Many of the papers relate to Berry's Australian career after he established the Chair of Anatomy at the University of Melbourne in 1905. They include volumes of cuttings, addresses, and articles on secondary education, university matters, and medical questions. In his last years in Melbourne Berry was involved in the question of the site of the Royal Melbourne Hospital.

DDX 97/1. Letter 17 Jan. 1880 from Charles Hunt, Sydney, to his brother and sister Mr and Mrs Rothwell describing the voyage from Plymouth and listing some Sydney prices.

DDX 140/7. Correspondence 1812-16 Thomas Holden [Holding] of Bolton with his wife and parents concerning his trial and transportation for seven years to New South Wales, including letters 1815 from Sydney referring to his wages, the price of food and clothing, and the natives, and asking his wife to sell his looms and clothes to pay for his passage home.

DDX 387/1-2. Letter 4 Aug. 1875 Daniel R. Gardner on board the *Loch Maree* in the Clyde describing the ship and preparations for the voyage to Melbourne; letter [1876?] to his wife from the vicinity of Cairo, written on his way home.

DDX 505. Letters 1840-58 from the step-brothers Richard Taylor and Simon Brown, convicts transported to New South Wales and Van Diemen's Land respectively in 1840 and 1841. Written chiefly to their father George Taylor of Burnley, Lancs., they relate to removal to the hulks, arrival in Australia, and progress there.

DDX 537. Letters 1840-6 Richard Boothman to his father at Colne concerning his trial and transportation to Van Diemen's Land, his efforts to prove his innocence, also his will 7 Aug. 1876, and account of solicitor's expenses 1878 regarding his estate.

DDX 627. Papers relating to Thomas Hodgson, yeoman of Yealand Conyers, Lancs., who died c.1872. His will 11 June 1872 cites Henry Smithes, merchant of London as an executor and the papers include letters of administration 4 Aug. 1903 of Eliza Smithes of the island of Motu Korea, district of Auckland, N.Z., granted to John Henry Hodgson of the same with a schedule of estate duty and a plan of the property on the Waikato River.

THE QUEEN'S LANCASHIRE REGIMENT
Peninsula Barracks, Warrington

See Capt. R. H. Raymond Smythies, *Historical Records of the 40th (2nd Somersetshire) Regiment now 1st Battalion The Prince of Wales Volunteers (South Lancashire Regiment) from its formation in 1717 to 1893*, Devonport 1894. Capt. Smythies's own copy bound in 2 vols. held in the Regimental Headquarters, contains manuscript letters, illustrations, and notes. The Regiment was amalgamated in 1958 with The East Lancashire Regiment to form The Lancashire Regiment (The Prince of Wales's Volunteers). In 1970 The Lancashire Regiment and The Loyal Regiment amalgamated to form The Queen's Lancashire Regiment. Numerical references below are to spine numbers.

526, 670-72, 697, 795. Records of Services. Six volumes together covering 1717-1908 with considerable overlapping in date coverage, and duplication. These give a synoptic history of the Regiment, its movements, action, and personnel.

696. Regimental Order Book 4 Feb. 1824 to 19 Jan. 1827, indexed.

695. Regimental Order Book 22 Oct. 1845 to 10 Oct. 1865, indexed.

66, 77. Two volumes of memorabilia and cuttings, the first including an undated article on Sergeant-Major Lucas, awarded the V.C. at Waitara, N.Z., in 1861; the second containing an original General Order to the Troops 7 Jan. 1858, Melbourne, and an article on the New Zealand campaign from the *New Zealand Herald* 13 June 1896.

25. Miscellaneous printed articles including one relating to Sergeant-Major Lucas.

Miscellanea: copies of guard reports of the 40th Regiment while in Melbourne, originals with the Royal Victorian Historical Society; items *c.*1860 including cuttings and manuscript maps, relating to the New Zealand War; items relating to the services of the Regiment 1845-77.

LEICESTERSHIRE

LEICESTER MUSEUMS, DEPARTMENT OF ARCHIVES
New Walk, Leicester

PRIVATE RECORDS

8D 43/4. Order 7 Jan. 1836 sentencing John Smith, convicted of felony, to be transported beyond the seas for seven years.

9D 43. Harris, Watts, and Bouskell papers; deeds and papers deposited on the amalgamation of two firms of solicitors including:

213/1-9. Birth certificates 1870-83 of the six children of Walter R. Hardy Higginson, one time farmer of Leicester and now pastoralist at Tawonga, Vic., and Ellen his wife; also his death certificate 1887 and death certificates [of his parents?] 1895 and 1896.

15D 57. Coltman letters, correspondence of a prominent Leicester Dissenting family of manufacturers including:

337. Letter 14 July 1852 Samuel Coltman and his wife from Duffield to his sister discussing the emigration to New Zealand of friends and relatives including Charles Lowndes.

1577 (1885). Duplicate certificate 31 Oct. 1818 with receipt for delivery of five convicts to the hulks at Woolwich by the Sheriff of Leicestershire.

LEICESTERSHIRE RECORD OFFICE
57 New Walk, Leicester

QUARTER SESSIONS RECORDS

Qs13/3. Transportation

Papers 1844-5 including letters, memos, and drafts relating to a petition by William Napier Reeve, an employee in the office of the Clerk of the Peace, on behalf of Samuel Chambers, a steam pump operator, convicted and sentenced to transportation to Australia for seven years. Reeve drew up the indictment in the belief that the charge would be quashed and felt a responsibility for what he saw as a miscarriage of justice. Details of the case are given.

NONCONFORMIST RECORDS

Leicestershire and Rutland Congregational Union Records

N/C/MB/13-14. Leicesterhire & Rutland Auxiliary to the London Missionary Society, Minute Books 1870-1919, 2 vols. These cover the activities of the auxiliary and include reports of the anniversaries or annual meetings when delegates from the churches in the county met to hear the reports of the directors and to meet the deputation from the parent society and invited missionaries, some of them from New Guinea and the Pacific. The minutes contain cuttings of their addresses when reported by the local press, e.g. 1873 Rev. G. Drummond of Samoa and Rev. W. G. Lawes of Savage Island and New Guinea.

PRIVATE RECORDS

Dalby MSS.

109-11. Three letters Nov.-Dec. 1811 from Lord Moira in London to the Rev. John Dalby at Castle Donington about the son of Mary Richmond sentenced to transportation to Botany Bay for fourteen years.

115, 116, 132. Three letters Apr. 1812 concerning the convict Percival Cook and the belief that all intervention on his behalf would be fruitless.

MRS D. V. CRAWFORD
91 Park Lane, Sutton Bonington, Loughborough

Letters of the Rev. R. B. Lyth 1829-56 and a letter 12 Dec. 1952 from M. L. Early to Miss Longstaff giving biographical information about the wife of the Rev. R. B. Lyth. A microfilm is in the Methodist Missionary Society, London.

LINCOLNSHIRE

LINCOLNSHIRE ARCHIVES OFFICE
The Castle, Lincoln

QUARTER SESSIONS RECORDS

H.QS. Records of the parts of Holland, County of Lincoln

H.QS.C/3. Financial records, returns 1835-43 of the expenses of criminal prosecution at Quarter Sessions and Assizes and for the conveyance of prisoners under sentence of transportation to the hulks or depots for convicts.

DIOCESAN RECORDS

N.R.L. Petitions for licences to be non-resident

N.R.L./19/2. Documents 1854-5 including the petition of the Rev. Michael Henry Becker, Rector of Barnoldby le Beck, to the Bishop of Lincoln, seeking a mission to Australia for two years for the British and Foreign Bible Society; includes licence of the Bishop 4 Jan. 1855.

PRIVATE RECORDS

Daubney

Daub.IV/4/8. Letter 22 Nov. 1849 Lord Yarborough to W. H. Daubney, Great Grimsby, stating he had seen Lord Grey who advised against going to Australia.

Elwes

Papers of Valentine Dudley Henry Carey Elwes.

2 Elwes 1/1. Correspondence 1854-5 with his mother referring to his arrival and stay in Perth, relatives there, his financial affairs, possibility of joining the army, and news of the colony.

2 Elwes 1/8. Papers 1849-88 of his sister Elien, Mrs Fitzgerald, wife of Gov. Fitzgerald, including: address 2 May 1849 to the Governor from a minister of religion on the bad influence of some women arrivals on the *Merope*; letter 12 July 1852 Polding to Gov. Fitzgerald; copy despatch 4 May 1853 from Sanford, Colonial Secretary's Office, Perth, to the Commandant *re* money for the Sisters of Mercy; copy 12 May 1853 of the reply of the Commandant, F. C. Irwin, and further despatch 13 May 1853 of Sanford claiming the Commandant had voted money for Protestant children but not for Catholic groups; letters 1855 V. C. Elwes to his sister relating to his voyage home via Mauritius.

2 Elwes 2/1. Two volume journal 1854-5 of a visit to Egypt followed by a voyage to Australia and back with a prolonged stay at Government House, Perth.

Fane

Fane 6/10/8F. Michel Family letters.

Letters 1866-74 to W. D. Fane from H. E. Michel referring to a visit to the west coast of New Zealand 1866 but concerned mainly 1869-70 with family affairs in Melbourne and in 1874 with the Tichborne trial and his unfulfilled expectation of being able to produce Arthur Orton; also thanks for an introduction to Sir George Bowen. There is a receipt July 1876 by Jane Michel for moneys on a life assurance policy of her late husband H. E. Michel and correspondence 1878-80 with W. Fane on the marriage of Charlotte Michel to Charles Goldspink, their visit to London and her death from measles in 1880.

Flinders

Flinders 2. Diary 1785-1802 of Matthew Flinders of Donington, father of Matthew Flinders the explorer, with references 1791, 1796-7 to his son's intended voyage and later promotion.

Lincolnshire

Flinders 3/2-10. Correspondence 1800-1 of Matthew Flinders with his father containing references to his brother Samuel's appointment to the *Investigator*, his sister Susan, his marriage with Miss Chappell and his father's disapproval. There are also references to the progress of the voyage and to George Bass.

Flinders 3/11-16. Correspondence 1803, 1805-7 of Matthew Flinders with his stepmother including letter 10 June 1803 telling of his circumnavigation of New Holland and letters from the Isle de France concerning his imprisonment without prospect of release.

Goulding
Personal papers 1880-1929 of R. W. Goulding.
Goulding 3/C. Correspondence from friends, mostly of Louth, but including:
Goulding 3/C/75. Sheets from the journal 12 Dec. 1899 to 1 Mar. 1900 of William Newman on a voyage to New Zealand including impressions of Adelaide and Melbourne. There are references to the non-observance of Sunday on board ship and to the purpose of his journey being to see old friends.
Goulding 3/C/60. Letter 1899 John Marshall on his mining activities in Queensland.
Goulding 3/C/59. Letter 1914 George Marshall on his life in Australia as a farm worker.
Goulding 3/C/89. Lena Ellen Playll, seventy-four letters 1901-19 including descriptions of teaching in various English schools 1901-11 and in Australia 1912-19.

Jarvis
Jarvis VA/2-4. Personal correspondence of Capt. G. R. P. Jarvis including seven letters 1809-10, 1814-17 from Lachlan Macquarie, his brother-in-law, referring to his preparations for departure to New South Wales, the voyage to Australia, the state of the colony, family news, and, on 18 Dec. 1817, to Macquarie's intention to return to England because of Bathurst's letters and his inadequate income.
Jarvis VA/12/72. Letter 29 Mar. 1847 Dorothea Morley, Winchester, to Jarvis, her brother, forwarding seeds from Van Diemen's Land sent by Lord Ogilvy's son.

Padley, Estate Agent's Deposit
Pad. 3/234. Plan 1853 of the Louth Park Estate, Hunter River, N.S.W., containing a general plan, an enlarged plan of the homestead and local sketch and key.

Stubbs, solicitors, Deposit
Stubbs 1/399/1. Disposal of the properties of Mathew and Amelia Akes on behalf of the brothers Matthew, Tom, and John Moss of South Australia, 1877-94, including account books and correspondence on the disposal of moneys to the Moss brothers and the will of Amelia Akes.

Tennyson D'Eyncourt
Miscellaneous letters including:
2 T.d'E. H41/45. 31 Mar. 1847 James Mayne Conilly, Portland Bay, N.S.W., to Charles D'Eynecourt asking him to use his influence to obtain for him an office in New South Wales.

Turnor
4 Turnor. Memoranda, reports, articles, processed circulars, and correspondence 1917-25 relating to empire land settlement including: article Jan. 1920 by C. Turnor and E. Jowett 'British Empire Land Settlement for Service Men'; letter 7 Feb. 1920 E. Jarrett to W. M. Hughes on the work of the Royal Colonial Institute in settling soldiers on the land; typed report Aug. 1922 'The Royal Colonial Institute and Imperial Migration'; typed article Feb. 1925 'For the information of the members of the London Board, Australian Farms Limited' by the Chairman of the Board, J. Sanderson, and copies of cables on the subject of the settlement of Tresco West;

processed statement 31 May 1925 regarding the progress of schemes under the Empire Settlement Act.

Diary 1919-20 Christopher Turnor of a visit to Australia, with entries on agriculture and farming.

Welby of Allington

LD 24/3/2/8. Bound volume of papers including letter 14 Aug. 1867 C. W. Howell, Secretary, P.&O. Company, to F. Hill, G.P.O., on service contracts, and with statement n.d. 'Australian Contracts and Australian Mail Service'.

Mossop and Bowser, solicitors, Deposit

H.D. 65/35/41. Assignment of mortgage c.1902, parties including William Smithson Cortes, Manly, N.S.W., doctor of medicine.

H.D. 65/35/42. Assignment of mortgage, Alice Weddell Hobbs, Jondalee near Cootamundra, N.S.W.

Miscellaneous Deposits

Misc. Dep. 28/7. Paper 1 Apr. 1854 issued by the Secretary of State's Office, Home Department, Whitehall, stating that John Thompson, convicted at Worcester Assizes 17 July 1846 and transported to Van Diemen's Land on the *Pestonjee Bomanjee*, died on the voyage.

Misc.Dep. 28/8-9. Declarations by John and Elizabeth Clay 30 Mar. 1854 relating to the Tomlinson family.

Massingberd of Gunby

M.G. 4/5/8. Journal 29 June 1832 to 22 Sept. 1833 of Peregrine Langton Massingberd. P. Langton Massingberd, his daughters Mary and Margaret, Mary's husband Hastings Neville, and their baby daughter, sailed for Van Diemen's Land via the Cape of Good Hope, on the *Edward Lombe*. The journal contains an explanation of the family's decision to emigrate to Van Diemen's Land and detailed descriptions of the voyage out, the colony, meetings with prominent people including Capt. James England, W. J. T. Clarke, A. F. Kemp, John Glover, Batman, and Gov. Arthur. They returned to England on the *Duckenfield* arriving on 22 Sept. 1833.

MIDDLESEX

See also Greater London Record Office (Middlesex).

A. W. ROBERTSON, ESQ.
Ranworth, St Lawrence Drive, Pinner

Letters collected primarily for their philatelic interest and including letters from Australia.*

1 Jan. 1829 John Foster, Macquarie River, V.D.L., containing news of his brother Henry, who is with him at Macquarie River, and his brother William in New South Wales.

11 Aug. 1829 Mrs Samuel R. Dawson, Claremont, V.D.L., giving impressions of the colony.

NORFOLK

A. H. R. MARTINDALE, ESQ.
Hill House, 64 Mount Pleasant, Norwich

Letters 1850-63 written by George Ewbank from South Australia, commenting on South Australian affairs, particularly the Burra Copper Mine.*

NORFOLK AND NORWICH RECORD OFFICE
Central Library, Norwich

An account entitled 'The Norfolk and Norwich Record Office' by the City and County Archivist was published in the journal of the British Records Association, *Archives* VIII No.38, Oct. 1967, pp.63-9. It includes a brief survey of records held and means of reference. See also Norfolk and Norwich Record Office 'Notes for the Assistance of Genealogists', compiled by Miss Jean M. Kennedy, duplicated. A card index is maintained of deposits other than official and ecclesiastical records, and typescript catalogues are made for individual collections.

PRIVATE RECORDS

HEA 570 Rolfe (Heacham) MSS.

The following printed papers relating to emigration to the Australian colonies are included:

HEA 570 257 X 5. *Female Emigration. Extract of a Letter from Hobart Town Van Diemen's Land dated 26 September 1834.*

Papers Relating to Emigration to the Australian Colonies ordered by the House of Commons to be Printed 27th March 1835; Committee for Promoting the Emigration of Females to the Australian Colonies . . . A Free Passage to Single Women and Widows, Government notice, London 30 Apr. 1835.

MS.2292, 2 E 2. Petition Oct. 1786 to the Secretary of State from the Mayor and Justices of the Peace for the Borough of Great Yarmouth requesting that a number of prisoners in the overcrowded gaol be included among the convicts being sent to Botany Bay. The names, ages, and occupations of eight prisoners are given.

NORTHAMPTONSHIRE

MUSEUM OF THE NORTHAMPTONSHIRE REGIMENT
Gibraltar Barracks, Barrack Road, Northampton

The Digest of Service 1740-1941 of the 48th Regiment of Foot contains a mention that the Regiment went to New South Wales and were there 1817-24.

NORTHAMPTONSHIRE RECORD OFFICE
Delapré Abbey, Northampton

PRIVATE RECORDS

CE(B) 46-7. Diaries by Dudley Cary Elwes including description of journey 1890-1

England to Australia and visits to Australian towns. Also an account of a ride from Rotorua to Napier, N.Z.

E(GB) 947-61, 980. Ledger, mementoes 1854-5 of Valentine Cary Elwes's visit to Perth, W.A.

GK 919. Will 1840 J. O. Davis mentioning land at Canning River, W.A.

ZA 1451. Log of Thomas Vincent Dickins, Daventry, describing a journey 1852-3 from Liverpool to Port Phillip.

ZA 1452. Fifty-three printed verses on 'The Log of the ship Norfolk' on her second return trip from Victoria, 1858.

E(GB) 944-5. Despatch books of Charles Fitzgerald as Governor of Gambier 1844-7, and of Western Australia 1848-51, 2 vols.

E(GB) 946. Copy of a despatch 20 Dec. 1849 concerning a native attack on Gov. Fitzgerald's party of five men.

Holthouse Papers. Holthouse Box 1061. Thirty letters 1881-91 from Dr T. LeGay Holthouse of Ballarat Asylum and Lying-in Hospital.

Wake Family Papers. Journal of a voyage to Port Phillip 1848 by Philip Wake containing a description of life on a cattle station at Janevale, 1848-52.

NORTHUMBERLAND

NORTHUMBERLAND RECORD OFFICE
Melton Park, North Gosforth, Newcastle-upon-Tyne

PRIVATE RECORDS

Blackett Ord (Whitfield) MSS.
NRO 324/A/32. Two letters 1822, 1824 Thomas Hobbes Scott, Whitfield, with notes on New South Wales, in papers of William Ord.

Ridley (Blagdon) MSS.
ZRI 25/49. Eleven documents referring to inquiries into conditions in New South Wales in the late 1820s, with particular reference to the punishments inflicted on convicts.

T. B. HUGHES, ESQ.
'Lawnswood', 1 King John's Court, Ponteland

The collection of family papers includes a small group relating chiefly to Bristow Herbert Hughes, grandfather of Mr T. B. Hughes. A few papers relate to brothers of B. H. Hughes, Herbert Bristow Hughes, and John Bristow Hughes, and to the son of B. H. Hughes, Ernest Horatio Burgess Hughes. The three brothers went to South Australia in the early 1840s. J. B. Hughes took up Bundaleer and later became a prominent public man in South Australia, H. B. Hughes and B. H. Hughes took up Booyoolee, both stations north of Adelaide near Gladstone. See *Australian Garden and Field* XXV, No.5, Oct. 1909, pp.I-XII, a copy of which is with the papers, together with cuttings concerning J. B. Hughes. Items particularly noted* are:

Northumberland

Family tree, typescript.

Memorandum of agreement of partnership 6 Nov. 1855 between H. B. Hughes and B. H. Hughes, 'stockholders of Boille'.

Balance sheet 1855 endorsed 'B.H.H. left Rocky River Nov 1855 & up to that time had active management of Stock & Runs'. On verso is a note of balance at 3 Sept. 1856 with comment by H. B. Hughes.

Letter 26 Apr. 1867 from B. H. Hughes, London, to H. B. Hughes in South Australia concerning sale of consols and remittance of proceeds for the credit of H. B. Hughes in Adelaide; also concerning the racehorse Leonidas and his pedigree.

Letter 23 May 1867 H. B. Hughes, Adelaide, to his sister Mrs White, Birkenhead, with notes on the Bristow pedigree. On the same sheet is a letter 23 May 1867 H. B. Hughes, Booyoolee, to his mother at Birkenhead describing his recent trip with his family from Adelaide to Booyoolee.

Other papers include correspondence, two letters on biographical matters; notes in the handwriting of E. H. B. Hughes, on the dates of arrival in South Australia of J. B. Hughes, B. H. Hughes, and H. B. Hughes and on their activities there; four letters Oct. 1897 to Mar. 1898 from E. H. B. Hughes written during his voyage to Australia and from Booyoolee; steerage ticket for E[H. B.] Hughes, Lund's Line of Steamers, *Bungaree*, Adelaide to London, leaving Adelaide on or about 18 June 1898.

Notebook containing notes on the Bristow and Hughes families and cuttings and papers including obituary notices of B. H. Hughes, H. B. Hughes, W. Bartley, and other relatives.

NOTTINGHAMSHIRE

NOTTINGHAM CITY LIBRARIES
Archives Department, South Sherwood Street, Nottingham

ATKEY MSS.

Papers of Sir Albert Atkey.
ATK/37. Personal letters Feb.-Dec. 1936 to Sir Albert and Lady Atkey of Nottingham during and after their visit to New Zealand and including a letter from the president of the Auckland Chamber of Commerce on how trade with Great Britain should be increased.

MISCELLANEOUS MSS.

M 3940. Power of Attorney 4 Apr. 1868 Isaac Mason Hill, Nelson, N.Z., to Mr Roby, Nottingham, to act *re* an intended indenture.

TC 2/84. Letter 10 Mar. 1855 Henry Austin, Melbourne, to his mother and sister with mention of the fall of rents and trade in Melbourne and his intention of going to the goldfields. Letter 22 Dec. 1852 Secretary of State's Office, Home Department, Whitehall, reporting that William Austin of Nottingham, transported to New South Wales in 1839 in the *Woodbridge* had died and was buried on 24 June 1840.

M 16471-3. Letters 18 July, 3 Oct. 1852 Thomas Russell Ross from Melbourne and

Bendigo to his parents, describing his voyage out, preparations for setting off to the goldfields including the prices of a number of articles and commodities and describing the diggings and his success. Also letter 12 May 1857 John William Till to Isabella Ross, Islington, telling of the death of her brother Thomas on 11 Apr. 1857 and burial at Maryborough.

NOTTINGHAMSHIRE RECORD OFFICE
County House, High Pavement, Nottingham

See *Guide to the Nottinghamshire County Record Office*, 1960.

PRIVATE RECORDS

DD 380/1. Letter 9 Nov. 1855 J. and R. Turner, Brighton, Vic., to parents in England with family details and mention that trade is still bad and that they hope to go to the diggings at Ballarat.

DDBB Bristowe of Beesthorpe Papers
   Family correspondence *c*.1800-31 including:

DDBB 113/107. Letter 24 June 1917 Leonard Hugh Bristowe, Yarragon, Vic., to his sister Mrs Georgina Garnet concerning his plans to return to England.

DDBB 113/108. L. H. Bristowe's application Feb. 1922 for nomination as a Brother of Charterhouse giving an outline of his career with a brief note on his time in Australia 1895-1917, in Melbourne and country districts. The eight attached references give some additional biographical detail.

DDH Hodgkinson and Beevor, solicitors, Collection
Papers of the Buck Family of Farndon.

DDH 151/91-8. Eight letters 1901-5 concerning S. C. H. Buck of New Zealand and the estate of his father J. P. Buck; mortgage of his interest in the estate of C. J. Parr, barrister and solicitor of Auckland, N.Z.; letters S. C. H. Buck to R. Hodgkinson concerning his father's death, return to England and tenancy matters.
Papers of Harvey of Balderston, Newark, and Lincolnshire.

DDH 154/142-5. Four items including letter 20 Jan. 1902 Henry Thompson and Sons, solicitors of Grantham, Lincs., to R. Hutchinson *re* amount payable to Samuel Hole on death of Mrs Hole, for whose estate George Harvey was trustee, and letter 29 Mar. 1902 Samuel Hole, Wondooba, Curlewis, N.S.W., to Robert Hodgkinson concerning monies due to him from the estate of George Harvey who died in 1879.
Papers of H. A. Irwin.

DDH 160/30. Letter 24 Feb. 1866 Dyson Lacy, St Helen's, Bowen, Q'ld, to H. A. Irwin asking him to surrender his trusteeship in an estate to an individual in Australia, and other news.
Wills, Settlements and Cognate Papers.

DDH 172/2. Probate will of Jane Andrews of Hobart who died at Nottingham 21 Nov. 1898 leaving her estate to her brothers John and Thomas Andrews of Hobart.

DDH 172/135, 148. Deed poll and power of attorney 30 Oct. 1878 between George Johnson, East Melbourne, Vic., and J. A. Swan, London, *re* the former's interest in his parents' wills. Nine receipts 1876-8 George Johnson and others of the family for specified shares under the wills of their parents.

DDH 172/173-4. Indenture, release of trusts 27 Dec. 1866, 8 Dec. 1874 William Newbound, Alexandra, N.Z., settler, and others.

DDH 177/139. Copy of deed poll, letter of attorney 22 Apr. 1897 of Ann Esam, Warrnambool, Vic., widow of Richard Mason of Lincoln.

DDWM Williamson & Co., Retford, solicitors, Collection

Nottinghamshire

Foster Family Papers: papers of H. P. Foster.

DDWM 4/146-62. Letters 1888-93 of the brothers T. P. and C. M. Foster, Australia, mainly to Thomas Bescoby, East Retford. The brothers settled in 1889 at Ulmarra on the Clarence River, N.S.W., but Thomas Foster later began business in Sydney. The letters refer initially to the transfer of monies to Australia and then to matters arising out of the estate of H. P. Foster and the payment to each of his share in the estate. One letter 14 Jan. 1892 from C. M. Foster to his uncle H. P. Foster mentions his approaching marriage to the daughter of the chief warder of Grafton gaol and his brothers' losses through flood and in Sydney trading.

CP Edward Smith Godfrey Papers

CP 5/4/382-3. Two letters 1832 to Edward Smith Godfrey, Clerk of the Peace, giving details of Lincolnshire transportation methods and the possibility of a joint scheme with Nottinghamshire.

UNIVERSITY OF NOTTINGHAM
Department of Manuscripts, University Park, Nottingham

For descriptions of some collections and accessions see *Report of the Keeper of the Manuscripts*, 1958/9- .

GALWAY MSS.

Papers of the Monckton and Arundell families.

G13230-47. Papers of Sir George Vere Arundell, 8th Viscount Galway, Governor General of New Zealand 1935-41.

G13231-2. Correspondence 1933-6 relating to the Oxford Society in New Zealand and the printed report of the Society for 1934-5.

G13233. Papers 1937-41 relating to Viscount Galway's appointment to the Privy Council.

G13234. Correspondence 1938-9 relating to the west window in the proposed Anglican Cathedral at Wellington, N.Z.

G13237. Letter 6 Mar. 1941 Lord Hardinge, Buckingham Palace, on Galway's return from New Zealand.

G13238. Letters 1941-2 D. E. Fouley, Government House, Wellington, relating to affairs in New Zealand.

G13239. Fragment of a letter from the Bishop of Wellington.

Ga 17-31. Papers of George Edmund Milnes, 7th Viscount Galway.

Ga 20/1-217. File box of correspondence 1877-1913 containing letters from various individuals including F. A. Monckton in New Zealand.

NEWCASTLE MSS.

The Newcastle MSS. are divided into two sections: personal papers, principally correspondence, and title deeds and estate papers. Main groups in the first section are the papers of Henry Pelham and of the 2nd, 4th, and 5th Dukes of Newcastle.

NeC 8779-14145 Papers of Henry Pelham Clinton, 5th Duke of Newcastle.

NeC 9552-10884b. Political Correspondence: Colonial Office 1852-4 and War Department 1854-5.

NeC 9555. Letter book 1852-4, incomplete, private letters, Colonial Department. Contains sections for New South Wales, Victoria, South Australia, Van Diemen's Land, and New Zealand including correspondence with Sir Charles FitzRoy on responsible government in New South Wales and the appointment of his successor Sir William Denison, Rev. J. Woolley on Sydney University, the Bishop of Melbourne on transportation, Sir Charles Hotham on his appointment as Governor of Victoria,

Henry Fox Young on political and constitutional affairs in South Australia, Sir William Denison, Sir George Grey containing references to gold and native affairs.

NeC 9557. Letter book 1852-4, incomplete, Colonial Department, colonial church.

NeC 9558-87. Miscellaneous papers and correspondence 1852-4 with memoranda on colonial governorships including comment on individual governors.

NeC 9588-99. Copies of letters 1852-3 from Newcastle to, inter alia, Sir William Denison, Van Diemen's Land, and copy despatches to Denison re the resolution of the government to put an end to transportation.

NeC 9600-10. Papers and correspondence 1852-4 relating to New Zealand including letters from Q. Mathias, F. A. Weld, C. J. Abraham, J. R. Godley, and J. E. FitzGerald.

NeC 9666-71. Letters 1853 from Charles Trevelyan, Treasury, to Newcastle including references to proposed depot and guardship for Melbourne, and the establishment of police at Melbourne to check desertion of seamen.

NeC 9672-80. Letters 1854-5 from Sir George Grey, Colonial Office, to Newcastle, War Department, mostly concerning Colonial Office business, relating inter alia to New South Wales and also including a letter from Lord Stanley with reference to the North Australian expedition and the employment of Mr Baines.

NeC 10764-830. Copies of letters 1854 Newcastle to various individuals including Sir Charles Hotham, Col. Lockyer, Sir Robert Gardiner and others; one states the Duke's intentions while colonial minister as to separation of Australian governments.

NeC 10885-11653. Political Correspondence, Colonial Office, 1859-64 including private letter books and general Colonial Office papers.

NeC 10885-8. Private letter books 1860-4, Series B containing copies of Newcastle's letters to colonial governors including governors of Australian colonies.

NeC 10905-12. General Colonial Office papers 1859-63 with references to New Zealand, A. Woods's proposal to abolish Emigration Commissioners; letter from Lord Shaftesbury on colonial bishops.

NeC 11038-72. Australia.

NeC 11038-44. Letters 1859-61 from Sir William Denison to E. Lytton (copy) and to Newcastle.

NeC 11045-6. Papers 1861 relating to Count P. E. Strzelecki, terms upon which land is granted to settlers in New South Wales and Van Diemen's Land 1826-9; papers relating to gold in New South Wales c.1840-53.

NeC 11047-51. Letters 1862 from Sir John Young, Governor of New South Wales, to Newcastle.

NeC 11052-8. Papers 1861-3 belonging to Sir John Young including letters from Newcastle.

NeC 11059-67. Papers 1861-5 belonging to Sir John Young.

NeC 11068-9. Papers 1863 re transportation especially relating to Western Australia.

NeC 11073-101. New Zealand.

NeC 11073-5, 11077-101. Papers 1860-4 concerning Maori Wars and native affairs.

NeC 11076. Memo 1861 on the New Zealand constitution.

NeC 11654-12810. Political Correspondence 1832-64.

NeC 12205-345. Miscellaneous correspondence, political and private, 1842-63 of the 5th Duke of Newcastle including letters from Sir John Young.

NeC 12423-34. Correspondence 1846-59 between Edward Cardwell and the 5th Duke of Newcastle; the letters from the Duke of Newcastle cover only 1850-2.

OSSINGTON MSS.

Papers of John Evelyn Denison, 1st Viscount Ossington, Speaker of the House of Commons.

Nottinghamshire

OsC 1-1836. Correspondence

OsC 29, 30, 197-201. Letters 1852 of Sir William Denison, Governor of Van Diemen's Land to his brothers John Evelyn and Henry; letters 1840 Henry Denison, Sydney, to J. E. Denison.

OsC 284-308. Letters 1846-54 mainly from Sir William Denison, Hobart, describing conditions in the colony, from Henry Denison, and one 29 June 1854 from W. Wentworth.

OsC 318. Letters 1, 24 June 1852 Sir William Denison, Hobart.

OsC 461, 463-6. Letters 1850 Henry Denison.

OsC 547. Letter 12 Jan. 1852 Sir William Denison, Hobart.

OsC 890. Reprint of article 3 Nov. 1860 in the *Indian Statesman*, Madras, on the careers of the Denison family particularly Sir William Denison.

OsC 949. Letter 24 Feb. 1863 Redmond Barry, Public Library of Victoria, to J. E. Denison.

OsC 1384. Letter 22 Apr. 1849 Sir William Denison, Hobart.

OsC 1800-15. Letters 1907 to Miss L. Denison from various State Parliamentary librarians concerning the receipt of *Notes from my Journal when Speaker of the House of Commons*, London 1899, by J. E. Denison.

OsD 1-24. Diaries, notebooks

OsD 10. Extracts from letters 1840-1 from Henry and Alfred Deakin in Australia.

OXFORDSHIRE

BODLEIAN LIBRARY
Oxford

The Bodleian Library, the library of the University of Oxford, is housed in several buildings. Western manuscripts are available in the Old Reading Room (Duke Humphrey's Library) and in Rhodes House Library, q.v. Readers who are not members of the University must be recommended and forms for this purpose are available on request. All readers are required to be formally registered.

There are two sets of published catalogues of manuscripts written in European languages, the 'Quarto Catalogues' and the 'Summary Catalogue'. The former, *Catalogus Codicum Manuscriptorum Bibliothecae Bodleianae*, Oxford 1853-98, 11 parts, comprise catalogues of a few large collections. Each part is provided with an index. A set of the indexes has been cut up, pasted on cards and filed in one alphabet. The latter, *A Summary Catalogue of Western Manuscripts in the Bodleian Library at Oxford, which have not hitherto been catalogued in the Quarto Series; with References to the Oriental and Other Manuscripts*, Oxford 1895-1953, 7 vols., includes Vol.I, 1953, *Historical Introduction and Conspectus of Shelf-Marks*, and Vol.VII, 1953, *Index*. It covers accessions to 1915 except for the catalogue of manuscripts relating to Oxford which covers accessions up to 1962. Typed descriptions of accessions since 1915 are kept with the 'Summary Catalogue'. A card index of these volumes is maintained. There is also a catalogue of the manuscripts of Oxford colleges and some colleges have deposited their manuscripts in the Bodleian. Parochial indexes of deposited ecclesiastical records are shelved near the Quarto Catalogues together with personal indexes of Oxfordshire and Berkshire probate records. A separate leaflet on manuscript genealogical sources in the library is available.

For a survey of the manuscript collections see H. H. E. Craster, *The Western Manuscripts in the Bodleian Library*, London 1921. The staff should be consulted with regard to uncatalogued accessions. All call numbers for manuscripts must include the name of the group of papers, e.g. Bryce U.S.A.19, Clarendon c.129, MSS. Eng.lett. c.189. The letters c, d, and e in call numbers indicate size.

RAWLINSON COLLECTION

See *Catalogi Codicum Manuscriptorum Bibliothecae Bodleianae Partis Quintae (Fasc.I-V)* ... *confecit Gulielmus D. Macray*, Oxford 1862-1900. Fasc.II includes an index to classes A-C, fasc.V is an index to class D. Most of the manuscripts concerning the Pacific relate to the western coast of South America. Two manuscripts record voyages across the Pacific:

MS. Rawlinson C869. Journal of a voyage in the *Townshend* through the Ladrones towards Macao, 18 June 1717 to 11 Jan. 1718. A description of islands, part of the Ladrones, is given on pp.1-2 and a list of officers of the *Townshend*, Capt. Charles Kesar, on pp.19-20.

MS. Rawlinson D813. A collection of small seventeenth century charts of seaports and coasts of islands, chiefly in South America and in the East Indian Archipelago, including, on ff.19-22, sketches of plants and fruits. A rough chart of the course of a ship across the Pacific from Le Maire Strait via various islands, New Ireland and New Guinea to Gilolo has been torn in two and bound up as ff.16 and 18.

MSS. ACLAND

Papers of Sir Henry Wentworth Acland, Bt. A manuscript list is available (1970). MS. Acland 140 ff.133-44. Letters 1883-5 from W. A. Dyke Acland, H.M.S. *Miranda*, Sydney, and 'at sea Samoa to Sydney'.

ASQUITH PAPERS

Permission to quote from these papers must be obtained from Mr Mark Bonham Carter, 49 Victoria Road, London, W.8. The typescript catalogue is provided with an index of names of correspondents including Sir Ian Hamilton, W. R. Birdwood, Andrew Fisher, and W. M. Hughes. Printed government papers 1886, 1892-4, 1901, 1906-16 are chiefly papers for Cabinet use, White Papers, Bills and related documents, including some Committee of Imperial Defence and Colonial Defence Committee papers. Photocopies of papers in Vols. 95-132 are at Cab.37 in the Public Record Office. Vol.132 includes Secretary's notes of Dardanelles Committee meetings June-Aug. 1915. Vol.133 contains papers 1914-24, chiefly typescript but some printed, among which are papers on the Dardanelles and Mesopotamia campaigns.

BRYCE PAPERS

The papers of James Bryce, Viscount Bryce of Dechmont, are partly uncatalogued (1970). There is a Calendar of Papers relating to the United States of America, with index, duplicated typescript, and a Calendar of Letters to and from English Corres-pondents, Part 1, duplicated typescript. The latter includes major English correspon-dents and a further part will follow. The following letters have been noted:

U.S.A.2 f.80. 25 July 1912 Bryce to C. W. Elliot, President of Harvard, concerning machinery in Australia for averting or settling strikes.

U.S.A.4 f.226. 12 Dec. 1893 from the literary editor of *The Nation* concerning *inter alia* the Hawaiian annexation imbroglio. Further references to Hawaii occur in

Oxfordshire

U.S.A.5 f.108, 19 Nov. 1893 from the editor of *The Nation*; U.S.A.9 f.139, 31 Mar. 1898 from Roosevelt who feared the United States would let Hawaii slip through their fingers; U.S.A.11 f.290, 1921 from H. Bingham concerning the Japanese problem in Hawaii. There are also two letters in U.S.A.23 f.235, 6 Sept. and 1 Oct. 1921 from Bryce to Bingham.

U.S.A.13 f.7a. Apr. 1921 from R. H. Dana concerning the Yap Island situation.

U.S.A.19 f.106. Letter 1913 from H. L. Stimson asking for information on woman suffrage in Australia.

U.S.A.20 f.83. Letter 1921 from C. F. Thwing concerning a visit to Australia and New Zealand.

U.S.A.22. Letters from Bryce to Americans include f.70, 23 Aug. 1887 to Jesse Macy mentioning *inter alia* proposal for direct election of senators in Australia, and f.154, 29 Aug. 1908 to Roosevelt concerning the reception of the United States fleet in Australia.

U.S.A. Embassy papers include: U.S.A.27 f.169, 13 Nov. 1907 to Bryce requesting him to afford all possible help to an Australian bacteriologist visiting the United States to study cattle diseases; U.S.A.31 f.77, cable in cipher 3 Feb. 1911 concerning Bryce's remaining at Washington and arrangements for his leave to visit Australia; U.S.A.33 f.179, 26 Sept. 1912 from Arthur, Duke of Connaught concerning the attachment of Australia and New Zealand to the imperial cause.

Papers not yet calendared (May 1970) include three boxes (C4, 6-7) containing Australian and New Zealand correspondence chiefly concerning federation and politics.

C.4. Letters 1887-1921 from Australia and New Zealand include:
Sir Edmund Barton, London, three letters Apr.-[June?] 1900 concerning the meeting to discuss the Commonwealth Bill.

G. B. Barton, Sydney, 18 June 1891 sending a draft of a federal constitution.

E. G. Blackmore, South Australia and Melbourne, a number of letters 1899-1905 concerning Federation and Commonwealth politics.

Rev. Dr George Brown, Sydney, three letters 1916, 25 Jan. mentioning the death of Chief Justice Way and answering Bryce's questions on Samoa and New Guinea; New Zealand to give up Samoa and Australia to have former German New Guinea; 12 June forwarding chapters of Brunsdon Fletcher's book about New Britain and commenting on the popularity of W. M. Hughes in England; 27 Nov. 1916 commenting on the mining strike and on Chinese and Indians in the Pacific.

Alfred Deakin, nine letters 1887, 1890-1908 concerning relations with the United Kingdom and Federation.

Letters chiefly on Australian politics from: C. Brunsdon Fletcher 1916-21; H. B. Higgins 1915-16; W. H. Irvine 20 Mar. 1920; Sir William MacGregor 26 Aug. 1911 and 23 Nov. 1912; E. G. Mackinnon, Clerk of Parliaments, Melbourne, 23 June 1903 asking Bryce's opinion on a question concerning the Australian constitution; W. Harrison Moore, several letters 1902-20 including a letter 22 Oct. 1905 commenting on Higgins's answers to Bryce's questions about Australian politics; Sir Henry Parkes, four letters 1891-5; C. H. Pearson, a few letters 1890-4 concerning imperial federation; S. T. Way, five letters 1891-4 and a letter 8 Jan. 1914 saying he will not fail to write about local events and suggesting an honorary Oxford degree be conferred on Dr George Brown for his scientific work; T. W. Young, 19 Dec. 1916 concerning the referendum on conscription and the coal strike.

Letters from New Zealand include:
W. B. Matheson 9 Apr. 1916 concerning an 'International Court' and 21 Jan. 1917

answering Bryce's letter about small holdings in New Zealand; Matheson was a small farmer in a bush district.

J. W. Salmond, 24 Feb. 1920 containing general comments on New Zealand.

C.6 includes a letter 11 July 1912 from Sir Edgeworth David urging the need for science fellowships in Australian universities.

C.7 includes: letter 17 Jan. 1900 from E. G. Blackmore, Clerk of Parliaments, South Australia, protesting against Chamberlain asking for delegates to go to the United Kingdom to explain legal and constitutional questions connected with the Commonwealth Bill; letter 4 Apr. 1900 from Sir Edmund Barton concerning such delegates; also duplicated typescript and printed papers concerning the Bill.

CLARENDON DEPOSIT

The Clarendon papers were deposited in the Bodleian Library by the 6th Earl of Clarendon on condition that no extracts from them shall be printed without his or his heirs' written consent. The Bodleian Library description lists two deposits, Clarendon and Clarendon (Irish). The lists give covering dates and some description of the contents of each volume or box. Some papers are damaged or fragile but a microfilm is available. The Bodleian Library also holds a microfilm of the papers of the 4th Earl which are in the Public Record Office (F.O.361), q.v. Papers of the 4th Earl deposited at the Bodleian Library include:

c.1-104. Letters received as Foreign Secretary 1853-6

c.4 Cabinet. 4 Dec. 1853 Lord Aberdeen, Sandwich Islands question.

c.14 Cabinet. 25 Sept., 2 Oct., 6, 7 Dec. 1855 Sir James Graham, co-operation with France in the Pacific, unsatisfactory nature of the conduct of the United States with regard to the Sandwich Islands.

c.16 France. 24 Mar. 1854 Denham, H.M.S. *Herald*, with enclosures, on French occupation of New Caledonia, the chagrin of the Australian colonies, his visit to the New Hebrides, praise of the missionaries, the need for a resident British consul in Fiji, whose function should extend to the New Hebrides.

c.24-5 United States. c.24, 6 Feb. 1854 concerning Irish influence in New York; 28 Mar. 1854 Mitchel's proclamation urging the Irish in the United States and Canada to rise against Great Britain, copy of proclamation printed in *New York Herald* 23 Mar. enclosed; c.25, 4 Sept., 29 Oct., 6 Nov., 4 Dec. 1854 concerning United States intentions towards the Sandwich Islands.

c.28. South America section includes 9 Feb. 1855 concerning Sandwich Islands with reference to letter from Capt. Harris.

c.44 United States. 4 Sept. 1855 saying the Irish movement of little consequence; 9 Dec. 1855 reports a meeting of the Irish Confederate Party in New York.

c.48 Cabinet. 2 Jan. 1856 opining that a Russian naval force in the Pacific with the possibility of American co-operation would be formidable.

c.82 Under Secretary etc. 15 Feb. 1858 from Labouchere concerning the Cocos Islands, saying it is impossible to indemnify Mr Ross for loss of trade, and suggesting the Dutch be informed that Britain would withdraw if the Dutch allowed trade into Batavia and engaged not to occupy the islands.

c.125-49. Letter books 1853-8, 1865-6, 1868-9

Most of the volumes have indexes at the end or beginning and are paged or foliated. A check of indexed volumes from 1854 revealed:

c.129 ff.195-7. 11 July 1854 to the British ambassador in the United States concerning moves by the United States to annex the Sandwich Islands and the bad effect these would produce in Britain, and directing the ambassador to do his utmost to prevent annexation.

c.178-226. Registers of letters in and out 1853-6

Each volume relates to correspondence with a particular country. A check of c.189-94 France, c.224-5 United States revealed entries in c.224-5:

c.224. Letters concerning the escaped convict Mitchel, the proposed annexation of the Sandwich Islands by the United States, Meagher's intention to land a force on the coast of Ireland, annexation of the island of Natividad by United States citizens of the Sandwich Islands, rumoured descent on the Irish coast by American ships of war.

c.225. Reports on a line of mail steamers in the Pacific Ocean, proposed annexation by the United States of the Sandwich Islands, Mitchel.

c.474-510. Correspondence as Foreign Secretary 1868-70

c.499. Box of loose papers from members of Cabinet. Folder 7 includes papers 1869-70 on the navy in the Pacific. A few papers Apr. 1869 concern instructions relating to discretionary powers granted to naval officers. There is a copy of a letter 22 Mar. 1870 concerning the Duke of Edinburgh in Australia and the Pacific.

c.500. Box of loose papers from members of Cabinet. Folder 1, letters from Granville include letters 22, 27 Aug. 1869 concerning letters of recommendation being given to persons going to the colonies.

c.520-61. General Correspondence and Miscellaneous Papers 1820-70

The papers include matter relating to the 4th Earl's general political career and his Presidency of the Board of Trade 1846-7, also scattered papers more properly relevant to papers relating to his service in Spain 1833-9, his terms as Foreign Secretary, and Ireland. Correspondence, especially letters from Gladstone 1859, 1864, 1866-8 and from Lord John Russell 1840-70 may repay examination.

c.549. Miscellaneous printed Command, Foreign Office, etc. papers including an unpublished Command Paper on New Zealand affairs in 1848.

c.555. Miscellaneous papers, drafts, letters, memoranda including No.27 an undated memo by Clarendon on the Anglo-French dispute over Tahiti.

CLARENDON DEPOSIT (IRISH)

Papers relating to the term of the 4th Earl as Lord Lieutenant of Ireland 1847-53 with a box of memoranda 1868-70. There is a Provisional List, typescript, but no index has been prepared (1970). A check of boxes or volumes likely to contain papers relating to Irish rebels transported to Australia revealed the following:

Box 12. Letters 1848 from Sir George Grey, also information on Irish rebels and other papers. Some letters from Grey at the Home Office concern transfer of convicts to hulks, the advisability of granting tickets of leave to convicts arriving in Van Diemen's Land, the treatment of O'Brien, and the escape of Doheny. Other papers include letters from Irish judges concerning commutation of capital sentences to transportation for life; return 27 Nov. 1848 from Dublin Castle showing the number of prisoners under sentence of transportation for previous October Quarter Sessions with place of sentence.

Box 53. Letters 1848-51 from Col. Balfe and other agents reporting on the 'war leaders'.

Box 76. Papers relating to police, sedition, and other subjects, many dated 1848.

Box 77. Miscellaneous letters and papers, mainly 1851, relating to trials and other subjects connected with rebels including:

10 Oct. 1851 from J. D. Balfe, Comptroller General's Office, Hobart, V.D.L., giving details of the activities of the 'Irish State Prisoners' especially O'Brien, their suspicions of him personally and as the suspected author of the *Letters of Dion*, Hobart 1851, published in pamphlet form; also describing the effect on Van Diemen's

Land of the gold rushes on the mainland and the need for convict labour. There is a postscript deploring the sending of Irish girls to Van Diemen's Land if untrained for domestic work.

Letter Books

Vols.1-3, 1847-9 include letters to Grey concerning unrest, Balfe's valuable services, trials of O'Brien, Meagher, and Mitchel.

Vol.4 includes many letters 1849 to Grey concerning the rebels and a few letters about the overcrowding of Irish gaols, the cessation of transportation, the need to give tickets of leave and even liberate prisoners of fairly good character.

ff.18-78. Letters 6 May to 9 July, scattered among these pages, concern the necessity of deciding what to do with the convicted rebels in view of agitation in favour of their release, difficulties connected with their transportation, the advisability of informing the Governor of Van Diemen's Land of the need for vigilance, and the possibility of Duffy's causing trouble as he 'understands the theory of agitation'.

ff.96-7. 22 July to the Lord Mayor of London concerning purchase of Irish land by the Corporation of London, defends Irish labourers and states that they adapted themselves in the colonies more readily than the English and Scots.

Vol.5 includes ff.33-4 letter 17 Nov. 1849 to Sir John Cam Hobhouse concerning the behaviour of Mr Jeffcott who resigned as Judge and left the colony of Port Phillip because of a doubt of the validity of his commission, but acted most honourably and was universally regretted in the colony; letter 30 Apr. 1850 to Grey concerning the activities of O'Donohue and the need for vigilance with regard to both O'Donohue and Mitchel.

CLOUGH PAPERS

MSS. Eng.lett. c.189-90, d.175-9, e.74-84 include correspondence of Clough with the Rev. J. P. Gell and with T. Arnold, the younger. Some of this correspondence relates to Gell's term in Van Diemen's Land and to Arnold's life in New Zealand and Van Diemen's Land.

The Correspondence of Arthur Hugh Clough, ed. by F. L. Mulhauser, Oxford 1957, 2 vols., includes App.III, Vol.2, pp.622-49, 'A Catalogue of all known letters'. Numerical references for letters in the Bodleian Library are to this Catalogue. Apart from a few quotations in footnotes, Mulhauser prints only one letter 24 Sept. to 22 Nov. 1849 from Arnold in New Zealand and otherwise omits all Clough's 'antipodistic' correspondence with Gell and Arnold. For 'antipodistic' correspondence with Arnold see *The New Zealand Letters of Thomas Arnold, the Younger, with Further Letters from Van Diemen's Land and Letters of Arthur Hugh Clough 1847-51*, ed. J. Bertram, Auckland 1966.

MSS. Eng.lett. c.189, 1829-40.

Mulhauser 1-107. Letters from Clough to Gell, Nos.90, 94, 3, 23 Oct. 1839 are farewell letters. Letters from Gell to Clough, Nos.79, 83, 89, 91, May-Oct. 1839 concern his preparations for departure for Van Diemen's Land, No.99, 3 Jan. 1840 his experiences during the voyage, and No.104, 9 Sept. 1840 from Hobart, his impressions of the colony.

MSS. Eng.lett. d.175, 1841-5, Mulhauser 108-217. Letters from Gell, Nos.111, 114, 15, 28 Feb. 1841, concern his visit to Adelaide to see his brother Arthur, an excursion hunting kangaroos, and his impressions of the Governor; Nos.122, 129, 139, 143, 150, 152, 173, 187, Aug. 1841 to Aug. 1845 concern his life in Van Diemen's Land, the conditions for clergymen, Sir John Franklin's troubles with his Colonial Secretary, Gell's difficulties in getting a college established, his low opinion of Sir John Eardley Wilmot, and the evils of the convict system.

Oxfordshire

MSS. Eng.lett. c.190, 1846-8, Mulhauser 218-326. Letter from Gell No.219, 10 Feb. 1846 condemning transportation.

MSS. Eng.lett. d.176, 1849-50, Mulhauser 327-413, include two letters from Gell lately returned from Van Diemen's Land, No.341, 9 Feb. 1849 and No.356, 8 Mar. 1849.

MSS. Eng.lett. d.177, 1851-3, Mulhauser 415-723, include Nos.421-5, 429-30, 433, 551, Clough's correspondence Nov. 1851 to Jan. 1852 with friends in England and letters to the 'Sydney Committee' concerning his application for the classical professorship at the University of Sydney. There is a brief reference to the 'Sydney Project', 1851, in MSS. Eng.lett. e.81, No.681, letter 29 Apr. 1853 from Clough to his future wife. The reference occurs in a chronology of his life enclosed in the letter.

GILPIN PAPERS

The papers and correspondence of Rev. William Gilpin.

MSS. Eng.misc. c.389-90. 2 vols. of letters to Gilpin arranged alphabetically by writer.

MSS. Eng.misc. c.389, ff.252-6 two letters from Rev. Richard Johnson; ff.252-4, 5 Nov. 1798, Sydney, N.S.W., mentions assistance from the Governor, the burning of the church by some who resented the Governor's orders about Sunday observance, the laying of foundations for a new church and beginning a church in Parramatta, plans for schools, and the state of the colony; ff.255-6, 15 Jan. 1802, London, concerns his memorial about his 'services & sufferings in New S. Wales' and his hopes of provision being made for him in the Church.

MARVIN PAPERS

MSS. Eng.lett. c.257 and various other numbers, list at MSS. Eng.lett. c.257. The papers of Francis Sydney Marvin, educationalist and historian, mainly letters to Marvin and a certain number to his wife. There is a handlist arranged in chronological order, giving addresses of writers. Writers include Frank B. Turner, Sydney, N.S.W., 1885-91 and John Sutherland, Vic., 1913.

MILNER PAPERS

Papers of Sir Alfred Milner, Viscount Milner, typescript list.

Vol.171. Papers relating to Australasia 1907-23, including Milner's correspondence 1919-21 as Secretary of State for the Colonies.

MONK BRETTON DEPOSIT

The papers are those of three generations of the Dodson family including papers of John William Dodson, 2nd Baron Monk Bretton.

Box 84. Miscellaneous Correspondence 1893-1930 includes letters relating to Monk Bretton's trip to Australia, 1904.

Box 86. Miscellaneous Colonial Office Papers 1895-1902 include letters about raising troops in Australia.

Box 98. Papers 1895-1904 relating to Australia, New Zealand, the Pacific, and the Far East include papers on Australian Federation, pamphlets, essays in Monk Bretton's hand on Australia, Australian trade, and Western Australia; also Colonial Office printed papers on the proposed incorporation of Fiji and New Zealand 1902 and labour traffic in the New Hebrides 1902.

Box 102. Printed papers 1901-2 relating to the colonies including papers on salaries of Australian governors and on the relationship of crown agents with various colonies.

Box 104. Printed papers relating to the Colonial Conference 1902.

Box 105. Papers 1902-8 relating to tariff reform.

PAPERS OF JOHN PALMER

MSS. Eng.lett. c.67-127. A series of out-letter books 1808-35 recording letters written by John Palmer from Calcutta, some volumes missing and others damaged by water or difficult to read. Nearly every volume has an index of addressees. Letters listed below were found chiefly by consulting these indexes. It is possible that a page by page search might reveal other letters of Australian interest.

c.83 pp.36-40. 1 Aug. 1813 to James Bell, Sydney, referring to his failure to manage the cargo of the *Frederick* or Blaxcell's debt and to his bad behaviour at the Derwent.

pp.305-6. 22 Jan. 1814 to P. Puget, Madras, referring to the arrival of the company's ship *Eliza* from Port Jackson and the Derwent.

c.84 pp.75-6. 15 Apr. 1814 to Isaac Golledge stating Palmer's willingness to inspect Mr McArthur's accounts with the estate of I. Golledge's father and to receive Mr Riley's assistance in the investigation.

pp.152-4, 201-3, 490-4. 5, 21 May, 6 Sept. 1814 to Gov. Macquarie saying that excellent shawls for Mrs Macquarie were being sent in the *Betsy*, and discussing the export of grain and spirits to New South Wales, wheat, sugars, and rum having been sent on the *General Browne*. Letter 6 Sept. 1814 thanking Macquarie for protecting persons introduced by Palmer, and referring *inter alia* to Palmer's fears that he would lose all his stake in New South Wales owing to the misconduct of his agents.

pp.495-501. 7 Sept. 1814 to P. Maitland, London, sketching *inter alia* the state of things in New South Wales and at the Derwent whence he had received letters, mentioning that J. R. O'Connor, just arrived at Sydney, confirmed the drunkenness and dishonesty of Bell.

c.85 pp.203-5. 19 Feb. 1817 to Col. Molle, Sydney, saying that he had ceased to expect anything from the Derwent or from William Collins's concerns elsewhere, that he thought well of Brown as a merchant and as a man, and rejoiced in the Governor's triumph over opposition.

pp.205-6. 19 Feb. 1817 to J. R. O'Connor, Sydney, referring to Lieut. Hyde's venture and trusting O'Connor would be returning soon to close the affairs of his New South Wales agency.

p.212. 23 Feb. 1817 to Gov. Macquarie presenting Capt. Faithfull.

c.87 p.164. 10 Oct. 1818 to Edward Riley, Sydney, concerning Howe's account with Bell, Riley's investigations about Bell agreed with O'Connor's previous statement.

pp.235-7. 22 Nov. 1818 to Molle, Madras, concerning his affairs.

c.89 pp.209-10. 12 Mar. 1820 to Gov. Macquarie presenting his friends Lieut. Irvine and Mr Harington.

c.90 pp.52-61. 21 May 1820 to Henry Trail, England, concerning *inter alia* the possibility of Bethune's connecting himself at Sydney with Jones and Riley and Palmer's refusal to provide capital; the likelihood that his protégé, Harington would be disappointed; Palmer's avoidance of all marine engagements of which the issue was not manifest.

pp.122-3. 10 June 1820 to T. Harington, Sydney, saying that Mr Riley would have told him of his proposition and that Harington's good sense would understand Palmer's negative.

pp.136-8. 14 June 1820 to Bethune, Sydney, hoping he was employed by Riley, Palmer being unlikely to send a consignment.

pp.239-47. 18 July 1820 to Maitland mentioning that New South Wales was overstocked and the Company's supplies thither were suspended.

c.100 p.202. 7 Feb. 1824 to Edward Riley, Sydney, asking him to deliver an enclosed letter to Capt. Walker and to exert himself to help Palmer in the cases of Walker, Murray, Burton, Collins, and others; stating that, except for dealings with Riley and Reid of Hobart, Palmer's concerns in the colony had been disastrous.

.110 pp.34-7. 16 May 1829 to Richard Jones, Sydney, wishing to interest him in the concerns of the *Navarino* and her large investment.

pp.291-2. 4 Aug. 1829 to J. Brown, Sydney, wishing him success 'altho' I doubt you have chosen the fairest Field for it'.

c.113 pp.341-4. 15 Mar. 1830 to Capt. G. Vine, Sydney, acknowledging his letters from the *Navarino* including letter from Vine and Goodsir concerning Rogers's will; also describing the failure of Palmer & Co. pp.399, 429, 432-3, 585. 25, 29 Mar., 22 Apr. 1830 to various persons including J. T. Goodsir and George Vine concerning the estate of Capt. J. Rogers.

c.115 p.75. 9 July 1830 to Capt. C. Swanston regretting injuries to Swanston owing to the failure of Palmer & Co. Further letters to Swanston pp.77, 99, 10, 16 July 1830.

pp.94-5. 13 July 1830 to Richard Jones, Sydney, concerning the failure of Palmer & Co. and presuming that his assignee would furnish Jones with power to settle matters affecting persons in New South Wales.

c.117 pp.67-8. 12 Apr. 1831 to Richard Jones, Sydney, concerning dividends on shares in Provident Society for Edward Riley's children; apparently Mr Walker had been aware of these subscriptions in 1826 but had forgotten to furnish requisite proof of identity.

MSS. Eng.lett. c.105-7. Chiefly business letters addressed to John Palmer but including some out-letters, private letters, and biographical material.

MSS. Eng.hist. c.301-2. Account books 1825-7.

MSS. PEARSON

Letters to Charles Henry Pearson, historian and Minister of Education in Victoria, Australia, MSS. Eng.lett., MSS. Eng.misc. may repay examination. They are listed by names of correspondents among lists of Collections. Letters connected with the Australian part of his career are in the State Library of Victoria, Melbourne. See J. Tregenza, *Professor of Democracy, the Life of Charles Henry Pearson, 1830-1894, Oxford Don and Australian Radical*, Melbourne 1968.

MSS. WILBERFORCE

The Wilberforce manuscripts mainly consist of the papers of Samuel Wilberforce but include a small quantity of the papers of William Wilberforce. A list with index was completed ready for typing early in 1970.

c.7-18. Correspondence 1822-73 of Samuel Wilberforce arranged chronologically. This collection consists of small groups of letters and includes letters from Bishop G. A. Selwyn in c.10-11; letter from Lady Jane Franklin in c.12; letters from Queen Emma of Hawaii in c.13, 15.

c.19. Letters c.1853-73 to Samuel Wilberforce concerning the church overseas. Letters relating to the church in Australia and New Zealand are at ff.181-263 and include letters from Hobhouse, Bishop of Nelson; Nixon, Bishop of Tasmania; Patteson, Missionary Bishop of Melanesia; Perry, Bishop of Melbourne; G. A. Selwyn, Bishop of New Zealand; Rev. Josiah Spencer, Missionary Priest of the Diocese of Grafton. At ff.66-7 there is a copy of a letter 12 July 1865 from Baroness Burdett-Coutts to the Archbishop of Canterbury concerning her guarantee to endow the bishoprics of Adelaide, S.A., and Cape Town.

c.20. Letters to Samuel Wilberforce concerning the church in Europe include: ff.12-52. Letters c.1860-70 relating to Honolulu, among which are letters from Queen Emma; Manley Hopkins, Hawaiian Consul General; Staley, Missionary Bishop of Honolulu.

d.13-17. Volumes of correspondence of William Wilberforce labelled 'Autographs'.

d.14 ff.30-2. 20 Sept. 1808 Rev. S. Marsden stating that he has completed the number of clergymen required for New South Wales and reporting news of the arrest of Gov. Bligh.

d.14 ff.36-9. 12 Mar. 1817 Rev. S. Marsden, Parramatta, giving news of the abandonment of the mission to Tahiti and the inauguration of the mission to New Zealand.

d.17 ff.318-20. 6 Feb. 1820 Rev. S. Marsden, Parramatta.

d.46 ff.1-68. Letters 1835-63 from Sir James Stephen to Samuel Wilberforce.

ff.39-40. 12 Nov. 1839 states that New Zealand was 'a foreign country of which we have recognised the independence', the government being unable to have anything to do with the New Zealand Company.

ff.53-6. 4 Mar. 1846 refers to difficulties of retaining in England prisoners sentenced to transportation.

ff.57-8. 27 Aug. 1846 concerns Joshua Hill, master of a merchant ship, who was removed from Pitcairn by Edward Russell.

ff.59-68. 23, 25, 30 Aug. 1853 concern colonial bishoprics.

MISCELLANEOUS MANUSCRIPTS

MSS. Eng.lett. e.90 f.41. Letter 15 June 1845 G. A. Selwyn, Auckland, concerning the church and general conditions in New Zealand.

MSS. Eng.lett. e.91 f.84. Letter 14 July 1879 H. J. C. Harper, Bishop of Christchurch, to I. G. Swayne thanking him for a contribution to the cathedral fund and commenting on the wages of skilled masons.

Deposit approved 1970. Courtney Mann Papers. See *The Mann Family*, compiled by H. M. Thorold and V. M. Mann, privately printed, 1950. The papers include letters 1889-1909* from Frederick Gother Mann, working as a surveyor in Western Australia. The letters comment on social and economic conditions.

RHODES HOUSE
Oxford

Rhodes House Library, part of the Bodleian Library, may be used by persons admitted there and by others provided with adequate recommendation. Applications should be addressed to the Superintendent. The Library's field includes the British colonies and Commonwealth, except India, Pakistan, and Burma. Since the inception in 1963 of the Oxford Colonial Records Project, deposits of manuscripts have greatly increased. For a published list of manuscripts including those relevant to this survey see L. B. Frewer, *Manuscript Collections (excluding Africana) in Rhodes House Library, Oxford*, 1970. Duplicated typescripts 'Accessions of Note' are compiled three times a year for meetings of the Library Committee and are available for distribution to institutions. A card catalogue of manuscripts is arranged by areas including Africa, America, Australia, British Empire, Pacific Islands, cards under each area being filed alphabetically by authors' names. For some collections, inventories and sometimes card indexes are compiled, e.g. the typescript description of Anti-Slavery Society and Aborigines Protection Society Papers and the card indexes to the Anti-Slavery Society's Secretaries' letters. Call numbers must always include the name of the group of manuscripts to which a manuscript belongs, e.g. MSS. Nathan 420-6, MSS. Africa t.7, MSS. Australia r.1.

MSS. NATHAN

The papers of Sir Matthew Nathan 1862-1938 are housed partly in the Bodleian Library. Relevant papers, MSS. Nathan 231-656, are at Rhodes House and include the following papers:

Oxfordshire

420-6. Pacific Cable Board 1910-15.

494-5. Oversea Settlement Committee 1919-20.

496-584. Sir Matthew Nathan's term as Governor of Queensland 1920-5.

585-7. Committee on Geophysical Surveying.

632-44. Civil Research Committee and Great Barrier Reef Expedition 1925-38.

648-56. Irrigation Research Committee 1928-30. MS. Nathan 652 contains replies from Australia, New Zealand, Fiji, and Gilbert and Ellice Islands to questionnaire.

MSS. AFRICA

t.7. Bourke, Sir Richard. Correspondence, letter books relating to his administration of the Cape of Good Hope, 31 vols. and summary of contents. Letters from Bourke include 31 Jan. 1836 from Parramatta, N.S.W., concerning Cape affairs and 4 Aug. 1845 to Spring Rice concerning Deas Thomson. Letters to Bourke include 3 Jan. 1832 presenting an address from the principal merchants of Cape Town congratulating Bourke on his appointment to New South Wales and asking him to promote the importation of Cape wines and spirits.

MSS. AUSTRALIA

r.1. Cutlack, A. J. 'Four years in Queensland and New South Wales', 1875, description of Brisbane, reminiscences of life on cotton and sugar plantations, on sheep stations, and as a steward on coastal steamers.

r.2. Hunt, Ebenezer. Diary 1852-3 of a voyage to Melbourne, journey to the gold diggings, and life there.

s.1. Phillips, J. R. Letter book 1850-5 containing correspondence with the Colonial Secretary of Western Australia. Phillips was Guardian of Aborigines.

s.2. Guard-book of miscellaneous papers containing: letter 9 May 1800 P. G. King to the Earl of Mornington concerning his arrival in Sydney and the import of spirits into the colony, photostat; letter 1839 T. P. Pratt, Bath, to Rev. W. Buckland containing advice on setting up as a squatter; 'Foreign & colonial stations of the British army', account c.1840 of Van Diemen's Land, signed St Hubert, with manuscript note that the account was offered to the 'United Service Magazine'; letter 25 Feb. 1831 J. P. Webber, Patterson's River, concerning the employment of convict labour, typescript copy; letter 1869-70 from J. H. Parrington, an emigrant from London to Brisbane, typescript copy.

s.3. O'Byrne, G. D. Reminiscences of three voyages to Australia and sixteen years' experience as a goldminer in Victoria; with 'The gold fields of Victoria, 1851' and 'The Stowaway', 3 pts. in 1 vol. 1889-91, typescript.

s.4-9 Sturt Papers
See Mrs N. G. Sturt, *Life of Charles Sturt*, London 1899.
Selections from s.4 vol.1, s.5 fol. vol. and s.6-9 have been microfilmed for the Australian Joint Copying Project.
s.4. Journals, letters and papers, chiefly 1828-46, connected with his expeditions of discovery in Australia, his overland journey to Adelaide in 1838, and his life in Australia, 2 vols. fol. and 8vo. The fol. vol. includes a pocket containing Sturt's manuscript charts of the 'great bend' of the Murray River, showing the course of the expedition 25 Jan. to 8 Feb. 1830; also a notebook entitled 'Flora of Norfolk Island' with manuscript inscription 'From Allan Cunningham to Charles Sturt on Norfolk Island in which they accidentally met in 1830'. The 8vo volume contains Sturt's journal 1844-5 written for his wife during his Central Australian expedition.
s.5. Correspondence and papers of the Sturt family chiefly of Charles Sturt, 1 fol.

vol., 1 notebook, and 4 boxes. The fol. vol. contains Charles Sturt's correspondence and papers 1841-69 including papers and correspondence 1855-8 concerning A. C. Gregory's North Australian Expedition. The notebook labelled s.5.b, contains miscellaneous questions and notes, some relating to Charles Sturt, and the boxes, labelled s.5.a, c-e, contain Sturt family letters, sketches, and photographs, letters 1895-1904 to Mrs N. G. Sturt, miscellaneous maps.

s.6. Maps including 'Map of the Country explored by the Central Australian Expedition', manuscript.

s.7. Notebook of Mrs N. G. Sturt containing transcripts of papers received by her after completion of her *Life of Charles Sturt*.

s.8. Printed items in the possession of Charles Sturt.

s.9. Calendar of Sturt papers, typescript.

MSS. BRITISH EMPIRE

s.16-24. British and Foreign Anti-Slavery Society and Aborigines Protection Society Papers

Papers to 1941 were acquired in 1951 and in 1961 the Rhodes Trustees made a further grant to the Society to ensure that papers to the end of the twentieth century should be handed over at ten year intervals. The collection is arranged in nine sections lettered A-J: A engraving plates, B photographs of African subjects, C in-letters to both Societies to c.1909, D later twentieth century correspondence, E minute books, F receipt files, G nineteenth and twentieth century correspondence and papers arranged by area called 'Territorial Section', H records relating to Africans in Europe, J cuttings, printed papers, and photographs. There is a description and guide to sections, duplicated typescript. A copy, filed at N.R.A. as Report 1095, contains also early N.R.A. notes on a part of the collection.

s.18. C1-166. In-letters of the two Societies to c.1909. Three card indexes have been made: to names of writers giving covering dates, places from which letters were written, volume and letter numbers; to areas from which letters were written with references to names of writers, called 'Territorial Index'; to names of officers and committee members. By tracing letters from the 'Territorial Index' to the index of writers and relevant volumes over 500 letters mostly 1860s to 1880s may be found relating to Australasia and the Pacific, written by missionaries, officials, and private persons, dealing chiefly with labour recruiting in Pacific Islands, the Maori land question, and Australian Aborigines.

s.19. D1-7. Twentieth century correspondence of the two Societies since 1909, some volumes or files having indexes. A search of selected volumes and files revealed correspondence relating to Pacific Islands and Australian Aborigines, for example: D6/1. Letters 1913 concerning taxation of natives of the Gilbert and Ellice Islands; 1911-16 concerning illicit recruiting in the New Hebrides.

D6/2. Letters 1916-26 concerning Pacific Islands.

D6/4-5. Letters 1934-9 concerning Australian Aborigines, some letters in D6/5 referring to a proposed Jewish settlement on Melville Island.

D7/13. Correspondence 1939-43 concerning Aborigines in Western Australia, compulsory military service in Tonga, Vestey Bros. and Melville Island, Australian Aborigines.

s.20. E1-5. A mixed collection containing Anti-Slavery minute books 1823-1935, memorials and petitions 1843-55, account books 1846-1941, minute book 1902-9 of the Aborigines Protection Society, out-letters 1869-99 of the Anti-Slavery Society.

s.22. G1-517. Territorial Section.

G97-101, 374-99. 'Australasia' including New Guinea and Pacific Islands. There are many letters and papers on Australian Aborigines, New Zealand, New Guinea,

Fiji, and the New Hebrides. G97-9, *c.*1843-*c.*1890 includes papers on Maconochie's plans and the Van Diemen's Land assignment system; G100-1 papers 1868-*c.*1890 relate to Pacific Islands, New Guinea, and Polynesian labour in Queensland; G374-99 papers 1911-37 include G391 papers 1908-14 on the Gilbert Islands and the Pacific Phosphates Company.

G360. Papers 1937-41 Cocos Islands.

The following sections of G may also repay examination:

G400-4, 1919-24 German mandated territories; G425, 1917-18 Empire resources; G434-42, 1912-44 international conferences concerning colonies; G444-81, 1922-35 League of Nations, slavery and labour; G510, 1930-45 mandatory system of trusteeship; G511, 1941-51 British colonial policy; G514-16 League of Nations and United Nations Organisation papers on labour and slavery.

s.100-21. Constitution, minutes of conferences, correspondence and papers 1947-61 of the Colonial Civil Servants Association.

s.123-206. Harlow, Vincent Todd. Transcripts used in his *Founding of the Second British Empire, 1763-1793*, London 1952-64, 2 vols.

s.240-75. Evans, Sir Geoffrey. Diaries 1906, 1909-63. Evans advised the Queensland government on cotton culture in the 1920s and visited Fiji and New Guinea.

s.285 C. W. W. Greenidge Papers

Box 7/3. An envelope marked 'Drummond Shiels' Australian papers' contains material on Australian Aborigines.

s.288. Grantham, Sir Alexander William G. H. Recollections including some 1945-7 as Governor of Fiji and High Commissioner for the Western Pacific, tape recording and typescript.

s.292. Marchant, Col. W. S. Papers including some 1942-3 relating to his service in the British Solomon Islands.

s.309. Two papers, one of which is: Solf, Wilhelm H., 'Samoa, the people, the missions and the Europeans', copy of a report 1907 prepared for the Imperial Colonial Office, Berlin, typescript.

s.314-18. Fell, T. E. Letters including letters and papers relating to service in Fiji 1920-2 and two cruises off Fiji 1921-4.

s.327-31. Seton, M. E., Lady. Personal household account books 1938-60, including account book in Fiji.

s.332 Creech Jones Papers

A duplicated typescript list gives a description of each paper preceded by a list of titles of files in each box. An index of persons, places, and subjects will be prepared. The papers consist of correspondence, printed papers, etc., including many connected with Creech Jones's interest in colonial policy and administration, the development of dependent peoples, his work as a member of the Colonial Office Advisory Committee on Education in the Colonies, and that as Chairman of the Fabian Colonial Bureau.

Box 27. Papers 1934-9 relating to Pacific territories. File 1, papers 1938 relating to Australia and to trade between Australia and the United Kingdom. File 3, papers relating to Fiji including correspondence July 1937 to Mar. 1938 between Henry Polak, Hon. Secretary and Treasurer of the Indian Overseas Association and Creech Jones about a clash in the Fijian Legislative Assembly between the Governor and Indian elected members. File 4, papers 1937-9 on Pacific Islands relating to phosphates exploitation, guano in the Gilbert and Ellice Islands and Pitcairn.

Boxes 34-43. Papers relating to Creech Jones's work for the Colonial Office Advisory Committee on Education in the Colonies. Box 41, file 2, papers 1938-9 on Fiji;

file 3, one item only, Annual Report 1937-8 of the Director of Education, Gilbert and Ellice Islands.

s.346. Hart-Davis, V. Personal reminiscences including some 1909-10 in Fiji, type-script.

s.352. Paton, W. B. Collection of cuttings and papers 1883-9 including invitations to functions in Australia during his visit in 1888.

s.357. Hailey, Malcolm, 1st Baron. Great Britain and her dependencies, c.1941, typescript. Addresses and correspondence of the 1st Baron Hailey at s.334-40, 342-3 may be worth examination.

s.358. Melville, E. Memo on the organisation and functions of the British Colonies Supply Mission being an extract from letter 16 Dec. 1943 to the Colonial Office, typescript. The memo gives some account of Commonwealth Missions in the United States including missions from Australia and New Zealand.

s.359. Cowell, H. R. Colonial history of the war 1939-45, economic section, type-script. Personal diary of the war, reports on economic affairs in the colonies, letters 1939-46.

s.365 Papers of the Fabian Colonial Bureau

A brief provisional typescript has been prepared, 1969. The Bureau was formed in October 1940 as an organisation independent of the Fabian Society. In 1958 its title was changed to Fabian Commonwealth Bureau and in 1962 the Fabian International Bureau and the Commonwealth Bureau merged to become the Commonwealth and Overseas Bureau. As well as boxes listed below, boxes 3-68 containing correspondence and papers on colonial policy, economics, social and educational development and boxes 170-80, Mauritius, other territories, French and Dutch colonies, may repay examination.

Boxes 1-2. Files 1929-43 of Arthur Creech Jones include a file on New Zealand in Box 1 and a number of files in Box 2 relating to colonial policy and mandates.
Box 149. File 1, 1952-61 relates to the Colombo Plan.
Box 167-8. Files 1939-60 relating to the South Pacific including files on Australian Aborigines; correspondence concerning Papua-New Guinea including letters from C. Belshaw; correspondence with H. E. Maude, Officer for Social Development, South Pacific Commission, chiefly on the co-operative movement; correspondence about Fiji.
Box 169. Papers 1940-60 include correspondence 1846-51 on the Antarctic.
Box 185. Cuttings 1963-5 sorted under headings including 'West Pacific'.

s.368. Milverton, Arthur Frederick, 1st Baron. Recollections 1969 of a colonial administrator 1908-47 including his term in Fiji and the Western Pacific 1936-8, tape recording and transcript.

MSS. INDIAN OCEAN

s.10-19. Dowbiggin Papers. The papers of Sir Herbert Layard Dowbiggin include s.12, diary 1937 of his tour Madras to London via the Pacific during which he visited Australia, New Zealand, and Pacific Islands, making notes on the police forces.

MSS. NEW ZEALAND

r.1. Burn, David. Seven letters 1849-63 from Auckland regarding affairs in New Zealand.

s.1. Guard-book of miscellaneous papers relating to New Zealand including government grant to George de Blaquiere of a parcel of land in Alexander East, Auckland, 1866; letter 1844 from Edward Wakefield to James Backhouse regarding missionaries and the massacre of settlers by the Raupero tribe; memo 17 July 1856 by Herman

Oxfordshire

Merivale on local government with letter 11 Feb. 1856 from H. Labouchere concerning proposed alterations in the constitution.

MSS. PACIFIC

r.1. Harrison, S. G. Diary 1924 of a journey from Fanning Island to recruit labour from the Gilbert and Ellice Islands, with letter 12 June 1966 giving some comment on this journey.

r.3. Leake, H. M. Land tenure and sugar estates in Fiji, c.1938, extracts, typescript. See also his *Land Tenure and Agricultural Production in the Tropics*, Cambridge 1927.

r.4. Fox-Strangways, V. Diary Jan.-Feb. 1942, last days of the defence force, Solomon Islands.

s.2-33. Codrington Papers. Papers of the Rev. R. H. Codrington, 'Apostle of the Pacific', include s.2 diaries; s.4 letters 1867-87 from Auckland, Norfolk Island, Mota; s.5-6 letters from natives in native languages; s.18 letters 1866-1925; s.22 material for a biography. Other papers, some printed, relate to the Melanesian Mission and there are also sermons, lectures, etc.

s.35. Armstrong, A. L. Minute n.d. to the Colonial Secretary, Fiji, regarding American forces in Tonga during World War II, typescript copy and photographs. The author was Agent and Consul in Tonga.

s.36. Boys Smith, H. G. 'Pacific Marine, an autobiographical story 1946-9', typescript with photographs of ships. The author was appointed by the Colonial Office in 1946 to raise a fleet of small ships for island communication for the Western Pacific High Commission.

s.37-9. Hopkins, G. H. E. Diary and correspondence 1923-5 connected with government service in Samoa, typescript with photographs.

s.40. Ashley, F. N. British Solomon Islands Protectorate, history, administration, native manners and customs, with associated papers and photographs 1931-8 accumulated as Resident Commissioner.

s.41. Walker, V. L. Letters 1878-86 to his mother from Australia and New Caledonia, also one letter 1887 H. Walker to his sister, xerox and original letters. V. L. Walker's letters refer to his brother Howard's business in the labour trade and its failure in 1886; letter 1887 from H. Walker, Mallicolo, mentions the murder of V. L. Walker at Pentecost Island.

s.43. Barrow, G. L. 'Outlying interlude, the Solomon Islands during World War II', typescript.

s.44. Barrow, G. L. 'The Condominium of the New Hebrides 1950', typescript.

s.45. Harper, S. W. 'Remembering Fiji, reminiscences 1886-1930', typescript.

s.57. Faddy, H. S. 'Introduction to my Fiji saga, three true Fiji stories', typescript.

s.61. Clemens, W. F. M. Diary 1942 (on loan) as District Officer, Guadalcanal, also fuller typescript copy with manuscript annotations Jan. 1941 to Dec. 1942 describing evacuation of the Solomon Islands and operations against the Japanese, with photographs.

s.68. Jack, H. W. 'Recommendations of the Committee appointed under the Birds, Game and Fish Protection Ordinance, Fiji, 1936'; 'Candlenuts', 1949, typescripts.

s.72. Chamberlain, G. D. Recommendations 1948, as Chief Secretary, for economy and improvement of the administration of the Western Pacific High Commission territories; notes on administrative developments 1950; notes and correspondence 1951 on proposed extensions of the QANTAS air service, typescripts.

s.73/1. Hill, J. A. C. Miscellaneous reports and memoranda as Administrative

Officer, Fiji, including: strike and arbitration at the Colonial Sugar Refining Company 1957; statement on disturbances 1959; diary Dec. 1957; development of local government 1957; duties and functions of Divisional Commissioners and District Officers 1963, typescripts.

s.73/2. McDougall, R. S. Fijian administration 1957, report to the Governor, typescript.

s.75. Grimble, Sir Arthur Francis. Investigation notes c.1920 on magic, poetry, and song making, Gilbert and Ellice Islands, typescript.

s.76. Kennedy, D. G. Marching rule in the British Solomon Islands Protectorate, a memo 1967 on the origin of the term, manuscript and typescript.

t.1. Protectorates in the South Pacific, the question of the Gilbert and Ellice Islands and the southern Solomons 1892-3, extracts from Colonial Office records.

UNCATALOGUED MSS. 1970

Bevington, E. R. 'The Things we do for England, if only England knew!', service 1930-50 in the Gilbert and Ellice Islands, Fiji and Brunei, typescript.

Cartland, B. C. Files of papers and correspondence 1947-54 on land in the Gilbert and Ellice Islands (on loan).

Firth, S. G. Guide to materials on the Pacific held at the Deutsches Zentralarchiv, Potsdam, 1970, typescript.

Hamilton, M. B. Reports and correspondence 1962-8, British Solomon Islands, dealing mainly with pensions and staff.

Kitto, K. Papers 1957-9, Department of Lands, British Solomon Islands.

CHRIST CHURCH
Oxford

SALISBURY PAPERS

The papers of the 3rd Marquess of Salisbury are on deposit in the Library. All inquiries should be addressed to the Librarian. Photographic reproduction has not been permitted to May 1970. The papers included a draft of Volume 5 of Lady Gwendolen Cecil's *Life of Robert, Marquis of Salisbury*, London 1921-32, 4 vols. Correspondence is arranged in classes lettered A-Z. A collection of draft letters by Salisbury, other than those in classes A, C, and D, is being built up from copies of drafts and notes scattered throughout the papers. There is a Guide and Calendar of Class A, 2 vols., duplicated typescript.

A Private Foreign Office Correspondence 1878-80, 1885-6, 1887-92, 1895-1900

A/8. Letters from France include 8/77, 8 Oct. 1879, 8/84, 88, 21 Nov., 5 Dec. 1879 containing references to the New Hebrides and other Pacific Islands.

A/9/33. 15 Feb. 1879 from Loftus, Berlin, expressing his delight at his appointment to New South Wales.

A/37/37. 8 Sept. 1885 from France mentioning the Carolines dispute.

A/43/32. 24 Nov. 1885 Salisbury to the Queen concerning appointments including Capt. Talbot to Tahiti.

A/44/5. 7 July 1885 Salisbury to Waddington in France concerning the Colonial Office proposal for definition of an area in the Pacific within which France and Britain would not create convict settlements.

A/44/17. 13 Jan. 1886 Salisbury to Malet in Berlin mentioning Samoa.

Oxfordshire

A/46/142. 27 Aug. 1891 Salisbury to the Queen mentioning Samoa.

A/56-60. Correspondence 1886-92 with representatives in France, see Lord Newton, *Lord Lyons, a Record of British Diplomacy*, London 1913, 2 vols. 56/1, 13, 15-17, 26-7, 41, 47, 54, 59-88 letters from France containing references to the New Hebrides and French foreign policy; 56/26-7 letters 16-18 Apr. 1887 on the policy of New South Wales and New Zealand regarding the New Hebrides and a proposal for a meeting in Paris between Australian delegates to the Colonial Conference, Lyons and French Ministers; 57/55, 16 Oct. 1888 from France, 20pp., on L. Pasteur's complaints against the New South Wales authorities (another reference to Pasteur occurs in 59/83, 25 Oct. 1888 to Paris); 58/4, 24 Jan. 1889 from France referring to alleged British annexations in the Tubuai Archipelago, France considering the Archipelago under her protection; 58/23, 19 Apr. 1889 from France mentioning Samoa; 59/5, 63, 70, 74, 83, 85, 116, letters 1887-91 to France concerning New Caledonia, some referring to escaped convicts, the New Hebrides, and Samoa; 60/41, 15 June 1889 from France refers to German-United States relations and Samoa.

A/61/31-2; 62/22, 24-5, 34, 37-40, 42-3, 49; 63/21-2; 64/1, 5, 51, 53, 102. Correspondence 1887-90 with representatives in Germany referring to Samoa.

A/77-8. Correspondence 1887-92 with representatives in the United States. 77, letters 1887-90 from the United States including 77/6-8, 23-4, 29, 52-3 concerning Samoa and 77/41, memo 10 Jan. 1890 by Pauncefote of action taken on various questions, Haiti, Hawaii, Merchant Shipping Convention; 78, letters 1891 from United States including: 78/15, mentioning Tonga, 78/16, concerning Tonga and the Rev. Shirley Baker, 78/19, referring to crimes at sea and sale of arms and spirits in the Western Pacific, 78/67 *re* desertion from British merchantmen, 78/68, draft by Pauncefote of Anglo-United States Treaty of recovery of deserters from merchantmen of either power while in the ports of the other, and referring to Liberia, Hawaii, Gilbert Islands, Canadian Fisheries, 78/75, 24 Jan. 1889 to United States mentioning Samoa and the Sackville incident, 78/87, 16 Nov. 1888 from United States, Sackville incident.

A/83-4. Correspondence 1895-1900 with the Queen. 83/129, 138 and 84/94, 105 refer to Samoa and the Anglo-German agreement; 83/163, 28 June 1900 concerns Australian Federation, Chamberlain's explanation of the term 'Commonwealth'; 84/95, 7 Feb. 1899 states *inter alia* that the adoption of Australian Federation is certain.

A/92. Correspondence 1895-1900 with the Colonial Office includes 92/52, 29 Sept. 1899 Salisbury to Chamberlain on a conversation with Hatzfeldt on Samoa, Tonga to be for Germany and 92/53, copy of memo 28 Sept. 1899 by Chamberlain on Samoa and terms of proposed bargain with Germany.

A/96. Private Secretary's memoranda 1895-1900. 96/61, 3 Sept. 1898 Balfour to Salisbury mentioning Samoa among other pending matters; 96/82, 8 Feb. 1899 H. White's annoyance at his failure to see Salisbury *re* Samoa.

A/98-102. Miscellaneous letters arranged alphabetically by correspondents. 99/30-2, 27 Dec. 1899 from A. Goldsborough concerning China and Samoa, missionary interests, with summary of draft reply endorsed by Salisbury; 99/63, 21 Dec. 1897 from Mrs E. M. Keays concerning native opposition in Hawaii to annexation by the United States and preference for annexation by Britain; 100/71, 12 Nov. 1899 from T. Fowler concerning the alleged forthcoming visit of the German Emperor to Oxford with minute by Bigge, 'Evidently the subterranean negotiations are not closed with the Samoan Question . . .'; 102/34, 23 Nov. 1897 from H. de R. Walker presenting a book on Australian democracy with minute by Bigge on Walker's past.

A/114-19. Correspondence 1896-1900 with representatives in France. 115/59, 6 July 1897 from France on the proposed visit to Paris by colonial premiers and undesirability of any attempt to promote Western Australian immigration interests, enclosure 115/60, 5 July 1897 from Chamberlain approving these interests, enclosure 115/61, 5 July 1897 Sir John Forrest to Chamberlain refusing to visit Paris.

A/120-2. Correspondence 1895-1900 with representatives in Germany. A number of letters deal with Anglo-German relations and colonial questions especially Samoa: 120/1, 121/24-5, letters from Germany, 122/55-6, 62, 64, 67-75, 77-80, 84, letters to Germany. 121/17, 3 Dec. 1898 from Germany reports *inter alia* rumour of proposed United States takeover in the Carolines; 122/81 n.d. is a list of 'Islands East and South East of Bougainville belonging to Germany in the Solomon Group' corrected by the Hydrographer.

A/139-40. Correspondence 1895-1900 with representatives in the United States. 140/15, 17 Mar. 1899 from United States, political bulletin discussing *inter alia* Samoa, 'open door' and 'spheres of influence'; 140/16, 29 May 1899 including anecdotes about Admiral Kautz; 140/22, 31 Oct. 1899 from Pauncefote concerning Samoa and the desirability of equal commercial treatment for Britain, the United States, and Germany.

B Cabinet and Other Official Papers

Almost all the papers, which include copies of bills, are printed. Copies exist in the Public Record Office in either printed or photographic form.

C Letter Books

C/1-4, private letter books relating to India; C/5-7, artificially created volumes made up of typescripts obtained by Lady Gwendolen Cecil from 'Secretary's notebook'. At the beginning of each volume is a list of letters. 7/393, 23 Dec. 1889 to Sir Henry Parkes pointing out the difficulties of establishing an Imperial Conference suggested by Parkes; 7/448, 13 Feb. 1892 to George Mackar, Bendigo, Vic., acknowledging a *History of Bendigo*, Melbourne 1891.

D Chiefly Copies of Letters from Salisbury

Twenty volumes containing for the most part typescript copies procured by Lady Gwendolen Cecil.

Volume III, D/16 letters 1852-82 to Rev. C. R. Conybeare. 16/1, 11 July 1852 off the Pacific coast of New Zealand, letter giving impressions of South Australia and Victoria, chiefly about the gold diggings, describing discontent in the colonies with the Colonial Office, the general violent opposition to transportation, the good conditions of convicts in Van Diemen's Land and stating that in his opinion bad convict administration had created the Australian League.

Volume VI, D/26 letters to Goschen. 26/8-10, 1, 8, 14 Oct. 1887 concern negotiations on the Suez Canal and New Hebrides.

Volume VIII, chiefly letters D/31, 1856-90 to the 4th Earl of Carnarvon. One letter 6 Nov. 1885 from Carnarvon has a postscript saying that Sir Samuel Wilson had asked Carnarvon to support his application for a peerage but he was unable to do so, Wilson being a successful Australian speculator.

Volume IX, D/32/1-126 are chiefly letters to Henry Holland, later Viscount Knutsford. 32/13, 14, 17-22, 27, 49 refer to the propositions and remonstrances of the Australian governments about the New Hebrides and negotiations at the Colonial Conference; 32/23, 18 July 1887 refers to the possible alteration of the Queen's title to include more distinctly the colonies; 32/29, 12 Nov. 1887 and 32/37-8,

12, 14 Jan. 1888 concern the New South Wales Divorce Bill; 32/33, 10 Dec. 1887 concerns the granting of responsible government to Western Australia; 32/34-5, 15 Dec. 1887 refer to suggestions that Germany take Samoa and England take Tonga; 32/40, 1 Feb. 1888 concerning *inter alia* Australian exhibits in Paris exhibition; 32/47, 25 Apr. 1888 concerning a peerage for Sir Arthur Gordon; 32/51, 20 June 1888 concerning Lord Carrington's telegram on Chinese immigration; 32/56, 12 Oct. 1888 refers *inter alia* to 'Savage Island' being a German sphere of influence; 32/57-8, 60, 20-26 Nov. 1888 concern the offer of the governship of Queensland to Sir H. Blake and objections thereto; 32/61 n.d. [Dec. 1888?] concerning a peerage for Sir Hercules Robinson; 32/64, 25 Jan. 1889 offers no objection to Knutsford's accepting the hospitality of the Agent General for Queensland; 32/104-5, 4, 30 Dec. 1891 concern the governorship of New Zealand and suggested candidates.

Volume XVI, D/74/1-43, letters 1851-81 to Mary Catherine Stanley, Countess of Derby, include 74/1-15 letters 1851-3 written during Lord Robert Cecil's voyage round the world, describing his impressions of Australia and New Zealand, especially the effects of gold discovery, the convict system, the Church of England, and affairs in New Zealand.

Volumes XVIII-XX, D/87 letters to Queen Victoria.

Volume XX, D/87/528, 29 Mar. 1889 reports conversations with Bismarck concerning Samoa and Zanzibar.

E-L Special Correspondence especially Class E Correspondence, Main Series

There is a card index to correspondents in classes E-H. Letters from the future 3rd Marquess about his voyage round the world in 1851-3, include the following:

Letters to the 2nd Marquess:
25 Sept. 1851, Cape Town, containing a brief mention of his voyage on the *Maidstone* and outlining his plan to go to Adelaide. Other letters from Cape Town are dated 16 Oct., 7 Nov., and 5 Dec. 1851.
10 Feb. 1852, Adelaide, commenting adversely on depression in the colony and on Gov. Young.
6 Apr. 1852, Melbourne, stating that travel was difficult because of the gold mania and that he had been to the goldfields and stayed a week.
19 Apr. 1852, Hobart, asking for money to be sent to Panama.
3 June 1852, Sydney, saying he had left Van Diemen's Land on 21 May after five weeks there, that he had a high opinion of the Governor, and that the Australian League consisted of a few fanatics.
16 July 1852, Auckland, saying he had arrived by the brig *Raven*, having found Sydney a disagreeable place with two plagues, the society and the mosquitoes.
2 Sept. 1852, Wellington, N.Z., where he was staying with Gov. Grey, describing New Zealand affairs.

Letters to Lady Blanche Balfour: 30 Sept. 1851, Cape Town; 9 July 1852, off Cape Maria van Diemen, giving impressions of South Australia, Victoria, and Van Diemen's Land.

To Lord Lothian, 1 June 1852, at sea between Hobart and Sydney, giving impressions of Melbourne and Van Diemen's Land.

To Lord Eustace Cecil, 12 July 1853, Hatfield, giving reminiscences of Canterbury, N.Z., and Sydney, N.S.W.

The following letters in Special Correspondence, addressed to Lord Salisbury, relate to Australasia and the Pacific; other correspondents in this section whose letters should repay examination are Viscount Cardwell, Sir Charles Dilke, and Sir Michael Hicks Beach.

Cavendish, Spencer Compton, 8th Duke of Devonshire. 8 Oct., 1, 4 Nov. 1899 reporting intrigues about Samoa.

Chamberlain, J. 16 Dec. 1895 mentioning the project of an exchange of territory with France and Germany including the abandonment in Britain's favour of Germany's claim to Samoa, 'The Australasian Colonies are very eager on this latter point'; 25 Nov. 1897 concerning appointments to Australian governorships and the possibility of giving Germany a free hand in Samoa in return for German New Guinea; 18 Sept. 1899 concerning bargaining with Germany and colonial indignation; 29 Sept. 1899 referring to the fate of Tonga; 22 Jan. 1900 concerning Australian Federation and the Queen's qualms about the title 'Commonwealth of Australia'.

Currie, Sir Philip. 29 Nov. 1899 stating there was no objection in the Foreign Office to Germany's having a preponderant influence in Samoa, Thurston's report being expected within a week and an official reply then being possible, the Colonial Office being against the proposal.

Fergusson, Sir James. 21 Mar., 1 Aug., 11, 24 Oct., 1 Nov. 1887, 17 May 1888 concerning the New Hebrides and Samoa, also 5 Oct. 1887 Salisbury to Fergusson on Consul Layard's reports from the New Hebrides.

Gathorne-Hardy, Gathorne, 1st Earl of Cranbrook. 24 Oct. 1887 requests advice on what he may say about the New Hebrides in a speech in Glasgow.

Gordon, Sir Arthur. 13 Nov. 1878 reporting a rumour that the German government intended to annex the Samoan group, 'the effect on Fiji would I fear be disastrous'; June, Aug. 1879 three letters concerning Tonga.

Goschen, G. J. 8 Oct. 1887 stating that 'Nothing can be more important than to settle the New Hebrides question'; 7 Oct. 1899 'from the strictly naval point of view we care little for the Samoan group'.

Heaton, Sir John Henniker. 24 Sept. 1884 asking Salisbury to rebut assertions in the Australian press that the Tory party is against Australian Federation; 26 Sept. 1884 remarking that Victoria 'though the youngest colony, has statesmen remarkable for impudence'.

Holland, Sir Henry. 23 Aug. 1887 enclosing two letters from Sir John Bates Thurston concerning Samoa.

Northcote, Sir Stafford Henry, 1st Earl of Iddesleigh. 20 Aug. 1886 asking if Cabinet should discuss the New Hebrides and other colonial disputes; 16 Dec. 1886, 7 Jan. 1887 concerning Samoa and Germany.

Parkes, Sir Henry. 2 Nov. 1889, 4 Feb. 1890 concerning the Imperial connection and the need for an Imperial Council.

Pauncefote, Sir Julian. 20 Dec. 1886, 7 Aug., 13 Sept. and three letters 1-7 Oct. 1887 concerning Samoa, the Suez Canal, and the New Hebrides, also five letters 30 Sept., 3, 5, 10, 16 Oct. 1887 concerning settlement of the New Hebrides crisis.

Quin, Windham Thomas Wyndham-, 4th Earl of Dunraven. 11 Apr. 1889 giving notice of questions in the Lords about the names of Commissioners to represent Britain at the Berlin Conference on Samoa.

Villiers, Victor Albert George Child-, 7th Earl of Jersey. 12 May 1891 forwarding copy of letter from an unnamed influential trader in Samoa, commenting on New South Wales opposition to the Federation Bill and enthusiasm in Victoria for the proposal; 11 Dec. 1892 informing Salisbury he intended to resign from the governorship of New South Wales, commenting on the electoral bill and on the prospects for Federation.

M-Z Miscellaneous Correspondence

The correspondents in these classes are of minor importance but some classes may possibly contain letters of interest to the field of this survey, e.g. M Political 1886-1903, Y Honours 1885-1902 arranged by ministries. There are name indexes on cards to Y 1885-6, 1887-92, 1895-1902.

MANCHESTER COLLEGE
Oxford

REV. W. SHEPHERD PAPERS

Vol.10, pp.9-15, contain papers and copies of papers concerning T. F. Palmer.*
p.9. Extract concerning the Life of Palmer by Mrs Ridyard, abridged from the *Monthly Magazine* 1804.
p.11. Copies of letters from T. F. Palmer: 23 Apr. 1794 from the *Surprize*; 16 Sept. 1795, 23 Apr., 16 Sept., 22 Nov. 1796 from New South Wales.
p.13. Letter 5 May 1796 from T. F. Palmer, New South Wales, to Jeremiah Joyce, enclosing a copy of the inscription for the tomb of J. Gerrald.
pp.14-15. Later papers concerning J. Gerrald.

NUFFIELD COLLEGE
Oxford

FABIAN SOCIETY RECORDS

The Society's official records including in-letters, miscellaneous manuscripts, minutes, reports, and publications. There is a brief typescript list called 'Catalogue I' and a more detailed typescript list called 'Catalogue II'. A second sequence of papers is listed in typescript. For a history of the Society see M. I. Cole, *The Story of Fabian Socialism*, London 1961, and E. R. Pease, *The History of the Fabian Society*, 3rd ed., London 1963. No full index to the papers has been prepared (May 1970).

A. Box Files, In-letters and Other Papers
    21 boxes.

A3-4. Letters 1891-1939 from Sidney Webb.
    The letters are filed in packets in chronological order. Box 3 includes: postcard 7 Aug. 1898, Auckland, N.Z., describing Auckland as 'charmingly English'; letter 16 Oct. 1898, Melbourne, 'Australia is more interesting than I thought but very backward . . . the England of 1850 plus a crude Individualistic Radicalism of moderate type', promising a report on Australia and referring to his American and New Zealand reports; letter 26 Dec. 1898 asking that the title of his lecture on 27 Jan. 1899 be 'Some Impressions of Australasia'.

A7. Lists of Members, printed with manuscript corrections. A check of one of the lists revealed only a few members in Australia and New Zealand.

A8. Local Societies includes a mutilated notebook listing Fabian Societies among which are: Melbourne, established Mar. 1895, Secretary J. Howlett Ross; New Zealand, established Jan. 1896, Secretary (Jan. 1898) O'Bryen Hoare; Dunedin, Secretary Mr Bastings, *Otago Daily Times*, a printed leaflet with this entry being entitled 'Dunedin Fabian Society 1897' and giving the names of office bearers and committee. A8 also includes packets of miscellaneous manuscript, typescript, and printed documents, some relating to the activities of New Zealand and South Australian Branches.

A21. Lectures and Conferences.

The contents are advertisements for meetings and lectures, tickets, and lists of tracts. A folder entitled 'Lectures' includes: advertisement for a public lecture by the Right Hon. Sir Charles W. Dilke on 'The Empire', Essex Hall, 12 Nov. 1897; advertisement with syllabus of six lectures at King's Hall beginning 13 Oct. 1922, lecture II 'The British Empire' by Sidney Webb advocating a 'Britannic Alliance' of autonomous nations.

B. Minute Books of the Executive and Other Committees

Executive Committee 23 Dec. 1885 to 29 June 1947, 19 vols. The minutes 28 Oct. and 11 Nov. 1898 include brief references to Sidney and Beatrice Webb's visit to New Zealand and Australia.

Fabian Society Meetings Minutes 15 Feb. 1896 to 14 June 1901, 7 vols. The minutes 27 Jan. 1899 describe Sidney Webb's address at that meeting entitled 'Some Impressions of Australasia', in which he contrasted the Australasian colonies with the United States, discussing 'Fabianism' in New Zealand, Queensland's 'Socialism in Our Time' and its results, the Labour Parties of Victoria, New South Wales, and South Australia, and Federalism and its difficulties.

Fabian Society Publishing Committee 26 Apr. 1893 to 3 Oct. 1938, 7 vols. At the meeting on 1 Mar. 1899 it was agreed that a Municipal Year Book be sent to the Victorian Socialist Party.

C. Bound Volumes of Fabian Tracts and Annual Reports

These include several sets of Annual Reports covering various periods between 1887 and 1944 and several sets of *Fabian News* 1891-1948.

ORIEL COLLEGE
Oxford

The college archives include:

CORRESPONDENCE OF THE REV. L. R. PHELPS, D.C.L.

The correspondence covers 1877-1936 and is housed (1968) in two large boxes. It once included nearly all letters received by Dr Phelps, including correspondence connected with his term as Provost of Oriel 1914-29, and also a considerable number of letters from Phelps collected after his death. See P. C. Lyon, *Report on the Correspondence of the Rev. L. R. Phelps, D.C.L., from 1877 to 1936*, Oxford 1939, which describes classified bundles of letters including twenty-six bundles of letters 1884-1933 from correspondents abroad, among them three bundles labelled 'America, Australia, etc.'. When examined in 1968 most of the bundles described by P. C. Lyon had been broken up and an examination of the contents of the two boxes revealed only two relevant letters:

25 July 1926, Dudley Struben, Government House, Sydney, N.S.W., staying with his uncle Sir Dudley de Chair describing his visits to Australian states.

23 July 1937, J. R. Darling, Geelong Church of England Grammar School, Corio, Vic., concerning unemployment and depressed economy in Australia and the need for retrenchment in the school; Darling considered that politics in Australia, the Labour Party, and democracy were failures and advised against emigration.

Oxfordshire

PITT RIVERS MUSEUM
Oxford

The library includes some manuscripts. In-letters relating to objects received are filed in pockets in Accession Books.

MAKERETI PAPERS

Maori notes, 6 boxes. Some of these notes are translated in *The Old-Time Maori*, *by Makereti, sometime Chieftainess of the Arawa Tribe known in New Zealand as Maggie Papakura*, collected and edited with a biography by T. K. Penniman, London 1938. The notes are in Maori and are the accumulation of a lifetime of study of Maori lore.

BALDWIN SPENCER PAPERS

Correspondence and field note books of Sir Walter Baldwin Spencer 1892-1929, 7 boxes and 1 roll of drawings. See *Spencer's Scientific Correspondence with Sir J. G. Frazer and Others*, ed. R. R. Marett and T. K. Penniman, Oxford 1932. The field notes and diaries were used by Spencer in his published works, see also *Spencer's Last Journey, being the Journal of an Expedition to Tierra del Fuego . . . with a memoir*, ed. R. R. Marett and T. K. Penniman, Oxford 1931.

Boxes 1-5. Scientific correspondence 1892-1929.

Box 1. Letters 1897-9 from Edward B. Tylor and letter 24 June 1927 from Spencer to Dr Marett; letters 1895-6 from W. A. Horn with copies of letters from Spencer to Horn; letters 1896-1904 Spencer to L. Fison; letters 1892-1923 from H. Balfour, W. E. Roth, A. C. Haddon, and others.

Box 2. Letters 1894-1901 from F. J. Gillen.

Box. 3. Correspondence 1880-1906 with various friends; letters and notes 1913-21 from Paddy Cahill.

Box 4. Correspondence 1897-1929 with H. Balfour including photograph of Spencer's house, Armadale, Melbourne; letters 1893-*c.*1917 from P. M. Byrne, C. Ernest Cowle, A. W. Howitt, W. E. Roth, J. Edge-Partington, and others.

Box 5. Letters *c.*1897-1903 Spencer to Sir James Frazer.

Boxes 6-7. Field notes and diaries 1896-1929.

Box 6. Field notes and diaries: Field notes, trip to MacDonnell Ranges, Nov. 1896 to Jan. 1897; with Cowle from Alice Springs via Undiara to Crown Point, Jan. 1897; journey with Gillen 1901-2, field notes and diary, 5 vols.; diary, motor trip with Gilruth, Pine Creek, and trip to Bathurst Island 1912, rough notes; diary of journey to Tierra del Fuego, Feb.-June 1929, with notes on Spencer's last journals by Sir James Frazer.

Box 7. Diaries: Commonwealth expeditions to Northern Australia, 1 June to 9 July 1911 and 30 Dec. 1911 to 7 Apr. 1912, with sketches.

Roll of ten water-colours entitled: 'Copies by Sir Baldwin Spencer of Australian designs for totemic ceremonies, etc.'. Facsimile size drawings.

WESTLAKE PAPERS

Papers of Ernest Westlake assembled in connection with his collection of stone implements from Tasmania; for data on this see the Museum's Accession Books. The papers include Westlake's manuscript of a work on his collection. There are also two folders of letters and notes and five notebooks, which include lists of Aboriginal words. The notebooks appear to date from about 1910. The letters and notes are of varying dates *c.*1889-*c.*1940 and include letters to Westlake *c.*1908-16 among which is a letter 5 Feb. 1911 J. W. Beattie, Hobart, asking Westlake's opinion on the manuscripts of George Augustus Robinson. There are also a few notes of reminiscences of Tasmanian Aborigines. A microfilm and photographs are in the Institute of Aboriginal Studies, Canberra.

UNIVERSITY COLLEGE
Oxford

ATTLEE PAPERS

The correspondence and papers 1939-*c*.1951 of Earl Attlee are deposited in the Library, University College. Application for permission to consult the papers must be made to the Librarian. The Library holds a typescript list, also a typescript list of files of biographical material, which Earl Attlee deposited in Churchill College, Cambridge.

The papers in the Library of University College are in forty-four boxes, eight containing correspondence and thirty-six containing papers connected with Earl Attlee's political career. An examination of the typescript list and letters connected with Australia and New Zealand revealed only short letters of a formal nature in boxes 4-7, correspondence 1945-51 arranged alphabetically by correspondents, and in boxes 8-9, correspondence 1939-50 with labour officials. Such letters sent congratulations or good wishes or request an interview. The collection of speeches 1940-50 in boxes 15-40 may repay examination, especially for speeches on the British Commonwealth.

OXFORDSHIRE COUNTY RECORD OFFICE
County Hall, Oxford

See *The Oxfordshire County Record Office and its Records*, 1938, and *Summary Catalogue of the Privately Deposited Records in the Oxfordshire County Record Office*, 1966. There are volumes containing manuscript indexes of personal names, place names, and subjects in Quarter Sessions records and card indexes of personal names, place names, and subjects in private records. Private records are listed in a card index arranged alphabetically by names of deposits.

PRIVATE RECORDS

Papers deposited by Mrs J. R. Bailey
Bailey I/1-30. Farm diaries 1930-60 of Capt. the Hon. Bertram Freeman-Mitford of Westwell include Bailey I/22 ff.37-40 a brief account of his tour Jan.-Mar. 1953 to sheep farms in Australia and New Zealand.

Papers deposited by Mrs R. H. Gretton
Misc.Gre.I. Register of convicts transported to Maria Island, V.D.L., 1815-32. Section for names with initial A has been torn out.

SHROPSHIRE

SALOP RECORD OFFICE
Shirehall, Abbey Foregate, Shrewsbury

PRIVATE RECORDS

465 Sandford of the Isle Collection

465/877-85. Documents concerning lands of Jonathan Sandford in Adelaide and elsewhere in South Australia including leases, surveys, and maps 1839-65.

465/886-900. Documents concerning lands of Humphrey Sandford in South Australia including deed 1873-4, plans 1880 and n.d., and pedigree of Australian cousins compiled 8 Feb. 1904 by Edward Sandford, barrister and solicitor, Melbourne, Vic.

465/906-8. Two letters 24 Oct. 1863 and 25 Jan. 1866 Edward Sandford, Melbourne, to his cousin Folliot Sandford, solicitor, Shrewsbury, concerning his legal career in Australia and his membership of the Sandford of the Isle family, with cutting 10 Jan. 1887 from the *Argus* concerning his son Arthur's successful medical studies in Edinburgh.

631 Marrington Collection

631/3/1-1228. Correspondence and personal papers of Rev. R. J. Davies.

631/3/237-8. Two letters: 12 Feb. 1863 Charles Snape, Warialda, N.S.W., to his uncle with references to the death of his brother Tom, medical practices in the area, pastoral conditions, losses from the recent drought, and his two brothers James and Philip; extract from a letter 27 Oct. 1862 widow of Thomas William Snape to Philip Snape giving details of her family history and life in Australia. Also copy of will 15 Jan. 1862 Thomas William Snape.

631/3/1229-3184. Price Family Personal Papers.

631/3/2292-314. Correspondence 1877-80 among Lewis R. Price, his sister Fanny Kay, and her younger son Lewis Kay in Australia, concerning the latter's financial straits and his unsuccessful importuning of his uncle for assistance; his interest in investing in a Queensland gold mine and production of cotton.

631/3/2523-4, 2544-9. Letter books and diaries of Lewis R. Price containing items relating to the affairs of his nephew.

731 Hill (Hawkstone) MSS.

731/V. Box of correspondence and papers 1870-9 concerning mines in Queensland. Letters and copies of letters between Hathorn of the Hawkstone Estate Office, mining engineers and managers, and the Hon. R. C. Hill, later 3rd Viscount Hill, concerning interests in gold mines at Ravenswood, Q'ld, where Hill had a lease of ten acres. Bristowe, the manager of the mines, had returned insufficient information and as a result Edwin Haste had been sent out to report on prospects and mining methods.

1040 Rear Admiral Robert Jenkins

1040/1-4. Log books 1854-6, 1863-5, 1868-9 and letter book 1868-93 of Rear Admiral Robert Jenkins. Jenkins, as commander of the *Miranda*, was on the Australia Station 1861-5; he participated in action against the Maoris, commanding the Thames, Tauranga, and Maketu expeditions and the reserve of the Naval Brigade in the assault of the Gate Pa, Tauranga, on 29 Apr. 1864.

1104 Watkins-Pitchford Collection

1104/Box 2. Contains letter 25 Jan. 1877 H. Richards, Hororata, Canterbury, N.Z., to Hubert Smith, Bridgnorth, Salop, with references to the New Zealand climate, a request for seed potatoes, and the suggestion that Smith invest in New Zealand land.

Hill Family Papers

Reminiscences of Mrs Cora von Bültzingslöwen relating particularly to her father Charles Hill and early years in New Zealand. Hill went to New Zealand from Java in 1863 as a bankrupt, intending to take up land in Dunedin of which he was trustee for his aunt Eliza Symons; this property was leased and the family lived at Nelson while Hill engaged in trade with Bali and Lombok, until they returned to Java in 1871.

SHREWSBURY BOROUGH LIBRARY
Castle Gates, Shrewsbury

CORBET (SUNDORNE) MSS.

18294. Four items were noted in the correspondence of Leighton and Frederick R. Pigott, sons of the Rev. John Dryden Pigott, Rector of Edgmond. Leighton Pigott joined the Navy, and one letter 31 Dec. 1854 Robert Bernard, M.D., surgeon, Valparaiso, to Mrs Pigott acquainted her of her son's death. Frederick R. Pigott went to Australia and a letter 4 June 1854 from Tamberoora, 170 miles north-west of Sydney, says he had been four months on the diggings and gives an account of his friendships and living conditions. On 20 Apr. 1855 he writes from Long Creek and speaks of his lack of success on Campbell's Creek. He seems to have disappeared for a letter 7 June 1876 from J. Brooke, Salop, recounts efforts to trace him.

HUNT COLLECTION

17590 (H/1220). Copy of indentures 14 Dec. 1884 between Mrs Florence Marianne Hunt, Bowen Bridge, Q'ld, widow, and various individuals in England *re* conveyance of estates in Shropshire.

SOMERSET

DOWNSIDE ABBEY
Stratton-on-the-Fosse, nr Bath

The records of this Benedictine house are (1969) not fully available for study, pending their transfer to a new Library and Archives Room. It is expected that they will be available after 1971 and interested scholars should then apply in writing to the Librarian for further information concerning content and use of the archives.

A calendar of papers in the archives of the monastery for 1366-1791 has been printed in early volumes of *The Downside Review*. These volumes can be traced from a consolidated index 1880-1906 in Vol.XXV. The records so listed are too early to be of direct relevance to this survey but the existence of later material is indicated by references to original documents in other articles in the *Review*. Vol.I, pp.91-102, 165-75, 241-9, 'Memoir of J. B. Polding' and Vol.XXI, pp.134-45, 'Some letters of Archbishop Polding' suggest there are documents concerning his appointment as vicar Apostolic in Australia, and his own letters to his Superior and friends in England, including a large number 1836-49, to his cousin, fellow-religious and general agent at home, Fr Paulinus Heptonstall. Vol.III, pp.1-27, 'Memoirs of R. B. Vaughan', points to letters of Archbishop Vaughan, while Vol.V, pp.285-6, 'Letter from Bishop

Ullathorne 1886', and Vol.VIII, pp.71-81, 'In Memoriam W. B. Ullathorne' point to letters of that Bishop. Vol.XXI, pp.177-83, contains a reprint of an article in *The Austral Light*, Melbourne, Feb. 1902, on Bishop Davis. An interesting article on New Caledonia appears in Vol.XVIII, 1899, pp.234-42, T. B. Fulton, 'A French Colony in the Antipodes'.

It is also known that there are papers relating to Francis Murphy and Henry Gregory at Downside Abbey.

MRS R. T. SNEYD
The Malt House, Hinton Charterhouse, nr Bath

SHERBROOKE PAPERS*

Papers 1819-96 of Robert Lowe, 1st Viscount Sherbrooke, and his first wife Georgiana, née Orred. They sailed for Sydney in June 1842 and returned to England in 1850. The papers relating to Australia are chiefly letters from Mrs Lowe and are a record of her husband's legal and political career in New South Wales. They describe their life in the colony and show her knowledge of her husband's work and her keen observation.

Georgiana Lowe to Mrs Sherbrooke: Jan. 1840; n.d. [Oct. 1844], Parramatta, with copy; also ten letters Dec. 1842 to Oct. 1846, Sydney.

n.d. [1842] Georgiana Lowe to 'My dear Aunt', written to announce her husband's decision to go to Australia.

n.d. [Dec. 1842] Georgiana Lowe, Sydney, to Agnes Lowe; also three letters 20 Nov., 22 Dec. 1843, 28 Jan. 1844.

20 July 1845, 4 May 1849 Georgiana Lowe, Sydney, to Rev. W. Whitley.

15 Aug. 1844 Robert Lowe, Sydney, to Mrs Sherbrooke.

30 Nov. 1846 Robert Lowe, Nelson's Bay, Sydney, to Rev. R. Michell.

Miscellanea: Cutting on Bronte House; small black exercise book containing 'Newspaper Scraps' many relating to Australia or of biographical interest; letter 28 July 1896 J. Chamberlain to Lady Sherbrooke containing reminiscences of Robert Lowe.

MRS H. E. COTTON
Lower Farm, West Bradley, Glastonbury

Diary 1885-6 of W. Allen describing his visit to Australia to report on the Hampton Plains Syndicate, also a transcript of most of the diary. Microfilms of the original diary in the Mitchell Library, Sydney, and State Library of Victoria.

MINISTRY OF DEFENCE, HYDROGRAPHIC DEPARTMENT
Creechbarrow House, Taunton

Applications to consult charts and documents should be made in writing to the Hydrographer of the Navy. Established by Order in Council 12 Aug. 1795 the Hydrographic Department was founded on a collection of charts and information collected by naval officers and civilian surveyors. The first Hydrographer, Alexander Dalrymple, was appointed in that year and publication of Admiralty charts began. Some naval officers had been submitting 'observations' about the ports they visited since at least 1760 and Dalrymple made it obligatory for all naval commanders to record in a ship's remark book navigational information about the ports and coasts they visited.

A list of important early hydrographic surveys in the possession of the Department has been issued: 'A Summary of Selected Manuscript Documents of Historic Importance preserved in the Archives of the Department', London, Hydrographic Department, Admiralty, 1950, Hydrographic Department Professional Paper No.13, duplicated typescript. This supersedes a list compiled in 1946, the entries having been rearranged in sections devoted to various areas. Copies have been distributed to major libraries. Entries in this list are not given below. Two indexes of Original Documents are maintained, the handwritten Numerical List, begun in 1826, and the Geographical Index which is regionally classified in both list and diagrammatic form.

The collection of maps and charts relating to Australasia and the Pacific is very large and includes many in manuscript from the seventeenth, eighteenth and nineteenth centuries. There are maps of the Pacific by Dampier, Anson, Byron, Wallis, and Carteret, and of Australasia by Cook, Flinders, P. P. King, and all the professional surveyors since active in these regions. The collection also includes a large number of manuscript maps by Antarctic explorers including Ross, Shackleton, and Scott. A number of land and river surveys are preserved. Examples for Australia and New Zealand are:

A 464. Solitary Island to Jervis Bay by John Oxley.

D 7976. The country east of Warnbro' and Cockburn Sounds, 1845.

D 7376/1-2. Explorations of De Grey River, Fortescue to Lyons Rivers, by F. T. Gregory, 1861, tracing.

D 8400. Port Darwin to Port Daly, overland track by W. P. Auld, 1865, tracing.

A 2787. Adelaide to Perth, overland track by J. Forrest, 1870, tracing.

A 5023. The Canning, Swan and Helena Rivers, hydrographic survey by Staff Commander Archdeacon, 1876, tracing.

L 5867. Track of an expedition south west of Nelson, Fox, Brunner, and Heaphy, 1846, tracing.

L 6980. Route of an expedition to Rud Peka Peka by Mr Naps, 1848, plan.

L 9295. Auckland Harbour topography, by J. L. Stokes, 1848, plan.

These are chiefly eye sketches designed as an aid to navigation; they are not always shown on the published charts. Some sketches show ports and buildings used by seamen as landmarks and the drawings of successive surveyors illustrate the development of towns.

Miscellaneous Papers

There are 106 bound volumes of miscellaneous papers which contain many early remark books, but they are not indexed. 29 volumes 1760-80, are bound in alphabetical order of ship's name. No records of the Pacific voyages of Cook and Wallis have been found in these volumes. The remaining 77 volumes, *c.*1790-1850, are bound by region; 69-71 (Ba 1-3) contain material relating to Australia and the Pacific Islands, e.g.:

Volume 69 (Ba 1) ff.281-404. Remark book 1801 of Acting Lieut. J. Murray in the *Lady Nelson* on a voyage of discovery in Bass Strait.

ff.411-583. Journal 1817-18 of the cutter *Mermaid*, P. P. King, on a voyage to the north and north-west coasts of Australia, two copies, one marked 'duplicate' in the same handwriting, received from Lieut. King, 1819. This contains some detailed descriptions of Aborigines.

ff.591-613. Flinders's chapters 6, 7, and 8, from his 'Memoir' 1805, with a preface dated Isle de France 14 May 1805, in his own hand.

ff.615-30. Remark book 1787-92 of the *Supply*.

ff.831-935. Observations 1803 by Lieut. J. Tuckey on the present constitution and judicial state of the colony of New South Wales and on the state of its defence, society, religions. Tuckey was on the *Calcutta* and refers to the activities of Irish priests and comments 'It also appears that a person of high trust in the colony was very deeply implicated, as one of the advisers of the rebels'.

Volume 71 (Ba 3) ff.93-6. Extract of a letter 3 June 1838 from Grey, Isle de France, relating to his experiences while exploring in north-western Australia. He describes his introduction of many new animals and plants.

ff.145-72. Remarks and observations 1813 on the coasts of New South Wales, Norfolk Island, and New Zealand by J. Oxley. There are references to the possibility of a flax and spars trade, and to sandalwood trade with Fiji.

ff.621-86. Journal 1830 of a tour of the islands of the South Seas in the *Seringapatam* which includes a detailed description of missionary activities on Tahiti and an account of a visit to Pitcairn with a list of inhabitants.

Original Documents

Documents, including some remark books, from which considerable information has been used for compiling published sailing directions. Examples are:

OD 10. Remark book 1841-2 of the *Beagle* on the Australian north-west coast.

OD 81. Remark book 1846-50 of Capt. Owen Stanley of H.M.S. *Rattlesnake* on the New Guinea coast.

OD 88. Journal 1860 of the exploratory cruise of the *Herald* in the Pacific.

OD 90. Remark book 1845-6 of H.M.S. *Fly* in Torres Strait.

OD 92. Account 1865 by Dr Belgrave Ninnis of an exploring expedition that examined the country between the Adelaide River and Port Darwin.

Remark Books

There are about 6,000 remark books *c*.1825-*c*.1909 arranged alphabetically by ships' names for each year.

Ships' Logs

A few ships' logs *c*.1832-53 include *Virago* 1852-3 and *Starling* 1835-41.

DATA BOOKS AND ANGLE BOOKS

These books contain technical information concerning Hydrographic surveys. They include Astronomical Observation Books 1825-88, 90 vols., and Data Books 1855-1946, 122 vols. These include Flinders's Book of Bearings taken from the *Investigator*.

MINUTE BOOKS AND CORRESPONDENCE

Minute Books 1825-1912 [1832-7 missing] with indexes.

Confidential Minute Books Nos.1-3 [No.4 missing] 1899-1911 with indexes.

Letter Books 1815-1916 containing copies of all out-letters including letters to surveyors, indexed.

In-letters. There are about 10,000 letters 1800-57 filed alphabetically by name of author and indexed in Historical Indexes (see below). In-letters include letters from Sir John Franklin as Governor of Tasmania, from Sir William Parry and P. P. King when Commissioners of the Australian Agricultural Company, and from J. S. Roe, first Surveyor-General of Western Australia. Some of these contain remarks about colonial affairs. Sir Everard Home's letters 1842-5 refer to FitzRoy's high abilities as Governor of New Zealand.

Letters from Surveyors. Most in-letters from surveyors 1823-66 are filed separately by name, 70 files, indexed in Historical Indexes (see below).

Miscellaneous Letter Files 1802-1946, mostly pre-1874. A number of in-letters and a few papers of historical interest have been filed separately, 55 files, indexed in Historical Indexes, e.g. Miscellaneous File No.6 with several letters from Flinders and Gov. P. G. King.

Historical Indexes. In the 1950s the Minute Books and Letters listed above were carefully examined and indexed for Vice-Admiral Sir Archibald Day's book *The Admiralty Hydrographic Service 1795-1919*, London 1967. There are fifteen volumes of this index including:

Index to Original Manuscripts and Records 1815-1905.
Index to Original Manuscripts and Records, name index to in-letters before 1857.
Index to Original Manuscripts and Records, chronological 1801-1905, 3 vols.
General and Chronological Index 1791-1925, with abstracts of surveyors' letters.

SOMERSET RECORD OFFICE
Obridge Road, Taunton

A card index of papers is maintained.

PRIVATE RECORDS

DD/MDL Medlycott Papers

The papers include the journals of Rear-Adm. Sir Mervyn Bradford Medlycott Jan. 1880 to Oct. 1881, 2 vols. Capt. Medlycott left Southampton for Callao via Panama by mail steamer in Jan. 1880, took command of H.M.S. *Turquoise* on 20 Feb., and on 3 July 1880 began a six months cruise of the Pacific Islands, visiting the Marquesas, Tahiti, Raiatea, and Mangaia, returning to Tahiti. A sketch plan of Medlycott's house in Papeete is in the journal, which also includes a detailed account of activities at Papeete and descriptions of islands visited. The *Turquoise* returned to the coast of South America in Jan. 1881. Medlycott comments on the war between Chile and Peru and on activities of the British Navy.

The papers also include two Night Order Books for H.M.S. *Turquoise* Oct. 1877 to Oct. 1881.

DD/SH Strachie MSS.

These include papers of Chichester Samuel Parkinson-Fortescue, Baron Carlingford, Under-Secretary for the Colonies 1857-8 and 1859-65. N.R.A. Report 8898 does not indicate that the papers contain material of interest to the field of this guide and no further index of the papers exists. They may repay examination.

DD/SF Sanford MSS.

DD/SF/3418 (Box 205). Estimate of sums required to defray expenses of the police force in Western Australia, 1846.

The bundles of general correspondence of W. A. Sanford (not listed in detail) include one or two letters written from H. A. Sanford in Perth.

MRS F. E. SPURWAY
Mounthouse, Halse, nr Taunton

PAPERS OF SIR ARTHUR HODGSON*

The papers include a journal 1838 in the *Royal George*, London to Sydney; head station killing and shearing tallies 1842-7; victualling tallies 1842; bale tallies, Hodgson and Elliott 1842, financial transactions 1839-47; diary on the *Walmer Castle*, Sydney to the West Indies 1848; account book 1860-2 of Sir Arthur Hodgson; map showing land owned by Arthur Hodgson at Eton Vale; pencil drawing of Eton Vale station with manuscript note on back 'Head Station, Eton Vale, Darling Downs, December 1st 1841'. There are also crayon portraits of Sir Arthur and Lady Hodgson.

MISSES A. AND E. BOND
Crossways, 1 Higher Kingston, Yeovil

Manuscript copy of a 'diary' written by John James Bond in 1915 chiefly from letters to his mother during his visit to Australia 1853-4. Bond sailed to Melbourne and Sydney 1853 in the *Lady Flora*, returning to Melbourne, he stayed for some months with his uncle at Benalla and later visited the goldfields. To the 'diary' he adds some details from Australian letters to him 1868-74. The original 'diary' is in the possession of Miss M. Bond, 19 Gleneagles Road, Greenside, Johannesburg, South Africa. Two of Bond's original letters 1853-4 are in the possession of Mrs G. C. Dunn, 2 Bishop's Cottage, Wootton Courtenay, near Minehead, but are now so frail that they cannot be handled and are not available for inspection. The manuscript copy of the 'diary', the original, and the two letters 1853-4 have all been microfilmed for the Australian Joint Copying Project.

STAFFORDSHIRE

SOUTH STAFFORDSHIRE REGIMENT
Whittington Barracks, Lichfield

RECORDS OF THE 80TH REGIMENT

Digest, Vol.1, 1793-1897; Vol.2, 1793-1899. Record of services of the Regiment including orders Sept. 1835 for the men to proceed to Chatham to act as guards on convict ships and the embarkation of the first such guard at Gravesend on 23 May 1836. On 11 July 1837 the Colours arrived in Sydney. Movements are recorded and tables include 'State of the 80th Regiment, Paramatta 16 July 1844', a list of personnel; 'List of officers 80th Regiment, Paramatta 16th July 1841'; 'Embarkation 80th Regiment from England for N.S. Wales' giving dates of embarkation and arrival and other details.

Roll 1804-81. 'Nominal and descriptive roll of the Eightieth Regiment' with entries for name, date of enlistment, age at enlistment, height, trade or occupation, place of birth, and remarks.

Record of Stations. List of dates of embarkation and disembarkation. The first section covers 1793-1905.

STAFFORDSHIRE RECORD OFFICE
Eastgate Street, Stafford

PRIVATE RECORDS

D258 Daniel Bate (Calverley) Documents

D258/M/B/8. Probable cost of tread wheels and machinery for two pairs of stones for Auckland Government, N.Z., 1880.

D260 Hatherton Collection

D260/M/E/430/37. Correspondence 1865-6 concerning Lord Hatherton's shares in the Queensland Land Company including references to properties at Inniskillen and Barcoo Plains.

D260/M/F/5/38. Correspondence 1894-5 Algernon Littleton, Tasmania, with his parents the 3rd Baron and Lady Hatherton relating to his financial affairs, farming experience, and work with the Tasmanian Gold Mining Co.

D260/M/F/5/80. Letters 1867 concerning the refusal of a pension for the widow of Lieut.-Col. Hassard, 57th Regiment, who was killed in New Zealand.

D554 Bill (Farley) MSS.

D554/103, 186. Papers 1880-1913 concerning an estate at Aberfeldie, N.Z., owned by Charles Bill and sold in 1913, including an account book 1880-1913 with entries for land bought, number of stock, purchases of seed, prices for produce of Aberfeldie Station, and papers at the time of the sale.

D593 Sutherland Papers

D593/N/1/2/1/8. Investment register 1861-92 with an index to stocks, and entries for investments in Queensland, South Australia, Victoria, Western Australia, New South Wales, and New Zealand.

D593/P/29/1/9, 12. Two letters 1886-7 Lady Stafford to Lady Alexandra Leveson-Gower including one in S.S. *Rome* after five weeks in Australia; letters 1888-90 from E. M. Broome including references to possible future appointments of Sir Frederick Broome, Governor of Western Australia.

D593/S/10/7. Granville Leveson-Gower, 1st Marquess of Stafford: documents, including copy of commission 20 Sept. 1790 of Arthur Phillip as Governor of New South Wales to remit sentences of transported felons.

D660 Manby and Steward, solicitors, Deposit

D660/20/3. Papers 1908-9 concerning the administration of the estates of George Pauton of Sydney, N.S.W., including a copy of his will.

D660/21/22. Personal papers and documents *re* the Woodward family.

D660/21/24. Two bundles of correspondence 1890-1909 concerning Frank Woodward of Canterbury, N.Z., mainly relating to his financial affairs and the forwarding of moneys to him.

D661 Dyott Family MSS.

D661/18/10-12. Miscellaneous manuscripts including: copy report 31 Aug. 1830 of Ensign Dale, 63rd Regiment, on a journey of exploration in the Swan River Valley, W.A.; 'Remarks suggested by a visit to the female factory, Parramatta, New South Wales, Nov. 30 1836' by William Palma and 'Remarks occasioned by a visit to the principal felons gaol in Sydney, New South Wales, Wednesday March 15 1837' by the same authors.

D661/19/7/6. Additional sheet 30 Oct. 1829 of *Tasmanian and Austral-Asiatic Review* reporting the court martial of Lieut. Carew, 63rd Regiment, for allowing a ship to be seized by convicts 30 Oct. 1829, printed.

Staffordshire

D683 Whitehouse (Sedgely) MSS.

D683/4/3/8. Two letters 1900 to Benjamin Whitehouse on the death of Charles Blake [?Charles Howard Whitehouse] in an accident in New South Wales.

D683/4/6. Three letters 1882, 1884, 1898 Susanna Matilda Whitehouse to her son Charles [?Charles Howard Whitehouse] in Australia.

D695 Harward and Evers, solicitors, Deposit

D695/1/11/14/3. Certificate 13 Dec. 1901 for Queensland Government Inscribed Stock in the names of Eliza Jane Moore and Walter John Fletcher.

D710 Alderman G. Shufflebotham Deposit

D710/26. Power of attorney 27 Mar. 1867 W. H. Gaunt, Beechworth, Vic., police magistrate, to Joseph Challinor, Leek.

D726 Business Archives Council (London) Deposit

Letters Patent 15 Dec. 1898 granted to Harold Boyd, Wiggington, Staffs., mining engineer, for an improvement in explosives, registered in the Patent Office of Tasmania.

D834 St Mary's, Stafford, Parish Records

D834/12/1-3. Pamphlets, papers, and photographs concerning missionary boats including D834/12/1, two letters 1931 Rev. W. F. France, Overseas Secretary, Society for the Propagation of the Gospel in Foreign Parts, written on his voyage to New Zealand, to the Archbishop of New Zealand and the Rev. L. Lambert, the Rectory, Stafford.

D834/15. Pictures and Drawings, including D834/15/1/1-2, photographs of Bishop Cowie of Auckland, N.Z.

D868 Sutherland Papers

D868/11/36. Letter 11 May 1806 [Grey?] to the 2nd Marquess of Stafford advocating the purchase for the nation of the South Sea Islands curiosities in the sale of the Leverian Museum.

D(W)1778 Dartmouth Papers

D(W)1778/III/342. Letter 14 Jan. 1776 Sir Harry Trelawney to the Secretary of the Society for Promoting Christian Knowledge concerning his not baptising Omiah of Otaheite.

D(W)1778/V/696. Letter 25 Sept. 1852 R. Dawson, Sydney, to Lord Dartmouth with references to his experience in coal mining in West Bromwich which would be useful in supplying Sydney with water, a plan to bring Nepean water to Sydney, cheaper alternatives, and a description of the area; also references to the son of Joseph Townsend now on the Australian gold fields, having worked in California, life in the colony for children, morals, and descriptions of life in the country and the effect of gold discoveries, 31pp.

WILLIAM SALT LIBRARY
19 Eastgate Street, Stafford

92/1-10 Kirby Manuscripts

92/8/64. Letter 20 May 1880 J. Barrett, Waimate, N.Z., to his sister on his life and conditions in New Zealand.

253/8/68. A printed catalogue [189?] of exhibits concerning the reputed convict ship *Success* and its world tour.

Hand, Morgan and Owen, solicitors, Collection

D1798/321. New Zealand Company, terms of purchase for a quantity of land in the Wellington district, John Ward, Secretary, New Zealand House, London 1843, printed; circular, Association for Promoting the Settlement of Otago by the Secretary of the Court of Directors, Thomas Cudbert Harington, New Zealand House, London 1849, printed.

SUFFOLK

BURY ST EDMUNDS AND WEST SUFFOLK RECORD OFFICE
Angel Hill, Bury St Edmunds

PARISH RECORDS

EL12 Barningham Parish Records

EL12/7/24. Notice 28 Mar. 1851 of meeting to consider allocation of Poor Rate money to defraying expenses of emigration of poor persons. Attached is a list of six bachelor labourers of the parish wishing to emigrate to Port Phillip, Australia, giving ages.

EL110 Mildenhall Parish Records

EL110/7/73. Letter 17 Dec. 1828 Keeper of Cambridge Town Gaol, to the Church-wardens and Overseers of the parish seeking help to provide necessaries for Sarah Pitchers and her child to be transported to New South Wales for seven years.

PRIVATE RECORDS

Robert Boby Ltd Papers

Tem/141/45. Deed 8 Mar. 1873 concerning transfer of Bury St Edmunds property to Robert Boby contains reference to parties including Thomas Pattle, postmaster of Castlemaine, Vic., and to the surviving children of the late William Pattle, brewer of Castlemaine.

Acc.941 Hervey Family Archives

Acc.941/56/92. The papers of Frederick William, 5th Earl and 1st Marquess of Bristol, contain an account of a visit to Pitcairn Island by Rodney Shannon 'Lieutenant aboard the King's Ship', [H.M.S. *Briton*], noting their arrival off the island 17 Sept. 1814 with references to Thursday October Christian and John Adams. Details are given of agriculture, the moral state of the settlement and an account of the reasons for Fletcher Christian's death.

IPSWICH AND EAST SUFFOLK RECORD OFFICE
County Hall, Ipswich

IPSWICH BOROUGH RECORDS

AI 2/29. Papers 1-9 Apr. 1789 relating to the transportation of Susana Hunt to New South Wales including contract for her conveyance to Botany Bay, and receipt for her transfer to the *Lady Juliana*.

PARISH RECORDS

FB 217 Old Newton Parish Records

FB 217/D1/3. Register of Baptisms and Burials, Vol.IV, 1755-1812, contains an entry 18 Feb. 1793 for the baptism of Valentine Blomfield, son of Thomas and Mary Blomfield, born 14 Feb. 1793, who later settled in the Monaro district of New South Wales.

FC 184 Halesworth Parish Records.
FC 184/N1/8. Log 1825-7 of the *Merope* kept by Commander G. Parkyn, during a voyage from India to China, thence to the Sandwich Islands and California and back to India. The remarks column contains varied information on shipboard routine including statistics on the weekly use of water and notes on the stowing of cargo.
FC 184/N1/10. List and accounts 1829-30 of the crew of the *Merope*.

PRIVATE RECORDS

HA 11 Rous Family Archives
HA 11/A15/9. 13. Papers of 3rd Earl of Stradbroke. Address 25 Mar. 1926 from Mayor and citizens of Melbourne expressing regret at the termination of his appointment as Governor of Victoria. Diary of Australian tour 24 July to 13 Sept. 1924.
HA 11/B1/7/2. Observations 5 Jan. 1833 on the introduction and cultivation in Ireland of New Zealand flax, *Phormium tenax*, by Capt. George Harris, R.N., printed. Copy forwarded to the Earl of Stradbroke 7 Oct. 1835.
HA 11/B5/4/1-8. Local and official papers 1835-6 of the Earl of Stradbroke, connected with the Poor Law but relating specifically to emigration to Australia. Eight items including: notice of the Committee for Promoting the Emigration of Females to the Australian Colonies and scheme by John Marshall for victualling such emigrants on the voyage; papers presented to the House of Commons Emigration Committee and printed extracts from letters of John Sullivan, surgeon superintendent of the emigrant ship *Canton*, also presented; circular from the Emigration Department of the Colonial Office concerning wages in Van Diemen's Land; letter to Lord Stradbroke giving particulars of the *Launceston* bound for Van Diemen's Land; advertisements for the emigrant ship *Amelia Thompson* and the ship *Camden*.
HA 11/B5/8. Circular 9 Aug. 1848 of Silver & Co., clothiers and outfitters, London, with list of clothes and other necessities for emigrants to Australia, addressed to the Earl of Stradbroke.
HA 11/B21/1-5. Papers 1846-50 relating to the convict James Lowe who had apparently arrived in New South Wales in 1838 and been sentenced at a Berrima circuit court in 1846 to fifteen years transportation for shooting with intent to murder. There are letters from him in Hobart to Lord Stradbroke seeking his liberty, testimonials of character, a cutting of the Berrima trial from the *Sydney Morning Herald* 11 Mar. 1846, and letters from officials relating to the case.

HA 28 Rope Collection
HA 28/50/23/7.6. Three letters Aug.-Dec. 1842, Charles S. Webber to George Mingay of Orford, Suffolk, dealing with the departure from Plymouth and voyage to Van Diemen's Land of the emigrant ship *Sir Charles Napier*. Webber was medical officer in charge.

HA 61 Loraine Family Archives
Family and Personal Records: Papers of Charles Acton Broke.
HA 61/436/330. Cutting 25 Dec. 1851 from the [*Sydney*?] *Morning Herald*. Article by Capt. Erskine late of H.M.S. *Havanna* on an excursion to the Australian goldfields by Hugh Hamilton, Walter Leslie, and Lieut. Pollard.
HA 61/436/345. Letters 26 Jan., 26 Mar. 1852 Hugh Hamilton, Assistant Gold Commissioner, Ophir Barracks, to his sister Anna Maria Broke containing reflections on his life since arrival in 1841 and references to Illawarra, Bathurst, and the Lachlan,

and to misadventures running stock on a property at Kirconnel between Bathurst and Sydney.

HA 61/436/346. Bundle containing letter 29 Mar. 1860 James Hamilton to his sister Anna Horton, Christchurch, N.Z., referring to his run on the River Taieri, in Otago.

HA 61/436/357-78. Papers including inventories 1877-8, c.25 items relating to William Charles Loraine, his voyage to Australia on the *Lord Warden*, his death on board 11 Apr. 1877 and disposal of his effects. Documents include a brief diary of the voyage, accounts and an agreement with Charles Frederick Birch for the latter to serve him as manservant on the voyage and for two years in Australia.

HA 67 Albemarle MSS.

HA 67/461/222. Stores and provisions demanded by Commodore G. Anson from the Chief Mandarin of the Province of Canton 18 Dec. 1742.

HA 67/461/228. Log 16 Sept. 1740 to 14 Jan. 1744 on Lord Anson's voyage round the world by Hon. Augustus Keppel in H.M.S. *Centurion*.

HA 67/461/229-30. Journal 1740-2 of Hon. Augustus Keppel in H.M.S. *Centurion* round the world, 2 vols. The journal is largely identical with HA 67/461/228.

HA 213:1287 Lingwood Papers

Papers relating particularly to Margaret Catchpole including 'Homespun Heroine: Portrait of Margaret Catchpole', c.1947, typescript, 246pp. This is a critique of the Rev. Richard Cobbold, *The History of Margaret Catchpole*, 2nd ed., London 1845, 2 vols. and to a lesser extent of later writings on her. Errors are corrected mainly from Suffolk sources, the whole providing additional information on the Catchpole story and on Cobbold and his publication, on theatrical productions of the story, on Elizabeth Cobbold, and on individuals mentioned in *The History*. The text of eleven letters from Margaret Catchpole is given, ten from Australia, originals or copies in the Mitchell Library, Sydney, and one from Ipswich Gaol, now at Christchurch Mansion, Ipswich.

IPSWICH BOROUGH LIBRARIES
Northgate Street, Ipswich

WOOLNOUGH COLLECTION

Vols.135, 136. Two volumes containing letters, cuttings and photographs relating to Margaret Catchpole. Correspondents include G. C. Johnson, Sydney, Gregory Mathews on the lyrebirds in the Ipswich Museum described as sent to Mrs Cobbold by Margaret Catchpole, Laurence Irving on the production of a play about Margaret Catchpole by Walter Frith at the Ipswich Lyceum on 6 Oct. 1910.

fS92. Letters and cuttings relating to Margaret Catchpole 1880-1958, 1 vol. Correspondents include Gregory Mathews writing on the burial certificate of Margaret Catchpole; A. G. Foster, J. Leigh Jones, H. Wright of the Mitchell Library, Sydney. There is also a copy of a pamphlet by F. J. Foakes Jackson, *St. Luke and a Modern Writer. A Study in Criticism*, Cambridge 1916. (The modern writer is the Rev. Richard Cobbold, author of *The History of Margaret Catchpole*, London 1845.)

A. H. LOWTHER-PINKERTON, ESQ.
Spring House, Alderton, Woodbridge

Letter 6 Sept. 1852 from John Adams, Pitcairn, son of the mutineer John Adams.*

Documents n.d. [?18th cent.] purporting to authenticate a club in the possession of Mr A. H. Lowther-Pinkerton, as the club which killed Capt. James Cook. The

Department of Ethnography at the British Museum has identified the club from a photograph as Tongan.

SURREY

NATIONAL ARMY MUSEUM
R.M.A. Sandhurst, Camberley

Collections relate to the British army to 1914, the Indian army to 1947, and colonial forces up to the time of self government. Entries for manuscript material are included in a card catalogue of books, articles, and archives divided into five sections: Biography, Regiments, Campaigns, Subjects, Places. Accession numbers are used as call numbers. In 1968 military manuscripts of the Royal United Service Institution were transferred to the Museum.

5105/70. Francis M. Lind. Eight diaries 1854-76. The first volume 13 Feb. 1854 to 31 July 1855 records a journey by the screw steamer *Formosa* from Calcutta to Sydney touching at King George Sound, Adelaide, and Port Phillip, followed by an account of travel through New England including a description of gold prospecting at Rocky River. Lind departed for Auckland 21 Feb. 1855 on the *William Denison* and left again for Sydney 12 Apr. The diary describes several journeys in the neighbourhood of Auckland, contacts with British army officers and comments on the Maoris and their traditions.

6409/87. List of kit carried by the Queensland Mounted Volunteers at the Boer War, printed.

6509/25. Lieut.-Col. R. Hickman Russell, 57th Foot, seven diaries covering campaigns in New Zealand and elsewhere including diary 1863-4.

6705/45. Scrapbook compiled by P. W. Reynolds containing some notes on early colonial forces in Australia and New Zealand.

6707/19. Birdwood Papers, including diaries 1882, 1886, 1889-90, 1892-1914, 1921-49. The diaries for 1915-20 are among the Birdwood papers deposited by the family in the Australian War Memorial, Canberra.

6807/255. Colonial Office print, Further Papers relative to the Affairs of New Zealand 1865.

6807/306-7, 313-14. Records of the Queen's Own Royal West Kent Regiment (50th/97th), 50th Foot 1756-1848 and 1757-1882, 1st Bn Queen's Own Royal West Kent Regiment 1849-1914, 1882-1913. Photocopy of the manuscript records in the possession of the Regiment. There is a similar copy in the War Office Library.

7001/6. Typescript nominal roll of the Soudan contingent 1885. Taken from Frank Hutchinson and Francis Myers, *The Australian Contingent. A History of the Patriotic Movement in New South Wales*, Sydney 1885.

MRS P. EDGECUMBE
C/o Mrs M. R. Croly, Heatherwood, Lower Bourne, Farnham

A volume of letters and papers 1880-1 including papers relating to the appointment of Sir John Henry Lefroy as Governor of Tasmania. The letters are to be placed in Lloyd's Bank, Farnham, Surrey.

SURREY RECORD OFFICE
County Hall, Penrhyn Road, Kingston upon Thames

BOARDS OF GUARDIANS RECORDS

Sample volumes were examined and references to pauper emigration were noticed including, in a minute book of the Guildford Union, BG 6/11/5, pp.92, 105, 16 Sept., 7 Oct. 1843, payments assisting emigrants to Australia.

PRIVATE RECORDS

80 Ravensbury Estate

80/5/36. Conveyance 23 Nov. 1863 between various persons including Joseph Schroder Moore, Melbourne, Vic.

203 Ashtead Manor and Howard Family

203/33/177a-b. Letter 7 June 1833 from Col. H. [W.?] Sorrell concerning assistance given him when he returned from Van Diemen's Land and asking for help in obtaining a position for one of his sons as Surveyor of Lands in one of the colonies, also letter 9 July 1833 from R. W. Hay saying he doubted he could help.

Acc.319 Goulburn Papers

Private and political papers of Henry Goulburn, Under-Secretary for War and the Colonies 1812-21; also family papers including those of his brother Frederick Goulburn, first permanent Colonial Secretary, New South Wales, deposited on loan by Maj.-Gen. E. H. Goulburn. Bundle numbers in N.R.A. Report 0777 are given below but will be revised when the papers have been listed in detail.

II/9/A/a. Packet containing *inter alia* despatch 1826 Bathurst to Darling concerning female convicts at Emu Plains, copy.

II/9/A/b. Bundle of papers 1837-63 labelled 'N.S.W.' and consisting of the correspondence of the executors of Maj. F. Goulburn. The papers chiefly concern the recovery of debts from Dr H. G. Douglass, partly from his properties in Illawarra, also from W. Cordeaux, W. C. Wentworth, W. Buchanan, S. Stephen, F. Stephen, Rev. M. D. Meares, and the estate of J. Oxley and including correspondence with Campbell & Co., Sydney.

II/9/E. Papers *c.*1819-39 of Maj. F. Goulburn including papers concerning his position as Colonial Secretary, New South Wales, notebooks *c.*1819-30 and correspondence with or concerning Rev. M. D. Meares, J. Norton, W. W. Burton, Campbell & Co., Dr H. G. Douglass, F. Forbes, and K. Barnes, also papers concerning W. C. Wentworth, W. Cordeaux, S. Stephen, and F. Stephen.

III/6. Letter n.d. Maj. F. Goulburn to H. Goulburn concerning a convict's wife.

III/9. Notes including some on New South Wales 1788-1834.

III/10. Chart 1817 of part of the interior of New South Wales by J. Oxley and plan 1817 of the Government Farm at Toongabbee signed James Meehan, Deputy Surveyor General, New South Wales.

Acc.661 Royal Philanthropic Society's School, Redhill, Surrey

Records are open if more than 100 years old. The Society helped numbers of boys from the school to emigrate and its records include considerable material on emigrants to Australia and New Zealand.

Finance (Working Ledger), emigration charges 1854-61. The boys are grouped by ship, and passage money and cost of outfit are recorded. An index of names, an aid in using the whole body of records, covers 1854-8.

Journals (Emigration Letter Book) 1857-*c.*1874. The Journals contain lengthy abstracts of in-letters including letters from Australia and New Zealand 1856-1860s. Names appear in full only in the letter books but many of the letters are printed in

Annual Reports. The printed *Annual Reports* are in two series, 1860-87, 6 vols., and 1878-1910, 5 vols.

Acc.705 Ware Family Papers

'The Autobiography of Martin Ware, 1818-1895, written out from his diaries by his wife', also the six diaries used. Ware was the friend of reformers and worked for Ragged Schools and the Shoeblack Society. Letters *c.*1850-70 from boys from these societies who emigrated to Australia and New Zealand are preserved among the papers.

Journal 1911-12 of Rev. Martin S. Ware, typescript copy. The journal contains comments on local worthies met during a world tour including Hawaii, Fiji, Australia, and New Zealand.

J. W. M. WILLIAMS, ESQ.
38 Fairfield South, Kingston upon Thames

Papers of the Rev. John Williams have been microfilmed by the Pacific Manuscripts Bureau, Research School of Pacific Studies, Australian National University.

Journal July-Aug. 1823 written by the Rev. John Williams and the Rev. Robert Bourne describing their missionary voyage to the Cook Islands, copy. Some passages are similar in content to passages in Williams's *A Narrative of Missionary Enterprises in the South Sea Islands*, London 1837, but the journal contains greater detail.

Letters from the Rev. John Williams: 9 Nov. 1822, Raiatea, to his family; 27 Feb. 1830, Raiatea, to A. Birnie; 17 June 1836, Portsea, to his sister; 14 July 1838, Capetown, to his sister.

Letter 10 Sept. 1829, Tamatoa, chief of Raiatea, to the President of the United States, copy.

Extract from the minutes of a meeting of the London Missionary Society 30 Mar. 1840 concerning the murder in the New Hebrides of Williams and James Harris, copy.

RICHMOND PUBLIC LIBRARY
Parkshot, Richmond

SLADEN PAPERS

The papers of Douglas Brooke Wheelton Sladen containing correspondence, cuttings, drafts, postcards, some in poor condition, 74 vols.

SLA.1-20. Personal

Literary and business correspondence 1880-1922. A number of relevant items were noted including:

SLA.1. Correspondence 1880, 1886, 1888 concerning Sladen's publications of Australian verse and ballads including letters and some original verse from authors in Australia, New Zealand, and elsewhere, and letters from his publishers. Correspondents include: F. W. L. Adams, Brisbane; Sarah Welch, Adelaide; E. A. Landor on Adam Lindsay Gordon; M. R. Wills, Auckland; Annie de Carl *re* poem by Henry Lawson; Jane A. Wilson, Wellington; Samuel Clarke Johnson, Christchurch; John Huybers sending 'The Dirge' by Tasma (Mrs Jessie Couvreur); D. J. Holdsworth, Sydney, on a publication by Kendall.

SLA.2. Letters 1892, 1895-6, 1902 to Sladen including: May 1895 J. Howlett Ross, Melbourne; 27 Apr. 1896 Mrs M. Braithwaite; 27 Oct. 1902 A. Musgrave, Vice-President of Port Moresby Reading Club; 16 May 1892 Sarah Welch, Adelaide, with verse.

SLA.7. Letter 29 May 1896 E. J. Jenkins, Sydney, introducing his friend Louis Becke, and a card from Becke.

SLA.11. Correspondence mainly 1910-12 including an undated speech on Adam Lindsay Gordon and an undated letter from Professor Petrini, Milan, *re* his own publication on English poetry in Australia.

SLA.12. Correspondence 1911-12 connected with *Adam Lindsay Gordon and His Friends*, Edith M. Humphris and Douglas Sladen, London 1912. Also letters: 9 Feb. 1912 Leon Brodsky requesting advice as a playwright; 13 Dec. 1912 Donald McKenzie sending some of his compositions for judgement; 29 Oct. 1912 J. Henniker Heaton on Australian poets.

SLA.13. Letters 1913 with reference to visit of the New Zealand All Black football team, the reaction in Australia to his book on Gordon; also letter to Alfred Deakin on the future of Empire and expressing the wish that Deakin would enter British politics.

SLA.15. Letters 1916-18 including 28 Apr. 1916 H. M. Hyndman *re* visit of W. M. Hughes, and 22 Dec. 1916 C. Mackellar on memories of Australia and Australians.

SLA.16. Letter 9 Mar. 1906 W. Cornwall, Registrar, University of Melbourne, *re* Sladen's proposed thesis 'Copyright Relations of Great Britain and the United States' for the degree of LL.B.

SLA.17. Letter 31 Jan. 1912 J. Howlett Ross, Melbourne, and two letters 1919 of George Gordon McCrae sending a copy of his *John Rous*, Melbourne 1918.

SLA.18. Correspondence 1919-20, 1930-9 including: 21 Sept. 1919 D. Sladen referring to his helping Sir John Monash in writing an account of his campaigns; copy letter 27 Oct. 1919 to G. Gordon McCrae on his book *John Rous*; two letters 8 Feb. 1930 to Andrew Fisher and G. Gordon McCrae on obtaining a posthumous decoration for the latter's son; 30 June 1920 Sir John Henniker Heaton seeking a copy of *A Century of Australian Song*, ed. D. Sladen, London 1888, to help him with his article on Kendall.

SLA.33-8. Literary and Business

General literary and business correspondence 1887-1920 including letters from Australian and New Zealand minor poets and correspondence 1919 concerning Sir John Monash, *Australian Victories in France in 1918*, London 1920.

SLA.39-40. Literary Agency

Correspondence with those for whom Douglas Sladen acted as a sort of literary agent, and with the publishers whom he approached.

SLA.41-74. Books and Literary Projects

SLA.59. Correspondence *c.*1911-12 with Edith M. Humphris about the composition of *Adam Lindsay Gordon and His Friends*, with letters from various people containing suggestions and recollections for inclusion in the publication.

SLA.70. Notes for *From Boundary Rider to Prime Minister: Hughes of Australia*, London 1916, a biography of W. M. Hughes by Sladen. The notes include: letters from Hughes, A. Fisher, H. M. and R. T. Hyndman, making extensive comments on the book and giving their estimate of Hughes's capabilities; correspondence concerning sale and review of the publication.

ROYAL BOTANIC GARDENS
The Library, Kew, Richmond

The Library's manuscript collection contains official and semi-official correspondence and official records in addition to collectors' journals and notes. See the catalogue of the Library, published as Royal Botanic Gardens, Kew, *Bulletin of*

Surrey

Miscellaneous Information, Additional Series III, 1899 (catalogue of manuscripts pp.776-90) and Supplement, *Bulletin of Miscellaneous Information, Additional Series III,* 1919 (catalogue of manuscripts pp.421-33). A card index of names of writers of letters is maintained. The Library houses a collection of illustrations of plants.

Elsewhere in the Royal Botanic Gardens there are: a collection of portraits and busts of botanists, see *Catalogue of Portraits of Botanists . . . in . . . the Royal Botanic Gardens,* 1906; botanical paintings by Marianne North, housed in the North Gallery, see *Official Guide to the North Gallery,* 5th ed., London 1892; five oil paintings by Thomas Baines (Museum No.1), four illustrating Gregory's North Australian Expedition 1855-6.*

OFFICIAL CORRESPONDENCE

This correspondence is in one continuous series although the letters *c.*1825-65 addressed to Sir William Jackson Hooker who became Director of Kew in 1841 are in Vols.I-LXXVI and the letters post 1865 addressed to succeeding Directors are continued in Vols.77-218. Official correspondence is not on open access until it is thirty years old.

Letters addressed to Sir William Jackson Hooker *c.*1825-65, 76 vols.

The volumes are arranged geographically, relevant volumes being: Vols.LXXII-LXXIV, Australian letters 1825-33, 1834-51, 1851-8; Vol.LXXV Australian and Pacific letters 1859-65; Vol.LXXVI New Zealand, Western Australian, and Tasmanian letters 1835-43. A manuscript index by Lady Hyacinth Hooker, 2 vols., lists each letter under correspondent's name, giving place of origin and, when known, date. Most correspondents are professional or amateur botanists. The subject matter is mainly botanical, description of new flora, exchange of specimens, but some letters include description of local conditions.

Sir William Jackson Hooker printed extracts from correspondence in *Botanical Miscellany,* London 1830-3, continued as *The Journal of Botany* 1834-42, *London Journal of Botany* 1842-8, and *Hooker's Journal of Botany and Kew Gardens Miscellany* 1849-57. A selection of letters from William Colenso is included in A. G. Bagnall and G. C. Petersen, *William Colenso,* Wellington 1948. A number of letters from G. Francis to Sir William J. Hooker are published in Barbara Best, *The Life and Work of George William Francis . . . 1800-1865,* Adelaide 1965. A selection of letters from R. C. Gunn, J. Jorgenson, and R. W. Lawrence has been published in 'Van Diemen's Land Correspondents . . . Letters to Sir W. J. Hooker 1827-49', ed. T. E. Burns and J. R. Skemp, *Records of the Queen Victoria Museum,* New Series No.14, Launceston, 1961. A microfilm and photoprints of a number of Dr G. Bennett's letters are in the Mitchell Library, Sydney.

Correspondents writing of Australia and the Pacific area include: F. M. Adamson 1853-5; W. Archer 1854-65; J. Armstrong 1830-45; J. Backhouse 1820, 1827, 1841-63; Sir Henry Barkly 1852-65; W. Baxter 1825, 1827; G. Bennett 1853-64; J. E. Bicheno 1820-42; J. C. Bidwill 1843-52; Sir George Ferguson Bowen 1861-5, six letters giving encouraging accounts of the development of Queensland; T. H. Braim, Principal of Sydney College 1845; Sir Thomas Makdougall Brisbane 1827, 1829; A. T. Brongniart 1826-62; J. Busby 1844-8; H. S. Chapman 1841-5; G. Clifton 1857-62, 12 Aug. 1858, 23 Nov. 1861 sending seeds from Gregory expedition; Rev. W. Colenso 1840-53, Sept. 1842, Paihia, Bay of Islands, letter written in form of journal Nov. 1841 to Feb. 1842 describing journey made in East Cape area, 68 pp.; A. Collie 1828, collection of specimens made on voyage of H.M.S. *Blossom;* H. Cuming 1831-58; A. Cunningham 1824-36, Vol.LXXII letter 6 including sketch map of journey from Parramatta to Liverpool Plains July 1825; R. Cunningham 1823-35, Vol.LXXVI letter 48 autobiographical sketch, unsigned, n.d., 27 pp.;

H. M. Denham 1852-8, H.M.S. *Herald*; Sir William Denison 1846-65; E. Dieffenbach 1842-4; J. Drummond 1839-60, 18 July 1842 account of early relations between natives and settlers; G. Francis 1835-65; Sir John Franklin 1827-41; C. Fraser 1824-31; Sir George Gipps 1843-62; Sir George Grey 1852-63; R. C. Gunn 1832-49; J. von Haast 1861-2; W. Hill 1859-65; W. Hillebrand 1857-65, 12 Apr. 1865, Honolulu, outlines objects of his forthcoming voyage as Commissioner for Immigration to China, India and the East Indies to obtain agricultural labour; R. B. Hinds 1842-3; Sir Everard Home 1846-51, 1853, H.M.S. *Calliope*, Sydney; J. Jorgenson 1834-40; J. Kidd 1845-6; J. King 1833; P. P. King 1840-52; C. Knight 1852-63; C. J. LaTrobe 1854-5; R. W. Lawrence 1830-3; L. Leichhardt Vol.LXXIII item 228, letter 20 May 1846, Sydney, describing his attempts to foster interest in botany, Vol.LXXIII item 239 'Scientific exploration of Dr. L. Leichhardt in N.S.W. 1842-4' being extracts from letters 23 June 1842, Sydney, 6 Jan. 1844, Bunya Bunya district, Archer's Station, 12 July 1844, Sydney, in French; A. A. Leycester 1859-61; J. Lhotsky 1842-8; W. Macarthur 1848-63, 5 Aug. 1844, Camden, soliciting interest on behalf of Leichhardt to have him appointed Colonial Botanist and Curator of Sydney Botanic Garden; T. W. MacDonnell 1844; J. MacGillivray 1848-54 concerning collection of specimens on voyage of H.M.S. *Rattlesnake*; A. MacLeay 1843-6; Sir George MacLeay 1859-64; W. Milne 1849-58, Mar.-July 1855 describing expedition of H.M.S. *Herald* including 6 Mar. 1855, Sydney, describing meeting with hostile natives in Fiji; Sir Thomas Livingstone Mitchell 1840-6; W. Mitten 1846-62; D. Monro 1852-4 describing country near Nelson; C. Moore 1842-65; Sir Ferdinand von Mueller 1853-65; F. W. Newman 1845; F. P. Pascoe 1844-6; Rev. T. Powell, Samoa, 1861-4; L. Preiss 1839-43. B. C. Seemann 1846-61; A. Sinclair 1839-61; J. Stirling 7 Sept. 1829 commenting on progress of Swan River colony, [copy?]; Capt. C. Sturt 1833-61, 1848-9 five letters; 1854-5 [England] nine letters discussing appointments of botanist to Gregory expedition; W. Swainson 1830-42; I. P. Townsend 1849; W. T. Locke-Travers 1860-4; E. J. Wakefield 1847, 1850; F. Wakefield 1851, 1864; C. Wilhelmi 1855-63; W. Woolls 1861. There are also many letters to Hooker from J. Lindley and G. Bentham, which would probably repay examination.

Letters addressed to the Director or others after 1865

Volumes are arranged geographically then chronologically and most volumes have an index to correspondents. As well as identification and exchange of seeds and specimens, much correspondence discusses the advisability of introducing economic plants to specific areas.

Vol.169, Australasia 1914-28. Includes letters from Australia, New Guinea, New Zealand, Pacific Islands.

Vol.170, Australia and Tasmania 1899-1914.

Vol.171, Queensland 1865-1900. ff.215-16, 10 Mar. 1866 Sir George Ferguson Bowen, Brisbane, relates Aboriginal legend about Bunya-bunya tree; ff.267-359, 1863-81 W. Hill including f.300, 30 Aug. 1873, Brisbane, explaining that the aim of the exploring expedition to the rivers north of Cardwell and to the islands around and in the vicinity of Rockingham Bay was to find land suitable for sugar cane. Other correspondents include: F. M. Bailey, J. Bancroft, L. A. Bernays, A. M. Cowan, P. MacMahon, Sir Anthony Musgrave, J. Pink, and W. Soutter.

Vol.172, South Australia, Tasmania, Western Australia 1865-1900. Writers include: F. Abbott, jnr, W. Archer, R. C. Gunn, M. Holtze, N. Holtze, G. W. Leake, Sir John Lefroy, G. Maxwell, R. M. Schomburgk, R. Tate.

Vol.173, New South Wales and Victoria 1865-1900. Includes: ff.4-5, 11 Nov. 1900 Peter Barlett, detailed description of Fiji Botanic Gardens; ff.32-3, 24 Oct. 1898 W. J. Farrer, Lambrigg, Tharwa, asking if Kew could identify samples to assist his finding the 'origin of our cultivated head-wheats'; ff.323-31, 1878-80 letters from J. J. Shillinglaw asking for information on J. Jorgenson and mentioning his projected work on Flinders including f.324, 30 Dec. 1833 W. J. Hooker, Glasgow, to R. C. Gunn describing his acquaintance with J. Jorgenson, copy; ff.328-9, 7 July 1805 Matthew Flinders, Isle de France, to his wife, lithograph. Other correspondents include: W. R. Guilfoyle, Prof. A. Liversidge, W. MacArthur, Sir George MacLeay, C. Moore, and C. Wilhelmi.

Vols.174-5, New Zealand 1854-1900. Include: ff.271-400, 1861-86 J. von Haast, letters reflecting his wide range of scientific interests and commenting on contemporary affairs; ff.406-684, 1861-89 J. Hector, including f.526 memo 44, 1868, for the Under-Colonial Secretary seeking information on child-bearing of natives, copy. Other correspondents include: Dr W. L. Buller, T. F. Cheeseman, Rev. W. Colenso, Sir George Grey, G. B. Hetley, T. Kirk, C. Knight, W. Mantell, W. Petrie, A. Sinclair, H. Travers, and W. T. Locke-Travers.

Vol.176, New Zealand, Miscellaneous 1864-1913. This volume is filed with official correspondence but contains miscellaneous papers similar to those in the section headed Volumes of Miscellaneous Reports.

Vol.177, New Zealand, New Guinea, and Pacific Islands 1892-1914. Correspondents include: T. F. Cheeseman, H. Travers, N.Z., Sir Everard Ferdinand im Thurn, Suva and London, Sir William MacGregor, British New Guinea, and writers from the Sandwich Islands.

Vol.178, Pacific Islands 1865-1900. Includes: ff.37-142, 1879-96 Sir John Thurston, Fiji, with comments on and description of contemporary affairs with special reference to the introduction of commercial crops; ff.188-94 J. Askin, Pacific Islands, including ff.190-4, 24 Sept. 1870, mission schooner *Southern Cross*, giving detailed description of Solomon Islands and natives. Other writers include: J. P. Storck, D. Yeoward, Fiji, Archdeacon R. B. Comins, Melanesian Mission, Norfolk Is., Rev. S. J. Whitmee, Samoa, and W. Hillebrand, Honolulu and Heidelberg, about Hawaiian flora.

Vol.218, Supplementary Foreign Letters 1865-1900. Includes some letters from Australia and New Zealand.

KEW COLLECTORS SERIES

This small collection includes letters to and from Sir Joseph Banks; descriptions of letters are given under the names of correspondents in *The Banks Letters*, ed. Dawson.

Armstrong, John. Papers 1837-40. ff.4-5, 23 Nov. 1839, Port Essington, and ff.6-7, 7 Dec. 1840, Lafang, letters describing difficulties he encountered at Port Essington; ff.13-38 list of specimens collected 1838-9.

Barclay, George. Documents 1835-41 relating to his voyage as botanist in H.M.S. *Sulphur*: instructions, journal, specimen lists, letters including pp.71-3, 20 July 1837, Oahu, Sandwich Is., pp.105-6, 13 June 1839, Aroori, Sandwich Is., both commenting on contemporary affairs.

Cunningham, Allan and Bowie, James. Correspondence 1814-18 among W. T. Aiton, Sir Joseph Banks, J. Bowie, and Cunningham relating to the appointments of the two latter as Kew collectors; pp.221-69, correspondence of Cunningham after his arrival in Australia including pp.224-8C, 24 Mar. 1817, Parramatta, to his brother, with detailed comment on transportation; pp.264-9, Dec. 1816 to Jan. 1817 Cunningham's journal.

Cunningham, Allan. Miscellaneous 1816-28, with index. Lists of specimens collected, list of journeys made, date and number of specimens collected.

Cunningham, Allan. 1817-23. Pencil title, 'An enum. of the plants collected during the several voyages of Survey of the Coasts of Terra Austs. on board H.M. Cutter *Mermaid* & H.M. Brig *Bathurst* under the command of Lieut. P. P. King. Commencing Decr. 1817 ending . . . 1822'. See also below under Maps.

Cunningham, Allan. Correspondence 1817-31, copies of forty-six letters to Sir Joseph Banks and W. T. Aiton and letters received from them 1817-24; copies of correspondence 1824-31 with W. T. Aiton, thirty-three letters from Cunningham, many with descriptions of country including his visits to New Zealand; 8 Nov. 1824, Parramatta, his journey with Oxley to Brisbane River.

Milne, William Grant. Documents 1852-9 relating to his appointment as botanist of H.M.S. *Herald*, letters and journal.

Papers relating to Kew collectors 1791-1865 with index. Notes with a few letters.

MISCELLANEOUS MANUSCRIPTS

Arranged alphabetically by author.

Backhouse, James. 'Recollections of the botany of New South Wales, Van Diemen's Land and their dependencies', n.d., 2 vols. Botanical descriptions arranged systematically.

Banks, Sir Joseph. Correspondence 1766-1820, 3 vols. and index. The index is entitled 'Banksian Letters, Preliminary Correspondence, Index to Correspondence, Compiled by B. Daydon Jackson 1906'. Descriptions of this correspondence are included under names of correspondents in *The Banks Letters* ed. Dawson. The letters have been guarded and rebound, Vol.1 in 3 parts, Vol.2 in 3 parts, Vol.3 in 1 part. Vol.3 is listed as Banksiana in the 1919 Supplement to the Catalogue of the Library. Copies of three letters to Banks listed in the 1899 catalogue, letters from Dr Solander, W. Anderson 24 Nov. 1776, and A. Cunningham 8 Nov. 1819, 'originals in the possession of Mr Enys', are now bound in the volumes. The volumes include the following letters: Vol.1 No.113 [25 Dec.] 1781 from W. W. Ellis, Kew, giving his reasons for publishing an account of Cook's voyage; No.245, 26 Sept. 1786 from S. Bacstrom asking to be sent out as a collector when convicts were transported to New Holland, one of several letters from Bacstrom in Vols.1 and 2; No.363, 20 Oct. 1789 from R. Molesworth concerning the fitting out of the *Gorgon* for New South Wales. Vol.2 No.20, 10 Oct. 1790 from D. Burton concerning his passage on the *Gorgon*, No.206; 17 Oct. 1798 from Correia de Serra informing Banks that R. Brown offered to go to New Holland in place of Mungo Park; No.251, 9 Nov. 1801 from W. Kent concerning three emus he had brought to England; No.281, 6 Nov. 1803 from Barrallier concerning his journey in the Blue Mountains; No.293, 27 Aug. 1804 from Bauer written on his way to Norfolk Island concerning his drawings and collections by himself and Brown.

Banks, Sir Joseph. A journey of Sir Joseph Banks on Cook's first voyage round the world in H.M.S. *Endeavour* 1768-71, 3 vols. A transcript of the copy of the original manuscript made by the Misses Turner, emended by J. D. Hooker for his edition, Sir Joseph Banks, *Journal . . . during Capt. Cook's first voyage in H.M.S. Endeavour in 1768-71*, London 1896.

Bentham, George. Collectors' accounts 1835-83. ff.10, 16 Drummond, Swan River collection.

Bentham, George. Diaries 1807-83, 20 vols. Vol.19, 1874-80, 26-30 Sept. 1878 mentions receipt of the last contribution for *Flora Australiensis*, London 1863-78, 7 vols., listing contributions from Victoria, South Australia, New South Wales, and Queensland, his payments to publishers, and the time taken to complete the work.

Bentham, George. Letters addressed to him by various people c.1829-83, 10 vols.

Surrey

Arranged alphabetically under writers' surnames. Vol.1 contains an index to all correspondents; relevant names noted are: W. Archer, J. C. Bidwill, A. Cunningham, R. D. Fitzgerald, C. Moore, R. M. Schomburgk, W. Woolls.

Bentham, George. Memoirs of botanists including A. Cunningham, C. Fraser, R. M. Schomburgk.

Challenger, H.M.S. Botanical letters and documents relating to the 1872-87 voyage.

Christian, Frederick W. List of names of trees and plants of the North and South Marquesas Islands c.1909.

Colenso, Rev. William. Botany of New Zealand, consisting of letters from Colenso to Sir William Hooker 1841-52 with lists of 6190 specimens sent to Hooker.

Cunningham, Allan. 'Congestiones plantarum minus cognitarum Australasiae', 1834. Quotes descriptions of plants found by Dampier, de Freycinet, and others on west and east coasts with comments and sketches.

Cunningham, Allan. 'Hortus Trianonus', 1826. This list, which belonged to A. Cunningham, includes Australasian plants.

Cunningham, Allan. Plants of New Zealand, 'Florae Insularum Novae Zelandiae praecursor etc.' n.d. Narrative of botanical exploration in New Zealand including A. and R. Cunningham's visits, with descriptive list of plants. Another volume similarly lettered, n.d. with index, consists of memoranda.

Darwin, Charles Robert. Letters to Professor Henslow 1831-7. Forty-four letters including Jan.1836, Sydney, giving his impressions of the colony, Galapagos Is., Tahiti.

Duthie, John Firminger. Letters from various botanists, 2 vols. with index. Includes letters from T. W. Naylor Beckett, N.Z., C. Moore, Sydney, and F. von Mueller.

Forsyth, William. Correspondence, 3 vols. Vol.2 ff.40-3, 23 Aug. 1790, Norfolk Is., unsigned letter describing despatch of people to Norfolk Island by Phillip because of lack of supplies at Sydney. Also describes breeding of mutton birds.

Guppy, Henry Brougham. Notes on Solomon Islands plants 1885.

Guppy, Henry Brougham. Miscellaneous notes, n.d., 2 vols.

Hemsley, Clara Edith. Catalogue of the plants of New Guinea, 1898, with some additions by I. H. Birkill.

Henslow, John Stevens. Correspondence, including two letters 13 Apr. 1838, 6 Mar. 1839 from A. Cunningham, Sydney.

Hill, Arthur William. Journeys to various countries 1902-37, 12 vols. They include diaries of visits to Australia and New Zealand 1927-8.

Hooker, Sir Joseph Dalton. Antarctic expedition correspondence 1839-45, 110 letters, original or copies, describing places visited. The letters are numbered consecutively: letters 24-44, 16 Aug. 1840 to 6 July 1841, V.D.L.; letter 45, 5 Aug. 1841, Sydney; letters 46-54, 24 Aug. to 23 Nov. 1841, Bay of Islands, N.Z.

Hooker, Sir Joseph Dalton. Antarctic Journal 18 May 1839 to 28 Mar. 1843.

Hooker, Sir Joseph Dalton. Botany of the Auckland Islands and Campbell Island. Descriptive notes and drawings.

Hooker, Sir Joseph Dalton. Correspondence 1839-45, 274 letters and papers relating to Ross's Antarctic expedition, correspondents include W. Colenso, R. Gunn, J. Jorgenson, W. J. MacLeay, J. S. Henslow, and many others.

Hooker, Sir Joseph Dalton. Letters and Journal 1839-43 containing botanical observations and descriptions of places and people; pp.129-226, 29 Mar. 1840 to 15

July 1841, letters from Hobart, V.D.L.; pp.237-74, 24 Aug. to 8 Oct. 1841, letters from Bay of Islands, N.Z.

Hooker, Sir Joseph Dalton. Antarctic botany, notes and drawings 1839-43.

Hooker, Sir Joseph Dalton. Letters to J. D. Hooker, 21 vols. The letters are bound in alphabetical order of correspondents including: F. M. Bailey, R. T. Baker, W. L. Bowen, T. F. Cheeseman, L. Cockayne, W. Colenso, W. R. Guilfoyle, Sir James Hector, H. J. W. Mahon, E. E. Morris, A. Morton, G. R. Mott, C. Mudd, and F. von Mueller.

Hooker, Sir Joseph Dalton. Correspondence concerning the transit of Venus expedition 1874-5, mainly about Kerguelen.

Hooker, Sir Joseph Dalton. Letters to Sir Joseph and Lady Hooker, 4 vols.

Lambert, Aylmer Bourke. Letters; Nos.29, 30 from John Egerley, N.Z., 1839.

Lindley, John. Letters 1807-65, 2 vols. Correspondents include: W. Macarthur, T. L. Mitchell, F. von Mueller, and R. C. Gunn.

MacGillivray, John. Voyage of H.M.S. *Rattlesnake*. Catalogue of botanical specimens collected 1847-9.

Mitten, William. Correspondence 1845-1905 including a few letters from W. Bell, T. Kirk, and Sir Ferdinand von Mueller and notebooks containing lists of specimens and where collected.

Mueller, Sir Ferdinand von. Correspondence with the Royal Botanic Gardens, Kew, and G. Bentham 1858-91, 3 vols. Vol.1, ff.1-43, n.d., unsigned notes on *Flora Australiensis*; Vol.3, ff.230-1, 24 Aug. 1887, Melbourne, von Mueller, President of Royal Geographical Society of Australasia (Victorian Branch) to Sir Joseph Dalton Hooker asking for donation towards projected expedition by Giles, signed by Council members of Central Australian Exploration Fund. Contemporary expeditions of botanical interest are mentioned.

Mueller, Sir Ferdinand von. Correspondence with the Royal Botanic Gardens, Kew, 1891-6.

Munro, William and Bentham, George. Correspondence on Australian grasses 1877.

Paterson, William. Letters 1777-1803 to William Forsyth; ff.34-9, 1791-2 Norfolk Island; ff.40-51, 1793-1803 Port Jackson.

Swainson, William. Ten pencil sketches of Australasian, chiefly New Zealand, trees 1847-52.

FERN LISTS

Lists 1857-91, 1867-1904, 2 vols. Both volumes are indexed under collector and place.

INWARDS AND OUTWARDS BOOKS

Books, sometimes called Record Books, 1793 to date, containing lists of collections of plants and seeds collected for and despatched from Kew Gardens. The volume for 1793-1809 contains entries for Banks's items from Botany Bay and for Bligh and his breadfruit.

PLANT LISTS

Lists, sometimes called Determination Lists, c.1811-1939, in volumes, and folders which will eventually be bound. Volumes are indexed under name of collector and area including areas in Australia, New Guinea, New Zealand, and Polynesia.

VOLUMES OF MISCELLANEOUS REPORTS

These bound folio volumes contain a miscellaneous collection of copies of government reports, despatches, official and private correspondence, parliamentary papers, and cuttings, dealing with economic botany. Each volume is indexed, usually under subject matter. Only those volumes containing some manuscript material are mentioned here: 1.2 Colonial Fruit, Correspondence 1866-96, 2 vols; 6.5 New Guinea, Fiji and Pacific Islands, Miscellaneous Reports 1850-1928; 7.1-7.7 Miscellaneous Reports and Correspondence *c.*1846-90 from New South Wales, Victoria, Queensland, Western Australia, and South Australia; 8 Miscellaneous Correspondence *c.*1843-1928 from New Zealand and Tasmania; 9.3 Reports and Correspondence *c.*1860-1919 from Fiji.

MAPS

Allan Cunningham. Charts and sketch maps of the north-east coast of Australia, Wide Bay, Brisbane River, Murray and Murrumbidgee Rivers, Castlereagh and Macquarie Rivers; 'A rough sketch of a portion of . . . N.S.W. . . . constructed from various observations taken during the progress of journeys performed in the winter months of 1827 and 1828' superimposed on Map of Interior Discoveries made in New South Wales by John Oxley 1824; map of journey Mar.-July 1827.

Dr Julius von Haast. 8B. Sketch map of Lake District (Middle Is.), N.Z., n.d. Coloured tracing on linen cloth.

8B. The Southern Alps of the Middle Island of New Zealand 1863.

J. S. Roe. 7.4A. Explorations in the interior of Western Australia between September 1848 and February 1849 by J. S. Roe, Surveyor General, 2 sheets.

Versteeg. 6.5B. Dutch expedition to New Guinea. Route taken by Mr Versteeg n.d. Printed, with MS. additions.

SUSSEX

P. S. LAURIE, ESQ.
30 Peartree Lane, Bexhill-on-Sea

Log of John Ord, master *Margaret*, 24 May 1850 to 9 Mar. 1852.* The log records part of a circumnavigation of the world, Liverpool to San Francisco, thence via Tahiti to Sydney and Bombay, and part of the voyage to China before returning to England. The second volume cannot be found at present (1969). The entries, mostly signed Jon. Bennett, are generally routine, but daily work on the ship, wages of crew, near-mutiny, desertions in San Francisco and Sydney, proceedings during brief calls at Juan Fernandez and Tahiti for water and in port are recorded. The ship touched at only a few islands while crossing the Pacific until Lady Elliot Island was sighted and two landings made, apparently for the purpose of taking samples of guano. The log records the movements of the ship in Port Jackson 18 June to 21 Aug. and details of the voyage north to Endeavour Strait and thence to Bombay.

WEST SUSSEX RECORD OFFICE
West Street, Chichester

See *A Descriptive Report on the Quarter Sessions, Other Official and Ecclesiastical Records in the custody of the County Councils of West and East Sussex*, 1954, and printed *Catalogues* of a number of collections including those referred to below. These should be consulted for all conditions of use of material. The relevant *Catalogues* are: *The Cobden Papers* ed. Francis W. Steer, 1964; *The Cobden and Unwin Papers* ed. Patricia Gill, 1967; *The Cowdray Archives*, Parts 1, 2 ed. A. A. Dibben, 1960, 1964; *The Goodwood Estate Archives* ed. Francis W. Steer and J. E. Amanda Venables, Vol.1, 1970, Vol.2, not yet published (Apr. 1970).

PRIVATE RECORDS

Cobden Papers

7-8. Three letters to Richard Cobden: 19 Jan. 1864 Sir George Ferguson Bowen on his position and life as colonial governor with reference to local labour and products; 5 Oct. 1864 Henry H. Brown, Taranaki, N.Z., on the taking of Maori land and the Maori Wars; 22 Feb. 1865 Archibald Michie, Minister of Justice for Victoria, saying that the *Shenandoah* is in Australian waters and it is believed there will be an attempt to embroil Australia with the Northern States in the American Civil War.

153. Letter 1 June 1926 Stanley V. Larkin, Sydney, to Emma Jane, daughter of Richard Cobden and wife of T. Fisher Unwin, referring to the present situation of free trade in Australia destroyed by a protectionist policy.

155. Two letters to T. Fisher Unwin: 30 Sept. 1903 Senator E. Pulsford, Melbourne, stating he does not know of any Cobden correspondence; 6 Oct. 1903 Sir Josiah Symon, Adelaide, stating he has no correspondence of the late Mr Cobden for the new book.

Cobden and Unwin Papers

971-2. Two letters 1883, 1892 Dorothy Richmond, Nelson, N.Z., to Emma J. C. Cobden containing domestic news and expressing a wish that she would come to New Zealand.

979. Correspondence 1879-91 with the Richmond family of Nelson, N.Z., including fifteen letters 1880-91 Dorothy Richmond to Lucy Elizabeth Margaret Cobden containing in 1881 a reference to her father's electioneering but mainly concerned with domestic news.

988. Letter 28 Feb. 1878 J. W. Longmuir, Sydney, to T. B. Potter, response to advertisement seeking papers of Richard Cobden.

Cowdray Archives

Family Papers

5080. Copy of order 1 Oct. 1867 of the Supreme Court of New Zealand, Canterbury District, for the sale of the estate and effects of Spencer Arthur Perceval of Leithfield in the province of Canterbury, a debtor.

5089-102. Legal documents 1874-5 concerning the payment of legacies under the will of George James, 6th Earl of Egmont, to his brother's children, Spencer Arthur Perceval, formerly of New Zealand, Augustus George Perceval of New South Wales, and Charles John Perceval, Victoria.

Goodwood Archives

Papers of Charles Lennox, 5th Duke of Richmond, Lennox and Aubigny, Parliamentary Papers.

638. Papers 1831-2 relating to plans for relieving the labouring poor by way of emigration including: 20 July 1831, House of Lords, Poor Law Committee, on the possibility of emigration including to Australia.

641. Papers 1831-2 relating to emigration including to Western Australia; also 16 Dec. 1831 'Royal instructions and despatches to the Governors of New South Wales, Van Diemen's Land and Western Australia as to the mode to be adopted in

disposing of Crown Lands and the means by which emigration may be facilitated', printed.

647-50. Jan.-Aug. 1832 Parliamentary letters and papers relating *inter alia* to emigration and including: letter Jan. 1832 J. W. Birch, Colonial Office, to Duke of Richmond, on emigration of Mrs Morgan to Sydney; letters 3, 26, 28 Apr. 1832 T. F. Elliot, on ships leaving for Van Diemen's Land and New South Wales and the inability to finance more female emigrants; 10 Feb. 1832 'Extract of a letter from the Swan River Settlement to Mr. George Blunden, Petworth'; 14 July 1832 T. F. Elliot, Colonial Office, sending an article by Edward Forster, Treasurer of the Refuge for the Destitute, 'Emigration of females to New South Wales and Van Diemen's Land'.

Among correspondence in the Goodwood Archives not yet listed by the Record Office, but listed in N.R.A. Report 0850, Box 43, Bundle 123 there are reports 1846-8 by Dr and Mrs Bowden from the hulk *Anson*, River Derwent, V.D.L., concerning female convicts.

ADD.MSS.2216-32. Deeds and Documents of 51 Tower St, Chichester, 1810-1938 2223. Conveyance 13 Oct. 1871 Mary and Alfred Barker of Baldina Keringa, Burra Burra, and Rev. George Septimus Gruggen, with witnesses Edward Arnold, solicitor, Chichester, Ralph Ingleby, solicitor, Adelaide, and John Nicholson, notary public, Adelaide.

6013. Letter 12 May 1860 R. W. Nutt, Melbourne, to Richard Cobden with condolences on the loss of his boy and references to the influence of his theories on economics in Australia.

ROYAL GREENWICH OBSERVATORY
Herstmonceux Castle, Hailsham

See the following lists:

List of the Royal Observatory Manuscripts, Part 1, 1675-1881. The title-page is printed and the list is duplicated typescript. Part 1 covers the terms of Astronomers Royal to 1881 and also the Board of Longitude Papers. Numbers 1-1333 have been assigned to the volumes or boxes.

Index to the MSS. of Nevil Maskelyne (Astronomer Royal 1765-1811) at the Royal Greenwich Observatory, [by E. G. Forbes], duplicated typescript.

Index of the Board of Longitude Papers at the Royal Greenwich Observatory, [by E. G. Forbes], duplicated typescript.

List of Christie Papers, typescript. A brief provisional list of non-current records 1881-*c*.1930. Includes papers of Sir William H. M. Christie, Astronomer Royal 1851-1910 and some papers of Sir Frank Dyson, Astronomer Royal 1910-33.

The documents described below are samples of the type of material existing in the records. They were found by checking the lists and indexes listed above and by looking through selected volumes on the shelves of series *c*.1835-*c*.1930. An index of personal or place names is added at the beginning of nearly all volumes, boxes, or files. Except where otherwise stated, the numbers given at the beginnings of the following entries are those assigned in 'List of Royal Observatory Manuscripts, Part 1, 1675-1881'.

136-303 MASKELYNE PAPERS
c.1743-*c*.1815, 168 vols.

269. Correspondence 1760-1808. A packet of twenty-four letters sewn together entitled 'The Rev. Mr. Maskelyne's Letters, relating to the Transits of Venus in 1761 and 1769 &c. &c.' includes 'Instructions for observing the Transit of Venus for

1769 by the Revd. Mr. Nevil Maskelyne, Astronomer Royal'; draft of letter of agreement 1 Mar. 1801 with John Crossley; draft letter of agreement with James Inman.

270. Correspondence 1766-1809. Forty-three letters including two letters 28 Jan., 3 Oct. 1807 from Bligh, Government House, Sydney, sending observations 9 Dec. 1806 of an eclipse of the sun, and observations 27 Sept. 1807 of a comet.

529-96 BOARD OF LONGITUDE PAPERS*

1713-1829, 68 vols. In addition to volumes from which papers listed below are selected, the following may also repay examination: 533-6, Confirmed Minutes 1737-1829; 537, Letter Books 1782-1810; 583, Correspondence, miscellaneous, arranged alphabetically by correspondent.

541-2. Instruments belonging to the Board, persons entitled to publications, receipt and delivery of presents and loans 1767-1828: ff.159-68, loan of instruments to Lieut. Dawes 1787-91; ff.169-80, loan of instruments to Dr Inman 1802; ff.193-230, receipts for instruments lent 1784-1828 including f.206, receipt 18 Oct. 1787 from Bligh for 'a Time-Keeper', the second made by Kendall.

545. Accounts 1776-1828: ff.54-64, William Bayly 1772-85; ff.191-8, John Crossley 1801-6; ff.202-4, William Dawes 1800.

576. Observatories 1786-1828: ff.215-31, the observatory at Parramatta 1822-9; ff.237-308, William Dawes's correspondence 1786-92 during the establishment of an observatory at Port Jackson, N.S.W.

579. Tides and trade winds 1780-1828: ff.170-3, Matthew Flinders, sending a chart of New Holland 1804.

584-7. Contain log books and observations of H.M.S. *Adventure* 1772-4 and H.M.S. *Resolution* 1772-5.

588. Captain Cook's journal, variation of compass, chronometers, rates 1776.

589. Captain Cook's last voyage, astronomical observations 1778-80.

592-3. Observations, *Investigator* log book, astronomical observations, calculations, reductions of calculations.

594. Includes calculations of observations apparently made in *Investigator* 1801 and 1802.

595. ff.80b-175, astronomical observations made in the *Providence* 1794-7.

596. ff.2-7, letters 1787-8 from Wales about the publication of Capt. Cook's observations; ff.8-12, letter 1796 from Vancouver about reducing his observations made on a voyage round the world; ff.13-36, memoranda and correspondence 1802-8 relating to Flinders's application for a reward; ff.37-67, correspondence 1811-14 relating to the recalculations of Flinders's observations and to Flinders's memorial; ff.68-90, papers relating to Flinders's voyages, Dawes's observations etc.; ff.171-256, Dr James Inman's observations at Port Jackson and on a voyage from Port Jackson.

597-1333 AIRY PAPERS

1835-*c*.1888, 737 vols. Each volume usually has an index and in-correspondence is accompanied by press copies of Airy's replies. The following papers have been noted:

737-53. Observatories 1835-62
737. Section 9, correspondence 1835-47 concerning the observatory at Parramatta. For correspondence 1849 see 739 Section 9.
738. Section 7, letter 27 Aug. 1847 from P. P. King, Port Stephen, referring to the wretched state of the instruments at Parramatta.

S

740. Section 17, correspondence 1851 concerning the purchase of an astronomical clock for South Australia; Section 23, contains one letter 1853 from J. Challis, Cambridge Observatory, forwarding a letter from Pell, 'Mathematical Professor' at the new University of Sydney, N.S.W., and a press copy of Airy's reply returning Pell's letter.

741. Section 1, correspondence 1853-4 concerning Sydney Observatory and time ball; Section 2, letter 21 Jan. 1853 from Denison concerning the Hobart Observatory.

742-4. Section 1 in each volume contains letters 1858-61 from Todd concerning the proposed observatory for Adelaide; 744 Section 14, letter 5 Apr. 1861 requesting Airy to inspect a 'Transit Circle' for Melbourne.

745. Section 13, two letters 1863, 1865 from Robert J. Ellery, Melbourne. Other correspondence 1869-75 with Ellery is in 746, Section 13, 747, Section 10, 748, Section 8. Sections 22-45, papers 1861-5 relate to the choice of an astronomer to succeed Rev. W. Scott in Sydney and the appointment of George Roberts Smalley, and include a draft code of instructions for the Astronomer at Sydney.

746. Section 4, letter 29 July 1867 from Todd, Adelaide. Other papers 1869-75 concerning Todd are in 748 Section 2, 749 Section 1. Section 21 contains papers 1866-7 relating to Sydney, repair of instruments, and part of letter from Smalley.

747. Section 13, letter 6 Aug. 1870 from J. L. Sinclair, Secretary of the Auckland, N.Z., Polytechnic Institution, concerning a proposed observatory, press copy of Airy's reply, letter 9 Mar. 1872 from J. L. Sinclair. Section 16, letter 5 Sept. 1871 from H. C. Russell, Sydney, also *Report of Government Observatory, Sydney* for 1871. Section 20, correspondence 1872 concerning a proposed observatory at Christchurch, N.Z.

748. Section 6 includes correspondence 1873-5 concerning a telescope for the University of Sydney.

750. Section 7 includes correspondence 1878-9 concerning the purchase of instruments for the Observatory, Wellington, N.Z.

751. Section 3 includes two letters July 1887 from H. C. Russell concerning records of the Observatory at Parramatta and reply from the Royal Observatory; it appears from correspondence that some Parramatta papers were kept by the Royal Society.

753. Papers 1855-62 relating to the Sydney Observatory.

754-76. Instruments 1833-87

762. Papers 1852-3 concerning the establishment of a large telescope in the southern hemisphere.

767-74. A few papers about instruments for Australia or New Zealand are included. 767 item 38 is a 'Catalogue' 1860 of the auction sale at Edinburgh of instruments belonging to the late General Sir Thomas Makdougall Brisbane. 770 Section 9 includes a letter 30 May 1871 from the Royal Society stating that the committee appointed to superintend the construction of the Melbourne telescope is about to publish a third concluding part of correspondence.

864-80. Transit of Venus 1874. The papers cover 1869-82 and include correspondence, information, charts, photographs of stations, papers concerning instruments, buildings, and stores. Many papers relate to the British establishment in the Sandwich Islands under Capt. Tupman, R.M.A., in Kerguelen's Land under Rev. S. J. Perry, and in New Zealand under Major Palmer, R.E.

905-6. University of Melbourne 1854-6, 2 vols. The papers include letters 26 Jan. 1854 and 11 Sept. 1856 from Sir Redmond Barry, Chancellor, the first requesting Airy's advice and the second thanking him for advice in the choice of professors.

907. University of Sydney 1851-2. Correspondence and papers 1851-2 concerning the choice of professors for the University of Sydney.

986-94. Geodesy

988. Section 7 contains letter 17 June 1830 from the Admiralty concerning base apparatus to be sent to New South Wales; Section 8, file of correspondence 1847-9 on the trigonometrical survey of Van Diemen's Land including correspondence with Denison. Section 18, file of correspondence 1850 with Lieut.-Col. Estcourt on the Australian Colonies Government Bill with printed copy of the Bill, including letters referring to the creation of a new province, Victoria, and the difficulties concerning the boundary.

990. Section 19, letter 24 Apr. 1861 from Ellery, Williamstown, Vic., concerning the geodetic survey of Victoria. Section 37, file of correspondence 1860 concerning the survey of Victoria, including copy of despatches 19 Feb. 1859 and 12 Mar. 1860 from Barkly.

1198-1203. Galvanic connections 1851-78

1198. Section 33, file of correspondence 1854-5 chiefly on galvanic communications at Adelaide and appointment of Charles Todd as Superintendent of the Electric Telegraph at Adelaide, including a tracing showing the telegraph line Adelaide to Port Adelaide and location of stations.

1199. Section 59, file of manuscript and printed papers 1853-7 on the Adelaide telegraph and on the proposed telegraph connection between Adelaide and Melbourne.

1204-11. Longitudes

1209. Section 10, extract from letter 24 Nov. 1866 from Charles Todd concerning determination of the boundary of the colonies of New South Wales, South Australia and Victoria.

1210. Section 5 contains letter 11 July 1877 from Todd concerning determination of the east and west boundaries of South Australia.

1211. Section 3, Australian and New Zealand longitudes 1878-81 including correspondence 1878 with Major W. M. Campbell; with and concerning Todd 1880-1, concerning Rockyside Observatory, Otago, N.Z., 1881; cutting from *Sydney Morning Herald* 18 June 1878 and offprint of paper read by John Tebbutt before the Royal Society of New South Wales 2 June 1880, both concerning the longitude of Sydney.

CHRISTIE PAPERS

1881-*c*.1930 As no new list with running numbers exists, old classification numbers are given for papers listed below. The following papers have been noted:

Q.5. Observatories, 7 boxes. The following files were noted:

Miscellaneous Astronomy 1890-1910. Includes letter 20 Jan. 1890 from W. Steadman Aldis, University College, Auckland, N.Z., asking about the minimum cost of an instrument to serve as a commencement of a national astronomical observatory, with remarks on the request and other papers.

Colonial Observatories 1891-1903. Section 8, Perth Observatory, General Correspondence 1901-3 includes correspondence with William Ernest Cooke, Government Astronomer, Western Australia.

Appointments 1907-13. Includes papers 1911-12 concerning appointment of Government Astronomer at Sydney with correspondence between Dyson and the Agent General for New South Wales and copies of applications from astronomers.

General Correspondence 1909-27. Includes letter 17 Nov. 1913 from Mary Proctor, Wellington, N.Z., to Dyson concerning the choice of a site for a Cawthron Observatory at Nelson; the letter refers to Duffield and the meteorological station at Canberra. Sydney, N.S.W. Correspondence 1913-24 with Cooke and Board of Visitors.

Z.2. Clocks, not Royal Observatory. A miscellaneous section includes letter 8 Dec. 1886 from E. Dent & Co. concerning a chronograph sent by Ellery from Melbourne to the late Colonial Exhibition. The same section also includes letter 13 Jan. 1891 from Henry Daly stating that the new clock for the Sydney Post Office tower is complete, that it has been made to Lord Grimthorpe's design, and suggesting that Christie and Grimthorpe inspect it together.

Z.8. Longitude and Latitude, 5 boxes arranged chronologically. Included in the papers is a sheet of notes headed 'Australian longitudes, C. Todd's Report 1886 Nov.'.

J. R. GREEN, ESQ.
Pondtail Farm, West Grinstead, Horsham

REV. JAMES LAMPARD GREEN PAPERS

Papers relating to the Pacific have been microfilmed for the Pacific Manuscripts Bureau, Research School of Pacific Studies, Australian National University, Canberra, and positive microfilm copies have been distributed to member libraries of the Bureau; see the Bureau's newsletter *Pambu*, No. 11, June 1969, p.8.

Certificate 6 Nov. 1860 of ordination of J. L. Green.

Diary 1 Jan. 1874 to 29 Dec. 1879.

Loose sheets, cover entitled in J. L. Green's handwriting 'Journal notes July 1884 to Aug. 1886. Some pages missing'. Extant pages have entries 12 Nov. 1884 to 20 Sept. 1886. Those for Aug.-Sept. 1886 describe Green's departure from Tahiti to his arrival in San Francisco on his homeward journey to England.

Letters from Rev. James Chalmers: 11 Aug., 28 Sept., 23 Oct., 16 Nov. 1875, Rarotonga; 5 Oct. 1880, Port Moresby, containing an account of an attack at Keakolo on a Chinese junk; 8 Jan. 1881, New Guinea; 29 Mar. 1881, New Guinea, describing the 'motley crowd' of old missionaries, gold diggers, bêche-de-mer fishers, and bird and plant collectors who 'risk New Guinea proper'; 18 Oct. 1884, Port Moresby; 17 Dec. 1884, New Guinea, containing references to annexation.

Miscellanea include: letter 17 July 1871 James H. Wodehouse, Honolulu, to Green congratulating him on his removal from Tahaa to Tahiti, and opining that the Pomare family were all bad; translation of letter 13 June 1883 from Terai, native missionary at Aloma, New Guinea, to J. L. Green, his family and friends, describing the character and customs of the Papuans with extract from an earlier letter 23 Apr. 1882; text of an address 'The Bible in the Pacific' possibly by a son of J. L. Green, p.5 referring to his father's revision of the Tahitian Bible; report of an appreciation of the work of J. L. Green in Tahiti taken from an address 16 May 1908 by Rev. C. Silvester Horne.

A. F. COGHLAN, ESQ.
Ludwell Grange, Horsted Keynes

Papers 1878-1929 of Sir Timothy Coghlan, New South Wales Government Statistician and, from 1905, Agent General for New South Wales in London.

In-letters 1879-1929 including: *c.*300 miscellaneous letters 1879-1929; eighteen letters 1905-8 from Alfred Deakin; fifty letters 1887-1920 from J. LeGay Brereton, Sir George Dibbs, R. E. O'Connor, B. R. Wise, Henry Parkes, Alfred Deakin, and Andrew Fisher; folder of congratulations on Coghlan's knighthood in 1914. There are letters of condolence on Coghlan's death in 1926 with these in-letters.

Letter books 30 Mar. to 30 Oct. 1906, 18 Dec. 1908 to 15 May 1911, 23 June 1911 to 17 June 1915, 3 vols. They contain *c.*800 copies of letters from Coghlan to friends, business associates, public service colleagues, and Federal and State politicians.

Other papers include: family correspondence with some letters from Coghlan but mainly letters to him from his wife; cuttings relating to Coghlan's career in Australia and London, seven volumes 1885-1920 and miscellaneous cuttings 1900-26; miscellanea including notification of honours and a folder of documents relating to Coghlan's patent of a method for the treatment of greasy wool; photographs.

HOVE CENTRAL LIBRARY
Church Road, Hove

AUTOGRAPH COLLECTION

Letter 16 Mar. 1891 John Billington to Mrs Carlton [Arlton], *re* her son Frank at Newcastle, Q'ld [?N.S.W.] whose ship S.S. *Victoria* was due in London.

Document 26 Dec. 1818 Frederick Augustus, Duke of York, to Duke of Wellington concerning the death sentence on four soldiers commuted to transportation for life to New South Wales.

WOLSELEY PAPERS

Papers of Garnet Joseph, 1st Viscount Wolseley. They include papers formerly in the Royal United Service Institution.

Autograph Collection includes: invitation 9 June 1886 from Sir George Bowen to a dinner at the Royal Colonial Institute to read his paper on the proposed Federation of the Empire; letter n.d. H. C. E. Childers introducing Gen. Scratchley on a mission from the government of Victoria; letter 21 Oct. 1882 King of Honolulu to Robert F. Synger, Foreign Office, with thanks for bringing contents of his letter to notice of Earl Granville, acknowledging gifts and mentioning Viscount and Lady Wolseley; three letters 1883-4 Sir Henry Parkes, 31 Oct. 1883 asking if Wolseley had been able to give consideration to the question of the defences of Sydney; letter 15 Aug. 1891 Thomas Humphrey Ward asking Wolseley to support his cousin Col. Sandwith for the command of the troops in New Zealand.

Scrapbook No.19. *The New South Wales Contingents to South Africa, Oct. 1899-June 1900*, Sydney 1900.

EAST SUSSEX RECORD OFFICE
Pelham House, Lewes

See *Descriptive Report on the Quarter Sessions, Other Official and Ecclesiastical Records in the custody of the County Councils of West and East Sussex, with a guide to the development and historical interest of the Archives*, 1954, and printed *Catalogues* of some of the deposited private collections.

QUARTER SESSIONS RECORDS

QCR Parliamentary Returns
QCR/1/EW6. Expenses of Criminal Prosecutions and Transport of Convicts to depots 1835-57; return of expenses of conveying convicts 1857-78. Three bundles of returns and associated documents for the Eastern and Western divisions of Sussex, based on Lewes and Chichester respectively.

RYE CORPORATION RECORDS

54. Returns 1836-51 of expenses of criminal prosecutions and transportation.
55. Circulars and papers 1847-68 on expenses of criminal prosecutions and transportation.

BOARDS OF GUARDIANS RECORDS

G13/75. Eastbourne Union

Register of emigrations 1899-1930 giving name, date of emigration and destination including a few emigrants to Australia and New Zealand, e.g. Staley family 21 Sept. 1923 to New Zealand.

PARISH RECORDS

233 Ashburnham Parish Records

233/37/4/17, 18, 33. Small printed poster 16 Feb. 1839 advertising emigration to New South Wales for married men of good character belonging to the Battle Union; two printed notices concerning free passages for emigrants to New South Wales, receipted 1838 and 1840 by John Marshall, Australian Emigration Agent for London.

PRIVATE RECORDS

3099 Ashburnham MSS.

Wentworth Goldfields Proprietary Company Limited, Lucknow, N.S.W., printed reports and statements of accounts to 30 Sept. 1893.

D677 Frewen MSS. Political and religious tracts 1623-1831

D677/9. *The Isle of Pines, or, a late discovery of a fourth island in Terra Australis Incognita*, [by Henry Nevile], 'printed by S.G. for Allen Banks and Charles Harper at the Flower-Deluice near Cripplegate Church', London 1668.

ADD.MS.2166 Tourle Family of Lewes 1708-1878

Copy n.d. of the *Morning Herald*, London, being notice of the marriage at Scone, Hunter River, N.S.W., of Thomas Tourle of Balala, N.S.W., to Helen M. Emma Moise, daughter of Rev. John Moise of Oxenhall, Glos.

Campion Archives

Papers 1924-31 of Col. Sir William Robert Campion, Governor of Western Australia, including: journals 1924-31 with brief entries only; visitors' books 1924-31; miscellaneous addresses to Sir William and souvenir documents.

LORD EGREMONT
Petworth House, Petworth

PETWORTH HOUSE ARCHIVES

See *The Petworth House Archives, A Catalogue*, Vol.I, ed. Francis W. Steer and Noel H. Osborne, Chichester 1968. Conditions of use of the collection are given in the *Catalogue*; material listed in it may generally be consulted in the West Sussex Record Office, West Street, Chichester, during normal office hours but only after written or telephone application at least one week in advance.

Relevant papers relate mainly to Col. George Wyndham and his interest in emigration and Australian settlement, particularly in South Australia.

Correspondence, General

P.H.A.1622. Letters July-Sept. 1845 from Capt. Logan, Rev. H. Foster, and Rev. John Cole to J. L. Ellis and from Ellis and Col. G. Wyndham to Rev. Thomas Sockett, Petworth, clarifying the conduct of W. H. Yaldwyn in connection with his sister-in-law Miss Bowles on a voyage to Australia in 1844.

Correspondence, Mainly Estate and Financial

P.H.A.729, 731, 734. Correspondence 1837-8 mainly of Col. G. Wyndham, Midhurst, with Rev. T. Sockett concerning assistance to several individuals, including three members of the Ayliffe family, to emigrate to Australia, with references to conditions of settlement particularly near Adelaide.

P.H.A.736. Col. G. Wyndham's Irish letter book 1839-43. References to Australia are found at pp.26, 117-18, the latter stating that for labourers Canada is greatly to be preferred as Australia is good only for great capitalists.

P.H.A.738. Letters July-Nov. 1840 mainly E. J. Wheeler to Rev. T. Sockett concerning investments in Australian development companies and land rents in Australia and including: plan for the Western Australian Company's new settlement at Australind; letter 2 Nov. 1840 to R. Currie, South Australia, on investments in the South Australia Company; correspondence concerning the forwarding by Mary Jacob of Morooroo, South Australia, of £45 as rent of John Jacob.

Emigration

P.H.A.136. Letters to George O'Brien Wyndham, 3rd Earl of Egremont: 5 Nov. 1829 Thomas Bannister, Swan River, on his recent arrival, the taking up of land and the state of the colony; 28 Aug. 1830 Thomas Henty, West Tarring, on horses bred by Egremont to send to the Swan River for market in the East Indies, and on his son who had taken up 60,000 acres at Leschenault south of the Swan River; 25 Sept. 1830 Thomas Bannister, Swan River, on progress in exploration, his taking up of land, a reference to Mr Peel's and Lieut.-Col. Lawton's establishments being defunct and asking for assistance in obtaining a post in the colony.

P.H.A.1054. Letters Oct. 1840, Carter and Burns, London, to Rev. T. Sockett regarding the application and appointment of Dr Thomas Ryan as Surgeon Superintendent on the *Portland Emigrant* leaving for Sydney.

P.H.A.1057. Letter 18 June 1838 T. F. Elliot, London, to Col. G. Wyndham thanking him for advice on emigrants prematurely selling up. Correspondence 1839 involving W. Labouchere, J. W. Brydone, and Col. G. Wyndham and including copy of despatch from Gov. Gipps to Lord Glenelg concerning four Irish families, tenants of Wyndham who claimed they wished to emigrate to South Australia but were sent to New South Wales.

P.H.A.1059. Poster 8 June 1838 advertising free emigration to Upper Canada or Australia for tenants and labourers in Col. G. Wyndham's Irish estates.

P.H.A.1060. Rough draft of letter 1838 from Col. G. Wyndham seeking a purchase of 1000 acres of good land in Sydney or Van Diemen's Land for a young man he was sending out with a small allowance. Letter 21 Dec. 1841 Thomas [Blair?], Brighton, to Wyndham saying that his son in Australia would like to purchase one of Lord Egremont's horses.

P.H.A.1063, 1066. Emigration expenses 1844 paid through Rev. T. Sockett and Col. G. Wyndham including sums towards passages to Port Phillip; two small account books including accounts between Wyndham and Sockett concerning emigration to Australia 1838-43.

P.H.A.1067. Documents and correspondence 1838-41 on the emigration of the Ayliffe family of Bovey Tracey, Devon, in 1838 to South Australia sponsored by Col. G. Wyndham, including bills and receipts for equipment, medicines, and prefabricated huts; letters from T. H. Ayliffe on his financial difficulties prior to departure and after arrival; and correspondence concerning Frederick Mitchell, Wyndham's agent in South Australia, and his resignation. Drafts 1852 on South Australian Banking Company in favour of the Ayliffes. Many of the bills bear the stamp of the Petworth Emigration Committee.

P.H.A.1068. Letter in French 20 Sept. 1838 Gauterton, London, to Col. G. Wyndham seeking his assistance in going to Australia. Letter 5 Nov. 1838 of Rev. T. Sockett saying Wyndham had succeeded to a large part of the property of the late Earl of Egremont; he wished to continue to support the Petworth Emigration Committee, had bought land in South Australia and was sending a large party there; he was to encourage people on his Irish estate to emigrate to Upper Canada or Australia.

P.H.A.1071. Miscellaneous correspondence including: 16 June 1840 Col. G. Wyndham to Rev. T. Sockett on forwarding Hereford and Devon bulls to a property on the Hunter River, N.S.W.; 29 Nov. 1840 Wyndham to J. W. Brydone regretting actions on land in Australia; 9 July 1841 Loughran and Hughes, London, to Wyndham on the receipt of South Australian wool which had fetched good prices; 6 June 1845 H. M. Lefroy, Surrey, to Wyndham sending a paper with suggestions for a better land system for Australia; 6 Jan. 1847 Capt. John Hart, Adelaide, to Wyndham on obtaining a pair of black swans, the arrival of five deer, and mining operations, saying he was sorry that the Australian Mining Company delayed sending out the land orders and so missed the area of the present Burra Burra Mine, but he had discovered a large copper deposit on Yorke Peninsula.

P.H.A.1072. Letters 1859-61 of the Ayliffe family at Adelaide and Stockport, S.A., to Lord Leconfield mainly seeking financial assistance but with references to local affairs.

Maps, Plans and Drawings

P.H.A.3492. 'The District of Adelaide, South Australia; As divided into Country Sections from the trigonometrical surveys of Col. Light, late Surveyor-General', John Arrowsmith, London, printed. Probably issued with Third Annual Report of the South Australian Colonisation Commissioners. Manuscript note on sections held by Col. G. Wyndham.

P.H.A.3493. 'The Special Survey of the Hutt River. Copied from a sketch drawn by John McDouall Stuart, Adelaide, 21st July 1842'. Shows sections including ten held by Col. G. Wyndham.

WARWICKSHIRE

BIRMINGHAM CITY LIBRARY
Reference Library, Ratcliffe Place, Birmingham 1

There is no single all-inclusive catalogue or index of manuscripts in the Library. The following material may be consulted in the Local Studies section of the Reference Library.

ALSTON COLLECTION

2. Bundle of correspondence and documents, 19th cent., concerning a disputed title to property involving the Egginton family; it includes letters and papers c.1824-40 concerning Walter Egginton tried at Quarter Sessions, Warwick, 1 Jan. 1824, and transported to New South Wales on the *Lady East*. Some of the letters were written by Walter Egginton himself to his family in Birmingham.

LEE COLLECTION

Bundle 574. Seventeen agreements 1881-91 for the sale of patents for improving cable tramways in Australia.

Bundle 1378. Two plans, engraved in London 1842-3, of Nelson, N.Z., showing settlement blocks.

NORTON COLLECTION

1007. Volume containing minutes of the Council of the Society for the Reform of Colonial Government 3 Jan. 1850 to 30 June 1851. The meeting 18 Jan. 1850 at which representatives of the Australian Governments were present, decided to limit the operations of the Society to the North American, South African, and Australian colonies and New Zealand. Matters coming before the Council were the draft Bill for the Better Government of New South Wales, the constitution of New Zealand, and the expediency of giving a second legislative chamber to the colonies of New South Wales and Victoria.

2785. Receipts c.1892-1908 from various banks and institutions for New Zealand stock.

CADDICK DIARIES

336851-62. Travel diaries 1895-1914 of Helen Caddick, one of the first Governors of Birmingham University and a Unitarian, twelve typescript volumes illustrated with photographs. The diaries are mainly descriptive, with little discussion of social or cultural conditions. Vol.3, 1893, Cape Colony, India, Japan, and Hawaii; Vol.4, 1895-6, Java and Australia, including the South Pacific and New Zealand; Vol.7, 1905, New Zealand, Panama, and Peru; Vol.11, 1912-13, Uganda and Australia; Vol.12, 1913-14, Australia, Philippines, China, and Burma.

STONE COLLECTION OF PHOTOGRAPHS

Included in this vast collection of photographs taken by Sir Benjamin Stone, sometime President of the National Photographic Record Association and of the Birmingham Photographic Association, are photographs of the following: 416, celebrations and ceremonies at the inauguration of the Australian Commonwealth in Sydney 1901; 417, various places in New Zealand 1878-87; 418, scenes and people in New Zealand 1878 including Maori chieftains, Pewi Maniapoto and Petra-te-Tuli; 483-4, places and people in the South Sea Islands c.1870-9 including Kealakekua Bay, Hawaii, showing the monument on the spot where Capt. Cook was killed.

UNIVERSITY OF BIRMINGHAM
The Main Library, P.O. Box 363, Birmingham 15

Manuscript collections are stored and produced for inspection in the Heslop Room of the Main Library building, where reproduced typescript handlists or catalogues of the collections are available. There are no detailed indexes but a summary card index of persons, places, and important topics is maintained. The index is constantly added to and will one day include all the Library's manuscript collections. The manuscript collections are readily available for inspection by scholars, who should first apply in writing to the Librarian.

JOSEPH CHAMBERLAIN COLLECTION

The papers of Joseph Chamberlain, Secretary of State for the Colonies 1895-1903. Most are bound into volumes and arranged in sections by subject matter or by major correspondents. Within the sections the papers are usually, but not always, in chronological order. JC16-22 were not deposited until May 1969; for these sections only general entries have been made below indicating where Australian and New Zealand material will be found. JC4/9 contains general press cuttings on colonial policy 1895-7.

JC5 Correspondence

5/67/1-132. Lord Salisbury 1887-99.

5/67/60. Letter 13 Jan. 1895 Lord Salisbury to Chamberlain concerning the reply to a loyal telegram from Australia.

5/67/106. Letter 22 Jan. 1899 Lord Salisbury to Chamberlain concerning Lord Beauchamp and Lord Tennyson proposed as Governors of New South Wales and South Australia respectively.

5/67/107. Letter 31 Jan. 1898 Lord Salisbury to Chamberlain about the visit of the Duke of York to New Zealand.

5/67/123-5, 127. Four letters 18-29 Sept. 1899 Lord Salisbury to Chamberlain concerning Samoa and German designs there.

JC9 Imperial Affairs

9/1/3/1-17. Australia 1895-1900. Includes letters to and from Sir Gerard Smith, Governor of Western Australia, speaking highly of Sir John Forrest and discussing the treatment of Aborigines, and the resignation of H. W. Venn, Commissioner of Railways; also letters from Lord Hopetoun and Lord Loch forwarding a letter 5 May 1897 from Alfred Deakin on the Senate in the new Federation.

9/1/4/1-2. Fiji 1897. Secret despatch 14 Dec. 1897 from Sir George O'Brien, Governor of Fiji, on the policy for governing 'through Native Chiefs'.

9/1/5/1-2. Pacific Cable Conference 1896-7. Two letters 6 Apr. 1896, 10 Jan. 1897 Lord Selborne to Chamberlain concerning Conference meetings which were not very successful.

9/6/3A/1-7. Imperial Penny Postage 1897-9. Includes correspondence and papers concerning delayed decision of Australia and New Zealand whether they would join the scheme.

9/6/3B/1-5. Agricultural Congress 1899. Includes references to the enthusiasm of Queensland's Agent General for the Congress to be held in London 1900.

9/6/3C/1-3. Anglo-French negotiations 1895. Correspondence mainly relating to Domenica but referring to Samoa and the New Hebrides.

9/6/3D/1-38. Miscellaneous correspondence 1895-9. Includes two letters Nov. 1897 from C. E. Borchgrevink about an interview with Chamberlain to discuss his Antarctic expedition; two letters Feb. 1898 concerning the invitation to the Prince of Wales to visit New Zealand, one being from the Prince of Wales saying that he himself would be willing to go; letter 7 Mar. 1899 from J. Henniker Heaton declining the K.C.M.G. but describing his services to Australasia especially with reference to the penny postage; copy letter 12 July 1895 to Lord Hopetoun anticipating a talk about his experiences in Australia; two copy letters May 1898 to Lord Hopetoun concerning the offer made to him of the Governor-Generalship of Canada; two letters July 1897 from Sir Edmund Monson, H.M. Ambassador in France, stating that Sir John Forrest and the Australian premiers intend to use their visit to Paris to promote mining interests in their colonies, with letter July 1897 from the Colonial Office on this matter.

9/7/1-57. Miscellaneous correspondence c.1895-9. Includes correspondence concerning the appointment of governors and honours bestowed on individuals, e.g. 15 Dec. 1896 from Lord Castletown concerning the possibility of the Governorship of New Zealand, June-Sept. 1895 from Sir Arthur Havelock, Governor of Ceylon, concerning promotion, and his appointment as Governor of Madras.

JC11 General Correspondence

11/30/1-234. Lord Salisbury 1900-2. Includes letters about the appointment of governors, honours bestowed on individuals, the German interest in Samoa, and Tonga.

11/39/1-165. Miscellaneous 1900-2.

11/39/44. Letter 19 Mar. 1901 from Sir Charles Dilke about a parliamentary question on the joint control of the New Hebrides, with copy of Chamberlain's reply 21 Mar. 1901 and a memo.

11/39/79. Letter 19 Jan. 1901 from Sir Arthur Havelock wishing to know when he will start for Australia.

11/39/81. Letter 26 Oct. 1901 from J. Henniker Heaton concerning penny postage to Australia.

JC14 Colonial Affairs

14/1/1/1-60. Australia 1900-2. Includes correspondence with Alfred Deakin about Sir John Dodds, Lieut.-Gov. of Tasmania; Sir John Forrest on Australian contributions to South Africa and on the Immigration Restriction Bill; Sir Walter James, Premier of Western Australia, concerning a Governor-General for Australia; Lord Hopetoun, concerning the Royal visit, the Alien Immigration Act, and Le Hunte, Governor of British New Guinea; Sir Gerard Smith, concerning his resignation; Lord Tennyson, concerning his expenses and appointments as Governor of South Australia.

14/1/2/1-7. New Zealand 1902-3. Mostly letters from Lord Ranfurly, Governor of New Zealand, about expenses and honours in connection with Dr Campbell and Mr Cadman.

14/2/3/1. Fiji 1901. Letter 6 May 1901 from Sir George O'Brien stating that he is unable to accept the Governorship of British Guiana.

JC17-20 Papers 1901-5. These include: 17/1/1-13, Colonial Conference 1902, documents and correspondence; 18/2/1-18, Australia 1903, documents and correspondence; 18/9/1-4, New Zealand 1903, correspondence; 19/1/1-8, Australia 1904, correspondence; 20/1/1-9, Australia 1905, correspondence.

JOHN GALSWORTHY COLLECTION

JG504. Sheet of notes in Galsworthy's hand dated 19 May 1925, Hampstead, answering the rhetorical question 'What comes into my mind when I think of New Zealand?' and stating that his recollections come from 'away back thirty two years'.

ADDITIONAL LETTERS

L.Add.755, 807, 828, 859, 862, 866. Correspondence and notes 1946-7 addressed to Alan Strode Campbell Ross, Professor of Linguistics at Birmingham University, in connection with his book *Ginger: a loan-word study*, London, Philological Society, 1952. The letters are from R. E. P. Dwyer, Papua, A. McKenzie, Samoa, Howard Hayden, Fiji, M. le Directeur de l'enseignment dans les établissements français d'Océanie, and G. E. Hard, Gilbert and Ellice Islands.

L.Add.1546-1629. Correspondence and notes 1958-62 addressed to Professor Campbell Ross on Pitcairniana, from many individuals in the United Kingdom, the Pacific, Australia, New Zealand, and elsewhere.

THE EARL OF DENBIGH
Pailton House, Rugby

The papers are at present (May 1970) being listed by the Warwickshire Record Office. They include the papers of Lieut.-Col. the Hon. William Henry Adelbert

Warwickshire

Feilding relating to the Feilding settlement in New Zealand 1871-2 and more especially to his preliminary survey work and executive involvement with the Australian Transcontinental Railway Syndicate liquidated in 1893, and with a proposed railway from Brisbane to Point Parker on the Gulf of Carpentaria. The papers include diaries of exploration, geological reports by Robert L. Jack, correspondence, reports, and Queensland Parliamentary Papers.

WARWICKSHIRE COUNTY RECORD OFFICE
Shire Hall, Warwick

BOARDS OF GUARDIANS RECORDS

Records 1826-c.1930 including Minute Books and General Ledgers. Headings in Ledgers include 'Emigration Expenses' and 'Emigration Loan Account'. The following scattered references were noted in a sample search of Ledgers and Minute Books 1848-57.

CR 51/1391. Southam Union, Minute Book 1847- . References relating to the emigration in 1849 of John Checkley with his wife and six children from the parish of Napton to Australia, including directions to obtain the sanction of the Poor Law Board, reference to sureties, the creation of a Napton Emigration Fund, disbursements to the overseers and churchwardens of Napton, and the contracting with a firm for their passage to Australia.

CR 51/1419. Southam Union, General Ledger 1848- . Details the costs of emigration of John Checkley.

CR 51/1585. Warwick Union, Minute Book 1849. Emigration of Abraham Murcott, labourer, with his wife and two children from the parish of Leamington to South Australia; and also John Harwood, iron moulder, out of employment, with his wife and two children.

CR 51/551-2. Rugby Union, Minute Books 1848-53. Emigration of Jane Essen and family of Kilsby parish in 1850.

CR 51/592-3. Rugby Union, General Ledgers 1848-52. Payments to the Emigration Commissioners towards the passage of the Essen family to Van Diemen's Land in 1850. Also payments to the Commissioners towards the passage of the Cotton family to New Zealand.

PARISH RECORDS

Southam, House of Industry. Copy of printed 'Notice to young women desirous of bettering their condition by emigration to New South Wales', issued by the Refuge for the Destitute, Hackney Rd, London.

PRIVATE RECORDS

CR 114A Seymour of Ragley Papers

Family and estate papers of the Marquesses of Hertford. The collection contains papers of Adm. Hugh Seymour, 5th son of the 1st Marquess; his son Adm. Sir George Francis Seymour, Admiral-of-the-Fleet, Commander-in-Chief Pacific Station 1844-8, and Sir George's son Francis Hugh George who became 5th Marquess in 1870. There is a typescript catalogue of the collection.

CR 114A/369-638. Sir George Francis Seymour
CR 114A/374/1-47. Personal diaries 1824-70 including diaries 1844-8, 5 vols.
CR 114A/411. Source book c.1847 for information about places in the Pacific, indexed, part autograph. Small memorandum book of George F. Seymour.
CR 114A/412-422B. Pacific Station.

CR 114A/412/1-2. Journal as Commander-in-Chief 14 May 1844 to 23 Mar. 1847, 2 vols. Visits to the Society and Sandwich Islands in the latter part of 1845 and to Sandwich Islands in July 1846. Matters dealt with in the journal include negotiations with the French authorities over the control of Pacific territories.

CR 114A/413. Signal log 21 July 1844 to 9 Aug. 1848 of ships on the Pacific Station.

CR 114A/414/1-2. Special order books 25 May 1844 to 29 Jan. 1848, indexed. Subjects include investigation of the losses of Mr Pritchard and orders to the ship having him on board; references to conduct to be observed by the ship's company in the islands.

CR 114A/415/1-2. Squadron letter books 24 Dec. 1844 to 9 July 1848, indexed. Subjects include instructions for conduct to be observed towards foreigners in official situations in the Sandwich Islands, queries concerning the expenses of the Commander of the *Basilisk* having Queen Pomare on board; approval of the action of Capt. Onslow on the *Daphne* in support against the Maoris in New Zealand.

CR 114A/416/1-2. Official letter books 14 May 1844 to 9 July 1848, registers of letters to the Admiralty, indexed. Despatch No.85 of 17 Dec. 1845 refers to information on the independence of the Society Islands collected from various sources.

CR 114A/417/1-2. Miscellaneous letter books 26 July 1844 to 8 July 1848, registers of letters mainly to consuls and other British officials on the Station, indexed. Addressees include: Governor Bruat, the King of the Sandwich Islands, Rear Admiral Hamelin, agents of the Hudson's Bay Company in Honolulu, Rev. Robert Thompson of Tahiti, Rev. Barff of Papeete, Queen Pomare, Rev. Platt at Raiatea, William Miller as H.M. Consul General in the Sandwich Islands.

CR 114A/418/1-4. Private letter books 19 Sept. 1844 to 23 Nov. 1850 including letters to Bruat and Hamelin.

CR 114A/419. Rough notebook 1844-6.

CR 114A/420. Miscellaneous memoranda for letters and orders c.1837-47.

CR 114A/421. Accounts and notes of visits and plans 1845-8.

CR 114A/422A. 'Memorandum on difficulties which occurred relative to the appropriation of the ships under my command during the first six months after my arrival in the Pacific. A detail of temporary perplexities only . . .', n.d. [c.1846].

CR 114A/422B. Chart n.d. of 'Track of Sir G. F. Seymour to and from N. America in 1840, and of H.M.S. Collingwood bearing his flag to and from the South Seas in 1844 and 1848'.

CR 114A/433. Miscellaneous précis of actions c.1850-7 including abstract of transactions in the Sandwich Islands 1849-55.

CR 114A/464. Chart of Taloo harbour in the island of Eimeo, from a Russian survey 1835, hand-drawn 1839.

CR 114A/508/1-13. Private letter books: summaries of letters sent 1834-70; 508/4-5, letter books 1840-9.

CR 114A/525/1-2. Letters received by Sir George F. Seymour from his nephew Frederick Beauchamp Paget Seymour, including three letters 1860 from H.M.S. *Pelorus* and Camp Waitare, concerning the campaign against the Maoris; letter 1862 *Pelorus*, Melbourne, mentioning he would cruise after American whalers if war declared between the Federal States.

CR 114A/526/2. Miscellaneous family letters including 7 Nov. 1845 from Sir George Seymour's son Francis with reference to Sir George Cockburn's approval of Seymour's conduct in the Pacific.

CR 114A/528B. Letter of invitation 1845 from Queen Pomare inviting Seymour to visit Tahiti.

CR 114A/533/8. Includes letter 30 Jan. 1861 containing an extract from letter 27 June 1855 from Capt. Charles Pasley on disturbances among the miners at

Ballarat and the intention of setting up an independent republic, and also the situation in New Zealand; printed circular 1 Aug. 1844 of London Missionary Society on the troubles in Tahiti; letter 19 May 1861 C. Barff, Huahine, to Seymour.

CR 114A/533/13. Copy letters 30 Oct., 2 Dec. 1860 from F. B. P. Seymour, New Zealand, to his uncle Sir George Seymour concerning the campaign against the Maoris; letters 29 Mar. 1854, 12 June 1856 William Miller, Honolulu, describing changes since Seymour was there and his efforts to defeat American annexation; letter 28 Nov. 1856 from A. S. Hammond concerning annexation by America.

CR 114A/533/19. Letter Dec. 1859 from F. B. P. Seymour, Melbourne.

CR 114A/637. Prints and drawings. Prospect of Auckland from the sea, including a key to various features.

CR 114A/639-837B. Francis Hugh George Seymour, 5th Marquess.

CR 114A/695/2-5. About eighty letters 1844-7 from Adm. Sir George F. Seymour and his wife describing preparations for departure and events on the Pacific Station.

CR 394 Hyett Freer (Frier), Farr, and Gwinnett Family MSS.

CR 394/107. Three letters 1858, 1860 E. Bartlett, Ballarat, on the goldfields and domestic affairs; six letters 1905-20 Annie Morley, Hawkes Bay and Hastings, N.Z., to her cousin Miss Farr. Also letter 3 May 1919 G. H. Bartlett to Miss Farr from the Suttor goldfields and letter 21 May 1852 Henry Chamberlaine, London, to Frederick Chamberlaine on his imminent departure for a 'distant land'.

CR 394/111. Fourteen letters 1913-33 including several from Annie Morley in New Zealand.

CR 895 Dormer of Grove Park

CR 895/63. Miscellaneous papers c.1830-50 with some original papers of the Tichborne family.

CR 895/100. Letters and papers c.1866-74, mainly legal, relating to the Tichborne and Dormer families with cuttings on the Tichborne trial.

CR 1012 Fernbank Deeds

Probates, executorship papers and correspondence 1834-95 relating to the Gibbs family of Snitterfield, including letters 1851-8 from Mrs M. A. Hunt, daughter of Mrs G. Gibbs from a farm near Adelaide, S.A., referring to newly discovered goldfields.

WESTMORLAND

See Cumberland, Westmorland and Carlisle Record Office.

WILTSHIRE

BRIGADIER A. W. A. LLEWELLEN PALMER
Manor House, Great Somerford, Chippenham

The papers of Charles Robert Wynn-Carrington, 1st Marquess of Lincolnshire, 1st Earl Carrington. The collection includes papers relating to Lord Carrington's term as Governor of New South Wales 1885-90. Correspondence with Sir Henry

Parkes is among the papers. Brigadier Llewellen Palmer has given permission for this correspondence and other relevant papers to be copied for the Australian Joint Copying Project.

LORD METHUEN
Corsham Court, Corsham

Correspondence 1851-5 of William Ayshford Sanford and Henry Ayshford Sanford during their residence in Western Australia.*

W. A. Sanford was Colonial Secretary in Western Australia 1851-5. His younger brother Capt. H. A. Sanford, already in the colony, was placed Jan. 1852 in charge of the building of a town and the making of thirty miles of road near Toodyay. By 1853 he had taken up land at Port Gregory where he called his farm Lynton after a property in Devon owned by his family. He had a share in neighbouring lead mines and in 1854-5 he and others engaged in whaling.

There are many references in the correspondence to the benefits of the convict system and also to the social problems of the colony. Letters from the brothers to their relatives in England describe their first impressions, and letters from H. A. Sanford to W. A. Sanford describe his pioneering enterprises at Port Gregory. The considerable number of letters to W. A. Sanford of an official or semi-official nature contain sidelights on colonial life of the 1850s, letters from relations in England to the brothers refer to their activities while in Western Australia, and finally there is a group of accounts 1851-5 of W. A. Sanford, including household bills. Letters to W. A. Sanford as Colonial Secretary include three letters from Gov. Fitzgerald, letters from Rev. J. Brown, Rev. G. P. Pownall, Rev. J. R. Wollaston and the Roman Catholic Bishop, from M. W. Clifton and W. P. Clifton concerning development at Australind and emigration, from W. Cowan, Guardian of Aborigines at York, and Capt. E. Y. W. Henderson, Comptroller General of Convicts. There are also letters 1854 from Dr W. H. Harvey, a visiting botanist writing from near Albury and from Melbourne and correspondence with J. W. Sillifant, Bunbury and Albury.

MISS J. DE LACY MANN
The Cottage, Bowerhill, nr Melksham

See *The Mann Family, Notes on Some Members of the Mann Family*, compiled by H. M. Thorold and V. M. Mann, privately printed 1950. The papers include a journal 1836 of James Saumarez Mann, H.M.S. *Victor* from Sydney to New Zealand and the Pacific Islands, among islands visited being Tahiti, where they called on the Queen with Pritchard as interpreter, and the Fiji Islands. There are a number of coastal profiles also maps with soundings of the island and harbour of Tongatabu. There is also a letter 11 Sept. 1836 J. S. Mann, Farm Cove, Port Jackson, to his sister describing Maoris and his experiences in Sydney social life. The journal and the letter have been microfilmed for the Australian Joint Copying Project.

WILTSHIRE RECORD OFFICE
County Hall, Trowbridge

See *Guide to the Wiltshire Record Office*, Part I, 1959, Part II, 1961.

QUARTER SESSIONS RECORDS

Bonds and contracts 1728-89 for the transportation of felons to the American colonies and plantations, Africa and Australia, 2 bundles. The second bundle contains twelve documents 1787-9 relating to transportation to New South Wales.

Wiltshire

BOARDS OF GUARDIANS RECORDS

Melksham Union. Minute books 1848-58. These contain a number of references to emigration to Australia.

PRIVATE RECORDS

Acc.9. Savernake Archives, Wiltshire Emigration Society. At a meeting in 1849 of the Marlborough District Association, a county emigration association to promote the emigration of labourers was proposed. This was set up as the Wiltshire Emigration Society which continued until 1851. Records of the Society include: minute book Oct. 1849 to 17 Dec. 1851 giving details of the development of the scheme, consultation with the Secretary of the Colonial Land and Emigration Commission, questions of finance, supply of clothing, and the selection of Chippenham as an assembly point for emigrants departing from Plymouth; register Dec. 1850 to May 1851 listing and giving particulars of candidates for emigration; accounts Jan.-Mar. 1851; cash account 29 Nov. 1850 to 27 May 1851; correspondence 14 Feb. to 4 June 1851 with the Colonial Land and Emigration Commission, London, c.43 letters.

Acc.533/50. Printed notice n.d. Committee for Promoting the Emigration of Females to the Australian Colonies, re passages to Hobart Town on the *Boadicea*.

Acc.865. Diary Oct. 1864 to 11 Nov. 1865 of William Chafyn Grove covering a voyage to Australia on the *Vimiera*; visits to Adelaide, Launceston and Hobart, and experience in New South Wales before departure for Ceylon and Bombay.

WORCESTERSHIRE

STANBROOK ABBEY
Callow End, Worcester

This Benedictine community of women possesses a few letters relevant to Catholicism in Australia, and particularly to the establishment of a convent in Parramatta, N.S.W., in 1848, the founder members of which were Dame Magdalene le Clerc, a nun from Stanbrook, and Sister Scholastica Gregory, a nun from the community at Princethorpe, and sister to Abbot Gregory. The Parramatta convent has since moved to Pennant Hills, N.S.W., and additional letters written to the Lady Abbess at Stanbrook by Mother Walburge Wallace who went to Australia in 1854 and became Prioress there at the first free election in 1864, have been transferred from Stanbrook to Pennant Hills.

Application for permission to use the following material at Stanbrook should be made to the Lady Abbess.

Circular n.d. from Archbishop Polding, concerning the state of Catholicism in Australia, with a note to the Lady Abbess in Polding's hand, written on it.

Letter 1847 Archbishop Polding to the Lady Abbess, written prior to his departure with the two nuns for Australia, comforting her on the loss of Dame Magdalene.

Farewell letter 1847 Dame Magdalene to the community, written immediately prior to her departure.

About forty letters 1848-c.1870 Dame Magdalene to the Lady Abbess on a variety of aspects of the life of the community in Australia. Some are printed by H. N. Birt, *Benedictine Pioneers in Australia*, London 1911, Vol.II.

Letter Aug. 1848 from a sister at Princethorpe to the Lady Abbess giving Sister Scholastica's first impressions of Australia, with a description of the monk's monastery in the Archbishop's Palace, and the Archbishop's own cell.

Copy letter Sept. 1849 Dr Davis at St Mary's, Sydney, to his mother giving a detailed account of his almost miraculous recovery from an apparently fatal illness.

Three letters June-Oct. 1855 Archbishop Polding to the Lady Abbess, during his visit to Europe, mentioning *inter alia* Australia and the Vatican Council.

Notes, drafts and copies of letters written by Dame Scholastica Gregory, Lady Abbess, concerning Abbot Gregory and his difficulties in Australia. Abbot Gregory visited Stanbrook frequently and made it his headquarters while in England 1861-2.

Letter 1867 Fr Edmund Athy, one of the original monks at St Mary's College, Lyndhurst, N.S.W., to Fr Prior [probably Downside], giving a general description of the voyage out to Australia (see *Benedictine Pioneers in Australia*, Vol.II, p.323). Also letter n.d. from Fr Athy describing the Archbishop's enthusiastic reception on his return to Australia.

Letter 1 May [1860] Bishop Serra to Dr Heptonstall referring to his recent visit to Stanbrook.

Three letters 1876 concerning Mother Walburge's visit to Stanbrook, one from Mother Walburge and one from Archbishop Vaughan to the Lady Abbess and one from the Lady Abbess to Archbishop Vaughan.

Copies of four letters 1874-87 Archbishop Ullathorne to Mrs Merewether, née Plunkett, in Sydney. The present location of the originals is not known. The letter 5 May 1874 mentions Archbishop Vaughan's 'very fine start in New South Wales', and Bishop Redwood ordained for New Zealand; the other three letters 24 Dec. 1884, 14 Apr. and 26 Dec. 1887 refer to his *Memoir of Bishop Willson*, London 1887.

Letter 1890 from Soeur Marie des Anges, one of three Princethorpe nuns who went out to Australia in 1856 and returned in 1861, to Dame Benedicta Anstey, the first Archivist at Stanbrook, written in French. It gives a succinct account of the early history of the Australian foundation and the failure of the Princethorpe mission there.

WORCESTERSHIRE RECORD OFFICE
Shirehall, Worcester

PRIVATE RECORDS

705:260 Harward & Evers, solicitors, Records
BA 4000/568. Papers 1869-1904 of James Weston Clulee, hawker and fishmonger of Dunedin, N.Z. Will, birth certificate, and certificate of marriage with Jessie Aitken and copies of register of births of his three children. Correspondence on his behalf with the Metropolitan and Birmingham Bank Ltd and with his brother concerning their father's estate.

705:349 Hampton Family Archives
Personal, semi-official, and political correspondence of Sir John Somerset Pakington, 1st Baron Hampton.
BA 3835/16 (xi). Miscellaneous letters 1852-3 relating to Australia and New Zealand including a letter from Sir George Grey on the new constitution for New Zealand; two letters from FitzRoy, Governor of New South Wales, and two letters from La Trobe, one referring to colonial policy under the Duke of Newcastle.
BA 3835/17 (i). Letter 28 Nov. 1852 from John Robert Godley giving the resolutions at a public meeting at Lyttelton, N.Z.

Worcestershire

BA 4732/2 (vi). Letter 19 Dec. 1854 from Arthur E. Kennedy referring to his Sierra Leone governorship and promotion to Western Australia.

BA 4732/2 (vii). Letter 5 Nov. 1855 from Lord Alfred Churchill on transportation, a Parliamentary issue, with references to his recent travels in the Australian colonies and visit to Port Arthur. Letter 2 June 1856 from Lord Harrowby with reference to transportation.

BA 4732/3 (vii). Copy of *Lyttelton Times* 25 Dec. 1852.

BA 4732/4 (iv). Correspondence 16 July 1866 to 4 Feb. 1867 chiefly from Alfred, Duke of Edinburgh, concerning appointments to the *Galatea* and arrangements for early part of the vessel's cruise.

705:462 Sir Granville Bantock Papers

BA 4664/10 (ii). Book of cuttings of Sir Granville Bantock, composer and conductor, during his Australian tour 1938-9 as Chairman of the Corporation of Trinity College of Music, London.

BA 4664/29. Book of welcome 15 Nov. 1938 from musicians, music teachers, and students of Victoria; an address with numerous signatures including Dr A. E. Floyd and W. A. Laver. Also a photograph album 1907 containing photographs of scenes and people in Kalgoorlie, Melbourne, and New Zealand.

705:550 Marcy, Hemingway & Sons, solicitors, Deposit

BA 4600/138 (xi). Papers 1863-8 relating to the death and estate of James Nash who died on 30 July 1867 at St Kilda, Melbourne, including his will, power of attorney from his father, Dr James Nash of Martley near Worcester to Klingender, Charsley and Liddle of Melbourne to act *re* the estate, with related correspondence.

BA 4600/202. Papers 1891-3 concerning the New Zealand estates of Viscount Cobham (Lord Lyttelton). Correspondence between Lord Cobham of Hagley Hall, Stourbridge, Worcs., and the manager of the estate, R. J. S. Harman of Harman & Stevens, Christchurch, N.Z., and also W. N. Marcy including statements of account for the year ending 14 Aug. 1892.

BA 4600/802 (ii). Legal documents and correspondence 1856-69 relating to the 'Lyttelton Trust Estate' in the Canterbury Settlement, N.Z., including a summary of the deed of gift 2 Dec. 1856 by which Frederick Earl Spencer gave his New Zealand properties to George William Lord Lyttelton in trust for the latter's son George William Spencer Lyttelton.

705:587 Ticehurst, Wyatt & Co., solicitors, Deposit

BA 5093/2 (v). Papers of the Boissier and Dumaresq families including correspondence and documents 1835-9, 1853 relating to lands in New Norfolk, V.D.L., held by Edward Dumaresq. Having mortgaged one property to Gabriel Cook of Van Diemen's Land, Dumaresq sought to pay off the mortgage, borrowing from Rev. P. M. Boissier of Malvern Wells, Worcs. There is also a report 1 Sept. 1835 of a Committee of Enquiry into Gen. Darling's conduct during his administration of New South Wales, read before the House of Commons on 1 Sept. 1835.

Cobham Family Papers

Letters to George William Lord Lyttelton including: letter 30 Nov. 1867 3rd Duke of Buckingham and Chandos, Secretary of State for the Colonies, to Lord Lyttelton about to visit New Zealand, unofficially seeking his aid as an intermediary in dealings with the colonial government; letter 26 Aug. 1843 from Sir George Graham of the Home Office concerning emigration; letter 16 Sept. 1874 from Anthony Trollope concerning his *Australia and New Zealand*, London 1873, 2 vols., with comments on the writing of this work and correction of some errors and impressions; letter 4 Aug. 1849 from Sir James Stephen with general reflections on colonial government after his withdrawal from active participation in colonial affairs.

YORKSHIRE

EAST RIDING COUNTY RECORD OFFICE
County Hall, Beverley

See Brief Guide to the Contents of the East Riding County Record Office, 3rd ed., 1966, duplicated typescript.

DDBH Baines of Bell Hall

DDBH/26/11-18. New Zealand correspondence, c.283 letters 1851-1909 many partly illegible. The letters are mainly to William Mortimer Baines but also to his wife Maryanne Verdon Baines; half of them fall within 1866-72. W. M. Baines arrived in New Zealand in 1850 where he had interests in land, timber, and mining. In 1868 he returned to England, followed by his wife and family in 1869. There are letters to his wife concerning her passage home and the rental of his Mount Eden property. Subsequent correspondence with agents, lessees, and others refer to the rental and management of this and other New Zealand properties, but much of the correspondence is from New Zealand friends or relatives giving family news and, indirectly, information on economic developments and affairs including references to the Thames goldfields. W. P. Fooks of Aratapu and Otahuhu is a principal correspondent until his death in 1873; there are also letters from members of the Dixon and Hunter families. Members of the Fooks, Dixon, and Hunter families went to Australia and there are letters from H. Fooks 1902-9, South Australia, and from A. H. Hunter and R. Hunter 1891, Ballina, N.S.W.

DDBH/27/4. Notes 1832-40 possibly on the Dixon family, Sydney, partly illegible.

DDBH/27/5. Diary Aug.-Dec. 1850 W. M. Baines of a voyage to New Zealand on the *Sir Edward Paget*.

DDBH/27/9. Recollections 19th cent. of life and conditions of early settlers in New Zealand, possibly by Maryanne Verdon Dixon (née Barnes), partly illegible.

DDCB Burton of Cherry Burton

DDCB/31/34. Probate copy of the will 8 Oct. 1861 of Sir Stuart Alexander Donaldson of Sydney, N.S.W., property includes estates in New South Wales and New Zealand.

DDEV Maxwell-Constable of Everingham

DDEV/60/31. Correspondence of Marmaduke Constable Maxwell of Terregles.

DDEV/60/31 viii. Letters 1862-70 mainly from nephews Robert, Wilfred, and Edward Constable Maxwell concerning their emigration to New Zealand. The correspondence includes a list of Robert's clothing and outfit before departure, letters describe the voyage and subsequent life on Stonyhurst Station with references to his plans for obtaining his own property. Letters to him include: 4 Mar. 1863 F. A. Weld, N.Z., saying his station manager appears satisfied with Robert; 24 Nov. 1865 from Hon. W. Petre, London, saying he has written to his agent in New Zealand to look out for another position for Robert. After 1866 Robert writes from Benmore Station where he was joined by his brothers: letters from all three give details of station life and prospects. Wilfred later worked on Booth Station and Edward went to Wellington. Other correspondents include F. A. Weld and H. J. Mathias of New Zealand.

DDEV/60/31 xi. Letters 1862-6 from various individuals concerning the affairs of his nephew Robert and his emigration to New Zealand.

DDFA Forbes-Adam (Beilby Lawley) of Escrick

DDFA/36. Beilby, 3rd Lord Wenlock.

DDFA/36/22-46. Public Office and Affairs. Miscellaneous items 1899-1901 including: notebook of Lord Wenlock with itinerary and details of world tour 1901 of Duke and Duchess of Cornwall and York in H.M.S. *Ophir*, with related papers.

DDHO Hotham of Dalton Hall

DDHO/10. Sir Charles Hotham.

DDHO/10/1. Correspondence 1853-5 mainly with the Duke of Newcastle on the offer of post as Governor of Victoria; also three letters after his arrival in Victoria including one 15 Aug. 1855 to his brother referring to the financial affairs of the colony, the gold and land questions, and his relations with the Victorian Government.

DDHO/10/15. Correspondence 1853-5 including: letter 9 Jan. 1854 Duke of Newcastle to Lieut.-Gov. La Trobe on the extraordinary expenses of sending out a governor where there is no established residence, and letters 20 Mar. 1854 and 1 May 1854 La Trobe to Newcastle on political affairs, the state of Victoria, accommodation for Hotham, and his personal desire to return to England as soon as possible; correspondence 1854 between Hotham and R. Airey, Horse Guards, obtaining the appointment of Richard Hotham as his A.D.C.; draft of secret and confidential despatch 27 Jan. 1855 Hotham to Secretary of State with reply 1 June 1855 concerning the use of secret service money to control the agitation against the government in the colony; statement 1 Feb. 1855 on the trials of prisoners from Ballarat.

DDHO/10/16-19. Copy despatch 29 Nov. 1853 Duke of Newcastle to Lieut.-Gov. La Trobe on the squatting question; memo n.d. Sir Charles Hotham on colonial finances; papers 1854 relating to the sale and shipping of furniture; book of cuttings 1854-60 relating to Hotham's governorship.

DDHO/10/20. Letter book 24 June 1854 to 6 Oct. 1855 containing despatches from the Secretaries of State dealing with punishment of convicts from Van Diemen's Land, Hotham's arrival and reception, financial conditions of the colony, Hotham's visit to the goldfields, the affair at Eureka including the trial of prisoners, constitutional changes and responsible government, and duties and customs in Victoria.

DDHO/10/21. Letter book 1854-6 containing despatches to the Secretaries of State concerning subjects mentioned in DDHO/10/20, also the Royal Commission on squatting, mail charges between England and Australia, report of Commission to inquire into laws and regulations on mining, Chinese immigration, the military in Victoria, guns for the battery, and the death of Sir Charles Hotham.

DDHO/10/22. Draft of speech [1855?] Sir Charles Hotham to the Legislative Council on the Bill for a new constitution.

DDHO/10/23. Copy of covering letter 23 Nov. 1855 Sir Charles Hotham to the Colonial Secretary, Melbourne, and a statement of his views on the position of the Governor under the new constitution.

DDHO/10/25. Memo 1855 on the Denominational School Board.

DDHO/10/26. Pamphlet 1855 'Three letters to Hon. James Frederick Palmer, Speaker of the Legislative Council of Victoria by J. F. Leslie Foster late Colonial Secretary', printed.

DDHO/10/28-9. Two memos 7 Feb. 1855 Sir Charles Hotham concerning the salary of Lieutenant Governor and the Governor's residence.

DDHO/10/31. Copy of despatch 6 Nov. 1855 Sir Henry Edward Young, Tasmania, to Sir William Molesworth on the privilege question in Tasmania.

DDHO/10/32-7. Cuttings 1855 from Melbourne papers.

DDHO/10/39-43. Papers and cuttings 1855-6 concerning the death of Hotham.

DDHO/13. Correspondence.

DDHO/13/19. Three letters July-Oct. 1878 Beaumont Hotham in New Zealand to his father Rev. F. H. Hotham and other members of the family.

DDSY Sykes of Sledmere
DDSY/23/260. Probate copy of the will 24 Jan. 1846 John Boyes late merchant of Antwerp and London: bequests include shares in the South Australian Banking Company and the South Australian Agricultural Company.
DDSY/72/95. Copy of a medical certificate 27 May 1853 on the health of Charles Simpson of Waratah, Co. Northumberland, N.S.W.

BRADFORD CITY LIBRARIES
Central Library, Prince's Way, Bradford 5

SPENCER STANHOPE MANUSCRIPTS

2748. Letter 10 May 1810 John Hillas, Sydney, to Walter Spencer Stanhope referring to a box of skins he was sending and mentioning disturbances under Gov. Bligh, Macquarie, Marsden, the hope that the New South Wales Corps would be put under arrest, and the confidence of the free settlers in the bearer of the letter, M. Mason, and in George Suttor. The letter is enclosed in letter 22 Nov. 1810 from M. Mason stating he had just arrived in England from New South Wales.

HEATON MANUSCRIPTS

A558. List of the eleven children of Henry Cryar Johnston and his wife Henrietta née Heaton, married in Victoria 18 Dec. 1864. A brief note is given on each, indicating marriage and children's names and addresses up to 1916.

N. J. A. CROSSE, ESQ.
C/o Sir James Hill & Sons Ltd, Bradford

Three incomplete pocket diaries of travels, cuttings, a genealogical table and miscellaneous material relating to Sir James Hill, founder of Sir James Hill & Sons Ltd, woolcombers and topmakers, Bradford. The firm established trading connections with Australia and New Zealand at the end of the nineteenth century. One of the diaries contains observations on Samoa and New Zealand 2-11 Sept. 1897. The cuttings mention Sir James and Lady Hill's world tours of 1897 and 1910. While in New Zealand in 1898 Sir James bought a tannery and fellmongery business which was placed in the hands of his younger brother, Walter Hill.

J. E. PICKLES & CO.
37 Chapel Street, Bradford

The firm in Australia was set up in 1916 as Joseph Pickles & Son Ltd, stuff merchants, warehousemen, general merchants and manufacturers agents. The Australian business was taken over in 1932 by Robert Reid and Co. and the Company was dissolved in 1936 although its name continued to be used by Robert Reid and Co.

Ledger sheets 1931-c.1955 covering the invoicing of dress material orders placed through the Australian firm and its successor.

C. E. WRANGHAM, ESQ.
Rosemary House, Catterick

WILLIAM WILBERFORCE PAPERS
Diary 1783-1833.
'Journal' 1785-1818 devoted to religious reflections.

Yorkshire

Correspondence, 7 boxes. Five boxes contain correspondence of William Wilberforce and two boxes correspondence of his sons R. I. and S. Wilberforce partly relating to their *The Life of William Wilberforce*, London 1838, 5 vols. Some of the letters are numbered and tied in packets, some sorting by names of correspondents has been done and there are a few typescripts of letters. Letters in boxes 'No.1' and 'No.2' have been numbered.

'Box No.1' includes: letter 9 Nov. 1797 Cadell and Davies to William Wilberforce concerning a new edition of *A Practical View of the Prevailing Religious System of Professed Christians*, London 1797, and referring to 'Wilberforce's wish that Mr. Dawes's Press [?William Dawes] might be engaged upon an Edition'; letter 12 July 1836 Rev. Robert Cartwright, Liverpool, N.S.W., to Rev. Samuel Marsden, Parramatta, explaining that he is anxious to repay the estate of William Wilberforce money advanced sixteen years ago for Mrs Cartwright's passage to Australia and asking for Marsden's help; letter 16 July 1836 Rev. Samuel Marsden to J. Coates transmitting Cartwright's letter, with comments, also postscript stating that James McArthur is the bearer of the letter and is taking to England a petition against emancipists serving on juries.

'Box No.2' in two parts includes: letters 15 Nov. 1786, 21 July 1796 Rev. John Newton to William Wilberforce referring to Wilberforce's influence in obtaining the appointment of Johnson in New South Wales; letter 14 Apr. 1817 William Wilberforce to William Hey expressing pleasure at news of the 'Success of ye Gospel in the South Sea Islands & in plantations in New Zealand'. Other correspondence with William Hey may repay examination.

Box labelled inside 'Wilberforce/Correspondence . . . .'. Packet containing letters 1786-1804 from Rev. John Newton chiefly to William Wilberforce includes an undated letter [1787] Newton to Sir Charles Middleton returning 'Mr. Wilberforce's letter', and referring to the previous collection by a friend of 'something more than £220' to outfit Johnson. Two other references to New South Wales have been noted in letters from Newton to Wilberforce: 1 Nov. 1786 referring to Johnson and undated letter [1789] apparently referring to the search for an assistant to Johnson which resulted in Crowther sailing in the *Guardian*.

Box labelled inside 'Wilberforce Papers, R. I. and William' includes family letters and correspondence with William Hey mostly listed and transcribed in typescript but including a letter not listed or transcribed, 28 Aug. 1835 James Stephen to R. I. Wilberforce concerning information to be included or omitted from the biography of their father by R. I. and Samuel Wilberforce.

A search of the papers at Rosemary House did not reveal William Wilberforce's letter to William Hey, Christmas Holidays 1809, referring to Marsden's visit to England, see *The Life of William Wilberforce*, Vol.3, p.40, nor letters from Marsden and Castlereagh to Wilberforce, see *Correspondence of W. Wilberforce Edited by his Sons R. I. . . . and S. Wilberforce*, London 1840, Vol.1, pp.195, 229; Vol.2, pp.3, 53, 183.

HULL CITY LIBRARIES
Local History Department, Albion Street, Hull

Local notes of the South Cave area, 2 vols. The volume dated 7 July 1894 compiled by William Richardson contains cuttings and manuscript copies of articles and includes:

pp.82-235. 'Life of Mr. T. Blossom written about the year 1847 . . . copied March 1895 from the original MS. book lent me by his son Mr. J. B. Blossom of 5 Park

Terrace, Waterloo, nr. Liverpool'. At p.231 there is a copy of the inscription or tombstone in North Cave Churchyard and on p.233 copies of two short newspaper notices of his return to England in 1844. Thomas Blossom served as a teacher in the South Sea Academy, retiring to England in 1844. See John Davies, *The History of the Tahitian Mission 1799-1830*, ed. C. W. Newbury for the Hakluyt Society, Cambridge 1961. The location of the original 'Life' is unknown.

LEEDS PUBLIC LIBRARIES
Archives Department, Sheepscar Branch Library, Chapeltown Road, Leeds 7

ARTHINGTON TRUST COLLECTION

AT/A/1-2. Minute books 1905-33 of the Robert Arthington Trust for the Extension of Mission Work including entries concerning missions in New Guinea.

AT/B/8. Arthington Fund No.2 (London Missionary Society), estimates, balance sheets and various general reports 1905-27, and special reports for missionary enterprises in north and south India and Papua including one 1927, for Aird Hill, Kikori, Papua, New Guinea.

AT/C/9, Series 1, 2; AT/D. Papers 1905-35 relating to Australian and New Zealand Baptist missions in India: reports, handbooks, and yearbooks.

EARL OF HAREWOOD ARCHIVES

Canning Papers. The following items were noted in this partially listed collection:
Packet 75. Correspondence 1822-7 of George Canning with, amongst others, Wilmot Horton, including letter and reply 9 July 1823 concerning the introduction of the New South Wales Bill in the House and Horton's urging that it be given priority; correspondence 1823-6 with Henry Goulburn including five letters 1823 on growing New Zealand flax in Ireland.

Packet 91. Correspondence 1822-7 of George Canning with miscellaneous correspondents, containing petition 22 July 1824 of George Gordon offering himself as Hebrew and English teacher in New South Wales.

ROBERT WALKER LETTERS

GA/Z41. Letters 28 Mar. 1853 and 8 June 1854 Robert Walker to his parents describing his arrival at Sydney, work on Coolondong Station in the Snowy Mountains owned by Mr Bradley, work on the gold diggings at Araluen and in the Ovens district, and his later employment as turnkey at the Goulburn gaol; letters 18 Feb., 18 Nov. 1864 to his brother describing conditions with mention of bushranging and farming failures and letter 28 Dec. 1867 from his daughter Jane Hannah Walker of Goulburn to her uncle near Leeds.

KIRBY, SON & ATKINSON, SOLICITORS, RECORDS

Acc.1306. A small group of miscellaneous documents in this collection contains a free pardon 14 Apr. 1856 by Gov. Henry Fox Young, Van Diemen's Land, for the convict Elisha Sinclair, sentenced at the York Assizes 1843.

YORKSHIRE PATENT STEAM WAGON CO.

Records including plans and specifications of No.1535, a steam wagon built in 1926, still preserved (1970) in working order at Invercargill, N.Z.

UNIVERSITY OF LEEDS
Brotherton Library, Leeds 2

BROTHERTON COLLECTION

Gosse Collection. For a list of correspondents see *A Catalogue of the Gosse Correspondence in the Brotherton Collection*, Leeds 1950. The correspondence includes nine letters 1927-8 Jack Lindsay to Sir Edmund Gosse in connection with the Fanfrolico Press.

BUSINESS RECORDS

The following firms were noted as having business dealings with Australia:

Jeremiah Ambler & Sons Ltd, Bradford

Combers, spinners, and weavers of all kinds of wool and hair. Established 1783. 1, Debtors' ledger 1849-60; 2, Creditors' ledger 1855-60; 3, Personal ledger 1861-80, separate index inserted; 4, Journal 1861-1933; 5, General ledger 1880-1929, separate index inserted; 6-9, Debtors' ledgers 1870-1914, separate indexes inserted; 10, Letter book 1895-*c.*1917; 11-13, Stock books 1888-1919; 14-15, Bought day books 1897-1914; 16-23, Sold day books 1903-14; 24, Envelope containing correspondence for 1828.

Robt Jowitt & Sons Ltd, Bradford

Wool merchants and top makers, wool combers, wool scourers, carbonisers and fellmongers. Established 1776. Sixty-six volumes 1775-1914: General ledgers 1775-1904; Customers' ledgers 1848-1904; Colonial and bank ledgers 1877-1904; Interest accounts 1876-94; Status report books 1881-1913; Cash books 1827-1907; Analysis of sales and purchases 1842-1909; Letter books 1802-59; Private business 1877-1909; Private ledgers 1806-1914; Letters.

John Raistrick & Sons, Bradford

1, Order book 1864-77; 2, Correspondence 1875-90 with W. H. Chard & Co., Sydney, and W. Peace and Co., Durban; 3, Wool ledger, etc. 1675-*c.*1834, in the possession of the Raistrick firm but owner unidentified.

John Reddihough Ltd, Bradford

Wool merchants and top makers. 1, Notebook containing balance sheets of John Reddihough 1875-92, woolstapler, Bradford; 2, Private ledger of John Reddihough 1898-1918; 3, Letter book of John Reddihough 1889-1922; 4, Wages book 1883-1906; 5-6, Two notebooks containing balance sheets 1882-97 of William Gawthorp and Co., commission woolcombers, Bradford; 7, General ledger 1894-1903; 8, General ledger 1906-19.

NORTH RIDING COUNTY RECORD OFFICE
County Hall, Northallerton

NONCONFORMIST RECORDS

ZT Religious Society of Friends Records, Richmond Monthly Meeting

ZT6/116. Epistles and queries referring to epistles 20-28 May 1896 from the yearly meeting of women in London to women in Australasia with appreciation of their efforts in the anti-opium cause, also referring to an epistle from the women's meeting of South Australia.

ZT16/54. Miscellaneous, containing a publicity pamphlet concerning James Backhouse's *A Narrative of a Visit to the Australian Colonies*, London 1843.

PRIVATE RECORDS

ZAW Pullein and Hutton Archives

Letters and papers 1867-74 mainly addressed to James Pullein of Clifton Castle, concerning a New Zealand sheep farming venture, the partnership of Tetley, Beaumont & Co., in which his nephew Frederick A. Pullein was involved. J. D. Tetley appears to have absconded and left the partners liable for undisclosed debts. The records include a copy of the deed of partnership 6 Apr. 1868 and letters from F. A. Pullein in New Zealand and from partners, their relatives, and interested parties in England, discussing the disappearance of Tetley and the question of legal liability, particularly towards the New Zealand Bank. In 1872 Dudley Beaumont, an English partner, went to New Zealand and had his connections with Tetley formally dissolved in the bankruptcy court.

ZBA Beresford-Pierse Papers

21/9. Sir John Poo Beresford's Naval Letters. These contain a group of letters 1814 concerning the convicts on the *Indefatigable* and their praise of conditions on board under Capt. Bowles.

ZFL Mauleverer Brown Archive

186, 188. Papers of William Gowan (later Mauleverer), captain in the service of the East India Company, and member of the provisional committee of the South Australian Land Company 1832 and the Committee of the South Australian Association 1834. Included are: printed papers 1830-2 relating to the South Australian venture; letters Mrs Elizabeth Fletcher, Edinburgh, to William Gowan, one letter 20 May 1833 seeking information on the 'Australian Company' and New South Wales; letter 28 Apr. 1823 Capt. Henry Cock, Hobart, to Capt. Gowan speaking of his arrival from the Cape and casting reflections on the conduct of Governor Sorell.

ZFW Wyvill of Constable Burton Archive

7/5. Letters and papers of the Price family including a testimonial 28 Aug. 1853 concerning John Banner Price, Commissariat Department of the Army, who had served in New South Wales, and correspondence 1885-8 between J. B. Price, his son Edwin Price and M. D'Arcy Wyvill concerning Edwin Price's difficulties in London and emigration to Australia.

COUNTY RECORD OFFICE NOTES AND TRANSCRIPTS

CRONT 99/33. File of notes and correspondence concerning ten convicts transported to New South Wales, by C. K. Croft-Andrew, County Archivist, Northallerton, in response to a request from A. J. Grey and J. Cobley of Sydney. Sources in York, Hull, Wakefield and Beverley were consulted as well as the records at Northallerton.

SHEFFIELD CITY LIBRARIES
Department of Local History and Archives, Central Library
Surrey Street, Sheffield

See *Guide to the Manuscript Collections in the Sheffield City Libraries, 1956* with *Supplements I and II 1956-1967*, 1968, also *Sheffield City Libraries, Catalogue of Business and Industrial Records*, 1968.

EM 930 ELMHIRST MUNIMENTS

Letter 17 Feb. 1845 Lawrence Potts, Maitland, N.S.W., to William Elmhirst describing his family affairs, his crops, trade with India in horses and including comments on different classes of convicts with the remark that the 'best men here are the London pickpockets—capital fellows for sheep'. The letter is published in Bulletin No.5, South Yorkshire Committee of the National Register of Archives, Oct. 1969.

Yorkshire

MD 2296-2339 EDGAR ALLEN & CO.

The records 1898-1941 of this iron foundry business consist principally of order books including:

MD 2315-33. Order books 1898-1935 for overseas contracts; MD 2315 Australasia 1923-9 gives details of orders, costs for various firms, principally John Chambers & Son, Wellington, also Noyes Bros., Melbourne; MD 2318 Colonial and Foreign 1907-16 and MD 2319-21 Colonial 1908-31 are likely to contain similar orders.

MD 2334-9. Miscellaneous volumes: wages books 1914-41, journal of accounts 1924-30, capital account 1918-30 and invoice books 1929-35.

MD 2366-78 CHRISTOPHER JOHNSON & CO.

This firm of cutlers was established in 1836.

MD 2366-75. Letter books 1849-1905; MD 2366, 1849-60; MD 2367-9 Foreign 1875-9, 1879-83, 1888-90; MD 2370-2 Exports 1875-8, 1878-80, 1887-8; MD 2373 London Office 1876-9; MD 2374-5 Australia 1883-90, 1897-1905. Early Australian letters are in the Foreign series.

MD 2376. Pattern and price lists: printed pattern books of the firm are held in the printed books section of the Library.

MD 2377. Papers of agent, Paul Rodgers including two letters and his account 1881-3 with the firm regarding expenses.

MD 2378. Typed note 22 Jan. 1850 on Thomas Johnson (brother of Christopher) and his Australian descendants.

SLPS 36 JAMES MONTGOMERY LETTERS

SLPS 36/404, 407, 435, 463, 473, 478, 489, 525, 528, 546. Letters from George Bennet of Highfield, Sheffield, missionary, to James Montgomery, including ten letters 1822-4 written from Huahine, Raiatea, Tahiti, Papara, Erineo [sic], Sydney, and Parramatta.

SSC SHEFFIELD SMELTING COMPANY

See *Two Hundred Precious Metal Years. A History of the Sheffield Smelting Company Limited 1760-1960*, London 1960.

SSC 39. Assay Ledger 1897-1939 including assays of material received from firms in Australia and New Zealand.

SSC 277. List 1903-4 of assayers, refiners, jewellers' material manufacturers, silversmiths and bullion dealers compiled for 'The Buyers & Sellers & Professions of the Commonwealth of Australia and New Zealand'.

SSC 320. Letter Mar. 1897 F. J. Greenway, Broken Hill, N.S.W., with notes of electrolytic refining of silver.

SSC 376. Rough tables including figures 1914-18 of sulphides and silver precipitates bought from Australia.

SSC 407. Notebook containing a carbon copy of the journal kept by J. W. Wilson and letters written by him during various business trips including a trip to Australia and New Zealand 1897.

SSC 408. Notebook containing an index to J. W. Wilson's journal 1896-7.

SSC 410. Letters 1896-7 received from J. W. Wilson while on his business trip to the United States of America, Australia and New Zealand, with copies of letters sent to him referring to the trip and to business affairs at the Sheffield Smelting Company.

SSC 421. List 31 Oct. 1896 of Australian and New Zealand customers.

SSC 422. Terms 17 Dec. 1896 offered to the Melbourne and Sydney Mints.

SSC 423. Notebook with rough notes of visits to firms in Sydney by J. W. Wilson on his Australian trip 1897.

SSC 424. Book containing brief notes of correspondence 1897-1900 with firms of refiners and smelters in Australia and New Zealand.

SSC 427. List of Commercial Councillors, Senior Trade Commissioners and Commissioners in various countries including Australia.

SSC 633. Agreement 1 June 1882 allowing James Powrie, Sydney, N.S.W., miner and mine owner, to buy the exclusive rights in Australia to a fume condensing plant patented by the Sheffield Smelting Co. and one of their chemists.

wh.M WHARNCLIFFE MUNIMENTS

Edward Stuart Wortley Papers

Wh.M 418/i, vii, x, xiii. Seven letters 1856-76 T. A. Browne (Rolf Boldrewood) from Melbourne, Narranderra, Wagga Wagga, and Gulgong, N.S.W., to Edward Stuart Wortley, 1st Earl Wharncliffe. The letters, written infrequently, often summarise events of several years. They refer to Browne's marriage, his pastoral ventures and losses on properties on the Murray and Murrumbidgee, and positions as police magistrate at Gulgong and warden of the goldfields at Mudgee; there are references to the bushranger Morgan and others, and to Australian politics.

Wh.M 457 a, b. Twelve letters 1851-3 from New Zealand to 2nd Baron Wharncliffe and notes on New Zealand by his son Edward Stuart Wortley.

Wh.M 458. Diary 1857 probably of Edward Stuart Wortley during his New Zealand tour.

WWM WENTWORTH WOODHOUSE MUNIMENTS

F66/14, 18. Two letters 1792, 1801 from D'Arcy Wentworth concerning his affairs in New South Wales.

F114/1-62. Sixty-two items 1791-1813, 1817, 1819, 1834 mainly letters to Earl Fitzwilliam and documents concerning D'Arcy Wentworth's various appointments, disputes over his pay, and his court martial. The chief correspondents are D'Arcy Wentworth himself and Charles Cookney; other correspondents include W. C. Wentworth, Philip Gidley King, John Hunter, Viscount Castlereagh, J. T. Campbell, and Col. Torrens. The documents include: questions put to Francis Oakes and replies re the conduct of D'Arcy Wentworth, 23 July 1807; letter 31 Oct. 1807 William Bligh to Mr Windham transmitting Oakes's deposition and saying he is suspending D'Arcy Wentworth; proclamation 27 Jan. 1808 announcing the cessation of martial law; 'Private copy of the Proceedings of a General Court Martial held on Mr. D'Arcy Wentworth taken by a Friend in Court', 18-21 July 1807; 'Statement of Proceedings on the affair of Lt. Governor Molle' addressed to the Right Hon. Earl Fitzwilliam and endorsed as received from Mr Wentworth June 1820; memo n.d. on the timber of New South Wales and Norfolk Island regarded for naval purposes.

F127/202. Letter 1828 Lady Frances Fitzwilliam giving details on report of D'Arcy Wentworth's death.

SPEAR AND JACKSON PAPERS

No.79. Bound volume containing the business diary 1905 of L. J. Combe during a visit to Australia and New Zealand.

JOSEPH GILLOTT PAPERS

MP 688-9. 199S, 200S, also classified items 042S and 780.73SST. Miscellaneous printed papers *c.*1887-1900, cuttings concerning the composer J. Gillott and annotated programs of his concerts in Australia.

AUTOGRAPHS

Book 2 F219. Letter [June 1772] Sir Joseph Banks to Edmund Burke thanking Burke for his active interest in his withdrawal from Cook's second voyage.

THE YORK AND LANCASTER REGIMENT
Regimental Headquarters and Museum, Endcliffe Hall, Sheffield

See *The York and Lancaster Regiment 1758-1919*, Vols.1-2, by Col. H. C. Wylly, London 1930, and Vol.3, 1919-53 by O. F. Sheffield, London 1956. See also Donald Creighton Williamson, *The York and Lancaster Regiment (65th and 84th Regiments of Foot)*, London 1968.

Digest of Service of the 65th Regiment of Foot, 1758-1873. This includes lengthy accounts of engagements in the Maori Wars.

Scrapbook (A/27) including a List of Officers and Men of the 65th Regiment, and years of service as at 18 May 1846.

Copy of return of NCO's and men who became non-effective and served in the Regiment in the field in New Zealand 1845-7 and 1860-6. Typescript prepared 1930.

WHITBY LITERARY & PHILOSOPHICAL SOCIETY
Whitby Museum, Pannett Park, Whitby

The Museum possesses a collection of documents, portraits and relics connected with Capt. James Cook including:

Letter 3 Jan. 1772, Capt. James Cook, Great Ayton, to Capt. William Hammond, see C. Preston, *Captain James Cook R.N., F.R.S., and Whitby*, Whitby 1965, p.26.

Captain James Cook, Journal 5 Aug. 1774 describing events at Tana in the New Hebrides, 1 page. Apparently a preliminary draft, see Whitby Literary and Philosophical Society, *Annual Report*, 1969, pp.15-17.

B. GODWARD, ESQ.
2 St Mary's, York

Mr Godward's library contains many rare prints and publications as well as manuscripts relating to New Zealand and the Pacific. Manuscripts include besides other letters:

Letters 1837-90 Newman family of Wesleyan missionaries to New Zealand, 300 letters.

THE EARL OF HALIFAX
Garrowby, Bishop Wilton, York

HICKLETON PAPERS

See N.R.A. Report 8128 'Catalogue of the Hickleton Papers, the Archives of the Wood family of Hickleton and Garrowby, Co. York, from 1634 to the Present Day'. The references given below are those used in this report. In June 1970 microfilming of the official and professional papers of the 1st Viscount Halifax was in progress.

A2. Personal Papers of the Wood Family

A2.89. Letters from Francis Lindley Wood, son of 1st Viscount Halifax, to his parents, including letters 1857-60 on H.M.S. *Iris*, South Africa, Australia, New Zealand.

A4. Official and Professional Papers, Wood Family

A4.50-180. Political correspondence of the 1st Viscount Halifax. N.R.A. Report 8128 includes an index of correspondents.

A4.56. 1844-75 from Lord John Russell, 1st Earl Russell, including Apr. 1847 discussing the New Zealand Company.

A4.65. 1846-72 from Fox Maule, 2nd Baron Panmure, 11th Earl of Dalhousie, including June 1854 concerning the separation of the War and Colonial Departments.

A4.66. 1846-64 from George Arbuthnot, Private Secretary to the 1st Viscount, 1846-52. The group includes Aug. 1851 relating to the New Zealand Company; Sept. 1852 relating to Australia; Feb. 1853 relating to the Australian Mint.

A4.70. 1846-61 from Sir James Graham including Nov. 1846 concerning Smith O'Brien.

A4.146. 1857-81 from Admiral William Loring, including Mar. 1857 in H.M.S. *Iris* about to leave for Australia, referring to Francis Lindley Wood; Apr. 1858 from Sydney concerning Cockatoo Island and troop movements; Feb.-Apr. 1860 concerning F. L. Wood, Australia, and the Maori War.

Wales and Isle of Man

CAERNARVONSHIRE

UNIVERSITY COLLEGE OF NORTH WALES
Department of Manuscripts, The Library, Bangor

BANGOR MSS.

3571-89. Papers relating mainly to William Jones of Glybcoed in Llanwenllwyfo. He went to Australia in 1852, worked on the Ballarat goldfields and returned in 1855 to the Isle of Man. There is a description of the voyage 4 Aug. to 27 Oct. 1852 from Liverpool to Melbourne; two letters 1853, Ballarat, to his parents describing stores and equipment taken to the goldfields, conditions, and prices there and referring to fellow Welshmen; gold licence issued 1854 to W. Jones; receipt 19 Sept. 1855 from Browne & Wingrove, refiners; two letters, one 1857 from William Selkirk, a Collins Street storekeeper, referring to conditions in Melbourne and giving information to Jones on mutual Australian acquaintances.

5708. Papers of J. Glyn Davies including typescript copy of letter 23 Sept. 1853 from Owen Davies, the Ovens diggings, Vic., to his nephews John and David Davies; also letter 1 Jan. 1938 from J. Glyn Davies, Cambridge, son of John Davies, referring to the discovery of the above transcript.

18415. Includes letter 10 Oct. 1909 in Welsh written from Tamworth, N.S.W., and an account 18 Mar. to 4 May 1909 in Welsh of a voyage from England to Sydney touching at Adelaide and Melbourne.

AMLWCH PAPERS

The collection relates to three generations all with the name of John Mathews. Papers relating to John Mathews II, surveyor in north Cardiganshire and south Merioneth include a letter book 1824-69 concerning *inter alia* his activities as emigration agent. Ten letters 1855-8, mainly to H. Walcott, London, have been noted concerning free passages to New South Wales and Victoria.

TY CALCH (ASHBY) MSS.

Correspondence of the two families of Prytherch of Dyffryn Gwyn, Trefdraeth, Anglesey, and Williams of Ty Calch, Bodergan. It contains one letter 20 Mar. 1832 from John Davies, missionary, to Rev. John Hughes of Pont Robert written from Haweis Town, Papara, Tahiti, describing his work there. The letter is published in J. H. Morris, *Hanes Cenhadaeth Dramor*, Caernarvon 1907.

CAERNARVONSHIRE RECORD OFFICE
County Offices, Caernarvon
See *Guide to the Caernarvonshire Record Office*, 1952.

PRIVATE RECORDS

M764. Lonfa House of Roberts, centennial dinner 2 May 1964 at Rangiora, N.Z., to honour the arrival of Robert Morris Roberts in Canterbury, N.Z., in 1862 and of his future wife in 1864: invitation form sent to family members with list of those attending and printed brochure giving list of family chiefs, biographical notes on the two pioneers and including two poems by T. E. L. Roberts.

M857. Xerox copy of diary 1887, in Welsh, of William Pritchard, joiner, an emigrant to Australia mentioning his arrival in Melbourne; miner's right 18 July 1887 to David Williams at Rockhampton, Q'ld.

M1410. Xerox copy of letter 26 Apr. 1867 Griffith T. Evans, an emigrant in Ballarat, Vic., to his father Thomas Evans, Bangor, with reference to the goldfields.

T

CARDIGANSHIRE

NATIONAL LIBRARY OF WALES
Aberystwyth

See *Annual Report* 1909- , and *Handlist of Manuscripts in the National Library of Wales* issued annually 1940- . Deposited collections are not listed in the *Handlist* but may be described in typescript schedules. Descriptive articles on some collections may be found in *The National Library of Wales Journal* issued twice yearly, 1939- .

NATIONAL LIBRARY OF WALES MANUSCRIPTS

N.L.W. MS.679 (U.C.W.39) Sermons, etc.

Includes printed translation of a portion of the Gospel according to St John into Tahitian by John Davies [*Te Evanelia A Ioane*, 2nd ed., Tahiti], Windward Mission Press, 1821. This translation may be by John Hughes, Methodist minister in Montgomeryshire and linguist.

N.L.W. MSS.2521-98 Pennant MSS.

Papers of Thomas Pennant and of his son David Pennant of Flintshire, including:
N.L.W. MS.2597 (Pennant 77). Miscellaneous Pamphlets and Papers. Pamphlets and papers on miscellaneous subjects including: *A Letter to . . . The Earl of Sandwich . . . from George Forster*, London 1778; autograph letter 28 Feb. 1778 The Earl of Sandwich to Daines Barrington concerning Forster.

N.L.W. MSS.2921-3018 Haverfordwest MSS.

N.L.W. MS.2982 (Haverfordwest 62). Correspondence including six miscellaneous letters 1854-95 from Australia and New Zealand mainly on legal matters. Correspondents are: Ann Evans, Sydney; Mrs L. Coghlan-Davis, Sydney; Thomas R. James, Christchurch, N.Z.; Charles Cozens, Ipswich, Q'ld; and William and John Rees on board the *Duncan Hoyle* at Melbourne.

N.L.W. MS.3291 Letters.

Miscellaneous letters including two in Welsh 25 May 1859, 24 June 1864, David Lloyd Thomas, Ballarat.

N.L.W. MS.3292 Letters.

Miscellaneous autograph letters including: 30 Jan. 1808 Rev. John Davies, Tahiti, to John Griffiths, Pont Robert, in Welsh with an introduction in English asking Griffiths to pass on the rest of the letter to Davies's parents if they are still alive; Apr. 1816 Pomare II, King of Otaheite, to Rev. John Davies; 30 Jan. 1844 John Davies, Papara, to Rev. John Hughes, Welshpool.

N.L.W. MS.4493 Robert Roberts, 'Y Sgolor Mawr'.

Papers 1852-84 including an address given by Roberts at an eisteddfod in Ballarat. See *The Life and Opinions of Robert Roberts, a Wandering Scholar*, ed. J. H. Davies, Cardiff 1923.

N.L.W. MSS.4796-807 Bridgwater MSS.

N.L.W. MS.4798 (Bridgwater 3). Charles Correspondence. Correspondence 1779-1813 of Thomas Charles and Sarah Jones (afterwards Charles); letters to Thomas Charles from John Davies of Tahiti and Thomas Haweis of London.

N.L.W. MSS.6238-53 Lleufer Thomas MSS.

N.L.W. MS.6243 (Lleufer Thomas 46). Letter in Welsh 12 Apr. 1859 John Thomas [West?], Daisy Hill, Melbourne, to his mother in Wales.

N.L.W. MSS.6511-615 Traherne-Mansel Franklen MSS.

Mainly collections of the Rev. John Montgomery Traherne of Glamorgan, including:

N.L.W. MS.6514 (Traherne-Mansel Franklen 4). Letters 1779-c.1783 by John Walters with poems written in the letters, one in Latin commemorating Capt. James Cook.

N.L.W. MSS.6798-848 Hartland MSS.

Manuscripts and notebooks of Edwin Sidney Hartland including MS.6816 (Hartland 26) and MSS.6833-4 (Hartland 43-4) containing material on Australian Aborigines.

N.L.W. MSS.7011-189 'Nefydd' MSS., (Group I).

Manuscripts and papers from the collection of William Roberts ('Nefydd'), of Blaenau, Monmouthshire, agent in South Wales for the British and Foreign School Society, including:

N.L.W. MSS.7163-6 ('Nefydd' 153-6). Autograph letters. Letters 1787-1930 addressed chiefly to 'Nefydd' and his father-in-law Daniel Jones, generally of personal, religious, or Baptist interest including letters from George Jared Jones, Melbourne.

N.L.W. MSS.7176-7 ('Nefydd' 166-7). Letters 1823-1917 addressed chiefly to 'Nefydd' with references to Baptist activities in Australia, including letters from George [Jared] Jones, Melbourne, Margaret and David Morris of Tarleton, Tas., and Lewis Thomas of Port Adelaide, S.A.

N.L.W. MSS.7355-98 Croesor MSS.

N.L.W. MS.7386 (Croesor 32) Sermons including sermons in Welsh 1864-6 by Daniel Jones written and preached at Ballarat.

N.L.W. MSS.9151-233 Hobley Griffith MSS.

N.L.W. MS.9216 (Hobley Griffith 66). Miscellaneous notes 19th-20th cents. including an account of the Australian bush traveller.

N.L.W. MSS.10275-94 Solva MSS.

N.L.W. MSS.10275-6 (Solva 1-2). Letters mainly addressed to Hugh Jones 'Cromwell O Went', Congregational minister, including letters 1869-71 John Davies, Melbourne, on the plight of Ellice John Jones, son of Hugh Jones; letters 1859-71 Ellice John Jones to his father on life in New South Wales.

N.L.W. MSS.10678-707 Eurwedd Williams MSS.

N.L.W. MS.10691 (Eurwedd Williams 14) Autobiography. Notes by T. Eurwedd Williams including names of emigrants from Dafen to Australia.

N.L.W. MS.10700 (Eurwedd Williams 23) General notes. A volume entitled 'Cyfrol V. Nodion Cyffredinol', Jan. to 27 Sept. 1928, including references to emigration to Australia.

N.L.W. MS.11138 Album of Richard Rees.

Album of memoranda c.1857 by Richard Rees, Unitarian minister, Glamorgan, consisting largely of letters to Rees including: 16 July 1843 Benjamin Samuda, Macintyre River, referring to a previous partnership in a property on the Hunter River and the current property where the numerous Aborigines were a danger; 4 Dec. 1852 John Samuda, Stoke-on-Trent, referring mainly to his brother Benjamin who had returned to Sydney from a second voyage to India trading horses.

N.L.W. MSS.12731-853 D. E. Jenkins MSS.

Manuscripts, notes, correspondence of the Rev. David Erwyd Jenkins, Calvinistic Methodist Minister, including:

N.L.W. MS.12852 (D. E. Jenkins 122). Miscellaneous notes including typescript notes on 'Emigration from Wales, 1760-1868' giving conjectural estimates of the number of Welsh emigrants to Australia 1826-68.

N.L.W. MSS.14455-7 Salter MSS.

Letters 1915-19 from Brigadier William A. Salter, Salvation Army, China, forming a journal in three volumes. Letter 25 Feb. 1917 and later letters mention fourteen officers sent to Peking from Australia and New Zealand; letter 3 May 1917 refers to Dr Morrison of the *Times*; letters 1919 describe the mission at Honolulu and conditions there as seen by Salter on his return journey to England.

N.L.W. MS.15078 Journal of a Voyage to Australia.

Journal 1865-6 in Welsh by J. Davies, Blaenafon, describing his voyage with his sister Elizabeth to Australia and their early days in Sydney.

N.L.W. MS.16799. Two typescript poems by T. H. Jones, University of Newcastle, N.S.W.

N.L.W. MS.19628. Drafts of fourteen published poems by T. H. Jones, all containing variations from the published form.

OTHER COLLECTIONS

Calvinistic Methodist Archives

16206. Letter in Welsh 20 Nov. 1811 John Davies, Tahiti, to his parents with covering letter 19 Nov. 1811, in English, to John Griffiths, Pont Robert.

16207-37. Letters 1818-45, one in English, from John Davies, Tahiti, to Rev. John Hughes, Pont Robert, with article Rev. A. Pearse, 'Tahiti of Today', Raiatea, Feb. 1885, printed.

J. Glyn Davies Collection

Ninety-seven letters 1856, 1892-9, 1939-40, 1951-2 relating to Australia and New Zealand have been noted, the chief correspondents being John Glyn Davies, his brother Frank Davies and his parents John and Gwen Davies. Letters 1897-8 by J. Glyn Davies, Auckland, refer to his stay in New Zealand and particularly to the shipment home of his sailing boat *Cymro*. Letters 1895-8 from Frank Davies refer to his employment on the *Cambrian Queen* and the *Annie Thomas* on voyages to Australia. Letters 1939-40 from Peggy Haddon Jones, Kapiti Island and Tongariro, N.Z., describe local fauna and her work as a teacher of music. Letters 1950-2 from B. Heaton, Cambridge, include reference to Frances and Nevil Norway [Shute] having emigrated to Australia.

Glansevern Collection

The collection includes correspondence 1847, 1859-92 concerning Edward Wingfield Humphreys, pastoralist and politician in New Zealand.

Letters 1836-1905 to Arthur Charles Humphreys-Owen, brother of Edward Wingfield Humphreys.

5789. Letter 30 Apr. 1892 Cyril G. Hawdon, Brighton, on death of E. W. Humphreys.

5832-43. Letters c.1883-92 but mostly undated, Alice Humphreys, wife of E. W. Humphreys, from New Zealand and London, giving personal and social news, and referring to financial matters, progress of the station, Edward's illness and death.

5845-911, 8157. Letters 1862-91 E. W. Humphreys mainly from Rock and Pillar Station, later named Garthmyl, Dunedin, relating chiefly to his sheep farming ventures and financial position in New Zealand, containing also references to personal, family, social, and political news.

5986. Letter 30 Apr. 1892 J. M. Lloyd, Castell Forwyn, expressing sympathy on the death of E. W. Humphreys.

5995-6005. Letters 1864-8 George Macfarlane, Christchurch, describing his voyage to New Zealand, his affairs and those of E. W. Humphreys in New Zealand.

6114-16. Letters 1878, 1891, n.d. John Studholme, Christchurch and London, *re* E. W. Humphreys's affairs.

Letters to Erskine Humphreys, father of Edward Wingfield Humphreys.

5405-11. Letters 1871-6 Alice Humphreys, mainly from Rock and Pillar Station, describing personal and social life, and farming progress.

5412. Letter 9 Mar. 1876 A. C. Humphreys-Owen, Paris, on his brother E. W. Humphreys's estate in New Zealand and the question of compelling him to live within a fixed income.

5426-49. Letters 1863-77 E. W. Humphreys, mainly from Rock and Pillar Station, describing his voyage out, giving personal news and reporting on his farming progress and financial matters, including his partnership with George Macfarlane.

5465. Letter 15 Aug. 1864 George Macfarlane on his purchase of sheep runs and investment in New Zealand, his agreements with E. W. Humphreys and intended partnership.

7770. Letter 6 Oct. 1868 J. Hawdon, Hagley Park, Christchurch, on the proposed marriage of his daughter with E. W. Humphreys; also family and personal news.
Letters to Edward Wingfield Humphreys.

7742-63, 8170. Letters 1859-89 from fourteen correspondents, mainly family members, including: 22 Dec. 1887 A. C. Humphreys-Owen, Glansevern, re a settlement to carry out their father's intentions; 1875 Erskine Humphreys despatching deeds of reconveyance and reassignment with reference to a partnership agreement; 1859 Fleetwood J. Edwards, Windsor House, referring to E. W. Humphreys's early years; 10 Dec. 1877 Australian Mortgage Land and Finance Co. Ltd re deed for station property; 2 June 1889 [N?] Campbell, Oamaru, on E. W. Humphreys's candidature for Christchurch North.

8156-7. Included in the group entitled Letters to Edward Wingfield Humphreys are two letters from E. W. Humphreys, 2 Oct. 1874, London, to his station manager Frank Pogson.
Miscellaneous.

3737. Letter 13 Nov. 1847 William Martin, lawyer, Auckland, N.Z., to Arthur James Johnes, barrister at Lincolns Inn, and uncle of E. W. Humphreys, referring to philological studies, law reform, and the New Zealand Company.

4901. Letter 16 Feb. 1884 A. C. Humphreys-Owen, London, to his cousin Rev. Robert Temple referring to frozen lamb sent from New Zealand by his brother Edward.

8027. Letter 7 Sept. 1881 E. W. Humphreys, Garthmyl, N.Z., to Rev. Robert Temple on receipt of legacy bequeathed by A. J. Johnes.
Herbert Stanley Jevons Collection
Part IV 80b. File of correspondence on Alberta and New Zealand 1937.

J. W. Jones Collection
Includes letters 1932-3 Baldwyn M. Davies, Treasurer, St David's Society of Blackstone, Q'ld, to J. W. Jones; and letters 1939, 1943 from Bill Roberts of Port Adelaide describing how he left Wales for Patagonia in 1906, came back to Blaenau Festiniog in 1915 and left next day for Australia where he was a government night watchman.

Timothy Lewis MSS. and Papers
The collection contains papers of Dr J. Gwenogvryn Evans including:
131-2. Notebook containing draft of part of a journal describing a storm on a voyage to Australia towards the end of 1881 and a notebook containing daily entries describing a voyage from Melbourne 4 Feb. to 7 Apr. 1882.

GLAMORGAN

BOARD OF TRADE, GENERAL REGISTER AND RECORD OFFICE OF SHIPPING AND SEAMEN
Llantrisant Road, Llandaff, Cardiff

The following classes of records which the Registry retains (May 1969) contain material helpful in specific searches into the history of ships or individuals travelling to or from Australasia. Requests for further information and application to study the records should be made direct to the Registrar-General.

Agreements and Crew Lists 1860-

Those for 1835-60, together with a few late eighteenth and early nineteenth century muster rolls, and also agreements and crew lists for ships of special interest or importance from 1860-1913, have been transferred to the Public Record Office, B.T.98 and 100. It is proposed that a sample of the post-1860 records will be selected for preservation in the Public Record Office, but the nature of this sample and the question of the disposal of the remaining records have not yet been agreed. The agreements and crew lists are in annual runs arranged by ship's registration number and not by port of registry. Ships registered in the dominions and colonies are included as well as ships registered in the United Kingdom and engaged in domestic and overseas trade.

Official Ships' Logs 1914-18, 1939-45, 1961-

In general, the practice has been to destroy logs after seven years, but those for the two World Wars and a number in which deaths and births at sea were recorded have survived. Logs relating to agreements which may be selected for preservation will also probably be preserved in future.

Central Register of Ships 1812-

Up to 1890 the registries are in bound volumes; from 1855-90 transactions subsequent to original registry are separately bound. After 1890 the documents are not separately bound but the transcript of the original registry and subsequent transactions are kept together and filed in ten-year runs after closing of the registry. Since this Central Register comprises an exact copy of the details held in each port of registry it is in effect a duplicate register, of particular use if the port of registry is not known or the local registers have been destroyed. The pre-1890 registries and transactions and all documents of closed registries, except those closed within the last ten years, will be transferred to the Public Record Office in the near future.

Certificates of Competency 1850-

These are registers and office copies of the certificates issued to seamen. Registers 1850-*c.*1900 will be transferred to the Public Record Office in the near future.

Registers of Deaths, Births and Marriages c.1854-

Deaths, births and marriages at sea in British ships are recorded in these registers, the majority of entries being deaths.

UNIVERSITY COLLEGE OF SWANSEA
The Library, Singleton Park, Swansea

LLANELLY TINPLATE WORKS RECORDS

Llanelly Associated Tinplate Company

Registered in 1939 the company was formed to acquire the Ashburnham, Kidwelly,

Old Castle, Teilo, and Western Tinplate Companies.

Ledgers, Journals, Day Books including Order Books and Sales Books, Minutes of Directors Meetings, Contracts Books, and Correspondence 1939-47, including: (xix) Correspondence.

19. Correspondence 1939-41 with Henry Gawler, Richmond, Vic., re loss of share certificate and payment of dividends.

30. Correspondence 15 May 1939 to 30 Dec. 1946 with Sir Evan Williams, Chairman, re redundancy, lacquering, tinplates to Australia.

53. Correspondence 17 Feb. 1942 to 25 Apr. 1947 W. E. Hughes Co. Ltd, London, re appointment of an agency in Australia.

Old Castle Iron and Tinplate Works

Minute Books, Registers, Ledgers, Journals, Day Books, Letter Books, Cash Books, Correspondence 1866-1947, including: (xii) General Correspondence.

31. Letter 30 May 1939 J. A. Dagleas to W. E. Phillips concerning the possible effects of tinplate manufacture in Australia. (xvi) Miscellaneous.

(e)17. Notes 1937-9 re Australian tinplate tariff inquiry.

(e)21. Tinplate manufacture in Australia, 31 May 1939.

Teilo Tinplate Works

Ledgers, Registers, Stock Records, Reports, Correspondence 1880-1947 but mainly 1935-46, including: (ix) Correspondence, miscellaneous letters 1935-47 including reference to Japanese competition in Australia, comparative Japanese and Welsh prices, cost sheets.

Western Tinplate Works

Ledgers, Day Books, Stock Records, Correspondence 1891-1950 but mainly 1934-47, including: (ix) Miscellaneous material c.1941-4 containing reports, sale contracts, correspondence, and export figures to Australia.

MONMOUTHSHIRE

MONMOUTHSHIRE COUNTY RECORD OFFICE
County Hall, Newport

See *Guide to the Monmouthshire Record Office*, 1959.

PRIVATE RECORDS

D460. Papers of Sir Alexander Murray Tulloch and Sir Alexander Bruce Tulloch, including:

Summary of arrangements c.1851 relating to the emigration of pensioners and their families to various specified colonies. In New Zealand the pensioners were to be used as military reservists, in Australia as convict guards.

Two letters c.1889 Arabella Tulloch, wife of General Sir Alexander B. Tulloch, Melbourne, to her son Angus and her mother-in-law.

Letter 1892 J. Richardson, Military Staff Office, Sydney, to Tulloch referring to his own state of health on service in New Zealand, the Sudan and Port Darwin, and to a commission reporting on him.

PEMBROKESHIRE

PEMBROKESHIRE RECORD OFFICE
The Castle, Haverfordwest

DX/32/1. Letter 4 Sept. 1883 A. J. Davies, Portsmouth Harbour, about to sail to Sydney in the *Rialto*, including description of life on board.

DX/72. Receipts 1899 from Arthur H. Nathan, Auckland and 9 Broad Street, London, to J. Sheriff, Takapuna.

ISLE OF MAN

MANX MUSEUM
The Library, Kingswood Grove, Douglas

MS.1016C. Transcripts n.d. [early 19th cent.] of letters and papers connected with Peter Heywood and his family including letters June-Sept. 1792 from Peter Heywood to his sister.

Scotland

FIFESHIRE

UNIVERSITY OF ST ANDREWS
The Library, St Andrews

There is an index of Western Manuscripts on slips filed in binders, with entries for names of authors, writers, and addressees of letters, and a few subjects.

LIBRARY CORRESPONDENCE

Letter 19 July 1879 from Arnott concerning J. G. Beaney.

MANUSCRIPTS

MS.LF1110 B4. Six autobiographical letters 1867-8 from Alexander Berry to Rev. George Walker, photographs of typed copies from the originals in the possession of Dr David Russell of Silverburn, Leven. Berry and Walker were fellow students at Cupar Burgh Grammar School and at St Andrews, see J. B. Salmond, 'After Many Days', *The Alumnus Chronicle*, No.42, June 1954, pp.5-12. Extracts are published in the *Fife News* 28 Feb., 7, 14 Mar. 1874 and in the *Fife Herald* 26 Feb., 5, 12 Mar. 1874.

MS.PR4877. Andrew Lang, 'Australian marriage systems, abstract of a paper on the marriage systems of Australian Aborigines read at a meeting of the Folk-Lore Society, Oxford, 25 Oct. 1902', published in *Folk-Lore*, Vol.13, 1902, pp.398-402.

MSS.5600-9012 Donaldson Papers

Papers of Sir James Donaldson, Principal of the United Colleges of St Salvator and St Leonard, 1886-1915.

5916. Letter 1886 concerning J. G. Beaney.

6312. Letter 1874 from J. Crauford, Lord Ardmillan, recommending W. Norrie for a teaching post in Dunedin, N.Z.

6579-620 include letters 1889-1909 from John Hay of Coolangatta and his brother Alexander Hay, and other papers concerning David Berry's bequest to the University.

7018, 7579, 7592-3, 7639, 8202, 8427, 8674, 8915. Letters 1888-1912 from Sir Henry Normand MacLaurin, Chancellor, University of Sydney.

7107, 7943, 8671, 8919. Letters 1878-1907 from Rev. W. M. Nicholson, Ravensburn, Dunedin.

7403. Letter 1880 from Rev. Michael Watt, Otago.

7597, 7649. Letters 1889, 1890 from D. McN. Stuart, University of New Zealand.

7856, 8207. Letters 1893, 1897 from Sir Anthony Colling Brownless.

8624. Letters 1909 from R. Arthur, M.L.C., New South Wales.

MSS.9013-30000 D'Arcy Wentworth Thompson Papers

The correspondence of Sir D'Arcy Wentworth Thompson, Professor of Natural History at St Andrews 1882-1948. An index of names of writers and addresses and of some subjects has been made on slips filed in binders.

9223-325. Fifty-eight letters 1923-45 from A. Martin Adamson including letters 1927-33 concerning his work with E. Philpott Mumford on a survey of entomology in Polynesian Islands sponsored by the Hawaiian Sugar Planters Association, the Bernice P. Bishop Museum, and the Association of Hawaiian Pineapple Packers. Letters 1928-32 describe collecting expeditions in Honolulu, Tahiti, and the Marquesas.

11655-8. Letters 1896-7 from H. Croft, consulting engineer, Victoria, B.C., concerning photographs of birds from Honolulu and other Pacific Islands.

11866, 21851. Letters 1885, 1910 from W. M. Bale, Melbourne.

12861. Letter 30 Apr. 1948 from Department of External Territories, Canberra, acknowledging recommendation of C. R. Stonor for a position in the Papua-New Guinea civil service.

12901-10. Include letters 1926-32 from J. S. Gardiner, Zoological Laboratory, Cambridge, and 11 Feb. 1924 from T. B. Robertson, University of Adelaide.

13189. Letter 1940 from M. D. Oeser.

13190-6, 23527. Letters 1938-46 from O. A. Oeser.

13911-50. Include letters from J. S. Gardiner.

14204-9. Letters 1891-8 from Professor W. A. Haswell, University of Sydney.

15551-5. Letters 1905-9 from A. F. Mackay.

18155-81. Correspondence 1911-38 with Professor W. J. Dakin, chiefly letters from Dakin.

20109-27. Letters 1895-1927 from C. Chilton, University of New Zealand.

20126. Letter 1927 from A. Crabb, Secretary, High Commissioner, New Zealand.

21427-8, 22654-9. Letters 1893-7 from G. M. Thomson, Dunedin.

21476-7. Letter 25 Mar. 1907 from E. H. Shackleton, Glasgow, concerning A. F. Mackay and copy of letter 21 Mar. 1907 from Thompson recommending Mackay.

21550-5. Letter 19 June 1933 from A. Martin Adamson concerning the termination of the entomological survey in the Pacific for the Hawaiian Sugar Planters Association, and letters 1933 from Sir Guy A. K. Marshall, Director of the Imperial Institute of Entomology concerning Adamson.

22538-40. Three letters 1893 from W. Baldwin Spencer.

24809-12. Letters 1893 from T. J. Parker, Otago University Museum.

25855-6. Letters 1945-6 from J. T. Salmon, Dominion Museum, Wellington.

MS.30017/95. Letter 1902 from R. J. Seddon.

UNIVERSITY OF ST ANDREWS
The University Muniments, St Andrews

Minutes of the Senate

Minutes 8 Dec. 1888, 12 Jan. 1889, 13 Apr. 1889 record negotiations and regulations under which qualified students from approved Australian and New Zealand colleges should be granted the degree of Bachelor of Divinity *in absentia*. A special volume of the muniments entitled 'Extract List of Graduates', Vol.2, 1880-1914 and lettered UY 342/2, records the conferring of degrees of Bachelor of Divinity *in absentia*. There are also entries in this volume recording the conferring of degrees of Hon. LL.D. and Hon. D.D. on a number of Australians and New Zealanders.

Minutes of the University Court

Minutes 1890-1906 record correspondence and transactions concerning the bequest 23 Sept. 1889 of £100,000 to the University by David Berry. The bequest was made to comply with the wishes of David Berry's elder brother Alexander who had studied medicine at St Andrew's University.

MIDLOTHIAN

HIGH COURT OF JUSTICIARY
Parliament Square, Edinburgh

Justiciary processes and papers 1800 to date are preserved in the High Court of Justiciary, those to 1799 having been transferred to the Scottish Record Office q.v. Consideration is being given to the transfer of additional records to the Scottish Record Office. The papers are arranged chronologically and include some circuit papers. Criminal registers exist for cases tried at Edinburgh 1537-1887 and, since 1887, for the separate circuits, Edinburgh, South, North, and Western. Processes and papers of a particular trial may be produced for students with satisfactory credentials if the name of person tried and date and place of trial are known.

NATIONAL LIBRARY OF SCOTLAND
George IV Bridge, Edinburgh

The Advocates' Library, founded in 1682, became the National Library of Scotland in 1925. See National Library of Scotland *Summary Catalogue of the Advocates' Manuscripts*, 1970; *Catalogue of Manuscripts Acquired since 1925, Volume I, Manuscripts 1-1800*, 1938, *Volume II, Manuscripts 1801-4000*, 1966, *Volume III, Manuscripts 4001-4940*, *Blackwood Papers 1805-1900*, 1968. Typescripts of Volume IV Manuscripts 4941-7000 and Volume V Manuscripts 7001-9000 are available. Volume VI Manuscripts 9001-   , is in progress (1970). Manuscripts acquired since 1925 and not yet catalogued are listed in an alphabetical index to accessions on slips. This index is kept in the Department of Manuscripts. See also National Library of Scotland *Annual Reports*, also *Accessions of Manuscripts 1959-1964*; a list covering 1965-9 is in preparation (1970).

ADVOCATES' MSS.

Adv.MS.17.1.18. Edward Robarts, Narrative of a voyage to the South Seas 1797-[1824?].* See extract of two letters from Capt. von Krusenstern, *Philosophical Magazine* XXII, 1805, pp.6-13, 116. Robarts set out on a whaling voyage and deserted. The narrative includes a vocabulary of the Marquesas language, descriptions of Tahiti and the Bay of Islands, N.Z., with a first hand account of Bruce. Robarts proceeded to Calcutta, then went to Van Diemen's Land and Sydney, and returned to India.

Adv.MSS.46.1.1-46.10.2, various numbers, Sir George Murray Papers

For a description by M. R. Dobie see *Journal of the Society for Army Historical Research*, Jan. 1931. The papers include Murray's correspondence and papers 1828-30 as Secretary of State for the Colonies, also letters 1815-43 from and concerning Sir Thomas Livingstone Mitchell and other letters 1831-45 relating to Australia. Selections have been microfilmed for the Australian Joint Copying Project.

46.8.6-8. Include, besides correspondence 1818-19 from and concerning Mitchell, 46.8.7 ff.57-60 establishment 1828 of the Secretary of State's Office, Colonial Department, with notes by Murray on distribution of duties; ff.109-10 letter 2 Nov. 1828 from the Duke of Wellington concerning a retiring allowance for the Archdeacon of New South Wales; ff.117-18 letter 24 Nov. 1828 W. Lake to the King concerning his loss of the appointment as Agent for the Civil Establishment for New South Wales with minute from the King to Murray.

46.8.9-15. Include papers and correspondence 1819-30 on convicts and on Australia, and 46.8.12-15 Murray's letter books 1826-30 while Secretary of State for the Colonies.

46.8.16-23. Include letters from Mitchell: 46.8.16 ff.11-16, 13 Apr. 1831 complaining of difficulties with Darling, ff.19-20, 5 Dec. 1831 from Liverpool Plains reporting hopes of new discoveries, ff.111-12, 25 May 1832 report on his expedition and on happy relations with Bourke; 46.8.21 ff.45-8, 8 Nov. 1841 from Felton Mathew, surveyor, Auckland, N.Z.; 46.8.23 ff.207-13 letter 31 Jan. 1842 from Capt. Stirling, H.M.S. *Indus*, with enclosures, concerning his work in Western Australia.

46.9.2-12. Include letters from Mitchell, also 46.9.2 ff.1-6 letter 1 Apr. 1842, New South Wales, unsigned, charging Col. Barney with corruption; ff.29-34 letter 5 Apr. 1842 from W. R. Govett, Devon, enclosing copies of letters from Mitchell and the Colonial Office supporting his application for further employment; 46.9.3 ff.197-203 letters 1842 concerning Felton Mathew; 46.9.6 ff.41-2 letter 10 Mar. 1842 from Mitchell concerning his difficulties with Gipps; ff.209-10 letter 6 May 1843 from Sir E. Hayes requesting an introduction in Australia for Mr Lewis Clarke, surveyor; 46.9.9 ff.171-2 letter 15 Apr. 1845 from Sir Eardley Wilmot, Hobart, concerning the departure of his son Lieut. H. Eardley Wilmot for New Zealand and stating that troops could not be spared from Van Diemen's Land; ff.183-4 letter 8 Aug. 1845 from Peter Brown, Perth.

Adv.MSS.80.1.1-80.7.14 Dundas of Dundas Papers

An index to these papers in six loose-leaf binders, is available in the Manuscripts Reading Room. Among Miscellaneous Papers and Books is 80.7.13, account of the mutiny on H.M.S. *Bounty* and the subsequent history of Pitcairn Island to 1841 by John Buffett who settled on Pitcairn as a school-teacher in 1823 succeeding John Adams.

MANUSCRIPTS ACQUIRED SINCE 1925

MSS.1-67 Melville Papers

Letters and documents received by Henry Dundas, 1st Viscount Melville, and his son Robert, 2nd Viscount, including some copies of replies or draft replies, see H. Furber, *Henry Dundas*, London 1931, G. W. T. Omond, *The Arniston Memoirs*, Edinburgh 1887.

6. Correspondence of Robert Dundas 1790-4 including letters relating to the State Trials of Thomas Muir and other Scottish Martyrs, see especially ff.50-1, 65-8, 127, 139-44, 151-8.

MS.98 Miscellaneous Letters and Documents

f.105, item xxxv. Letter 16 Apr. 1794 Thomas Muir to George Dyer concerning his solicitor, William Moffat.

MS.170 Goodsir Papers

ff.68-85. 'The Lakes Fisheries' and the 'Closed Grounds Question by Chrysophrys', apparently articles defending fishermen on the Gippsland Lakes, Vic., the writer having been a resident of the area for eight years.

ff.86-112. Articles for the *Australian*, a Brisbane paper, about an excursion to fish hatcheries near Stirling, written during the International Fisheries Exhibition 1882. The second article is signed 'G'.

MSS.351-4 Melville Papers

351 f.15. Report on Friends of the People and on Joseph Gerrald, 1794.

MS.546 Miscellaneous Letters and Documents

Item vi, four letters 1784-94 of Alexander Abercromby, Lord Abercromby, Senator of the College of Justice, to Henry Dundas, afterwards 1st Viscount Melville. In the letter of 4 Mar. 1794 he forwarded a copy (missing) of the notes he took at the trial of T. F. Palmer.

MSS.665-6 Carlyle Collection
666 ff.265-6. Letter 2 Dec. 1879 D. Buchanan, Sydney, in praise of Carlyle's 'French Revolution'.

MSS.668-84 Constable Collection
Correspondence of Archibald Constable, publisher, his firm, family, and other papers.
683. Articles and memoranda of literary, historical, and topical interest, including ode inscribed to Thomas Muir.

MSS.1002-3 Miscellaneous Letters
1003 ff.37-8. Letter 1797 from Thomas Muir.

MSS.1041-79 Melville Papers
1051 ff.43-95. Includes papers 1789, 1793 and n.d. concerning transportation of convicts including the sentence of T. F. Palmer and list 14 Nov. 1793 of male convicts under sentence of transportation in Edinburgh gaol including T. Muir.
1068 ff.40-53. Note 2 Nov. 1792 from Dalrymple enclosing extracts of a letter 25 May 1792 from Lieut. J. McCluer, H.M.S. *Panther* concerning the expedition to the Pelew Islands and New Guinea.
ff.56-65. Letter 3 Feb. 1794 from Dalrymple enclosing extract of a letter 23 Jan. 1793 from Lieut. J. McCluer concerning the Pelew Islands.
ff.86-96. Letter 21 Dec. 1795 Dalrymple to the Secret Committee of the East India Company concerning *inter alia* visits to New Guinea by Capt. Forrest 1771 and Capt. Rees, *Northumberland*, Indiaman, 1783 and enclosing extract of letter from Lieut. McCluer advocating a route to China via Timor instead of round New Holland.

MSS.1763-77 Carlyle Collection
1766-73 include letters 1849-c.1880 C. G. Duffy to Carlyle: 1766 ff.243-4; 1768 ff.10-11, 23 May 1861 introducing Parkes; 1768 ff.31-3, 36-7, 308-9; 1770 ff.75-6, 233-4; 1772 f.176; 1773 ff.160-1, 230-9; 1777 ff.182-3.
1770 ff.29-30, 1772 ff.120-1. Letters 19 Apr. 1871 and 27 Sept. 1876 David Buchanan, Sydney, to Carlyle.
1777 ff.170-1, 23 July 1892 C. G. Duffy to Mrs Carlyle; f.189 n.d. A. H. Richards, Melbourne, to Duffy.

MSS.1847-62 Brown Correspondence
Correspondence of the Brown family, chiefly of Gen. Sir George Brown.
1847 ff.141-55. Letters and papers 1846-7 of Lieut.-Col. R. H. Wynyard including letters to Brown from Sydney, Parramatta, and New Zealand.

MSS.2264-505 Cochrane Papers
Correspondence and papers, private and official, 1799-1856 of Admiral the Hon. Sir Alexander Forrester Inglis Cochrane and of his son Admiral Sir Thomas John Cochrane.
2378-426. Correspondence of Adm. Sir Thomas John Cochrane as second in command 1842-5 and Commander-in-Chief 1845-6 of the East Indies Station.
2413-14. 'Admiralty Enclosures' 1844-6 include an article 1845 on a stockade of the Maori chief Heke.
2414 ff.52-63, 104-9. Correspondence July 1845 concerning the conveyance of Capt. Grey from South Australia to New Zealand.
ff.138-42. Letter 13 Nov. 1845 from Capt. J. Everard Home, H.M.S. *North Star*, Bay of Islands, N.Z., enclosing copy of letter from Heke.
ff.191-3. Letters Mar. 1846 from H.M.S. *Hazard* complaining of the 'traitorous

conduct' of the Venerable Archdeacon Henry Williams in connection with the Maoris.

ff.202-10, 274-9. Letters Dec. 1845 and Jan. 1846 from Capt. C. Graham, H.M.S. *Castor*, Bay of Islands.

MSS.2543-55 Lithgow Papers
    Correspondence and papers of Maj.-Gen. Stewart A. Lithgow with a few earlier letters of his family.

2543-4. Correspondence 1785-1893 includes ff.39-48 several letters 1853 from Edwin Lithgow at the Australian goldfields, Campbell's Creek Diggings, Port Phillip, Woodend, Mount Macedon, and Williamstown.

MSS.2835-78 Brown Correspondence
    Letters and papers of Gen. Sir George Brown and of other members of his family.
2846 ff.93-8. Letter 4 Apr. 1848 Pitt, Auckland, concerning Heke.
2851 ff.59-64. Letter 27 Sept. 1852 Lieut.-Col. R. H. Wynyard describing the state of the colony.
2853 ff.13-14. Letter 18 Sept. 1853 R. Nickle, Sydney, concerning his salary and costs of living in Australia.

MS.3011 Melville Papers
    Papers 1793-9 relating to sedition. The papers include ff.1-48, notes of the speeches and opinions of the Court at the trial of Sinclair for sedition at Edinburgh 1794; ff.49-70, memo for Dundas on the trial of Muir for sedition at Edinburgh 1793.

MS.3278 Miscellaneous
ff.196-8, item xlix. Two letters 11 May 1889, Honolulu, and n.d., Vailima, Robert Louis Stevenson to R. D. Blackmore describing his life in Samoa and mentioning a journey from Sydney with Rev. Hunt, missionary in Savaii; ff.199-200 letter 11 Aug. 1894 R. L. Stevenson to W. E. Adams.

MSS.3824-9 Thomas Muir
    Material relating to Thomas Muir, presented 1950 by J. W. Earnshaw, Sydney.
3825. Typed copies of letters written by Thomas Muir at Monterey, California, originals in Seville.

MS.3833. Letters 1799-1824 Lachlan Macquarie, Governor of New South Wales, to his brother Charles Macquarie.*

MSS.3874-920 Letters to Sir Walter Scott 1796-1831
3892 ff.146-7. 1 June 1821 Ebenezer Knox, Sydney, thanking Scott for his letter to Gov. Macquarie and stating he was Principal Superintendent of a government agricultural establishment three miles from Sydney and had had an interview with Mr Bigge.
3893 ff.41-2. 14 Aug. 1821 George Harper, Sydney, then in the Commissary's Department; ff.165-6, 24 Nov. 1821 Gov. Macquarie thanking Scott for his letter delivered by Harper and for the present of his works, inviting Scott to Mull and sending him a copy of the history of Michael Howe, the bushranger of Van Diemen's Land.
3894 f.59. 14 Feb. 1822 George Harper, Sydney, concerning his grant of land which he had named Abbotsford, and offering a brace of black swans, emus, or kangaroos; another letter 31 Jan. 1823 from Harper is in MS.3896 ff.21-2.
3900 ff.286-7. 25 June 1825 Sir Thomas Brisbane referring to W. Harper and Ebenezer Knox, 'least said soonest mended', stating that Mr Pretgel was a benefit to the colony, having agricultural skill and steadiness, and describing Oxley's explorations.
3901 f.168. 22 Nov. 1825 Andrew Murray, Government Garden, Parramatta,

stating he had been eight years in the colony and served Mr McArthur four years. Two letters 1813 from Andrew Murray are in MS.3884 ff.77, 284.

MSS.5794-6 Diaries of the 9th Marquess of Lothian 1852-7, 1870, 1876
5794. 'Log of the ship *Resolute*, 700 tons for Australia, Capt. Lewis', journal 1852-7 describes the voyage, travels in New South Wales and the continued voyage to Hong Kong via New Caledonia.

MSS.6337-46 R. W. Lloyd Collection
The papers 1789-1947 mostly concern mountaineering.
6344 ff.36-62. Letters 1924-34 to Henry Cockburn, Alpine Club, London, concerning his membership of the New Zealand Alpine Club.

MSS.6362-401 Henry Mackenzie Correspondence and Manuscripts 1755-1887
6366 ff.34-7. Letter 24 Mar. 1810 Elizabeth Paterson, Sydney, to W. G. Mackenzie describing Macquarie's landing, 1 Jan., an excursion to the Cow Pastures and recalling W. G. Mackenzie's visit; ff.38-9 letter n.d. E. Paterson to W. G. Mackenzie, *Lady Barlow*, concerning the return of a greyhound.

MS.7180 Constance Frederica Gordon-Cumming, Journal 1874-6
The author accompanied Sir Arthur and Lady Gordon to Fiji in 1875. At Galle they shipped Chinamen at £10 a head to work in Australia, mostly on the new gold diggings at Cooktown, and in Sydney they met Lucy Osburn of the Sydney Hospital. See C. F. Gordon-Cumming, *At Home in Fiji*, Edinburgh 1881.

MSS.7530-8022 Church of Scotland, Foreign Mission Committee
Surviving mission records of the churches, which reunited in 1929 to form the Church of Scotland, were deposited in 1953. Cataloguing is well advanced (1970) and a typescript 'Draft Catalogue' has been made. The records 1822-1929 consist mainly of letter books of the Conveners and Secretaries of the various Foreign Mission Committees, containing letters to missionaries and to supporters and others in Great Britain; they also include some in-correspondence and a few minute books, account books, diaries, volumes of cuttings, and other miscellanea.

The only surviving in-letters connected with the New Hebrides are in MS.7854 ff.80-2, three letters from Rev. Frederick G. Bowie 24 June, 9 Sept. 1922, and 23 Feb. 1923 written while he was in Scotland, all referring to his translation work. Existing letter books do not include letter books of the Reformed Presbyterian Church, and those of the Free Church of Scotland are not yet indexed. Letter books for 1876-1920 are at MSS.7748-69.

MS.8790. Undated note Robert Louis Stevenson to Professor Threlfall, Sydney University, asking for the address of his uncle, the wine-merchant.

MS.9770. Papers 1910-39 of Rev. R. L. Turner including the following papers from Papua: six letters 1910, 1928, 1932, 1933, 1938 from Mrs Edith E. Turner, Papua, describing missionary work; two letters 1939 from R. L. Turner; 'A visit to the Home of the Gods', typescript; 'Taking up the Collection in Papua', typescript; 'An Extraordinary Week', 4-10 May 1932, by R. L. Turner; 'The Ethnology of Papua (British New Guinea) with special reference to the Motu and neighbouring tribes', 4 lectures, typescript.

Acc.3993. Church of Scotland, Colonial Committee, Minutes 1836-89, 16 vols.
Minutes of the Assembly Committee in Edinburgh including reports from the Glasgow Sub-committee and Abstracts of proceedings of the Advisory Committee covering various periods. The Abstracts devote sections to various areas including Australia, Van Diemen's Land, and New Zealand. In a check of volumes 1-4, 1836-50, references were noted to the appointment of ministers and school teachers

in Hobart and New South Wales, and arrangements for emigration, also to correspondence with Rev. J. D. Lang.

Acc.4633. Letters, mainly to Rev. John Bonar, Convener of the Colonial Committee of the Free Church, 1 vol. with index of writers. Letters from Australasia 1851-4 include letters from George Machie, Alexander Salmon, William McIntyre, William McLeod, Arthur Sherriff, and Arthur Paul. Some letters were published, though not in full, in *The Home and Foreign Missionary Record of the Free Church of Scotland*, Edinburgh 1850-6, 6 vols. Letters show the relationship of the Free Church in Australia and New Zealand with the Free Church in Scotland and describe pastoral work and social conditions.

Acc.4070 Rosebery Papers

The correspondence and papers 1860-1936, mostly political, of Archibald Philip Primrose, 5th Earl of Rosebery, are a recent accession in the National Library of Scotland. The papers are filed temporarily in 117 large foolscap size boxes. A draft inventory has been prepared and cataloguing is in progress.

A check of box 46 containing letters from the Marquess of Ripon 1885-1906 disclosed a few letters 1894 concerning the Colonial Conference, South Australian, Victorian, and New South Wales Governors, and Samoa and New Zealand. A check of boxes 88-9, letter books 1894-1902, disclosed several letters on closer union in the Empire, letter 26 Mar. 1894 to Lord Kimberley concerning Hawaii and the Necker Island project, letters about Governors in Australia, and letter 4 Dec. 1899 to the Hon. Edmund Barton.

REGISTRAR GENERAL
General Register Office, New Register House, Edinburgh

BIRTHS, MARRIAGES, AND DEATHS

Registers of births, marriages, and deaths in the custody of the Registrar General, General Register Office, include statutory records commencing 1 Jan. 1855 and old parochial registers of the parishes of the Church of Scotland prior to that date. A complete set of all registers of births, marriages, and deaths created by statute since 1 Jan. 1855 is held at General Register Office. General indexes are available for each year. For the parochial registers of baptisms, proclamations of banns and marriages, and burials prior to 1 Jan. 1855, there are some local indexes, but there is no general index for the whole of Scotland, and the completeness of the records varies from parish to parish. Searches can be made, varying fees being payable according to the type of search and time necessary. Only searches for a specific entry, during which not more than twenty years need be searched, are undertaken by the staff.

For registers of baptisms, marriages, and burials prior to 1 Jan. 1855 other than those of the Church of Scotland, applications should be made as follows: for records of the Roman Catholic Churches, to individual parishes; for records of the Episcopal Church, to the Official Registrar of Births, Marriages and Deaths, Episcopal Churches, 56 Frederick Street, Edinburgh; for records of the Free Church of Scotland to The Principal Clerk, Free Church of Scotland, 15 North Bank Street, Edinburgh.

SCOTTISH RECORD OFFICE
H.M. General Register House, Edinburgh 2

The Scottish Record Office contains, besides the surviving Scottish central records to 1707, records of the central courts of law, records of the modern Scottish departments of state, local records, church records, and private muniments. See M. Livingstone, *Guide to the Public Records of Scotland*, Edinburgh 1905, list of accessions published in the *Scottish Historical Review* 1947, and lists in the *Annual Reports of the Keeper of the Records of Scotland* 1950- . Printed, typescript, or manuscript lists and indexes are available and card indexes are in progress. There are also typescript 'Source Lists' on some subjects, e.g. Australia and New Zealand, 2 lists, Emigration, 2 lists.

Archives remaining in private custody are described in reports prepared for the National Register of Archives (Scotland) which is based in the Scottish Record Office. See also National Register of Archives (Scotland) *Reports* 1947- .

WILLS AND DEEDS

Before 1823 wills and inventories were recorded with the Commissary Clerks of the various districts and their records are now in the custody of the Scottish Record Office, but after 1823 wills were recorded with the Sheriff Clerks of the respective sheriffdoms. Some Sheriff Court records are deposited in the Record Office but others are still in the custody of the Sheriff Clerks.

The 'List of Commissary Records', typescript, prepared by the Record Office, has an introductory note including mention of the series of indexes to Testaments published by the Scottish Record Society, amended and supplemented by typescript indexes prepared by the Record Office. Indexes of Deeds maintained by the Record Office include 'An Alphabetical Index to the Register of Deeds and Probative Writs, 1770- '.

JUSTICIARY OFFICE

In general, Justiciary records to 1799 are in the Scottish Record Office and records from 1800 to date are in the Justiciary Office q.v. The Scottish Record Office has compiled a 'Repertory of Justiciary Records', typescript; it has also compiled an index of Justiciary Precognitions 1830-77, and an index to Justiciary Precognitions 1824-9 is in preparation (June 1970).

Information concerning trials of persons transported to Australia may be found in the following records:

Books of Adjournal 1584-1797. These contain reports of some trials of persons transported to Australia.

High Court Minute Books 1576/7-1799.

Receipt Books of Justiciary 1708-1800.

Justiciary Responde Books 1755-1808.

Registers of Criminal Letters 1647-1799.

Lord Advocate's Department Journals 1818-28.

North, West, and South Circuit Minute Books beginning 1708, the North Circuit Minute Books ending in 1800, the West in 1799, and the South in 1798. The North Circuit Minute Book No.39, 1793, includes Minutes of the Trial of Thomas Fyshe Palmer 12 Sept. 1793 with list of the jury and list of witnesses. The minutes of 13 Sept. 1793 record the verdict.

Appeal Books for the North, West, and South Circuits beginning 1748, the North Circuit Appeal Book ending 1798, the West 1799, and the South 1803.

Enrolments of Civil Causes for the North, West, and South Circuits beginning 1748, the North ending 20 Sept. 1798, the West 27 Apr. 1808, and the South 19 Sept. 1815.

Justiciary Processes and Papers to 1799. These are arranged in chronological order. They include circuit material. Seven boxes contain papers relating to the 'Scottish Martyrs', Thomas Fyshe Palmer, Joseph Gerrald, Maurice Margarot, Thomas Muir, and William Skirving, tried for sedition 1793-4.

Midlothian

There is no subject index to the Court of Session Processes. The papers listed were found from Australian and New Zealand headings in the personal name index which includes companies. Searchers having names of others concerned with Australasian affairs or commercial ventures may find additional material in the records.

Australian Mortgage Co. 1888 (1st Div. A.2/2).

Mortgage Co. of South Australia Ltd 1902 (1st Div. S.24/5); 1903 (1st Div. S.24/6); 1904 (1st Div. S.28/1c); 1904 (1st Div. M.22/6).

New Zealand and Australian Land Co. 1881 (Currie McNeill N.7/3); 1888 (1st Div. M.4/1).

New Zealand Meat Preserving Co. Ltd 1883 (Currie McNeill N.9/2).

Scottish West Australian Land Syndicate 1896 (1st Div. S.14/1).

Scottish and New Zealand Investment Co. Ltd 1898 (1st Div. S.18/4); 1903 (1st Div. S.25/20); 1904 (1st Div. S.27/11).

EMIGRATION

See Source Lists No.6 and No.19, Emigration, typescript. Two groups of papers are relevant to Australia and New Zealand.

The records of the Department of Agriculture and Fisheries for Scotland include 'Emigration Files' AF51/1-175, 1885-1926/31, covering all aspects of emigration from Scotland. The following files relate to Australia and New Zealand:

AF51/157, 1888-9. Proposals for crofter emigration to Western Australia.
AF51/158, 1886-9. Proposals for crofter emigration to New Zealand.
AF51/161, 1890-1. Proposals for emigration of fishermen to Tasmania.

Other papers relating to emigration occur in a deposit of which there is a typescript inventory in List of Deposited Muniments, Vol.5, pp.216-22, entitled 'Inventory of Papers relating to Highland Destitution and Highland Emigration transmitted in 1856 and 1868 by Sir C. E. Trevelyan, of the Treasury, London, and Sir John McNeill'.

Highland Destitution. A number of volumes and boxes of Treasury correspondence and papers 1783-51 and 1846-52.

Highland and Island Emigration Society.
In-letters, minutes of meetings of committees, and miscellaneous papers 1852-9.
Treasury Minute Books 20 Jan. 1852 to 11 Jan. 1859; letter books of Sir Charles Edward Trevelyan, 4 vols.
List of Emigrants 1852-7, a folio volume containing a list of emigrants assisted to Australia by the Society.*
Promissory Note Book 1852, containing the names of those granted promissory notes.
'Minute Book' Jan.-July 1852, letter book.

REGISTER HOUSE SERIES

RH15/103. Report on the affairs of the Australian Company of Edinburgh, 1845.

PRIVATE MUNIMENTS

See *Annual Reports of the Keeper of the Records of Scotland. Annual Report . . . 1966*, 1967, includes App.6, List of Gifts and Deposits to date. See also typescript handlists and inventories.

GD1/395 Riddell Papers
GD1/395/25. Papers 1848-54 connected with Drummond Riddell, member of the Executive Council, New South Wales.*

GD1/471/1. Account of voyage 1871-2 by Alexander Strathern of Blantyre in the *Loch Tay* from Glasgow to Melbourne and back to Liverpool, with details of his stay in Australia.

GD1/486/1. Letter 1896 from Gov. Boyle of New Zealand to John Rodger on death of his brother Andrew Rodger at Timaru.

GD1/553 New Zealand and Australian Land Co. Ltd
These records are deposited on indefinite loan. The thirty year closure rule applies and any request for relaxation should be made to the Company's registered office, 22 Charlotte Square, Edinburgh. There is a typescript list of the records and of the plans accompanying them.
GD1/553/1-18. Minute books of the New Zealand and Otago Agricultural and Land Investment Association Ltd 1862-8, Canterbury and Otago Association Ltd 1865-77, New Zealand and Australian Land Co. Ltd 1866-1962.
GD1/553/19-30. Ledgers of the Canterbury and Otago Association Ltd 1865-6 and of the New Zealand and Australian Land Co. Ltd 1866-1944.
GD1/553/31-611. Day books, balance sheets, letter books, records of estates, land and wool sales.
GD1/553/612. Cash book 1862-5 of the Glasgow Association.
GD1/553/613. Papers 1879-84 concerning the liquidation of the City of Glasgow Bank.
GD1/553/614-20. Miscellaneous pamphlets and papers.

GD18 Clerk of Penicuik Muniments
The muniments include letters to Sir George Clerk, and other papers. Those listed below have been microfilmed for the Australian Joint Copying Project.
GD18/3549. Letter 13 June 1843 Patrick Neill pressing claims for promotion of Robert Neill, Commissariat Department, Albany, with sketches of Albany and two natives, also letter 16 Sept. 1842 from R. Neill, King George Sound; Treasury minute 14 Jan. 1840.
GD18/3578. Statement of quantities and prices of wheat and flour imported into New South Wales and Van Diemen's Land 1841-3.
GD18/3620. Letter 1 Aug. 1844 T. Dacre Lacy, Guernsey, enclosing copy of extract of letter 1 May 1844 from his son Edward Lacy, mate on H.M.S. *Cormorant* describing a visit to Tahiti and attacking the French seizure of the island.
GD18/3755. Rough notes of queries and answers concerning freight rates for copper ore from South Australia to Britain 1845.
GD18/4250. Letters 1792, 1793 James Clerk, letter 12 Dec. 1793, H.M.S. *Queen Charlotte*, mentioning midshipman Peter Heywood, one of the mutineers in the *Bounty*.
GD18/4297-9. Letters 1843-5 Lieut. Henry Clerk, R.A., concerning his employment at the Ordnance Magnetic Establishment at the Cape, suggesting his employment in Van Diemen's Land or St Helena and including a copy of his official letter 28 June 1845 reporting on his voyage to the Antarctic in the *Pagoda* and visit to King George Sound.
GD18/5591. Letter 26 June 1844 William Bell, Glasgow, concerning G. E. Clerk's share in a station on the 'Mitti Mitti'; Bell was connected with the firm of Bell and Buchanan, Melbourne.
GD18/5592, 5596. Letters 1844-5 Lord Stanley stating that he was unable to offer

G. E. Clerk any office in the Australian colonies as all patronage was in the hands of the governors.

GD18/5602/1. Letter 1 Aug. 1846 G. E. Clerk, Sydney, stating he was a partner with two gentlemen named Lockhart, they had bought cattle and had 'right & title' to a station on the Little River, tributary of the Hume, incomplete.

GD18/5602/2-14. Letters 1847-60 G. E. Clerk, Edinburgh and Canada, concerning his becoming a Roman Catholic, the possibility of returning to Australia; a letter 1857 concerns the sale of Tallandoon Station, N.S.W.

GD18/5607. Letter 22 July 1857 W. M. Bell & Co., Melbourne, concerning sale of G. E. Clerk's interest in Tallandoon.

GD18/5608. Letters 1858 Alexander Clerk, Auckland, N.Z.

GD18/5790. Half yearly return 1 Jan. 1847 of stock at Tallandoon, signed Charles Lockhart.

GD18/5792. Letters and accounts 1857 W. M. Bell & Co., Melbourne, concerning the sale of Tallandoon.

GD21 Cuninghame of Thorntoun Papers
   The following papers have been microfilmed for the Australian Joint Copying Project.

GD21/465. Letters 1846-54 from Christian [?Christina] Cuninghame, Victoria, describing life in Australia.

GD21/475. Letter 14 Aug. 1859 William Macredie, Melbourne, to Miss Cuninghame, Devon, giving an account of the wreck of the steamer *Admilla* near Cape Northumberland and enclosing bill of exchange of Colonial Bank of Australasia, Melbourne, 1859.

GD21/482. Letters 1876-9, some long and detailed, George Wrey to his aunt Mrs C. E. Stuart, Reading, describing travels including journeys 1877-9 in Australia and New Zealand. Wrey bought a farm, Feilding, Poatatau, Co. Manawatu near Auckland, and he refers to the effect in New Zealand of the failure of the Glasgow Bank, and to his own investment of £13,000.

GD21/484. Letters 1879-83 G. Wrey to Mrs C. E. Stuart. Four letters 26 Aug. to 30 Oct. 1882 concern a visit to New Zealand.

GD25 Ailsa Muniments
GD25/Box 42, folder 9. Letters 1811-12,* business and estate matters, to the Earl of Cassilis include letters Jan.-June 1811 concerning John Hutchinson transported to New South Wales for forgery and letter 27 Nov. 1812 from Gov. Macquarie acknowledging recommendation of Hutchinson, who arrived in the *Guildford* 18 Jan. 1812, now employed by Simeon Lord to conduct a glass, pottery, and hat manufactory.

GD45 Dalhousie Muniments
   The following papers have been microfilmed for the Australian Joint Copying Project.

GD45/8/15. Letter 3 Mar. 1847 from Lord Grey enclosing copy of letter 16 Oct. 1846 from Sir George Grey to Gladstone concerning mutiny at Porirua and conditions of service in New Zealand.

GD45/8/28. Memo n.d. on reduction of forces in Australia and settlement of discharged men.

GD45/8/97. Reports 1851 from the Governor of New South Wales on discovery of gold, printed.

GD45/8/114. Memo n.d. on corps of military labourers for South Australia and Western Australia.

GD45/8/115. Memo n.d. on local companies of prisoners in New Zealand.

GD45/8/120. Memo n.d. by Capt. L. Cowell on discontent among troops in Australia.

GD45/8/358. Correspondence and memos 1856 on New Zealand, printed.

GD45/8/390. Despatches 1856, Secretary of State for the Colonies to the Governor of New Zealand, printed.

GD45/14/548. Letters 1817-32 Lord Ramsay from the Cape, Australia, Canada, and India, with letter 28 Nov. 1830 Lauderdale Maule, Sydney Barracks, describing life in the colony, stating that there were 'villainies' and that Gov. Darling was unpopular.

GD46 Seaforth Muniments

GD46/13/184, 197, 206. Papers relating to emigration to North America and to the Australian colonies.*

GD46/13/198. Letter 4 Feb. 1836 George Mackenzie, London, to J. A. S. Mackenzie, M.P., concerning an application by a shepherd named Tweedie anxious to emigrate to New South Wales, and referring to his brother John Mackenzie in New South Wales.

GD51 Melville Castle Muniments

GD51/1/479. Letter 28 July 1792 W. Brereton to George Rose suggesting cargoes of timber from New South Wales to China and the sending of several hundred Chinese labourers to New South Wales.

GD51/1/481/1-4. Letter 5 Jan. 1793 David Ross to Henry Dundas concerning the renewal of the contract of his eldest son's firm, Lambert and Ross, Calcutta, for the supply of necessaries to New South Wales enclosing copy of letter 24 Oct. 1791 Gov. Phillip to Lambert, Ross, and Biddulph.

GD51/1/593. Letter 5 Feb. 1792 Dr John Millar to Henry Dundas with observations on medical arrangements and reference to the voyages of Capt. Cook.

GD51/2/456. Letter 15 Aug. 1812 James Phillip Inglis, recently appointed master of colonial brig *Emu*, to Lord Melville concerning an affray between some of his crew and an impress party.

GD51/2/617. Letter 24 July 1820 Sir Hew Dalrymple concerning a free passage to New South Wales for George Thomson and family with related correspondence.

GD51/2/704. Remarks 1826-7 on coasts and headlands of Australia and New Zealand made by Capt. Richard Saunders Dundas in H.M.S. *Warspite*, copy.

GD51/2/744. Letters 1860 Commodore William Loring to Maj.-Gen. Pratt, commanding H.M. forces, Taranaki, respecting authority over naval brigade, copies.

GD51/3/66/1-2. Letter 21 July 1796 Rev. T. Haweis enclosing copy of his letter 20 July 1796 to Court of Directors outlining the purpose of a missionary society to work in the South Sea Islands.

GD51/3/276-8, 281, 283. Correspondence 1807 concerning the *Lady Madelina Sinclair*, William Osbourne, refusal of East India Company to permit ships proceeding to Botany Bay to touch at any port in India and refusal to allow Osbourne to bring to England cargoes from Canton and Bengal when returning from Botany Bay.

GD51/6/1395, 2284. Applications for employment 21 Jan. 1800 and 2 July 1828 containing references to plantations in New South Wales.

GD64 Campbell of Jura Papers

GD64/1/324. Papers 1840-2 concerning the affairs of William Cadell, late of New South Wales, relating to rental of stock from Mrs Hely and payments to her.*

GD64/1/371. Letter 25 Jan. 1859 John Rutherford, 'Rossella', Gardiner's Creek, Melbourne, to R. D. Campbell of Jura, concerning squatters being obliged to buy their land or have it sold by public auction.*

GD64/3/5. Letters 1835-61 A. C. McDougall, Port Phillip, Dunolly, Charlotte Plains, Loddon River, to R. D. Campbell of Jura, his attorney.*

Midlothian

GD68 Murray of Lintrose Writs and Papers

The following papers have been microfilmed for the Australian Joint Copying Project.

GD68/2/91-102. Letters and papers 1838-90 concerning land in the Murray district, Western Australia, including a bond 1838 by David Smyth Murray, St Leonards, W.A., to George and Luke Leake of Perth, W.A.

GD68/2/140, 143-6. Letters 1839-48 relating to the Murray and Stirling families in Western Australia.

GD68/2/147. Letter 1852 L. A. Hankey, Kent, to D. S. Murray, Mandurah, Murray River, concerning proposed introduction of convicts into Western Australia.

GD68/2/169. Speech n.d. by a member of the Murray family at Lintrose on his return from Australia.

GD80 Macpherson of Cluny Papers

GD80/962. Letters and papers 1855-66 concerning estate in Australia of Col. Duncan Macpherson deceased.*

GD112 Breadalbane Muniments

A handlist is available. The following letters relevant to the field of this guide were noted.

15 Dec. 1834 R. W. R. Davidson, Sydney, concerning his claim for promotion in the Surveyor General's Department.*

20 Aug. 1841 R. G. Jameson, Aberdeen, concerning the evils resulting from suspension of emigration and stating that his interests are in New Zealand and he has accomplished his object in placing the affairs of the New Zealand Company in fair train.*

15 Aug. 1845 W. E. Cormack, Auckland, referring to the 'fraud of the Treaty of Waitangi' and the necessity of a more honourable management of the Maoris.*

GD146 Robertson of Kindeace Papers

GD146/Box 18. Two bundles of abstracts of accounts and bills 1842-4 for Maj. Robertson's Company of 96th Regiment at Auckland, New South Wales, and Launceston.*

GD156 Elphinstone Muniments

GD156/Box 67. Journal 1884-5 of travels in Australia, New Zealand, and the Pacific.

GD161 Buchanan of Leny Collection

GD161/Box 19. Memo c.1815-23 on New Zealand, its climate and people, urging that it be made a British colony and settled.

GD174 McLaine of Lochbuie Papers

Papers 1782-1839 relating to Lachlan Macquarie, Governor of New South Wales, and his immediate family.*

GD219 Murray of Murraythwaite Papers

GD219/306. Letters 1853-4 from Henry William Murray, Wellington, N.S.W., on sheep farming, commenting on the low state of morals in the colony.

GD232 Fraser Stodart & Ballingall Papers

GD232/18. Letters 1920-3 from Mrs Bell, Australia.

GD240 Bruce and Kerr Papers

A handlist is available.

Box 8, bundle 8. Letter 5 Aug. 1819 Gov. Macquarie to Gen. Balfour expressing his wish to return home.

GD248 Seafield Muniments

GD248/351/7, 687/2, 692/1, 693/2, 701/3. Five letters 1794-1801 from John Grant,

Rio de Janeiro and New South Wales. The letters describe his voyage to New South Wales on a convict ship, his discovery of a plot to seize the ship, the ringleaders being Skirving and Palmer, his appointment as clerk to John McArthur. There are references to the cruelty and oppression of Gov. King's rule.

NATIONAL REGISTER OF ARCHIVES (SCOTLAND)

The National Register of Archives (Scotland) is compiling reports on documents in private possession in Scotland. Preliminary inquiries concerning collections listed below should be addressed to the Secretary, National Register of Archives (Scotland) at the Scottish Record Office where a card index of reports is maintained. Copies of reports are also available in the National Register of Archives, Quality House, Quality Court, Chancery Lane, London, W.C.2, and in the Institute of Historical Research, Senate House, University of London, W.C.1.

Brodie. The manuscripts include letters 1843-50 to William Brodie from his sister Louisa and her husband H. Cotton, concerning Cotton's work on irrigation and trigonometrical survey in Tasmania.

N. A. Cochrane-Patrick of Ladyland, Beith, Ayrshire. Cardboard box 'A'. Correspondence including letters 1847-53 from Christina Cuninghame (Cuninghame of Thorntoun) while in Australia.
Wooden box 'D'. Papers including letters 1842-4 from Christina Cuninghame in Australia.

Messrs Davidson and Garden, advocates, Aberdeen. Papers of Capt. D. Forbes consisting of accounts and letters concerning trading voyages to the East, including letters 1865-70 from Alexander Matheson and Matheson and Company, Hong Kong.

Earl of Dundonald. Box 4. Letters 1832 Jemima Young to Hon. Arthur Cochrane concerning Pitcairn Island.

Viscount Elibank. The papers of Gideon Murray, 2nd Viscount Elibank, include a journal 1899-1901 of his career as private secretary to the Lieutenant Governor of New Guinea and as colonial administrator in New Guinea.

Earl of Haddington, Tyninghame House, Prestonkirk, East Lothian. There are two series of boxes of manuscripts in the muniment room. Series 2, box 8 contains *inter alia* a bundle of printed papers including a prospectus 1832 of the Australian Company concerning the conveyance of settlers.

Earl of Home, Coldstream. Letter 23 Jan. 1781 from one of the officers of H.M.S. *Rattlesnake* describing the ship's voyages and containing an account of the death of Capt. Cook.

Colonel Hope of Luffness, Aberlady. Political and administration papers of George W. Hope as Under-Secretary at the Colonial Office 1837-47. The correspondence 1841-5 includes letters concerning emigration, colonial appointments and other matters relating to Australia and New Zealand. There is also a small wooden box labelled 'Old Papers', among which are papers and newspapers 1841-5 relating to New Zealand.

Macleod. Box 33B, Papers 1853-6 relating to the sale of the *Glendale* including a list of emigrants sailing on the *Glendale* 1855 for South Australia. Box 36, Two boxes of papers c.1846-55 on the potato famine. Printed papers in box 2 include *Letters from Australia on the Business of the Highland and Island Emigration Society*, 1852. Box 63, Letters including letter 1853 from A. Wauchope, Mordun, Armidale, N.S.W., concerning emigrants from Skye to New South Wales.

Midlothian

W. H. Robertson-Aikman of the Ross, Lanarkshire. India and East India Company Papers:

Chart of the east coast of New Guinea and New Zealand, 1791.

Chart of 'the island to the eastward of New Guinea shewing what appears to be the best route from Botany Bay to China', by George Robertson, 1792.

Instructions by the owners of the *Lord Castlereagh*, trading to the East Indies, to Capt. G. Robertson *c*.1802, printed and manuscript.

Log by Henry Aikman in the East India Company ship *Orwell* from London to Madras, Singapore, and China and return 1836-7, and of the *Eleanor* to Sydney, 1841.

UNIVERSITY OF EDINBURGH
The Library, George Square, Edinburgh

Edinburgh University Library, *Index to Manuscripts*, Boston, Mass., 1864, 2 vols., reproduces in page form the typed slips of the Library's dictionary catalogue. The typed slips in loose-leaf binders are retained and to them additions are made.

L.O.A.126/33, 144/3, 214/10, 222/3, 240 f.11. Letters 1867-76 from T. and T. F. Halliwell in Australia and New Zealand to their uncle J. O. Halliwell-Phillips.

Gen.855. J. H. Ashworth. Journals including journal 1914 of visit to Australia.

Gen.140-153. A. Berriedale Keith Papers and Correspondence 1896-1941, 14 boxes. The papers include correspondence with government departments, private persons and newspapers consulting Professor Berriedale Keith on constitutional matters concerning the British Commonwealth and Australian states.

Gen.715/5. Lord Augustus Loftus, correspondence 1848-90. Microfilm in the Mitchell Library, Sydney.

Gen.119. Notes by Sir Charles Lyell on the earthquake in New Zealand in 1855 made after conversations in London in 1856 with W. Roberts, Royal Engineers, W. Mantell, and F. A. Weld.

Gen.768/1/35, 92. Letters 28 Nov. 1881, 23 Feb. 1895 to William Marwick, N.S.W., from his uncle John in Sydney mentioning Australian conditions, cricket, and exports of Australian produce.

Dc.7.123. J. Mitchell, 'Journal of a voyage to New South Wales & from there to England . . . 7 Apr. 1822 to the 11th May 1823 by James Mitchell, Surgeon'. Refers to his last voyage to New South Wales on the convict ship *Neptune* 1820-1, manuscript in the New College Library, Edinburgh University q.v. Includes descriptions of Sydney, excursion to Mr Oxley's seat, meetings with Rümker and Mudie, visit to Sir John Jamison and tobacco growing. Microfilm in the Mitchell Library, Sydney.

Gen.523. Sir Roderick Impey Murchison Papers include:

523/4. Letter 6 Nov. 1870 from F. von Mueller concerning the Murchison River; other letters 1855-6 of Australian interest including letters Jan.-Mar. 1855 from E. H. Hargraves, London, concerning gold in Australia and New Zealand and letters Jan.-Nov. 1855 from W. B. Clarke.

523/6. Papers *c*.1850-5 concerning gold in Australia including letters 28 Aug. 1852 from W. T. Smith, Sydney, claiming he discovered gold in New South Wales in 1848.

Gen.835/5/11. Letter 9 May 1834 Benjamin Townsend to his father T. Townsend about plans for emigrating to Australia.

DK.2.41. Correspondence of Benjamin Wyatt.

f.97. Letter 21 Feb. 1843 from Mrs A. M. Barker, Langshaw, Roxburghshire, referring to her second son William who went to Australia two years before and was 'tending his flocks on the Darling Downs'.

UNIVERSITY OF EDINBURGH
The Library, New College, Mound Place, Edinburgh

In 1962 New College Library became the Theological Library of the Faculty of Divinity of the University of Edinburgh. There is an incomplete catalogue of manuscripts on slips filed in loose-leaf binders. The catalogue of manuscripts on pp.933-9 of the Library's *Catalogue of Printed Books and Manuscripts*, Edinburgh 1868, does not list any items of Australian, New Zealand, or Pacific Islands interest.

Burns, William. Letter to Henry Dunlop concerning the projected colony at Port Cooper, N.Z. This document was missing in Oct. 1966.

Chalmers Papers. The papers of the Rev. Dr Thomas Chalmers, first moderator of the Free Church of Scotland, are a large collection not yet catalogued (1966). Research has not so far revealed any letters from Australian correspondents although it seems probable that he was acquainted with the Rev. J. D. Lang and other ministers and teachers in New South Wales and Van Diemen's Land.

Menzies, Archibald. 'Narrative of the exploration of the Sandwich Islands and ascent of the highest mountain', journal 15 Jan. to 16 Feb. 1794.

Mitchell, James. Journal 1820-1 as surgeon on the *Neptune* including a description of stay in Sydney July-Sept. 1820 mentioning Commissioner Bigge, a visit to Oxley's property, and giving an account of New South Wales.

Preston, Rev. David. History of the colonial mission of the Church of Scotland, c.1930. Accounts of missions include brief accounts of the sending of Presbyterian ministers and teachers to New South Wales, Tasmania, Victoria, Queensland, South Australia, Western Australia, New Zealand, Fiji, and the New Hebrides. No sources are given.

Northern Ireland

PUBLIC RECORD OFFICE OF
NORTHERN IRELAND
May Street, Belfast

See Deputy Keeper of the Records, *Reports* 1924- . Typescript and processed schedules of a number of collections are held and there are extensive card indexes. Official archives have been deposited since the establishment of the Government of Northern Ireland in 1921 but considerable quantities of official records *c.*1830-1921 were transferred to Belfast in the 1920s.

DEPOSITS

D207/67/58. Letter 24 Nov. 1823 from Sir Thomas Brisbane, Government House, Parramatta, giving an account of New South Wales.

D268/5-8. Letters *c.*1850 from Thomas Vogan, Australia.*

D560. Diary 1848-58 of John Martin, containing a journal of a voyage from Ireland to Australia in the convict ship *Mountstuart Elphinstone.**

D618/209, 268. Correspondence *c.*1905 between Mary C. Savage, Sydney, and Savage Armstrong concerning the Savage family in Australia.*

D664. Papers 1823-62 of Lord John George de la Poer Beresford, Primate of All Ireland, including: D664/D/77, letter 1853 referring to the Speaker of the Melbourne Parliament; D664/D/81, letter referring to Sir Charles Hotham and an estate in Victoria.

D718. Letters 1871-86 from Charles Barton, Sydney, N.S.W., including a detailed account of his voyage from England to Australia 1884.*

D721. Letter 1908 from 'Dan' Rathgar, Barolin, Bundaberg, Q'ld, relating to children born in Australia.*

D724. Release of lands 1884 Co. Cavan, Robert Haig, Melbourne, Vic., to executors of the estate of Mrs Jane Haig, Kensington Park Road, Middlesex.*

D780. Records *c.*1900-*c.*1940 of linen industry, including trade with Australia.

D834. Includes typescript extracts 1809-11 from the journals kept by Ensign Alexander Huey, 73rd Regiment of Foot, in which he describes the regiment's voyage from England to Sydney, his personal impressions of Australia and his own return voyage to England. The original journals are in the possession of Lady Macdonald-Tyler, Limavady, Co. Londonderry, q.v.

D869. Diary 1839-43 of a member of the crew of H.M.S. *Terror* during the Antarctic expedition of James Clark Ross.

D921. Collins & Collins, solicitors, Newry, Co. Down. Testamentary papers 1910-12 relating to various families and to Francis McVerry, Fremantle, formerly of Newry.

D953. Correspondence and papers *c.*1860-*c.*1900 relating to the business activities of William Whigham of Mullahglass, Co. Armagh, in San Francisco and Tahiti.

D955. Martin, King, French & Ingram, solicitors, Limavady, Co. Londonderry. The papers include correspondence 1822-4, 1866-80 of Sampson Lawrence and his family, Coleraine and Castlemaine, Vic., the later letters referring to gold-mining, events in Castlemaine, and in Australia in general. There is also a report 1839 of the death in a mining accident of William Lawrence, Surveyor of Distilleries, Glenmore, [Vic.?].

D957/3. Journal 1861 of Charles Elliott, Moira, Co. Down, on his voyage to Melbourne in the *Prince of the Seas.**

Antrim

D961. Legal and miscellaneous papers including an address 1853 to Andrew Newton, Cookstown, Co. Tyrone, on his emigration to New Zealand.

D965. Letter 1905 from Hugh Rea, Otago, N.Z.

D975. Correspondence, legal papers and domestic accounts 1839-60 relating to the Verner family in Heidelberg, Vic., in Carrickfergus, Co. Antrim, and in Belfast.*

D985. Letters from John Milliken including one 1884 Peat's Ferry, N.S.W., and two 1887 Failford, N.S.W.*

D986. Letter 1894 from an emigrant, Goulburn, N.S.W., discussing prospects of employment in Australia for artists and illustrators.*

D1003. Letters 1842 from William McDonald, Salt Water Creek, Tas., describing the outward journey to Tasmania and conditions there.

D1004. Letter 1857 from William Waugh, Melbourne, Vic., concerning the arrival of Hugh Waugh in Australia, his employment, and the state of trade in general.*

D1022. Personal diaries and papers c.1882-c.1950 of Sir Ernest Clark. Restricted access.

D1071 Papers of the Marchioness of Dufferin and Ava

The majority of the papers were created by Frederick, 1st Marquess of Dufferin and Ava.

D1071 H/U/28-39. Papers relating to private investments including five papers 1895-8 concerning Western Australian gold mines.

D1071 H/U/45. Bundle of papers 1901-2 concerning Munro-Ferguson.

D1071 H/W4/37. Letter 9 July 1883 from J. Henniker Heaton, Sydney, asking Lord Dufferin to go to Australia to organise a federation, 'we have no great politician capable of bringing about federation'.

D1071 J/A/6. Papers of Hariot, Lady Dufferin, including letters of condolence Feb.-Mar. 1902 from Australia and New Zealand on the death of the Marquess of Dufferin and Ava.

D1071 J/A/16A-C. Three letters July-Oct. 1918 from the future 4th Marquess written from Sydney describing life with his aunt.

D1099. Letter 1875 from Daniel R. Gardner describing a voyage from England to Australia.

D1114. Letters 1833, 1852 from J. Foster, Parramatta, N.S.W.*

D1189. Records of Belfast firms dealing in flax, jute, and linen. The records 1920-47 of William McCullough & Co., linen merchants, include letter books 1934-8 of their Australian and New Zealand agents.

D1191. Accounts, correspondence 1847-1936 of Gribbon & Son, linen manufacturers, Coleraine, Co. Londonderry, including sales books 1910-22 for Australia.

D1193. Accounts, correspondence, order books c.1882-c.1950 of the Broadway Damask Co. Ltd, Belfast, including details of sales c.1900-c.1950 to Brisbane, Melbourne, Sydney, and in particular, Auckland, N.Z.

D1197. Typescript copy of an article dealing with the career of F. C. Irwin, Commandant and Governor of Western Australia*; modern annotated copies of letters 1808-44 relating to F. C. Irwin and the Swan River Settlement.*

D1294. Genealogical notes relating to the Lutton family of Co. Armagh and Co. Down, a branch of which emigrated to Australia in 1842.*

D1310. Passage ticket 28 Feb. 1855 belonging to Charles Wilson for journey by Black Ball Line from Melbourne to Liverpool.*

D1326. L'Estrange & Brett, solicitors, Belfast, documents mainly concerned with legal disputes and in many cases with bankruptcy proceedings. They include papers 1885-1913 of H. J. Neill, wine and spirit business, Belfast and Craigavad, and papers 1882-1918 of J. & J. McConnell Ltd, distillery, Belfast, both having Australian connections.

D1384. Correspondence 1844-75 of the Doody family, Ballymena. These include letters from a married sister, Margaret Fuller, Adelaide, and letters discussing the emigration 1851-2 of John, William, and Ann Jane Doody from Liverpool to Australia.

D1401. Includes letters from and relating to William Legg in Melbourne, Vic., in the 1870s.

D1414. Includes diary 1858 of an emigrant voyage from Glasgow to Australia probably kept by William Bates of Strabane.

D1415/C1-6. Papers of Viscount Craigavon including photograph albums, with commentary by Lady Craigavon illustrating sea cruises 1929-39, some to Australia and New Zealand.

D1420. Includes letters from Hugh Maguire in Melbourne 1852-4, and Back Creek, Vic., 1860 describing his work as a goldminer, the unrest at Ballarat, and the opening of new goldfields near Back Creek.

D1454. Includes a typescript copy of letter 1847 describing life on Pitcairn Island.

D1497. Includes letter 1860 from Thomas Graham, Melbourne.

D1504. Letter books and accounts 1902-23 of Strain & Elliot, later W. J. Strain, linen manufacturers, Belfast, with details of the firm's overseas contracts *inter alia* with Melbourne.

D1560. Letters 1866-8 from William Cherry, working on sheep stations near Melbourne.

D1626. Correspondence and testamentary papers of the Steele-Nicholson family of Co. Down, including two letters 1861-2 from Victoria.

D1627. Genealogical notes and correspondence c.1930 from members of the Buchanan family in Ireland, America, and Australia concerning claims on the alleged estate of James Buchanan, 15th President of the United States of America.

D1692. Includes letters 1904-13 from Dr Alexander McKelvey employed in the lunatic asylum in Auckland, N.Z., commenting on the quality of Masonic lodges there in 1904 and the strike of 1913.

D1700. Crawford papers including diary of Capt. Frederick Crawford, Ulster Volunteer Force, of a visit to Melbourne in 1892.

D1727. Includes two letters 1917 from an Australian prisoner of war in Germany.

D1729. Family correspondence c.1858-c.1880 received by Jane Graham of Limerick and Melbourne mostly from her father, Rev. James Moffitt of Clones.

D1745. Papers of the Nolan and Adams families, Dungiven, Co. Londonderry, including letter 1863 from Robert Nolan, Richmond, N.S.W.

D1746. Documents relating to the McClure family of Belfast, including: letter 1865 from John McClure, Invercargill, N.Z., commenting on conditions in New Zealand and on the discovery of gold on the west coast, also mentioning he 'was beaten ten months ago for the seat for this district in the Provincial Council' but had been asked to stand for the House of Representatives.

D1757. Papers including letters 1878, 1881 from Elizabeth Macready in Christchurch, N.Z., describing her voyage out, farming techniques and produce in Canterbury,

L

and her own career as a rather superior servant. Letter 1903 from Robert Cheyne, Melbourne, Vic., with comments on land values there and the cost of living.

D1854. Papers of the Earls of Annesley, including albums of photographs of Pacific Islands 1894-6 by Lieut. Gerald Sowerby, R.N.; also log books and papers of Gerald Sowerby while serving in the Pacific 1894-9.

D1864. Copies of letters 1902-13 from Dr James C. Nicholson as a Presbyterian medical missionary in the New Hebrides.

D1905/3/23/6. Letter 1896 Gordon T. Smith concerning a farm near Melbourne, and his marriage.

D1908. Papers of the Earl of Lanesborough, Swithland Hall, Leics. Correspondence includes two letters 1838, 1840 from Cavendish Butler, a disillusioned government servant in New South Wales.

D1913. Crawford family papers including about forty letters 1881-4 between Alexander Crawford on the Murchison River, W.A., and Elizabeth Mathews, his cousin and later his first wife, in Lintons, Vic., with details about the hazards of sheep farming and trouble with the Aborigines; family correspondence 1857-66 of Rev. Thomas Crawford of Drumcliff, Co. Sligo, including letter 1866 from his son Adair, Sydney.

D1944/9/1. Log book c.1850 of William Fleming in the *Fear Not* bound for Australia.

D1978. Shean & Dickson, solicitors, Belfast, documents including correspondence c.1934 involving the Hawaiian Trust Co. Ltd.

D1998. Photographs of Sergeant Robert Ross's service with the New Zealand Expeditionary Force in Egypt and France during the 1st World War.

D2066. Photograph album c.1890 of the Sands and Dickey families in Sydney, N.S.W., and Auckland, N.Z.

D2137. Correspondence, draft speeches, articles and memoranda c.1840-68 of John Martin. Includes letter 17 June 1849 to Thomas Meagher in the *Mount Elphinstone* in Cork harbour, describing conditions on board; also letters from Martin in Sydney and Hobart. Correspondents include W. S. O'Brien, P. O'Donohue, K. O'Doherty, and P. J. Smyth.

D2298. Wilson & Simms, solicitors, Strabane, Co. Tyrone. McCarter Estate papers including: D2298/19/2/4, letter 23 Oct. 1862 from John McCrae, Melbourne, containing comments on Australia; D2298/19/3, two letters 1882-3 from Rev. William Gillies, The Manse, Timaru, N.Z.

COPIES

T413. Transcripts of letters from John Mitchel in Van Diemen's Land and the United States including letter 1852 describing attitude of colonists to Irish political prisoners.*

T634. Account of emigrant voyage from Belfast to Melbourne 1852-3, probably by Samuel Pillow.* Transcript from Raeburn MS., County Museum, Armagh.

T1280. Typescript biography of Dr John Patterson of Strabane, Co. Tyrone, who emigrated to Australia in 1838 where he became Immigration Agent in Melbourne.* Letter 1845 Mrs Foote, Table Top, N.S.W., to her father Dr Patterson in which she describes sheep farming.*

T1370. Letters 1882-99 from A. Wilson, Pennsylvania, and James Wilson, Melbourne, with testamentary papers 1900-4 relating to J. Wilson's estate.*

T1396. Correspondence 1868-1915 between members of the Gass family, Markethill,

Co. Armagh, including letters from emigrants in Goulburn, N.S.W., and genealogical notes 1828-1926 relating to the Gass family.*

T1440. Chambers family papers and genealogical notes 1862-1941 including correspondence 1916-17 relating to the death of William Hugh Chambers in New Zealand.

T1454, T1469. Robb family papers and genealogical notes c.1700-c.1900 including letters 1862-78 from various members of the Robb family who emigrated to New South Wales and elsewhere.*

T1457. Letter 1856 Maxwell Lipper, Honolulu, describing conditions in Honolulu and referring to John Montgomery and Dr McKibbin, former Belfastmen, then resident in Honolulu.

T1488. Letters 1874-6 from John and Ann Sherry and Mathew and Mary Madill, Clunes, Vic.

T1489. Includes correspondence 1833-47 between James N. Richardson, Lisburn, Co. Antrim, and Edward Pease, Darlington, Yorks. The letters are principally concerned with family affairs and with the Society of Friends, and include a comment on the future of the Society of Friends in Van Diemen's Land.

T1504. Correspondence of J. E. Mansfield including letter 1890 from R. Motherell, Sydney, giving an account of the journey out to Australia and his work as a ballroom decorator.*

T1542. Includes letters: 1893 Dan Quigley, Teralba, N.S.W., concerning family affairs; c.1896 William Bell, Sydney, about conditions in Australia.*

T1552. Letters 1890-1907 from William Quinn, Broken Hill, N.S.W., and Kalgoorlie, W.A., describing the strike of goldminers in Kalgoorlie; letters 1903-6 from Patrick Quinn, North Wairoa, N.Z., mentioning his employment as a gum digger.*

T1555. Letter 1847 from Mary Muirhead, Port Phillip, describing life on a sheep farm; letters 1849 George Adams, London, describing his voyage to Australia in 1848 as a ship's doctor, and his experiences in Australia.*

T1590. Title deeds and papers 1853-1903 relating to property at Kilrea, Co. Londonderry, of the Millen family with a reference to the emigration to Australia of Joseph Millen in the 1850s.

T1611. Seven letters 1876-1903 from members of the Gilmore family, Tauranga, N.Z.

T1639. Documents including letter 1855 from William Kerr, Liverpool, describing his passage to England and commenting on his intended emigration to Australia.

T1698. Includes: letters 1879-80 from William Cardwell, Christchurch, N.Z.; description of John Cardwell's emigrant voyage to New Zealand in 1881; genealogical notes 1820-1900 relating to the Cardwell family.

T1701. Includes letters 1854-7 from Noah Dalway describing his experiences as a gold miner at Forest Creek, Melbourne, and at Ballarat, Vic.

T1769. Documents including diary of Elizabeth Anketell during her voyage to Australia in 1865.*

T1779. Includes extracts from the *Londonderry Sentinel* c.1830 describing the Swan River Settlement in Australia.

T1790. Letters received by Elizabeth Carlisle of Forkhill, Co. Armagh, including letters 1856 from her son William in Williamstown, Vic.

T1806. Includes passenger ticket for the Bell family, sailing from Liverpool to Melbourne, Vic., in 1852.

T1917. Diary of John Sayers during the voyage from Belfast to Australia in 1875;

letter 1887 from John Sayers, Melbourne, giving details of property values in the city.

T1923. Typescript copy of diary kept by Samuel Shaw of Saintfield, Co. Down, during an emigrant voyage to Sydney, N.S.W., 1877-8.

T1927. Documents including letter and cartoon relating to the 1937 Australian election.

T1935. Detailed description 1838 of shipboard conditions, written after the first few days on an emigrant voyage from Londonderry to Australia.

T1956. Documents relating to William Orr, Creevery, Co. Antrim, wrongfully convicted of robbery in 1799, transported to New South Wales, and eventually pardoned; genealogical notes 1769-1860 relating to the Orr family of Creevery.

T1978. Papers including letters from J. N. Armstrong, New Plymouth, N.Z., to his sister in Dublin: 1859 describing the drilling of militia with Enfield rifles, a fire in New Plymouth and his own success as a farmer; 1861 touching family affairs but mainly concerned with Bishop Selwyn's peace-making efforts among the Taranaki; 1865 giving some details of skirmishing with the Maoris around Wanganui.

T2018/40. Letter 13 Aug. 1895 Charles H. Webb, Sussex Square, Wellington, N.Z., to Mrs Andrew Lowry, Raphoe, concerning the death of her husband.

T2052. Miscellaneous letters 1851-9 including the following*: 1853-7 John and Mary Getty, Taughey, Co. Antrim, to James Getty, Melbourne, Vic.; 1851, 1857 James Irvine, Victoria and New South Wales; 1857 John Garry, Melbourne, Vic.; 1859 Ed. Weaver, Kilmore, Vic.; agreement of James Getty, Kilmore, Vic.

T2080. Correspondence 1821-1919 of the Workman family of Belfast including letter 25 July 1835 from William Keir, Perth, W.A.

T2093. Irwin family papers including genealogical notes and correspondence 1829-49 of F. C. Irwin as Commandant of the Swan River Settlement, W.A.

T2207. Papers including lecture notes compiled by Miss P. Cowan as Secretary of the Ulster Branch of the Overseas League, referring to the important part played by Ulstermen in the history and settlement of the United States, Canada, Australia, New Zealand, South Africa, and other places.

T2393. Correspondence of the Wyly family including letters 1856-1948 from members of the family in Adelaide, Melbourne, and Sydney, and letters 1923-48 from Geoff Whitby, Perth.

T2479. Two volume notebook May 1825 to Nov. 1826 compiled by Richard Beechey, in H.M.S. *Blossom*. A description is given of visits to several island groups of the Pacific. The second volume contains a collection of twenty-four drawings by Richard Beechey including views of Pacific Islands.

T2502. Letters 1860-c.1863 from William and J. Purse. The latter writes from Melbourne and the former from the Victorian goldfields at Happy Valley and Scarsdale giving details of his work connected with contracting for the sinking of shafts, including references to machinery and equipment.

Mic.46. Letters from Annie Magill, later Mrs Arthur Wallace, including 1892-1900 about twenty letters as a married woman at Kergunyah Station, N.S.W.

Mic.64. Memoir describing life in Australia c.1852-67 by Robert Cochran of Melbourne; journal 1867-8 by Cochran including description of his voyage from Australia to England in 1867.

Mic.66. Family papers of the Peebles and Williamson families including two letters 1870 from George McLean near Sydney with references to goldmining and store keeping.

Public Record Office (Northern Ireland)

Mic.109. Diary, 5 vols., by Major Parkins Hearle, Royal Marines, including one diary Jan.-Dec. 1896 in H.M.S. *Orlando* at Australian ports, New Zealand, and Fiji. A further diary Jan.-Dec. 1897 covers Major Hearle's service in Australian waters until his return to England in 1897 on the P. & O. liner *Ballarat*.

Mic.111/C. Letters 1831-48 from James and Adam Sloane in Tasmania. There is a description of the voyage out from Leith to Tasmania 1830-1. The brothers seem to have been concerned with a general store in Hobart and there is reference to sheep farming.

Mic.134. Diary *c.*1871 of Robert William Von Steiglitz describing his experiences in Australia.

QUEEN'S UNIVERSITY OF BELFAST
The Library, Belfast

WILLIAM MAZIERE BRADY PAPERS

MS.1/130-4. Family notes *c.*1882-91 of William Maziere Brady; diaries 1871, 1885-6; a traveller's impressions of Australia *c.*1886 by W. M. Brady.

GEORGE RUSSELL, (AE) PAPERS

Correspondence of George Russell with T. F. O'Rahilly and other papers Apr.-Aug. 1927 all dealing with a proposed Higgins Fund to aid the study of Celtic literature, to be set up by Mr Justice H. B. Higgins of Melbourne.

LONDONDERRY

LADY MACDONALD-TYLER
The Umbra, Magilligan, Limavady

Journal May 1809 to Apr. 1810 kept by Ensign Alexander Huey, 73rd Regiment, in H.M. Store Ship *Dromedary*, which carried Governor and Mrs Macquarie to New South Wales.

Journal 29 Oct. 1810 to 21 Feb. 1811 kept by Ensign Alexander Huey on a voyage from New South Wales to London via New Zealand and Cape Horn carrying despatches from Macquarie, probably on the brig *Atalanta*.

The two journals have been copied in typescript and entitled 'The voyage of the 73rd Regiment of Foot'. Photographic copies of the typescript have been placed in the National Library of Australia, Canberra, and the Mitchell Library, Sydney. In May 1969 the family papers were put away and could not be consulted but the originals of these two journals should be among the papers.

Republic of Ireland

CORK

CORK COUNTY LIBRARY
Courthouse, Cork

BOARDS OF GUARDIANS RECORDS

The records include minute books of a number of Unions, some of which are indexed, e.g. Mallow Union Minute Book 1848-9. References to emigration with no destination specified were found at pp.286, 301, 304, 311, and 327. Entries were also noted at pp.367, 376, 393, 398: 9, 15, 30 Mar. 1859 referring to Margaret and Mary Murphy accompanying their mother to Australia provided they are in good health and clothed for the voyage.

DUBLIN

ALL HALLOWS COLLEGE
Drumcondra, Dublin

All Hallows College was established in 1842 to train priests to serve the Irish emigrating to the United States and Australasia. Microfilms of most of the archives are held by the National Library of Ireland, Dublin.

The material of particular interest in the archives of the College consists of overseas missionary correspondence 1842-77, two out-letter books 1857-61 in the hand of Dr Bartholomew Woodlock, Rector of the College, and two publications which contain early missionary letters, the originals of which in most cases no longer exist, *Annual Reports* 1848-58, and *Annals* 1859-63 of All Hallows College. The 'Typed calendar of the overseas missionary correspondence of All Hallows College, 1842-77' by Patrick F. Murray, with indexes, 1956, describes all the letters, a number of which relate to Australia and New Zealand.

The archives of the College also include students' registers, 3 vols; correspondence *c.*1877-90 at present unlisted and unsorted; account books dating from the foundation of the College; correspondence dealing with College administration; and a manuscript history by Dr Woodlock from the foundation of the College to 1854. The successor to the *Annals*, the *All Hallows Annual*, contains items of missionary correspondence up to the present day.

The overseas missionary correspondence 1842-77 is divided by geographical area, one section being devoted to Australasia, and then alphabetically by diocese. There is also a miscellaneous section. The Calendar lists 522 letters in its Australasian section but occasional items relating to the area were noted in the United States section and under South Africa and Mauritius. Most of the *c.*160 letters in the miscellaneous section are also relevant. The bulk of the correspondence consists of letters from bishops of the various dioceses addressed to successive Rectors. The correspondence includes reports of progress and descriptions of the missions, conditions, requests for students, faculties for ordination, the payment of free places at All Hallows, procuring of books, passages of priests and payments towards expenses, sickness, the suitability of priests, their movements, the education question, and accounts of travel on board emigrant ships. The miscellaneous section contains:

correspondence 1858-60 with the Colonial Land and Emigration Commission relating particularly to the question of the appointment of religious or secular instructors and teachers on board convict or emigrant ships, individual appointments, and instructions for the guidance of chaplains; letters 1845-69 mainly to the Rev. Thomas Heptonstall who acted as agent for a number of Australian and New Zealand bishops on matters of emigration, arranging the passages of priests, obtaining from the Rector faculties and permission for mass to be said on board, and similar matters to those occurring in the correspondence with the Colonial Land and Emigration Society.

GENEALOGICAL OFFICE (OFFICE OF ARMS)
Dublin Castle, Dublin

The Office of the Ulster King of Arms was transferred from British to Irish administration 1 Apr. 1943 when it was renamed the Genealogical Office. The Office is under the immediate direction of the Director of the National Library of Ireland. Material in the Office is described in *Manuscript Sources for the History of Irish Civilization*, ed. R. J. Hayes, Boston, Mass., 1965. For an article by T. V. Sadleir on on the Ulster Office records see *The Genealogists' Magazine*, Vol.6, June 1934, No.10. Card indexes to names supersede bound indexes; there is no subject approach to the records. The records are mainly grants and confirmations of arms to named individuals, and registered pedigrees. They are in volumes, most having contemporary name indexes.

NATIONAL LIBRARY OF IRELAND
Kildare Street, Dublin

The manuscript holdings of the Library to MS.13651 are described in *Manuscript Sources for the History of Irish Civilization*, ed. R. J. Hayes, Boston, Mass., 1965. Cards for this work were prepared in the National Library and accessions since publication are described on cards in the same style and filed in the same sequences. For description of acquisitions in general see *Reports of the Council of Trustees of the National Library of Ireland*, 1899- . See also the report of the Librarian 1877-98 in *Report of the Trustees of the Department of Science and Art*.

NATIONAL LIBRARY OF IRELAND MANUSCRIPTS

MSS.267-8. Journal 3 Jan. 1852 to 3 Apr. 1855 kept by Rockfort Maguire in H.M.S. *Plover* on the Behring Strait Arctic Expedition, including a journey from London to Honolulu via Panama.

MSS.426-67. William Smith O'Brien Papers

MS.427/158. Letter 1 Mar. 1832 Malacky Lins, convict employed by Henry Brooks, Liverpool, N.S.W., to his wife discussing prices and prospects.

MSS.426/42, 428/319-20, 429/462, 483, 565. Correspondence 1830-8 with William Hutt containing references to emigration, E. G. Wakefield, South Australia, New Zealand, and O'Brien's dispute with Spring Rice. There is also reference to Hutt having considered applying for the Governorship of South Australia.

MS.430/654, 656-9. Four letters June 1839 from R. Wilmot Horton regarding an allegation against him by E. G. Wakefield, and the applicability of the 'South Australian principle' to the removal of surplus population in Ireland; letter June 1839 from O'Brien giving his opinion on the latter.

MS.431/731, 734, 736-7, 742, 746, 748-50, 754, 757, 764, 800, 821, 837, 868.

Miscellaneous correspondence 1840-2 mainly relating to emigration to the Australian colonies and New Zealand. Correspondents include: George Hyde, S. Walcott, Secretary of the Land and Emigration Board, E. G. Wakefield, R. Torrens, John O'Sullivan, Goulburn, N.S.W., V. Denham Pinnock, Sydney, and John Hutt, Perth.

MS.442. Correspondence 1848 relating to the Young Ireland Movement and to O'Brien's trial.

MS.443. Correspondence and papers relating to O'Brien's trial and transportation. MS.443/2548-818 contain correspondence June 1849 to May 1852 of O'Brien, in Ireland and at Maria Island, Port Arthur, and New Norfolk, with prison officials, his family, and others.

MS.445/2819-980. Correspondence 28 June 1852 to 7 Sept. 1857 including letters from O'Brien at New Norfolk, letters to him from T. B. McManus, J. Martin, P. J. Smyth concerning Mitchel's escape, K. I. O'Doherty concerning Meagher's escape, J. O'Shannessy on Australian politics, C. Gavan Duffy on O'Brien's pardon, T. F. Meagher congratulating him on his return, and J. Motherwell concerning C. Gavan Duffy's arrival in Victoria.

MS.446/2981, 3014, 3073, 3097. Letters 1857-9 from C. Gavan Duffy on politics in Australia, H. G. Brock and J. B. Motherwell on C. Gavan Duffy in Victoria.

MS.449/3400. Journal 31 Oct. 1849 to 20 Mar. 1853 by O'Brien written for his wife describing his arrival at Hobart Town in the *Swift*, his life at Maria Island, Port Arthur, and New Norfolk, and conditions in the colony.

MS.449/3402. Letter n.d. R. R. Torrens to H.M. Colonisation Commissioners concerning a plan for aiding and directing emigration from Ireland to the British colonies.

MSS.450-1. Pocket diaries of O'Brien 1852, [1853?] containing brief daily entries.

MSS.532-66. Monteagle Papers

The two main sections consist of twenty-one letter books 1836-40 relating to contemporary politics and government administration, and eight register books 1835-9 of letters received. The following entries were noted:

MS.556 p.6. Richard Harris, a convict, requesting 1838 that his wife be sent to him in Van Diemen's Land.

MS.561 pp.1, 42, 44, 46. References to correspondence 1835 with Sir Richard Bourke and p.47 with Col. Arthur.

MSS.913-14. Letters 1893-1918 Michael Davitt and others to William O'Brien concerning contemporary politics including: 16 Oct. 1895 Davitt, Coolgardie, with references to his tour of Australia, expected departure for New Zealand and return home in January.

MS.2059. Copy of diary 1856-75 of Francis Maybury of Avonmore, a retrospective account of his voyage in 1856 to Adelaide on the *Cheapside* and subsequent years on the goldfields at Castlemaine and Daylesford, continued as a diary at Avonmore with some comments on the Australian years.

MS.2071. Three letters of T. F. Meagher: 25 Dec. 1848, 18 June 1849 from Richmond Prison, to Mrs Sergeant at Waterford; 27 Aug. 1851 from Lake Sorell, Tas., to Mr Sergeant saying he is 'doomed for life in this hateful land'.

MS.2298. 'The Irish background of Peter Lalor'. Typescript copy of a paper 2 Dec. 1948 read to the Illawarra Historical Society, N.S.W., by Dr T. J. Kiernan.

MS.2642. Fifty-nine letters 1845-55 W. Smith O'Brien to C. Gavan Duffy relating mainly to the Young Ireland Movement and including three letters 1851-2 from New Norfolk referring to his plans, the conditions of prisoners in Van Diemen's Land, Patrick O'Donohue's imprisonment and release, congratulations to Duffy on his election success; three letters 1854-5 from Brussels with references to the Irish in Victoria.

MS.3016. Convict register 1849-50 of an Irish prison including detailed particulars of prisoners transported to Van Diemen's Land. There are some entries for convicts removed 1850-2 to the *Hyderabad*, *Blenheim*, *Lord Dalhousie*, and *Rodney*, all bound for Van Diemen's Land, and 1853 to the *Robert Small* bound for Western Australia.

MS.3224. Letters 1851-8 from John Martin, T. F. Meagher and his wife, and W. Smith O'Brien from Tasmania, Paris and Ireland, to the Connell family of Tasmania, with cutting 3 Sept. 1948 from *The Irish Press* on the provenance of the letters.

MSS.3225-7. Hickey Collection

The collection of Fr William Hickey relates to the Young Irelanders and includes material presented by the son of P. J. Smyth and Mrs Eva O'Doherty.

MS.3225. Typescript copies of papers *c.*1884-1900 on the Young Irelanders including biographies of Joseph Brenan and John Mitchel by Michael Cavanagh and obituary notices of Mrs T. F. Meagher, J. E. Pigot and P. J. Smyth.

MS.3226. Typescript copies of correspondence 1834-84 between prominent Young Irelanders and their friends including letters written in Tasmania.

MS.3227. Typescript copies of letter 1865 T. F. Meagher to his father and of letter Aug. 1855 C. Gavan Duffy to K. I. O'Doherty congratulating him on his marriage; also typescript notes *c.*1945 on Fr W. Hickey and his collection on the Young Irelanders.

MS.3753. Pocket diary of Robert C. Levinge containing description of his voyage from Gravesend to Brisbane 23 Nov. 1870 to 29 Feb. 1871 and description 1 Jan. to 12 Aug. 1875 of work on a cattle station in the area of Yandilla, Q'ld.

MS.3900. Two letters from T. F. Meagher: 27 Aug. 1851, 28pp., Lake Sorell, V.D.L., to Sir Colman O'Loghlen describing conditions, the life of the Irish political prisoners and the escape of T. B. McManus, see National Library of Ireland, *Trustees Report*, 1937-8, pp.17-22; 2 Oct. 1851, Lake Sorell, to Stephen Curtis, Waterford.

MS.3923. Journal 9 July to 24 Aug., 13 Oct. 1849 by W. Smith O'Brien in H.M.S. *Swift*.

MS.4760. Miscellaneous items mid-19th cent. relating to C. Gavan Duffy including lists of jurors at his trial, with counsel's notes.

MS.5159. Maurice Lenihan Papers 1845-85 including contemporary notes on the trial of T. F. Meagher and his imprisonment.

MSS.5756-8. Charles Gavan Duffy Papers

Correspondence 1840-54, 1842-92 of C. Gavan Duffy with people prominent in literary and political affairs.

MS.5886. Narratives of the Rising of 1848 by R. O'Gorman, T. B. McManus, and J. Kavanagh.

MSS.7477-795. Larcom Papers

The papers include MSS.7689, 7695-6, 7698, 7723, 7728, 7731 containing cuttings 1862-8 relating to Fenianism, *inter alia* Fenians in Australia and New Zealand, Irish nationalists, and later cuttings relating to C. Gavan Duffy as Premier of Victoria.

MSS.8005, 8098. Charles Gavan Duffy Papers

MS.8005. Letters 1855-1901 to Gavan Duffy from various persons including many literary and political figures.

MS.8098. Correspondence of Gavan Duffy with Cassell, Potter and Galpin, T. Fisher Unwin, and M. H. Gill concerning his published books.

MS.8216. P. J. Smyth Papers

MS.8216/1. Seven letters from P. J. Smyth including copy of letter 23 Oct. 1884 to H. T. Evans with comments on John Mitchel's escape.

MS.8216/2. Note 8 Mar. 1884 by P. J. Smyth on Meagher's escape.

MS.8216/26. Incomplete letter n.d. from Henry Hunter *re* property in Van Diemen's Land.

MS.8221. Petition 1840 for a free passage to Australia for Mary Mulvany wishing to join her husband Morris Mulvany transported from Tipperary in 1830; with related papers and letter 1840 relating to convict E. Harding.

MS.8404. Minute of protest Nov. 1848, Colonial Secretary, W.A., against the 'Scourging Ordinance' of Col. Irwin, late Acting Governor.

MSS.8473-8. Bourke Papers

Include correspondence 1820-54 of Sir Richard Bourke containing: letters 1842-3 from W. Smith O'Brien; letters *c.*1826, 1831, 1841-54 from Thomas Spring Rice, 1st Lord Monteagle; correspondence 1837-8 with R. Therry with references to 'Mudie's slanders'.

MSS.8506, 8557. William O'Brien Papers

MS.8506. Copies by William O'Brien of his own letters 1914-24 on political matters to various people including letter 18 Feb. 1924 to Dr Mannix, Melbourne, Vic.

MS.8557. Correspondence 1895-1928 on current political questions including cable 19 Apr. 1918 from Archbishop Kelly, Sydney, on behalf of the Australian hierarchy calling for Home Rule and opposing conscription in Ireland.

MSS.8562-75. Lalor Papers

MS.8564. Letters 1855-87 from Peter Lalor in Australia, with cutting from *The Argus* containing article by him about his connection with the Eureka affair.

MS.8566. Correspondence 1848-78 of Richard Lalor including letters from Australia, one 2 Dec. 1874 from Domenic Dillon.

MSS.8653-66. William Smith O'Brien Papers

MS.8653. Letters 1836-60 W. Smith O'Brien to his wife Lucy including forty-one letters 1849-54 mainly from places in Van Diemen's Land; also letter 1 Sept. 1849 in H.M.S. *Swift* and one 1854 from Geelong.

MS.8654. Letters 1838-59 Lucy O'Brien to her husband mainly with family and personal news.

MS.8655. Correspondence 1819-63 including letters 1849-53 from W. Smith O'Brien to his family and a few letters from Lord John Russell to Sir Lucius O'Brien concerning the case of W. Smith O'Brien.

MS.8657. Letters 1849-64 to W. Smith O'Brien including letters from J. B. Dillon and John Martin.

MS.8659. Journal 9 July to 29 Oct. 1849 W. Smith O'Brien written for his wife.

MS.8660. [Draft?] letter *c.*1850 C. Gavan Duffy concerning memorial for O'Brien's unconditional release.

MS.8662. Letters 1848-9 Emma Barton and others to Mrs Lucy O'Brien concerning her husband's arrest and other matters.

MS.8666. Miscellaneous papers 1840-59 including letters 7 Mar. 1850 and 24 Nov. 1852 from W. Smith O'Brien to Augustine Barton and a copy of the 'Reply from the Dock' by T. F. Meagher.

MS.8935. Padraic Colum Papers

Typescript copy, early 20th cent., of Hawaiian language lessons prepared by W. J. Coelho.

MSS.9049-50. Addresses 1846-59 presented to W. Smith O'Brien.

Dublin

MS.9728. Memoir of T. F. Meagher, with diary, correspondence, and speeches compiled for publication 1869 by Frederick Kearney.

MS.9760. Luke Cullen Papers
Papers, early 19th cent., written by Br Luke Cullen relating to the life of Michael Dwyer.

MSS.10497-533. Hickey Papers
MS.10497. Includes letters 1908-9 from P. W. Joyce referring to poems and music by Eva Kelly [Eva O'Doherty].
MS.10498. Thirteen letters c.1907 from Eva O'Doherty, Norwood, [Toowong?], Q'ld, relating to her writings and circumstances.
MS.10500. Papers of P. J. Smyth including: letter 10 Aug. 1853 from P. J. Smyth, Sydney; letter 23 Mar. 1861 to Smyth advising against speculating in Tasmania; fifteen letters from P. J. Smyth, one referring to Mitchel's escape.
MS.10501. Includes items 1872-8 among them letters from C. F. and Mary Dease, Melbourne and Sydney, and letters from C. Gavan Duffy, London; also letters 1859 from John Regan and his wife, Hobart, concerning Smyth's properties in Tasmania.
MS.10510. Patriotic verse, 19th cent., including verse by W. Smith O'Brien 'Songs in Exile' and 'To My Country' written while imprisoned on Maria Island.
MS.10511. Letters 1846-8 Thomas Reilly, Albany, New York, one referring to his wish to emigrate to New South Wales.
MS.10515. Letters 1850-8 from W. Smith O'Brien including letters to John Martin and K. I. O'Doherty, also papers 1846-50 concerning his verse 'To My Country'.
MS.10520. Letters 1848-65 to 'Eva' including six letters 1856-65 from John Martin, one from C. Gavan Duffy, and one from James Stephens, Paris, hoping to be an overseas correspondent for an Australian newspaper.
MS.10521. Biographical sketch of 'Eva' by D. F. McCarthy.
MS.10522. Letters c.1849-54 to K. I. O'Doherty including letters from J. Martin, T. B. McManus, and R. Willson, Bishop of Hobart, concerning Meagher's escape and O'Doherty's obtaining a place at St Mary's Hospital, Hobart.

MSS.11017-257. Papers of Richard Southwell Bourke, 6th Earl of Mayo
MS.11183. Memo 13 Aug. 1852 on the appointment of Roman Catholic priests as instructors in convict ships to Australia, giving reasons for the practice being discontinued, including an extract from Rev. Dr P. B. Geoghegan's report on the system from his experience in the *London* in Dec. 1850, and a list of instructors appointed to convict ships from Ireland 1848-52.

MS.11705. Biographical notes, letters and cuttings c.1957-60 relating to the Irish in Australia compiled by Alan Queale in Australia and forwarded to Dr Edward MacLysaght, see E. Lysaght, *More Irish Families*, Galway and Dublin 1960.

MS.13334. Notes etc. c.1900 compiled by J. C. M. Weale towards a study of Michael Dwyer.
Weale spent some years in Australia c.1890 and became acquainted with Irish residents in Sydney brought together through the establishment of the Land League aided by William Redmond.

MSS.13345-417. Monteagle Papers
MS.13400. Correspondence, papers, and documents 1833-57 on emigration, particularly to Australia. There are c.100 letters 1850-3 to Lady Monteagle from emigrants whose passages to Australia she had assisted, offering thanks, describing Australian conditions and their progress, refunding monies, and asking that relatives may join them. Miscellaneous accounts and expenses and statistics of emigration are

598

included; also some correspondence from individuals in Ireland seeking to emigrate, and from the Colonial Land and Emigration Office, London. There are also letters to the 1st Baron Monteagle, among them letters 1846-8 relating to the Select Committee of the House of Lords on Emigration and earlier papers 1836-8 including: letter 13 Feb. 1836 W. W. Whitmore referring to his waiting on Spring Rice with Col. Torrens to urge wider application of the principle of settlement in South Australia; document 1837, 66pp., by Richard M. Muggeridge, emigration agent for the Poor Law Commission on emigration as a source of relief in Ireland; memo 29 Jan. 1838 by T. F. Elliot, Agent General for Emigration, on his department. Papers 1846-8 include: 'A Plan of Colonization from Ireland' by John Ham referring to Swan River and South Australia; a statistical table 'Emigration 1848' giving details of English, Scottish and Irish emigration to Australia. Other letters include Oct. 1848 from Col. W. Macarthur, Cavan, Ireland, replying to Monteagle's request for advice on a family settling in Australia; 14 July 1842 Edward Macarthur to the Earl of Ripon on the advantage of emigration to New South Wales; Oct. 1848 and 8 Feb. 1849 from Caroline Chisholm referring to Lady Monteagle's interest in emigration and giving an account of the successful settlement of three Irish emigrants. Three items refer to the approach to Monteagle in 1851 by the New South Wales Association for Preventing the Revival of Transportation.

MS.13798. Rolleston Papers
Account-book 1862, 1866 of Lieut. H. Rolleston in Ceylon and New South Wales; papers Dec. 1864 concerning complaints against Rolleston while in service against the Maoris.

MSS.15164-280. John Redmond Papers
A collection of c.9000 items 1882-1919 relating mainly to Irish political affairs.

MS.15181. Letters 1900-17 from Joseph Devlin, among them letters describing Devlin's Australian and New Zealand tour with J. T. Donovan 1906-7 as representatives of the Irish Parliamentary Party at Westminster; letter 29 Jan. 1906 refers to the return of J. W. Walsh from Australia and includes some personal details.

MS.15186(3). Two letters Dec. 1882 from C. Gavan Duffy, London, commending Redmond's visit to Australia to Francis Longmore, M.P., and Robert Byrne, M.P.

MS.15206(8). Letters 1902-9 mainly from Cardinal Moran. The 1902 correspondence relates to the honouring of visiting colonial premiers by the Irish Parliamentary Party and Redmond's plan that Edmund Barton and Laurier be persuaded to make statements in support of Home Rule. A letter from Denis F. O'Haran is included containing personal references to Forrest of Western Australia and Seddon of New Zealand.

MS.15235(1). Letters 1900-7 from Irish Home Rule organisations in Melbourne, Sydney, Brisbane, Adelaide and Perth forwarding funds in support of the Irish Parliamentary Party and inviting a further visit. There are also two letters 1905 from H. B. Higgins referring to his Home Rule motion in the Australian Federal Parliament and support received from Hugh Mahon.

MS.15235(3). Letters 1902, 1907: Edward McGowan referring to Rev. W. J. Larkin and Sir Patrick Buckley; P. M. Twomey, Acting Secretary, Irish National Federation, Wellington, N.Z.; Denis F. O'Haran, Auckland, N.Z., saying that on behalf of Cardinal Moran and the Central Committee in Sydney, he is placing drafts on London for transmission to Redmond.

OTHER COLLECTIONS
Joly Collection
Principally a book collection of Dr J. R. Joly it also contains a group of manuscripts and additional manuscript material found within printed works. The Joly Collection

Dublin

is described in *The Irish Book Lover*, XII, Mar.-Apr. 1921, pp.99-101, and the manuscript group is listed in *Report of the Council of Trustees of the National Library of Ireland, 1932-3*.

MS.J.7-8. Capt. James Cook, 'A journal of the proceeding of His Majesty's Sloop the Resolution in a voyage on discoveries towards the South Pole and round the world . . . 1772, 3, 4, and 5'. Copy of Cook's journal of the second voyage 9 Apr. 1772 to 29 July 1775 in two folio volumes, 416 and 558pp., being a later variant of the two Cook holograph journals and three copies described in *The Journals . . . of Cook*, ed. Beaglehole, II, pp.cxv-clvii. The manuscript is in the hand of Cook's clerk on the *Resolution* during the third voyage.

MS.J.10. Joseph Cockfield (pseud. 'A Christian') and others. Letters to John Hawkesworth, editor, *An Account of the Voyages . . . Commodore Byron . . . and Captain Cook*, London 1773. This is a transcription with occasional margin notes of fifty-six letters published in the *Publick Advertiser* 5 June to 10 Dec. 1770, dealing with the controversy over the exemplification of Divine Providence by the voyages.

A. Kippis, *The Life of Captain James Cook*, London 1788. Bound in at p.1 is a bill of exchange marked 'Cape of Good Hope 28th Nov. 1776' signed by Cook and addressed in his hand to the Commissioners for Victualling the Navy, Lond.; it is an order to pay Mr Abraham Chison at Amsterdam the sum of six hundred Rix dollars for provisions for the *Resolution* and *Discovery*.

J. R. Forster, *Observations made during a voyage round the world . . .*, London 1778. There are two copies: one has marginal notes by an Irish reader of the volume, the second contains at p.102 a single leaf manuscript on the origin of fresh water yielding ice at sea (cf. *The Journals . . . of Cook*, ed. Beaglehole, II, pp.645-6).

W. Bligh, *A narrative of the mutiny . . . and the subsequent voyage . . .*, London 1790. Contains a cutting of an article on Pitcairn Island *c.*1814 with manuscript note *c.*1831 referring to Bligh's return to England in 1790, his voyage 1791-3 and the fate of the mutineers who remained in the *Bounty*.

An autograph letter 24 Apr. 1791 from William Bligh is listed as attached to Bligh's *A voyage to the South Sea . . . in His Majesty's ship the Bounty . . . including an account of the mutiny*, London 1792, but was not found.

PUBLIC RECORD OFFICE OF IRELAND
Four Courts, Dublin

See Margaret Griffith, *A Short Guide to the Public Record Office of Ireland*, Dublin, Stationery Office, 1952, revised edition 1964, also accession lists printed in *Reports of the Deputy Keeper of the Public Records of Ireland*, Nos.55- , Dublin 1928- .

The records were almost entirely destroyed in the explosion and fire of 1922. The records prior to this date are described in H. Wood, *A Guide to the Records Deposited in the Public Record Office of Ireland*, Dublin, Stationery Office, 1919. Surviving records are listed in appendices to the 55th and subsequent *Reports of the Deputy Keeper of the Public Records of Ireland*.

M.2802. Draft despatches 1857-60 from the Governor of South Australia to Lord Stanley.

M.3532. Advertisement 1852 for ships sailing to Australia.

M.3733. Volume of accounts 1874-1910 relating to sheep on a farm called Coolnabucca.

M.5385. Affidavit relating to the goods in Ireland of C. T. Bagot, probate granted 1896 in New South Wales.

M.7052(3). Mining licence 1858 of Edmund Morony.

Frazer Collection. Nos.16-18. Brief of John E. Pigot, counsel for the defendants, lists of jurors and information 1848 in the case of The Queen *v.* W. Smith O'Brien and T. F. Meagher.

ROYAL IRISH ACADEMY
Dawson Street, Dublin

MS.12.P.9. Manuscript book of materials for an autobiography of Thomas Francis Meagher, covering his life and political career before transportation to Australia.

MS.12.P.19. Letters and papers of Charles Gavan Duffy including letter n.d., 44pp., from T. F. Meagher concerning his escape from Van Diemen's Land, the treatment of Irish prisoners, the anti-transportation movement, and the opening of the new Legislative Council sittings.

R. R. MADDEN PAPERS

MS.24.N.1. Papers of Dr R. R. Madden, Colonial Secretary in Western Australia 1847-9 including: letters 1849-50 from various people concerning the Roman Catholic Mission in Western Australia including letters from Bishop Brady of Perth and Archbishop Polding of Sydney; draft n.d. of letter from R. R. Madden giving an account of the state of the colony; correspondence and papers 1846-9 of Bishop Brady; papers 1829-33 relating to the setting up of a colony on the Swan River and proposed prospectus for the settlement of the Victoria district, W.A.; papers concerning the Aborigines in Western Australia including an Aboriginal vocabulary; address to R. R. Madden on his departure from Western Australia Jan. 1849 with papers concerning his office; miscellaneous papers 1829, 1848 concerning Aborigines, land regulations; papers 1840-9 concerning the Wesleyan Mission, and policy towards Aboriginal children in Western Australia; letters 1849 Rev. John Smithies to R. R. Madden; papers of James Stokes concerning claims on the government for damage sustained by the suppression of his distillery in 1849; various papers 1828-49 concerning settlement in Western Australia and the Western Australian Company.

MS.24.O.5-8. Four volumes, mainly cuttings and unpublished essays, by Dr Madden but including: extract of letter 28 Oct. 1851 from Thomas Meagher; letter 21 Mar. 1848 from R. R. Madden acquainting the Acting Governor of Western Australia with his arrival at Fremantle in the barque *Orient*, and note on a gold cup presented to W. S. O'Brien by the inhabitants of Victoria Sept. 1855.

MS.24.O.9-11. Three volumes of correspondence of R. R. Madden including a letter from him on the education of the poor of all religious denominations, with reference to New South Wales.

MS.24.O.12-13. Two volumes of literary, historical, political, and travel notes by R. R. Madden including notes on South Polar discoveries.

STATE PAPER OFFICE
Dublin Castle, Dublin

Established in 1702 the State Paper Office was the repository of the Chief Secretary's Office. The principal office of the Irish executive under the Lord Lieutenant, this continued in existence beyond the Act of Union in 1800 until the foundation of the Irish Free State in 1922, and came to include several government departments whose records also came into the State Paper Office. Under the Public Records (Ireland) Act 1867 provision was made for the transfer of records of the State Paper

Dublin

Office to the Public Record Office, Dublin, q.v. Those transferred prior to 1922 were destroyed in the explosion and fire of that year. For the limited current transfers see 'Index to State Papers in the Public Record Office', typescript. Extant records are described in 'State Paper Office. Short Guide', typescript 1967-8. The papers are under reorganisation (1970).

I RECORDS OF THE CHIEF SECRETARY'S OFFICE

I.2. Rebellion Papers 1790-1807, 67 cartons.

These include reports from officials and private individuals throughout the country describing the procedure of arrests and trials. There are many sentences to transportation or death sentences commuted to transportation for life. There is a calendar in four volumes with slip index.

I.3. State of the Country Papers 1790-1831, 71 cartons.

There are three series: numbered papers 1796-1831 with calendar, 2 vols.; papers arranged by year, 1790-1831; papers 1821, 1825-9, 1830- , now (1970) among C.S.O. Registered Papers and entitled Outrage Papers.

I.4. Official Papers 1790-1922, 149 vols., 1000 cartons.

This class is being reorganised. It contains: Official Papers 1790-1831, 144 cartons; calendar, 2 vols. with card index, in which documents of Australian interest may be found under the headings prisons and prisoners, commissioners of accounts, naval, finance, and miscellaneous; Official Papers formerly entitled Unregistered Papers, 1832-80, 403 cartons and index, 4 vols.; Official Papers, MA, i.e. Miscellaneous Assorted 1832-82, 55 cartons with calendar and index; Official Papers 1800-1921, 147 vols., 398 cartons with list of items.

I.5. Registered Papers 1818-1924, 347 vols., 3800 cartons.

These include: in-correspondence concerning government administration and covering a wide range of subjects, e.g. convicts, petitions, and emigration; Outrage Papers 1832-52; police reports 1853- ; Fenian papers 1858-83, see 'State Paper Office. C.S.O. Registered Papers 1867, Calendar of Papers Relating to Fenians and Fenianism'. There are contemporary registers and index volumes to the Registered Papers. For a general description of Chief Secretary's Office Registered Papers see B. MacGiolla Chiolle, 'Fenian documents in the State Paper Office', *Irish Historical Studies*, xvi, No.63, Mar. 1969, p.259.

I.6. Letter Books 1801-1921, 555 vols.

These include: private and official correspondence books 1789-93, 1806-55; abstracts of correspondence 1801-46 etc.

II POLICE AND CRIME RECORDS

II.2. Fenian Papers 1857-83, 12 vols., 40 cartons.

These include: 'F' papers 1866-74, 14 cartons; police reports 1857-65, 3 cartons; Fenians, arrests and discharges 1866-8, 4 vols., 2 cartons; crown briefs 1865-9, 1 vol., 11 cartons; Fenian photographs and descriptions 1866-80, 1 vol., 4 cartons; 'A' files 1864-8, 1877-83, formerly listed as 'Consular Despatches', 5 cartons. The records include references to Fenianism in Australia, particularly Fenians transported to Western Australia, e.g. 'F' series, f.5246 return 10 Dec. 1868 of all persons at present in custody under convictions in Ireland for Fenian offences, half the number in custody in Western Australia having been sent out in 1867, with a short memorandum of each case. Other papers list Fenians, including individuals in Australia, to whom clemency might be shown. There are transmitted reports from Australian authorities including f.5505 copy of despatch Jan. 1870 from the Governor of New South Wales, forwarded to the Chief Secretary, stating that a 'pic-nic' for the released Western Australian Fenians who had recently reached Sydney, had been banned.

III RECORDS OF DEPARTMENTS OF THE CHIEF SECRETARY'S OFFICE

III.1. Convict Department 1778-1924, 75 vols., 1212 cartons.

The records include: Convict Papers 1836-1922, 1192 cartons; Convict Reference Books 1836-1924, 16 vols.; Criminal Index Books 1841-1920, 17 vols.; Letter Books 1845-1921, 21 vols.; Miscellaneous papers, registers 1876-1919, 3 vols.; Prisoners' Petitions and Cases 1778-1836, 20 cartons.

The main series is the Convict Papers, the unit of which is an individual file. The first 412 cartons cover 1836-67. The Convict Reference Books are registers of the Convict Papers. In conjunction with the Registers of Convicts Sentenced to Transportation (see IV below) or independently, the Convict Reference Books can be used to locate the papers of individual convicts transported to Australia. There are also unregistered papers containing further documents on transportation. In the series of papers designated 'Free Settlers', papers were noted in 1839-43, 1846-7, 1850, containing memorials, petitions, letters mainly concerning the wives and families of convicts seeking, and on occasion obtaining, free passages to Australia, including letters of convicts themselves.

IV GENERAL PRISON BOARD RECORDS 1836-1928

377 vols., 897 cartons. These include: Convict returns 1848-56, 1878-9, 12 cartons; Convicts Sentenced to Transportation, Registers, 1836-57, 15 vols.; Correspondence 1851-1900, 453 cartons; Correspondence Registers 1850-1900, 100 vols.; Letter books 1843-78, 32 vols.

UNIVERSITY OF DUBLIN
Trinity College Library, Dublin

MSS.868-9 (N4.1-13) SIRR PAPERS

Papers of Major Henry C. Sirr, town major or head of police in Dublin 1798-1826, relating chiefly to the Rebellion 1798-1804. There is a list and index. The papers contain letters, informations, warrants, and petitions. Vols.8-12 include thirteen documents 1801-3 relating to Michael Dwyer and his associates, also to the information of Thomas Devoy relating to John Carroll, later transported to Botany Bay, and petition 9 June 1800 of Mathias McElray in the *Anne* at Cork, bound for Botany Bay.

MS.872 (G2.19A) PROCEEDINGS OF COURTS MARTIAL 1798

Volume containing copies of court martial proceedings in 1798 at Drogheda, Slane, Trim, Dublin, and Loughlinstown, including courts martial of prisoners sentenced to transportation. There is a list of contents.

MSS.873, 1469-73 (S3.19-22) MADDEN PAPERS

A collection of papers relating to the United Irishmen. There is a list and index. S3.22. Courts martial held at Wexford 1799, 1800 including the trials of five men sentenced to transportation.

MSS.1827-36 LECKY CORRESPONDENCE

Correspondence of W. E. H. Lecky, historian and essayist. There is a list and index. Letters 1865-97 include letters from Henry Parkes, G. W. Rusden, and Charles Gavan Duffy on Federation and the Australian constitution, literary matters, English politics, and Irish affairs. Other correspondents are: H. J. Wrixon, Melbourne, Daniel Bishopp Ryan, N.S.W., F. W. Hutton, Christchurch, N.Z., James Bonwick, Surrey, England, P. D. Phillips, Melbourne, Sam Hodgkinson, Invercargill, N.Z., Lord Brassey and Sidwell Shotton, Vic., S. J. Way, S.A., and A. H. Barlow, Brisbane.

MSS.2919-22 (L7.) BOURKE FAMILY PAPERS

There is a list and index. The collection of printed and manuscript material includes a letter from Capt. Edmund Bourke concerning his appointment to H.M.S. *Gannet* to be employed on the Pacific Station.

MSS.3147-54 DOWDEN CORRESPONDENCE

There is a list and index. This correspondence of Edward Dowden, critic and Professor of English Literature at Trinity College, Dublin, includes letter 2 Apr. 1884 from M. Tomkins, Newcastle, N.S.W., telling of his father's acquaintance with the poet Shelley, invitation 1 Sept. 1905 in Latin, to Edward Dowden to attend the fiftieth anniversary celebrations of the University of Melbourne.

MSS.3391-413 (N1.11-16, N5.12-27, N6.1) O'REILLY PAPERS

There is a list and index.

MS.3396 (N1.16). Letter 3 Apr. 1930 W. J. Williams, British Consulate, Tahiti, to Capt. S. C. Beresford Mudey [*sic*] informing him of the death of Myles John Beresford O'Reilly (The O'Reilly) on 9 Jan. 1928 and his burial at Papeete, with note 16 Aug. 1929 on The O'Reilly by Cyril Beresford Mundey; also seven photographs 1923 of O'Reilly and his house at Papeete and cutting from *The Hamilton Spectator*, Vic., 26 Aug. 1897 containing a speech of O'Reilly.

MS.3412 (N5.27). Nine letters 1853-4 from George O'Reilly to his father and Myles G. O'Reilly giving an account of his voyage from New York to Port Phillip, his journey to Bendigo and experiences on the diggings.

HARVEY CORRESPONDENCE

Twenty-two letters 1854-5 from Dr William Henry Harvey, Professor of Botany at Trinity College, Dublin 1856-66, to relatives. These describe his visits to Australia, Tonga, and Fiji, often giving botanical details and descriptions of places, people, customs, and events.

MISCELLANEOUS DEEDS 9 (2071)

Conditional Pardon 31 Dec. 1847 of James Scully sentenced to transportation for life, signed by Gov. FitzRoy.

FRANCISCAN HOUSE OF STUDIES
The Library, Dún Mhuire, Seafield Road, Killiney

MSS.E.25. Letters and papers of Rev. Richard Joachim Hayes, O.F.M., including fourteen letters 1799-1825 Michael Hayes, transported to Australia in 1799, to his family in Ireland. Also three letters 1831-3 F. Girard, Sydney, Hayes's son-in-law, to Patrick Hayes and the family in Ireland. All letters have been published in *The Past* 6, 1950, pp.45-103, the organ of the Ui Ceinnsealaigh Historical Society.

MSS.M: Irish Franciscan Notebook 12. Notes Mar. 1879 to June 1880 by Rev. M. A. Holohan on the Catholic Church in Australia and the will of Rev. P. F. O'Farrell also a missionary in Australia.

KILDARE

MAJOR J. DE BURGH
Oldtown, Naas

The de Burgh family papers include:

Letter 4 Aug. 1841 Henry de Burgh to his mother written shortly after his arrival in Western Australia.

Journal of Henry de Burgh 7 Apr. 1831 to 13 Jan. 1844 describing his voyage to Western Australia in the *James Matthews* in 1831 and his life in the York district.

Copies of both these items are in the State Library of Western Australia. The family papers have not been fully examined for documents of Australian interest and may contain other relevant material.

TIPPERARY

CASHEL DIOCESAN ARCHIVES
Thurles

Microfilms of the two collections noted below are held in the National Library of Ireland, Dublin.

ARCHBISHOP LEAHY PAPERS

Papers 1833-72 of Dr Patrick Leahy, Archbishop of Cashel 1857-75. See Dom Mark Tierney, O.S.B., 'Calendar of the Papers of Dr. Leahy', 1965-6, processed. The papers include:

1862/33. Printed circular letter 1 Nov. 1862, Melbourne, signed by the Australian hierarchy, dealing with parish matters.

1862/47. Letter 24 Dec. 1862 Dr J. A. Goold, Melbourne, to Dr Leahy sending £100 for the relief of the poor in the Cashel diocese being part of a collection made by the clergy of Melbourne.

1863/66. Printed circular letter 10 Sept. 1863 Archbishop of Sydney and Bishops of Hobart and Melbourne giving the resolutions of the Australian hierarchy concerning foreign clergymen coming to make collections in their dioceses referring especially to visiting clergy from England, Ireland, and Scotland.

1868/10. Letter 28 Jan. 1868 Dr William Lanigan, Bishop of Goulburn, N.S.W., giving Leahy faculties to promote orders for his diocese and to transact business for him; also details of his diocese and of the lonely life of priests.

1868/56. Letter 10 Aug. 1868 Dr Lanigan concerning priests for his diocese and other matters and enclosing letter explaining the shortage of priests on the mission, the difficulties of travel and his having to attend a Synod summoned by the Archbishop of Sydney.

ARCHBISHOP CROKE PAPERS

Papers 1841-1902 of Thomas William Croke, Bishop of Auckland 1870-5 and afterwards Bishop of Cashel. See Dom Mark Tierney, O.S.B., 'Calendar of the

Tipperary

Papers of Dr. Croke', 1965, processed. Letters 1870-5 from Bishop Croke to his sister, Mother Joseph Croke, give news of his appointment and comment on diocesan affairs. After 1875 there are letters from various correspondents referring to Australian bishops and affairs and letters from political figures including C. Gavan Duffy.

1849/1. Notebook 1849-75 giving the full text of sermons with date and occasion, the majority preached in Auckland.

1853/1. Documents 22 July 1853 appointing James Croke Solicitor General for the colony of Victoria.

1856/1. Printed booklet, Auckland 9 Mar. 1856, of regulations for the priests of Auckland, written and signed by Bishop Pompallier containing some manuscript notes.

1856/2. Letters Patent 25 Nov. 1856 granting James Croke a pension for life.

1866/5. Letter 20 July [1866?] Dr Matthew Quinn, Bishop of Bathurst in the *Empress*, Queenstown harbour, appointing Croke his Vicar-General to transact business in Ireland.

1870/7. Report 10 July 1870 Mgr Simeoni, Rome, to Croke on the situation in Auckland.

1870/9. Printed and corrected proof copy of an address 27 July 1870, Bishop Croke, Villa of the Irish College, Rome, to the clergy and laity of his diocese of Auckland.

1870/18. 'Journal of my administration of the Diocese of Auckland' 17 Dec. 1870 to 10 Jan. 1874, Bishop Croke's record of events connected with his duties there.

1871/1. 'The Directory for the Clergy of the diocese of Melbourne', 1871 with manuscript notes in margin by Bishop Croke giving account of his episcopal activities.

1882/3. Letter 19 Apr. 1882 Dr J. Murray to Croke recommending Fr James Ryan returning to Cashel after nine years in New South Wales.

1883/8. Legal document 1883 for the conveyance of property in Auckland from Dr Croke to the Bishop of Auckland.

1888/30. Letter 8 Sept. 1888 Mother Ignatius Croke, Bathurst, to her sister.

1891/64. Letter 13 July 1891 members of the New Zealand Irish National Federation, Ahaura, West Coast, N.Z., sending a donation towards the Evicted Tenants Fund.

Index

Spelling of personal and place names follows that of standard reference books and may differ from spelling in the text, which follows that in the manuscript. Full Christian names and dates of birth and death are given only if easily ascertained. Professional titles, Admiral, Capt., Bp, Rev., Dr, etc. and any description such as merchant, are not given unless necessary to distinguish between persons of the same name or when Christian names have not been found. Titled persons are entered under their family names with any necessary references. Entries for papers still in the possession of the holders of titles are however under the titles.

Index

Index

Index

315, 316, 318, 328, 424, 485, 512, 515, 544; collection, 319
Bacon, Anthony (1796-1864), 39
Bacon, Lady Charlotte, wife of General Anthony, 39
Bacstrom, S., 515
Badenach, John, 156
Bagot, C. T. (d.1894), 600
Bagshawe, T. W., 400
Bailey, Frederick Manson (1827-1915), 513, 517
Baillie, Alexander Dundas Ross Wishart Cochrane-, see Cochrane-Baillie
Bain, George, 258
Bainbridge, Oliver, 242
Baines, Maryanne Verdon (Barnes), Mrs William Mortimer, 539
Baines, Thomas (1822-75), 328, 335, 337, 371, 471, 512
Baines, William Mortimer, 539
Baines of Bell Hall papers, 539
Baird, Sir John Lawrence, Viscount Stonehaven (1874-1941), 76
Baker, Charles, 71
Baker, I. C., 68
Baker, Richard Thomas (1854-1941), 517
Baker, Shirley Waldemar (1835-1903), 70, 71, 488
Baldwin, Stanley, 1st Earl Baldwin of Bewdley (1867-1947): papers, 385
Baldwin, Sir William, 21
Bale, W. M., 563
Balfe, John Donnellan (1816-80), 476, 477
Balfour, Andrew F., 356
Balfour, Arthur James, 1st Earl of Balfour (1848-1930), 273, 488; papers, 72-4, 244
Balfour, Lady Blanche, 490
Balfour, Cecil Charles (1849-81), 74
Balfour, Charles, 3
Balfour, Henry (1863-1939), 494
Balfour, James, 3
Balfour, James (1830-1913), 391
Balfour, Nisbet (1743-1823), 576
Ball, Henry Lidgbird (d.1818), 27
Ball, John Thomas (1815-98), 425
Ballarat, s.s., 589
Ballarat, Vic.: goldfield, 405, 424, 533-4, 540, 553; diocese, 151; Asylum and Lying-in Hospital, 467
Ballarat anti-transportation petition 1864, 331
Balleny, John, 337
Bampton, William, 80, 107
Bancroft, Joseph (1838-94), 513
Bank of Australasia, 34, 388
Bank of New South Wales, 297, 299
Bank of South Australia, 417
Banking, 149-50, 291; Australia, 33, 42, 52; New South Wales, 278; New Zealand, 278, 293; Victoria, 4; see also Savings banks

Bankruptcy, 300
Banks, Sir Joseph (1743-1820), 19, 20, 23, 78-88 passim, 156, 158, 159, 171, 176, 183, 279, 326, 341, 342, 343, 355, 362, 397, 413, 420, 452; papers, 12, 515; plants collected at Botany Bay, 517; recommends transportation of convicts to Botany Bay, 135
Banks, Sarah Sophia, 452
Banksian Herbarium, 84, 88
Bannerman, David Armitage (b.1886), 83
Bannerman, Sir Henry Campbell-, see Campbell-Bannerman
Bannister, Saxe (1790-1877), 25, 33, 39, 258, 365, 410
Bannister, Thomas, 527
Bantock, Sir Granville Ransome (1868-1946), 538
Baptist Church: Australia, 555; missions, 543
Baranov, Alexander Andrevich (1746-1819), 82
Baratta Station, S.A., 121
Barazer, Frenchman, report on Pacific Islands 1851, 172
Barbara, ship, 187
Barclay, Edward, 457
Barclay, George (fl.1835-41), 83, 514
Barcoo River, Qld, 417
Barff, Charles (1792-1866), 37, 95, 96, 533, 534
Barham, 1st Baron, see Middleton, Sir Charles
Baring, Evelyn, 1st Earl of Cromer (1841-1917): papers, 242
Baring, Francis, 3rd Baron Ashburton (1800-68), 425
Baring, Sir Francis Thornhill, Baron Northbrook (1796-1866), 394
Baring, Thomas, 4
Barker, Mrs A. M., 578
Barker, Alfred, 520
Barker, Frederic (1808-82), 156, 407
Barker, Mary, 520
Barker, Mary, nurse, 67, 124
Barker, Robert Edward, 173
Barker, William, 578
Barklamb family, Benalla, Vic., 382
Barkly, Ann (Pratt), Lady, 379
Barkly, Sir Henry (1815-98), 4, 66, 120, 345-6, 361, 437, 446, 512, 523; papers, 379
Barlee, Sir Frederick Palgrave (1827-84), 141
Barlett, Peter, 513
Barlow, Andrew Henry (1837-1915), 604
Barlow, Charles James (1848-1912), 169
Barnard, Edward, 156, 296, 450
Barnard, Thomas, 377
Barnes, K., 509
Barnes, William, 28
Barney, George (1792-1862), 53, 566

615

ⓧ Richard Brydges Beatty was 17 when he began
his voyage as midshipman under his brother
Captain Frederick Beechey on H.M.S. Blossom

Index

Index

Index

222-3; *see also* British colonies; headings under Imperial

British Empire, *see* British colonies; British Commonwealth; British dominions; Great Britain; and headings under Imperial

British Empire Delegations' Conference, Geneva (1927), 76

British Empire Statistical Conference (1920) 1921, 287

British Expedition to Dutch New Guinea (1909-11), 335

British Exploration of Australia Ltd, 416

British Graham Land Expedition, 334, 400

British Imperial Trans-Antarctic Expedition (1914-16), 295, 336, 337, 399

British National Antarctic Expedition (1901-4), 86, 334, 335, 336, 342, 399; drawings and paintings, 337

British New Guinea, 240, 335, 577; C.O. records, 210, 214, 221; economic development, 214; languages, 321

British Ornithologists' Union, 299; Expedition to New Guinea (1908-11), 334

British Relief Expedition (1903-4), *see* British [Antarctic] Relief Expedition

British Sovereign, H.M.S., 174

British Women's Emigration Association, 113

Brittain, A. H., 332

Britton, Henry, 266

Broadway Damask Co. Ltd, 584

Brock, H. G., 595

Brockman, Frederick S., 323

Broderip, William John (1789-1859), 27, 157

Brodie, Sir Benjamin Collins, senior, Bt (1783-1862), 157

Brodie, William, 577

Brodsky, Leon, 511

Brogden, James, 432

Broke, Anna Maria, 506

Broke, Charles Acton: papers, 506-7

Broken Bay, N.S.W.: drawings and paintings, 19; maps and charts, 13, 18

Broken Hill, N.S.W., 419, 420

Bromby, Charles Henry (1814-1907), 56, 57, 62, 448

Brongniart, Adolph Theophile (1801-76), 512

Brooke, J., 497

Brooker, Francis, 109

Brookhill Hall collection, 409-10

Brooking, Elizabeth, 165

Brooks, G. H., 368

Brooks, Henry, 594

Brooksbank, S., 254

Broome, E. M., 503

Broome, Sir Frederick Napier (1842-96), 503

Broome, W. A., 89

Brougham, Henry Peter, 1st Baron

Brougham and Vaux (1778-1868), 24, 39; papers, 365

Brougham, John, 365

Brougham, P. R., 365

Broughton, Eliza C., 450

Broughton, William (1768-1821), 313

Broughton, William Grant (1788-1853), 49, 53, 54, 55, 91, 154, 157, 177, 221, 273, 309, 351, 352, 382

Broughton, William Robert (1762-1821), 16

Broughton de Gyfford, 2nd Bt, *see* Hobhouse John Cam

Broughton papers, 25

Brown, Alfred Henry (1860-1932), 317

Brown, Alfred Reginald Radcliffe- (1880-1955), 395

Brown, G. H., 422

Brown, Sir George (1790-1865), 567, 568

Brown, George (1835-1917), 22, 369, 474

Brown, George (*fl.*1881 Christchurch, N.Z.), 417

Brown, Henry H., 519

Brown, Henrietta (1851-1907), 317

Brown, J. (*fl.*1815), 479, 480

Brown, James, 535

Brown, James L., 452

Brown, John, 405

Brown, John, servant of Queen Victoria, 262

Brown, John George, 130

Brown, Peter, 566

Brown, R. W. B., 409

Brown, Robert (1773-1858), 38, 79, 84, 85, 87, 157, 158, 401, 515; papers, 20-1, 83-4

Brown, Robert Neal Rudmose-, *see* Rudmose-Brown

Brown, Simon, convict, 460

Brown, William (*fl.*1857 Sydney, N.S.W.), 157

Brown, William, author of *New Zealand and its Aborigines*, 34

Brown, emigration agent, 434

Brown & Co., 388

Brown River, Tas., 413

Browne, Denis, 25

Browne, Fielding (1789-1871), 365

Browne, J. R. [or T. R.], artist, 166

Browne, Thomas Alexander (1826-1915), 547

Browne, Sir Thomas Gore (1807-87), 267, 331, 425

Browne, William Henry (1800-77), 154

Browne, artist, on goldfields, 327

Browne & Wingrove, 553

Browning, Robert (1812-89), 64, 65

Brownless, Sir Anthony Colling (1817-97), 371, 563

Brownrigg, Sir Robert (1759-1833), 309

Brownrigg, William (1711-1800), 156

Bruat, Armand-Joseph (1796-1855), 37, 533

620

Index

Business records, 129-31, 149-50, 346, 350-1, 365-6, 367-8, 379, 387-92 *passim*, 403, 416, 432, 451, 453-4, 541-7 *passim*, 558-9, 572, 573, 585; *see also* Companies; names of companies and firms
Bussell, John Garrett, 460
Butcher, Benjamin, 335
Bute, 2nd Marquis of, *see* Stuart, John
Butler, Cavendish, 586
Butler, Samuel (1835-1902), 23, 25, 398; papers, 29, 46-8
Butler, Weeden, 15
Butter, 180
Buxton, P. A., 361
Buxton, Sydney Charles, 42, 51
Buxton, Sir Thomas Fowell (1786-1845), 410, 411
Buxton, Sir Thomas Fowell, 3rd Bt (1837-1915), 424
Buxton family, 413
Buzacott, Aaron (1800-64), 96, 97
Byng, Frederick Gerald (1784-1871), 269
Byng, Julian Hedworth George, Viscount Byng of Vimy (1862-1935), 272
Byrne, P. M., 494
Byrne, Robert, (*b*.1882), 599
Byrne, trader (*fl*.1862), 29
Byron, John (1723-86), 108, 170, 174, 499

C

Cabinet Office records, 199-208
Cabinet papers, 73-4, 240, 386
Cable communications, *see* Telegraphic communications
Cable tramways, 529
Cáceres, Francisco de, 78
Cadbury, John (1801-89), 316
Cadbury, John, junior, 320
Caddick, Helen, 529
Caddick diaries, 529
Caddy, J. P., 438
Cadell, William, 575
Cadell and Davies, 542
Cadman, Mr, 531
Cahill, Paddy, 494
Cairns, William Wellington (1828-88), 264
Cakobau (*c*.1817-83), 166, 213, 262, 264
Calandoon, N.S.W., 442
Calapoda Cretensis, *see* Sideri, Georgio
Calcutta, H.M. storeship, 64, 441, 442, 500
Caley, ['Cayley'], George (1770-1829), 13, 20, 83, 84
Callaghan, Eliza, *see* Batman
Calvert, James (1813-92), 165
Calvert, Mary (Fowler), Mrs James, 165
Calypso, H.M.S., 172
Cambon, Pierre Paul (1843-1924), 244
Cambrian, H.M.S., 173
Cambrian Queen, ship, 556

Cambridge Anthropological Expedition to Torres Strait (1898), 362
Camden, 2nd Earl and 1st Marquess of, *see* Pratt, John Jeffreys
Camden, mission ship, 97
Camden, ship, 506
Camden, N.S.W., 171
Cameron, Cyril St Clair (1857-1941), 310
Cameron, Donald, 436
Cameron, Sir Duncan Alexander (1808-88), 41, 43
Campbell, Charles (1810-88), 157, 265
Campbell, Sir Francis, 386
Campbell, George Douglas, 8th Duke of Argyll (1823-1900), 57, 270
Campbell, I., Ensign, 457
Campbell, James, 25
Campbell, John, Major, 426
Campbell, John (1802-86), 154
Campbell, John Thomas (1770?-1830), 547
Campbell, [N.?], of Oamaru, N.Z., 557
Campbell, Peter, 49
Campbell, Robert (1769-1846), 28, 157, 279, 379, 388
Campbell, Robert, & Company, 416; *see also* Campbell & Co.
Campbell, S. T., 450
Campbell, W. L., 382
Campbell, W. M., 523
Campbell, William Douglas (1770-1827), 259
Campbell, Dr, 531
Campbell, Mr, representative of Burns, Philp, 243
Campbell & Co. Sydney, 380, 509; *see also* Campbell, Robert, & Co.
Campbell of Jura papers, 575
Campbell-Bannerman, Sir Henry (1836-1908), 41; papers, 35-6, 77
Campbell's Creek, N.S.W., goldfield, 497
Campbelltown, N.S.W., 372
Camperdown, 2nd Viscount Duncan of, *see* Haldane-Duncan, Robert Dundas
Campion, Sir William Robert, 526
Canada, convict ship, 22
Canadian exiles (1839), 234
Candlenuts, 486
Candolle, Augustin Pyrame de (1778-1841), 79
Cann, F. C., 408
Cannan, Edwin (1861-1935): papers, 357
Canning, George (1770-1827), 269, 411; papers, 543
Canning, Stratford, 1st Viscount Stratford de Redcliffe (1786-1880): papers, 242
Canning, Thomas, ticket of leave, 128
Canning River, W.A., 467; hydrographic survey, 499
Canoes, 25, 81, 175, 387
Canowie Station, S.A., 121

622

Index

Index

Index

Index

Index

Index

Index

Index

Index

Index

Hamilton, William Henry (1790?-1870), 390

Hamilton-Gordon, Arthur Charles, 1st Baron Stanmore, *see* Gordon

Hamilton-Gordon, George, 4th Earl of Aberdeen, *see* Gordon

Hamilton-Gordon, George Arthur Maurice, 2nd Baron Stanmore, *see* Gordon

Hamley, J. O., 18

Hammond, A. S., 534

Hammond, William, 176

Hammond, William (*fl.*1772 Hull), 548

Hamond, Sir Andrew Snape (1738-1828), 20

Hampden, 2nd Viscount, *see* Brand, Henry Robert

Hampton, John Stephen (1810?-69), 57

Hampton, 1st Baron, *see* Pakington, Sir John Somerset

Hampton family archives, 537

Hampton Plains, W.A., 498

Hampton Plains Syndicate, 498

Hampton Properties Ltd, 403

Hanbury, Mrs F. C., 445

Hanislaus, hulk, 110

Hankey, L. A., 576

Hankey, Sir Maurice Pascal Alers, 1st Baron Hankey (1877-1963), 201, 206

Hankey, Thomson (1805-93), 48

Hankinson, Robert Mitford, 346

Hannah and Eliza, whaling vessel, 258

Hao Island, Tuamotu Archipelago: chart, 26

Harbutt, Mary Jane (Dixon), Mrs William (1813-85), 97

Harbutt, William (1809-66), 96, 97

Harcourt, Sir William George Granville Venables Vernon (1827-1904), 61

Hard, G. E., 531

Hardcastle, J., 94

Harding, E., convict, 597

Harding, Sir Edward John (1880-1954), 327

Hardisty, Joseph, 137, 138

Hardwicke, Earls of, *see* Yorke, Charles Philip, 4th Earl of; Yorke, Philip, 2nd Earl of; Yorke, Philip, 3rd Earl of

Hardwicke, Thomas, 13

Hardwicke papers, 24-5

Hardy, Arthur, 358, 359

Hardy, Gathorne Gathorne-, 1st Earl of Cranbrook, *see* Gathorne-Hardy

Hardy, J. N., 426

Hardy, John, convict, 423

Hardy, Marmaduke, 358

Hare, Alexander, 26

Harewood, 2nd Earl of, *see* Lascelles, Henry

Harewood, 6th Earl of, *see* Lascelles, Henry George Charles

Harewood archives, 543

Hargrave, Lawrence (1850-1915), 81, 321

Hargraves, Edward Hammond (1861-91), 578

Harington, Thomas Cudbert (1798-1863), 53, 157, 426, 428, 479

Harlow, V. T., *Founding of the Second British Empire, 1763-1793*, 484

Harman, R. J. S., 538

Harman & Stevens, Christchurch, N.Z., 538

Harmsworth, Alfred Charles William, Viscount Northcliffe (1865-1922), 244

Harper, Arthur Paul (1865-1955), 335

Harper, George (1802?-41), 568

Harper, Henry John Chitty (1804-93), 355, 382, 481

Harper, Robert, & Co., 389

Harper, Rosamund, 335

Harper, S. W., 486

Harper, William, 568

Harrier, H.M.S., 438

Harris, Ann Jane (Hobbs), Mrs George Prideaux Robert, 64

Harris, Charles Miller, 86

Harris, George, 506

Harris, George Prideaux Robert (1775-1810): papers, 64

Harris, Rev. J., New Hebrides, 45

Harris, James, missionary, 97

Harris, James, ship's surgeon, 176

Harris, James, 1st Earl of Malmesbury (1746-1820), 23, 420

Harris, Richard, convict, 595

Harrison, Benjamin, the younger (1808-87), 55

Harrison, G., 313

Harrison, John Turner, 235

Harrison, S. G., 486

Harrowby, 2nd Earl of, *see* Ryder, Dudley

Hart, Frederick, 130

Hart, Miss H., 114

Hart, John (1809-73), 268, 528

Hart, William Hamilton, 130

Hart-Davis, V., 485

Hartland, Edwin Sidney, 555

Hartley, John, 110

Hartwell papers, 383

Hartwood Station, N.S.W., 432

Harvey, George, 469

Harvey, John H., 335

Harvey, William, 176

Harvey, William Henry (1811-66), 535, 604

Harwood, John, 532

Hassall, Rowland (1768-1820), 95, 97

Hassard, Lieut.-Col., 503

Haste, Edwin, 496

Hastings, Francis Rawdon, 1st Marquis of Hastings, 2nd Earl of Moira (1754-1826), 462

Haswell, William Aitcheson (1854-1925), 564

Index

Herbert, Harriet H., 113
Herbert, Henry Howard Molyneux, 4th Earl of Carnarvon (1831-90), 52, 72, 161, 459, 489; papers, 262-8
Herbert, Sir Robert George Wyndham (1831-1905), 55, 59, 266, 270, 323, 441
Herbert, Sidney, 1st Baron Herbert of Lea (1810-61), 37, 57
Herbertson, J. J. W., 207
Hercules, convict ship, 21, 35
Hereford, ship, 176
Hermannsburg Mission, N.T., 395
Herschel, Sir John Frederick William, 1st Bt (1792-1871), 57, 339, 402
Herschel, Sir William (1738-1822), 341
Hertford, 5th Marquess of, *see* Seymour, Francis George Hugh
Hertslet, Sir Edward (1824-1902), 45
Hervey, Frederick William, 5th Earl and 1st Marquess of Bristol (1769-1849), 505
Hervey family archives, 505
Hervey Islands, *see* Cook Islands
Hesse, F., 455
Hetley, G. B., 514
Hewett, Anderson J., 439
Hewett family, 439
Hey, William, 542
Heywood, Peter (1773-1831), 560, 573
Hickey, William (1787?-1875): papers, 596, 598
Hickleton papers, 548-9
Hicks, Johnson, 277
Hicks & Creeth, *see* Creeth, Hicks & Creeth
Hicks Beach, Sir Michael Edward, 9th Bt and 1st Earl St Aldwyn (1837-1916), 491; papers, 436
Hicks Beach, Susan, 436
Hides, John G., 335
Higgins, Edward, 442
Higgins, Henry Bournes (1851-1929), 474, 589, 599
Higginson, Ellen, Mrs Walter R. Hardy, 461-2
Higginson, Walter R. Hardy (d.1887), 461-2
High Commission for the Western Pacific, *see* Western Pacific High Commission
High Commissioners in London, 201
High Court of Admiralty records, 186-7
Highflyer, ship, 174, 176
Highland and Island Emigration Society, 572, 577
Hill, Alexander Staveley (1825-1905), 451
Hill, Sir Arthur William (1875-1941), 516
Hill, Charles, 497
Hill, Edward S. ['C. S.'], 87
Hill, F., 465
Hill, Frank Harrison (1830-1910), 44
Hill, Henry, 306

Hill, Isaac Mason, 468
Hill, J. A. C., 486-7
Hill, J. W., 94
Hill, Sir James, 541
Hill, John, 71
Hill, Joshua (*b*.1773), 336, 481
Hill, Julia (Thomas), Mrs Henry, 306
Hill, Matthew Davenport (1792-1872), 365
Hill, Richard (1782-1836), 352, 354
Hill, Sir Rowland (1795-1879), 27, 112, 119, 345, 364
Hill, Rowland Clegg, 3rd Viscount Hill (1833-95), 496
Hill, Stanley, 445
Hill, Samuel (*fl*.1844), 40
Hill, Walter (1820-1904), 513
Hill, Walter (*fl*.1898 N.Z.), 514
Hill family papers, 497
Hill (Hawkstone) manuscripts, 496
Hillas, John, 541
Hillebrand, Wilhelm, 513, 514
Hillier collection, 395
Hills, John Francis (1868-1948), 318
Hilston, D., 438
Himalaya, ship, 172, 433
Hindmarsh, Sir John (1785-1860), 364, 413, 415, 435
Hindmarsh, Mary, 330
Hinds, Richard Brinsley (*d*. before 1861), 86, 513
Hindson, Matthew, 450
Hindu, ship, 388
Hinemoa legend, N.Z., 18
Hinks, Arthur Robert (1873-1945), 322
Hitchcock, M., 83
Hitchings, Michael S., 90
Hoare, Charles James (1781-1865), 157
Hoare, O'Bryen, 492
Hoare, Sir Samuel John Gurney, 2nd Bt, Viscount Templewood (1880-1959), 393-4
Hoare & Co., 379
Hoare papers, 126
Hobart, Robert, Baron Hobart, 4th Earl of Buckinghamshire (1760-1816), 279, 383
Hobart, Tas., 38, 160, 169, 451, 586, 595; Government House, 297, 329, 415; painting, 22
Hobbs, Alice Weddell, 465
Hobhouse, Edmund (1817-1904), 23, 155, 161, 354, 480
Hobhouse, Henry (1854-1937), 30, 411
Hobhouse, John Cam, 2nd Baron Broughton-de-Gyfford (1786-1869), 25, 477
Hobley-Griffith manuscripts, 555
Hobson, Edmund Charles (1814-48), 325
Hobson, William (1793-1842), 33, 274, 341, 418
Hobson's Bay, Port Phillip, Vic.: chart, 109

Index

w

Index

Index

Index

Land: Australian colonies, 34, 38, 291, 329, 426, 528, (New South Wales), 257, 279, 426, (Van Diemen's Land), 29, (Western Australia), 527; Fiji, 69, 235, 239; Gilbert and Ellice Islands, 98, 487; New Guinea, 263; New Zealand, 90, 91, 236, 496; Crown, 211, 329, 458, 459, 520; legislation, 29, 329; policy (Australian colonies), 136, 360, 411, 446, (Fiji), 72; grants, 31, 219, 221, (Gladstone Colony), 212, (New South Wales), 28, 158, 279, 378, 410-3, 471, (New Zealand), 53, 485, (Norfolk Island), 28, (South Australia), 330, (Van Diemen's Land), 329, 378, 410-13, 426, 471; regulations (New SouthWales), 412, (New Zealand), 381, (South Australia), 433, (Victoria), 575, (Western Australia), 601; sales, 40, 136, 158, (Fiji), 69, (New South Wales), 411, 412, (New Zealand), 33, 40, 49, 215, 274, 276, 504, (South Australia), 224, (Western Australia), 364; settlement, 464, (Van Diemen's Land), 329, (Western Australia), 43, see also Soldier settlement, Squatters; speculation (Victoria), 433; survey (Van Diemen's Land), 329; tenure (Fiji), 486; titles, 278, (New Zealand), 53, 58; values, 411, (New Zealand), 422, (Victoria), 586
Land and Emigration Board, see Board of Colonisation Commissioners (South Australia); Colonial Land and Emigration Commission
Land and Emigration Commission, see Colonial Land and Emigration Commission
Land League, Australia, 598
Landor, E. A., 510
Lane, William, 94
Lanesborough, Earl of: papers, 586
Lang, Andrew (1844-1912), 563
Lang, J., 443
Lang, John Dunmore (1799-1878), 4, 56, 331, 410, 411, 426, 427, 428, 570
Lang, John Thomas, 386
Langara, Cayetana de, 29
Langham, Fred, 71, 166, 394
Langley, Sir Walter: papers, 243
Lanigan, William (b.1820), 605
Lansbury, George (1859-1940): papers, 360
Lansdowne, 5th Marquess, see Petty-Fitzmaurice, Henry Charles Keith
La Pérouse, Jean-François de Galaup, Comte de (1741-88), 12, 16, 234, 397
La Pilar, ship, 17
Larcom, Arthur, 243
Larcom papers, 596
La Recherche, French ship, 85, 361, 362
Larkin, Stanley V., 519
Larkin, W. J., 599

Larkins, J., 389, 390-1
Larnac, Comte de, 37
Lascelles, Sir Frank Cavendish (1841-1920): papers, 243
Lascelles, Henry, 2nd Earl of Harewood (1767-1841): archives, 543
Lascelles, Henry George Charles, 6th Earl of Harewood (1882-1947), 272
Latham, Alfred, 59
La Trobe, Charles Joseph (1801-75), 57, 427, 428, 435, 513, 537, 540
La Trobe family, 10
Lauderdale, 8th Earl of, see Maitland, James
Launceston, emigrant ship, 506
Laurier, Sir Wilfrid (1841-1919), 599
Lausanne Conference (1932), 206
Lavaud, Governor of Tahiti, 456
Laver, William Adolphus (1866-1940), 538
Lavinia, schooner, 174
Law, Andrew Bonar (1858-1923), 5, 73, 272; papers, 7-8
Law, John, 26
Law, international, 363; officers, 219, 238, 251, 256, 263
Lawes, William George (1839-1907), 95, 462
Lawley, Sir Arthur, 6th Baron Wenlock (1860-1932), 540
Lawley (fl.1854), 49
Lawn, George, 357
Lawrence, Effingham, 350
Lawrence, Sir Henry Montgomery (1806-57), 140
Lawrence, Honoria, 140
Lawrence, James, 389
Lawrence, Robert William (1807-33), 512, 513
Lawrence, Sampson, 583
Lawrence, William, 583
Lawrence, William Effingham (1781-1841), 350
Lawrence, William Nicholl (b.1859), 95
Lawrenny Estate, Tasmania, 449
Lawry, Walter (1793-1859), 164
Lawson, G., 424
Lawson, Hannah, Mrs, 102
Lawson, Henry (1867-1922), 510
Lawson, Joseph, 424
Lawson, Nelson, 102
Lawson, Thomas, 424
Lawson, William (1774-1850), 102, 450
Lawton, Lieut.-Col., 527
Layard, Sir Austen Henry (1817-94): papers, 28-9
Layard, Edgar Leopold, 71, 213, 265, 266, 491
Leach, William Elford (1790-1836), 156
Lead and lead mining, 6, 359, 388, 391, 535
League of Nations, 76, 201, 202, 244-5, 484

654

Index

M

Index

Index

Index

Mennonites, 318
Menzies, Archibald (1754-1842), 21, 78, 158, 159, 579
Menzies, Sir Charles (1783-1866), 379
Merchant Shipping Convention, 488
Merchant ships, 168-82 *passim*, 277-90 *passim*, 558; crew agreements, 287; passenger lists, 286-7; *see also* names of ships
Merchants' Trust Company Ltd, 150
Meredith, George (1777-1856), 410
Merewether, Edward Christopher (1815-93), 57
Merewether, Kate Amelia (Plunkett), Mrs Francis Lewis Shaw, 537
Meridian, ship, 442
Meridian, proposed measurement (1823), 30
Meriton, Walter, 40
Merivale, George Montagu, 129
Merivale, Herman (1806-74), 66, 276, 428, 446, 485-6
Mermaid, H.M. cutter, 85, 107
Merope, barque (1888), 171
Merope, ship (1825-7), 506
Merope, ship (1849), 463
Merret, J., 18
Meryon, Charles (1821-68): papers, 25
Mesopotamia campaign, 473
Messer, A. B., 438
Messer, J. C., 438
Messenger, schooner, 337
Meteorology, 341; Antarctic regions, 341, 370, 399; Hawaiian Islands, 341; New South Wales, 341; Northern Territory, 341; Tasmania, 341, 343; Victoria, 341; *see also* Climate
Metge, Alice Joan, 324
Methodist Church: registers of births, deaths and marriages, 246; Australia, 162-7 *passim*; New Zealand, 162-7 *passim*
Methodist Missionary Society, 10, 32, 162-7, 548; in New Zealand, 162-7 *passim*; in Pacific Islands, 110, 162-7 *passim*, (Fiji), 265
Methodist New Connexion, 166
Methven, Robert, 181
Michel, Charlotte, *see* Goldspink, Mrs Charles
Michel, Henry Edward, 31, 463
Michel, J., General, 31
Michel, Jane, Mrs Henry Edward, 463
Michel family, 463
Michelsen, Oscar, 362
Michie, Sir Archibald (1813-99), 55, 519
Micronesia: languages, 362
Middleton, Alfred E., 23
Middleton, Sir Charles, 1st Baron Barham (1726-1813), 542
Miklouho-Maclay, Nicolaus Nicolaevitch de (1846-88), 61, 71
Mildmay, Sir Henry, 22

Milford Haven, 1st Marquess of, *see* Mountbatten, Louis Alexander
Military survey: Australia, 309; Fiji, 309; New Guinea (Anglo-German boundary), 309, (Australian-Dutch boundary), 309
Militia, N.Z., 588
Mill, Hugh Robert (1861-1950): papers, 400
Mill, John Stuart (1806-73), 25; papers, 358
Millar, John, 575
Millar, Robert, 110
Millard, James, 405
Millard, Thomas, 34
Millard, William, 366
Millechamp, Lawrence, 174
Millen, Joseph, 587
Miller, Annie, 124
Miller, Frederick (*d.*1862), 95
Miller, George Galway, 410
Miller, Hugh (1802-56), 120
Miller, J. F., 15, 19
Miller, John, 177
Miller, T. F., 175
Miller, William (*fl.*1838 Sydney, N.S.W.), 309
Miller, William (1795-1861), British consul, Honolulu, 138, 533, 534
Milliken, John, 584
Millionaire Ltd, 416
Mills, George G., 411, 412
Mills, J. R., 236
Mills, Lilian (McClymont), Mrs William (*d.*1861), 96
Mills, Thomas, convict, 381
Mills, William (1811-76), 96
Milne, Sir Arthur, 265
Milne, R. G., 456, 457
Milne, William Grant (*d.*1866), 513, 515
Milner, Alfred, Viscount Milner (1854-1925), 7, 8, 357, 478
Milnes, Robert Offley Ashburton Crewe-, *see* Crewe-Milnes
Milton, Viscountess (1812-83), 160
Milverton, 1st Baron, *see* Richards, A. F.
Mimosa, 344
Minchin, William (1774?-1821), 302
Minerals: Australia, 120, 429, (New South Wales), 22, (South Australia), 330, (Western Australia), 66, 221; New Zealand, 429; rights, 211
Minerva, convict ship, 14, 302
Minerva, whaling vessel, 258
Mines and mining: Australian colonies, 530; Queensland, 408, 496; South Australia, 423, 528; Victoria, 66; Western Australia, 283; licences, 30, 553, 601
Mingay, George, 506
Minorca, convict ship, 22
Minto, 4th Earl of, *see* Elliot, Gilbert John Murray Kynymond

662

Index

Index

Neville, Mary (Massingberd), Mrs Hastings, 465
Neville, Samuel Tarratt (1837-1921), 91
New Australia Settlement, 239, 557
New Britain, 66, 474; exploration, 332; languages, 22, 362
New Caledonia, 46, 80, 147, 172, 236, 242, 364, 384, 394, 498; Anglo-French relations, 488; annexation by France, 29, 172, 475; Isle of Pines, 18, 526; language, 361
New England, N.S.W., 508
New Georgia, Solomon Islands, 27; drawings, 80
New Guinea, 17, 235, 236, 240, 483-4, 518; 16th century, 78; 17th-18th centuries, 129, 567; 1801-50, 356; 1871-80, 50, 55, 263, 266, 438; 1881-90, 63, 66, 69, 269, 270, 271, 524; 1891-1900, 95; 20th century, 241, 334, 474; agriculture, 484; annexation, 46, 52, 263, 265, 270, 332, 524, (by Germany), 44, 49, 70, 235, 270, 271, (by Queensland), 61; Australian interest in, 49, 61, 69, 70, 71, 263, 265, 270, 271 passim; boundaries, 238; F.O. correspondence, 235; coastal survey, 500; drawings and paintings, 356; Maclay Coast, 71; maps and charts, 12, 79, 309; natives, 483-4, (government policy), 61, (ill treatment), 242; languages, 81, 95, 321, 362, 363; photographs, 330; proposed colonisation by a company, 71, 265; R.N., Australia Station records, 196; Spanish voyages, 13; trade, 23, 148, 205; see also German New Guinea; Netherlands New Guinea; Papua
New Hebrides, 44, 210, 214, 240, 326, 486; 17th century, 11, 16; 1801-50, 169, 364; 1851-1900, 62, 66, 170, 241, 266, 394, 475, 491 passim; 20th century, 204, 205, 237, 241, 243, 244, 273, 586; Anglo-French relations, 71, 74, 486, 487, 488, 530, 531; Australian interest in, 46, 205, 488, 489; defence, 307; drawings, 18; languages, 107, 363; New Zealand interest in, 205, 488; proposed Belgian colonisation, 29; maps, 17; see also Eromanga
New Hebrides Association, 29
New Holland (name used to c.1820), 17, 18, 370; maps and charts, 12, 79, 327; see also Australia
New Holland Roman Catholic Mission, 371
New Ireland, 86; languages, 81
New Norcia, W.A., 359
New Norfolk, Tas., 595
New Plymouth, N.Z., 149; map, 20
New South Shetland, Antarctic, 19
New South Wales: 1788-1800, 15, 16, 18, 136, 159, 210, 214-22 passim, 279, 478, 509; 1801-50, 3, 24, 53, 279, 363-4, 365, 372, 378, 382, 389, 410-11, 467, 500, 509, 516, 575, 579, 583; 1851-1900, 382, 438, 471, 482, 504, 547, 576; accounts, 190, 199, 230, 254, 296, 300; administration, 67, 314; agriculture, 13, 28, 268; boundaries, 523; civil service, 156, 410-13; coastal survey, 500; currency, 251; defence, 215, 312, 428, (naval), 26; drawings and paintings, 14, 87-8; economic conditions, 31, 390; elections, 446; exploration by land, 331, 341, 416, 421, 512, 515; finance, 3, 251; government, 215, 274, 426, 470; health and medical services, 192; law courts, 411; legislation, 211, 258; Legislative Council, 411, 443; maps and charts, 13, 14, 18, 19, 21, 499, 509; newspapers, 51, 411; Parliament, 51, 55, see also Legislative Council; politics, 263, 264, 384, 498; prices, 13, 460; public works, 297; settlement, 26, 51, 67, 215, 247-53 passim, 291, 383, see also Immigration and emigration, Land settlement; settlers, 13, 411, (relations with convicts), 39; shipping, 22, 27, 144, 148, 278-81 passim, 308-13 passim; statistics, 215, 524-5; Supreme Court, 259; trade, 3, 27, 39, 259, 279, 360, 411, 412, 479-80, 575, (China), 143, 147, 148, 387-92 passim, (France), 281, (India), 144, 146, 148, 412, 575, (Netherlands Indies), 252, (Pacific Islands), 182, (Fiji), 500, (west coast of America), 182, 279
New South Wales Association for Preventing the Revival of Transportation, 599
New South Wales Bill (1823), 411, 543
New South Wales Church and School Corporation, 450
New South Wales Corps, 14, 26-7, 302-12 passim, 541
New South Wales Divorce Bill (1888), 490
New South Wales Gold Mines, 445
New South Wales Veteran Corps (Invalid Company), 303, 304, 305, 306
New Ulster, province, New Zealand, 54
New York Island, Gilbert and Ellice Islands, see Washington Island
New Zealand, 47, 92, 135, 166, 209-27 passim, 261, 425-31 passim, 459, 483-4, 547; before 1800, 19, 140, 192; 1801-50, 133, 136, 169, 192, 234-5, 274, 392, 394, 398, 401, 413, 425, 452, 459, 477, 481, 515, 577, 594; 1851-60, 267, 276, 404, 408, 444, 447, 470, 471, 477, 485, 490, 534, 549, 568; 1861-70, 23, 44, 45, 50, 59, 60, 108, 141, 160, 170, 270, 408, 438, 447, 463, 471, 485, 497, 514, 549, 585; 1871-80, 174, 264, 265, 266, 369,

Index

Nightingale Training School, 123-5
Nimrod, Antarctic vessel, 336
Nimrod, ship (1827), 407
Ninnis, Aubrey Howard, 337
Ninnis, Belgrave, 500
Nisbet, Henry (1818-76), 96
Niue (Savage Island), 98, 238, 490; language, 99
Nixon, Francis Russell (1803-79), 54, 55, 57, 58, 62, 151, 155, 405, 429, 459, 480
Nixon, J. H., 419
Nobbs, George Hunn (1799-1884), 348
Noble, E., 67
Noel, Emilia F., 160
Nolan, Robert, 585
Nonconformists, 444; records, 245
Noon, Henry, & Co., 368
Norfolk, colonial sloop, 14, 18
Norfolk, ship, 467
Norfolk Island, 15, 20, 52, 66, 80, 86, 91, 92, 159, 211, 214, 221, 251, 261, 262, 266, 267, 319, 328, 380, 500; accounts, 230; agriculture, 28; constitution, 42; drawings and paintings, 88; measles epidemic, 262; penal settlement, 273, 274; pines, 339
Norie, W. F., 181
Norman, George Warde (1793-1882), 450
Norman, Henry (1859-1925), 176
Norman, Sir Henry Wylie (1826-1904), 42
Norman, Herman, 450
Norman, Richard, 450
Normanby, 1st Marquess of, *see* Phipps, Sir Constantine Henry
Normanby, 2nd Marquess of, *see* Phipps, Sir George Augustus Constantine
Norries, W., 563
Norris, H., 12
Norrish family, 418
North, Frederick (1839-1927), 172
North, Marianne (1830-90), 512
'North Australia', *see* Gladstone Colony
North Australian Expedition (1855-6), 269, 335, 371, 471, 483, 513; paintings, 512
North Star, H.M.S., 567
North West Kimberley Exploring Expedition (1901), 323
Northampton, 2nd Marquis of, *see* Compton, Spencer Joshua Alwyne
Northampton, ship, 147
Northbrook, Baron, *see* Baring, Sir Francis Thornhill
Northcliffe, Viscount, *see* Harmsworth, Alfred Charles William
Northcote, Alice (Stephen), Lady (d.1934), 243
Northcote, Henry Stafford, Baron Northcote (1846-1911), 35, 73, 74, 77, 273

Northcote, Sir Stafford Henry, 1st Earl of Iddesleigh (1818-87), 491; papers, 74
Northern Australia: drawings and paintings, 337; settlement, 28, 74
Northern Territory, Australia, 42, 55, 80, 212, 216; Fort Dundas, 80; map, 63
Northumberland, 2nd Duke of, *see* Percy, Sir Hugh
Northumberland, Indiaman, 567
Northwood, William, 378
Norton, James (1795-1862), 509
Norton, 1st Baron, *see* Adderley, Sir Charles Bowyer
Norton collection, 529
Norway, Frances, 556
Norway, Nevil (Shute, pseud. 1899-1960), 556
Norway: F.O. correspondence, 234, 238
Norwegian-British-Swedish Antarctic Expedition (1949-52), 400
Notcutt, W. R., 397
Nott, Henry (1774-1844), 97, 98, 456
Nott, John, 457
Novar, Viscount, *see* Munro-Ferguson, Sir Ronald Craufurd
Novikoff, Olga, Mrs, 61
Noyes Bros, Melbourne, Vic., 546
Nunn, Elizabeth Mary, *see* Starr
Nunn, Fred, 419
Nursing profession, 67, 123-5
Nutt, R. W., 520

O

Oakden, Georgiana (Cowie), Mrs Philip, 458
Oakden, Philip, 406
Oakes, Francis (1770-1844), 97, 547
O'Brien, Sir George, 530, 531
O'Brien, Sir Lucius ['Lucien'], 275, 597
O'Brien, Lucy, Mrs William Smith, 597
O'Brien, William Smith (1803-64), 275, 459, 476, 477, 549, 586, 596-601 *passim*; journal on *Swift*, 596; papers, 594-5, 597; trial, 601
Observatories: Australia, 340-3 *passim*; 425, 521-3 *passim*, Parramatta, 383; New Zealand, 522, 523
Observer, Fremantle, W.A., 330
O'Byrne, G. D., 482
Ocean, convict ship, 62
Ocean, ship (1881), 389
Ocean Chief, clipper, 451
Ocean Island, Gilbert and Ellice Islands, 46, 351
Ocean Steamship Company Ltd, 454
Oceana, s.s., 333, 335
Oceania, ship, 374
Oceanography, 82, 86, 343
O'Connell, Daniel (1775-1847), 347, 459
O'Connor, F. W., 361

Index

Oxford Society, N.Z., 470
Oxley, John Joseph William Molesworth (1785?-1828), 331, 499, 500, 515, 568, 578, 579; chart of the interior of New South Wales (1817), 509; map of New South Wales (1824), 518
Oysters, 376

P

Pacific Cable, 42, 89, 357
Pacific Cable Board (1910-15), 482
Pacific Cable Conference (1896-7), 530
Pacific Islanders Protection Bill, 61, 263-4, 266
Pacific Islands, 17, 18, 19, 64, 81, 82, 93-100 *passim*, 135, 162-6 *passim*, 210, 216, 234-9 *passim*, 291, 387, 437-8, 483, 484, 588; 1801-50, 136, 173, 425, 500, 535, 588; 1851-1900, 160, 170, 174, 271, 501, 576; 20th century, 237, 443; administration of justice, 61, 71, 263, 264, 446; annexation, 31, 194, 218, 240, 243; arms traffic, 235, 237, 488; Australian interest in, 49, 60; F.O. records, 234-44 *passim*; defence, 201, 203-6 *passim*, 267, 310; discovery, 13, 16-18 *passim*, 78; drawings and paintings, 12, 396, 588; German records, 487; languages, 334, 361, 362, 387, 486; liquor traffic, 235, 488; maps and charts, 15, 79, 499; naval bases, 200; New Zealand interest in, 60; photographs, 332, 529; territorial changes after World War I, 204, 240, 241; trade, 27, 103, 204, 228-30, 237, 238, 239, 265, 323, 387-92 *passim*; *see also* Indentured labour, Melanesia, Micronesia, Polynesia, South West Pacific, names of island groups and names of islands, names of navigators and ships
Pacific Islands Company, 350-1
Pacific Ocean, 437-8, 586, 588; difference in level with Atlantic Ocean, 342; exploration, 13-18 *passim*, 188, 199, 234, 384, 500; maps and charts, 79, 499; shipping, 141, 208, 239, 244, 323; trade, 323; *see also* South West Pacific; names of navigators and ships
Pacific Phosphate Co., 46, 351, 484
Pacific Steam Navigation Co., 366
Pacifism, 363
Packet boats, 115-18 *passim*
Paddon, James (*c.*1812-61), 390, 391, 394
Page, Mr, 123
Page and Moody deposit, 439, 440
Paget, Sir Henry William, 1st Marquis of Anglesey, 2nd Earl of Uxbridge (1768-1854), 425
Pagoda, H.M. barque, 343, 573
Paine, John, 117

Pakington, Sir John Somerset, 1st Baron Hampton and 1st Bt (1799-1880), 36, 276, 428, 446, 537
Palaeontology, *see* Fossils
Palatinate of Lancaster records, 459-60
Palau Islands, 16, 18, 235, 238, 243, 567; drawings and paintings, 438
Palliser, Henry St Leger Bury, 197
Palliser, Miss, 112
Palliser Islands, Tuamotu Archipelago: chart, 109
Palma, William, 503
Palmer, George (*fl.*1823), 28
Palmer, George (*fl.*1874), 266
Palmer, Henry Spencer (1838-93), 522
Palmer, Sir James Frederick (1803-71), 540
Palmer, John (1742-1818), 119
Palmer, John (1760-1833), 183, 258, 313
Palmer, John, of Calcutta, 479-80
Palmer, John Linton, 336
Palmer, Sir Roundell, 1st Earl of Selborne (1812-95), 70
Palmer, Lady Sophia, 39
Palmer, Thomas Fyshe (1747-1802), 110, 377, 378, 492, 567, 577
Palmer, William Waldegrave, 2nd Earl of Selborne (1859-1942), 530
Palmer, Wilson & Co., 28
Palmer River goldfield, Qld, 264
Palmerston, 3rd Viscount, *see* Temple, Henry John
Palolo, 325
Palsy (*fl.*1772 Landerneau, France), 374
Paluma, H.M.S., 173
Panaitan (Prince's Island), 361
Panama Line, 58
Pancher, Jean Armand Isidore, 158
Pandanus, 81
Pandora, H.M.S., 108, 196
Panmure, 2nd Baron, *see* Maule, Fox
Panopticon, 21, 22, 363
Panther, H.M.S., 18, 567
Papakura, Maggie (Makereti), Maori chieftainess, 494
Papehia, Isaiah, Cook Islander, 96, 97
Papermakers, 252
Papua, 95, 96, 210, 214, 322, 335, 485, 524, 569; exploration by air, 335; genealogies, 324; languages, 321, 362, 363; photographs, 100; trade, 287; *see also* Netherlands New Guinea; New Guinea
Paraguay: F.O. correspondence, 234
Parbury, *see* Lamb and Parbury
Parbury & Co., 389
Paris Exhibition (1888), 490
Parish records, 245; Berkshire, 381; Dorset, 421-2; Gloucestershire, 435; Hertfordshire, 445; Ipswich and East Suffolk, 505-6; London, 122-3; Southampton, 439; Warwickshire, 439; Scotland, 570

Index

Index

Poynter, William (1762-1827), 269, 372-3
Prado y Tovar, Diego de, 17
Pratt, George (1817-74), 98, 99
Pratt, John Jeffreys, 2nd Earl and 1st Marquess of Camden (1759-1840), 451
Pratt, T. P., 482
Pratt, Sir Thomas Simson (1797-1879), 575; papers, 379
Precedence, 211, 226, 446
Pre-fabricated houses, 432, 527
Preiss, Johann August Ludwig (1811-83), 513
Prendergast, Sir James (1826-91), 50
Prerogative Court of Canterbury records, 183, 187-8
Presbyterian Church: Australia, 241, 331; *see also* Church of Scotland
President, convict ship, 196
Press, *see* Newspapers
Preston, David, 579
Preston, Jenico William Joseph, 14th Viscount Gormanston (1837-1907), 43
Pretgel (*fl.*1825), 568
Price, C., 330
Price, Edwin, 545
Price, John Banner, 545
Price, John Washington, 14
Price, Lewis R., 496
Price, William, 397
Price family, 496
Prideaux, Francis Grevile, 434
Priestley, Joseph (1733-1804), 110
Priestley, Sir Raymond Edward (*b.*1866), 370, 399
Prima Donna, ship, 390
Prime Ministers' papers, 202
Primrose, Archibald Philip, 5th Earl of Rosebery (1847-1929), 41, 62, 271, 570
Prince Alfred Hospital, Sydney, 125
Prince, Edward, 398
Prince Edward Islands (Indian Ocean), 173
Prince of the Seas, ship, 583
Prince of Wales's Island, *see* Rangiroa, Tuamotu Archipelago
Prince Regent, ship, 239
Prince William Henry, ship, 97
Prince's Island, *see* Panaitan
Princesa, Spanish frigate, 109
Pring, Samuel William, 174
Pringle, Sir John, Bt (1707-82), 12
Pringlea antiscorbutica, 83
Prison Commission records, 247, 255-6
Prisons, 250, 357; Australian colonies, 402, 411, 503; *see also* Panopticon
Pritchard, George (1796-1883), 37, 40, 45, 95, 98, 267, 456, 533, 535
Pritchard, William, 553
Privateers, from U.S., 197
Privy Council, 45, 104, 105; records, 256-61
Prize cases, 186, 187, 269
Prize Courts, 107, 288, 300, 301

Probate records, 183, 187-8, 232; Scotland, 571
'Proclamation Tree', Glenelg, S.A., 330
Proctor, Mary, 523
Propaganda, 208
Property: deceased estates, 294, 300; *see also* Real estate
Prosser, Charles John, 34
Prossor, James George, 268
Protestant South Australian Emigration Community, 364
Protozoa, 83
Prout, John Skinner (1806-76), 81, 82, 83
Providence, H.M.S., 170
Provincial Councils, New Zealand, 265
Prytherch family, 553
Psychical research, 370
Public finance, 290-9, 293; Australia, 267, 299, New Zealand, 264; *see also* finance under names of states
Public health, 256
Public Library of New South Wales, 386
Puckey, William (*b.*1776), 97
Puget, P., 16, 479
Pukahinahina (Gate Pa), 424, 496
Puket tin dredging, N.Z., 150
Pullein, Frederick A., 545
Pullein, James, 544
Pullein and Hutton archives, 544
Pulsford, E., 519
Purari Delta, New Guinea, 96
Purcell, Brab I., 323
Purcell-Buret, Theobald John Claud (*b.*1879), 172
Purse, J., 588
Purse, William, 588
Purves, James (1734-95), 110-11
Pusey, Philip (1799-1855), 381
Pycroft, Henry T., 56
Pylades, H.M.S., 172, 438
Pyramus, H.M.S., 74

Q

Qantas Airways Ltd, 486
Quaife, Barzillai (1798-1873), 40
Quarantine, 246, 257, 261; Australia, 181
Quarter Sessions records, 185; Chester, Cheshire, 404; Dorchester, Dorset, 421; Essex, 431; Exeter, Devon, 418; Hereford, 441; Hertford, 444; Kent, 448-9; Lancashire, 459; Leicester, 462; Lincoln, 463; Middlesex, 126-7; Southampton, 439-40; Sussex, East Sussex, Lewes, West Sussex, Chichester, 518, 525; Wiltshire, 535; *see also* Sessions records
Queale, Alan, 598
Queen Charlotte, H.M.S., 18
Queen of Avon, barque, 454
Queen's School, Tasmania, 414
Queensland, 210, 214, 216, 220, 221, 222, 267, 446, 482, 512, 519; choice of

Index

677

Index

Index

Index

Index

Soutter, W., 513
Sowerby, Gerald, 586
Sowerby, James (1757-1822), 88
Sowerby, James de Carle (1787-1871), 158
Spain: Archivo General de Indias, Seville, 78; Archivo Real de Simancas, 78; F.O. correspondence, 234, 235-6
Spaniards in the Pacific, 13, 14, 16-18, 81, 234, 235-6
Spanish relics at Point Piper, Port Jackson, N.S.W., 81
Sparke, J. G., 246
Sparke family, 418
Sparkes, Samuel, 422
Sparks, Octavius Batten, 422
Sparks, Thomas Maber, 422
Sparks, William, 422
Spaulding, T. C., 175
Spear and Jackson Papers, 547
Speedwell, ship, 107
Spence, John C., 302
Spence, Mr (*fl.*1789), 159
Spencer, Frederick, 4th Earl Spencer (1798-1857), 538
Spencer, John Elgar, 449
Spencer, Josiah, 480
Spencer, Sir Walter Baldwin (1860-1929), 564; papers, 494; photographs of Aranda tribe, 395
Spencer Stanhope manuscripts, 541
Sperling family correspondence, 432
Sperm whale, 325
Sphinx, H.M.S., 438
Spicer, Louisa, 96
Spielbergen, Joris van, 78
Spiritualism, 370
Spöring, Herman Diedrich (*d.*1771), 15, 19
Spooner, Gerard William, 151
Sprigg, George, 376
Spring-Rice, Ellen Mary (Frere), Lady Monteagle (*d.*1869), 598-9
Spring-Rice, Sir Cecil Arthur (1859-1918), 270
Spring-Rice, Thomas, 1st Baron Monteagle (1790-1866), 430, 459, 482, 594, 597; papers, 595, 598-9
Spry, John Hume (1777/8-1854), 123
Spurge, John, 182
Squatters and squatting, 4, 215, 482, 540, 575
Squirrel, introduced into N.S.W., 375
Stafford, Sir Ernest William (1819-1901), 63
Stafford, 1st Marquess, *see* Leveson-Gower, Granville
Stafford, 2nd Marquess, *see* Leveson-Gower, George Granville, 1st Duke of Sutherland
Stafford, Lady, wife of 5th Marquess, 503
Stag, ship, 174
Staley, Thomas Nettleship (1823-98), 59

Stalker, W., 81, 88
Stallard, Mrs, 176
Stamfordham, Baron, *see* Bigge, Arthur John
Stanhope, Edward (1840-93), 62, 269, 310
Stanhope, Philip Henry, 5th Earl Stanhope (1805-75), 57, 68
Stanhope, Walter Spencer, 541
Stanley, Arthur Lyulph, 5th Baron Stanley of Alderley and 5th Baron Sheffield of Roscommon (1875-1931), 3, 7
Stanley, Catherine, 405
Stanley, Charles Edward (1819-49), 404, 405
Stanley, Edward (1779-1849), 410
Stanley, Edward George Geoffrey Smith, 14th Earl of Derby (1799-1869), 31, 32, 33, 39, 57, 177, 274, 309, 393, 402, 413, 415, 427, 446, 573-4; papers, 458-9
Stanley, Edward Henry, 15th Earl of Derby (1826-93), 46, 49, 61, 263-70 *passim*, 459, 471
Stanley, Eliza (Clayton), Mrs Charles Edward (*d.*1901), 381, 404, 405
Stanley, Louisa Dorothea, 405
Stanley, Mary Catherine, Countess of Derby, widow of 2nd Marquess of Salisbury (*d.*1900), 490
Stanley, Owen (1811-50), 157, 169, 172, 404-5, 500
Stanley of Alderley papers, 404-5
Stanmore, 1st Baron, *see* Gordon, Sir Arthur Charles Hamilton-
Stanmore, 2nd Baron, *see* Gordon, George Arthur Maurice Hamilton-
Stanmore collection, 394, 395; papers, 69-72
Stanton, George Henry (1835-1905), 155
Stapleton, Ann, 378
Star of Devon, ship, 173
Starling, H.M.S., 500
Starr, Elizabeth Mary (Nunn), Mrs Stephen, formerly Mrs George Kidman, 419
Starr, Stephen, 419
State aid to religion: Australian colonies, 62, 351, 352
State Library of Victoria, 262
Statesman, ship, 390
Station life, 377, 418, 422, 432, 436, 437, 443, 467, 482
Station records, *see* Admiralty: Station records
Stavers, Capt., 87
Stawell, Sir William Foster (1815-89), 265
Steam: communication, 136, 178, 181-2, 221, 292, 368, 426, 446, 476; navigation, 8, 32, 38, 57, 77, 175
Stecher, H., 367

Index

Index

689

Index

W

Index

Walker, George Washington (1800-59), 316, 318, 319, 328, 445
Walker, Henry de Rosenbach, 488
Walker, Howard, 486
Walker, James John (1851-1939), 333
Walker, Jane Hannah, 543
Walker, ['Walter'], John, of Whitby, 334, 436
Walker, Robert, 543
Walker, V. L., 486
Walker, W. Maitland, 423
Walker, William (1800-55), 354
Walker, Capt. (*fl.*1824), 479
Walker, Capt. *King George* (*fl.*1817), 16
Walker, Mr (*fl.*1831), 480
Wallace, Alexander, 432
Wallace, Alfred Russel (1823-1913), 29, 88, 160, 376, 386, 398
Wallace, Annie (Magill), Mrs Arthur, 588
Wallace, Arthur O., 432
Wallace, Robert B., 390
Wallace, Mother Walburge, 536-7
Wallah Wallah copper mines, N.S.W., 450
Wallich, George Charles (1815-99), 371
Wallis, James (1809-95), 163
Wallis, Samuel (1728-95), 14, 109, 174, 343, 370, 499
Wallis Island, *see* Uvea
Walmer Castle, ship, 176, 502
Walsh, J. W., 599
Walsh, John, 243
Walsh, William, 31
Walsingham, 2nd Baron, *see* Grey, Thomas de
Walter family papers, 382
Walters, John (1759-89), 555
Walton, Izaak (*fl.*1860), 443
Wanigera, Papua, 81
War Cabinet (1916-19), 200, 244
War criminals, World War I, 300
War Office: separation from Colonial Office, 549; Library, 508; papers, 430; records, 301-14, (W.O.6 index), 217
Warburton, Alicia (Mant), Mrs Peter Egerton- (*d.*1892), 406
Warburton, Augusta (Spencer), Mrs George Edward Egerton- (*d.*1871), 406
Warburton, Emma (Croxton), Mrs Rowland Egerton- (*d.*1881), 406
Warburton, George Drought (1816-57), 432
Warburton, George Edward Egerton- (1819-89), 406
Warburton, Peter Egerton- (1813-89), 406
Warburton, Richard Egerton- (1840-1917), 406
Warburton, Rowland Egerton- (1778-1846), 406
Warburton, Rowland Eyles Egerton- (1804-91), 406

Ward, E. M., 341
Ward, James, 175
Ward, John (1805-90), 394, 504
Ward, John M., 393
Ward, Joseph & Co., 390
Ward, Sir Joseph George, 1st Bt (1856-1930), 7, 73, 272, 360, 376
Ward, Thomas Humphrey, 525
Ward, William Humble, 2nd Earl of Dudley (1867-1932), 42
Wardi, Chaim, 367
Wardroper, Mrs S. E., 67, 123, 124, 125
Ware, Martin, 510
Ware, Martin S., 510
Ware family papers, 510
Warrants, 221
Warspite, H.M.S., 196
Washington (Disarmament) Conference (1921-2), 200, 206
Washington Island, Gilbert and Ellice Islands, 351
Wassenaar, ship, 130
Water Lily, ship, 444
Water supply and sewerage, Sydney, N.S.W., 438, 504
Waterfield, William (1795-1868), 364
Waterhouse, Frederick George (1815-98), 87
Waterhouse, George Marsden (1824-1906), 335
Waterhouse, Henry (1770-1812), 182, 183
Waterhouse, Jabez Bunting, 163
Waterhouse, Jane B., 163
Waterhouse, John (*d.*1842), 166
Waterhouse, William, 182-3
Waterhouse family letters, 182-3
Watkin, James (1805-86), 163
Watkins, Francis, 369
Watkins-Pitchford collection, 496
Watling, Thomas (*b.*1762), 87, 88
Watlington, J. W. Perry, 432
Watson, John, 33
Watson, John Christian (1867-1941), 273
Watson, Joshua (1771-1855): papers, 155
Watson, Robert, 428
Watson-Taylor, George (*d.*1841), 410
Watt, Michael, 563
Watts, John (1821-1902), 87, 383
Watt's Peninsula, N.Z., 381
Wattle bark, 344
Wauchope, A., 577
Waugh, Hugh, 584
Waugh, William, 584
Way, Sir Samuel James (1836-1916), 50, 474, 604
Weale, J. C. M., 598
Weather, *see* Climate; Drought; Meteorology
Weaver, Charles Thomas (*d.*1874), 309
Weaver, Ed., 588
Webb, Charles H., 588
Webb, E. N., 400

Index

332; Farrer's research, 513-4; import into Australia, 479, 573; prices (1813), 13; supplies, 201, 202, 203

Wheat Commission (1916-17), 203, 293

Wheat Supplies Commission, *see* Wheat Commission

Wheeler, Charles (*d.*1840), 319

Wheeler, Daniel (1771-1840), 315, 316; collection, 319

Wheeler, E. J., 527

Wheeler, Gerald Clair William Camden, 363

Wheeler, Jane (Brady), Mrs Daniel, 319

Wheeler, Joseph, 436

Wheelwright, William, 366

Whigham, William, 583

Whitaker, Sir Frederick (1812-91), 70, 382

Whitbread, Samuel (1758-1815): papers, 378

Whitby, Geoff, 588

Whitby, George, 125

Whitby, John, 125

White, Sir Cyril Brudenell Bingham (1876-1940), 77

White, H., 488

White, John (1756?-1832), 86, 159

White, Margaret, 409

White, Samuel (1835-80), 409

White, Susanna Matilda, Mrs, 504

White (Hughes), Mrs, 468

'White Australia' Policy, 73, 202, 240

White Star Line, 454

Whitehouse, Benjamin, 504

Whitehouse, Charles Howard [alias Charles Blake?], 504

Whitehouse (Sedgeley) manuscripts, 504

Whitley, Mr, 38

Whitmee, Samuel James (1838-1925), 96, 97, 98, 100, 514

Whitmore, W. W., 599

Whitney, George, 123

Whitney family, 123

Whitson, W. Gilchrist, 325

Whittell, Henry Rawes, 404

Whytehead, Robert Yates, 398

Whytehead, Thomas (1815-43): papers, 398

Whytlaw, John, 34

Wickham, Sir Henry Alexander (1846-1928), 327

Wickstead, J. F., 353

Widdowson, William, 417

Wigg, Montagu John Stone-, 449

Wilberforce, William (1759-1833), 22, 80, 94, 150, 398-9, 411; papers, 541-2, 480-1

Wilcocks, James Blackmore, 366

Wild, Frank, 399

Wild, John James, 84

Wilhelmi, Carl, 513, 514

Wilkins, Sir George Hubert (1888-1958), 400; *Undiscovered Australia*, 88

Wilkinson, Charles Smith (1843-91), 87

Wilkinson, David, 70, 72, 213

Wilkinson, Frederick W., 352

Wilkinson papers, 3

Willemoes-Suhm, Rudolf von (1847-75), 84, 326

William, John, 451

William, whaling vessel, 159

William Denison, ship, 508

William Light district, Adelaide: map, 528

Williams, Anthony, 365

Williams, David, 553

Williams, Sir Evan, 559

Williams, Francis (1780?-1831), 344

Williams, Henry (1782-1867), 91, 568

Williams, John (1796-1839), 38, 94, 97, 98, 364, 456, 510

Williams, John Brown, 165

Williams, John Chauner, 97

Williams, Mary (Chauner), Mrs John (*d.*1852), 97

Williams, Ralph Vaughan, *see* Vaughan Williams

Williams, Samuel Tamatoa, 97, 98

Williams, T. Eurwedd, 555

Williams, Thomas (1815-91), 157

Williams, Thomas, M.L.C., South Australia, 382

Williams, W. J., 604

Williams, William (1800-78), 27, 87, 91, 380

Williams, chief mate *Nassau*, 175

Williams, Rev. (*fl.*1836 nr Reading), 381

Williams family of Ty Calch, 553

Williams family of Warfield papers, 382

Williamson, James (1758-1826), 313

Williamson, Robert Wood, 322

Willis, Alfred (1836-1920), 151

Willis, G., 125

Willis, John Walpole (1793-1877), 53, 54, 136

Willis family papers, 381

Willoughby, Sarah (Callaghan, Eliza, alias Thompson), formerly Mrs John Batman (*d.*1852), 127

Wills, M. R., 510

Wills, 183, 187-8, 232, 292, 300; Scotland, 571; *see also* Property: deceased estates

Willson, Robert William (1794-1866), 373, 598

Wilmot, H. Eardley-, *see* Eardley Wilmot

Wilmot, Sir John Eardley Eardley-, 1st Bt, *see* Eardley-Wilmot

Wilmot, Sir John Eardley Eardley-, 2nd Bt, *see* Eardley-Wilmot

Wilmot Horton, Sir Robert John, *see* Horton

Wilmoth, Leslie James (1881-1963), 329

Wilsden, F. W., 336

Wilshere, William, 377

Wilson, A., 586

Index

6, 290; gift of money to France from New South Wales, 245; hospitals, Australian, Digswell House, Hertfordshire, 445; naval operations, history, 43, 195; New Zealand troops, 245, 586; Peace Conference (1919-20), 74, 233, 240-1, 245; political and economic effects on Australia, 131; prisoners, 223, 242, 585; reparations, 6, 219; shipping, 73, 181, 244; trade and trade with the enemy, 204, 222, 223, *see also* Import restrictions (1916); war graves on Gallipoli, 6; war diaries, 308; Western Pacific High Commission correspondence, 216; *see also* Anzac
World War II (1939-45), 485; New Zealand troops, 172; operations in the Pacific, 396, (Solomon Islands), 486; (Tonga), 486; prisoners, 233, 241; shipping, 180, 181; war criminals, 139; Western Pacific High Commission correspondence, 216
Worms, 83
Worth, Henry John (*b.*1803), 165, 172
Wortley, John Stuart-, 2nd Baron Wharncliffe, *see* Stuart-Wortley
Woureddy, Tasmanian Aboriginal, 324
Wrecks, 103, 168, 169, 189, 192
Wrey, George, 574
Wright, Alfred (1831-1901), 320
Wright, Arthur, 415
Wright, Henry, 376
Wright, Hugh, 507
Wrixon, Sir Henry John (1839-1913), 603
Wulbier, W. R., 449
Wyatt, Benjamin: correspondence, 578
Wykeham-Martin manuscripts, 449
Wyld, F. H., 152
Wyly family, 588
Wyndham, George, 1st Baron Leconfield (1787-1869), 526-7, 528
Wyndham, Sir George O'Brien, 3rd Earl of Egremont (1751-1837), 527
Wyndham-Quin, Windham Thomas, 4th Earl of Dunraven and Mount-Earl, *see* Quin
Wynn-Carrington, Charles Robert, 1st Marquess of Lincolnshire, 1st Earl Carrington (1843-1928), 44, 49, 490; papers, 534-5
Wynyard, Robert Henry (1802-64), 567, 568
Wyvill, M. D'Arcy, 545

X

X-rays, 339-40

Y

Yaldwyn, W. H., 526
Yandella, Qld, 596

Yanko Station, Jerilderie, N.S.W.: map, 328
Yap Islands, 474
Yarborough, 2nd Earl of, *see* Pelham, Charles Anderson Worsley
Yea, Vic., 443
Yeoward, D., 514
Yonge, Charlotte Mary, *Life of John Coleridge Patteson*, 63
York, Duke of, Prince George, Duke of Cornwall and York, *see* George V
York district, W.A., 605
Yorke, Charles Philip, 4th Earl of Hardwicke (1799-1873), 24-5, 173
Yorke, Philip, 2nd Earl of Hardwicke (1720-90), 24
Yorke, Philip, 3rd Earl of Hardwicke (1757-1834), 24
Yorkshire, ship, 424
Yorkshire Motor Car Manufacturing Co. Ltd, 368
Yorkshire Patent Steam Wagon Co.: records, 543
Youl, Sir James Arndell (1810-1904), 429, 430
Young, [Capt.?] (*fl.*1875), 336
Young, D. H. W., 193
Young, Dorcas, Pitcairn Islander: sketch, 336
Young, Ethel, 328
Young, Sir Frederick (1817-1913), 328
Young, George, *Life and Voyages of Captain James Cook*, 456
Young, George Frederick, 33, 331
Young, Sir Henry Edward Fox (1808-70), 268, 280, 430, 471, 490, 540, 543
Young, Jemima, 577
Young, Jess, 263
Young, Sir John, 2nd Bt, Baron Lisgar (1807-76), 33, 51, 58, 59, 346, 428, 446
Young, T. W., 474
Young Irelanders, 234, 459, 476, 477, 595, 596, 601; attitude of Australian colonists, 586; *see also* MacManus, Terence Bellew; Martin, John; Mitchel, John; Meagher, Thomas Francis; O'Brien, William Smith; O'Doherty, Kevin Izod; O'Donohoe, Patrick; Irish Exiles
Younghusband, W., and Co., 454
Yriarte, Bernardo de, 14
Yule, Charles Bampfield, 169, 381

Z

Zacharin, M., 367
Zandwill, Israel, 367
Zapican, Miguel, 17
Zélée, French ship, 334
Zenaida, ship, 86
Zinc concentrates, 283, 284
Zinc Products Association Pty Ltd, 284
Zingari, ship, 389

696

Designed by Arthur Stokes

Text set in Monotype Baskerville
and printed on Warrens Bookman Thin
by John Sands Sydney Pty. Ltd. Halstead Press Division